The Adventures in Literature Program

ADVENTURES FOR READERS: BOOK ONE
Teacher's Manual
Test Booklet
Reading/Writing Workshop, Grade 7

ADVENTURES FOR READERS: BOOK TWO
Teacher's Manual
Test Booklet
Reading/Writing Workshop, Grade 8

ADVENTURES IN READING
Teacher's Manual
Test Booklet
Reading/Writing Workshop, Grade 9

ADVENTURES IN APPRECIATION
Teacher's Manual
Test Booklet
Reading/Writing Workshop, Grade 10

ADVENTURES IN AMERICAN LITERATURE
Teacher's Manual
Test Booklet
Lessons in Critical Reading and Writing:
Henry James's *Washington Square* and *Daisy Miller*

ADVENTURES IN ENGLISH LITERATURE
Teacher's Manual
Test Booklet
Lessons in Critical Reading and Writing:
Shakespeare's *Hamlet*

ADVENTURES IN MODERN LITERATURE
Teacher's Manual
Test Booklet

ADVENTURES IN WORLD LITERATURE
Teacher's Manual
Test Booklet
Lessons in Critical Reading and Writing:
Three Masters of Russian Fiction

JAMES APPLEGATE

Wilson College, Chambersburg, Pennsylvania
Chinese and Japanese Literatures, The Renaissance,
The Age of Rationalism, Romanticism and Realism,
Modern Short Stories

GORDON BROWNE

Cape Cod Community College, Hyannis, Massachusetts
Sumerian Literature, Indian Literature,
Persian-Arabic Literature, The Middle Ages,
Introduction to Modern Europe and Africa

GRETCHEN C. HANKINS

Southwest Miami High School, Miami, Florida
Hebrew Literature, Greek Literature
Roman Literature, Modern Poetry

THOMAS M. FOLDS

The Metropolitan Museum of Art, New York, New York
Fine Arts Program

M. ELINOR BROWN

Fordham Liberal Arts College, New York, New York
Fine Arts Program

ADVENTURES
in World Literature

CLASSIC  EDITION

Harcourt Brace Jovanovich

New York   Chicago   San Francisco   Atlanta   Dallas   *and*   London

JAMES APPLEGATE is Professor and Chairman of English at Wilson College, Chambersburg, Pennsylvania. He received the A.B. and Ph.D. degrees from The Johns Hopkins University and has taught at the University of Rochester and Elmira College. He has published articles in scholarly journals and participated in the Commission on English publications "End-of-the-Year Examinations in English, Grades 9–12" and "12,000 Students and Their English Teachers" (1963, 1968).

GORDON BROWNE is an Associate Professor of English at Cape Cod Community College in Hyannis, Massachusetts. A graduate of Harvard College and Northwestern University, he has taught in independent secondary schools in the Midwest and has worked as a free-lance writer. His short stories and articles have appeared in magazines here and in Europe. For many years he has been a Reader of the English Composition Test for the College Entrance Examination Board.

GRETCHEN C. HANKINS has been head of the English Department at Southwest Miami High School since 1958. She is a graduate of the College of Notre Dame of Maryland and the University of Miami. In 1959 she instituted and has since taught a humanities-oriented Honors English 12 course at Southwest Miami High School. She has taught secondary students in Florida and Ohio and has been an instructor at various English and humanities institutes held for secondary teachers in Florida and Alabama.

THOMAS M. FOLDS is Dean of Education at The Metropolitan Museum of Art in New York. A graduate of Yale College and Yale School of Fine Arts, Mr. Folds has been an instructor of English and Art Director at Phillips Exeter Academy, New Hampshire, and a Professor of Art and Chairman of the Department of Art at Northwestern University.

M. ELINOR BROWN is an Assistant Professor in the Fine Arts Department at Fordham Liberal Arts College. She is a graduate of Boston University and Radcliffe Graduate School. She has been a lecturer at the Boston Museum of Fine Arts, the Museum of the Rhode Island School of Design, and The Metropolitan Museum of Art in New York.

Front cover: Mosaic peacock in City Palace,
Udaipur, near New Delhi, India (Shostal, N.Y.).

Coin used as colophon courtesy of The American Numismatic Society.

Copyright © 1970 by Harcourt Brace Jovanovich, Inc.

PRINTED IN THE UNITED STATES OF AMERICA
ISBN 0-15-335395-3

CONTENTS

Part 1   The Ancient World

SUMERIAN AND HEBREW LITERATURES

GREEK LITERATURE

ROMAN LITERATURE

Part 2   The East

INDIAN LITERATURE

CHINESE AND JAPANESE LITERATURES

PERSIAN–ARABIC LITERATURE

Part 3   Europe to 1914

THE MIDDLE AGES

THE RENAISSANCE

THE AGE OF RATIONALISM

ROMANTICISM AND REALISM

Part 4   *Modern Europe and Africa*

MODERN EUROPE AND AFRICA

The Fine Arts Program

PART 1

THE ANCIENT WORLD

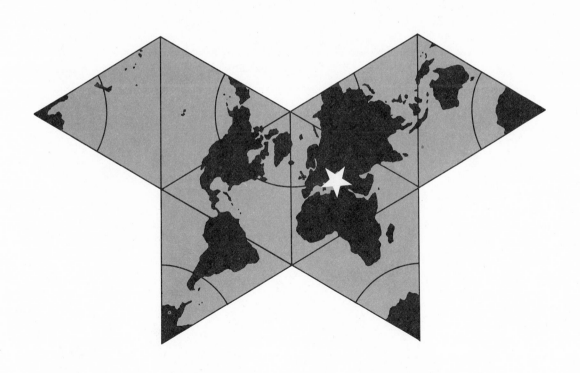

SUMERIAN AND HEBREW LITERATURES

c. 2000 B.C. – c. 100 B.C.

MESOPOTAMIA, a word that means "between the rivers," is the name given by the Greeks to an ancient region in the Middle East which covered generally the greater part of present-day Iraq. East and west, it occupied the valley between the Tigris and Euphrates rivers and extended beyond their further banks. The northern limits were formed by the mountains of Asia Minor and the southern limits by the Persian Gulf, where the two rivers formed a delta before flowing into the sea.

Although to modern Americans Mesopotamia is one of the least known regions of the world, historically it is one of the richest and most fascinating. Mesopotamia has been called the cradle of civilization. The writers of Genesis (see page 20) placed the Garden of Eden, the earthly paradise, there. It was there, from the Tigris-Euphrates valley, that the patriarch of the Jewish people, Abraham, led his family and his flocks in the direction of the Promised Land. And it was back to Mesopotamia that his descendants were taken in the days of the Babylonian captivity. To the north of Mesopotamia is Mount Ararat, where Noah's ark went aground. To the west, along the eastern shore of the Mediterranean, is the land of the Phoenicians, the traders and seamen who transmitted their alphabet to us. Along this eastern shore of the Mediterranean is the birthplace of Jesus Christ, and here lie sites sacred to Judaism and Christianity. To the south and west are the Arabian peninsula and the great Arabian desert, the holy city of Mecca and the birthplace of Islam. Over to the east are the vales and mountains through which the people known as Aryans moved east into

India and west into Persia, giving their name to the region we know as Iran. To the east, too, across the desert and hills of the Iranian plateau, where the religion of Zoroaster arose, is the fabled city of Samarkand, the home of the fourteenth-century Mongol conqueror Tamerlane.

It was in this area of southwest Asia, and in the land of Egypt, that the first three thousand years of western history were acted out. Not until the high tide of the Persian Empire had beaten in vain against the inhospitable shores of Greece did Europe become the site of major events in world history.

Men have lived in Mesopotamia continuously for twelve thousand years, leaving so many traces of their existence that it has been possible to reconstruct several vanished cultures. For countless generations, men of this region had kept themselves alive by hunting and food-gathering. But at last they discovered the relationship between sowing seed and harvesting a crop. With that, agriculture was born. It happened earlier, perhaps, in Mesopotamia than anywhere else. Here, too, at much the same time as in the valleys of the Nile in Egypt and of the Indus in India, the life of cities—which we call civilization—made its appearance. For this to be possible, an accepted and efficient form of government was required, accompanied by advanced technical skills, including metallurgy and the corresponding scientific and mathematical insights. Finally, before the dim reaches of prehistory could yield to the more glaring light of our own historical period, a system of writing had to be created.

THE SUMERIANS

We owe this achievement to the Sumerians, or, as they were called in the Old Testament, Chaldeans. They had come to Mesopotamia—no one knows from where—perhaps between 5000 B.C. and 4000 B.C., and speaking a language related to no other known tongue, to settle in the marshlands of the delta formed by the Euphrates and the Tigris. They dug canals to drain the area and to provide irrigation for the new fields of rich mud. Since there was no stone in this delta region, and virtually no timber, the Sumerians not only grew their crops in mud and built their houses of it, but they also used it to make an excellent grade of pottery. With the pottery and other manufactured goods, the Sumerians carried on a thriving trade. The delta mud also provided them with the clay tablets on which they recorded their financial transactions and their laws, their myths and their literature, and their science, which included astronomy, chemistry, and zoology. The wedge-shaped marks which could easily be scratched into the still-wet clay with a pointed stick or stylus are called *cuneiform* (from the Latin word *cuneus,* meaning "wedge"), the name that has come to be used for this system of writing. Thanks to their superior culture, both material and

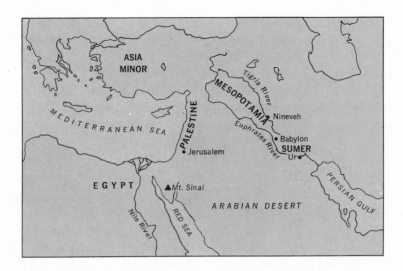

intellectual, the gifted Sumerians exerted a strong influence on their neighbors and set an enduring stamp on the whole culture of the region.

The Sumerians built many flourishing cities. Each was erected around a great temple-mound, built to honor the local deity, who was considered the actual owner of the city. Each city-state was ruled by a high priest acting as the earthly representative of the local god. Since each locality had its god, the Sumerian pantheon was made up of a number of divinities, no one of whom held undisputed sway over the others. The Sumerian religion was chiefly made for this world, and the fortunes of a god waxed and waned with those of his city. The afterlife was seen by the Sumerians as some vague and shadowy existence. Rewards for good behavior were meted out on earth; the Sumerians had no expectation of a paradise to come. Yet, one individual or another, seeking eternal values or (like Gilgamesh) facing his own death, must have found little comfort in the Sumerian religion.

In addition to the Sumerians, other peoples lived in Mesopotamia and along its borders, many of whom spoke Semitic languages. Successively, various peoples dominated the territory during the twenty-five centuries that separated the origins of Mesopotamian civilization from its conclusive defeat by Cyrus the Great of Persia in 539 B.C. Some time after 2300 B.C. the Sumerians were conquered by a Semitic people who established a new and magnificent capital city on the banks of the Euphrates River. The city was called Babylon, meaning "gate of the gods," and these new settlers became known as Babylonians. The Babylonians subjected the Sumerians politically, but they adopted the Sumerian culture as their own. Babylon reached the peak of its glory around 1800 B.C. under the reign of Hammurabi, its sixth monarch, famed for his code of laws. Hammurabi made his own Semitic tongue the official language of his kingdom and he raised the Babylonian gods to supremacy over the old Sumerian deities. Under him, Babylon became the religious and cultural center of western Asia. Even after it was conquered by the militaristic Assyrians, Babylon was looked up to as the source of culture. Though the Assyrians produced little literature of their own, they did preserve in great libraries copies of Babylonian and Sumerian works inscribed on clay tablets.

When her enemies combined to destroy Assyria in 612 B.C., Babylon rose once again to enjoy about seventy years of further glory. Under the reign of Nebuchadnezzar, the city was rebuilt and adorned with fairy-tale palaces and temples in glazed multicolored bricks, terraced gardens, and a great spiral tower that is supposed to be the original "Tower of Babel" (Babel was the Hebrew name for Babylon). Nebuchadnezzar is the king who destroyed Jerusalem and kept the Jews captive in Babylon for seventy years (see Psalm 137, page 35). Babylon lost its independence forever when it fell to Cyrus the Great of Persia, but it remained a center of trade and culture for several centuries, until a new port was dug at a more favorable site on the Euphrates. After that, Babylon fell into ruins.

It should be borne in mind that all the many cultures of this region had the same basic characteristics; hence they may truly be regarded as one "Su-

The Sumerian plaque (c. 2630 B.C.), showing two figures of a king with his children, was probably made for a temple brick-laying rite. The Hebrew manuscript is from Ecclesiastes and dates from the first century B.C.

merian-Babylonian" culture. It was from this Sumerian-Babylonian culture that we acquired the system of time measurement that we still use, the sciences of mathematics and astronomy, and the great tragic epic about Gilgamesh, the king of the Mesopotamian city of Uruk (see page 12).

Even after the Sumerian language ceased to be spoken, it was preserved as a written language. Thus, for a while, Sumerian occupied a position rather like that of Latin in western Europe. The earliest texts of the *Epic of Gilgamesh* are in the Sumerian language, even though most of them were written down long after the Semitic conquest of the Sumerians.

JEWISH HISTORY

Jewish history also begins in Mesopotamia. The first event occurred in about 1800 B.C., when Abraham, a native of the city of Ur of the Chaldees, departed for the land of the Canaanites, a part of Palestine lying between the River Jordan and the Mediterranean. The people of Abraham did not long remain in this new land, for we later find them living much farther to the south, in Egypt. The biblical story of Joseph, Abraham's great-grandson, explains how the Jews came to settle in Egypt.

The favorite of his father Jacob, Joseph was victimized by his jealous older brothers. They sold him out of Canaan into slavery, and Joseph was taken to Egypt. There, by a strange mixture of good and bad fortune, of uprightness, shrewdness, and skill in interpreting the Pharaoh's dreams, Joseph rose to be Egypt's first minister. Eventually, he invited his father, and also his brothers, whom he forgave, to settle in Egypt to escape a famine in Canaan.

Several centuries later, the Jews found themselves reduced to slavery in Egypt and abominably treated by the reigning Pharaoh. A Jewish leader, Moses, arose and led his people out of Egypt, across the Red Sea, and into the Sinai Peninsula. This exodus might have happened in the thirteenth century B.C. Moses died in the wilderness of Sinai, but under his successors, the Jewish people again entered the Promised Land. Gradually, over a period of about two hundred years, the invading Hebrews strengthened their position in battles with other tribes that thickly populated the area—Moabites, Ammonites, Edomites, and especially the Canaanites, who occupied most of Palestine. King David, who reigned from about 1013 B.C. to 973 B.C., finally broke the Philistines' control over the coastal lands of Palestine and captured the old city of Jebus, which, as Jerusalem, became the capital of a strong united Hebrew kingdom. David's son and successor Solomon, who reigned until about 933 B.C., beautified Jerusalem with many handsome buildings. One of the great achievements of Solomon was the centralization of all worship in the magnificent Temple of Jerusalem which he had built as an appendage to the royal palace.

All this cost a great deal of money, however, and the taxes imposed produced serious discontent. After King Solomon's death, the kingdom split into two parts—Israel, later called Samaria, and Judah. It was about this time that the prophets began to warn of dreadful things to come. Samaria, though larger and wealthier than Judah, suffered from political instability. In 721 B.C. it was conquered by the Assyrians, then the great imperialist power in the region, and many of the inhabitants were deported. For some reason the Assyrians did not press their advantage against the kingdom of Judah. Though Judah did not have the internal weaknesses of Samaria, it fell nevertheless to the next expansionist power, Babylonia, in 586 B.C. Jerusalem and the Temple were destroyed, and more of the Jews were led into captivity. Yet these Jews in exile in Babylon managed to preserve their identity. When Cyrus the Great of Persia overthrew the Babylonians in 539 B.C., many of the Jews returned to Palestine. Jerusalem was rebuilt, and the defiled Temple was subsequently restored.

This new Jewish state recognized the overlordship of Persia. As empires waxed and waned, a whole succession of overlords was recognized: Alexander the Great of Macedonia, the Ptolemies of Egypt, and the Seleucids of Syria. Yet there was little internal change until, in 168 B.C., the Seleucid king Antiochus IV decided to suppress the Jewish religion. The reaction to this was a highly successful rebellion, led by various members of the Maccabees family. By 142 B.C. complete independence had been won, and later military campaigns regained all the historical territory of Palestine.

With this, we have reached the end of the Old Testament period. What lay ahead was control of the Jewish state by the Romans, sometimes by direct administration and sometimes through puppet kings like the half-Jewish Herod the Great. In A.D. 70, the city of Jerusalem and the Temple, the center of all Jewish religious life, were once again destroyed.

THE JEWISH RELIGION

According to Hebrew tradition, the first patriarch of the Jews, Abraham, received God's command to depart and to found "a great nation." Other nations had sought to demonstrate their greatness by acting with cruelty and selfishness. But the nation Abraham founded was told to seek a different kind of greatness, and the result would be that, as God told Abraham, "in thee shall all families of the earth be blessed."

The calling of Abraham is mentioned for the first time in the twelfth chapter of Genesis, at the beginning of the Old Testament. The earlier chapters of Genesis (see page 20) have a different story to tell. According to Genesis, God created the world and set Adam and Eve to live happily and forever in the Garden of Eden. But, because of their pride in wanting to be like God, they were expelled from the Garden, and their fall brought about the fall of all mankind. Other sins followed, and men became so wicked that only Noah and his family were allowed to escape drowning in the flood that God sent to cover the whole earth. The children of Noah spread out to repopulate the earth, but once again God had to punish man, this time also for the sin of pride: by building a lofty tower, men thought they could reach heaven. Until then everyone had spoken the same language, but now God spread confusion and interrupted the work of the builders by giving to each of them a different language.

Thus the task of nation-building allotted to Abraham, and the promise made him, represented a very necessary reconciliation between God and man and also set a new goal for man. The rest of the Old Testament is an account of how men tried to carry out God's will—and how, all too often, men's own willfulness and wickedness led them astray. Clearly, the history contained in the Old Testament is told with a stress different from that of the history books. History deals with events that have great political, economic, or cultural importance. But the Old Testament offers us religious history. It is the book of but one people among the many peoples who lived at that time and in that region—a people who at no time play a major political role. The mighty theme that unifies the Old Testament is the slowly evolving relationship between this people, the Jews, and God.

We said that each city of the Sumerians and, indeed, of the other Mesopotamian peoples, had its own god. Yet we cannot speak of the Jews and of "their" god, because their god is Yahweh (meaning "Creator," "Eternal"), the one, universal God, creator of the universe and father of all mankind. While the Bible does not tell us why Abraham was ordered to leave Mesopotamia along with his family, we can be sure that living in a new country set them apart and made it easier for them to stay aloof from the old beliefs and the worship of many gods. But even then, there were many relapses into paganism. The Old Testament rigorously condemns these pagan practices as abominations, yet at times they exercised a strange fascination. On one occasion, the great leader Moses, after a long absence from his people's midst, discovered the Jews, under the guidance of his own brother Aaron, idolatrously dancing around a golden calf.

Through their thundering denunciations of greed, injustice, and ceremonialism, the prophets of Israel, through the centuries, helped the Hebrews develop a purer and highly ethical monotheism. Around the eighth century B.C., the greatest Hebrew prophets emerged and began through their writings to develop another aspect of the Jewish religion, the hope of a Messiah to come, one who would save Israel. At times the prophets speak of the Messiah, the "Anointed One," as a great warrior king; at other times as the suffering servant of his people. Isaiah says that he "hath no form nor comeliness"; he is "despised and rejected of man . . . the Lord hath laid on him the iniquity of us all."

The Bible is a collection of many books. Indeed, the very name comes from *biblia,* the plural of the Greek word *biblion,* "a book." The Christian Bible consists of the Old and New Testaments. The Old Testament—the Bible of the Jews—was written in Hebrew, except for a very few passages in Aramaic, another Semitic tongue which, about 400 B.C., replaced Hebrew as the spoken language of the Jews. The New Testament, which presents the life and teachings of Jesus Christ and reveals something of the concerns of the first Christian communities, was written entirely in Greek.

The word *testament,* as it is used here, means a covenant or solemn agreement by which God promises to bless those who obey him. Early covenants in the Old Testament were God's promises to Noah and Abraham and, through them, to all mankind. But the covenant that gives the Old Testament its name was entered into on Mount Sinai. There Moses, who sometime before 1200 B.C. had led the people of Israel out of their persecution in Egypt, heard the promise: "Now therefore, if ye will obey my voice indeed, and keep my covenant, then ye shall be a peculiar treasure unto me above all people . . ." Moses descended from the mountain to consult the people of Israel. They replied: "All that the Lord hath spoken we will do." That was the old covenant entered into by the Jews. The New Testament, as the name indicates, contains the "new convenant" between God and mankind, established by Christ and ratified by his death.

The contents of the Old Testament were written and assembled over many hundreds of years. Its first part, which is also the earliest, consists of the five books of the Pentateuch, a Greek term meaning "five scroll-jars"—for at one time the five scrolls on which the work is written were kept in jars. The earliest events in Jewish history to which reference is made in Genesis (see page 20), the first of the five books, date back to about 1800 B.C. Scholars tend to think that the Pentateuch was written down in its present form by the fifth century B.C. and is the work of several writers, although throughout the centuries Jews and Christians alike have regarded Moses as its sole author. In addition to the historical content, these five books contain detailed instructions, including the Ten Commandments, on how Jews must worship and how they should conduct themselves in all activities of life. The Hebrew name for these five books, indeed, is *Torah,* usually translated as "The Law." The Torah is held in such reverence that no copy is ever destroyed.

Another main division of the books of the Old Testament consists of the prophetic works. When some people today hear of prophecy and prophets, they may be inclined to think of fortunetellers rather than of those extraordinary men, the Old Testament prophets. The prophets did not in the least resemble fortunetellers. It was their burning desire to call the rulers and people of Israel to repent and to lead a purer life. The prophets rose up from nowhere, with no external signs of authority, with no earthly power or religious institution behind them, and relied solely on the force of their words. They claimed divine inspiration: "Thus saith the Lord!" The major prophets are Isaiah, Jeremiah, and Ezekiel. The first of them saw the collapse of one of the two Jewish kingdoms. The second lived through the destruction of Jerusalem and of the Temple erected by King Solomon. Ezekiel himself lived in exile in Babylon. Despite the immense lapse of time, the denunciations and visions of the prophets still move us. More than that, they come to life and resound for us, too, when it appears that our own age is woefully "out of joint."

The remaining books of the Old Testament are quite varied in character. Some, like those already discussed, relate history or recount visions. The Book of Psalms (see page 30) is filled with hymns of praise and supplication that are intensely lyrical, as is the luxuriant imagery of the Song of Solomon. The Book of Ruth (see page 24) is a tender pastoral; Proverbs, a collection of maxims. The Book of Jonah, classed as a prophetical work, is quietly ironical about this would-be draft-dodger of a prophet, and Ecclesiastes is deeply questioning. A special position is occupied by the Book of Job, for Job dares to question the righteousness of God's treatment of man and wishes to understand the reason for his own suffering. God gives Job an answer in a reply that is magnificent in its poetry, yet that God does not reveal the answer to Job's question is significant. Here the Hebrew writers suggest that there never will be an explanation for human suffering which man can understand.

The Bible, we have said, has a mighty theme, since it traces Israel's developing relationship with God and states both the promises made to man and the demands made of him. But the greatness at the heart of a book exists and actually becomes visible only by means of great writing, and this the Bible provides in plenty. In the English-speaking world especially, where "the Bible" means the King James version of 1611, the Bible has been an inspiration to writers in every century. Up to our own day, familiarity with the Bible's major and minor personages and episodes was taken for granted, even when the readers had little education. To understand fully much of the literature of the past, we need to know the Bible. It is even better to read the Bible on its own account, because it presents men and women whom God confronts with eternal human problems, who must take the right turn or suffer the consequences of taking a wrong one. The Bible's central, permanent, human significance lies in the fact that it keeps these records of a distant past fresh and alive for us.

The Epic of Gilgamesh

The *Epic of Gilgamesh* is one of man's most ancient literary works. The fragmentary stories of Gilgamesh, which have been brought together to make up the epic, probably predate the Golden Age in Greece by as much as that cultural landmark predates the discovery of America. The oldest written fragments of the Gilgamesh stories have been dated from before 2000 B.C., and these seem to record material that was in an even more ancient oral tradition. But whatever the age of the epic, it was preserved to our day only because the great Assyrian emperor Assurbanipal, in the seventh century B.C., had the epic transcribed on twelve clay tablets as a part of the vast library at his capital city of Nineveh. When Nineveh was conquered and utterly destroyed by the Medes and the Babylonians in 612 B.C., that library was buried under the rubble. It was not rediscovered until the nineteenth century, when English archeologists found and carried off to the British Museum for translation some 25,000 clay tablets. Among these tablets, most of which record the business transactions of a thriving commercial center, were the twelve tablets containing the epic. They were not complete or unbroken, and the process of filling in missing details from other written fragments found in other places still continues. But the main outlines of the story of Gilgamesh—a hero once known and admired in many parts of the ancient Middle East—now seem complete and clear.

The story begins with Gilgamesh in his mature manhood, already the restless, dynamic king of the city of Uruk and a semidivine being of great strength who is exhausting his subjects by his sheer energy and ambition. The subjects call for the help of the gods, who answer their petition by creating a match for Gilgamesh, a wild man named Enkidu, who was reared among wild beasts. Lured from his natural life and gradually civilized, Enkidu reaches the city of Uruk, where he and Gilgamesh engage in a titanic wrestling match. Gilgamesh wins, and the two men become close friends.

Together Enkidu and Gilgamesh pursue several heroic adventures, one to the cedar mountain where they cut down the dark forest and kill its guardian Humbaba, an evil demon; another against the monstrous Bull of Heaven, sent by the gods to punish Gilgamesh for rejecting the advances of Ishtar, the goddess of love and war. Though the two men kill the bull, a council of the gods decides one of them must immediately die. Enkidu is chosen and is visited with a disease which soon proves fatal.

Now Gilgamesh, bereft of his friend and tormented by the knowledge that he, too, like all mortals, must some day die, sets out on a journey to find the one man whom the gods have made immortal, Utnapishtim, a "Babylonian Noah," one of Gilgamesh's forefathers. From Utnapishtim, Gilgamesh hopes to learn the secret of eternal life.

The following selections from the epic recount the major episodes of Gilgamesh's journey into the world of the immortals.

be silent, how can I rest? He is dust and I shall die also and be laid in the earth forever." Again Gilgamesh said, speaking to Utnapishtim, "It is to see Utnapishtim whom we call the Faraway that I have come this journey. For this I have wandered over the world, I have crossed many difficult ranges, I have crossed the seas, I have wearied myself with traveling; my joints are aching, and I have lost acquaintance with sleep which is sweet. My clothes were worn out before I came to the house of Siduri. I have killed the bear and hyena, the lion and panther, the tiger, the stag and the ibex, all sorts of wild game and the small creatures of the pastures. I ate their flesh and I wore their skins; and that was how I came to the gate of the young woman, the maker of wine, who barred her gate of pitch and bitumen against me. But from her I had news of the journey; so then I came to Urshanabi the ferryman, and with him I crossed over the waters of death. Oh, father Utnapishtim, you who have entered the assembly of the gods, I wish to question you concerning the living and the dead, how shall I find the life for which I am searching?"

Utnapishtim said, "There is no permanence. Do we build a house to stand forever, do we seal a contract to hold for all time? Do brothers divide an inheritance to keep forever, does the flood-time of rivers endure? It is only the nymph of the dragonfly who sheds her larva and sees the sun in his glory. From the days of old there is no permanence. The sleeping and the dead, how alike they are, they are like a painted death. What is there between the master and the servant when both have fulfilled their doom? When the Annunaki, the judges, come together, and Mammetun, the mother of destinies, together they decree the fates of men. Life and death they allot but the day of death they do not disclose."

.   .   .

[Now Utnapishtim tells Gilgamesh the story of how he came to possess everlasting life. It seems that at one time an assembly of the gods decided to let loose a flood and destroy mankind. But Utnapishtim was warned of the plan by one kind god and was ordered to build a boat. This he did, and when the deluge came and all the world was smashed by a raging tempest, Utnapishtim rode out the storm in safety. On the seventh day the dreadful storm was ended, and when Utnapishtim looked out upon the earth he saw that all mankind, except himself and his wife, had been turned into clay. Even the gods were now shocked at what they had done, and as reparation they took Utnapishtim and his wife to live forever with them in their home.]

The Return

UTNAPISHTIM said, "As for you, Gilgamesh, who will assemble the gods for your sake, so that you may find that life for which you are searching? But if you wish, come and put it to the test: only prevail against sleep for six days and seven nights." But while Gilgamesh sat there resting on his haunches, a mist of sleep like soft wool teased from the fleece drifted over him, and Utnapishtim said to his wife, "Look at him now, the strong man who would have everlasting life, even now the mists of sleep are drifting over him." His wife replied, "Touch the man to wake him, so that he may return to his own land in peace, going back through the gate by which he came." Utnapishtim said to his wife, "All men are deceivers, even you he will attempt to deceive; therefore bake loaves of bread, each day one loaf, and put it beside his head; and make a mark on the wall to number the days he has slept."

So she baked loaves of bread, each day one loaf, and put it beside his head, and she marked on the wall the days that he slept; and there came a day when the first loaf was hard, the second loaf was like leather, the third was soggy, the crust of the fourth had mold, the fifth was mildewed, the sixth was fresh, and the seventh was still on the embers. Then Utnapishtim touched him and he woke. Gil-

The Search for Everlasting Life

BITTERLY Gilgamesh wept for his friend Enkidu; he wandered over the wilderness as a hunter, he roamed over the plains; in his bitterness he cried, "How can I rest, how can I be at peace? Despair is in my heart. What my brother is now, that shall I be when I am dead. Because I am afraid of death I will go as best I can to find Utnapishtim whom they call the Faraway, for he has entered the assembly of the gods." So Gilgamesh traveled over the wilderness, he wandered over the grasslands, a long journey, in search of Utnapishtim, whom the gods took after the deluge; and they set him to live in the land of Dilmun, in the garden of the sun; and to him alone of men they gave everlasting life.

At night when he came to the mountain passes Gilgamesh prayed: "In these mountain passes long ago I saw lions, I was afraid and I lifted my eyes to the moon; I prayed and my prayers went up to the gods, so now, O moon god Sin, protect me." When he had prayed he lay down to sleep, until he was woken from out of a dream. He saw the lions round him glorying in life; then he took his axe in his hand, he drew his sword from his belt, and he fell upon them like an arrow from the string, and struck and destroyed and scattered them.

So at length Gilgamesh came to that great mountain whose name is Mashu, the mountain which guards the rising and the setting sun. Its twin peaks are as high as the wall of heaven and its paps reach down to the underworld. At its gate the Scorpions stand guard, half man and half dragon; their glory is terrifying, their stare strikes death into men, their shimmering

From *The Epic of Gilgamesh*, an English version by N. K. Sandars. Reprinted by permission of Penguin Books Ltd.

halo sweeps the mountains that guard the rising sun. When Gilgamesh saw them he shielded his eyes for the length of a moment only; then he took courage and approached. When they saw him so undismayed the Man-Scorpion called to his mate, "This one who comes to us now is flesh of the gods." The mate of the Man-Scorpion answered, "Two thirds is god but one third is man."

Then he called to the man Gilgamesh, he called to the child of the gods: "Why have you come so great a journey; for what have you traveled so far, crossing the dangerous waters; tell me the reason for your coming?" Gilgamesh answered, "For Enkidu; I loved him dearly, together we endured all kinds of hardships; on his account I have come, for the common lot of man has taken him. I have wept for him day and night, I would not give up his body for burial, I thought my friend would come back because of my weeping. Since he went, my life is nothing; that is why I have traveled here in search of Utnapishtim my father; for men say he has entered the assembly of the gods, and has found everlasting life. I have a desire to question him concerning the living and the dead." The Man-Scorpion opened his mouth and said, speaking to Gilgamesh, "No man born of woman has done what you have asked, no mortal man has gone into the mountain; the length of it is twelve leagues of darkness; in it there is no light, but the heart is oppressed with darkness. From the rising of the sun to the setting of the sun there is no light." Gilgamesh said, "Although I should go in sorrow and in pain, with sighing and with weeping, still I must go. Open the gate of the mountain." And the Man-Scorpion said, "Go, Gilgamesh, I permit you to pass through the mountain of Mashu and through the high ranges; may your feet carry you safely home. The gate of the mountain is open."

When Gilgamesh heard this he did as the Man-Scorpion had said, he followed the sun's road to his rising, through the mountain. When he had gone one league the darkness became thick around him, for there was no light, he could see nothing ahead and nothing behind him. After two leagues the darkness was thick and there was no light, he could see nothing ahead and nothing behind him. After three leagues the darkness was thick, and there was no light, he could see nothing ahead and nothing behind him. After four leagues the darkness was thick and there was no light, he could see nothing ahead and nothing behind him. At the end of five leagues the darkness was thick and there was no light, he could see nothing ahead and nothing behind him. At the end of six leagues the darkness was thick and there was no light, he could see nothing ahead and nothing behind him. When he had gone seven leagues the darkness was thick and there was no light, he could see nothing ahead and nothing behind him. When he had gone eight leagues Gilgamesh gave a great cry, for the darkness was thick and he could see nothing ahead and nothing behind him. After nine leagues he felt the north wind on his face, but the darkness was thick and there was no light, he could see nothing ahead and nothing behind him. After ten leagues the end was near. After eleven leagues the dawn light appeared. At the end of twelve leagues the sun streamed out.

There was the garden of the gods; all round him stood bushes bearing gems. Seeing it he went down at once, for there was fruit of carnelian with the vine hanging from it, beautiful to look at; lapis lazuli leaves hung thick with fruit, sweet to see. For thorns and thistles there were hematite and rare stones, agate, and pearls from out of the sea. While Gilgamesh walked in the garden by the edge of the sea, Shamash[1] saw him, and he saw that he was dressed in the skins of animals and ate their flesh. He was distressed, and he spoke and said, "No mortal man has gone this way before, nor will, as long as the winds drive over the sea." And to Gilgamesh he said, "You will never find the life for which you are searching." Gil-

---

[1] **Shamash:** the all-knowing and just Sun God.

gamesh said to glorious Shamash, "Now that I have toiled and strayed so far over the wilderness, am I to sleep and let the earth cover my head forever? Let my eyes see the sun until they are dazzled with looking. Although I am no better than a dead man, still let me see the light of the sun."

Beside the sea she lives, the woman of the vine, the maker of wine; Siduri sits in the garden at the edge of the sea, with the golden bowl and the golden vats that the gods gave her. She is covered with a veil; and where she sits she sees Gilgamesh coming toward her, wearing skins, the flesh of the gods in his body but despair in his heart, and his face like the face of one who has made a long journey. She looked, and as she scanned the distance she said in her own heart, "Surely this is some felon; where is he going now?" And she barred her gate against him with the crossbar and shot home the bolt. But Gilgamesh, hearing the sound of the bolt, threw up his head and lodged his foot in the gate; he called to her, "Young woman, maker of wine, why do you bolt your door; what did you see that made you bar your gate? I will break in your door and burst in your gate, for I am Gilgamesh who seized and killed the Bull of Heaven, I killed the watchman of the cedar forest, I overthrew Humbaba who lived in the forest, and I killed the lions in the passes of the mountain."

Then Siduri said to him, "If you are that Gilgamesh who seized and killed the Bull of Heaven, who killed the watchman of the cedar forest, who overthrew Humbaba that lived in the forest, and killed the lions in the passes of the mountain, why are your cheeks so starved and why is your face so drawn? Why is despair in your heart and your face like the face of one who has made a long journey? Yes, why is your face burned from heat and cold, and why do you come here wandering over the pastures in search of the wind?"

Gilgamesh answered her, "And why should not my cheeks be starved and my

face drawn? Despair is in my heart and my face is the face of one who has made a long journey, it was burned with heat and with cold. Why should I not wander over the pastures in search of the wind? My friend, my younger brother, he who hunted the wild ass of the wilderness and the panther of the plains, my friend, my younger brother who seized and killed the Bull of Heaven and overthrew Humbaba in the cedar forest, my friend who was very dear to me and who endured dangers beside me, Enkidu my brother, whom I loved, the end of mortality has overtaken him. I wept for him seven days and nights till the worm fastened on him. Because of my brother I am afraid of death, because of my brother I stray through the wilderness and cannot rest. But now young woman, maker of wine, since I have seen your face do not let me see the face of death which I dread so much."

She answered, "Gilgamesh, where are you hurrying to? You will never find that life for which you are looking. When the gods created man they allotted to him death, but life they retained in their own keeping. As for you, Gilgamesh, fill your belly with good things; day and night, night and day, dance and be merry, feast and rejoice. Let your clothes be fresh, bathe yourself in water, cherish the little child that holds your hand, and make your wife happy in your embrace; for this, too, is the lot of man."

But Gilgamesh said to Siduri, the young woman, "How can I be silent, how can I rest, when Enkidu whom I love is dust, and I too shall die and be laid in the earth forever." He said again, "Young woman, tell me now, which is the way to Utnapishtim, the son of Ubara-Tutu? What directions are there for the passage; give me, oh, give me directions. I will cross the Ocean if it is possible; if it is not I will wander still farther in the wilderness." . . .

[The young woman sends Gilgamesh down in the woods, to find Urshanabi, the ferryman. He brings the hero across the Ocean and over the waters of death.]

So Urshanabi the ferryman brought Gilgamesh to Utnapishtim, whom they call the Faraway, who lives in Dilmun at the place of the sun's transit, eastward of the mountain. To him alone of men the gods had given everlasting life.

Now Utnapishtim, where he lay at ease, looked into the distance, and he said in his heart, musing to himself, ". . . That man who comes is none of mine; where I look I see a man whose body is covered with skins of beasts. Who is this who walks up the shore behind Urshanabi, for surely he is no man of mine?" So Utnapishtim looked at him and said, "What is your name, you who come here wearing the skins of beasts, with your cheeks starved and your face drawn? Where are you hurrying to now? For what reason have you made this great journey, crossing the seas whose passage is difficult? Tell me the reason for your coming."

He replied, "Gilgamesh is my name, I am from Uruk, from the house of Anu." Then Utnapishtim said to him, "If you are Gilgamesh, why are your cheeks so starved and your face drawn? Why is despair in your heart and your face like the face of one who has made a long journey? Yes, why is your face burned with heat and cold; and why do you come here, wandering over the wilderness in search of the wind?"

Gilgamesh said to him, "Why should not my cheeks be starved and my face drawn? Despair is in my heart and my face is the face of one who has made a long journey. It was burned with heat and cold. Why should I not wander over the pastures? My friend, my younger brother who seized and killed the Bull of Heaven and overthrew Humbaba in the cedar forest, my friend who was very dear to me and who endured dangers beside me, Enkidu, my brother whom I loved, the end of mortality has overtaken him. I wept for him seven days and nights till the worm fastened on him. Because of my brother I am afraid of death; because of my brother I stray through the wilderness. His fate lies heavy upon me. How can I

gamesh said to Utnapishtim the Faraway, "I hardly slept when you touched and roused me." But Utnapishtim said, "Count these loaves and learn how many days you slept, for your first is hard, your second is like leather, your third is soggy, the crust of your fourth has mold, your fifth is mildewed, your sixth is fresh, and your seventh was still over the glowing embers when I touched and woke you." Gilgamesh said, "What shall I do, O Utnapishtim, where shall I go? Already the thief in the night has hold of my limbs, death inhabits my room; wherever my foot rests, there I find death."

Then Utnapishtim spoke to Urshanabi the ferryman: "Woe to you Urshanabi, now and forever more you have become hateful to this harborage; it is not for you, nor for you are the crossings of this sea. Go now, banished from the shore. But this man before whom you walked, bringing him here, whose body is covered with foulness and the grace of whose limbs has been spoiled by wild skins, take him to the washing-place. There he shall wash his long hair clean as snow in the water, he shall throw off his skins and let the sea carry them away, and the beauty of his body shall be shown, the fillet [1] on his forehead shall be renewed, and he shall be given clothes to cover his nakedness. Till he reaches his own city and his journey is accomplished, these clothes will show no sign of age, they will wear like a new garment." So Urshanabi took Gilgamesh and led him to the washing-place, he washed his long hair as clean as snow in the water, he threw off his skins, which the sea carried away, and showed the beauty of his body. He renewed the fillet on his forehead, and to cover his nakedness gave him clothes which would show no sign of age, but would wear like a new garment till he reached his own city, and his journey was accomplished.

Then Gilgamesh and Urshanabi launched the boat on to the water and

boarded it, and they made ready to sail away; but the wife of Utnapishtim the Faraway said to him, "Gilgamesh came here wearied out, he is worn out; what will you give him to carry him back to his own country?" So Utnapishtim spoke, and Gilgamesh took a pole and brought the boat to the bank. "Gilgamesh, you came here, a man wearied out, you have worn yourself out, what shall I give you to carry you back to your own country? Gilgamesh, I shall reveal a secret thing, it is a mystery of the gods that I am telling you. There is a plant that grows under the water, it has a prickle like a thorn, like a rose; it will wound your hands, but if you succeed in taking it, then your hands will hold that which restores his lost youth to a man."

When Gilgamesh heard this he opened the sluices so that a sweet-water current might carry him out to the deepest channel; he tied heavy stones to his feet and they dragged him down to the water-bed. There he saw the plant growing; although it pricked him he took it in his hands; then he cut the heavy stones from his feet, and the sea carried him and threw him on to the shore. Gilgamesh said to Urshanabi the ferryman, "Come here, and see this marvelous plant. By its virtue a man may win back all his former strength. I will take it to Uruk of the strong walls; there I will give it to the old men to eat. Its name shall be 'The Old Men Are Young Again'; and at last I shall eat it myself and have back all my lost youth." So Gilgamesh returned by the gate through which he had come, Gilgamesh and Urshanabi went together. They traveled their twenty leagues and then they broke their fast; after thirty leagues they stopped for the night.

Gilgamesh saw a well of cool water and he went down and bathed; but deep in the pool there was lying a serpent, and the serpent sensed the sweetness of the flower. It rose out of the water and snatched it away, and immediately it sloughed its skin and returned to the well. Then Gilgamesh sat down and wept, the tears ran

---

[1] **fillet:** a narrow headband or ribbon.

down his face, and he took the hand of Urshanabi; "O Urshanabi, was it for this that I toiled with my hands, is it for this I have wrung out my heart's blood? For myself I have gained nothing; not I, but the beast of the earth has joy of it now. Already the stream has carried it twenty leagues back to the channels where I found it. I found a sign and now I have lost it. Let us leave the boat on the bank and go."

After twenty leagues they broke their fast, after thirty leagues they stopped for the night; in three days they had walked as much as a journey of a month and fifteen days. When the journey was accomplished they arrived at Uruk, the strong-walled city. Gilgamesh spoke to him, to Urshanabi the ferryman, "Urshanabi, climb up on to the wall of Uruk, inspect its foundation terrace, and examine well the brickwork; see if it is not of burnt bricks; and did not the seven wise men lay these foundations? One third of the whole is city, one third is garden, and one third is field, with the precinct of the goddess Ishtar. These parts and the precinct are all Uruk."

This too was the work of Gilgamesh, the king, who knew the countries of the world. He was wise, he saw mysteries and knew secret things, he brought us a tale of the days before the flood. He went a long journey, was weary, worn out with labor, and returning engraved on a stone the whole story.

The Death of Gilgamesh

THE DESTINY was fulfilled which the father of the gods, Enlil of the mountain, had decreed for Gilgamesh: "In nether-earth the darkness will show him a light; of mankind, all that are known, none will leave a monument for generations to come to compare with his. The heroes, the wise men, like the new moon have their waxing and waning. Men will say, 'Who has ever ruled with might and with power like him?' As in the dark month, the month of shadows, so without him there is no light. O Gilgamesh, this was the meaning of your dream. You were given the kingship, such was your destiny, everlasting life was not your destiny. Because of this do not be sad at heart, do not be grieved or oppressed; he has given you power to bind and to loose, to be the darkness and the light of mankind. He has given unexampled supremacy over the people, victory in battle from which no fugitive returns, in forays and assaults from which there is no going back. But do not abuse this power, deal justly with your servants in the palace, deal justly before the face of the Sun."

> The king has laid himself down
> and will not rise again,
> The Lord of Kullab will not rise
> again;
> He overcame evil, he will not
> come again;
> Though he was strong of arm he
> will not rise again;
> He had wisdom and a comely
> face, he will not come again;
> He is gone into the mountain, he
> will not come again;
> On the bed of fate he lies, he will
> not rise again,
> From the couch of many colors
> he will not come again.

The people of the city, great and small, are not silent; they lift up the lament, all men of flesh and blood lift up the lament. Fate has spoken; like a hooked fish he lies stretched on the bed, like a gazelle that is caught in a noose. Inhuman Namtar [1] is heavy upon him, Namtar that has neither hand nor foot, that drinks no water and eats no meat.

· · · ·

Gilgamesh, the son of Ninsun, lies in the tomb. At the place of offerings he weighed the bread-offering, at the place

[1] **Namtar:** Fate, pictured as a demon from the underworld.

of libation he poured out the wine. In those days the lord Gilgamesh departed, the son of Ninsun, the king, peerless, without an equal among men, who did not neglect Enlil his master. O Gilgamesh, lord of Kullab, great is thy praise.

FOR STUDY AND DISCUSSION

1. As these selections from the epic open, Gilgamesh is grieving for Enkidu. In what way is he also grieving for himself? What might be the reason for Gilgamesh's killing the lions of the mountain passes? What might this act tell about his state of mind?

2. Gilgamesh's trip through the mountain Mashu is described simply but with considerable dramatic effectiveness. What phrases are repeated over and over again? What is the effect of this repetition? What small variations in phrasing are used? How do they contribute to the dramatic effect? This whole passage, describing a fearful enterprise which Gilgamesh begins with confident energy, endures in terror, and completes with relieved success, is told with great understatement. Does a hero seem more or less heroic when his deeds are understated? Why?

3. A familiar device found in any literature which has been in the oral tradition is that of repetition, particularly repetition of questions and answers. What examples of such repetition can you find in the passage describing the meeting between Siduri and Gilgamesh?

4. Although Siduri eventually gives Gilgamesh directions for crossing the Ocean and the waters of death, she first tells him that he will never find eternal life. In a famous passage, she advises him to seek the familiar pleasures of men, "for this, too, is the lot of man," she says. What are these pleasures? Could a man like Gilgamesh ever find satisfaction in them? Could most men? Explain.

5. Why did Utnapishtim resort to the trick of the loaves to prove to Gilgamesh how long he had slept? This incident, in which Gilgamesh is unable to stay awake, has great sym-

bolic significance. What might Gilgamesh's inability to fight off sleep symbolize?

6. What might Gilgamesh's loss of the magic flower symbolize? To what use did he intend to put the magic flower? What does this intention say about Gilgamesh's character?

7. The theme of this portion of the epic is the mortality of man. Is the tone of the story angry, pessimistic, optimistic, accepting? Cite passages of the story to support your answer. Did the people who told this story seem to believe in the possibility of a happy afterlife? Explain. Some people feel that awareness of the fact of death makes life more precious, more to be enjoyed. Others feel that the inevitability of death poisons all of life's pleasures. Find passages from the story in which Gilgamesh reveals his feelings about this question.

8. What does the term *epic* mean? In what ways does the story of Gilgamesh qualify as an epic?

FOR COMPOSITION

Many works of literature are based on the quest-myth: the story of the hero who sets out on a long and difficult journey to search for something, perhaps for a real object of great value, perhaps for something intangible. In the *Epic of Gilgamesh,* the hero quests for immortality. Write a brief essay showing how some modern story is based on the quest-myth. You might choose something from the printed media (perhaps even a comic strip), or something from the visual media, a movie or a television show. In your essay, consider these questions: What was the hero searching for? What series of adventures did the quest lead him through? Did he succeed in his quest? Was he rewarded when his quest was over? Did he discover anything through his quest, perhaps a true vision of himself, perhaps a secret knowledge of something concealed or forbidden to most people? In what ways did this quest and its outcome resemble that of Gilgamesh?

Genesis

The first five books of the Old Testament deal generally with the history of the Jews up to the death of Moses. Genesis, the first book of the Old Testament, is a book about "beginnings": the beginning of the world, the creation of man, the emergence of evil, the cause of the flood, the origins of languages. From these stories of remote universal beginnings, Genesis moves into more particular concerns, into the beginnings of the Jewish people and the lives of their great forefathers, Abraham, Isaac, Jacob, and Joseph.

Genesis and the four historical books that follow it are thought to be based on about four separate narratives. The first contributor is believed to have lived in the period around 950 B.C., the last in the period around 550 B.C. The compiling and editing of these ancient narratives was carried out gradually by later Hebrew writers. The Pentateuch, as these five books are called, did not take its final form until relatively late, perhaps not until 400 B.C.

The first three chapters of Genesis follow. They appear here in a modern translation that was made directly from the Hebrew, the original language of the Old Testament.

Creation

WHEN GOD set about to create heaven and earth—the world being then a formless waste, with darkness over the seas and only an awesome wind sweeping over the water—God said, "Let there be light." And there was light. God was pleased with the light that he saw, and he separated the light from the darkness. God called the light Day, and he called the darkness Night. Thus evening came, and morning—first day.

God said, "Let there be an expanse in the middle of the water to form a division between the waters." And it was so. God made the expanse, and it divided the water below it from the water above it. God called the expanse Sky. Thus evening came, and morning—second day.

God said, "Let the water beneath the sky be gathered into a single area, that the dry land may be visible." And it was so. God called the dry land Earth, and he called the gathered waters Seas. God was pleased with what he saw, and he said, "Let the earth burst forth with growth: plants that bear seed, and every kind of fruit tree on earth that bears fruit with its seed in it." And it was so. The earth produced growth: various kinds of seed-bearing plants, and trees of every kind bearing fruit with seed in it. And God was pleased with what he saw. Thus evening came, and morning—third day.

From *Genesis (Anchor Bible)*, translated, with an introduction and notes by E. A. Speiser, copyright © 1964 by Doubleday & Company, Inc. Reprinted by permission of the publisher.

God said, "Let there be lights in the expanse of the sky, to distinguish between day and night; let them mark the fixed times, the days and the years, and serve as lights in the expanse of the sky to shine upon the earth." And it was so. God made the great lights, the greater one to dominate the day and the lesser one to dominate the night—and the stars. God set them in the expanse of the sky to shine upon the earth, to dominate the day and the night, and to distinguish between light and darkness. And God was pleased with what he saw. Thus evening came, and morning—fourth day.

God said, "Let the waters teem with swarms of living creatures, and let birds fly above the earth across the expanse of the sky." And it was so. God created the great sea monsters, every kind of crawling creature with which the waters teem, and all kinds of winged birds. And God was pleased with what he saw. God blessed them, saying, "Be fertile and increase; fill the waters in the seas, and let the birds multiply on earth." Thus evening came, and morning—fifth day.

God said, "Let the earth bring forth various kinds of living creatures: cattle, creeping things, and wild animals of every kind." And it was so. God made various kinds of wild animals, cattle of every kind, and all the creeping things of the earth, whatever their kind. And God was pleased with what he saw.

Then God said, "I will make man in my image, after my likeness; let him subject the fish of the sea and the birds of the sky, the cattle and all the wild [animals], and all the creatures that creep on earth."

And God created man in his image;
In the divine image created he him,
Male and female created he them.

God blessed them, saying to them, "Be fertile and increase, fill the earth and subdue it; subject the fishes of the sea, the birds of the sky, and all the living things that move on earth." God further said, "See, I give you every seed-bearing plant on earth and every tree that bears fruit; they shall be yours for food. And to all the animals on land, all the birds of the sky, and all the living creatures that crawl on earth [I give] all the green plants as their food." And it was so. God looked at everything that he had made and found it very pleasing. Thus evening came, and morning—sixth day.

Now the heaven and the earth were completed, and all their company. On the seventh day God brought to a close the work that he had been doing, and he ceased on the seventh day from all the work that he had undertaken. God blessed the seventh day and declared it holy, for on it he ceased from all the work which he had undertaken.

Such is the story of heaven and earth as they were created.

The Story of Eden

AT THE TIME when God Yahweh made earth and heaven—no shrub of the field being yet in the earth and no grains of the field having sprouted, for God Yahweh had not sent rain upon the earth and no man was there to till the soil; instead, a flow would well up from the ground and water the whole surface of the soil—God Yahweh formed man from clods in the soil and blew into his nostrils the breath of life. Thus man became a living being.

God Yahweh planted a garden in Eden, in the east, and placed there the man whom he had formed. And out of the ground God Yahweh caused to grow various trees that were a delight to the eye and good for eating, with the tree of life in the middle of the garden and the tree of knowledge of good and bad.

A river rises in Eden to water the garden; outside, it forms four separate branch streams. The name of the first is Pishon; it is the one that winds through the whole land of Havilah, where there is gold. The gold of that land is choice; there is bdellium [1] there, and lapis lazuli. The name of the second river is Gihon; it is the one that winds through all of the land of Cush. The name of the third river is Tigris; it is the one that flows east of Asshur. The fourth river is the Euphrates.

God Yahweh took the man and settled him in the garden of Eden, to till and tend it. And God Yahweh commanded the man, saying, "You are free to eat of any tree of the garden, except only the tree of knowledge of good and bad, of which you are not to eat. For the moment you eat of it, you shall be doomed to death."

God Yahweh said, "It is not right that man should be alone. I will make him an aid fit for him." So God Yahweh formed out of the soil various wild beasts and birds of the sky and brought them to the man to see what he called them; whatever the man would call a living creature, that was to be its name. The man gave names to all cattle, all birds of the sky, and all wild beasts; yet none proved to be the aid that would be fit for man.

Then God Yahweh cast a deep sleep upon the man and, when he was asleep, he took one of his ribs and closed up the flesh at that spot. And God Yahweh fashioned into a woman the rib that he had removed from the man, and he brought her to the man. Said the man,

This one at last is bone of my bones and flesh of my flesh.

She shall be called Woman, for she was taken from Man. Thus it is that man leaves his father and mother and clings to his wife, and they become one flesh.

The Fall of Man

THE TWO of them were naked, the man and his wife, yet they felt no shame. Now the serpent was the sliest of all the

[1] **bdellium** (del′ē·əm): probably crystal, pearl, or amber.

wild creatures that God Yahweh had made. Said he to the woman. "Even though God told you not to eat of any tree in the garden . . ." The woman interrupted the serpent, "But we may eat of the trees in the garden! It is only about the fruit of the tree in the middle of the garden that God did say, 'Do not eat of it or so much as touch it, lest you die!' " But the serpent said to the woman, "You are not going to die. No, God well knows that the moment you eat of it your eyes will be opened and you will be the same as God in telling good from bad."

When the woman saw that the tree was good for eating and a delight to the eye, and that the tree was attractive as a means to wisdom, she took of its fruit and ate; and she gave some to her husband and he ate. Then the eyes of both were opened and they discovered that they were naked; so they sewed fig leaves together and made themselves loincloths.

They heard the sound of God Yahweh as he was walking in the garden at the breezy time of day; and the man and his wife hid from God Yahweh among the trees of the garden.

God Yahweh called to the man and said to him, "Where are you?" He answered, "I heard the sound of you in the garden; but I was afraid because I was naked, so I hid." He asked, "Who told you that you were naked? Did you, then, taste of the tree from which I had forbidden you to eat?" The man replied, "The woman whom you put by my side— it was she who gave me of that tree, and I ate." God Yahweh said to the woman, "How could you do such a thing?" The woman replied, "The serpent tricked me, so I ate."

God Yahweh said to the serpent:

"Because you did this,
    Banned shall you be from all cattle
    And all wild creatures!
    On your belly shall you crawl
    And on dirt shall you feed
    All the days of your life.

I will plant enmity between you and
the woman,
And between your offspring and hers;
They shall strike at your head,
And you shall strike at their heel."

To the woman he said:

"I will make intense
Your pangs in childbearing.
In pain shall you bear children;
Yet your urge shall be for your hus-
band,
And he shall be your master."

To the man he said: "Because you
listened to your wife and ate of the tree
from which I had forbidden you to eat,

Condemned be the soil on your ac-
count!
In anguish shall you eat of it
All the days of your life.
Thorns and thistles
Shall it bring forth for you,
As you feed on the grasses of the
field.
By the sweat of your face
Shall you earn your bread,
Until you return to the ground,
For from it you were taken:
For dust you are
And to dust you shall return!"

The man named his wife Eve, because
she was the mother of all the living. And
God Yahweh made shirts of skins for the
man and his wife, and clothed them.

God Yahweh said, "Now that the man
has become like one of us in discerning
good from bad, what if he should put out
his hand and taste also of the tree of life
and eat, and live forever!" So God
Yahweh banished him from the garden of
Eden, to till the soil from which he was
taken. Having expelled the man, he stationed east of the garden of Eden the
cherubim and the fiery revolving sword to
guard the way to the tree of life.

FOR STUDY AND DISCUSSION

CREATION

1. What two phrases are most often repeated in this account? What characteristics
of God do the Hebrew writers emphasize by
repeating these phrases?

2. In what lines do the Hebrew writers
stress that God ordained order and purpose
in the universe? How would they explain the
disorder man sees around him? How would
you explain the line "And God made man in
his image"? According to this account, what
is the position of man in relation to God? to
nature?

THE STORY OF EDEN

1. Genesis was not the work of an individual. From studying textual differences,
Biblical scholars have agreed that "Creation"
and "The Story of Eden," for example, show
the work of two different writers. In "The
Story of Eden" man, not the universe, is the
center of interest. Compare the ways the creation of man is described in these two accounts.
What significances can you find in the differences and in the similarities? According to
"The Story of Eden," why did God create
woman? What attitude toward marriage does
this account reveal?

2. What attitude of God toward man do the
Hebrew writers stress in this story?

THE FALL OF MAN

1. The center of interest in this account is
perhaps the tree of knowledge. How does
the serpent tempt Eve to eat of this tree? Do
you think the serpent is distorting what God
said? Explain.

2. What part does a serpent play in the *Epic
of Gilgamesh* (see page 17)? How is the
magic plant in that epic similar to the fruit of
the forbidden tree in Eden? Was what Adam
and Eve desired similar in any way to what
Gilgamesh desired and quested for? Explain.

3. What problems that still puzzle mankind
find answers in this chapter? How do the
Hebrew writers establish a concept of a God
who is just?

The Book of Ruth

Although the opening lines of this famous story place it in the time when the judges ruled Israel, perhaps about 1100 B.C., scholars believe it was actually written some seven hundred years later, after the time when the Jewish people had returned to their homeland from a long and bitter captivity in Babylon. The Hebrew prophets of this time, fearful that the Jews would assimilate with the pagans around them, were condemning mixed marriages and advocating the expulsion of all foreign wives. It is possible that the author of the Book of Ruth was moved by the intolerance of the times to write this story, in which he emphasizes compassion toward outsiders who accept the faith of Israel.

The land of Moab, Ruth's home, was near Israel. The Moabite religion, however, was a pagan one, probably consisting of idol-worship which was an abomination to Israel. Naomi and her family were devout Hebrews, from the district of Bethlehem and the tribe of Judah.

The representation of ancient Israelite customs in the story of Ruth is authentic and unusually revealing. One of these customs is the so-called levirite marriage (from *levir,* Latin for "brother-in-law"), according to which a man was duty-bound to marry his brother's widow or the widow of his next of kin if the dead man had had no sons. The first male child born to the childless widow would, for legal purposes, be regarded as the dead husband's son.

This translation of the Book of Ruth is taken from the King James Bible.

CHAPTER 1

Now it came to pass in the days when the judges ruled that there was a famine in the land. And a certain man of Bethlehem-Judah went to sojourn in the country of Moab, he, and his wife, and his two sons.

And the name of the man was Elimelech, and the name of his wife Naomi, and the name of his two sons Mahlon and Chilion, Ephraphites of Bethlehem-Judah. And they came into the country of Moab and continued there.

And Elimelech, Naomi's husband died; and she was left, and her two sons.

And they took them wives of the women of Moab; the name of the one was Orpah, and the name of the other Ruth: and they dwelled there about ten years.

And Mahlon and Chilion died also, both of them; and the woman was left of her two sons and her husband.

Then she arose with her daughters-in-law, that she might return from the country of Moab: for she had heard in the country of Moab how that the Lord had visited his people in giving them bread.

Wherefore she went forth out of the place where she was, and her two daughters-in-law with her; and they went on the way to return unto the land of Judah.

And Naomi said unto her two daughters-in-law, "Go, return each to her mother's house: the Lord deal kindly with you, as ye have dealt with the dead and with me. The Lord grant you that ye may find rest, each of you in the house of her husband." Then she kissed them; and they lifted up their voice and wept.

And they said unto her, "Surely we will return with thee unto thy people."

And Naomi said, "Turn again, my daughters: why will ye go with me? Are there yet any more sons in my womb, that they may be your husbands?

"Turn again, my daughters, go your way; for I am too old to have a husband. If I should say I have hope, if I should have a husband also tonight and should also bear sons, would ye tarry for them till they were grown? Would ye stay for them from having husbands? Nay, my daughters; for it grieveth me much for your sakes that the hand of the Lord is gone out against me."

And they lifted up their voice and wept again: and Orpah kissed her mother-in-law, but Ruth clave unto her.

And she said, "Behold, thy sister-in-law is gone back unto her people and unto her gods: Return thou after thy sister-in-law."

And Ruth said, "Entreat me not to leave thee or to return from following after thee: for whither thou goest, I will go; and where thou lodgest, I will lodge: thy people shall be my people, and thy God my God: where thou diest, will I die, and there will I be buried: the Lord do so to me, and more also, if ought but death part thee and me."

When she saw that she was steadfastly minded to go with her, then she left speaking unto her.

So they two went until they came to Bethlehem. And it came to pass, when they were come to Bethlehem, that all the city was moved about them, and they said, "Is this Naomi?"

And she said unto them, "Call me not Naomi, call me Mara: [1] for the Almighty hath dealt very bitterly with me. I went out full, and the Lord hath brought me home again empty: why then call ye me Naomi, seeing the Lord hath testified against me, and the Almighty hath afflicted me?"

So Naomi returned, and Ruth the Moabitess, her daughter-in-law, with her, which returned out of the country of Moab: and they came to Bethlehem in the beginning of barley harvest.

CHAPTER 2

AND NAOMI had a kinsman of her husband's, a mighty man of wealth, of the family of Elimelech; and his name was Boaz.

And Ruth the Moabitess said unto Naomi, "Let me now go to the field and glean ears of corn after him in whose sight I shall find grace." And she said unto her, "Go, my daughter."

And she went, and came, and gleaned in the field after the reapers: and her hap [2] was to light on a part of the field belonging unto Boaz, who was of the kindred of Elimelech.

And, behold, Boaz came from Bethlehem and said unto the reapers, "The Lord be with you." And they answered him, "The Lord bless thee."

Then said Boaz unto his servant that was set over the reapers, "Whose damsel is this?"

[1] **Mara:** a Hebrew name meaning "bitter." *Naomi* means "sweet."
[2] **hap:** luck.

And the servant that was set over the reapers answered and said, "It is the Moabitish damsel that came back with Naomi out of the country of Moab. And she said, 'I pray you, let me glean and gather after the reapers among the sheaves': so she came, and hath continued even from the morning until now, that she tarried a little in the house."

Then said Boaz unto Ruth, "Hearest thou not, my daughter? Go not to glean in another field, neither go from hence, but abide here fast by my maidens. Let thine eyes be on the field that they do reap, and go thou after them: have I not charged the young men that they shall not touch thee? And when thou art athirst, go unto the vessels, and drink of that which the young men have drawn."

Then she fell on her face and bowed herself to the ground and said unto him, "Why have I found grace in thine eyes, that thou shouldest take knowledge of me, seeing I am a stranger?"

And Boaz answered and said unto her, "It hath fully been showed me all that thou hast done unto thy mother-in-law since the death of thine husband: and how thou hast left thy father and thy mother, and the land of thy nativity and art come unto a people which thou knewest not heretofore. The Lord recompense thy work, and a full reward be given thee of the Lord God of Israel, under whose wings thou art come to trust."

Then she said, "Let me find favor in thy sight, my lord; for that thou hast comforted me, and for that thou hast spoken friendly unto thine handmaid, though I be not like unto one of thine handmaidens."

And Boaz said unto her, "At mealtime come thou hither, and eat of the bread, and dip thy morsel in the vinegar." And she sat beside the reapers: and he reached her parched corn, and she did eat, and was sufficed, and left.

And when she was risen up to glean, Boaz commanded his young men, saying, "Let her glean even among the sheaves, and reproach her not. And let fall also some of the handfuls on purpose for her, and leave them, that she may glean them, and rebuke her not."

So she gleaned in the field until even, and beat out that she had gleaned: and it was about an ephah [1] of barley.

And she took it up and went into the city: and her mother-in-law saw what she had gleaned: and she brought forth and gave to her what she had reserved after she was sufficed.

And her mother-in-law said unto her, "Where hast thou gleaned today? and where wroughtest thou? Blessed be he that did take knowledge of thee." And she showed her mother-in-law with whom she had wrought, and said, "The man's name with whom I wrought today is Boaz."

And Naomi said unto her daughter-in-law, "Blessed be he of the Lord, who hath not left off his kindness to the living and to the dead." And Naomi said unto her, "The man is near of kin unto us, one of our next kinsmen."

And Ruth the Moabitess said, "He said unto me also, 'Thou shalt keep fast by my young men, until they have ended all my harvest.'"

And Naomi said unto Ruth her daughter-in-law, "It is good, my daughter, that thou go out with his maidens, that they meet thee not in any other field."

So she kept fast by the maidens of Boaz to glean unto the end of barley harvest and of wheat harvest; and dwelt with her mother-in-law.

---

[1] **ephah** (ē′fə): a little more than a bushel.

CHAPTER 3

THEN NAOMI her mother-in-law said unto her, "My daughter, shall I not seek rest for thee, that it may be well with thee? And now is not Boaz of our kindred, with whose maidens thou wast? Behold, he winnoweth barley tonight in the threshingfloor. Wash thyself therefore, and anoint thee, and put thy raiment upon thee, and get thee down to the floor: but make not thyself known unto the man, until he shall have done eating and drinking. And it shall be, when he lieth down, that thou shalt mark the place where he shall lie, and thou shalt go in and uncover his feet and lay thee down; and he will tell thee what thou shalt do."

And she said unto her, "All that thou sayest unto me I will do."

And she went down unto the floor and did according to all that her mother-in-law bade her.

And when Boaz had eaten and drunk and his heart was merry, he went to lie down at the end of the heap of corn: and she came softly and uncovered his feet and laid her down.

And it came to pass at midnight, that the man was afraid and turned himself: and, behold, a woman lay at his feet.

And he said, "Who art thou?" And she answered, "I am Ruth thine handmaid: spread therefore thy skirt over thine handmaid; for thou art a near kinsman."

And he said, "Blessed be thou of the Lord, my daughter: for thou hast showed more kindness in the latter end than at the beginning, inasmuch as thou followedst not young men, whether poor or rich. And now, my daughter, fear not; I will do to thee all that thou requirest: for all the city of my people doth know that thou art a virtuous woman. And now it is true that I am thy near kinsman: howbeit, there is a kinsman nearer than I. Tarry this night, and it shall be in the morning that if he will perform unto thee the part of a kinsman, well; let him do the kinsman's part: but if he will not do the part of a kinsman to thee, then will I do the part of a kinsman to thee, as the Lord liveth: lie down until the morning."

And she lay at his feet until the morning: and she rose up before one could know another. And he said, "Let it not be known that a woman came into the floor."

Also he said, "Bring the vail¹ that thou hast upon thee, and hold it." And when she held it, he measured six measures of barley and laid it on her: and she went into the city.

And when she came to her mother-in-law, she said, "Who art thou, my daughter?" And she told her all that the man had done to her.

And she said, "These six measures of barley gave he me; for he said to me, 'Go not empty unto thy mother-in-law.'"

Then said she, "Sit still, my daughter, until thou know how the matter will fall: for the man will not be in rest until he have finished the thing this day."

¹ **vail:** cloak.

CHAPTER 4

THEN WENT Boaz up to the gate and sat him down there: and, behold, the kinsman of whom Boaz spake came by; unto whom he said, "Ho, such a one! turn aside, sit down here." And he turned aside and sat down.

And he took ten men of the elders of the city and said, "Sit ye down here." And they sat down.

And he said unto the kinsman, "Naomi, that is come again out of the country of Moab, selleth a parcel of land, which was our brother Elimelech's. And I thought to advertise thee, saying, Buy it before the inhabitants and before the elders of my people. If thou wilt redeem it, redeem it: but if thou wilt not redeem it, then tell me, that I may know: for there is none to redeem it beside thee; and I am after thee." And he said, "I will redeem it."

Then said Boaz, "What day thou buyest the field of the hand of Naomi, thou must buy it also of Ruth the Moabitess, the wife of the dead, to raise up the name of the dead upon his inheritance."

And the kinsman said, "I cannot redeem it for myself, lest I mar mine own inheritance: redeem thou my right to thyself; for I cannot redeem it."

Now this was the manner in former time in Israel concerning redeeming and concerning changing, for to confirm all things; a man plucked off his shoe, and gave it to his neighbor: and this was a testimony in Israel.

Therefore the kinsman said unto Boaz, "Buy it for thee." So he drew off his shoe.

And Boaz said unto the elders and unto all the people, "Ye are witnesses this day, that I have bought all that was Elimelech's, and all that was Chilion's and Mahlon's, of the hand of Naomi. Moreover, Ruth the Moabitess, the wife of Mahlon, have I purchased to be my wife, to raise up the name of the dead upon his inheritance, that the name of the dead be not cut off from among his brethren and from the gate of his place: ye are witnesses this day."

And all the people that were in the gate and the elders said, "We are witnesses. The Lord make the woman that is come into thine house like Rachel and like Leah,[1] which two did build the house of Israel: and do thou worthily in Ephratah, and be famous in Bethlehem. And let thy house be like the house of Pharez, whom Tamar bare unto Judah,[2] of the seed which the Lord shall give thee of this young woman."

So Boaz took Ruth, and she was his wife: and when he went in unto her, the Lord gave her conception, and she bare a son.

And the women said unto Naomi, "Blessed be the Lord, which hath not left thee this day without a kinsman, that his name may be famous in Israel. And he shall be unto thee a restorer of thy life and a nourisher of thine old age: for thy daughter-in-law, which loveth thee, which is better to thee than seven sons, hath born him."

And Naomi took the child and laid it in her bosom and became nurse unto it.

And the women her neighbors gave it a name, saying, "There is a son born

---

[1] **like Rachel and like Leah:** the wives of Jacob. Their sons by Jacob were among his twelve sons whose names were given to the twelve tribes of Israel.

[2] **Pharez, whom Tamar bare unto Judah:** Tamar, like Ruth, had been left a childless widow (see Genesis 38). Judah was her father-in-law.

to Naomi"; and they called his name Obed: he is the father of Jesse, the father of David.

Now these are the generations of Pharez: Pharez begat Hezron, and Hezron begat Ram, and Ram began Amminadab, and Amminadab begat Nahshon, and Nahshon begat Salmon, and Salmon begat Boaz, and Boaz begat Obed, and Obed begat Jesse, and Jesse begat David.

FOR STUDY AND DISCUSSION

1. Why does Ruth's decision to return to Bethlehem with Naomi show unusual devotion? What character in the story acts as a foil to Ruth? How does Naomi return Ruth's devotion in a very practical way?

2. In biblical times, a wealthy farmer, like Boaz, would permit the poor to pick up grain that his reapers had dropped. How did Boaz treat Ruth?

3. Is the characterization in the story simple or complex? Do Naomi, Ruth, and Boaz seem sympathetic and realistic or are they idealized and unreal? Explain.

4. In what stylistic ways does this story differ from the stories taken from Genesis?

5. Through what incidents and details does the author emphasize the values he feels to be important, such as hospitality, courtesy, modesty, generosity, respect for custom and tradition?

6. David, of course, was one of the greatest kings of Israel. What gentle irony may be involved in the closing announcement, appended to this story, concerning the descendants of Ruth's child?

HEBREW NAMES

The ancient Hebrews regarded names not only as labels but also as symbols, as keys to the nature of things. Look up the following names in a dictionary, all from one of the first three chapters of Genesis or from the Book of Ruth. Explain what they tell about the nature of the thing or being named: Adam, Eve, Eden, Yahweh, Bethlehem, Judah, Naomi, Ruth, David, Israel.

How do people in today's cultures show that they are aware of the social and political power of names? How do parents choose names for a child? What various names are you known by? In what symbolic ways, other than by names, do people describe themselves to others?

THE TRANSLATION

This translation of the Book of Ruth was completed in 1611 by a commission of eminent scholars and churchmen, appointed by King James I to work on an English translation of the Bible. The work of the commission entailed comparing various English editions of the Bible then in existence with the old Latin, Greek, and Hebrew texts. The translation that resulted, regarded as one of the masterpieces of English literature, represents the culmination of many efforts over several centuries to provide the English people with the Bible written in their own tongue. The King James translation, as it has been called, reflects, of course, linguistic usages of seventeenth-century English, many of them antiquated today:

An eighth personal pronoun was used; *thou* was its singular nominative form. This pronoun was used in the early part of the seventeenth century to address familiars. Today it survives in some prayers.

Certain verb endings were obligatory with this eighth pronoun: "thou goest," "thou hast," "thou art," "thou wert," "thou wilt."

After singular subjects or after the pronouns *it, he,* or *she,* a verb could take *–s* or *–th:* "he dies or dieth," "he has or hath."

The verb *do* was used differently from the way it is used today: "Go not to glean in another field" would be today *"Do* not (or *don't)* go to glean in another field"; and "she *did* eat" would be today "she ate."

Some words commonly used in 1611 have since disappeared altogether from the spoken language. For example: *wherefore, unto, clave* (past tense of *cleave), whither.*

Examine the Book of Ruth closely and find examples of these seventeenth-century linguistic usages. Then "translate" the first chapter of the story into modern English. Do not alter the meaning of the story.

The Book of Psalms

The two titles associated with this book of the Old Testament suggest something about the form and nature of biblical poetry. The word *psalm* is derived from the Greek word *psalmos,* which means "a plucking of strings," and indicates that biblical poetry was sung. The Hebrew name for the book, *tehillim,* means "praise-songs," and the purpose of many of the 150 poems is to sing praise to God.

The Book of Psalms reflects a wide range of emotions and covers many themes. Though over half of the psalms are ascribed to King David (1040? B.C.–970? B.C.), it is believed that nearly all of them are of a much later date. The final compilation of the psalter might not have been made until the third and second centuries B.C. The psalms were intertwined in the ritual of Israelite life. Some were part of the liturgy for Temple worship; some were sung to celebrate battles or coronations; some were used in family or individual devotions.

Psalms of various types have been included here. To show how language and literary style have changed over the last five hundred years, three famous English translations are included of Psalm 23. All the other psalms are from the English translation completed in 1611 for King James.

Psalm 8

O Lord our Lord, how excellent is thy name in all the earth!
Who hast set thy glory above the heavens.

Out of the mouth of babes and sucklings hast thou ordained strength
   because of thine enemies,
That thou mightest still the enemy and the avenger.

When I consider thy heavens, the work of thy fingers,   5
The moon and the stars, which thou hast ordained;

What is man, that thou art mindful of him?
And the son of man, that thou visitest him?

For thou hast made him a little lower than the angels,
And hast crowned him with glory and honor.   10

Thou madest him to have dominion over the works of thy hands;
Thou hast put all things under his feet:

All sheep and oxen,
Yea, and the beasts of the field;

The fowl of the air, and the fish of the sea,   15
And whatsoever passeth through the paths of the seas.

O Lord our Lord, how excellent is thy name in all the earth!

Three Translations of Psalm 23

(Translated by John Wycliffe)

The Lord gouerneth me, and no thing schal faile to me; in the place of pasture there he hath set me. He nurschide me on the watir of refreischyng; he conuertide my soule. He ledde me forth on the pathis of riȝtfulnesse; for his name. For whi thouȝ Y schal go in the myddis of schadewe of deeth; Y schal not drede yuels, for thou art with me. Thi ȝerde and thi staf; tho han coumfortid me. Thou hast maad redi a boord in my siȝt; aȝens him that troblen me. Thou hast maad fat myn heed with oyle; and my cuppe, fillinge greetli, is ful cleer. And thi merci schall sue me; in alle the daies of my lijf. And that Y dwelle in the hows of the Lord; in to the lengthe of daies.

(The King James Translation)

The Lord is my shepherd;
I shall not want.

He maketh me to lie down in green pastures:
He leadeth me beside the still waters.

He restoreth my soul: 5
He leadeth me in the paths of righteousness for his name's sake.

Yea, though I walk through the valley of the shadow of death, I will fear
   no evil: for thou art with me;
Thy rod and thy staff they comfort me.

Thou preparest a table before me in the presence of mine enemies:
Thou anointest my head with oil; my cup runneth over.   10

Surely goodness and mercy shall follow me all the days of my life:
And I will dwell in the house of the Lord for ever.

Yahweh is my shepherd,
    I shall not lack.
In green meadows he will make me lie down;
Near tranquil waters will he guide me,   .
    to refresh my being.   5
He will lead me into luxuriant pastures,
    as befits his name.
Even though I should walk
    in the midst of total darkness,
I shall fear no danger   10
    since you are with me.
Your rod and your staff—
    behold, they will lead me.
You prepare my table before me,
    in front of my adversaries.   15
You generously anoint my head with oil,
    my cup overflows.
Surely goodness and kindness will attend me
    all the days of my life;
And I shall dwell in the house of Yahweh   20
    for days without end.

Psalm 104

Bless the Lord, O my soul.
O Lord my God, thou art very great;
Thou art clothed with honor and majesty.

Who coverest thyself with light as with a garment:
Who stretchest out the heavens like a curtain: 5

Who layeth the beams of his chambers in the waters:
Who maketh the clouds his chariot:
Who walketh upon the wings of the wind:

Who maketh his angels spirits;
His ministers a flaming fire: 10

Who laid the foundations of the earth,
That it should not be removed for ever.

Thou coveredst it with the deep as with a garment:
The waters stood above the mountains.

At thy rebuke they fled;   15
At the voice of thy thunder they hasted away.

They go up by the mountains;
They go down by the valleys unto the place which thou hast founded for
   them.

Thou hast set a bound that they may not pass over;
That they turn not again to cover the earth.   20

He sendeth the springs into the valleys,
Which run among the hills.

They give drink to every beast of the field:
The wild asses quench their thirst.

By them shall the fowls of the heaven have their habitation,   25
Which sing among the branches.

He watereth the hills from his chambers:
The earth is satisfied with the fruit of thy works.

He causeth the grass to grow for the cattle,
And herb for the service of man: 30
That he may bring forth food out of the earth;

And wine that maketh glad the heart of man,
And oil to make his face to shine,
And bread which strengtheneth man's heart.

The trees of the Lord are full of sap;   35
The cedars of Lebanon, which he hath planted;

Where the birds make their nests:
As for the stork, the fir trees are her house.

The high hills are a refuge for the wild goats;
And the rocks for the conies.°   40

He appointed the moon for seasons:
The sun knoweth his going down.

Thou makest darkness, and it is night:
Wherein all the beasts of the forest do creep forth.

40. **conies:** probably rabbits.

The young lions roar after their prey,   45
And seek their meat from God.

The sun ariseth, they gather themselves together,
And lay them down in their dens.

Man goeth forth unto his work
And to his labor until the evening.   50

O Lord, how manifold are thy works!
In wisdom hast thou made them all:
The earth is full of thy riches.

So is this great and wide sea,
Wherein are things creeping innumerable, both small and great beasts. 55

There go the ships:
There is that leviathan,° whom thou hast made to play therein.

These wait all upon thee;
That thou mayest give them their meat in due season.

That thou givest them they gather: 60
Thou openest thine hand, they are filled with good.

Thou hidest thy face, they are troubled:
Thou takest away their breath, they die, and return to their dust.

Thou sendest forth thy spirit, they are created:
And thou renewest the face of the earth.   65

The glory of the Lord shall endure for ever:
The Lord shall rejoice in his works.

He looketh on the earth, and it trembleth:
He toucheth the hills, and they smoke.

I will sing unto the Lord as long as I live: 70
I will sing praise to my God while I have my being.

My meditation of him shall be sweet:
I will be glad in the Lord.

Let the sinners be consumed out of the earth,
And let the wicked be no more.   75
Bless thou the Lord, O my soul.
Praise ye the Lord.

---

57. **leviathan:** probably a whale, something few Israelites ever saw.

Psalm 137

By the rivers of Babylon, there we sat down,
Yea, we wept, when we remembered Zion.

We hanged our harps upon the willows in the midst thereof.

For there they that carried us away captive required of us a song;
And they that wasted us required of us mirth, saying, Sing us one of the
    songs of Zion.   5

How shall we sing the Lord's song in a strange land?

If I forget thee, O Jerusalem, let my right hand forget her cunning.

If I do not remember thee, let my tongue cleave to the roof of my mouth;
If I prefer not Jerusalem above my chief joy.

Remember, O Lord, the children of Edom in the day of Jerusalem;   10
Who said, Raze it, raze it, even to the foundation thereof.

O daughter of Babylon, who art to be destroyed;
Happy shall he be, that rewardeth thee as thou has served us.

Happy shall he be, that taketh and dasheth thy little ones against the stones.

Psalm 139

O Lord, thou hast searched me, and known me.

Thou knowest my downsitting and mine uprising,
Thou understandest my thought afar off.

Thou compassest my path and my lying down,
And art acquainted with all my ways.   5

For there is not a word in my tongue,
But, lo, O Lord, thou knowest it altogether.

Thou has beset me behind and before,
And laid thine hand upon me.

Such knowledge is too wonderful for me;   10
It is high, I cannot attain unto it.

Whither shall I go from thy spirit?
Or whither shall I flee from thy presence?

If I ascend up into heaven, thou art there:
If I make my bed in hell, behold, thou art there.   15

If I take the wings of the morning,
And dwell in the uttermost parts of the sea;

Even there shall thy hand lead me,
And thy right hand shall hold me.

If I say, Surely the darkness shall cover me;   20
Even the night shall be light about me.

Yea, the darkness hideth not from thee;
But the night shineth as the day:
The darkness and the light are both alike to thee.

For thou hast possessed my reins: 25
Thou hast covered me in my mother's womb.

I will praise thee; for I am fearfully and wonderfully made:
Marvelous are thy works; and that my soul knoweth right well.

My substance was not hid from thee, when I was made in secret,
And curiously wrought in the lowest parts of the earth.   30

Thine eyes did see my substance, yet being unperfect;
And in thy book all my members were written,
Which in continuance were fashioned,
When as yet there was none of them.

How precious also are thy thoughts unto me, O God!   35
How great is the sum of them!

If I should count them, they are more in number than the sand:
When I awake, I am still with thee.

Surely thou wilt slay the wicked, O God:
Depart from me therefore, ye bloody men.   40

For they speak against thee wickedly,
And thine enemies take thy name in vain.

Do not I hate them, O Lord, that hate thee?
And am not I grieved with those that rise up against thee?

I hate them with perfect hatred: 45
I count them mine enemies.

Search me, O God, and know my heart:
Try me, and know my thoughts:

And see if there be any wicked way in me,
And lead me in the way everlasting.   50

PSALM 8

1. What contrasting thoughts and images is the psalmist setting forth in lines 1–4?

2. Is the question in lines 5–8 rhetorical or is it answered? Support your answer by referring to the psalm. What do the verbs in lines 6 and 8 suggest about God? What noun in line 5 suggests the enormous power of God?

3. What definite evidence is set forth in this psalm to show the importance of man? How do these ideas compare with those in the chapters of Genesis (page 20)?

PSALM 23: KING JAMES TRANSLATION

1. What two roles close to the lives of the ancient Hebrews are assigned to God in this psalm? In what position does the psalmist cast himself?

2. Where does a pronoun shift take place in the psalm, in reference to God? Can you see any significance in this shift?

3. What is the psalmist's mood here? What feeling does he express toward God? In what images does he picture paradise or eternal life?

4. It was a custom among the Jews to show respect or hospitality toward a man by pouring oil on his head, since his hair and beard might be dusty from the roads or fields. The psalmist refers to this custom in line 10. What else is the psalmist confident God will do for him, according to lines 9–10?

PSALM 104

1. What images in lines 4–11 describe God and his workings?

2. What details in this psalm refer to things and wonders that would be familiar to the ancient Israelites? What lines show an awareness of order and purpose in the universe?

3. This psalmist uses many lines to describe earth and sea life. In all these descriptions, what is the underlying theme? What lines in the psalm seem to sum up this theme?

PSALM 137

1. To what historical event does this psalm refer? What two emotions are dominant in the psalm? At what point does the mood of the psalmist change sharply?

2. Why might the question asked in line 6 arouse strong feelings today, in view of the subsequent history of the Jewish people?

3. What powers does the psalmist say he should be deprived of if he forgets Jerusalem? Why would the specified punishments seem particularly appropriate?

PSALM 139

1. What images in lines 1–26 best describe the presence of God with the psalmist? How does the psalmist feel about God's presence?

2. Line 27 is a famous one. Why does the psalmist praise God when he looks on man? Compare this psalm with Psalm 8. Which one seems more personal, and why?

3. According to the psalmist, how does God feel about man? How does this contrast with the way the Babylonians thought the gods treated man, in the *Epic of Gilgamesh* (page 13)?

THE PSALMS AS LITERATURE

Several literary techniques are characteristic of the psalms. Perhaps their outstanding feature is the use of repetition, or parallelism, of thought.

Sometimes almost precisely the same thought recurs in the same or succeeding lines: "I will sing unto the Lord as long as I live: I will sing praise to my God while I have my being." On other occasions, a cause-and-effect harmony is achieved: "I cried unto the Lord with my voice; And he heard me out of his holy hill." Another form of parallelism often used is contrast, or antithesis: "Weeping may endure for a night, but joy cometh in the morning."

Another significant poetic element of the psalms is their striking visual images. These may change swiftly from pictures of everyday life, such as "The righteous shall flourish like the palm tree: He shall grow like a cedar in Lebanon," to soaring descriptions that challenge the imagination, such as speaking of God as one "who maketh the clouds his chariot: Who walketh upon the wings of the wind." Emotions are likewise visualized and personified. Instead of saying "My sorrow was turned into joy," the psalmist says, "Thou hast turned for me my mourning into dancing: thou hast put off my sackcloth, and girded me with gladness."

Examine the psalms in this unit closely, and identify lines which use the different poetic techniques illustrated above.

COMPARING TRANSLATIONS

John Wycliffe, in the fourteenth century, gave impetus to the first English translation of parts of the Bible. His purpose was to provide a Bible that could be understood by the common people of England. To achieve this, he used not a literary language but the straightforward and simple language spoken by the people, which incorporated many words derived from the old Anglo-Saxon. (Wycliffe's translation of Holy Writ into the vulgar English tongue scandalized most churchmen, and, in the interests of orthodoxy, the early manuscripts of his Bible, all hand-done, were systematically destroyed, some in huge bonfires.)

The King James translation, made in the seventeenth century, was the product of scholars whose diction and literary style were influenced by the Elizabethan poets.

The Anchor Bible's Psalms were published in 1965. The translation was made directly from Hebrew and the aim was to convey the meaning of the original language.

1. In the Wycliffe version, do you think the psalm was recognized as a poem? Explain.

2. Which translation uses phrases that sound most poetic? For example, compare the effects of "in the myddis of schadewe of deeth"; "through the valley of the shadow of death"; and "in the midst of total darkness." (Does familiarity influence your choice?)

3. Trace several words that change in each version. For example: *nurschide* (Wycliffe), *leadeth* (King James), and *guide* (Anchor). Does such variation in word choice seem to alter meaning? Explain.

4. Do certain word choices of the Anchor translation seem more relevant to twentieth-century English speakers? Explain.

GREEK LITERATURE

c. 800 B.C. – c. A.D. 200

A YOUNG BOY of intellectual promise was once asked by Socrates, Greek philosopher and teacher of the fifth century B.C., if he had thought a great deal. The boy quickly and modestly replied no, but at least, he said, he had wondered a great deal. The answer that Socrates allegedly gave the boy has become proverbial: "Wisdom," he replied, "begins in wonder."

It may have been almost two hundred years before Socrates' time that there had evolved among the peoples of Greece this spirit of inquiry so much admired by the great teacher. Here men, in a manner never known in the world before, began to observe the marvels of the universe and the mysteries of their own natures. They began to reflect and to give voice to their questionings.

Since Hebrew and Greek elements, in their different ways, played such major roles in shaping Western thought, it is tempting to contrast them. For the Bible, too, asks questions. "What is man?"—that, perhaps, is the great biblical question. "What is man," asks the psalmist, "that thou art mindful of him?" But at the center of the Bible is concern with man's relationship to God. In Greek culture there is no overall parallel to this Jewish absorption in the divine-human relationship. Perhaps the noblest Greek is Socrates; but he was an ethical genius, not a religious one. No thundering Old Testament prophet, for example, fired with divine inspiration, would have used Socrates' careful, rational steps in arriving at a definition of virtue.

Socrates raised basic ethical questions. Other Greeks posed other questions, no less basic. What are things made of? "Of water," Thales suggested. "Of fire!" declared Heraclitus. For his part, Democritus thought that everything was constructed of atoms.

In the arts the Greeks showed the same drive to seek answers to questions and solutions to problems. Greek sculptors struggled to conceive and reveal, in their marble-hewn statues, the standard or the ideal of human beauty, and they represented the gods as imposing human beings. Greek architects sought, in the temples they constructed, to achieve a splendid equilibrium of boldly planned regularities. Yet, since these regularities would have remained lifeless if the builders had cared for nothing else, they made their structures come vibrantly alive by introducing scarcely noticeable variations.

In public affairs, in the same way, the Greeks arrived at a conception of the ideal citizen, the freely acting individual who could win everlasting fame by striving, and even sacrificing himself, for what fundamentally mattered: the public good. Our notions of fame and of patriotism, even today, cannot be separated from the ideal of citizenship worked out by the Greeks. The "pursuit of excellence" discussed today is the most recent link in a chain that begins with the notion of virtue or excellence that is summed up in the Greek word *arete*.

The writings of the Greek philosopher Plato (427? B.C.–347? B.C.) (see page 131), came at the very outset of Western philosophy's long career and have never been surpassed in depth and subtlety. *Platonic, Neo-Platonic, Platonist*—the repetition of these terms throughout the centuries reflects the continued influence of Plato's philosophical idealism on Western thinking.

The philosopher Aristotle (384 B.C.–322 B.C.) was Plato's pupil. In our technological age, Aristotle appears more down to earth than does Plato, more scientific in his outlook because he was more prepared to measure his theories against the available evidence. Where Plato's interests centered upon ethical problems, Aristotle was most interested in exploring the biological and physical sciences. Today Aristotle's most widely read work is his *Poetics* (see page 168), which sets forth the principles of drama, based on the special conditions and limitations of the Greek theater.

Aristotle is also the author of a book on morals, the *Nichomachaean Ethics* (addressed to his son), which outlines the portrait of the "great-souled" or "magnanimous" man. Both directly and indirectly, Aristotle's conclusions have had a remarkable influence on our ideals of manhood: from the "Renaissance man" of the sixteenth century, to the traditional nineteenth-century English "gentleman," to the "well-rounded man" of our own day.

A similar conception of human greatness is provided in the funeral oration pronounced by the Athenian statesman Pericles (see page 126). Whenever,

in any later age, a statesman has formulated his conception of greatness for his nation and its citizens, he inevitably challenges comparison with this great speech. It is well to bear in mind that in 429 B.C., within a year of delivering the address, Pericles was dead, carried off by a disease spread during the Peloponnesian War. It is well to recall too that Athens went on to lose this war and that its unavoidable outcome was Athenian and Greek decadence.

THE HEROIC AGE OF GREEK HISTORY

A word, first of all, about a people who preceded the Greeks in the eastern Mediterranean. By 2000 B.C., a remarkable civilization had arisen on the none too fertile mountainous island of Crete. This island, 160 miles long, is some sixty miles south of mainland Greece. Only since the beginning of our own twentieth century have excavations revealed the true extent of this Minoan civilization, as it is called. The word *Minoan* is formed from the name of the legendary King Minos of Crete. Each year this king was said to have exacted from Athens a tribute of twelve youths and maidens, who were fed to the Minotaur, a beast which was half man and half bull. According to Homer's epic poem the *Iliad,* King Minos had reigned in Crete several generations before the Greeks went to war against Troy.

Minoan civilization was the first major civilization to take root on European soil. It reached its peak about 1950 B.C. and came to a sudden and mysterious end about 1350 B.C. Remains of magnificent palaces, wall paintings, various kinds of pottery, and beautiful jewelry all point to a vigorous, prosperous, varied, and cosmopolitan culture. These archeological remains also testify that the Minoans spoke a Semitic language and that they maintained connections with the much older civilizations of Egypt and Mesopotamia.

The Minoan national sport of bull-leaping (c. 1500 B.C.). The toreador has somer-saulted over the bull's head. His lady comrade will break his fall.

Meanwhile, vigorous tribes of herdsmen from the north were making their way down into mainland Greece, beginning around the seventeenth century B.C. In a whole long series of invasions, these tribes—Achaeans, Arcadians, Aeolians, and Ionians—pushed ever farther south. The fair-haired Achaeans, one of the names used in Homer's *Iliad,* became the Mycenaeans of history and archeology. They inhabited the town of Mycenae in eastern Greece, the town ruled by the warrior-king Menelaus of the *Iliad.* They were the most enterprising and aggressive of the Greeks during the heroic age of Greece's history, the age which Homer idealizes in the *Iliad* and the *Odyssey.* Later Greeks looked up to the great, hardy heroes of this age—Agamemnon, Achilles, Odysseus, Menelaus—as their ancestors.

Sometime after 1400 B.C. the Mycenaeans gained control in Crete, a move which further exposed them to the strong influence of the much more advanced Minoan culture. Archeological discoveries show that the adventuresome Mycenaeans also crossed over to Asia Minor and fought at the site of the rich commercial center of Troy, overthrowing this city by about 1180 B.C.

A last wave of invasions into the Greek peninsula occurred about 1100 B.C., when the more barbaric Dorians scattered or conquered the other tribes and enslaved the earlier, more civilized settlers. With that, the heroic age was over, and a cultural "dark age" separates it from the later period characterized by the rise of the Greek city-states. Nevertheless, the disruptive invasion of the warlike and crude Dorians—who themselves settled in southern Greece, in the Peloponnesus—served to spread the Greek peoples more widely throughout the Aegean world. As a result of this invasion, the Aegean islands were settled, as was the coast of Asia Minor. At a later period, so many Greek colonies were formed in southern Italy and

Sicily that the region was called, in Latin, *Magna Graecia*. Other Greeks settled along the North African coastline, in southern France, and on the shores of the Black Sea.

By the time Homer wrote his poems, around the eighth century B.C., the Greeks had developed a script for their own essentially Indo-European language. For an alphabet they borrowed from the Phoenicians, a Semitic people whose trading activities had brought them into the Mediterranean. In adapting the Phoenician alphabet to their own spoken language, the Greeks devised markings for vowel sounds, for which Semitic languages have no symbols, and they reversed the Oriental method of writing from right to left.

THE RISE OF THE CITY-STATES

The next period of Greek history may be thought of as extending from 800 B.C. to 500 B.C. What chiefly characterized it was the founding of a large number of city-states. The Greeks, who did not think of themselves as one people, never established any higher level of political unity than these city-states, each of which, with the land around it, led its own independent existence. (In practice, of course, no small state could overlook the wishes of a more powerful neighbor, and sometimes an alliance of city-states was dominated by the most powerful among them.)

Kings were the first to exercise power in the Greek city-states. They were succeeded by a landed aristocracy and, later, by the middle classes, who—since their wealth was derived from buying and selling—greatly strengthened their position after the introduction of coined money in about 680 B.C. Conflict between the classes became acute after 650 B.C. In most city-states the aristocratic regimes were overthrown and "tyrants" seized power. (They were not necessarily "tyrannical" as we understand the word, for the word *tyrant* in Greek simply refers to a man who has used irregular means to reach the top, whose power is absolute but not necessarily dictatorial.) By about 500 B.C., the tyrants too had nearly all disappeared. With so many opportunities to exercise power and to influence rulers, with so many contrasting political systems, and with men's interests and passions so deeply involved in public affairs, it need not surprise us that many Greek thinkers pondered over problems of constitution-building and statecraft; the political theories of Plato, for instance, stimulate controversy even today.

Though each free man was a citizen only of his own small city-state (women were not regarded as citizens nor, of course, were the slaves), the Greeks recognized and fully sensed their common bonds. They called themselves Hellenes, because they looked on themselves as descendants of one ancient hero, Hellen, the son of two mythical survivors of the great deluge that in the earliest times had destroyed the rest of mankind. To owe an emotional allegiance to Hellas, the name the Greeks gave to the Greek-speaking world, set one off from the surrounding "barbarian" world with its babble of non-Greek tongues. The unity among the Greeks found expression in various institutions. In the religious sphere, a number of shrines, among them that of Apollo at Delphi, received universal veneration. At Delphi, the priests of Apollo advised statesmen on matters of state. Another bond, no less religious, was created through the four Panhellenic Games, in which Greeks from all over Greece participated. The greatest prestige was enjoyed by the games held at Olympia every four years, in honor of Zeus. The Greeks used the supposed date of the very first Olympian Games, 776 B.C., as the starting point for their calendar.

The *Iliad* and *Odyssey* of Homer also served to maintain a feeling of unity among the Greeks. The deeds of the heroes in these epics were told not merely to entertain but to inspire and challenge young men to imitate the great accomplishments and noble outlooks of their ancestors of the heroic age. Homer's epic stories also helped to sort out the tangled and often conflicting tales of the gods, which the Greeks, with their differing tribal pasts and their varying contacts with other peoples, had been telling for several centuries.

THE CLASSICAL PERIOD

The period extending from 499 B.C. to 338 B.C., the classical period of Greek history, was marked from the beginning by the dominant position attained by two city-states, Athens and Sparta. Sparta, which was the more conservative of the two, was dominated by the Dorians, the last and most ruthless of the tribes invading Greece. Sparta had been prominent in the outburst of choral lyric poetry that occurred in the seventh century B.C., but a succession of slave revolts had so seriously threatened the state that its rulers determined to transform Sparta into a permanent armed camp. From his earliest moments, the destiny of every Spartan was subjected to the requirements of the state. Frail babies were exposed on a mountaintop and left to die. At the age of seven, boys left home to be brought up by the state in Spartan fashion, with plain living, hard physical training, the endurance of pain, and unquestioning obedience as the universal lot. Even after marriage, young men continued to live in barracks, so there was little family life. Girls, too, practiced gymnastics so that they could bear strong sons for their state. Thus Sparta became an impressive military power.

Thucydides, the fifth century B.C. Greek historian (see page 125), put the following speech into the mouth of a Corinthian envoy. He is addressing the Spartan assembly, which was considering whether to declare war on Athens. The envoy's words describe the Athenians and Spartans of Thucydides' own day. Thucydides himself was an Athenian. (Lacedaemon was another name for Sparta.)

● "You have never considered, O Lacedaemonians, what manner of men are these Athenians with whom you will have to fight, and how utterly unlike yourselves. They are revolutionary, equally quick in the conception and in the execution of every new plan; while you are conservative—careful only to keep what you have, originating nothing, and not acting even when action is most necessary. They are bold beyond their strength; they run risks which prudence would condemn; and in the midst of misfortune they are full of hope. Whereas it is your nature, though strong, to act feebly; when your plans are most prudent, to distrust them; and when calamities come upon you, to think that you will never be delivered from them. They are impetuous and you are dilatory; they are always abroad, and you are always at home. For they hope to gain something by leaving their homes; but you are afraid that any new enterprise may imperil what you have already. When conquerors, they pursue their victory to the utmost; when defeated, they fall back the least. Their bodies they devote to the country as though they belonged to other men; their true self is their mind, which is not truly their own when employed in her service. When they do not carry out an intention which they have formed, they seem to have sustained a personal bereavement; when an enterprise succeeds, they have gained a mere installment of what is to come; but if they fail, they at once conceive new hopes and so fill up the void. With them alone to hope is to have, for they lose not a moment in the execution of an idea. This is the lifelong task, full of danger and toil, which they are always imposing upon themselves. None enjoy their good things less, because they are always seeking for more. To do their duty is their only holiday, and they deem the quiet of inaction to be as disagreeable as the most tiresome business. If a man should say of them, in a word, that they were born neither to have peace themselves nor to allow peace to other men, he would simply speak the truth."—THUCYDIDES

(Sparta did fight Athens and won, after a war that lasted nearly thirty years, from 431 B.C.–404 B.C. Sparta was hampered, however, by a rigid, unimaginative military outlook, and her period of dominance was a short one.)

In the modern Western world, Athens is looked on as the center of the most amazing civilization ever to have sprung into being. The other Greek city-states are neglected by comparison, and this distorts our picture of Greece. Nevertheless, Athens in its own day was recognized as outstanding, politically and culturally. At a time so remote that the only accounts we have of the occurrence are legendary, the whole region of Attica was united

The quotation from Thucydides, translated by Catherine B. Avery, from the entry "Athens" from *The New Century Classical Handbook* edited by Catherine B. Avery, copyright © 1962 by Meredith Corporation. Reprinted by permission of Appleton-Century-Crofts.

with the city, and Athenian citizenship was granted to all free men. We should bear in mind, however, that even at its peak in the fifth century B.C., Athens, by far the largest of the Greek cities, probably counted no more than 43,000 male adult citizens. In Greek eyes, 10,000 was the ideal number, for then all could participate in public life, and no one need remain an *idiotes,* an uninvolved private citizen.

Athens had a checkered political history. Monarchy gave way to democracy, which was replaced by a tyranny. Democracy once again came to the fore, and by about 500 B.C. the aristocratic faction had been decisively defeated by the common people. This was timely indeed, for Athens and all Greece were on the brink of a desperate struggle whose outcome was to affect the course of world history.

The Greek-populated cities of Asia Minor had revolted against their overlord, the Persian Emperor Darius, and had received help from mainland Greece. Darius resolved to conquer mainland Greece in revenge. Lest he be diverted from his goal of conquest, Darius ordered that every time he dined, a servant should repeat three times, "Sire, remember the Athenians!" His successors shared Darius' ambition. The Persian Wars began in 499 B.C. and may be said to have ended in 479 B.C., though hostilities still erupted from time to time before the Persians finally abandoned their aim and thus said farewell to any hope of establishing themselves in Europe. At one stage of the war, the Persians entered Athens and virtually destroyed the city, but in the long run the greater adaptability and ingenuity of the Greeks wore down the "Persian Goliath." It was a splendid beginning for the great age of Greek history, marked by the glorious victory of the Athenians at Marathon in 490 B.C. and by the no less glorious stand made by a handful of Spartans at Thermopylae ten years later. Among the Greek city-states, the main beneficiary of these wars was Athens, which had acted vigorously as wartime 'leader and subsequently became the chief naval power. Athens proceeded to run in double harness a policy of democracy at home and of economic penetration and imperialist expansion abroad. Everything, it seemed, conspired or was induced to enhance the prestige of Athens. The very destruction of the town itself created the occasion to rebuild it in unmatched splendor. (Some of the heavy expenses incurred were met by Athens' allies. They had entrusted the common war chest to Athens and now saw their contributions used for Athens' own purposes.) Learned men came to Athens from the other Greek cities, for it was the undisputed intellectual center of Greece. The patriotic enthusiasm of the population was maintained during and after the Persian Wars by the democratic expansion of the dramatic festivals, which retained their overall religious character while serving to strengthen the sense of civic and national unity. The similar expansion of the athletic festivals had the same function.

THE PELOPONNESIAN WAR

It is, perhaps, sad to relate—for there are scholars even today who react emotionally to these events of long ago—that Greek and Athenian promise and achievement were short-lived. The Greeks did not take the right historical turning, which could only have been the unification of all Greece as a nation. This could have been brought about by Athens. But it was made impossible by the rivalry of Athens and Sparta—and also, no doubt, by the insufficiently broad vision of the Athenian leaders, Pericles among them, and by the resentments aroused by selfish Athenian policies. After long and bitter dissension, war broke out between Sparta and Athens. This, the Peloponnesian War, lasted from 431 B.C. to 404 B.C. The outcome was victory for Sparta, but a more significant consequence was the weakening of Greece as a whole. There was no immediate extinction of Greece's cultural prestige—only her inevitable assignment to a supporting role on the stage of history. What lay ahead was conquest by Philip of Macedon, who defeated the Athenians in 338 B.C., the even more severe overlordship of his son Alexander, and, after the collapse of Alexander's huge and hastily assembled empire, eventual subordination to the last empire builders of the ancient world, the Romans. In defeat there can be, of course, a kind of victory. The Romans were awed by Greek culture, and placed themselves under Greek tutelage in matters of poetry, art, and refinement. However, the Greeks felt that they were living, henceforward, in a backwater.

THE ILIAD AND THE ODYSSEY

The earliest surviving works of Greek literature are Homer's two epics, which romanticize heroic, powerful men, whose exploits and sufferings are the direct concern of the gods. Available as raw material for these epics

This vase (fifth century B.C.) depicts a scene from the *Odyssey*. Odysseus, tied to the mast, listens to the sirens' seductive song.

was, undoubtedly, a large store of separate poetic narratives about early heroes, which wandering bards had for centuries chanted before audiences to the accompaniment of harplike instruments called lyres. The two epics, the *Iliad* (see page 52) and the *Odyssey*, skillfully sorted out and unified this raw material. Though they were probably composed in the eighth century B.C., during the otherwise generally "dark age" of Greek cultural history, the text of the poems makes it clear that the events take place in the preceding heroic age. As for the authorship, antiquity attributed both works to one man, Homer. Nothing whatever is known about Homer, but tradition pictures him as a blind wandering bard. Other theories of authorship have been put forward in more recent, skeptical ages, but the prevailing view today is that both the *Iliad* and the *Odyssey* were written by the same highly gifted author. In any event, the question of authorship is much less absorbing than the poems themselves.

Homer's epics also represented a step forward in Greek religious beliefs. In the course of a few centuries, the different tribes that had invaded the Greek peninsula had come in contact with one another and with many alien peoples. The coherence that these tribes' primitive religious concepts might have once possessed had been lost. Eventually Greeks could only tremble before vague, dimly sensed supernatural forces that were both threatening and chaotic, but with which they had to deal. Homer, in his epics, called the "Bibles" of the Greeks, clarified, arranged, humanized, and in some degree explained the many tangled and conflicting myths. Thus he provided his audience with a clearer frame of reference for their own speculations on things divine. Also, generations of Greeks found in Homer's poems a concept of *arete*. Here was the kind of life that they themselves might strive to lead. Here also were heroic models to imitate.

LYRIC POETRY

From about the seventh to the fifth centuries B.C., a new form of poetry began to flourish among the Greeks, a form in which the poet's main concern was no longer the telling of a great story of a past heroic age. Poetry expressing personal emotions and reflecting the interests of daily life arose, partly as a result of the Greeks' ever-increasing stress on the individual man. The poet, whose function so far had been to celebrate the heroes of old, grew more aware of his own existence in his own changing age; he grew self-conscious in the best sense of the term.

The lyric poets of this period lived in all parts of Greece and wrote in a number of dialects, but the greatest number were from the cities of Asia Minor and the islands of the Aegean. Their output was probably immense, but only a minute percentage of it has survived. Except for the odes of Pindar (522? B.C.–443 B.C.) (see page 112), only fragments of the lyrics of this era are extant. Many of them were preserved only because philosophers or teachers of public speaking of the time included quotations from the poems in their own written works.

Another flowering of Greek lyric poetry occurred about a century later, during what has come to be called the Hellenistic Age. This period began with the conquests of Alexander the Great of Macedon (356 B.C.–323 B.C.) and ended about two hundred years later with the conquest by Rome.

Much of the poetry of subsequent ages has been influenced by the forms originated by the Greeks. Unfortunately, the melody and rhythm, the subtle distinctions in word meaning, and the harmonious balance of words and phrases, so characteristic of Greek poetry, are lost in English translation. The English tradition in poetry has usually stressed lavish use of adornment, but Greek poets wrote directly, simply, and economically—stimulating rather than overpowering the imagination. Greek poets did not use rhyme schemes, or highly ornate language, or complex symbols. Deeply concerned with music, the Greeks must have thought that the sound of a lyric was as essential as its words. The spirit of Greek poetry can probably be best rendered by the simplest of translations, but only faint echoes of its lovely sounds can be heard in English translations.

While the Greeks distinguished among a number of types of poetry (epic, lyric, elegiac, etc.) and various subtypes, their classifications are not of main importance. It is worth noting one very real distinction, however. Certain of the Greek lyrics were written to be sung by a chorus while others were written to be sung by one person only. The choral lyrics were more dignified and were bound up with state occasions and with religious ceremonies in the different city-states. Pindar, for example, is the great name in this domain of poetry. His poems celebrated the victors in the Olympian Games and were sung by a civic chorus at the games themselves.

THE DRAMA

The immediate successor to the outburst of lyric poetry was the drama. While fifth-century B.C. Greece was incomparably rich in the many varieties of human expression, including philosophy, history, oratory, sculpture, and architecture, the drama is considered by many to be the supreme Greek achievement.

Greek theater originated in religious festivals. For the Athenian public, ceremonies dedicated to Dionysus, the god of the joyous life, the god of the vine and of fertility, were held seasonally, probably five times a year, in winter and in spring. As these ceremonies became increasingly popular, the Greeks built imposing theaters in which to present them. At the sanctuary of Dionysus in Athens, an enormous outdoor amphitheater, accommodating

A pug-nosed Silenus, tutor and companion of the god of wine, looks over the Theater of Dionysus in Athens, built about 340 B.C.

more than 25,000 spectators, was erected. There, the traditional spectacles of men dressed as satyrs, dancing and singing in honor of the god, gradually gave way to dramatic stories based on the myths and interpreted by actors. Eventually, a carefully chosen jury awarded prizes to the best playwrights and actors.

Of course, all this did not come about at once. The ceremonies to honor Dionysus originally had been presented almost exclusively by choruses, of about fifty men chanting songs of praise to Dionysus, which were interspersed with narrations of the old myths. Then, in the sixth century B.C., a writer named Thespis apparently called for one man to step out and converse with the rest of the chorus; Thespis is therefore credited with inventing the role of the actor. Later, according to Aristotle, the dramatist Aeschylus inaugurated the use of two actors. This decreased the importance of the chorus and increased, through dialogue, the realistic enactment of a story. When the dramatist Sophocles introduced three actors to the stage, drama, in the form we know it today, was definitely established.

Three of the most revered authors of tragic drama in the history of Western literature—Aeschylus, Sophocles, and Euripides—lived in fifth-century B.C. Athens. These Athenian dramatists posed questions in their plays which challenged not only the Greeks but all succeeding generations as well: Can man exert free will and determine his own actions? Can the dilemma be resolved when the "rights" of two individuals conflict? What explanation can be given for pain and suffering inflicted on the innocent and the just? What is man's responsibility in accepting a universal moral law?

Tragedy in the classical sense was neither a depressing nor a despairing experience for a Greek audience. Despite the sufferings of the protagonist, emphasis was on the dignity of man, on his ability to follow the dictates of his conscience with integrity, to meet his fate with courage, and, most important, to learn wisdom through suffering. Having witnessed the fall of a flawed but heroic character and then recognizing the nobility of the human spirit, the Greek audience could leave a tragedy with heightened, relieved feelings.

Aeschylus (525 B.C.–456 B.C.) lived through the period when the Greeks successfully repelled the might of the Persian Empire. He took part in the Battle of Marathon and possibly in other battles also. In his famous trilogy of plays about the House of Atreus, Aeschylus considers the problem of evil as it repeats itself in several generations, by exploring the blood feud that haunted the family of King Agamemnon. Agamemnon was murdered by his vengeful wife on his return from the Trojan War; his wife was slain in revenge by their son; and their son in turn was pursued relentlessly by the avenging deities, the Furies. Despite the dreadful events which Aeschylus recounts in the seven tragedies that have come down to us, despite the conflicts and cruel dilemmas in which his people are engaged, he impresses us as having an elevated vision of human life. The Athenians of his time, as well as the rest of the Greeks, sensed that they were on the threshold of a great epoch, and Aeschylus embodied and ennobled this feeling.

Sophocles (496? B.C.–406 B.C.), as author of more than 120 tragedies, was even more productive than Aeschylus, who wrote about ninety plays. However, only seven of Sophocles' dramas survive. The most admired playwright of his day and the winner of some twenty prizes for his dramas, Sophocles moved on a plane equal to the other great men of his time, and himself carried out political, military, and ceremonial tasks. Thus, when Sophocles writes of the harsh dilemmas of power as they confront, for example, the king in his *Antigone* (see page 140), he is acquainted with these problems from the inside. Sophocles' life presents an answer to those who ask if an outstanding writer can possibly also be an outstanding man of action.

Sophocles' somewhat younger contemporary, Euripides (480? B.C.–406? B.C.), never enjoyed this great public favor. Euripides was much more the outsider, a brilliant psychologist who viewed the conduct of man and the role of the gods with penetrating skepticism. Expert though he was in probing the depth of human motives, Euripides was nevertheless extremely sensitive to human suffering. The *Trojan Women*, for example, represents the predicament of the defenseless women of Troy as the Greeks sacked their city. *Medea* is a portrait of a proud, barbaric woman driven to murder her children by her desire for vengeance against her husband. As Aeschylus coincides with the splendid opening of Athenian glory, so Euripides coincides with its bitter decline, which was being brought about in the battles of the Peloponnesian War.

The Iliad

HOMER

The events of the *Iliad* take place in the twelfth century B.C., in the tenth year of the Trojan War, during the Greek siege of the city of Troy in Asia Minor. The siege of Troy was a real historical event, probably caused by fierce competition for trade and sea control. But Homer based his story on oral tradition, and in the *Iliad* the Trojan War is the result of the sensational abduction of a beautiful woman. The Greeks of Homer's day were completely familiar with this legendary explanation of why their ancestors had set sail in their warships to attack a powerful Asian city, for the folk tales and songs from which Homer drew his story had been popular in Greece for centuries.

The legend about the cause of the war begins with a gold apple, inscribed "To the Fairest." Three goddesses were said to be vying for the prize: Hera, Athena, and Aphrodite. The gods themselves refused to become involved in the potentially flammable beauty contest, and so a handsome but naive young man named Paris, a prince of Troy, was chosen as judge. Each goddess offered Paris a bribe to choose her; he named Aphrodite because her offer was the most appealing: the most beautiful mortal woman in the world for his wife. Not only did Paris' decision bring down on him and his people the wrath of the two rejected goddesses, but it paved the way for war, since the most beautiful woman in the world was Helen, the wife of Menelaus, king of Mycenae in Greece; heedless of the consequences, Paris seized his lovely prize, and, with her full consent, the pair sailed back to Troy.

Bound to help Menelaus by oaths of loyalty, a group of Greek chieftains banded together, some of them reluctantly, under the leadership of Menelaus' brother, Agamemnon. With a fleet of over a thousand ships, they sailed across the Aegean Sea to the coast of Asia Minor to attack the well-fortified city of Troy, in the hopes of recovering Helen.

The Greeks were said to have laid siege to Troy for ten years. During this time their army was encamped on the plains outside the city walls. Occasionally, for diversion and for supplies, the warriors left their camp to plunder nearby towns, a means of livelihood that was regarded as legitimate in the Homeric age. Troy itself, however, remained intact because the Greeks could not penetrate its high, strong walls.

The *Iliad* opens as the war enters its tenth year, and it closes several weeks later. The story revolves around two main characters: Achilles, the bravest and handsomest warrior in the Greek army, and his enemy Hector, the honorable warrior-prince of the Trojans. The cause of the tragedy central to the *Iliad* is human anger, that of Achilles.

Taking sides with either the Trojans or the Greeks are the gods. Although men battle, it is the gods who decide on the outcome of the war. The Greeks' gods may seem unjust and sometimes even immoral to us. Yet if we could put ourselves in the place of eighth-century B.C. Greeks, we would realize that Homer's gods and goddesses represented, for them, a step forward. Divinities of the past had often been terrifying beings, sometimes represented as beasts, unapproachable by man, except perhaps through the mediation of priests. These divinities had cared little for man, and his chief hope in escaping their terrible wrath lay in performing magical rites or in making human sacrifice. The gods in Homer's epics, though definitely not perfect beings, were nevertheless humanized, interested in men, and accessible to them.

GENERAL RULES OF PRONUNCIATION

The *ch* in Greek words is always pronounced like *k,* as in Achaeans (ə·kē'ənz). The *c* is pronounced like *s* before *e, i, y,* and *ae,* as in Oceanus (ō·sē'ə·nəs), and *g* in the same position is pronounced like *j,* as in Aegean (i·jē'ən). Elsewhere, *c* is pronounced like *k,* as in Clytemnestra (klī'təm·nes'trə), and *g* is pronounced as in go. A final *e* is always pronounced, as in Niobe (nī'ə·bē).

The traditional spelling of Greek names in English goes back to the Latin spelling of the name, not to the original Greek. More recently, some translators and commentators have preferred to turn to the Greek form. Here are examples of both forms, the Greek being given first: Hephaistos / Hephaestus; Herakleitos / Heraclitus; Herakles / Hercules; Phoibos / Phoebus.

Some translators use special devices to indicate stress or vowel quality (Antigonē, aretê, Callínus), but these are individual preferences and not standard practice.

NAMES IN THE ILIAD

GODS AND GODDESSES

Aphrodite: goddess of love and beauty. Because Paris judged her fairest of all immortals, she favors the Trojan prince.

Apollo: son of Zeus; patron of arts; the god of light—the physical light that dispels darkness and the spiritual and moral light that dispels ignorance. Sometimes called Phoebus (fē'bəs) Apollo, *phoebus* meaning "bright." He helped to build Troy.

Ares: god of war; son of Zeus and Hera. He often helps the Trojans.

Athena: daughter of Zeus; goddess of wisdom, arts, and crafts. Because of Paris' judgment against her, she is an enemy of the Trojans and a protectress of Achilles. Sometimes called Pallas Athena.

Hephaestus: god of fire; the craftsman and blacksmith of the gods, who makes their armor and arms at a divine forge.

Hera: wife of Zeus; the white-armed queen of the gods. Because of Paris' judgment against her, she despises the Trojans.

Hermes: messenger of the gods.

Poseidon: god of the sea; brother of Zeus.

Zeus: the king-god; wielder of the thunderbolt and lightning, who draws the lots of men from two urns and weighs out man's fate on golden scales.

Achilles: greatest of the Greek warriors; the son of Peleus (pēl'yо̄о̄s), a mortal, and the goddess Thetis; leader of the Myrmidons.

Agamemnon: commander-in-chief of the Greek army; brother of Menelaus, both of whom are sons of Atreus (ā'trо̄о̄s).

Ajax: prince of Salamis, an island near Athens.

Menelaus (men'ə·lā'əs): king of Mycenae; Helen's wronged husband.

Odysseus: cleverest of the Greeks; son of Laertes (lā·ûr'tēz); king of Ithaca, an island off the western coast of Greece.

Patroclus: Achilles' best friend.

Andromache (an·drom'ə·kē): young wife of Hector.

Cassandra: daughter of Priam; has prophetic powers.

Hecuba: wife of Priam.

Hector: eldest son of Priam; foremost Trojan warrior.

Paris: also called Alexander; handsome son of Priam; Hector's brother, who stole Helen from Menelaus.

Priam (prī'əm): aged king of Troy.

Briseis (brī·sē'is): captive girl given to Achilles.

Chryseis (krī·sē'is): captive girl given to Agamemnon.

Homer never speaks of the Greeks as Greeks, for that name originated in Italy a thousand years later. He refers to his people by their old sectional or tribal names: Danaans (see line 5), Achaeans (see line 10), or Argives (see line 30). All of these tribes were temporarily united by war.

The city of Troy is referred to often as Ilium. *Iliad* means the "tale of Ilium."

FROM *Book 1: The Quarrel*

[As Book 1 of Homer's epic opens, a terrible disease is raging through the Greek camp. It has been caused by the god Apollo, who is angry at Agamemnon, chief of the Greek army. During a foray into a nearby town, the Greeks had taken several captives, among them a beautiful young girl named Chryseis, whose father is a priest of Apollo. The girl had been awarded to Agamemnon as a prize. Chryseis' father had made his way into the Greek camp and offered Agamemnon rich ransom for his daughter's release, but the vain and selfish Greek chieftain had sent him away. Apollo, disgusted at the treatment of one of his priests, rained shafts of pestilence down upon the Greeks.]

. . .

For nine days the deadly shafts
Of the god sped through the army, but on the tenth day
The white-armed goddess Hera put into the heart
Of Achilles to call the men to the place of assembly,
For it distressed her to see the Danaans dying.   5
When they were assembled and seated, fleet-footed Achilles
Stood up in their midst, and spoke:
    "Now, O son
Of Atreus,° it seems that we shall be baffled and driven
Back home, if indeed we escape with our lives from the war
And pestilence too that plague the Achaeans. But come,   10
Let us consult some prophet or priest, or some reader
Of dreams—for even a dream is from Zeus—someone
Who may be able to tell us why Phoebus Apollo
Rages so fiercely. If it is because of a hecatomb°
Or vow unperformed, perhaps the god will accept   15
The savor of sacrificed lambs and goats without blemish
And change his mind about plaguing us all this way."
    When he had spoken and sat down again, up stood
Calchas, son of Thestor, he who was far
The best reader of ominous birds,° who knew what was   20
And had been and things that were to be, and who had
By means of the keen prophetic vision given
To him by Apollo guided the Achaean ships
To Ilium. Now, with all good intentions, he addressed
The assembly:
    "Zeus-loved Achilles, you bid me explain   25
The wrath of far-smiting Apollo. Therefore I will.
But first you must make up your mind and swear to defend me,
Swear that you'll be both willing and quick with word
And hand. For I fear I am going to anger a man
Who rules with might over all the Argives, and from whom   30

---

8. **son of Atreus:** that is, Agamemnon.   14. **hecatomb:** a great sacrifice to the gods, originally a hundred oxen.   20. **ominous birds:** birds believed to bear omens.

Composite of excerpts from *The Iliad of Homer,* translated by Ennis Rees, © copyright 1963 by Ennis Rees. Reprinted by permission of Random House, Inc.

The Achaeans take orders. A king, you know, is always
More lordly when angry at a low-ranking man. Even
If he swallows his wrath at the time, in his heart he nurses it
Still, till he has his revenge. So decide whether you
Will protect me."
    Then swift Achilles answered him thus: 35
"Be bold, and tell us what you can of the god's mind and will,
For by Zeus-loved Apollo I swear to you that so long
As I live on earth and have my sight, no one
Shall hurt you here by the hollow ships, no one
In the Danaan host, though you mean Agamemnon himself,   40
Who claims to be far the best of all the Achaeans."
    At this the peerless prophet took heart, and spoke:
"It's not for a hecatomb or broken vow that he blames us,
But because Agamemnon insulted his priest by not
Accepting the ransom and giving the man his daughter.   45
Thus the far-smiting god has given us woes,
And will continue to give them. He will not remove
This loathsome plague till we return to her father
His wide-eyed daughter—nor can we accept any ransom—
And we must carry to Chryse a holy hecatomb.   50
Only then can we hope to change the mind of Apollo."
    When he had spoken and sat down again, the son
Of Atreus, the wide-ruling wager of war Agamemnon,
Stood up in a rage among them. His black heart boiled
With wrath and his eyes were like fire when it blazes. Fixing   55
Calchas with an evil scowl, he railed at him thus:
"Prophet of misery! you've still got your first good thing
To foretell for me. Unhappy events you always
Enjoy predicting, but never yet have you prophesied
Anything pleasant, much less brought it to pass.   60
And now in the midst of this Danaan meeting you go on
Spouting your oracles, telling the men it's because
Of me that the far-darting god is inflicting these woes
Upon them, because I refused the royal ransom
For the darling daughter of Chryses, since I much prefer   65
To have her at home with me. I would rather have her,
In fact, then Clytemnestra, my wife. For this girl is quite
Her equal, just as tall and good looking, just as
Smart and clever with her hands. Even so, I want
To give the girl back, if that is the thing to do.   70
I prefer the men safe and well, not sick and dying.
But you must prepare a prize for me at once.
For me to be the only Argive here
Without some gift of honor would hardly be right!
As you can see, my prize is going elsewhere."   75
    Then Achilles, noble and strong, answered him thus:
"Renowned son of Atreus, most covetous of men, how
Can the gallant Achaeans give you a prize? If there
Is some large public treasure, we've yet to learn where it is,
And the plunder we took from the cities we sacked has already   80

Been divided. Nor can we rightly take these things back
From the people. But you, give up the girl as the god
Demands. We Achaeans will recompense you three
And four times over, if Zeus ever wills that we sack
The well-walled city of Troy."

And lordly Agamemnon   85
Spoke in reply: "Though you be, O godlike Achilles,
A man of great valor, don't try to outwit me like that,
For I'll not be persuaded or gotten the best of by you!
Do you tell me to give the girl back so that you can keep
What you've got while I sit here with nothing? If the gallant   90
Achaeans give me a prize to my liking, and equal
To the one I am losing, all right—but if they do not,
Then I myself will come and take your gift
Of honor, or that of Ajax, or I'll seize and bear off
The prize of Odysseus. Wrathful indeed will be   95
The man to whom I make that visit! But this
We can think about later. Right now let us launch a black ship
On the sacred sea, get enough rowers together,
And put on board a hecatomb along with the girl,
The lovely Chryseis herself. And let one of our leaders   100
Take charge, either Ajax, or Idomeneus, or godly Odysseus,
Or, son of Peleus, you yourself, most dreaded
Of men, that so you may offer gifts and appease
The far-working god."

Then swift Achilles, scowling
At him, replied: "You greedy-minded shamelessness   105
Incarnate! how can any decent Achaean want to
Take orders from you, to go where you tell him to go
Or battle his best with hostile men? I didn't
Come here to fight because of the Trojan spearmen.
They've never done me any harm, never rustled my cattle   110
Or horses, or plundered in fertile Phthia° a harvest
Of mine, for between here and there lie a great many things—
Shadowy mountains and crashing sea. But we
Came here with you, the incredibly shameless, in an effort
To gratify you! to get satisfaction for Menelaus   115
And you! covetous cur that you are. All this
You turn your back on and choose to forget, and now
You threaten to take my prize of prestige, the gift
I got from the sons of Achaeans and for which I labored
So much. Whenever we warriors sack a populous   120
Trojan city, my share of the booty is never
Equal to yours. True, I get more, much more,
Than my share of chaotic battle, but when it comes
To dividing the loot, your portion is always far larger
Than mine. Worn out with fighting, I go back to my ships   125
And with me take some pitiful little prize
Allotted to me—little, but mine. Now, though,

---

111. **Phthia** (thī′ə): Achilles' home in northern Greece.

I'll go back to Phthia, for I would much rather take all
My beaked ships and go home than stay on here in disgrace
To heap up wealth for you!"
      And the king of men   130
Agamemnon answered him thus: "Go on and run,
If you feel the urge so strongly. I do not beg you
To stay on my account. I've others here
Who honor and respect me, including the best of all counselors,
Zeus himself. Of all the god-nurtured leaders,   135
You are most hateful to me, for strife is always
Dear to your heart, and battles and fighting. And if
You're so full of valor, that's the gift of a god.
So take your ships and your men and go lord it over
The Myrmidons° at home. I have no regard for you,   140
Nor do I care how angry you are. But see now
How you like this. Since Phoebus Apollo is taking
Chryseis from me, I'm returning her with a ship
And men of mine—but I myself will come
To your lodge and take your prize, the lovely Briseis,   145
That once and for all you may know how greatly I
Exceed you in power and excellence, and another man
Will think twice before calling himself my equal and right
In my presence comparing himself with me!"
    He spoke,
And the pain from his words went deep in the son of Peleus,   150
Rending the heart in his shaggy breast two ways
As to what he should do, whether to draw the sharp sword
By his thigh, break up the meeting, and kill the son
Of Atreus, or swallow his rage and control his temper.
While he was thus divided in mind and heart,   155
With that huge sword of his half drawn from the scabbard,
Pallas Athena came down from the sky, sent
By white-armed Hera, the goddess whose heart held equal
Love and concern for both of the angry men.
Standing behind him, she caught the son of Peleus   160
By a handful of tawny hair and made herself visible
To him alone, nor could any of the others see her.
Astonished, Achilles turned, and as he looked
In the blazing blue eyes of the goddess he knew her at once
For Pallas Athena, and his words came winged with surprise: 165
    "Why, O daughter of aegis-bearing Zeus,° do you come again
Now? Can it be that you wanted to witness the hubris
And gross overreaching of Atreus' son Agamemnon?
Well let me say this, and believe me I mean what I say.
That arrogant pride of his may shortly cost him   170
His life!"

---

140. **Myrmidons:** the people of Phthia, followers of Achilles. 166. **aegis-bearing Zeus:** the aegis (ē′jis) was the breastplate of Zeus. It was made from the hide of a goat that had suckled Zeus (from the Greek *aigis,* meaning "goatskin").

And the bright-eyed goddess Athena replied:
"I came down from the sky to help you control
Your wrath, if only you will obey, and the goddess
White-armed Hera sent me, for her heart holds equal
Love and concern for both of you. So come,   175
No fighting, and don't draw your sword. Wound him with words
Instead, and tell him just how it will be. And now
I say this to you, and I too mean what I say.
On account of this arrogant insult, splendid gifts
Worth three times as much as what you may lose will one day   180
Be given to you. So hold yourself back, and obey us."
     Then Achilles, swift of foot, answered her thus:
"No man, O goddess, can ignore the word of two
Such powers, no matter how wrathful his heart may be.
To obey is surely better. The gods hear all   185
The prayers of him who heeds them."
                    He spoke, and restrained
His mighty hand on the silver hilt. Then obeying
The word of Athena he thrust the long blade back into
The scabbard. And the goddess left for Olympus and the palace
Of aegis-bearing Zeus, to mingle with the other gods there.   190
     And again Achilles, wrathful as ever, spoke violent
Words to the son of Atreus: "You drunken sot!
With the greedy eyes of a dog and the heart of a deer!
You never have courage enough to arm yourself
For battle along with the rest of us, or go   195
With the best Achaeans on a crafty ambush. You'd rather
Die than do either! You much prefer to go
Through this huge camp and seize for yourself the gift
Of anyone here who disagrees with you, you wretched
Devourer of what we win! And truly, the men   200
You rule are also worthless, or this, O son
Of Atreus, would be the last of your arrogant insults.
But I'll make something clear right now, and swear a great oath.
I swear by this staff I hold—which no longer has bud
Or leaf since it left its stump in the mountains, nor ever   205
Grows green again and blooms since the sharp bronze stripped it
Of foliage and bark, but which now the sons of Achaeans
Bear in their hands, they who are judges among us
And uphold the laws of God—by this staff I swear
A great oath that surely someday a desperate need   210
For Achilles shall come upon all the sons of Achaeans,
Nor will you be able to help them at all, no matter
How grieved you are, when man-killing Hector is cutting them
Down by the dozen. Then, I say, you'll rend
Your heart with wrath and remorse for failing to honor   215
The best Achaean of all!"
     So saying, Achilles
Dashed to the ground the staff with its studs of bright gold,
And sat down, while opposite him the son of Atreus
Went on venting his rage. Then among them up stood

Nestor, the silver-tongued speaker of Pylos,° from whose   220
Lips the words flowed sweeter than honey. Since he
First saw the light, two generations of mortal
Men had come and gone in sacred Pylos,
And now among the third he was the king.
In an effort to help, he addressed the assembly: 225
  "For shame!
Surely now great grief comes on the land
Of Achaea. But think how glad it would make King Priam
And all of his sons along with the other Trojans
To learn of this wrangling between you—you that among
The Danaans stand first in counsel and warfare. But listen   230
To me. Both of you are younger than I,
And in other days I have campaigned with mightier
Men than you, nor did they ever belittle
Or disregard me. Never since have I seen such warriors,
Nor ever again shall I see such heroes as Peirithous   235
Was and Dryas, marshaler of men, and Caeneus
And Exadius and Polyphemus, godlike in his might, and that equal
Of the immortal gods, Theseus, son of Aegeus.
Of all men reared on earth, these were the strongest.
The strongest, I say, and with the strongest they fought—   240
With the monstrous mountain Centaurs, and the slaughter they there
Performed was terrible indeed. I came a long way
From distant Pylos and mingled with those very men,
For I came at their summons. And in the war I did
My personal share of the fighting. There are today   245
No mortals alive on earth who would be fit
To fight with those men. Still, they listened to me
And took my advice. And you too would do better to harken
And heed. You, Agamemnon, are a man of great power,
But don't try taking that girl away. Leave her   250
Alone, the prize of him to whom the Achaeans
Gave her. And you, O son of Peleus, do not
Presume to pit your might in strife against
A sceptered king, who derives his power from Zeus
And therefore has no common glory. You   255
Are the son of a goddess and valiant indeed, yet he
Is the mightier man, since he rules over more people.
Check your rage, Atrides°—in fact, I beg you
To extinguish the wrath of yours against Achilles,
Who in the moil of horrible war is the mightiest   260
Mainstay we Achaeans have."
  And ruling Agamemnon
Replied: "All that you say, O aged one,
Is just and wise enough, but this man wants
To be higher than anyone else. He wants to rule
Over all—to be king, I tell you, and give orders to all.   265
Well I know one, at least, who won't take orders

220. **Pylos:** a city in southern Greece.   258. **Atrides** (ə·trī′dēz): son of Atreus; that is,
Agamemnon.

From him! So the immortal gods made him
A mighty spearman—does that give him the right
To go around spouting insults?"
    Then the gifted Achilles
Interrupted, saying: "Indeed, for if I yielded   270
To you in all things, no matter what you commanded,
I would be called a coward and good for nothing.
So boss the others about, but give no more orders
To me! I'm through with doing what you say. And here
Is something else that you will do well to remember.   275
I will not fight with you or anyone else
For the girl, since you do but take what you gave. But of all
That I'll have left by that swift black ship of mine,
I warn you not to take away anything else!
Go on and try, if you like, so that all may learn   280
I mean business—and see how soon your black blood covers
My spear!"
    When the violent words had all been spoken,
The two men arose and broke up the meeting beside
The Achaean ships. Achilles strode off to his shelters
And well-balanced ships along with Patroclus and all   285
The rest of his comrades. But the son of Atreus ordered
Others to drag a swift ship down into the sea
And he picked out twenty oarsmen. Then they drove on board
For the god the hecatomb of cattle and brought Chryseis
Of the lovely cheeks and put her aboard. And Odysseus,   290
Resourceful as ever, mounted the deck and took charge.
    When all were embarked and sailing the foamy sea-lanes,
Atreus' son commanded the army to wash,
And they purified themselves in the salt sea-water and offered
To Apollo appeasing hecatombs of bulls and goats   295
By the shore of the unresting sea. And the plentiful smoke
Curled up in the sky and eddying with it the savor.
    While the men were busy with offerings throughout the camp,
Agamemnon proceeded to fulfill his threat to Achilles.
He called his heralds and nimble squires, Talthybius   300
And Eurybates, and spoke to them thus: "Go to the lodge
Of Peleus' son Achilles, take the hand
Of the beautiful-cheeked Briseis, and bring her to me.
And if he refuses to give her, I myself will go
With more men and take her, which will be far more painful for him." 305
    With this harsh order he sent them away on their mission,
And they, reluctant, walked off along the beach
Of the desolate sea till they came to the shelters and ships
Of the Myrmidons. They found Achilles sitting by his lodge
And black ship, nor was he glad to see them. Frozen   310
With fear and embarrassment, they stood in awe of the prince,
Unable to speak a word or ask a question.
But he knew very well what they wanted and spoke to them, saying:
    "Come here, good heralds, and welcome. You bear the words
Of God and men, and my quarrel is not with you,   315

But Agamemnon, who sent you here for the girl Briseis.
So come, god-sprung Patroclus, bring out the girl
And give her to these men to take back with them. And in
That day when I shall be desperately needed to save
The Achaeans from shameful destruction, these two shall witness   320
For me before blissful gods and mortal men
And the stupid king himself. For surely his rage
Will be the ruin of him yet. If he wants his Achaeans to fight
With both success and survivors, he had better try looking
Before as well as behind!"

      He spoke, and Patroclus   325
Obeyed his dear friend. He led from the lodge Briseis,
Lovely of face, and gave her to go with the men.
And back they went down the line of Achaean ships
And with them the unwilling girl. Now Achilles, weeping,
Withdrew from his comrades, and sitting down by himself   330
On the beach by the silvery surf he looked out over
The wine-dark sea, stretched out his arms, and fervently
Prayed to his own dear mother:
      "Since, O Mother,
You bore me, though only to live for a few short years,
Surely Olympian Zeus should have given me honor,   335
But now that high-thundering god has given me quite
The reverse. For truly the son of Atreus, imperial
Agamemnon, has grossly insulted me. He has robbed me
Of my gift of honor and now he keeps her himself!"

      Thus in tears he spoke, and far down in the sea,   340
Sitting by her ancient father, his goddess mother
Heard him. And quickly she left the gray sea like a mist
And sank down in front of her weeping son, gently
Caressed him, called him by name, and said:
      "My child,
Why are you crying? What sorrow has entered your heart?   345
Keep it in no longer. Speak out, and share it with me."
      Then moaning, swift-footed Achilles spoke to her thus:
"You know. Why should I tell it to one who already
Knows all about it? We went out to Thebe, the sacred
City of Eetion,° destroyed and plundered it all,   350
And brought the booty back here. This the sons
Of Achaeans divided farily among them, and they chose
For the son of Atreus the fair-cheeked daughter of Chryses.
But he, as a priest of far-smiting Apollo, came
To the speedy ships of the gallant bronze-clad Achaeans   355
To ransom his daughter, and the ransom he bore was boundless.
In suppliant hands on a staff of gold he carried
The fillets of far-darting Apollo, and he pleaded with all
The Achaeans, especially with the two sons of Atreus,
Marshalers of many:
      "'O sons of Atreus and you other   360

---

350. **Eetion** (ē·ē′ti·on): king of Thebe (thē′bē), a city near Troy.

Well-greaved° Achaeans, may the gods who live on Olympus
Allow you to sack the city of Priam and reach
Your homes in safety. But reverence the son of Zeus,
Apollo who strikes from afar—take this ransom
And return my precious daughter.'
    "All the other Achaeans   365
Supported the priest and shouted to reverence him
And accept the splendid ransom. But Atreus' son
Agamemnon was far from pleased. Roughly he sent him
Away, threatening him harshly. And back he went,
A very angry old man, and Apollo, who loves him dearly,   370
Sent a shaft of sickness against the Argives.
His arrows flew through the wide Achaean camp,
And more and more people were dying. Then a prophet whom we
Could depend on told us the mind and will of the god
Who smites from afar, and I was the first to suggest   375
That we try to appease him. At this a great rage gripped
Agamemnon, and he uttered a threat that has now been fulfilled.
For already the quick-eyed Achaeans are taking one girl
To Chryse aboard a swift ship along with gifts
For the god, and heralds have come to my lodge and taken   380
The other, Briseis, my gift from the sons of Achaeans.
But if you really have power, protect your own son.
If you ever did or said anything that gladdened
The heart of Zeus, go now to Olympus and plead
With him. Many times in the halls of my father I have heard you   385
Glory in telling how you were the only immortal
To help lord Zeus of the dark and lowering sky
And rescue him from shame when other Olympians—
Hera, Poseidon, and Pallas Athena—plotted
To bind him fast. Then, O goddess, you came   390
And untied him, but first with all speed you summoned to lofty
Olympus him of the hundred hands, known as
Briareus to the gods, but Aegaeon to all mankind,
A monster even more powerful than his father Poseidon.
He crouched by the side of Cronos' son,° exulting   395
In his reputation, and the blessed gods were afraid
Of him and made no attempt to bind Zeus again.
Go sit by his side and remind him of this, and embrace
His knees in earnest prayer for him to support
The Trojans; but as for their foes, the Achaeans, may he trap them   400
Between the sterns of their ships and litter the beach
With dead and dying men, that all may share
The reward of their king, and that Atreus' son, imperial
Agamemnon, may know how blind he was to give
No honor at all to the bravest and best of Achaeans!"   405
    Then Thetis, weeping, replied: "My child, my child,
Why did I raise you to all this misery? I only

---

361. **Well-greaved:** well-protected by armor. Greaves were worn on the legs to protect the
area below the knees.   395. **Cronos' son:** Zeus.

Wish that you might have stayed by your ships and escaped
All grief and tears, for the life allotted to you
Is short, not long at all. And now not only   410
Will you die young, but you have to suffer as well,
And more than anyone else. Hence, back home
In our halls, I bore you to a fate most miserable. But I
Will go in person to snowy Olympus and tell
This grievance of yours to Zeus, the lover of lightning,   415
In hope of his help. Meanwhile, you remain
By the swift seagoing ships, and go on in your wrath
Against the Achaeans and your utter refusal to fight.
For yesterday Zeus departed for the stream of Oceanus°
To attend a feast of the excellent Ethiopians, and all   420
The other gods went with him. In twelve days he
Will be back on Olympus, and then to the brazen-floored palace
Of Zeus I will go, and embrace his knees in prayer.
I believe I shall win him over."
　　　　With this she left him
There on the beach, resentful and brooding on account of   425
The fair-gowned woman they had forcefully, spitefully
Taken from him.
　　　　　　　　　　　. . .

[Without Achilles' help, the Greeks are at a grave disadvantage against the Trojans, who are led by their great warrior Hector. As Book 3 opens, the Greek and
Trojan armies confront each other on the dusty plain outside Troy.]

FROM *Book 3: The Duel*

When each battalion had been drawn up with its captain,
The Trojans advanced with clamor and clang like the noise
Of birds, the clangor of cranes that rises toward heaven
When they flee the storms of winter and floods of beating
Rain and fly with loud cries toward the stream of Oceanus   5
To offer in battle at dawn terrible slaughter
And death to men of the Pygmies.° The Achaeans, however,
Came on with no cries at all, but breathing might
And full of resolve to aid and defend one another.
　　　　As when the South Wind covers the peaks of a mountain   10
With a mist no shepherd loves, but that thieves prefer
To night, since through it a man can see but a stone's throw
Ahead, so now from beneath their feet a thick
Dust cloud arose as swiftly they went on the double
Across the plain.
　　　　When the two advancing armies   15
Drew near each other, out from the Trojan ranks
Stepped godlike Paris, also called Alexander,

419. **Oceanus:** a sea thought to surround the earth. Near it, supposedly, lived the Ethiopians.
7. **cranes . . . Pygmies:** It was believed that the cranes were at war with the Pygmies, a race
of tiny men. The Greek word *pygme* means the length of the arm from the elbow to knuckles.

With a leopard skin on his shoulders along with his sword
And bent bow. Then shaking two bronze-headed spears he challenged
The best of the Argives to come out and meet him in grim   20
And single combat.
     And no sooner did King Menelaus,
The favorite of Ares, catch sight of him there, coming out
Of the crowd and swaggering along with great strides, than he
Was as glad as a starving lion that happens upon
The large carcass of an antlered stag or wild goat and greedily   25
Gulps away, despite the frantic efforts
Of darting dogs and lusty young hunters. So now
Menelaus rejoiced when first his eyes fell on Prince
Alexander, for he thought that vengeance on the sinner was finally
His. And at once he leaped in full armor from his car   30
To the ground.
     But when Prince Alexander saw who it was
Who appeared to accept his challenge, his spirit collapsed
And back he shrank mid a crowd of comrades, seeking
To save his life. Like a man who comes on a snake
In a mountain ravine and springs back pale and trembling   35
And gives the snake plenty of room, so Prince Alexander
Feared Atreus' son, and cringing shrank back in the ranks
Of lordly Trojans.
     But Hector saw and tried
To shame him with words of reproach: "Despicable Paris,
Handsome, deceitful, and crazy for women, would you   40
Had never been born, or had died unmarried! Indeed,
I really wish that you had, since such would have been
Much better than what you are now—an object of scorn
Looked down on by others. Surely the longhaired Achaeans
Will laugh loud and long, saying that a prince is our champion   45
Because he's good looking, though he be both woefully gutless
And weak. Aren't you the one who rounded up
Your trusty cronies and took off in your seagoing ships
Across the deep to mingle with strangers and bring back
From a distant country a comely, voluptuous woman,   50
The daughter-in-law of a nation of spear-wielding warriors,
But a cause of terrible harm to your father and city
And all the people—aren't you the strong man who took her,
A joy to your foes and an utter disgrace to yourself?
And can it be that now you refuse to stand up   55
To the fighting Menelaus? You would soon find out what kind
Of fighter he is whose glamorous wife you have.
When you're lying down there in the dust you won't be helped
By that lyre of yours nor the gifts Aphrodite gave you,
Your handsome face and pretty hair. But truly   60
The Trojans are just as afraid, or you would already
Have paid for all the evil you've done—paid
By donning that tunic of stone which rocks from their hands
Would have furnished!"
     And godlike Alexander replied: "Hector,

You chide me no more than is right and not a bit more   65
Than you should. Yours is a tireless heart and unyielding,
Like an ax that serves the blow of a skillful shipwright
As he sends it down through a log to shape a ship's timber.
So the heart in your breast bears all before it, but do not
Reproach me for the winsome gifts of golden Aphrodite.   70
The gods give wonderful gifts no man can choose
For himself, and such are not to be scorned or discarded.
But now, if you really insist on my doing battle
With Ares-loved Menelaus, have all other Trojans
And men of Achaea sit down, and put us together   75
Out there in the middle to fight for Helen and all
Her treasures. And whoever is stronger and wins, let him take
Both wealth and woman and carry them home, while you others
Swear oaths of faith and friendship and solemnize all
With sacrifice, that you may remain in the fertile land   80
Of Troy, and they return to their thoroughbred horses
And beautiful women in Achaea and grassy Argos."°
     Then Hector rejoiced, and stepping out between
The two armies he gripped his spear by the middle and held
The Trojan line back till all were seated. Meanwhile,   85
The longhaired Achaeans kept trying to strike him with arrows
And stones, but now the king of men Agamemnon
Raised his voice in command:
     "Enough, Argives!
No more shooting, you men of Achaea! for it seems
That bright-helmeted Hector has something to say."
     He spoke,   90
And they ceased their shooting and hurling and quickly grew quiet.
Then Hector spoke between the two armies: "From me,
O Trojans and well-greaved Achaeans, hear the proposal
Of Paris, who began this miserable war. He says
For all other Trojans and men of Achaea to lay   95
Their excellent arms on the bountiful earth, and that he,
Out here in the middle, will fight with fierce Menelaus
For Helen and all her treasures. And whoever is stronger
And wins, let him take both wealth and woman and carry them
Home, while we others swear oaths of faith and friendship   100
And solemnize all with sacrifice."
     So Hector, and no one
Answered a word till among them out spoke Menelaus
Of the fierce battle-scream: "Hear also me, as one
Whose heart has borne more pain than any of yours.
Now I think that Trojans and Argives should part,   105
Since you have already suffered sorrows enough
Because of my quarrel, which Alexander began.
For one of us two, death and doom are allotted.
So let one of us die, and you others part
With all speed. But first bring two lambs, a white ram and black ewe   110

82. **Argos:** a city on the plain of Argolis in Greece.

For Earth and the Sun, and we'll bring another for Zeus.
And some of you go for the powerful Priam, that he too
May swear and sacrifice, for he has haughty, unscrupulous
Sons, and we do not want any proud overreacher
To spoil the oaths we swear in God's name. The hearts   115
Of young men are often unstable, but whenever an old man
Is present, he thinks of the future as well as the past,
And so both parties benefit greatly."
     He spoke,
And both sides rejoiced, hoping to cease their miserable
Fighting. They reined their chariots back in the ranks,   120
Stepped down, and took off their armor, which they laid on the ground
Beside them with not much space between. And Hector
Sent two heralds to bring the lambs from the city
As fast as they could and to summon King Priam, while ruling
Agamemnon dispatched Talthybius to the hollow ships   125
With orders to bring a lamb, and he did not ignore
His royal commander.
     Meanwhile Iris° arrived
With a message for white-armed Helen, and she came in the likeness
Of her sister-in-law Laodice, the loveliest daughter
Of Priam and the wife of lord Helicaon, son   130
Of Antenor. Helen she found in the hall, weaving
A web of double width and of iridescent
Purple. And in it she wove not a few of the battles
That the horse-breaking Trojans and bronze-clad Achaeans had suffered
At the hands of Ares on her account. Standing   135
Close by her side, nimble Iris spoke to her, saying:
     "Come, my dear, that you may see an incredible
Thing that the horse-breaking Trojans and bronze-clad Achaeans
Have done. They who but lately were eager to clash
On the plain and tearfully tear each other to pieces   140
Have now called off the battle and are sitting quietly
Out there, leaning back on their shields, with their long spears fixed
In the ground beside them. But Paris and fierce Menelaus
Are to use their long spears to fight each other for you,
And you will be called the dear wife of whichever one wins."   145
     These words of the goddess aroused in the heart of Helen
An irresistible yearning for her former husband,
Her city, and parents. Quickly she veiled herself
In shining white linen, and softly crying hurriedly
Left her chamber, not by herself but attended   150
By two of her handmaids, Aethra, daughter of Pittheus,
And heifer-eyed Clymene. And quickly they came in sight
Of the Scaean Gates.°
     There in the council of Priam
Sat the elders of Priam's people, Panthous and Thymoetes,
Clytius, Lampus, and Hicetaon, scion of Ares,   155

---

   127. **Iris:** a messenger of the gods.   153. **Scaean** (sē′ən) **Gates:** the northwest gates of the walled city of Troy.

And two other men of wisdom, Ucalegon and Antenor.
Too old for battle, these elders were excellent speakers,
And now they sat on the wall like forest cicadas
That sit on a tree and sing with their lily voices.
Even so, the leaders of Troy sat on the turreted   160
Wall, and when they saw Helen approaching spoke softly
One to another in these words winged with wonder:
　　"Surely no one could blame either side for suffering
So much and so long for such a woman, for she
In appearance is terribly like an immortal goddess!   165
But still, though lovely she is, let her go home
With the ships and not be left here as a curse to both us
And our children."
　　So they, but Priam spoke to her, saying:
"Come here, dear child, and sit before me, that you
May see your former husband, your kinsfolk and friends.   170
I certainly don't blame you. The gods alone
Are to blame for hurling upon me this tearful war
With Achaeans. But tell me the name of yonder huge
Achaean, that chieftain so valiant and tall. To be sure
There are others at least a head taller than he, but never   175
Have I laid eyes on a man so truly handsome
And regal. That man has the look of a ruler, of one
Who is king indeed."
　　And glamorous Helen replied:
"You I regard with respect and reverence, you
My own dear father-in-law. But now I wish   180
It had been my good fortune to die when I came here
With your son, deserting my marriage chamber and daughter
So precious, my blood relations and circle of charming
Friends. But that wasn't to be. Instead, I weep out
My life little by little. Now, though, I will answer   185
Your question. Yonder Achaean is Atreus' son,
Great Agamemnon, a high-ranking king and mighty
Spearman. And as sure as ever there was such a man
He was once the brother-in-law of bitch-hearted me."
　　She spoke, and the old man marveled, saying: "O happy   190
Son of Atreus, born lucky, god-blessed man,
How very many young men of Achaea are under
Your rule! I journeyed once to the viny land
Of Phrygia° where I saw huge hosts of Phrygian warriors
With their glancing-swift horses, the armies of Otreus and royal   195
Mygdon, encamped along the banks of the river Sangarius.
And I was an ally of theirs and numbered among them
That day when the man-matching Amazons° came. But not even
They were so numerous as are the quick-eyed Achaeans."
　　Next the old man noticed Odysseus, and said: 200
"Come, dear child, tell me who that man is too.

　194. **Phrygia** (frij´ĭ·ə); a district east of Troy.   198. **Amazons:** a tribe of female warriors
who, during the Trojan War, were allies of Troy.

He's a good head shorter than Atreus' son Agamemnon
But broader through shoulders and chest. His armor lies
On the bountiful earth while he goes up and down
Through the ranks like the leading ram in a herd. To me   205
That's what he is like, a wooly ram that paces
His way through a truly large flock of silvery-white sheep."
        And Zeus-born Helen° answered again: "That
Is the son of Laertes, resourceful Odysseus, who was raised
In rocky Ithaca. He's a cunning and clever man,   210
Both wily and wise."
        Then the grave Antenor answered
Her thus: "What you say, my lady, is true indeed.
For some time ago the brilliant Odysseus was here
With Ares' own Menelaus to confer about you,
And I was their host. I welcomed them in my halls   215
And got to know what they look like and how they think.
Whenever they mixed in a meeting with Trojans, Menelaus
Stood head and shoulders above Odysseus, but when
They were seated Odysseus was the more majestic. And when
They stood before all to weave the words of wise counsel,   220
Menelaus' words were few, but fluently uttered,
Clear, and to the point. Though the younger man,
He was surely no rambler or bungler with words. But whenever
Resourceful Odysseus got up, he would stand looking down,
His eyes fixed hard on the ground, nor would he gesture   225
At all with the staff he held. He would hold it rigid,
Like a man who wasn't all there. You would, in fact,
Have thought him a sullen and foolish fellow. But when
He spoke, that great voice of his poured out of his chest
In words like the snowflakes of winter, and then no other   230
Mortal could in debate contend with Odysseus.
Nor did we care any longer how he looked."
        Then the old man, noticing Ajax, asked: "And who
Is that other manly Achaean, the one so tall
And knightly, whose head and broad shoulders tower above   235
The Argives?"
        And exquisite Helen of the flowing gowns:
"That's the enormous Ajax, a very fortress
Of Achaean valor. And over there Idomeneus
Stands like a god mid the men and captains of Crete.
Many times, on journeys from Crete, he stayed at our house,   240
And my warrior lord, Menelaus, welcomed him warmly.
And now I see many other quick-eyed Achaeans
Whom I know well enough and could name, but two of their martial
Commanders I cannot see, horse-mastering Castor
And Pollux, good in a fistfight, my own blood brothers,   245
For all of us had the same mother. Either they didn't come
With the men from dear Lacedaemon,° or else they came

---

208. **Zeus-born Helen:** Supposedly, Helen was the daughter of Zeus and of Leda, a mortal
woman.   247. **Lacedaemon** (las′ə·dē′mən): Sparta, Helen's original home.

All the way in their seagoing ships but are now too ashamed
To mingle with others in battle on account of the vile
And insulting things the soldiers say about me." 250
    Thus Helen, but they already lay in the close
Embrace of the life-giving earth back home in Lacedaemon,
Their own dear country.

    ·   ·   ·

[The duel between Paris and Menelaus is inconclusive. The two armies then break the truce and clash, disregarding their sacred oaths. As the war rages, Achilles sulks in his quarters, his anger at Agamemnon still smoldering. But the Greeks press hard, and eventually the Trojan soldiers find themselves backed up to their gates. At this point, Hector enters the city to speak some final words to his family before returning to the crisis on the battlefield. At the beginning of the selection from Book 6 which follows, he takes leave of Paris and Helen.]

FROM *Book 6: Hector and Andromache*

    ·   ·   ·

    Then tall bright-helmeted Hector: "You're kind
To ask me to sit, Helen, but don't. I cannot accept.
Already my spirit is spoiling to fight for the Trojans,
Who always miss me keenly when I am not
On the field. But try to hurry this husband of yours, 5
And may he himself make haste and catch up with me
Before I leave the city. Meanwhile, I want
To go home and briefly look in on my servants and family,
The wife I love and my baby son, whom I
May never, for all I know, come back to again, 10
Since any time the gods may hurl me down
Beneath the hands of Achaeans."
    So saying, Hector
Left them, his helmet flashing, and quickly arrived
At his comfortable home. But there he did not find
His white-armed wife Andromache. She, with the baby 15
And one of her pretty-robed women, had gone to stand
On the wall, and there she was now, weeping and frantically
Anxious. When Hector saw that his excellent wife
Was out, he stopped on the threshold and spoke to the maids:
    "Tell me truly, women. Where did Andromache go 20
When she left the house? Is she visiting one of my elegant
Sisters or sisters-in-law, or has she gone
To the shrine of Athena, where the other fair-braided women
Of Troy are making their vows to the awesome goddess?"
    Then the busy housekeeper answered him thus: "Hector, 25
To tell the truth you so urgently ask for, your wife
Has not gone to see any one of your elegant sisters
Or sisters-in-law, nor has she gone to the shrine
Of Athena, where the other fair-braided women of Troy
Are making their vows to the awesome goddess. She heard 30

The Trojans were yielding to the powerful men of Achaea
And ran from the house toward the great city wall like a woman
Half out of her senses, and the nurse took the baby and followed."
    The housekeeper spoke, and Hector rushed from the palace
And back through the well-laid streets the way he had come,   35
Striding down through the great city. But just as he got
To the Scaean Gates, through which he intended to pass
On his way to the plain, his wife came running to meet him,
His gifted wife Andromache, daughter of hearty
Eetion, who lived at the foot of wooded Mount Placus   40
In Hypoplacian Thebe and ruled the men
Of Cilicia.° His daughter it was whom Hector had married,
And now she met her helmeted husband, and with her
The nurse came holding the child, great Hector's dear son,
A laughing baby fair as any bright star.   45
His father called him Scamandrius, but others Astyanax,
Or Lord of the City, with reference to his tall father
On whom alone the safety of all depended.
Hector smiled at the sight of his son, but Andromache
Fairly grew to his arm, and weeping spoke thus: 50
    "Ah, Hector, possessed by a demon, your might as a fighter
Will be the death of you yet. Nor do you pity
Your baby boy and my unfortunate self,
So soon to be your widow, for any time now
The Achaeans will gang up and kill you, I know. But I   55
Would be better off in my grave, were I to lose you,
For once you have met your fate, never again
Can there be any warmth in my life, nor anything else
But pain. I have no father, no lady mother.
My father was killed by fierce Achilles when he   60
So utterly sacked the Cilicians' teeming city,
High-gated Thebe. He killed Eetion, yes,
But even his spirit recoiled at stripping that king
Of his armor. So him he burned in his richly wrought bronze
And heaped a high barrow above him, and all about it   65
The mountain nymphs, daughters of Zeus of the aegis,
Planted elm trees. And the seven brothers I had
At home went down to Hades the very same day,
For right in the midst of their shuffling cattle and silvery
White sheep, quick-footed Achilles killed them all.   70
But here he brought my mother the Queen, torn
From below our wooded Mount Placus along with the rest
Of the spoils. Then having extorted a ransom past counting,
He let her go to her father's house where she died
A victim of arrow-scattering Artemis.° So you,   75
My Hector, are father and mother to me, and brother
And manly husband. Have pity, then, and stay
Right here on the wall, or truly your son will soon

---

42. **Cilicia** (si·lish′ə): a province in Asia Minor. Thebe was a city there.   75. **Artemis:** goddess of the hunt and sister of Apollo. Sudden death in women was attributed to Artemis' arrows.

Be an orphan, your wife a miserable widow. And order
The army to make a stand at the fig tree, where the city   80
Is best assaulted and the wall most easily scaled.
Three times already their bravest men have charged there,
Led by the two Ajaxes, world-famous Idomeneus,
Atreus' sons, and strong Diomedes—all
Kept trying to get at us there, as if some knowing   85
Seer had told them our weakness, or they themselves
Had guessed it."
     Then great bright-helmeted Hector replied:
"I too, my dear, have all these things on my mind.
But how could I face the men of Troy, or their wives
Of the trailing gowns, if I were to skulk like a coward   90
And stay away from the battle? Nor does my own spirit
Urge me to do so, since I have learned to be valiant
Always and fight mid the foremost champions of Troy,
To win and uphold the king my father's glory
As well as my own. For this one thing in heart   95
And soul I know: the day of ruin shall surely
Come for holy Troy, for Priam and all
The people of Priam, who wielded the good ashen spear.
But when I think of the suffering the Trojans will have to
Endure, of Hecuba's grief and that of King Priam,   100
And of my many brave brothers who shall on that day
Go down in the dust, slain by those who hate them,
I am not troubled so deeply as at the thought
Of your grief when some bronze-clad Achaean leads you off
Weeping and puts an end to your freedom. Then   105
In Argos you'll weave at the loom of somebody else
And carry water for her from the spring Messeis
Or Hypereia,° unwillingly always, but forced
To do as you're told. Then someone, seeing your tears,
Will say: 'Look there at the wife of Hector, the best   110
In battle of all the horse-taming Trojans in the war
We fought about Ilium!' So then will someone remark.
And stabbing new grief will surely be yours to think
Of losing that man who could have held off the day
Of your bondage. But I'd much rather be dead, with earth   115
Heaped high above me, than hear your screams as warriors
Drag you away to a life of slavery!"
     So saying,
Resplendent Hector reached out to take his son,
But the baby cried and clung to the fair-belted nurse,
Afraid of the way his own father looked, with all   120
That bronze and the horsehair crest dreadfully waving
On top of his helmet. This made them both laugh, his father
And lady mother, and quickly resplendent Hector
Took off his helmet and laid the dazzling thing down.
Then he took the baby and kissed him, bounced him a bit   125

108. **Messeis** (mes·ē′is) . . . **Hypereia** (hī′pə·rī′ə): wellsprings in Greece.

In his arms, and prayed this prayer to all of the gods:
    "O Zeus and you other immortals, grant that my son
May be, like myself, outstanding among the Trojans,
As strong as I and as brave, and a mighty ruler
Of Ilium. And may it be said of him someday, as home   130
He comes from battle, 'There goes a much better man
Than his father.' Let him be bearing the bloodstained bronze
Of an enemy slain, and may he rejoice the heart
Of his mother."
    He prayed, and placed the child in the arms
Of his wife, and she held him close in her fragrant bosom,   135
Laughing and crying at once. Seeing her so,
Her husband felt deep compassion and gently caressed her,
Saying: "Poor haunted one, do not be overly
Anxious. No man in the world can hurl me to Hades
Before my appointed time comes. And no man, valiant   140
Or vile, can escape his fate ordained, once he's been
Born. So go to the house and keep yourself busy
With the loom and spindle, and see that your maids are busy.
War is for men, my dear, for all men here
In Ilium, but most of all for me."   145
    So saying,
Resplendent Hector picked up his helmet with the horsehair
Plume, and his dear wife started for home, shedding
Big tears and often looking behind her. But soon
She arrived at the comfortable home of man-killing Hector
And found her numerous maids inside. Her coming   150
Made all of them join her in wailing lament for Hector.
So there in his house they mourned for Hector still living,
For none of them thought he would ever return, once
He fell into the violent hands of Achaeans.
    Now Paris
Did not linger long in his palace, but trusting his swiftness 155
Of foot he donned his elaborate bronze and set out.
As when a horse at the manger eats his fill
Of barley, breaks his halter, and thunders away
On the plain, eager to splash in the rippling river—
He throws back his head, and his mane streams over his shoulders 160
As he exults in his splendor and gallops full speed
For the grazing grounds of mares—so Priam's son Paris
Strode down from the citadel heights, laughing aloud
To himself and bright as the sun in his glittering armor.
Rapidly walking, he quickly caught up with his brother,   165
Brave Hector, just on the point of turning away
From where he had talked with his wife. Then handsome Paris
Spoke first:
    "Surely, old fellow, I've held you back,
And you so anxious to get there. I took too long,
I know, and wasn't as fast as you told me to be."   170
    And Hector, his helmet flashing, made this reply:
"My playful brother, no right-thinking man would belittle

Your prowess in battle. You're brave enough when you want
To be, but only too often you let yourself go
And don't seem to care. That attitude pains me deeply,   175
Nor does it help when I hear the Trojan fighters
Insulting you right and left, the men who suffer
Hard battle on your account. But come, let us go.
We'll make all this up to each other yet, if only
Zeus grants us the power to rid our Trojan land   180
Of the well-greaved Achaeans. Then we shall mix in our halls
The bowl of deliverance to the heavenly gods everlasting."

[In the battles that follow, Hector fights fiercely for the Trojans, and the tide of
war begins to turn once again. As fear grows in the Greek camp, Agamemnon admits that he has wronged Achilles. He sends a delegation to offer amends and ask
Achilles and his comrades to return to the battle. Achilles remains aloof, however,
and nurses his anger with stubborn pride.
    The defenses that the Greeks have built on the shores now are broken, and the
Trojans threaten to burn the Greek ships. At this point, Achilles' best friend,
Patroclus, grieving for the suffering of the Greeks, pleads with Achilles at least to
permit him to rejoin the fighting. Achilles, fearing that if the ships are burned all
escape will be cut off, agrees, clothes his friend in his own famous armor, and sends
him into the battle along with the rest of his warriors. The battle rages, and as bodies
of both Trojans and Greeks litter the bloody field, Patroclus breaks away and heads
for the walls of Troy. But then the god Apollo, the powerful supporter of the Trojans, interferes and strikes Patroclus from his horse. As the great warrior stands
dazed, Hector drives his spear through Patroclus and strips Achilles' armor from the
body of the fallen man.
    On hearing of Patroclus' death, Achilles is overcome with grief and rage. Vowing
to avenge his friend and renouncing his anger at Agamemnon, he returns to the battle
and performs miraculous feats of heroism, as the retreating Trojan forces are
slaughtered mercilessly. Achilles would now enter Troy, but Apollo interferes again
and, by taking the form of a Trojan, momentarily distracts Achilles and lures him
into pursuit. As Book 22 opens, the exhausted Trojan soldiers take advantage of
Achilles' absence from the field and stampede through the gates of the city to take
refuge behind its high walls. One Trojan remains outside the city: Hector.]

Book 22: The Death of Hector

        So throughout the city they rested like panic-worn fawns,
Exhausted from heat and running, slaking their thirst
And cooling off as they leaned on the marvelous battlements.
Meanwhile, the Achaeans, leaving their shields on their shoulders,
Drew near the wall, and Hector, bound fast in the bonds   5
Of treacherous fate, stood waiting outside the city
In front of the Scaean Gates. Then Phoebus Apollo
Revealed himself to Achilles, spitefully saying:
        "What, O son of Peleus, can you possibly think
You're achieving, you a mere mortal hotly pursuing   10
Me, an immortal god? You rage so madly
That still you have not perceived that I'm an immortal.

But have you no interest in further slaughter of Trojans,
Whom you were routing in panic, but who have now
Poured into the city while you were sprinting out here? 15
You'll never kill me, since I am not fated to die."
　　　Then greatly enraged, fleet-footed Achilles replied:
"You've duped me, O far-working god, most ruthless of all
The immortals—duped me by leading me here, away
From the wall. Else many a Trojan now in the city 20
Would surely lie out on the plain with a bloody mouthful
Of dirt. You've robbed me of truly great glory and cheaply
Saved those you favor, since you have no fear of revenge
To come. O would that I had the power to wreak
Vengeance on you as I saw fit!"
　　　So saying, Achilles 25
Was off for the city, still thinking great deeds, and he ran
With the speed of a prize-winning horse in a chariot race,
A powerful stallion that stretches himself full length
As lightly he gallops across the wide plain. So Achilles
Churned hard his quick feet and knees.
　　　The ancient Priam 30
Was first to see him as on he came toward the city,
Brilliantly flashing bright as the star that rises
In autumn to outshine all of the myriad others
That burn in the blackness of night—the star men call
The Dog of Orion, most brilliant of all, but wrought 35
As a sign of bad days, for he is the bringer of much
Deadly fever upon wretched mortals. So now the bronze flashed
On the chest of charging Achilles. And the old one groaned
A great groan and violently beat his gray head with his hands,
As he screamed a plea to his precious son still standing 40
Before the high gates, determined and anxious to clash
With Achilles. To him old Priam, reaching out both
Of his arms, called pitifully:
　　　"Hector, I beg you, dear child,
Don't stand there alone and wait for the charge of that man,
Or death at his hands may soon be yours, since he 45
Is far stronger than you—and a savage! If only the gods
Loved him no better than I do! Then quickly the dogs
And vultures would feast on his unburied corpse, thus lifting
Some measure of terrible grief from my heart. For he
Has deprived me of many brave sons, either slaughtering them 50
Or selling them off as slaves to distant islands.
Right now I miss two more of my sons, Lycaon
And Polydorus, nowhere to be seen mid the Trojans
Gathered within the city, even those two boys
The Princess Laothoe bore me. If they still live 55
In the Argive camp, we'll do all we can to ransom
Those two with bronze and gold, since there is plenty
At home that ancient Altes, a king of high fame,
Sent with his daughter Laothoe. But if already
They're dead and in Hades' halls, great grief shall come 60

On the hearts of their mother and me, from whom their lives sprang.
The rest of the Trojans will not grieve so long—unless
You also go down at the hands of Achilles! Come then,
My son, put walls between you and him, that you
May yet save the men and women of Troy, instead 65
Of giving great glory to Peleus' son and losing
Your own sweet life. Moreover, have pity on miserable
Me, wretched but still quite able to feel!
Think of the grinding fate Father Zeus is preparing
For me, to kill me in feeble old age, after I 70
Have seen countless horrors—my sons in the throes of death,
My daughters and daughters-in-law dragged off by loathsome
Achaean hands, their marriage chambers wrecked
And despoiled, and their babies dashed to the ground in the heat
Of horrible war. Myself last of all, with the life 75
Ripped out of my limbs by slash or thrust of sharp bronze,
Shall hungry dogs tear further—my own table hounds
Brought up in my halls to guard the gate of my palace.
Gone mad from lapping their master's blood, they'll loll
In my courts. A young man cut down in battle may 80
Very well lie exposed, though the mangling bronze has done
Its worst on his body. Dead and naked though such
A young warrior lie, nothing is seen that is not
Noble and fair. But when savage dogs defile
The gray head and beard and the privy parts of an old man 85
Fallen—surely nothing more foul than this can come upon
Wretched mortals!"
    So saying, old Priam tore
Gray hairs from his head, but he could not persuade the heart
Of his son. And then, beside the old king, Hector's mother,
Wailing and shedding hot tears, undid the front 90
Of her gown and holding out one of her breasts, spoke these words
Winged with entreaty:
    "Hector, my child, have
Some regard for this, and pity your mother, if ever
I quieted your crying by giving you suck at this breast.
Remember all this, my precious child, and fight 95
Yonder savage from inside the walls. Do not be so heartless
As now to stand there and face him. For if he should kill you,
I'll never be able, my darling, to whom I gave life,
To so much as mourn your dead body laid out on a bed,
Nor shall your rich-gifted wife, but far over there 100
By the Argive ships fast dogs shall devour you completely!"
    Thus the two wept and called out to their much-loved son,
Beseeching him over and over, but they could do nothing
To change Hector's heart as there he stood and awaited
The clash with gigantic Achilles. And as a bright snake 105
Of the mountains, swollen and fierce from its diet of deadly
Poisons, waits in his lair for a man, balefully
Glaring forth and coiling about within,
So Hector, his courage unquenched, would not give ground,

But leaned his bright shield against the wall's jutting tower 110
And, deeply troubled, spoke thus to his own great spirit:
   "Ah misery! if now I take cover within the gates
And the walls, Polydamas ° surely will be the first
To reproach me, since he is the one who urged me to lead
The Trojans back into Troy during the dread 115
Accursed night when great Achilles came forth. But I
Wouldn't listen, much to the sorrow of many, and now
That I've all but destroyed the troops through my own stubborn pride,
I can't face the men and gown-trailing women of Troy,
Lest some low fellow should say: 'Great Hector put all 120
Of his trust in his own brute strength and destroyed the whole army!'
So they will surely remark, but it were far better
For me to face and slay Achilles and so
Return home in triumph, or now to die bravely myself
In front of the city. But what if I lay my bossed shield 125
And thick helmet down and, leaning my spear on the wall,
Go out unarmed to meet the matchless Achilles
And promise him that we'll give to Atreus' sons
To carry away both Helen and all the shiploads
Of treasure Prince Paris brought home to Troy—thus starting 130
The war—and say that I'll have the elders of Troy
Swear a strong oath for the Trojans that we will divide
With the Argives all of the treasure that this lovely city
Contains? But why do I argue these things with myself?
Let me not be so foolish as thus to approach him 135
Only to have him completely refuse to pity
Or hear me at all, but kill me instead, unarmed
As some helpless woman, my bronze lying back by the wall.
This, I fear, is hardly the time for a lengthy
Chat with Achilles by oak tree or rock, such as 140
A boy and his girl might have with each other—boy
And his girl indeed! Much rather, let us now clash
With no further delay, that we may find out to whom
The Olympian wills the high glory."
      As thus he debated,
Achilles, peer of the plume-waving war god, loomed up 145
Before him hefting his spear of Pelian ash,°
That awesome bronze-bladed shaft, above his right shoulder,
While all about him his marvelous armor was flashing
Like leaping flames or the rising sun. Then Hector
Took but one look before trembling seized him all over, 150
Nor did he dare hold his ground, but leaving the gates
Behind him, he fled in fear with the son of Peleus,
Putting his faith in his speed as a runner, hot
In pursuit. As a hawk of the mountains, fastest of fowls,
Darts with shrill screams in pursuit of a trembling dove, 155
Hungry to kill her, so now Achilles sped on

---

113. **Polydamas** (pō·lid′ə·məs): a Trojan leader.   146. **Pelian ash:** wood cut from trees on
Mount Pelion, one of the highest mountains in Greece.

In his furious wrath, and Hector before him ran swiftly
Beneath the wall of the Trojans. Past the place
Of lookout and the wind-swayed wild fig tree they ran, always
Out from the wall along the wagon-made road,   160
And came to the two fair-burbling fountains, where those
Two springs jet up that feed deep-swirling Scamander.°
Hot water flows from the one, and over its stream
Steam rises like smoke from a blazing fire, while even
In summer the other runs cold as hail or chill snow   165
Or hard-frozen ice itself. And there by those fountains
Are handsome wide washing-troughs where the wives and fair daughters
Of Trojans had washed glossy clothes in the days of peace
Before the Achaeans came.
     By these they dashed,
One fleeing, the other pursuing. A good man led   170
The race, but the one in pursuit was far the stronger
And came swiftly on, for now it was not for any
Mere hide or sacrificed bull that they strove, such as men
Most usually race for, but now it was for the life
Of horse-breaking Hector. And as when hard-hoofed, prize-winning   175
Stallions wheel fast around the turn-posts, and some
Fine prize is put up, a tripod° perhaps, or a woman,
In games for a warrior dead, so now these two
Swiftly circled the city of Priam three times, while all
The gods gazed down on their race. Then the Father of men   180
And immortals was first to speak out among them, saying:
    "Look now, truly a much-cherished man I see
Being chased about the high walls, and my heart grieves greatly
For Hector, who often has burned for me the thigh-pieces
Of oxen high on the crags of many-ridged Ida°   185
And on the citadel heights. But now great Achilles
Is chasing him swiftly about Priam's city. Come then,
You gods, think and decide whether we shall save him
From death, or slay him at last, brave man though he is,
At the hands of raging Achilles, Peleus' son."   190
    Then the goddess Athena, her blue eyes blazing, answered him
Thus: "O Father, lord of the dazzling bolt
And darkly ominous cloud, what are you saying!
Can it be that you really wish to deliver a mortal,
One long foredestined by fate, from dolorous death?   195
Well, do as you like, but don't suppose for one moment
That all of us like what you do!"
    Then Zeus, god of gales,
Replied: "Why so grim, my Tritogeneia?°
Dear child, I was not altogether in earnest in what
I said, and surely I want to be gentle with you.   200
Do as you please, and restrain yourself no longer."

[HOMER CONTINUES ON PAGE 87]

162. **Scamander** (skə·man′dər): main river of the Trojan plain. 177. **tripod**: a bronze altar,
used in sacrifices. 185. **Ida**: a mountain near Troy. 198. **Tritogeneia** (trī′tō·jē·nī′ə): Athena.
Some say it means "Tritoborn." Athena was born near Lake Tritonis in a part of Africa.

Sumerian, Greek, and Roman Art

The works of art in this section span a period of more than two thousand years—from the Sumerian culture of ancient Mesopotamia to the time of the Roman Emperor Constantine. During this period many great civilizations flourished and crumbled to dust. In the visual arts, as in literature, each culture developed its own form of expression.

We do not know the name and rank of the little bearded man (PLATE 1) who was found in an ancient Sumerian temple. With his hands folded in prayer, he has stood offering perpetual worship to his god for over 4,000 years. The sculptor gave him a painted beard and inlaid eyes of lapis lazuli to make him look more lifelike, but there is still something strange and inhuman about him. Even the three-dimensional design of the figure is abstract and geometrical rather than organic and human. Note, for example, the cylindrical form of the lower part of the body.

All pre-Greek peoples portrayed man in an abstract or diagrammatic way. Not until the fifth century B.C. did Greek sculptors learn to carve lifelike statues based on an understanding of human anatomy and proportion. The most perfect examples of this great classic period in Greek art are the statues and relief carvings of the Parthenon. Erected on the Acropolis of Athens, the Parthenon (PLATE 2) was dedicated to Athena Parthenos, the powerful goddess of the Athenians. A rectangular building surrounded by columns, it was designed as part of an ambitious building program under Pericles in the fifth century B.C. Although this marble temple seems to be a perfect example of geometric regularity, many lines in the building are curved to correct optical illusions. For example, the columns swell slightly in the middle, and they are narrower at the top than at the bottom to avoid the appearance of falling outward. The top step rises about $4\frac{1}{2}$ inches from end to middle; otherwise it would appear to sag. These refinements of design, in addition to the perfection of the workmanship, make the Parthenon one of the great architectural masterpieces of all time.

The beautifully carved sculptured frieze which runs around the building wall inside the columns shows a procession of Athenians marching from the lower city to the Acropolis to honor Athena. On the east side of the

Parthenon, the frieze shows the maidens of Athens presenting a new robe to Athena in the presence of the Olympian deities. The fragment illustrated in Plate 3A shows several gods and goddesses watching the ceremony. Although the carving on this frieze is never more than $2\frac{1}{2}$ inches deep, you can perceive the solid muscle and flesh of their beautifully formed bodies under the rippling flow of soft garments.

Rome conquered Greece and was captivated by Greek art and culture. But the Romans were practical men who preferred the real to the ideal, especially in their own portraits. The Roman desire for an exact likeness in portrait statues may have been due to their veneration of wax ancestor images made from death masks. The marble portrait shown as Plate 4B was probably made with the help of a life mask. After making an impression in wax or plaster, the details of the likeness were transferred to stone. Notice how the sculptor revealed all the individual traits of this man's face with unsparing realism, giving us a forceful portrait of this stern Roman.

Under Augustus, sculptors copied and adapted Greek works and developed an imperial Roman style distinguished by a new grace and elegance. Official portraits of Augustus were often based on statues of Greek gods. The marble head of Augustus (Plate 4A) was once part of such a statue. Though it may seem strikingly different from the figure of a Greek god shown in Plate 3B, it was also intended to suggest a godlike being and thus was somewhat idealized.

Wherever the Romans conquered, they built impressive monuments and public buildings. One of the several basic types of Roman architecture is the amphitheater. Another basic design, one used for churches, is the *basilica*. An oblong structure, usually curved at one end, it was a large hall for the law courts in ancient Rome. An arched structure, called a *vault*, roofed over the immense spaces of these great halls. In the Basilica of Constantine (Plate 5), the vaults of the side aisles stand 87 feet high. The pieces jutting out at the top of this magnificent ruin once supported a central vault 120 feet high. Using unskilled labor, the Romans built these vast structures of brick or rubble held together by cement. This method of construction was faster and cheaper than the Greek system of building with marble. Later, the Romans concealed their brick construction with a colorful surface of mosaics or marble.

Many Roman houses were preserved intact under the ashes of Vesuvius when it erupted in A.D. 79. Paintings from these houses (Plate 6) reveal what they looked like, inside and out. The painting from the bedroom wall of a villa at Boscoreale, near Pompeii, shows the courtyard of a large house with its balconies and colonnades, even its potted plants. Through paintings like this, sculpture, architecture, and literature, we can know the Romans more fully and intimately than any other ancient people.

PLATE 1. *Standing Male Figure.* Sumerian, about 2600 B.C. From Shrine II of the Square Temple at Tell Asmar. White gypsum statuette, height: 11¾ inches. (The Metropolitan Museum of Art, Fletcher Fund, 1940)

PLATE 2A. IKTINOS and KALLIKRATES (Greek, 5th century B.C.): *The Parthenon.* 448–42 B.C. Marble temple on the Acropolis in Athens.

PLATE 2B. Detail from the Parthenon, showing the exterior northwest corner.

PLATE 3A. *Poseidon, Apollo and Artemis.* Greek, 5th century B.C. From the frieze on the east wall of the Parthenon. Marble, height: 40 inches. (Acropolis Museum, Athens)

PLATE 3B. *Dionysus.* Greek, about 438–32 B.C. From the east pediment of the Parthenon. Marble, over life-size. (By courtesy of the Trustees of the British Museum, London)

PLATE 4A. *Portrait Head of Augustus.*
Graeco-Roman, A.D. 1st century. Marble, height: 17 inches. (Courtesy, Museum of Fine Arts, Boston, Pierce Fund)

PLATE 4B. *Portrait of a Man.* Roman, before 31 B.C. Marble, life-size. (The Metropolitan Museum of Art, New York, Rogers Fund, 1912)

PLATE 5. *Basilica of Constantine*. Roman, A.D. 310–13. Adjoins the Forum Romanum, Rome.

PLATE 6. *Wall Painting*. Pompeian, 1st century B.C. Panel II from the villa at Boscoreale. Fresco, average height: 8 feet. (The Metropolitan Museum of Art, New York, Rogers Fund, 1903)

So saying, he started Athena, who needed no urging,
And down she went darting from high on the peaks of Olympus.
　　　But fast Achilles, ceaselessly running, pressed hard
Upon Hector. And as when a hound in the mountains jumps　　　205
The fawn of a deer and chases him hotly through glade
And winding gorge, relentlessly tracking him down
Whenever he cowers in hiding beneath a dense thicket,
So Hector now could not escape Achilles.
As often as he endeavored to make a dash　　　210
For the lofty Dardanian Gates,° hoping his fellows
Above on the wall might cover his effort with showers
Of shafts till he gained the protection of well-built bastions,
Achilles would cut him off and turn him back
Toward the plain, while he himself continued to run　　　215
On the city-side of the course. And as in a dream
A man is unable to chase one who wishes to flee,
And both, though struggling to run, remain rooted fast,
So that neither gains on the other, so now Achilles
Could not overtake Hector, nor could swift Hector　　　220
Escape. But how did the Trojan manage to keep
Away for so long from the fierce fates of death? Only
With help from Apollo, who came for the last and final
Time to inspire him with strength and quicken his knees.
And Achilles signaled his men with shakes of his head　　　225
Not to hurl their bitter missiles at Hector, lest someone
Else might win the glory of bringing him down,
And he himself come second. But when for the fourth
Time around they reached the fair fountains, Father Zeus
Lifted his golden scales and set on the pans　　　230
Two fates of forever-sad death, one for Achilles
And one for horse-breaking Hector. Then by the middle
He took the balance and raised it, and down all the way
To Hades' house sank the death-day of Hector, whereat
Apollo left him. But bright-eyed Athena came up　　　235
To Achilles and spoke to him these winged words:
　　　"Now, finally,
Zeus-loved resplendent Achilles, I've hope that we two
Will cut Hector down, no matter how hungry for battle
He is, and bear to the ships great glory for all
The Achaeans. For now he cannot escape us, not even　　　240
If far-working Phoebus suffers tremendously for him
And grovels in his behalf before Father Zeus
Of the aegis. So take your stand and get back your breath,
While I go persuade your quarry to fight with you
Man to man."
　　　So spoke Athena, and Peleus' son, gladly　　　245
Obeying, stood where he was, leaning upon

---

211. **Dardanian Gates:** gates of the city, named for Dardanus, a son of Zeus and legendary
founder of a city which later became part of Troy.

His bronze-bladed shaft of ash. Athena left him
And came up to shining Hector, assuming the form
And weariless voice of his brother Deiphobus. Standing
Beside him, she spoke to him these words winged with beguilement: 250
    "Dear brother, surely fleet-footed Achilles has sadly
Abused you, chasing you thus around Priam's city.
But come, let us now stand against him and beat back his charge
Together."
    To which great Hector, his bronze helmet flashing:
"Deiphobus, you've always been my favorite brother 255
By far, of all the sons that were born to Priam
And Hecuba. Now, though, I'm sure I shall hold you dearer
Than ever, since you have dared to come out and help me,
While all the others stay back of the lofty walls."
    To him then the goddess bright-eyed Athena replied: 260
"Dear brother, believe me, our father and queenly mother
And all of the comrades about me earnestly pleaded
With me to stay where I was, so fearfully do
They all tremble before Achilles. But my heart was deeply
Pained by piercing sorrow for you. So now 265
Let us charge straight at him and fight, nor let there be
Any sparing of spears, that we may know at once
Whether Peleus' son is going to cut us both down
And carry our bloodstained armor back to the ships,
Or whether he shall go down beneath the bronze point 270
Of your spear."
    With these guileful words Athena induced him
To fight, and when they got within range of each other,
Huge Hector, his bronze helmet flashing, spoke first to Achilles:
"No longer, O Peleus' son, will I flee before you,
As I have done three times around the great city 275
Of Priam, without the heart to stand up to your charge.
For now my spirit says fight with you face to face,
Whether I kill or be killed. Come then, let us
Invoke our gods to sanction this pact between us,
For they will witness and guard our covenant best. 280
If Zeus allows me to outlast you and rob you
Of life, I'll do to your corpse no foul defilement.
But when I have stripped off your armor, Achilles,
I'll give your dead body back to the host of Achaeans—
And you do the same for me."
    Then savagely scowling 285
At him, fast-footed Achilles replied: "Hector,
You madman, don't stand there babbling to me of covenants.
There are no faithful oaths between lions and men,
Nor do wolves and lambs have any oneness of heart,
But they are always at fatal odds with each other. 290
So too it is not to be thought that we can ever
Be friends, nor shall there be any peace between us
Till one or the other has fallen and glutted with blood
The battling Ares, him of the tough hide shield!

Recall every jot of your warrior's prowess, for now   295
Is the time to show your courage and skill as a spearman.
Escape for you there is none, but Pallas Athena
Shall soon bring you down with this long lance of mine.
And now you shall pay all at once for the grief I endured
For my comrades, whom you in your raging killed with the spear."   300
    So saying, he poised his long-shadowing spear and hurled it,
But shining Hector, looking straight at him, escaped,
For he saw it coming and crouched, so that the bronze point
Flew over his head and embedded itself in the earth.
But Pallas Athena snatched it up, without   305
Hector's knowledge, and gave it back to Achilles. And Hector,
His people's commander, spoke thus to the great son of Peleus:
    "You missed, O godlike Achilles. It seems that Zeus
Has not yet informed you concerning the day of my doom,
Though surely you thought that he had. You thought by your glibness   310
And cunning of speech to fill me with terror of you
And completely deprive me of courage and strength. But you'll not
Plant your spear in my back as I flee, but as I
Charge down straight upon you, drive it clean through my chest—
If God has granted you that. Look out now and avoid,   315
If you can, my keen-cutting bronze. Here's hoping you take
The whole shaft into your hard flesh! Surely this war
Would be lighter for Trojans, if you, their greatest scourge,
Were dead."
    Then poising his shade-making spear, he cast,
Nor did he miss, but struck full upon the shield   320
Of Achilles, from which a long way it rebounded, enraging
Hector, since his swift shaft had flown from his hand
In vain. And now, since he had no second ash spear,
He stood in deep consternation, then shouted to him
Of the dazzling white shield, Deiphobus, asking a long spear   325
Of him. But he was nowhere around, and Hector,
Aware now of just what had happened, spoke thus:
    "So be it.
Surely the gods have summoned me deathward. For I
Thought sure that the hero Deiphobus stood right behind me,
Whereas he is safe on the other side of the wall,   330
And Athena has tricked me. Now evil death is at hand
For me, not far off at all, nor is there any
Way out. Such, I believe, has always been
Zeus's pleasure, and that of his far-shooting son Apollo,
Who have in the past been willing and eager to help me.   335
Now, though, my doom is surely upon me. But let me
Not die without a huge effort, nor let me dishonorably
Die, but in the brave doing of some great deed
Let me go, that men yet to be may hear of what happened."
    So saying, he drew the keen blade that hung by his side,   340
A sword both heavy and long. Then bracing himself
He charged at Achilles, plunging upon him like some
Huge high-flying eagle that dives through dark clouds to seize

On the plain a tender lamb or cowering hare.
Even so, Hector plunged, his sharp sword held high. And Achilles,   345
Seething with savage wrath, met the advance
With one of his own, protecting his chest with his intricate,
Exquisite shield and tossing his head, so that all
The gold plumes that Hephaestus had thickly set in the crest
Of that four-horned helmet shook with a gorgeous glitter.   350
And from the bronze point of the spear that Achilles balanced
In his right hand there went forth a gleam like that
Which glints amid stars in the blackness of night from Hesperus,
Fairest of all the stars set in wide heaven.
Hefting that powerful spear, he scanned the form   355
Of his foe to find the spot where a spear was most likely
To pierce the firm flesh of Hector. He saw that his armor
Of bronze covered him all the way, the beautiful
Gear he had stripped from mighty Patroclus when he
Cut him down. But there where the collarbones separate neck   360
And shoulders, there at his throat, most fatal of targets,
Appeared a spot unprotected by bronze. So there,
As on him he charged, great Achilles drove in his spear,
And the point went through his soft neck and stuck out behind.
Even so, the ashen shaft, heavy with cleaving bronze,   365
Failed to sever the windpipe. Hence Hector could still say words
And answer his foe. Dying, he sprawled in the dust,
And shining Achilles exulted above him, vaunting:
    "Hector, I dare say you thought while stripping Patroclus
That you would be safe, nor did you have one thought of me,   370
Since I was not there and since you are a very great fool!
Behind at the hollow ships that man had a helper,
One mightier far than himself to avenge him—me,
The man who unstrung those knees of yours. Now dogs
And birds will ravin on° your shredded corpse, defiling   375
You utterly. Meanwhile, Achaeans shall hold for Patroclus
A high and fitting funeral."
    Then Hector, his bronze helmet
Gleaming, his small strength rapidly draining, answered:
"I beg you, Achilles, by your own knees and parents
And life, do not allow me thus to be eaten   380
By dogs at the ships of Achaeans. Instead, accept
What you want of our plentiful bronze and gold, a ransom
My father and queenly mother will gladly give you,
If only you'll give back my body, that Trojans and wives
Of Trojans may give me my due of funeral fire."   385
    Then blackly scowling at him, fast-footed Achilles
Replied: "Do not beg me by knees or by parents,
You dog! I only wish I were savagely wrathful
Enough to hack up your corpse and eat it raw—
In view of what you have done—but no man alive   390
Shall keep the dogs from your head, not even if here

375. **ravin on:** feed on.

They should bring and weigh out a ransom ten or twenty times
What you are worth and promise still more, not even
If Priam, descended of Dardanus, should tell them to pay
Your weight in gold—not even then should your 395
Queenly mother lay you on a bed and mourn you, the son
Whom she herself bore, but dogs and birds shall devour you,
Bones and all!"
        Then noble bright-helmeted Hector,
Rapidly dying, replied: "I know you, Achilles,
All too well, and clearly foresee what you'll do, 400
Nor was there a chance of my changing your mind. The heart
In your breast is solid iron. But think what you're doing,
Or one day I may bring the gods' wrath on you, when Paris
And Phoebus Apollo destroy you there, great valor
And all, at the Scaean Gates."
        As thus he spoke, 405
The final moment arrived, and his soul flew forth
From his body and quickly journeyed to Hades, bewailing
Her lot as one too soon bereft of youth
And manly vigor. And now to the corpse of his foe,
God-gifted Achilles spoke thus:
        "Die—and as 410
For my own fate, I'll accept that whenever Zeus wills
To fulfill it, Zeus and the other immortal gods."
        He spoke, and drawing the bronze from Hector's throat,
He laid it aside and started to strip from his shoulders
The armor, sticky with blood. And the other sons 415
Of Achaeans ran up all around and gazed at the wondrously
Handsome body of Hector, nor did a man
Approach him without inflicting a wound in his flesh,
And many a one, with a glance at his neighbor, would say:
        "Aha! fierce Hector is not even nearly so hard 420
To handle now as when he hurled blazing fire
On the ships!"
        So saying, a man would step in and stab
Hector's body. At last, having stripped him of bronze, swift Achilles
Stood up among the Achaeans and spoke to them, saying:
"O friends, captains and counselors of the Argives, 425
Now that the gods have enabled us thus to destroy
This man, who has done more damage than all of the others
Together, come, let us make a tour with our weapons
Around Priam's city and see what the Trojans intend
To do next, whether they will desert their high town, now that 430
Their champion is dead, or whether they've made up their minds
To stay on without Hector's help. But what kind of talk
Is this? Back at the ships lies a dead man unwept
And unburied, Patroclus, whom I will never forget
So long as my knees are quick and I am one 435
Of the living. And though all phantoms else in Hades'
House forget their dead, even there will I
Remember my precious comrade. But come, you sons

Of Achaeans, singing our song of triumph, let us
Go back to the hollow ships, bearing this body. 440
Today we have won tremendous renown, for we
Have slain royal Hector, whom Trojans have always lauded
Throughout the city as if the man were a god."
    So saying, he set about foully defiling the body
Of noble Hector. Piercing behind the tendons 445
Of both of his feet between heel and ankle, he pulled through
And tied leather throngs and bound them fast to his chariot,
Leaving the head to drag. Then lifting the famous
Armor aboard, he mounted the car himself
And lashed the team on, and they unreluctant took off 450
At a gallop. And dust billowed up on either side
Of the dragging Hector, as his black hair trailed out
In the dirt and the once so handsome head was defiled
With foul dust. For Zeus had now committed the man
To the hands of his foes to suffer disgrace and defilement 455
There in the land of his fathers.
        Thus was his head
All filthied with dust, and his mother, seeing him so,
Tore at her hair and, screaming, flung wildly off
Her shimmering veil. And his dear father pitifully groaned,
While the people around them and those throughout the city 460
Took up the mournful wail. Nor could they have grieved
Any more had all looming Troy been wreathed in flames
From walls to the citadel heights. And the people had all
They could do to keep old Priam, grief-frenzied, from rushing
Out through the lofty Dardanian Gates. He begged them 465
All, groveling in dung of horses and calling
Each man by his name, crying:
        "Release me, my friends,
And though you don't want to, allow me to go from the city
Alone to the ships of Achaeans. I'll pray to this unfeeling
Monster, this worker of horrors, to have some regard 470
For my age and for himself in the eyes of his fellows.
He too, you know, has a father, Peleus, a man
Like myself, who sired and reared him to be a great scourge
To the Trojans, to me most of all, so many have been
My sons cut off by him in the flower of youth. 475
Yet not for them all do I mourn so much, great
Though my grief surely is, as I now mourn for one only,
Keen sorrow for whom will bring me down at last
To Hades' dark house—sorrow, I say, for Hector.
Ah that he might have died in my arms. Then his mother 480
And I might at least have found some relief in weeping
And wailing, she who bore him ill-fated, and I
His father."
        So spoke old Priam, sobbing, and with him
His grieving people joined in. And Hector's mother,
Old Hecuba, led in their vehement keening the women 485
Of Troy, crying: "My child, how wretched I am!

Why should I go on alive in this terrible anguish
Of mine, now that you're gone forever? You
My constant glory both night and day in the city
And ever a blessing to all of the men and women   490
Of Troy, who greeted you quite as they would a god,
While you were alive. But now death and fate have finally
Caught up with you."
    Thus Hecuba wailed through her tears.
But Hector's wife knew nothing of what had occurred,
Since no one had gone to tell her that her dear husband   495
Remained outside the gates. She was weaving a web
In an inner room of the high-roofed house, a scarlet
Web of double width through which she artfully
Sprinkled a pattern of flowers. And now she called
Through the house to her girls with the beautiful braids to set   500
A large three-legged cauldron over the fire, that there
Should be a hot bath for Hector when he returned
From the fighting—poor innocent one, who had no idea
That far from all baths strong fire-eyed Athena had cut
Hector down by the hand of Achilles. But then she heard   505
The shrieks and groans from the wall, and shaking all over
She dropped the shuttle to earth and spoke once again
To her fair-braided handmaids:
    "Two of you, come go with me,
That I may see what has happened. For that was the voice
Of my husband's reverenced mother, and my heart leaps   510
To my mouth and my knees are frozen beneath me. Surely
Some horror is close at hand for the children of Priam.
O far from my ears may such news always be,
But I am terribly fearful that great Achilles
Has cut brave Hector off from the city and driven him   515
Out on the plain, and most likely ended by now
The fatal pride that has for so long possessed him.
For Hector would never lag back in the throng of fighters,
But always insisted on charging well out in front
And never allowed any man to outdo him in daring."   520
    So saying, Andromache rushed from the hall like a woman
Gone mad, her heart wildly pounding, and with her went two
Of her handmaids. But when she had joined the crowd on the wall,
She stopped and looked toward the plain, and there she saw Hector
Ruthlessly dragged by fast horses away from the city   525
And toward the hollow ships of Achaea. Then darkness
Night-black came over her eyes and enclosed her, as backward
She fell, flinging far off her shining headdress,
Her fair coronet, her snood and woven fillet,°
And with them the veil that Aphrodite the golden   530
Had given to her on the day that Hector, he
Of the flashing helmet, had led her forth as his bride
From Eetion's house, having given innumerable gifts

529. **fillet:** hairband.

To her father. Now round her crowded her husband's sisters
And sisters-in-law and in her dead faint they held her   535
And tried to revive her. When she came to and her spirit
Returned to her breast, she lifted her voice in lament
Mid the women of Troy, sobbing:
     "Ah Hector, what misery
Is mine! To one fate, it seems, we were born, you
Here in Troy in Priam's house, I at the foot   540
Of wooded Mount Placus in Thebe in the house of Eetion,
Who raised me, the unlucky father of one whose fate
Is even more cruel. I heartily wish he had never
Sired me. Now you are going to Hades' house
In the hidden depths of the earth, leaving me here   545
In bitter anguish, a widow in your spacious halls,
And your son is still just a baby, the son we two
So unluckily had. For now you can be no help to him,
Hector, nor he any pleasure to you. And though
He survives this tear-fraught war with Achaeans, he'll always   550
Have plenty of labor and woe to endure, for others
Will take all his land. A fatherless son is cut off
From the friends of his childhood. He goes about with his head
Hanging down and his cheeks wet with tears, and when in his need
He comes where the friends of his father are feasting and plucks   555
At one's cloak or another's tunic, someone out of pity
Holds out his cup for a moment, just long enough
To wet the child's lips but leave his palate still dry.
And up comes a boy whose parents are still alive
And beats him away from the feast with his fists, jeering: 560
'Get out of here fast! You've no father feasting with us.'
Then, crying, back to his widowed mother the little one
Runs—our little Astyanax, who always before
On his father's lap ate only rich mutton and marrow,
And who, when he was through playing and sleepy, would lie   565
On a bed in the arms of his nurse, a lovely soft bed,
Where he would sleep well with his little heart full of good cheer.
Now, though, with no father, he'll suffer innumerable evils—
My precious Astyanax, Lord of the City, so called
By the Trojans because you alone, my husband, protected   570
Their gates and high walls. But now by beaked ships, far away
From your parents, slick-wriggling worms shall devour you, the dogs
Having eaten their fill, all feasting on your naked body—
Though in your halls you've plenty of handsome fine clothes,
Which now I shall burn to ashes, since you'll never lie   575
In any of them, and such at least I can do
In your honor for all of the men and women of Troy."
    So she through her tears, and the women all added their wails.

[After slaying Hector, Achilles prepares for Patroclus' ceremonial funeral. Into
a huge fire the Greeks throw twelve slain Trojan princes and the bodies of sacrificed animals. After Patroclus' body is burned, elaborate athletic contests are held,
a custom in funeral services for distinguished men. As Book 24 opens, Achilles is

still so enraged at Hector's killing of his friend that he refuses to relinquish the body of Hector for proper burial. This is a particularly offensive form of revenge, for these people believed that a body must be buried with certain rites before its soul could find rest. Each day the wrathful Achilles drags Hector's defiled body around the tomb of Patroclus. This shameful treatment of an honorable man offends Zeus, and he finally orders Achilles to give up the body to Priam. The aged king, bowed with grief and bearing rich ransom to exchange for his son's body, is escorted to the Greek camp by the god Hermes, who is in disguise.]

FROM *Book 24: Priam and Achilles*

. . .

When they came to the trench and the wall round the ships, the guards
Had just begun fixing supper, but Hermes quickly
Put them to sleep and, thrusting the bars back, opened
The gates. Then into the camp he drove the old king,
And with them they brought the wagon of glorious gifts   5
For Achilles. Soon they arrived at his lodge, the lofty
Shelter the Myrmidon men had built for their chief,
Hewing out beams of pine and roofing it over
With reed-shaggy thatch from the fields. And they had built round it
For him a spacious courtyard high fenced with stakes   10
Closely set, with a gate strongly locked by means of one bar
Across it. This huge beam of pine it took three Achaeans
To move back and forth, though Achilles could handle the thing
By himself. Once there, luck-bringing Hermes opened
The gate for old Priam and drove him inside, and with them   15
They brought the marvelous gifts for the swift son of Peleus.
Then stepping down, Hermes spoke thus to the king:
        "Old sire, I that have come to you thus am a god
Everlasting—Hermes, sent by the Father° to act
As your guide. But now I'll go back without letting Achilles   20
See me, for it would be wrong for an immortal god
To be so openly welcomed by mortal men.
But you yourself go in and, embracing the knees
Of Peleus' son, make your plea in the name of his father,
Lovely-haired mother, and son, that you may stir   25
The depths of his soul."
        So saying, Hermes took off
For the heights of Olympus, and Priam sprang down from the car
To the ground and, leaving Idaeus° in charge of the horses
And mules, strode straight for the lodge where Zeus-loved Achilles
Sat. And inside he found him, apart from all comrades   30
But two, the hero Automedon, and Alcimus, scion
Of Ares, who busily waited upon him, since he
Had just finished eating and drinking, and still the table
Had not been removed. Great Priam came in unnoticed
By any, till coming up close to Achilles he threw   35

19. **the Father:** Zeus.   28. **Idaeus** (ī·dē′əs): Priam's messenger.

His arms round his knees and kissed his dread hands, the murderous
Hands that had killed so many of his precious sons.
And as when thick darkness of soul comes down on a man
And killing another he flees from his own dear country
And comes to some foreign land and the house of a man   40
Of bountiful wealth, and wonder grips all who see him
A suppliant there, so now Achilles was seized
With exceeding amazement at sight of sacred Priam,
And those who were with him marveled and looked at each other.
Then Priam made his plea, beseeching him thus: 45
  "Remember, Achilles, O godlike mortal, remember
Peleus your father, a man of like years as myself,
Far gone on the path of painful old age. Very likely
His neighbors are grinding him down, nor is there one there
To keep from him ruin and destruction. However, so long   50
As he hears you're alive, his heart can daily be glad
In the hope that he shall yet see his dear son returning
From Troy. But I am without good fortune completely,
Since though I begot the best sons in the whole wide country
Of Troy, yet now not even one is left!   55
When the sons of Achaeans arrived, I had fifty sons
Of my own, nineteen from the womb of one mother, the rest
Borne to me by women of mine in the palace. But though
They were many, furious Ares has unstrung the knees
Of all, and the only one left me, who all by himself   60
Protected the city and people, fell to your spear
Some days ago as he was defending his country—
Hector my son, and now I have come to the ships
Of Achaea to pay you a ransom for him, and I bring
With me a load of treasure past counting. Have awe   65
Of the gods, O Achilles, and pity on me, remembering
Your dear father. I am indeed even more
To be pitied than he, for I have endured what no other
Earth-dwelling mortal has—to reach out my hand
To the face of him who slaughtered my precious sons!"   70
  Such was his plea, and he stirred in Achilles a yearning
To weep for Peleus his father, and taking the hand
Of old Priam he gently pushed him away. Then the two of them
Thought of their losses, and Priam sobbed sorely for man-killing
Hector, the old king huddling in front of Achilles,   75
Whose weeping was now for his father and now for Patroclus,
And throughout the lodge arose the sound of their grief.
But when great Achilles had found some relief in lamenting,
And longing for such had gone out of his body and soul,
He suddenly sprang from his chair, and filled with pity   80
For Priam's gray head and gray beard, he raised the old king
By the hand and spoke to him these winged words:
  "Wretched sire,
Many indeed are the horrors your soul has endured.
But how could you ever have come here alone to the ships
Of the Argives to look in the eyes of the man who has killed   85

Your many brave sons? Surely your heart is of iron!
But come, sit down in a chair, and we'll both let our grief,
Great though it is, lie quiet in our hearts. Cold crying
Accomplishes little. For thus have the sorrowless gods
Spun the web of existence for miserable mortals—with pain   90
Woven in throughout! There stand by the threshold of Zeus
Two urns, one full of evils, the other of blessings.
To whomever Zeus, the lover of lightning, gives
A portion from each, that man experiences
Both evil and good, but to whomever Zeus gives nothing   95
But of the grievous, that man is reviled by gods
And men and hounded by horrible hunger all over
The sacred earth. Take Peleus my father for instance.
No man ever had more glorious god-bestowed gifts
Than he from the time of his birth, for he surpassed all   100
In wealth and good fortune, was king of the Myrmidon people,
And though but a mortal himself, the gods gave a goddess
To him for a wife. But even on him the immortals
Brought evil enough, since there in his halls no plentiful
Offspring of princes was born, but only one son,   105
And he undoubtedly doomed to die young. Nor can I
So much as look after him as he ages, since far,
Very far from home I live in the country of Troy,
A plague to you and your children. And you, old sire,
We hear were once happy, for you, because of your wealth   110
And your sons, were the first of mortals in all the great space
That lies between Lesbos, south in the sea, where Macar
Was king long ago, and Phrygia off to the north
And the free-flowing Hellespont. Since, though, the heavenly gods
Brought on you this baneful war, your city has been   115
Surrounded by havoc and dying men. But you
Must bear up, nor can you afford to grieve without ceasing.
You'll not thereby do anything good for your son.
Before you bring him back to life, you'll suffer a fate
Little less unhappy yourself!"   120
      To which the old Priam:
"By no means ask me to sit, O god-nourished man,
So long as Hector lies mid the lodges uncared for.
Release him to me at once, that I may see him
Myself, and take the great ransom we bring to you
For his body. May you enjoy it all and come   125
Even yet to the land of your fathers, since you now have spared me
To live on for a while beholding the light of the sun."
      Then scowling at him, quick-footed Achilles spoke sternly:
"Do nothing else to provoke me, old man! I myself,
With no help from you, have already agreed to give   130
Hector back, for Zeus has sent word to me by the mother
Who bore me, the briny old sea-ancient's daughter. And don't think
I haven't known all along about you—that you
Were guided here by some god to the swift-sailing ships
Of Achaeans. For certainly no mere mortal, no matter   135

How young and strong, would ever dare enter this camp.
He could not get by the guards, nor could he easily
Push back the bar of my gate. So say nothing else,
Old man, to make me feel any worse, or I
May forget to spare even you mid the lodges, and so break   140
The strict law of Zeus."
      At this the old king was gripped
By a wordless terror and watched as Achilles sprang
Through the door of the lodge like a lion, not by himself,
But accompanied by the two squires, the hero Automedon
Followed by Alcimus, two that Achilles honored   145
Beyond all his comrades, save only the dead Patroclus.
These then unharnessed the horses and led
The herald inside, the old king's aged town crier,
And gave him a seat, and from the wagon they took
The boundless ransom for Hector. They left, however,   150
Two cloaks and a well-woven tunic, that these Achilles
Might use to wrap up the dead and so give him back
To be borne to his home. Then Achilles called for handmaids
To wash and anoint the dead body, bidding them do it
Where Priam could not see his son, for Achilles feared   155
That his guest might not be able to hold back his wrath,
And so he might lose his own temper and kill the old man,
Thus sinning against Zeus's law. When the handmaids had washed
The body and rubbed it with oil and put about it
A tunic and beautiful cloak, Achilles himself   160
Lifted it onto a bier and helped his companions
Lift it onto the wagon. Then groaning, he called
On his precious friend by name:
    "Do not be angry
At me, O Patroclus, if even in Hades' halls
You hear that I've given Prince Hector back to his father,   165
For not unbefitting at all was the ransom he gave me,
And you may be sure of getting your due share of that."
    So spoke great Achilles, then went back inside and sat down
In his richly wrought chair by the opposite wall from old Priam,
To whom he spoke thus: "Your son, old sire, has now   170
Been released to you as you have requested and lies
On a bier, and you yourself shall see him tomorrow
At daybreak while carrying him away—but let us
Not neglect supper, for even the lovely-haired Niobe°
Ate, though her twelve children all died in her palace,   175
Six daughters and six lusty sons. Shaft-showering Artemis
Brought down the daughters, while Phoebus Apollo put arrows
Through all of the sons with his silver bow, both of them
Wrathful with her for comparing herself with their own mother
Leto, Niobe saying that Leto had only   180

174. **Niobe** (nī′ə·bē): a woman whose children were killed by the goddess Artemis and the
god Apollo because she boasted of her superiority to their mother, Leto. Niobe was then
turned into a pillar of stone, from which her tears are still said to flow. This pillar of stone is
on a mountain called Sipylus in Asia Minor.

Two children while she herself had borne many. So they,
Though only two, destroyed all twelve of hers.
And there for nine days they lay in their blood unburied,
For Cronos' son Zeus turned all of the people to stones.
On the tenth, however, the heavenly gods held the funeral,   185
And Niobe, weary of weeping, remembered to eat.
And now somewhere mid the crags in the desolate hills
Of Sipylus, where, men say, the nymphs go to bed
When they tire of dancing about the stream Achelous,
Niobe stands and, though solid stone, broods   190
On her god-sent disasters. So come, my royal old sire,
And let us likewise remember to eat, and later,
Back in your city, you may lament your dear son
With innumerable tears."
        So saying, Achilles sprang up
And slaughtered a silvery white sheep, which his comrades flayed   195
And made ready in every detail, skillfully cutting
The carcass into small pieces, which meat they spitted
And roasted well, and drew it all from the spits.
Then Automedon served them the bread, setting it forth
In exquisite baskets, while swift Achilles apportioned   200
The meat, and they reached out and ate of the good things before them.
But when they had eaten and drunk as much as they wanted,
Priam, descended of Dardanus, sat there and marveled
At mighty Achilles, thinking how huge and handsome
He was, a man in the image of gods everlasting,   205
And likewise Achilles marveled at Priam, looking
Upon his fine face and listening to what he said.
When both had looked on each other enough, old Priam
The godlike spoke thus:
        "Show me my bed, now, Achilles,
O nobleman nurtured of Zeus, that we may enjoy   210
A night of sweet sleep. For never once have my lids
Come together in sleep since my son lost his life at your hands,
But always I've mourned, miserably brooding on
My innumerable sorrows and groveling in dung on the ground
Of my high-walled courtyard. Now, though, I've tasted some food   215
And drunk flaming wine. Till now, I had tasted nothing."
        He spoke, and Achilles ordered his comrades and handmaids
To place two beds in the portico and cover them
With fine purple robes, light spreads, and fleecy warm blankets,
And the girls went out with torches and made the beds.   220
Then Achilles, fast on his feet, spoke to King Priam,
Somewhat bitterly saying:
        "My dear aged friend,
You'll have to sleep outside, since one of the counselors
Of the Achaeans may come to consult me, as often
They do, and as they should. But if one of these   225
Were to catch sight of you through the fast-flying blackness of night,
He might very well go straight to King Agamemnon,
Commander-in-chief of the army, and so there would be

A delay in my giving back the body. But come,
Tell me frankly. How long would you like for the funeral rites   230
Of Prince Hector, that I myself may hold back from battle
And keep back the others also?"
          And the godlike old king:
"If you really want me to give noble Hector his full
Funeral rites, this, O Achilles, is what you could do
To help me. You know how we're penned in the city and also   235
How far the terrified Trojans must go for wood
From the mountains. Let us, then, mourn for him in our halls
For nine days, then burn him and hold the funeral feast
On the tenth, and on the eleventh build a barrow°
For him. Then on the twelfth we'll fight again,   240
If we must."
          To which fleet-footed, noble Achilles:
"So be it, my ancient Priam, just as you wish.
I'll hold back the battle for all the time you request."
          So saying, he clasped the old king's right wrist, in a gesture
Of friendly assurance. Then there in the porch of the lodge   245
The old ones retired, the herald and Priam, their hearts
Ever thoughtful. But Achilles slept in one corner of the spacious,
Strongly built lodge, and beside him lay Briseis,
Lovely of face.
          Now all other gods and mortal
Wearers of horsehair-plumed helmets slept soundly all night,   250
Overcome by soft sleep, but not on help-bringing Hermes
Could sleep get a grip, as he pondered within his mind
How he could get King Priam away from the ships
Unseen by the powerful guards at the gate. Standing close
By the head of his bed, he spoke to him, saying:
          "Old sire,   255
To sleep this way in the midst of your foes, it must be
You have no idea of possible harm, now that
Achilles has spared you. True, you have ransomed your son,
And great was the ransom you paid. Just think what the sons
You left in the city would have to pay for your life—   260
Three times as much at least—if Atreus' son
Agamemnon should find that you're here and the other Achaeans
Get word!"
          At this the old king was afraid and awakened
His herald. And Hermes harnessed the horses and mules
For them and drove the two old ones quietly out   265
Through the slumbering camp, nor did anyone know of their going.
          When they came to the ford of the fair-flowing river, the swirling
Xanthus,° that immortal Zeus begot, then Hermes
Left for Olympus, just as crocus-clad Dawn
Was scattering light over earth. And the king and his herald   270
With moaning and wailing drove the two horses on
Toward the town, and the mules came on with the dead. Nor were

___

239. **barrow:** a mound of earth or stones built over a grave.   268. **Xanthus** (zanʹthəs).

They noticed by any, no man or brightly-sashed woman,
Until Cassandra, lovely as golden Aphrodite,
Having gone to the heights of Pergamus,° stronghold of Troy,   275
Saw her dear father coming on in the car with his herald,
The aged town crier, beside him. And then she saw
What they brought on the bier in the mule-drawn wagon.
     Screaming,
She roused the whole town, crying to all in her grief:
     "Come, you men and women of Troy, you   280
That took such delight in welcoming Hector back
From battle alive, since he was the whole city's joy
And pride. Come, I say, and look at him now!"
     She called, and soon not one man or woman was left
In the town, for unbearable grief seized all, and close   285
By the gates they met Priam bringing the corpse of his son.
Hector's dear wife and royal mother rushed up
To the wheel-spinning wagon, and touching the head of the dead
They wailed and tore at their hair, while the people crowded
Around them and wept. And now all day long till sunset   290
They would have stayed outside the gates, lamenting
And weeping for Hector, had not the old king, still
In the chariot, spoken thus to his people:
     "Make way
For the mules to pass through. Later, when I've brought him home,
You may weep to your heart's content."
     He spoke, and the crowd   295
Opened up, making way for the wagon. Once at the palace
They laid Hector out on a corded bed and seated
Beside him singers to lead in the dirge, and they chanted
The funeral song with the women responding in chorus.
Then white-armed Andromache led their lament, holding   300
The head of man-killing Hector close in her arms,
And wailing:
     "My husband, early indeed you have left us,
Me a widow in your spacious halls, your son
Still a baby, the son we two so unluckily had,
Who now I think will never live to be grown,   305
Since long before that this city shall topple in ruins.
For you, my husband, are dead, you that protected
The town and kept from harm its excellent wives
And little children. These, I fear, shall soon
Be riding the hollow ships, and I among them—   310
And you, my child, must go with me to where you shall toil
For some monstrous master, or have some Achaean seize
Your small arm and hurl you down from the wall to a miserable
Death, being bitter at Hector for killing his brother,
Perhaps, or his father, or else his son, since many,   315
Many Achaeans have bitten the dusty huge earth
At the hands of brave Hector, for your father was not at all gentle

275. **Pergamus:** the citadel, or fortress, of Troy.

In horrible war—so now the people are mourning
For you, Hector, throughout the city, and grief beyond words
You have brought on your parents, but I far more than all others   320
Have nothing left but miserable sorrow. For you
As you died neither stretched out your arms to me from the bed,
Nor did you say any word of sweet love that I
Might have kept in my heart through long days and nights of weeping."
        Thus she spoke in her wailing, and all of the women   325
Responded, moaning and weeping. Then Hecuba took up
The dirge and led the vehement keening, crying:
"Hector, the dearest by far to my heart of all
My children, you when alive were also dear
To the gods, and so they have cared for you now, though your fate   330
Was to die as you did. Whenever swift-footed Achilles
Took other children of mine, he sold them as slaves
Beyond the barren and unresting sea, into Samos,
Imbros, and Lemnos,° lost in the haze. But when
With his tapering bronze he had taken your life, he dragged you   335
Daily about his comrade Patroclus' barrow—
Patroclus, whom you, my son, slew—though even this
Did not resurrect his friend. But now you lie
Fresh as the dew in our palace, like one merely sleeping,
Or one whom silver-bowed Phoebus Apollo has slain   340
With his gentle shafts."
        Even so she spoke in her wailing,
And roused the passionate keening. Then Helen was third
To lead the lament, crying: "O Hector, dearest
By far to my heart of all my husband's brothers,
My husband is Paris the godlike, who brought me to Troy—   345
Would I had died first! Now this is the twentieth year
Since I left my own country, but never once have I heard
From you an evil word or an ugly. In fact,
When the others reproached me here in the palace, some brother
Of yours, a sister, or a well-dressed sister-in-law,   350
Or even your mother—your father was kind to me always,
A father to me as well—at such times you
Would turn them away and restrain them with your gentle spirit
And courteous words. Hence now I weep for you
And my own luckless self, grieving at heart, for now   355
No longer is anyone left in wide Troy that is gentle
Or loving to me. All shudder whenever I pass."
        Such was her wailing lament, and the numberless crowd
Reechoed her moans. Then the old King Priam spoke
Mid his people, saying: "Bring wood, you men of Troy,   360
Into the city, and have no dread in your hearts
Of a treacherous Argive ambush, for Achilles truly
Assured me when he sent me forth from the hollow black ships
That he would do us no harm till the twelfth morning came."
        Such were his words, and they harnessed their oxen and mules   365

334. **Samos, Imbros, and Lemnos:** large islands in the Aegean Sea.

To wagons and rapidly gathered in front of the city.
Then for nine days they carted in wood, a supply
Unspeakably great, but when the tenth man-lighting morning
Arrived, they carried brave Hector forth, and laying
Him down on top of the pyre threw flame upon it.   370
     But as soon as young rose-fingered Dawn appeared the next day,
The people gathered about Hector's pyre, and when
They had quenched with sparkling wine whatever still burned,
His grieving brothers and friends, weeping big tears
All the while, collected Hector's white bones. These they placed   375
In a golden box, which they wrapped in soft purple robes
And laid away in a hollowed-out grave. This they closed
With huge stones laid side by side and over it, rapidly
Working, they heaped his high barrow, setting guards round about
To prevent a surprise attack from the well-greaved Achaeans.   380
When the barrow was done, they returned to the palace of Priam,
The Zeus-nurtured king, where they feasted a glorious feast.
     Even so they buried Prince Hector, tamer of horses.

FOR STUDY AND DISCUSSION

THE QUARREL

1. In Book 1, find several reasons for Achilles' anger. Identify those which are based on specific grievances and those which are mainly about honor.

2. What role does Nestor play in the argument? What advice does he give Agamemnon and Achilles? How does each receive his counsel?

3. What is the relationship between Achilles and Thetis? How does she promise to help him?

4. In the conversation between mother and son, what fate for Achilles is alluded to which strongly motivates his wrath? Why is Achilles more concerned with his own honor than with supporting the Greek cause? Do you think Achilles was justified in his wrath and in his subsequent withdrawal from battle? Explain.

THE DUEL

1. Usually in the *Iliad* we hear only from the great warriors or the Olympian gods. But in this book the elder citizens of Troy state their feelings about the war. How do their opinions compare with those expressed by Paris, Hector, and Priam?

2. What do we learn about Helen's character? Is she sensitive, observant, selfish, kindhearted? In what way is she a pathetic figure? Refer to her speeches in your answers.

HECTOR AND ANDROMACHE

1. Hector's parting from Andromache is a rare tender scene in the *Iliad*. What is Hector's feeling toward his wife and son? What is his attitude toward war and glory? How does his attitude differ from that of Achilles? How does Andromache feel about the war?

2. Do Hector's conversations with Paris in Book 3 and with Andromache in Book 6 show him to be consistent in his attitudes toward war and duty? Explain.

THE DEATH OF HECTOR

1. In rejoining the battle, Achilles rejects the possibility of a long, peaceful life for the certainty of glory. Is this decision in keeping with Achilles' character? At what other time has he shown himself to be greatly concerned with personal honor?

2. At the climactic meeting of Hector and Achilles, Hector turns and runs away. It has been suggested that Hector, realizing his inferiority to Achilles in battle, hoped he could tire Achilles. Do you find any evidence in the poem to support this view? What other reasons can you give for Hector's puzzling action?

3. How is Hector's running from Achilles different from Paris' shrinking from Menelaus in Book 3? What part did the gods play in Hector's downfall?

4. The Greeks greatly prized the quality they called *arete,* which means "courage,

pride, dignity, and nobility of deed." Do Achilles and Hector display any or all of these characteristics? Explain.

PRIAM AND ACHILLES

Why is the meeting between Achilles and Priam included in the epic? Which character claims your sympathies by the time this scene ends?

GENERAL

1. Three societies are represented in the *Iliad*—that of the camp, of the city, and of the mountaintop. Identify the members of these three societies. Contrast the natures of the societies and the motivations of each with regard to the war.

2. Do you think the human characters of the *Iliad* are merely puppets of the Olympian gods, or do they exercise any freedom of choice or action? Give reasons for your answer. Homer seems to use the activities of the gods as a means of explaining what is puzzling about human behavior and events. Richmond Lattimore says that the gods may represent "projections of feelings or activities in the observed world." Thus Ares, god of war, might also represent war itself or even the brutal forces in man which drive him to make war. List at least three incidents in the epic in which the gods play a vital, manipulative part, and tell how a modern-day novelist or TV scriptwriter would handle such incidents.

3. Since Homer does not appear to make value judgments on the actions of the characters, how do we form an estimate of their worth? Give examples referring to Achilles, Hector, Agamemnon, Helen, Priam.

4. Homer's eighth century B.C. audience was an aristocratic one. His epics celebrate the deeds of nobles, and they were written to be recited in nobles' halls. What kinds of heroes are celebrated in contemporary folk tradition? Do these heroes reflect the interests of democratic nonaristocratic society? If so, in what ways?

CLASSICAL CONVENTIONS

Certain poetic characteristics which originated in the Greek epics are also to be found in later epics, such as Virgil's *Aeneid* and Milton's *Paradise Lost* (see page 629). These are known as classical conventions and include the use of the following techniques:

1. The epic opens with an invocation to the Muse and a statement of the theme. The *Iliad* opens with the following invocation. What three themes are stated in these lines?

● Sing, O Goddess, the ruinous wrath
   of Achilles,
   Son of Peleus, the terrible curse that
   brought
   Unnumbered woes upon the Achaeans and hurled
   To Hades so many heroic souls,
   leaving
   Their bodies the prey of dogs and carrion birds.
   The will of Zeus was done from the
   moment they quarreled,
   Agamemnon, son of Atreus, and godlike Achilles.—HOMER

2. The epic plunges immediately *in medias res* (into the middle of things), and uses flashbacks to remind the audience of related events that are not included in the epic. Homer reminds the audience of some of these events by means of Calchas' speech. How else, in Book 1, are earlier events narrated?

3. The epic retells events which have already occurred in the epic. About one third of the epic is repetitious. Identify such repetition in Book 1. How is the necessity for this repetition rationalized?

4. The epic uses long speeches rather than rapid-fire dialogue to present the characters' conversations. Count the lines of at least three speeches in Book 1.

5. The epic uses a figure of speech known as the Homeric simile. In the Homeric simile, one element in a comparison is described at far greater length than the other. These extended similes compare an event in the epic with some occurrence in nature or in everyday life which would be familiar to the audience. In Book 3 (page 64, lines 2–7), the noise of the advancing Trojans is compared at length with the noise of cranes. Find at least three other Homeric similes. Tell if you think they are effective, and why.

6. The epic uses another figure of speech known as the stock epithet. A stock epithet is a descriptive adjective or a descriptive phrase that is repeatedly used with, or in place of, a name. A well-known example of a stock epithet, used by Homer, is "wine-dark sea." What epithets are used here to describe gods and goddesses and mortal men and women? Explain the effect of each.

ARCHILOCHUS

Archilochus led a turbulent life during the seventh century B.C., a time marked by uprisings against the nobility. He became a soldier of fortune, but during a particularly savage battle he deserted and lost all honor at home. His next years were lived in miserable exile, until his poetry won him an Olympian prize and extensive fame. The two virtues he praises in the following poem were of supreme importance to the Greeks.

Courage and Moderation

[handwritten: courage of whole person]

[handwritten arrow] Heart, my heart, so battered with misfortune far beyond your strength,
up, and face the men who hate us. Bare your chest to the assault
of the enemy, and fight them off. Stand fast among the beamlike spears.
Give no ground; and if you beat them, do not brag in open show,
nor, if they beat you, run home and lie down on your bed and cry.
Keep some measure in the joy you take in luck, and the degree
you give way to sorrow. All our life is up and down like this.

[handwritten: Can't be sure your fortune (good or bad) will stay. Do not allow them to dissuade or persuade you.]

CALLINUS

Callinus lived at about the same time as Archilochus. He was a citizen of Ephesus in Asia Minor. In the following poem, which is the only major fragment of his poetry that survives, he urges his fellow citizens to resist the barbarian hordes from the Crimea.

A Call to Arms

How long will you lie idle, and when will you find some courage,
you young men? Have you no shame of what other cities will say,
you who hang back? You think you can sit quiet in peacetime.
This is not peace, it is war which has engulfed our land.

"Courage and Moderation" by Archilochus from *Greek Lyrics*, rev. ed., translated by Richmond Lattimore, © 1960 by Richmond Lattimore. Reprinted by permission of The University of Chicago Press.
"A Call to Arms" by Callinus from *Greek Lyrics*, rev. ed., translated by Richmond Lattimore, © 1960 by Richmond Lattimore. Reprinted by permission of The University of Chicago Press.

A man, as he dies, should make one last throw with his spear.   5
It is a high thing, a bright honor, for a man to do battle
 with the enemy for the sake of his children, and for his land
and his true wife; and death is a thing that will come when the spinning
 Destinies make it come. So a man should go straight on
forward, spear held high, and under his shield the fighting   10
 strength coiled, ready to strike in the first shock of the charge.
When it is ordained that a man shall die, there is no escaping
 death, not even for one descended from deathless gods.
Often a man who has fled from the fight and the clash of the thrown spears
 goes his way, and death befalls him in his own house,   15
and such a man is not loved nor missed for long by his people;
 the great and the small alike mourn when a hero dies.
For all the populace is grieved for the high-hearted warrior
 after his death; while he lives, he is treated as almost divine.
Their eyes gaze on him as if he stood like a bastion before them.   20
 His actions are like an army's, though he is only one man.

[handwritten: don't know when death will come, so do your best now / take things as they come / leave an honorable reputation]

SEMONIDES

Semonides, who lived during the late seventh century B.C., was one of the early
writers of satire. The "blind poet" he refers to in line 1 is Homer.

[handwritten: carpe diem. / life is undependable so / seize the day]

Brevity of Life

[handwritten: Homer]

One verse by the blind poet of Chios is indelible:
"The life of man is like a summer's leaf."
Yet few who hear these words take them into their heart,
for hope is rooted in every youthful soul,
the lovely flower of youth grows tall with color,   5
life will have no end,
or there is no place for growing old, for death;
and while in health, no fear of foul disease.
Poor fools! in islands of illusion,
for men have but a day of youth and life.   10
You few who understand know when death is near
the food you give your soul must be supreme.

ALCAEUS

Alcaeus, who lived in the sixth century B.C., was a much-admired poet. He and the attractive woman poet Sappho lived on the island of Lesbos, and some legends maintain that he was hopelessly in love with her.

State is being compared to a ship.

A Nation at Sea

I can't tell you which way the gale has turned
for waves crash in from west and east, and we
are tossed and driven between, our black ship
    laboring under the giant storm.

The sea washes across the decks and maststep   5
and dark daylight already shows through long rents
in the sails. Even the halyards slacken as
    windward waves coil above the hull.

What sore labor to bail the water we've shipped!
Let us raise bulwarks and ride out the storm,   10
heeding my words: "Let each man now be famous."
    Yet base cowards betray the state.

"A Nation at Sea" by Alcaeus from *Greek Lyric Poetry,* translated by Willis Barnstone, copyright © 1962, 1967 by Bantam Books, Inc. Reprinted by permission of the publisher.

SAPPHO

[handwritten top-left: why assume from this is written from a woman's point of view]

Called by Plato "the tenth Muse," Sappho is often considered to be the supreme woman poet of any time. Few of her poems are extant, but critics have no doubts concerning her greatness. Her poems deal almost exclusively with personal relationships, and they are generally acclaimed the most sensitive, delicate, and passionate of Greek lyrics. Sappho lived on the island of Lesbos during the sixth century B.C.

Sappho directed many poems to the women who attended the school she seems to have run. The Anaktoria referred to in the first poem that follows is a woman. Apparently she had once been loved by a man who later became the lover of the speaker in the poem. In the second "letter," it becomes clear that the man has left both women. Perhaps he is dead.

[handwritten left: this ist wrong]

[handwritten left: jealousy loss anguish]

Three Letters to Anaktoria

[handwritten: close friend or relative]

1

[handwritten: present tense "I"]

I set that man above the gods and heroes—
all day, he sits before you face to face,
like a cardplayer. Your elbow brushes his elbow—
if you should speak, he hears.

[handwritten: affected or contact]

The touched heart madly stirs,
your laughter is water hurrying over pebbles— *[handwritten: soft murmur / metaphor]*
every gesture is a proclamation,
every sound is speech . . . *[handwritten: says something]*   5

Refining fire purifies my flesh!
I hear you: a hollowness in my ears   10
thunders and stuns me. I cannot speak.
I cannot see. *[handwritten: blinded]* *[handwritten: helpless]*

I shiver. A dead whiteness spreads over
my body, trickling pinpricks of sweat.
I am greener than the greenest green grass— *[handwritten: new, fresh, healthy]*   15
I die!

[handwritten left margin: Each stanza is a thought]
[handwritten left: so angry that cannot see or speak / symbol of death]

[handwritten right: because he has accomplished feat: gets to be w/ Anaktoria & so lucky, has power by getting Anaktoria, can do what writer couldn't]

[handwritten: direct address, confrontation]

[handwritten top margin: Difference 'tween self & society - Perhaps parallels bizarre contrasting relationship w/ Anak. society's norms]

For some the fairest thing on the dark earth is Thermopylae
and the Spartan phalanx lowering lances to die—
Salamis and the half-moon of Athenian triremes
sprinting to pin down the Persian fleet;
nothing is as fair as my beloved. *[handwritten: similie]*   5

[handwritten: You know]
I can easily make you understand this:
dwell on the gentleness of his footstep,
the shimmer of his shining face fairer than ten thousand *[handwritten: metaphor]*
barbarous scythe-wheeled Persian chariots,
or the myriad hanging gardens in Persepolis.   10
[handwritten: great memories of Sappho]

[handwritten: Anaktoria] Helen forgot her husband and dear children
to cherish Paris, *[handwritten: man]*
the loveliest of mortals, *[handwritten: man]*
the murderer of Troy— *[handwritten: Sappho? friendship?]*
she bestowed her heart far off. *[handwritten: man]*   15
[handwritten: Anak]

How easily a woman is led astray!   *[handwritten: → slaves]*
She remembers nothing of what is nearest at hand:
her loom, her household, her helots . . . *[handwritten: close friend]*
Anaktoria, did you cherish my love, *[handwritten: respect my emotions]*
when the Bridegroom was with you?   *[handwritten: or consider]*   20

A woman seldom finds what is best—
no, never in this world,
Anaktoria! Pray
for his magnificence I once pined to share . . . *[handwritten: giving him up to her]*
to have lived is better than to live!   25

[handwritten: did she kill one of them? suicide?]

The moon slides west,
it is midnight,
the time is gone—
I lie alone!

[handwritten: not just angry Anak. does not accept, appreciate her love. society does not either]

Four Fragments

1

Hesperos, you bring home all the bright dawn disperses,
bring home the sheep,
bring home the goat, bring the child home to its mother.

2

Off in the twilight hung the low full moon,
And all the women stood before it grave,
As round an altar. Thus at holy times
The Cretan damsels dance melodiously
With delicate feet about the sacrifice,
Trampling the tender bloom of the soft grass.

3

Round about me hum the winds of autumn,
Cool between the apple boughs: and slumber,
Flowing from the quivering leaves to earthward,
Spreads as a river.

4

I could not hope
to touch the sky
with my two arms.

SIMONIDES

Simonides (c. 556 B.C.–c. 468 B.C.) was the most versatile of the Greek lyric poets, a master of practically every form of poetry known in his time. The first poem that follows treats one of the Greek myths with tender pathos. According to this myth, an oracle informed a certain king that he would be killed by the son of his daughter Danae. When Danae bore a son named Perseus, her father placed Danae and the infant boy in a chest and cast them to the mercy of the waves.

Numbers 1 and 4 by Sappho from *Greek Lyric Poetry,* translated by Willis Barnstone, copyright © 1962, 1967 by Bantam Books, Inc. Reprinted by permission of the publisher.
Numbers 2 and 3 by Sappho, translated by William Ellery Leonard, from *A Son of Earth* by William Ellery Leonard. Copyright 1928 by The Viking Press, Inc., © renewed 1956 by Charlotte Charlton Leonard. Reprinted by permission of The Viking Press, Inc.

Danae and the Infant Perseus
Imprisoned in a Chest on the Sea

A tilting sea and thundering winds
tossed the carved chest and filled Danae
with terror; she cried
and placed her arm lovingly around
Perseus, saying: "My child, I suffer   5
and yet your heart is calm; you sleep
profoundly in the blue dark of night
and shine in our gloomy bronze-ribbed boat.
Don't think of the heaving saltwave
that seeps in through airholes and drenches   10
your hair, nor of the clamoring gale;
but lying in our seaviolet blanket
keep your lovely body close to mine.

If you knew the horror of our plight,
your gentle ears would hear my words.   15
But sleep, my son, and let
the ocean sleep and our great troubles end.
I ask you, father Zeus,
rescue us from our fate; and should
my words seem too severe, I beg you please   20
remember where we are, and forgive
my prayer."

humble

Arete

There is one story
that Virtue has her dwelling place above rock walls hard to climb
with a grave chorus of light-footed nymphs attendant about her,
and she is not to be looked upon by the eyes of every mortal,
only by one who with sweat, with clenched concentration
and courage, climbs to the peak.

"Danae and the Infant Perseus . . ." by Simonides from *Greek Lyric Poetry,* translated by Willis Barnstone, copyright © 1962, 1967 by Bantam Books, Inc. Reprinted by permission of the publisher.
"Arete" by Simonides from *Greek Lyrics,* rev. ed., translated by Richmond Lattimore, © 1960 by Richmond Lattimore. Reprinted by permission of The University of Chicago Press.

Pindar (522? B.C.–443 B.C.) is best known for his choral lyrics honoring the victors in athletic contests, their families, and their cities. Usually, Pindar weaves mythological stories into his poems, to lift them above the particular occasion and inspire his audience with pride, not only in one athlete but in a total culture and tradition. To fully appreciate Pindar's poems you would have to re-create the splendor of the athletic festivals, the now-lost music that accompanied the choral recitation of the odes, the fervent civic patriotism of the spectators, the pride they took in the display of perfect physical beauty.

appealing to civic pride

"Olympia 11" honors Agesidamos, winner of boys' boxing at the contest held at Olympia in 476 B.C. Agesidamos was a citizen of Lokris, a Greek city in southern Italy. This ode is one of Pindar's shortest, and it lacks the usual mythological allusions.

Olympia 11

There is a time when men need most favoring
gales; there is a time for water from the sky,
rain, child of cloud.
But if by endeavor a man win fairly, soft-spoken songs
are given, to be a beginning of men's   5
speech to come and a true seal on great achievements.

Abundant is such praise laid up for victories
Olympian. My lips have good will
to marshal these words; yet only
by God's grace does a man blossom in the wise turning of his thought.   10
Son of Archestratos, know
that for the sake, Agesidamos, of your boxing

I shall enchant in strain of song a glory upon
your olive wreath of gold
and bespeak the race of the West Wind Lokrians.   15
There acclaim him; I warrant you,
Muses, you will visit no gathering cold to strangers   *hospitality*
nor lost to lovely things   *aesthetic sense*
wise but deep to the heart in wisdom, and spearmen also. No thing, neither
   devious fox   *good warriors*
nor loud lion, may change the nature born in his blood.   20

well rounded

From *Odes of Pindar,* translated by Richmond Lattimore, © 1947 by Richmond Lattimore. Reprinted by permission of The University of Chicago Press.

athelete's winning is almost not up to him

THEOCRITUS

After the death of Pindar, lyric poetry was supplanted in importance by other forms, such as tragedy, comedy, and historical and philosophical prose. It was not until after the beginning of the Hellenistic Age that lyric poetry returned to prominence with a group of "Alexandrian" poets, so-called because many of them lived in Alexandria, in Egypt, the center of Greek culture in the East. Theocritus, who wrote in the early decades of the third century B.C., is generally considered the greatest of these Alexandrian poets. He originated a type of poetry called *pastoral,* which describes country scenes with artful simplicity and which expresses a genuine love of nature and rural life. The following passage, taken from a longer poem, describes a beautiful drinking cup or bowl promised by a goatherd to a shepherd in return for a song.

The Ivy Bowl

Above, along the rim, the ivy tendril
Trails sinuous, rejoicing in its fruit,
Gold clustered berries laid between the leaves.
Within, a woman, cloaked and circleted,
Fair as some god might fashion, stands enwrought,   5
While at her side two lovers vie in speech
To win her favor, fair with flowing locks.
Now this one speaks, now that; and yet their words
Touch not her heart; but now she looks on one
And smiles, now turns her thought to heed the other;   10
Both toil in vain, love-stricken, hollow-eyed.
And next engraved an aged fisherman
Stands on a rugged rock and eagerly
Draws close his heavy net to make a cast;
Strongly he toils, till all about his neck   15
Stand out the sinews—gray, wave-worn and old;
Yet, as he labors, seems his strength a boy's.
Hard by, a carven vineyard, where the vines
Droop with empurpled clusters, and a child
Sits idly on a loose stone wall to guard   20
The ripening grapes; and see, two wily foxes
Lurk near, one ravaging the grapes and one
Intent, uncaught, to steal the poor lad's bread
From his unguarded wallet; but the child,
Gathering asphodel and rush to plait   25
A pretty cricket cage, cares naught for vines
Or wallet—all his joy is in his task.
And all about the cup the pliant stems
Of the acanthus spread their leaves—a marvel
To please a goatherd's eyes and dazzle thine!   30

"The Ivy Bowl" from *The Idylls of Theocritus in English Verse,* translated by W. Douglas P. Hill. Published by The Shakespeare Head Press, Oxford: 1959. Reprinted by permission of Basil Blackwell, Publisher.

Three Alexandrian Epigrams

The word *epigram,* which comes from a term meaning "inscription," was used by the Greeks to refer to almost any brief poem. For many centuries, the epigram was a popular literary form. Often elegantly expressed, these lines were frequently used as inscriptions on monuments or tombs.

The author of the first epigram that follows is anonymous. The second is by Callimachus, who was the arbiter of literary taste in Alexandria during the third century B.C. Lucian (c. A.D. 120–c. A.D. 200), the author of the third epigram, was born in Syria but traveled extensively, trying various occupations which included law and ghostwriting. For twenty years he lived in Athens, where he became famous for his irreverent satire.

Unhappy Dionysius

(Anonymous)

Here lie I, Dionysius of Tarsus,
Who lived for sixty years and never married.
Would that my father hadn't.

wish he'd never been born

CALLIMACHUS

Elegy for Heraclitus

They told me, Heraclitus, they told me you were dead,
They brought me bitter news to hear and bitter tears to shed.
I wept as I remembered how often you and I
Had tired the sun with talking and sent him down the sky.

And now that thou art lying, my dear old Carian guest,
A handful of gray ashes, long, long ago at rest,
Still are thy pleasant voices, thy nightingales, awake:
For Death, he taketh all away, but these he cannot take.

remembers

LUCIAN

On Early Death

A child I was, Callimachus, five years of age,
    With heart still free from care,
When pitiless Hades snatched me from the light.
Mourn not my early passing from this stage!
    Had I of life brief share?
Brief share had I too of its evil plight.

FOR STUDY AND DISCUSSION

1. What imagery does Archilochus use in the address to his own heart or soul? How does the attitude expressed in this poem compare with the attitude expressed by Homer's heroes in the *Iliad?* Cite specific passages from the *Iliad* in answering.

2. In "A Call to Arms," what three reasons does the speaker give in urging the young men to fight? What two different ways of meeting death does he describe? Point out the lines which clearly describe the poet's attitude toward death. What does he suggest are the compensations for death?

3. In "Brevity of Life," what metaphor is used for youth? What is the poet's attitude toward youth? What might be the "food you give your soul"? To what should it be supreme?

4. "A Nation at Sea" is one of the first poems to use the famous metaphor of the ship of state. What words reveal that the ship is a metaphor for the state? How may the different images in the poem be applied to a country in distress?

5. In the first letter to Anaktoria, how does the speaker stress the intensity of her feeling? How does the intensity increase as the poem proceeds? In the second letter, the speaker makes several historical and mythological allusions. Explain these allusions. How would you paraphrase line 25?

6. In Sappho's fragment 1, who or what is Hesperos? What adjectives best describe the mood of this poem? For what purpose might such a song have been sung?

7. What occasion is being described in the second fragment?

8. In the third fragment, how do the winds of autumn sound? How do they feel? Paraphrase the lines that describe the approach of sleep.

9. What idea is Sappho expressing in the fourth fragment?

10. What images are used in Simonides' poem about Danae? Describe Danae's attitude toward her son, toward their situation, and toward Zeus. What error is Danae anxious to avoid committing?

11. In "Arete," is the poet describing a physical or a spiritual struggle? How does the struggle described in this poem compare with the struggle waged by Achilles in the *Iliad?*

12. "Olympia 11" honors the winner of a boxing match. Do you find in the poem any images suggesting the color and excitement of the match? Explain. What is Pindar most interested in glorifying? What attributes of man does Pindar seem to believe are most praiseworthy? How does the tone of Pindar's ode contrast with Sappho's lyrics?

13. In "The Ivy Bowl," what three scenes on the bowl are described in detail? What three stages of life do they represent? What motifs weave between the scenes and unify them?

FOR COMPOSITION

The ancient Greeks revealed certain attitudes toward the good life, toward death, and toward immortality. Write a brief composition examining the Greek attitude toward these problems, based on the evidence in the poems in this section. In your final paragraph, assess the relevance of the Greek attitude to the present day and to your own life.

Fables

AESOP

Although many legends are told about the life of the sixth-century B.C. fabulist Aesop (Aesopos), nothing is known that can be accepted as certain. According to a later Greek tradition reported by Herodotus, Aesop was a slave who, after being set free, traveled extensively to many parts of Greece and to foreign lands and eventually met a violent death at Delphi. Other traditions assert that he was not a Greek at all, but a Lydian from Asia Minor. Because the reports about him are so vague and contradictory, some modern scholars have suggested that no such person ever existed. Nevertheless, the Greeks thought of him as a real person, tended to attribute all fables to him, and gave him credit for inventing this kind of tale.

In the fables, we see the faults and foibles of mankind illustrated, usually, but not always, by the actions of animals. Given the tendency of the Greeks toward self-examination and their enjoyment of debate, it is probable that the fables were popularly used to exemplify specific points in arguments rather than to teach general moral precepts. Their style is consistently straightforward, realistic, and terse: the scene is set, the action related, and the result clearly stated.

animals a characters
realistic, simple style
has a moral

life oriented
Satyrical in tone

The Goatherd and the Wild Goats

A GOATHERD DROVE his goats out to pasture, and when he saw some wild goats mingling with them as evening came on, he drove them all into his cave. The next day a big storm came up, and since he couldn't take them to the usual pasture, he fed them inside. To his own goats he gave a small amount of feed, just enough to stave off their hunger, but he gave piles of food to the others to get them to stay with him. After the storm, when he took them all out to pasture, as soon as the wild goats got to the mountains, they ran away. As the herdsman was complaining of their ingratitude for leaving him after getting more than their share of feed, they turned around and said, "That's why we are all the more cautious. If you took better care of us, who came to you only yesterday, than you did of your old flock, obviously, if any others come to you, you'll prefer them to us."

"The Goatherd and the Wild Goats," "The Wayfarers and the Bear," "The Lion and the Mouse Who Returned a Favor" by Aesop from *Aesop Without Morals,* translated by Lloyd W. Daly. Reprinted by permission of A. S. Barnes & Company, Inc.

The Wayfarers and the Bear

Two FRIENDS were traveling along the same road. When a bear suddenly appeared, one of them quickly climbed a tree and hid. The other was about to be caught but fell down on the ground and played dead. When the bear put its muzzle up close and smelled all around him, he held his breath, for they say that the animal will not touch a dead body. When the bear went away, the man up in the tree asked him what the bear had said in his ear. He replied, "Not to travel in the future with friends who won't stand by you in danger."

The Lion and the Mouse Who Returned a Favor

WHILE A LION was sleeping, a mouse ran over his body. The lion awoke, seized the mouse, and was on the point of devouring him. When the mouse begged the lion to let him go and said that if he were spared he would repay him in gratitude, the lion smiled and released him. But it turned out that it wasn't long until the lion's life was saved thanks to the mouse. When he was caught by some hunters and tied to a tree with a rope, the mouse heard his groans, came to his aid, gnawed through the rope, and set him free, with the remark, "You once laughed at me because you didn't expect to get any return for your favor to me, but now you know that even mice can show their gratitude."

FOR STUDY AND DISCUSSION

1. Two of these fables have animal characters. Do these creatures exhibit animal or human characteristics? Explain. How do various forms of modern media make use of animal characters?

2. In later collections of fables, a moral tag that might begin "This fable teaches that . . ." was added at the end of each fable. Here, these fables appear without stated morals. Formulate a moral in one or two sentences for each of these fables. Can each fable illustrate more than one moral?

3. Which, if any, of these fables tell stories that are already familiar to you? In your opinion, what characteristics of these fables make them so popular and widely known?

FOR COMPOSITION

Make up a fable of your own that reflects modern life. Write a moral for the fable on the back of your paper, and exchange fables with a classmate. After your classmate has added his own moral at the end of the fable, compare the two morals. Do they differ in content or just in wording? Does one moral hold more authority than the other? Can your fable illustrate more than one moral?

The History of the Persian Wars

HERODOTUS

Cicero, the Roman statesman and orator, called Herodotus (c. 484 B.C.–c. 424 B.C.) "the father of history." Herodotus' great work, the *History of the Persian Wars,* is indeed the first historical narrative of the Western world. Previously, accounts of the past had been conveyed principally through the recitation of legends. Herodotus used the word *historia* to mean investigation and research.

Herodotus surely must have been filled with boundless curiosity, since he traveled widely at a time when travel was dangerous and difficult. He spent most of his lifetime sailing the Black Sea, traveling deep into the enormous Persian Empire, penetrating far up the Nile River, and venturing at least as far west as Sicily. His historical methods included interviewing eyewitnesses and key persons and examining old manuscripts and inscriptions; thus he absorbed all the information available to him. To criticize Herodotus as being naive or credulous because he tells wondrous stories of Indian ants bigger than foxes, of mares giving birth to rabbits, of cattle that backed up as they ate, and of sheep whose tails were so large they were supported on wheeled carts is to do him an injustice. His system required that he do this. "For myself," he says, "my duty is to report all that is said, but I am not obliged to believe it all."

Of the nine books into which the *History* is divided, only the last three recount the events of the war. The first six trace the causes of the war (which, according to Herodotus, stretch back into mythical times) and give information about the social customs, religious observances, and legends of the time. Although Herodotus aimed at an objective account of the war itself, there is no doubt where his sympathies lay. He saw the war as a struggle between an Oriental tyrant and the free men of Greece. His theme was to show the inevitable humiliation of the Persians who had offended the gods by an arrogant belief in their own invincibility. However, Herodotus essentially deals with men and events on a humanistic rather than a pietistic level.

The Persian Wars began in the following way. Athens had aided a number of Greek cities in Asia Minor that were in unsuccessful revolt against their Persian rulers. Darius, the Persian emperor, was so enraged at this meddling in Persian affairs that he ordered the invasion of Greece. But the Persian attempts at conquest failed. After a humiliating defeat by a small Athenian army on the plain of Marathon, Darius withdrew his forces. Before he could organize another invasion, he died. Xerxes, his son, spent years in preparation and gathered an enormous army with troops from all over the Persian Empire, an army which Herodotus generously estimates at more than two million men. In 480 B.C. hordes of Persians swept through the northern passes of Greece. So vast was the army, Herodotus reports, that it drank whole rivers dry, and whenever it ate two meals, the city that fed it was ruined. The central and southern Greek city-states, aware of the approaching danger, could not decide what to do. Sparta, far to the south, had the foremost warriors in Greece, but it was the time of an important religious feast and Sparta was unwilling to send her men away at this particular time. Finally, however, the Spartans ordered a select band of three hundred men (later joined by a small number of other Greek forces) to march north under the command of their king, Leonidas. Their mission was to help hold the strategic northern mountain pass at Thermopylae, in the district of Melis, until the Greeks to the south could mobilize a larger force. The stand made by the three hundred Spartans is considered one of the most heroic defenses in military history.

digression

*Biased, put himself in it.
Written to give individual's
accounts; human interest,
personal*

Thermopylae

Informal, personal tone

XERXES ENCAMPED at Melis in Trechis, while the Greeks settled down to wait at the pass which most Greeks call Thermopylae, though the locals refer to it as Pylae. One army controlled all the country to the north as far as Trechis, the other kept guard to the south and west.

The Greek army that faced the Persians in the pass was composed of the following nations: 300 Spartan hoplites;[1] 1,000 Tegeans and Mantineans—500 of each; 120 Orchomeneans; 1,000 from the rest of Arkadia; 400 from Corinth; 200 from Phleius; 80 from Mycenae; 700 Boeotians and Thespians; 400 Thebans.

Additional strength was supplied by the Locrian Opuntians, who came with the whole of their army, and the Phokians, who sent a thousand men. They had been persuaded to come by messages from the Greeks which said that they were the advance force of the main army, the rest of which was expected any day, while the sea was policed by the combined fleets of Athens, Aegina, and many other states—so that there was no danger involved. The invader was no more than human, and no

man was born without some potential for misfortune in his make-up. The present aggressor, mortal as he was, must surely fail in his aim. The Opuntians and Phokians, when they heard this, sent men to fight at Trechis.

subjected

When they first arrived, the allies all had their own generals with them, but the most distinguished, and the one who was made commander-in-chief, was Leonidas, the Spartan, who had come to the throne of Sparta almost by accident. He had two elder brothers—Kleomenes and Dorieus—and it never entered his head that one day he would be king. But Kleomenes died without a son to inherit his title, and Dorieus was killed in Sicily, so the throne reverted to Leonidas. He had brought an army of picked men to Thermopylae, all in the prime of life, and all with children at home. He had a special reason for taking the Thebans I mentioned, whose commander was Leontiades. He strongly suspected them of Persian sympathies. So he ordered them into battle, hoping they would come out into the open and either reject or accept alliance with Greece. They sent troops, but remained pro-Persian at heart.

Sparta sent on the advance party with Leonidas in case the allies lost heart at the sight of the Spartan delay and decided to surrender. Given a lead, however, they would follow. But having done this, the Spartans intended to hold their traditional festival (it was the time of the Karneia) and bring up their main army later, leaving only a light garrison for the city. The other allies had similar plans—for the Olympic games were due—and so, con-

---

[1] **hoplites:** heavily armed foot soldiers, from the Greek word *hoplon,* meaning "shield."

"Thermopylae" from *The Struggle for Greece* by Herodotus, translated by Kenneth Cavander. Reprinted by permission of The Folio Society Ltd.

vinced that the battle at Thermopylae would not be decided for a long time, they sent only a skeleton force.

But as the Persian attack grew imminent the Greeks at Thermopylae began to panic and talk in terms of surrender. Most of the Peloponnesians wanted to retire to their own country and hold the Isthmus; Leonidas, the Phokians, and the Locrians, highly incensed by this idea, voted to keep their present position and send a message to the various cities to ask for help, since their small force could not cope with the Persian army.

While they were debating, Xerxes sent a mounted scout to spy out the Greek strength, where and what they were doing. While he was still in Thessaly he had heard that the army at Thermopylae was a small band whose leaders were the Spartans under Leonidas, a descendant of the great warrior Herakles. The scout came close up to the Greek lines, reconnoitered the ground, and examined the camp, though not all of it, for he could not see the men drawn up behind the wall they had raised to guard the pass. But he counted the men outside, who had their weapons propped up against the wall and happened at this moment to be the Spartans. Some of them were exercising, others combing their hair. The scout was stupefied when he saw their numbers, but having made an exact count he retreated at his leisure—no one followed him, no one even took the slightest notice of him. When he delivered his information to Xerxes, the king was unable to understand what was happening. He could not grasp the fact that the Greeks were prepared to fight to the last man. Their tactics seemed ridiculous to him, and he sent for Demaretos,[1] who was still with him, and asked him what the Spartans were doing.

"When we started this invasion," Demaretos said, "I gave you my estimate of these men, and you laughed at me. It is very difficult for me to maintain the truth

[1] **Demaretos:** an exiled king of Sparta who had gone over to Persia and become an adviser to Xerxes.

when it contradicts you, my king, but you must listen again. These men have come to fight with you for this pass, and they are preparing for that. It is their custom, on the eve of a dangerous adventure, to dress their hair. Believe me when I say that if you overcome these men, and the ones they have left behind in Sparta, there is no other people in the world who will offer any resistance to your soldiers. You are going to meet the noblest and the bravest men in Greece."

Xerxes was frankly incredulous and again asked how they could fight his army.

"Sir," replied Demaretos, "if I am wrong, never believe a word I say again."

Even this did not convince Xerxes, who waited for four days, always expecting the Greeks to retreat. But on the fifth day, when they were still there and appeared to be persisting in their stupidity and conceit, he lost his patience and sent off the Medes and Kissians, with instructions to take them alive and bring them before him.

The Medes attacked at the charge, and many were killed; a second charge was made, and they were cut down in their hundreds—but they would not be driven back. All the same, it was clear to everyone, and especially to Xerxes, that his army contained plenty of men, but very few soldiers. The battle lasted throughout that day. The slaughter of Medes was ghastly and they were at last withdrawn from the fighting line and replaced by the Persians, led by Hydarnes. These troops were called the King's Immortals and were expected to finish off the Greeks easily. But when they came to grips they did no better than the Medes—exactly the same, in fact—for they were fighting in a confined space, and using shorter spears than the Greeks, so that their numbers were no use to them.

The Spartans fought a masterly battle. They were battle-scarred men of long experience fighting raw recruits, and they showed it. Without warning they would turn and run—the Persians would give a shout and follow noisily. Then, just as the Persians were catching up, the Spartans would double back on their tracks and face them, inflicting fearful casualties with almost no loss to themselves.

The Persians had attacked in waves, they had tried every formation they knew, but they had failed to take the pass and were forced to retreat. Three times during the day, I was told, the king, who was watching from a special throne, leaped to his feet in terror for the safety of his army. The next day, the Persians again came off worse. They had hoped that the Greeks would be feeling the effect of their wounds and would have no spirit left for a fight. But there they were, only a few hundred of them, but exactly in place, never stirring an inch from their order of battle, and refusing to give ground. Only the Phokians were not to be seen—they were up in the mountains guarding the path. And so, on the second day, the Persians had no better luck than in the previous engagement. Once again they had to retreat.

Xerxes was desperate. While he was racking his brains for an answer, a man from Melis asked for audience with him; his name was Epialtes, and, hoping for a large reward, he told Xerxes about the path leading to Thermopylae through the hills—information which proved fatal to the Greeks left to hold the pass alone. Afterward he was so afraid of what the Spartans might do to him that he fled to Thessaly, and a price was put on his head by the Pylagoroi [1] who had met at Pylaia. His death came some time later, at the hands of Athenades, a man from Trechis, when he came home to Antikyra. In fact, Epialtes was killed for a different reason (which I shall describe later), but Athenades was nonetheless greatly honored by the Spartans. There is another story which says that it was a Karystian called Onetes and someone from Antikyra, Korydallos, who showed the Persians how to cross the mountain. I don't believe this, and my evi-

Herodotus

dence is the fact that the Greek Pylagoroi put the price on Epialtes' head, not on Onetes and Korydallos—and the Pylagoroi should have had the most exact information. I am sure, too, that this was the reason for Epialtes' exile. Onetes might possibly have betrayed the path if he had been very familiar with the country, but I shall put Epialtes on record as the one who gave away the secret.

Epialtes' offer delighted Xerxes, who immediately became enthusiastic about the idea. He selected Hydarnes and his soldiers for the mission and the forces left the camp as lights were being lit. The path was originally found by the Melians who invaded Phokis at the time when the Phokians had used the war with Thessaly as a pretext for walling up the pass. The Melians had entered Phokis by the alternative route to help the Thessalians. Its use had been known ever since.

This was the path taken by the Persians. Crossing the Asopos, [2] they marched all through the night, keeping the mountains of Oite on their right, and the hills of Trechis on their left. At dawn they found themselves on top of the mountain near the very place where the Phokians were holding the path with a thousand hoplites —guarding the way to the heart of their country. They had volunteered for the duty, while Leonidas held the pass down below. The Persians had come up unobserved through thick oak forests, and the Phokians only realized they were approaching when, through the silence of the night, they heard the sound of feet scuffling through leaves. The Phokians rushed to throw on their armor, but the enemy were on top of them. The sight of these men scrambling into armor astonished the Persians; they had expected no opposition and here they were faced with an army. Hydarnes, alarmed at the thought he might be facing Spartans, asked Epialtes what country these soldiers came from. When he was told Phokis, he ordered the Persians into battle formation.

---

[1] **Pylagoroi:** deputies sent to a league of Greek states.

[2] **Asopos:** a river.

The Phokians, subjected to a barrage of arrows, retired quickly to the crest of the mountain, convinced that the attack was directed solely against them. They were prepared for a fight to the death, but the Persians, led by Epialtes and Hydarnes, ignored them and hurried past down the mountainside.

The first time the Greeks at Thermopylae knew what was in store for them was at dawn that day, when their seer,[1] Megisties, looked at the omens and deserters arrived with the news of the Persian detour. This news came while it was still night and, as soon as day broke, three lookouts came running down from the hills. What were the Greeks to do? Some wanted to leave the position, others opposed this, and agreement seemed impossible. Finally they split; one half went off to disperse to their respective cities, while the rest settled down with Leonidas for the siege. It is reported that Leonidas himself ordered the others away. He refused to dishonor Sparta by deserting the post they had come to guard, but he said there was no reason why the rest should be sacrificed. In this case, my own opinion is that when Leonidas saw his allies losing heart at the unpleasant prospect before them—certain death for everyone—he ordered the others away, though he himself scorned such an easy way out. To him it was dishonorable to retreat. His stand brought him great glory, and the might of Sparta was undiminished by the losses they suffered. For at the outbreak of war, the Pythia[2] had told the Spartans that they would either see their land devastated or lose one of their kings. The oracle was couched in verse:

Men of the broad fields of
  Sparta, either your great city

And its name of strength will
  smoke beneath Persian fire,
Or you will go in mourning for a
  king of the blood of Herakles.
The bull's muscle, the lion's jaws
  shall not beat him back,
For he carries the powers of
  Zeus, and will not be stopped
Till one of these is utterly consumed.

Leonidas must have had this prophecy in mind and wished to be remembered with unique glory in Sparta, and that was why he dismissed his allies rather than let them quarrel, disband, and separate without discipline. Think, for instance, of the priest who foretold all this to the army, Megisties, said to have been descended from Melampus;[3] he was certainly sent away by Leonidas so that he should not die with the rest of them. But in spite of this, he refused to go, and let his son, who was serving with him and was his only child, leave in his place.

When the allies who were dismissed had obeyed Leonidas' order to retreat, only the Thespians and the Thebans were left to keep the Spartans company, the latter very much against their will. Leonidas kept them principally as hostages. The Thespians were more enthusiastic; they refused to desert Leonidas and his men now, determined to stay and die with him. Their general was Demophilos.

At daybreak Xerxes poured a libation,[4] waited until about the time when the marketplace grows full, and then launched his main attack. This was part of a carefully arranged plan. The descent from the mountain is shorter and the ground more quickly covered than the way round as you ascend. Xerxes' Persians moved forward, and the Greeks with Leonidas, now marching to their death, came much farther out than ever before into the broader

---

[1] **seer:** a priest who could read omens in the condition of the intestines of sacrificial animals.

[2] **Pythia:** the priestess at the temple of Apollo at Delphi. People came from all over Greece to hear the Pythia, in a trance, utter the god's prophecies. The words spoken by the Pythia were put into verse by the priests of the temple.

[3] **Melampus:** in mythology, the first mortal who had the power to foretell the future.

[4] **libation:** a liquid, such as wine, poured out in a religious ceremony. The liquid might be poured on a sacrificial victim or on the ground.

part of the pass. In previous engagements they had guarded the barricade and made quick sorties into the narrow part of the gorge. But now, fighting outside the narrows, the Persians fell in their scores, for the officers stood behind, lashing them on and beating them forward, forward all the time. Many fell into the sea and were drowned, many more were trampled to death by their comrades. It was indiscriminate carnage. The Greeks knew that they were doomed now that the Persians had discovered a way round the hill, and put forth their last ounce of strength, utterly desperate, utterly unsparing of their lives. By now most of their spears were shattered, and they had to butcher the Persians with swords. Leonidas fell in this battle. He had proved himself a great and brave man, and so had many other noble Spartans—whose names I have taken, because they deserved to be remembered, as in fact I took the names of all the three hundred.

Two brothers of Xerxes were also killed, and a fierce struggle between Persians and Greeks took place over the corpse of Leonidas. At last, after beating back the Persians four times, the Greeks dragged it away by sheer courage, and the battle raged on.

And then, all at once, the men with Epialtes arrived. When the Greeks saw them approaching they knew that the day was lost; all except the Thebans crowded back into the narrowest part of the gorge, leapt over the wall, and entrenched themselves there in a small hill at the entrance where a stone lion now stands to commemorate Leonidas. Here they fought with daggers—if they were lucky enough to have any left—or with bare hands and teeth, until the overwhelming Persian attack engulfed them, reduced the wall to ruins on one side, and surrounded the hill from the other.

In all the heroism on the part of the Spartans and the Thespians one man is especially remembered—Dienekes, a Spartan. Before the battle began, one of the Trechinians told him that when the

Persians fired their bows there were so many arrows that it was like a cloud passing over the sun; quite unperturbed, Dienekes remarked that this only showed what fools the Persians were. If what his Trechinian friend said was true, it was good news for the Greeks—the Persians were giving them a chance to fight in the shade instead of the heat of the sun. This is only one of the many memorable remarks attributed to Dienekes. After him, two brothers, Alpheos and Maron, are said to have fought with conspicuous bravery, and the hero among the Thespians proved to be Dithyrambos.

They were buried where they fell, and so an epitaph was written for those who died before obeying Leonidas' order to retreat:

> Four thousand from the Peloponnese.
> Once fought here with three million.

The Spartans were given their own epitaph:

> Friend, tell the Spartans that we lie here
> Because we obeyed their orders.

FOR STUDY AND DISCUSSION

1. The Spartans perished to the last man; why then has the story of the Battle of Thermopylae been told for so many centuries? What other heroic defenses have men made in the centuries since Thermopylae?

2. The Roman poet Horace (page 204) wrote in the first century B.C. that "it is sweet and right to die for one's country." How can this be applied to the Greeks at Thermopylae? Two thousand years later, American writer Ernest Hemingway disagreed with Horace, saying that "in modern war there is nothing sweet nor fitting in dying. You will die like a dog, for no good reason." Do you think Hemingway was right or wrong? Explain. What characteristics of modern wars might explain the emergence of attitudes like Hemingway's?

3. What details does Herodotus use to make his account interesting and real? What does this brief passage from the *History* tell you about Greek attitudes and customs?

4. Sometimes in his *History,* Herodotus digresses, departing from his subject to discuss some other matter. What digressions does Herodotus make in the selection you have just read? Do such digressions make you lose interest in a historical narrative, or do they sometimes add to the interest? Give reasons for your answer.

5. Do you think that Herodotus was a carefull historian? Did he seem to weigh carefully all the evidence to get at the truth? Give details from the selection to support your answer.

6. In your opinion, does the account of the Battle of Thermopylae show Herodotus to be a sensitive observer of human nature? What human traits are revealed through the events narrated in this selection?

FOR COMPOSITION

In speaking of those British fliers who held off a German invasion of England during the early years of World War II, Winston Churchill said, "Never in the field of human conflict was so much owed by so many to so few." In a brief composition, explain the relevance that this statement has to the Battle of Thermopylae. Explain also what meaning this battle can have for the modern world. Some people maintain that the modern world is so complex that the actions of one person or a small group can have very little significance. In your composition tell if you think that the Battle of Thermopylae can be used to argue against this view.

The History of the Peloponnesian War

THUCYDIDES

Thucydides (c. 460 B.C. – c. 401 B.C.) belonged to a wealthy and prominent Athenian family. When he was about thirty, war broke out between Athens and Sparta and dragged on for almost thirty years. The war involved almost every city and state in Greece and ended with the defeat of Athens and the irreparable weakening, not of Athens alone, but of all Greece. In 424 B.C. Thucydides was placed in charge of a fleet in the northern Aegean. His failure to relieve a town under siege by the Spartans cost him his post, and from that time until the end of the war, twenty years later, he was an exile from Athens—whether voluntarily or involuntarily is not known.

Even before his exile, Thucydides wanted to write the history of the conflict. His exile gave him the opportunity to travel widely in search of information, which he sought not only from the Athenians and their allies but also from the Spartans and their allies. In this regard he resembles Herodotus. But where Herodotus was generally content to set down everything that was told to him, Thucydides carefully examined all the material he collected: "As to the deeds done in the war," he wrote, "I have not thought myself at liberty to record them on hearsay from the first informant or on arbitrary conjecture. My account rests either on personal knowledge or on the closest possible scrutiny of each statement made by others. The process of research was laborious, because conflicting accounts were given by those who had witnessed the several events, as partiality swayed or memory served them." Thucydides thus set himself a standard of rigorous accuracy, and he adhered to it with remarkable success.

He was no storyteller, no entertainer, but an objective critic of his time, who believed that his writing could be of utmost importance to the future. Viewing human nature as unchanging, Thucydides thought that if men could realize the causes and futility of war, they would forever shun it as a solution to their problems. In speaking of the Athenian defeat in Sicily—the result of an ill-advised and poorly led campaign—he summarized the death of many Greek soldiers on the battlefield and the suffering of others as captives in Sicilian salt mines with the words, "Having done what men could, they suffered what men must."

Thucydides did not live to complete his history. The seven completed books (and an eighth that appears to be a first draft) carry the story down to 411 B.C., some seven years before the end of the war. His exile from Athens ended with the end of the war in 404 B.C., and he is believed to have died about three years later, with seeming suddenness and possibly by violence.

It was customary for Thucydides to quote speeches of generals and statesmen in his histories. The greatest Athenian statesman was Pericles. In the passage reproduced below, Thucydides gives the speech delivered by Pericles on an annual ceremonial occasion, the public funeral for the burial of the bones of the Athenian war dead of the previous year—in this instance, the first year of the Peloponnesian War. We have no way of knowing with what degree of accuracy Thucydides reports the speech. At all events, as it stands it is a magnificent expression of praise for the noble qualities that the Athenians admired, and it still moves men today. But the record of Athens as a colonizing imperial power and the sorry course of the war itself are sufficient to indicate that these stirring words do not tell the whole story of Athens or present a picture that all the citizens of other Greek cities would have been willing to accept as true.

The Funeral Oration of Pericles

MOST OF THOSE who have spoken here before me have commended the lawgiver who added this oration to our other funeral customs; it seemed to them a worthy thing that such an honor should be given at their burial to the dead who have fallen on the field of battle. But I should have preferred that, when men's deeds have been brave, they should be honored in deed only, and with such an honor as this public funeral, which you are now witnessing. Then the reputation of many would not have been imperiled on the eloquence or want of eloquence of one, and their virtues believed or not as he spoke well or ill. For it is difficult to say neither too little nor too much; and even moderation is apt not to give the impression of truthfulness. The friend of the dead who knows the facts is likely to think that the words of the speaker fall short of his knowledge and of his wishes; another who is not so well informed, when he hears of anything which surpasses his own powers, will be envious and will suspect exaggeration. Mankind are tolerant of the praises of others so long as each hearer thinks that he can do as well or nearly as well himself, but, when the deed is beyond him, jealousy is aroused and he begins to be incredulous. However, since our ancestors have set the seal of their approval upon the practice, I must obey, and to the utmost of my power shall en-

"Funeral Oration of Pericles" by Thucydides, translated by Benjamin Jowett.

deavor to satisfy the wishes and beliefs of all who hear me.

"I will speak first of our ancestors, for it is right and becoming that now, when we are lamenting the dead, a tribute should be paid to their memory. There has never been a time when they did not inhabit this land, which by their valor they have handed down from generation to generation, and we have received from them a free state. But if they were worthy of praise, still more were our fathers, who added to their inheritance, and after many a struggle transmitted to us, their sons, this great empire. And we ourselves assembled here today, who are still most of us in the vigor of life, have chiefly done the work of improvement and have richly endowed our city with all things, so that she is sufficient for herself both in peace and war. Of the military exploits by which our various possessions were acquired, or of the energy with which we or our fathers drove back the tide of war, Hellenic or barbarian, I will not speak; for the tale would be long and is familiar to you. But before I praise the dead, I should like to point out by what principles of action we rose to power, and under what institutions and through what manner of life our empire became great. For I conceive that such thoughts are not unsuited to the occasion, and that this numerous assembly of citizens and strangers may profitably listen to them.

"Our form of government does not enter into rivalry with the institutions of others. We do not copy our neighbors, but are an example to them. It is true that we are called a democracy, for the administration is in the hands of the many and not of the few. But while the law secures equal justice to all alike in their private disputes, the claim of excellence is also recognized; and when a citizen is in any way distinguished, he is preferred to the public service, not as a matter of privilege, but as the reward of merit. Neither is poverty a bar, but a man may benefit his country whatever be the obscurity of his condition. There is no exclusiveness in our public life, and in our private intercourse we are not suspicious of one another, nor angry with our neighbor if he does what he likes; we do not put on sour looks at him which, though harmless, are not pleasant. While we are thus unconstrained in our private intercourse, a spirit of reverence pervades our public acts; we are prevented from doing wrong by respect for authority and for the laws, having an especial regard to those which are ordained for the protection of the injured, as well as to those unwritten laws which bring upon the transgressor of them the reprobation of the general sentiment.

"And we have not forgotten to provide for our weary spirits many relaxations from toil; we have regular games and sacrifices throughout the year; at home the style of our life is refined; and the delight which we daily feel in all these things helps to banish melancholy. Because of the greatness of our city, the fruits of the whole earth flow in upon us; so that we enjoy the goods of other countries as freely as of our own.

"Then again, our military training is in many respects superior to that of our adversaries. Our city is thrown open to the world, and we never expel a foreigner or prevent him from seeing or learning anything of which the secret if revealed to an enemy might profit him. We rely not upon management or trickery, but upon our own hearts and hands. And in the matter of education, whereas they from early youth are always undergoing laborious exercises which are to make them brave, we live at ease and yet are equally ready to face the perils which they face. And here is the proof. The Lacedaemonians [1] come

into Attica [2] not by themselves, but with their whole confederacy following; we go alone into a neighbor's country; and although our opponents are fighting for their homes and we on a foreign soil, we have seldom any difficulty in overcoming them. Our enemies have never yet felt our united strength; the care of a navy divides our attention, and on land we are obliged to send our own citizens everywhere. But they, if they meet and defeat a part of our army, are as proud as if they had routed us all, and when defeated they pretend to have been vanquished by us all.

"If then we prefer to meet danger with a light heart but without laborious training, and with a courage which is gained by habit and not enforced by law, are we not greatly the gainers? Since we do not anticipate the pain, although, when the hour comes, we can be as brave as those who never allow themselves to rest; and thus too our city is equally admirable in peace and in war. For we are lovers of the beautiful, yet with economy, and we cultivate the mind without loss of manliness. Wealth we employ, not for talk and ostentation, but when there is a real use for it. To avow poverty with us is no disgrace; the true disgrace is in doing nothing to avoid it. An Athenian citizen does not neglect the state because he takes care of his own household; and even those of us who are engaged in business have a very fair idea of politics. We alone regard a man who takes no interest in public affairs, not as a harmless but as a useless character; and if few of us are originators, we are all sound judges of a policy. The great impediment to action is, in our opinion, not discussion, but the want of that knowledge which is gained by discussion preparatory to action. For we have a peculiar power of thinking before we act and of acting too, whereas other men are courageous from ignorance but hesitate upon reflection. And they are surely to be esteemed the bravest spirits who, having the clearest sense both of the pains and

[1] **Lacedaemonians** (lăs´ə·di·mō´nē·ənz): Spartans.

[2] **Attica:** the region of Greece surrounding Athens.

pleasures of life, do not on that account shrink from danger. In doing good, again, we are unlike others; we make our friends by conferring, not by receiving, favors. Now he who confers a favor is the firmer friend, because he would fain by kindness keep alive the memory of an obligation; but the recipient is colder in his feelings, because he knows that in requiting another's generosity he will not be winning gratitude but only paying a debt. We alone do good to our neighbors, not upon a calculation of interest but in the confidence of freedom and in a frank and fearless spirit.

"To sum up: I say that Athens is the school of Hellas, and that the individual Athenian in his own person seems to have the power of adapting himself to the most varied forms of action with the utmost versatility and grace. This is no passing and idle word, but truth and fact; and the assertion is verified by the position to which these qualities have raised the state. For in the hour of trial Athens alone among her contemporaries is superior to the report of her. No enemy who comes against her is indignant at the reverses which he sustains at the hands of such a city; no subject complains that his masters are unworthy of him. And we shall assuredly not be without witnesses; there are mighty monuments of our power which will make us the wonder of this and of succeeding ages; we shall not need the praises of Homer or of any other panegyrist whose poetry may please for the moment, although his representation of the facts will not bear the light of day. For we have compelled every land and every sea to open a path for our valor and have everywhere planted eternal memorials of our friendship and of our enmity. Such is the city for whose sake these men nobly fought and died; they could not bear the thought that she might be taken from them; and every one of us who survive should gladly toil on her behalf.

"I have dwelt upon the greatness of Athens because I want to show you that we are contending for a higher prize than those who enjoy none of these privileges, and to establish by manifest proof the merit of these men whom I am now commemorating. Their loftiest praise has been already spoken. For in magnifying the city I have magnified them and men like them whose virtues made her glorious. And of how few Hellenes can it be said as of them, that their deeds when weighed in the balance have been found equal to their fame! It seems to me that a death such as theirs has been gives the true measure of a man's worth; it may be the first revelation of his virtues, but is at any rate their final seal. For even those who come short in other ways may justly plead the valor with which they have fought for their country; they have blotted out the evil with the good and have benefited the state more by their public services than they have injured her by their private actions. None of these men were enervated by wealth or hesitated to resign the pleasures of life; none of them put off the evil day in the hope, natural to poverty, that a man, though poor, may one day become rich. But, deeming that the punishment of their enemies was sweeter than any of these things and that they could fall in no nobler cause, they determined at the hazard of their lives to be honorably avenged and to leave the rest. They resigned to hope their unknown chance of happiness; but in the face of death they resolved to rely upon themselves alone. And when the moment came they were minded to resist and suffer, rather than to fly and save their lives; they ran away from the word of dishonor, but on the battlefield their feet stood fast, and in an instant, at the height of their fortune, they passed away from the scene, not of their fear but of their glory.

"Such was the end of these men; they were worthy of Athens, and the living need not desire to have a more heroic spirit, although they may pray for a less fatal issue. The value of such a spirit is not to be expressed in words. Anyone can discourse to you forever about the advantages of a brave defense which you know already. But instead of listening to him I would have you day by day fix your eyes upon the greatness of Athens, until you become filled with the love of her; and when you are impressed by the spectacle of her glory, reflect that this empire has been acquired by men who knew their duty and had the courage to do it, who in the hour of conflict had the fear of dishonor always present to them, and who, if ever they failed in an enterprise, would not allow their virtues to be lost to their country, but freely gave their lives to her as the fairest offering which they could present at her feast. The sacrifice which they collectively made was individually repaid to them; for they received again each one for himself a praise which grows not old, and the noblest of all sepulchers— I speak not of that in which their remains are laid, but of that in which their glory survives and is proclaimed always and on every fitting occasion, both in word and deed. For the whole earth is the sepulcher of famous men; not only are they comemorated by columns and inscriptions in their own country, but in foreign lands there dwells also an unwritten memorial of them, graven not on stone but in the hearts of men. Make them your examples, and esteeming courage to be freedom and freedom to be happiness, do not weigh too nicely the perils of war. The unfortunate who has no hope of a change for the better has less reason to throw away his life than the prosperous who, if he survives, is always liable to a change for the worse, and to whom any accidental fall makes the most serious difference. To a man of spirit, cowardice and disaster coming together are far more bitter than death striking him unperceived at a time when he is full of courage and animated by the general hope.

"Wherefore I do not now commiserate the parents of the dead who stand here; I would rather comfort them. You know that your life has been passed amid manifold vicissitudes; and that they may be deemed fortunate who have gained most honor, whether an honorable death like

theirs, or an honorable sorrow like yours, and whose days have been so ordered that the term of their happiness is likewise the term of their life. I know how hard it is to make you feel this, when the good fortune of others will too often remind you of the gladness which once lightened your hearts. And sorrow is felt at the want of those blessings, not which a man never knew, but which were a part of his life before they were taken from him. Some of you are of an age at which they may hope to have other children, and they ought to bear their sorrow better; not only will the children who may hereafter be born make them forget their own lost ones, but the city will be doubly a gainer. She will not be left desolate, and she will be safer. For a man's counsel cannot have equal weight or worth when he alone has no children to risk in the general danger. To those of you who have passed their prime, I say, 'Congratulate yourselves that you have been happy during the greater part of your days; remember that your life of sorrow will not last long, and be comforted by the glory of those who are gone. For the love of honor alone is ever young, and not riches, as some say, but honor is the delight of men when they are old and useless.'

"To you who are the sons and brothers of the departed I see that the struggle to emulate them will be an arduous one. For all men praise the dead, and, however preeminent your virtue may be, hardly will you be thought, I do not say to equal, but even to approach them. The living have their rivals and detractors, but when a man is out of the way, the honor and good will which he receives is unalloyed. And, if I am to speak of womanly virtues to those of you who will henceforth be widows, let me sum them up in one short admonition: To a woman not to show more weakness than is natural to her sex is a great glory and not to be talked about for good or for evil among men.

"I have paid the required tribute, in obedience to the law, making use of such fitting words as I had. The tribute of deeds has been paid in part; for the dead have been honorably interred, and it remains only that their children should be maintained at the public charge until they are grown up: this is the solid prize with which, as with a garland, Athens crowns her sons living and dead, after a struggle like theirs. For where the rewards of virtue are greatest, there the noblest citizens are enlisted in the service of the state. And now, when you have duly lamented, everyone his own dead, you may depart."

FOR STUDY AND DISCUSSION

1. Oratory is called the art of persuasion. Besides commemorating the war dead, what is the purpose of Pericles' oration? What emotions might this speech have aroused?

2. The speech may be logically divided into five parts. What are they? Identify the sections with appropriate headings.

3. How does Pericles win the sympathetic attention of his listeners in his introduction? In what way does the conclusion of the speech echo the thoughts in the introduction?

4. How does Pericles contrast Athens with Lacedaemon?

5. Periclean Athens was a man's world. Women lived a secluded life and their inferior status was not questioned. How do Pericles' words to the women of Athens strikingly reflect this attitude?

6. It has been said that the Age of Pericles was a time when man, spiritually, physically, and mentally, came closest to achieving balance and harmony with himself and his world. What sentences from this oration express this idea most eloquently?

The Dialogues

[handwritten marginalia: Spoke of shadow world (Earth) but form world (Heaven) as more real, which stalled scientific research w/ talk of mystic stuff]

[handwritten marginalia: Saw math as necessary to all thought]

Most of the works of Plato (427? B.C. – 347? B.C.), though showing poetic gracefulness, are written in the form of argumentative dialogues. The principal speaker and shrewd challenger in these conversations is usually Socrates, Plato's teacher and "elderly friend." Plato's dialogues have immortalized his teacher, for Socrates left no writings of his own, even though he is still regarded as the supreme teacher of all time. "I have heard Pericles and other great orators, and I thought they spoke well," said Plato, "but my soul was not stirred by them . . . I am conscious that if I did not shut my ears against him [Socrates], . . . I should grow old sitting at his feet."

Plato's voluminous works show a fine mind seeking honestly for solutions to the problems of his society. One of Plato's own famous political works is his *Republic,* in which he sets forth in brilliant detail his own theory of the ideal state, to be governed by philosopher-kings, men chosen for their wisdom and ability.

Plato spent most of his life as a teacher in Athens. At the age of sixty, he was given the unusual chance to test some of his ideas; he was invited to Syracuse in Greece to train its young ruler, Dionysius, to be a philosopher-king. Dionysius was a poor pupil, however, and he lost enthusiasm over the first subject Plato introduced, which was geometry (Plato saw mathematics as necessary for the attainment of higher philosophical truth). As Plato was returning home after his bad experience at the Syracuse court, it is said, his ship was intercepted and the wealthy aristocrat was captured and put up for sale in a slave market on an island off the southeastern coast of Greece. He was supposedly bought by a former pupil, who helped him return to Athens, which he never left again. Over the entrance to the school he founded was the sentence "Let no one who is without geometry enter here."

THE TRIAL OF SOCRATES

[handwritten marginalia: used "Socratic method: allowing students to form own opinions, question pre-set methods]

Plato was present at the trial of Socrates. The great teacher, who was now about seventy years old, was required to answer charges of teaching false religion (because he believed in one God) and of corrupting the minds of the young (because he urged his students to think questions through honestly for themselves rather than mime the clever, useful, but empty proverbs given to them by their elders, who were mainly interested in material success). Plato gives an account of the trial in the *Apology,* which is largely a monologue, supposedly delivered by Socrates.

We might have expected Socrates to defend his life and teachings, but instead of doing so he attacked the judges in his three speeches, insisted on honoring the law, and upheld to the end his personal integrity.

The jury consisted of a panel of 501 citizens; in the absence of lawyers, plaintiff and defendant delivered their own speeches. At the conclusion of Socrates' first oration, the jury balloted, found him guilty by a vote of 280 to 221, and condemned him to death. It was customary for the defendant then to propose a counterpenalty, after which the jury would pronounce its decision. Socrates refused to beg for mercy; instead, he ironically suggested that his services to Athens merited a pension, and he refused to admit any possibility of guilt by proposing a punishment. At this, the jury voted the death penalty by a much larger majority. (Socrates' conviction is the only recorded case of an Athenian's being sentenced to death for his beliefs.)

Socrates' final address to the court is reproduced here.

Handwritten note at top: "The unexamined life is not worth living."

FROM THE *Apology*

Handwritten annotations: "—not quite an apology." "Informal, almost spontaneous style"

NOT MUCH TIME will be gained, O Athenians, in return for the evil name which you will get from the detractors of the city, who will say that you killed Socrates, a wise man; for they will call me wise, even although I am not wise, when they want to reproach you. If you had waited a little while, your desire would have been fulfilled in the course of nature. For I am far advanced in years, as you may perceive, and not far from death. I am speaking now not to all of you, but only to those who have condemned me to death. And I have another thing to say to them: You think that I was convicted because I had no words of the sort which would have procured my acquittal—I mean, if I had thought fit to leave nothing undone or unsaid. Not so; the deficiency which led to my conviction was not of words—certainly not. But I had not the boldness or impudence or inclination to address you as you would have liked me to do, weeping and wailing and lamenting, and saying and doing many things which you have been accustomed to hear from others and which, as I maintain, are unworthy of me. I thought at the time that I ought not to do anything common or mean when in danger: nor do I now repent of the style of my defense; I would rather die having spoken after my manner than speak in your manner and live. For neither in war nor yet at law ought I or any man to use every way of escaping death. Often in battle there can be no doubt that if a man will throw away his arms, and fall on his knees before his pursuers, he may escape death; and in other dangers there are other ways of escaping death, if a man is willing to say and do anything. The difficulty, my friends, is not to avoid death, but to avoid unrighteousness; for that runs

Handwritten note in left margin: "you will be sorry that you killed me"

faster than death. I am old and move slowly, and the slower runner has overtaken me, and my accusers are keen and quick, and the faster runner, who is unrighteousness, has overtaken them. And now I depart hence condemned by you to suffer the penalty of death—they too go their ways condemned by the truth to suffer the penalty of villainy and wrong; and I must abide by my award—let them abide by theirs. I suppose that these things may be regarded as fated—and I think that they are well.

And now, O men who have condemned me, I would fain prophesy to you; for I am about to die, and in the hour of death men are gifted with prophetic power. And I prophesy to you who are my murderers, that immediately after my departure punishment far heavier than you have inflicted on me will surely await you. Me you have killed because you wanted to escape the accuser, and not to give an account of your lives. But that will not be as you suppose: far otherwise. For I say that there will be more accusers of you than there are now; accusers whom hitherto I have restrained: and as they are younger they will be more inconsiderate with you, and you will be more offended at them. If you think that by killing men you can prevent someone from censuring your evil lives, you are mistaken; that is not a way of escape which is either possible or honorable; the easiest and noblest way is not to be disabling others, but to be improving yourselves. This is the prophecy which I utter before my departure to the judges who have condemned me.

Friends, who would have acquitted me, I would like also to talk with you about the thing which has come to pass, while the magistrates are busy, and before I go to the place at which I must die. Stay then a little, for we may as well talk with one another while there is time. You are my friends, and I should like to show you the meaning of this event which has happened to me. O my judges—for you I may truly call judges—I should like to tell you of a wonderful circumstance. Hitherto the

From the *Apology* by Plato, translated by Benjamin Jowett.

divine faculty, of which the internal oracle [1] is the source, has constantly been in the habit of opposing me even about trifles, if I was going to make a slip or error in any matter; and now as you see there has come upon me that which may be thought, and is generally believed to be, the last and worst evil. But the oracle made no sign of opposition, either when I was leaving my house in the morning, or when I was on my way to the court, or while I was speaking, at anything which I was going to say; and yet I have often been stopped in the middle of a speech, but now in nothing I either said or did touching the matter in hand has the oracle opposed me. What do I take to be the explanation of this silence? I will tell you. It is an intimation that what has happened to me is a good and that those of us who think that death is an evil are in error. For the customary sign would surely have opposed me had I been going to evil and not to good.

Let us reflect in another way, and we shall see that there is great reason to hope that death is a good; for one of two things —either death is a state of nothingness and utter unconsciousness, or, as men say, there is a change and migration of the soul from this world to another. Now if you suppose that there is no consciousness, but a sleep like the sleep of him who is undisturbed even by dreams, death will be an unspeakable gain. For if a person were to select the night in which his sleep was undisturbed even by dreams, and were to compare with this the other days and nights of his life, and then were to tell us how many days and nights he had passed in the course of his life better and more pleasantly than this one, I think that any man, I will not say a private man, but even the great king will not find many such days or nights, when compared with the others. Now if death be of such a nature, I say that to die is gain; for eternity is then only a single night. But if death is the journey to another place, and there, as men say, all the dead abide, what good, O my friends and judges, can be greater than this? If indeed when the pilgrim arrives in the world below he is delivered from the professors of justice in this world and finds the true judges who are said to give judgment there, Minos and Rhadamanthus and Aeacus and Triptolemus,[2] and other sons of God who were righteous in their own life, that pilgrimage will be worth making. What would not a man give if he might converse with Orpheus and Musaeus and Hesiod and Homer?[3] Nay, if this be true, let me die again and again. I myself, too, shall have a wonderful interest in their meeting and conversing with Palamedes,[4] and Ajax[5] the son of Telamon, and any other ancient hero who has suffered death through an unjust judgment; and there will be no small pleasure, as I think, in comparing my own sufferings with theirs. Above all, I shall then be able to continue my search into true and false knowledge; as in this world, so also in the next; and I shall find out who is wise, and who pretends to be wise and is not. What would not a man give, O judges, to be able to examine the leader [6] of the great Trojan expedition; or Odysseus[7] or Sisyphus,[8] or numberless others,

nab at accuses

---

[1] **internal oracle:** Socrates believed he was constantly guided by a divine inner voice which warned him against evil acts and wrong choices.

[2] **Minos and Rhadamanthus** (rad′ə·man′thəs) **and Aeacus** (ē′ə·kəs) **and Triptolemus:** heroes in Greek mythology who, because of their great deeds or just lives, were after death made judges in Hades, the world of the dead.

[3] **Orpheus and Musaeus** (mōō·zē′us) **and Hesiod** (hē′sē·əd) **and Homer:** Greek poets, some real, some mythical.

[4] **Palamedes** (pal′ə·mē′dēz): in Greek legend, a hero who fought in the Trojan War. He was unjustly accused of treachery and stoned to death.

[5] **Ajax:** another hero of the Trojan War. Feeling that the armor of the slain Achilles had been unjustly awarded to Odysseus and not to himself, Ajax went mad.

[6] **leader:** that is, Agamemnon, commander-in-chief of the Trojan forces.

[7] **Odysseus:** cleverest of the Trojan warriors, the hero of Homer's *Odyssey*.

[8] **Sisyphus** (sis′ə·fəs): in Greek mythology, a great man who was punished in Hades by eternally having to roll up a hill a huge stone that always rolled down again just as it got to the top.

men and women too! What infinite delight would there be in conversing with them and asking them questions! In another world they do not put a man to death for asking questions: assuredly not. For besides being happier than we are, they will be immortal, if what is said is true.

Wherefore, O judges, be of good cheer about death, and know of a certainty, that no evil can happen to a good man, either in life or after death. He and his are not neglected by the gods; nor has my own approaching end happened by mere chance. But I see clearly that the time had arrived when it was better for me to die and be released from trouble; wherefore the oracle gave no sign. For which reason, also, I am not angry with my condemners, or with my accusers; they have done me no harm, although they did not mean to do me any good; and for this I may gently blame them.

Still I have a favor to ask of them. When my sons are grown up, I would ask you, O my friends, to punish them; and I would have you trouble them, as I have troubled you, if they seem to care about riches, or anything, more than about virtue; or if they pretend to be something when they are really nothing—then reprove them, as I have reproved you, for not caring about that for which they ought to care and thinking that they are something when they are really nothing. And if you do this, both I and my sons will have received justice at your hands.

The hour of departure has arrived, and we go our ways—I to die, and you to live. Which is better God only knows.

FROM THE *Phaedo*

[The following selection is the conclusion of the dialogue that is supposed to be the conversation held by Socrates with several of his disciples during the last hours of his life. The dialogue is narrated by Phaedo, one of the disciples. Plato was apparently not present because of illness. As this selection opens, Socrates has just spoken to his friends of his belief in the immortality of the soul and of his views on the afterlife. Evening and death approach as Socrates continues to speak to the group of men gathered about him.]

WHEREFORE, SIMMIAS, seeing all these things, what ought not we to do that we may obtain virtue and wisdom in this life? Fair is the prize, and the hope great!

"A man of sense ought not to say, nor will I be very confident, that the description which I have given of the soul and her mansions is exactly true. But I do say that, inasmuch as the soul is shown to be immortal, he may venture to think, not improperly or unworthily, that something of the kind is true. The venture is a glorious one, and he ought to comfort himself with words like these, which is the reason why I lengthen out the tale. Wherefore, I say, let a man be of good cheer about his soul, who having cast away the pleasures and ornaments of the body as alien to him and working harm rather than good, has sought after the pleasures of knowledge; and has arrayed the soul, not in some foreign attire, but in her own proper jewels, temperance, and justice, and courage, and nobility, and truth—in these adorned she is ready to go on her journey to the world below, when her hour comes. You, Simmias and Cebes, and all other men will depart at some time or other. Me already, as a tragic poet would say, the voice of fate calls. Soon I must drink the poison; and I think that I had better repair to the bath first, in order that the women may not have the trouble of washing my body after I am dead."

When he had done speaking, Crito said: "And have you any commands for us, Socrates—anything to say about your children, or any other matter in which we can serve you?"

"Nothing particular, Crito," he replied; "only, as I have always told you, take care of yourselves; that is a service which you may be ever rendering to me

From the *Phaedo* by Plato, translated by Benjamin Jowett.

and mine and to all of us, whether you promise to do so or not. But if you have no thought for yourselves and care not to walk according to the rule which I have prescribed for you, not now for the first time, however much you may profess or promise at the moment, it will be of no avail."

"We will do our best," said Crito. "And in what way shall we bury you?"

"In any way that you like; but you must get hold of me and take care that I do not run away from you."

Then he turned to us and added with a smile: "I cannot make Crito believe that I am the same Socrates who has been talking and conducting the argument; he fancies that I am the other Socrates whom he will soon see, a dead body—and he asks, How shall he bury me? And though I have spoken many words in the endeavor to show that when I have drunk the poison I shall leave you and go to the joys of the blessed—these words of mine, with which I was comforting you and myself, have had, as I perceive, no effect upon Crito. And therefore I want you to be surety for me to him now, as at the trial he was surety to the judges for me: but let the promise be of another sort; for he was surety for me to the judges that I would remain, and you must be my surety to him that I shall not remain, but go away and depart; and then he will suffer less at my death and not be grieved when he sees my body being burned or buried. I would not have him sorrow at my hard lot or say at the burial, Thus we lay out Socrates, or, Thus we follow him to the grave or bury him; for false words are not only evil in themselves, but they infect the soul with evil. Be of good cheer then, my dear Crito, and say that you are burying my body only, and do with that whatever is usual, and what you think best."

When he had spoken these words, he arose and went into a chamber to bathe; Crito followed him and told us to wait. So we remained behind, talking and thinking of the subject of discourse, and also of the greatness of our sorrow; he was like a father of whom we were being bereaved, and we were about to pass the rest of our lives as orphans. When he had taken the bath, his children were brought to him (he had two young sons and an elder one); and the women of his family also came, and he talked to them and gave them a few directions in the presence of Crito; then he dismissed them and returned to us.

Now the hour of sunset was near, for a good deal of time had passed while he was within. When he came out, he sat down with us again after his bath, but not much was said. Soon the jailer, who was the servant of the Eleven,[1] entered and stood by him, saying: "To you, Socrates, whom I know to be the noblest and gentlest and best of all who ever came to this place, I will not impute the angry feelings of other men, who rage and swear at me, when, in obedience to the authorities, I bid them drink the poison—indeed, I am sure that you will not be angry with me; for others, as you are aware, and not I, are to blame. And so fare you well, and try to bear lightly what must needs be—you know my errand." Then bursting into tears he turned away and went out.

Socrates looked at him and said: "I return your good wishes and will do as you bid." Then turning to us, he said, "How charming the man is. Since I have been in prison he has always been coming to see me, and at times he would talk to me and was as good to me as could be, and now see how generously he sorrows on my account. We must do as he says, Crito; and therefore let the cup be brought, if the poison is prepared: if not, let the attendant prepare some."

"Yet," said Crito, "the sun is still upon the hilltops, and I know that many a one has taken the draught late, and after the announcement has been made to him, he has eaten and drunk and enjoyed the society of his beloved; do not hurry—there is time enough."

Socrates said: "Yes, Crito, and they of whom you speak are right in so acting, for

[1] **the Eleven:** governors of Athens.

they think that they will be gainers by the delay; but I am right in not following their example, for I do not think that I should gain anything by drinking the poison a little later: I should only be ridiculous in my own eyes for sparing and saving a life which is already forfeit. Please then to do as I say, and not to refuse me."

Crito made a sign to the servant, who was standing by; and he went out, and having been absent for some time, returned with the jailer carrying the cup of poison. Socrates said: "You, my good friend, who are experienced in these matters, shall give me directions how I am to proceed."

The man answered: "You have only to walk about until your legs are heavy, and then to lie down, and the poison will act."

At the same time he handed the cup to Socrates, who in the easiest and gentlest manner, without the least fear or change of color or feature, looking at the man with all his eyes, Echecrates,[1] as his manner was, took the cup and said: "What do you say about making a libation[2] out of this cup to any god? May I, or not?"

The man answered: "We only prepare, Socrates, just so much as we deem enough."

"I understand," he said; "but I may and must ask the gods to prosper my journey from this to the other world—even so—and so be it according to my prayer."

Then raising the cup to his lips, quite readily and cheerfully he drank off the poison. And hitherto most of us had been able to control our sorrow; but now when we saw him drinking and saw, too, that he had finished the draught, we could no longer forbear, and in spite of myself my own tears were flowing fast; so that I covered my face and wept, not for him, but at the thought of my own calamity in having to part from such a friend. Nor was I the first; for Crito, when he found himself unable to restrain his tears, had got up, and I followed; and at that moment, Apollodorus, who had been weeping all the time, broke out in a loud and passionate cry which made cowards of us all.

Socrates alone retained his calmness: "What is this strange outcry?" he said. "I sent away the women mainly in order that they might not misbehave in this way, for I have been told that a man should die in peace. Be quiet then, and have patience."

When we heard his words we were ashamed, and refrained our tears; and he walked about until, as he said, his legs began to fail, and then he lay on his back, according to the directions, and the man who gave him the poison now and then looked at his feet and legs; and after a while he pressed his foot hard and asked him if he could feel; and he said, "No"; and then his leg, and so upward and upward, and showed us that he was cold and stiff. And he felt them himself and said: "When the poison reaches the heart, that will be the end."

He was beginning to grow cold about the groin, when he uncovered his face, for he had covered himself up, and said— they were his last words—he said: "Crito, I owe a cock to Asclepius;[3] will you remember to pay the debt?"

"The debt shall be paid," said Crito; "is there anything else?"

There was no answer to this question; but in a minute or two a movement was heard, and the attendants uncovered him; his eyes were set, and Crito closed his eyes and mouth.

Such was the end, Echecrates, of our friend; concerning whom I may truly say, that of all the men of his time whom I have known, he was the wisest and justest and best.

---

[1] **Echecrates** (e·kek′rə·tēz): another disciple, to whom Phaedo is telling the story of Socrates' death.

[2] **libation:** an offering to the gods, in this case made by pouring a drop from the drinking cup to the ground.

[3] **Asclepius** (as·klē′pē·əs): the god of health and medicine. Socrates may mean that he owes the god an offering because he is about to recover from the sickness called life. But this is far from certain.

APOLOGY

1. How does Socrates justify his refusal to plead for his life? At the end of the first paragraph, Socrates says his accusers are "condemned by the truth." What does he mean? What prophecy does he make about the judges who condemned him?

2. What two views of death does Socrates present? What arguments does Socrates present to prove that death is a good from either point of view? In the course of his discussion of death, what biting comments does he make about his accusers?

3. Explain Socrates' statement that "no evil can happen to a good man, either in life or after death" (page 134).

4. What does Socrates ironically ask his accusers to do for his sons?

5. What comments can you make about Socrates' character after reading this selection? Give at least three words that can be used to describe him.

PHAEDO

1. How do Socrates' views on death, as presented in the *Phaedo,* correlate with his views expressed in the *Apology?* Give details to support your answer.

2. Crito asks Socrates a practical question about his burial. With what humorous remarks does Socrates answer his anxious disciple?

3. What do you learn about Socrates' relations with his friends and followers from this dialogue? What do you learn about Socrates from the jailer's speech?

4. Do you think the *Apology* is a dramatically effective work? Give reasons for your answer.

5. Homer's *Iliad* gives a portrait of Achilles, a great hero. Plato's writings give a portrait of Socrates, a hero, too, but of quite a different sort. In what ways is Socrates a hero? How is he different from the kind of hero Achilles represents? Which type of hero would be more admired by people today? Why?

6. The *Epic of Gilgamesh* (page 13) was told in ancient Mesopotamia at least 1500 years before Socrates' time. Gilgamesh, as you might remember, was searching for immortality, for the meaning of death. How does Gilgamesh's attitude toward death differ from Socrates'? How would you account for the difference in attitudes? How does Socrates' attitude resemble the Judeo-Christian attitude? How might a person's attitude toward death and what it means affect the way he lives out his life?

7. On page 15 in the Gilgamesh epic, a young woman tells Gilgamesh how man can find happiness. Contrast this general philosophy with Socrates' statements about what man should seek for and how he should regard riches, as found in the *Apology* and the *Phaedo.* Are both of these philosophical attitudes toward happiness and its attainment evident in modern life? Explain.

FOR COMPOSITION

A number of quotations from the *Dialogues* have become famous. Write a short essay in which you discuss the meaning and pertinence of one of the following quotations.

Know thyself.
Wisdom begins in wonder.
The unexamined life is not worth living.
No evil can happen to a good man, either in life or after death.

Antigone

SOPHOCLES

(Translated by Dudley Fitts and Robert Fitzgerald)

Sophocles (496? B.C.–406 B.C.) was a prominent, patriotic citizen of Athens in its greatest period, the brilliant and creative Age of Pericles. Renowned as a playwright and greatly esteemed, Sophocles conformed to the ideal of Athenian citizenship by taking an active part in public life. He was twice elected a general and was also one of the ten special commissioners who for a time directed the city's affairs.

The theater of Greece in the fifth century B.C. was a distinct, and in many ways dissimilar, ancestor of today's theater. Performances took place in daylight, outdoors, on a stage half-surrounded by rising tiers of seats. Stage sets were almost nonexistent. The actors, all of whom were men, were masked and each usually played several parts. Their gestures and body movements were controlled and stately. Although sensational and bloody outrages were usually included in the plots of the dramas, these were never enacted on stage but were reported to the audience through the speeches of the actors. Parts of the plays were written to be sung by a chorus, which usually represented the city elders and revealed their attitude toward the tragedy (a similar device is still used in opera). The chorus sometimes performed stylized dances to the accompaniment of a flute. Most of the Greek plays were based on the myths. Hence the audience knew the plots beforehand and the element of surprise was largely excluded. The audience's interest was instead riveted on the struggle of the hero who, unconscious of his fate, heads into inevitable doom. All these characteristics helped create a formal, ceremonial atmosphere which makes Greek drama almost totally different from modern drama.

Sophocles is given credit for making several technical innovations in the theater. Previous dramatists had used only two actors; Sophocles raised the number of actors to three. He also added painted sets. But all lovers of drama since the fifth century B.C. have esteemed Sophocles as more than a technical innovator. He was a master of dramatic construction who could bring the action of a play to its climax without a single wasted motion. He was also a great poet. But most of all, he was a Greek, who could contemplate the world's exaltations and terrors without flinching. The poet Matthew Arnold paid tribute to Sophocles as one who "saw life steadily and saw it whole." It is this capacity to hold the balance firmly between conflicting opposites that has kept Sophocles' name alive for more than two thousand years.

THE BACKGROUND OF ANTIGONE

Antigone was apparently first performed in 441 B.C. It is one of three plays which together are known as the Oedipus cycle. The three plays are based on a group of tragic legends about Oedipus, king of Thebes, and his sons and daughters.

Since Sophocles' Athenian audience was thoroughly familiar with these legends about Oedipus, the dramatist did not need to relate them in detail. The Athenians knew about Oedipus' tragic fate, to which references are made throughout the play. They knew that when Oedipus was born, an oracle had foretold that he would slay his own father and marry his mother. To prevent this, his father, the king of Thebes, exposed the infant Oedipus to die on a mountainside. But the baby was rescued by a shepherd and brought up as the son of the ruler of Corinth, a neighboring state. When Oedipus was a grown man, he set off to verify his identity by consulting the oracle at Delphi. Learning there of the terrible prophecy, he resolved never to return home, as he believed his parents to be the king and queen of Corinth. At a crossroads he met another traveler, argued with him, and in a fit of temper, killed him. Calming his temper, Oedipus eventually came to the city of Thebes and found that its king had recently been killed in a foreign land. By correctly answering a riddle set to him by the Sphinx, a terrible creature who had been menacing the Thebans, Oedipus won the hand of the widowed queen of Thebes, Iocaste, and became king of Thebes himself.

Iocaste and Oedipus had four children—two daughters, Antigone and Ismene, and two sons, Eteocles and Polyneices. Oedipus and Iocaste ruled Thebes in harmony for many years until a plague struck the city. Desperate, Oedipus consulted the oracle for advice and was told that the plague would not lift until the murderer of the former king of Thebes was found and punished. In anguish, Oedipus soon learned not only that the man he had killed at the crossroads was the king of Thebes, but also that this same man was his own long-lost father. The horrifying extent of the tragedy gradually unfolded as Oedipus realized that he had also, as the oracle had long ago predicted, married his own mother. Iocaste hanged herself when she learned the truth. Oedipus tore his eyes from his head and exiled himself forever from Thebes.

Athenian audiences also knew that, after Oedipus' death, his two sons, Eteocles and Polyneices, agreed to rule Thebes in alternate years. Eteocles ruled first, and when his term was ended he refused to let Polyneices take the throne, claiming his brother's temper was too violent. Polyneices raised an army from the city of Argos and attacked Thebes. The Thebans defended their seven gates successfully against the Argive army, but in the course of battle Eteocles and Polyneices slew each other.

The play *Antigone* begins on the day after the battle. Creon, the uncle of Polyneices and Eteocles, has been made king of Thebes. He is faced with the task of restoring order to the strife-torn city. In his eyes Polyneices is an enemy to Thebes and must be denied burial. This is an offensive punishment to the Greeks, for their holiest law—to which all Greeks are bound—requires the performance of certain burial rites. The soul of the man whose corpse is left to decay in the open, on whose behalf no libation of wine is poured out for the gods, will be condemned to eternal unrest. To Polyneices' sister Antigone, however, the dictates of divine law and the ties of blood are stronger than the man-made laws of the state. She decides to act against Creon's prohibition.

Characters in Antigone

ANTIGONE
ISMENE } *daughters of Oedipus, former king of Thebes*

CREON, *king of Thebes, uncle of Antigone and Ismene*

HAIMON, *his son, engaged to Antigone*

EURYDICE, *wife of Creon*

TEIRESIAS, *a blind prophet*   GUARDS

A SENTRY   SERVANTS

CHORUS, *made up of about fifteen elders of Thebes*

SCENE: *Before the palace of* CREON, *king of Thebes. A central double door, and two lateral doors. A platform extends the length of the façade, and from this platform three steps lead down into the "orchestra," or chorus-ground.*

TIME: *Dawn of the day after the repulse of the Argive army from the assault on Thebes.*

Prologue

[ANTIGONE *and* ISMENE *enter from the central door of the palace.*]

ANTIGONE. Ismene, dear sister,
    You would think that we had already suffered enough
    For the curse on Oedipus:
    I cannot imagine any grief
    That you and I have not gone through. And now—   5
    Have they told you of the new decree of our King Creon?
ISMENE. I have heard nothing: I know
    That two sisters lost two brothers, a double death
    In a single hour; and I know that the Argive army
    Fled in the night; but beyond this, nothing.   10
ANTIGONE. I thought so. And that is why I wanted you
    To come out here with me. There is something we must do.
ISMENE. Why do you speak so strangely?
ANTIGONE. Listen, Ismene:
    Creon buried our brother Eteocles   15
    With military honors, gave him a soldier's funeral,
    And it was right that he should; but Polyneices,
    Who fought as bravely and died as miserably—
    They say that Creon has sworn
    No one shall bury him, no one mourn for him,   20
    But his body must lie in the fields, a sweet treasure
    For carrion birds to find as they search for food.
    That is what they say, and our good Creon is coming here
    To announce it publicly; and the penalty—
    Stoning to death in the public square!
                                    There it is,   25
    And now you can prove what you are:
    A true sister, or a traitor to your family.
ISMENE. Antigone, you are mad! What could I possibly do?
ANTIGONE. You must decide whether you will help me or not.

ISMENE. I do not understand you. Help you in what?   30
ANTIGONE. Ismene, I am going to bury him. Will you come?
ISMENE. Bury him! You have just said the new law forbids it.
ANTIGONE. He is my brother. And he is your brother, too.
ISMENE. But think of the danger! Think what Creon will do!
ANTIGONE. Creon is not strong enough to stand in my way.   35
ISMENE. Ah sister!
      Oedipus died, everyone hating him
      For what his own search brought to light, his eyes
      Ripped out by his own hand; and Iocaste died,
      His mother and wife at once: she twisted the cords   40
      That strangled her life; and our two brothers died,
      Each killed by the other's sword. And we are left:
      But oh, Antigone,
      Think how much more terrible than these
      Our own death would be if we should go against Creon   45
      And do what he has forbidden! We are only women,
      We cannot fight with men, Antigone!
      The law is strong, we must give in to the law
      In this thing, and in worse. I beg the dead
      To forgive me, but I am helpless: I must yield   50
      To those in authority. And I think it is dangerous business
      To be always meddling.
ANTIGONE.   If that is what you think,
      I should not want you, even if you asked to come.
      You have made your choice, you can be what you want to be.
      But I will bury him; and if I must die,   55
      I say that this crime is holy: I shall lie down
      With him in death, and I shall be as dear
      To him as he to me.
               It is the dead,
      Not the living, who make the longest demands:
      We die forever . . .
                   You may do as you like,   60
      Since apparently the laws of the gods mean nothing to you.
ISMENE. They mean a great deal to me; but I have no strength
      To break laws that were made for the public good.
ANTIGONE. That must be your excuse, I suppose. But as for me,
      I will bury the brother I love.
ISMENE.   Antigone,   65
      I am so afraid for you!
ANTIGONE.   You need not be:
      You have yourself to consider, after all.
ISMENE. But no one must hear of this, you must tell no one!
      I will keep it a secret, I promise!
ANTIGONE.   Oh tell it! Tell everyone!
      Think how they'll hate you when it all comes out   70
      If they learn that you knew about it all the time!
ISMENE. So fiery! You should be cold with fear.
ANTIGONE. Perhaps. But I am doing only what I must.

ISMENE. But can you do it? I say that you cannot.
ANTIGONE. Very well: when my strength gives out, I shall do no more.   75
ISMENE. Impossible things should not be tried at all.
ANTIGONE. Go away, Ismene:
    I shall be hating you soon, and the dead will, too,
    For your words are hateful. Leave me my foolish plan:
    I am not afraid of the danger; if it means death,   80
    It will not be the worst of deaths—death without honor.
ISMENE. Go then, if you feel that you must.
    You are unwise,
    But a loyal friend indeed to those who love you.

[*Exit into the palace.* ANTIGONE *goes off, left. Enter the* CHORUS.]

Parados *

CHORUS. Now the long blade of the sun, lying   [STROPHE 1]
    Level east to west, touches with glory
    Thebes of the Seven Gates. Open, unlidded
    Eye of golden day! O marching light
    Across the eddy and rush of Dirce's stream,°   5
    Striking the white shields of the enemy
    Thrown headlong backward from the blaze of morning!
CHORAGOS.° Polyneices their commander
    Roused them with windy phrases,
    He the wild eagle screaming   10
    Insults above our land,
    His wings their shields of snow,
    His crest their marshaled helms.

CHORUS. Against our seven gates in a yawning ring   [ANTISTROPHE 1]
    The famished spears came onward in the night;   15
    But before his jaws were sated with our blood,
    Or pinefire took the garland of our towers,
    He was thrown back; and as he turned, great Thebes—
    No tender victim for his noisy power—
    Rose like a dragon behind him, shouting war.   20
CHORAGOS. For God hates utterly
    The bray of bragging tongues;
    And when he beheld their smiling,
    Their swagger of golden helms,
    The frown of his thunder blasted   25
    Their first man from our walls.

* **Parados:** the "parade," or song accompanying the entrance of the Chorus. The strophe (strŏ′fē) and antistrophe (an·tis′trə·fē) are balanced stanzas chanted by the Chorus. It faces first, for the strophe, in one direction and then, for the antistrophe, in the other.   5. **Dirce's stream:** Dirce, an early queen of Thebes, was murdered and her body thrown into the stream that bears her name.   8. **Choragos** (kŏ·rā′gəs): the leader of the Chorus.

CHORUS. We heard his shout of triumph high in the air   [STROPHE 2]
        Turn to a scream; far out in a flaming arc
        He fell with his windy torch, and the earth struck him.
        And others storming in fury no less than his   30
        Found shock of death in the dusty joy of battle.
CHORAGOS. Seven captains at seven gates
        Yielded their clanging arms to the god
        That bends the battle line and breaks it.
        These two only, brothers in blood,   35
        Face to face in matchless rage,
        Mirroring each the other's death,
        Clashed in long combat.

CHORUS. But now in the beautiful morning of victory   [ANTISTROPHE 2]
        Let Thebes of the many chariots sing for joy!   40
        With hearts for dancing we'll take leave of war:
        Our temples shall be sweet with hymns of praise,
        And the long night shall echo with our chorus.

Scene I

CHORAGOS. But now at last our new king is coming:
        Creon of Thebes, Menoikeus' son.
        In this auspicious dawn of his reign
        What are the new complexities
        That shifting fate has woven for him?   5
        What is his counsel? Why has he summoned
        The old men to hear him?

[*Enter* CREON *from the palace, center. He addresses the* CHORUS *from the top step.*]

CREON. Gentlemen: I have the honor to inform you that our ship of state, which recent storms have threatened to destroy, has come safely to harbor at last, guided by the merciful wisdom of Heaven. I have   10 summoned you here this morning because I know that I can depend upon you: your devotion to King Laios° was absolute; you never hesitated in your duty to our late ruler Oedipus; and when Oedipus died, your loyalty was transferred to his children. Unfortunately, as you know, his two sons, the princes Eteocles and Polyneices,   15 have killed each other in battle; and I, as the next in blood, have succeeded to the full power of the throne.

    I am aware, of course, that no ruler can expect complete loyalty from his subjects until he has been tested in office. Nevertheless, I say to you at the very outset that I have nothing but contempt   20 for the kind of governor who is afraid, for whatever reason, to follow the course that he knows is best for the state; and as for the man who

12. **Laios** (lā′yəs): the father of Oedipus.

sets private friendship above the public welfare—I have no use for him, either. I call God to witness that if I saw my country headed for ruin, I should not be afraid to speak out plainly; and I need hardly 25 remind you that I would never have any dealings with an enemy of the people. No one values friendship more highly than I; but we must remember that friends made at the risk of wrecking our ship are not real friends at all.

These are my principles, at any rate, and that is why I have 30 made the following decisions concerning the sons of Oedipus: Eteocles, who died as a man should die, fighting for his country, is to be buried with full military honors, with all the ceremony that is usual when the greatest heroes die; but his brother Polyneices, who broke his exile to come back with fire and sword against his na- 35 tive city and the shrines of his fathers' gods, whose one idea was to spill the blood of his blood and sell his own people into slavery— Polyneices, I say, is to have no burial: no man is to touch him or say the least prayer for him; he shall lie on the plain, unburied; and the birds and the scavenging dogs can do with him whatever they like. 40

This is my command, and you can see the wisdom behind it. As long as I am king, no traitor is going to be honored with the loyal man. But whoever shows by word and deed that he is on the side of the state—he shall have my respect while he is living, and my rever- ence when he is dead. 45

CHORAGOS. If that is your will, Creon son of Menoikeus,
    You have the right to enforce it: we are yours.
CREON. That is my will. Take care that you do your part.
CHORAGOS. We are old men: let the younger ones carry it out.
CREON. I do not mean that: The sentries have been appointed. 50
CHORAGOS. Then what is it that you would have us do?
CREON. You will give no support to whoever breaks this law.
CHORAGOS. Only a crazy man is in love with death!
CREON. And death it is; yet money talks, and the wisest
    Have sometimes been known to count a few coins too many. 55

[*Enter* SENTRY *from left.*]

SENTRY. I'll not say that I'm out of breath from running, King, because
    every time I stopped to think about what I have to tell you, I felt like
    going back. And all the time a voice kept saying, "You fool, don't you
    know you're walking straight into trouble?"; and then another voice:
    "Yes, but if you let somebody else get the news to Creon first, 60
    it will be even worse than that for you!" But good sense won out, at
    least I hope it was good sense, and here I am with a story that makes
    no sense at all; but I'll tell it anyhow, because, as they say, what's
    going to happen's going to happen, and—
CREON. Come to the point. What have you to say? 65
SENTRY. I did not do it. I did not see who did it. You must not punish me
    for what someone else has done.
CREON. A comprehensive defense! More effective, perhaps,
    If I knew its purpose. Come: what is it?
SENTRY. A dreadful thing . . . I don't know how to put it— 70
CREON. Out with it!

SENTRY.   Well, then;
    The dead man—
                    Polyneices—

[*Pause. The* SENTRY *is overcome, fumbles for words.* CREON *waits impassively.*]

                            out there—
                                    someone—
    New dust on the slimy flesh!

                [*Pause. No sign from* CREON.]

    Someone has given it burial that way, and
    Gone—   75

            [*Long pause.* CREON *finally speaks with deadly control.*]

CREON. And the man who dared do this?
SENTRY.   I swear I
    Do not know! You must believe me!
                            Listen:
    The ground was dry, not a sign of digging, no,
    Not a wheeltrack in the dust, no trace of anyone.
    It was when they relieved us this morning; and one of them,   80
    The corporal, pointed to it.
                            There it was,
    The strangest—
                    Look:
    The body, just mounded over with light dust: you see?
    Not buried really, but as if they'd covered it
    Just enough for the ghost's peace. And no sign   85
    Of dogs or any wild animal that had been there.

    And then what a scene there was! Every man of us
    Accusing the other: we all proved the other man did it,
    We all had proof that we could not have done it.
    We were ready to take hot iron in our hands,   90
    Walk through fire, swear by all the gods,
    It was not I!
    I do not know who it was, but it was not I!

[CREON'S *rage has been mounting steadily, but the* SENTRY *is too intent
    upon his story to notice it.*]

    And then, when this came to nothing, someone said
    A thing that silenced us and made us stare   95
    Down at the ground: You had to be told the news,
    And one of us had to do it! We threw the dice,
    And the bad luck fell to me. So here I am,
    No happier to be here than you are to have me:
    Nobody likes the man who brings bad news.   100
CHORAGOS. I have been wondering, King: can it be that the gods have
        done this?

CREON (*furiously*). Stop!
  Must you doddering wrecks
  Go out of your heads entirely? "The gods!"
  Intolerable!   105
  The gods favor this corpse? Why? How had he served them?
  Tried to loot their temples, burn their images,
  Yes, and the whole state, and its laws with it!
  Is it your senile opinion that the gods love to honor bad men?
  A pious thought!—
                        No, from the very beginning   110
  There have been those who have whispered together,
  Stiff-necked anarchists, putting their heads together,
  Scheming against me in alleys. These are the men,
  And they have bribed my own guard to do this thing.
  (*Sententiously*)
  Money!   115
  There's nothing in the world so demoralizing as money.
  Down go your cities,
  Homes gone, men gone, honest hearts corrupted,
  Crookedness of all kinds, and all for money!
                        (*To* SENTRY) But you—!
  I swear by God and by the throne of God,   120
  The man who has done this thing shall pay for it!
  Find that man, bring him here to me, or your death
  Will be the least of your problems: I'll string you up
  Alive, and there will be certain ways to make you
  Discover your employer before you die;   125
  And the process may teach you a lesson you seem to have missed:
  The dearest profit is sometimes all too dear:
  That depends on the source. Do you understand me?
  A fortune won is often misfortune.
SENTRY. King, may I speak?
CREON.   Your very voice distresses me.   130
SENTRY. Are you sure that it is my voice, and not your conscience?
CREON. By God, he wants to analyze me now!
SENTRY. It is not what I say, but what has been done, that hurts you.
CREON. You talk too much.
SENTRY.   Maybe; but I've done nothing.
CREON. Sold your soul for some silver: that's all you've done. 135
SENTRY. How dreadful it is when the right judge judges wrong!
CREON. Your figures of speech
  May entertain you now; but unless you bring me the man,
  You will get little profit from them in the end.
                        [*Exit* CREON *into the palace.*]
SENTRY. "Bring me the man"—!   140
  I'd like nothing better than bringing him the man!
  But bring him or not, you have seen the last of me here.
  At any rate, I am safe!   [*Exit* SENTRY.]

Ode I *

CHORUS. Numberless are the world's wonders, but none   [STROPHE 1]
    More wonderful than man; the storm-gray sea
    Yields to his prows, the huge crests bear him high;
    Earth, holy and inexhaustible, is graven
    With shining furrows where his plows have gone   5
    Year after year, the timeless labor of stallions.

    The lightboned birds and beasts that cling to cover,   [ANTISTROPHE 1]
    The lithe fish lighting their reaches of dim water,
    All are taken, tamed in the net of his mind;
    The lion on the hill, the wild horse windy-maned,   10
    Resign to him; and his blunt yoke has broken
    The sultry shoulders of the mountain bull.

    Words also, and thought as rapid as air,   [STROPHE 2]
    He fashions to his good use; statecraft is his,
    And his the skill that deflects the arrows of snow,   15
    The spears of winter rain: from every wind
    He has made himself secure—from all but one:
    In the late wind of death he cannot stand.

    O clear intelligence, force beyond all measure!   [ANTISTROPHE 2]
    O fate of man, working both good and evil!   20
    When the laws are kept, how proudly his city stands!
    When the laws are broken, what of his city then?
    Never may the anarchic man find rest at my hearth,
    Never be it said that my thoughts are his thoughts.

Scene II

[*Reenter* SENTRY, *leading* ANTIGONE.]

CHORAGOS. What does this mean? Surely this captive woman
    Is the princess, Antigone. Why should she be taken?
SENTRY. Here is the one who did it! We caught her
    In the very act of burying him.—Where is Creon?
CHORAGOS. Just coming from the house.

[*Enter* CREON, *center.*]

CREON.   What has happened?   5
    Why have you come back so soon?
SENTRY (*expansively*).   O King,
    A man should never be too sure of anything:

---

* **Ode:** a song chanted by the Chorus. An ode separates one scene from the next.

I would have sworn
That you'd not see me here again: your anger
Frightened me so, and the things you threatened me with;   10
But how could I tell then
That I'd be able to solve the case so soon?

No dice-throwing this time: I was only too glad to come!

Here is this woman. She is the guilty one:
We found her trying to bury him.   15
Take her, then; question her; judge her as you will.
I am through with the whole thing now, and glad of it.
CREON. But this is Antigone! Why have you brought her here?
SENTRY. She was burying him, I tell you!
CREON *(severely).*   Is this the truth?
SENTRY. I saw her with my own eyes. Can I say more?   20
CREON. The details: Come, tell me quickly!
SENTRY.   It was like this:
After those terrible threats of yours, King,
We went back and brushed the dust away from the body.
The flesh was soft by now, and stinking,
So we sat on a hill to windward and kept guard.   25
No napping this time! We kept each other awake.
But nothing happened until the white round'sun
Whirled in the center of the round sky over us:
Then, suddenly,
A storm of dust roared up from the earth, and the sky   30
Went out, the plain vanished with all its trees
In the stinging dark. We closed our eyes and endured it.
The whirlwind lasted a long time, but it passed;
And then we looked, and there was Antigone!
I have seen   .   35
A mother bird come back to a stripped nest, heard
Her crying bitterly a broken note or two
For the young ones stolen. Just so, when this girl
Found the bare corpse, and all her love's work wasted,
She wept, and cried on heaven to damn the hands   40
That had done this thing.
                          And then she brought more dust
And sprinkled wine three times for her brother's ghost.

We ran and took her at once. She was not afraid,
Not even when we charged her with what she had done.
She denied nothing.
                    And this was a comfort to me,   45
And some uneasiness: for it is a good thing
To escape from death, but it is no great pleasure
To bring death to a friend.
                          Yet I always say
There is nothing so comfortable as your own safe skin!

CREON (*slowly, dangerously*). And you, Antigone,   50
    You with your head hanging—do you confess this thing?
ANTIGONE. I do. I deny nothing.
CREON (*to* SENTRY).   You may go.   [*Exit* SENTRY.]
(*To* ANTIGONE) Tell me, tell me briefly:
    Had you heard my proclamation touching this matter?
ANTIGONE. It was public. Could I help hearing it?   55
CREON. And yet you dared defy the law.
ANTIGONE.   I dared.
    It was not God's proclamation. That final justice
    That rules the world below makes no such laws.

    Your edict, King, was strong,
    But all your strength is weakness itself against   60
    The immortal unrecorded laws of God.
    They are not merely now: they were, and shall be,
    Operative forever, beyond man utterly.

    I knew I must die, even without your decree:
    I am only mortal. And if I must die   65
    Now, before it is my time to die,
    Surely this is no hardship: can anyone
    Living, as I live, with evil all about me,
    Think death less than a friend? This death of mine
    Is of no importance; but if I had left my brother   70
    Lying in death unburied, I should have suffered.
    Now I do not.
             You smile at me. Ah Creon,
    Think me a fool, if you like; but it may well be
    That a fool convicts me of folly.
CHORAGOS. Like father, like daughter: both headstrong, deaf to reason!   75
    She has never learned to yield.
CREON.   She has much to learn.
    The inflexible heart breaks first, the toughest iron
    Cracks first, and the wildest horses bend their necks
    At the pull of the smallest curb.
                  Pride? In a slave?
    This girl is guilty of a double insolence,   80
    Breaking the given laws and boasting of it.
    Who is the man here,
    She or I, if this crime goes unpunished?
    Sister's child, or more than sister's child,
    Or closer yet in blood—she and her sister   85
    Win bitter death for this!
          (*To servants*) Go, some of you,
    Arrest Ismene. I accuse her equally.
    Bring her: You will find her sniffling in the house there.

    Her mind's a traitor: crimes kept in the dark
    Cry for light, and the guardian brain shudders;   90

But how much worse than this
Is brazen boasting of barefaced anarchy!
ANTIGONE. Creon, what more do you want than my death?
CREON.   Nothing.
     That gives me everything.
ANTIGONE.   Then I beg you: kill me.
     This talking is a great weariness: your words   95
     Are distasteful to me, and I am sure that mine
     Seem so to you. And yet they should not seem so:
     I should have praise and honor for what I have done.
     All these men here would praise me
     Were their lips not frozen shut with fear of you.   100
     (Bitterly)
     Ah the good fortune of kings,
     Licensed to say and do whatever they please!
CREON. You are alone here in that opinion.
ANTIGONE. No, they are with me. But they keep their tongues in leash.
CREON. Maybe. But you are guilty, and they are not.   105
ANTIGONE. There is no guilt in reverence for the dead.
CREON. But Eteocles—was he not your brother too?
ANTIGONE. My brother too.
CREON.   And you insult his memory?
ANTIGONE (softly). The dead man would not say that I insult it.
CREON. He would: for you honor a traitor as much as him.   110
ANTIGONE. His own brother, traitor or not, and equal in blood.
CREON. He made war on his country. Eteocles defended it.
ANTIGONE. Nevertheless, there are honors due all the dead.
CREON. But not the same for the wicked as for the just.
ANTIGONE. Ah Creon, Creon,   115
     Which of us can say what the gods hold wicked?
CREON. An enemy is an enemy, even dead.
ANTIGONE. It is my nature to join in love, not hate.
CREON (finally losing patience). Go join them, then; if you must have your
          love,
     Find it in hell!   120
CHORAGOS. But see, Ismene comes:

[Enter ISMENE, guarded.]

     Those tears are sisterly, the cloud
     That shadows her eyes rains down gentle sorrow.
CREON. You too, Ismene,
     Snake in my ordered house, sucking my blood   125
     Stealthily—and all the time I never knew
     That these two sisters were aiming at my throne!
                                                  Ismene,
     Do you confess your share in this crime, or deny it?
     Answer me.
ISMENE. Yes, if she will let me say so. I am guilty.   130
ANTIGONE (coldly). No, Ismene. You have no right to say so.
     You would not help me, and I will not have you help me.

ISMENE. But now I know what you meant; and I am here
    To join you, to take my share of punishment.
ANTIGONE. The dead man and the gods who rule the dead   135
    Know whose act this was. Words are not friends.
ISMENE. Do you refuse me, Antigone? I want to die with you:
    I too have a duty that I must discharge to the dead.
ANTIGONE. You shall not lessen my death by sharing it.
ISMENE. What do I care for life when you are dead?   140
ANTIGONE. Ask Creon. You're always hanging on his opinions.
ISMENE. You are laughing at me. Why, Antigone?
ANTIGONE. It's a joyless laughter, Ismene.
ISMENE.   But can I do nothing?
ANTIGONE. Yes. Save yourself. I shall not envy you.
    There are those who will praise you; I shall have honor, too.   145
ISMENE. But we are equally guilty!
ANTIGONE.   No more, Ismene.
    You are alive, but I belong to death.
CREON (to the CHORUS). Gentlemen, I beg you to observe these girls:
    One has just now lost her mind; the other,
    It seems, has never had a mind at all.   150
ISMENE. Grief teaches the steadiest minds to waver, King.
CREON. Yours certainly did, when you assumed guilt with the guilty!
ISMENE. But how could I go on living without her?
CREON.   You are.
    She is already dead.
ISMENE.   But your own son's bride!
CREON. There are places enough for him to push his plow.   155
    I want no wicked women for my sons!
ISMENE. O dearest Haimon, how your father wrongs you!
CREON. I've had enough of your childish talk of marriage!
CHORAGOS. Do you really intend to steal this girl from your son?
CREON. No; death will do that for me.
CHORAGOS.   Then she must die?   160
CREON (ironically). You dazzle me.
                        —But enough of this talk!
(To GUARDS) You, there, take them away and guard them well:
    For they are but women, and even brave men run
    When they see death coming.
                    [Exeunt ISMENE, ANTIGONE, and GUARDS.]

Ode II

CHORUS. Fortunate is the man who has never tasted God's vengeance!
                                            [STROPHE 1.
    Where once the anger of heaven has struck, that house is shaken
    Forever: damnation rises behind each child
    Like a wave cresting out of the black northeast,
    When the long darkness under sea roars up   5
    And bursts drumming death upon the windwhipped sand.

I have seen this gathering sorrow from time long past

[ANTISTROPHE 1]

Loom upon Oedipus' children: generation from generation
Takes the compulsive rage of the enemy god.
So lately this last flower of Oedipus' line   10
Drank the sunlight! but now a passionate word
And a handful of dust have closed up all its beauty.

What mortal arrogance   [STROPHE 2]
Transcends the wrath of Zeus?
Sleep cannot lull him, nor the effortless long months   15
Of the timeless gods: but he is young forever,
And his house is the shining day of high Olympos.
All that is and shall be,
And all the past, is his.
No pride on earth is free of the curse of heaven.   20

The straying dreams of men   [ANTISTROPHE 2]
May bring them ghosts of joy:
But as they drowse, the waking embers burn them;
Or they walk with fixed eyes, as blind men walk.
But the ancient wisdom speaks for our own time: 25
Fate works most for woe
With folly's fairest show.
Man's little pleasure is the spring of sorrow.

Scene III

CHORAGOS. But here is Haimon, King, the last of all your sons.
Is it grief for Antigone that brings him here,
And bitterness at being robbed of his bride?

[Enter HAIMON.]

CREON. We shall soon see, and no need of diviners.
—Son,
You have heard my final judgment on that girl: 5
Have you come here hating me, or have you come
With deference and with love, whatever I do?
HAIMON. I am your son, Father. You are my guide.
You make things clear for me, and I obey you.
No marriage means more to me than your continuing wisdom.   10
CREON. Good. That is the way to behave: subordinate
Everything else, my son, to your father's will.
This is what a man prays for, that he may get
Sons attentive and dutiful in his house,
Each one hating his father's enemies,   15
Honoring his father's friends. But if his sons
Fail him, if they turn out unprofitably,

What has he fathered but trouble for himself
And amusement for the malicious?
                                        So you are right
Not to lose your head over this woman.   20
Your pleasure with her would soon grow cold, Haimon,
And then you'd have a hellcat in bed and elsewhere.
Let her find her husband in hell!
Of all the people in this city, only she
Has had contempt for my law and broken it.   25

Do you want me to show myself weak before the people?
Or to break my sworn word? No, and I will not.
The woman dies.
I suppose she'll plead "family ties." Well, let her.
If I permit my own family to rebel,   30
How shall I earn the world's obedience?
Show me the man who keeps his house in hand,
He's fit for public authority.
                                I'll have no dealings
With lawbreakers, critics of the government:
Whoever is chosen to govern should be obeyed—   35
Must be obeyed, in all things, great and small,
Just and unjust! O Haimon,
The man who knows how to obey, and that man only,
Knows how to give commands when the time comes.
You can depend on him, no matter how fast   40
The spears come: He's a good soldier, he'll stick it out.

Anarchy, anarchy! Show me a greater evil!
This is why cities tumble and the great houses rain down,
This is what scatters armies!

No, no: Good lives are made so by discipline.   45
We keep the laws then, and the lawmakers,
And no woman shall seduce us. If we must lose,
Let's lose to a man, at least! Is a woman stronger than we?
CHORAGOS. Unless time has rusted my wits,
   What you say, King, is said with point and dignity.   50
HAIMON (boyishly earnest). Father:
   Reason is God's crowning gift to man, and you are right
To warn me against losing mine. I cannot say—
I hope that I shall never want to say!—that you
Have reasoned badly. Yet there are other men   55
Who can reason, too; and their opinions might be helpful.
You are not in a position to know everything
That people say or do, or what they feel:
Your temper terrifies them—everyone
Will tell you only what you like to hear.   60
But I, at any rate, can listen; and I have heard them
Muttering and whispering in the dark about this girl.
They say no woman has ever, so unreasonably,

Died so shameful a death for a generous act:
"She covered her brother's body. Is this indecent?   65
She kept him from dogs and vultures. Is this a crime?
Death?—She should have all the honor that we can give her!"

This is the way they talk out there in the city.

You must believe me:
Nothing is closer to me than your happiness.   70
What could be closer? Must not any son
Value his father's fortune as his father does his?
I beg you, do not be unchangeable:
Do not believe that you alone can be right.
The man who thinks that,   75
The man who maintains that only he has the power
To reason correctly, the gift to speak, the soul—
A man like that, when you know him, turns out empty.

It is not reason never to yield to reason!

In flood time you can see how some trees bend,   80
And because they bend, even their twigs are safe,
While stubborn trees are torn up, roots and all.
And the same thing happens in sailing:
Make your sheet fast, never slacken,—and over you go,
Head over heels and under: and there's your voyage.   85
Forget you are angry! Let yourself be moved!
I know I am young; but please let me say this:
The ideal condition
Would be, I admit, that men should be right by instinct;
But since we are all too likely to go astray,   90
The reasonable thing is to learn from those who can teach.
CHORAGOS. You will do well to listen to him, King,
    If what he says is sensible. And you, Haimon,
    Must listen to your father—both speak well.
CREON. You consider it right for a man of my years and experience   95
    To go to school to a boy?
HAIMON.   It is not right
    If I am wrong. But if I am young, and right,
    What does my age matter?
CREON. You think it right to stand up for an anarchist?
HAIMON. Not at all. I pay no respect to criminals.   100
CREON. Then she is not a criminal?
HAIMON. The city would deny it, to a man.
CREON. And the city proposes to teach me how to rule?
HAIMON. Ah. Who is it that's talking like a boy now?
CREON. My voice is the one voice giving orders in this city!   105
HAIMON. It is no city if it takes orders from one voice.
CREON. The state is the King!
HAIMON.   Yes, if the state is a desert.

[Pause]

CREON. This boy, it seems, has sold out to a woman.

HAIMON. If you are a woman: My concern is only for you.

CREON. So? Your "concern"! In a public brawl with your father!　110

HAIMON. How about you, in a public brawl with justice?

CREON. With justice, when all that I do is within my rights?

HAIMON. You have no right to trample on God's right.

CREON *(completely out of control)*. Fool, adolescent fool! Taken in by a
　　woman!

HAIMON. You'll never see me taken in by anything vile.　115

CREON. Every word you say is for her!

HAIMON *(quietly, darkly).*　　　　　And for you.
　　And for me. And for the gods under the earth.

CREON. You'll never marry her while she lives.

HAIMON. Then she must die—But her death will cause another.

CREON. Another?　120
　　Have you lost your senses? Is this an open threat?

HAIMON. There is no threat in speaking to emptiness.

CREON. I swear you'll regret this superior tone of yours!
　　You are the empty one!

HAIMON.　　　　　　　　If you were not my father,
　　I'd say you were perverse.　125

CREON. You girlstruck fool, don't play at words with me!

HAIMON. I am sorry. You prefer silence.

CREON.　　　　　　　　Now, by God—!
　　I swear, by all the gods in heaven above us,
　　You'll watch it, I swear you shall!
　　　　　　　(To the SERVANTS*)* Bring her out!
　　Bring the woman out! Let her die before his eyes!　130
　　Here, this instant, with her bridegroom beside her!

HAIMON. Not here, no; she will not die here, King.
　　And you will never see my face again.
　　Go on raving as long as you've a friend to endure you.

　　　　　　　　　　　　　　　[Exit HAIMON.*]*

CHORAGOS. Gone, gone.　135
　　Creon, a young man in a rage is dangerous!

CREON. Let him do, or dream to do, more than a man can.
　　He shall not save these girls from death.

CHORAGOS.　　　　　　　　These girls?
　　You have sentenced them both?

CREON.　　　　　　　　No, you are right.
　　I will not kill the one whose hands are clean.　140

CHORAGOS. But Antigone?

CREON *(somberly).*　　　　I will carry her far away
　　Out there in the wilderness and lock her
　　Living in a vault of stone. She shall have food,
　　As the custom is, to absolve the state of her death.
　　And there let her pray to the gods of hell:　145
　　They are her only gods:
　　Perhaps they will show her an escape from death,

Or she may learn,
though late,
That piety shown the dead is pity in vain.   [*Exit* CREON.]

Ode III

CHORUS. Love, unconquerable   [STROPHE]
    Waster of rich men, keeper
    Of warm lights and all-night vigil
    In the soft face of a girl:
    Sea-wanderer, forest-visitor!   5
    Even the pure Immortals cannot escape you,
    And mortal man, in his one day's dusk,
    Trembles before your glory.

    Surely you swerve upon ruin   [ANTISTROPHE]
    The just man's consenting heart,   10
    As here you have made bright anger
    Strike between father and son—
    And none has conquered but love!
    A girl's glance working the will of Heaven:
    Pleasure to her alone who mocks us,   15
    Merciless Aphrodite.°

Scene IV

CHORAGOS (*as* ANTIGONE *enters, guarded*). But I can no longer stand in
    awe of this,
    Nor, seeing what I see, keep back my tears.
    Here is Antigone, passing to that chamber
    Where all find sleep at last.
ANTIGONE. Look upon me, friends, and pity me   5
    Turning back at the night's edge to say
    Good-by to the sun that shines for me no longer;
    Now sleepy death
    Summons me down to Acheron,° that cold shore:
    There is no bridesong there, nor any music.   10
CHORUS. Yet not unpraised, not without a kind of honor,
    You walk at last into the underworld;
    Untouched by sickness, broken by no sword.
    What woman has ever found your way to death?
ANTIGONE. How often I have heard the story of Niobe,°   15

16. **Aphrodite:** goddess of love.
9. **Acheron** (ak'ə·ron): in Greek mythology, one of the rivers surrounding Hades.
15. **Niobe** (nī'ə·bē): To punish her extravagant boasting, the gods slew all Niobe's children
and turned her into a column of stone from which her tears still continue to pour.

Tantalos' wretched daughter, how the stone
Clung fast about her, ivy-close; and they say
The rain falls endlessly
And sifting soft snow; her tears are never done.
I feel the loneliness of her death in mine. 20
CHORUS. But she was born of Heaven, and you
Are woman, woman-born. If her death is yours,
A mortal woman's, is this not for you
Glory in our world and in the world beyond?
ANTIGONE. You laugh at me. Ah, friends, friends, 25
Can you not wait until I am dead? O Thebes,
O men many-charioted, in love with fortune,
Dear springs of Dirce, sacred Theban grove,
Be witnesses for me, denied all pity,
Unjustly judged! and think a word of love 30
For her whose path turns
Under dark earth, where there are no more tears.
CHORUS. You have passed beyond human daring and come at last
Into a place of stone where justice sits.
I cannot tell 35
What shape of your father's guilt appears in this.
ANTIGONE. You have touched it at last: that bridal bed
Unspeakable, horror of son and mother mingling:
Their crime, infection of all our family!
O Oedipus, father and brother! 40
Your marriage strikes from the grave to murder mine.
I have been a stranger here in my own land:
All my life
The blasphemy of my birth has followed me.
CHORUS. Reverence is a virtue, but strength 45
Lives in established law: That must prevail.
You have made your choice,
Your death is the doing of your conscious hand.
ANTIGONE. Then let me go, since all your words are bitter,
And the very light of the sun is cold to me. 50
Lead me to my vigil, where I must have
Neither love nor lamentation; no song, but silence.

[CREON *interrupts impatiently.*]

CREON. If dirges and planned lamentations could put off death,
Men would be singing forever.
      (To the SERVANTS) Take her, go!
You know your orders: take her to the vault 55
And leave her alone there. And if she lives or dies,
That's her affair, not ours: Our hands are clean.
ANTIGONE. O tomb, vaulted bride-bed in eternal rock,
Soon I shall be with my own again
Where Persephone° welcomes the thin ghosts underground: 60

60. **Persephone** (pər·sef'ə·nē): queen of Hades.

And I shall see my father again, and you, Mother,
And dearest Polyneices—
                                              dearest indeed
To me, since it was my hand
That washed him clean and poured the ritual wine;
And my reward is death before my time!   65

And yet, as men's hearts know, I have done no wrong,
I have not sinned before God. Or if I have,
I shall know the truth in death. But if the guilt
Lies upon Creon who judged me, then, I pray,
May his punishment equal my own.

CHORAGOS.   O passionate heart,   70
Unyielding, tormented still by the same winds!
CREON. Her guards shall have good cause to regret their delaying.
ANTIGONE. Ah! That voice is like the voice of death!
CREON. I can give you no reason to think you are mistaken.
ANTIGONE. Thebes, and you my fathers' gods,   75
And rulers of Thebes, you see me now, the last
Unhappy daughter of a line of kings,
Your kings, led away to death. You will remember
What things I suffer, and at what men's hands,
Because I would not transgress the laws of heaven.   80
(To the GUARDS, *simply)* Come: let us wait no longer.
                                    [*Exit* ANTIGONE, *left, guarded.*]

Ode IV

CHORUS. All Danae's° beauty was locked away   [STROPHE 1]
In a brazen cell where the sunlight could not come:
A small room, still as any grave, enclosed her.
Yet she was a princess, too,
And Zeus in a rain of gold poured love upon her.   5
O child, child,
No power in wealth or war
Or tough sea-blackened ships
Can prevail against untiring destiny!

And Dryas' son° also, that furious king,   [ANTISTROPHE 1]   10
Bore the god's prisoning anger for his pride:
Sealed up by Dionysos in deaf stone,
His madness died among echoes.
So at the last he learned what dreadful power
His tongue had mocked: 15

1. **Danae:** a princess, whose father imprisoned her in a bronze tower. Zeus loved her and visited her in the form of a shower of gold (see also page 111). 10. **Dryas' son:** a king named Lycurgos, who disapproved of the revels of Dionysos and attacked the god. As punishment, some legends say, he was driven mad and imprisoned in stone.

For he had profaned the revels,
And fired the wrath of the nine
Implacable Sisters° that love the sound of the flute.

And old men tell a half-remembered tale°   [STROPHE 2]
Of horror done where a dark ledge splits the sea   20
And a double surf beats on the gray shores:
How a king's new woman, sick
With hatred for the queen he had imprisoned,
Ripped out his two sons' eyes with her bloody hands
While grinning Ares° watched the shuttle plunge   25
Four times: four blind wounds crying for revenge,

Crying, tears and blood mingled—piteously born,   [ANTISTROPHE 2]
Those sons whose mother was of heavenly birth!
Her father was the god of the North Wind
And she was cradled by gales,   30
She raced with young colts on the glittering hills
And walked untrammeled in the open light;
But in her marriage deathless Fate found means
To build a tomb like yours for all her joy.

Scene V

[*Enter blind* TEIRESIAS, *led by a boy. The opening speeches of* TEIRESIAS
should be in singsong contrast to the realistic lines of CREON.]

TEIRESIAS. This is the way the blind man comes, Princes, Princes,
    Lock-step, two heads lit by the eyes of one.
CREON. What new thing have you to tell us, old Teiresias?
TEIRESIAS. I have much to tell you: Listen to the prophet, Creon.
CREON. I am not aware that I have ever failed to listen.   5
TEIRESIAS. Then you have done wisely, King, and ruled well.
CREON. I admit my debt to you.° But what have you to say?
TEIRESIAS. This, Creon: You stand once more on the edge of fate.
CREON. What do you mean? Your words are a kind of dread.
TEIRESIAS. Listen, Creon: 10
    I was sitting in my chair of augury, at the place
    Where the birds gather about me. They were all a-chatter,
    As is their habit, when suddenly I heard
    A strange note in their jangling, a scream, a
    Whirring fury; I knew that they were fighting,   15

---

    18. **nine Implacable Sisters:** the Muses, goddesses of the arts and sciences.   19. **a half-remembered tale:** The details that follow refer to an ancient myth about King Phineus of Thrace, who imprisoned his first wife, Cleopatra, daughter of the North Wind god. Cleopatra's two sons were blinded by the king's new wife.   25. **Ares:** god of war, a creator of strife.

    7. **my debt to you:** Teiresias served as an instrument of the gods in determining Oedipus' fate and was thus indirectly responsible for Creon's ascension to the throne.

Tearing each other, dying
In a whirlwind of wings clashing. And I was afraid.
I began the rites of burnt-offering at the altar,
But Hephaistos° failed me: Instead of bright flame,
There was only the sputtering slime of the fat thighflesh   20
Melting: The entrails dissolved in gray smoke,
The bare bone burst from the welter. And no blaze!

This was a sign from heaven. My boy described it,
Seeing for me as I see for others.

I tell you, Creon, you yourself have brought   25
This new calamity upon us. Our hearths and altars
Are stained with the corruption of dogs and carrion birds
That glut themselves on the corpse of Oedipus' son.
The gods are deaf when we pray to them, their fire
Recoils from our offering, their birds of omen   30
Have no cry of comfort, for they are gorged
With the thick blood of the dead.
                                O my son,
These are no trifles! Think: all men make mistakes,
But a good man yields when he knows his course is wrong,
And repairs the evil. The only crime is pride.   35

Give in to the dead man, then: Do not fight with a corpse—
What glory is it to kill a man who is dead?
Think, I beg you:
It is for your own good that I speak as I do.
You should be able to yield for your own good.   40
CREON. It seems that prophets have made me their especial province.
    All my life long
    I have been a kind of butt for the dull arrows
    Of doddering fortunetellers!
                                No, Teiresias:
    If your birds—if the great eagles of God himself   45
    Should carry him stinking bit by bit to heaven,
    I would not yield. I am not afraid of pollution:
    No man can defile the gods.
                                Do what you will,
    Go into business, make money, speculate
    In India gold or that synthetic gold from Sardis,   50
    Get rich otherwise than by my consent to bury him.
    Teiresias, it is a sorry thing when a wise man
    Sells his wisdom, lets out his words for hire!
TEIRESIAS. Ah Creon! Is there no man left in the world—
CREON. To do what?—Come, let's have the aphorism!   55
TEIRESIAS. No man who knows that wisdom outweighs any wealth?
CREON. As surely as bribes are baser than any baseness.
TEIRESIAS. You are sick, Creon! You are deathly sick!

19. **Hephaistos:** god of fire.

CREON. As you say: It is not my place to challenge a prophet.
TEIRESIAS. Yet you have said my prophecy is for sale.   60
CREON. The generation of prophets has always loved gold.
TEIRESIAS. The generation of kings has always loved brass.
CREON. You forget yourself! You are speaking to your king.
TEIRESIAS. I know it. You are a king because of me.
CREON. You have a certain skill; but you have sold out.   65
TEIRESIAS. King, you will drive me to words that—
CREON.   Say them, say them!
       Only remember: I will not pay you for them.
TEIRESIAS. No, you will find them too costly.
CREON.   No doubt. Speak:
       Whatever you say, you will not change my will.
TEIRESIAS. Then take this, and take it to heart!   70
       The time is not far off when you shall pay back
       Corpse for corpse, flesh of your own flesh.
       You have thrust the child of this world into living night,
       You have kept from the gods below the child that is theirs:
       The one in a grave before her death, the other,   75
       Dead, denied the grave. This is your crime;
       And the Furies° and the dark gods of hell
       Are swift with terrible punishment for you.

       Do you want to buy me now, Creon?
                                   Not many days,
       And your house will be full of men and women weeping,   80
       And curses will be hurled at you from far
       Cities grieving for sons unburied, left to rot
       Before the walls of Thebes.

       These are my arrows, Creon: They are all for you.

       (To BOY) But come, child: Lead me home.   85
       Let him waste his fine anger upon younger men.
       Maybe he will learn at last
       To control a wiser tongue in a better head.   [Exit TEIRESIAS.]

CHORAGOS. The old man has gone, King, but his words
       Remain to plague us. I am old, too,   90
       But I cannot remember that he was ever false.
CREON. That is true . . . It troubles me.
       Oh it is hard to give in! But it is worse
       To risk everything for stubborn pride.
CHORAGOS. Creon: Take my advice.
CREON.   What shall I do?   95
CHORAGOS. Go quickly: free Antigone from her vault
       And build a tomb for the body of Polyneices.
CREON. You would have me do this?

---

77. **Furies:** three winged goddesses who avenge unpunished crimes, especially those that
go against the ties of kinship.

CHORAGOS.   Creon, yes!
    And it must be done at once: God moves
    Swiftly to cancel the folly of stubborn men.   100
CREON. It is hard to deny the heart! But I
    Will do it: I will not fight with destiny.
CHORAGOS. You must go yourself, you cannot leave it to others.
CREON. I will go.
                —Bring axes, servants:
    Come with me to the tomb. I buried her, I   105
    Will set her free.
                Oh quickly!
    My mind misgives—
    The laws of the gods are mighty, and a man must serve them
    To the last day of his life!   [*Exit* CREON.]

Paean *

CHORAGOS. God of many names   [STROPHE 1]
CHORUS.   O Iacchos
                          son
    of Kadmeian Semele°
                          O born of the Thunderer!°
    Guardian of the West
                    Regent
    of Eleusis' plain°
                    O Prince of maenad° Thebes
    and the Dragon Field° by rippling Ismenos:°   5

CHORAGOS. God of many names   [ANTISTROPHE 1]
CHORUS.   the flame of torches
    flares on our hills
                    the nymphs of Iacchos
    dance at the spring of Castalia:°

    from the vine-close mountain
                          come ah come in ivy:
    Evohe evohe!° sings through the streets of Thebes   10

CHORAGOS. God of many names   [STROPHE 2]

---

* **Paean** (pe′ən): a song of praise, in this case to the god Dionysos, in whose honor the
Greeks presented their dramas. In line 1, the god is called **Iacchos** (ē′ə·kəs). 2. **Kadmeian
Semele:** Semele, mother of Dionysos, was the daughter of King Kadmos, founder of Thebes.
the Thunderer: Zeus, father of Dionysos. 4. **Eleusis'** (i·lōō′sis) **plain:** the city of Eleusis was
famed for secret religious rites held in honor of Dionysos. **maenad** (mē′nad): A maenad is a
priestess of Dionysos. Thebes itself is spoken of here as a priestess. 5. **Dragon Field:** King
Kadmos was said to have sown dragon's teeth to grow the race of warriors who populated
Thebes. **Ismenos** (is·mē′nus): a river that flows by Thebes. 8. **Castalia:** a fountain, sacred
to the Muses. 10. *Evohe* (ē·vō′ē): a cry of joy, like an "alleluia," sounded at Dionysian
festivals.

CHORUS.   Iacchos of Thebes
        heavenly child
                of Semele, bride of the Thunderer!
        The shadow of plague is upon us:
                                come
        with clement feet
                oh come from Parnasos°
        down the long slopes
                        across the lamenting water   15

CHORAGOS. Io° Fire! Chorister of the throbbing stars!   [ANTISTROPHE 2]
        O purest among the voices of the night!
        Thou son of God, blaze for us!
CHORUS. Come with choric rapture of circling Maenads
        Who cry *Io Iacche!*
                    God of many names!   20

Exodos *

[*Enter* MESSENGER, *left.*]

MESSENGER. Men of the line of Kadmos, you who live
        Near Amphion's° citadel:
                        I cannot say
        Of any condition of human life "This is fixed,
        This is clearly good, or bad." Fate raises up,
        And fate casts down the happy and unhappy alike: 5
        No man can foretell his fate.
                            Take the case of Creon:
        Creon was happy once, as I count happiness;
        Victorious in battle, sole governor of the land,
        Fortunate father of children nobly born.
        And now it has all gone from him! Who can say   10
        That a man is still alive when his life's joy fails?
        He is a walking dead man. Grant him rich,
        Let him live like a king in his great house:
        If his pleasure is gone, I would not give
        So much as the shadow of smoke for all he owns.   15
CHORAGOS. Your words hint at sorrow; what is your news for us?
MESSENGER. They are dead. The living are guilty of their death.
CHORAGOS. Who is guilty? Who is dead? Speak!
MESSENGER.   Haimon.
        Haimon is dead; and the hand that killed him
        Is his own hand.
CHORAGOS.   His father's? or his own?   20
MESSENGER. His own, driven mad by the murder his father had done.

---

14. **Parnasos:** a mountain, one peak of which was sacred to Dionysos.   16. **Io** (ī′ō): Hail!
* **Exodos:** the final, or exit, scene.   2. **Amphion** (am·fī′on): a former ruler of Thebes.

CHORAGOS. Teiresias, Teiresias, how clearly you saw it all!

MESSENGER. This is my news; you must draw what conclusions you can
    from it.

CHORAGOS. But look: Eurydice, our queen:
    Has she overheard us?   25

        [*Enter* EURYDICE *from the palace, center.*]

EURYDICE. I have heard something, friends:
    As I was unlocking the gate of Pallas'° shrine,
    For I needed her help today, I heard a voice
    Telling of some new sorrow. And I fainted
    There at the temple with all my maidens about me.   30
    But speak again; whatever it is, I can bear it:
    Grief and I are no strangers.°

MESSENGER.   Dearest lady,
    I will tell you plainly all that I have seen.
    I shall not try to comfort you: What is the use,
    Since comfort could lie only in what is not true?   35
    The truth is always best.
                  I went with Creon
    To the outer plain where Polyneices was lying,
    No friend to pity him, his body shredded by dogs.
    We made our prayers in that place to Hecate°
    And Pluto,° that they would be merciful. And we bathed   40
    The corpse with holy water, and we brought
    Fresh-broken branches to burn what was left of it,
    And upon the urn we heaped up a towering barrow
    Of the earth of his own land.
                When we were done, we ran
    To the vault where Antigone lay on her couch of stone.   45
    One of the servants had gone ahead,
    And while he was yet far off he heard a voice
    Grieving within the chamber, and he came back
    And told Creon. And as the king went closer,
    The air was full of wailing, the words lost,   50
    And he begged us to make all haste. "Am I a prophet?"
    He said weeping. "And must I walk this road,
    The saddest of all that I have gone before?
    My son's voice calls me on. Oh quickly, quickly!
    Look through the crevice there, and tell me   55
    If it is Haimon, or some deception of the gods!"

    We obeyed; and in the cavern's farthest corner
    We saw her lying:
    She had made a noose of her fine linen veil
    And hanged herself. Haimon lay beside her,   60
    His arms about her waist, lamenting her,

---

27. **Pallas:** Pallas Athena, goddess of wisdom.   32. **Grief and I...:** Megareus, the older son of Eurydice, had died in the battle for Thebes.   39. **Hecate:** goddess associated with the dead and the underworld.   40. **Pluto:** god of the underworld.

His love lost under ground, crying out
That his father had stolen her away from him.

When Creon saw him the tears rushed to his eyes
And he called to him: "What have you done, child? Speak to me.   65
What are you thinking that makes your eyes so strange?
O my son, my son, I come to you on my knees!"
But Haimon spat in his face. He said not a word,
Staring—
          And suddenly drew his sword
And lunged. Creon shrank back, the blade missed; and the boy,   70
Desperate against himself, drove it half its length
Into his own side and fell. And as he died
He gathered Antigone close in his arms again,
Choking, his blood bright red on her white cheek.
And now he lies dead with the dead, and she is his   75
At last, his bride in the houses of the dead.

[*Exit* EURYDICE *into the palace.*]

CHORAGOS. She has left us without a word. What can this mean?
MESSENGER. It troubles me, too; yet she knows what is best.
      Her grief is too great for public lamentation,
      And doubtless she has gone to her chamber to weep   80
      For her dead son, leading her maidens in his dirge.
CHORAGOS. It may be so; but I fear this deep silence.

[*Pause*]

MESSENGER. I will see what she is doing. I will go in.

[*Exit* MESSENGER *into the palace.*]

[*Enter* CREON *with attendants, bearing* HAIMON's *body.*]

CHORAGOS. But here is the king himself: oh look at him,
      Bearing his own damnation in his arms.   85
CREON. Nothing you say can touch me any more.
      My own blind heart has brought me
      From darkness to final darkness. Here you see
      The father murdering, the murdered son—
      And all my civic wisdom!   90

      Haimon my son, so young, so young to die,
      I was the fool, not you; and you died for me.
CHORAGOS. That is the truth; but you were late in learning it.
CREON. This truth is hard to bear. Surely a god
      Has crushed me beneath the hugest weight of heaven,   95
      And driven me headlong a barbaric way
      To trample out the thing I held most dear.

      The pains that men will take to come to pain!

[*Enter* MESSENGER *from the palace.*]

MESSENGER. The burden you carry in your hands is heavy,
      But it is not all: You will find more in your house.   100

CREON. What burden worse than this shall I find there?

MESSENGER. The queen is dead.

CREON. O port of death, deaf world,
Is there no pity for me? And you, angel of evil,
I was dead, and your words are death again.   105
Is it true, boy? Can it be true?
Is my wife dead? Has death bred death?

MESSENGER. You can see for yourself.

[*The doors are opened, and the body of* EURYDICE *is disclosed within.*]

CREON. Oh pity!
All true, all true, and more than I can bear!   110
O my wife, my son!

MESSENGER. She stood before the altar, and her heart
Welcomed the knife her own hand guided,
And a great cry burst from her lips for Megareus dead,
And for Haimon dead, her sons; and her last breath   115
Was a curse for their father, the murderer of her sons.
And she fell, and the dark flowed in through her closing eyes.

CREON. O God, I am sick with fear.
Are there no swords here? Has no one a blow for me?

MESSENGER. Her curse is upon you for the deaths of both.   120

CREON. It is right that it should be. I alone am guilty.
I know it, and I say it. Lead me in
Quickly, friends.
I have neither life nor substance. Lead me in.

CHORAGOS. You are right, if there can be right in so much wrong.   125
The briefest way is best in a world of sorrow.

CREON. Let it come,
Let death come quickly, and be kind to me.
I would not ever see the sun again.

CHORAGOS. All that will come when it will; but we, meanwhile,   130
Have much to do. Leave the future to itself.

CREON. All my heart was in that prayer!

CHORAGOS. Then do not pray any more: the sky is deaf.

CREON. Lead me away. I have been rash and foolish.
I have killed my son and my wife.   135
I look for comfort; my comfort lies here dead.
Whatever my hands have touched has come to nothing.
Fate has brought all my pride to a thought of dust.

[*As* CREON *is being led into the house, the* CHORAGOS *advances and speaks directly to the audience.*]

CHORAGOS. There is no happiness where there is no wisdom;
No wisdom but in submission to the gods.   140
Big words are always punished,
And proud men in old age learn to be wise.

PROLOGUE AND PARADOS

1. In the Prologue, what is revealed of Antigone's character? How is she contrasted to Ismene? What conflicts set them apart from one another? Explain especially the conflict between two kinds of law. What lines refer to this conflict?

2. What expectations for the future of the city of Thebes are expressed by the citizens who, as the Chorus in the Parados, recount the recent victory? How does their attitude contrast with the premonitions of Antigone and Ismene in the Prologue? What images are used in the Parados to describe the battle to the audience?

SCENE I AND ODE I

1. How does Creon justify his decision that the body of Polyneices must lie unburied? Do you believe that the Chorus is convinced he is acting rightly? Explain. What light is thrown on Creon's character, in the course of Scene I? What distinguishes his reaction to the news brought by the sentry from the reaction of the Chorus?

2. What portrait of man emerges in the Ode? What limit is set to man's mastery of all things? What place does law have in the life of man? Compare and contrast Ode I with Psalm 8 (see page 30).

SCENE II AND ODE II

1. Find the lines that reveal the sentry's attitude toward the important events he has become involved in. How do the sentry's reactions add to the force of the play?

2. How does Creon seek to justify his actions? How does Antigone justify hers? To what extent do you agree with Antigone's suggestion that Creon may actually be a fool? What attitude to Creon appears to lie behind the cautious remarks of the Choragos?

3. In Ode II, the Chorus expresses grave forebodings, without mentioning any name but that of Oedipus. How has the "anger of heaven" struck Oedipus' house? What does the Chorus mean by saying that "Man's little pleasure is the spring of sorrow" (line 28)?

SCENE III AND ODE III

1. What may Creon's lengthy self-justification indicate about his feelings? What view of authority does Haimon urge on his father? At one point Creon cries "The state is the King!"

What does Haimon answer? What does this answer mean? What, in your opinion, motivates Creon's change of plan, at the end of the scene?

2. Does the Chorus, in Ode III, consider Haimon's attitude to be carefully thought out or to be based mainly on emotion? Explain. What, according to the Chorus, is the power of love, and what, or whose, purpose does it serve? How does Ode III contrast with and complement Ode I?

SCENE IV AND ODE IV

1. What lines in this scene foreshadow future developments?

2. How does the Chorus, in Scene IV and especially in Ode IV, succeed in discovering a sort of glory in Antigone's fate, treating it as godlike rather than as the lot of a human being? Do you think that any of Antigone's own words, throughout the play, suggest that she has been partly motivated by thoughts of future glory? Consider in particular her words in Scene IV and her words to Ismene in the Prologue and Scene II.

SCENE V, PAEAN, AND EXODOS

1. Teiresias tells Creon that the "only crime is pride." How does Creon show that he is indeed guilty of this? In Ode II (line 20) the Chorus suggests that Antigone, too, is guilty of pride. In what ways might this be true? Could Creon's treatment of Teiresias be considered an offense to the gods? Explain. What finally persuades Creon to reverse his position?

2. Try to account for the insertion, and the actual contents, of the Paean at this point in the play.

3. The last words of the play (lines 139–42), uttered by the Choragos, express one of its major themes. Find at least five other lines throughout the play that also refer to this theme.

GENERAL

1. *Antigone* has been read, acted, and admired for more than two thousand years. What features of the play do you think appeal most strongly to audiences today?

2. Antigone was determined to risk death to insure the eternal rest of her dead brother. What character in the *Iliad* exhibits this same determination for the same reason?

3. *Antigone*, which presents a sympathetic picture of an individual who defies the law of

the king for the sake of family and religious obligations, was highly regarded by both rulers and common people in its own day. What does this reveal about the way the Athenians of the fifth century B.C. felt about the ties of family and the unrecorded laws of God? Find passages in Pericles' funeral oration (page 126) that discuss recorded and unrecorded law.

4. In the *Apology* (page 132), Socrates says "The difficulty, my friends, is not to avoid death, but to avoid unrighteousness; for that runs faster than death." How does this statement apply to *Antigone?* What other attitudes expressed in the *Apology* can be applied to *Antigone?*

TRAGEDY AND THE TRAGIC HERO

As the philosopher Aristotle observed in his *Poetics,* Greek tragedy is concerned with imitating some tragic, realistic action that will arouse pity and fear in the viewer and so purge him of an accumulation of upsetting emotions. This is the purpose of tragedy, this emotional purging or cleansing of the viewer, and the catharsis, as it is called, brings a kind of pleasure. Aristotle also observes how fear and pity may be aroused:

●Fear and pity may be aroused by spectacular means; but they may also result from the inner structure of the piece, which is the better way, and indicates a superior poet. For the plot ought to be so constructed that, even without the aid of the eye, he who hears the tale told will thrill with horror and melt to pity at what takes place. This is the impression we should receive from hearing the story of the *Oedipus.* But to produce this effect by the mere spectacle is a less artistic method, and dependent on extraneous aids. Those who employ spectacular means to create a sense not of the terrible but only of the monstrous are strangers to the purpose of tragedy; for we must not demand of tragedy any and every kind of pleasure, but only that which is proper to it. And since the pleasure which the poet should afford is that which comes from pity and fear through imitation, it is evident that this quality must be impressed upon the incidents.

Let us then determine what are the cir-

cumstances which strike us as terrible or pitiful.

Actions capable of this effect must happen between persons who are either friends or enemies or indifferent to one another. If an enemy kills an enemy, there is nothing to excite pity either in the act or the intention—except so far as the suffering in itself is pitiful. So again with indifferent persons. But when the tragic incident occurs between those who are near or dear to one another— if, for example, a brother kills, or intends to kill, a brother, a son his father, a mother her son, a son his mother, or any other deed of the kind is done—these are the situations to be looked for by the poet. He may not indeed destroy the framework of the received legends—the fact, for instance, that Clytemnestra was slain by Orestes and Eriphyle by Alcmaeon—but he ought to show invention of his own and skillfully handle the traditional material.—ARISTOTLE

1. Does *Antigone* arouse terror and pity through spectacular visual means? How are the violent events that take place in the play made known to the audience? Is this method effective? Why?

2. How is violence handled in contemporary drama, in TV, in movies, on stage? Which method of handling spectacle do you feel is most effective? What is the purpose of violent spectacle in contemporary dramatic forms? Do you agree with Aristotle about the purpose of spectacle in the Greek tragedies? If not, what do you think its purpose is?

The hero of a Greek tragedy, observed Aristotle, is neither completely virtuous nor utterly villainous, but has "a character between these two extremes—that of a man [or a woman] who is not preeminently good and just, yet whose misfortune is brought about not by vice or depravity, but by some error of judgment or frailty." The tragic hero (or heroine) is "one who is highly renowned or prosperous," so that his fall from good fortune will be great enough to arouse the audience's emotions. In *Antigone,* it is not easy to decide who is the tragic hero. Traditionally, the role has been assigned to Antigone herself. Some critics argue, however, that Creon is the real tragic hero and that his role is the more dramatic.

3. In deciding who is truly the tragic hero or heroine in *Antigone,* you should first consider whether the play is constructed to arouse

From Book XIV of the *Poetics* by Aristotle, translated by Benjamin Jowett.

greater pity or terror for Antigone's situation or for Creon's. About which of the two can it be said that his (or her) misfortune is brought about by some error or frailty? If the frailty in character is one of pride, who suffers more acutely as a result of it—Creon or Antigone? When you have finished the play, which character has aroused greater emotions in you? On which character is your pity focused?

4. The noted classical scholar H. D. F. Kitto has suggested that *Antigone* is built on a "double foundation," and that the play's "center of gravity does not lie in one person, but between two." But Kitto also observes that "of the two, the significant one to Sophocles was always Creon." Do you agree or disagree? Support your answer with specific references to the play.

5. Think of at least four contemporary dramatic works you have seen recently, either on TV, in the movies, or on the stage, two of which you would classify as tragic, and two as comic. How is the hero's world and his relationship to it portrayed in *Antigone* and in the other works you have classified as tragic? in those you have classified as comic? How do the plots of the tragedies differ from those of the comedies? Is the misfortune in the tragic works caused by some error or frailty in the hero, as in *Antigone?* If not, what is the cause of the misfortune?

FOR COMPOSITION

1. The last four lines, spoken by the Choragos, embody a principal theme of the play:

> There is no happiness where there is no wisdom;
> No wisdom but in submission to the gods.
> Big words are always punished,
> And proud men in old age learn to be wise.

Write a composition discussing how these lines may be applied to Antigone; to Creon; to the Chorus itself. Is the viewpoint they express reflected in any of the other Greek works you have read in this unit? Explain, giving specific references.

2. American drama critic Walter Kerr has called *Antigone* "a battle of hopelessly locked horns." The conflict between human law, enacted to create order in society, and divine law, as interpreted by the individual conscience, has recurred throughout history. Present in a composition an example of this conflict, taken from literature, movies, history, or current events. How does *Antigone* deepen your understanding of this conflict?

ROMAN LITERATURE

c. 100 B.C. – c. A.D. 180

T HE ROMANS are credited with a lesser gift for literature and the arts than was possessed by the Greeks, but are held to have outranked the Greeks by far in such practical achievements as soldiering and road-building, and as organizers and administrators of an empire. Yet, in the construction of that highly practical, "consumer-oriented" literary work called the national legend, the Romans exhibited an amazing skill. Even today we cannot overlook Rome's legendary history, for little solid information has come down to us about the earliest centuries of Rome's existence.

THE BEGINNINGS OF ROME

The fantastic elements in Rome's national legend are placed, naturally, at the remotest point in time. While they are most notably presented in Virgil's great epic poem, the *Aeneid,* other authors had preceded Virgil (70 B.C.–19 B.C.) in the task of national self-glorification, and it is probable that by the third century B.C. these legends were widely believed. They played their part, consequently, in filling Roman citizens with the ambitions, the drive, and the persistence that would make a reality of Rome's "manifest destiny." Rome, by Virgil's time, in the final years of the last century B.C., had become the most impressive empire of antiquity.

In order to attribute to themselves the noblest possible beginning, the Romans turned to those revered literary works of Greece, the *Iliad* (see page 52) and the *Odyssey* of Homer. For their own purposes, the Romans added details that had no counterpart in Homer. They related a story about Aeneas, a son-in-law of King Priam of Troy. Aeneas' father was a Trojan prince; his mother was the goddess Venus. Aeneas fled from the flaming ruins of Troy carrying his aged father on his back and leading his small son

Romans made this Etruscan statue of a she-wolf their emblem. In Roman legend, such a wolf nursed Romulus and Remus. (The boys were added in the Renaissance.)

by the hand. His divinely appointed task was to establish a remnant of the Trojan people on Italian soil, and so plant a seed—this is Virgil's vision of things—that would grow into the huge spreading oak of the Roman Empire.

Before reaching Italy, Aeneas landed on the African shore near Carthage, where he visited Queen Dido and won her love. But duty compelled him to abandon her and push on to Italy. She, in despair, committed suicide. Aeneas saw Dido again when he was taken alive to visit his father in Hades. Here, however, the ghost of Dido turned away from him, eternally irreconcilable. This is the fanciful background which legend provided for the very real struggle to the death that opposed Rome and Carthage toward the end of the third century B.C.

Shortly after Virgil wrote his epic, a Greek writer named Plutarch (A.D. 46?–A.D. 120?), who lived for a time in Rome, presented some of the conflicting views concerning the naming of the city. Here is one of the popular stories.

● Those very authors, too, who, in accordance with the safest account, make Romulus give the name of the city, yet differ concerning his birth and family. For some say he was son to Aeneas and Dexithea, daughter of Phorbas, and was, with his brother Remus, in their infancy, carried into Italy, and being on the river when the waters came down in a flood,

From Plutarch, the Dryden translation, from *Great Books of the Western World*. Reprinted by permission of Encyclopaedia Britannica.

all the vessels were cast away, except only that where the young children were, which being gently landed on a level bank of the river, they were both unexpectedly saved, and from them the place was called Rome.—PLUTARCH

Legend even fixes the exact time and date when Romulus later established his settlement: April 27, 753 B.C., at about 8:00 A.M.

What of the real events? Compared with the lands of the eastern Mediterranean, the Italian peninsula had long remained a backward area, of little interest to outsiders. Various Greek cities, as we have seen, established flourishing colonies in southern Italy and Sicily. On the mainland, the most substantial group was formed by the confederated cities of the Etruscans, who inhabited a region in central Italy. They achieved a rather high level of civilization and were skilled in metal-working, art, and architecture. Their language remains entirely mysterious.

The Eternal City began, probably by the eighth century B.C., as an unimpressive settlement on the east bank of the Tiber, facing the superior power of the Etruscans on the farther bank. The settlement grew, and its first seven rulers—again we have only tradition to rely on—were kings. The fifth and seventh of these, and perhaps the sixth also, were not Romans but Etruscans. In the sixth century B.C., the Romans expelled their Etruscan king, Tarquin, to set up a republican government. Tarquin more than once attempted to regain his throne, but the Romans fought bitterly for their freedom. At length, Tarquin allied himself with another Etruscan noble, and together they marched with their armies on Rome. Livy (59 B.C.–A.D. 17), the Roman historian, retells the legend of how the Romans foiled this formidable Etruscan attack.

When the enemy appeared, the Romans all, with one accord, withdrew from their fields into the city, which they surrounded with guards. Some parts appeared to be rendered safe by their walls, others by the barrier formed by the river Tiber. The bridge of piles almost afforded an entrance to the enemy, had it not been for one man, Horatius Cocles; he was the bulwark of defense on which that day depended the fortune of the city of Rome. He chanced to be on guard at the bridge when Janiculum was captured by a sudden attack of the enemy. He saw them as they charged down on the run from Janiculum, while his own people behaved like a frightened mob, throwing away their arms and quitting their ranks. Catching hold first of one and then of another, blocking their way and conjuring them to listen, he called on gods and men to witness that if they forsook their post it was vain to flee; once they had left a passage in their rear by the bridge, there would soon be more of the enemy on the Palatine and the Capitol than on Janiculum. He therefore warned and commanded them to break down the bridge with steel,

From "Horatius at the Bridge" from *Roman History Book II* by Livy, translated by B. O. Foster. Reprinted by permission of Harvard University Press and Loeb Classical Library.

with fire, with any instrument at their disposal; and promised that he would himself receive the onset of the enemy, so far as it could be withstood by a single body. Then, striding to the head of the bridge, conspicuous among the fugitives who were clearly seen to be shirking the fight, he covered himself with his sword and buckler and made ready to do battle at close quarters, confounding the Etruscans with amazement at his audacity. Yet were there two who were prevented by shame from leaving him. These were Spurius Larcius and Titus Herminius, both famous for their birth and their deeds. With these he endured the peril of the first rush and the stormiest moment of the battle. But after a while he forced even these two to leave him and save themselves, for there was scarcely anything left of the bridge, and those who were cutting it down called to them to come back. Then, darting glances of defiance around at the Etruscan nobles, he now challenged them in turn to fight, now railed at them collectively as slaves of haughty kings, who, heedless of their own liberty, were come to overthrow the liberty of others. They hesitated for a moment, each looking to his neighbor to begin the fight. Then shame made them attack, and with a shout they cast their javelins from every side against their solitary foe. But he caught them all upon his shield and, resolute as ever, bestrode the bridge and held his ground; and now they were trying to dislodge him by a charge, when the crash of the falling bridge and the cheer which burst from the throats of the Romans, exulting in the completion of their task, checked them in mid-career with a sudden dismay. Then Cocles cried, "O Father Tiberinus, I solemnly invoke thee; receive these arms and this soldier with propitious stream!" So praying, all armed as he was, he leaped down into the river, and under a shower of missiles swam across unhurt to his fellows, having given proof of valor which was destined to obtain more fame than credence with posterity. The state was grateful for so brave a deed; a statue of Cocles was set up in the comitium, and he was given as much land as he could plow around in one day. Private citizens showed their gratitude in a striking fashion, in the midst of his official honors, for notwithstanding their great distress, everybody made him some gift proportionate to his means, though he robbed himself of his own ration.

—LIVY

We may surmise that the Etruscans for a time had exercised a degree of domination over Rome that the Romans felt too ashamed to admit. The Romans acquired, at all events, a lasting hatred of the office and title of king. The assassination of Julius Caesar, many centuries later, was motivated in part by the conviction that he intended to make himself king.

THE REPUBLIC

Having rid themselves of the last of the Etruscan kings, the Romans established a republic in 509 B.C. It lasted until 27 B.C. Its history was a long tale of territorial expansion, with astonishingly few major setbacks or catastrophes on the way—though the Gauls did occupy the city at least once, in 390 B.C. In seeking to explain Roman history after this event, we must attribute to the Romans a greater realism and more grinding persistence than was possessed by any of their rivals. By 272 B.C., all Italy south of the Rubicon was in Roman hands, and by 27 B.C. Rome controlled the entire Mediterranean region. Outside Italy, Roman armies had to wage three tough and lengthy wars, known as the Punic Wars, before at last, in 146 B.C., their rival city of Carthage was utterly destroyed.

The internal history of Rome, for two centuries, was characterized by constant struggle between the patricians, members of old aristocratic Roman families, who at first kept all public offices for themselves, and the plebeians (from the Latin *plebs,* "common people"), the descendants of later settlers. The plebeians, who at one time threatened to found a city of their own, gradually gained an increasing share in the exercise of power, and in 300 B.C. the last restriction against them was removed. However, a new "class" distinction arose, that between the families (both plebeian and patrician) whose members monopolized political offices and those whose members were excluded.

The clash of patrician and plebeian had one important, far-reaching effect on the concept and practice of law. In view of the patricians' tendency to go back on oral agreements that had been reached after long, bitter dispute, the plebeians demanded that the laws be recorded. This was done in 451 B.C.–450 B.C., and the resulting first code of Roman law was chiseled in the marble of the Twelve Tablets. This was the beginning of a process that led eventually to the much more ambitious codification of Roman law in the sixth century A.D. This code is still the basis of the legal system in many European countries (and also in Louisiana, a former French colony).

Roman conquests, especially following the Punic Wars, brought about vast and unforeseeable changes in society. The sturdy republican freeman and small farmer began to find the conditions of his livelihood undermined and sometimes, under a heavy burden of debt, he sank into slavery. He could not compete with the cheap, large-scale production of grain, which was achieved in huge new estates with the use of slave labor. Many ruined farmers flocked to the city of Rome to find jobs. These unemployed were called the proletariat. (The word comes from *proles,* "offspring," and the suggestion is that the propertyless individuals served the state only by breeding.) By the time of the empire, the government was keeping this populace quiet by providing them with free grain and free entertainment—sensational, bloody contests involving men and animals.

The last years of the republic were also beset by especially serious political problems, for which a solution was sought in no fewer than four civil wars. The Roman Republic was governed by a system which included a senate, appointed for life, and two consuls—the chief executives—elected for one-year terms. Voting rights could be exercised by any citizen, but only in Rome itself. These methods of government, which had proved adequate for a small city, did not match the needs of a growing colossus. A constant struggle for power on the part of the senatorial and military leaders brought on the wars, marked by terrorism and bloodshed.

Meanwhile, as Roman armies pushed ever farther from home, the citizen-soldiers were replaced by full-time professional troops, loyal primarily to their commander, to the man they knew, rather than to the state, which was for them only a hazy abstraction. Far from home, an army commander could make major decisions entirely on his own and could transfer enormous wealth to his own pockets. And he could dream even vaster dreams of personal power. By far the most successful of these army commanders was Julius Caesar (102 B.C.–44 B.C.). His astounding successes as a military leader and statesman set his seal on the world and are not likely to be forgotten. Caesar established Roman military domination in the west, his armies going even so far as England. To build up popularity at home he recorded his victories in admirably sober narratives and sent them as bulletins back to Rome. Caesar's seeming modesty in referring to himself in the third person, and his apparent objectivity, put his actions in the best possible light. The following is his account of his first expedition to Britain.

> ● These matters being arranged and finding the weather favorable for his voyage, he set sail about the third watch and ordered the cavalry to march forward to the farther port and there embark and follow him. As they performed this rather tardily, he himself reached Britain with the first squadron of ships, about the fourth hour of the day, and there saw the forces of the enemy drawn up in arms on all the hills. The nature of the place was this: The sea was bounded by mountains so close to it that a javelin could be thrown from their summits upon the shore. Considering this by no means a fit place for disembarking, he remained at anchor till the ninth hour, for the other ships to arrive there. Having in the meantime assembled the lieutenants and military tribunes, he told them both what he had learned from Volusenus and what he wished to be done, and enjoined them (as the principle of military matters and especially maritime affairs, which have a quick and uncertain action, required) to perform everything at a nod and at the instant. He dismissed them, and meeting with favorable wind and tide at the same time, he gave the signal, the anchor was weighed, and he advanced about seven miles from that place and stationed his fleet near an open and level shore.
>
> But the natives, seeing the plan of the Romans, sent forward their cavalry and charioteers, a class of warriors of whom it is their practice to make great use in battle, and following with the rest of their

From "First Expedition to Britain," from *Gallic Wars* by Julius Caesar, translated by Eugene Burdock. Reprinted by permission of Barnes & Noble, Inc.

A Roman war galley, loaded with infantry on the top deck. Most of Rome's ships were rowed by slaves, which left the soldiers fresh and with an advantage over the enemy's tired crew. Note the crocodile on the prow.

forces, endeavored to prevent our men from landing. The latter found this very difficult because our ships, on account of their great size, could be stationed only in deep water, and our soldiers, in places unknown to them, with their hands full and oppressed with a large and heavy weight of armor, had at the same time to leap from the ships, stand amid the waves, and encounter the enemy; whereas the enemy, either on dry ground or advancing a little way into the water, free in all their limbs, in places thoroughly familiar, could confidently throw their weapons and spur on their horses, which were accustomed to this kind of service. Dismayed by these circumstances and altogether untrained in this mode of battle, our men did not all exert the same vigor and eagerness which they had been wont to exert in engagements on dry ground.

When Caesar observed this, he ordered the ships of war, the appearance of which was somewhat strange to the barbarians and whose handling was quicker, to be withdrawn a little from the transport vessels, rowed ahead, and stationed toward the open flank of the enemy, whereupon the enemy were to be beaten off and driven away, with slings, arrows, and engines; this plan was of great service to our men, for the barbarians, startled by the form of our ships and the motions of our oars and the nature of our artillery, which was strange to them, stopped and shortly after retreated a little. And while our men were hesitating, chiefly because of the depth of the sea, the man who carried the standard of the tenth legion, after praying to the gods that the matter might turn out favorably to the legion, shouted, "Leap down, fellow soldiers, unless you wish to betray your eagle to the enemy. I, for my part, will have done my duty to my country and general." When he had said this in a loud voice, he leaped from the ship and proceeded to bear the eagle toward the enemy. Then our men, encouraging one another not to incur so great a disgrace, all leaped from the ship. When those in the nearest vessels saw them, they speedily followed and approached the enemy.

The battle was vigorously fought on both sides. Our men, however, as they could neither keep their ranks, get firm footing, nor follow their standards, and as men from different ships rallied around whatever standards they met, were thrown into great confusion. But the enemy were acquainted with all the shoals and when from the shore they saw a few coming from a ship one by one, they spurred on their horses and attacked them while embarrassed, many of the enemy surrounding a few of our men while others threw their weapons upon our collected forces on their exposed flank. When Caesar observed this, he ordered the warships' boats and the spy-boats to be filled with soldiers, and sent them up to the aid of those whom he had observed in distress. Our men, as soon as they got good footing on dry ground and all their comrades had joined them, made an attack upon the enemy and put them to flight but could not pursue them very far, because the cavalry had not been able to maintain their course at sea and reach the island. This alone was lacking to Caesar's accustomed success.—JULIUS CAESAR

Soaring ambitions to seize control of Rome, which was torn by riots and fighting, forced two army commanders into a head-on collision—Pompey, who commanded in the east, against Caesar, who commanded in the west. The victor in this power struggle was Julius Caesar, who defeated Pompey in 45 B.C. Caesar became dictator for life—but he did not grow old in office. On the Ides of March, March 15, 44 B.C., he was assassinated by a conspiracy of senators who disliked his reforms and feared his power. The leaders of the conspiracy, Brutus and Cassius, found it advisable to flee from Rome. Defeated in battle in 42 B.C., they committed suicide shortly afterward. The victors and new heirs to power were Mark Antony and Octavian, Julius Caesar's grandnephew and adopted son. But these victors promptly fell out with each other, and there ensued more years of civil war. Antony set himself up in the east, where he succumbed to the charms of Queen Cleopatra of Egypt. Octavian defeated their navy in 31 B.C., and Antony and Cleopatra, in the following year, committed suicide and left Octavian in undisputed control.

THE EMPIRE

Octavian scrupulously maintained the *forms* of republican rule but concentrated all power in his own hands by having himself appointed to one office after another. The Roman Empire was born in 27 B.C., when Octavian was given the name Augustus (meaning "of good omen") and the title Imperator. Originally, this title meant nothing more than "leader," but as it was used by Augustus' successors, it gave rise to the English word *emperor* and to related words in other modern languages. The month of August was named after Augustus, just as July had already been named after Julius Caesar. Every precinct of the city had a shrine dedicated jointly to Rome and to Augustus. Augustus' long and just reign ended with his death in A.D. 14.

While there were periods of sound rule under later effective and conscientious emperors, one basic problem was never solved and so led to countless other problems. This was the problem of orderly succession. Rome had become a monarchy in effect, but not in name and never by acknowledgment. Consequently, no standard, universally recognized method of designating a new ruler could even be proposed. The struggle to reach the top inevitably led to rivalries, plots, and assassinations. These produced harrowing results and deplorable emperors in the forty years following the death of Augustus. The next four emperors were Tiberius, Caligula, Claudius, and Nero. It has been said that an arch-deceiver was succeeded by a madman, and a fool by a monster. Some of the worst men ever to rule anywhere came during these years to have power of life and death over many millions of human beings.

An account of these times was written, from a chronologically safe vantage point, by Suetonius (c. A.D. 69–c. A.D. 140). It is impossible to distinguish, in what he relates, the ghastly truth from malevolent gossip. The subject of the following passage is the Emperor Claudius (10 B.C.– A.D. 54).

> ● He gave frequent and grand dinner parties, as a rule in spacious places, where six hundred guests were often entertained at one time. He even gave a banquet close to the outlet of the Fucine Lake and was well-nigh drowned when the water was let out with a rush and deluged the place. He always invited his own children to dinner along with the sons and daughters of distinguished men, having them sit at the arms of the couches as they ate, after the old-time custom. When a guest was suspected of having stolen a golden bowl the day before, he invited him again the next day, but set before him an earthenware cup.
>
> He was eager for food and drink at all times and in all places. Once when he was holding court in the forum of Augustus and had caught the savor of a meal which was preparing for the Salii in the temple of Mars hard by, he left the tribunal, went up where the priests were, and took his place at their table. He hardly ever left the dining room until he was stuffed and soaked; then he went to sleep at once, lying on his back with his mouth open, and a feather was put down his throat to

From "The Emperor Claudius" from *The Lives of the Caesars* by Suetonius, translated by J. C. Rolfe. Reprinted by permission of The Loeb Classical Library and Harvard University Press.

relieve his stomach. He slept but a little at a time, for he was usually awake before midnight; but he would sometimes drop off in the daytime while holding court and could hardly be roused when the advocates raised their voices for the purpose. . . . He was greatly devoted to gaming, even publishing a book on the art, and he actually used to play while driving, having the board so fitted to his carriage as to prevent his game from being disturbed.

That he was of a cruel and bloodthirsty disposition was shown in matters great and small. He always exacted examination by torture and the punishment of parricides at once and in his presence. When he was at Tibur and wished to see an execution in the ancient fashion, no executioner could be found after the criminals were bound to the stake. Whereupon he sent to fetch one from the city and continued to wait for him until nightfall. At any gladiatorial show, either his own or another's, he gave orders that even those who fell accidentally should be slain, in particular the net-fighters, so that he could watch their faces as they died. When a pair of gladiators had fallen by mutually inflicted wounds, he at once had some little knives made from both their swords for his use. He took such pleasure in the combats with wild beasts and of those that fought at noonday that he would go down to the arena at daybreak, and after dismissing the people for luncheon at midday, he would keep his seat and, in addition to the appointed combatants, he would for trivial and hasty reasons match others, even of the carpenters, the assistants, and men of that class, if any automatic device or pageant or anything else of the kind had not worked well. He even forced one of his pages to enter the arena just as he was, in his toga. . . .

No suspicion was too trivial, nor the inspirer of it too insignificant, to drive him on to precaution and vengeance, once a slight uneasiness entered his mind. One of two parties to a suit, when he made his morning call, took Claudius aside, and said that he had dreamed that he was murdered by someone; then a little later, pretending to recognize the assassin, he pointed out his opponent, as he was handing his petition. The latter was immediately seized, as if caught red-handed, and hurried off to execution. It was in a similar way, they say, that Appius Silanus met his downfall. When Messalina and Narcissus had put their heads together to destroy him, they agreed on their parts and the latter rushed into his patron's bedchamber before daybreak in pretended consternation, declaring that he had dreamed that Appius had made an attack on the emperor. Then Messalina, with assumed surprise, declared that she had had the same dream for several successive nights. A little later, as had been arranged, Appius, who had received orders the day before to come at that time, was reported to be forcing his way in, and as if this were proof positive of the truth of the dream, his immediate accusation and death were ordered. And Claudius did not hesitate to recount the whole affair to the senate next day and to thank the freedman for watching over his emperor's safety even in his sleep.—SUETONIUS

Historically, our knowledge of Rome's later collapse leads us to search for seeds of decay even in the empire's most flourishing years. While we do this, we should not forget that in the second century A.D. the line of Good Emperors spread peace throughout the empire. Rome strengthened her grip on the outlying regions, acted to ensure law and order at home, improved communications, and fostered commerce and industry.

Nevertheless, the empire began slowly to disintegrate and decay. Politically, its structure became obsolete. It was too large and unwieldly, and poor supervision resulted in corruption and inefficiency. Rome became a city of the very rich and the very poor. The rich entertained in exotic villas, with gourmet dinners of nightingale tongues costing ten thousand dollars and more, while the poor were supported by the state and kept docile with public spectacles of violence. These bloody fights to the death in the arenas took place between men and beasts, or, worse, between condemned criminals or war prisoners. The family, long the backbone of Roman life, began to break up as divorce became more common. Sexual mores became lax, manners declined, and manliness and self-respect were lost as politicians and writers rendered servile flattery to the emperor and his court.

Since literature is our central concern, it is not necessary to trace in more detail the slow decline of Rome, which the English historian Edward Gibbon made the subject of a book, *The Decline and Fall of the Roman Empire*. Latin works of pagan Rome which were written after the second century A.D. have not come, in most instances, to occupy a prominent place in world literature.

The date usually given for the end of the Roman Empire is A.D. 476, the year when a barbarian-mercenary in the Roman army seized rule of Italy.

Urban problems, first century A.D. This marble relief shows a city in Italy. On the left, crowded inside the city walls, are the tenements of the poor. In the suburbs to the right sprawl the spacious villas of the rich.

This date refers to the end of the empire of the west, with Rome as its capital. (The empire before this had split into two parts, east and west.) The empire of the east, or the Byzantine Empire, continued in existence until 1453, when the invading Turks brought about its collapse by seizing its capital, Constantinople, today the Turkish city of Istanbul.

What must be stressed is not this ending of the Roman Empire in time, but the extraordinary degree to which Rome, as a concept, as a glorious past, and almost, it might be said, as a state, did survive or leap across the centuries of chaos and cultural decline that were to afflict western Europe. The Roman roads survived and were not matched by new roads of equal excellence until the eighteenth century. Roman law, creatively adapted, left its indelible mark. Yet, extending far beyond these or any other aspects of administration and statehood, the idea and ideal of Roman unity lived on in men's minds. Thus Charlemagne, the powerful king of the Franks, had himself consecrated "Emperor of the Romans" in the presence of Pope Leo III in the year A.D. 800. In A.D. 962 the Holy Roman Empire was born, when Otto the Great of Saxony was crowned Roman Emperor by Pope John XII. The Holy Roman Empire maintained its shadowy existence until 1806. Yet in 1804 Napoleon, in a ceremony that deliberately echoed the coronation of Charlemagne 1,004 years before, snatched the crown from the Pope's hands and crowned himself "Emperor of the French."

This was not all. Unlike the pale unreality of the Holy Roman Empire, which was ultimately extinguished, the institution known as the Roman Catholic Church has led across the centuries, and continues to lead, a vigorous existence. The Christian Church became the official church of the Roman Empire in A.D. 380. By embodying the principle of the unity of Christendom, the Church for a long time offered to the peoples of Europe the only appeal to unity transcending regional and national barriers.

ROMAN RELIGION

The earliest gods of Rome were associated with its rural existence: rain, crops, and so forth. As the modest village on the Tiber pushed beyond its original narrow boundaries, incorporating new territories and larger populations, these rural deities took on functions more in keeping with the requirements of an aggressive, expansion-minded state. Two of the major gods, during the early period of this state religion, were Jupiter and Mars. Jupiter had originally been the spirit of the sky, and Mars was at first the spirit associated with both agriculture and war. The month of March, the first month of the year until Julius Caesar reformed the calendar, became Mars' month. When Greek cultural influences exerted themselves, parallels were established between the Greek and Roman gods, as between Jupiter and Zeus, Mars and Ares. This pairing obscures the marked dissimilarities

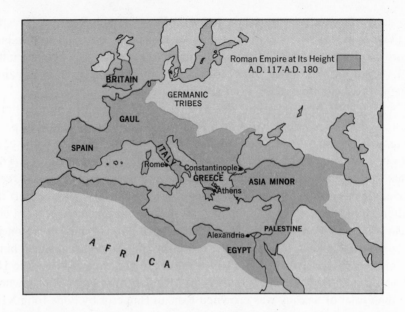

in the religious outlook of the two peoples. Roman religion, in official hands, grew increasingly formal and ritualistic. Within this framework, dogma, personal belief, and individual fervor counted for little. What mattered was observance of the externals. It is interesting to note, too, that originally the Romans had not told stories about the gods: they had no mythology. They had worshiped awesome, shadowy "spirits" that dwelt in trees or rocks or in localities—spirits of the earth, not of the heavens. Mythology is a later importation from Greece, and the Roman contribution to mythology, coming even later, seldom penetrates below the level of frivolous, charming, or sentimental fiction.

Rome's early appropriation of the gods for official purposes left unsatisfied the religious urges latent in any community. Nor did the traditional family religious practices—worship of the household gods called the lares and penates—answer this need. This is shown by the fact that, from an early date in the history of the republic, cults were imported from abroad: the cult of the fertility goddess Isis from Egypt, for example, and that of the sun god Mithras from Persia. (The latter cult found many devotees among Roman legionaries.) These unofficial cults are known as mystery religions. They promised, often through conflicting practices, both an escape from suffering and eventual individual salvation—concerns remote indeed from the aims of the official religious practices.

Promises of release from anxiety were also made by the various philosophical "schools" in the last century of the republic. The Epicureans said that the object of life is to seek pleasure and avoid pain. But the Stoics disagreed. They said that the object of life is to seek tranquillity and that tranquillity can be achieved through moderation in all things. Marcus Aurelius (A.D. 121–A.D. 180) wrote a series of now-famous *Meditations* on Stoicism. It should be borne in mind that Marcus Aurelius, though the Roman emperor, wrote his *Meditations* in Greek, which, in itself, no doubt pointed to a lessening of Roman self-confidence. A philosopher of distinction, Aurelius was one of the very few men in history to attain the position of philosopher-king. In the view of the historian Edward Gibbon, his reign is "the only period of history in which the happiness of a great people was the sole object of government." From this earthly happiness Aurelius took care to exclude all Christians, however. He regarded them as menacing subversives, fit only to be persecuted and killed. Here are two of his meditations.

> ● Every moment think steadily, as a Roman and as a man, to do what thou hast in hand with perfect and simple dignity and feeling of affection and freedom and justice, and to give thyself relief from all other thoughts. And thou wilt give thyself relief, if thou doest every act of thy life as if it were the last, laying aside all carelessness and passionate aversion from the commands of reason, and all hypocrisy and self-love and discontent with the portion which has been given to thee. Thou seest how few the things are which, if a man lays hold of, he is able to live a life which flows in quiet and is like the existence of the gods; for the gods on their part will require nothing from him who observes these things.
>
> How small a part of the boundless and unfathomable time is assigned to every man! For it is very soon swallowed up in the eternal. And how small a part of the whole substance! And how small a part of the universal soul! And on what a small clod of the whole earth thou creepest! Reflecting on all this, consider nothing to be great, except to act as thy nature leads thee and to endure that which the common nature brings.—MARCUS AURELIUS

This hodgepodge of religious cults and philosophies, one often contradicting another, along with the political and social instability of the times, could produce tension and uncertainties about existence that might overwhelm anyone. A Roman could well feel that his inner world and the world around him were chaotic and menaced. As we now know, the great new hope came to the individual and to the multitudes neither from Isis, nor from Mithras, nor from any of the rational philosophies, but from the Christian religion.

LATIN LITERATURE

Like all peoples at the preliterate stage, the Romans of the young republic had developed an oral literature. But whatever chants or ballads may have been composed or listened to, little is known about them, and there is

From the *Meditations of Marcus Aurelius,* translated by George Long.

no evidence that the Romans were entranced, as the Greeks of the heroic age had been, by any such imaginative mirrorings of their life and feelings. With the adaptation of the Etruscan alphabet to Latin, the language spoken by the Romans, the way was opened for a recorded literature. No complete work survived from the earliest period, but we have names of authors and titles of works, and the fragments or single lines that later commentators cited and discussed.

The impact made by Greek culture and literary achievement on educated Romans can scarcely be overstated. Just how great this impact was is demonstrated not only by the numerous translations made from the Greek, but even more strikingly by the translators' abandonment of their native meters, based on stress, and the adaptation to Latin of the very different, less flexible language of the Greek meters, based on syllable length. The adoption of syllabic meters determined the whole future course of Latin poetry up to and into the Christian era.

In every culture, it would seem, works in prose represent a later development than poetry. In Rome, the prestige of the Greek historians so undermined the local writers' self-confidence that the creation of Latin prose was even further delayed. The first Roman historians felt obliged to write in Greek, even when they had to apologize for their poor handling of the language. An end was put to this by Cato the Censor (234 B.C.–149 B.C.). He combined a narrowly patriotic outlook and a dislike of what he considered Greek nonsense with great energy and versatility as a writer. Though he refused on principle to record in his history the names of the generals, he did pass on to posterity the name of the bravest elephant in the Carthaginian army: Surus.

At least as important as history, in Roman eyes, was oratory. Political controversy, from the earliest days, had been intense, and law and legal disputation acquired great importance. So it was natural for the Romans to adapt to their own needs Greek rhetorical treatises and practices. Cicero (106 B.C.–43 B.C.), the great orator of the classical period of Roman literature, was the most prominent in a long line of orators. His example, directly and indirectly, still counts.

The most popular branch of literature in ancient Rome was the drama. Here, too, the Greek example and Greek plays in translation had a dominating influence. But the earliest dramatist whose works are available to us, Plautus (c. 254 B.C.–184 B.C.), though strongly influenced by the Greeks, unmistakably revealed his own vigorous personality and his sense of the knockabout goings on that would appeal to a Roman popular audience. His echoing, alliterative, swashbuckling lines are very much his own, and not much like anything the Greeks had attempted. Though Plautus' comedies are not often acted today, they are, in a sense, as alive as they ever were, for the stock situations and the gags utilized by Plautus continue, in the

The Appian Way as it looks today, part of the empire's vast highway network.

hands of more recent dramatists, to amuse and titillate audiences. His successor as a writer of comedies was Terence (c. 195 B.C.–159 B.C.), who was an African. Though Terence came to Rome as a slave, his master had him educated and later set him free. His comedies were much more polished, more "Greek" than those of Plautus. They appealed to the educated class but were not nearly so well liked by the general public.

The Golden Age of Latin literature is seen as extending over the years from 70 B.C. to A.D. 14, from the closing years of the republic to the death of Augustus. The first thirty years or so are known as the Ciceronian period, and the remaining years as the Augustan. The earlier period was stormy, and its literature, not surprisingly, reflects the individual boldness and decisiveness that the circumstances of the time made necessary. Cicero played a remarkable dual role. Deeply and dangerously involved in public affairs at the highest level, he also was a productive and wide-ranging writer (see page 194). The link between the man of action and the man of words was constituted by his great speeches, since these were at the same time dazzling literary compositions and significant deeds.

Two outstanding poets grace the periods. About the life of Lucretius (c. 96 B.C.–55 B.C.) nothing precise is known. Did he suffer from recurrent insanity? Did he commit suicide? No well-founded answer can be given. His great poem is *De Rerum Natura* ("Of the Nature of Things"). In it Lucretius tries to give a true rational picture of the world and by doing so to free men from superstitious fears. The work of Catullus (c. 84 B.C.–c. 54 B.C.) offers a striking contrast to Lucretius' epic, for Catullus' poems are brief, concentrated, and intensely personal (see page 189).

In the later period, after Augustus had established himself in power, the new writers were more sedate, less adventurous. They lived in a time of fulfillment, in a mature age, when state and writer could serve and enhance each other. Writers clearly understood that they could become accepted by "the establishment," and they acted accordingly.

Central to the culture of the time, and supreme in all Latin literature, is the poet Virgil (see page 198). By birth a poor provincial, he nevertheless rose to be the associate of the great and very great, including the Emperor Augustus. Since his patrons believed in him and provided him with a comfortable livelihood, Virgil could work scrupulously and slowly (his average

Shopping in Rome, first century A.D. The customers appear to be paying close attention to the salestalk. Pillows, sashes, and fabrics hang from the rod above. The streets of Rome were jammed with such small shops.

rate was not more than three or four lines daily) on the *Aeneid,* which would celebrate Rome's divinely decreed mission to impose unity, peace, and civilization on the world, and the triumphant fulfillment of the divine command under Augustus Caesar. Augustus himself had encouraged Virgil to undertake the project. When the poet died before he could, as he had planned, devote three years to polishing the masterpiece, the emperor took steps to have the poem properly edited. (The emperor had good literary taste, but he also had an unerring instinct for all that could enhance his own prestige and add to the luster of his reign.)

Horace (65 B.C.–8 B.C.) (see page 204), like Virgil, was of humble provincial origin. His acceptance in the circle of the elect was the work, in part, of Virgil, who presented the timid young poet to the wealthy and powerful Maecenas. (The name *Maecenas* is now often used as a noun to designate someone of considerable wealth who supports literature and the arts.)

Ovid (43 B.C.–A.D. 17) was much more the playboy. Uninterested in any occupation but idleness, play, and versification, he poured out a steady stream of works, frivolous for the most part. Most influential of his works is his retelling of the myths, called the *Metamorphoses* (see page 208), which has served as a source of mythological lore for centuries. At the age of fifty, Ovid was still a man about town when the blow fell: banishment to a barbarous town on the Black Sea. There Ovid spent a wretched, self-pitying ten years, and there he died. Why had he been banished? It is generally thought that the Emperor Augustus, who wanted to elevate the moral tone of a luxury-loving Roman society, frowned on Ovid's writings as immoral and tending to undermine that purpose.

On the whole, the prose writers of Augustus' reign were no match for the poets. Oratory, under despotism, lost the vital function it had exercised during more turbulent times. Historians, too, found it hazardous to write frankly of the immediate past and turned to safer, more distant, historical themes. By far the greatest historian was Livy (59 B.C.–A.D. 17), who showed himself to be bolder than his lesser brethren—or surer of his connections. His history of Rome (see page 201), though it begins uncontroversially with the remote past, in the course of its 142 books moves on to deal with the events of Livy's own lifetime—and the emperor's. Yet Livy continued to enjoy Augustus' favor even after he had dared to present Brutus and Cassius, the assassins of Julius Caesar, as men of distinction and heroes.

The Silver Age of Roman literature succeeded the Golden Age, the moment of cleavage being the death of Augustus in A.D. 14. It closed sometime during the middle of the second century A.D. The atmosphere of the Silver Age was, in general, not conducive to the free exercise of literary talents. For many years, the government of Rome was either morally corrupt or cruel and despotic, or both, and society for the most part fawned over each emperor. Many writers were forced to flatter rulers whom they feared and who often set themselves up as censors, as Caligula did, or as poets, as Nero did. Although more competent emperors ruled at intervals, the moral deterioration continued. Some writers, moved by moral indignation, used their talents in writing satire.

Martial (A.D. 40–A.D. 104) is noted for clever poems (see page 213) which give a clear if unflattering portrait of his times. Satire was polished to a higher degree by Juvenal (c. A.D. 60–A.D. 140) who, with blazing hatred, saw vice and sham wherever he looked. Included in his biting attacks were hypocritical philosophers who didn't practice what they preached, and women with shallow intellectual pretensions who affected Greek ways. In his most famous poem, "The Vanity of Human Wishes," Juvenal says that all the gifts man prays for may bring sorrow; in his best-known line, Juvenal asks only for "a sound mind in a sound body."

The great prose writer of the time was the historian Tacitus (A.D. 55?–A.D. 120?). In contrast to the patriotic historian Livy of several generations earlier, Tacitus revealed undisguised and sometimes extreme disgust of Rome (see page 216).

During the centuries that followed the Silver Age, the most significant achievements in Latin were made by Christian writers. St. Jerome (c. A.D. 340–A.D. 420), who was to become the patron saint of translators, translated the Bible, from Genesis to Acts, into Latin. This version is now known as the Vulgate. St. Augustine (A.D. 354–A.D. 430), from North Africa, wrote his vastly impressive historical-philosophical work, the *City of God,* and his autobiographical work, the *Confessions,* in Latin. Latin became the language of the western Church and remained, throughout the Middle Ages, the accepted means of communication between temporal rulers as well as between ecclesiastics. Only with the rise of national states in western Europe did Latin, as a written language, slowly begin to lose ground to the various vernacular tongues. During the Renaissance there was a revival of Ciceronian Latin among learned men. Inevitably, this did not spread beyond the learned and, by discrediting the sort of Latin that had been used without self-consciousness or embarrassment throughout the Middle Ages, it contributed to the rise of the modern vernaculars for purposes of written communication.

CATULLUS

During the troubled years of the civil wars, when most writers were chiefly concerned with politics and public statements, one personal, lyric voice was heard. Catullus (c. 84 B.C.–c. 54 B.C.) came to Rome as a naive and talented youth to join the literary circles of the city. He is considered the finest love poet since Sappho and the only Roman writer to convey so directly his emotional experiences.

A large number of Catullus' 116 poems are addressed to the notorious and fickle Roman matron, Clodia, whom he calls Lesbia. (Such pseudonyms were fashionable in the love poetry of the day.) That Clodia was as faithless as she was beautiful, as well as some years his senior, did not discourage Catullus. His poems range in tone from tentative hope to cynical disillusionment, as he records the course of his love through the brief years of his brilliant and tempestuous career.

Two Translations of Poem Number 3

(Translated by Horace Gregory)

Dress now in sorrow, O all
you shades of Venus,
and your little cupids weep.

My girl has lost her darling sparrow;
he is dead, her precious toy   5
that she loved more than her two eyes,
O, honeyed sparrow following her
as a girl follows her mother,
never to leave her breast, but tripping
now here, now there, and always singing   10
his sweet falsetto
song to her alone.

Now he is gone; poor creature,
lost in darkness,
to a sad place   15
from which no one returns.

O ravenous hell!
My evil hatred rises against your power,
you that devour
all things beautiful;   20
and now this pitiful, broken sparrow,
who is the cause of my girl's grief,
making her eyes weary and red with sorrow.

Numbers 3 and 51 from *The Poems of Catullus* translated by Horace Gregory, 1934, Covici Friede. Reprinted by permission of Crown Publishers, Inc.

Ye Cupids, droop each little head,
Nor let your wings with joy be spread;
My Lesbia's favorite bird is dead,
  Whom dearer than her eyes she loved.
For he was gentle and so true,   5
Obedient to her call he flew,
No fear, no wild alarm he knew,
  But lightly o'er her bosom moved:

And softly fluttering here and there,
He never sought to clear the air,   10
But chirruped oft and, free from care,
  Tuned to her ear his grateful strain.
Now having passed the gloomy bourne
From whence he never can return,
His death and Lesbia's grief I mourn,   15
  Who sighs, alas! but sighs in vain.

Oh! curst be thou, devouring grave!
Whose jaws eternal victims crave,
From whom no earthly power can save;
  For thou hast ta'en the bird away:
From thee my Lesbia's eyes o'er flow,   20
Her swollen cheeks with weeping glow;
Thou art the cause of all her woe,
  Receptacle of life's decay.

51

He is changed to a god he who looks on her,
godlike he shines when he's seated beside her,
immortal joy to gaze and hear the fall of
    her sweet laughter.

All of my senses are lost and confounded;   5
Lesbia rises before me and trembling
I sink into earth and swift dissolution
    seizes my body.

Limbs are pierced with fire and the heavy tongue fails,
ears resound with noise of distant storms shaking   10
this earth, eyes gaze on stars that fall forever
    into deep midnight.

This languid madness destroys you, Catullus,
long day and night shall be desolate, broken,
as long ago ancient kings and rich cities   15
    fell into ruin.

70

My woman says that she would rather wear the wedding veil for me
than anyone: even if Jupiter himself came storming after her;
that's what she says, but when a woman talks to a hungry,
ravenous lover, her words should be written upon the wind
and engraved in rapid waters.

[handwritten: doubt]

[handwritten: her word means nothing]

75

[handwritten: despair, close to giving up]

You are the cause of this destruction, Lesbia,
that has fallen upon my mind;
this mind that has ruined itself
by fatal constancy.
And now it cannot rise from its own misery
to wish that you become
best of women, nor can it fail
to love you even though all is lost and you destroy
all hope.

101

[handwritten: farewell to bro.]

Over many lands and many seas I have traveled,
only to stand by a tomb, brother, to weep what is lost.
Give you death's last gift, tears, words of sorrowful parting,
tears to the careless earth, words to the silent dead.
But since fate has taken you, you, your very self, from me,   5
brother, pitied, beloved, gone from me in your youth,
these rites now I pay, from olden time taught our fathers,
weeping pay to the dead what to the dead is due.
Wet with a brother's tears, receive from my hand the last tribute.
And forever, my dear, greeting—forever good-by.   10

Numbers 70 and 75 from *The Poems of Catullus* translated by Horace Gregory, 1934, Covici Friede. Reprinted by permission of Crown Publishers, Inc.
Number 101 by Catullus from *The Roman Way* by Edith Hamilton, copyright 1932 by W. W. Norton & Company, Inc., copyright renewed 1960 by Edith Hamilton. Reprinted by permission of the publisher.

NUMBER 3

How would you characterize the tone of this poem? Is Catullus mourning over the death of the sparrow or over his lover's red and tired eyes? Explain your answer. How does the poem indirectly compliment Lesbia?

NUMBERS 51, 70, AND 75

1. Compare Catullus' poem number 51 with Sappho's first letter to Anaktoria, page 108.

2. What different stages in Catullus' feeling for Lesbia do poems 51, 70, and 75 convey? Do you think he gives a realistic or a romantic portrayal of his sentiments? Justify your answer.

NUMBER 101

The final line of this poem is as famous in Latin as it is in English: *Atque in perpetuum, frater, ave atque vale.* How would you explain the apparent contradiction in this line?

COMPARING TRANSLATIONS

The first translation of poem number 3, by contemporary poet Horace Gregory, is a fairly literal translation; the second, by the nineteenth-century Romantic poet Byron, is a free adaptation, clearly more Byron than Catullus. Cite the ways in which the translations differ in use of rhyme and meter, in poetic diction, and in general effect. What is the difference in effect between "lost in darkness" (line 14 of Gregory's translation) and "gloomy bourne" (line 13 of Byron's translation); between "making her eyes weary and red with sorrow" and "her swollen cheeks with weeping glow"? All in all, which version seems to convey most adequately what you think are Catullus' feelings? State reasons for your answer.

On Duties

CICERO

Greatest of all Roman orators, Cicero (106 B.C.–43 B.C.) exerted an enormous influence, not only with his oratory but also with his vigorous writings. His orations and his philosophical works are expressed in such eloquent and forceful Latin that his style was widely imitated by subsequent prose writers. In fact, as recently as the nineteenth century, Ciceronian prose served as a model of speaking and writing for English schoolboys. Cicero's ideas had an equally wide effect, for the English moral code which for centuries indicated proper conduct for the well-bred gentleman received inspiration from Cicero's ethical precepts.

Cicero lived in a time of civil strife and engaged actively in a political career. He served ably as consul at one time and took the side of those working for orderly government. His orations against the reckless politician Catiline, who had attempted to seize the government by violence, are still famous as examples of brilliant invective. For over a year, Cicero was forced into exile because he incurred the hostility of the First Triumvirate—Caesar, Pompey, and Crassus. After his return to Italy, he took little part in public life. When in 49 B.C. Pompey and Caesar began their battle for supreme control of the state, Cicero, after great uncertainty as to his duty, championed Pompey. Though Caesar was victor, he generously refused to have Cicero severely punished. Cicero went through another period of understandable indecision after Caesar was assassinated in 44 B.C., but when the confusion began to clear he roared his denunciations of Antony, who, with Octavian, was seeking and won dictatorial control of Rome. Antony and Octavian (later the Emperor Augustus) were less generous with political enemies than Caesar was. They put Cicero's name on the top of the proscription list. Proscription was a cold-blooded way of getting rid of potential troublemakers, for it offered rewards for the murder of the men whose names were listed. Several rough Roman soldiers, only too eager for the money on his head, tracked down the aged Cicero and attacked him as he was trying to leave Italy by boat. Cicero met his brutal death with composure and courage. The murderers severed his head and hands and brought them back to Antony, who displayed the grisly trophies in the Forum.

Partly because of the reverence in which Cicero was held by succeeding generations, fifty-seven complete orations survive, some 800 letters, as well as a considerable number of philosophical treatises.

The following selection is from the books which Cicero addressed to a son, who never lived up to his expectations.

Duties of the Individual to the State

THOSE WHOM NATURE has endowed with the capacity for administering public affairs should put aside all hesitation, enter the race for public office, and take a hand in directing the government; for in no other way can a government be administered or greatness of spirit be made manifest. Statesmen, too, no less than philosophers—perhaps even more so—should carry with them that greatness of spirit and indifference to outward circumstances to which I so often refer, together with calm of soul and freedom from care, if they are to be free from worries and lead a dignified and self-consistent life. This is easier for the philosophers; as their life is less exposed to the assaults of fortune, their wants are fewer; and if any misfortune overtakes them, their fall is not so disastrous. Not without reason, therefore, are stronger emotions aroused in those who engage in public life than in those who live in retirement, and greater is their ambition for success; the more, therefore, do they need to enjoy greatness of spirit and freedom from annoying cares.

If anyone is entering public life, let him beware of thinking only of the honor it brings; but let him be sure also that he has the ability to succeed. At the same time, let him take care not to lose heart too readily through discouragement nor yet to be overconfident through ambition. In a word, before undertaking any enterprise, careful preparation must be made.

Most people think that the achievements of war are more important than those of peace; but this opinion needs to be corrected. For many men have sought occasions for war from the mere ambition for fame. This is notably the case with men of great spirit and natural ability, if they are adapted to a soldier's life and fond of warfare. But if we will face the facts, we shall find that there have been many instances of achievement in peace more important and no less renowned than in war.

How highly Themistocles,[1] for example, may be extolled—and deservedly—and however much more illustrious his name may be than Solon's,[2] and however much Salamis[3] may be cited as witness of his most glorious victory—a victory glorified above Solon's statesmanship in instituting the Areopagus[4]—yet Solon's achievement is not to be accounted less illustrious than his. For Themistocles' victory served the state once and only once; while Solon's work will be of service forever. For through his legislation the laws of the Athenians and the institutions of their fathers are maintained. And while Themistocles could not readily point to any instance in which he himself had rendered assistance to the Areopagus, the Areopagus might with justice assert that Themistocles had received assistance from it; for the war was directed by the counsels of that senate which Solon had created. . . .

There are, therefore, instances of civic courage that are not inferior to the courage of the soldier. Nay, the former calls for even greater energy and greater devotion than the latter.

That moral goodness which we look for in a lofty, high-minded spirit is secured, of course, by moral, not by physical, strength. And yet the body must be trained and so disciplined that it can obey the dictates of judgment and reason in attending to business and in enduring toil. But that moral goodness which is our

---

[1] **Themistocles:** Athenian statesman and military commander.

[2] **Solon:** Athenian lawmaker.

[3] **Salamis:** In the Bay of Salamis, the Greeks won a naval victory over the Persians (480 B.C.).

[4] **Areopagus** (ar′ē·op′ə·gəs): the highest court of ancient Athens.

From *De Officiis* by Cicero, translated by Walter Miller. Reprinted by permission of Harvard University Press and Loeb Classical Library.

theme depends wholly upon the thought and attention given to it by the mind. And in this way, the men who in a civil capacity direct the affairs of a nation render no less important service than they who conduct its wars. By their statesmanship oftentimes wars are either averted, or terminated; sometimes also they are declared. Upon Marcus Cato's [1] counsel, for example, the Third Punic War was undertaken, and in its conduct his influence was dominant, even after he was dead. And so diplomacy in the friendly settlement is more desirable than courage in settling wars on the battlefield; but we must be careful not to take that course merely for the sake of avoiding war rather than for the sake of public expediency. War, however, should be undertaken in such a way as to make it evident that it has no other object than to secure peace.

But it takes a brave and resolute spirit not to be disconcerted in times of difficulty or ruffled and thrown off one's feet, as the saying is, but to keep one's presence of mind and one's self-possession and not to swerve from the path of reason.

Now all this requires great personal courage; but it calls also for great intellectual ability by reflection to anticipate the future, to discover some time in advance what may happen, whether for good or for ill, and what must be done in any possible event, and never to be reduced to having to say "I had not thought of that."

These are the activities that mark a spirit, strong, high, and self-reliant in its prudence and wisdom. But to mix rashly in the fray and to fight hand to hand with the enemy is but a barbarous and brutish kind of business. Yet when the stress of circumstances demands it, we must gird on the sword and prefer death to slavery and disgrace.

As to destroying and plundering cities, let me say that great care should be taken that nothing be done in reckless cruelty or wantonness. And it is a great man's duty in troublous times to single out the guilty for punishment, to spare the many, and in every turn of fortune to hold to a true and honorable course. For whereas there are many, as I have said before, who place the achievements of war above those of peace, so one may find many to whom adventurous, hotheaded counsels seem more brilliant and impressive than calm and well-considered measures.

We must, of course, never be guilty of seeming cowardly and craven in our avoidance of danger; but we must also beware of exposing ourselves to danger needlessly. Nothing can be more foolhardy than that. Accordingly, in encountering danger we should do as doctors do in their practice. In light cases of illness they give mild treatment; in cases of dangerous sickness they are compelled to apply hazardous and even desperate remedies. It is, therefore, only a madman who, in a calm, would pray for storm; a wise man's way is, when the storm does come, to withstand it with all the means at his command, and especially when the advantages to be expected in case of a successful issue are greater than the hazards of the struggle.

The dangers attending great affairs of state fall sometimes upon those who undertake them, sometimes upon the state. In carrying out such enterprises, some run the risk of losing their lives, others their reputation and the good will of their fellow citizens. It is our duty, then, to be more ready to endanger our own than the public welfare and to hazard honor and glory more readily than other advantages.

Many, on the other hand, have been found who were ready to pour out not only their money but their lives for their country and yet would not consent to make even the slightest sacrifice of personal glory—even though the interests of their country demanded it. For example, when Callicratidas,[2] as Spartan admiral in the Peloponnesian War, had won many signal successes, he spoiled everything

---

[1] **Marcus Cato:** Roman statesman, known as Cato the Elder.

[2] **Callicratidas** (ka′li·krat′ə·dəs): Spartan admiral, killed in battle in 406 B.C.

at the end by refusing to listen to the proposal of those who thought he ought to withdraw his fleet from the Arginusae[1] and not to risk an engagement with the Athenians. His answer to them was that "the Spartans could build another fleet if they lost that one, but he could not retreat without dishonor to himself." And yet what he did dealt only a slight blow to Sparta; there was another which proved disastrous, when Cleombrotus[2] in fear of criticism recklessly went into battle against Epaminondas.[3] In consequence of that the Spartan power fell.

How much better was the conduct of Quintus Maximus![4] Of him Ennius[5] says:

One man—and he alone—restored our state by delaying.
Not in the least did fame with him take precedence of safety;
Therefore now does his glory shine bright, and it grows ever brighter.

This sort of offense must be avoided no less in political life. For there are men who for fear of giving offense do not dare to express their honest opinion, no matter how excellent.

Those who propose to take charge of the affairs of government should not fail to remember two of Plato's rules: first, to keep the good of the people so clearly in view that regardless of their own interests they will make their every action conform to that; second, to care for the welfare of the whole body politic and not in serving the interests of some one party to betray the rest. For the administration of the government, like the office of a trustee, must be conducted for the benefit of those entrusted to one's care, not of those to whom it is entrusted. Now, those who care for the interests of a part of the citizens and neglect another part, introduce into the civil service a dangerous element—dissension and party strife. The result is that some are found to be loyal supporters of the democratic, others of the aristocratic, party, and few of the nation as a whole.

As a result of this party spirit bitter strife arose at Athens, and in our own country not only dissensions but also disastrous civil wars broke out. All this the citizen who is patriotic, brave, and worthy of a leading place in the state will shun with abhorrence; he will dedicate himself unreservedly to his country, without aiming at influence or power for himself; and he will devote himself to the state in its entirety in such a way as to further the interests of all. Besides, he will not expose anyone to hatred or disrepute by groundless charges, but he will surely cleave to justice and honor so closely that he will submit to any loss, however heavy, rather than be untrue to them, and will face death itself rather than renounce them.

A most wretched custom, assuredly, is our electioneering and scrambling for office. Concerning this also we find a fine thought in Plato: "Those who compete against one another," he says, "to see which of two candidates shall administer the government are like sailors quarreling as to which one of them shall do the steering." And he likewise lays down the rule that we should regard only those as adversaries who take up arms against the state, not those who strive to have the government administered according to their convictions. This was the spirit of the disagreement between Publius Africanus[6] and Quintus Metellus:[7] there was in it no trace of rancor.

---

[1] **Arginusae** (är′ji·nyo͞o′sē): a group of small islands off the coast of Asia Minor.

[2] **Cleombrotus:** regent of Sparta early in the fifth century B.C.

[3] **Epaminondas** (i·pam′ə·non′dəs): Theban general and statesman.

[4] **Quintus Maximus:** Quintus Fabius Maximus, known as Cunctator, "the delayer," because he foiled the enemy in the Second Punic War by avoiding direct combat.

[5] **Ennius** (en′ē·əs): Roman epic poet, only fragments of whose work survive.

[6] **Publius Africanus:** Scipio the Younger, called Africanus after his capture of Carthage in 146 B.C., which ended the Third Punic War.

[7] **Quintus Metellus:** Roman general, and a political rival of Publius Africanus.

Neither must we listen to these who think that one should indulge in violent anger against one's political enemies and imagine that such is the attitude of a great-spirited, brave man. For nothing is more commendable, nothing more becoming in a preeminently great man than courtesy and forbearance. Indeed, in a free people, where all enjoy equal rights before the law, we must school ourselves to affability and what is called "mental poise"; for if we are irritated when people intrude upon us at unseasonable hours or make unreasonable requests, we shall develop a sour, churlish temper, prejudicial to ourselves and offensive to others. And yet gentleness of spirit and forbearance are to be commended only with the understanding that strictness may be exercised for the good of the state; for without that, the government cannot be well administered. On the other hand, if punishment or correction must be administered, it need not be insulting; it ought to have regard to the welfare of the state, not to the personal satisfaction of the man who administers the punishment or reproof.

We should take care also that the punishment shall not be out of proportion to the offense and that some shall not be chastised for the same fault for which others are not even called to account. In administering punishment it is above all necessary to allow no trace of anger. For if anyone proceeds in a passion to inflict punishment, he will never observe that happy mean which lies between excess and defect. This doctrine of the mean is approved by the Peripatetics [1]—and wisely approved, if only they did not

[1] **Peripatetics:** disciples of the Greek philosopher Aristotle or of his teachings, so called because Aristotle walked about while lecturing (from *peripatetikos,* "to walk around").

speak in praise of anger and tell us that it is a gift bestowed on us by nature for a good purpose. But in reality, anger is in every circumstance to be eradicated; and it is to be desired that they who administer the government should be like the laws, which are led to inflict punishment not by wrath but by justice. . . .

FOR STUDY AND DISCUSSION

1. What characteristics does Cicero look for in one who has "greatness of spirit"? Why, according to Cicero, is it easier for a philosopher to exhibit these qualities than for a politician to do so? Do you agree? Explain.

2. What example does Cicero cite to demonstrate why the achievements of peace are more important than achievements in war?

3. What part does physical strength play in aiding the development of moral greatness? On what occasion does Cicero believe it necessary to engage in war?

4. What comments does Cicero make on the desire of men for personal glory? How does he demonstrate that it sometimes leads to disaster for the state?

5. What two rules, as stated by Plato regarding the affairs of government, does Cicero hold to be essential?

6. Compare Cicero's comment on the evils of "scrambling for office" with present-day political conventions and campaigns. What rules of conduct do you think should be adopted by politicians for dealing with men of opposing beliefs?

7. Compare the feelings Cicero expresses for the state with those expressed by the Athenian Pericles (page 126). Is the idea of the individual and of his freedom stressed by Cicero as it was by Pericles? Explain.

FOR COMPOSITION

Review Cicero's essay, listing the main points necessary to ethical political conduct. Write an essay applying these points to contemporary problems of government.

VIRGIL

The universally acknowledged sublime artist of Roman poets, Virgil (70 B.C.–19 B.C.) expresses in his poetry two major themes—a majestic vision of world order and peace in his epic poem the *Aeneid,* and an abiding love for the simple joys and rewards of nature and honest toil in his earlier poems about the countryside he knew in his youth. The *Eclogues* (or *Bucolics*) include ten short pastorals, influenced by the Greek poet Theocritus (see page 113); the *Georgics* consist of four didactic poems, which encourage a return to the simple virtues of agrarian life.

Much of Virgil's life was spent under the patronage of such wealthy sponsors of literature as Maecenas, Pollio, and, later, even the Emperor Augustus himself. It was only natural that the poet should lend his talent to subjects which emphasized the glorification of the Roman dream.

Because of Virgil's genius, Romans considered him the voice of their greatness and the inspiration for their statesmen, soldiers, and schoolchildren. This reverence was carried over into the Christian era, when Virgil was considered a veritable prophet who foreshadowed the coming of Christianity.

People still argue about the identity of the boy in the following poem. The eclogue was written and dedicated to Pollio, who was then consul, in 40 B.C., when the wives of Rome's rulers, Octavian (later Augustus) and Antony, were both expecting children. It is supposed that Virgil is referring to the son awaited by one of them, most likely by Octavian, since it is also believed that this text is a revision of the original, completed by Virgil some years after Octavian became emperor in 27 B.C. Others have called this the Messianic Eclogue, believing that Virgil is prophesying the coming of Christ, born during Octavian Augustus' reign of peace.

The Fourth Eclogue

Muses
Muses of Sicily
Now let us sing a serious song
There are taller trees than the apple and the crouching tamarisk
If we sing of the woods, let our forest be stately   5

Now the last age is coming
As it was written in the Sybil's book°
The great circle of the centuries begins again
Justice, the Virgin, has returned to earth
With all of Saturn's court°   10
A new line is sent down to us from the skies
And thou, Lucina,° must smile

---

7. **the Sybil's book:** The destiny of Rome is supposed to have been revealed in nine books written by a prophetess, or sybil.   10. Saturn was the Roman god of agriculture. In mythology, his reign established an earlier Golden Age.   12. **Lucina:** in Roman mythology, the goddess presiding over childbirth.

"Fourth Eclogue" by Virgil, translated by James Laughlin, © 1957 by James Laughlin. Reprinted by permission of James Laughlin.

Smile for the birth of the boy, the blessed boy
For whom they will beat their swords into plowshares
For whom the golden race will rise, the whole world new   15

Smile, pure Lucina, smile
Thine own Apollo will reign
And thou, Pollio
It is in thy term this glorious age begins
And the great months begin their march   20
When we shall lose all trace of the old guilt
And the world learn to forget fear
For the boy will become divine
He will see gods and heroes
And will himself be seen by them as god and hero   25
As he rules over a world of peace
A world made peaceful by his father's wisdom

For thee, little boy, will the earth pour forth gifts
All untilled, give you gifts
First the wandering ivy and foxglove   30
Then colocasia and the laughing acanthus
Uncalled the goats will come home with their milk
No longer need the herds fear the lion
Thy cradle itself will bloom with sweet flowers
The serpent will die   35
The poison plant will wither
Assyrian herbs will spring up everywhere

And when thou art old enough to read of heroes
And of thy father's great deeds
Old enough to understand the meaning of courage   40
Then will the plain grow yellow with ripe grain
Grapes will grow on brambles
Hard old oaks drip honey
Yet still there must remain some traces of the old guilt
That lust that drives men to taunt the sea with ships   45
To circle cities with walls
And cut the earth with furrows
There must be another Tiphys°
Another Argo carrying picked men
And there must be a war, one final war   50
With great Achilles storming a last Troy

But when thou hast grown strong and become a man
Then even the trader will leave the sea
His pine ship carry no more wares
And everywhere the land will yield all things that life requires 55
No longer need the ground endure the harrow
Nor the vine the pruning hook

---

48. **Tiphys** (tī´fĭs): in Greek legend, the helmsman on the ship *Argo* that carried a fifty-man crew of the greatest heroes in Greece on the quest for the Golden Fleece.

The farmer can free his oxen from the yoke
Then colored cloths no longer will need lying dyes
For the ram in the field will change his own fleece   60
To soft purple or saffron yellow
Each grazing lamb will have a scarlet coat

    "Onward, O glorious ages, onward"
    Thus sang the fatal sisters to their spindles
    Chanting together the unalterable Will°   65

Go forward, little boy, to thy great honors
Soon comes thy time
Dear child of gods from whom a Jupiter will come
See how for thee the world nods its huge head
All lands and seas and endless depths of sky   70
See how the earth rejoices in the age that is to be
O may my life be long enough to let me sing of thee
With strength enough to tell thy deeds
With such a theme not even Thracian Orpheus° could outsing me
No Linus° either, though Apollo prompted him   75
Help from Calliope° herself could not make Orpheus' song the best
And even Pan, with Arcady as judge°
Yes Pan, would fall before me when I sang of thee

Learn, little boy, to greet thy mother with a smile
For thee she has endured nine heavy months   80
Learn, little boy, to smile
For if thou didst not smile
And if thy parents did not smile on thee
No god could ask thee to his table
No goddess to her bed.   85

---

65. A reference to the three goddesses of destiny who saw that the threads of each man's fate were spun out according to the gods' will. 74. **Thracian Orpheus:** Orpheus, the son of the King of Thrace, was the greatest musician in Greek legend. 75. **Linus:** another great musician, the teacher of Orpheus. Some say he was the son of Apollo. 76. **Calliope** (kə·lī′ə·pē): chief of the nine muses in Greek mythology, the inspiration of epic poetry. 77. Pan was the god of the woodlands, a musician who played melodies as sweet as the songs of nightingales on his reed pipes. Pan was born in Arcady, a mountainous district in Greece. In one myth, a mountain in Arcady acted as a judge in a musical contest between Pan and Apollo.

FOR STUDY AND DISCUSSION

1. Cite specific lines that might tell why this has been called the Messianic Eclogue.

2. Justice, in line 9, was often personified as a goddess. What image has Virgil created in lines 9–10? What do the words *again* (line 8) and *returned* (line 9) imply?

3. Some claim that this eclogue was influenced by the Hebraic prophecies. In line 14 the translator has used an expression from the writings of the prophet Isaiah (Chapt. 2: 4). What does this line mean? What would be the characteristics of a "golden" race (line 15)?

4. What do you think is meant by the "old guilt" (lines 21 and 44)?

5. What images characteristic of an ideal, paradisical state are found in lines 28–43?

6. Lines 44–51 say that before the age of peace is complete, certain things must recur. What are these things and why will they recur?

History of the Roman Republic

LIVY

Livy (59 B.C.–A.D. 17), the most significant prose writer of the Augustan Age, was primarily a moral historian. His purpose was to show the qualities of the early heroes and ancient institutions that had contributed to the greatness of Rome. He earnestly desired to teach an ethical lesson to his own generation, which he feared was becoming corrupt and luxury-loving. Because of this lofty, didactic purpose, similar to Virgil's, Livy chose the material which best suited his intent. Consequently, he is considered a romantic rather than a realistic historian.

Livy's *History of the Roman Republic* begins with the divine origin of Rome, includes many legendary tales of early patriots, and continues until A.D. 9. More interested in style than in facts, Livy departed from the accepted prose standards of Cicero's day and wrote a spirited, vivid, at times almost poetic prose.

It is believed that Livy's extraordinary task occupied some forty years of his life. Unfortunately, his vast *History* was abridged by the Romans and the original was neglected. As a result, only thirty-five of the original 142 books are extant.

The following selection from the *History* relates two incidents, which are probably part history, part legend. The incidents are set during the sixth century B.C., when the Romans drove out their last king, a tyrant named Tarquin. In an attempt to regain his throne, Tarquin formed an alliance with Porsinna, the king of the Etruscans. According to legend, these enemy armies would have entered Rome easily had not a Roman named Horatius held them off till his countrymen hacked down the bridge across the Tiber (see page 172). As this selection opens, Porsinna and his armies are outside Rome. They have blockaded the city, so that a famine has resulted.

Scaevola and Cloelia

THE BLOCKADE went on notwithstanding. The corn was giving out, and what there was cost a very high price, and Porsinna was beginning to have hopes that he would take the city by sitting still, when Gaius Mucius, a young Roman noble, thinking it a shame that although the Roman people had not, in the days of their servitude when they lived under kings, been blockaded in a war by any enemies, they should now, when free, be besieged by those same Etruscans whose armies they had so often routed, made up his mind that this indignity must be avenged by some great and daring deed. At first he intended to make his way to the enemy's camp on his own account. Afterward, fearing that if he should go unbidden by the consuls and without anyone's knowing it, he might chance to be arrested by the Roman sentries and brought back as a deserter—a charge which the state of the city would confirm—he went before

From "Scaevola and Cloelia" from *Roman History Book II* by Livy, translated by B. O. Foster. Reprinted by permission of Harvard University Press and Loeb Classical Library.

the senate. "I wish," said he, "to cross the river, senators, and enter, if I can, the enemy's camp—not to plunder or exact reprisals for their devastations. I have in mind to do a greater deed, if the gods grant me their help."

The Fathers approved. Hiding a sword under his dress, he set out. Arrived at the camp, he took up his stand in the thick of the crowd near the royal tribunal. It happened that at that moment the soldiers were being paid; a secretary who sat beside the king, and wore nearly the same costume, was very busy, and to him the soldiers for the most part addressed themselves. Mucius was afraid to ask which was Porsinna, lest his ignorance of the king's identity should betray his own, and following the blind guidance of fortune, he slew the secretary instead of the king. As he strode off through the frightened crowd, making a way for himself with his bloody blade, there was an outcry, and thereat the royal guards came running in from every side, seized him, and dragged him back before the tribunal of the king.

But friendless as he was, even then, when fortune wore so menacing an aspect, yet as one more to be feared than fearing, "I am a Roman citizen," he cried; "men call me Gaius Mucius. I am your enemy, and as an enemy I would have slain you; I can die as resolutely as I could kill. Both to do and to endure valiantly is the Roman way. Nor am I the only one to carry this resolution against you. Behind me is a long line of men who are seeking the same honor. Gird yourself, therefore, if you think it worth your while, for a struggle in which you must fight for your life from hour to hour with an armed foe always at your door. Such is the war we, the Roman youths, declare on you. Fear no serried ranks, no battle; it will be between yourself alone and a single enemy at a time."

The king, at once hot with resentment and aghast at his danger, angrily ordered the prisoner to be flung into the flames unless he should at once divulge the plot with which he so obscurely threatened him. Whereupon Mucius, exclaiming

"Look, that you may see how cheap they hold their bodies whose eyes are fixed upon renown!" thrust his hand into the fire that was kindled for the sacrifice.

When he allowed his hand to burn as if his spirit were unconscious of sensation, the king was almost beside himself with wonder. He bounded from his seat and bade them remove the young man from the altar. "Do you go free," he said, "who have dared to harm yourself more than me. I would invoke success upon your valor, were that valor exerted for my country; since that may not be, I release you from the penalties of war and dismiss you scathless and uninjured." Then Mucius, as if to requite his generosity, answered, "Since you hold bravery in honor, my gratitude shall afford you the information your threats could not extort. We are three hundred, the foremost youths of Rome, who have conspired to assail you in this fashion. I drew the first lot; the others, in whatever order it falls to them, will attack you, each at his own time, until fortune shall have delivered you into our hands."

The release of Mucius, who was afterward known as Scaevola,[1] from the loss of his right hand, was followed by the arrival in Rome of envoys from Porsinna. The king had been so disturbed, what with the hazard of the first attack upon his life, from which nothing but the blunder of his assailant had preserved him, and what with the anticipation of having to undergo the danger as many times more as there were conspirators remaining, that he voluntarily proposed terms of peace to the Romans. In these terms Porsinna suggested, but without effect, that the Tarquinii should be restored to power, more because he had been unable to refuse the princes this demand upon their behalf than that he was ignorant that the Romans would refuse it. In obtaining the return of their lands to the Veientes[2] he was suc-

[1] **Scaevola** (sē'vō·lə): The name means "left-handed."
[2] **Veientes** (vē·yen'tēz): inhabitants of Veii, an Etruscan city.

cessful; and the Romans were compelled to give hostages if they wished the garrison to be withdrawn from Janiculum. On these terms peace was made, and Porsinna led his army down from Janiculum and evacuated the Roman territory. The Fathers bestowed on Gaius Mucius, for his bravery, a field across the Tiber, which was later known as the Mucian Meadows.

Now when courage had been thus distinguished, even the women were inspired to deeds of patriotism. Thus the maiden Cloelia,[1] one of the hostages, eluded the sentinels when it chanced that the Etruscans had encamped not far from the bank of the Tiber, and heading a band of girls swam the river and, under a rain of hostile darts, brought them all back in safety to their kinsmen in Rome. When this had been reported to the king, he was at first enraged and sent emissaries to Rome to demand that the hostage Cloelia be given up, for he made no great account of the others. Then, admiration getting the better of anger, he asserted that her feat was a greater one than those of Cocles [2] and Mucius and declared that although in case the hostages were not returned he should regard the treaty as broken, yet if she were restored to him he would send her back safe and inviolate to her friends.

Both parties kept their word. The Romans returned the pledge of peace, as the treaty required; and the Etruscan king not only protected the brave girl but even honored her, for after praising her heroism he said that he would present her with half the hostages and that she herself should choose the ones she wished. When they had all been brought out, it is said

---

[1] **Cloelia** (klē′li·ə).

[2] **Cocles:** Horatius, the defender of the bridge. Horatius had lost one eye; *Cocles* means "one-eyed."

that she selected the young boys, because it was not only more seemly in a maiden, but was unanimously approved by the hostages themselves, that in delivering them from the enemy she should give the preference to those who were of an age which particularly exposed them to injury. When peace had been established, the Romans rewarded this new valor in a woman with a new kind of honor, an equestrian statue, which was set up on the summit of the Sacred Way, and represented the maiden seated on a horse.

FOR STUDY AND DISCUSSION

1. Point out specific passages in which Livy seems to be emphasizing the virtues most revered by the ancient Romans. What qualities, for instance, are exemplified in Gaius Mucius?

2. What insight does this selection give into the position of women in ancient Rome? Compare Cloelia with Antigone (page 140). How do the motives of the women differ?

3. How is Rome's enemy, Porsinna, treated by Livy? Do Porsinna's reactions to the actions of Scaevola and Cloelia make these young heroes even more admirable? Explain your answers.

FOR COMPOSITION

Clearly, Livy held to the theory that if we wish to find out what values a people hold most high, we should examine the legends preserved from their early history. Write an essay in which you examine several of the most popular legends preserved from the early history of the United States. Explain what values they are pointing to, and tell whether you believe these values are still esteemed. Do you find that the values pointed out by these American legends are different from those pointed out in the two legends retold by Livy in the text? Do you believe that the values of a nation can legitimately change?

HORACE

The son of a freed slave, Horace (65 B.C.–8 B.C.) received a first-rate education through his father's efforts. He fought along with Brutus in the civil wars and found his small landholdings confiscated in the resettlement that followed. However, he proved to be remarkably resilient and soon became friendly with the literary patrons surrounding Augustus. Horace assumed a position as a man about town, genially critical of the follies of society, possessing the sense of humor to take neither himself nor anyone else too seriously, and in his poetry calling for common-sense resignation and moderation in personal conduct.

Consequently, Horace's poetry tends to moralize. His sentiments are seldom profound. His genius lies in the way he expresses his ideas rather than in their content. Although he has been cleverly imitated by later poets, Horace's own unique style has never been successfully captured in translation.

Horace's poems range through an imposing array of light and serious subjects, including praise of Augustus and comments on contemporary events *(Epodes* and *Odes),* satires and conversations in verse *(Epistles* and *Satires),* and a poem about poetry-writing and literary criticism *(Art of Poetry).*

The poems that follow are from his *Odes.* The first of these is about Cleopatra. The queen of Egypt had used her charms on Julius Caesar and Mark Antony, both of whom had helped her maintain her rule of Egypt and had given her extensive territory. When Octavian (later Augustus) defeated Antony in a sea battle in 31 B.C., the great queen, then thirty-nine years old, ended her life to escape being taken back to Rome as part of the conqueror's booty. After her death, Egypt was annexed to the Roman Empire.

The Fall of Cleopatra

Drink we now, and dancing round,
Press with footsteps free the ground;
Pour we now the rosy wine,
And, in honor of the gods,
Comrades, in their own abodes   5
Pile we the banquet on each holy shrine.

Sin it were ere now to pour
Forth the cellar's generous store;
While the haughty queen of Nile,
With her base and scurvy crew,   10
Dared unbridled to pursue
Wild hopes, and drunk with fortune's favoring smile,

"The Fall of Cleopatra" (Odes I, 37) by Horace, translated by The Earl of Derby.

Madly dreamed the Capitol°
Soon should totter to its fall,
And the Empire's self should die;   15
But her spirit quailed awhile,
When of all the ships of Nile
From Rome's avenging fires scarce one could fly.

Then assailed her stricken soul
Frenzied with the wassail bowl   20
Terrors true, and wild despair,
When (as falcon from above
Pounces on the timorous dove,
Or hunters o'er Haemon's snow° the hare)

Oar and sail incessant plying   25
As he marked her galleys flying,
Caesar urged her headlong race:
Deeming that his wondrous prize
Soon would gladden Roman eyes,
And bound in chains his haughty triumph grace.   30

Nobly she to death resigned,   *not a coward*
Not with woman's shrinking mind,
Gazed upon the deadly knife;
Nor within some friendly creek
Basely lurking, did she seek   35
To save from death a now dishonored life.   *committed suicide rather than publicly ridiculed*

On her prostrate citadel
Dared her dauntless eye to dwell:
Firm of purpose, calm she stood,
Holding with unflinching grasp,   40
To her breast applied the asp,
Whose venom dire she drank through all her blood.

Sternly resolute she died;
Nor could stoop her royal pride,
That, reserved to swell a show,   45
She a woman and a queen,
Should be led like captive mean
Through streets of Rome to grace her conquering foe.

---

13. **Capitol:** the temple of Jupiter, built on the highest of Rome's seven hills.   24. **Haemon's snow:** here, a reference to the Haemus range, now called the Balkans, in Bulgaria.

Opposite of Arete p. 111

Don't stick your neck out — it might get chopped off

Almost saying — mediocrity is safer

Stay w/ crowd, don't draw attention

The Golden Mean

Receive, dear friend, the truths I teach;
So shalt thou live beyond the reach
  Of adverse fortune's power;
Not always tempt the distant deep,
Nor always timorously creep   5
  Along the treacherous shore.

He that holds fast the golden mean,
And lives contentedly between
  The little and the great,
Feels not the wants that pinch the poor,   10
Nor plagues that haunt the rich man's door,
  Embittering all his state.

The tallest pines feel most the power
Of winter blasts; the loftiest tower
  Comes heaviest to the ground;   15
The bolts that spare the mountain's side,
His cloud-capped eminence divide,
  And spread the ruin round.

The well-informed philosopher
Rejoices with a wholesome fear   20
  And hopes, in spite of pain;
If winter bellows from the north,
Soon the sweet spring comes dancing forth,
  And nature laughs again.

What if thine heaven be overcast,   25
The dark appearance will not last;
  Expect a brighter sky.
The God that strings the silver bow,
Awakes sometimes the muses too,
  And lays his arrows by.   30

If hindrances obstruct thy way,
Thy magnanimity display,
  And let thy strength be seen;
But Oh! if fortune fill thy sail
With more than a propitious gale,   35
  Take half thy canvas in.

"The Golden Mean" (Odes II, 10) by Horace, translated by William Cowper.

can't depend on a long life

Do what you can w/ the time you have

Carpe Diem

Strive not, Leuconoe,° to know what end
The gods above to me or thee will send:
Nor with astrologers consult at all,
That thou mayst better know what can befall;
Whether thou liv'st more winters, or thy last   5
Be this, which Tyrrhen° waves 'gainst rocks do cast.
Be wise! Drink free, and in so short a space
Do not protracted hopes of life embrace:
Whilst we are talking, envious time doth slide;
This day's thine own; the next may be denied.   10

1. **Leuconoe** (lyoo·kō′nō·ē): a woman friend. 6. **Tyrrhen** (tir′ēn) **waves:** a reference to the Tyrrhenian Sea, a part of the Mediterranean, southwest of Italy.

FOR STUDY AND DISCUSSION

THE FALL OF CLEOPATRA

What is Horace's mood in this poem? How does Horace characterize Cleopatra? Does the picture of the queen in lines 9–15 contrast with that presented in lines 31–48? Explain.

THE GOLDEN MEAN

1. What is the "golden mean"? What images does the poet use to describe it? How do the ideas in stanzas four and five relate to the golden mean?

2. The god referred to in the fifth stanza is Apollo, often called the "Lord of the Silver Bow." Explain Horace's allusion to Apollo here.

3. The doctrine of the golden mean has sometimes been labeled one of "golden medi-ocrity." Do you think such a label can be justified? Explain.

4. Does the attitude of the speaker in "Arete" on page 111 necessarily contrast with that expressed by Horace in this poem? Explain why or why not.

CARPE DIEM

1. *Carpe diem*, a Latin phrase for "seize (or enjoy) the day," is often quoted for widely differing purposes. Is the thought of this poem consistent with the ideas in "The Golden Mean"? Does the poem necessarily advocate an "eat, drink, and be merry" way of life? Explain.

2. Can you see any likenesses or differences between the attitudes in this poem and those in the poem by the Greek lyricist Semonides on page 106?

"Carpe Diem" (Odes I, 11) by Horace, translated by Thomas Hawkins.

The Metamorphoses

OVID

Bridging the gap from the Golden to the Silver Age of Roman literature, the writings of Ovid (43 B.C.–A.D. 17) add considerable lightness and cleverness to the poetry of his time. Most of Ovid's life was spent in Rome. He never attached himself to the intellectual literary figures who flocked around the emperor, but instead associated with the more notorious members of Rome's jaded fast set.

Ovid considered himself an expert on the theory of love, and his first works deal with the use of cosmetics by ladies *(A Lady's Toilet Directions)*, with the techniques for making amorous conquests *(Art of Love)*, and later for disposing of them *(Cures of Love)*. This light verse graphically portrayed the amoral atmosphere of decadent Roman society and perhaps offended Augustus, who, in his old age, was trying to improve the moral tone of his people.

However, Ovid's most noteworthy achievement was compiling the Greek and Roman mythological tales in the fifteen books which he called the *Metamorphoses*. The framework of the episodes is loosely suggested by the title, as each of the tales ingeniously involves some sort of transformation. (The transformations are not included in the parts of the two tales that follow; in these cases, the "shape-changes" are tacked onto the ends of the stories.) Even medieval moralists managed to attach some worthy allegorical meaning to the *Metamorphoses*. Ovid's influence on subsequent literature has been impressive, as authors of all ages have used his writings as a reference work for mythological allusions and tales.

FROM *Book 8: The Story of Daedalus and Icarus*

[Daedalus is a famous architect from Athens, who is held prisoner along with his young son Icarus by King Minos on the island of Crete.]

· · ·

Homesick for homeland, Daedalus hated Crete
And his long exile there, but the sea held him.
"Though Minos blocks escape by land or water,"
Daedalus said, "surely the sky is open,
And that's the way we'll go. Minos' dominion   5
Does not include the air." He turned his thinking
Toward unknown arts, changing the laws of nature.

"The Story of Daedalus and Icarus" from *The Metamorphoses* by Ovid, translated by Rolfe Humphries. Reprinted by permission of Indiana University Press.

He laid out feathers in order, first the smallest,
A little larger next it, and so continued,
The way that panpipes rise in gradual sequence.   10
He fastened them with twine and wax, at middle,
At bottom, so, and bent them, gently curving,
So that they looked like wings of birds, most surely.
And Icarus, his son, stood by and watched him,
Not knowing he was dealing with his downfall,   15
Stood by and watched and raised his shiny face
To let a feather, light as down, fall on it,
Or stuck his thumb into the yellow wax,
Fooling around, the way a boy will, always,
Whenever a father tries to get some work done.   20
Still, it was done at last, and the father hovered,
Poised, in the moving air, and taught his son:
"I warn you, Icarus, fly a middle course:
Don't go too low, or water will weigh the wings down;
Don't go too high, or the sun's fire will burn them.   25
Keep to the middle way. And one more thing,
No fancy steering by star or constellation,
Follow my lead!" That was the flying lesson,
And now to fit the wings to the boy's shoulders.
Between the work and warning the father found   30
His cheeks were wet with tears, and his hands trembled.
He kissed his son (*Good-by,* if he had known it),
Rose on his wings, flew on ahead, as fearful
As any bird launching the little nestlings
Out of high nest into thin air. *Keep on,*   35
Keep on, he signals, *follow me!* He guides him
In flight—O fatal art!—and the wings move
And the father looks back to see the son's wings moving.
Far off, far down, some fisherman is watching
As the rod dips and trembles over the water,   40
Some shepherd rests his weight upon his crook,
Some plowman on the handles of the plowshare,
And all look up, in absolute amazement,
At those airborne above. They must be gods!
They were over Samos, Juno's sacred island,   45
Delos and Paros toward the left, Lebinthus
Visible to the right, and another island,
Calymne, rich in honey. And the boy
Thought *This is wonderful!* and left his father,
Soared higher, higher, drawn to the vast heaven,   50
Nearer the sun, and the wax that held the wings
Melted in that fierce heat, and the bare arms
Beat up and down in air, and lacking oarage
Took hold of nothing. *Father!* he cried, and *Father!*
Until the blue sea hushed him, the dark water   55
Men call the Icarian now. And Daedalus,
Father no more, called "Icarus, where are you!
Where are you, Icarus? Tell me where to find you!"

A little like Frankenstein

And saw the wings on the waves and cursed his talents,
Buried the body in a tomb, and the land   60
Was named for Icarus.

. . .

leaving Hell   *like Lot's wife in genesis—pilar of salt*

FROM *Book 10: The Story of Orpheus and Eurydice*

[Ovid arranged his stories with some thought to chronological order, and in the previous story the god of marriage, Hymen, had presided at a wedding on the island of Crete.]

He turned around either because he loved her + had to look

or

because he didn't like her + wanted to send her back

So Hymen left there, clad in saffron robe,
Through the great reach of air, and took his way
To the Ciconian country, where the voice
Of Orpheus called him, all in vain. He came there,
True, but brought with him no auspicious words,   5
No joyful faces, lucky omens. The torch
Sputtered and filled the eyes with smoke; when swung,
It would not blaze: Bad as the omens were,
The end was worse, for as the bride went walking
Across the lawn, attended by her naiads,°   10
A serpent bit her ankle, and she was gone.
Orpheus mourned her to the upper world,
And then, lest he should leave the shades untried,
Dared to descend to Styx,° passing the portal
Men call Taenarian. Through the phantom dwellers,   15
The buried ghosts, he passed, came to the king
Of that sad realm, and to Persephone,
His consort, and he swept the strings, and chanted:
"Gods of the world below the world, to whom
All of us mortals come, if I may speak   20
Without deceit, the simple truth is this:
I came here, not to see dark Tartarus,°
Nor yet to bind the triple-throated monster,
Medusa's offspring, rough with snakes.° I came
For my wife's sake, whose growing years were taken   25
By a snake's venom. I wanted to be able
To bear this; I have tried to. Love has conquered.
This god is famous in the world above,
But here, I do not know. I think he may be
Or is it all a lie, that ancient story   30
Of an old ravishment, and how he brought
The two of you together? By these places

10. **naiads** (nā′adz): water nymphs.   14. **Styx:** one of the rivers surrounding the underworld.   22. **Tartarus:** the underworld.   24. A reference to Cerberus, the three-headed dog who guarded the entrance to Hades.

"The Story of Orpheus and Eurydice" from *The Metamorphoses* by Ovid, translated by Rolfe Humphries. Reprinted by permission of Indiana University Press.

All full of fear, by this immense confusion,
By this vast kingdom's silences, I beg you,
Weave over Eurydice's life, run through too soon.   35
To you we all, people and things, belong,
Sooner or later, to this single dwelling
All of us come, to our last home; you hold
Longest dominion over humankind.
She will come back again, to be your subject,   40
After the ripeness of her years; I am asking
A loan and not a gift. If fate denies us
This privilege for my wife, one thing is certain:
I do not want to go back either; triumph
In the death of two."
                      And with his words, the music   45
Made the pale phantoms weep: Ixion's wheel°
Was still, Tityos' vultures° left the liver,
Tantalus° tried no more to reach for the water,
And Belus' daughters° rested from their urns,
And Sisyphus° climbed on his rock to listen.   50
That was the first time ever in all the world
The Furies° wept. Neither the king nor consort
Had harshness to refuse him, and they called her,
Eurydice. She was there, limping a little
From her late wound, with the new shades of hell.   55
And Orpheus received her, but one term
Was set: He must not, till he passed Avernus,°
Turn back his gaze, or the gift would be in vain.

They climbed the upward path, through absolute silence,
Up the steep murk, clouded in pitchy darkness,   60
They were near the margin, near the upper land,
When he, afraid that she might falter, eager to see her,
Looked back in love, and she was gone, in a moment.
Was it he, or she, reaching out arms and trying
To hold or to be held, and clasping nothing   65
But empty air? Dying the second time,
She had no reproach to bring against her husband,
What was there to complain of? One thing, only:
He loved her. He could hardly hear her calling

---

46. **Ixion's** (ik·sī'ənz) **wheel:** Ixion was condemned to be tied to a perpetually revolving fiery
wheel. (All of these legendary characters named in lines 46–50 are confined to Tartarus, with
its gates of bronze and its triple wall. Those punished here in endless torture had committed
crimes against the gods.) 47. **Tityos' vultures:** Because of his crime against Leto, mother of
Apollo, Tityos was condemned to be pecked at by vultures. 48. **Tantalus:** a king who cut
up his son and served him to the gods to test their omniscience. He was condemned to stand
in water up to his neck and be surrounded by splendid food, both of which remained forever out
of his reach. 49. **Belus' daughters:** forty-nine women who murdered their husbands and were
condemned forever to fill and refill leaky jars. 50. **Sisyphus** (sis'ə·fəs): a man condemned to
roll uphill a huge stone that always rolled down again just before it reached the top. 52. **Furies:** goddesses who carried out the gods' vengeance on mortals. 57. **Avernus:** entrance to
Hades.

Farewell! when she was gone.

The double death   70
Stunned Orpheus, like the man who turned to stone
At sight of Cerberus, or the couple of rock,
Olenos and Lethaea,° hearts so joined
One shared the other's guilt, and Ida's mountain,
Where rivers run, still holds them, both together.   75
In vain the prayers of Orpheus and his longing
To cross the river once more; the boatman Charon
Drove him away. For seven days he sat there
Beside the bank, in filthy garments and tasting
No food whatever. Trouble, grief, and tears   80
Were all his sustenance. At last, complaining
The gods of hell were cruel, he wandered on
To Rhodope and Haemus,° swept by the north winds,
Where, for three years, he lived without a woman,
Either because marriage had meant misfortune   85
Or he had made a promise. But many women
Wanted this poet for their own, and many
Grieved over their rejection. . . .

73. **Olenos and Lethaea:** Olenos took upon himself his wife's sin of excessive pride in her beauty. They were both turned to rocks on Mount Ida.   83. **Rhodope** (rod′ə·pē) **and Haemus:** mountains.

FOR STUDY AND DISCUSSION

DAEDALUS AND ICARUS

1. What details make the construction of the wings seem realistic?

2. What chilling hints of imminent disaster are included in the poem?

3. Do the boy and his father seem to be believable human beings? Do you feel pity and sorrow for them? If so, what details in the poem evoke these feelings?

4. The introduction states that medieval moralists attached some worthy allegorical meaning to the *Metamorphoses*. What meaning might moralists have drawn from this legend?

ORPHEUS AND EURYDICE

1. What event is described in lines 1–8? The god Hymen carried a flaming torch to the nuptials he presided over. What ill-omened event occurred in connection with this torch?

2. Why did Orpheus descend to the underworld? Find lines throughout the poem that describe the underworld. What kind of place was it? Compare Orpheus' journey with that made by the Sumerian hero Gilgamesh (see page 13). Journeys to an underworld are found in other ancient literatures; are any extraordinary journeys found in modern literature or in TV and movie scripts? Explain and discuss.

3. Orpheus was the greatest musician in mythology. According to line 18, his plea to the king and queen of Hades was sung to the strumming of his lyre. What effect does Orpheus' song have on the people in Hades?

4. What agreement is reached between the king of the underworld and Orpheus? What human reactions cause Orpheus to violate the pact? What similar incident is found in the Gilgamesh story?

5. What meaning might the moralists have seen in the story of Orpheus and Eurydice?

6. Modern readers see rich psychological meaning in Ovid's stories, which illustrate the causes and effects of extreme human passions. What psychological plight might be illustrated in the "case study" of Orpheus?

MARTIAL ~~Satyrist~~

Satire was a strong and original weapon in the hands of certain Roman poets. The reign of four infamous emperors had made the most obsequious flattery necessary to the survival of poets; but as the morals of Roman society seemed to deteriorate past salvation, writers became more daring in condemning the abuses of the time. Whereas Horace's satire had been good-humored and restrained, the cynical epigrams of Martial (A.D. 40–A.D. 104) castigated both individuals and society as the Silver Age declined late in the first century A.D.

Martial came to Rome from Spain to seek his fortune, but when his influential friends fell into disfavor, he was forced to eke out a miserable existence by writing epigrams. Close to 1600 of these brief verses remain. They are not great poetry, but they make up a remarkable sketchbook of the seamy life of Roman society during the corrupt reign of Domitian. Sometimes Martial's verses are like greeting-card sentiments; sometimes they have rare moments of tenderness or sincerity; sometimes they sound like the comments of a modern gossip columnist. However, restricted as was Martial's talent, he is the widely acclaimed and often imitated master of the epigram—that form of short verse with the "sting in its tail."

A Total Abstainer

Though you serve richest wines,
Paulus, rumor opines

That they poisoned your four wives, I think.
It's of course all a lie;
None believes less than I—
No, I really don't care for a drink.

Man's Inhumanity to Man

That your trees may be bold
When the weather grows cold;
That their buds may be nipped by no breeze,
In hothouses faced
To the south they're encased   5
And enjoy the warm sunlight at ease.
In a cell I am bunked
With one window—defunct;
If he slept there old Boreas° would sneeze.
If this is the best   10
That you'll do for a guest,
Why, the next time I'll visit your trees.

9. **Boreas:** the north wind.

"A Total Abstainer," "Man's Inhumanity to Man," "To Quintus" by Martial, translated by Paul Nixon from *A Roman Wit.* Reprinted by permission of Houghton Mifflin Company.

To Quintus

don't forget my birthday (handwritten)

Your birthday I wished to observe with a gift;
You forbade and your firmness is known.
    Every man to his taste:
    I remark with some haste,
May the third is the date of my own.

The Blind

criticizing his taste in ugly women (handwritten)

he (handwritten)   *she* (handwritten)

Quintus loves Thais. Which? Thais the blind.   *he's judging her beauty* (handwritten)
As she wants one eye, he wants both, I find.

Galla's Hair

catty (handwritten)

The golden hair that Galla wears
    Is hers; who would have thought it?
She swears 'tis hers, and true she swears,
    For I know where she bought it.

Thou Mother Dead

different tone (handwritten)

Thou Mother dead, and thou my Father's shade,
To you I now commit the gentle maid,
    Erotion, my little love, my sweet;
    Let not her shuddering spirit fear to meet
The ghosts, but soothe her lest she be afraid.   5
How should a baby heart be undismayed
To pass the lair where Cerberus° is laid?
    The little six-year maiden gently greet.
Dear reverend spirits, give her kindly aid
And let her play in some Elysian glade,°   10
    Lisping my name sometimes—and I entreat,
    Lie softly on her, kindly earth; her feet,
Such tiny feet, on thee were lightly laid.

7. **Cerberus:** the three-headed dog guarding the entrance to Hades. 10. **Elysian glade:**
in the land of the blessed dead, a place of bliss where good souls and heroes go after death.

"Galla's Hair" by Martial, translated by Sir John Harrington.
"Thou Mother Dead" by Martial, translated by J. A. Pott, from *The Twelve Books of Epigrams,* edited by Pott and Wright.
Reprinted by permission of Routledge & Kegan Paul Ltd.

The Meanes to Attaine Happy Life

Martiall, the thinges that doe attain
The happy life, be these I finde,
The riches left, not got with pain; *— it's best to inherit it, not earn*
The fruitfull ground, the quiet minde,
good harvest
compatible friends
The egall frend; no grudge, no strife;   5
No charge of rule, nor governaunce; *— no tyranny*
Without disease, the healthful life;
The houshold of continuance:
The meane dyet, no delicate fare; *— moderation*
Trew wisedome joynde with simplenesse;   10
The night discharged of all care;
Where wine the witte may not oppresse. *— don't drink in excess*
faithful but don't argue
The faithfull wife, without debate;
Such slepes as may begile the night;
Contented with thine owne estate, *— not envious of others* 15
Ne wish for death, ne feare his might. *— don't wish for or fear death*

FOR STUDY AND DISCUSSION

FIVE EPIGRAMS

1. How is Martial's wit demonstrated in his punch lines?

2. Virgil wrote during a time of nationalism, when patriotism was high. Contrast the feelings expressed in the eclogue on page 198 with those expressed in Martial's epigrams.

3. Three famous Alexandrian epigrams are on pages 114–15. Do these epigrams differ in tone and poetic feeling from Martial's? Explain.

4. Could any of these biting epigrams apply to contemporary life? Explain.

THOU MOTHER DEAD

1. How does the tone of this poem differ from that of the epigrams?

2. What use of personification conveys poignancy to the poem?

3. Compare this poem to Catullus' lament for his brother (page 191). Which poem is expressed more formally? Can you think of any reason why this might be so?

THE MEANES TO ATTAINE HAPPY LIFE

1. What qualities does this poet see as necessary for a happy life? Compare them with those advocated by Horace in "The Golden Mean" and "Carpe Diem" (pages 206 and 207).

2. Despite the archaic spellings, you should be able to understand the mid-sixteenth-century translation of this poem. If you have difficulty, read the poem aloud. Then rephrase each line of the poem into modern colloquial English.

"The Meanes to Attaine Happy Life" by Martial, translated by Henry Howard, from *The Twelve Books of Epigrams,* edited by Pott and Wright. Reprinted by permission of Routledge & Kegan Paul Ltd.

The Annals

TACITUS

[handwritten: attacked Roman emperors — they were all nuts anyway]

[handwritten: simply criticizing]

While Livy, writing earlier, had stressed the sturdy virtues of the Romans' fore-fathers, Tacitus (A.D. 55?–A.D. 120?) stressed with bitterness the vicious excesses of the imperial court and the fawning corruption of the senate. This is not surprising, for Tacitus lived as a boy under the evils of Nero's reign, and as an adult under the cruelties of Domitian's.

Tacitus wrote two great historical works, of which only fragments have survived. The *Annals* depict events from the death of Augustus to the death of Nero, and the *Histories* continue to the death of Domitian. Tacitus also wrote a detailed account of the Germanic tribes, which gives us the fullest and earliest extant record of Germany and its primitive people.

[handwritten: personal, slanted, particular accounts]

[handwritten: not a good source]

Tacitus was a masterful and compelling stylist. His writings show great dramatic skill and a talent for vivid character studies. However, Tacitus' works have several shortcomings. So acutely aware was he of private immorality and public decay that he often neglected stirring events happening in the Empire as a whole in favor of bitter railing at the corruption in Rome itself. Tacitus was accurate in dealing with facts and he was evidently sincere, but he often imputed false motives to people, so that his interpretation of Roman imperial history is narrow and prejudiced. Unfortunately, Tacitus' interpretation became the generally accepted view of later historians. Modern scholars, through a more critical study of Tacitus himself and of contemporary data, have given a more balanced view of the early Empire and its administrators.

The characteristics of Tacitus' style are seen in the following report about the burning of Rome in A.D. 64, during the reign of Nero. Besides revealing Tacitus' own feeling toward the emperor and describing the holocaust, this account also records for the first time the reactions of first-century pagan Rome toward the new Christian religion.

[handwritten: tries to keep tone neutral but personal stuff come through]

The Burning of Rome

[handwritten: Tacitus believes this probably]

AND NOW CAME a calamitous fire— whether it was accidental or purposely contrived by the emperor remains uncertain, for on this point authorities are divided—more violent and more destructive than any that ever befell our city. It

From "The Burning of Rome" by Tacitus, translated by G. G. Ramsay.

began in that part of the Circus[1] which adjoins the Palatine and Caelian hills.[2] Breaking out in shops full of inflammable merchandise, it took hold and gathered strength at once; and being fanned by the wind soon embraced the entire length of the Circus, where there were no mansions with protective walls, no temple enclosures, nor anything else to arrest its course. Furiously the destroying flames

[1] **Circus:** Circus Maximus, a great arena used for chariot races.
[2] **Palatine and Caelian** (sē'lē·ən) **hills:** two of the seven hills in Rome. The emperor's palace was on the Palatine.

[handwritten: burnout]

swept on, first over the level ground, then up the heights, then again plunging into the hollows, with a rapidity that outstripped all efforts to cope with them, the ancient city lending itself to their progress by its narrow tortuous streets and its misshapen blocks of buildings. The shrieks of panic-stricken women; the weakness of the aged and the helplessness of the young; the efforts of some to save themselves, of others to help their neighbors; the hurrying of those who dragged their sick along, the lingering of those who waited for them—all made up a scene of inextricable confusion.

Many persons, while looking behind them, were enveloped from the front or from the side; or having escaped to the nearest place of safety, found this, too, in possession of the flames, and even places which they had thought beyond their reach in the same plight with the rest. At last, not knowing where to turn or what to avoid, they poured into the roads or threw themselves down in the fields: some having lost their all, not having even food for the day; others, though with means of escape open to them, preferred to perish for love of the dear ones whom they could not save. And none dared to check the flames; for there were many who threatened and forced back those who would extinguish them, while others openly flung in torches, saying that they had their orders—whether it was really so, or only that they wanted to plunder undisturbed.

At this moment Nero was at Antium.[1] He did not return to the city until the flames were approaching the mansion which he had built to connect the Palatine with the Gardens of Maecenas; nor could they be stopped until the whole Palatine, including the palace and everything around it, had been consumed. Nero assigned the Campus Martius and the Agrippa monuments for the relief of the fugitive and houseless multitude. He threw open his own gardens also and put up temporary buildings for the accommodation of the destitute; he brought up provisions from Ostia and the neighboring towns; and he reduced the price of corn to three sesterces [2] the peck. But popular as these measures were, they aroused no gratitude; for a rumor had got abroad that at the moment when the city was in flames Nero had mounted upon a stage in his own house and, by way of likening modern calamities to ancient, had sung the tale of the sack of Troy.

Not until the sixth day was the fire got under, at the foot of the Esquiline hill, by demolishing a vast extent of buildings, so as to present nothing but the ground, and as it were the open sky, to its continued fury. But scarcely had the alarm subsided, or the populace recovered from their despair, when it burst out again in the more open parts of the city; and though here the loss of life was less, the destruction of temples and porticoes of pleasure was still more complete. And the scandal attending this new fire was the greater that it broke out in the property owned by Tigellinus,[3] in the Aemilian quarter; the general belief being that Nero had the ambition to build a new city to be called after his own name. For of the fourteen regions into which Rome was divided only four remained intact. Three were burnt to the ground; in the other seven, nothing remained save a few fragments of ruined and half-burnt houses.

To count up the number of mansions, of tenements, and of temples that were destroyed would be no easy matter. Among the oldest of the sacred buildings burnt was that dedicated by Servius Tullius to the Moon, and the Great Altar and fane [4] raised by Evander to the Present Hercules. The temple vowed by Romulus to Jupiter, the Stayer of Flight; the Royal palace of Numa; the Temple of Vesta, with the Household Gods of the Roman people, were all destroyed; added to these

---

[1] **Antium** (an′shi·um): a seaside town about thirty-two miles south of Rome, and Nero's birthplace. The modern name is Anzio.

[2] **sesterces** (ses·tûr′sēz): A sesterce was a silver piece, worth about five cents.

[3] **Tigellinus:** Nero's worthless friend, who joined and encouraged the emperor in his cruelties and debaucheries.

[4] **fane** (fān): sanctuary or temple.

were the treasures won in numerous battles, and masterpieces of Greek art, as well as ancient and genuine monuments of Roman genius which were remembered by the older generation amid all the splendor of the restored city and which could never be replaced. Some noted that the nineteenth of July, the day on which the fire began, was also the day on which the Senonian Gauls [1] had taken and burnt the city; others were so curious in their calculations as to discover that the two burnings were separated from one another by exactly the same number of years, of months, and of days.

Nero profited by the ruin of his country to erect a palace in which the marvels were not to be gold and jewels, the usual and commonplace objects of luxury, so much as lawns and lakes and mock wildernesses, with woods on one side and open glades and vistas on the other. His engineers and masters-of-works were Severus and Celer, men who had the ingenuity and the impudence to fool away the resources of the Empire in the attempt to provide by art what nature had pronounced impossible.

For these men undertook to dig a navigable canal, along the rocky shore and over the hills, all the way from Lake Avernus to the mouths of the Tiber. There was no other water for supplying such a canal than that of the Pontine marshes; and even if practicable, the labor would have been prodigious, and no object served. But Nero had a thirst for the incredible, and traces of his vain attempt to excavate the heights adjoining Lake Avernus are to be seen to this day.

The parts of the city unoccupied by Nero's palace were not built over without divisions, or indiscriminately, as after the Gallic fire, but in blocks of regular dimensions, with broad streets between. A limit was placed to the height of houses; open spaces were left; and colonnades were added to protect the fronts of tenements, Nero undertaking to build these at his own cost and to hand over the building

sites, cleared of rubbish, to the proprietors. He offered premiums also, in proportion to the rank and means of the owners, on condition of mansions or tenements being completed within a given time; and he assigned the marshes of Ostia for the reception of the rubbish, which was taken down the Tiber in the same vessels which had brought up the corn. Certain parts of the houses were to be built without beams, and of solid stone, Gabian or Alban, those stones being impervious to fire. Then as water had often been improperly intercepted by individuals, inspectors were appointed to secure a more abundant supply, and over a larger area, for public use; owners were required to keep appliances for quenching fire in some open place; party walls were forbidden, and every house had to be enclosed within walls of its own.

These useful measures added greatly to the appearance of the new city; and yet there were not wanting persons who thought that the plan of the old city was more conducive to health, as the narrow streets and high roofs were a protection against the rays of the sun, which now beat down with double fierceness upon broad and shadeless thoroughfares.

Such were the measures suggested by human counsels; after which means were taken to propitiate the gods. The Sibylline books [2] were consulted and prayers were offered, as prescribed by them, to Vulcan,[3] to Ceres,[4] and to Proserpine.[5] Juno [6] was supplicated by the matrons, in the Capitol first, and afterward at the nearest point upon the sea, from which water was drawn to sprinkle the temple and image of the goddess; banquets to the goddesses and all-night festivals were celebrated by married women.

---

[2] **Sibylline books:** nine ancient books, supposedly written by the Sybil, or prophetess. These books reveal the destiny of Rome.

[3] **Vulcan:** Roman god of fire.

[4] **Ceres** (sir'ēz): Roman goddess of grain and harvest.

[5] **Proserpine** (prō·sûr'pə·nē): Ceres' daughter, and the wife of Pluto, king of Hades.

[6] **Juno:** in Roman mythology, wife of Jupiter, and queen of the gods.

[1] **Senonian Gauls:** barbarians from northern Italy who captured and burned Rome about 390 B.C.

But neither human aid, nor imperial bounty, nor atoning-offerings to the gods could remove the sinister suspicion that the fire had been brought about by Nero's order. To put an end therefore to this rumor, he shifted the charge onto others and inflicted the most cruel tortures upon a body of men detested for their abominations, and popularly known by the name of Christians. This name came from one Christus, who was put to death in the reign of Tiberius by the Procurator Pontius Pilate; but though checked for the time, the detestable superstition broke out again, not in Judea only, where the mischief began, but even in Rome, where every horrible and shameful iniquity, from every quarter of the world, pours in and finds a welcome.

First those who acknowledged themselves of this persuasion were arrested; and upon their testimony a vast number were condemned, not so much on the charge of incendiarism as for their hatred of the human race. Their death was turned into a diversion. They were clothed in the skins of wild beasts and torn to pieces by dogs; they were fastened to crosses, or set up to be burned, so as to serve the purpose of lamps when daylight failed. Nero gave up his own gardens for this spectacle; he provided also Circensian games,[1] during which he mingled with the populace or took his stand upon a chariot, in the garb of a charioteer. But guilty as these men were and worthy of direst punishment, the fact that they were being sacrificed for no public good, but only to glut the cruelty of one man, aroused a feeling of pity on their behalf.

Meanwhile Italy was ransacked for contributions. The provinces and allied peoples were rifled, as well as the states which are called "free." Even the gods had to submit to being plundered. The temples in the city were despoiled and emptied of the gold consecrated at triumphs or vowed by past generations in times of panic or prosperity. As for Asia [2]

and Achaia,[3] not offerings only, but the very images of the gods were carried off by Acratus and Secundus Carrinas, who were sent out to those provinces for the purpose. The former was a freedman ready for any kind of villainy; the latter was a man whose lips were tinged with Greek learning but who had no real culture in his heart.

We are told that Seneca [4] craved leave to withdraw to a remote country retreat to avoid the odium of such sacrilege; on this being denied him, he pretended to be suffering from some muscular ailment and shut himself up in his own chamber. Other accounts say that Nero ordered poison to be administered to him by one of his own freedmen, called Cleonicus; but that Seneca escaped the trap, either by the man's avowal or by his own precaution in adopting a simple diet of natural fruits, and slaking his thirst from running water.

[3] **Achaia** (ə·kē′ə): here, Greece.
[4] **Seneca:** Nero's minister of state, a Stoic philosopher. He retired from office in A.D. 62.

FOR STUDY AND DISCUSSION

1. What details does Tacitus use for human interest?

2. Cite the specific passages in which Tacitus makes a subjective judgment on a person or occurrence. What evidence does he offer to substantiate his opinions? What passages reveal Tacitus' cynicism toward Nero and the corruption of Rome?

3. What line from Tacitus has been corrupted to the familiar remark, "Nero fiddled while Rome burned"? What does Tacitus actually say about Nero's actions? If Nero was responsible for setting the fire, what motive might he have had for giving aid to the victims? How would you describe Tacitus' characterization of Nero?

4. From this account, how well informed does Tacitus seem to be about the beliefs of Christianity? How does he account for his prejudice against the Christians? On what ground does Tacitus express indignation about their persecution?

5. Compare the "tone of voice" used by Livy (page 201) and Tacitus in their respective histories.

[1] **Circensian** (sûr·sen′shən) **games:** games held in the Circus, or arena.
[2] Asia Minor.

The Letters

PLINY

Although Pliny the Younger (A.D. 62?–A.D. 114?) spent most of his life in public service, the picture he paints of Roman life in the first century is considerably more attractive than that depicted by Tacitus. In his ten books of *Letters,* Pliny reveals himself as a charming and kindly, though a worldly and vain man, who views the world with a wholesome optimism so refreshingly different that it does not seem possible that the corruption seen by his contemporaries could have existed in the same era.

Letter-writing was highly developed by the Romans. Pliny's letters, although apparently personal in nature, were carefully polished and edited—written, no doubt, with the possibility of publication in mind.

In two letters, written at the request of Tacitus, Pliny relates his eyewitness account of the eruption of Vesuvius. The first letter describes the death by asphyxiation of his uncle, Pliny the Elder, a famous naturalist and naval commander. In the second letter, which follows, the younger Pliny continues the story of his own experiences during the catastrophe. Pliny's home was located at the fashionable seaside town of Misenum, about twenty miles from the vicinity of Vesuvius, so he escaped personal injury. As immediate as the following account may appear, the letter was written some twenty-seven years after the eruption occurred, which was on August 24, A.D. 79.

The Eruption of Vesuvius

To CORNELIUS TACITUS:

The letter which, in compliance with your request, I wrote to you concerning the death of my uncle, has raised, you say, your curiosity to know not only what terrors, but what calamities I endured when left behind at Misenum (for there I broke off my narrative).

From "The Eruption of Vesuvius" by Pliny, translated by Melmoth-Hutchinson from *Loeb Classical Library.* Reprinted by permission of Harvard University Press.

"Though my shocked soul recoils, my tongue shall tell." [1]

My uncle having set out, I gave the rest of the day to study—the object which had kept me at home. After which I bathed, dined, and retired to short and broken slumbers. There had been for several days before some shocks of earthquake, which the less alarmed us as they are frequent in Campania; but that night they became so violent that one might think that the world was not being merely shaken, but turned topsy-turvy. My mother flew to my chamber; I was just rising, meaning on my part to awaken her, if she was asleep.

[1] A quotation from Virgil's *Aeneid,* Book II, line 12.

We sat down in the forecourt of the house, which separated it by a short space from the sea. I know not whether I should call it courage or inexperience—I was not quite eighteen—but I called for a volume of Livy, and began to read, and even went on with the extracts I was making from it, as if nothing were the matter. Lo and behold, a friend of my uncle's who was just come to him from Spain appears on the scene; observing my mother and me seated, and that I have actually a book in my hand, he sharply censures her patience and my indifference; nevertheless I still went on intently with my author.

It was now six o'clock in the morning, the light still ambiguous and faint. The buildings around us already tottered, and though we stood upon open ground, yet as the place was narrow and confined, there was certain and formidable danger from their collapsing. It was not till then we resolved to quit the town. The common people follow us in the utmost consternation, preferring the judgment of others to their own (wherein the extreme of fear resembles prudence), and impel us onward by pressing in a crowd upon our rear. Being got outside the houses, we halt in the midst of a most strange and dreadful scene. The coaches which we had ordered out, though upon the most level ground, were sliding to and fro and could not be kept steady even when stones were put against the wheels. Then we beheld the sea sucked back, and as it were repulsed by the convulsive motion of the earth; it is certain at least the shore was considerably enlarged and now held many sea animals captive on the dry sand. On the other side, a black and dreadful cloud, bursting out in gusts of igneous serpentine vapor now and again, yawned open to reveal long fantastic flames, resembling flashes of lightning but much larger.

Our Spanish friend already mentioned now spoke with more warmth and instancy: "If your brother—if your uncle," said he, "is yet alive, he wishes you both may be saved; if he has perished, it was his desire that you might survive him.

Why therefore do you delay your escape?" We could never think of our own safety, we said, while we were uncertain of his. Without more ado our friend hurried off and took himself out of danger at the top of his speed.

Soon afterward, the cloud I have described began to descend upon the earth and cover the sea. It had already begirt the hidden Capreae,[1] and blotted from sight the promontory of Misenum. My mother now began to beseech, exhort, and command me to escape as best I might; a young man could do it; she, burdened with age and corpulency, would die easy if only she had not caused my death. I replied I would not be saved without her, and taking her by the hand, I hurried her on. She complies reluctantly and not without reproaching herself for retarding me. Ashes now fall upon us, though as yet in no great quantity. I looked behind me; gross darkness pressed upon our rear and came rolling over the land after us like a torrent. I proposed, while we yet could see, to turn aside, lest we should be knocked down in the road by the crowd that followed us and trampled to death in the dark. We had scarce sat down when darkness overspread us, not like that of a moonless or cloudy night, but of a room when it is shut up and the lamp put out. You could hear the shrieks of women, the crying of children, and the shouts of men; some were seeking their children, others their parents, others their wives or husbands, and only distinguishing them by their voices; one lamenting his own fate, another that of his family; some praying to die, from the very fear of dying; many lifting their hands to the gods; but the greater part imagining that there were no gods left anywhere and that the last and eternal night was come upon the world.

There were even some who augmented the real perils by imaginary terrors. Newcomers reported that such or such a building at Misenum had collapsed or taken

---

[1] **Capreae** (kap'ri·ē): Capri, an island off the coast of Italy.

fire—falsely, but they were credited. By degrees it grew lighter; which we imagined to be rather the warning of approaching fire (as in truth it was) than the return of day. However, the fire stayed at a distance from us; then came darkness and a heavy shower of ashes; we were obliged every now and then to rise and shake them off, otherwise we should have been buried and even crushed under their weight. I might have boasted that amid dangers *gravitas* so appalling not a sigh or expression of fear escaped from me, had not my support been founded in that miserable, though strong, consolation that all mankind were involved in the same calamity and that I was perishing with the world itself.

At last this dreadful darkness was attenuated by degrees to a kind of cloud or smoke and passed away; presently the real day returned, and even the sun appeared, though lurid as when an eclipse is in progress. Every object that presented itself to our yet affrighted gaze was changed, covered over with a drift of ashes, as with snow. We returned to Misenum, where we refreshed ourselves as well as we could, and passed an anxious night between hope and fear; though indeed with a much larger share of the latter, for the earthquake still continued, and several enthusiastic people were giving

rumors a grotesque turn to their own and their neighbors' calamities by terrible predictions. Even then, however, my mother and I, notwithstanding the danger we had passed and that which still threatened us, had no thoughts of leaving the place till we should receive some tidings of my uncle. — *pietus — duty to relatives*

And now, you will read this narrative, so far beneath the dignity of a history, without any view of transferring it to your own; and indeed you must impute it to your own request, if it shall appear scarce worthy of a letter. Farewell. *tries to be humble*

FOR STUDY AND DISCUSSION

1. What idea consoles Pliny from fear of death? What attitude does Pliny take in describing the reactions of the common people to the disaster?

2. What can you determine about the character of Pliny from his comments on his own reactions to the disaster? How does Pliny want to reveal himself in this letter? Support your comments with evidence from the letter.

FOR COMPOSITION

Write a letter relating a personal experience as you would tell it to a historian. Furnish background explanation, such as would be necessary if you knew the letter would be published. You are the speaker in the letter; how will you characterize yourself?

PART 2
THE EAST

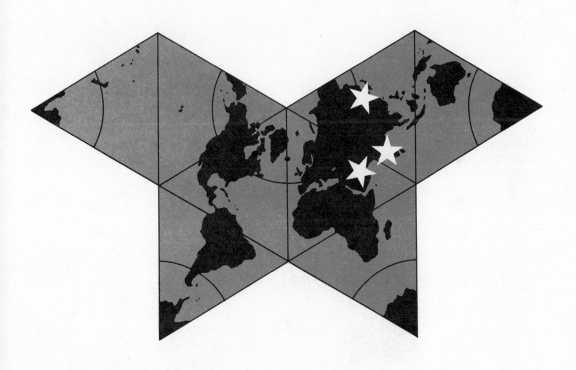

INDIAN
LITERATURE
c. 1000 B.C. – c. 200 B.C.

I N THE SHADOWY HISTORY of the first half of the second millennium B.C., we dimly discern great migrations of peoples, moving in families, tribes, clans, and nomadic nations, from established homes to new and richer lands. The ancestors of Homer's heroes make their first appearance in Greece and their first contact with the rich Minoan civilization of Crete. Abraham, his flocks, and family set out from Ur toward the land of Canaan. And farther east, sometime before 1500 B.C., people known as Aryans enter India from the northwest and begin a process of conquest and cultural absorption which is to continue for over a thousand years.

The Aryans are Europeans, probably from southern Russia, who for reasons unknown to us, left their homes to move in several directions. The two major nations which they established, however, resulted from their eastward movement onto the Iranian Plateau and into the Punjab of India. Their name, despite Hitler's use of it as a racial label, is properly a linguistic one. Both the ancient language of Iran and the Sanskrit language of India are branches of the Aryan family of languages. Other related languages, which, like Aryan, descended from a parent language known as Indo-European, include Greek, Latin, and, more recently, English.

To enter India, the Aryans had to cross some of the most rugged and varied terrain on earth. The Indian subcontinent is bounded on the north by the Himalayas, the world's highest mountains. Other chains of mountains come down from the Himalayas to the coasts, to the Arabian Sea on the west and to the Bay of Bengal on the east. Though there are ancient trade routes through high passes in all these mountains, they still represent a formidable barrier to invaders.

Within this encircling mountainous barrier, northern India is watered, and sometimes flooded, by three great rivers, the Indus, the Ganges, and the Brahmaputra. Not only does rainfall tend to be seasonal, but it also varies greatly in amount from place to place, being generally heavier in the east than in the west. Despite the aridity of the Indian Desert south of the Punjab, northern India is one of the most highly cultivated and heavily populated areas in the modern world. Its soil and climate must have been attractive to the ancient Aryans.

The Vindhya Mountains, running east and west across the Indian peninsula, divide northern India, where the Aryans first settled, from the rest of the country. The geography and climate of the southern section range from mountains to coastal plains, from temperate climates to tropical ones.

Like the Greeks who conquered the Minoans, the Aryans found in India a civilization more advanced than their own. Modern explorations in the valley of the great Indus River have revealed remains of vast cities and commercial centers. Although the very existence of these ancient cities was unsuspected till their discovery in the early 1920's, subsequent research at two of them, Harappa and Mohenjo-Daro, has uncovered a highly developed civilization which may have reached its peak as early as 2300 B.C. Its cities were densely populated and contained well-organized public facilities. There is evidence of extensive trade with contemporary Mesopotamian civilizations to the west. Quite sophisticated artwork has been uncovered, and a fully developed system of writing has been found. Yet many mysteries remain. Unfortunately, the writing has so far not been deciphered. Scholars are still uncertain who the people who created this civilization actually were. Some conjecture that these city builders were themselves invaders who replaced yet earlier peoples, but where they might have come from and when no one really knows.

What is clear is that the Aryans were quite different from the people they found already in India. The Aryan newcomers were a simple, agricultural people with no interest in urban centers except for the commercial wealth found in them. Their earliest songs and stories record the endless fighting accompanying their conquest and make frequent references to cities destroyed. They did not occupy the cities they captured, and it was several centuries before they began to develop cities of their own. Though there are no historical documents to indicate with certitude the way the Aryan conquest advanced, historians have pieced together from references in their songs and stories some impressions of the pattern of development.

The earliest age is called the Vedic period, from the name given to the collections of religious hymns, chants, and rituals which make up the literature of these times. The Vedic period covers nearly a thousand years, which saw the Aryans conquer the Punjab first, spend a relatively long time consolidating their conquest, and then move farther east and south to establish their

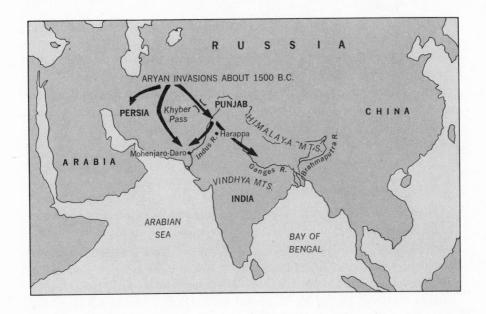

cultural center near the site of the modern city of Delhi. A number of quite stable kingdoms grew up along the routes of their progress and continued as separate political units, either within or without the empire structures that various kings tried now and again to build. Later advance of the Aryans through the Ganges Valley and toward the west coast of India forced the native peoples south ahead of them. Even today the descendants of these refugees from the Aryan invasions are recognizable minority groups in the south of India; several have still preserved their own languages, which are quite distinct from the dialects that have developed from the Sanskrit. The Aryan movement toward the west coast brought them in touch with Phoenician traders and Phoenician writing, which became the source of their own form of script when writing developed among them, probably around 800 B.C.

By the latter part of the sixth century B.C., which usually is considered to mark the end of the Vedic period, the northern two thirds of what is modern India and Pakistan were under Aryan domination, and movement south was continuing. Great religious and political ferment marked the close of this first historical period. Gautama Buddha (c. 563 B.C.–c. 483 B.C.) and other religious reformers were carrying on their ministry, and two major new religions, Jainism and Buddhism, both building on traditional Hinduism, came into being. At the same time, many of the ancient smaller states were being absorbed into larger states. The establishment of a handful of dynasties ruling substantial kingdoms was the political pattern.

The invasion of India by Alexander the Great in 327 B.C. was the first of a series of foreign invasions which continued for several hundred years thereafter. Some, like Alexander's, came from the northwest, while others, like the Tokharian invasion in the first century A.D., came from central Asia. None of these invasions, however, significantly disrupted the cultural continuity of India, and when there came a period with no major foreign powers on the scene, and when native empire building began anew under the Guptas in the early fourth century A.D., the so-called classical period of Indian history was in full flower, its high polish and sophistication never concealing its roots in the Vedic Age.

LITERATURE OF THE VEDIC PERIOD

The literature of the Aryan settlers in India is classified by these same two labels, the Vedic and the classical. As previously indicated, the Vedic period coincides with the advance of the Aryans into India and lasts approximately one thousand years. During most of this time, the literature was preserved by oral transmission; it was written down much later. The most important literary materials of the Vedic period are the Vedic hymns which give the period its name. The word *veda* means "knowledge" and came to mean specifically "sacred knowledge." The Vedic hymns, whose origin was said to be divinely inspired, represented the accumulated sacred wisdom of the ancient Aryans. Along with some chants and ritual formulas, the Vedic hymns are gathered into four collections called Samhitas.

Of the four Samhitas, the oldest and most purely poetic is the *Rig Veda* (see page 235), containing over one thousand hymns. These are poems of praise to the beauty of the earth and the wonder of existence. Many of them personify phenomena of nature as gods, as the Aryans groped for an understanding of the mysterious powers they sensed behind manifestations of nature. These hymns are not expressions of an organized religious philosophy or practice, but they represent the beginning of such a faith.

Indeed, the Vedic period is a period of religious synthesis and evolution. Some ideas, such as the concept of transmigration of souls, were adopted from the peoples the Aryans were conquering or displacing. The Aryans' own relatively primitive ancestor and nature worship was evolving complex rituals, sacrifices, and other practices of its own. The eventual product of such borrowings and development would be the infinitely varied way of life known as Hinduism, a way of life which recognizes no distinction between the secular and the religious, and which is still vital today.

The other three Samhitas reflect the early development of the religious traditions and practices just mentioned. The *Sama Veda* turns many of the verses of the *Rig Veda* into hymns to be sung in the practice of certain rituals. The *Yajur Veda,* which includes material composed considerably later, is a collection of formulas for sacrifices, mostly in prose. Finally, the *Atharva Veda,* which contains much later materials than the other three, reflects the change from the ancient practice of having tribal leaders direct religious rites to the establishment of a separate priestly class. The *Atharva Veda* is a collection of magic spells and sorcery which the priests might perform to ward off disease or demons or other dangers.

Attached to each of the Vedas were several kinds of commentary, composed by the priests during the Vedic period. The *Brahmanas* sought to explain the connections between the Vedic hymns and the elaborate sacrificial ceremonials which gradually developed. The *Aranyakas* were intended as aids to meditation on the Vedas to be used by hermits. The *Upanishads* (see page 239) turned attention away from ceremonials to a search for the mystical experience of that reality which the priests sensed to underlie the earlier Vedic appreciation of nature. In general, the *Brahmanas* concern themselves with ritual while the *Aranyakas* and *Upanishads* turn away from ritual to philosophical speculation. All these commentaries, along with the Samhitas, constitute Hindu scriptures.

Scholarly works called Sutras (meaning "threads" or "clues") are practical rules written by famous teachers and organized into six categories. The Sutras are really collections of maxims or precepts, concise and practical applications of the Vedic wisdom.

From the Samhitas, the commentaries on them, and the Sutras come the complex and varied religious beliefs and practices which comprise Hinduism.

THE HINDU RELIGION

It is impossible to define Hinduism. There is no body of dogma, no creed, no ritual or other practices to which all Hindus give assent. Hindu beliefs and practices are as varied as the Indian people themselves. Two Hindu beliefs, however, are constantly reflected in Indian literature and need to be understood. These are the concepts of caste and transmigration.

The Aryans made few class distinctions among their own peoples, and these were distinctions of function more than status. The society of the sophisticated peoples they conquered, however, seems to have been rigidly stratified. As time passed, the accommodation of conqueror and conquered to each other involved accepting parts of each other's cultures and beliefs. The caste system may have grown from such an accommodation. The Aryans recognized the functions of priests, or Brahmans; of warriors and rulers, or Kshatriyas; and of traders and farmers, or Vaishyas. Later, they created the caste of the Sudras, probably from among the conquered people, who were to perform the menial tasks of life. Eventually, the belief became established that these four castes were divinely ordained.

From this beginning, literally hundreds of hereditary sub-caste divisions developed in a complicated social system. Each caste had its rules, chiefly concerning food, marriage, and, to a certain extent, occupation. The possibility of pollution by contact with someone of a lower caste became a subject of concern. Excluded from society altogether were the so-called untouchables, persons who supposedly could pollute others by touch, by proximity, or, in some cases, even by sight. For example, one group of untouchables was permitted to move about and work only at night, for even the sight of them "polluted" higher castes. Modern India has tried to eliminate caste from its social system but has not been wholly successful in uprooting this ancient tradition.

Transmigration holds that a person's soul progresses from body to body, in one reincarnation after another, until his soul is sufficiently purified to be united with Brahman, the ultimate spiritual reality, the essence of all things. If a person leads a good life, that is, if he faithfully carries out the duties of the caste he is born into, he is reincarnated after his death into a slightly higher caste; but if he leads a bad life, if he is unfaithful to the rules for his caste, he is reborn into a lower caste, perhaps even into the body of an animal or insect. The life that is closest to union with Brahman is that of the highest caste, the priestly life, which is spent in meditation and so is free from material concerns. When a person has achieved this kind of spiritual perfection, when he has become indifferent to the material world of the senses, his reincarnations end and he is ready for union with Brahman, the goal of his spiritual journey. This migration toward perfection would take a long time; the lower castes were told that no Sudra could escape to a higher caste without undergoing hundreds or even thousands of reincarnations.

In the light of the way Hinduism evolved, it is not surprising that there are many Hindu cults and sects. The pantheon of nature gods of the *Rig Veda* gradually diminished in general importance, but many of the deities continued to have local importance as objects of cult worship. Brahma the Creator, Vishnu the Protector, and Siva the Destroyer became the major deities. Each deity, however, has a number of manifestations and accompanying names which might be objects of cult worship. Further, most deities have wives and possibly children around whom further cults might form. Thus, Ganapati, a son of Siva, is associated with agricultural cults. In addition, Vishnu's various mythological and historical appearances invite the development of cults. Vishnu was said to be incarnated as Rama, the hero of the *Ramayana,* and as the historical figure Buddha. Buddhism is derived from Hinduism, then, but with its own emphasis and its own prophet.

LITERATURE OF THE CLASSICAL PERIOD

The second period in Indian literature, as in Indian history, is called the classical period. It may be thought of as beginning with the end of the Vedic period and continuing through the first millennium A.D. The striking fact

The Hindu hero Krishna fights Kaliya, while the monster's snake-wives plea for his life (an eighteenth-century illustration). Kaliya was a looter-killer in Krishna's village. Indians see this as an encounter between good and evil.

about the literature of this period is that it is based on an artificial convention. Nearly everyone recognizes that language changes, sometimes so extensively that over a period of time earlier forms become unintelligible to later readers. Often the earlier language has dissolved into a number of dialects which become themselves separate languages, just as Latin gradually turned into French, Spanish, Italian, and Portuguese. This same sort of dialectical change occurred in the Sanskrit of India. But even as these dialectical changes were taking place in the ordinary use of the language, Sanskrit as a literary language became frozen. The reasons for this are not known, but the fact is clear that by the time the dramatist Kalidasa wrote, about A.D. 500, he was using a language which was preserved only among the scholars and literary men of the court. It is as if we spoke the English that we do now, but our authors wrote in the Old English used by the author of *Beowulf*.

The freezing of the Sanskrit literary language seems to have occurred in the sixth century B.C., about the time that Buddha was beginning his ministry. It is interesting to observe that most of his teachings were expressed in a dialect of Sanskrit rather than in Sanskrit itself. He, of course, was trying to reach people other than the scholars and courtiers and used, therefore, a dialect of ordinary speech.

Though some of the familiar dialects developed extensive literatures of their own, the Sanskrit continued to be regarded as the instrument for the noblest literary expression. Indeed, in the court drama, only the noblest figures, the hero and leading male characters, were given lines to speak in Sanskrit, while women and minor male characters used one of the less elevated Prakrit dialects.

However artificial the language, the literature written in it in the classical period is rich indeed. Like the Greeks, the Hindus had two great national epics, both in Sanskrit. The *Mahabharata* (see page 247) is the longest poem in any language, running to over 100,000 verses. Its authorship is attributed to one Vyasa, meaning "the arranger." Whether such a person actually existed or not, the name is appropriate, for the poem is a vast collection of narrative, theology, philosophy, ethics, and history, gathered from many sources. Despite digressions, there is a major story line in the poem, a mythical account of the struggle for empire between two heroic families, who are cousins.

One of the most famous sections of the *Mahabharata* is the "Bhagavad-Gita" (the "song of the holy one"), which is an extended conversation between the warrior Arjuna and Krishna, an incarnation of the god Vishnu. Arjuna, before battle, recognizes many of those he must kill as kinsmen and old friends. In despair, he exclaims "I will not fight!" Krishna's reply to Arjuna occupies the rest of the "Bhagavad-Gita" and presents a comprehensive Hindu view of the nature of action and duty, the meaning of life and of detachment, and the aims toward which men struggle in this life.

The second epic poem, attributed to the poet Valmiki, is the *Ramayana,* by far the most popular and widely known work in India. Based on an episode in the *Mahabharata,* the *Ramayana* tells the story of the prince Rama, a model of perfect nobility. In order to protect the honor of his father, who has been tricked into promising his throne to Rama's younger brother, Rama gives up his claim to the throne and withdraws with his wife, Sita, and his brother, Lakshmana, to an ascetic life in the wilderness. Here they are happy until evil demons begin to annoy them. At last Ravana, the demon king, carries Sita off with him to his island city of Lanka. Sita, the ideal wife and woman, firmly resists the efforts of Ravana to win her love and affirms her faith that Rama will at last rescue her. Rama succeeds in gathering an army to conquer Lanka, but after the victory he and Sita are separated by suspicions raised about her purity. Faithful and patient, she endures a trial by fire to prove her innocence. When Rama returns to his father's city, however, and is made king by acclamation, his people again raise doubts about Sita, and Rama and Sita have to endure another long separation before they are finally and happily reunited. The popularity of this tale has made Sita the revered symbol of womanly virtue and devotion throughout all India.

Two other important poetic forms followed these heroic epics. The first was the Puranas, long didactic poems (containing some four hundred thousand verses) which give legendary accounts of creation, of the ages of mankind, of genealogies of gods and kings. *Purana* means "that which lives from ancient times," and the material is the stuff of myths and sagas. Its purpose, however, is to give instruction. The cyclic nature of human experience is a common idea in these writings, and men are exhorted always to be ready to build again after calamity or disaster. Love, altruism, and self-sacrifice, even the values of nature, science, and art, are among the many subjects dealt with in these miscellanies.

The second major poetic form was an artificial epic known as the Kavya. Modeled on the *Ramayana* but using more elaborate artistic devices and much more complicated verse forms, these poems, too, took their subjects from ancient and traditional material. Their purposes were artistic rather than didactic, however. They were not popular with the great mass of people, but were very much enjoyed by the highly educated at the courts where they were composed. Kalidasa, the great dramatist and author of several of the most famous of the Kavyas, was reported to be but one of nine poets maintained at the court of his patron, the king Vikramaditya. The Kavyas were written for the entertainment of such courts.

So, too, was the drama, one of the outstanding literary achievements of the classical period. It is not known when plays were first performed at court. There is persuasive evidence of the existence of some forms of dramatic performance as early as the second century B.C., but where and how they originated is a mystery. Certain similarities to Greek drama have led some scholars to suggest that the drama came to India with Alexander the Great, but most modern scholars agree that it probably sprang from native sources and material. Dance, song, and recitation have their places in it, and these may be extensions of dramatic elements in ancient ritual and in the dialogue pattern of some of the Vedic literature. Traditionally, the Hindus themselves credit the sage Bharata, whose name is the Sanskrit word for "actor," with the creation of drama and with authorship of the earliest treatises on dramatic art. Whatever its source, Sanskrit drama, by the time it reached its climax in the works of Kalidasa, had become a rich and highly developed art form.

The outstanding characteristic of the best Indian drama is its idyllic beauty, a lyrical, poetic quality which permeates all the lines and action on the stage. Brief lyrical or epigrammatic verses frequently interrupt the prose dialogue. The subject matter is love or heroism, and no matter what tragic elements there may be in the plot, the plays always end happily. No unbecoming or violent emotion or action occurs on stage. Here there is a resemblance to the Greek practice of having all violent action occur offstage and be reported by messengers. But the Indian drama ignores the unities which the Greek drama adheres to, and it lacks the dramatic inevitability which characterizes the best of the Greek tragedies. Indian drama is light; it is sensuous; and in its highest achievement, *Shakuntala,* it is iridescently beautiful.

The didactic purposes of the Puranas appear in yet another literary form, the beast fables. The Indian beast fables, in which animals are personified and speak with one another and with men, are among the most ancient in the world's literature. They are foreshadowed, perhaps, in some passages of the Vedic literature, in the *Upanishads* particularly, where animals are occasionally given the ability to speak and act like men in order to drive home some satiric or didactic point. The popularity of the beast fables was already established by the time Buddhist teachers in the sixth century B.C. used them to illustrate their sermons.

The significant achievement of the classical period, as far as these ancient stories are concerned, was to bring them together into several collections, told in a consistent style and tone and given unity by the imposition of a frame story. Thus, the introduction to the *Panchatantra,* the most famous collection (see page 253), makes the whole collection a lesson in statecraft by imposing a frame story about the education of a king's thick-witted sons. The language of these collections is generally simple and direct, though occasionally the artistic devices of the Kavyas appear. The narratives are punctuated with brief, epigrammatic verses, somewhat like the verses used in the drama. Of all the literature of the classical period, these stories come closest to being popular literature and certainly have had the widest circulation in translation in other lands.

The student approaching Sanskrit literature for the first time will inevitably find much that seems strange to him in content, form, and style. But if he watches for its close awareness of nature, its intellectual subtlety, its sensuousness and appreciation of beauty, and its consistent didactic purpose, he will begin to understand why its introduction into Europe in the Romantic period of the late eighteenth and early nineteenth centuries was greeted with enthusiasm and delight by literary men and students all over the Western world.

An old ceremonial dipper. The bowl is silver and the handle, incorporating a dragon, is ivory. The art of ivory carving reached a high level in India.

The Rig Veda

The *Rig Veda,* or *Rik Veda,* is a collection of over one thousand hymns, the most ancient of the Vedic literature. The name is derived from two Sanskrit words, *ric* meaning "hymn" or "praise," and *veda* meaning "knowledge." The oldest of the hymns may have been composed even before the Aryans invaded India, before 1500 B.C.; the most recent may date from several hundred years after the invasion. A rigid ritual of memory-training enabled the holy men and priests to preserve the hymns in the oral tradition until they were at last written down.

The *Rig Veda* contains not only the oldest Vedic hymns but also the most purely lyrical. Many are nature hymns, like "To Night," which is included here. Such hymns, though addressed to personified qualities in nature, express the Aryans' sense of identity with the natural world more than they deify natural phenomena.

It is possible to trace the progress of the Aryan conquest through the Vedic hymns. Some early hymns call for unity and strength in battle, for support of the gods in overcoming the cities of the enemy. As the Aryan success grows, however, and peace begins to come, the hymns are concerned with good rains for the crops and for rich harvests. The hymn "To Pushan," which also follows, shows this kind of concern. Clearly, this hymn is addressed to a kind of guardian spirit of the shepherds.

To Night

With all her eyes the goddess Night looks forth approaching many a spot:
She hath put all her glories on.

Immortal, she hath filled the waste, the goddess hath filled height and depth:
She conquers darkness with her light.

The goddess as she comes hath set the Dawn her sister in her place: 5
And then the darkness vanishes.

So favor us this night, O thou whose pathways we have visited
As birds their nest upon the tree.

The villagers have sought their homes, and all that walks and all that flies,
Even the falcons fain for prey.   10

"To Night," translated by Ralph T. H. Griffith, from *The Wisdom of China and India,* edited by Lin Yutang, copyright 1942 by Random House, Inc. Reprinted by permission of the publisher.

Keep off the she-wolf and the wolf; O Urmya,° keep the thief away:
Easy be thou for us to pass.

Clearly hath she come nigh to me who decks the dark with richest hues:
O morning, cancel it like debts.

These have I brought to thee like kine. O Night, thou child of heaven,   15
   accept
This laud as for a conqueror.

> 11. **Urmya** ($\overline{oo}$rm′yə): the personification of night.

To Pushan, God of Pasture

Pushan, God of golden day,
Shorten thou the shepherd's way,
Vanquish every foe and stranger,
Free our path from every danger;
Cloud-born Pushan, evermore,   5
Lead us as you led before!

Smite the wild wolf, fierce and vile,
Lurking in the dark defile,
Smite the robber and the thief,
Stealing forth to take our life;   10
Cloud-born Pushan, evermore,
Lead us as you led before!

Chase him, Pushan, in thy wrath,
Who infests the lonely path,
Robber with his ruthless heart,   15
Slayer with his secret dart;
Child of clouds, for evermore,
Lead us as you led before!

Trample with thy heavy tread,
On the darksome man of dread,   20
On the low and lying knave,
Smooth-tongued double-dealing slave;
Child of clouds, for evermore,
Lead us as you led before!

Thou dost pathless forests know,   25
Thou canst quell the secret foe,
Thou didst lead our fathers right,
Wonder-worker, orb of light;

"To Pushan, God of Pasture" (anonymous), translated by Romesh Dutt.

Grant from thy unfailing store
Wealth and blessings evermore!   30

Thou hast treasures manifold,
Glittering weapons, arms of gold;
Foremost of the sons of light,
Shepherds' god and leader bright;
Grant from thy unfailing store   35
Wealth and blessings evermore!

Lead us through the dark defile
Past pursuers dread and vile,
Lead us over pleasant ways
Sheltered by thy saving grace,   40
Lead us o'er this trackless shore,
And we follow evermore!

Where the grass is rich and green,
And the pasture's beauteous seen,
And the meadow's soft and sweet,   45
Lead us, safe from scorching heat,
Blessings on thy servants pour,
And we follow evermore!

Fill our hearts with hope and courage,
Fill our homes with food and forage,   50
Save us from a cruel fate,
Feed us and invigorate;
We are suppliants at thy door,
And we follow evermore!

Heart and voice we lift in praise,   55
Chant our hymns and pious lays,
From the Bright One, good and gracious,
Ask for food and pasture spacious;
Shepherds' god! Befriend the poor,
And we follow evermore!   60

FOR STUDY AND DISCUSSION

TO NIGHT

1. The Aryans felt that night is as much a
valued part of nature as is day. Find the lines
in this poem in which night is spoken of not
in terms of darkness but in terms of light.
What are the special virtues and characteristics of night suggested in this hymn? In what
mood or state of mind does one love the night?
How does the fifth stanza suggest something
of this mood?

2. The second stanza speaks of night as
having filled the void of space. Thus, in order
to fill a "nothing," night must be a "something."
Is that "something" a goddess in the sense
that Aphrodite and Athena, for example, are
goddesses? What kind of entity, then, is night?

3. In another translation of this hymn, the
second stanza reads: "Darkness she drives
away with light. She fills the valleys and the
heights." * Which translation offers the
grander conception of the night? Why do you
think so?

* From *A History of Sanskrit Literature* by
Krishna Chaitanya. Reprinted by permission of
Asia Publishing House.

1. What are the dangers from which the shepherds ask protection in this hymn? What are the blessings they seek? How do these compare with the dangers and blessings that a Greek or biblical herdsman might have been concerned with? Compare this hymn with the Hebrew hymns of praise on pages 30–36.

2. What can you learn from this poem about the countryside through which the Aryans moved? Point out the lines in the poem which justify your answers.

3. Generally the gods in the *Rig Veda,* unlike the Greek Olympians, were not individu-ally characterized. Indeed, the same qualities are often assigned to more than one deity. Are there any distinctive traits assigned to Pushan? If so, what are they?

4. The translator has taken some liberties with the original form of this hymn. For example, he has imposed a highly regular English metrical pattern and rhyme scheme on the original verse. Also, he makes extensive use of double or compound labels and descriptions. Thus, the wolf in stanza two is described as both "fierce and vile," and in the same stanza Pushan is asked to smite "the robber and the thief." How many examples of this technique do you find? What effect does it produce?

The Upanishads

The *Upanishads* are the most famous and valued of the philosophical commentaries on the Vedas, the sacred hymns of the ancient Aryans. Complex and mystical, the *Upanishads* were composed by priests, or Brahmans, sometime between 1000 B.C. and 500 B.C. For years these commentaries survived through oral transmission; the 108 that have been preserved are considered central to Hindu scriptures.

The word *upanishad* literally means "sitting near devotedly," which suggests a picture of a young and earnest disciple studying religious truth at the feet of a great holy man. This picture gives us additional insight into the way these ancient writings have come down to us.

Varying in length from a few words to many pages, the *Upanishads* do not offer a coherent order of religious thought. Rather, they offer statements of individual perceptions and experiences, often inconsistent and incomplete, but all seeking to express the inexpressible nature of reality. Where the early Vedic hymns tend to identify some phenomenon of the external world—wind or night or fire, for example—as a deity and source of power in the universe, the *Upanishads* turn inward to seek the essence of all external phenomena and of man himself. The two fundamental concepts of the *Upanishads* are Brahman, the central principle of the universe, and Atman, called Self in this translation, which is the basis of human selfhood. One of the most famous insights of the *Upanishads* is promulgated in the selection called Chandogya, with the equation of these two principles—"that art thou," in which "that" is Brahman and "thou" is Atman.

In addition to their profound and provocative speculations, the *Upanishads* are widely celebrated for the literary excellence of the imagery, analogies, and anecdotes with which they express their difficult concepts.

The titles of the following three *Upanishads* (Kena, Chandogya, and Aitareya [1]) might be either the word that opens the commentary in the original Sanskrit or the name of its otherwise anonymous priest-author.

---

[1] **Aitareya** (ī·tə·rā′yə).

Kena

The power behind every activity of nature and of man is the power of Brahman. To realize this truth is to be immortal.

> *May quietness descend upon my limbs,*
> *My speech, my breath, my eyes, my ears;*
> *May all my senses wax clear and strong.*
> *May Brahman show himself unto me.*
> *Never may I deny Brahman, nor Brahman me.*
> *I with him and he with me—may we abide always together.*
> *May there be revealed to me,*
> *Who am devoted to Brahman,*
> *The holy truth of the Upanishads.*
> *OM . . . Peace—peace—peace.*[1]

A T WHOSE BEHEST does the mind think? Who bids the body live? Who makes the tongue speak? Who is that effulgent Being that directs the eye to form and color and the ear to sound?

The Self is ear of the ear, mind of the mind, speech of speech. He is also breath of the breath and eye of the eye. Having given up the false identification of the Self with the senses and the mind, and knowing the Self to be Brahman, the wise, on departing this life, become immortal.

Him the eye does not see, nor the tongue express, nor the mind grasp. Him we neither know nor are able to teach. Different is he from the known, and different is he from the unknown. So have we heard from the wise.

That which cannot be expressed in words but by which the tongue speaks—know that to be Brahman. Brahman is not the being who is worshiped of men.

That which is not comprehended by the mind but by which the mind comprehends—know that to be Brahman. Brahman is not the being who is worshiped of men.

That which is not seen by the eye but by which the eye sees—know that to be Brahman. Brahman is not the being who is worshiped of men.

That which is not heard by the ear but by which the ear hears—know that to be Brahman. Brahman is not the being who is worshiped of men.

That which is not drawn by the breath but by which the breath is drawn—know that to be Brahman. Brahman is not the being who is worshiped of men.

If you think that you know well the truth of Brahman, know that you know little. What you think to be Brahman in your self, or what you think to be Brahman in the gods—that is not Brahman. What is indeed the truth of Brahman you must therefore learn.

I cannot say that I know Brahman fully. Nor can I say that I know him not. He among us knows him best who understands the spirit of the words "Nor do I know that I know him not."

He truly knows Brahman who knows him as beyond knowledge; he who thinks that he knows, knows not. The ignorant think that Brahman is known, but the wise know him to be beyond knowledge.

He who realizes the existence of Brahman behind every activity of his being—whether sensing, perceiving, or thinking—he alone gains immortality. Through knowledge of Brahman comes power. Through knowledge of Brahman comes victory over death.

Blessed is the man who while he yet

---

[1] The syllable *OM*—symbol of Brahman, or God—is, to Hindus, divine; and in their rituals it is uttered with a solemn resonance, indefinitely prolonged. Our typographical form for the recurrent benediction (OM . . . Peace—peace—peace) is intended to suggest as nearly as possible the mode in which it is intoned.—(Translators' note)

Kena, Chandogya, and Aitareya from *The Upanishads, Breath of the Eternal*, translated by Swami Prabhavanada and Frederick Manchester. Published in the Mentor paperback edition by The New American Library, Inc. Reprinted by permission of the Vedanta Society of Southern California.

lives realizes Brahman. The man who realizes him not suffers his greatest loss. When they depart this life, the wise, who have realized Brahman as the Self in all beings, become immortal.

Once the gods won a victory over the demons, and though they had done so only through the power of Brahman, they were exceedingly vain. They thought to themselves, "It was we who beat our enemies, and the glory is ours."

Brahman saw their vanity and appeared before them. But they did not recognize him.

Then the other gods said to the god of fire: "Fire, find out for us who this mysterious spirit is."

"Yes," said the god of fire, and approached the spirit. The spirit said to him: "Who are you?"

"I am the god of fire. As a matter of fact, I am very widely known."

"And what power do you wield?"

"I can burn anything on earth."

"Burn this," said the spirit, placing a straw before him.

The god of fire fell upon it with all his might, but could not consume it. So he ran back to the other gods and said: "I cannot discover who this mysterious spirit is."

Then said the other gods to the god of wind: "Wind, do you find out for us who he is."

"Yes," said the god of wind, and approached the spirit. The spirit said to him: "Who are you?"

"I am the god of wind. As a matter of fact, I am very widely known. I fly swiftly through the heavens."

"And what power do you wield?"

"I can blow away anything on earth."

"Blow this away," said the spirit, placing a straw before him.

The god of wind fell upon it with all his might, but was unable to move it. So he ran back to the other gods and said: "I cannot discover who this mysterious spirit is."

Then said the other gods to Indra, great-est of them all: "O respected one, find out for us, we pray you, who he is."

"Yes," said Indra, and drew nigh to the spirit. But the spirit vanished, and in his place stood Uma, God the Mother, well adorned and of exceeding beauty. Beholding her, Indra asked:

"Who was the spirit that appeared to us?"

"That," answered Uma, "was Brahman. Through him it was, not of yourselves, that you attained your victory and your glory."

Thus did Indra, and the god of fire, and the god of wind come to recognize Brahman.

The god of fire, the god of wind, and Indra—these excelled the other gods, for they approached nearest to Brahman and were the first to recognize him.

But of all gods Indra is supreme, for he approached nearest of the three to Brahman and was the first of the three to recognize him.

This is the truth of Brahman in relation to nature: Whether in the flash of the lightning, or in the wink of the eyes, the power that is shown is the power of Brahman.

This is the truth of Brahman in relation to man: In the motions of the mind, the power that is shown is the power of Brahman. For this reason should a man meditate upon Brahman by day and by night.

Brahman is the adorable being in all beings. Meditate upon him as such. He who meditates upon him as such is honored by all other beings.

A Disciple:

Sir, teach me more of the knowledge of Brahman.

The Master:

I have told you the secret knowledge. Austerity, self-control, performance of duty without attachment—these are the body of the knowledge. The Vedas are its limbs. Truth is its very soul.

He who attains to knowledge of Brahman, being freed from all evil, finds the Eternal, the Supreme.

OM ... Peace—peace—peace.

FROM *Chandogya*

Brahman is all. From Brahman come appearances, sensations, desires, deeds. But all these are merely name and form. To know Brahman one must experience the identity between him and the Self, or Brahman dwelling within the lotus of the heart. Only by so doing can man escape from sorrow and death and become one with the subtle essence beyond all knowledge.

> *May quietness descend upon my limbs,*
> *My speech, my breath, my eyes, my ears;*
> *May all my senses wax clear and strong.*
> *May Brahman show himself unto me.*
> *May I never deny Brahman, nor Brahman me.*
> *I with him and he with me—may we abide always together.*
> *May there be revealed to me,*
> *Who am devoted to Brahman,*
> *The holy truth of the Upanishads.*
> *OM ... Peace—peace—peace.*

. . .

WHEN SVETAKETU [1] was twelve years old, his father Uddalaka [2] said to him, "Svetaketu, you must now go to school and study. None of our family, my child, is ignorant of Brahman."

Thereupon Svetaketu went to a teacher and studied for twelve years. After committing to memory all the Vedas, he returned home full of pride in his learning.

His father, noticing the young man's conceit, said to him: "Svetaketu, have you

[1] **Svetaketu** (svā·tə·kä′tōō).
[2] **Uddalaka** (ōōd·də·lä′kə).

asked for that knowledge by which we hear the unhearable, by which we perceive the unperceivable, by which we know the unknowable?"

"What is that knowledge, sir?" asked Svetaketu.

"My child, as by knowing one lump of clay, all things made of clay are known, the difference being only in name and arising from speech, and the truth being that all are clay; as by knowing a nugget of gold, all things made of gold are known, the difference being only in name and arising from speech, and the truth being that all are gold—exactly so is that knowledge, knowing which we know all."

"But surely those venerable teachers of mine are ignorant of this knowledge; for if they had possessed it, they would have taught it to me. Do you therefore, sir, give me that knowledge."

"Be it so," said Uddalaka, and continued thus:

"In the beginning there was Existence, One only, without a second. Some say that in the beginning there was nonexistence only, and that out of that the universe was born. But how could such a thing be? How could existence be born of nonexistence? No, my son, in the beginning there was Existence alone—One only, without a second. He, the One, thought to himself: Let me be many, let me grow forth. Thus out of himself he projected the universe; and having projected out of himself the universe, he entered into every being. All that is has its self in him alone. Of all things he is the subtle essence. He is the truth. He is the Self. And that, Svetaketu, THAT ART THOU."

"Please, sir, tell me more about this Self."

"Be it so, my child:

"As the bees make honey by gathering juices from many flowering plants and trees, and as these juices reduced to one honey do not know from what flowers they severally come, similarly, my son, all creatures, when they are merged in that one Existence, whether in dreamless sleep or in death, know nothing of their past or present state, because of the ignorance enveloping them—know not that they are merged in him and that from him they came.

"Whatever these creatures are, whether a lion, or a tiger, or a boar, or a worm, or a gnat, or a mosquito, that they remain after they come back from dreamless sleep.

"All these have their self in him alone. He is the truth. He is the subtle essence of all. He is the Self. And that, Svetaketu, THAT ART THOU."

"Please, sir, tell me more about this Self."

"Be it so, my son:

"The rivers in the east flow eastward, the rivers in the west flow westward, and all enter into the sea. From sea to sea they pass, the clouds lifting them to the sky as vapor and sending them down as rain. And as these rivers, when they are united with the sea, do not know whether they are this or that river, likewise all those creatures that I have named, when they have come back from Brahman, know not whence they came.

"All those beings have their self in him alone. He is the truth. He is the subtle essence of all. He is the Self. And that, Svetaketu, THAT ART THOU."

"Please, sir, tell me more about this Self."

"Be it so, my child:

"If someone were to strike once at the root of this large tree, it would bleed, but live. If he were to strike at its stem, it would bleed, but live. If he were to strike at the top, it would bleed, but live. Pervaded by the living Self, this tree stands firm and takes its food; but if the Self were to depart from one of its branches, that branch would wither; if it were to depart from a second, that would wither; if it were to depart from a third, that would wither. If it were to depart from the whole tree, the whole tree would wither.

"Likewise, my son, know this: The body dies when the Self leaves it—but the Self dies not.

"All that is has its self in him alone. He is the truth. He is the subtle essence of all. He is the Self. And that, Svetaketu, THAT ART THOU."

"Please, sir, tell me more about this Self."

"Be it so. Bring a fruit of that Nyagrodha tree."

"Here it is, sir."

"Break it."

"It is broken, sir."

"What do you see?"

"Some seeds, extremely small, sir."

"Break one of them."

"It is broken, sir."

"What do you see?"

"Nothing, sir."

"The subtle essence you do not see, and in that is the whole of the Nyagrodha tree. Believe, my son, that that which is the subtle essence—in that have all things their existence. That is the truth. That is the Self. And that, Svetaketu, THAT ART THOU."

"Please, sir, tell me more about this Self."

"Be it so. Put this salt in water, and come to me tomorrow morning."

Svetaketu did as he was bidden. The next morning his father asked him to bring the salt which he had put in the water. But he could not, for it had dissolved. Then said Uddalaka:

"Sip the water, and tell me how it tastes."

"It is salty, sir."

"In the same way," continued Uddalaka, "though you do not see Brahman in this body, he is indeed here. That which is the subtle essence—in that have all things their existence. That is the truth. That is the Self. And that, Svetaketu, THAT ART THOU."

"Please, sir, tell me more about this Self," said the youth again.

"Be it so, my child:

"As a man may be blindfolded and led away and left in a strange place; and as, having been so dealt with, he turns in every direction and cries out for someone to remove his bandages and show him the way home; and as one thus entreated may loose his bandages and give him comfort; and as thereupon he walks from village to village, asking his way as he goes; and as he arrives home at last—just so does a man who meets with an illumined teacher obtain true knowledge.

"That which is the subtle essence—in that have all beings their existence. That is the truth. That is the Self. And that, O Svetaketu, THAT ART THOU."

"Please sir, tell me more about this Self."

"Be it so, my child:

"When a man is fatally ill, his relations gather round him and ask, 'Do you know me? Do you know me?' Now until his speech is merged in his mind, his mind in his breath, his breath in his vital heat, his vital heat in the Supreme Being, he knows them. But when his speech is merged in his mind, his mind in his breath, his breath in his vital heat in the Supreme Being, then he does not know them.

"That which is the subtle essence—in that have all beings their existence. That is the truth. That is the Self. And that, O Svetaketu, THAT ART THOU."

.   .   .

Aitareya

Brahman, source, sustenance, and end of the universe, partakes of every phase of existence. He wakes with the waking man, dreams with the dreamer, and sleeps the deep sleep of the dreamless sleeper; but he transcends these three states to become himself. His true nature is pure consciousness.

> *May my speech be one with my mind, and may my mind be one with my speech.*
> *O thou self-luminous Brahman, remove the veil of ignorance from before me, that I may behold thy light.*
> *Do thou reveal to me the spirit of the scriptures.*

> *May the truth of the scriptures be ever present to me.*
> *May I seek day and night to realize what I learn from the sages.*
> *May I speak the truth of Brahman.*
> *May I speak the truth.*
> *May it protect me.*
> *May it protect my teacher.*
> *OM . . . Peace—peace—peace.*

BEFORE CREATION, all that existed was the Self, the Self alone. Nothing else was. Then the Self thought: "Let me send forth the worlds."

He sent forth these worlds: *Ambhas,* the highest world, above the sky and upheld by it; *Marichi,* the sky; *Mara,* the mortal world, the earth; and *Apa,* the world beneath the earth.

He thought: "Behold the worlds. Let me now send forth their guardians." Then he sent forth their guardians.

He thought: "Behold these worlds and the guardians of these worlds. Let me send forth food for the guardians." Then he sent forth food for them.

He thought: "How shall there be guardians and I have no part in them?

"If, without me, speech is uttered, breath is drawn, eye sees, ear hears, skin feels, mind thinks, sex organs procreate, then what am I?"

He thought: "Let me enter the guardians." Whereupon, opening the center of their skulls, he entered. The door by which he entered is called the door of bliss.[1]

The Self being unknown, all three states of the soul are but dreaming—waking, dreaming, and dreamless sleep. In each of these dwells the Self: The eye is his dwelling place while we wake, the mind is his dwelling place while we dream, the lotus of the heart is his dwelling place while we sleep the dreamless sleep.

[1] The sages declare that this door of bliss, the highest center of spiritual consciousness, technically known as the Sahashrara, the thousand-petaled lotus, is situated in the center of the brain. When the yogi's mind, absorbed in meditation, reaches this center, he realizes his unity with Brahman.—(Translators' note)

Having entered into the guardians, he identified himself with them. He became many individual beings. Now, therefore, if an individual awake from his threefold dream of waking, dreaming, and dreamless sleep, he sees no other than the Self. He sees the Self dwelling in the lotus of his heart as Brahman, omnipresent, and he declares: "I know Brahman!" [1]

Who is this Self whom we desire to worship? Of what nature is this Self?

Is he the self by which we see form, hear sound, smell odor, speak words, and taste the sweet or the bitter?

Is he the heart and the mind by which we perceive, command, discriminate, know, think, remember, will, feel, desire, breathe, love, and perform other like acts?

Nay, these are but adjuncts of the Self, who is pure consciousness. And this Self, who is pure consciousness, is Brahman. He is God, all gods; the five elements—earth, air, fire, water, ether; all beings, great or small, born of eggs, born from the womb, born from heat, born from soil; horses, cows, men, elephants, birds; everything that breathes, the beings that walk and the beings that walk not. The reality behind all these is Brahman, who is pure consciousness.

All these, while they live, and after they have ceased to live, exist in him.

The sage Vamadeva, having realized Brahman as pure consciousness, departed this life, ascended into heaven, obtained all his desires, and achieved immortality.

FOR STUDY AND DISCUSSION

KENA

1. There are three major divisions in this brief *Upanishad*. Do they all have the same purpose? If so, what is it? In your judgment, which division comes closest to achieving its purpose?

2. A statement like "He truly knows Brahman who knows him as beyond knowl-

[1] The Mandukya *Upanishad* designates this experience as "The Fourth," transcending the three states and differing from them in kind.—(Translators' note)

edge . . ." is called a paradox, that is, a statement which seems to be self-contradictory. Why would paradox be a device frequently employed in this kind of writing?

3. The third division of this *Upanishad* is an anecdote, a form frequently used in Hindu scriptures. In the anecdote, does the concept of Brahman seem the same as in the other divisions of the piece? In what ways does it differ? Does the use of the anecdote itself contribute to these differences? If so, how?

CHANDOGYA

1. This *Upanishad* uses analogies, or comparisons, to try to explain the inexplicable. In the analogies which use the lump of clay and the nugget of gold, what is being defined? What aspects or qualities of Brahman are being compared in the other analogies?

2. According to this *Upanishad,* could a man come to knowledge of Brahman and still maintain awareness of his separate, individual identity? Which of the analogies most clearly answers this question?

3. The brief account of creation given here seems to suggest that Brahman is eternal, changeless, and beyond the knowledge of human senses. Can men know anything except through the senses? Explain your answer.

AITAREYA

1. This brief *Upanishad* contains one of the many Hindu creation stories. In what ways does this creation story differ from that in the selection from the Chandogya *Upanishad?* How does this story compare with the biblical creation stories (see pages 20–23)?

2. Two important Hindu ideas are the concepts of *karma*—the belief that one is responsible for the effects of his own acts in every incarnation—and of transmigration. These two concepts together make possible a belief in the strict justice of the universe, for the acts of one lifetime may see their inevitable effects fulfilled in a later existence. The combination of these two ideas would seem to provide for what we of the West would call the immortality of the soul. But is this what is meant in the final paragraph when Vamadeva is said to have achieved "immortality"? How does transmigration differ from the concept of immortality presented in the *Upanishads?* Is it an optimistic or pessimistic religious belief that seeks the loss of individual identity and earthly existence in a mystical

union with Ultimate Reality? Explain your answer.

3. Ralph Waldo Emerson (1803–1882), American poet-philosopher, was attracted by Hindu scriptures. His poem "Brahma," originally entitled "Song of the Soul," follows. It is an example of what might almost be called an American *Upanishad*. According to this poem, how real is what we ordinarily call reality? (The "sacred Seven" in line 14 refers to the greatest Hindu saints.)

● If the red slayer think he slays,
   Or if the slain think he is slain,
They know not well the subtle ways
   I keep, and pass, and turn again.

Far or forgot to me is near;
   Shadow and sunlight are the same;
The vanished gods to me appear;
   And one to me are shame and fame.

They reckon ill who leave me out;
   When me they fly, I am the wings;
I am the doubter and the doubt,
   And I the hymn the Brahmin sings.

The strong gods pine for my abode,
   And pine in vain the sacred Seven;
But thou, meek lover of the good!
   Find me, and turn thy back on heaven.

—RALPH WALDO EMERSON

FOR COMPOSITION

1. In a paragraph, explain what you understand by the equation "That art thou."

2. The Master says that knowledge of Brahman can come from austerity, self-control, and performance of duty without attachment. In an essay, explain how these values might affect man's attitude toward "progress" and his relationship to the material world.

The Mahabharata

The *Mahabharata* [1] is the older of the two great Indian epics, dating from about 300 B.C. Though its main narrative is attributed to a sage called Vyasa, about whom nothing is known, many nameless scribes added to the story, making the total work a compendium of treatises on theology, history, government, and ethics—fragments of nearly every kind of literature and thought. Much of subsequent Indian literature finds its material in this diversity in the *Mahabharata*.

Episodic and varied as it is, the *Mahabharata* does have one major plot, the story of the bloody battle for power between families of cousins, the Kauravas and the Pandavas. The blood relationships and mutual affections of the contending cousins add pathos to their inability to resolve their differences peacefully. This pathos becomes tragedy as, in the fury of battle, the finer qualities of warriors on both sides are brutalized, and they commit hideous and unrestrained violence against one another. The Pandavas are ultimately victorious, but their victory is at so bitter a cost that it brings them little joy. Years later the warriors of both sides are reconciled in heaven.

The actual fighting lasts only eighteen days. The episode which follows occurs near the end of the war and includes the fulfillment of a hideous oath of revenge by Bhima, one of the most powerful of the Pandavas. Bhima had sworn to drink the blood of his cousin, who had molested the wife of the five Pandava brothers.

The quarrel between the two families began when Duryodhana, the eldest of the Kauravas, became jealous of his cousins, the Pandavas, after his father gave them a piece of his kingdom as their own. On the advice of his uncle, a gambler, Duryodhana challenged the eldest of the Pandava brothers to a dice game. This brother, who was addicted to gambling but unskilled in it, staked and lost first his wealth, then himself and his brothers, and finally their wife. (She lived with each Pandava brother in turn, an arrangement resulting from the order of the Pandavas' mother that all the brothers should share in whatever good came to one.) When the Pandavas' wife was lost in the gambling, one of the Kaurava brothers insulted her by trying to disrobe her before the whole court. This brought down on him the terrible curse of Bhima. The king restored the kingdom to the Pandavas, but another gambling match lost the land for them again, and, as another condition of the new bet, the Pandava brothers spent twelve years in exile. When they later sought the restoration of their kingdom again, war resulted.

The epic is divided into sections which bear the names of the characters whose exploits are especially described. The title of this section from the epic means "Karna's Book," Karna being one of the heroes of the Kaurava family. The section which precedes this one is called "Drona Parva," "Drona's Book." Drona was the preceptor of both the Pandavas and the Kauravas. Fighting for the Kauravas, he was killed by the Pandava Dhrstadyumna through treachery.

---

[1] *Mahabharata* (mə·hä·bä′rə·tə).

KAURAVAS AND THEIR ALLIES

Duryodhana (dur·yō′də·nə): eldest of the hundred sons of King Dhrtarastra.

Duhsasana (duh·shä′sə·nə): second of the hundred sons; the Kaurava who dishonored the wife of the Pandavas.

Karna: son of Vikartana, the sun god; brother of the Pandavas but allied to Duryodhana because of a generous gift of land from him.

Drona: preceptor of the Kauravas and Pandavas who fought on the side of the Kauravas; killed before this selection of the epic opens.

Asvatthama (ash·vat·tä′mə): son of Drona.

Krpa (kri′pə): brother-in-law of Drona.

Krtavarma (krit′ə·vər·mə): ally of Duryodhana.

Salya (shal′yə): king of Madra; holds reins of Karna's chariot in this story.

the Samsaptakas: band of warriors pledged to kill the Pandava Arjuna.

Sakuni (shə·ku′ni): uncle of Duryodhana, who advised him to take advantage of Yudhisthira's weakness for gambling.

Uluka (u·lōō′kə): son of Sakuni.

PANDAVAS AND THEIR ALLIES

Yudhisthira: king of the Pandavas; eldest of the five brothers; son of the god of justice; had a weakness for gambling.

Arjuna: third Pandava; son of Indra, king of the gods. Arjuna is greatest of the Pandavas.

Bhima (bē′mə): second and strongest of the Pandavas; son of Vayu, god of the winds; the warrior who has sworn revenge on Duhsasana.

Nakula: fourth Pandava.

Sahadeva: fifth Pandava; like Nakula, son of Asvins, who are the twin physicians of heaven.

Yuyutsu

Draupadi (drou′pə·de): wife to all five Pandava brothers.

Dhrstadyumna (drisht·əd·yum′nə): brother of Draupadi.

Sikhandi (shik′hən·dē): sister of Draupadi; temporarily granted manhood so that she might gain revenge on one of the Kauravas.

Krsna (krish′nə): said to be an incarnation of Vishnu, one of the holiest of celestials; holds reins of Arjuna's chariot in this story.

FROM *Books 67–69: Karna Parva*

WHEN the mighty bowman Drona was slain, the Kaurava host became pale-faced and gloomy. Seeing his own forces standing as if paralyzed and lifeless, King Duryodhana said to them, "Relying on the strength of your arms, I have challenged the Pandavas to this battle. Victory or death is the lot of all warriors. Why wonder then at the fall of Drona? Let us resume the fighting in all directions, encouraged by the sight of the lofty-minded Karna, the son of Vikartana, mighty bowman and wielder of celestial weapons, who is roving about in the field of battle.

From *The Mahabharata, An English Version Based on Selected Verses* by Chakravarthi V. Narasimham. Reprinted by permission of Columbia University Press.

Permit me to remind you that it was he who slew Ghatotkaca,[1] that creator of illusions, with the indomitable Sakti weapon."[2] Then all those kings, headed by Duryodhana, quickly installed Karna as commander in chief, and bathed him according to rites with golden and earthen pitchers of holy water.

As the sixteenth day dawned, Karna summoned the Kaurava forces to battle with loud blasts on his conch. He arranged his army in the form of a makara,[3] and proceeded to attack the Pandavas, desirous of victory. On the Pandava side, Arjuna, whose car was drawn by white horses, formed a counterarray in the shape of a half-moon.

The day's fighting was marked by many duels, between Bhima and Asvatthama, Sahadeva and Duhsasana, Nakula and Karna, Uluka and Yuyutsu, Krpa and Dhrstadyumna, and Sikhandi and Krtavarma. While they were thus engaged, the sun disappeared behind the western mountains. Then both sides retired from the field and proceeded to their own encampments.

Before the fighting began on the seventeenth day, Karna said to Duryodhana, "Today, O King, I will go forth and battle with the famous Pandava, Arjuna. Either I shall slay that hero, or he shall slay me. You are aware of his energy, weapons, and resources. My bow, known by the name of Vijaya, is the greatest of all weapons. It was made by Visvakarma[4] in accordance with Indra's[5] wishes, and is a celestial and excellent weapon. On this count I believe I am superior to Arjuna.

"Now you must know," continued Karna, "in what respect Arjuna is superior to me. Krsna, born of the Dasarha race, who is revered by all people, is the holder of the reins of his horses. He who is verily the creator of the universe thus guards Arjuna's car. On our side Salya, who is the ornament of all assemblies, is of equal heroism. Should he take over the duties of my charioteer, then victory will surely be yours. Let the irresistible Salya, therefore, act as my charioteer."

Duryodhana thereupon went to see Salya. Humbly approaching the Madra prince, he affectionately spoke these words to him: "You have heard what Karna has said, namely that he chooses you, foremost of princes, as his charioteer. Therefore, for the destruction of the Pandavas, and for my own good, be pleased to become Karna's charioteer. As that foremost of charioteers, Krsna, counsels and protects Arjuna, so should you support Karna at all times."

Salya replied, "You are insulting me, O Duryodhana, or surely you must doubt my loyalty, since you so readily request me to do the work of a charioteer. You praise Karna and consider that he is superior to us. But I do not consider him to be my equal in the field of battle. Knowing that I can strike down the enemy, why do you wish to employ me in the office of charioteer to the lowborn Karna?"

Duryodhana replied to Salya with great affection and high respect. Desirous of achieving his main objective, he addressed him in a friendly manner, saying sweetly, "O Salya, what you say is doubtless true. However, in making this request I have a certain purpose. Even as Karna is reckoned to be superior to Arjuna in many ways so are you, in the opinion of the whole world, superior to Krsna. As the high-souled Krsna is expert in the handling of horses, even so, O Salya, are you doubly skilled. There is no doubt about it."

Thus flattered, Salya said, "O Duryodhana! As you tell me that among all these troops there is none but myself who is more accomplished than Krsna, I am pleased with you. I therefore agree to act as the charioteer of the famous Karna while he is engaged in battle with Arjuna, foremost of the Pandavas. But there is one condition on which I accept your pro-

---

[1] **Ghatotkaca:** a demon, son of Bhima and a demon mother.

[2] **Sakti** (shak'ti) **weapon:** *Sakti* literally means "power." Here it is the name of a missile.

[3] **makara:** a standard battle formation.

[4] **Visvakarma:** the celestial architect and weaponmaker.

[5] **Indra:** king of the celestials.

posal: that I shall give vent in Karna's presence to such expressions as I may wish." Duryodhana, who was accompanied by Karna, readily accepted this condition, saying, "So be it."

After Salya had taken over as his charioteer, Karna said to him, "Today I shall fearlessly fight Krsna and Arjuna, foremost among all wielders of weapons. My mind is, however, troubled by the curse of Parasurama, that best of Brahmanas.[1] In my early days, desirous of obtaining a celestial weapon, I lived with him in the disguise of a Brahmana. But, O Salya, in order to benefit Arjuna, Indra, the king of the gods, took on the horrible form of an insect and stung my thigh. Even so, I remained motionless for fear of disturbing my preceptor. When he woke up, he saw what had happened. He subsequently learned the deception I had practiced on him and cursed me, that the invocation for the weapon I had obtained by such trickery would not come to my memory at the time of dire need.

"Once while wandering in the forest," Karna continued, "I accidentally killed the sacrificial cow of a Brahmana. Although I offered him seven hundred elephants with large tusks, and many hundreds of male and female slaves, the best of Brahmanas was still not pleased, and although I begged for forgiveness, he said: 'O suta,[2] what I have prophesied will happen. It cannot be otherwise.' He had said, 'Your wheel shall fall into a hole.' In this battle, while I am fighting, that will be my only fear."

During the fighting on that day there was a dreadful and thrilling battle between Karna and the Pandavas which increased the domain of the god of death. After that terrible and gory combat only a few of the brave Samsaptakas survived. Then Dhrstadyumna and the rest of the Pandavas rushed toward Karna and attacked him. As a mountain receives heavy rain-

fall, so Karna received those warriors in battle. Elsewhere on the battlefield Duhsasana boldly went up to Bhima and shot many arrows at him. Bhima leapt like a lion attacking a deer, and hurried toward him. The struggle that took place between these two, incensed against each other and careless of life, was truly superhuman.

Fighting fiercely, Prince Duhsasana achieved many difficult feats in that duel. With a single shaft he cut off Bhima's bow; with six shafts he pierced Bhima's driver. Then, without losing a moment, he pierced Bhima himself with many shafts discharged with great speed and power, while Bhima hurled his mace at the prince. With that weapon, from a distance of ten bow-lengths, Bhima forcibly dislodged Duhsasana from his car. Struck by the mace and thrown to the ground, Duhsasana began to tremble. His charioteer and all his steeds were slain, and his car too was smashed to pieces by Bhima's weapon.

Then Bhima remembered all the hostile acts of Duhsasana toward the Pandavas. Jumping down from his car, he stood on the ground, looking steadily on his fallen foe. Drawing his keen-edged sword, and trembling with rage, he placed his foot upon the throat of Duhsasana and, ripping open the breast of his enemy, drank his warm lifeblood, little by little. Then, looking at him with wrathful eyes, he said, "I consider the taste of this blood superior to that of my mother's milk, or honey, or ghee,[3] or wine, or excellent water, or milk, or curds, or buttermilk."

All those who stood around Bhima and saw him drink the blood of Duhsasana fled in terror, saying to each other, "This one is no human being!" Bhima then said, in the hearing of all those heroes, "O wretch among men, here I drink your lifeblood. Abuse us once more now, beast, beast, as you did before!"

Having spoken these words, the victorious Bhima turned to Krsna and Arjuna, and said, "O you heroes, I have ac-

[1] **Parasurama ... Brahmanas:** Parasurama is a warrior-sage. The Brahmanas are members of the priestly caste.
[2] **suta:** charioteer.

[3] **ghee:** a butterlike substance made from buffalo milk.

complished today what I had vowed in respect of Duhsasana! I will soon fulfill my other vow by slaying that second sacrificial beast, Duryodhana! I shall kick the head of that evil one with my foot in the presence of the Kauravas, and I shall then obtain peace!" After this speech, Bhima, drenched with blood, uttered loud shouts and roared with joy, even as the mighty Indra of a thousand eyes after slaying Vrtra.[1]

Fleeing in the face of Arjuna's onslaught, the broken divisions of the Kauravas saw Arjuna's weapon swelling with energy and careering like lightning. But Karna destroyed that fiery weapon of Arjuna with his own weapon of great power which he had obtained from Parasurama. The encounter between Arjuna and Karna became very fierce. They attacked each other with arrows like two fierce elephants attacking each other with their tusks.

Karna then fixed on his bowstring the keen, blazing, and fierce shaft which he had long polished and preserved with the object of destroying Arjuna. Placing in position that shaft of fierce energy and blazing splendor, that venomous weapon which had its origin in the family of Airavata[2] and which lay within a golden quiver covered by sandal dust, Karna aimed it at Arjuna's head. When he saw Karna aim that arrow, Salya said, "O Karna, this arrow will not succeed in hitting Arjuna's neck! Aim carefully, and discharge another arrow that may succeed in striking the head of your enemy!" His eyes burning in wrath, Karna replied, "O Salya, Karna never aims an arrow twice!"

Thereupon Karna carefully let loose that mighty snake in the form of an arrow, which he had worshiped for many long years, saying, "You are slain, O Arjuna!" Seeing the snake aimed by Karna, Krsna, strongest among the mighty, exerted his whole strength and pressed down Arjuna's chariot with his feet into the earth. When the car itself had sunk into the ground, the

steeds, too, bent their knees and laid themselves down upon the earth. The arrow then struck and dislodged Arjuna's diadem, that excellent ornament celebrated throughout the earth and the heavens.

The snake said, "O Krsna! Know me as one who has been wronged by Arjuna. My enmity toward him stems from his having slain my mother!"

Then Krsna said to Arjuna, "Slay that great snake which is your enemy." Thus urged by Krsna, Arjuna asked, "Who is this snake that advances of his own accord against me, as if right against the mouth of Garuda?"[3] Krsna replied, "While you were worshiping the fire god at the Khandava forest, this snake was ensconced within his mother's body, which was shattered by your arrows." As the snake took a slanting course across the sky, Arjuna cut it to pieces with six keen shafts, so that it fell down on the earth.

Then, because of the curse of the Brahmana, Karna's chariot wheel fell off, and his car began to reel. At the same time, he forgot the invocation for the weapon he had obtained from Parasurama. Unable to endure these calamities, Karna waved his arms and began to rail at righteousness, saying, "They that are conversant with virtue say that righteousness protects the righteous! But today righteousness does not save me."

Speaking thus, he shed tears of wrath and said to Arjuna, "O Pandava! Spare me for a moment while I extricate my wheel from the earth! You are on your car while I am standing weak and languid on the ground. It is not fair that you should slay me now! You are born in the Ksatriya order.[4] You are the scion of a high race. Recollect the teachings of righteousness, and give me a moment's time!"

Then, from Arjuna's chariot, Krsna said, "It is fortunate, O Karna, that you now remember virtue. It is generally true that those who are mean rail at Providence when they are afflicted by distress,

---

[1] **Vrtra** (vri′trə): a demon.

[2] **Airavata** (ī·rä′və·tə): a mythical serpent.

[3] **Garuda:** the Indian eagle, the traditional enemy of snakes.

[4] **Ksatriya** (kish′ə·tri·yə) **order:** the warrior caste.

but forget their own misdeeds. You and Duryodhana and Duhsasana and Sakuni caused Draupadi, clad in a single garment, to be brought into the midst of the assembly. On that occasion, O Karna, this virtue of yours was not in evidence! When Sakuni, skilled in dicing, vanquished Yudhisthira who was unacquainted with it, where was this virtue of yours? Out of covetousness, and relying on Sakuni, you again summoned the Pandavas to a game of dice. Whither then had this virtue of yours gone?"

When Krsna thus taunted Karna, Arjuna became filled with rage. Remembering the incidents to which Krsna alluded, he blazed with fury and, bent upon Karna's speedy destruction, took out of his quiver an excellent weapon. He then fixed on his bow that unrivaled arrow and charged it with mantras.[1] Drawing his bow Gandiva, he quickly said, "Let this shaft of mine be a mighty weapon capable of speedily destroying the body and heart of my enemy. If I have ever practiced ascetic austerities, gratified my preceptors, and listened to the counsels of well-wishers, let this sharp shaft, so long worshiped by me, slay my enemy Karna by that truth!"

Having uttered these words, Arjuna discharged for the destruction of Karna that terrible shaft, that blazing arrow fierce and efficacious as a rite prescribed in the Atharva of Angiras,[2] and invincible against the god of death himself in battle. Thus sped by that mighty warrior, the shaft endowed with the energy of the sun caused all the points of the compass to blaze with light. The head of the commander of the Kaurava army, splendid as the sun, fell like the sun disappearing in the blood-red sunset behind the western hills. Cut off by Arjuna's arrow and deprived of life, the tall trunk of Karna, with blood gushing from every wound, fell down like the thunder-riven summit of a mountain of red chalk with crimson

streams running down its sides after a shower of rain.

Then from the body of the fallen Karna a light, passing through the atmosphere, illumined the sky. This wonderful sight was seen by all the warriors on the battlefield. After the heroic Karna was thus thrown down and stretched on the earth, pierced with arrows and bathed in blood, Salya, the king of the Madras, withdrew with Karna's car. The Kauravas, afflicted with fear, fled from the field, frequently looking back on Arjuna's lofty standard which blazed in splendor.

FOR STUDY AND DISCUSSION

1. In this selection, you probably observed many similarities to the *Iliad* (page 55). For example, in the *Iliad* the distinctions between men and gods are not always clear, and supernatural effects play a large part in the action. Find passages in "Karna Parva" which illustrate these characteristics.

2. Consider, too, the attitude toward fate in both epics. Is the prophecy concerning Karna's chariot and his inability to remember the invocation for his weapon like the prophecy that promised Achilles a short but heroic life? If you see differences between the two kinds of "fated" events, what are they?

3. The pride of Salya, the diplomacy of Duryodhana, the vengeance of Bhima, all have their parallels in the *Iliad*. What are these parallels? Is the heroic tone of this tale similar to that of the *Iliad*? Discuss its use of the same elevated style, the same larger-than-life characters, the same rejection of the petty and trivial incidents of life. Compare and contrast the Achilles-Hector battle with the Karna-Arjuna battle.

4. It is typical of the *Mahabharata* that at the height of the battle, when Karna's chariot is crippled and he forgets the invocation for his magic weapon, Karna should consider the moral question of whether the righteous are protected from harm by their righteousness. Furthermore, he appeals to Arjuna, in the name of righteousness, to give him time to prepare to defend himself. Does this suggest a broader artistic purpose for the *Mahabharata* than merely recording heroic events? What might that broader purpose be? Is that purpose shared by the *Iliad* or other epics you have read? Explain your answers.

---

[1] **mantras:** incantations, charms, and spells.
[2] **Atharva of Angiras:** Atharva was the fourth Veda, the collection of magic spells. Angiras was a sage credited with preparing various magic spells.

The Panchatantra

The *Panchatantra* is the most famous of the Indian story cycles. Its age is not certainly known, but some scholars believe the collection as we now have it goes back as far as the beginning of the second century B.C. The stories were first translated into a foreign language—Middle Persian—in the sixth century A.D., and since that time the *Panchatantra* has been a world classic. It has appeared in some two hundred versions in more than fifty different languages and has influenced the literatures of many lands. The fables of La Fontaine (see page 626), of seventeenth-century France, for example, owe a clear debt to the *Panchatantra*.

Like many subsequent story collections, such as *The Thousand and One Nights* (see page 343), Chaucer's *Canterbury Tales* (see page 435), and Boccaccio's *Decameron* (see page 507), the *Panchatantra* establishes its unity through a frame story, presented as the introduction. The frame story tells that a Brahman, a priest, is attempting to teach within six months the art of statecraft to two rather stupid and spoiled princes. The five headings under which the Brahman divides his course of study are Loss of Friends, Winning of Friends, Crows and Owls (international relations), Loss of Gains, and Ill-Considered Action. The stories in the *Panchatantra* (the word means "five books") are grouped under these five headings. Though the stories, which are frequently interlocked and overlapping, are told in prose, it is the witty, epigrammatic verses, usually quoted from sacred writings, which give the *Panchatantra* much of its special flavor and appeal.

Four stories from the *Panchatantra* follow.

The Ungrateful Man

IN A CERTAIN TOWN lived a Brahman whose name was Sacrifice. Every day his wife, chafing under their poverty, would say to him: "Come, Brahman! Lazybones! Stony-Heart! Don't you see your babies starving, while you hang about, mooning? Go somewhere, no matter where, find some way, any way, to get food, and come back in a hurry."

At last the Brahman, weary of this refrain, undertook a long journey, and in a few days entered a great forest. While wandering hungry in this forest, he began

"The Ungrateful Man," "The Cave That Talked," "How Supersmart Ate the Elephant," "The Lion-Makers" from *Panchatantra*, translated by Arthur W. Ryder, © 1925, renewed © 1953 by the Misses Mary E. Ryder and Winifred M. Ryder. Reprinted by permission of The University of Chicago Press.

to hunt for water. And in a certain spot he came upon a well, overgrown with grass. When he looked in, he discovered a tiger, a monkey, a snake, and a man at the bottom. They also saw him.

Then the tiger thought: "Here comes a man," and he cried: "O noble soul, there is great virtue in saving life. Think of that, and pull me out, so that I may live in the company of beloved friends, wife, sons, and relatives."

"Why," said the Brahman, "the very sound of your name brings a shiver to every living thing. I cannot deny that I fear you." But the tiger resumed:

"To Brahman-slayer, impotent,
To drunkard, him on treason bent,
To sinner through prevarication,
The holy grant an expiation:
While for ingratitude alone
No expiation will atone."

And he continued: "I bind myself by a triple oath that no danger threatens you from me. Have pity and pull me out." Then the Brahman thought it through to this conclusion: "If disaster befalls in the saving of life, it is a disaster that spells salvation." So he pulled the tiger out.

Next the monkey said: "Holy sir, pull me out too." And the Brahman pulled him out too. Then the snake said: "Brahman, pull me out too." But the Brahman answered: "One shudders at the mere sound of your name, how much more at touching you!" "But," said the snake, "we are not free agents. We bite only under orders. I bind myself by a triple oath that you need have no fear of me." After listening to this, the Brahman pulled him out too. Then the animals said: "The man down there is a shrine of every sin. Beware. Do not pull him out. Do not trust him."

Furthermore, the tiger said: "Do you see this mountain with many peaks? My cave is in a wooded ravine on the north slope. You must do me the favor of paying me a visit there some day, so that I may make return for your kindness. I should not like to drag the debt into the next life." With these words he started for his cave.

Then the monkey said: "My home is quite near the cave, beside the waterfall. Please pay me a visit there." With this he departed.

Then the snake said: "In any emergency, remember me." And he went his way.

Then the man in the well shouted time and again: "Brahman! Pull me out too!" At last the Brahman's pity was awakened, and he pulled him out, thinking: "He is a man, like me." And the man said: "I am a goldsmith and live in Baroch. If you have any gold to be worked into shape, you must bring it to me." With this he started for home.

Then the Brahman continued his wanderings but found nothing whatever. As he started for home, he recalled the monkey's invitation. So he paid a visit, found the monkey at home, and received fruits sweet as nectar, which put new life into him. Furthermore, the monkey said: "If you ever have use for fruit, pray come here at any time." "You have done a friend's full duty," said the Brahman. "But please introduce me to the tiger." So the monkey led the way and introduced him to the tiger.

Now the tiger recognized him and, by way of returning his kindness, bestowed on him a necklace and other ornaments of wrought gold, saying: "A certain prince whose horse ran away with him came here alone, and when he was within range of a spring, I killed him. All this I took from his person and stored carefully for you. Pray accept it and go where you will."

So the Brahman took it, then recalled the goldsmith and visited him, thinking: "He will do me the favor of getting it sold." Now the goldsmith welcomed him with respectful hospitality, offering water for the feet, an honorable gift, a seat, hard food and soft, drink, and other things, then said: "Command me, sir. What may I do for you?" And the Brahman said: "I have brought you gold. Please sell it." "Show me the gold," said the goldsmith, and the other did so.

Now the goldsmith thought when he saw it: "I worked this gold for the prince." And having made sure of the fact, he said: "Please stay right here, while I show it to somebody." With this he went to court and showed it to the king. On seeing it, the king asked: "Where did you get this?" And the goldsmith replied: "In my house is a Brahman. He brought it."

Thereupon the king reflected: "Without question, that villain killed my son. I will show him what that costs." And he issued orders to the police: "Have this Brahman scum fettered, and impale him tomorrow morning."

When the Brahman was fettered, he remembered the snake, who appeared at once and said: "What can I do to serve you?" "Free me from these fetters," said the Brahman. And the snake replied: "I will bit the king's dear queen. Then, in spite of the charms employed by any great conjurer and the antidotes of other physicians, I will keep her poisoned. Only by the touch of your hand will the poison be neutralized. Then you will go free."

Having made this promise, the snake bit the queen, whereupon shouts of despair arose in the palace, and the entire city was filled with dismay. Then they summoned dealers in antidotes, conjurers, scientists, druggists, and foreigners, all of whom treated the case with such resources as they had, but none could neutralize the poison. Finally, a proclamation was made with beat of drum, upon hearing which the Brahman said: "I will cure her." The moment he spoke, they freed him from his fetters, took him to the king, and introduced him. And the king said: "Cure her, sir." So he went to the queen and cured her by the mere touch of his hand.

When the king saw her restored to life, he paid the Brahman honor and reverence, then respectfully asked him: "Reveal the truth, sir. How did you come by this gold?" And the Brahman began at the beginning and related the whole adventure accurately. As soon as the king comprehended the facts, he arrested the goldsmith, while he gave the Brahman a thousand villages and appointed him privy counselor. But the Brahman summoned his family, was surrounded by friends and relatives, took delight in eating and other natural functions, acquired massive merit by the performance of numerous sacrifices, concentrated authority by heedful attention to all phases of royal duty, and lived happily.

The Cave That Talked

THERE WAS ONCE a lion in a part of a forest and his name was Rough-Claw. One day he found nothing whatever to eat in his wanderings, and his throat was pinched by hunger. At sunset he came to a great mountain cave and went in, for he thought: "Surely, some animal will come into this cave during the night. I will hide and wait."

Presently the owner of the cave, a jackal named Curd-Face, came to the door and began to sing: "Cave ahoy! Cave aho-o-oy!" Then after a moment's silence, he continued in the same tone: "Hello! Don't you remember how you and I made an agreement that I was to speak to you when I came back from the world outside and that you were to sing out to me? But you won't speak to me today. So I am going off to that other cave, which will return my greeting."

Now when he heard this, the lion thought: "I see. This cave always calls out a greeting when the fellow returns. But today, from fear of me, it doesn't say a word. This is natural enough. For

> The feet and hands refuse to act
>   When peril terrifies;
> A trembling seizes every limb;
>   And speech unuttered dies.

"I will myself call out a greeting, which he will follow to its source, so providing me with a dinner."

The lion thereupon called out a greeting. But the cave so magnified the roar that its echo filled the circuit of the horizon, thus terrifying other forest creatures as well, even those far distant. Meanwhile the jackal made off, repeating the stanza:

> "Joy comes from knowing what
>   to dread,
> And sorrow smites the dunder-
>   head:
> A long life through, the woods
>   I've walked,
> But never heard a cave that
>   talked."

How Supersmart Ate the Elephant

THERE WAS ONCE a jackal named Supersmart in a part of a forest. One day he came upon an elephant that had died a natural death in the wood. But he could only stalk about the body; he could not cut through the tough hide.

At this moment a lion, in his wanderings to and fro, came to the spot. And the jackal, spying him, obsequiously rubbed his scalp in the dust, clasped his lotus paws, and said: "My lord and king, I am merely a cudgel-bearer, guarding this elephant in the king's interest. May the king deign to eat it."

Then the lion said: "My good fellow, under no circumstances do I eat what another has killed. I graciously bestow this elephant upon you." And the jackal joyfully replied: "It is only what our lord and king has taught his servants to expect."

When the lion was gone, a tiger arrived. And the jackal thought when he saw him: "Well, I sent one rascal packing by doing obeisance. Now, how shall I dispose of this one? To be sure, he is a hero, and therefore can be managed only by intrigue. For there is a saying:

Where bribes and flattery would fail,
Intrigue is certain to avail.

And indeed, all creatures are held in bondage by heart-piercing intrigue. As the saying goes:

Even a pearl, so smoothly hard
    and round,
Is fastened by a thread and
    safely bound,
After a way to pierce its heart
    is found."

So he took his decision, went to meet the tiger, and slightly stiffening his neck, he said in an agitated tone: "Uncle, how could you venture into the jaws of death? This elephant was killed by a lion, who put me on guard while he went to bathe. And as he went, he gave me my orders. 'If any tiger comes this way,' he said, 'creep up and tell me. I have to clear this forest of tigers, because once, when I had killed an elephant, a tiger helped himself while my back was turned, and I had the leavings. From that day I have been death on tigers.'"

On hearing this, the tiger was terrified, and said: "My dear nephew, make me a gift of my life. Even if he is slow in returning, don't give him any news of me." With these words he decamped.

When the tiger had gone, a leopard appeared. And the jackal thought when he saw him: "Here comes Spot. He has powerful teeth. So I will use him to cut into this elephant hide."

With this in mind, he said: "Well, nephew, where have you been this long time? And why do you seem so hungry? You come as my guest, according to the proverb:

A guest in need
Is a guest indeed.

Now here lies this elephant, killed by a lion who appointed me its guardian. But for all that, you may enjoy a square meal of elephant meat, provided you cut and run before he gets back."

"No, uncle," said the leopard, "if things stand so, this meat is not healthy for me. You know the saying:

A man to thrive
Must keep alive.

Never eat a thing that doesn't sit well on the stomach. So I will be off." "Don't be timid," said the jackal. "Pluck up courage and eat. I will warn you of his coming while he is yet a long way off." So the leopard did as suggested, and the jackal, as soon as he saw the hide cut through, called out: "Quick, nephew, quick! Here comes the lion." Hearing this, the leopard vanished also.

Now while the jackal was eating meat through the opening cut by the leopard, a second jackal came on the scene in a great rage. And Supersmart, esteeming him an equal whose prowess was a known quantity, recited the stanza:

Sway patrons with obeisance;
    In heroes raise a doubt;
Fling petty bribes to flunkeys;
    With equals, fight it out—

made a dash at him, tore him with his fangs, made him seek the horizon, and himself comfortably enjoyed elephant meat for a long time.

The Lion-Makers

IN A CERTAIN TOWN were four Brahmans who lived in friendship. Three of them had reached the far shore of all scholarship, but lacked sense. The other found scholarship distasteful; he had nothing but sense.

One day they met for consultation. "What is the use of attainments," said they, "if one does not travel, win the favor of kings, and acquire money? Whatever we do, let us all travel."

But when they had gone a little way, the eldest of them said: "One of us, the fourth, is a dullard, having nothing but sense. Now nobody gains the favorable attention of kings by simple sense without scholarship. Therefore we will not share our earnings with him. Let him turn back and go home."

Then the second said: "My intelligent friend, you lack scholarship. Please go home." But the third said: "No, no. This is no way to behave. For we have played together since we were little boys. Come along, my noble friend. You shall have a share of the money we earn."

With this agreement they continued their journey, and in a forest they found the bones of a dead lion. Thereupon one of them said: "A good opportunity to test the ripeness of our scholarship. Here lies some kind of creature, dead. Let us bring it to life by means of the scholarship we have honestly won."

Then the first said: "I know how to assemble the skeleton." The second said: "I can supply skin, flesh, and blood." The third said: "I can give it life."

So the first assembled the skeleton, the second provided skin, flesh, and blood. But while the third was intent on giving the breath of life, the man of sense advised against it, remarking: "This is a lion. If you bring him to life, he will kill every one of us."

"You simpleton!" said the other, "it is not I who will reduce scholarship to a nullity." "In that case," came the reply, "wait a moment, while I climb this convenient tree."

When this had been done, the lion was brought to life, rose up, and killed all three. But the man of sense, after the lion had gone elsewhere, climbed down and went home.

FOR STUDY AND DISCUSSION

THE UNGRATEFUL MAN

This story is from the course on the Loss of Friends. What point is the teacher trying to make to his pupils?

THE CAVE THAT TALKED

This story, from the course on Crows and Owls (international relations), contains one of the most popular themes in folk literature—the outwitting of the powerful and dangerous by the weak and vulnerable. What conditions of life make this a popular theme? The jackal's very life depends on his using his wits to stay alive. Is this true for some people, too? for all people? Under what conditions of life does it cease to be true?

HOW SUPERSMART ATE THE ELEPHANT

Does this story about Supersmart, from the course on Loss of Gains, teach the same ideas as "The Cave That Talked"? What, if anything, is added to those teachings in the story of Supersmart?

THE LION-MAKERS

1. What is the difference between scholarship and sense as they are presented here? Does this story, from the course on Ill-Considered Action, constitute an attack on education and learning? Can scholarship and sense exist together? Explain your answers.

2. Is the lesson of this story at all applicable to modern society? Has our technology manufactured any "lions"? If so, name some. How would sense deal with these lions?

FOR COMPOSITION

Think of a lesson in the art of statecraft that might be taught to some young man who will become a modern-day ruler. Then, in 500 to 750 words, write a beast fable, set in modern times, which illustrates this lesson.

CHINESE AND JAPANESE LITERATURES

c. 1000 B.C. – c. A.D. 1800

IN CHINA, to be educated has been to be a poet. Ministers of state, it is said, recited appropriate verses when they viewed a scenic mountain, and diplomats quoted passages from China's ancient *Book of Songs* (see page 271) to suit contemporary situations. All Chinese political officials, in fact, for at least thirteen hundred years, had to qualify for their posts by passing a literary examination which tested, among other things, their ability to compose original verse in the traditional forms. Po Chü-i (A.D. 772–A.D. 846) (see page 288) was a prominent government official and also the most popular poet of the great T'ang period. In his poem congratulating a friend and fellow-poet on his appointment to the Water Board, Po recalls that a famous fifth century poet, Ho Hsün, had also held this position.

● Since the day that old Ho died the sound of recitation has ceased;
Secretaries have come and secretaries gone, but none of them cared for poetry.
Since Ho's day their official journeys have remained unsung;
The lovely precincts of the head office have waked no verse.
For long I grieved to see you kept in the same humble post;
I trembled lest the art of high song should sink to its decline.
Today when I heard of your appointment as Secretary of the Water Board
I was far more pleased than when myself I became secretary to a Board.
—PO CHÜ-I

"Since the day that old Ho died . . ." by Po Chü-i from *The Life and Times of Po Chü-i*, translated by Arthur Waley. Reprinted by permission of George Allen & Unwin Ltd.

The tradition did not die under the Communist regime of the twentieth century. Mao Tse-tung (1893–   ), writes poetry in the ancient style, as seen in this poem, "On the Pei-Tai River."

● Heavy rain on the northland
　White surf surges toward the sky,
　Fishing boats adrift beyond the Ch'in-huang Isle.
　Only water in sight,
　How does one tell directions?

　The past has been gone for over a thousand years,
　When the Emperor Wu of the Wei Dynasty ordered his army northward
　To pass by the Chieh-shih Hill, as history tells us.
　Again the rustling autumn wind now, but
　What a changed world! —MAO TSE-TUNG

Mao here is thinking of revolution and conquest, as many others ambitious of rule in China have done; and he is thinking that the world in which he hopes to win his own ambitions is different from the world in which dynastic struggles of the past have taken place. It is characteristically Chinese that Mao poetizes his thoughts, that he thinks of his political situation in terms of rain and fishing boats and the autumn wind.

CHINESE POETRY

More than a hobby or a recreation, poetry to the Chinese is an exercise of the mind and spirit. Traditionally, cultured Chinese have made a pleasant formal occasion of viewing the cherry blossoms in spring (see the poem on page 295) and the red maple leaves in autumn, of moon-watching or mountain-visiting. Like the observance of such occasions, the writing of poems and the painting of sketches are exercises in contemplation, in which nature and one's own being are felt and enjoyed and perhaps in some way better understood.

Most Chinese poetry, then, is intended to express in words the impression of a moment. Words are chosen with care to call up for the reader the total experience of the moment: a sight or sound or feeling and the thought and emotion that go with it. The words in the poem suggest more than they actually say; the poet tries to *evoke* the experience rather than define it or moralize from it. In effect, the poet invites the reader to join him in experiencing a passing moment, which by means of the poem is caught and held until its full significance sinks in.

The images that the poet focuses attention upon are mostly drawn from nature, and they are significant both for what they express about the natural

"On the Pei-Tai River" by Mao Tse-tung from *20th Century Chinese Poetry*, translated by Kai-yu Hsu, copyright © 1963 by Kai-yu Hsu. Reprinted by permission of Doubleday & Company, Inc.

world itself and for the connection they suggest or express between the natural world and the world of men. Tu Fu (A.D. 712–A.D. 770) (see page 277) makes this connection explicit: "The processes of nature resemble the business of men." But such connections between man and nature can be assumed and sought even when they are not directly stated. Sometimes common associations suggest the significance of nature images; for example, for most people a bare bough usually evokes autumn as well as the passing of human life. Often conventional symbolism is utilized; for example, the bamboo traditionally symbolizes longevity and the butterfly stands for joy.

Chinese poems are written in a very strict form, which defines the number of syllables in a line, the rhyme, and often the tone or pitch of the syllables. Part of the reader's pleasure comes from recognizing how skillful the poet has been in making a richly suggestive statement within the limits set by the form. Thus, the effect of most Chinese (and Japanese) poems is partly due to a sort of high artificiality, similar to that encountered in much Western poetry written during the Renaissance. (In Japan, the haiku represents an extreme in this tradition of poetry: seventeen syllables, three lines, a single image, and a suggestion rippling out from the center as far as the power of the poet's words and the reader's sensitivity can carry it.)

English translations can reveal little of this aspect of Chinese poetry because there are basic differences in the languages. Connecting words essential to Western languages are omitted in Chinese poetry. Lines which in Chinese read:

TIN	CH'EUNG	tei	fut	ling	T'AU	FAN
sky	long	earth	wide	sierra	head	divide

hui	kwok	LEI	KA	kin	paak	WAN
go	country	leave	home	see	white	cloud

are translated into English as:

> The sierra divides the vast heaven above and the wide earth below
> Far away from country and home appear the same white clouds.

Furthermore, an English translation cannot imitate the pitch pattern of the original; the first of the Chinese lines just cited, for example, has the three middle syllables on a medium pitch and the first two and last two (in capital letters) on higher or lower tones.

Worthy of note is not only the close link in China, as in Japan, between poetry and song, but more especially the connection between poetry and painting. This is due in large measure to the pictorial nature of the writing and, conversely, to the calligraphic quality of the painting.

"Sky long, earth wide, etc." from *Chinese Literature: A Historical Introduction* by Ch'ën Shou-Yi, copyright © 1961 by The Ronald Press Company, New York. Reprinted by permission of the publisher.

What has been said about the Chinese poetic tradition does not, of course, cover all the poems written by hundreds of poets in thousands of years; it describes only the dominant strain that has persisted with surprising consistency through the long history of Chinese poetry.

JAPANESE POETRY

Japanese poetry has derived its attitudes and its style so directly from the Chinese that it can be considered as belonging to the same tradition. Chinese influence was strong from the beginning of written Japanese literature. The Japanese had no written form of their language until about the fifth century A.D., when Chinese characters were adopted for it. The earliest collections of Japanese poetry were made in the eighth century, and these included poems written in the Chinese language by Japanese poets.

But most Japanese poets eventually adapted to their own language the forms and the manner of Chinese poetry. Japanese poetry is more than merely imitative, but the differences between it and Chinese poetry reflect the differences in culture and language. Even though Japanese took its written characters from the Chinese script, the Japanese language itself is quite distinct from the Chinese. Japanese is unaccented, and it does not have the variations in pitch so essential to Chinese. With the exception of words ending in an *n* sound, all Japanese words end in a vowel, giving the language a fluid sound somewhat like Italian. Japanese prosody is based entirely on the number of syllables in a verse unit. The real quality of Japanese poetry depends upon subtleties of phrasing and of play upon the meanings of words. Thus, much of its distinctiveness from Chinese poetry disappears in translation.

CHINESE PROSE

While Chinese prose appears to be as old a written form as poetry, the long, continuous tale or novel did not develop until about the eleventh century A.D. Behind it lay centuries of oral narration and an old tradition of Buddhist moral tales and stories of miracles. The eighteenth-century Chinese novel *Dream of the Red Chamber,* an immensely long family chronicle, has been widely read in the West. Marked by unflagging vigor and psychological penetration, it is one of the great works of world literature. Yet it should be mentioned that until quite recently the novel was regarded in China as a subordinate literary form quite unworthy to be ranked beside poetry—and, furthermore, of not the slightest use to youths who hoped, through a devoted study of poetry, to qualify for a tenured position in the civil service.

Drama, too, may be said to have arisen in China in the eleventh century A.D. There had previously existed a long tradition of entertainments involving singing, dancing, and impersonation, together with the reenactment of historical events. But before the eleventh century no one had hit on the idea of adhering to a consistent plot. The plays that were then evolved did not, however, abandon the lively dancing and singing. Indeed, as the drama developed and spectacles of unimaginable length were staged, the plot tended to get swamped among such external elements as gorgeous costuming, orchestral music, and thrilling acrobatic dancing. Only of recent years and under Western influence have "normal" plays, as we would regard them, been written and produced.

JAPANESE PROSE

As with poetry, the rest of Japanese literature is an outgrowth of Chinese, but it, too, has distinct marks of its own. The first Japanese literature might be the *Record of Ancient Matters,* compiled in A.D. 712 for the emperor, who wanted an account of creation and of the ancient Japanese empire. This record embodies the teachings of Shintoism, which held that the Japanese were descendants of the sun goddess and were all members of one family, ruled by the emperor, who mediated between the divinity and his subjects. *The Tale of Genji,* a famous novel about a Japanese prince and the languid life of the court, was written by Lady Murasaki in the eleventh century A.D. In the seventeenth and eighteenth centuries a form of drama called kabuki developed to please the wealthy merchants in Japan's cities. Kabuki, which featured popular and comic themes, was developed because the common class was bored with the solemn Nō dramas, semi-religious morality plays used to teach Zen. This form of Buddhism stresses self-discipline, concentration, and self-reliance, and every word and gesture of the Nō actors had to conform to a set of formal rules.

ORIENTAL PHILOSOPHIES

Most Chinese and most Japanese literature expresses a cast of thought that bears the imprint of three religious philosophies that have dominated the Orient for about twenty-five centuries. These philosophies derive from three masters who were very closely contemporary: Confucius (551 B.C.–479 B.C.), whose honorific name, K'ung Fu-tzu, has been Latinized as Confucius; Lao-tzu, a much more shadowy figure, perhaps born around 570 B.C.; and the Buddha, of India, a reformer of the Hindu religion, usually said to have been born about 563 B.C. and to have died in 483 B.C.

The teachings of Confucius were dominant for several centuries in China. Confucius was concerned with the right ordering of society, with men's relationships with one another. He was not interested in theology, nor in

A modern kabuki ("popular") actor, a participant in an old hereditary art.

mysticism, nor in life after death, things which he held beyond human comprehension. Living in a time of social and political disorder, when the Chou dynasty was crumbling and warlords were cropping up all over, Confucius was most interested in reestablishing a good, well-regulated life here on earth. This good life, he preached, depended on order and stability, and order and stability depended on good government. As an example of good government, he looked back to China's ancient feudal system. He traveled for three years looking for a ruler who would let him try out his political theories, but he was unsuccessful. However, the books of Confucian teachings, the *Analects,* which were gathered by his disciples were soon established—along with the *Book of Songs*—as the basis of Chinese education and have remained so until modern times.

Unlike Confucianism, the philosophy of Taoism, derived from Lao-tzu, held that the less government the better and, in fact, advised men to withdraw from the distractions of public life. Taoism paid no heed to codes of proper behavior or to one's duties in life, which were the foundations of Confucianism. On the contrary, Taoism taught that man should seek understanding by turning his back on the world, by passively accepting a simple life, and by contemplating Tao—the indescribable force which governs and unifies all nature. A true guide to existence, says the Taoist, may be discovered by contemplating such a natural phenomenon as water, which humbly takes the lowliest place and yet in the end fills all out and flows conqueringly onward.

These two elements of thought which originated in China—one sensible and practical and conservative, the other mystic and unworldly—created a climate receptive to the spread of Buddhism, introduced from India during the Han dynasty (202 B.C.–A.D. 220), where it had already flourished for centuries. Buddhism, with its ethical commandments and its way of life that called for the renunciation of desire and which promised perfect peace, established a strong position in China and later in Japan, where the Zen school of Buddhism originated. Zen combines Buddha's teachings with the Taoist emphasis on meditation and nonaction. (*Zen* is the Japanese word for "meditation.") Zen disciples are ever alert for immediate and abrupt enlightenment, the idea being that a person can have a direct perception of the whole universe through the sudden perception of one moment in the present.

Although these three philosophies remained distinct, with their own temples and followers, the sympathies and cross-influences among them were considerable enough to produce what can be thought of, with some oversimplification, as an Oriental cast of thought. (In the West, similarly, the merging of Hebraic, Greek, Roman, and Christian traditions has created a world view that characterizes Western or European-American thought, in spite of great differences among sects and individuals.)

Oriental religious philosophy might be defined roughly as a compound of the Confucian emphasis upon reverence for the past, courtesy, ritual, and codes of conduct; of the Taoist emphasis upon the simple life and the search for the harmonizing force in nature; and of the Buddhist emphasis upon the renunciation of desire and the search for enlightenment, the transcendent, intuitive, direct experience of deity or of truth.

YIN AND YANG

A retrospective glance at China's long history strengthens the conviction that the Chinese have the capacity to endure, to absorb, and, time and again, to rise up vigorously out of chaos and disaster. This capacity must be attributed to China's nourishing cultural roots that plunge deep in the soil of reality. The Chinese see permanence as possible only through the acceptance of inevitable change. Traditionally, they have explained all phenomena, cosmic and human, as arising from the dynamic interplay of two opposing forces. These forces have many manifestations: light and dark, mountain and valley, heaven and earth, male and female. The basic terms for the two forces are yang and yin. They are represented by an age-old symbol, which today appears on the flag of South Korea. In order to visualize the notion that these elements are not locked in sterile opposition, that they are not mutually exclusive, each is shown as containing a "seed" of the other. A person who holds the yin-yang philosophy can endure evil times; better days will come, he knows, for within evil is always the seed of good.

Left, a rubbing from a stone inscription, first century A.D. Each symbol stands for a word or an idea. The characters here are considered so perfect that they have been imitated for thousands of years. Right, the yin-yang symbol.

Because of this accepting attitude, the Chinese approach to matters of principle, and to possible compromises with principle, is very different from the less flexible approach that characterizes the West. Chinese rationality has been much less self-assertive, much less ready to claim exclusive mastery. Quite to the contrary, it is closely linked with all the other factors in a given situation including those—perhaps the most fundamental—of which we are only dimly aware and which find expression, if at all, in metaphors and symbols, never in direct statement.

CHINESE HISTORY

China, as a coherent pattern of culture, has been in existence longer than any other. The first of the many dynasties to rule over China is said to have come to power in 1994 B.C. But if this first dynasty is practically lost in the mists of time, with the next, the Shang, from the sixteenth to eleventh centuries B.C., we find ourselves on firm historical ground. As for writing, the earliest Chinese specimens date from the fourteenth century B.C., when characters were scratched into molds and incised on tortoise shells and animal bones. The year 1028 B.C. marked the beginning of the great Chou dynasty, which the Chinese later came to regard as their classical period. In this vast expanse of time—for the dynasty was not extinguished until 256 B.C.—countless advances were made in agriculture, technology, and the arts.

It would be out of place here to name China's succeeding dynasties— the last dynasty did not collapse until 1912—or to try to trace even in barest outline the history of a civilization now in the closing years of its fourth millennium. More importantly and more feasibly, stress should be laid on certain constant or recurring features of Chinese history. One situation often repeated has been the establishment of strong central authority under an emperor. The other situation is characterized, naturally, by reaction— the breakdown of central authority, followed by a period of warring kingdoms or by the arbitrary rule of numerous warlords. Reversals of this sort, at least in their initial stages, are actually sanctioned by an age-old Chinese conviction that a ruler, through negligence or the abuse of his authority, can

This fierce winged lion stands guard over a tomb near Nanking, China. It dates from A.D. 518.

forfeit "the mandate of heaven." In that event, his subjects may legitimately overthrow him, for his rule has become unlawful.

Another recurrent feature in Chinese history has been invasion—usually across its land frontiers. Mongols, Tibetans, and many other peoples have ravaged the land, sometimes set up their leader as emperor, and even established long-lasting dynasties. Time and again, however, foreign rulers discovered that the Chinese could rule themselves far better than could any invader who tried to introduce newfangled plans of his own. So the invader maintained both the Chinese pattern of government—the selection of government officials by means of literary examinations, as one example—and the Chinese world view that underlay everything else. As a consequence, the descendants of the foreign usurper became, in dress, manners, and way of thinking, indistinguishable from the rest of China's inhabitants.

One of the two most recent invasions of China was only partly territorial. In the nineteenth and early twentieth centuries, the Western powers (Great Britain, France, Germany, and Russia, with the United States appearing late on the scene) obtained from the decaying Chinese empire "concessions"—actual parcels of Chinese soil over which the Chinese government lost all authority. Foreign nationals also enjoyed, everywhere in China, extraterritorial status—that is, they could not be called to the Chinese courts to account for their possible misdeeds. One outburst of Chinese rage against these indignities was the Boxer Rebellion of 1900, which was rapidly crushed by the Western powers.

The impact of the West on China was not only territorial, however. It was ideological also. The modern Western world first revealed itself to the Chinese as a firmly established and expanding network of commercial exchanges, backed by capitalism's unrivaled productivity and capacity for discovering and exploiting raw materials. Later the Chinese learned that not all Westerners completely admired or supported this capitalistic system. The Russian Revolution of 1917 demonstrated to them that an ideology, that of Karl Marx, could inspire an attempt to develop a new and different system, based on the dictatorship of the proletariat, with Communism as a perhaps remote ideal goal. The Chinese themselves, after a certain point, ceased to regard this split in the Western world as a subject for debate or contemplation only. Some sought to modernize China within a capitalist framework. Others, between 1924 and 1928, unsuccessfully tried to communize China. In 1949, a second attempt culminated in the setting up of the People's Republic of China under the Communist leader Mao Tse-tung.

JAPANESE HISTORY

The people inhabiting the islands that make up Japan would appear to be mainly Mongoloid in origin, with a mixture of Malayan. The presence of this Malayan element is presumed not only because of Japanese physical characteristics, but also because Japanese creation myths have much in common with those found among the islanders of Polynesia. For centuries, too, the Japanese had to fight against barbarians in the land. These were the Ainu, a people with Caucasian features who today live in Japan in tribes, as wards of the state, confined to certain restricted areas.

The earliest historical references to the Japanese islands are found in Chinese and Korean documents. The Japanese themselves acquired Chinese writing early in the fifth century A.D., and about a century later, Japan was introduced to the rich Chinese culture when Buddhism spread from China to Japan. Buddhism became an extremely important element in Japanese life, though at first the Buddha's teaching about after-life deeply disturbed the Japanese, who had had no experience with such teachings before. However, Buddhism did not replace the native Japanese religion of Shintoism, which teaches the existence of many gods whom men can satisfy by carrying out certain rituals. Shintoism, which also calls for ancestor worship, has maintained itself right up to the present and is closely interwoven with patriotic emotions in Japan.

The multiple tribal system of Japanese life first moved toward some measure of central control in A.D. 646. While a bureaucracy on the Chinese model was set up, there was one significant difference: only members of the aristocracy could seek appointments within it. What this strengthened, with lasting impact on the whole of Japanese history, was the preponderant political role reserved for the aristocracy. With the rarest of exceptions, the emperor, often placed on the throne while still a child, remained a puppet whose strings were pulled by the leading aristocratic warrior family or clan. The real power came eventually to be centered in the office of the shogun, the aristocrat who was the chief officer for the emperor and who himself was often dictated to by the family in power. The office of shogun was not abolished until 1867.

At the local level, a feudal system developed. Power there was held by warrior-landlords who had their own soldiers, called samurai, to keep order. The samurai developed their own code of behavior and were much like the knights of medieval Europe.

The aristocrats, the landlords, and the samurai were widely separated from the commoners—the agricultural and commercial classes. There was no possibility allowed for an individual to move from one social class to another. In one of the lowest classes were the merchants, despised creatures whose minds were thought to be fixed on monetary gain. It may be noted that they succeeded in this aim and that, having done so, they were responsible for the rise of an impressive popular culture that developed an extensive literature, the kabuki form of drama, and the art of the multicolor woodcut. The ruling class was either contemptuous of all this, or unaware of it. Outside the community altogether were the outcasts, who performed such unpleasant tasks as executing criminals. (Outcasts were given the vote in 1871, but popular prejudice against them has remained powerful.)

One method used to stifle any curiosity the Japanese emperor might feel about real issues in the real world was to fill his day with religious and court ceremonials and with a multiplicity of delights. A fascinating portrait of life in this hothouse atmosphere can be found in Lady Muraski's eleventh-century novel, *The Tale of Genji,* or in the *Pillow Book* by another woman writer, Sei Shōnagon. (In men's eyes, for some time, the Japanese language was good enough only for the ladies. Men wrote in Chinese. As a result, there was a splendid flowering of works in verse and prose written by aristocratic Japanese women.)

The sixteenth century was a particularly critical time in Japanese history. During an epoch of internal turmoil and uncertainty, the Western world made its first impact on Japan in the form of Portuguese and Dutch sailors and merchants, and in the form of Christianity. The Jesuit missionary from Spain, St. Francis Xavier, arrived in Japan in 1549 and remained for two years. In short order, however, Japanese Christians were subjected to ruthless persecution. Christianity vanished and, for all practical purposes, ceased to be a factor in Japanese life.

In 1630 almost all of Japan's contacts with the West were deliberately severed, for the shogun and the people he represented feared both the "subversive" effects of such contacts and the danger of invasion. The shogun practically closed Japan's doors to Europe, and Japanese were forbidden to leave their country under pain of death. Only after 1850, and largely because of persistent pressure from the United States, did Japan become more accessible to the West. Finally, in 1867, the whole shogunate system broke down. A new, able emperor came to the throne and, under the name of Meiji, transformed imperial power from a fiction to a reality. Feudalism was abolished. Western scientific and technological skills were avidly acquired, universal education was introduced, and with amazing speed Japan created an impressive industrial economy. An island empire feeling the effects of overcrowding, Japan's appearance on the world stage was affirmed by a series of expansionist military undertakings. Militarists and extreme nationalists were in control in 1937 when Japan entered into a pact with Hitler's Germany and Mussolini's Italy. With her attack on Pearl Harbor in 1941, Japan brought the United States into World War II.

Japanese defeat was followed by seven years of American occupation and tutelage. Emperor worship was abolished. A new constitution was ratified. Freed from militaristic preoccupations, the Japanese, ever since the war, have devoted their remarkable energies and discipline to making their nation one of the most heavily industrialized and most successful trading powers in the world.

The selections from Chinese and Japanese literatures which are included in this unit do not represent what is being written in these countries today. Many of the selections here are taken from early writers and represent some of the themes and literary forms that characterize Oriental literature of the past.

As with all peoples, the older literatures of China and Japan in some ways reflected the conditions of society, but this element has been unusually slight in the poetry, and even the fiction has traditionally been more occupied with love stories or tales of the supernatural than with realistic social or psychological problems. However, a considerable body of the poetry of China's great age in the T'ang dynasty dealt with themes of social criticism in a relatively realistic style.

Twentieth-century writers in China and Japan, largely because of the influence of Western literature and because of the dislocations and sufferings caused by war, have gone even further in this direction. Many of them have been educated in America or Europe, and following both the Western example and their own inclination to democratize literature, they have increasingly adopted the vernacular language—the speech used by the uneducated as well as by the educated for ordinary purposes—instead of the formal literary language of the ancient tradition. The realistic short story, often an episode of social injustice or of violence, has become an important literary type.

Their traditional regard for poetry is not dead, however. A poem by Chinese poet Wen I-to (1898–1946), called "The Confession," describes the position of the modern poet, who has a nostalgia for the beauties and wisdom of the old poetry but who feels that he must use his poetic art to examine the unpleasant realities of life.

● It's no joke at all, I'm not that sort of poet.
Though I adore the sheen of white quartz,
Though I love green pines, vast seas, the glimmer of sunset on a crow's
   back,
The dusky sky interwoven with the wings of bats,
Though I adore heroes and high mountains,
The flags of nations waving in the wind,
All colors from saffron to the heavy bronze of chrysanthemums,
Remember my food is a pot of old tea.

You should be afraid: there is another person in me:
His imagination is a gnat's and he crawls through muck. —WEN I-TO

"The Confession" by Wen I-to translated by Ho Yung from *Contemporary Chinese Poetry,* edited by Robert Payne. Reprinted by permission of Routledge & Kegan Paul Ltd.

The Book of Songs

The *Book of Songs,* an anthology of 305 poems, contains the earliest recorded poetry in Chinese. The poems themselves probably date back to 1000 B.C. or earlier, but the compilation was made several centuries later. Known to the Chinese as *Shih Ching* (song-word scripture), these poems began to be used around 500 B.C. by Confucius and his disciples to illustrate his moral teachings. Up till the present day, Chinese schoolchildren have had to memorize all 305 poems for use on social and political occasions. Two songs from the *Shih Ching* are included here. Both are laments of the common man, who has been forced to take up arms for a war lord. The hardship of war is a recurring theme in later Chinese poetry.

36

How few of us are left, how few!
Why do we not go back?
Were it not for our prince and his concerns,
What should we be doing here in the dew?

How few of us are left, how few!
Why do we not go back?
Were it not for our prince's own concerns,
What should we be doing here in the mud?

167

We plucked the bracken, plucked the bracken
While the young shoots were springing up.
Oh, to go back, go back!
The year is ending.
We have no house, no home   5
Because of the Hsien-yün.
We cannot rest or bide
Because of the Hsien-yün.

"Song 36" and "Song 167" from *Book of Songs,* translated from the Chinese by Arthur Waley. Reprinted by permission of George Allen & Unwin, Ltd.

We plucked the bracken, plucked the bracken
While the shoots were soft.   10
Oh, to go back, go back!
Our hearts are sad,
Our sad hearts burn,
We are hungry and thirsty,
But our campaign is not over,   15
Nor is any of us sent home with news.

We plucked the bracken, plucked the bracken;
But the shoots were hard.
Oh, to go back, go back!
The year is running out.   20
But the king's business never ends;
We cannot rest or bide.
Our sad hearts are very bitter;
We went, but do not come.

What splendid thing is that?   25
It is the flower of the cherry tree.
What great carriage is that?
It is our lord's chariot.
His war chariot ready yoked,
With its four steeds so eager.   30
How should we dare stop or tarry?
In one month we have had three alarms.

We yoke the teams of four,
Those steeds so strong,
That our lord rides behind,   35
That lesser men protect.
The four steeds so grand,
The ivory bow-ends, the fish-skin quiver.
Yes, we must be always on our guard;
The Hsien-yün are very swift.   40

Long ago, when we started,
The willows spread their shade.
Now that we turn back
The snowflakes fly.
The march before us is long,   45
We are thirsty and hungry,
Our hearts are stricken with sorrow,
But no one listens to our plaint.

CH'Ü YÜAN

Ch'ü Yüan (c. 343 B.C.–c. 290 B.C.) has been called the first distinguished man of letters in China's long annals. He was an important counselor at court, but political intrigues drove him into exile, and exile made him a poet.

Battle

"We grasp our battle spears: we don our breastplates of hide.
The axles of our chariots touch: our short swords meet.
Standards obscure the sun: the foe roll up like clouds.
Arrows fall thick: the warriors press forward.
They menace our ranks: they break our line.   5
The left-hand trace horse is dead: the one on the right is smitten.
The fallen horses block our wheels: they impede the yoke horses!"
They grasp their jade drumsticks: they beat the sounding drums.
Heaven decrees their fall: the dread Powers are angry.

The warriors are all dead: they lie on the moor-field.   10
They issued but shall not enter: they went but shall not return.
The plains are flat and wide; the way home is long.
Their swords lie beside them: their black bows, in their hand.

Though their limbs were torn, their hearts could not be repressed.
They were more than brave: they were inspired with the spirit of "Wu."°
Steadfast to the end, they could not be daunted.   16
Their bodies were stricken, but their souls have taken Immortality—
Captains among the ghosts, heroes among the dead.

15. **"Wu"**: military genius.

"Battle" by Ch'ü Yüan from *Translations from the Chinese* by Arthur Waley, copyright 1919 and renewed 1947 by Arthur Waley. Reprinted by permission of Alfred A. Knopf, Inc. and Constable Publishers, London.

WU TI

Wu Ti (157 B.C.–87 B.C.) was the sixth emperor of the Han dynasty; he came to the throne as a young man of sixteen and reigned until his death at seventy. Though Wu Ti had more significance as patron of literature than as a poet, his poem that follows is famous. Li Fu-jen was a woman whom the emperor loved. She had just died.

Li Fu-jen

The sound of her silk skirt has stopped.
On the marble pavement dust grows.
Her empty room is cold and still.
Fallen leaves are piled against the doors.
    Longing for that lovely lady
How can I bring my aching heart to rest?

T'AO CH'IEN

For a time T'ao Ch'ien (A.D. 372–A.D. 427) was a minor official, but corruption and intrigue disgusted him with court life. He finally resigned his public office and withdrew to a simple life, writing poetry and growing flowers.

1

Shady, shady the wood in front of the hall:
At midsummer full of calm shadows.
The south wind follows summer's train:
With its eddying puffs it blows open my coat.
I am free from ties and can live a life of retirement.   5
When I rise from sleep, I play with books and harp.
The lettuce in the garden still grows moist:
Of last year's grain there is always plenty left.

Self-support should maintain strict limits:
More than enough is not what I want.   10
I grind millet and make good wine:
When the wine is heated, I pour it out for myself.
My little children are playing at my side,
Learning to talk, they babble unformed sounds.
These things have made me happy again   15
And I forget my lost cap of office.
Distant, distant I gaze at the white clouds:
With a deep yearning I think of the sages of antiquity.

2

I built my hut in a zone of human habitation,
Yet near me there sounds no noise of horse or coach.
   Would you know how that is possible?
A heart that is distant creates a wilderness round it.
I pluck chrysanthemums under the eastern hedge,   5
Then gaze long at the distant summer hills.
The mountain air is fresh at the dusk of day:
The flying birds two by two return.
In these things there lies a deep meaning;
Yet when we would express it, words suddenly fail us.   10

Substance, Shadow, and Spirit

High and low, wise and simple, all busily hoard up the moments of life. How
   greatly they err!
Therefore I have to the uttermost exposed the bitterness both of Substance
   and Shadow and have made Spirit show how, by following Nature, we
   may dissolve this bitterness.

Substance speaks to Shadow:

Heaven and Earth exist forever:
Mountains and rivers never change.
But herbs and trees in perpetual rotation   5
Are renovated and withered by the dews and frosts:
And Man the wise, Man the divine—
Shall he alone escape this law?
Fortuitously appearing for a moment in the World
He suddenly departs, never to return.   10
How can he know that the friends he has left
Are missing him and thinking of him?

Only the things that he used remain;
They look upon them and their tears flow.
Me no magical arts can save, 15
Though you may hope for a wizard's aid.
I beg you listen to this advice—
When you can get wine, be sure to drink it.

Shadow replies:

There is no way to preserve life.
Drugs of Immortality are instruments of folly. 20
I would gladly wander in Paradise,
But it is far away and there is no road.
Since the day that I was joined to you
We have shared all our joys and pains.
While you rested in the shade, I left you a while: 25
But till the end we shall be together.
Our joint existence is impermanent:
Sadly together we shall slip away.
That when the body decays Fame should also go
Is a thought unendurable, burning the heart. 30
Let us strive and labor while yet we may
To do some deed that men will praise.
Wine may in truth dispel our sorrow,
But how compare it with lasting Fame?

Spirit expounds:

God can only set in motion: 35
He cannot control the things he has made.
Man, the second of the Three Orders,
Owes his precedence to Me.
Though I am different from you,
We were born involved in one another: 40
Nor by any means can we escape
The intimate sharing of good and ill.
The Three Emperors were saintly men,
Yet today—where are they?
P'eng lived to a great age, 45
Yet he went at last, when he longed to stay.
And late or soon all go:
Wise and simple have no reprieve.
Wine may bring forgetfulness,
But does it not hasten old age? 50
If you set your hearts on noble deeds,
How do you know that any will praise you?
By all this thinking you do Me injury:
You had better go where Fate leads—
Drift on the Stream of Infinite Flux, 55
Without joy, without fear:
When you must go—then go,
And make as little fuss as you can.

TU FU

The early years of the T'ang Dynasty (A.D. 617–A.D. 907) were something of a golden age, a period of prosperity and splendor at court, during which literature and art flourished. But in 755 A.D. a political rebellion shattered the peace and brought the dynasty to the edge of extinction. The resultant chaos and terror were to last ten years. Tu Fu (A.D. 712–A.D. 770) was one of the minor officials who lost his position in the disturbance, and much of the rest of his life was spent in a search for some post that would help him support his family. During one of the times that Tu Fu was away from home seeking work, his young son died of starvation.

The first three poems of Tu Fu included here represent the refinement of his art in the traditional manner, but the fourth strikes a satiric and realistic note that was new to Chinese poetry. Understandably, Tu Fu was critical of the luxury of the court and of the oppression which made it possible.

Jade Flower Palace

The stream swirls. The wind moans in
The pines. Gray rats scurry over
Broken tiles. What prince, long ago,
Built this palace, standing in
Ruins beside the cliffs? There are   5
Green ghost fires in the black rooms.
The shattered pavements are all
Washed away. Ten thousand organ
Pipes whistle and roar. The storm
Scatters the red autumn leaves.   10
His dancing girls are yellow dust.
Their painted cheeks have crumbled
Away. His gold chariots
And courtiers are gone. Only
A stone horse is left of his   15
Glory. I sit on the grass and
Start a poem, but the pathos of
It overcomes me. The future
Slips imperceptibly away.
Who can say what the years will bring?   20

Loneliness

A hawk hovers in air.
Two white gulls float on the stream.
Soaring with the wind, it is easy
To drop and seize
Birds who foolishly drift with the current.
Where the dew sparkles in the grass,
The spider's web waits for its prey.
The processes of nature resemble the business of men.
I stand alone with ten thousand sorrows.

Night in the House by the River

It is late in the year;
Yin and Yang struggle
In the brief sunlight.
On the desert mountains
Frost and snow   5
Gleam in the freezing night.
Past midnight,
Drums and bugles ring out,
Violent, cutting the heart.
Over the Triple Gorge the Milky Way   10
Pulsates between the stars.
The bitter cries of thousands of households
Can be heard above the noise of battle.
Everywhere the workers sing wild songs.
The great heroes and generals of old time   15
Are yellow dust forever now.
Such are the affairs of men.
Poetry and letters
Persist in silence and solitude.

[TU FU CONTINUES ON PAGE 287]

MASTERPIECES OF WORLD ART

Chinese and Japanese Art

China's ancient civilization attained a continuity of artistic accomplishment unparalleled in the West. Chinese art, moreover, is so exquisitely subtle and sophisticated that Western art often seems crude by comparison.

Ancestor worship was an important factor in Chinese culture. In order to placate the spirits of ancestors and provide for their needs in the next world, the prehistoric Chinese developed elaborate funeral rituals involving human sacrifice. During these bloody burials, the ancient Shang and Chou rulers placed magnificent bronze vessels in the tombs of the nobles along with their favorite horses and retainers. Some of these ceremonial bronzes, which represent the culmination of a long development in bronze casting, are more than 3,500 years old. In perfection of form and mastery of technique, they are unsurpassed. The bronze *ting* shown in PLATE 1B was made like a tripod so that it could be placed over a fire to heat food. By looking carefully at the decoration, you will see a mask called a *t'ao t'ieh,* or glutton.

In later periods, statuettes were substituted for the human and animal sacrifices. The many figurines found in the tombs of the T'ang dynasty (A.D. 617–907) give us a vivid picture of Chinese life. Birds, camels, merchants, acrobats, dancing girls, and musicians were modeled in clay and either painted or glazed with bright colors. The dignified Chinese lady shown in PLATE 1A has the typical T'ang glazes of white, yellow, and green.

The word *porcelain* was first used by Marco Polo to describe certain wares he saw being made at the court of Kublai Khan. About 900 years old, the olive-green bowl carved with dragons (PLATE 2A) is a special type of porcelain called *celadon.* Celadon was popular with Eastern rulers because they believed it would reveal the presence of poison by cracking. During succeeding centuries, Chinese potters perfected the shapes of their vases and invented numerous colorful glazes. A lemon yellow vase (PLATE 2B) made in the early eighteenth century is an example of the elegant forms produced under the Emperor Yung Cheng.

Although Chinese emperors and scholars valued porcelains greatly, they regarded painting as the foremost art, along with poetry and calligraphy.

Chinese painting is really a branch of calligraphy, and is therefore very different from European painting. The Chinese painter learned a vocabulary of brushstrokes for trees, water, rocks, and other subject matter. By changing the size of the brush, the density of the ink, or the speed of the stroke, he could create different effects at will. *The Five-Colored Parakeet* (PLATE 3) by Emperor Hui-tsung is painted on silk and mounted on paper in the form of a scroll. At the beginning of the scroll the emperor wrote a poem telling how he enjoyed watching his pet bird and listening to its speech, "its tone most beautiful." The parakeet is perched on a flowering apricot tree. Just to the right of the bird is the emperor's signature. The red marks in the upper part of the painting are the seals of former owners.

Japanese painters were strongly influenced by Chinese art until the twelfth century, when a distinctive Japanese style emerged, characterized by delicacy of feeling, vigorous brushwork, and clean-cut design. *The Burning of the Sanjo Palace* (PLATE 4) is a handscroll that should be looked at by unrolling a few feet at a time. It depicts a battle between two powerful Japanese families for control of the puppet emperor. A long inscription at the beginning of the scroll tells how the Minamoto clan invaded the Sanjo palace, set it on fire, and kidnapped the emperor. The scene illustrated is just to the left of the burning palace. There is wild confusion as the mounted warriors rush through the gateway. Flaming timbers appear at the lower right where bodies of court ladies are heaped up in a well. The vivid color and action of this great epic painting of Japanese history is akin to that of a modern comic strip.

The sumptuous screen by Korin shown in PLATE 5 was perfectly suited to the luxurious palaces where the major concerns of the nobility were painting, poetry, and gazing at cherry blossoms. In Korin's design, the island of Matsushima, outcroppings of rock off the Japanese coast, are recognizable although superbly abstracted. Gold leaf and rich deep colors were applied on a background of warm yellow paper. In boldness of design, feeling for spacing, and decorative quality, Korin's screen is the quintessence of Japanese art.

An even bolder Japanese design is seen in the print of a dancer by Kiyonobu (PLATE 6). After the black lines were printed from a wood block, the red color was added by hand. In a later development, colors were printed from separate wood blocks—one for each color. Japanese prints first came to Europe after Commodore Perry opened Japan to foreign trade in 1853. Painters like Whistler, Degas, and Van Gogh were profoundly influenced by their bright colors and bold designs. Undoubtedly, the history of nineteenth-century European painting would be vastly different were it not for the impact of Japanese art.

PLATE 1A. *Lady with Phoenix Headdress*. Chinese, A.D. 8th century, T'ang Dynasty. Terra-cotta pottery, height: 17⅜ inches. (Courtesy, Museum of Fine Arts, Boston, Bequest of Charles B. Hoyt)

PLATE 1B. *Ting Vessel*. Chinese, 11th century B.C., late Shang or Early Chou Dynasty. Bronze, height: 7½ inches. (The Metropolitan Museum of Art, New York, Gift of Mrs. John Marriott, Mrs. John Barry Ryan, Gilbert W. Kahn, Roger Wolfe Kahn, 1949)

281

PLATE 2. A(left). *Bowl with Relief Design of Dragons in Waves*. Chinese, Sung Dynasty, A.D. 960–1280. Porcelaneous ware with celadon glaze, diameter: 10½ inches. (The Metropolitan Museum of Art, New York, Rogers Fund, 1917)

B(right). *Pear-shape Bottle*. Chinese, Ch'ing Dynasty, Yung Cheng period, A.D. 1723–1735. Porcelain with lemon-yellow glaze, height: 8 inches. (The Metropolitan Museum of Art, New York, Bequest of Benjamin Altman, 1913)

PLATE 3. Attributed to HUI TSUNG (Chinese, A.D. 1082–1135): *Five-Colored Parakeet on the Branch of a Blossoming Apricot Tree*. Executed during Hui Tsung's reign as Emperor of the Northern Sung Dynasty, A.D. 1101–26. Handscroll, colors on silk, 21 x 49¼ inches. (Courtesy, Museum of Fine Arts, Boston, Maria Antoinette Evans Fund)

PLATE 4. *The Burning of the Sanjo Palace.* Japanese, A.D. 12th-13th century, Kamakura period. Detail from the handscroll, *Heiji Monogatari.* Ink and color on paper; height 16¾ inches, width of entire handscroll: 23 feet. (Courtesy, Museum of Fine Arts, Boston, Fenollosa-Weld Collection)

PLATE 5. OGATA KORIN (Japanese, A.D. 1658–1716): *Wave Screen (Isle of Matsushima)*. A.D. late 17th century, Early Edo (Tokugawa) period. Color and gold on paper, $24\frac{3}{16}$ x $61\frac{11}{16}$ inches. (Courtesy, Museum of Fine Arts, Boston, Fenollosa-Weld Collection)

PLATE 6. Attributed to TORRII KIYONOBU I (Japanese, A.D. 1664–1729): *Woman Dancer*. About A.D. 1708, Early Edo (Tokugawa) period. Print, 21¾ x 11½ inches. (The Metropolitan Museum of Art, New York, Harris Brisbane Dick Fund, 1949)

Pretty Women

There is a freshness in the air this Third of Third, a spring festival day.
I see by the Meandering River of Ch'ang-an many fair women
With distant looks but frequent smiles, sweet and real.
With delicacy of complexion and symmetry of form,
They appear in silken dresses embroidered with golden peacocks   5
Or silvery unicorns, dazzling in the sunshine of late spring.
What do they wear on their heads?
Kingfisher headdresses with jade leaves over the temples.
What do you see on their backs?
Pearl-trimmed capes cut perfectly to fit.   10
You can spot the Imperial relatives among those rainbow-screens—
Among them the Lady of Kuo and the Lady of Ch'in.
The purple steak of dromedary hump, broiled in a shining pan,
The white meat of raw fish served on crystal plates,
Are not inviting enough to the satiated palate.   15
All that is cut with fancy and prepared with care is left untouched.
Palace messengers come on light steeds, galloping without dust,
Continuously bringing the rarest delicacies from His Majesty's kitchens.
Strings and pipes now accompany the feasting with music, weird enough
To move ghosts—not to mention the hoard of guests and retainers, each of
     commanding importance.   20
You see the last comer, who approaches leisurely on his horse,
Dismounts near the screens, and steps on the flowery carpet.
Willow catkins drop like snow to confuse the white frogbit;°
A bluebird flies away with a pink kerchief in its beak.
The Prime Minister is so powerful, his mere touch will scorch.   25
Approach not, lest you anger him.

23. **frogbit:** an aquatic floating herb, with small white flowers.

"Pretty Women" (#XLVIII) by Tu Fu from *Tu Fu: China's Greatest Poet,* edited and translated by William Hung. Reprinted by permission of Harvard University Press.

PO CHÜ–I

Po Chü-i (A.D. 772–A.D. 846) was the leader of a group of poets, a generation or two younger than Tu Fu, with their own program of political and literary reform. Like Tu Fu, Po Chü-i was a critical observer of the injustices of the T'ang court. Civil wars, foreign invasions, and these abuses at the court made the days in which he was born evil, as he says in the poem that follows. The failure he refers to in the same poem may have been one of the temporary reversals he suffered in his career as a government official and reformer. Po was ultimately successful, however, and he achieved a position of considerable eminence before his death. In changing posts, Po traveled a great deal, and he made several trips through the spectacular gorges of the Yangtze River.

Alarm at First Entering the Yangtze Gorges

Above, a mountain ten thousand feet high:
Below, a river a thousand fathoms deep.
A strip of green, walled by cliffs of stone:
Wide enough for the passage of a single reed.
At Chü-t'ang a straight cleft yawns: 5
At Yen-yü islands block the stream.
Long before night the walls are black with dusk;
Without wind white waves rise.
The big rocks are like a flat sword:
The little rocks resemble ivory tusks.   10
We are stuck fast and cannot move a step.
How much the less, three hundred miles?
Frail and slender, the twisted bamboo rope:
Weak, the dangerous hold of the towers' feet.
A single slip—the whole convoy lost: 15
And *my* life hangs on *this* thread!
I have heard a saying "He that has an upright heart
Shall walk scathless through the lands of Man and Mo."°
How can I believe that since the world began
In every shipwreck none have drowned but rogues?   20
And how can I, born in evil days
And fresh from failure, ask a kindness of fate?
Often I fear that these untalented limbs
Will be laid at last in an unnamed grave!

18. **Man and Mo:** dangerous savages.

MEI YAO-CH'EN

Mei Yao-ch'en (1002–1060) and the next poet, Ou-yang Hsiu (1007–1072), were both minor officials in the court during the Sung dynasty, and both were poets and historians. Since they were close friends, they may be referring to each other in the following poems.

An Excuse for Not Returning the Visit of a Friend

Do not be offended because
I am slow to go out. You know
Me too well for that. On my lap
I hold my little girl. At my
Knees stands my handsome little son.   5
One has just begun to talk.

The other chatters without
Stopping. They hang on my clothes
And follow my every step.
I can't get any farther   10
Than the door. I am afraid
I will never make it to your house.

OU–YANG HSIU

Spring Day on West Lake

The lovely spring breeze has come
Back to the Lake of the West.
The spring waters are so clear and
Green they might be freshly painted.
The clouds of perfume are sweeter   5
Than can be imagined. In the
Gentle east wind the petals
Fall like grains of rice. This old
Military counselor,
Moved by the spring, is filled with   10
Troubled thoughts. His white hairs, like
This poem, are a salute of
Autumn to spring. He offers
The lake a cup of wine. He
Thinks of his comrades on the   15

Frontiers of heaven, ten thousand
Miles away. The spring moves the
  hearts
Of all men alike. Snow melts
From the passes. The mountains
Turn green. Flowers cover the   20
Riverbanks. Under the full
Moon of April young men welcome
The spring with wine and love. But
Me, once more greeting the spring,
My head is white. I am in   25
A strange land, in the midst of
People whose ways are not mine.
The soft east wind is the only
Familiar thing from the old days.

THE BOOK OF SONGS

1. What is known about the fierce tribe called the Hsien-yün comes mostly from number 167 and from a few other poems. How much can you learn about them from the details of this poem? What tragic, universal experiences of war and injustice are evoked by these two ancient poems?

2. What can you infer about the identity of the speakers in numbers 36 and 167?

3. What references to the natural world, or images drawn from nature, are used in numbers 36 and 167? What effect do such images have on these poems?

4. Both of these poems use repetition. Number 36 changes only one bit of phrasing and one key word. What is the effect of the repetition? What is the significance of the words that are emphasized by *not* being repeated?

5. Number 167 falls into two parts, with repetition in the first part only. What are the two main divisions of the poem? Do you see any reason that repetition should be used only through the first part? What other differences do you observe between the two parts?

CH'Ü YÜAN

1. How does "Battle" differ from song number 167 from the *Book of Songs* in its attitude toward war and in the attitude it tries to arouse in the reader? What details contribute to these differences in the two poems?

2. Compare the images of and attitudes toward battle found here with those of other war poems in this volume. For example, consider the poems by Callinus and Semonides on pages 105 and 106.

WU TI

How does Wu Ti use images of the natural world to express personal sadness and desolation over the loss of Li Fu-jen?

T'AO CH'IEN

1. In the first of these poems (number 1), what details convey the idea expressed in line 10: "More than enough is not what I want"? What do the speaker's thoughts suggest about the "sages of antiquity," as contrasted with the men who held power in his own day?

2. Compare and contrast the "deep meaning" mentioned in line 9 of poem number 2

with the last two lines of William Wordsworth's "Ode: Intimations of Immortality":

To me the meanest flower that blows can give
Thoughts that do often lie too deep for tears.

3. T'ao Ch'ien expresses a Taoist outlook (see page 263) in "Substance, Shadow, and Spirit." How would you define the way he uses the word *hoard* in the first line? Describe the poet's philosophy of life in terms of the dialogue he presents here. (Pay particular attention to lines 18 and 54–58.)

4. How does T'ao's philosophy contrast with traditional Judeo-Christian thought?

TU FU

1. In "Jade Flower Palace," how does the description of the ruined palace recall details of the palace as it once was? What do you understand by the image of the organ pipes in line 8? What uses are made of contrasts between natural and man-made things?

2. In "Loneliness," explain the analogy drawn between the speaker and the nonhuman creatures. What does this analogy imply about the speaker and the reasons for his sorrow?

3. In "Night in the House by the River," which force is winning the struggle between Yin and Yang? What details of the poem point to an answer to that question? What significance do you read in the opposition between the "bitter cries . . . of households" and the "noise of battle"? What commentary do lines 12–16 make on "the affairs of men"? What effect do the last two lines have on the feeling and understanding that the rest of the poem has created?

4. In "Pretty Women," the Third of Third refers to the third day of the third half-month of the year, counting from a date early in February. The festival, then, would be in early March. What are the clues to the poet's attitude toward the festival and the women— that is, how do his details and the way he presents them lead you to understand this poem as a criticism of the court rather than as a celebration of its splendor?

PO CHÜ-I

Fear is something we must all come to terms with. Po's poem is a frank expression of physical fear. Where is the speaker standing in relation to the Yangtze gorges? What lines express the speaker's sense of insignificance?

MEI YAO-CH'EN

"An Excuse" is clearly not an expression of profound thought or feelings. What, instead, does it express? What interest and pleasure does this kind of poem hold, to make it worth the poet's writing and your reading?

OU-YANG HSIU

1. In "Spring Day on West Lake," the poet describes a scene in a way that helps you to imagine almost any pleasant spring day near almost any pleasant lake. How does the poet give interest to this general description? How does he create an individualized impression?

2. How does the identity of the speaker in "Spring Day on West Lake" affect the impression conveyed by the scene? What is the effect of the speaker's initially using the third person and later the first person?

FOR COMPOSITION

1. "Jade Flower Palace" is similar in theme to the following sonnet, "Ozymandias," written in the nineteenth century by Percy Bysshe Shelley.

I met a traveler from an antique land
Who said: Two vast and trunkless legs of
    stone
Stand in the desert. Near them, on the sand,
Half sunk, a shattered visage lies, whose
    frown,
And wrinkled lip, and sneer of cold com-
    mand
Tell that its sculptor well those passions read
Which yet survive, stamped on these life-
    less things,
The hand that mocked them and the heart
    that fed;
And on the pedestal these words appear:
"My name is Ozymandias, king of kings:
Look on my works, ye Mighty, and despair!"
Nothing beside remains. Round the decay
Of that colossal wreck, boundless and bare
The lone and level sands stretch far away.
                    —PERCY BYSSHE SHELLEY

In an essay, describe the similarities in theme and describe how the two treatments differ. In coming to your conclusions, you may want to consider these questions. What are the differences in tone and feeling between the two poems? How are these differences related to the different images the poems use to express the theme?

2. The following version of a popular ballad is sung by contemporary folk singer Pete Seeger. In an essay, compare and contrast the two ancient Chinese poems from the *Book of Songs* with this ballad. Comment on the use of repetition for certain effects; on the kinds of attitudes expressed; on the use of nature images. Tell which poem of the three has the greatest appeal for you, and try to explain why.

Where have all the flowers gone,
    Long time passing?
Where have all the flowers gone,
    Long time ago?
Where have all the flowers gone?
The girls have picked them every one.
When will they ever learn?
When will they ever learn?

Where have all the young girls gone,
    Long time passing?
Where have all the young girls gone,
    Long time ago?
Where have all the young girls gone?
Married young men every one.
When will they ever learn?
When will they ever learn?

Where have all the young men gone,
    Long time passing?
Where have all the young men gone,
    Long time ago?
Where have all the young men gone?
Gone for soldiers every one.
When will they ever learn?
When will they ever learn?

Where have all the soldiers gone,
    Long time passing?
Where have all the soldiers gone,
    Long time ago?
Where have all the soldiers gone?
Gone to graveyards every one.
When will they ever learn?
When will they ever learn?

Where have all the graveyards gone,
    Long time passing?
Where have all the graveyards gone,
    Long time ago?
Where have all the graveyards gone?
Growing flowers every one.
When will they ever learn?
When will they ever learn?

Poems from Japanese Collections

Ancient Japanese poetry has been preserved in a number of collections. Little is known of most of the poets themselves: their names and perhaps the time when they lived, sometimes not even that much. The first two poems that follow come from the earliest compilations, made in the eighth century: one called *Man'Yōshū* ("Collection of Ten Thousand Leaves") and the other, *Kaifūsō* ("Fond Recollections of Poetry"). The other poems are from collections of various dates, up to the thirteenth century. Most of these poems are not titled in the originals.

ŌTOMO YAKAMOCHI (c. A.D. 716–A.D. 785)

In obedience to the Imperial command,
Though sad is the parting from my wife,
I summon up the courage of a man,
And dressed for journey, take my leave.
My mother strokes me gently;   5
My young wife clings to me, saying,
"I will pray to the gods for your safekeeping.
Go unharmed and come back soon!"
As she speaks, she wipes with her sleeves
The tears that choke her.   10
Hard as it is, I start on my way,
Pausing and looking back time after time;
Ever farther I travel from my home,
Ever higher the mountains I climb and cross,
Till at last I arrive at Naniwa of wind-blown reeds.   15
Here I stop and wait for good weather,
To launch the ship upon the evening tide,
To set the prow seaward,
And to row out in the calm of morning.
The spring mists rise round the isles,   20
And the cranes cry in a plaintive tone,
Then I think of my far-off home—
Sorely do I grieve that with my sobs
I shake the war arrows I carry
Till they rattle in my ears.   25

On an evening when the spring mists
Trail over the wide sea,
And sad is the voice of the cranes
I think of my far-off home.

Thinking of home,   30
Sleepless I sit,
The cranes call amid the shore reeds,
Lost in the mists of spring.

Poem ("The Departure of the Warrior") by Ōtomo Yakamochi from *Man'Yōshū*. Reprinted by permission of Columbia University Press. Translation made by the Japanese Classics Translation Committee under the auspices of the Nippon Gakujutsu Shinkōkai. The poet Ralph Hodgson was among those responsible for the translation.

KI NO SUEMOCHI

(early eighth century, A.D.)

By the southern woods I have built my hut;
I drop my hook from the north lake banks.
Sporting birds dive when I draw near;
Green duckweed sinks before my gliding boat.
The quivering reeds reveal the fish below;
By the length of my line I know the bottom's depth.
With vain sighs I dangle the tempting bait
And watch the spectacle of avaricous hearts.

(Anonymous)

Can this world
From of old
Always have been so sad,
Or did it become so for the sake
Of me alone?

SŌJŌ HENJŌ

(A.D. 815– A.D. 890)

The weeds grow so thick
You cannot even see the path
That leads to my house:
It happened while I waited
For someone who would not come.

Poem ("Watching Fish in the Water") by Ki no Suemochi, translated by Burton Watson from *Anthology of Japanese Literature,* edited by Donald Keene. Reprinted by permission of Burton Watson.
Anonymous poem ("Sadness") translated by Donald Keene from *Anthology of Japanese Literature: From the earliest era to the mid-nineteenth century,* compiled and edited by Donald Keene, copyright © 1955 by Grove Press, Inc. Reprinted by permission of the publisher.
Poem ("Waiting") by Sōjō Henjō, translated by Donald Keene from *Anthology of Japanese Literature: From the earliest era to the mid-nineteenth century,* compiled and edited by Donald Keene, copyright © 1955 by Grove Press, Inc. Reprinted by permission of the publisher.

THE PRIEST MANSEI
(c. A.D. 720)

To what shall I compare
This world?
To the white wake behind
A ship that has rowed away
At dawn!

PRINCESS SHIKUSHI
(died 1201)

The blossoms have fallen.
I stare blankly at a world
Bereft of color:
In the wide vacant sky
The spring rains are falling.

THE PRIEST JAKUREN
(died 1202)

The hanging raindrops
Have not dried from the needles
Of the fir forest
Before the evening mist
Of autumn rises.

Poem ("The World") by Mansei, translated by Arthur Waley in *Anthology of Japanese Literature*, edited by Donald Keene. Reprinted by permission of George Allen & Unwin, Ltd.
Poem ("The Blossoms Have Fallen") by Princess Shikushi, translated by Donald Keene from *Anthology of Japanese Literature: From the earliest era to the mid-nineteenth century*, compiled and edited by Donald Keene, copyright © 1955 by Grove Press, Inc. Reprinted by permission of the publisher.
Poem ("The Hanging Raindrops") by The Priest Jakuren from *One Hundred Poems from the Japanese*, translated by Kenneth Rexroth. All Rights Reserved. Reprinted by permission of New Directions Publishing Corporation.

1. The poem by Ōtomo Yakamochi tells a story up through line 19. When the speaker rows out "in the calm of morning," the poem tells no more of the story. What is the rest of the poem concerned with? What lines in the poem are repeated, with variations? Describe the effect of these repetitions and of the variations. What significance do you see in them? Both cranes and wild ducks conventionally symbolize good fortune and married happiness; what do such associations add to the effect of the poem?

2. Does the last line of the poem by Ki no Suemochi come as a surprise? Why?

3. What meaning do you find in the comparison of this world to the wake of a ship, in the poem by Mansei?

4. What do you take to be the contrasting states indicated by the raindrops and the mist, in the poem by Jakuren?

5. Compare the use of nature imagery in these seven poems with that in the Chinese poems.

Japanese Haiku

The haiku, developed as a distinct form in the sixteenth century, reflects certain emphases in the Zen philosophy. The haiku is still widely used in Japan, and it has had a significant influence upon American and European poets of this century. Sometimes the pleasure of haiku is the pleasure of puzzle-solving. Chiefly, however, haiku holds our interest as a kind of pure poetry, from which every nonessential element, such as storytelling or obvious philosophizing, has been eliminated.

The haiku has three lines. Those written in Japanese have five syllables in the first and third lines and seven syllables in the second line. Within this rigid form, the Japanese poet creates an impression of a moment by establishing an often surprising comparison between two dissimilar objects. In the following haiku, for instance, images of the moon and a fan are brought together.

> ● If to the moon
>   one puts a handle—what
>   a splendid fan!
>   —SŌKAN (1465–1553)

This may suggest for some readers a picture of the full moon seen behind a branch, and the association of moon and fan may enhance the beauty and coolness of each object. In the following haiku, cherry trees and humans are compared.

> ● On top of skeletons
>   they put a gala dress, and then—
>   the flower-viewing!
>   —ONITSURA (1660–1738)

Both the cherry trees and the fashionable viewers have disguised their skeletons. This haiku may remind the reader of the Zen teaching that any beautiful scene or object, like man himself, is transitory.

All haiku by Sōkan, Bashō, Sora, Buson, Gyōdai, and Issa, and the two haiku by Onitsura beginning "On top of skeletons" and "They blossom, and then" from *An Introduction to Haiku*, translated by Harold G. Henderson, copyright © 1958 by Harold G. Henderson. Reprinted by permission of Doubleday & Company, Inc.
The haiku by Onitsura beginning "Even stones in streams" from *Haiku Harvest*, translated by Peter Beilenson and Harry Behn. Reprinted by permission of Peter Pauper Press, Inc.

BASHŌ
(1644–1694)

1

On a journey, ill,
    and over fields all withered, dreams
      go wandering still.

2

Clouds come from time to time—
    and bring to men a chance to rest
      from looking at the moon.

3

Poverty's child—
    he starts to grind the rice
      and gazes at the moon.

4

The winds of fall
    are blowing, yet how green
      the chestnut burr.

SORA
(1648–1710)

Up the barley rows,
    stitching, stitching them together,
      a butterfly goes.

ONITSURA
(1660–1738)

1

They blossom, and then
    we gaze, and then the blooms
      scatter, and then . . .

2

Even stones in streams
    of mountain water compose
      songs to wild cherries

BUSON
(1715–1783)

1

For me who go,
    for you who stay—
      two autumns.

2

Morning haze:
    as in a painting of a dream,
      men go their ways.

GYŌDAI
(1732–1793)

The falling leaves
fall and pile up; the rain
beats on the rain.

ISSA
(1762–1826)

1	2
What a red moon! And whose is it, children?	This Dewdrop World— a dewdrop world it is, and still, although it is . . .

FOR STUDY AND DISCUSSION

1. Most haiku create tiny pictures. What pictures does each haiku create?

2. Identify the images that are brought together in each haiku. What associations do they have for you? What emotion does each haiku produce?

3. The revered Bashō, a Zen practitioner, was deeply philosophical. Asked on his deathbed for a poem summarizing his philosophy, he refused, but during the night he dreamed, and when he woke he said that a poem (number 1) had come to him. What attitude does Bashō express in his farewell to the world?

4. Unhappy and poor, Issa was often in revolt against the social conventions of his time. Do you find a note of protest in the first haiku under his name? Explain. The second haiku by Issa was written upon the death of his last surviving child. The first line of this haiku is from a scripture which compares the transitoriness of life to the transitoriness of dew. Does Issa find comfort in the line of scripture? Explain.

FOR COMPOSITION

Compose an unrhymed poem of three lines, in the style of the haiku, which brings together two dissimilar images, perhaps suggested by one of the following pairs. What can one image illumine about the other?

a. sand, city streets
b. riverbank, mother and child
c. guitar, tree
d. flower, rifle
e. thundercloud, parting lovers

Chinese and Japanese Anecdotes

One way to gain insight into the religious and philosophical thought of China and Japan is through their anecdotes, which are intended to convey indirectly the teachings or the character of a religious master, such as Confucius or the Taoist Chuang Tzu. Many anecdotes have their origin in the sayings attributed to the religious masters; others are of indeterminate origin. For Zen Buddhism, in particular, anecdotes are a useful means for the student to gain insight into the nature of this philosophy, which seeks enlightenment, or *satori,* only through receptivity to experience. Zen, distrustful of words, has no doctrine or written documents to define it.

Though the anecdotes are pointed and often amusing, they may scarcely seem to belong to the category of literature at all. But many of them have something of the relationship to storytelling that the haiku have to poetry, although the anecdotes seldom show the artistry of the haiku. The anecdote focuses upon a single significant event or saying and surrounds it with only enough narration and description to make the point understandable and dramatically vivid. Its purpose is to amuse, satirize, or enlighten.

Cats and Parrots

Early in the eighth century the usurping Empress Wu taught cats and parrots to drink from the same dish, but her belief that she had brought about the millennium was very soon shattered.

The Invitation

A CERTAIN MAN who had plenty of money but no education was advised to engage a tutor for his son so that the boy might have the advantages which his father had missed. The tutor arrived and after the first day's lesson the lad came to his father and said: "Father, why should you waste money on a teacher? I have now learned all the rudiments of writing and counting and the rest is simple. He has today explained that one horizontal

stroke stands for *one,* and two strokes mean *two;* in fact, this reading and writing business is now quite clear to me." The father was delighted at his son's intelligence and rapid progress, and dismissed the tutor.

A day or two later the boy was told to write an invitation to his father's old friend, Mr. Million, asking him to dine. At noon the father went to the study to see why the note was not forthcoming. "Father," protested the boy, looking up tired and disheveled from his task, "could you not have invited some other friend to dine? Here have I been working since dawn and up till now I have written only five hundred strokes. I can't think how long it is going to take to write a million."

Dragons

The SURNAME Dragon-Keeper was conferred on a man who was greatly interested in dragons. He knew their tastes and habits and kept a pair in captivity.

Now dragons and men are very different creatures, but thinking he was allowing them to follow their natural instincts, Master Dragon-Keeper gave his pets a pond in the palace to bask in, though the

"Cats" (retitled: "Cats and Parrots"); "The Invitation"; "Dragons" by Lu Kuei Meng; "The Fawn" by Liu Tsung-Yuan; "Fox Outfoxed" from the *Chinese Times;* "The Butterfly"; "The Tortoise" by Chuang Tzu from *The Dragon Book,* compiled and edited by E. D. Edwards. Published by William Hodge & Company. Reprinted by permission of David Higham Associates, Ltd.

hundred rivers and the four oceans are not large enough for them to sport in; and he fed them with tidbits, though the great whales in the vasty deep could not satisfy their appetite. Still, they grew very tame and were quite content to remain where they were.

One morning a wild dragon appeared, whom they eagerly hailed, saying, "What are you doing? To lie torpid between heaven and earth in the great ocean when it is cold and rise to the surface when it is warm is surely a dull existence? You really should come here and live comfortably with us."

The wild dragon tossed his head proudly and laughed. "What," he cried, "all cramped up like you? I am endowed by nature with a crest and horns and a scaly body; I have power to lie hidden in the springs or fly through the sky; mine is the spirit which blows the clouds along and rides upon the wind; it is my business to crush the proud and to moisten the thirsty; I see beyond the limitless; I rest in the regions outside the bounds of space; I go wherever I will, hampered by no boundaries and in whatever form I please. Is not this supreme felicity? As for you, if you are satisfied in a puddle no bigger than a hoofprint, insensible as mud, and no better than earthworms, led by your appetites, hoping for plenty to eat and drink, then, though your appearance is like mine, your pleasures are very different. He who fawns upon man, hoping to profit thereby, will be strangled and his flesh made into mincemeat; it is only a matter of time. I pity you and would lend you a hand, and would you entice me also to enter the snare? No, indeed, you will not escape."

So saying, the wild dragon flew away, and before long the others actually were made into mincemeat for a rich man's table.—LU KUEI MENG

The Fawn

A HUNTER CAUGHT a live fawn and carried it home. When he opened the door his dogs, tails up and hungry for blood, came running out and leaped at the deer. Out of pity for the little creature, their master drove them off, and after that he made a practice of carrying it in his arms among the dogs every day until they grew accustomed to it, and by degrees he even taught them to play without harming it. After a time, the dogs were trained, and the deer, growing up among them, forgot it was a deer and felt they were its friends. It would push its way among them and lie down in the most friendly manner, and the dogs, fearing their master, behaved perfectly, even though they sometimes licked their lips.

About three years later the deer went out one day by itself, and, seeing some dogs in the road, ran up to play with them. The strange dogs, in fierce delight, tore it in pieces and lay about the road devouring it.

So the little fawn died, uncomprehending.—LIU TSUNG-YUAN

Fox Outfoxed

ONE EVENING a man was returning home when he overtook a young man on the road. They saluted each other and entered into conversation, but there was something in the young man's appearance which excited the other's suspicions, and he resolved to be on his guard. They talked freely on various subjects, and the young man proved an agreeable companion; finally, he begged his fellow traveler to give him a night's lodging as he was far from home. The request was readily granted. The young man then made several inquiries regarding his friend's home, asking particularly if he kept dogs. No, his friend kept no dogs; so he was comforted.

"My greatest fear," he said "is dogs; what is yours?"

"Oh!" said the other, "my great terror is money; the sight of it makes me shake and tremble."

By this time they had reached the house. The owner carefully closed the front gate behind them and called to his dog, which in a moment came bounding toward him, but, on seeing the guest, rushed at him open-mouthed. Quick as lightning, however, that individual changed into a fox, bounded over the wall and was gone.

That night the man was aroused by a noise at the open window, and looking up saw the fox with a large bag of money in his hand, grinning at him maliciously. The man sprang up in seeming terror, and the fox pelted him with handful after handful of money, while he ran about the room crying piteously for mercy, to the fox's great delight. This continued night after night, until the fox grew weary and the man became rich.—*Chinese Times*

The Butterfly

THE PHILOSOPHER Chuang Tzu dreamed he was butterfly, and when he woke up he said he did not know whether he was Chuang Tzu who had dreamed he was a butterfly, or a butterfly now dreaming that it was Chuang Tzu.

The Tortoise

THE PHILOSOPHER Chuang Tzu was fishing on the bank of a river when a messenger appeared with an invitation from the king of Ch'u offering him the post of prime minister. Without taking his eyes from the river, the philosopher replied: "They say that the king has in his treasury the shell of a supernatural tortoise; if the tortoise had been allowed to choose, would it have preferred to adorn a king's treasury or to continue to wag its tail in the mud of its native marsh?" "It would have preferred to remain wagging its tail in the mud," said the messenger. "And I, too," answered Chuang Tzu, "prefer to live obscure but free. To be in office often costs a man his life and always costs his peace of mind. Go back to the king and say that I will continue to wag my tail in the mud."—CHUANG TZU

TWO VERSIONS OF A CONFUCIAN ANECDOTE

Bad Government

WHEN CONFUCIUS was traveling through a wild district he one day heard a woman wailing and sent one of his disciples to inquire the cause of her grief. She paused in her weeping to explain that her father-in-law, her husband, and her son had in turn been killed by a tiger which haunted that place. "Then why do you stay here?" asked the messenger in surprise. "Because there is no bad government here," replied the woman simply. "Alas!" said Confucius, on hearing the explanation, "bad government is more destructive than tigers."

The Tyrant and the Tiger

CONFUCIUS ONCE passed by the foot of the Tai Mountain. There he saw a woman crying her heart out beside a newly finished grave.

The Master stopped and listened. Then he sent Tselu [1] over to inquire of the mourner, saying, "You cry as if you are in great sorrow."

"True!" the woman answered. "First my uncle was killed by the tiger; then my husband was killed by the tiger; and now my son—he also died at the mouth of the tiger."

"Why, then," the Master asked, "didn't you leave the place and go somewhere else?"

"But there is no tyrant here!" was the woman's reply.

Confucius turned to Tselu and said: "Mark it, my lad! A tyrant is worse than a tiger."

[1] **Tselu:** a disciple.

"Bad Government" from *The Dragon Book*, compiled and edited by E. D. Edwards. Published by William Hodge & Company. Reprinted by permission of David Higham Associates, Ltd.
"The Tyrant and the Tiger," translated by George Kao, from *Chinese Wit and Humor*, edited by George Kao, copyright 1946 by Coward-McCann, Inc. Reprinted by permission of the publisher.

FIVE ZEN ANECDOTES

A Cup of Tea

Nan-in, a Japanese master during the Meiji era (1868–1912), received a university professor who came to inquire about Zen.

Nan-in served tea. He poured his visitor's cup full and then kept on pouring.

The professor watched the overflow until he no longer could restrain himself. "It is overfull. No more will go in!"

"Like this cup," Nan-in said, "you are full of your own opinions and speculations. How can I show you Zen unless you first empty your cup?"

The Moon Cannot Be Stolen

Ryokan, a Zen master, lived the simplest kind of life in a little hut at the foot of a mountain. One evening a thief visited the hut only to discover there was nothing in it to steal.

Ryokan returned and caught him. "You may have come a long way to visit me," he told the prowler, "and you should not return empty-handed. Please take my clothes as a gift."

The thief was bewildered. He took the clothes and slunk away.

Ryokan sat naked, watching the moon. "Poor fellow," he mused, "I wish I could give him this beautiful moon."

"A Cup of Tea," "The Moon Cannot Be Stolen," "The Gates of Paradise," "Calling Card," and "A Parable," from *101 Zen Stories* from *Zen Flesh, Zen Bones,* edited by Paul Reps. Reprinted by permission of Charles E. Tuttle Co., Inc.

The Gates of Paradise

A soldier named Nobushige came to Hakuin and asked: "Is there really a paradise and a hell?"

"Who are you?" inquired Hakuin.

"I am a samurai," the warrior replied.

"You, a soldier!" exclaimed Hakuin. "What kind of ruler would have you as his guard? Your face looks like that of a beggar."

Nobushige became so angry that he began to draw his sword, but Hakuin continued: "So you have a sword! Your weapon is probably much too dull to cut off my head."

As Nobushige drew his sword Hakuin remarked: "Here open the gates of hell!"

At these words the samurai, perceiving the master's discipline, sheathed his sword and bowed.

"Here open the gates of paradise," said Hakuin.

Calling Card

Keichu, the great Zen teacher of the Meiji era, was the head of Tofuku, a cathedral in Kyoto. One day the governor of Kyoto called upon him for the first time.

His attendant presented the card of the governor, which read: Kitagaki, Governor of Kyoto.

"I have no business with such a fellow," said Keichu to his attendant. "Tell him to get out of here."

The attendant carried the card back with apologies. "That was my error," said the governor, and with a pencil he scratched out the words Governor of Kyoto. "Ask your teacher again."

"Oh, is that Kitagaki?" exclaimed the teacher when he saw the card. "I want to see that fellow."

A Parable

BUDDHA told a parable in a Sutra: [1]

A man traveling across a field encountered a tiger. He fled, the tiger after him. Coming to a precipice, he caught hold of the root of a wild vine and swung himself down over the edge. The tiger sniffed at him from above. Trembling, the man looked down to where, far below, another tiger was waiting to eat him. Only the vine sustained him.

Two mice, one white and one black, little by little started to gnaw away the vine. The man saw a luscious strawberry near him. Grasping the vine with one hand, he plucked the strawberry with the other. How sweet it tasted!

[1] **Sutra:** one of a collection of stories that embody the wisdom of Buddha.

FOR STUDY AND DISCUSSION

1. The first two anecdotes seem to be mere jokes, but each has a pointed observation to make about human nature. In each case, what is that observation?

2. Both "Dragons" and "The Fawn" illustrate a Taoist principle about man and his relationship with nature. According to these anecdotes, what effect can man have on the natural scheme of things?

3. Chinese folk legends often tell of animals and humans changing shape. The fox is a familiar character, used traditionally as a symbol of craftiness and evil and therefore a favorite disguise for evil spirits. In the light of this traditional symbolism, what significance do you attribute to the anecdote of the fox?

4. Chuang Tzu (fourth century B.C.) was the chief exponent of Taoist philosophy, said to have been established a century earlier by Lao-tzu. What do the anecdotes about Chuang Tzu reveal of his character and of Taoist beliefs about the nature of human existence?

5. The anecdote about the tortoise makes a point similar to the moral of "Dragons," but there is an important difference—perhaps even a contradiction—between their attitudes. What is it?

6. Traditionally, the butterfly symbolizes

joy and the tortoise longevity. How, then, are these two animals appropriate choices for these anecdotes?

7. Point out the differences in the ways the one anecdote about Confucius is told. Do the differences affect its meaning?

8. Anecdotes about Confucius were often told to illustrate one of the master's sage sayings. What observation is Confucius offering in this anecdote? Is his observation applicable today? Explain.

9. Concerning "A Cup of Tea," what attitudes and ideas would a university professor be likely to have that would prevent him from understanding the Zen ideas reflected in these anecdotes?

10. After reading the anecdote, what new meaning do you find in the title "The Moon Cannot Be Stolen"?

11. In "The Gates of Paradise," what definition is conveyed by *paradise* and *hell?*

12. In "Calling Card," what do you understand the governor's real error to have been?

13. How would you express the abstract idea that "A Parable" conveys? What might the details—the tiger, the precipice, the vine, the mice, the strawberry—symbolize?

14. Read the beast fables from Greece and India (pages 116 and 253). Define the essential characteristics of this kind of story. What is its particular appeal that might explain its use in different times and places? Would the fables of one culture be readily understandable by people of other cultures? Explain.

FOR COMPOSITION

1. Some of these anecdotes might express attitudes toward life that are surprising or that are contradictory to your own way of thinking. Write an essay explaining the difference between the way you would be likely to approach a particular problem and the way the philosopher of the anecdote would have you approach it. What truth and value do you find in his attitude and in your own?

2. Choose a popular maxim—"Beauty is in the eyes of the beholder," "Truth is stranger than fiction," "Enough is better than too much or too little," etc.—and write an anecdote to convey it without stating the idea directly. Notice particularly how the details you use to fill out your story force you to think more precisely about the general idea you are working with.

The Cricket Boy

P'U SUNG-LING

Chinese writer P'u Sung-ling (1640–1715) was fascinated by stories of the mysterious and supernatural. This story is one of a large collection of such stories that he made in 1679 under the title *Records of the Strange*. Most of them he presumably created out of story elements in popular folklore. As the story points out, crickets are caught and caged as pets by Chinese boys, and adults match the insects in fights and races. In popular superstition, crickets are associated with good fortune and friendly spirits, as in the Western superstition that a cricket on the hearth brings luck to the house.

WHEN KITI, a boy of eleven, came home with his father after a day's fruitless search for crickets, he had a most wonderful feeling—the discovery of his father as a play companion. Kiti was an extremely impressionable child. Once, when he was five, his father held a stick to punish him for something, and Kiti's face turned so pale with fright that his father let the stick drop out of his hand. He had always had a great fear of his father, a taciturn man of forty-five.

He was small for his age, about the size of other children of nine or ten, and the jacket which his mother had made for him a year ago, thinking he would grow up quickly, still seemed ample and long. His slim, childish figure was accentuated by a disproportionately large head and a pair of big, black, playful eyes and plump round cheeks. He jumped and skipped, rather than walked normally, and he was still very much a child in his emotions. When his brother was Kiti's age, he was

already a great help to his mother, but not Kiti. Now the brother was dead and his only sister was married into a family in another town. Kiti was perhaps pampered by his mother, a sad but strongly built woman, who could be made to smile only by Kiti's unusual pranks and wiles. He still retained many childish ways in his looks and smiles, and in the intense joys and sorrows of childhood.

Kiti loved crickets as only boys can love, and, with a child's keen enthusiasm and poetic imagination, he found in the beauty and delicacy of the insect something utterly perfect, noble, and strong. He admired the cricket's complicated mandibles and thought that no animal of a larger size in this world had such a lacquered, armored body and legs. He thought that if an animal the size of a dog or pig had such a beautiful outfit—no, there was no comparable animal. Crickets had been his passion since his early childhood. Like all village children, he had played with them and had come to know the worth of a cricket by the sound of its creak, the size and angle of its legs, and the proportion and shape of its head and body. There was a northern window in his room, adjoining a back garden, and as he lay in bed listening to the song of the crickets, it seemed to him the most pleasing music in the world. It represented to him all that was good and strong and beautiful in this world. Confucius and Mencius he learned quickly from his teacher, who was now his own father, and forgot just as quickly; but this song of the crickets he understood and remembered. He had heaped a pile of bricks and stones under the window for the purpose of attracting them. No grownup seemed to understand this—certainly not his cold and severe father—but today for the first time, he had come out with Kiti and run over the mountainside to look for a champion fighter.

There had been a memorable incident when Kiti was six. He had brought a cricket to the classroom, and the teachers discovered it and crushed it. Kiti was so furious that when the teacher turned his back, Kiti leaped from his chair, saddled on his back, and pummeled the teacher with all the strength of his small fists, to the amusement of the students, until the teacher had to shake him down.

That afternoon, he had watched his father silently making a hand net with a bamboo handle for catching crickets. When the net was made, his father had said to him, "Kiti, bring that bamboo box. We will go to the southern hills." It was beneath the scholar's dignity to announce that he was going to catch crickets.

But Kiti understood. He went out with his father and felt as if he were on a New Year holiday. It was like an answer to a child's prayer. He had gone out to catch crickets, but had never had the luxury of a proper net. Furthermore, he had never been allowed to go to the southern hills, about a mile and a half away, where he knew there were plenty of crickets.

It was July and the day was hot. The father and child, net in hand, ran all over the foothill slopes, making their way through thickets, jumping over ditches, turning over and peeping under stones, listening for that most important sound, the clear, metallic chirp of a good champion. They had found no worthy champion, but they had found each other as companions. That was a wonderful new sensation for Kiti. He had seen his father's eyes shine when they heard a clear, sharp note, and heard him curse under his breath when they lost one in the underbrush. On their way back, his father was still uttering sighs of regret over missing the beautiful one. For the first time, his father had become human, and he loved his father then.

His father had not bothered to explain why he suddenly took an interest in crickets, and Kiti, though secretly delighted, saw no reason to ask. But when they got home he saw his mother standing at the door, waiting for them to return for supper.

"Did you catch any?" asked his mother anxiously.

"No!" The father's reply was solemn and heavy with disappointment.

Kiti wondered greatly about it. That night he asked his mother, when they were alone, "Tell me, Mother, does Father love crickets, too? I thought I was the only one."

"No, he does not. He has to do it."

"Why? For whom?"

"For the emperor. Your father is the head of the village. He received an order from the magistrate to catch a good fighter. Who dares disobey the emperor?"

"I do not understand." Kiti was still more puzzled.

"Nor do I. But your father has to catch a good one within the next ten days, or he will lose his job and be fined. We are too poor to pay, and he may have to go to jail if he fails."

Kiti gave up trying to understand and asked no more questions. He only knew that it was something of terrible importance.

At this time, there was a great craze for cricket fights among the ladies of the court, with heavy betting going on, and culminating in the annual mid-autumn championship contests. It was perhaps an old tradition at the court, for the last premier of the Sung dynasty was known to have been watching his cricket fights when the armies of Genghis Khan marched into the capital. The district of Hwayin where Mr. Cheng lived was not known for producing the best fighters, but a year ago an alert magistrate of the province had obtained a good champion and sent it to the court. A prince had written a letter to the governor of the province asking him to send more champions for the annual mid-autumn contest, and the governor had issued an order to all his magistrates to send their choicest selections from the districts to him. What had been a private request from a prince had become an edict of the emperor, as far as the common people were concerned. The price of good crickets skyrocketed and one magistrate was known to have offered as much as a hundred dollars for a good champion. Cricket fights had also become a popular pastime among the local people, and those who had champions were reluctant to part with them for any price.

Some heads of villages had taken the occasion to extort money from the people to buy crickets for the emperor, calling it the "crickets' levy." Mr. Cheng could have collected one or two hundred dollars from the villagers, pocketed half of it, and with the other half bought a cricket from the town. He, however, would do nothing of the kind. If it was his duty to submit a champion, he would go and catch it himself.

Kiti shared his father's anxiety and felt important because his child's pastime had now become a dignified, grown-up affair. He watched his father's expression, as they were taking a rest in the cool shade. His father took out his pipe, lighted it, and his eyebrows danced a little as he puffed. He seemed to want to say something but paused and puffed away at his pipe, opened his mouth, and then stopped to puff again. Finally, he said with an almost guilty expression on his face, "Kiti, you can catch a good champion for me. It is worth a lot of money."

"How, Father?"

"You see, son, there is a national championship at the imperial palace on mid-autumn festival. The winner will be awarded a big prize by the emperor."

"Really—by the emperor himself?" exclaimed Kiti. "Does the emperor love crickets, too?"

"Yes," replied the father reluctantly, as if a shameful confession had been forced from his lips.

"Hey, Father, we might catch a good fighter and win the national championship!" Kiti was greatly excited. "Will you be able to see the emperor?"

"No, I will send the cricket through the magistrate and then through the governor, if it is good enough. It has got to be good. There is a big award in silver for the champion owner."

"Father, we will catch one, and we will be rich!"

It was difficult to repress the child's enthusiasm. But the father, having told him an important secret, looked serious once more. They got up and continued the search. Kiti now felt it was his responsibility to catch a champion fighter for his father, and for his mother as well because he had often heard her complain about being poor.

"I will catch one and fight and fight till we win," said the child.

The father was now glad that Kiti knew so much about crickets and was able to help him. For three days, they could not find a champion, but on the fourth day they had a streak of good luck. They had gone over the top of the hill and descended on the farther side where there was a deep thicket and heavy underbrush. Far down the slope was an ancient tomb site. The outline of the tomb, some fifty feet across, was clearly visible. Kiti suggested going down to the tomb where they might catch some good crickets, especially because the sand there was reddish yellow. They followed a small brook and reached the site where a great many stone slabs lay about, showing the outlines of the ancient tomb. Their hope was justified. The crickets were singing on that July afternoon, not a few, but dozens of them in concert. Kiti's senses were sharpened. A frog suddenly leaped from the grass under his feet and disappeared into a hole, from which sprang out a big, beautiful insect, hopping away in long, powerful strides. The big cricket disappeared into an underground hole protected by stone slabs. The father and son crouched down and listened with bated breath to the rich, resonant chirp. Kiti took a long blade of grass and tried to stir the insect out of the hole, but it stopped its singing. They were sure now that the prize champion was in that hole, but the crack was too small even for the child's small hands to reach down through it. The father tried to smoke it out without success. Then Kiti went to fetch some water to pour down the hole, while the father held the net in readiness outside the entrance.

In a few seconds, the cricket sprang neatly into their net. He was a beauty, of the kind called "blackneck," with wide jaws, slender body, and powerful legs bent at a high angle. His whole body was of a fine and deep reddish-brown lacquer finish. Their labor was rewarded.

They returned home happily and placed their prize in an earthen jar on a table in the father's room, carefully covered with a sheet of copper-wire netting. Mr. Cheng would take it to town the next day to present it to the magistrate. He instructed his wife to guard it carefully against neighbors' cats, and he went out to get some chestnut meat to feed it. Nobody was to touch it while he was away.

Kiti was excited beyond measure. He could not help coming into the room to listen to the insect's chirp and stare at it in sheer joy.

Then a tragedy happened. There was for a time no noise whatever in the jar. Kiti tapped it and still there was no sign of a movement. The cricket was apparently gone. He could not see into the dark jar, so he took it near the window and removed the wire net slowly to look, when out hopped the cricket and landed on a bookshelf. Kiti was desperate. He closed the window quickly and started to chase the insect around the room. In his excitement he neglected to use the net, and by the time he had caught the cricket under his palm, he had crushed its neck and broken one of its legs.

Kiti was pale with terror. His mouth was dry and he was without tears. He had destroyed what had promised to be a national champion.

"You accumulated debt of ten generations!" scolded his mother. "You are going to die! When your father returns, I do not know what he will do to you!"

Kiti's face was deathly white. He finally broke into sobs and ran away from the house.

At suppertime Kiti still had not returned. His father was enraged and mortified, and threatened to give him a sound thrashing when he returned. The parents thought that he was hiding away, afraid to return, but believed that he would come home when he was hungry.

Toward ten o'clock, there was still no sign of Kiti, and the anger of the parents had turned into anxiety for him. They went out with a lantern into the night to search for him, and toward midnight they found Kiti's body at the bottom of a well.

When the child was brought out, he was apparently lifeless. There was a big wound on his head, but a trickle of fresh blood was still oozing from a cut on his forehead. It was a shallow well, but his whole body was drenched. They dried him and bandaged him, laying him on the bed, and were glad to find that his heart was still beating. Only a feeble breath indicated that the child was still alive. The shock was apparently so great that Kiti remained unconscious for a whole day, hovering between life and death. That evening they heard him mumbling in his sleep, "I have killed the champion—the blackneck, the blackneck!"

The next morning, Kiti could take some soup, but he was a changed child. All life seemed to have gone out of him. He could not recognize his father and mother. His sister, hearing of the incident, came to visit him, and he made no sign of recognition. An old doctor told them that he had been badly frightened and that his illness was too deep to be cured by medicines. The only coherent words Kiti said were, "I have killed him!"

Happy that Kiti was at least alive and hopeful of an eventual recovery, Mr. Cheng remembered that he had still four more days in which to catch another fighter. He had a faint hope that if he could catch a good one and show it to Kiti, it might help to cure him. After all, there were plenty of crickets in the ancient tomb site. He slept lightly and at dawn he heard a chirp in his house. He got up and traced the sound to the kitchen, where he saw a small cricket resting high up on the wall.

A strange thing now happened. As the father stood looking at it, he thought how small and probably useless it was for such a loud chirp. But with three loud chirps the little one hopped down onto his sleeve, as if asking to be caught.

The father captured it and examined it slowly. It had a long neck and a plum-flower design on its wings. It might be a good fighter, but it was so small. He would not dare to offer it to the magistrate.

A neighboring young man had a local champion which had won every bout in the village. He had put a high price on it, but he had found no buyer, so he brought it to Mr. Cheng's house, intending to sell it to him.

When Mr. Cheng suggested a match, the young man took a look at the little cricket and covered his mouth in laughter. The two insects were placed inside a cage, and Cheng felt ashamed of his cricket and wanted to withdraw. The young man insisted on a fight to show his insect's prowess, and Cheng, thinking it would be no great sacrifice if the little one should be killed or maimed, yielded. The two insects now stood facing each other inside a basin. The little one stood still while the big one

opened its fangs and glowered as if eager for combat. The young man teased the little one with a pig's bristle to provoke it, but it remained unmoved. Again he prodded it, repeatedly, and suddenly the little fellow sprang into action, and the two insects fell at each other. In an instant, they saw the small cricket tilt its tail, raise its feelers, and with a powerful leap sink its jaws into the opponent's neck. The young man quickly lifted the cage and called the fight off in the hope of saving his pet. The little cricket raised its head and chirped triumphantly.

Cheng was greatly pleased and amazed, but while he was admiring his new find, along with his family, a cock came along unnoticed by them, and pecked at the prize. The little cricket hopped away, chased by the cock and in immediate reach of its claws. Cheng thought all was lost. Then he saw the cock shaking its head repeatedly and observed that the little cricket had perched safely on the cock's neck and was harassing it from that position. They were all astounded and delighted.

Now confident of the little cricket's fighting power, Cheng decided to present it to the magistrate, telling him the story. The magistrate was far from impressed and was very skeptical, but he gave the insect a trial. The cricket won every fight over others collected in his office. He tried it again on a cock, and the little "plum-flower wing" repeated his tactic of landing on the cock's neck, to everybody's astonishment. Satisfied with the district champion, the magistrate put it in a copper-wire cage and sent it to the governor. It was already the last day of July, and he dispatched it on horseback.

The father waited and hoped; one cricket had brought on his son's illness, another one might cure him. Then he heard that the little cricket had become the provincial champion, and his hopes went higher. It would take probably a month before he heard the results of the national championship match.

"Huh!" said Kiti's mother to her husband when she was told of the little cricket's fighting tactics. "Is it not just like Kiti riding on the teacher's back and pommeling him from behind?"

Kiti did not recover from his shock. Most of the time he was asleep and his mother had to force food down his mouth with a spoon. The first few days, his muscles twitched and he perspired heavily. The doctor came again and after hearing the symptoms announced that Kiti had burst his gall bladder in fright, and said that his yang-yin system of internal secretions had turned backward. His three spiritual and seven animal spirits had been frightened away. It would take a long and slow cure to restore his vitality.

After three days, Kiti suffered another fit of paroxysms. Then his head seemed clearer for a day—it was the last day of July, his mother remembered clearly—and he could even smile when he said to his mother, "I have won!" His eyes stared vacantly.

"You have what?"

"I have won."

"Won what?"

"I do not know. I must win." He seemed to be still in a delirium.

Then his spirit left him again, and he fell into a profound coma for half a month.

At dawn, on the morning of August the eighteenth, Kiti's mother heard him calling, "Mother, I am hungry!"

It was the first time Kiti had called his mother since the incident. She jumped out of bed, called her husband, and they went in together to see their boy.

"Mother, I am hungry."

"My darling child. you are well again!" The mother wiped her eyes with the hem of her jacket.

"How are you feeling?" asked the father.

"I am feeling fine, Father."

"You have slept a long time."

"Have I? How long?"

"About three weeks. You scared us."

"Was it that long? I did not know any-thing. Father, I did not mean to hurt that champion. I was trying to capture him for you." Kiti's voice was perfectly normal, and he spoke as if the incident had happened only a day ago.

"Do not worry, Kiti," said the father. "While you were ill, I caught a better champion. He was small, but a terribly good fighter. The magistrate accepted it and sent it to the governor. I hear that he has won every fight."

"Then you have forgiven me?"

"Of course I have. Do not worry, son. That plucky little fighter may be a national champion yet. Now put your mind at rest, and soon you will be able to get up."

The family was happy once more. Kiti had a good appetite and only complained that his thighs were sore.

"That is very strange," said his mother.

"I feel, Mother, as if I had run and jumped hundreds of miles."

His mother massaged his legs, while Kiti kept on saying that his thighs were stiff.

In a day, Kiti was able to get up and walk a few steps. On the third day after his recovery, father, mother, and the boy were sitting by the lamp after supper, eating chestnuts.

"This is like the chestnut meat I had at the palace," Kiti remarked casually.

"Where?"

"At the imperial palace," Kiti replied, not knowing how strange his words must have sounded in his parents' ears.

"You must have been dreaming."

"No, Mother, I was there. Now I remember All the ladies were dressed in red and blue and gold, when I came out of my golden cage."

"Did you dream that when you were ill?"

"No, it was true. Believe me, Mother, I was there."

"What did you see?"

"There were men with long beards and there was one I thought must be the emperor. They had come to see me. I only thought of Father and said to myself that

I must win. When I was let out of the cage, I saw a big fellow. He had very long feelers and I got frightened, until the fight started. Night after night, I fought with only one idea, that I must win for Father. On the last night, I met a redhead. He was fearful to look at. I was not afraid any more. I went at him, but when he came at me, I leaped away. I was in perfect form and felt very light and alert. I tore at his tail and bit off one of his front legs. He got mad and came at me with open fangs. I thought I was done for, but I bit him somewhere. Then he became confused. I saw his eye was bleeding. I sprang on his neck and finished him."

Kiti told all this so realistically that his parents listened in silence, knowing that he was perfectly sincere in describing what he had seen in his dreams.

"And you have won the national championship?" asked the father.

"I think I did. I wanted to so much. I only thought of you, Father."

The parents did not know whether to believe his story or not. The child was not lying, they knew. They would wait and see.

The little cricket, sent in a golden cage by the imperial system, had reached the capital just one day before the contests began. The governor was risking a great deal in submitting such a small cricket to the prince. If the insect gave a good account of itself, well and good, but if it failed, he stood a chance of being ridiculed for being in his dotage. He trembled at the thought. The official document of three thousand words accompanying the cricket was something unusual, both apologetic and bombastic at the same time.

"My friend is mad," said the prince, after reading his letter.

"Why not give it a trial?" remarked his wife, the emperor's daughter.

The plucky little fighter fought with supercricket powers. As far as they could see, he had shown no fear when put in a basin opposite the other provincial champions.

After the first night in which he felled a champion almost twice his size, the little plum-flower wing was regarded as a marvel and became the talk of the court.

Night after night, the little one won. It was true that he had the advantage of lightness and agility. While no champion could get at him, he always harassed the big fellows by his lightning attacks and bit the opponent here and there before he came in with deadly accuracy for a crushing bite. His accomplishments seemed incredible.

The contests lasted five nights from August fourteenth to August eighteenth. On the last night he became the champion. The next morning, the little champion had completely disappeared from his cage.

When the news reached Kiti's family, the father wept, and they were all overjoyed. The father put on his best gown and took Kiti along to the magistrate. He was told that he would be made an honorary member of the district college with monthly stipends for his support.

The family fortunes turned, and Kiti eventually was able to go to college. Kiti not only felt embarrassed to have his story told, but he stopped watching cricket fights altogether. He could not stand it.

Later he became a hanlin and was able to support his parents in ease and comfort in their old age. Mr. Cheng, now a proud grandfather, never tired of telling the story of his son, which grew better and better every time, and he always ended with the words, "There are many ways of showing filial piety. When one's heart is good, the spirits of heaven and earth will show mercy to them that love their parents."

FOR STUDY AND DISCUSSION

1. Although the author probably got this story from popular folklore, he has told it artfully. Trace the stages by which he develops the strange identity between the boy and the little "plum-flower wing" cricket: what is the first hint he gives that there is something unusual about this cricket? At what point do you suspect that the boy *is* the cricket? At what

point are you sure? What details in the plot became more significant when you recognize the identity between the boy and the cricket?

2. We are held in suspense in this story by wondering how certain problems will be resolved. What are the problems developed in this strange tale? How does the writer lead us to expect now one and now another solution to these problems? How are all the problems resolved by the final revelation of the supernatural connection between boy and cricket?

3. The mother in the story is not a well-developed character. Like the reader, she wonders what is happening and how it will turn out. The father, though, is given distinct characteristics and a part to play in the events of the story. How is he contrasted with the boy? Does this contrast make the story more dramatic and intense than it would be if he were only an onlooker, like the mother?

4. The first paragraph draws attention to the significance of the father. The last paragraph rounds the story off on sound Confucian principles. If one or both of these paragraphs were eliminated, how would the story be affected?

PERSIAN–ARABIC LITERATURE

c. A.D. 850 – c. A.D. 1350

Y OU HAVE ALREADY READ of the Aryan progress into India, beginning early in the second millennium B.C. (page 225). The Aryan movement westward to the Iranian plateau was very similar, apparently, though it reached natural and cultural barriers fairly early at the Zagros Mountains east of the Tigris River and temporarily halted there. Names of persons and places give clues to indicate that some Aryan tribes spurted farther west quite early, even as far as Syria and the Mediterranean, but they seem to have been destroyed or absorbed in the endless wars that swept across Mesopotamia and the eastern shore of the Mediterranean. Most of the Iranian Aryans stayed on the plateau, developing separate tribal areas of control and influence. Scholars have identified more than a dozen major tribal groups, and some of these groups had significant histories of their own. Thus, the Medes who joined with the Babylonians to smash the Assyrian Empire and to destroy its capital city of Nineveh in 612 B.C. were Aryans from the northwestern part of Iran. The Parthians who built an empire in the east after the fall of the Persian Empire were also Aryans. Indeed, one of the Middle Iranian languages from which modern Persian derives was called Pahlavi, which means "Parthian."

THE PERSIANS AND ZOROASTRIANISM

The tribal group which gave the name *Persian* to the empire and later to the nation of Iran settled in Persis (now Fars), a region in southwestern Iran bordering the Persian Gulf. From this people sprang Cyrus the Great and Darius I, the powerful emperors who built the Persian Empire in the sixth and fifth centuries B.C. till it stretched from the Indus River on the east to Libya and Macedonia on the west. Though this extensive empire was not a unified state, it was well administered by provincial governors called satraps and by a professional civil service. Its distant parts were linked together by roads and by an efficient postal system. In fact, the famous inscription on the main post office in New York City is a quotation from the Greek historian Herodotus, commenting on the Persian postal system.

> ● Neither snow nor rain nor heat nor gloom of night stays these couriers from the swift completion of their appointed rounds.—HERODOTUS

Perhaps the major cultural influence of this Persian Empire was religious. When the Aryans came into Iran, they brought with them the same polytheism that we have seen in the Vedic period of India. But a great prophet named Zarathustra, called Zoroaster in Greek, arose in eastern Iran in the region of Bactria, preaching an elevated religious and ethical system. Just when he was born or where is not clear, but Zoroaster seems to have been an historical figure whose teachings were already widespread by the sixth century B.C. He placed all of the awe-inspiring, good qualities of a deity in a being known as the Wise Lord, Ahura-Mazda, whose will to good is in constant conflict with Ahriman, the spirit of evil. Some of the ancient Aryan folk gods appear as angelic assistants to one or the other of these two great powers. Ahura-Mazda, later called Ormazd, is the embodiment of truth and law, while the evil spirit is the embodiment of falsehood. Man, as a creation of Ormazd, is accountable to him. If man does more good than evil in his life, he is rewarded at death by eternal life in paradise. If he does more evil than good, he goes to hell. If in the strict accounting which each man faces at death, his good and evil deeds balance, he passes into an intermediate stage of existence where he stays until the final judgment, when Ormazd will finally overcome Ahriman forever.

Zoroastrianism set an ethical standard for men well above the primitive religions which it at first displaced. As a result, the Persians felt that the expansion of their empire was a civilizing process for their neighbors. When the advance of Hellenism and then of Roman political power overwhelmed their empire, the Persians still strove to resist the corruption of their religious-cultural life. In fact, the latter part of their prolonged struggle against Rome was directed as much against the unwanted Christian and Jewish influence, introduced by cosmopolitan Roman administration, as against Roman political domination. Through changing fortunes and intermittent peace and war, the Persians' defense of their religion and culture continued, from the time of Alexander in the fourth century B.C. until both the Roman Empire and the Persians themselves were enfeebled in the seventh century A.D. At this point the long conflict was settled by an entirely new, outside influence, the Arabs.

The Arabs are a Semitic people whose home on the Arabian Peninsula was largely sheltered from the impact of world events. Yet Arabs in the southeast had come under Persian influence, and those of the northwest had been exposed to Roman, Jewish, and Egyptian influences. Some Ethiopian colonies seem to have existed in the southwest part of the peninsula well into the Christian era.

Although in earlier times, perhaps as early as 800 B.C., there had been thriving Arab kingdoms in the south and west, prospering from the trade between Egypt and India, these kingdoms fell into decay when an overland trade route in the north was developed. By A.D. 600 some Arabs were farmers, some were urban dwellers in the remaining commercial centers, but most were nomads in an ancient tribal tradition. Traveling the arid landscape with their flocks, they lived with a nomad's awareness of the mystery and majesty of the world of nature, of which man seems so insignificant a part. This awareness appears over and over again in Arabic poetry and imagery.

In A.D. 600, then, there was neither political unity nor religious orthodoxy in Arabia. Yet, within fifty years, the Arabs had acquired religious and political unity and embarked on conquests and conversions which were to carry them across North Africa into Spain and southern France, north and west to Constantinople, and east across Persia into northern India. All of this enterprise stemmed from the growth of Islam, often called Mohammedanism in the West.

The prophet Mohammed began his public ministry in A.D. 613, though he had been gathering a small group of close followers for three years before that. The religion he preached was a revealed religion, like Judaism and Christianity, of which it purports to be a final extension. Mohammed claimed to receive his teachings on morals, law, ethics, and doctrine direct from God. While in a trance, he would recite God's words to scribes who copied them down. These revelations were gathered and arranged after Mohammed's death into the holy book of Islam, the Koran. The revelations are not arranged chronologically in the Koran, but by length, with the longest first. This means that many of the earliest revelations come late in the book, for the revelations tended to increase in length as Mohammed gained power. The revelations are arranged in surahs, or chapters. Because they are often ambiguous, they have inspired a great quantity of interpretive literature. The revelations are generally presented as if God is speaking through the prophet, as is typified in this early surah, number eighty-one:

> ● When the sun shall be folded up, and when the stars shall fall; and
> when the mountains shall be made to pass away; and when the camels

From *The Koran*, translated by George Sale.

ten months gone with young shall be neglected; and when the wild beasts shall be gathered together; and when the seas shall boil; and when the souls shall be joined again to their bodies; and when the girl who hath been buried alive shall be asked for what crime she was put to death; and when the books shall be laid open; and when the heaven shall be removed; and when hell shall burn fiercely; and when paradise shall be brought near; every soul shall know what it hath wrought. Verily I swear by the stars which are retrograde, which move swiftly and which hide themselves; and by the night, when it cometh on; and by the morning, when it appeareth; that these are the words of an honorable messenger, endued with strength, of established dignity in the sight of the possessor of the throne, obeyed by the angels under his authority, and faithful; and your companion Mohammed is not distracted. He had already seen him in the clear horizon; and he suspected not the secrets revealed unto him. Neither are these the words of an accursed devil. Whither, therefore, are you going? This is no other than an admonition unto all creatures; unto him among you who shall be willing to walk uprightly; but ye shall not will, unless God willeth, the Lord of all creatures.—KORAN

Islam means "submission," that is, to the will of God. The religion emphasizes the unity of God ("There is no god but Allah, and Mohammed is his prophet") and makes Mohammed the final prophet of God's revelation, though it recognizes such earlier prophets as Moses and Jesus. Like Christianity, Islam asserts there is a Day of Judgment coming, but it rejects the Christian concept of the Trinity. The power, unity, and goodness of God are expounded in the Koran. A belief in angels, which are pure, sexless creatures who serve God, and in jinn, which are both male and female creatures created from fire who stand somewhere between men and angels, is expected of true believers. Every believer is obliged to recite the creed given in parentheses above, to offer prayers five times daily, to fast at certain seasons, to make gifts of alms, and, if at all possible, to make a pilgrimage to Mecca sometime during his life. The practice of Islam tends to emphasize ascetic personal discipline. For example, the use of strong drink is forbidden. Generosity and hospitality in social relationships and faithful adherence to Islamic law are also stressed. This law establishes legal, ethical, religious, and familial duties.

Only twenty years after Mohammed had begun his public ministry and had called on his followers to spread his truth abroad, the first Arab forces had moved into Persia. By A.D. 650 their conquest of Persia was complete as far east as Balkh, in modern Afghanistan. Shortly thereafter, large Arab garrisons were in Samarkand, projecting further invasions into Central Asia. Zoroastrianism, though officially tolerated, largely disappeared except among certain Persian refugees who fled to Bombay in India, where they

فاذا ازداد العصير نصفه فهذا الشراب موافق لوجع الحلق والجنب والرئين

والاسترخاء الرقيق، ومن كان له مغص غليظ في حلقه يصفي اللون ويكثر القيء م

وليبس له غائله موافق للمثانه والكلا ع ع ع

Prescription for coughs, from an Arabic translation of the Greek (c. 1200).

still live and are known as Parsees, "people of Persis." Most Persians became Mohammedans. Persian customs and traditions became mixed with Arab customs. Even the languages became intertwined in a verbal mix which eventually produced modern Persian, much as modern English has grown from a verbal mix of Anglo-Saxon, French, Latin, and several other languages.

After the death of Mohammed in A.D. 632, the rule of the Moslem lands was placed in the hands of one of his close followers, Abu Bekr, who came to be called the caliph, or "successor." The ruling place of Abu Bekr and his successors, called the caliphate, was at Medina, the city which had originally welcomed Mohammed. Later the caliphate was moved to Damascus and still later to Baghdad. Here Persian influence was strong and was shown in increased luxury, in a revival of Persian literature, and in the use of government practices borrowed from the old empire. It was in Baghdad, under the line of caliphs known as the Abbasids, that the brilliant intellectual and material civilization which spread over the entire Moslem world by the tenth century had its center. Many a Christian crusader, marching out from medieval Europe to try to capture the Holy Land from the Mohammedans or to oust the Moors from Spain, would be attracted by the wealth and grace of that Moslem civilization, even while he rejected its religious base.

PERSIAN-ARABIC LITERATURE 315

A Persian literary flowering had begun in the extreme northeast provinces of Iran in the ninth century A.D., when the Samanid dynasty produced nearly autonomous provincial rulers, more Persian than Arabic in spirit, who spurred a renewal of interest in Persian history and traditions and acted as patrons for a great number of court poets. Though much of the poetry consisted of eulogies of doubtful quality, some excellent poetry came out of this early period. The first major poet of the Persian literary revival was Dakiki (d. A.D. 975), who expressed unabashed enthusiasm for the traditions of Persian history, including even some Zoroastrian ideas. It was his unfinished work on historical materials which Firdawsi, a few years later, was to structure into the Persian national epic, *Shah-Nama* (see page 327). Firdawsi was but one of some four hundred poets at the court of his patron, the sultan Mahmud ibn Sabuktagin. This large number of court poets illustrates the extent of the literary interest of Persian provincial rulers and explains why, along with the historical poetry, there was also a burst of superb lyric poetry. Many of these Persian lyrics were in praise of the comfortable life and its sensuous pleasures. To some extent, Moslem puritanism had chilled traditional Persian enthusiasms for wine, women, and song, but these enthusiasms now had renewed poetic expression.

In the same period, far to the west in Moorish Spain, where Islam had again met another culture and been modified by it, other poets were writing graceful, acutely observant lyrics in Arabic. These poets were developing to the level of high art the brief verse forms which Arab poets had utilized

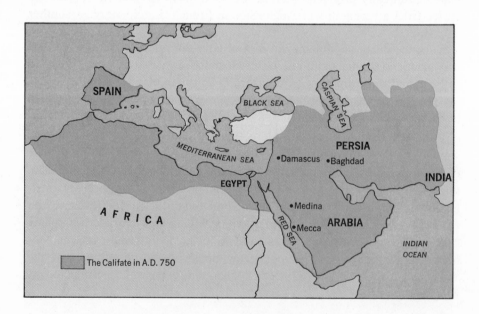

AFRICA

SPAIN

BLACK SEA

CASPIAN SEA

MEDITERRANEAN SEA

PERSIA

•Damascus •Baghdad

EGYPT

INDIA

•Medina

RED SEA

•Mecca   ARABIA

INDIAN OCEAN

The Califate in A.D. 750

for many years. The sharp, precise nature imagery of this Arabic poetry quite significantly influenced much Persian poetry. The following brief poem, "The Shooting Star," by tenth-century poet Ibn Sara (see also page 351) illustrates the sort of imagery with which the Moorish poets, writing in Arabic, were so skillful.

> The watch-star saw a devil-spy, that came
>   On evil work,
>   At heaven's gate lurk
> And leaped against him in a path of flame;
>
>   And seemed a burning cavalier
>   Whose swift career
> Unbinds his turban till it streams
> Behind, so jeweled that it gleams.—IBN SARA

One of the traditional Persian poetic forms was the rubai, a metrically complex four-line poem which lent itself well to the brief, pithy type of expression of which the Persians were fond. It is said that the rubai form was so much admired at the court of Mahmud, Firdawsi's patron, that extemporaneous composition of rubaiyat (the plural of rubai) was a favorite pastime for courtiers and commoners alike. The well-known works of Omar Khayyam in the eleventh century (see page 334) came, then, from a firmly established poetic tradition.

Contemporaneous with the secular poetry just described was a substantial body of mystical, religious verse written by Persian adherents to Sufism. Sometimes regarded as heretical, Sufism was an old branch of Islam which emphasized withdrawal from the ordinary aspirations of human life in order to achieve spiritual union with God. Although the Sufis followed an ascetic, contemplative discipline, their poetic language, strangely enough, was the language of the senses, given mystic significance. Thus, wine was a symbol for the mystic doctrine or experience, and the vintner was the teacher; the tavern, of course, was the place of teaching. The language of romantic love was frequently used to talk about the love of God for men or of men for God. "The Beloved" was a term for God, and "the Lover" for man. This use of language has its parallel in the West where, in the Middle Ages, a substantial body of poetry which sounded like secular love poetry was actually addressed to the Virgin Mary.

The two outstanding Sufi writers were unquestionably the thirteenth-century Persian poets Sa'di of Shiraz and Rumi of Balkh (see pages 340 and 353). Sa'di's collection of didactic tales is called the *Gulistan*. Rumi's two major poetic works are his *Diwan* in nearly 40,000 couplets, and his

"The Shooting Star" by Ibn Sara from *Arabic Andalusian Casidas*, translated by Harold Morland. Phoenix Press-Neville Braybooke Editions: London, 1949. Reprinted by permission of Phoenix Press.

A sultan and his court decorate a Persian bowl (thirteenth century).

Mathnawi in 25,000. The latter, which the poet left unfinished, is, like the *Gulistan,* a collection of didactic stories in verse.

If the thirteenth century saw a climax of Persian poetic achievement, it also saw the beginning of the end of an era. The first of the Mongol invasions of Iran under Genghis Khan occurred in 1220. The Mongol incursions in the east coincided with the invasion of Christian crusaders in the west. Baghdad fell to the Mongols in 1258. The looting of this rich center of the arts and of graceful living only foretold the destruction of Eastern cities that was to proceed almost without interruption for the next 250 years, as one conqueror after another swept across Iran and its western neighbors. The end of the great age of Persian classical literature was at hand. Just two more major poets were to appear, Hafiz of Shiraz (see page 354), whose life spanned much of the fourteenth century, and Jami of Kharjird, whose life spanned much of the fifteenth. These two were the last of the great Persian lyricists in the classic tradition.

The puritanical qualities of Islam explain in part, perhaps, why Arabic literature does not present the same variety and richness that are found in Persian literature. As already indicated, Arabic lyric poetry flourished in the eighth through tenth centuries especially, and popular romantic tales circulated at the same time. These tales, however, were considered mere popular entertainment, not literature. The most significant Arabic writings were in philosophy, religion, and science. In the West, probably the only truly famous Arabic literary work is *The Thousand and One Nights* (see page 343), which the Moslems themselves do not dignify as serious literature, despite the delight it has brought to millions of people through the centuries.

Islamic and Indian Art

Perhaps because our heritage is primarily Greco-Roman, we are not fully aware of the magnitude of Islamic civilization. Islamic conquests, which were broader in extent than those of the Roman Empire, enabled Islamic culture to flourish in a world that stretched from Spain to India. Today evidence of early Islamic culture is still visible in the architecture and the decorative arts of the Middle East.

The Mosque of Sultan Ahmed (PLATE 1A), built in the early seventeenth century, was inspired by Hagia Sophia, one of the best known examples of Byzantine architecture—a perfect blend of Roman and Eastern styles. Inside the building, the windows at the base of the great central dome and the semidome (PLATE 1B) admit quantities of light in every direction. The light is reflected and dispersed by the tiles covering the mosque's interior. Because of the predominant color of the tiles, this is known as the Blue Mosque.

Because Mohammed, the founder and prophet of Islam, considered sculpture and painting forms of creation and creation the privilege of God alone, images of animals and people were generally not used in decorations of Moslem buildings or objects intended for religious use. They were often used, however, in secular art. The Moslems developed a distinctive decorative art in which rhythmic patterns on geometric, floral, or calligraphic motives make dynamic abstract designs. Stylized leaves and tendrils turn and twist endlessly to form the arabesques that are so typical of Islamic art. These fanciful designs usually cover the entire surface either of the page of a book, the pile of a carpet, or the wall of a mosque. An elaborate palmette design decorates the surface of an incense burner in the form of a cat (PLATE 2B). Perforations to permit the passage of the incense fumes were cleverly made part of the design. Around the neck and chest of the cat is inscribed the name of the maker, Ja'far ibn Muhammad ibn 'Ali.

Because of its important function in recording the word of God as revealed in the Koran, calligraphy (ornamental handwriting) was more highly esteemed by Moslems than painting. As the calligrapher wrote the text of the *Shah-Nama* (PLATE 4), he left spaces for the painting. This illustrated version of Firdawsi's great epic, made after the Mongol conquest, shows an interesting combination of Persian and Chinese styles. The hills in the background are from Chinese landscape painting, and the figures are from the Persian tradition. Alexander and his companions are dressed in contemporary Mongol costume of the fourteenth century.

Although the technique of making knotted carpets was known as early as the fifth century B.C., it was not until the sixteenth century that this art was perfected by the Persians. Famous for their vivid colors and intricate designs, Persian rugs required a small army of workers to spin, dye, and weave the wool or silk into scenes depicting floral fantasies, animal combats, or royal hunts. Animal and floral motives are combined with exquisite skill in the Persian carpet (PLATES 2A and 3) presented by Peter the Great of Russia to Leopold I of Austria. It is interesting to note that there are from five to seven hundred hand-tied knots of silk in each square inch of this carpet. Each knot was cut by hand, and the pile which results feels like velvet.

Northwest India was conquered gradually by the Moslems. By the time they had subdued the Punjab in the eleventh century, Buddhism had declined and Hinduism was the main religion of India. Although later worshipped as a god, the Buddha was a real Indian prince who lived in the sixth century B.C. Because as a young man he wore heavy earrings which stretched his ears, statues always show him with elongated ear lobes.

You will notice in PLATE 5 two other distinguishing marks on images of the Buddha: the *urna* and the *ushnisha*. The urna was originally a tuft of hair between his eyes, marking the sacred spot where the third eye of a Hindu god like Siva appears (PLATE 6). The ushnisha is the bump on the head usually indicated by a knot of hair.

Whether the subject is the Buddha or a Hindu deity, Indian sculptures always show a supple body in a graceful pose, with the hands in meaningful gestures called *mudras*. The Buddha points his hand downward to call the earth to witness the truth of his teaching. Siva's upraised hand, palm outward, means "Fear not." Hindu images are not intended to represent gods, but to evoke thoughts of their divine energy. Gods like Siva (PLATE 6) are given as many arms as necessary to carry their divine attributes and to make the mudras. As you look at this statue, imagine Siva beating the drum and whirling in a wild dance as he destroys the world with fire. This will help you to understand the concept of the divine fury of destruction that must precede a new creation—for, according to Hindu belief, not only is the soul reincarnated many times, but the world also is destroyed and created again and again. Siva, shown here as the destroyer, is also the creator.

PLATE 1A. *Mosque of Sultan Ahmed*. Turkish, 1607–14. Istanbul.

PLATE 12. Detail from the Mosque of Sultan Ahmed, showing the interior mosiac domes.

PLATE 2A. Detail from PLATE 3.

PLATE 2B. JA'FAR IBN MUHAMMAD IBN 'ALI (Persian, 12th century): *Incense Burner in the Form of a Cat.* 1181–82, Seljuk period. From Tay-abad, Khurasan, Iran. Bronze, height: 33½ inches. (The Metropolitan Museum of Art, New York, Rogers Fund, 1951)

PLATE 3. *Animal Rug.* Iranian, last half of the 16th century, Safavid period. Silk Kashan carpet, 7 feet 10 inches by 5 feet 10½ inches. (The Metropolitan Museum of Art, New York, Bequest of Benjamin Altman, 1913)

PLATE 4. *Alexander Slaying a Dragon.* Mongol Persian, about 1330. From Firdawsi's *Shah-Nama.* Miniature from an illuminated manuscript, 6⅛ x 11½ inches. (Courtesy, Museum of Fine Arts, Boston, Ross Collection)

PLATE 5. *Seated Buddha.* Siamese, Sinhalese type, 14th-15th century. Bronze, height: about 30 inches. (Courtesy, Museum of Fine Arts, Boston, Frederick L. Jack Fund)

PLATE 6. *Siva as Natarja Dancing upon an Apasmara Purusa.* South India, 15th century. Bronze with greenish patina, height: 36 inches. (Courtesy, Museum of Fine Arts, Boston, Marianne Brimmer Fund)

The Shah-Nama

FIRDAWSI

Abu'l-Qasim Mansur ibn Hasan (A.D. 941?–A.D. 1020), who took the penname Firdawsi, meaning "belonging to Paradise," is a national hero of Iran whose verses are quoted by Iranian schoolchildren. He took over the incomplete work of the earlier poet Dakiki, and under the patronage of the sultan Mahmud ibn Sabuktagin completed the monumental epic, *Shah-Nama,* or "book of kings." This work is a compilation and retelling of the history and legends of ancient Persia, lore which was in danger of being lost under the impact of the Mohammedan conquest. Firdawsi labored on his epic for thirty-five years, and his final work ran to 60,000 couplets. His idiom was Persian; he carefully avoided the Arabic words and phrases which were already flooding the Persian language. Firdawsi's efforts to preserve the heritage of an ancient, proud people made him a national hero.

Firdawsi is also remembered for one magnificent gesture of contempt. The sultan Mahmud had promised him 1,000 gold coins for every 1,000 verses of the *Shah-Nama.* Firdawsi wished to use his pay to benefit the town of Tus, where he had been born. When time for payment came, Mahmud's treasurer convinced the sultan that 60,000 gold pieces was too large a sum and persuaded him to send Firdawsi 60,000 pieces of silver instead. Enraged, Firdawsi gave a third of the money to the person who was to deliver the manuscript to the sultan, a third to the keeper of the baths, and a third to a beer seller in payment for a glass of beer. He then sent the sultan a blistering satiric poem about stingy princes. The resulting wrath of the sultan caused Firdawsi to flee the country, but his satiric poem is now usually printed as a preface to the *Shah-Nama.*

The selection which follows is an excerpt from the legend about a miraculously strong warrior-hero named Rustam, one of many heroes in the *Shah-Nama.* This part of the legend tells about Rustam's meeting with his son Suhrab, a son Rustam did not even know existed. Suhrab, however, had been told by his mother that his father was Rustam, the famed warrior of Iran. The young man set out to find his father, hoping to identify him by certain features which his mother had carefully described to him. Suhrab joined the Turkmans, people from the eastern Caspian, with whom the Persians were warring, knowing that at some time, if he became sufficiently famous himself, he must meet his great father. It was his plan then to reveal himself and to be united with Rustam. As this selection opens, Suhrab has challenged the Persians to send one warrior to meet him in single combat. He hopes the Persian who comes to meet him will be his father. And Rustam it turns out to be, for although the warrior is aging, he does not want men to think he is afraid to peril his fame. However, Rustam refuses to identify himself to his challenger, and he rides to the fight in unmarked armor.

The result is what follows here—a story that is as close to true tragedy as Persian literature comes.

FROM *Rustam and Suhrab*

The bright sun shone, the raven night flew low,
Great Rustam donned his tiger-skin cuirass
And mounted on his fiery dragon-steed.
Two leagues divided host from host, and all
Stood ready-armed. The hero with a casque   5
Of iron on his head came on the field.
Suhrab on his side reveling with comrades
Had thus addressed Human:° "That lion-man,
Who striveth with me, is as tall as I am
And hath a dauntless heart. He favoreth me   10
In shoulder, breast, and arm, and thou wouldst say
That some skilled workman laid us out by line.
His very feet and stirrups move my love
And make me blush, for I perceive in him
The marks whereof my mother spake. Moreover   15
My heart presageth that he must be Rustam,
For few resemble him. I may not challenge
My sire or lightly meet him in the combat."
    Human said: "Rustam oft hath countered me:
This charger is like his, except in action."   20
    At sunrise, when they woke, Suhrab arrayed
Himself in mail and, mirthful though resolved,
Set forward shouting, ox-head mace in hand.
He greeted Rustam smiling, thou hadst said
That they had passed the night in company: 25
"How went the night? How is't with thee today?
Why so intent on strife? Fling down thine arrows
And scimitar, and drop the hand of wrong.
Let us dismount and, sitting, clear our faces
With wine, and, leaguing in God's sight, repent   30
Our former strife. Until some other cometh
To battle, feast with me because I love thee,
And weep for shamefastness. In sooth thou comest
From heroes and wilt tell me of thy stock,
For as my foe thou shouldst not hide thy name.   35
Art thou the famous Rustam of Zabul,
The son of valiant Zal the son of Sam?"
    Then Rustam: "Young aspirant! heretofore
We talked not thus but spake last night of wrestling.
I am not to be gulled, attempt it not.   40
Though thou art young I am no child myself,
But girt to wrestle, and the end shall be
According to the will of Providence.
I have known ups and downs and am not one

8. **Human:** an older warrior-companion of Suhrab.

"Rustam and Suhrab" by Firdawsi, translated by Arthur and Edmond Warner from *The Shah-Nama of Firdawsi*. Reprinted by permission of Routledge & Kegan Paul Ltd.

To practice guile upon."

                Suhrab replied: 45
"Old man! if thou rejectest my proposals . . . !
I wished that thou shouldst die upon thy bed,
And that thy kin should tomb thy soulless corpse,
But I will end thee if it be God's will."
   They lighted, tied their chargers to a rock,   50
And cautiously advanced in mail and casque
With troubled hearts. They wrestled like two lions
Until their bodies ran with sweat and blood.
From sunrise till the shadows grew they strove
Until Suhrab, that maddened elephant,   55
Reached out, up-leaping with a lion's spring,
Caught Rustam's girdle, tugged amain as though,
Thou wouldst have said, to rend the earth, and shouting
With rage and vengeance hurled him to the ground,
Raised him aloft and, having dashed him down,   60
Sat on his breast with visage, hand, and mouth
Besmirched with dust, as when a lion felleth
An onager,° then drew a bright steel dagger
To cut off Rustam's head, who seeing this
Exclaimed: "Explain I must! O warrior   65
That takest lions captive and art skilled
With lasso, mace, and scimitar! the customs
And laws of arms with us are not as yours.
In wrestling none may take a foeman's head
The first time that his back is on the ground,   70
But having thrown him twice and won the name
Of lion then he may behead the foe:
Such is our custom."
                Thus he sought to 'scape
The dragon's clutches and get off with life.
The brave youth hearkened to the old man's words.   75
In part through confidence, in part through fate,
In part no doubt through magnanimity,
Suhrab let Rustam go, turned toward the plain,
Pursued an antelope that crossed his path,
And utterly forgot his recent foe.   80
When he was far away, Human came up
As swift as dust and asked about the fight.
He told Human what had been said and done,
Who cried: "Alas! young man! art thou indeed
So weary of thy life? Woe for thy breast,   85
Mien, stature, stirrups, and heroic feet!
The mighty lion whom thou hadst ensnared
Thou hast let go and all is still to do.
Mark how he will entreat thee on the day
Of battle owing to thy senseless act.   90
A king once spake a proverb to the point:

      63. **onager** (on'ə·jər): wild ass.

'Despise not any foe however weak.' "
He took the very life out of Suhrab,
Who standing sorrowing and amazed replied:
"Let us dismiss such fancies from our hearts,   95
For he will come to fight with me tomorrow,
And thou shalt see a yoke upon his neck."
He went to camp in dudgeon° at his deed.
When Rustam had escaped his foeman's clutch
He was again as 'twere a mount of steel.   100
He went toward a rivulet as one
Who having fainted is himself again.
He drank and bathed, then prayed to God for strength
And victory, not knowing what the sun
And moon decreed, or how the turning sky   105
Would rob him of the crown upon his head.
    The tale is told that Rustam had at first
Such strength bestowed by Him who giveth all
That if he walked upon a rock his feet
Would sink therein. Such puissance° as that   110
Proved an abiding trouble, and he prayed
To God in bitterness of soul to minish
His strength that he might walk like other men.
According to his prayer his mountain-strength
Had shrunk, but face to face with such a task,   115
And pierced by apprehension of Suhrab,
He cried to God and said: "Almighty Lord!
Protect Thy slave in his extremity.
O holy Fosterer! I ask again
My former strength."
                    God granted him his prayer,   120
The strength which once had waned now waxed in him.
He went back to the field perturbed and pale
While, like a maddened elephant, Suhrab,
With lasso on his arm and bow in hand,
Came in his pride and roaring like a lion,   125
His plunging charger flinging up the soil.
When Rustam saw the bearing of his foe
He was astounded and gazing earnestly
Weighed in his mind the chances of the fight.
Suhrab, puffed up with youthful arrogance,   130
On seeing Rustam in his strength and grace,
Cried: "Thou that didst escape the lion's claws!
Why com'st thou boldly to confront me? Speak!
Hast thou no interests of thine own to seek?"
They tied their steeds while fate malignantly   135
Revolved o'erhead, and when dark fate is wroth
Flint rocks become like wax. The two began
To wrestle, holding by their leathern belts.
As for Suhrab thou wouldst have said: "High heaven

98. **dudgeon:** displeasure, anger.   110. **puissance** (pyōō′ə·səns): power, potency.

Hath hampered him," while Rustam, reaching, clutched   140
That warrior-leopard by the head and neck,
Bent down the body of the gallant youth,
Whose time was come and all whose strength was gone,
And like a lion dashed him to the ground;
Then, knowing that Suhrab would not stay under,   145
Drew lightly from his waist his trenchant sword
And gashed the bosom of his gallant son.
    Whenever thou dost thirst for blood and stain
Therewith thy glittering dagger, destiny
    Will be athirst for thy blood and ordain   150
Each hair of thine to be a sword for thee.
    Suhrab cried: "Ah!" and writhed. Naught recked he then
Of good or ill. "I am alone to blame,"
He said to Rustam. "Fate gave thee my key.
This hump-backed sky reared me to slay me soon.   155
Men of my years will mock me since my neck
Hath thus come down to dust. My mother told me
How I should recognize my father. I
Sought him in love and die of my desire.
Alas! my toils are vain, I have not seen him.   160
Now wert thou fish, or wrapped like night in gloom,
Or quit of earth wast soaring like a star,
My father would avenge me when he seeth
My pillow bricks.° Some chief will say to Rustam:
'Suhrab was slain and flung aside in scorn   165
While seeking thee.' "
              Then Rustam grew distraught,
The world turned black, his body failed; o'ercome
He sank upon the ground and swooned away;
Till coming to himself he cried in anguish:
"Where is the proof that thou art Rustam's son?   170
May his name perish from among the great,
For I am Rustam! Be my name forgotten,
And may the son of Sam sit mourning me!"
    He raved, his blood seethed, and with groans he plucked
His hair up by the roots, while at the sight   175
Suhrab sank swooning till at length he cried:
"If thou indeed art Rustam, thou hast slain me
In wanton malice, for I made advances,
But naught that I could do would stir my love.
Undo my breastplate, view my body bare,   180
Behold thy jewel, see how sires treat sons!
The drums beat at my gate, my mother came
With bloodstained cheeks and stricken to the soul
Because I went. She bound this on mine arm
And said: 'Preserve this keepsake of thy father's   185

---

164. **pillow bricks:** blocks of wood or stone, hollowed to fit the head, used as bed pillows. Those belonging to a slain warrior would be returned to his family with the rest of his belongings.

And mark its virtue.' It is mighty now,
Now when the strife is over and the son
Is nothing to his sire."
                        When Rustam loosed
The mail and saw the gem he rent his clothes,
And cried: "Oh! my brave son, approved by all   190
And slain by me!"
                        With dust upon his head
And streaming face he rent his locks until
His blood ran down.
                        "Nay, this is worse and worse,"
Suhrab said. "Wherefore weep? What will it profit
To slay thyself? What was to be hath been."   195
    When day declined and Rustam came not back
There went forth twenty trusty warriors
To learn the issue. Both the steeds were standing
Bemoiled with dust, but Rustam was not there.
The nobles, thinking that he had been slain,   200
Went to Kaus ° in consternation saying:
"The throne of majesty is void of Rustam!"
    A cry went up throughout the host and all
Was in confusion. Then Kaus bade sound
The drums and trumpets, Tus° came, and the Shah   205
Said to the troops: "Dispatch a messenger
That he may find out what Suhrab hath done,
And if there must be mourning through Iran.
None will confront him with brave Rustam dead.
We must attack in force and speedily."   210
    While clamor raged, Suhrab said thus to Rustam:
"The Turkmans' case is altered since my day
Is done. Use all thine influence that the Shah
May not attack them. They approached Iran
Through trust in me, and I encouraged them.   215
How could I tell, O famous paladin!°
That I should perish by my father's hand?
Let them depart unscathed, and treat them kindly.
I had a warrior in yonder hold
Caught by my lasso. Him I often asked   220
To point thee out. Mine eyes looked ever for thee.
He told me all but this. His place is void.
His words o'ercast my day, and I despaired.
See who he is and let him not be harmed.
I marked in thee the tokens that my mother   225
Described, but trusted not mine eyes. The stars
Decreed that I should perish by thy hand.
I came like lightning and like wind I go.
In heaven I may look on thee with joy."
    Then Rustam choked, his heart was full of fire,   230

___

201. **Kaus:** king of Iran. 205. **Tus:** probably troops from the area called Tus. 216. **paladin:** knight.

His eyes of tears. He mounted quick as dust
And came with lamentations to the host
In grievous consternation at his deed.
The Iranians catching sight of him fell prostrate
And gave God praise that Rustam had returned;   235
But when they saw the dust upon his head,
His clothes and bosom rent, they questioned him:
"What meaneth this? For whom art thou thus troubled?"
  He told the fearful deed, and all began
To mourn aloud with him. His anguish grew.   240
He told the nobles: "I have lost today
All strength and courage. Fight not with Turan:°
I have done harm enough."

242. **Turan:** the Turkmans.

FOR STUDY AND DISCUSSION

1. Suhrab is convinced that his opponent is his father Rustam. What makes him think so? Why does he permit himself to fight despite his feeling that he may be fighting Rustam?

2. Suhrab and Rustam are hero-warriors with much in common with other hero-warriors you have read about. What are some of the qualities they share with the heroes of the *Iliad* or of the *Mahabharata*? Rustam saves his life by tricking Suhrab. Is this proper heroic behavior? Were such tricks used in the *Iliad*? Explain your answers. Does the use of such a trick by a hero say anything about the values of the society to whom he is a hero? If so, what?

3. At the very moment at which Rustam stabs Suhrab, the story is interrupted by four lines of didactic verse, beginning in line 148 with "Whenever thou dost thirst for blood . . ." What does the presence of such an interruption indicate about the author's purpose? What is its effect on the story?

4. The dying Suhrab declares that what has happened is the work of fate, but this is little comfort to his father. For which of these characters do you feel the greater sympathy? Why? Has human will played as large a part in the tragedy as has fate? What passages support your answer?

5. Consider the frequent animal images used in this excerpt. What animals are used? Who or what are compared to these animals? What do these comparisons suggest about the Persians' view of their heroes? about their natural environment?

The Rubaiyat

OMAR KHAYYAM

(Translated by Edward Fitzgerald)

Omar Khayyam (d. A.D. 1123), whose full name was Ghias uddin Abul Fath Omar ibn Ibrahim al-Khayyam, was a noted Persian mathematician and astronomer from Nishapur. The name *Khayyam* means "tentmaker" and probably derives from his father's trade. One of the very wise men of his time, Omar Khayyam was a member of a committee appointed by Sultan Malik-Shah which made extensive astronomical observations and reformed the Moslem calendar with remarkable accuracy.

Though admired by his contemporaries as a scientist, Omar Khayyam was not highly regarded as a poet. In many of his verses he urged his readers to enjoy the present moment and to let the future take care of itself. He praised the pleasures of wine and other worldly delights. He appeared to reject both the austerity of orthodox Moslem thought and the emotionalism of the Sufis, the rather unorthodox religious mystics of his day. Some scholars have seen similarities between Omar Khayyam's work and the work of Sufi poets and have suggested that his use of language was symbolic and that he was, in reality, very like the Sufis in outlook. Most readers, however, accept Omar Khayyam as he presents himself—a worldly devotee of sensuous pleasure, an epicurean.

Each rubai, or four-line stanza of this poem, should be regarded as a separate epigram. The poet seems to have composed them over an extended period of his life, and their arrangement is based more on rhyme patterns than on any continuity of thought or sense.

These verses enjoyed only modest popularity in their native Persia, but in the hands of their English translator, who infused them with great lyric power, they became in the West the best-known and best-loved Persian poetry. The translation was the most distinguished literary achievement of Edward Fitzgerald (1809–1883) in his career as language student, translator, and country gentleman. He was often free in his translation and sacrificed literary accuracy to try to catch the spirit of the original as he interpreted it. The selections which follow are taken from Fitzgerald's fifth version. He is supposed to have made the translation from a fifteenth-century Persian manuscript. It is questionable that an authoritative manuscript of the original *Rubaiyat* exists today.

1

Wake! For the Sun, who scattered into flight
The Stars before him from the Field of Night,
Drives Night along with them from Heaven, and strikes
The Sultan's Turret with a Shaft of Light.

2

Before the phantom of False morning died,
Methought a Voice within the Tavern cried,
   "When all the Temple is prepared within,
Why nods the drowsy Worshiper outside?"

7

Come, fill the Cup, and in the fire of Spring
Your Winter garment of Repentance fling:
   The Bird of Time has but a little way
To flutter—and the Bird is on the Wing.

12

A Book of Verses underneath the Bough,
A Jug of Wine, a Loaf of Bread—and Thou
   Beside me singing in the Wilderness—
Oh, Wilderness were Paradise enow!

13

Some for the Glories of This World; and some
Sigh for the Prophet's Paradise to come;
   Ah, take the Cash, and let the Credit go,
Nor heed the rumble of a distant Drum!

14

Look to the blowing Rose about us—"Lo,
Laughing," she says, "into the world I blow,
   At once the silken tassel of my Purse
Tear, and its Treasure on the Garden throw."

15

And those who husbanded the Golden grain,
And those who flung it to the winds like Rain,
   Alike to no such aureate Earth are turned
As, buried once, Men want dug up again.

16

The Worldly Hope men set their Hearts upon
Turns Ashes—or it prospers; and anon,
   Like Snow upon the Desert's dusty Face,
Lighting a little hour or two—is gone.

17

Think, in this battered Caravanserai*
Whose Portals are alternate Night and Day,
  How Sultan after Sultan with his Pomp
Abode his destined Hour, and went his way.

21

Ah, my Beloved, fill the Cup that clears
TODAY of Past Regrets and Future Fears:
  Tomorrow!—Why, Tomorrow I may be
Myself with Yesterday's Seven Thousand Years.

22

For some we loved, the loveliest and the best
That from his Vintage rolling Time hath pressed,
  Have drunk their Cup a Round or two before,
And one by one crept silently to rest.

23

And we, that now make merry in the Room
They left, and Summer dresses in new bloom
  Ourselves must we beneath the Couch of Earth
Descend—ourselves to make a Couch—for whom?

24

Ah, make the most of what we yet may spend,
Before we too into the Dust descend;
  Dust into Dust, and under Dust to lie
Sans Wine, sans Song, sans Singer, and—sans End!

25

Alike for those who for TODAY prepare,
And those that after some TOMORROW stare,
  A Muezzin from the Tower of Darkness cries
"Fools! your Reward is neither Here nor There."

26

Why, all the Saints and Sages who discussed
Of the Two Worlds so wisely—they are thrust
  Like foolish Prophets forth; their Words to Scorn
Are scattered, and their Mouths are stopped with Dust.

---

* **Caravanserai:** in Oriental countries, an inn with an enclosed court for sheltering caravans.

27

Myself when young did eagerly frequent
Doctor and Saint, and heard great argument
    About it and about: but evermore
Came out by the same door where in I went.

28

With them the seed of Wisdom did I sow,
And with mine own hand wrought to make it grow;
    And this was all the Harvest that I reaped—
"I came like Water, and like Wind I go."

29

Into this Universe, and *Why* not knowing
Nor *Whence,* like Water willy-nilly flowing;
    And out of it, as Wind along the Waste,
I know not *Whither,* willy-nilly blowing.

30

What, without asking, hither hurried *Whence?*
And, without asking, *Whither* hurried hence!
    Oh, many a Cup of this forbidden Wine
Must drown the memory of that insolence!

48

A Moment's Halt—a momentary taste
Of BEING from the Well amid the Waste—
    And Lo!—the phantom Caravan has reached
The NOTHING it set out from—Oh, make haste!

71

The Moving Finger writes; and, having writ,
Moves on: nor all your Piety nor Wit
    Shall lure it back to cancel half a Line,
Nor all your Tears wash out a Word of it.

72

And that inverted Bowl they call the Sky,
Whereunder crawling cooped we live and die,
    Lift not your hands to *It* for help—for It
As impotently moves as you or I.

Yet Ah, that Spring should vanish with the Rose!
That Youth's sweet-scented manuscript should close!
    The Nightingale that in the branches sang,
Ah, whence, and whither flown again, who knows!

99

Ah, Love! could you and I with Him conspire
To grasp this sorry Scheme of Things entire,
    Would not we shatter it to bits—and then
Remold it nearer to the Heart's Desire!

100

Yon rising Moon that looks for us again—
How oft hereafter will she wax and wane;
    How oft hereafter rising look for us
Through this same Garden—and for *one* in vain!

101

And when like her, oh, Saki, you shall pass
Among the Guests Star-scattered on the Grass,
    And in your joyous errand reach the spot
Where I made One—turn down an empty Glass!

TAMAM

FOR STUDY AND DISCUSSION

1. Although the *Rubaiyat* is a collection of separate epigrams, a few major ideas seem to recur in them. One recurring idea is that all things human are impermanent, be they pleasures, achievements, or human life itself. Which rubai seems to express this idea most strongly? Does Omar Khayyam regard the transitory nature of life in the same way Gilgamesh did? (See especially the paragraph beginning "She answered," on page 15.) How do their attitudes differ?

2. Another major idea that recurs in the *Rubaiyat* is that man should seize joy while he can. Which rubai expresses this idea most effectively? How is this idea related to Omar Khayyam's concern with the swift passage of time? Cite passages which show this relationship.

3. How does rubai 48 appear to deny a divine plan or meaning in human life? Are there other verses that contradict this one? Does the poet seem to believe that life is meaningless, or does he believe that its meaning is beyond human comprehension? Is Omar Khayyam a pessimist? Cite passages that support your answers. What do verses 29, 30, and 72 contribute to this discussion?

COMPARING TRANSLATIONS

A number of early Persian intellectuals were much influenced by Greek rationalism, most notably the philosopher Avicenna, of whom Omar Khayyam was a follower. Such men found Moslem orthodoxy narrow and confining. A subtle rebellion against the rigid Moslem puritanism is found in the widespread use of wine images in Persian poetry: the Koran forbids the use of alcoholic beverages, while Persian Zoroastrianism permits it. Fitzgerald, a good and prudent Victorian, amends some of the wine imagery in his free translation. Thus for rubai 58, Fitzgerald translates:

● And lately, by the Tavern Door agape,
  Came shining through the Dust an Angel Shape
  Bearing a Vessel on his Shoulder; and
He bid me taste of it; and 'twas—the Grape!
    (Translated by Edward Fitzgerald)

Another, more literal, translation of Omar's verse, however, reads:

● Drunken by the winehouse I passed yester-night;
  an old man I saw, drunk, and a pitcher on [his] shoulder;
  I said, "Why hast thou not before God shame?"
He said, "Generous is God: Drink wine!"
    (Translated by Arthur Arberry)

Omar's dissolute scene, with its ironic humor in the final line, has become Fitzgerald's ghostly and mysteriously suggestive scene. What parts of Fitzgerald's verse have parallels in the literal translation? What wholly new elements has Fitzgerald introduced? Describe the effect produced by each translation. To what extent does it appear that Fitzgerald is a translator and to what extent a creative poet?

"Rubai LVIII" (from *Rubaiyat*) from *Omar Khayyam, A New Version Based on Recent Discoveries,* translated by Arthur J. Arberry. Reprinted by permission of John Murray (Publishers) Ltd.

The Gulistan

SA'DI

Scholars have few certain facts about the life of Sa'di. He seems to have been born around 1200 at Shiraz and to have received a splendid education either there or in Baghdad. He lived in a time of great upheaval in the Islamic world, with Mongols invading from the east and crusaders coming from the west to threaten all order and security. One story in the *Gulistan* seems to indicate that for a time Sa'di was himself held a prisoner of war by the crusaders. He was eventually ransomed, and out of gratitude he married his benefactor's daughter, a marriage which proved very unhappy. Sa'di appears, too, to have traveled extensively, perhaps as far as India, and to have made a number of pilgrimages to Mecca. He was devoutly religious and was associated with the ascetic, mystical Sufi sect of Islam. Like many other Sufis, he seems to have made poverty his way of life. He died around 1290.

The *Gulistan,* which means "rose garden," is a collection in eight chapters of a group of moral tales, in purpose not unlike those in the *Panchatantra* (page 253). Not all of the stories are original with Sa'di. Many undoubtedly came from ancient and familiar sources. Collections of such stories were fairly common in Sa'di's day. The popularity of the *Gulistan,* however, was immediately and persistently established, for its stories are not only didactic but also entertaining. Sa'di brings to his narratives and to his bits of verse a lightness of touch, a worldliness still gilded with innocence, and a contempt for hypocrisy—qualities which have made the stories popular in the scores of languages into which they have been translated. These qualities are found in the selections included here. Note that Sa'di uses quotations from the Koran, bits of verse of his own composition, and any other kind of wise saying he thinks will make clear the moral point of his stories.

FROM *The Manners of Kings*

1

I HEARD a padshah [1] giving orders to kill a prisoner. The helpless fellow began to insult the king on that occasion of despair,

[1] **padshah:** king.

with the tongue he had, and to use foul expressions according to the saying:

Who washes his hands of life
Says whatever he has in his heart.

When a man is in despair, his tongue becomes long and he is like a vanquished cat assailing a dog.

In time of need, when flight is no more possible,
The hand grasps the point of the sharp sword.

When the king asked what he was saying, a good-natured vizier replied: "My lord, he says: 'Those who bridle their anger and forgive men; for Allah loveth the beneficent.'"[1]

The king, moved with pity, forbore taking his life, but another vizier, the antagonist of the former, said: "Men of our rank ought to speak nothing but the truth in the presence of padshahs. This fellow has insulted the king and spoken unbecomingly." The king, being displeased with these words, said: "That lie was more acceptable to me than this truth thou hast uttered because the former proceeded from a conciliatory disposition and the latter from malignity; and wise men have said: 'A falsehood resulting in conciliation is better than a truth producing trouble.'"

> He who the shah follows in what
>   he says,
> It is a pity if he speaks anything
>   but what is good.

The following inscription was upon the portico of the hall of Feridun:

> O brother, the world remains
>   with no one.
> Bind the heart to the Creator, it
>   is enough.
> Rely not upon possessions and
>   this world
> Because it has cherished many
>   like thee and slain them.
> When the pure soul is about to
>   depart,
> What boots it if one dies on a
>   throne or on the ground?

7

A padshah was in the same boat with a Persian slave who had never before been at sea and experienced the inconvenience of a vessel. He began to cry and to tremble to such a degree that he could not be pacified by kindness, so that at last the king became displeased as the matter could not be remedied. In that boat there

happened to be a philosopher, who said: "With thy permission I shall quiet him." The padshah replied: "It will be a great favor." The philosopher ordered the slave to be thrown into the water so that he swallowed some of it, whereupon he was caught and pulled by his hair to the boat, to the stern of which he clung with both his hands. Then he sat down in a corner and became quiet. This appeared strange to the king who knew not what wisdom there was in the proceeding and asked for it. The philosopher replied: "Before he had tasted the calamity of being drowned, he knew not the safety of the boat; thus also a man does not appreciate the value of immunity from a misfortune until it has befallen him."

> O thou full man, barley bread
>   pleases thee not.
> She is my sweetheart who ap-
>   pears ugly to thee.
> To the huris [2] of paradise purga-
>   tory seems hell.
> Ask the denizens of hell. To them
>   purgatory is paradise.

> There is a difference between him whose
>   friend is in his arms
> And him whose eyes of expectation are
>   upon the door.

FROM *On the Excellence of Contentment*

7

Two Khorasani dervishes [3] traveled together. One of them, being weak, broke his fast every second night whilst the other, who was strong, consumed every day three meals. It happened that they were captured at the gate of a town on

[1] a quotation from the Koran.

[2] **huris:** beautiful virgins provided in Paradise for all the faithful.

[3] **Khorasani dervishes:** A dervish was a member of a Moslem order, devoted to poverty and chastity. Khorasan is a region in the north and northeast of Iran.

suspicion of being spies; whereon each of them was confined in a closet and the aperture of it walled up with mud bricks. After two weeks it became known that they were guiltless. Accordingly the doors were opened and the strong man was found to be dead whilst the weak fellow had remained alive. The people were astonished, but a sage averred that the contrary would have been astonishing because one of them having been voracious possessed no strength to suffer hunger and perished, whilst the other who was abstemious merely persevered in his habit and remained safe.

> When eating little has become
> the nature of a man
> He takes it easy when a calamity
> befalls him.
> But when the body becomes
> strong in affluence
> He will die when a hardship
> overtakes him.

19

I never lamented about the vicissitudes of time or complained of the turns of fortune except on the occasion when I was barefooted and unable to procure slippers. But when I entered the great mosque of Kufah with a sore heart and beheld a man without feet I offered thanks to the bounty of God, consoled myself for my want of shoes, and recited:

> A roast fowl is to the sight of a
> satiated man
> Less valuable than a blade of
> fresh grass on the table.
> And to him who has no means
> nor power
> A burnt turnip is a roasted fowl.

FOR STUDY AND DISCUSSION

1. These four brief tales are clearly didactic. Is the wisdom they teach intended to help men get along in this world or in the next? What makes you think so?

2. The second and fourth stories make similar points. Write a moral that would apply to both of them.

3. The first story seems to say that a pleasant lie is preferable to an unpleasant truth when its purpose is the reconciliation of men who are at odds. Is this an idea that is morally acceptable in our society? Explain.

4. This first story may also be read as a comment on truth and motives. Why is the prisoner telling the truth? Why does the padshah prefer the first vizier's story? Explain how the motives of the two viziers and the prisoner might be related to the padshah's attitude toward truth. According to this story, under what conditions are men most likely to tell the truth?

5. The third story seems to suggest that poverty and other forms of suffering build strength. Is this true? If so, why do most men aspire to wealth and comfort? Do you infer from this story that the East has an attitude toward misfortune different from the West?

The Thousand and One Nights

The collection of folk tales and fairy tales known as *The Thousand and One Nights,* or *The Arabian Nights' Entertainment,* has Indian, Persian, and Arabic origins and appears in many different versions in different times and places. The frame story, which is fairly stable, tells of a sultan, Shahriyar, who takes a new wife each night and kills her the next dawn, because he is convinced that no woman can be faithful. Held in suspense, however, by the entertaining stories told to him by one of these wives, named Shahrazad, the sultan postpones her execution day after day until, after a thousand and one nights of storytelling, he abandons his plans for execution and remains happily married to his artful entertainer. This frame story seems to have been attached to a collection of tales translated into Arabic from Persian as early as A.D. 850, but it was not until the end of the eighteenth century that an unknown Egyptian compiler brought together the collection as we know it now.

In the meantime, many of the tales had become known to European readers in the early eighteenth century through a translation done by a talented French story-teller, Antoine Galland. Because of their simple style and their fantastic content, the tales had no significant place in serious Moslem literature, but they were immediately popular in Europe and became the best-known and most widely read works of Arabic literature.

Unlike the didactic tales in the *Gulistan,* the stories of *The Thousand and One Nights* do not have any serious purpose. The sole purpose of the Arabian Nights stories is entertainment. Their combination of superstitions, fantasies, satire, and sly humor—all so typical of Eastern folk literature—beguiles and delights the reader. Some of the stories, like the Sindbad stories, seem to have had separate existences as story cycles at one time. Some others derive from particular locales, like the many Baghdad tales that have Haroun Al-Rashid as their hero. Still others, like the story of Ma'aruf the Cobbler, are sophisticated social satire which were added to the collection quite late.

The selection included here is a part of one of the oldest and simplest stories in the collection. It combines Moslem superstition with Persian and Indian folklore. The technique of interlocking stories is typical of the whole collection and was regularly employed earlier, in such Indian collections as the *Panchatantra* (see page 253).

The Fisherman
and the Jinnee

ONCE UPON A TIME there was a poor fisherman who had a wife and three children to support.

He used to cast his net four times a day. It chanced that one day he went down to the sea at noon and, reaching the shore, set down his basket, rolled up his shirt sleeves, and cast his net far out into the water. After he had waited for it to sink, he pulled on the cords with all his might; but the net was so heavy that he could not draw it in. So he tied the rope ends to a wooden stake on the beach and, putting off his clothes, dived into the water and set to work to bring it up. When he had carried it ashore, however, he found in it a dead donkey.

"By Allah, this is a strange catch!" cried the fisherman, disgusted at the sight. After he had freed the net and wrung it out, he waded into the water and cast it again, invoking Allah's help. But when he tried to draw it in he found it even heavier than before. Thinking that he had caught some enormous fish, he fastened the ropes to the stake and, diving in again, brought up the net. This time he found a large earthen vessel filled with mud and sand.

Angrily the fisherman threw away the vessel, cleaned his net, and cast it for the third time. He waited patiently, and when he felt the net grow heavy he hauled it in, only to find it filled with bones and broken glass. In despair, he lifted his eyes to heaven and cried: "Allah knows that I cast my net only four times a day. I have already cast it for the third time and caught no fish at all. Surely He will not fail me again!"

With this the fisherman hurled his net

From *The Thousand and One Nights*, translated by N. J. Dawood. Reprinted by permission of Penguin Books Ltd.

far out into the sea and waited for it to sink to the bottom. When at length he brought it to land he found in it a bottle made of yellow copper. The mouth was stopped with lead and bore the seal of our master Solomon, son of David. The fisherman rejoiced and said: "I will sell this in the market of the coppersmiths. It must be worth ten pieces of gold." He shook the bottle and, finding it heavy, thought to himself: "I will first break the seal and find out what is inside."

The fisherman removed the lead with his knife and again shook the bottle; but scarcely had he done so when there burst from it a great column of smoke which spread along the shore and rose so high that it almost touched the heavens. Taking shape, the smoke resolved itself into a jinnee of such prodigious stature that his head reached the clouds, while his feet were planted on the sand. His head was a huge dome and his mouth as wide as a cavern, with teeth ragged like broken rocks. His legs towered like the masts of a ship, his nostrils were two inverted bowls, and his eyes, blazing like torches, made his aspect fierce and menacing.

The sight of this jinnee struck terror to the fisherman's heart; his limbs quivered, his teeth chattered together, and he stood rooted to the ground with parched tongue and staring eyes.

"There is no god but Allah and Solomon is His Prophet!" cried the jinnee. Then, addressing himself to the fisherman, he said: "I pray you, mighty Prophet, do not kill me! I swear never again to defy your will or violate your laws!"

"Blasphemous giant," cried the fisherman, "do you presume to call Solomon the Prophet of Allah? Solomon has been dead these eighteen hundred years, and we are now approaching the end of time. But what is your history, pray, and how came you to be imprisoned in this bottle?"

On hearing these words the jinnee replied sarcastically: "Well, then; there is no god but Allah! Fisherman, I bring you good news."

"What news?" asked the old man.

"News of your death, horrible and prompt!" replied the jinnee.

"Then may heaven's wrath be upon you, ungrateful wretch!" cried the fisherman. "Why do you wish my death, and what have I done to deserve it? Have I not brought you up from the depths of the sea and released you from your imprisonment?"

But the jinnee answered: "Choose the manner of your death and the way that I shall kill you. Come, waste no time!"

"But what crime have I committed?" cried the fisherman.

"Listen to my story, and you shall know," replied the jinnee.

"Be brief, then, I pray you," said the fisherman, "for you have wrung my soul with terror."

"Know," began the giant, "that I am one of the rebel jinn who, together with Sakhr the Jinnee, mutinied against Solomon, son of David. Solomon sent against me his vizier, Asaf ben Berakhya, who vanquished me despite my supernatural power and led me captive before his master. Invoking the name of Allah, Solomon adjured me to embrace his faith and pledge him absolute obedience. I refused, and he imprisoned me in this bottle, upon which he set a seal of lead bearing the Name of the Most High. Then he sent for several of his faithful jinn, who carried me away and cast me into the middle of the sea. In the ocean depths I vowed: 'I will bestow eternal riches on him who sets me free!' But a hundred years passed away and no one freed me. In the second hundred years of my imprisonment I said: 'For him who frees me I will open up the buried treasures of the earth!' And yet no one freed me. Whereupon I flew into a rage and swore: 'I will kill the man who sets me free, allowing him only to choose the manner of his death!' Now it was you who set me free; therefore prepare to die and choose the way that I shall kill you."

"O wretched luck, that it should have fallen on my lot to free you!" exclaimed the fisherman. "Spare me, mighty jinnee, and Allah will spare you; kill me, and so shall Allah destroy you!"

"You have freed me," repeated the jinnee. "Therefore you must die."

"Chief of the jinn," cried the fisherman, "will you thus requite good with evil?"

"Enough of this talk!" roared the jinnee. "Kill you I must."

At this point the fisherman thought to himself: "Though I am but a man and he is a jinnee, my cunning may yet overreach his malice." Then, turning to his adversary, he said: "Before you kill me, I beg you in the Name of the Most High engraved on Solomon's seal to answer me one question truthfully."

The jinnee trembled at the mention of the Name, and, when he had promised to answer truthfully, the fisherman asked: "How could this bottle, which is scarcely large enough to hold your hand or foot, ever contain your entire body?"

"Do you dare doubt that?" roared the jinnee indignantly.

"I will never believe it," replied the fisherman, "until I see you enter this bottle with my own eyes!"

Upon this the jinnee trembled from head to foot and dissolved into a column of smoke, which gradually wound itself into the bottle and disappeared inside. At once the fisherman snatched up the leaden stopper and thrust it into the mouth of the bottle. Then he called out to the jinnee: "Choose the manner of your death and the way that I shall kill you! By Allah, I will throw you back into the sea, and keep watch on this shore to warn all men of your treachery!"

When he heard the fisherman's words, the jinnee struggled desperately to escape from the bottle, but was prevented by the magic seal. He now altered his tone and, assuming a submissive air, assured the fisherman that he had been jesting with him and implored him to let him out. But the fisherman paid no heed to the jinnee's entreaties and resolutely carried the bottle down to the sea.

"What are you doing with me?" whimpered the jinnee helplessly.

"I am going to throw you back into the

sea!" replied the fisherman. "You have lain in the depths eighteen hundred years, and there you shall remain till the Last Judgment! Did I not beg you to spare me so that Allah might spare you? But you took no pity on me, and He has now delivered you into my hands."

"Let me out," cried the jinnee in despair, "and I will give you fabulous riches!"

"Perfidious jinnee," retorted the fisherman, "you justly deserve the fate of the king in the tale of Yunan and the doctor.

"What tale is that?" asked the jinnee.

THE TALE OF KING YUNAN AND DUBAN THE DOCTOR

It is related (began the fisherman) that once upon a time there reigned in the land of Persia a rich and mighty king called Yunan. He commanded great armies and had a numerous retinue of followers and courtiers. But he was afflicted with a leprosy which baffled his physicians and defied all cures.

One day a venerable old doctor named Duban came to the king's capital. He had studied books written in Greek, Persian, Latin, Arabic, and Syriac, and was deeply versed in the wisdom of the ancients. He was master of many sciences, knew the properties of plants and herbs, and was above all skilled in astrology and medicine. When this physician heard of the leprosy with which Allah had plagued the king and of his doctors' vain endeavors to cure him, he put on his finest robes and betook himself to the royal palace. After he had kissed the ground before the king and called down blessings upon him, he told him who he was and said: "Great king, I have heard about the illness with which you are afflicted and have come to heal you. Yet will I give you no potion to drink, nor any ointment to rub upon your body."

The king was astonished at the doctor's words and asked: "How will you do that? By Allah, if you cure me I will heap riches upon you, and your children's chil-

dren after you. Anything you wish for shall be yours and you shall be my companion and my friend."

Then the king gave him a robe of honor and other presents and asked: "Is it really true that you can heal me without draught or ointment? When is it to be? What day, what hour?"

"Tomorrow, if the king wishes," he replied.

The doctor took leave of the king, and hastening to the center of the town rented for himself a house, to which he carried his books, his drugs, and his other medicaments. Then he distilled balsams and elixirs, and these he poured into a hollow polo stick.

Next morning he went to the royal palace and, kissing the ground before the king, requested him to ride to the field and play a game of polo with his friends. The king rode out with his viziers and his chamberlains, and when he had entered the playing field the doctor handed him the hollow club and said: "Take this and grasp it firmly. Strike the ball with all your might until the palm of your hand and the rest of your body begin to perspire. The cure will penetrate your palm and course through the veins and arteries of your body. When it has done its work, return to the palace, wash yourself, and go to sleep. Thus shall you be cured; and peace be with you."

The king took hold of the club and, gripping it firmly, struck the ball and galloped after it with the other players. Harder and harder he struck the ball as he dashed up and down the field, until his palm and all his body perspired. When the doctor saw that the cure had begun its work, he ordered the king to return to the palace. The slaves hastened to make ready the royal bath and hurried to prepare the linens and the towels. The king bathed, put on his nightclothes, and went to sleep.

Next morning the physician went to the palace. When he was admitted to the king's presence he kissed the ground before him and wished him peace. The king hastily rose to receive him; he threw his arms round his neck and seated him by his side.

For when the king left the bath the previous evening, he looked upon his body and rejoiced to find no trace of the leprosy. His skin had become as pure as virgin silver.

The king regaled the physician sumptuously all day. He bestowed on him robes of honor and other gifts, and when evening came gave him two thousand pieces of gold and mounted him on his own favorite horse. And so enraptured was the king by the consummate skill of his doctor that he kept repeating to himself: "This wise physician has cured me without draught or ointment. By Allah, I will load him with honors and he shall henceforth be my companion and trusted friend." And that night the king lay down to sleep in perfect bliss, knowing that he was clean in body and rid at last of his disease.

Next morning, as soon as the king sat down upon his throne, with the officers of his court standing before him and his lieutenants and viziers seated on his right and left, he called for the physician, who went up to him and kissed the ground before him. The king rose and seated the doctor by his side. He feasted him all day, gave him a thousand pieces of gold and more robes of honor, and conversed with him till nightfall.

Now among the king's viziers there was a man of repellent aspect, an envious, black-souled villain, full of spite and cunning. When this vizier saw that the king had made the physician his friend and lavished on him high dignities and favors, he became jealous and began to plot the doctor's downfall. Does not the proverb say: "All men envy, the strong openly, the weak in secret?"

So, on the following day, when the king entered the council chamber and was about to call for the physician, the vizier kissed the ground before him and said: "My bounteous master, whose munificence extends to all men, my duty prompts me to forewarn you against an evil which threatens your life; nor would I be any-thing but a base-born wretch were I to conceal it from you."

Perturbed at these ominous words, the king ordered him to explain his meaning.

"Your majesty," resumed the vizier, "there is an old proverb which says: 'He who does not weigh the consequences of his acts shall never prosper.' Now I have seen the king bestow favors and shower honors upon his enemy, on an assassin who cunningly seeks to destroy him. I fear for the king's safety."

"Who is this man whom you suppose to be my enemy?" asked the king, turning pale.

"If you are asleep, your majesty," replied the vizier, "I beg you to awake. I speak of Duban, the doctor."

"He is my friend," replied the king angrily, "dearer to me than all my courtiers; for he has cured me of my leprosy, an evil which my physicians had failed to remove. Surely there is no other physician like him in the whole world, from East to West. How can you say these monstrous things of him? From this day I will appoint him my personal physician and give him every month a thousand pieces of gold. Were I to bestow on him the half of my kingdom, it would be but a small reward for his service. Your counsel, my vizier, is the prompting of jealousy and envy. Would you have me kill my benefactor and repent of my rashness, as King Sindbad repented after he had killed his falcon?"

THE TALE OF KING SINDBAD AND THE FALCON

Once upon a time (went on King Yunan) there was a Persian king who was a great lover of riding and hunting. He had a falcon which he himself had trained with loving care and which never left his side for a moment; for even at nighttime he carried it perched upon his fist, and when he went hunting took it with him. Hanging from the bird's neck was a little bowl of gold from which it drank. One day the king ordered his men to make ready for a hunting expedition and, taking with him his falcon, rode out with his courtiers. At length they came to a valley where they laid the hunting nets. Presently a gazelle fell into the snare, and the king said: "I will kill the man who lets her escape!"

They drew the nets closer and closer round the beast. On seeing the king the gazelle stood on her haunches and raised her forelegs to her head as if she wished to salute him. But as he bent forward to lay hold of her, she leaped over his head and fled across the field. Looking round, the king saw his courtiers winking at one another.

"Why are they winking?" he asked his vizier.

"Perhaps because you let the beast escape," ventured the other, smiling.

"On my life," cried the king, "I will chase the gazelle and bring her back!"

At once he galloped off in pursuit of the fleeing animal, and when he had caught up with her, his falcon swooped upon the gazelle, blinding her with his beak, and the king struck her down with a blow of his sword. Then dismounting he flayed the animal and hung the carcass on his saddle-bow.

It was a hot day and the king, who by this time had become faint with thirst, went to search for water. Presently, however, he saw a huge tree, down the trunk of which water was trickling in great drops. He took the little bowl from the falcon's neck and, filling it with this water, placed it before the bird. But the falcon knocked the bowl with its beak and toppled it over. The king once again filled the bowl and placed it before the falcon, but the bird knocked it over a second time. Upon this the king became very angry and, filling the bowl a third time, set it down before his horse. But the falcon sprang forward and knocked it over with its wings.

"Allah curse you for a bird of ill omen!" cried the king. "You have prevented yourself from drinking and the horse also."

So saying, he struck the falcon with his sword and cut off both its wings. But the bird lifted its head as if to say: "Look into the tree!" The king raised his eyes and saw in the tree an enormous serpent spitting its venom down the trunk.

The king was deeply grieved at what he had done and, mounting his horse, hurried back to the palace. He threw his kill to the cook, and no sooner had he sat down, with the falcon still perched on his fist, than the bird gave a convulsive gasp and dropped down dead.

The king was stricken with sorrow and remorse for having so rashly killed the bird which had saved his life.

When the vizier heard the tale of King Yunan, he said: "I assure your majesty that my counsel is prompted by no other motive than my devotion to you and my concern for your safety. I beg leave to warn you that, if you put your trust in this physician, it is certain that he will destroy you. Has he not cured you by a device held in the hand? And might he not cause your death by another such device?"

"You have spoken wisely, my faithful vizier," replied the king. "Indeed, it is quite probable that this physician has come to my court as a spy to destroy me. And since he cured my illness by a thing held in the hand, he might as cunningly poison me with the scent of a perfume. What should I do, my vizier?"

"Send for him at once," replied the other, "and when he comes, strike off his head. Only thus shall you be secure from his perfidy."

Thereupon the king sent for the doctor, who hastened to the palace with a joyful heart, not knowing what lay in store for him.

"Do you know why I have sent for you?" asked the king.

"Allah alone knows the unspoken thoughts of men," replied the physician.

"I have brought you here to kill you," said the king.

The physician was thunderstruck at these words and cried: "But why should you wish to kill me? What crime have I committed?"

"It has come to my knowledge," replied the king, "that you are a spy sent here to cause my death. But you shall be the first to die."

Then he called out to the executioner, saying: "Strike off the head of this traitor!"

"Spare me, and Allah will spare you!" cried the unfortunate doctor. "Kill me, and so shall Allah kill you!"

But the king gave no heed to his entreaties. "Never will I have peace again," he cried, "until I see you dead. For if you cured me by a thing held in the hand, you will doubtless kill me by the scent of a perfume or by some other foul device."

"Is it thus that you repay me?" asked the doctor. "Will you thus requite good with evil?"

But the king said: "You must die; nothing can now save you."

When he saw that the king was determined to put him to death, the physician wept and bitterly repented the service he had done him. Then the executioner came forward, blindfolded the doctor and, drawing his sword, held it in readiness for the king's signal. But the doctor continued to wail, crying: "Spare me, and Allah will spare you! Kill me, and so shall Allah kill you!"

Moved by the old man's lamentations, one of the courtiers interceded for him with the king, saying: "Spare the life of this man, I pray you. He has committed no crime against you, but rather has he cured you of an illness which your physicians have failed to remedy."

"If I spare this doctor," replied the king, "he will use his devilish art to kill me. Therefore he must die."

Again the doctor cried: "Spare me, and Allah will spare you! Kill me, and so shall Allah kill you!" But when at last he saw that the king was fixed in his resolve, he said: "Your majesty, if you needs must kill me, I beg you to grant me a day's delay, so that I may go to my house and wind up my affairs. I wish to say farewell to my family and my neighbors and instruct them to arrange for my burial. I must also give away my books of medicine, of which there is one, a work of unparalleled virtue, which I would offer to you as a parting gift, that you may preserve it among the treasures of your kingdom."

"What may this book be?" asked the king.

"It holds secrets and devices without number, the least of them being this: that if, after you have struck off my head, you turn over three leaves of this book and read the first three lines upon the left-hand page, my severed head will speak and answer any questions you may ask it."

The king was astonished to hear this and at once ordered his guards to escort the physician to his house. That day the doctor put his affairs in order and next morning returned to the king's palace. There had already assembled the viziers, the chamberlains, the nabobs, and all the chief officers of the realm, so that with their colored robes the court seemed like a garden full of flowers.

The doctor bowed low before the king; in one hand he had an ancient book and in the other a little bowl filled with a strange powder. Then he sat down and said: "Bring me a platter!" A platter was instantly brought in, and the doctor sprinkled the powder on it, smoothing it over with his fingers. After that he handed the book to the king and said: "Take this book and set it down before you. When my head has been cut off, place it upon the powder to stanch the bleeding. Then open the book."

The king ordered the executioner to behead the physician. He did so. Then the king opened the book, and, finding the pages stuck together, put his finger to his mouth and turned over the first leaf. After much difficulty he turned over the second and the third, moistening his finger with his spittle at every page, and tried to read. But he could find no writing there.

"There is nothing written in this book," cried the king.

"Go on turning," replied the severed head.

The king had not turned six pages when the venom (for the leaves of the book were poisoned) began to work in his body. He fell backward in an agony of pain, crying: "Poisoned! Poisoned!" and in a few moments breathed his last.

"Now, treacherous jinnee," continued the fisherman, "had the king spared the physician, he in turn would have been spared by Allah. But he refused, and Allah brought about the king's destruction. And as for you, if you had been willing to spare me, Allah would have been merciful to you, and I would have spared your life. But you sought to kill me; therefore I will throw you back into the sea and leave you to perish in this bottle!"

FOR STUDY AND DISCUSSION

1. The stories here include a number of sly tricks, such as the one used by the fisherman to get the jinnee back into the bottle. At the same time, these stories record a high level of suspicion, such as King Yunan's suspicion of the doctor. What other tricks are used in the stories? How is suspicion used in the stories? Is there a relationship between these two elements? What is it? Is admiration for such cunning characteristic of other Eastern literature? Consider "Rustam and Suhrab" (page 328) and the *Panchatantra* (page 253), for examples. Is such cunning admired in Western literature? Cite examples to support your answer.

2. Interlocking stories are typical of *The Thousand and One Nights*. How are these stories connected? Is their arrangment plaus-

ible? Can you think of any other device which might have been used to bring together many different stories into a single collection? Remember that all of these stories are written to fit within the frame story of Shahrazad. How is the story of the fisherman a frame story for the other tales included here?

3. What sort of person is the fisherman? Is there any humor in the way he is characterized or in his behavior? If so, what is the source of the humor? Is there any humor associated with the jinnee?

4. What is presented here is a selection from a much longer story. In the rest of the story the fisherman is finally persuaded to release the jinnee again. The story then goes on to relate several very strange adventures, ending with the fisherman happy, the wealthiest man of his day. Is this the sort of ending you would expect for this story? Why? What kind of literature leads to such ". . . and they lived happily after" endings? What is the modern equivalent of this kind of story?

LANGUAGE AND VOCABULARY

1. A number of words are often not translated when Persian and Arabic literature is retold in English. Look up the following Persian or Arabic words in a standard dictionary so that you may be sure you know what they mean:

shah	jinnee (or genie)
sheik	muezzin
vizier (or vezier)	sultan
caliph	cadi

2. Some common English words were originally borrowed from Persian or Arabic. *Algebra*, for example, was borrowed from Arabic. See if you can discover its derivation and meaning in Arabic. For an interesting and surprising example of borrowing, look up the derivation of the English word *check* in the *Oxford English Dictionary* or in any good etymological dictionary.

IBN SARA

For seven hundred years, from the eighth to the fifteenth century, the Moslems dominated Spain, where they established the exotic Spanish-Arabic culture which we call Moorish. Poetry flourished; an anthology of Spanish-Arabic poetry published in the tenth century contained 20,000 verses. Ibn Sara, who lived in the tenth century, was one of the Moorish poets.

Pool with Turtles

Deep is the pool whose overflow
  In the cool bright showers
Is like an eye weeping below
Lashes of quivering flowers.

Look—the merry turtles sport
  Like Christians to the field
That sidle, frolic, and cavort
Bearing a casual shield.

AL–THURTHUSI

Al-Thurthusi lived in the twelfth century and was another famous lyricist of Moorish Spain.

Lines to His Absent Love

I look endlessly at the sky,
Hoping to see the star you see.
I go to meet travelers coming from all sides,
Hoping to encounter someone who has scented your fragrance.
I face the winds,   5
Hoping they carry your message.
I walk aimlessly along the ways,
Hoping to hear a song which tells of you.
I look at the faces of the women whom I meet,
Without any special intention,   10
Hoping only to find a touch of your beauty in theirs.

"Pool with Turtles" by Ibn Sara from *Arabic Andalusian Casidas*, translated by Harold Morland. Phoenix Press-Neville Braybooke Editions: London, 1949. Reprinted by permission of Phoenix Press.
"Lines to His Absent Love" by Al-Thurthusi from *Islamic Literature: An Introductory History with Selections* by Najib Ullah, copyright © 1963 by Najib Ullah. Reprinted by permission of the publisher, Washington Square Press, Inc.

KISA'I OF MERV

Merv was once a great center of Arabic culture in Central Asia. Kisa'i, born around A.D. 904, was a Moslem, one of the earliest Persian religious poets.

In His Old Age

... Did I come into this world
Just to say some things and to do some others,
To sing, to be joyful, and enjoy wealth?
In this animal way I have spent my life,
Being enslaved by wife and family.   5
What have I gained and what is there left for my empty hands
Except to count with my fingers
My innumerable sins ...

I am sold to envy
And dominated by greed;   10
I am the target of events
And the prey of want.

Alas, the glory of youth!
Alas, the beauty of life,
The handsome face   15
And its bygone charms.
Where are all those treasures?
Where are all those loves?
Where is all that strength?
And where those happy moments?   20

Now my hair is turned white as milk
And my heart has turned black as tar;
Now my face is bluish and gloomy and my body as curved as a horseshoe,
Now I am trembling night and day from the fear of death
Like a crying baby confined in his cradle.   25

Yes, time has passed
And happiness is left behind.
We will pass away
And become the tales of children ...

Dates

(FROM *The Thousand and One Nights*)

We grow to the sound of the wind
Playing his flutes in our hair.

Palm tree daughters,
Brown flesh Bedouin,
Fed with light   5
By our gold father;

We are loved of the free-tented,
The sons of space, the hall-forgetters,
The wide-handed, the bright-sworded
Masters of horses.   10

Who has rested in the shade of our palms
Shall hear us murmur ever above his sleep.

RUMI

Jalal Al-Din Muhammad Ibn Muhammad (1207–1273), called Rumi, was a much-revered Sufi saint, mystic, and poet. Many devout students became his disciples and attributed to him a number of remarkable events. According to one story, a follower once bade Rumi farewell before going on a journey. When the traveler arrived at his destination, he found his master composed and waiting for him. A poem like the following may have been responsible for this anecdote.

O Blessed Hour

O blessed hour, when thou and I
Together sit within this hall:
Two forms, two shapes then, thou and I—
Two bodies, and a single soul.

"Dates" from *The Thousand and One Nights*, translated by E. P. Mathers. Reprinted by permission of Houghton Mifflin Company.
"O Blessed Hour" by Rumi from *Classical Persian Literature*, translated by A. J. Arberry. Reprinted by permission of George Allen & Unwin, Ltd.

The garden's luster and the trill   5
  Of deathless birds such life bestow,
The hour when thou and I at will
  Into that flower garden go!

The stars that wheel upon their way
  Lean down to look upon us then,   10
And like some moon we shed our ray
  To lighten them and other men.

And thou and I no more remain,
  But rapt in ecstasy sublime
Soar far beyond the tale inane   15
  Of "Thou" and "I" and selfhood's clime.

The sky's brave birds that fly so free
  On me and thee all envious gaze
That we should laugh so merrily
  Together, in such wondrous ways.   20

But not so wonderful is it
  As that ourselves, who separate grace
Iraq and Khorasan, should sit
  Together in this secret place.

HAFIZ

Shams ud-din Muhammad (1326?–1389), known as Hafiz, a name meaning "one who knows the Koran by heart," was the most famous and popular of all Persian lyric poets, even in his own lifetime. A Sufi, he wrote mystical religious verse that used the language of human love.

Ode

A grievous folly shames my sixtieth year—
  My white head is in love with a green maid;
    I kept my heart a secret, but at last
  I am betrayed.
Like a mere child I walked into the snare;   5
  My foolish heart followed my foolish eyes;
    And yet, when I was young—in ages past—
  I was so wise.

From *Odes from the Divan of Hafiz,* translated by Richard Le Gallienne. Reprinted by permission of The Society of Authors as the literary representative of the Estate of Richard Le Gallienne.

If only she who can such wonders do
  Could from my cheeks time's calumny erase,   10
    And change the color of my snow-white locks—
Give a young face
To my young heart and make my old eyes new,
  Bidding my outside tell the inward truth!
    O 'tis a shallow wit wherewith time mocks   15
An old man's youth!

  Ah! it was always so with us who sing!
    Children of fancy, we are in the power
      Of any dream, and at the bidding we
    Of a mere flower;   20
Yet, Hafiz, though full many a foolish thing
  Ensnared thy heart with wonder, never thou
    Wert wont imagination's slave to be
As thou art now.

FOR STUDY AND DISCUSSION

IBN SARA

1. This brief lyric is by a Moorish poet who has had experience with Christian warriors. What picture of such warriors does he present? What is suggested by the image of the "casual shield"? Why is that image appropriate to this poem?

2. This poem is composed of two similes. What are they? Do they seem appropriate? Why are the flowers above the pool called "lashes"?

AL-THURTHUSI

1. The poet mentions five ways in which he tries to have some contact with his absent love. What are they? Would he actually know if he saw the star she sees? What "message" might the winds carry? Does he mean to suggest that songs have been written about his love? Or are all of these exaggerated statements of his longing for his love? Explain. Contrast this poem with the poems of parting by some of the Chinese and Japanese poets, perhaps the one by Yakamochi on page 292.

2. In line 4, what would be the effect on the poem if the word *odor* were substituted for *fragrance?*

KISA'I OF MERV

1. In looking back at his life what specific faults does Kisa'i find? What do you think he would like to have done differently? Has he been a worse man than most men, or does age make him more aware of his regrets? Is his attitude at all like that of Gilgamesh (page 13)? Why does he consider youth to be a happy time?

2. What does the poet mean in line 9 when he says he is "sold to envy"? in line 11 when he says he is "the target of events"? What are the "treasures" he asks the location of in line 17? Why does he fear death if his present life is so dreadful, if "happiness is left behind"? What is the meaning of the last two lines?

3. According to the poet, what purpose is there to life? Cite specific lines to support your opinion. What does he consider worthwhile in life? Contrast Kisa'i's attitude toward life and its purpose with the attitude expressed in Fitzgerald's translation of Khayyam (page 334).

DATES

1. Who is speaking in this poem? Who is "our gold father"? This poem suggests the feeling of spaciousness and freedom associated with the desert. What words or lines contribute to that feeling? What words or phrases suggest the personality of the nomadic peoples who lived in the desert? Does the poem make their lives seem exciting? How?

2. There are two metaphors used in the first two lines. What are they? Does either of them have an echo anywhere else in the poem?

3. An epithet is a word or phrase applied to a person to describe one of his or her attributes. For example, "the great" in "Alexander the Great" is an epithet. The anonymous author of this poem uses several epithets to

describe two different things. What are the epithets? What do they describe? Are some of the epithets also metaphors? Which ones?

RUMI

1. On the surface, this poem seems to be a love poem, but, as the fourth stanza indicates, the ecstasy experienced by two lovers might be used as a symbol of the ecstasy experienced by the soul in mystical union with God. In what ways is the Mohammedan experience described here like the Hindu experience of the *Upanishads* (page 240)? In what ways is it different? Point out the lines in the poem which reveal the similarities and differences. Does the fifth stanza sound like the *Upanishads?* Explain.

2. Is the garden into which "thou and I" go a real place or a symbol? How does the final stanza give an indication of what the garden is? If "flower garden" is used symbolically, of what is it a symbol?

3. When Rumi says, "And like some moon we shed our ray," what is the source of the light which they reflect? What sort of light is it? The loss of self-awareness is a part of the Hindu mystical experience. Is Rumi talking about that here? What lines justify your answer?

HAFIZ

1. In the final stanza, addressing himself by name as Persian lyric poets often did, Hafiz says something about poets in general. What does he mean when he says of poets, "we are in the power of any dream, and at the bidding we of a mere flower"? What might a flower bid a poet do? What pleases a poet?

2. If we read this poem only as a love poem, we see an older man's pained but still amused annoyance with himself at having fallen in love with a young girl. The poet's attitude is, perhaps, best summarized in the last two lines of the second stanza. Explain what those lines mean.

3. If, as with other Sufi poetry, we read this as a religious poem, what sort of experience is the subject of the poem? Has the poet, in the uncertainties of his years, developed a longing for the pure religious ardor of his youth? Or is there some other interpretation of the youth-age attraction? What do the last two lines of the first stanza suggest? Are they ironic or not? Explain. What wisdom does youth have that age does not?

4. Does this poet have the same attitude toward growing old that Kisa'i of Merv (page 352) has? If they are different, how do they differ?

PART 3

EUROPE TO 1914

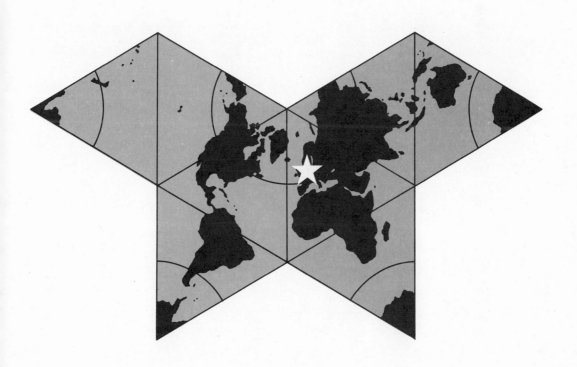

THE
MIDDLE AGES
c. A.D. 500 – c. 1500

THE COLLAPSE of the one-world superstate known as the Roman Empire coincided with the general collapse of Greco-Roman culture in Western Europe. Though the eastern half of the empire with its capital at Byzantium (now Istanbul, Turkey) continued a flourishing culture, the West entered a new era. This has been variously named by historians as the Dark Ages, the Middle Ages—suggesting, somewhat contemptuously, a thousand-year valley between the cultural pinnacles of the ancient and modern worlds—or the medieval period, a term derived from Latin which means the same thing as Middle Ages. This era is usually considered to last from roughly A.D. 500 to 1500, though the succeeding epoch, the Renaissance, clearly began before 1500 in some parts of Europe, such as Italy, and came much later than 1500 in other parts, such as Russia.

To use a single label like *medieval* for this whole thousand years is imprecise. The name Dark Ages does belong, perhaps, to the era up to A.D. 1000. This was the period when barbarian Germanic tribes moved across Europe, establishing by force of arms their areas of political dominance. With the exception of a few men like Charlemagne, the great ninth-century leader of the Franks, the Germanic tribespeople were generally rough, crude, and illiterate, only recently introduced to Christianity, if they were Christianized at all. Their hero was their warrior-leader and their chief interest and pride were in feats of arms. Even of Charlemagne it is reported:

● He made attempts at writing, too, and was accustomed to surround his pillows on his bed with tablets and notebooks for this purpose, so

From "Charlemagne: His Studies and Habits," from *Vita Karoli* by Einhard, translated by H. E. Wedeck from *Putnam's Dark and Middle Ages Reader*, edited by Harry E. Wedeck. Reprinted by permission of G. P. Putnam's Sons.

that when he had any spare time he would train his hand to form letters. But he met with little success in these efforts because he had started too late in life.—EINHARD

Nevertheless, though the flame of Western culture flickered and grew very dim during these Dark Ages, it did not entirely go out. A literate clergy preserved many documents of the past, mostly in Latin translations and commentaries. Later, other old documents were rediscovered by the crusaders and through trade contacts with Byzantium and the Arab East. Thus, some cultural continuity was maintained, and the later Middle Ages (sometimes called the High Middle Ages), far from being dark, was one of the great periods of cultural achievement in the West. In art, architecture, music, literature, philosophy, and theology there were major accomplishments. The last two developed in large part from a synthesis of Christian teachings and the works of Aristotle, who was so highly regarded by medieval scholars that they referred to him simply as "the Philosopher."

Now we can see with more perspective that the medieval period, in fact, was far from static. It opened with the collapse of the Roman Empire and closed with the establishment of modern nation-states; it opened with most men living a rural, agricultural life and ended with the growth of vast cities, commercial centers, and far-flung trade routes; it opened with Latin the one written language of the educated and ended with literatures written in many vernacular tongues; it opened with Christian unity and ended in the diversity of the Reformation; it opened with limited knowledge even of Europe and ended with the discoveries of vast new worlds to the west.

FEUDALISM

Politically, the Middle Ages was like the shattered fragments of a glass hemisphere which had been the Roman Empire. After the fall of the empire, more than a thousand separate units existed in northern Europe alone. Many of these were not natural, geographic, or social units, but simply areas that a particular chief or warlord could control by arms. In time, these units achieved some loose patterns of organization through the feudal contracts made between vassals and their suzerains, or lords.

These feudal contracts developed chiefly in two ways. The breakdown of the Roman Empire and the absence of organized national governments left every man at the mercy of his more powerful neighbors. Many landowners, in exchange for the protection of a powerful neighbor, made certain agreements: to pay a portion of the yield of their lands; to provide a certain number of soldiers from among their families or workers; and to perform whatever other duties and homage were required to secure the protection they sought. These landowners became vassals to their protecting lords, in a relationship which time and mutual advantage often made,

A world map, from a Spanish manuscript of the Book of Revelation (A.D. 787).

for all practical purposes, permanent and hereditary. Often the protecting lord was himself vassal to a yet more powerful lord, who might himself be, in turn, vassal to a great prince. Thus, theoretically at least, the feudal system grew, like a pyramid, from a broad base upward toward a single figure at the top, a king, who in his turn recognized God as his sovereign. But this was theory only, and even in England and France, where kingly power first eventually expanded enough to establish nation-states, the feudal framework was far less orderly than the theory suggests.

Feudal contracts grew in a second way. Conquering princes would reward valued allies with grants of territory which they were to administer for the prince. Though these grants still belonged in theory to the prince, in fact they often became the private domains of the barons and dukes who were the grantees. A variant of this practice is exemplified by the division of Charlemagne's empire into three parts as an inheritance for his three grandsons. Though one was still designated emperor over them all, three separate kingdoms developed in fact.

A special word should be said of the serfs, the peasants who were at the very bottom of the feudal social scale. Though some might be house servants, serfs generally worked the land. They were not enslaved in the sense that certain Greeks and Romans had been enslaved, nor in the sense that Africans were to be enslaved later in the New World. But the serfs were not free, either, for generally they were bound to the land on which they worked; they owed service to the master of the land and they passed with the land from owner to owner. The extent to which the serfs had rights like those had by free men, and the extent to which those rights were protected, varied greatly from place to place.

In the feudal relationships, then, loyalties were generally personal, not national. A serf was bound to his landlord, a landlord to his lord, a knight to his prince, a prince to his king, but the individual man, certainly the educated man at least, eventually felt himself to be a citizen of a united Christendom which included all Europe. Whereas during the earlier Dark Ages few men ventured more than ten miles from their birthplaces, by the High Middle Ages men traveled widely in Europe. The educated exchanged books and letters, and scholars often went wherever they could find students, just as certain philosophers of Greece had done. The great unifying force which gave men this sense of world citizenship was the Christian Church.

THE CHRISTIAN CHURCH

The Church was the one paramount fact of medieval life. Every man was a member or was, like the Jews of Europe, barred from full participation in the life of his time. The great genius of the Church was that it preached a uniform set of beliefs and values while still absorbing the natural diversity of human understandings and interests, abilities and aspirations. This achievement of unity in diversity was maintained without really serious challenge up to the time of Martin Luther, in the sixteenth century. Not that there were not numerous heresies and heretical tendencies; there were, but the Church had the wisdom and the power to divert and absorb them or to repress them.

If the medieval man sometimes seems gullible or superstitious to us, it is in part because we do not fully understand his attitude toward his religion.

The medieval Christian never forgot that the world he lived in was God's world and that God was at work in it. Though God generally operated the world according to regular patterns—rain dampened, fire burned, water ran downhill, etc.—there was no reason that an omnipotent and loving God might not change the patterns for some purpose if he wished to. The natural and the supernatural worlds were far more intimately related for the medieval man than they seem to be to most of us. For example, unlike modern Christians, medieval man believed for many years in trial by combat, in having an accused man fight his accuser, for surely God would give victory to the innocent and let punishment fall on the guilty, no matter which was the stronger or more experienced warrior. This certainty that God was closely interested in even the most trivial aspects of his life gave medieval man an enviable security, even when he faced what seems to us a perilously insecure kind of life, filled, as it might be, with violence, plague, famine, and unexpected reversals of fortune. At the same time, man in the Middle Ages was certain that this world was only a place of pilgrimage, a testing ground to see whether he would win eternal heaven or be condemned to eternal hell. This attitude encouraged a man to feel that the life he knew was the life that God, in his mysterious ways, intended him to have and that his main purpose in life was not to improve his lot or to solve social and political problems. The modern idea of progress, of moving toward an ever better world, would have been incomprehensible in the Middle Ages.

SCHOLASTICISM

Learning underwent a dramatic change during medieval times. The only literate persons were at first in the Church, and their early writing shows an interest limited to religious and philosophical matters. Churchmen sought to describe God's ways with men, or to comment on what had already been written by others. The many commentaries on the works of Aristotle are examples.

The later medieval period, however, had become intellectually active and more versatile, with substantial achievements made in formal thought. At the peak of the Middle Ages, Roger Bacon argued the value of inductive reasoning, which became the basis for the modern scientific method. Astrology, alchemy, and other pseudosciences prepared the way for the development of modern science. Theological and philosophical debate was endless and spirited, and much of it was on a high intellectual level. Out of such debate came the great intellectual achievement of the Middle Ages, the philosophical system known as scholasticism, of which St. Thomas Aquinas (1225?–1274) was the supreme exponent.

Scholasticism is characterized by great logical skill and subtlety. Like all of medieval thought, whether that of scholars or of simple folk, it has as its unquestioned premise Christian doctrine as interpreted by the Church fathers. To this was added a rather uncritical acceptance of the philosophical and scientific theories of Aristotle, whose works became better and better known in the Middle Ages as new translations taken from Arabic sources became available. Scholasticism was in a sense a compromise. The Christian Church has always held a firm position about both worlds, the natural and the supernatural. It preaches the importance of life after death but makes clear that one's earthly life influences the nature of one's eternal life. In the same way, scholasticism appeals to the use of human reason, but it holds that reason must be subject to the authority of the Church. If reason and faith seem to be in conflict, it is because reason has been used incorrectly. The scholastics hold that proper use of reason will lead to the same truths which the Church has come to through faith and revelation—or, at least, that these truths would not be contradictory to reason. St. Thomas makes this conviction of scholasticism clear in the passage that follows.

A portion of the embroidery recording the Norman invasion of England, 1066.

● Now, although the truth of the Christian faith which we have discussed surpasses the capacity of the reason, nevertheless that truth that the human reason is naturally endowed to know cannot be opposed to the truth of the Christian faith. For that with which the human reason is naturally endowed is clearly most true; so much so that it is impossible for us to think of such truths as false. Nor is it permissible to believe as false that which we hold by faith, since this is confirmed in a way that is so clearly divine. Since, therefore, only the false is opposed to the true, as is clearly evident from an examination of their definitions, it is impossible that the truth of faith should be opposed to those principles that the human reason knows naturally.

Furthermore, that which is introduced into the soul of the student by the teacher is contained in the knowledge of the teacher—unless his teaching is fictitious, which it is improper to say of God. Now, the knowledge of the principles that are known to us naturally has been implanted in us by God; for God is the author of our nature. These principles, therefore, are also contained by the divine wisdom. Hence, whatever is opposed to them is opposed to the divine wisdom, and, therefore, cannot come from God. That which we hold by faith as divinely revealed, therefore, cannot be contrary to our natural knowledge.

—THOMAS AQUINAS

CHRONICLES

As might be expected, secular writing developed slowly in the Middle Ages. There was some historical commentary written in the Dark Ages, but the kind of self-consciousness which believes that an orderly record of the events of daily life is worth preserving came slowly in a medieval world whose eyes were fixed on eternity. When history came, it came first through the chronicles.

The chronicles are records of events, kept in chronological order. The most ancient of these tend to be strictly local, the work of a monk who chronicled the events in the immediate neighborhood of his monastery or the events he had heard about from a passer-by. Though some chronicles contain valuable historical information, they lean toward fantastic interpretations and superstitious nonsense, as in this example from the annals of the German town of Xanten for the year 838.

> ● The winter was rainy and very windy and on January 21 thunder was heard and likewise on February 16 there were great claps of thunder and the intense heat of the sun scorched the earth, and in certain districts of the land an earthquake occurred, and the fiery shape of a dragon was seen in the air. In the same year a wicked heresy arose. In the same year on the fifth night before the birth of the Lord a great crash of thunder was heard and lightning was seen and in many ways the misery and misfortunes of men increased every day.—ANONYMOUS

Later, the chronicles began to have broader scope, to try to encompass more realistic history and more widely significant events. By the late Middle Ages, other largely secular works, though not numerous, were being written on government, on the deportment of holy hermits, on travel.

THE ORAL TRADITION

Popular literature developed quite apart from the scholastics or the chroniclers, however. Much of the early popular literature of the Middle Ages is in what is called the "oral tradition." We have a record of some of this popular literature today only because a few literate persons, priests or monks or others of the Church, finally wrote down the stories that they had heard. In most cases, however, we know of no author or even group of authors to whom we can credit a particular work.

The subject matter of this early material is the subject matter of most early literatures of whatever culture. There are stories about the warriors and heroes of the tribe or region or clan, and, as in ancient Greece, there are stories of gods and goddesses. These early stories, myths, and legends, despite their frequently fantastic natures, often reveal much about the character of the people who told them. The sort of person who was their hero, for example, tells us the values which that people held. Note the qualities of the Germanic hero Siegfried that are revealed in this brief account of his death by treachery.

> ● Siegfried was sore athirst and bade push back the table, that he might go to the spring at the foot of the mountain. Falsely had the knights contrived it. The wild beasts that Siegfried's hand had slain

From "News Chronicle" translated by H. E. Wedeck from *Putnam's Dark and Middle Ages Reader*, edited by H. E. Wedeck. Reprinted by permission of G. P. Putnam's Sons.
From *The Fall of the Nibelungs*, Everyman's Library Edition, translated by Margaret Armour. Reprinted by permission of E. P. Dutton & Co., Inc., and J. M. Dent & Sons Ltd., Publishers.

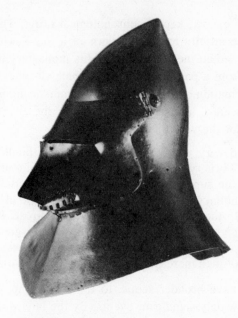

A knight's helmet from the late Middle Ages. Armor eventually became so heavy that knights had to be hauled onto their horses.

they let pile on a wagon and take home, and all they that saw it praised him.

Foully did Hagen break faith with Siegfried. He said, when they were starting for the broad lime tree, "I hear from all sides that none can keep pace with Kriemhild's husband when he runneth. Let us see now."

Bold Siegfried of the Netherland answered, "Thou mayst easily prove it, if thou wilt run with me to the brook for a wager. The praise shall be to him that winneth there first."

"Let us see then," said Hagen the knight.

And stark Siegfried answered, "If I lose, I will lay me at thy feet in the grass."

A glad man was King Gunther when he heard that!

Said Siegfried further, "Nay, I will undertake more. I will carry on me all that I wear—spear, shield, and hunting gear." Whereupon he girded on his sword and his quiver in haste. Then the others did off their clothes, till they stood in their white shirts, and they ran through the clover like two wild panthers; but bold Siegfried was seen there the first. Before all men he won the prize in everything. He loosed his sword straightway and laid down his quiver. His good spear he leaned against the lime tree; then the noble guest stood and waited, for his courtesy was great. He laid down his shield by the stream. Albeit he was sore athirst, he drank not till that the king had finished, who gave him evil thanks.

The stream was cool, pure, and good. Gunther bent down to the water and rose again when he had drunk. Siegfried had gladly done the like, but he suffered for his courtesy. Hagen carried his bow and his sword out of his reach and sprang back and gripped the spear. Then he spied for the secret mark on his vesture; and while Siegfried drank from the stream, Hagen stabbed him where the cross was, that his heart's blood spurted out on the traitor's clothes. Never since hath knight done so wickedly. He left the spear sticking deep in his heart and fled in grimmer haste than ever he had done from any man on this earth afore.

When stark Siegfried felt the deep wound, he sprang up maddened from the water, for the long boar spear stuck out from his heart. He thought to find bow or sword; if he had, Hagen had got his due. But the sore-wounded man saw no sword and had nothing, save his shield. He picked it up from the water's edge and ran at Hagen. King Gunther's man could not escape him. For all that he was wounded to the death, he smote mightily that the shield well-nigh brake, and the precious stones flew out. The noble guest had fain taken vengeance.

Hagen fell beneath his stroke. The meadow rang loud with the noise of the blow. If he had had his sword to hand, Hagen had been a dead man. But the anguish of his wound constrained him. His color was wan; he could not stand upright; and the strength of his body failed him, for he bare death's mark on his white cheek. Fair women enow made dole for him.—ANONYMOUS

CHIVALRY AND THE ARTHURIAN LEGENDS

As the above excerpt suggests, the warrior-leader of the early Middle Ages was occupied chiefly with violence. Though he might have a territory to govern or administer, he was still likely to be chiefly interested in his own skills in feats of arms. Yet there was a clear tension between his ambitions, his desires, his pleasure in combat, and the Christian faith which he espoused. Out of this tension and other moderating influences grew the way of life, shared by all feudal upper classes in the West, known as chivalry, a term derived from the word *chevalier,* the French word for "knight."

Chivalry set the rules for the game of war. It required that a knight who would defend his honor must do so by honorable means; it set limits on the scope and nature of revenge that could be taken for real or fancied insults; it demanded that the warrior fight fairly, even with the Moslem infidels, that he love God, and that he be loyal to his king or prince, if he had one. Christian humility, kindness and politeness to those of lower station, and generosity with the world's goods were added requirements which refined personal behavior. When a knight failed to uphold the standards of chivalry, he might do penance by undertaking special tasks, such as participating in a Crusade or performing some religious duty. Unquestionably, chivalry was a civilizing influence in the Middle Ages, as suggested in the following account of a medieval king of the twelfth century, Henry II of England.

● When his mind was undisturbed and he was not in an angry mood, he spoke with great eloquence, and, what was remarkable in those days, he was well learned. He was also affable, flexible, and facetious and, however he smothered his inward feelings, second to no one in courtesy. Withal, he was so clement a prince that when he had subdued his enemies, he was overcome himself by his pity for them. Resolute in war and provident in peace, he so much feared the doubtful fortune of the former that, as the comic poet writes, he tried all courses before he resorted to arms. Those whom he lost in battle he lamented with more than a prince's sorrow, having a more humane feeling for the soldiers who had fallen than for the survivors; and bewailing the dead more than he cared for the living. In troublesome times no man was more courteous, and when all things were safe, no man more harsh. Severe to the unruly, but clement to the humble; hard toward his own household, but liberal to strangers; profuse abroad, but sparing at home; those whom he once hated he would scarcely ever love, and from those he loved he seldom withdrew his regard. . . .

He was a great maker of peace, and kept it himself; a liberal almsgiver, and an especial benefactor to the Holy Land. He loved the humble, curbed the nobility, and trod down the proud; filling the hungry with good things, and sending the rich empty away; exalting the meek, and putting down the mighty from their seat.—GIRALDUS CAMBRENSIS

In the later Middle Ages, an additional element, the concept of courtly love, was added to the chivalric ideals of Christian humility and knightly valor. Each knight was devoted to a "lady." She was rarely his wife, but rather was likely to be an aristocratic lady whom he could never hope to marry, or someone he saw only from a distance or only heard about. Yet the performance of valorous deeds to honor one's lady became another chivalric ideal. Indeed, in the tales most taken up with themes of courtly love, a knight's every thought might well be devoted to his lady.

● Aucassin was armed and on his horse, as you have heard and understood. God, how becoming the shield was at his neck and the helmet on his head and the belt of his sword on his left hip. The lad was big and strong and handsome and noble and well turned out, and the horse which he rode, quick and rapid; and the lad had ridden him straight through the middle of the gate.

Now don't you believe that he was thinking of taking oxen or cows or goats, or that he would strike some knight or another strike him. Nothing like that! Not once did it occur to him. But he thought so much of Nicolette, his sweet love, that he forgot the reins and all that he had to do. And the horse that had felt the spurs carried him into the thick of the battle and hurled him right into the midst of his enemies. They grabbed him from all sides; so did they take him. And they re-

From "The Character of King Henry II, of England," by Giraldus Cambrensis, translated by T. Wright from Putnam's *Dark and Middle Ages Reader*, edited by Harry E. Wedeck.
Excerpt from "Aucassin et Nicolette," translated by Edward F. Moyer and Carey DeWitt Eldridge, from *World Masterpieces*, Vol. I edited by Mack et al., copyright 1937 by Robert W. Linker and reprinted with his permission.

lieved him of his shield and lance; so did they quickly lead him away a prisoner. And they went along, already considering what death they would make him die.

And when Aucassin heard them: "Ah, God," said he, "sweet creature! Are these my mortal enemies who are holding me here and who now will cut off my head? And after my head is cut off, never will I speak to Nicolette, my sweet love, whom I love so much. Yet I have here a good sword, and I'm riding a good fresh war horse. If now I don't defend myself for her sake, never may God help her if she loves me any more."

The lad was big and strong, and the horse on which he sat was lively. And he snatched his sword and began to strike right and left and cut through helmets and nosepieces and fists and arms and made a slaughter round about him, like the wild boar when the dogs attack him in the forest. And so did he strike down ten knights and wound seven, and rode quickly out of the thick of things. So did he come galloping back, sword in hand.—ANONYMOUS

·The chief literary expression of chivalric ideals is, of course, in the stories relating to King Arthur and the Knights of the Round Table. Historically, there was no king of England named Arthur, but there was apparently

A manuscript illustration of an early knighthood ceremony. Initially, a noble could simply be dubbed by a full-fledged knight, after proving himself in battle. Later, the initiation was made into a religious ceremony.

a Celtic cavalry leader named Arturius who helped to defend the land against the Anglo-Saxon invasions of the sixth century. Around this figure seem to have gathered most of the hero stories in the Celtic oral tradition, with the result that by the twelfth century, Arthur was so firmly established in tradition as a king that Geoffrey of Monmouth so recorded him in his *History of the Kings of Britain*. Later writers added the Round Table idea and some of the supernatural traditions about Arthur's birth and death.

Numerous and varied tales about Arthur and his knights spread through the oral tradition in England, Wales, and particularly in France, where the concept of courtly love was introduced. The major Arthurian tales were brought together in the late Middle Ages, in the fifteenth century, by Sir Thomas Malory in his book *Le Morte d'Arthur* ("The Death of Arthur"). Malory arranges the tales so as to give an account of Arthur's life and adventures from birth to death. The various episodes encompass the full range of chivalry, from its early, vigorous style when Arthur is presented as a true and valiant hero, to its later, decadent form when the emphasis is on courtly love, when Arthur becomes a rather pathetic old man whose wife Guinevere betrays him for the love of his knight Lancelot.

COLLECTIONS OF TALES

In *Le Morte d'Arthur* the character of Arthur provides the unifying force that holds together many different stories from many different sources. In the literature of India, however, in the *Panchatantra* (see page 253) and in the literature of the Middle East, in *The Thousand and One Nights* (see page 343), we see stories brought together with a different, more sophisticated organization. These other stories might be organized to illustrate a principle, an idea, or even a type of story.

A number of such collections of tales and stories were made during the late Middle Ages. The stories might be familiar folk tales, tales borrowed from ancient sources, or, in a very few cases, original creations of the author. Quality, of course, tended to vary widely according to the collector's skill in selection and in narration. One of the most important of these collections was *The Canterbury Tales* (see page 435) by Geoffrey Chaucer (1340?–1400).

LITERATURE IN THE VERNACULARS

Though an educated man, Chaucer wrote in his own English vernacular rather than in Latin, the traditional language of the learned. Folk literature and stories which were part of the oral tradition had always been told in the vernaculars spoken by the ordinary people, but most writings had been in Latin. Secular literature, however, increasingly abandoned Latin, and by the late Middle Ages literatures written in the various languages which characterize Europe today had begun to emerge. Dante Alighieri (1265–1321), the great Florentine poet, wrote his *Divine Comedy* (see page 400) in the Tuscan dialect of Italy. In France, the *Song of Roland* (see page 377) and the chivalric romances had appeared in various French dialects. And Chaucer, by writing his own English dialect, the dialect of London, helped to determine for all future writers what the literary language of England would be.

Brief poems continued to be composed in both the vernacular languages and in Latin, depending on the subject matter and intentions of the poet. Religious lyrics were written in Latin. There exists, for example, an extensive body of such poetry addressed to the Virgin Mary, who inspired considerable poetic adoration during the Middle Ages.

Of the vernacular poetry, one of the most popular forms was the ballad (see pages 467–71), which might well be considered the medieval musical equivalent of the short story. Ballad subjects were, more often than not, the sort of stories announced by today's newspaper headlines—about domestic crime, murder, disaster, lust, and love. Ballads seem to have developed early as a narrative form, perhaps in the fourteenth century, and to have enjoyed widespread popularity throughout all of Western Europe.

Because the most popular ballads were preserved for many generations as part of the oral tradition, one story may now be found in many different countries and in multiple forms. Many old European ballads traveled across the Atlantic to the United States as this country was settled, and they are still sung here. One of the most famous of these ballads is the tabloid crime story "Lord Randall," which probably originated in Italy (as "The Poisoned Man") during the Middle Ages and which has been found in various versions in parts of the United States in this century. The ballad form has been so widely popular that later "literary ballads," composed in imitation of the authentic medieval ballads, have enjoyed great vogue.

A special word should be said about Provençal poetry and the troubadours. In southern France, northern Italy, and northern Spain, beginning in the eleventh century, lyric poems, especially love lyrics, were composed by a large group of talented poets called troubadours who wrote in their vernaculars. (The word *troubadour* is from a Provençal verb, meaning "to compose" or "to invent.") Many of these poets were persons of high station, like William, Duke of Aquitaine (see page 458). Others were dependents at some noble court. Whatever their rank, they apparently wrote out of a fairly old tradition of vernacular poetry and experimented freely to produce the light, graceful lyric forms for which they are known. It was among these poets and courtiers that the concept of courtly love was developed and spread throughout Europe. They exerted substantial influence on other lyricists, and on Dante, who pays them grateful respect at several points in his writing.

The Prose Edda

SNORRI STURLUSON

Snorri Sturluson (1179–1241), the son of a great Icelandic chieftain, wrote several famous sagas of Norse-Icelandic kings. These heroic tales were part of an already ancient Icelandic tradition. The *Prose Edda*—*edda* probably means "poetics" or "the poetic art"—was designed as a handbook to tell poets how to compose in the style of the Viking skalds (early Icelandic poets), a style which Snorri Sturluson himself had mastered. Divided into three parts, the book offers rules of poetic diction with many illustrative stories and examples.

Not only are the stories of the *Edda* of interest in their own right, but they are among the best accounts we have of the pre-Christian mythology shared by such Teutonic peoples as the Germans, the Norse, and the people of Iceland. That Odin (called Wotan by the Germans), king of the gods, should be the god of both wisdom and war tells us something of the values of these Teutonic people.

As with other mythologies, the Greek and Hindu, for example, the stories of the *Edda* relate the actions of anthropomorphic deities, like Odin, Hoenir, and Loki; and of semidivine heroes, like Sigurd. Loki is the highly unreliable god of fire, while Hoenir is a deity who helped create the first man and woman from trees, by giving them reason and motion. Odin, as was said before, is the king of the gods and the divinity that bestows wisdom and reigns over wars.

The gods in these stories are referred to collectively as Aesir, a word which means simply "gods" in Old Norse but which Snorri Sturluson interpreted to mean "men of Asia." Sturluson was writing on pagan subjects in Christian times. He protected himself against the charge of propagating paganism by making clear that these pagan "gods" actually represented early kings and chieftains, who had been deified by Teutonic peoples from western Asia. Our knowledge of the movements of Germanic peoples like the Goths, and the appearance in these stories of historical characters like Atli, who is identified as Attila the Hun, lend credence to Sturluson's claim. Furthermore, there is an account as late as the ninth century A.D. of the actual deification of a Swedish king.

The Aesir are generally associated with war, in contrast to another group of Teutonic gods called the Vanir, who are usually associated with peace and plenty and who may be the gods originally worshiped by those people whose lands were overrun by the Teutonic tribes.

The selection which follows is from the second part of the *Prose Edda*, the Skaldskaparmal, which means "poetic diction." The skalds had used a number of standard phrases called *kennings,* which substituted an epithet for the actual name of an object. For example, a ship might be referred to as a "horse of the sea" and the sea as its "field." Such kennings were generally of two types: those, like the ones just mentioned, which were merely standard metaphors borrowed from nature, and those which alluded to the myths and legends of the Norse deities. In the Skaldskaparmal,

Snorri Sturluson explains many of this latter type of kenning by telling the stories associated with them.

He introduces a character named Aegir, a great magician, who attends a festival with the gods, at which he asks the explanation for some of the kennings. In the selection that follows, Aegir is asking the questions, and the explanations in the form of stories are given by Bragi, who is the son of Odin and also, appropriately, the Norse god of poetry.

This selection contains three separate but related stories, each explaining various kennings used by the skalds for "gold." You may recognize the last story about Sigurd as an early version of the adventures of the great Germanic warrior (usually called Siegfried, see page 365), who continues as a hero of legend, myth, drama, and opera up to the present time.

The Niflung Hoard

WHAT IS THE REASON for calling gold 'otter's ransom'?"

"It is said that when the Aesir, Odin and Loki and Hoenir, were exploring the whole world, they came to a river and went along it to a waterfall, and by the waterfall was an otter which was eating a salmon it had caught there and it was half asleep. Loki picked up a stone and flung it at the otter, striking it on the head. Then Loki boasted of his catch—with one throw he had bagged an otter and a salmon. They took the salmon and the otter away with them and came to a farm, which they entered. The farmer living there was called Hreidmar. He was a powerful man with much skill in magic. The Aesir asked the farmer for lodgings there for the night, saying that they had plenty of food, and they showed him their catch. When Hreidmar saw the otter, however, he called his sons Fafnir and Regin, and told them that their brother, Otter, had been killed, and also who had done the deed. Then father and sons attacked the Aesir and made them prisoner and bound them, telling them that the otter was

Hreidmar's son. The Aesir offered to pay as large a ransom as Hreidmar himself should demand, and those terms were agreed on and confirmed by oath. Then the otter was flayed, and Hreidmar took the skin and told them that they had to fill it and completely cover it into the bargain with red gold. That would reconcile them. Odin then sent Loki to the world-of-dark-elves, and he came to the dwarf called Andvari. He was in a pool in his fish shape, and Loki, seizing him, exacted as ransom all the gold he had in his rock dwelling. When they got there, the dwarf produced all the gold he possessed and it was a very great sum of money, but he kept back in his hand a little gold ring. Loki noticed this and told him to give him the ring. The dwarf begged him not to take it from him, saying that if only he were allowed to keep it he could by its means become wealthy again. Loki said that he was to be left without a single penny and, taking the ring from him, was going away, when the dwarf declared that the ring would destroy everyone who owned it. Loki replied that that was all to the good, adding that the prophecy should be fulfilled, provided that he himself pronounced it in the ears of those about to take over the ring.

"He went away and came to Hreidmar and showed the gold ring to Odin. When Odin saw it he admired it for its beauty and kept it back, although he paid the gold to Hreidmar. Hreidmar stuffed the skin to bursting and when it was full raised it up

"The Niflung Hoard," translated by Jean I. Young from *The Prose Edda* by Snorri Sturluson. Reprinted by permission of the University of California Press.

on end. Then Odin went up to it to cover it with gold and, this done, he asked Hreidmar to look and see if the skin was not completely hidden. Hreidmar took a good look at it and caught sight of one whisker. He ordered this to be concealed or otherwise, he said, their agreement would be at an end. Then Odin drew the ring from his finger and concealed the whisker, saying that now they had paid the otter's ransom. When, however, Odin had taken his spear and Loki his shoes and there was no reason they should be afraid, Loki declared that what Andvari had said should hold good, that that ring and that gold would destroy whosoever owned them. That has been the case ever since. Now you know why gold is called otter's ransom or the forced payment of the Aesir or metal-of-strife."

"Is anything more known about this gold?"

"Hreidmar accepted the gold as ransom for his son, and Fafnir and Regin asked for some of it as a ransom for their brother. Hreidmar did not give them a single penny of it. The brothers were wicked enough to kill their father for the gold. Then Regin asked Fafnir to go shares in the gold, but Fafnir replied that there was little likelihood that he would share with his brother the gold for which he had killed his father, and he told Regin to go away or else he would meet with Hreidmar's fate. Fafnir had taken a helmet which had been Hreidmar's and was wearing it; this struck fear into all beholders and was called the helmet of terror. He also had the sword known as Hrotti. Regin owned a sword called Refil. He took to flight, but Fafnir went up on to Gnita Heath and, making a lair there, turned himself into a dragon and lay down on the gold.

"Then Regin went to King Hjalprek in Ty and became his smith there. He adopted as his foster son Sigurd, son of Sigmund, son of Volsung and Hjordis, Eylimi's daughter. On account of his family, strength, and courage, Sigurd was the most famous of all warrior-kings. Regin told him where Fafnir was lying on the gold and egged him on to seek the treasure. Regin made the sword called Gram. This was so sharp that, when Sigurd thrust it into running water, he cut in two a lock of wool carried against the blade by the current. With the same sword, Sigurd clove Regin's anvil to the stock. After that Sigurd and Regin went to Gnita Heath and Sigurd dug pits in Fafnir's path and sat down in one. When Fafnir, crawling on his way down to the water, came over the pit, Sigurd ran him through with his sword and that was his death. Then Regin came and said that Sigurd had killed his brother, and offered him terms on condition that he took Fafnir's heart and roasted it over a fire. Regin himself lay down and drank Fafnir's blood and then went to sleep. When Sigurd thought the heart he was roasting was done, he touched it with his finger to see how tender it was, and the juice from it ran on to his finger, burning it, so he put this into his mouth. When the blood came on to his tongue, however, he understood the language of birds and knew what the nuthatches sitting in the branches were saying. One said:

> There sits Sigurd
> blood-bespattered;
> Fafnir's heart
> roasts at the fire;
> wise that liberal prince
> would appear to me
> should he eat
> that shining heart.

> There lies Regin, said another,
> revolving in his mind
> how to betray
> the lad who trusts him;
> in wrath he is collecting
> crooked words together,
> he longs, contriver-of-evil,
> to avenge his brother.

Then Sigurd went up to Regin and killed him, and afterwards to his horse, which was called Grani, and rode until he came to Fafnir's lair. There he took the gold and making it into packs put it on Grani's back, mounted himself and rode on his way.

"Now you know the story explaining why gold is called Fafnir's abode or lair, or the metal of Gnita Heath, or Grani's burden.

"Sigurd rode on then until he came to a hall on a mountain. In it was sleeping a woman in helmet and coat of mail. He drew his sword and cut the mail-coat from her. Then she woke up and said she was called Hild. Her name was Brynhild and she was a valkyrie.[1] Sigurd rode away from there and came to a king called Gjuki. His wife was called Grimhild and their children were Gunnar, Hogni, Gudrun, and Gudny. Gotthorm was Gjuki's stepson. Sigurd stayed there for a long time and married Gudrun, Gjuki's daughter, and Gunnar and Hogni became sworn brothers of Sigurd. Soon after, Sigurd and the sons of Gjuki went to ask Atli Budlason for his sister, Brynhild, as Gunnar's wife. She lived at Hindafjall and there was a rampart of flame round her hall. She had vowed only to marry that man who dared ride through the flames. Sigurd and the Gjukungar—they are also called the Niflungar—rode up on to the mountain and Gunnar was to ride through the rampart of flame. He had a horse called Goti but it did not dare leap into the fire. Sigurd and Gunnar then changed shapes and also names, because Grani would not move under any man but Sigurd, and Sigurd, vaulting on to Grani, rode the rampart of flame. That evening he married Brynhild but, when they went to bed, he drew the sword Gram from its sheath and laid it between them. In the morning when he got up and dressed, however, he gave Brynhild as a wedding present the gold ring Loki had taken from Andvari, receiving another from her in exchange. Then Sigurd jumped on to his horse and

[1] **valkyrie:** one of the maidens who ride through the air and choose heroes from among those slain in battle to carry off to Valhalla.

rode back to his companions. He and Gunnar changed shapes again and went back to Gjuki with Brynhild. Sigurd had two children by Gudrun, Sigmund and Svanhild.

"On one occasion Brynhild and Gudrun went down to the water to wash their hair. When they reached the river, Brynhild waded out further from the bank, saying that she was not going to use the water in which Gudrun had rinsed her hair for her own head, since she had the more valiant husband. Gudrun went into the river after her then and said that she had a right to wash her hair in water higher up the river, since she had a husband whom neither Gunnar nor anyone else in the world could match in courage, because he had killed Fafnir and Regin and had inherited the property of both. Then Brynhild answered: 'Sigurd did not dare ride the rampart of flame: Gunnar did—that counts for more.' Gudrun laughed then and said: 'You think it was Gunnar who rode the flames? The man you slept with was the one who gave me this gold ring, and the ring you are wearing and which you received as a wedding gift is called Andvari's treasure, and I don't think that Gunnar got it on Gnita Heath.' At that Brynhild was silent and went home.

"Afterward she urged Gunnar and Hogni to kill Sigurd but, because they were his sworn brothers, they persuaded their brother Gotthorm to kill him. He ran Sigurd through with a sword while he was sleeping, but, when Sigurd felt the wound, he hurled the sword after Gotthorm so that it cut him asunder through the middle. Sigurd and his three-year-old son called Sigmund, whom they also killed, perished there. After that, Brynhild fell on her sword and she was burned with Sigurd. Gunnar and Hogni, however, took Fafnir's inheritance then and Andvari's treasure and ruled the country.

"Brynhild's brother, Atli Budlason, married Gudrun, once the wife of Sigurd, and they had children together. King Atli invited Gunnar and Hogni to stay with him and they went on this visit. Before leaving home, however, they hid the gold that was Fafnir's inheritance in the Rhine, and it has never been found since. King Atli had troops to oppose them and these fought Gunnar and Hogni and took them prisoner. King Atli had Hogni's heart cut out of him while he was still living and that was his death. He had Gunnar flung into a snake pit. A harp was procured for him in secret and, because his hands were tied, he played it with his toes in such a way that all the snakes went to sleep, but for one adder, which made for him, and gnawing its way through the cartilage of his breastbone, thrust its head through the hole and buried its fangs in his liver until Gunnar was dead. Gunnar and Hogni are called Niflungar or Gjukungar; for this reason gold is called the treasure or inheritance of the Niflungar."

FOR STUDY AND DISCUSSION

1. There is in these stories an uncertainty about which characters are gods, which are men, and which, like Achilles in the *Iliad* (see page 55), are somewhere in between. Try to classify Andvari, Hreidmar, and Sigurd, and as many of the other characters as possible, into one of these three categories.

2. Clearly, such confusion indicates a relatively primitive cultural level, in which great heroes are given supernatural qualities. In addition, what connection can you see between such confusion and the fact that these stories were told orally for many years before they were written down?

3. How do the Norse gods differ from the Greek deities in the *Iliad?* Are they as powerful? Consider, for example, Hreidmar's demands on Odin, Loki, and Hoenir. Is there more emphasis on magic here than in Greek mythology? Explain. What do the differences between their gods show about the differences between Greek and Norse attitudes toward such values as justice, honesty, and moderation?

4. Vengeance is a major theme running through these stories. How many examples of it do you find? What sorts of people attach a great deal of importance to revenge? For what sorts of offense did the characters in these stories seek revenge? Was there any way other than killing that a demand for revenge could be satisfied?

5. From analyzing the character of the hero Sigurd, what do you infer were the values the Norsemen admired? Are any of these values still admired? How does Sigurd compare with the heroes in the *Iliad?*

6. Folk literature is generally characterized by directness, by action, and by a minimum of description and characterization. In what ways do these stories conform to these characteristics? Point out specific illustrations from the stories to support your answer. Did the *Epic of Gilgamesh* (see page 13) and the *Iliad* show the same characteristics? Are they more "literary" than these stories? Explain your answers.

FOR COMPOSITION

Write a paragraph of no more than 150 words in which you comment on the way Gunnar and Hogni honor their relationship to Sigurd as "sworn brothers." Explain what their behavior shows about the Viking sense of honor.

The Song of Roland

The *Song of Roland,* which might be called the national epic of France, is based on historical fact. In the year A.D. 778, Charlemagne, King of the Franks, was returning to France following an unsuccessful campaign against the Moslem Saracens in Spain. While his army was passing through the Pyrenees Mountains, the rear guard was attacked and wiped out by the local Basque inhabitants, in the valley of Roncesvalles. A number of songs about the incident grew up and spread over France in succeeding years, attaching themselves to the name of one of Charlemagne's leaders, named Hrodland, or Roland. By the latter part of the eleventh century, when the *Song of Roland* was actually composed in the form in which we have it today, the real historical events had largely been obscured or altered: the Basques had been replaced by Saracens; Roland had become a nephew of Charlemagne; the treachery of Ganelon had been introduced; and many other alterations of historical fact had been written in. But the heroic epic we are left with is a great one, and its hero, Roland, has become the model of the perfect Christian knight.

Before the following selection from the epic opens, Ganelon, Roland's stepfather, had become envious of Roland's reputation and angered because Roland recommended him for dangerous duty as Charlemagne's ambassador to the Saracen King Marsil. In his jealousy and anger, Ganelon treacherously encouraged King Marsil to attack the rear guard of Charlemagne's army with an overwhelming force— 400,000 Saracens against 20,000 Franks. He then persuaded Charlemagne to place Roland in command of the rear guard. As the following selection begins, Olivier, Roland's dearest friend and brother in arms, is trying to sight the approaching enemy.

FROM *Roncesvalles*

THE ENEMY

84

Sir Olivier° to the peak hath clomb,
Looks far on the realm of Spain therefrom;
He sees the Saracen power arrayed —
Helmets gleaming with gold inlaid,
Shields and hauberks° in serried row, 5
Spears with pennons that from them flow.

1. **Olivier** (here pronounced au·lǐ·vir′). 5. **hauberks** (hô′bûrks): long coats of chain mail.

From "The Song of Roland" translated by John O'Hagan from *The Harvard Classics,* Vol. 49, edited by Charles W. Eliot. Reprinted by permission of Crowell Collier and Macmillan, Inc.

He may not reckon the mighty mass,
So far their numbers his thought surpass.
All in bewilderment and dismay,
Down from the mountain he takes his way,   10
Comes to the Franks the tale to say.

85

"I have seen the paynim,"° said Olivier.
"Never on earth did such host appear:
A hundred thousand with targets bright,
With helmets laced and hauberks white,   15
Erect and shining their lances tall;
Such battle as waits you did ne'er befall.
My Lords of France, be God your stay,
That you be not vanquished in field today."
"Accursed," say the Franks, "be they who fly   20
None shall blench from the fear to die."

ROLAND'S PRIDE

86

"In mighty strength are the heathen crew,"
Olivier said, "and our Franks are few;
My comrade, Roland, sound on your horn;
Karl° will hear and his host return."   25
"I were mad," said Roland, "to do such deed;
Lost in France were my glory's meed.
My Durindana° shall smite full hard,
And her hilt be red to the golden guard.
The heathen felons shall find their fate;   30
Their death, I swear, in the pass they wait."

88

"Roland, Roland, yet wind one blast!
Karl will hear ere the gorge be passed,
And the Franks return on their path full fast."
"I will not sound on mine ivory horn: 35
It shall never be spoken of me in scorn,
That for heathen felons one blast I blew;
I may not dishonor my lineage true.
But I will strike, ere this fight be o'er,
A thousand strokes and seven hundred more,   40

12. **paynim** (pā′nim): pagans, that is, the Moslems.   25. **Karl:** Charlemagne (Charles the Great); *Karl* is German for "Charles."   28. **Durindana:** Roland's unbreakable sword, said to be the sword that had belonged to the Trojan hero Hector.

And my Durindana shall drip with gore.
Our Franks will bear them like vassals brave
The Saracens flock but to find a grave."

89

"I deem of neither reproach nor stain.
I have seen the Saracen host of Spain,   45
Over plain and valley and mountain spread,
And the regions hidden beneath their tread.
Countless the swarm of the foe, and we
A marvelous little company."
Roland answered him, "All the more   50
My spirit within me burns therefore.
God and his angels of heaven defend
That France through me from her glory bend.
Death were better than fame laid low.
Our emperor loveth a downright blow."   55

92

Archbishop Turpin,° above the rest,
Spurred his steed to a jutting crest.
His sermon thus to the Franks he spake:
"Lords, we are here for our monarch's sake;
Hold we for him, though our death should come;   60
Fight for the succor of Christendom.
The battle approaches—ye know it well,
For ye see the ranks of the infidel.
Cry *mea culpa,*° and lowly kneel;
I will assoil° you, your souls to heal.   65
In death ye are holy martyrs crowned."
The Franks alighted and knelt on ground;
In God's high name the host he blessed,
And for penance gave them—to smite their best.

94

Roland rideth the passes through,   70
On Veillantif, his charger true;
Girt in his harness that shone full fair,
And baronlike his lance he bare.
The steel erect in the sunshine gleamed,

---

56. **Archbishop Turpin:** Archbishop of Rheims. Though he dies in battle in this tale, he was once considered the author of a popular, pseudoliterary history of Charlemagne. He was a historical figure, a contemporary of Charles. 64. *mea culpa:* Latin for "my fault," a reference to the Act of Contrition, said by a penitent. 65. **assoil:** absolve.

With the snowwhite pennon that from it streamed;   75
The golden fringes beat on his hand.
Joyous of visage was he, and bland,
Exceeding beautiful of frame;
And his warriors hailed him with glad acclaim.
Proudly he looked on the heathen ranks,   80
Humbly and sweetly upon his Franks.
Courteously spake he, in words of grace—
"Ride, my barons, at gentle pace.
The Saracens here to their slaughter toil:
Reap we, today, a glorious spoil,   85
Never fell to monarch of France the like."
At his words, the hosts are in act to strike.

95

Said Olivier, "Idle is speech, I trow;
Thou didst disdain on thy horn to blow.
Succor of Karl is far apart;   90
Our strait he knows not, the noble heart:
Not to him nor his host be blame;
Therefore, barons, in God's good name,
Press ye onward, and strike your best,
Make your stand on this field to rest;   95
Think but of blows, both to give and take,
Never the watchword of Karl forsake."
Then from the Franks resounded high—
"Montjoie!"° Whoever had heard that cry
Would hold remembrance of chivalry.   100
Then ride they—how proudly, O God, they ride!—
With rowels° dashed in their coursers' sides.
Fearless, too, are their paynim foes.
Frank and Saracen, thus they close.

108

Mingled and marvelous grows the fray,   105
And in Roland's heart is no dismay.
He fought with lance while his good lance stood;
Fifteen encounters have strained its wood.
At the last it brake; then he grasped in hand
His Durindana, his naked brand.   110
He smote Chernubles'° helm upon,
Where, in the center, carbuncles shone:
Down through his coif and his fell of hair,

---

99. **Montjoie** (mônt·zhwä'): medieval war cry of the Franks, meaning "Mount Joy." Its origin is not definitely known. 102. **rowels:** the toothed wheels that are parts of spurs. 111. **Chernubles:** a Saracen knight.

Betwixt his eyes came the falchion° bare,
Down through his plated harness fine,   115
Down through the Saracen's chest and chine,
Down through the saddle with gold inlaid,
Till sank in the living horse the blade,
Severed the spine where no joint was found,
And horse and rider lay dead on ground.   120
"Caitiff,° thou camest in evil hour;
To save thee passeth Mohammed's power.
Never to miscreants like to thee
Shall come the guerdon° of victory."

147

Roland and Olivier then are seen   125
To lash and hew with their falchions keen;
With his lance the archbishop thrusts and slays,
And the numbers slain we may well appraise;
In charter and writ is the tale expressed—
Beyond four thousand, saith the geste.°   130
In four encounters they sped them well:
Dire and grievous the fifth befell.
The cavaliers of the Franks are slain
All but sixty, who yet remain;
God preserved them, that ere they die,   135
They may sell their lives full hardily.

THE HORN

148

As Roland gazed on his slaughtered men,
He bespake his gentle compeer again:
"Ah, dear companion, may God thee shield!
Behold, our bravest lie dead on field!   140
Well may we weep for France the fair,
Of her noble barons despoiled and bare.
Had he been with us, our king and friend!
Speak, my brother, thy counsel lend,
How unto Karl shall we tidings send?"   145
Olivier answered, "I wist not how.
Liefer death than be recreant now."

149

"I will sound," said Roland, "upon my horn,
Karl, as he passeth the gorge, to warn.
The Franks, I know, will return apace."   150

114. **falchion:** a sword with a broad, slightly curved blade. 121. **Caitiff:** scoundrel.
124. **guerdon:** reward. 130. **geste:** a romance or tale. There were many told about Roland.

Said Olivier, "Nay, it were foul disgrace
On your noble kindred to wreak such wrong;
They would bear the stain their lifetime long.
Erewhile I sought it and sued in vain;
But to sound thy horn thou wouldst not deign.   155
Not now shall mine assent be won,
Nor shall I say it is knightly done.
Lo! both your arms are streaming red."
"In sooth," said Roland, "good strokes I sped."

152

Archbishop Turpin their strife hath heard,   160
His steed with the spurs of gold he spurred,
And thus rebuked them, riding near:
"Sir Roland, and thou, Sir Olivier,
Contend not, in God's great name, I crave.
Not now availeth the horn to save;   165
And yet behoves you to wind its call,
Karl will come to avenge our fall,
Nor hence the foemen in joyance wend.
The Franks will all from their steeds descend;
When they find us slain and martyred here,   170
They will raise our bodies on mule and bier,
And, while in pity aloud they weep,
Lay us in hallowed earth to sleep;
Nor wolf nor boar on our limbs shall feed."
Said Roland, "Yea, 'tis a goodly rede."°   175

153

Then to his lips the horn he drew,
And full and lustily he blew.
The mountain peaks soared high around;
Thirty leagues was borne the sound.
Karl hath heard it, and all his band.   180
"Our men have battle," he said, "on hand."
Ganelon rose in front and cried,
"If another spake, I would say he lied."

154

With deadly travail, in stress and pain,
Count Roland sounded the mighty strain.   185
Forth from his mouth the bright blood sprang,
And his temples burst for the very pang.
On and onward was borne the blast,
Till Karl hath heard as the gorge he passed,

---

175. **rede:** advice.

And Naimes° and all his men of war.   190
"It is Roland's horn," said the emperor,
"And, save in battle, he had not blown."
"Battle," said Ganelon, "is there none.
Old are you grown—all white and hoar;
Such words bespeak you a child once more.   195
Have you, then, forgotten Roland's pride,
Which I marvel God should so long abide,
How he captured Noples° without your hest?
Forth from the city the heathen pressed,
To your vassal Roland they battle gave,   200
He slew them all with the trenchant glaive,°
Then turned the waters upon the plain,
That trace of blood might none remain.
He would sound all day for a single hare:
'Tis a jest with him and his fellows there;   205
For who would battle against him dare?
Ride onward—wherefore this chill delay?
Your mighty land is yet far away."

155

On Roland's mouth is the bloody stain,
Burst asunder his temple's vein;   210
His horn he soundeth in anguish drear;
King Karl and the Franks around him hear.
Said Karl, "That horn is long of breath."
Said Naimes, " 'Tis Roland who travaileth.
There is battle yonder by mine avow.   215
He who betrayed him deceives you now.
Arm, sire; ring forth your rallying cry,
And stand your noble household by;
For you hear your Roland in jeopardy."

156

The king commands to sound the alarm.   220
To the trumpet the Franks alight and arm;
With casque and corselet and gilded brand,
Buckler and stalwart lance in hand,
Pennons of crimson and white and blue,
The barons leap on their steeds anew,   225
And onward spur the passes through;
Nor is there one but to other saith,
"Could we reach but Roland before his death,
Blows would we strike for him grim and great."
Ah! what availeth!—'tis all too late.   230

---

190. **Naimes** (nīm): a Frankish duke and advisor to Charlemagne.   198. **Noples:** in Spain.
201. **glaive** (glāv): broadsword.

165

When the heathen saw that the Franks were few,
Heart and strength from the sight they drew;
They said, "The emperor hath the worse."
The Algalif° sat on a sorrel horse;
He pricked with spurs of the gold refined,   235
Smote Olivier in the back behind.
On through his harness the lance he pressed,
Till the steel came out at the baron's breast.
"Thou hast it!" the Algalif, vaunting, cried,
"Ye were sent by Karl in an evil tide.   240
Of his wrongs against us he shall not boast;
In thee alone I avenge our host."

166

Olivier felt the deadly wound,
Yet he grasped Hauteclère, with its steel embrowned;
He smote on the Algalif's crest of gold,   245
Gem and flowers to the earth were rolled;
Clave his head to the teeth below,
And struck him dead with the single blow.
"All evil, caitiff, thy soul pursue.
Full well our emperor's loss I knew;   250
But for thee—thou goest not hence to boast
To wife or dame on thy natal coast,
Of one denier° from the emperor won,
Or of scathe to me or to others done."
Then Roland's aid he called upon.   255

167

"Sir, my comrade, anear me ride;
This day of dolor shall us divide."

168

Roland looked Olivier in the face —
Ghastly paleness was there to trace;
Forth from his wound did the bright blood flow,   260
And rain in showers to the earth below.
"O God!" said Roland, "is this the end
Of all thy prowess, my gentle friend?

234. **Algalif:** uncle and counselor of King Mansil. 253. **denier** (də·nir´): former silver coin of France.

Nor know I whither to bear me now:
On earth shall never be such as thou.   265
Ah, gentle France, thou art overthrown,
Reft of thy bravest, despoiled and lone;
The emperor's loss is full indeed!"
At the word he fainted upon his steed.

170

Olivier feeleth his throe begin;   270
His eyes are turning his head within,
Sight and hearing alike are gone.
He alights and couches the earth upon;
His *mea culpa* aloud he cries,
And his hands in prayer unto God arise,   275
That he grant him paradise to share,
That he bless King Karl and France the fair,
His brother Roland o'er all mankind;
Then sank his heart, and his head declined,
Stretched at length on the earth he lay —   280
So passed Sir Olivier away.
Roland was left to weep alone:
Man so woeful hath ne'er been known.

172

When passed away had Roland's swoon,
With sense restored, he saw full soon   285
What ruin lay beneath his view.
His Franks have perished all save two—
The archbishop and Walter of Hum alone.

174

In Roland's sorrow his wrath arose,
Hotly he struck at the heathen foes,   290
Nor left he one of a score alive;
Walter slew six, the archbishop five.
The heathens cry, "What a felon three!
Look to it, lords, that they shall not flee.
Dastard is he who confronts them not;   295
Craven, who lets them depart this spot."
Their cries and shoutings begin once more,
And from every side on the Franks they pour.

175

Count Roland in sooth is a noble peer;
Count Walter, a valorous cavalier;   300
The archbishop, in battle proved and tried,
Each struck as if knight there were none beside.
From their steeds a thousand Saracens leap,
Yet forty thousand their saddles keep;
I trow they dare not approach them near,   305
But they hurl against them lance and spear,
Pike and javelin, shaft and dart.
Walter is slain as the missiles part;
The archbishop's shield in pieces shred,
Riven his helm, and pierced his head;   310
His corselet of steel they rent and tore,
Wounded his body with lances four;
His steed beneath him dropped withal:
What woe to see the archbishop fall!

176

When Turpin felt him flung to ground,   315
And four lance wounds within him found,
He swiftly rose, the dauntless man,
To Roland looked and nigh him ran.
Spake but, "I am not overthrown—
Brave warrior yields with life alone."   320
He drew Almace's burnished steel,
A thousand ruthless blows to deal.
In after time, the emperor said
He found four hundred round him spread —
Some wounded, others cleft in twain;   325
Some lying headless on the plain.
So Giles the saint,° who saw it, tells,
For whom High God wrought miracles.
In Laon cell the scroll he wrote;
He little weets° who knows it not.   330

177

Count Roland combateth nobly yet,
His body burning and bathed in sweat;
In his brow a mighty pain, since first,
When his horn he sounded, his temple burst;
But he yearns of Karl's approach to know,   335
And lifts his horn once more—but oh,
How faint and feeble a note to blow!
The emperor listened and stood full still.

327. **Giles the saint:** probably a monk of St. Gall who wrote the *Gesta Karali,* "the deeds of Charlemagne," a highly anecdotal and marvelous work.   330. **weets:** a form of the archaic verb *to wit,* meaning "to have knowledge of."

"My lords," he said, "we are faring ill.
This day is Roland my nephew's last;   340
Like dying man he winds that blast.
On! Who would aid, for life must press.
Sound every trump our ranks possess."
Peal sixty thousand clarions high,
The hills reecho, the vales reply.   345
It is now no jest for the heathen band.
"Karl!" they cry, "it is Karl at hand!"

178

They said, " 'Tis the emperor's advance,
We hear the trumpets resound of France.
If he assail us, hope in vain;   350
If Roland live, 'tis war again,
And we lose for aye the land of Spain."
Four hundred in arms together drew,
The bravest of the heathen crew;
With serried power they on him press,   355
And dire in sooth is the count's distress.

179

When Roland saw his coming foes,
All proud and stern his spirit rose;
Alive he shall never be brought to yield:
Veillantif spurred he across the field,   360
With golden spurs he pricked him well,
To break the ranks of the infidel;
Archbishop Turpin by his side.
"Let us flee, and save us," the heathen cried;
"These are the trumpets of France we hear—   365
It is Karl, the mighty emperor, near."

181

The heathens said, "We were born to shame.
This day for our disaster came:
Our lords and leaders in battle lost,
And Karl at hand with his marshaled host;   370
We hear the trumpets of France ring out,
And the cry *Montjoie!* their rallying shout.
Roland's pride is of such a height,
Not to be vanquished by mortal wight°;
Hurl we our missiles, and hold aloof."   375
And the word they spake, they put in proof,

374. **wight:** person.

They flung, with all their strength and craft,
Javelin, barb, and plumèd shaft.
Roland's buckler was torn and frayed,
His cuirass broken and disarrayed, 380
Yet entrance none to his flesh they made.
From thirty wounds Veillantif bled,
Beneath his rider they cast him, dead;
Then from the field have the heathen flown:
Roland remaineth, on foot, alone. 385

THE LAST BENEDICTION OF THE ARCHBISHOP

182

The heathens fly in rage and dread;
To the land of Spain have their footsteps sped;
Nor can Count Roland make pursuit—
Slain is his steed, and he rests afoot;
To succor Turpin he turned in haste, 390
The golden helm from his head unlaced,
Ungirt the corselet from his breast,
In stripes divided his silken vest;
The archbishop's wounds hath he staunched and bound,
His arms around him softly wound; 395
On the green sward gently his body laid,
And, with tender greeting, thus him prayed:
"For a little space, let me take farewell;
Our dear companions, who round us fell,
I go to seek; if I haply find, 400
I will place them at thy feet reclined."
"Go," said Turpin; "the field is thine—
To God the glory, 'tis thine and mine."

185

Dead around him his peers to see,
And the man he loved so tenderly, 405
Fast the tears of Count Roland ran,
His visage discolored became, and wan,
He swooned for sorrow beyond control.
"Alas," said Turpin, "how great thy dole!"

186

To look on Roland swooning there, 410
Surpassed all sorrow he ever bare;
He stretched his hand, the horn he took —
Through Roncesvalles there flowed a brook —

A draught to Roland he thought to bring;
But his steps were feeble and tottering,   415
Spent his strength, from waste of blood —
He struggled on for scarce a rood,
When sank his heart and drooped his frame,
And his mortal anguish on him came.

187

Roland revived from his swoon again;   420
On his feet he rose, but in deadly pain;
He looked on high, and he looked below,
Till, a space his other companions fro,
He beheld the baron, stretched on sward,
The archbishop, vicar of God our Lord.   425
Mea culpa was Turpin's cry,
While he raised his hands to heaven on high,
Imploring paradise to gain.
So died the soldier of Charlemagne —
With word or weapon, to preach or fight,   430
A champion ever of Christian right,
And a deadly foe of the infidel.
God's benediction within him dwell!

THE DEATH OF ROLAND

189

Roland feeleth his death is near,
His brain is oozing by either ear.   435
For his peers he prayed—God keep them well;
Invoked the angel Gabriel.
That none reproach him, his horn he clasped;
His other hand Durindana grasped;
Then, far as quarrel° from crossbow sent,   440
Across the march° of Spain he went,
Where, on a mound, two trees between,
Four flights of marble steps were seen;
Backward he fell, on the field to lie;
And he swooned anon, for the end was nigh.   445

190

High were the mountains and high the trees,
Bright shone the marble terraces;
On the green grass Roland hath swooned away.

440. **quarrel:** an arrow with a four-edged head.   441. **march:** border.

A Saracen spied him where he lay:
Stretched with the rest he had feigned him dead,   450
His face and body with blood bespread.
To his feet he sprang, and in haste he hied —
He was fair and strong and of courage tried,
In pride and wrath he was overbold —
And on Roland, body and arms, laid hold.   455
"The nephew of Karl is overthrown!
To Araby bear I this sword, mine own."
He stooped to grasp it, but as he drew,
Roland returned to his sense anew.

191

He saw the Saracen seize his sword;   460
His eyes he oped, and he spake one word—
"Thou art not one of our band, I trow,"
And he clutched the horn he would ne'er forego;
On the golden crest he smote him full,
Shattering steel and bone and skull,   465
Forth from his head his eyes he beat,
And cast him lifeless before his feet.
"Miscreant, makest thou then so free,
As, right or wrong, to lay hold on me?
Who hears it will deem thee a madman born;   470
Behold the mouth of mine ivory horn
Broken for thee, and the gems and gold
Around its rim to earth are rolled."

195

That death was on him he knew full well;
Down from his head to his heart it fell.   475
On the grass beneath a pine tree's shade,
With face to earth, his form he laid,
Beneath him placed he his horn and sword,
And turned his face to the heathen horde.
Thus hath he done the sooth° to show,   480
That Karl and his warriors all may know,
That the gentle count a conqueror died.
Mea culpa full oft he cried;
And, for all his sins, unto God above,
In sign of penance, he raised his glove.   485

480. **sooth:** truth.

196

Roland feeleth his hour at hand;
On a knoll he lies towards the Spanish land.
With one hand beats he upon his breast:
"In thy sight, O God, be my sins confessed.
From my hour of birth, both the great and small,   490
Down to this day, I repent of all."
As his glove he raises to God on high,
Angels of heaven descend him nigh.

197

Beneath a pine was his resting place,
To the land of Spain hath he turned his face,   495
On his memory rose full many a thought—
Of the lands he won and the fields he fought;
Of his gentle France, of his kin and line;
Of his nursing father, King Karl benign —
He may not the tear and sob control,   500
Nor yet forgets he his parting soul.
To God's compassion he makes his cry:
"O Father true, who canst not lie,
Who didst Lazarus raise unto life again,
And Daniel shield in the lions' den;   505
Shield my soul from its peril, due
For the sins I sinned my lifetime through."
He did his right-hand glove uplift—
Saint Gabriel took from his hand the gift;
Then drooped his head upon his breast,   510
And with claspèd hands he went to rest.
God from on high sent down to him
One of his angel Cherubim—
Saint Michael of Peril of the sea,
Saint Gabriel in company—   515
From heaven they came for that soul of price,
And they bore it with them to paradise.

FOR STUDY AND DISCUSSION

1. Roland is generally regarded as the prototype of the perfect Christian knight. List at least three of Roland's qualities that would personify such a knight.

2. It sometimes surprises modern readers to find an official of the Church, like Archbishop Turpin, a warrior as well. On the basis of what you have read here, how do you believe medieval men justified this common practice?

3. The chivalric code gave great attention to the concept of personal honor. Find examples in which concern for honor determines the conduct of Roland and Olivier.

4. What is the actual cause of Roland's death? Can you see any reasons for having him die this way? How does the cause of his death relate to his not re-sounding the horn?

5. Contrast Roland and Achilles (see page 55) as examples of tragic heroes. What fault do they share? How do their codes of honor differ?

6. Like other *chansons de geste*, this epic portrays superbly the values of the feudal military class. Describe and comment on these values. Does Roland submit to religion as a guide to life, or does he seem to use it as an excuse for fighting? Explain.

Compare the two translations of stanza 87 below. The first is from the translation used in the text; the second from another translation.

● "O Roland, sound on your ivory horn,
To the ear of Karl shall the blast be borne:
He will bid his legions backward bend,
And all his barons their aid will lend."
"Now God forbid it, for very shame,
That for me my kindred were stained with blame,
Or that gentle France to such vileness fell:
This good sword that hath served me well,
My Durindana such strokes shall deal,
That with blood encrimsoned shall be the steel.
By their evil star are the felons led;
They shall all be numbered among the dead." * *(Translated by John O'Hagan)*

● "Roland, dear comrade, wind your ivory horn!
And Charles, though far away in France, shall hear,
With all his host shall come to succor us."
But Roland answered, saying: "God forbid
That I bring low my kindred, or become
The instrument of my dear land's dishonor.
Nay, rather shall I draw my sword, my tried
And trusted Durendal, and you shall see
Drenched in red blood the gleaming blade thereof.

The wretched Paynims here in Ronceval
Shall meet their doom—I pledge you, they shall die!"°
(Translated by Frederick Luquiens)

What effect do the rhyming couplets of the text's translation have on the movement of the narrative? The diction of the unrhymed translation is simpler. Compare such phrases as "with blood encrimsoned" and "drenched in red blood"; "gentle France to such vileness fell" and "my dear land's dishonor." Which use of language, in your opinion, tells the story better? Which translation makes you feel as if you are reading something from an old oral tradition? Why does that translation have this effect? Point out other differences in the diction of these two translations.

FOR COMPOSITION

1. In a paragraph of no more than 150 words, explain whether or not you believe that in this story death was a defeat for the hero. Give reasons for your answer. Compare Roland's attitude toward death with that of Gilgamesh (see page 13).

2. In going from the tale of Sigurd to the tale of Roland, we go from an account of a pagan hero to an account of a Christian knight. In an essay of no more than 500 words, analyze the differences and similarities that you find in these heroes and in the tone and content of their stories.

* From "The Song of Roland" translated by John O'Hagan from *The Harvard Classics,* Vol. 49, edited by Charles W. Eliot. Reprinted by permission of Crowell Collier and Macmillian, Inc.

° Stanza from the *Song of Roland,* translated by Frederick Bliss Luquiens, copyright 1952 by The Macmillan Company. Reprinted by permission of the publisher.

Perceval

CHRÉTIEN DE TROYES

Few facts are known about the life of Chrétien de Troyes, one of the most famous of French medieval poets, except that he lived in the twelfth century, was a native of Champagne, and wrote five of the most popular of the long romances concerned with knights of King Arthur's court. He apparently depended on traditional Celtic or Breton materials, perhaps already put into French by an earlier poet, but the lightness and freshness of the narratives are his own.

Unlike the two epics you have just read, which present great events or heroic deeds told in elevated style, romances are simply long narratives of exciting or marvelous adventures, told to entertain. The selection which follows comes from *Perceval, or the Story of the Grail,* a romance which Chrétien wrote at the request of Philip, Count of Flanders. It tells the story of a crude, naive young Welshman who becomes the most famous knight of his day. The passage which follows appears early in the story, when Perceval is seeking to become a knight.

MEANWHILE, THE YOUTH rode on until he saw a charcoal-burner approaching, driving an ass before him. "Carl,[1] you there, driving the ass, show me the shortest way to Carlisle. They tell me that there King Arthur, whom I want to see, makes knights."

"Young sir, in that direction there is a castle standing by the sea. If you go there, good friend, you will find King Arthur in the castle, both happy and sad."

"Now tell me what I want to know, how the king can be both happy and sad."

"I will tell you very quickly. King Arthur with all his army has fought with King Rion, and the King of the Isles was beaten, and it is that which makes King Arthur glad. He is angry with his companions who have gone back to their castles where they find it pleasanter to live, and he does not know what has happened to them. That makes the king sad."

The youth did not care a penny for the information, except that he took the road which the charcoal-burner had shown. He saw a splendid, strong castle, well situated above the sea, and presently descried issuing from the gate an armed knight bearing a golden cup in his hand. With his left hand he held his lance, bridle, and shield, and the golden cup in his right. His arms, all scarlet, became him well. The youth, seeing the fresh, handsome arms, was pleased and said to himself: "By my faith, I will ask the king for these. If he gives them to me, I shall be well satisfied, and a curse on him who would want any others!"

At once, feeling impatient to reach the court, he rode rapidly toward the castle until he met the knight, who stopped him for a moment and asked: "Young sir, where are you going, tell me?"

---

[1] **Carl:** "peasant," from an Old Norse word for "freeman."

"I am going to court to ask the king for these arms of yours."

"Young sir, it is right for you to do so. Go quickly and return. Tell the evil king if he will not hold his land as my vassal, let him yield it, or let him send someone out to defend it against me, for I declare that it is mine. Let him believe you by this token that just now I seized in his presence, the cup I am carrying, with all the wine he was drinking."

The knight might better have found someone else to take the message, for the youth did not listen to a word, but hastened to the court where the king and the knights were seated at their repast. He rode into the hall, which was on the ground level, paved and as long as wide. King Arthur sat at the head of the table, sunk in thought; all the rest talked and amused themselves, save him who remained pensive and mute. The youth advanced, but he did not know whom to greet, for he did not recognize the king. Yonet, holding a knife in his hand, came to meet him. The newcomer said: "Young sir, you there, with the knife in your hand, show me who is the king."

Yonet was very courteous and replied: "Friend, behold him there."

The youth rode at once toward the king and greeted him as best as he knew how. The king remained brooding and uttered no word. Again the youth spoke; still the king brooded and uttered no sound.

"By my faith," said the youth then, "this king never made a knight! When I cannot drag a word out of him, how could he make a knight?"

Preparing to depart, the youth turned the head of his hunter, but, like an idiot, he had brought him so close to the king that actually the horse knocked the cap off his head onto the table. The king raised his head, turned toward the youth, and, dismissing his cares, said: "Good brother, welcome! Pray do not take it ill that I met your greeting with silence. Anger kept me from replying. My worst enemy, who hates and terrifies me most, has even here laid claim to my land and is so

mad as to threaten to take it, whether I will or no. He is called the Red Knight of the Forest of Quinqueroi. The queen had come to sit with me in order to see and comfort these wounded knights. That knight would not have roused my anger, whatever he said, but he snatched the cup before me and raised it so wildly that all the wine with which it was filled poured over the queen. That was a vile and churlish deed! Therefore the queen, burning with sorrow and anger, has gone to her chamber, where she will die. So help me God, I do not believe she can escape alive."

The youth did not care an onion for what the king said; nor did his grief nor the queen's humiliation make any impression. "Make me a knight, sir King," said he, "because I am eager to be gone."

The eyes in the countenance of the young barbarian were bright and smiling. Though no one who saw him thought him other than mad, all found him handsome and noble. "Friend, ' said the king, "dismount and give your hunter to this squire, who will care for it and perform your pleasure. I vow to God that your request shall be granted, to my honor and to your profit."

The youth answered: "The knights I met in the glade did not dismount, and you want me to dismount? But knight me quickly and then I will go."

"Ah," said the king, "dear good friend, I will do it gladly, to your profit and my honor."

"By the faith I owe my Maker, good sir King," said the youth, "I will never be a knight unless I am a red knight. Give me the arms of the man I met outside the gate who was carrying away your golden cup."

The seneschal,[1] who was wounded, was angry at what he heard and said: "Friend, you are right. Go at once and take away his arms, for they are yours. You were no fool when you came here to get them."

"Kay," said the king, "in God's name, I beg you. You are too ready to mock and

[1] **seneschal** (sen′ə·shəl): the official in charge of feasts, etc.

do not care who is the butt. It is unbecoming a gentleman. If the youth is simpleminded, he is still, I think, well born. If he has been thus trained by a boorish master, he may yet prove brave and wise. It is churlish to make a jest of others and to promise without giving. A gentleman should not promise anything that he cannot or will not bestow, for he earns the ill will of him who, but for that promise, would be his friend and who, after the promise is made, expects it to be kept. You should learn that it is better to refuse outright than to rouse vain expectations. To tell the truth, he mocks and deceives himself who promises and does not fulfill, for he loses the heart of his friend."

Thus the king rebuked Kay. As the youth departed, ... Yonet, who knew all the shortest passages and was eager to bring news to the court, ran alone through a garden beside the hall and descended through a postern till he came to the road just where the Red Knight was waiting for a knightly adventure. The Welsh youth now approached at high speed to seize his arms. The knight, while waiting, had set down the golden cup on a block of brown stone. As soon as the youth came within hearing, he cried: "Lay down your weapons! Carry them no longer, for King Arthur sends you this order!"

The knight inquired: "Young sir, does no one dare to come here to uphold the king's cause? If so, do not hide it from me."

"What the devil! Are you jesting with me, sir knight, that you have not yet stripped off my arms? Take them off at once, I command you."

"Young sir, I ask you whether anyone is coming on the king's behalf to fight with me."

"Sir knight, take off the arms at once, or I will take them off myself, for I will not let you keep them longer. Understand me, I will strike you if you make me talk any more about it."

Then the knight was furious, raised his lance with both hands, and gave the youth a blow across the shoulders with the butt, so that he made him crouch over the neck of his horse. The youth, enraged in his turn when he felt himself bruised by the stroke, aimed as well as he could at the knight's eye and let fly a javelin. It struck him through the eye and brain, so that he saw and heard no more, and the blood and brains oozed out at the nape of his neck. With the agony his heart stopped, and he fell full length to the earth. The youth alighted, laid the lance aside, took the shield from his neck, but could not remove the helm from his head, for he did not know how to grasp it. He sought to ungird the sword, but he did not know how, and he could not draw it from the sheath, but grasped the sheath and pulled and pulled.

Yonet began to laugh when he saw the youth so occupied. "What is it, friend?" he said; "what are you doing?"

"I do not know. I thought your king had given me these arms, but I will have to cut up the dead man for chops before I can get any of them, for they stick so to the body that the inside and the outside seem to be of one piece; they hold together so fast."

"Do not vex yourself," said Yonet, "for I will separate them if you wish."

"Do so then at once," said the youth, "and give them to me without delay."

Yonet promptly stripped the body, even down to the toes, removing coat and hose of mail, helmet, and every other piece of armor. But the youth would not take off his own garments, nor, in spite of anything Yonet said, would he put on the comfortable padded silk tunic which the knight had worn under his coat of mail; nor would he remove the brogues from his own feet, but said: "What the devil! are you mocking me? Change my good clothes that my mother made for me the other day for the clothes of this knight? Do you wish me to put off my thick shirt of hemp for this soft thin one, and my jacket that keeps out the water for this that will not stop a drop? Shame on his neck who would exchange his good clothes for another's bad ones!"

It is a hard task to teach a fool. The lad would take nothing but the arms and would heed no request. Yonet laced the mail hose on his legs, attached the spurs to his brogues, then put on the coat of mail so that none ever looked better, fitted the helm over the padded skullcap becomingly, and showed how to gird on the sword so that it swung loosely. Then he placed the lad's foot in the stirrup and made him mount the war horse. The youth had never seen a stirrup before and was not used to spurs but only to whip or willow switch. Yonet brought the shield and lance and handed them over to him. Before Yonet departed, the youth said: "Friend, take my hunter and lead him away, for he is a very good one. I give him to you because I have no more need of him. And take the cup to the king and greet him for me. . . ."

Yonet replied that he would return the cup to the king and carry the message faithfully. So the two parted. Yonet entered through the door the hall where the barons were gathered, bringing the cup back to the king, and said: "Sire, rejoice now, for your knight who was here returns your cup to you."

"Of what knight do you speak?" said the king, who was still in a rage of anger.

"In God's name, sire," said Yonet, "I speak of the youth who but now departed."

"Do you speak," said the king, "of the Welsh youth who asked me for the red-colored arms of the knight who has many times done all he could to humiliate me?"

"Sire, indeed it is he."

"How did he recover my cup? Did the knight love him or prize him so much that he yielded it of his free will?"

"Nay; rather, the youth made him pay dearly, for he killed the knight."

"How was that, good friend?"

"Sire, I know only that the knight struck the youth a painful blow with his lance, and the youth struck him back with a javelin through the eyehole so that the blood and the brains flowed out behind and hurled him dead to the earth."

Then the king said to the seneschal: "Ah, Kay, what harm you have done me today! By your evil tongue, so ready with idle chatter, you have driven away a knight who this day has done me great service."

. . . Meanwhile, the youth, without a pause, went spurring through the forest till he came to a plain bordering a river which was wider than a crossbow shot, for all the water of the countryside flowed through its bed. He crossed a meadow toward the great rushing river but he did not descend into it, for he saw that it was very deep and black and swifter than the Loire. So he followed the bank. Opposite, there was a tall cliff whose base was washed by the stream, and on the side which sloped toward the sea there stood a noble, strong castle. Where the river entered the bay the youth turned to the left and saw the towers of the castle, which seemed to him to grow out of the castle. In the middle stood a huge and mighty keep. Toward the bay, where the river fought with the tide, stood a strong barbican,[1] and the waves beat against its foot. At the four corners of the walls, built of hard stone, there were four low turrets, strong and fair. The castle was finely situated and well furnished within. In front of a round outwork a bridge of sandstone and limestone was built across the river, strong, high, with battlemented parapets, and in the middle a tower. At the near end was a drawbridge, fitted for its purpose, to serve as a passageway by day and as a closed gate by night. The youth proceeded to the bridge.

On it a lord, clad in an ermine robe, was pacing for his pleasure, and he waited the approach of the newcomer. He was holding for dignity's sake a short staff, and near him were two squires without mantles. The newcomer remembered well his mother's lesson, for he bowed to the lord and said: "Sir, my mother taught me that."

"God bless you, fair brother!" said the lord, who perceived that the stranger was

[1] **barbican:** outer fortification.

uncouth and silly of speech, and he added: "Fair brother, whence have you come?"

"Whence? From King Arthur's court."

"What did you do there?"

"The king made me a knight, good luck to him!"

"A knight? God save me, but I did not think that at this time his mind was on such things. I thought rather that he was concerned with other matters than making knights. Now tell me, gentle brother, who gave you these arms?"

"The king gave them to me."

"Gave them? How?"

The youth related what you have already heard; to retell it would be tedious and futile, for no story gains by repetition. The lord then asked what he did with his horse.

"I make him run up hill and down dale, just as I used to make the hunter I had in my mother's house."

"Tell me also, fair friend, what you can do with your arms."

"I know well how to put them on and take them off, just as the squire did who put them on me and took them off the knight whom I had killed. And they are so light to wear that they do not tire me at all."

"By God's soul," said the lord, "that I am glad to hear. Now tell me, if it does not annoy you, what errand brought you here."

"Sir, my mother taught me to go to men of rank to get their advice and to trust it, because good comes to those who believe them."

The lord replied: "Fair brother, blessed be your mother, for she gave you sound counsel. But have you more to say?"

"Yes."

"What?"

"Only this and no more: that you give me lodging tonight."

"Gladly," said the lord; "but grant me a favor which will bring you much good."

"What is it?"

"That you take your mother's advice and mine."

"By my faith, I grant it."

"Then dismount."

The youth dismounted, and one of the two squires who had come up took his horse and the other removed his arms, so that he stood in his rude costume, with the brogues and in the ill-made and ill-fitting coat of buckskin which his mother had given him. The lord then had the sharp steel spurs which the youth had brought attached to his own feet, mounted the horse, hung the shield by the strap around his neck, grasped the lance, and said: "Friend, now take a lesson in arms and watch how to hold a lance and how to spur and check a horse."

Then he displayed the pennon and showed how to hold the shield, a little forward so that it touched the horse's neck. He laid the lance in rest and pricked the horse, worth a hundred marks, which no other surpassed for ardor, speed, and strength. The lord was skilled in the management of shield, horse, and lance, since he had been trained in it from boyhood. All that he did delighted the youth, and when he had finished his expert tilting before the youth, who had watched it closely, he returned with his lance upright and inquired: "Friend, would you too like to know how to manage lance and shield and how to spur and control a horse?"

The youth answered at once that he did not care to live another day or to own wealth or lands before he had learned how to do the same. The lord said: "Dear good friend, what one does not know one can learn if he will take the pains. Every profession demands effort, heart, and practice; every knowledge comes by these three. But since you have never done these things nor seen others do them, you cannot be shamed or blamed if you do not know how."

Then the lord caused the youth to mount, and he began to carry lance and shield as adroitly as if he had passed all his days in tourneys and wars and had journeyed throughout the world seeking battle and adventure. For it came to him by nature, and when nature teaches and the heart attends, nothing can be too hard.

With the aid of these two, the youth performed so well that it greatly pleased the lord, and he said in his heart that if his pupil had devoted all his life to arms, he would have become a master. When the youth had carried out the exercise, he returned to the lord with his lance erect as he had seen it held, and said: "Sir, did I do well? Do you think that I will learn it if I take pains? My eyes have never seen anything that I am so eager to master. I long to know as much about it as you do."

"Friend," said the lord, "if you set your heart on it, you will learn without any difficulty."

Three times the lord mounted and three times showed all he knew of the handling of arms till he thought it was enough, and three times he made the youth mount. After the last he said: "Friend, if you met a knight and he struck you, what would you do?"

"I would strike him back."

"And if your lance broke?"

"Then there would be nothing to do but to attack him with my fists."

"Friend, never do that."

"What should I do?"

"You must use your sword and fence with him."

Then the lord planted the lance in the ground, for he wished to teach him how to defend himself with the sword or to attack with it, as circumstances required. He grasped the sword and said: "In this way you should defend yourself if anyone assails you."

"As for that, so God save me, no one knows more than I, because I have often practiced on cushions and shields at my mother's house until I was tired out."

"Then let us go inside," said the lord, "for there is no other lodging, and, whoever may object, you will enjoy no mean hospitality tonight."

Then, as the two went in, side by side, the youth said to his host: "Sir, my mother taught me that I should never be long in the company of anyone without knowing his name; so, as my mother taught me, I would ask your name."

"Fair sweet friend," said the lord, "my name is Gornemant of Gohort."

They entered hand in hand, and as they mounted the steps a squire of his own accord came running with a short mantle, which he cast over the youth that he might not, after the heat of exercise, take a bad cold. The buildings of the lord were rich and large, his servants pleasant to look upon, and an excellent meal was prepared. So the knights washed and sat down to eat. The lord seated the youth beside him and caused him to eat from the same dish. I will not say how many courses they had or what they were, but they had plenty to eat and drink; I do not need to tell more of the repast.

. . . Early on the morrow the lord arose and went where he found the youth lying in bed, and brought him as a present a shirt and breeches of fine linen, hose dyed red, and a tunic of indigo silk woven in India. He told him to put them on, saying: "Friend, if you trust me, dress yourself in the clothes you see here."

The youth answered: "Fair sir, surely you could give me better advice, for the clothes that my mother made me, are they not better than these, and yet you wish me to put these on?"

"Young sir," said the lord, "by my head, they are worse. You promised me, good friend, when I brought you here that you would obey all my orders."

"I will do so," said the youth; "I will not oppose you."

Without a pause he donned the new clothes and left those of his mother. The lord, bending over, fastened on his heel the right spur, such was the custom for him who made a knight. Many squires were present and each, as opportunity offered, helped in the arming. The lord took the sword, girded it on the youth, kissed him, and said that with the sword he had given him the highest order that God had made and decreed—namely, the stainless order of knighthood. He continued: "Remember this, fair brother, I pray you: If it happens that in combat with a knight you gain the upper hand and he is unable to defend himself longer, have mercy on him and do not kill him wittingly. Beware also of talking too much and of gossiping. No one can talk too much without saying something rude. The wise man declares: 'He who talks too much commits sin.' Therefore, fair brother, I forbid you to talk overmuch. Moreover, I beg you, if you find man or woman, whether damsel or lady, in distress, advise them so far as you can and if you have the power to help. One more thing I would have you learn, and do not despise it, for it is not to be scorned. Go to the minster [1] and pray to him who made all things to have mercy on your soul and to keep you a good Christian in this earthly life."

The youth said to the lord: "Good sir, may you be blessed by all the apostles of Rome! That is what I once heard my mother say."

"Now, fair brother," said the lord, "hereafter do not keep saying that your mother taught you this or that. Till now I do not blame you at all, but, begging your pardon, I ask that henceforth you correct yourself, for if you persist you will be taken for a fool. So I pray you, avoid it."

"What shall I say then, good sir?"

"You may say that the vavasor [2] who buckled on your spur taught you so."

The youth promised that he would never as long as he lived utter a word of any other master, for he saw clearly that the lord's teaching was good. His host then made the sign of the cross over him and, with hand uplifted, said: "Fair sir, God preserve you! Adieu, and may he guide you. . . ."

[1] **minster:** monastery.
[2] **vavasor:** a principal vassal, just below a baron.

FOR STUDY AND DISCUSSION

1. Perceval is obviously, at this point in the story, little more than a country bumpkin. For example, his rudeness in answering the wandering knight's questions mark him as lacking exposure to fine company. Is it possible to see, in spite of this, some of the qualities which will make him a good knight? Explain your answer.

2. What does Perceval's expertise with the javelin indicate about his interests? How does it show his individuality as a knight?

3. According to this source, what were the steps involved in "making a knight"? How do Roland's values (see page 377) compare with those taught to Perceval? Are there any indications in the story that Perceval is as religious as Roland was? Explain.

4. Chrétien de Troyes had a good sense of comedy, which gives a pleasant lightness to his style. Part of his humor results from the contrast between the impressive and the ridiculous. For example, how does the magnificence of the knights contrast with the conversations they have with Perceval? Also, there is good use of comic detail, as when Perceval's horse knocks the king's cap off. Find other examples of these humorous devices. Does such humor seem out of place in an Arthurian tale, or does it help to serve a purpose? Explain your answers.

5. What other details in the story make the characters, especially Perceval, seem real? What details make the youth a typical adolescent?

6. In this account of knightly adventure, very little space is given to fighting, but what little description we have is typically bloody. Does such gory detail seem out of place here? Does it suggest something about the sources the author relied on? Explain.

7. How does this account compare with other stories about Arthur you have read? How does it differ in tone from the selection from the *Song of Roland?*

The Divine Comedy

DANTE ALIGHIERI

Dante Alighieri (1265–1321) was born in Florence of an old and moderately distinguished family. From an early age he wrote poetry and associated himself with the literary people of Florence, but his life was not limited to the pursuit of the arts. His was a time of political turbulence, and Florence was torn by civil war three times during his residence there. He may have participated in the fighting at least once himself. Certainly he became deeply involved in the political life of the city and, as an elected official, sought to end Florence's civil strife, going so far on one occasion as to exile his best friend and some of his wife's relatives because of their part in the conflict. Dante was strongly opposed to the involvement of the Pope and the Church in political conflicts. He came to wish for a strongly renewed Roman Empire as the temporal authority over men and for a purified Church as the spiritual authority for men. In 1301, while Dante was out of Florence on an official mission, the city was seized by his political enemies, and in his absence he was sentenced to die. He never returned to his beloved city but lived the rest of his life in exile. Where he lived and whether he saw his wife and children again after leaving Florence are not surely known. What is known is that he died in Ravenna, where he is buried, and that during his exile he completed his great poetic achievement, the *Divine Comedy,* which shows the influence of his political beliefs and experiences.

The *Divine Comedy* is the supreme and culminating work of medieval thought. This complex, symbolic poem is considered by many people to be the greatest poem ever written in any language. In three canticles, Dante tells of an imaginary journey which takes him through hell, purgatory, and heaven. In the course of his journey, Dante gives expression to nearly every major intellectual conception achieved in the Middle Ages.

The first canticle, Inferno, which tells of Dante's trip through hell, is the best known and most graphically dramatic of the three canticles. The beginning of the canticle finds Dante, symbolizing mankind, lost in the "dark wood" of worldliness and sin. In heaven his plight is observed. Through the intercession of the Virgin Mary and of Dante's dead love Beatrice, the spirit of Virgil (whom Dante sees as the greatest poet who lived before the time of Christ) is summoned from limbo to lead Dante on the journey that can save him. Virgil, symbolizing human reason, is to lead Dante through hell and purgatory. Because human reason can take a man only so far, Virgil must let Beatrice, symbolizing divine revelation, lead Dante through heaven. What Dante learns of sin in viewing the hopeless agonies of hell, of renunciation in viewing the trials of purgatory, and of joy in viewing the glories of heaven will turn him forever from error.

Canto 3: The Entrance

[As this canto opens, Dante stands with Virgil, whom he calls Master, in a kind of vestibule to hell. This is the place allotted to those who were opportunists in life, persons who took no moral positions, either good or bad, but instead pursued their own advantages. Punishments in eternity are symbolically appropriate to the sin being punished; thus the opportunists are welcome neither in heaven nor in hell. They spend eternity on the edge of hell, pursuing an eternally circling and elusive banner, symbolic of their own imagined advantages. Stung by wasps and hornets, symbolic of their guilty consciences, they move endlessly through filth formed by tears, blood, and putrid matter, filth which symbolizes the moral filth of their lives.

Dante and Virgil are now before this vestibule to hell, reading the inscription on the gate to the underworld.]

THROUGH ME YOU GO INTO THE CITY OF GRIEF,
   THROUGH ME YOU GO INTO THE PAIN THAT IS ETERNAL,
   THROUGH ME YOU GO AMONG PEOPLE LOST.

JUSTICE MOVED MY EXALTED CREATOR;
   THE DIVINE POWER MADE ME,   5
   THE SUPREME WISDOM, AND THE PRIMAL LOVE.

BEFORE ME ALL CREATED THINGS WERE ETERNAL,
   AND ETERNAL I WILL LAST.
   ABANDON EVERY HOPE, YOU WHO ENTER HERE.

These words of a dark coloring   10
   I saw written above a gate; whereupon I said,
   "Master, their meaning is hard for me."

Then he spoke like one who understands:
   "Here you must give up all distrust,
   here all cowardice must end.   15

We have come to the place where I said
   that you would see the woeful people
   who have lost the good of the intellect."

And after he had taken me by the hand,
   with a cheerful look which comforted me,   20
   he drew me within the secret place.

There, sighs, lamentations, and deep wailings
   resounded through the starless air,
   so that at first I began to weep.

From "Inferno" from *The Divine Comedy* by Dante Alighieri, translated by H. R. Huse, Rinehart Edition, copyright 1954 by H. R. Huse. Reprinted by permission of Holt, Rinehart and Winston, Inc.

Diverse tongues, horrible languages,
　　words of pain, accents of rage,
　　voices loud and hoarse, and the sounds of blows

made a tumult which moved forever
　　in that air unchanged by time,
　　as sand eddies in a whirlwind.

And I said, my head girt with horror,
　　"Master, what is it that I hear,
　　and who are these people so overcome by pain?"

Then he to me, "This miserable fate
　　afflicts the wretched souls of those
　　who lived without infamy and without praise.

They are joined with that choir of wicked angels
　　who were neither rebellious
　　nor faithful to God, but for themselves.

The heavens, to remain beautiful, drove them out,
　　nor would deep hell receive them
　　lest the wicked gain pride by comparison."

And I, "Master, what is so burdensome
　　that it makes them lament loudly?"
　　He answered, "Briefly I will tell you.

They have no hope of death,
　　and their blind life is so debased
　　that they are envious of every other lot.

The world does not grant them any fame;
　　pity and justice° alike disdain them.
　　Let us not speak of them, but look and pass on."

And I, looking, saw a banner
　　which, circling, moved so fast
　　that it seemed to scorn all rest,

and behind it came such a throng of people
　　that I never would have believed
　　that death could have undone so many.

After I had recognized some of them,
　　I saw and knew the shade of him
　　who, through cowardice, made the great refusal.°

25

30

35

40

45

50

55

60

---

50. **pity and justice:** heaven and hell.　60. This reference is generally believed to be to
Pope Celestine V, who, fearing his own soul would be corrupted by worldliness, abdicated in
favor of Pope Boniface VIII, who became a political enemy of Dante's and who represented
to him the worst sort of evil secularization of the Church.

At once I understood and was certain
    that this was the sect of the wicked
    displeasing both to God and to his enemies.

These wretches, who had never really lived,   65
    were naked and stung constantly
    by hornets and wasps that were there.

These made their faces stream with blood
    which, mixed with tears, was consumed
    by loathsome maggots at their feet.

When I began to look farther on   70
    I saw people on the shore of a great river;
    whereupon I said, "Master, now grant

that I should know who they are
    and what makes them so ready to pass over,
    as I discern through the faint light."   75

And he to me, "These things will be known to you
    when we stay our steps
    on the sad bank of the Acheron."°

Then with eyes ashamed and lowered,
    fearing that my words might have offended him,   80
    I kept from speaking until we reached the stream.

And behold! coming toward us in a skiff
    an old man, white with ancient locks,
    shouting, "Woe to you, depraved spirits;

hope not ever to see heaven.   85
    I come to take you to the other shore
    into eternal darkness, into heat and cold.

And you there, living soul,
    get away from these who are dead."
    But when he saw that I did not leave,   90

"By another way, at other ports," he said,
    "you will come ashore, not here;
    a lighter boat will carry you."

And my guide, "Charon,° do not be disturbed;
    this is wished for where the power is   95
    to do what is wished;° and ask no more."

78. **Acheron:** the river which encircles the edge of hell. In Greek mythology, it is also one
of the rivers of the underworld.   94. **Charon** (kâr′ən): the ferryman who carries the dead
across the Acheron into hell. Dante has also retained him from classical mythology.
95–96. **where the power is to do what is wished:** that is, heaven. The names of Christ, God, and
heaven are never uttered in hell.

Then were quieted the woolly cheeks
    of the boatman of the livid marsh
    who, around his eyes, had rings of flame.

But those weary and naked souls   100
    changed color and gnashed their teeth
    as soon as they heard the cruel words.

They cursed God and their parents,
    the human race, and the place, time, and seed
    of their begetting and of their birth.   105

Then, all together they withdrew,
    weeping loudly, to the accursed shore
    which awaits every man without fear of God.

Charon the demon, with eyes like glowing coals,
    beckoning to them, gathered them in,   110
    and hit with an oar any who delayed.

As in autumn the leaves fall
    one after the other, until the branch
    sees all its spoils upon the ground,

so, the evil seed of Adam   115
    fell to that shore, one by one, and at signals,
    as the falcon does at its recall.

Thus they go over the dark water,
    and before they have landed on the other shore,
    again on this side a new crowd assembles.   120

"My son," said the courteous master,
    "those who die in the wrath of God
    gather here from every country,

and they are ready to pass the river,
    for divine justice so spurs them   125
    that fear is changed into desire.°

Along here no good spirit ever passes;
    therefore, if Charon complains of you,
    you can understand what his words imply."

When he had ended, the dark country   130
    trembled so that from fright
    my memory bathes me still with sweat.

---

126. Dante is saying that the condemned sinners have actually chosen hell; they have free will and were free to sin or not to sin.

The tearful land produced a blast
        which flashed a crimson light
        conquering all my senses;   135

and I fell, like one overcome by sleep.

FROM *Canto 4: Limbo*

[Dante's hell is like a deep funnel which winds down to the very center of the
earth. Around this abysmal cavity run nine ledges, or circles, which grow ever narrower as the cavity bores deeper into the earth. On each circle is carried out the
punishment of a certain kind of sin. The first circle of hell is called limbo, which is
the eternal home of the virtuous pagans. According to Dante's theology, these good
persons could not go to heaven because they were not baptized Christians. Virgil
himself belongs in limbo. There is no physical suffering in limbo, only a sad awareness that here one will be eternally excluded from the beatific vision, from the
presence of God.

As this canto opens, Dante is awakened from his faint. He finds that he and
Virgil have crossed the Acheron and are on the brink of limbo.]

        The deep sleep into which I fell was broken
                by heavy thunder, so that I started,
                like one awakened by force,

        and having risen, I glanced around
                and looked intently with rested eyes   5
                to discover where I was.

        In truth, I found myself on the brink
                of the dolorous valley of the abyss
                which resounds with the sound of countless cries.

        It was so dark, deep, and cloudy   10
                that in looking toward the bottom
                I could discern nothing.

        "Now, let us go into the blind world,"
                the poet began all pale,
                "I will be first and you second."   15

        And I, noticing his color, said,
                "How shall I come if you are afraid,
                you who always comfort me in my doubt?"

        And he to me, "The anguish
                of the people down there paints on my face   20
                the pity which you mistake for fear.

Let us go, for the long way impels us."
    Thus he moved on and made me enter
    the first circle which girds the abyss.

Here, so far as one could tell by listening,   25
    there was no lament, but only sighs
    which made the eternal air tremble.

They came from the sadness without torment
    felt by the great crowd
    of children and of women and of men.   30

My good master said to me, "You do not ask
    what spirits these are. Now,
    I want you to know before you go farther

that they did not sin, but having merit
    was not enough, for they lacked baptism,   35
    which is a portal of the faith you hold;

and if they lived before Christianity
    they did not worship God rightly;
    among such as these am I myself.

For such defects, not for other faults,   40
    are we lost and afflicted only
    in that we live in longing without hope."

Great grief gripped my heart when I heard this,
    for I knew that people of much worth
    were in that limbo in suspense.   45

"Tell me, Master, tell me, sir," I began,
    wishing to be assured of the faith
    that destroys every error,

"did any ever through his own merit
    or another's leave here to be blessed?"   50
    And he, understanding my veiled speech, answered,

"I was new in this condition
    when I saw a Powerful One
    crowned with the sign of victory.°

54. This is a reference to a tradition (based on I Peter 3:19) that Christ, here called the Powerful One, before his resurrection, descended into limbo to release the souls of the ancient Hebrews who had believed in his coming. This would have occurred in A.D. 33, after the crucifixion. Virgil died in 19 B.C. The "sign of victory" is the cross, the means by which Christ conquered death.

He took from here our first parent,
    Abel his son, and Noah,
    obedient Moses, the lawgiver,   55

the patriarch Abraham, and David, the king,
    Israel with his father and his sons,
    and Rachel for whom he did so much,   60

and many others, and he made them blessed,
    and I wish you to know that before then
    no human souls were ever saved."

We did not stop because of his remarks,
    but kept passing through the forest—   65
    the forest, I mean, of crowded spirits.

Our way had not yet taken us far
    after my slumber when I saw a light
    which dispelled a hemisphere of darkness.

We were still distant from the glow   70
    but not too far for me to discern
    that notable people occupied that place.

"O you who honor every science and art," I said,
    "who are these whose great merit
    separates them from the others?"   75

And he answered, "The deserved fame
    which still honors them in your life
    gains favor in heaven and thus promotes them."

Meanwhile a voice was heard, saying,
    "Honor the greatest poet;   80
    his shade which had left is returning."

When this voice was silent
    I saw four great figures come to us,
    their faces neither sad nor gay.

My good master began to speak: 85
    "See that one with sword in hand,
    coming ahead of the others as their lord.

He is Homer, the sovereign poet;
    the other, following, is Horace, the satirist;
    Ovid is the third, and Lucan the last.   90

Since each shares with me the title 'poet'
    which the single voice pronounced,
    they do me honor and in doing this do well."

Thus I saw assembled the school
    of that lord of the lofty song who soars   95
    above the others like an eagle.

After they had talked together a little
    they turned to me with signs of greeting,
    and my master smiled at that.

And still more honor they showed me   100
    by making me one of their group,
    so that I was the sixth among such sages.

Thus we continued toward the light,
    speaking of matters concerning which silence
    is as fitting now as speech was then,   105

and we arrived at the foot of a noble castle,
    seven times encircled by high walls,
    defended all around by a fair rivulet.

. . .

Canto 5: Francesca da Rimini

[The castle is the Castle of Wisdom or Fame. Its seven walls perhaps signify the moral and intellectual virtues, all of which could be attained by good nonbelievers. Here Dante meets many famous figures of Greek and Roman times. He cannot stay long, however, and soon moves downward, away from limbo and its light of human reason, toward the darkness by which hell proper is characterized.

In keeping with a concept borrowed from Aristotle, Dante places the sins of the flesh on the upper circles of hell, where punishment is mildest; the sins of anger in the middle circles; and the sins resulting from an abuse of reason at the lowest circles, where the torment is greatest.

In the second circle of hell are the spirits of those whose sin was an excess of sexual passion. Among the spirits whom Dante meets in this circle are two tragic lovers, Francesca and Paolo. Francesca da Rimini, a niece of Dante's patron, had been murdered with her lover, Paolo Malatesta, by her husband Giovanni (who was also Paolo's older brother), when he found the lovers together. They are in hell because they were murdered so suddenly that they had no time to repent of their sin.

As this canto opens, Dante enters the second circle of hell.]

Thus I descended from the first circle
    down to the second which encloses less space
    but so much more pain that it moves to tears.

There Minos° stands, horrible and snarling,
    examining the offenses, judging,   5
    and sending down as he girds himself—

4. **Minos:** the semibestial judge of the damned. Minos is also one of the judges of Hades in classical mythology.

I mean that when an ill-born soul
    comes before him, it confesses wholly,
    and that discerner of sin,

seeing what place in hell belongs to it,   10
    encircles himself with his tail as many times
    as the degrees he wants it to descend.

Always many stand in front of him;
    they come in turns to their judgment,
    confess and hear, and then are hurled below.   15

"O you who come to the painful refuge,"
    Minos said when he saw me,
    interrupting the work of his great office,

"consider how you entered and in whom you trust;
    do not let the breadth of the entrance deceive you."   20
    And my guide to him, "Why do you cry out?

Do not impede his fated going.
    It is wished for where the power is
    to do what is wished; so ask no more."

Now I begin to hear the sad notes of pain,   25
    now I have come to where
    loud cries beat upon my ears.

I have reached a place mute of all light,
    which roars like the sea in a tempest
    when beaten by conflicting winds.   30

The infernal storm which never stops
    drives the spirits in its blast;
    whirling and beating, it torments them.

When they come in front of the landslide,
    they utter laments, moans, and shrieks;   35
    there they curse the divine power.

I learned that to such a torment
    carnal sinners are condemned
    who subject their reason to desire.

And, as starlings are borne by their wings   40
    in the cold season, in a broad and dense flock,
    so that blast carries the evil spirits.

Here, there, up, and down, it blows them;
    no hope ever comforts them
    of rest or even of less pain.   45

And as cranes go chanting their lays,
    making a long line of themselves in the air,
    so I saw coming, uttering laments,

shades borne by that strife of winds.
    I asked, "Master, who are these people   50
    whom the black air so punishes?"

"The first of those about whom
    you want to know," he said to me,
    "was an empress over many peoples,

by the vice of luxury so subdued   55
    that she made lust lawful in her decrees
    to take away the blame she had incurred.

She is Semiramis° who, we read,
    succeeded Ninus, her spouse;
    she held the land that now the Sultan rules.   60

The other is she who killed herself
    after breaking faith with the ashes of Sichaeus;°
    next comes luxurious Cleopatra.

See Helen for whom
    so many bad years revolved, and the great Achilles   65
    whose last battle was with love.°

See Paris, Tristan,"°—and he pointed out and named
    more than a thousand shades
    whom love had taken from our life.

After I had heard my teacher   70
    name the knights and ladies of olden times,
    pity overcame me, and I felt dismayed.

I began, "Poet, willingly would I speak
    with those two° who go together
    and seem so light upon the wind."   75

And he to me, "Wait until they come closer,
    then entreat them by the love
    which impels them and they will come."

---

58. **Semiramis:** a legendary queen of Assyria. 62. **she . . . Sichaeus:** a reference to Dido, legendary queen of Carthage, who had vowed faith to her dead husband Sichaeus, but broke her vow and fell in love with Aeneas. When Aeneas abandoned her, she threw herself on a funeral pyre. 66. According to a legend popular in the Middle Ages, Achilles deserted the Greek army in order to marry a Trojan princess, but was killed when he went to the temple for the wedding. 67. **Tristan:** According to a medieval legend, Tristan fell in love with Iseult, a young princess who was to marry his uncle; ultimately, Tristan and Iseult died together. 74. **those two:** that is, Francesca and Paolo.

As soon as the wind brought them to us,
    I raised my voice, "O wearied souls,   80
    come speak to us if it is not forbidden."

As doves summoned by their desire,
    with wings raised and firm, sail through the air,
    borne on to their sweet nest by their will alone,

so those spirits moved from the band where Dido is,   85
    coming to us through the malignant air,
    so responsive were they to my affectionate cry.

"O living creature, gracious and benign,
    going through the dark air
    visiting us who stained the earth with blood,   90

if the king of the universe were friendly to us
    we would pray to him for your peace,
    since you pity our perverse evil.

Whatever you are pleased to hear from us or say
    we will relate and listen to,   95
    while the wind, as now, is silent.

The city where I was born
    lies on the shore where the Po descends
    with all its tributaries to find peace.

Love which flames quickly in noble hearts   100
    was kindled in this soul by the fair body
    taken from me; the manner still offends.

Love that exempts no one beloved from loving
    caught me so strongly with his charm
    that, as you see, it still does not leave me.   105

Love led us to one death together.
    Caina° waits for him who quenched our lives."
    These words were borne from them to us.

When I heard those afflicted souls
    I bent down my face, and held it low so long   110
    that the poet said, "Of what are you thinking?"

When I answered I began, "Alas!
    how many sweet thoughts, what desire
    led them to the woeful pass!"

---

107. **Caina:** or "Cain's hell," level of hell reserved for murderers of kin.

Then I turned to them and said,   115
    "Francesca, your suffering
    makes me weep with sorrow and with pity,

But tell me, at the time of the sweet sighs,
    by what means and how love permitted you
    to know the dubious desires."   120

And she to me, "There is no greater pain
    than to recall a happy time in misery
    and this your teacher knows;

but if to learn the first root of our love
    you have such desire, I will answer   125
    like one who speaks and weeps.

One day for our delight we were reading
    about Lancelot, how love constrained him;
    alone we were and without any suspicion.

Several times that reading made our glances meet   130
    and changed the color of our faces;
    but one moment alone overcame us.

When we read how the fond smile°
    was kissed by such a lover,
    he, who never will be separated from me,   135

kissed me, on my lips, all trembling.
    A Gallehaut was the book and he who wrote it.°
    That day we read no farther."

While one spirit was saying this
    the other wept, so that from pity   140
    I fainted, as if I had been dying,

and I fell, as a dead body falls.

Canto 10: Farinata degli Uberti

[Virgil and Dante continue downward till they come to the walls of the city of
Dis, which marks the division between upper and lower hell. It is in lower hell that
the sins of violence and fraud are punished. Here, the travelers first encounter punishments involving fire.

133. **smile:** of Guinevere, King Arthur's wife who deceived her husband to love Lancelot.
137. **Gallehaut was the book and he who wrote it:** The Italian for *Gallehaut* is *Galeotto,* which
is also the word for "pander," that is, a go-between for lovers, one who urges on the passions between secret lovers. The book was thus a kind of "pander" between Paolo and Francesca.

Dante peopled hell with the shades of all kinds of people, including many well known to him personally. In the passage that follows, Dante and Virgil are walking among various heretics who denied the immortality of the soul and are condemned to spend eternity in fiery tombs. Two of them speak to Dante. One is Farinata degli Uberti, who died a year before Dante's birth. Farinata was the famous leader of the political party which Dante and his forebears opposed. The other man in the fiery tomb is Cavalcante dei Cavalcanti, whose son, Guido, is a poet and Dante's close friend.]

Now along a solitary path
    between the city wall and the torments,
    my master makes his way, and I behind him.

"O supreme genius, you who through the impious circles
    turn me as you please," I began,   5
    "speak to me and satisfy my wishes.

The people lying in the sepulchers,
    might they be seen?—all the lids
    are raised and no one guards them."

And he to me, "All will be locked in   10
    when they return from Jehoshaphat°
    with the bodies they have left above.

On this side is the burial place
    of Epicurus and of all his followers
    who hold that the soul dies with the body.   15

But concerning the question you ask
    you will soon be satisfied,
    and also as to the wish you keep silent."

And I, "Good guide, I hide my thought
    only to speak little; not long ago   20
    you disposed me to do that."

"O Tuscan, you who through the city of fire
    go alive, speaking thus modestly,
    may it please you to remain in this place.

Your speech shows you a native   25
    of that noble fatherland
    to which, perhaps, I was too harmful."

Suddenly this sound came
    from one of the tombs, so that, startled,
    I drew closer to my guide.   30

---

11. **Jehoshaphat:** the place where all souls, reunited with their bodies, will assemble on Judgment Day.

He said to me, "Turn around! what are you doing?
　　See Farinata, who has stood erect;
　　from the waist upward, wholly, you can see him!"

I had already fixed my eyes on his,
　　and he lifted up his chest and head,　　　　　　　　　35
　　as if he had scorn for hell,

and the bold and ready hands of my guide
　　pushed me among the sepulchers to him,
　　saying, "Let your words be well chosen."

When I was at the foot of his tomb　　　　　　　　　　40
　　he looked at me a little; then, almost disdainfully,
　　he asked, "Who were your ancestors?"

I, desirous to obey, did not hide them,
　　but revealed them all,
　　whereupon he raised his brows a little　　　　　　　45

and said, "Fiercely were they adverse
　　to me and to my ancestors and to my party,
　　so that twice I scattered them."

"If they were driven out, they came back from every side,"
　　I answered him, "both the first and the second time,　　50
　　but yours did not learn well that art!"

Now beside him there arose to sight
　　a shade visible down to his chin;
　　I believe he had risen on his knees.

He looked around me as if anxious　　　　　　　　　　55
　　to see if someone else were with me,
　　but when this expectation was wholly spent,

weeping he said, "If through this blind prison
　　you go because of the greatness of your mind,
　　where is my son? why is he not with you?"　　　　　60

And I to him, "By myself I do not come;
　　Virgil, waiting there, guides me,
　　whom perhaps your Guido held in disdain."

His words and the manner of his punishment
　　had already revealed his name to me;　　　　　　　65
　　therefore my reply was so complete.

Rising suddenly he cried, "What did you say?
　　he *held?* Does he not live still?
　　Does not the sweet light strike his eyes?"

When he was aware of some delay 70
    before I answered, he fell back supine
    and showed himself no more.

But that other magnanimous one, at whose instance
    I had stopped, did not change his expression,
    nor move his head, nor bend his body. 75

"And if," he said, continuing his first remark,
    "they have badly learned that art,
    it torments me more than this bed.

But not fifty times will be rekindled
    the face of her° who rules here 80
    before you will know the hardness of that art!°

And—so may you return sometime to the sweet world—
    tell me why the people are so fierce
    against my kindred in all their laws."

Then I to him, "The slaughter and havoc 85
    which dyed the Arbia red
    cause such prayers to rise in our temple."

Sighing he shook his head and said,
    "In that I was not alone, nor certainly
    would I and the others have moved without cause, 90

but I was alone when all the rest
    agreed to wipe out Florence:
    I defended her openly before all."

"So may your descendants sometime have rest,"
    I replied, "please solve for me this puzzle 95
    which has now entangled my judgment.

It seems that you see, if I hear rightly,
    what the future brings,
    but for the present have a different vision."

"Like those with imperfect sight, 100
    we see things far from us," he said,
    "so much light the Supreme Ruler still allows,

but when they come close, or exist, our minds
    do not perceive them, and without news from others,
    we know nothing of your human state. 105

80. **her:** Hecate, the moon. 81. Dante spent the last years of his life as a political exile
from Florence. He wrote the *Divine Comedy* while in exile. Here he puts in the mouth of
Farinata the prophecy of his exile, for he is writing the poem as if the events occurred when
he was thirty-five.

Therefore you can understand that our knowledge
    will be wholly dead after that moment
    when the gates of the future are closed."

Then, as if sorry for my fault,
    I said, "Now please tell that fallen one   110
    that his son is still joined with the living,

and if I was silent at his question,
    let him know it was because my thoughts
    were confused by the error you have corrected."

Already my master was calling me back,   115
    so that I begged the spirit more hastily
    to tell me who was with him.

He said, "With more than a thousand I lie;
    here is the second Frederick
    and the Cardinal; of the others I am silent."   120

Then he hid himself, and toward the ancient poet
    I turned my steps, meditating
    about the prophecy hostile to me.

My guide moved on and, as we were going,
    he said to me, "Why are you so bewildered?"   125
    and I satisfied his request.

"Let your mind retain what you have heard
    against you," that sage commanded me,
    "and now listen to this," and he raised his finger:

"When you face the sweet light   130
    of her whose fair eyes see everything°
    you will learn from her the journey of your life."

Then he turned his steps to the left;
    we went from the wall toward the center
    along a path which goes into a valley   135

which even up there stifled us with its stench.

131. **her whose fair eyes see everything:** Beatrice, but this is in fact an error on Virgil's part, for it is another character who makes the prophecy. But here among the heretics who were wrong in thinking that death ended everything, error abounds. Both Farinata and Cavalcante have been deceived in several ways, Dante himself has been confused, and now, finally, even Virgil, reason itself, is in error.

FROM *Canto 26: Ulysses*

[Each of the lower circles of hell is subdivided to deal with specific kinds of a general classification of sin. The eighth *bolgia*, or ditch, of the circle containing those guilty of fraud holds the evil counselors. Among the great flames in this ditch Dante finds Ulysses (Latin for "Odysseus"). The story which Ulysses tells here about his last voyage is not from the *Odyssey*, which ends with Ulysses' being reunited with his family, but is Dante's own invention. He based the story on a brief passage in Book XI of the *Odyssey*, in which a seer tells Ulysses that death will come to him "from the sea," a prophecy which hints that the great mariner did not remain with his family, but made one last, fatal voyage.]

. . .

We departed, and over the steps
    which stones had made for our descent,
    my guide remounted, and drew me up,

and continuing our solitary way
    over the stones and rocks of the bridge,   5
    feet did not advance without help from hands.

I grieved then, and now I grieve again
    when I direct my thought to what I saw,
    and I control my mind more than usual

so that virtue alone may guide it.   10
    Thus, if a kindly star or something better°
    has given an advantage, it may not be harmful through abuse.

As a peasant who is resting on a slope
    in the season when the sun that lights the world
    keeps his face least hidden from us—   15

at the hour when gnats take the place of flies—
    sees fireflies down below in the valley,
    perhaps where he gathers grapes or plows;

so, with as many flames the eighth bolgia
    was all resplendent, as I noticed   20
    when I came to where I could see the bottom.

And, as he who avenged himself with the bears°
    saw the chariot of Elijah depart
    when the horses rose erect to heaven—

11. **something better:** divine grace. 22. This stanza and the next refer to an Old Testament story, in which Elisha watched Elijah taken up to heaven in a fiery chariot. Later, some children mocked Elisha, and at the prophet's curse, bears appeared and devoured them. (See II Kings 2:11–24.)

for he could not follow so closely with his eyes   25
     that he could see anything except the flame itself,
     like a little cloud rising upward—

so each light moved through the ditch,
     none revealing what it hid,
     and yet each concealed a sinner.   30

I was standing on the bridge leaning out to see,
     so that if I had not held to a rock,
     without being pushed I would have fallen,

and my guide, who saw me so attentive, said,
     "Within the fires are the spirits;   35
     each is wrapped in what is burning him."

"Master," I answered, "through hearing you
     I am more certain, but already I was aware
     that this was so, and wished to ask

who is in the fire which comes so divided at the top   40
     that it seems to rise from the pyre
     on which Eteocles was placed with his brother."°

He answered, "In that flame Ulysses and Diomed°
     are tortured, and thus they go together
     in punishment as in their battles.   45

They groan within their flame for the ambush
     of the horse which was the portal
     through which came the noble ancestors of the Romans.

Also they weep for the art on account of which
     Deidamia still grieves for Achilles,   50
     and they suffer, too, for the Palladium."

"If they can speak within those fires," I said,
     "Master, I beg you earnestly and beg again
     (and may my prayer be worth a thousand)

that you do not deny our waiting   55
     until the horned flame comes here;
     you see how my desire bends me toward it!"

42. Eteocles and his brother slew one another. According to one writer, when their bodies
were placed together on a funeral pyre, the flames which burned them drew apart, so great was
their hatred for each other. (See *Antigone*, page 140.)   43. **Ulysses and Diomed:** These Greeks
who fought against Troy would be guilty on three counts: tricking the Trojans to take the
wooden horse within their walls, a ruse which led to the destruction of Troy and the flight of
Aeneas, the father of the Roman race; tricking Achilles to abandon his lover Deidamia and
join the Greek army to attack Troy; and stealing the Palladium, a statue of the goddess Pallas
Athena on which the fate of Troy depended.

And he to me, "Your request is worthy
    of praise; therefore I grant it,
    but see that your tongue keeps silent.   60

Let me speak, for I have conceived
    what you want to know. Since they were Greeks,
    they might shy away from your words."

When the flame had come to where
    time and place seemed best to my guide,   65
    I heard him speak in these terms:

"O you two within one fire,
    if I merited thanks from you while I lived,
    if I deserved much or little

when in the world I wrote the lofty verses,   70
    do not move, but let one of you tell
    where, lost, he went to die."

The greater horn of the ancient flame
    began to shake, murmuring like a fire
    struggling in the wind,   75

then moving the tip here and there,
    as if it were a tongue speaking,
    it formed words and said:

"When I left Circe° who detained me
    more than a year near Gaeta°   80
    before Aeneas had named it thus,

neither fondness for my son, nor pity
    for an old father, nor the love for Penelope°
    which should have made her happy,

could overcome in me the desire I had   85
    to gain experience of the world
    and of the vices and the worth of men.

I set out on the high, open sea,
    with only one ship, and with that little company
    by which I was not deserted.   90

Both coasts I saw as far as Spain,
    down to Morocco and the island of Sardinia,
    and the others that are bathed in that sea.

---

79. **Circe** (sûr′sē): an enchantress who had kept Ulysses prisoner.   80. **Gaeta:** a town in southeastern Italy. Aeneas had earlier called it Caieta.   83. **Penelope:** Ulysses' wife.

I and my companions were old and slow
    when we came to that narrow pass°   95
    where Hercules set up his landmarks

so that men should not venture beyond.
    On the right I left Seville,
    and on the other side had already passed Ceuta.

'O brothers,' I said, 'you who   100
    through a thousand perils have come to the West,
    to the brief vigil of our senses

which is left, do not deny
    experience of the unpeopled world
    to be discovered by following the sun.   105

Consider what origin you had;
    you were not created to live like brutes,
    but to seek virtue and knowledge.'

With this little speech I made my companions
    so eager for the journey   110
    that scarcely then could I have held them back,

and, having turned our stern to the morning,
    we made wings of our oars for the mad flight,
    always gaining on the left.

The night already saw the stars   115
    of the other pole, and ours° so low
    it did not rise from the ocean floor.

Five times the light upon the moon
    had shone and been extinguished
    since we started on the deep way,   120

when a mount° appeared to us,
    dim in the distance, and which seemed
    higher than any I had ever seen.

We rejoiced; but soon our joy changed to sorrow,
    for, from the new land a whirlwind arose   125
    which struck the prow of our ship.

---

95. **narrow pass:** Gibraltar.   116. **ours:** the North Star.   121. This is the mount of purgatory. Where Dante envisions hell as a deep pit, narrowing at each level toward the bottom, he sees purgatory as just the opposite, a mountain peak, rising in narrowing levels toward heaven.

Three times it made it whirl with all the water;
    the fourth time it lifted high the stern
    and made the prow go down, as pleased Another,°

until at last the sea closed over us."   130

Canto 34: Satan

[His experiences in the lowest levels of hell teach Dante that he must not feel sympathy with sin or sinner if he is to be in harmony with divine justice. In this last canto of the Inferno, Dante and Virgil have reached the frozen pit of hell. It is dominated by the gigantic winged figure of Satan.]

"*Vexilla Regis prodeunt inferni*°
    toward us, therefore, look ahead,"
    my master said, "and try to discern him."

As, when a thick mist covers the land
    or when night darkens our hemisphere,   5
    a windmill, turning, appears from afar,

so now I seemed to see such a structure;
    then because of the wind, I drew back
    behind my guide, for there was no other protection.

Already—and with fear I put it into verse—   10
    I was where the shades are covered in the ice
    and show through like bits of straw in glass.

Some were lying, some standing erect,
    some on their heads, others on their feet,
    still others like a bow bent face to toes.   15

When we had gone so far ahead
    that my master was pleased to show me
    the creature that once had been so fair,°

he stood from in front of me, and made me stop,
    saying, "Behold, Dis! Here is the place   20
    where you must arm yourself with courage."

How faint and frozen I then became,
    do not ask, reader, for I do not write it down,
    since all words would be inadequate.

129. **Another:** God.
    1. A distortion of a medieval hymn: "On march the banners of the king—of hell."   18. **creature that once had been so fair:** Lucifer.

I did not die and did not stay alive:
     think now for yourself, if you have the wit,
     how I became, without life or death.   25

The emperor of the dolorous realm
     from mid-breast protruded from the ice,
     and I compare better in size   30

with the giants than they do with his arms.
     Consider how big the whole must be,
     proportioned as it is to such a part.

If he were once as handsome as he is ugly now,
     and still presumed to lift his hand against his Maker,   35
     all affliction must indeed come from him.

Oh, how great a marvel appeared to me
     when I saw three faces on his head!
     The one in front was fiery red;

the two others which were joined to it   40
     over the middle of each shoulder
     were fused together at the top.

The right one seemed between white and yellow;
     the left was in color like those
     who come from where the Nile rises.   45

Under each two great wings spread
     of a size fitting to such a bird;
     I have never seen such sails on the sea.

They had no feathers and seemed
     like those of a bat, and they flapped,   50
     so that three blasts came from them.

Thence all Cocytus° was frozen.
     With six eyes he wept, and over his three chins
     he let tears drip and bloody foam.

In each mouth he chewed a sinner with his teeth   55
     in the manner of a hemp brake,
     so that he kept three in pain.

To the one in front the biting was nothing
     compared to the scratching, for at times,
     his back was stripped of skin.   60

[DANTE CONTINUES ON PAGE 431]

52. **Cocytus** (kō·sī′təs): another river of hell, also in Greek mythology.

The Middle Ages

During the twelfth century, as the cities in northern France began to grow and prosper, the cathedral became the center of urban life and culture. The famous cathedral at Chartres (PLATE 1) is a magnificent example of early Gothic architecture that has much of its original sculpture and stained glass windows still intact today. A building of stone and glass of an entirely new kind, it was erected from A.D. 1194 to 1220 during a period of intense religious fervor.

By reducing the solid walls to a skeletal system of lofty pillars and flying buttresses, the Gothic builders were able to free large surfaces for the multi-colored windows which filled the church with a mysterious radiance. The superb windows of Chartres depict scenes from the life of Christ and the saints as well as deeds of kings and heroes and the labors of daily life. Each window is made up of many small pieces of glass steeped in jewelled hues of ruby and sapphire, held together by strips of lead, and supported by iron bars (PLATE 3). Rivalling the brilliantly colored windows, hundreds of painted statues once adorned the interior and exterior of the church. The sculptures of the great doorways, now weathered to the original stone color, possess marvelous grace and beauty. Infinitely rich in subject matter, these carvings portray many forms of vegetation and wildlife, domestic animals, creatures of fantasy, and man in his secular and spiritual aspects.

The western entrance of Chartres Cathedral, called the "Royal Portal," is flanked by statues of Biblical kings and queens (PLATE 2), representing the royal ancestors of Christ. The heads of these figures, with their cheerful expressions, are more natural than their elongated bodies, which are confined to the shapes of columns. Even the folds of their embroidered robes are predominantly vertical, like grooves in a column. Standing at the entrance of the cathedral, crowned and holding sacred books, they are part of the architecture, part of the decoration, and part of the pleasing illustrations for the teachings of the church.

Gothic sculpture was by no means limited to the stone carvings of the cathedral. Sculptors and craftsmen lavished prodigious amounts of time and skill on making chalices, reliquaries, and many other types of metal vessels for use in church services. A splendid example of the goldsmith's craft is the chalice made for Abbot Suger (PLATE 4A) who was regent of France during the Second Crusade. The ancient Roman cup, carved from a single piece of sardonyx, was mounted in gold and silver-gilt and set with pearls and precious gems. The gracefully curved handles terminate in what appears to be the *fleur de lis* (lily), the royal emblem of France.

The bronze aquamanile (PLATE 4B) in the form of Samson and the lion was used for ritual washing of the hands. In the top of Samson's head there is a small opening for filling it with water. The spout for pouring the water is under the lion's ear. The lion, a handsome beast with a powerful body, has every curl of his mane carefully arranged in a decorative pattern. Samson, sitting astride his back, wears a richly embroidered cloak and pointed shoes, the fashionable costume of a medieval prince of the thirteenth century.

Manuscript painting gives us an opulent vision of courtly life in medieval Europe. One of the outstanding masterpieces of this exquisite art is the *Book of Hours (Très riches heures)* made for the Duke of Berry, brother of the King of France. One of the most lavish art patrons in history, he built twenty castles and filled them with rare and costly works of art. The Duke of Berry's *Book of Hours* is a combination prayerbook and religious calendar. The page for January (PLATE 5) shows the duke at a New Year's feast. Sitting at the center of the table, directly under his coat of arms, he is surrounded by members of his court. The slender, richly dressed courtiers are painted in vivid colors, and there is such a wealth of detail in the portrayal of the setting that a small painting of this sort could be examined with prolonged pleasure by the leisured nobility. Notice especially the upper left corner where scenes from the Trojan War appear in a tapestry hanging on the wall.

Woven of brightly colored woolen threads, tapestries were used to cover the cold stone walls of medieval castles and churches. The tapestry shown in PLATE 6 was made for Anne of Brittany in honor of her marriage to Louis XII, King of France. This textured picture, called *The Unicorn Is Brought to the Castle*, portrays the king and queen surrounded by members of the court, standing before the castle gate to receive a slain unicorn brought by a hunter. The unicorn, a fantastic creature who could outrun the fastest horse, could be captured only with the help of a pure and virtuous lady like Anne of Brittany. So the story goes. One of a set of seven tapestries which feature the hunt of the unicorn, this tapestry is one of the finest masterpieces of medieval art in the world.

424

PLATE 1. *Chartres Cathedral.* French, Gothic; begun 1145, partially destroyed by fire 1194, rebuilt 1194–1260.

PLATE 2. Detail from Chartres Cathedral, showing four of the sculptured figures from the jamb of the west portals; often called the Royal Portals, they were begun about 1145.

PLATE 3. Detail from Chartres Cathedral, showing a portion of a stained glass window.

PLATE 4B. *Samson and the Lion*. German, 13th century. Bronze aquamanile, height: 13 inches. (Courtesy, Museum of Fine Arts, Boston, Benjamin Shelton Fund)

PLATE 4A. *Chalice of the Abbot Suger*. French, about 1140. From the Abbey of Saint-Denis at Paris. Sardonyx (agate), gold, silver gilt, gems and pearls; height: $7\frac{17}{32}$ inches. (National Gallery of Art, Washington, D.C., Widener Collection)

PLATE 5. POL DE LIMBOURG AND HIS BROTHERS (French, about 1385–1416): *January.*
1415. From *Les Très Riches Heures du Duc de Berry*. Miniature from the illuminated manuscript,
9½ x 6 inches. (Musée Condé, Chantilly, France)

PLATE 6. *The Unicorn is Brought to the Castle.* Franco-Flemish, late 15th century. Number 6 in the series, *The Hunt of the Unicorn,* from the Chateau de Verteuil. Wool and silk tapestry; entire tapestry is 12 feet 1 inch by 12 feet 5 inches. (The Metropolitan Museum of Art, New York, The Cloisters Collection, Gift of John D. Rockefeller, Jr., 1937)

"The soul up there with the greatest punishment,"
    said my master, "is Judas Iscariot. His head
    is inside the mouth, and he kicks with his legs.

Of the other two whose heads are down,
    the one hanging from the black face is Brutus;   65
    see how he twists and says nothing.

The other who seems so heavy set is Cassius.°
    But night is rising again now,
    and it is time to leave, for we have seen all."

When my guide was ready, I embraced his neck,   70
    and he took advantage of the time and place
    so that when the wings were wide open

he caught hold of the shaggy sides
    and descended from tuft to tuft
    between the tangled hair and the frozen crust.   75

When we were at the place where the thigh
    revolves on the swelling of the haunches,
    my guide, with effort and with difficulty,

turned his head to where he had had his feet,
    and grappled the hair, like one mounting,   80
    so that I thought he was returning into Hell.

"Hold fast, for by such stairs,"
    my master said, panting like one weary,
    "we must depart from so much evil."

Then he came through the opening in a rock   85
    and put me on its edge, sitting,
    and climbed toward me with wary steps.

I raised my eyes and thought
    that I would find Lucifer as I had left him,
    but saw him holding up his legs,   90

and if I then became perplexed,
    let dull people imagine who do not see
    what the point was that I had passed.

"Get up on your feet," said my master,
    "the road is long and the path rough, and already   95
    the sun has returned to mid-tierce."°

67. **Cassius:** one of the conspirators, along with Brutus, who plotted the assassination of
Caesar. 96. **mid-tierce:** 7:30 A.M.

The place where we were
    was no palace hall, but a natural dungeon,
    dark and with an uneven floor.

"Before I uproot myself from the abyss, Master,"   100
    I said when I was standing,
    "speak to me a little to dispel my error.

Where is the ice? And how is Satan planted
    so upside down? And how in such a short time
    has the sun made its way from evening to morning?"   105

And he to me, "You still imagine you are
    on the other side of the center where I grasped the hair
    of the wicked monster that pierces the world.

You were over there as long as I descended;
    when I turned, you passed the point   110
    to which all weights are drawn.

Now you have arrived in the hemisphere
    opposite that which dry land covers
    and at whose summit° was consumed

the man° who was born and lived without sin.   115
    You have your feet on a little circle
    which forms the other face of Giudecca.°

Here it is morning when it is evening there,
    and Satan who made a ladder for us
    with his hair is still as he was before.   120

On this side he fell from heaven, and the earth here,
    through fear, made a veil for itself
    of the sea and came to our hemisphere,

and perhaps the land° which shows on this side,
    to flee from him, rushed up   125
    and left this passageway empty."

There is a place as remote
    from Beelzebub as his tomb extends,
    not known by sight, but by the sound

of a little stream which descends in it   130
    along the hollow of a rock which it has eaten out
    with a slow and winding course.

---

114. **summit:** Jerusalem.   115. **the man:** Christ.   117. **Giudecca:** the lowest level of hell where traitors to lords and benefactors are punished.   124. **the land:** purgatory.

My guide and I started on that hidden way
    to return to the bright world,
    and, without caring for any rest,   135

we climbed, he first and I second,
    until I saw, through a round opening,
    the beautiful things that heaven bears,

and came forth to see again the stars.

FOR STUDY AND DISCUSSION

1. How are the punishments in the Inferno symbolically appropriate to the sin being punished?

2. Why might Dante have used Charon and Minos and other pre-Christian historical and mythological figures in his description of hell?

3. Scholars of the Middle Ages knew the Roman writers much better than the Greek writers. This is why Homer is the only Greek whom Dante lists among the great poets. On what basis does Dante place himself among these great poets? Is he merely vain, or does he see himself as continuing their tradition? Explain your answers.

4. Some readers have often misinterpreted the Francesca and Paolo story (Canto 5) as a romantic tale which shows that love can conquer death and hell. Refute this interpretation, using evidence from the selection.

5. Guinevere and Lancelot are, of course, representatives of the tradition of courtly love. Why is it especially appropriate that Francesca and Paolo should have been reading about them when they were "overcome"?

6. Several times during the journey through hell, Virgil censures Dante for the sympathy he shows suffering sinners. In the cantos here, where does Dante show such sympathy? In Dante's view of the workings of divine justice, why would Virgil's censure be justified?

7. In Canto 10, Farinata shows concern for his reputation among the living, and Cavalcante wonders that Dante should apparently be honored more than his own poet son. Does their concern with worldly esteem seem consistent with their present state of existence?

Does their obvious interest in affairs on earth seem convincing? Dante's astronomy placed the earth at the center of the universe, and his theology made man just slightly lower than the angels. Do these facts give any clues to answers to the questions above? Explain your answers.

8. Unlike the souls in hell, the souls in purgatory eventually go to heaven, after being purified of their sins. Ulysses' ship (see Canto 26) would have landed on the mount of purgatory had it not been sunk. Why was it necessary for Dante to write the shipwreck into his story? What theological idea would have been violated if Ulysses had landed on purgatory? Why was Ulysses in hell?

9. How would you explain the assignment of Judas, Brutus, and Cassius to the very pit of hell, in the jaws of Satan himself (Canto 34)?

10. One measure of a poet's talent is his ability to use language appropriate to his subject. Find passages which, even in translation, make it clear that Dante is fully capable of doing this. What images present most vividly the horror of various sinners' conditions? Which passages convey most strongly Dante's terror of eternal damnation?

11. In hell the names of heaven, God, and Christ are never uttered. What are some of the circumlocutions Dante uses to avoid these names? What is the dramatic effect of such phrases and of Dante's avoidance of the names?

12. Many readers are surprised to find that Dante pictures the very pit of hell as a frozen place. Puritan writer John Milton, in *Paradise Lost* (see page 629), pictures it as a fiery place, as in these lines (61–75) from Book I:

A dungeon horrible on all sides round
As one great furnace flamed, yet from those
    flames
No light but rather darkness visible
Served only to discover sights of woe,
Regions of sorrow, doleful shades, where
    peace
And rest can never dwell, hope never comes
That comes to all; but torture without end
Still urges, and a fiery deluge, fed
With everburning sulphur unconsumed:
Such place Eternal Justice had prepared
For those rebellious, here their prison or-
    dained
In utter darkness, and their portion set
As far removed from God and light of
    Heaven
As from the center thrice to the utmost pole.
O how unlike the place from whence they
    fell!—JOHN MILTON

Which symbolic matter—ice or fire—seems most appropriate to you to represent that point in man's experience which is farthest from God, which is the very center of evil? Why? Would Dante's Satan be as frightful a figure as he is if he were not stationary, frozen in ice of his own making? How does the following poem, "Fire and Ice," by contemporary American poet Robert Frost, influence your thinking on this question?

Some say the world will end in fire,
Some say in ice.
From what I've tasted of desire
I hold with those who favor fire.
But if it had to perish twice,
I think I know enough of hate
To say that for destruction ice
Is also great
And would suffice.
                        —ROBERT FROST

FOR COMPOSITION

In ancient literature there are a number of myths and legends about men who travel into the land of the immortals or the land of the dead. Among those in ancient literature who make such trips are Gilgamesh (see page 13), Odysseus (in Book 11 of the *Odyssey*), Aeneas (in Book 6 of the *Aeneid*), and Orpheus (see page 210). Look up one of these stories; then in a composition of no more than 750 words, compare and contrast Dante's journey with that of the other man. Describe the differences and similarities in their journeys and in their experiences.

The Canterbury Tales

GEOFFREY CHAUCER

Geoffrey Chaucer (1340?–1400) spent his life in a great variety of positions in the service of the English crown. His education was planned to prepare him for the civil service, and he had experience as a functionary in a great household, as a soldier, as a diplomat, and as a civil servant. Though he maintained a home in the bustling, growing city of London all his life, his duties took him to France, Italy, and, perhaps, other parts of Europe. This wide experience apparently introduced Chaucer to medieval people in all their variety—in all their diverse occupations and social levels, in all their follies and weaknesses, and in all their aspirations and strengths. It is this variety, spiced by Chaucer's own acute observation and satiric but genial humor, which we find in the Canterbury pilgrims.

Chaucer's plan for *The Canterbury Tales* was to present a group of men and women, representing nearly every social class in England, on a pilgrimage to and from Canterbury. Along the way, each pilgrim was to tell four stories, two on the road to Canterbury and two on the road back. Though Chaucer died before the whole plan was completed, he left for all time the most unforgettable collection of characters in medieval literature and a superb group of stories.

Chaucer borrowed the tales from many sources and used as a structural device the frame story, a popular device also found in *The Thousand and One Nights* (see page 344) and in Boccaccio's *Decameron* (see page 507). Unlike Boccaccio, Chaucer tried to make each tale appropriate to the character of the person telling it.

Chaucer himself narrates the General Prologue to the tales. The scene is set in the Tabard, an inn in a suburb of London known as Southwark, in about 1387. The narrator is to set off on a sixty-mile trip on horseback to the cathedral at Canterbury, to the popular shrine of Thomas à Becket, the archbishop who had been murdered in 1170 for refusing to relinquish ecclesiastical power to the state. Thomas was canonized in 1172, and King Henry II, accepting responsibility for the crime, did penance at the martyr's tomb.

FROM *The General Prologue*

When in April the sweet showers fall
And pierce the drought of March to the root, and all
The veins are bathed in liquor of such power
As brings about the engendering of the flower,

From *The Canterbury Tales* by Geoffrey Chaucer, translated by Nevill Coghill. Reprinted by permission of Penguin Books Ltd.

When also Zephyrus° with his sweet breath   5
Exhales an air in every grove and heath
Upon the tender shoots, and the young sun
His half course in the sign of the Ram has run,
And the small fowl are making melody
That sleep away the night with open eye   10
(So nature pricks them and their heart engages),
Then people long to go on pilgrimages
And palmers° long to seek the stranger strands
Of far-off saints, hallowed in sundry lands,
And specially, from every shire's end   15
In England, down to Canterbury they wend
To seek the holy blissful martyr, quick
To give his help to them when they were sick.
   It happened in that season that one day
In Southwark, at the Tabard, as I lay   20
Ready to go on pilgrimage and start
For Canterbury, most devout at heart,
At night there came into that hostelry
Some nine and twenty in a company
Of sundry folk happening then to fall   25
In fellowship, and they were pilgrims all
That toward Canterbury meant to ride.
The rooms and stables of the inn were wide;
They made us easy, all was of the best.
And shortly, when the sun had gone to rest,   30
By speaking to them all upon the trip
I soon was one of them in fellowship
And promised to rise early and take the way
To Canterbury, as you heard me say.
   But nonetheless, while I have time and space,   35
Before my story takes a further pace,
It seems a reasonable thing to say
What their condition was, the full array
Of each of them, as it appeared to me
According to profession and degree,   40
And what apparel they were riding in;
And at a Knight I therefore will begin.

There was a *Knight,* a most distinguished man,
Who from the day on which he first began
To ride abroad had followed chivalry,   45
Truth, honor, generousness, and courtesy.
He had done nobly in his sovereign's war
And ridden into battle, no man more,
As well in Christian as in heathen places,
And ever honored for his noble graces.   50
   When we took Alexandria, he was there.

---

5. **Zephyrus:** the west wind.   13. **palmers:** pilgrims who had visited the Holy Land and who wore crossed branches of palm to show it.

He often sat at table in the chair
Of honor, above all nations, when in Prussia.
In Lithuania he had ridden, and Russia,
No Christian man so often, of his rank.   55
When, in Granada, Algeciras° sank
Under assault, he had been there, and in
North Africa, raiding Benamarin;
In Anatolia he had been as well
And fought when Ayas° and Attalia° fell,   60
For all along the Mediterranean coast
He had embarked with many a noble host.
In fifteen mortal battles he had been
And jousted for our faith at Tramissene°
Thrice in the lists, and always killed his man.   65
This same distinguished knight had led the van
Once with the Bey of Balat,° doing work
For him against another heathen Turk;
He was of sovereign value in all eyes.
And though so much distinguished, he was wise   70
And in his bearing modest as a maid.
He never yet a boorish thing had said
In all his life to any, come what might;
He was a true, a perfect gentle-knight.
    Speaking of his equipment, he possessed   75
Fine horses, but he was not gaily dressed.
He wore a fustian° tunic stained and dark
With smudges where his armor had left mark;
Just home from service, he had joined our ranks
To do his pilgrimage and render thanks.   80

    He had his son with him, a fine young *Squire,*
A lover and cadet, a lad of fire
With locks as curly as if they had been pressed.
He was some twenty years of age, I guessed.
In stature he was of a moderate length,   85
With wonderful agility and strength.
He'd seen some service with the cavalry
In Flanders and Artois and Picardy
And had done valiantly in little space
Of time, in hope to win his lady's grace.   90
He was embroidered like a meadow bright
And full of freshet flowers, red and white.
Singing he was, or fluting all the day;
He was as fresh as is the month of May.
Short was his gown, the sleeves were long and wide;   95
He knew the way to sit a horse and ride.

---

56. **Algeciras** (al'jə·sir'əs): a city besieged and taken from the Moorish king of Granada
in 1344.   60. **Ayas:** in Armenia, taken from the Turks in about 1367.   **Attalia:** on the south
coast of Asia Minor, taken soon after 1352.   64. **Tramissene:** in western Algeria.   67. **Bey
of Balat:** governor of Balat, in Turkey.   77. **fustian:** a sturdy kind of cotton cloth.

He could make songs and poems and recite,
Knew how to joust and dance, to draw and write.
He loved so hotly that till dawn grew pale
He slept as little as a nightingale.   100
Courteous he was, lowly and serviceable,
And carved to serve his father at the table.

          . . .

    There also was a *Nun,* a Prioress.
Her way of smiling very simple and coy.
Her greatest oath was only "By St. Loy!"°   105
And she was known as Madam Eglantyne.
And well she sang a service, with a fine
Intoning through her nose, as was most seemly,
And she spoke daintily in French, extremely,
After the school of Stratford-atte-Bowe;°   110
French in the Paris style she did not know.
At meat her manners were well taught withal;
No morsel from her lips did she let fall,
Nor dipped her fingers in the sauce too deep;
But she could carry a morsel up and keep   115
The smallest drop from falling on her breast.
For courtliness she had a special zest,
And she would wipe her upper lip so clean
That not a trace of grease was to be seen
Upon the cup when she had drunk; to eat,   120
She reached a hand sedately for the meat.
She certainly was very entertaining,
Pleasant and friendly in her ways, and straining
To counterfeit a courtly kind of grace,
A stately bearing fitting to her place,   125
And to seem dignified in all her dealings.
As for her sympathies and tender feelings,
She was so charitably solicitous
She used to weep if she but saw a mouse
Caught in a trap, if it were dead or bleeding.   130
And she had little dogs she would be feeding
With roasted flesh, or milk, or fine white bread.
And bitterly she wept if one were dead
Or someone took a stick and made it smart;
She was all sentiment and tender heart.   135
Her veil was gathered in a seemly way,
Her nose was elegant, her eyes glass-gray;
Her mouth was very small, but soft and red,
Her forehead, certainly, was fair of spread,
Almost a span across the brows, I own;   140
She was indeed by no means undergrown.
Her cloak, I noticed, had a graceful charm.

105. **St. Loy:** a French saint known for his impeccable manners. 110. **the school of Stratford-atte-Bowe:** a convent in England.

She wore a coral trinket on her arm,
A set of beads, the gaudies° tricked in green,
Whence hung a golden brooch of brightest sheen   145
On which there first was graven a crowned A,
And lower, *Amor vincit omnia.*°

· · ·

   A *Monk* there was, one of the finest sort
Who rode the country; hunting was his sport.
A manly man, to be an Abbot able;   150
Many a dainty horse he had in stable.
His bridle, when he rode, a man might hear
Jingling in a whistling wind as clear,
Aye, and as loud as does the chapel bell
Where my lord Monk was Prior of the cell.   155
The Rule of good St. Benet or St. Maur°
As old and strict he tended to ignore;
He let go by the things of yesterday
And took the modern world's more spacious way.
He did not rate that text at a plucked hen   160
Which says that hunters are not holy men
And that a monk uncloistered is a mere
Fish out of water, flapping on the pier,
That is to say, a monk out of his cloister.
That was a text he held not worth an oyster;   165
And I agreed and said his views were sound;
Was he to study till his head went round
Poring over books in cloisters? Must he toil
As Austin° bade and till the very soil?
Was he to leave the world upon the shelf?   170
Let Austin have his labor to himself.
   This Monk was therefore a good man to horse;
Greyhounds he had, as swift as birds, to course.
Hunting a hare or riding at a fence
Was all his fun, he spared for no expense.   175
I saw his sleeves were garnished at the hand
With fine gray fur, the finest in the land,
And on his hood, to fasten it at his chin
He had a wrought-gold cunningly fashioned pin;
Into a lover's knot it seemed to pass.   180
His head was bald and shone like looking glass;
So did his face, as if it had been greased.
He was a fat and personable priest;
His prominent eyeballs never seemed to settle.
They glittered like the flames beneath a kettle;   185
Supple his boots, his horse in fine condition.

144. **gaudies:** In a rosary ("beads"), every eleventh bead, called a gaud, is larger; it stands for the recitation of an Our Father.   147. ***Amor vincit omnia:*** Latin for "Love conquers all."   156. **St. Benet or St. Maur:** St. Benedict or St. Maurus, who was Benedict's disciple. Benedict drew up a rule of behavior for religious orders.   169. **Austin:** St. Augustine, who warned his monks against sloth.

He was a prelate fit for exhibition,
He was not pale like a tormented soul.
He liked a fat swan best and roasted whole.
His palfrey was as brown as is a berry.   190

    There was a *Friar,* a wanton one and merry,
A Limiter,° a very festive fellow.
In all Four Orders° there was none so mellow
So glib with gallant phrase and well-turned speech.
He'd fixed up many a marriage, giving each   195
Of his young women what he could afford her.
He was a noble pillar to his Order.
Highly beloved and intimate was he
With county folk within his boundary,
And city dames of honor and possessions;   200
For he was qualified to hear confessions,
Or so he said, with more than priestly scope;
He had a special license from the Pope.
Sweetly he heard his penitents at shrift
With pleasant absolution, for a gift.   205
He was an easy man in penance-giving
Where he could hope to make a decent living;
It's a sure sign whenever gifts are given
To a poor Order that a man's well shriven,
And should he give enough he knew in verity   210
The penitent repented in sincerity.
For many a fellow is so hard of heart
He cannot weep, for all his inward smart.
Therefore instead of weeping and of prayer
One should give silver for a poor Friar's care.   215
He kept his tippet° stuffed with pins for curls,
And pocketknives, to give to pretty girls.
And certainly his voice was gay and sturdy,
For he sang well and played the hurdy-gurdy.
At singsongs he was champion of the hour.   220
His neck was whiter than a lily flower
But strong enough to butt a bruiser down.
He knew the taverns well in every town
And every innkeeper and barmaid too
Better than lepers, beggars, and that crew.   225
For in so eminent a man as he
It was not fitting with the dignity
Of his position, dealing with a scum
Of wretched lepers; nothing good can come
Of dealings with the slum-and-gutter dwellers,   230
But only with the rich and victual-sellers.
But anywhere a profit might accrue

192. **Limiter:** a friar who begged for alms, licensed to raise money within local limits by hearing confessions.   193. **Four Orders:** the four orders of mendicant, or begging, friars: Dominicans, Franciscans, Carmelites, and Augustinians.   216. **tippet:** hood or sleeve of a friar's robe.

Courteous he was and lowly of service too.
Natural gifts like his were hard to match.
He was the finest beggar of his batch,   235
And, for his begging-district, payed a rent;
His brethren did no poaching where he went.
For though a widow mightn't have a shoe,
So pleasant was his holy how-d'ye-do
He got his farthing from her just the same   240
Before he left, and so his income came
To more than he laid out. And how he romped,
Just like a puppy! He was ever prompt
To arbitrate disputes on settling days°
(For a small fee) in many helpful ways,   245
Not then appearing as your cloistered scholar
With threadbare habit hardly worth a dollar,
But much more like a doctor or a Pope.
Of double-worsted was the semicope
Upon his shoulders, and the swelling fold   250
About him, like a bell about its mold
When it is casting, rounded out his dress.
He lisped a little out of wantonness
To make his English sweet upon his tongue.
When he had played his harp, or having sung,   255
His eyes would twinkle in his head as bright
As any star upon a frosty night.
This worthy's name was Hubert, it appeared.

There was a *Merchant* with a forking beard
And motley dress; high on his horse he sat,   260
Upon his head a Flemish beaver hat
And on his feet daintily buckled boots.
He told of his opinions and pursuits
In solemn tones, and how he never lost.
The sea should be kept free at any cost   265
(He thought) upon the Harwich-Holland range,
He was expert at currency exchange.
This estimable Merchant so had set
His wits to work, none knew he was in debt,
He was so stately in negotiation,   270
Loan, bargain, and commercial obligation.
He was an excellent fellow all the same;
To tell the truth I do not know his name.

An *Oxford Cleric,* still a student though,
One who had taken logic long ago,   275
Was there; his horse was thinner than a rake,
And he was not too fat, I undertake,
But had a hollow look, a sober stare;

---

244. **settling days:** days appointed for settling disputes by arbitration. The clergy took an active part in such proceedings.

The thread upon his overcoat was bare.
He had found no preferment in the church   280
And he was too unworldly to make search
For secular employment. By his bed
He preferred having twenty books in red
And black, of Aristotle's philosophy,
To having fine clothes, fiddle, or psaltery.   285
Though a philosopher, as I have told,
He had not found the stone for making gold.°
Whatever money from his friends he took
He spent on learning or another book
And prayed for them most earnestly, returning   290
Thanks to them thus for paying for his learning.
His only care was study, and indeed
He never spoke a word more than was need,
Formal at that, respectful in the extreme,
Short, to the point, and lofty in his theme.   295
The thought of moral virtue filled his speech
And he would gladly learn, and gladly teach.

. . .

There was a *Franklin°* with him, it appeared;
White as a daisy petal was his beard.
A sanguine man, high-colored and benign,   300
He loved a morning sop of cake in wine.
He lived for pleasure and had always done,
For he was Epicurus' very son,
In whose opinion sensual delight
Was the one true felicity in sight.   305
As noted as St. Julian° was for bounty
He made his household free to all the county.
His bread, his ale were finest of the fine
And no one had a better stock of wine.
His house was never short of bake-meat pies,   310
Of fish and flesh, and these in such supplies
It positively snowed with meat and drink
And all the dainties that a man could think.
According to the seasons of the year
Changes of dish were ordered to appear.   315
He kept fat partridges in coops, beyond,
Many a bream and pike were in his pond.
Woe to the cook whose sauces had no sting
Or who was unprepared in anything!
And in his hall a table stood arrayed   320
And ready all day long, with places laid.
As Justice at the Sessions none stood higher;
He often had been Member for the Shire.

287. **the stone for making gold:** Medieval alchemists were looking for a stone or substance, called the philosopher's stone, that could transmute a baser metal into gold. 298. ***Franklin:*** a landholder, though not a noble. 306. **St. Julian:** patron saint of hospitality.

A dagger and a little purse of silk
Hung at his girdle, white as morning milk.   325
As Sheriff he checked audit, every entry.
He was a model among landed gentry.

. . .

They had a *Cook* with them who stood alone
For boiling chicken with a marrowbone,
Sharp flavoring-powder, and a spice for savor.   330
He could distinguish London ale by flavor,
And he could roast and seethe and broil and fry,
Make good thick soup and bake a tasty pie.
But what a pity—so it seemed to me,
That he should have an ulcer on his knee.   335
As for blancmange, he made it with the best.

. . .

A worthy *woman* from beside *Bath* city
Was with us, somewhat deaf, which was a pity.
In making cloth she showed so great a bent
She bettered those of Ypres and of Ghent.   340
In all the parish not a dame dared stir
Toward the altar steps in front of her,
And if indeed they did, so wrath was she
As to be quite put out of charity.
Her kerchiefs were of finely woven ground;   345
I dared have sworn they weighed a good ten pound,
The ones she wore on Sunday, on her head.
Her hose were of the finest scarlet red
And gartered tight; her shoes were soft and new.
Bold was her face, handsome, and red in hue.   350
A worthy woman all her life, what's more
She'd had five husbands, all at the church door,
Apart from other company in youth;
No need just now to speak of that, forsooth.
And she had thrice been to Jerusalem,   355
Seen many strange rivers and passed over them;
She'd been to Rome and also to Boulogne,
St. James of Compostella° and Cologne,
And she was skilled in wandering by the way.
She had gap-teeth, set widely, truth to say.   360
Easily on an ambling horse she sat
Well wimpled up, and on her head a hat
As broad as is a buckler or a shield;
She had a flowing mantle that concèaled
Large hips, her heels spurred sharply under that.   365
In company she liked to laugh and chat
And knew the remedies for love's mischances,
An art in which she knew the oldest dances.

358. **St. James of Compostella:** a pilgrimage center in Spain.

A holy-minded man of good renown
There was, and poor, the *Parson* to a town, 370
Yet he was rich in holy thought and work.
He also was a learned man, a clerk,
Who truly knew Christ's gospel and would preach it
Devoutly to parishioners and teach it.
Benign and wonderfully diligent, 375
And patient when adversity was sent
(For so he proved in great adversity)
He much disliked extorting tithe or fee,
Nay rather he preferred beyond a doubt
Giving to poor parishioners round about 380
From his own goods and Easter offerings.
He found sufficiency in little things.
Wide was his parish, with houses far asunder,
Yet he neglected not in rain or thunder,
In sickness or in grief, to pay a call 385
On the remotest, whether great or small,
Upon his feet, and in his hand a stave.
This noble example to his sheep he gave,
First following the word before he taught it,
And it was from the gospel he had caught it. 390
This little proverb he would add thereto
That if gold rust, what then will iron do?
For if a priest be foul in whom we trust
No wonder that a common man should rust;
And shame it is to see—let priests take stock— 395
A dirty shepherd and a snowy flock.
The true example that a priest should give
Is one of cleanness, how the sheep should live.
He did not set his benefice to hire
And leave his sheep encumbered in the mire 400
Or run to London to earn easy bread
By singing masses for the wealthy dead,
Or find some brotherhood and get enrolled.
He stayed at home and watched over his fold
So that no wolf should make the sheep miscarry. 405
He was a shepherd and no mercenary.
Holy and virtuous he was, but then
Never contemptuous of sinful men,
Never disdainful, never too proud or fine,
But was discreet in teaching and benign. 410
His business was to show a fair behavior
And draw men thus to heaven and their Saviour,
Unless indeed a man were obstinate;
And such, whether of high or low estate,
He put to sharp rebuke to say the least. 415
I think there never was a better priest.
He sought no pomp or glory in his dealings,

No scrupulosity had spiced his feelings.
Christ and his twelve apostles and their lore
He taught, but followed it himself before.   420

    There was a *Plowman* with him there, his brother.
Many a load of dung one time or other
He must have carted through the morning dew.
He was an honest worker, good and true,
Living in peace and perfect charity,   425
And, as the gospel bade him, so did he,
Loving God best with all his heart and mind
And then his neighbor as himself, repined
At no misfortune, slacked for no content,
For steadily about his work he went   430
To thrash his corn, to dig or to manure
Or make a ditch; and he would help the poor
For love of Christ and never take a penny
If he could help it, and, as prompt as any,
He paid his tithes in full when they were due   435
On what he owned, and on his earnings too.
He wore a tabard° smock and rode a mare.

          . . .

    The *Miller* was a chap of sixteen stone,°
A great stout fellow big in brawn and bone.
He did well out of them, for he could go   440
And win the ram at any wrestling show.
Broad, knotty, and short-shouldered, he would boast
He could heave any door off hinge and post,
Or take a run and break it with his head.
His beard, like any sow or fox, was red   445
And broad as well, as though it were a spade;
And, at its very tip, his nose displayed
A wart on which there stood a tuft of hair
Red as the bristles in an old sow's ear.
His nostrils were as black as they were wide.   450
He had a sword and buckler at his side,
His mighty mouth was like a furnace door.
A wrangler and buffoon, he had a store
Of tavern stories, filthy in the main.
His was a master hand at stealing grain.   455
He felt it with his thumb and thus he knew
Its quality and took three times his due—
A thumb of gold, by God, to gauge an oat!

437. **tabard:** short-sleeved.   438. **stone:** a unit of weight in England, equal to about fourteen pounds.

He wore a hood of blue and a white coat.
He liked to play his bagpipes up and down   460
And that was how he brought us out of town.

. . .

He and a gentle *Pardoner*° rode together,
A bird from Charing Cross of the same feather,
Just back from visiting the Court of Rome.
He loudly sang "Come hither, love, come home!"   465
The summoner sang deep seconds to this song,
No trumpet ever sounded half so strong.
This Pardoner had hair as yellow as wax.
Hanging down smoothly like a hank of flax.
In driblets fell his locks behind his head   470
Down to his shoulders which they overspread;
Thinly they fell, like rattails, one by one.
He wore no hood upon his head, for fun;
The hood inside his wallet had been stowed,
He aimed at riding in the latest mode;   475
But for a little cap his head was bare
And he had bulging eyeballs, like a hare.
He'd sewed a holy relic on his cap;
His wallet lay before him on his lap,
Brimful of pardons come from Rome all hot.   480
He had the same small voice a goat has got.
His chin no beard had harbored, nor would harbor,
Smoother than ever chin was left by barber.
I judge he was a gelding, or a mare.
As to his trade, from Berwick down to Ware   485
There was no pardoner of equal grace,
For in his trunk he had a pillowcase
Which he asserted was Our Lady's veil.
He said he had a gobbet of the sail
St. Peter had the time when he made bold   490
To walk the waves, till Jesu Christ took hold.
He had a cross of metal set with stones
And, in a glass, a rubble of pigs' bones.
And with these relics, any time he found
Some poor up-country parson to astound,   495
On one short day, in money down, he drew
More than the parson in a month or two,
And by his flatteries and prevarication
Made monkeys of the priest and congregation.
But still to do him justice first and last   500
In church he was a noble ecclesiast.
How well he read a lesson or told a story!

462. **Pardoner:** a preacher, licensed by the Pope to raise money to support the Church.
For each offering of money, the pardoner issued an indulgence, which meant that the contributor was absolved of doing some of the public penance still due after his sins were privately confessed. The granting of indulgences was often abused, and unlicensed pardoners
abounded, selling fake relics for their own profit.

But best of all he sang an Offertory,
For well he knew that when that song was sung
He'd have to preach and tune his honey-tongue   505
And (well he could) win silver from the crowd.
That's why he sang so merrily and loud.

. . .

FROM *The Pardoner's Tale*

[The idea that the pilgrims should entertain one another on the road to Canterbury by telling stories is the innkeeper's. He proposes that the pilgrim who tells the
tale that is best "in profit and in pleasant interest" should have a meal at the expense of the other travelers, back in the Tabard, after the pilgrimage is over. When
his turn comes up, the Pardoner chooses to tell a familiar folk tale which he uses in
his sermons to illustrate a maxim from the New Testament: *Radix malorum est
cupiditas,* "Greed is the root of evil." With candid brazenness, the Pardoner proclaims that he always preaches against avarice—the very vice he makes his living
from.]

It's of three rioters I have to tell
Who long before the morning service bell
Were sitting in a tavern for a drink.
And as they sat, they heard the hand bell clink
Before a coffin going to the grave;   5
One of them called the little tavern knave
And said "Go and find out at once—look spry!—
Whose corpse is in that coffin passing by;
And see you get the name correctly too."
"Sir," said the boy, "no need, I promise you;   10
Two hours before you came here I was told.
He was a friend of yours in days of old,
And suddenly, last night, the man was slain,
Upon his bench, face up, dead drunk again.
There came a privy thief, they call him Death,   15
Who kills us all round here, and in a breath
He speared him through the heart, he never stirred.
And then Death went his way without a word.
He's killed a thousand in the present plague,
And, sir, it doesn't do to be too vague   20
If you should meet him; you had best be wary.
Be on your guard with such an adversary,
Be primed to meet him everywhere you go,
That's what my mother said. It's all I know."
The publican joined in with, "By St. Mary.   25
What the child says is right; you'd best be wary,
This very year he killed, in a large village
A mile away, man, woman, serf at tillage,
Page in the household, children—all there were.
Yes, I imagine that he lives round there.   30

GEOFFREY CHAUCER   447

It's well to be prepared in these alarms,
He might do you dishonor." "Huh, God's arms!"
The rioter said, "Is he so fierce to meet?
I'll search for him, by Jesus, street by street.
God's blessed bones! I'll register a vow!   35
Here, chaps! The three of us together now,
Hold up your hands, like me, and we'll be brothers
In this affair, and each defend the others,
And we will kill this traitor Death, I say!
Away with him as he has made away   40
With all our friends. God's dignity! Tonight!"
    They made their bargain, swore with appetite,
These three, to live and die for one another
As brother-born might swear to his born brother.
And up they started in their drunken rage   45
And made toward this village which the page
And publican had spoken of before.
Many and grisly were the oaths they swore,
Tearing Christ's blessed body to a shred;
"If we can only catch him, Death is dead!"   50
    When they had gone not fully a half a mile,
Just as they were about to cross a stile,
They came upon a very poor old man
Who humbly greeted them and thus began,
"God look to you, my lords, and give you quiet!"   55
To which the proudest of these men of riot
Gave back the answer, "What, old fool? Give place!
Why are you all wrapped up except your face?
Why live so long? Isn't it time to die?"
    The old, old fellow looked him in the eye   60
And said, "Because I never yet have found,
Though I have walked to India, searching round
Village and city on my pilgrimage,
One who would change his youth to have my age.
And so my age is mine and must be still   65
Upon me, for such time as God may will.
    "Not even Death, alas, will take my life;
So, like a wretched prisoner at strife
Within himself, I walk alone and wait
About the earth, which is my mother's gate,   70
Knock-knocking with my staff from night to noon
And crying, 'Mother, open to me soon!
Look at me, mother, won't you let me in?
See how I wither, flesh and blood and skin!
Alas! When will these bones be laid to rest?   75
Mother, I would exchange—for that were best—
The wardrobe in my chamber, standing there
So long, for yours! Aye, for a shirt of hair
To wrap me in!' She has refused her grace,
Whence comes the pallor of my withered face.   80
    "But it dishonored you when you began

To speak so roughly, sir, to an old man,
Unless he had injured you in word or deed.
It says in holy writ, as you may read,
'Thou shalt rise up before the hoary head   85
And honor it.' And therefore be it said
'Do no more harm to an old man than you,
Being now young, would have another do
When you are old'—if you should live till then.
And so may God be with you, gentlemen,   90
For I must go whither I have to go."
    "By God," the gambler said, "you shan't do so,
You don't get off so easy, by St. John!
I heard you mention, just a moment gone,
A certain traitor Death who singles out   95
And kills the fine young fellows hereabout.
And you're his spy, by God! You wait a bit.
Say where he is or you shall pay for it,
By God and by the Holy Sacrament!
I say you've joined together by consent   100
To kill us younger folk, you thieving swine!"
    "Well, sirs," he said, "if it be your design
To find out Death, turn up this crooked way
Toward that grove. I left him there today
Under a tree, and there you'll find him waiting.   105
He isn't one to hide for all your prating.
You see that oak? He won't be far to find.
And God protect you that redeemed mankind,
Aye, and amend you!" Thus that ancient man.
    At once the three young rioters began   110
To run, and reached the tree, and there they found
A pile of golden florins on the ground,
New-coined, eight bushels of them as they thought.
No longer was it Death those fellows sought,
For they were all so thrilled to see the sight,   115
The florins were so beautiful and bright,
That down they sat beside the precious pile.
The wickedest spoke first after a while.
"Brothers," he said, "you listen to what I say.
I'm pretty sharp although I joke away.   120
It's clear that fortune has bestowed this treasure
To let us live in jollity and pleasure.
Light come, light go! We'll spend it as we ought.
God's precious dignity! Who would have thought
This morning was to be our lucky day?   125
    "If one could only get the gold away,
Back to my house, or else to yours, perhaps—
For as you know, the gold is ours, chaps—
We'd all be at the top of fortune, hey?
But certainly it can't be done by day.   130
People would call us robbers—a strong gang,
So our own property would make us hang.

No, we must bring this treasure back by night
Some prudent way, and keep it out of sight.
And so as a solution I propose   135
We draw for lots and see the way it goes.
The one who draws the longest, lucky man,
Shall run to town as quickly as he can
To fetch us bread and wine—but keep things dark—
While two remain in hiding here to mark   140
Our heap of treasure. If there's no delay,
When night comes down we'll carry it away,
All three of us, wherever we have planned."
      He gathered lots and hid them in his hand
Bidding them draw for where the luck should fall.   145
It fell upon the youngest of them all,
And off he ran at once toward the town.
      As soon as he had gone the first sat down
And thus began a parley with the other:
"You know that you can trust me as a brother;   150
Now let me tell you where your profit lies;
You know our friend has gone to get supplies
And here's a lot of gold that is to be
Divided equally amongst us three.
Nevertheless, if I could shape things thus   155
So that we shared it out—the two of us—
Wouldn't you take it as a friendly turn?"
      "But how?" the other said with some concern,
"Because he knows the gold's with me and you;
What can we tell him? What are we to do?"   160
      "Is it a bargain," said the first, "or no?
For I can tell you in a word or so
What's to be done to bring the thing about."
"Trust me," the other said, "you needn't doubt
My word. I won't betray you, I'll be true."   165
      "Well," said his friend, "you see that we are two,
And two are twice as powerful as one.
Now look; when he comes back, get up in fun
To have a wrestle; then, as you attack,
I'll up and put my dagger through his back   170
While you and he are struggling, as in game;
Then draw your dagger, too, and do the same.
Then all this money will be ours to spend,
Divided equally of course, dear friend.
Then we can gratify our lusts and fill   175
The day with dicing at our own sweet will."
Thus these two miscreants agreed to slay
The third and youngest, as you heard me say.
      The youngest, as he ran toward the town,
Kept turning over, rolling up and down   180
Within his heart the beauty of those bright
New florins, saying, "Lord, to think I might

Have all that treasure to myself alone!
Could there be anyone beneath the throne
Of God so happy as I then should be?"   185
    And so the fiend, our common enemy,
Was given power to put it in his thought
That there was always poison to be bought,
And that with poison he could kill his friends.
To men in such a state the devil sends   190
Thoughts of this kind and has a full permission
To lure them on to sorrow and perdition;
For this young man was utterly content
To kill them both and never to repent.
    And on he ran, he had no thought to tarry,   195
Came to the town, found an apothecary
And said, "Sell me some poison if you will,
I have a lot of rats I want to kill
And there's a polecat, too, about my yard
That takes my chickens and it hits me hard;   200
But I'll get even, as is only right,
With vermin that destroy a man by night."
    The chemist answered, "I've a preparation
Which you shall have, and by my soul's salvation
If any living creature eat or drink   205
A mouthful, ere he has the time to think,
Though he took less than makes a grain of wheat,
You'll see him fall down dying at your feet;
Yes, die he must, and in so short a while
You'd hardly have the time to walk a mile,   210
The poison is so strong, you understand."
    This cursed fellow grabbed into his hand
The box of poison and away he ran
Into a neighboring street, and found a man
Who lent him three large bottles. He withdrew   215
And deftly poured the poison into two.
He kept the third one clean, as well he might,
For his own drink, meaning to work all night
Stacking the gold and carrying it away.
And when this rioter, this devil's clay,   220
Had filled his bottles up with wine, all three,
Back to rejoin his comrades sauntered he.
    Why make a sermon of it? Why waste breath?
Exactly in the way they'd planned his death
They fell on him and slew him, two to one.   225
Then said the first of them when this was done,
"Now for a drink. Sit down and let's be merry,
For later on there'll be the corpse to bury."
And, as it happened, reaching for a sup,
He took a bottle full of poison up   230
And drank; and his companion, nothing loth,
Drank from it also, and they perished both.

There is, in Avicenna's° long relation
Concerning poison and its operation,
Trust me, no ghastlier section to transcend   235
What these two wretches suffered at their end.
Thus these two murderers received their due,
So did the treacherous young poisoner too.

O cursed sin! O blackguardly excess!
O treacherous homicide! O wickedness!   240
O gluttony that lusted on and diced!
O blasphemy that took the name of Christ
With habit-hardened oaths that pride began!
Alas, how comes it that a mortal man,
That thou, to thy Creator, him that wrought thee,   245
That paid his precious blood for thee and bought thee,
Art so unnatural and false within?
    Dearly beloved, God forgive your sin
And keep you from the vice of avarice!
My holy pardon frees you all of this,   250
Provided that you make the right approaches,
That is with sterling, rings, or silver brooches.
Bow down your heads under this holy bull!
Come on, you women, offer up your wool!
I'll write your name into my ledger; so!   255
Into the bliss of heaven you shall go.
For I'll absolve you by my holy power,
You that make offering, clean as at the hour
When you were born . . . That, sirs, is how I preach.
And Jesu Christ, soul's healer, aye, the leech   260
Of every soul, grant pardon and relieve you
Of sin, for that is best, I won't deceive you.
    One thing I should have mentioned in my tale,
Dear people. I've some relics in my bale
And pardons too, as full and fine, I hope,   265
As any in England, given me by the Pope.
If there be one among you that is willing
To have my absolution for a shilling
Devoutly given, come! and do not harden
Your hearts but kneel in humbleness for pardon;   270
Or else, receive my pardon as we go.
You can renew it every town or so
Always provided that you still renew
Each time, and in good money, what is due.
It is an honor to you to have found   275
A pardoner with his credentials sound
Who can absolve you as you ply the spur
In any accident that may occur.
For instance—we are all at fortune's beck—

233. **Avicenna:** an Arabian physician (A.D. 980–1037) who wrote a work on medicines that
includes a chapter on poisons.

Your horse may throw you down and break your neck.   280
What a security it is to all
To have me here among you and at call
With pardon for the lowly and the great
When soul leaves body for the future state!

THE GENERAL PROLOGUE

1. The Prologue of Chaucer's *Canterbury Tales* is one of the most vivid pictures we have of the people and institutions of fourteenth-century England, but it is also a commentary on human nature in general. What general characteristics of human nature can you find in the descriptions of the Squire? the Merchant? the Franklin? the Miller?

2. Compare Chaucer's descriptions of the Monk, the Friar, the Parson and the Pardoner, and tell what comments he is making on the condition of the Church in England in his time. Do you think Chaucer himself was irreligious? Why or why not?

3. There is some question whether Chaucer's treatment of the Prioress is meant to be serious or satiric. What do you think? Support your answer with quotations from the description. Does the association of the Latin phrase (on the brooch) with the Prioress seem at all ambiguous? Explain.

4. Critics say that Chaucer's treatment of even the worst villains in the group is humorous, gentle, and without venom. Find quotations that support or refute this statement.

5. Chaucer's success in depicting his pilgrims derives in large part from his ability to select descriptive details which characterize them. For example, notice what the Squire's apparel reveals about him, what the Monk's favorite amusements reveal about him. Find the descriptive details that reveal something about the character of the woman from Bath, of the Plowman, and of the Pardoner.

THE PARDONER'S TALE

1. Why is the Latin text used by the Pardoner particularly ironic?

2. In the Pardoner's Tale, what did the old man mean when he told the young revelers that they would find Death by the oak tree? How does this tale depend on a misunderstanding caused by the use of personification?

3. What might the old man himself represent? What evidence do you find to support your answer?

4. If the Pardoner's Tale were indeed used as a sermon, how effective would it be with the type of people the Pardoner would probably have as listeners? Support your answer by reference to what he tells you about his congregations.

5. Chaucer's version of the story of the three revelers, an ancient tale which scholars have traced back to India, is much admired as an example of skillful storytelling. Does its effectiveness depend more on plot or on characterization? How does Chaucer achieve suspense? How much does irony contribute to the effectiveness of this story? What other qualities contribute to its success? Can you imagine the tale used as part of a sermon?

ORIGINS OF SURNAMES

1. A list of Chaucer's pilgrims shows that many English surnames are derived from the names of professions; common examples are Miller, Franklin, and Reeve. What was the work of each of these? Make a list of as many such surnames as you can think of. You should have no trouble discovering ten or fifteen, and with a little ingenuity you should find many, many more. In each case, find out what the work was that the person in that profession did.

2. Some names have come from other languages the same way. Thus, Shoemaker and Schumacher are the same name. Miller, Moeller, Mueller, and Molinari all mean the same thing in different languages. How many other such names can you find?

THE TRANSLATION

Chaucer wrote in Middle English, a language which we can clearly recognize as our own but which is still far enough from modern English to be difficult to read. Below are the opening lines of the Pardoner's Prologue as Chaucer wrote them. Aside from differences in spelling and form, most of Chaucer's words are still in use.

● "Lordynges," quod he, "in chirches whan I
 preche,
I peyne me to han an hauteyn speche,
And rynge it out as round as gooth a belle,
For I kan al by rote that I telle.
My theme is alwey oon, and evere was—
Radix malorum est Cupiditas."
—GEOFFREY CHAUCER

1. What modern words correspond to *quod, peyne, han, kan, oon?*

2. Compare Chaucer's version with the translation of these lines which follows. Why is the translation longer? What forced the translator to use the extra lines? How well does the translation duplicate the form of Chaucer's verse? How well does it catch the sense of the original?

● "My lords," he said, "in churches where I
 preach
I cultivate a haughty kind of speech
And ring it out as roundly as a bell;
I've got it all by heart, the tale I tell.
I have a text, it always is the same
And always has been, since I learnt the
 game,
Old as the hills and fresher than the grass,
Radix malorum est cupiditas."
—GEOFFREY CHAUCER

From *The Canterbury Tales* by Geoffrey Chaucer, translated by Nevill Coghill. Reprinted by permission of Penguin Books Ltd.

The Wanderer

(Anonymous)

The translator of this poem, and of the following riddle, has tried to imitate the alliterative character of Anglo-Saxon verse, which is evidence of the strong oral tradition behind it. Both lyrics date from before A.D. 950.

Oft to the wanderer,   weary of exile,
Cometh God's pity,   compassionate love,
Though woefully toiling   on wintry seas
With churning oar   in the icy wave,
Homeless and helpless   he fled from fate.   5
Thus saith the wanderer   mindful of misery,
Grievous disasters,   and death of kin:
   "Oft when the day broke,   oft at the dawning,
Lonely and wretched   I wailed my woe.
No man is living,   no comrade left,   10
To whom I dare fully   unlock my heart.
I have learned truly   the mark of a man
Is keeping his counsel   and locking his lips,
Let him think what he will!   For, woe of heart
Withstandeth not fate;   a failing spirit   15
Earneth no help.   Men eager for honor
Bury their sorrow   deep in the breast.
   "So have I also,   often in wretchedness
Fettered my feelings,   far from my kin,
Homeless and hapless,   since days of old,   20
When the dark earth   covered my dear lord's face,
And I sailed away   with sorrowful heart,
Over wintry seas,   seeking a gold-lord,
If far or near   lived one to befriend me
With gift in the mead hall   and comfort for grief.   25
   "Who bears it, knows   what a bitter companion,
Shoulder to shoulder,   sorrow can be,
When friends are no more.   His fortune is exile,
Not gifts of fine gold;   a heart that is frozen,
Earth's winsomeness dead.   And he dreams of the hall-men,   30
The dealing of treasure,   the days of his youth,
When his lord bade welcome   to wassail and feast.
But gone is that gladness,   and never again
Shall come the loved counsel   of comrade and king.
   "Even in slumber   his sorrow assaileth,   35
And, dreaming he claspeth   his dear lord again,

Head on knee, hand on knee,   loyally laying,
Pledging his liege   as in days long past.
Then from his slumber   he starts lonely-hearted,
Beholding gray stretches   of tossing sea,   40
Sea birds bathing,   with wings outspread,
While hailstorms darken,   and driving snow.
Bitterer then   is the bane of his wretchedness,
The longing for loved one: his grief is renewed.
The forms of his kinsmen   take shape in the silence;   45
In rapture he greets them;   in gladness he scans
Old comrades remembered.   But they melt into air
With no word of greeting   to gladden his heart.
Then again surges   his sorrow upon him;
And grimly he spurs   his weary soul   50
Once more to the toil   of the tossing sea.
   "No wonder therefore,   in all the world,
If a shadow darkens   upon my spirit
When I reflect   on the fates of men—
How one by one   proud warriors vanish   55
From the halls that knew them,   and day by day
All this earth ages   and droops unto death.
No man may know wisdom   till many a winter
Has been his portion.   A wise man is patient,
Not swift to anger,   nor hasty of speech,   60
Neither too weak,   nor too reckless, in war,
Neither fearful nor fain,   nor too wishful of wealth,
Nor too eager in vow—   ere he know the event.
A brave man must bide   when he speaketh his boast
Until he know surely   the goal of his spirit.   65
   "A wise man will ponder   how dread is that doom
When all this world's wealth   shall be scattered and waste
As now, over all,   through the regions of earth,
Walls stand rime-covered   and swept by the winds.
The battlements crumble,   the wine halls decay;   70
Joyless and silent   the heroes are sleeping
Where the proud host fell   by the wall they defended.
Some battle launched   on their long, last journey;
One a bird bore   o'er the billowing sea;
One the gray wolf slew;   one a grieving earl   75
Sadly gave   to the grave's embrace.
The warden of men   hath wasted this world
Till the sound of music   and revel is stilled,
And these giant-built structures   stand empty of life.
   "He who shall muse   on these moldering ruins,   80
And deeply ponder   this darkling life,
Must brood on old legends   of battle and bloodshed,
And heavy the mood   that troubles his heart:
'Where now is the warrior?   Where is the war horse?
Bestowal of treasure,   and sharing of feast?   85
Alas! the bright ale cup,   the byrny-clad warrior,
The prince in his splendor   —those days are long sped

In the night of the past,   as if they never had been!'
And now remains only,   for warriors' memorial,
A wall wondrous high   with serpent shapes carved.   90
Storms of ash spears   have smitten the earls,
Carnage of weapon,   and conquering fate.
   "Storms now batter   these ramparts of stone;
Blowing snow   and the blast of winter
Enfold the earth;   night shadows fall   95
Darkly lowering,   from the north driving
Raging hail   in wrath upon men.
Wretchedness fills   the realm of earth,
And fate's decrees   transform the world.
Here wealth is fleeting,   friends are fleeting,   100
Man is fleeting,   maid is fleeting;
All the foundation of earth   shall fail!"
   Thus spake the sage   in solitude pondering.
Good man is he   who guardeth his faith.
He must never too quickly   unburden his breast   105
Of its sorrow, but eagerly   strive for redress;
And happy the man   who seeketh for mercy
From his heavenly Father,   our fortress and strength.

A Riddle

(Anonymous)

This Anglo-Saxon lyric is written in a form that was popular from the eighth century on. Such verse riddles, usually about objects familiar in country life, cover a wide range of subjects and are characterized by vivid detail. Who or what is speaking?

My attire is noiseless   when I tread the earth,
Rest in its dwellings   or ride its waters.
At times my pinions   and the lofty air
Lift me high   o'er the homes of men,
And the strength of the clouds   carries me far
High over the folk.   My feathers gay
Sound and make music,   swinging shrill,
When no longer I linger   by field or flood,
But soar in air,   a wandering spirit.

WILLIAM, DUKE OF AQUITAINE

By cunning and might, William (1071–1127), Count of Poitou and Duke of Aquitaine, established his sway over all Provence—the southern third of medieval France. He is also known as the first of the troubadours, those composers of love lyrics who flourished in southern France and in parts of Italy and Spain from the eleventh to the thirteenth centuries. Said to have lost 300,000 men on the First Crusade, William wrote poetry as a form of relaxation.

A Song of Nothing

I'll make some verses just for fun
Not about me nor anyone,
Nor deeds that noble knights have done
   Nor love's ado—
I made them riding in the sun.   5
   (My horse helped, too.)

When I was born I cannot say;
I am not sad, I am not gay,
I am not stiff nor dégagé;
   What can I do?   10
Long since enchanted by a fay
   Star-touched I grew.

Dreaming for living I mistake
Unless I'm told when I'm awake.
My heart is sad and nigh to break   15
   With bitter rue—
And I don't care three crumbs of cake
   Or even two.

I have a lady, who or where
I cannot tell you, but I swear   20
She treats me neither ill nor fair
   But I'm not blue
Just so the Normans stay up there
   Out of Poitou.

I have not seen yet I adore   25
This distant love; she sets no store
By what I think and furthermore
   ('Tis sad but true)
Others there are, some three or four,
   I'm faithful to.   30

"A Song of Nothing" by William, Duke of Aquitaine, translated by Thomas G. Bergin from *Medieval Literature in Translation*, edited by Charles W. Jones. Reprinted by permission of Thomas G. Bergin.

So ill I am that death I fear;
I nothing know but what I hear;
I hope there is a doctor here,
   No matter who.
If he can cure me I'll pay dear,   35
   If not, he's through.

I've made the verse; if you'll allow
I think I'll send it off right now
To one who'll pass it on somehow
   Up in Anjou;   40
He'd tell me what it means, I vow,
   If he but knew.

FRANCIS OF ASSISI

Of all the great saints of the medieval Church, Francis (1182–1226) was one of its truly popular and heroic figures. Born to a life of ease in Assisi in Italy, Francis was hardly out of his teens when he gave away all he owned to help the poor. His great achievement was the founding of the Order of Franciscan Friars, who ministered to the poor and despised, and who observed vows of poverty, chastity, and obedience. "Fear not," Francis told these followers, "that you are small and seem foolish. Have confidence in the Lord who vanquished the world." Francis is one of the earliest lyricists to write in the Italian language.

Canticle of the Sun

O most high, almighty, good Lord God, to thee belong praise, glory, honor, and all blessing!

Praised be my Lord God with all his creatures; and specially our brother the sun, who brings us the day, and who brings us the light; fair is he, and shining with a very great splendor: O Lord, he signifies to us thee!

Praised be my Lord for our sister the moon and for the stars, the which he has set clear and lovely in heaven.

Praised be my Lord for our brother the wind and for air and cloud, calms and all weather, by the which thou upholdest in life all creatures.

Praised be my Lord for our sister water, who is very serviceable unto us, and humble, and precious, and clean.

Praised be my Lord for our brother fire, through whom thou givest us light in the darkness; and he is bright, and pleasant, and very mighty, and strong.

"Canticle of the Sun" by Francis of Assisi, translated by Matthew Arnold.

Praised be my Lord for our mother the earth, the which doth sustain us and keep us, and bringeth forth divers fruits, and flowers of many colors, and grass.

Praised be my Lord for all those who pardon one another for his love's sake, and who endure weakness and tribulation; blessed are they who peaceably shall endure, for thou, O most Highest, shall give them a crown!

Praised be my Lord for our sister, the death of the body, from whom no man escapeth. Woe to him who dieth in mortal sin! Blessed are they who are found walking by thy most holy will, for the second death shall have no power to do them harm.

Praise ye, and bless ye the Lord, and give thanks unto him, and serve him with great humility.

Pastourelle Motet

(Anonymous)

Over there in the meadow
Rejoice and sing
Marion and Robin
With the fresh green spring.
She calls to him, "Sweetheart,
Come hither to me,
Robin, Robin, Robin,
Look how lovely I be!"

"Pastourelle Motet" (anonymous), translated by Claude Colleer Abbott. Published in *Early Mediaeval French Lyrics* by Oxford University Press. Reprinted by permission of the publisher.

A king and poet, Thibaud (1201–1253) as a child had known Chrétien. Thibaud spent the year from 1239 to 1240 on a Crusade in Palestine. When he returned to Navarre, he ruled so well for the rest of his life that he was known as *le Bon.*

Crusader's Farewell

Lady, the fates command, and I must go—
   Leaving the pleasant land so dear to me:
Here my heart suffered many a heavy woe;
   But what is left to love, thus leaving thee?
Alas! that cruel land beyond the sea!   5
   Why thus dividing many a faithful heart,
Never again from pain and sorrow free,
   Never again to meet, when thus they part?

I see not, when thy presence bright I leave,
   How wealth, or joy, or peace can be my lot;   10
Ne'er yet my spirit found such cause to grieve
   As now in leaving thee: And if thy thought
Of me in absence should be sorrow-fraught,
   Oft will my heart repentant turn to thee,
Dwelling, in fruitless wishes, on this spot,   15
   And all the gracious words here said to me.

O gracious God! to thee I bend my knee,
   For thy sake yielding all I love and prize;
And O how mighty must that influence be,
   That steals me thus from all my cherished joys!   20
Here, ready, then, myself surrendering,
   Prepared to serve thee, I submit; and ne'er
To one so faithful could I service bring,
   So kind a master, so beloved and dear.

And strong my ties—my grief unspeakable!   25
   Grief, all my choicest treasures to resign;
Yet stronger still the affections that impel
   My heart toward him, the God whose love is mine.
That holy love, how beautiful! how strong!
   Even wisdom's favorite sons take refuge there;   30
'Tis the redeeming gem that shines among
   Men's darkest thoughts—forever bright and fair.

"Crusader's Farewell" by Thibaud, King of Navarre, translated by Edgar Taylor.

Let's Away with Study

(Anonymous)

This poem is from the *Carmina Burana,* a collection of Latin lyrics composed by wandering students in the thirteenth century. These songs are generally light-hearted and irreverent. The students extol pleasure and satirize or parody the classics and the liturgy, which were the subjects of their studies. Most of these wanderers had been turned down for preferment, or were "spoiled priests," so the satire in their songs is understandable.

Let's away with study,
  Folly's sweet.
Treasure all the pleasure
  Of our youth:
Time enough for age   5
  To think on truth.
So short a day,
And life so quickly hasting,
And in study wasting
  Youth that would be gay!   10

'Tis our spring that slipping,
  Winter draweth near,
  Life itself we're losing,
  And this sorry cheer
Dries the blood and chills the heart,   15
  Shrivels all delight.
Age and all its crowd of ills
  Terrifies our sight.
So short a day,
And life so quickly hasting,   20
And in study wasting
  Youth that would be gay!

Let us as the gods do,
  'Tis the wiser part:
Leisure and love's pleasure   25
  Seek the young in heart,
Follow the old fashion,
  Down into the street!
Down among the maidens,
  And the dancing feet!   30

"Let's Away with Study" translated by Helen Waddell from *Medieval Latin Lyrics,* edited by Helen Waddell. Reprinted by permission of Constable Publishers, London.

So short a day,
And life so quickly hasting,
And in study wasting
    Youth that would be gay!

There for the seeing   35
    Is all loveliness,
White limbs moving
    Light in wantonness.
Gay go the dancers,
    I stand and see,   40
Gaze, till their glances
    Steal myself from me.
So short a day
And life so quickly hasting,
And in study wasting   45
    Youth that would be gay!

FRANÇOIS VILLON

François Villon (1431–1463?), a university graduate, poet, and criminal, spent most of his adult life fleeing convictions and arrests. Villon wrote the following epitaph for himself and his friends while they waited to be hanged for implication in several robberies. The sentence was commuted to banishment, and thereafter Villon disappeared from history.

Ballade of the Gibbet

Brothers and men that shall after us be,
    Let not your hearts be hard to us:
For pitying this our misery
    Ye shall find God the more piteous.
    Look on us six that are hanging thus,   5
And for the flesh that so much we cherished
How it is eaten of birds and perished,
    And ashes and dust fill our bones' place,
Mock not at us that so feeble be,
    But pray God pardon us out of his grace.   10

Listen, we pray you, and look not in scorn,
    Though justly, in sooth, we are cast to die;
Ye wot no man so wise is born
    That keeps his wisdom constantly.
    Be ye then merciful, and cry   15

"Ballade of the Gibbet" by François Villon, translated by Andrew Lang.

To Mary's Son that is piteous,
That his mercy take no stain from us,
    Saving us out of the fiery place.
We are but dead, let no soul deny
    To pray God succor us of his grace.   20

The rain out of heaven has washed us clean,
    The sun has scorched us black and bare,
Ravens and rooks have pecked at our eyes,
    And feathered their nests with our beards and hair.
    Round are we tossed, and here and there,   25
This way and that, at the wild wind's will,
Never a moment my body is still;
    Birds they are busy about my face
Live not as we, nor fare as we fare;
    Pray God pardon us out of his grace.   30

                    L'ENVOY

Prince Jesus, master of all, to thee
We pray hell gain no mastery,
    That we come never anear that place;
And ye men, make no mockery,
    Pray God pardon us out of his grace.   35

THE WANDERER

1. What is the present lot of the wanderer? What was his former position? What is he seeking?

2. This is a poem within a poem. The inner poem discusses the power of fate, and the opening and closing sections discuss the power of faith. It is possible that the outer poem—that is, the opening and closing sections—may have been added to an earlier poem by a Christian monk, who was recording this poem for future generations. Do the additions weaken the expression of grief in the inner poem, or do the two parts merge to make one effective poem? Does the inner poem show Christian influence, or is it pagan? What makes you think so?

3. A line of Anglo-Saxon poetry, as illustrated in this poem and in the riddle which follows, is in two short segments, each having two accented syllables. The segments are separated by a short pause (caesura). The two segments are unified by alliteration; at least one word in the first segment alliterates with one in the second. Locate the accents, the caesura, and the alliteration in several lines of the poem. How does this poetic technique influence the emphasis of your reading?

A RIDDLE

This anonymous Anglo-Saxon riddle is about a wild swan. What does the existence of such riddles suggest to you about medieval men and their amusements? What does the subject matter of this riddle suggest about their manner of life?

A SONG OF NOTHING

1. In the first stanza, this poem obviously satirizes poets in general. How is this done? What other things or ideas are satirized?

2. What is the poet's attitude toward the conventions of courtly love? Where does this attitude show itself? How does the poet make his attitude clear?

3. Some elements in this poem are pure nonsense. Which are these? Do they suggest that nonsense humor is much the same in all ages? Explain.

4. Normandy and Anjou were other duchies of medieval France. Their rulers were rivals to William, who ruled Poitou (Poitiers) and Aquitaine. What humorously practical at-

titude does William reveal about his political fortunes?

5. William was the ruler of a substantial part of France. If you found that a candidate for President of the United States wrote poetry as a hobby, would you regard his candidacy with more or less favor? Why?

CANTICLE OF THE SUN

1. Compare this song with the Hebrew psalms on pages 30–36. What is the advantage, if any, in the way the praises are catalogued in Francis' song?

2. What things in nature does St. Francis mention as being worthy of special thanks? Why might Francis use terms of kinship for these natural forces—even for death?

PASTOURELLE MOTET

A *pastourelle* is a medieval verse form which presents in dialogue the wooing of a simple girl, generally a country girl, by someone of a higher station. The man might be a knight, a scholar, or a poet. His suit usually includes a request to go with the girl into the countryside, and it was frequently interrupted by the girl's unwillingness or by the appearance of her relatives. This poem is not, strictly speaking, consistent with the usual pattern of a *pastourelle,* but it has some of its elements, especially the pastoral environment and mood, the delight in love, and the use of dialogue.

1. In what ways is this poem pastoral? How does the poet suggest the spirit and feeling of spring?

2. *Motet* is the diminutive for "word" in Old French. How can the term be applied to this lyric?

CRUSADER'S FAREWELL

1. Two kinds of love are discussed in this poem. What are they? Which one does the poet consider to be stronger?

2. Which kind of love seems to be spoken of with more heartfelt emotion by the poet? Cite words and phrases to support your answer.

3. What decision has the crusader been forced to make? Why does his decision seem appropriate for him personally? Would it be appropriate for any medieval man? Explain.

LET'S AWAY WITH STUDY

1. The student's eternal conflict is represented here. What arguments are used by the speakers to support their decision to cast study aside? Do they sound familiar? Explain.

2. In the last two stanzas the speakers make particularly effective use of imagery. What quick but graphic pictures do they select to evoke the feeling of pleasure? Which words are most pictorial?

3. What, if anything, does the refrain contribute to this song? Why do you suppose it was used?

BALLADE OF THE GIBBET

1. Villon wrote this verse with the assumption that the reader would see before him the hanging bodies of the criminals left out in public to decay. What specific pictures of the corpses does Villon present? Do these pictures suggest that hanging bodies were a familiar or an unfamiliar sight in medieval times? Explain.

2. Six corpses left hanging in the open would seem horrifying to us. How did medieval people seem to regard them? What customs of contemporary times will horrify someone from another era?

3. What effect do the refrain and envoy have on the poem?

4. What archaic words are used in this translation? How do these words affect the poem?

COMPARING TRANSLATIONS

1. Like the original in Anglo-Saxon, the modern English translation of "The Wanderer" by Charles Kennedy does not rhyme. Below are rhymed lines from another, older translation. Are they more or less effective in evoking the appropriate mood? Why?

● Still the lone one and desolate waits for his
    Maker's ruth—
  God's good mercy, albeit so long it tarry, in
    sooth.
  Careworn and sad of heart, on the watery
    ways must be
  Plow with the hand-grasped oar—how long?
    —the rime-cold sea,
  Tread thy paths of exile, O Fate, who art
    cruelty. (*Translated by Emily Hickey*)

Lines from "The Wanderer," translated by Emily Hickey, and "The Swan," translated by Herbert Brougham, from *Select Translations from Old English Poetry,* edited by Albert S. Cook and Chauncey B. Tinker. Reprinted by permission of Harvard University Press.

Looking only at the word choice this time, compare the lines below, from the same translation, with the corresponding section in the translation by Charles Kennedy. What words in the translation below are so literary that they destroy the simplicity which is so much a part of Anglo-Saxon poetry? What words or phrases has Kennedy used in place of the ones you have found? Are they better? If so, in what way?

● Behind the dear and doughty there standeth
    now a wall,
  A wall that is wondrous high, and with won-
    drous snakework wrought,
  The strength of the spears hath fordone the
    earls and hath made them naught,
  The weapons greedy of slaughter, and she,
    the mighty Wyrd;
  And the tempests beat on the rocks, and the
    storm wind that maketh afeard . . .
          (*Translated by Emily Hickey*)

2. Below is another translation of the riddle about the wild swan. Which translation, the one below or the one on page 457 in the text, has the form and the word choice which you think is most nearly appropriate to Anglo-Saxon poetry? Give specific illustrations to support your answer.

● My robe is noiseless while I tread the earth,
  Or tarry 'neath the banks, or stir the shal-
    lows;
  But when these shining wings, this depth
    of air,
  Bear me aloft above the bending shores
  Where men abide, and far the welkin's
    strength
  Over the multitudes conveys me, then
  With rushing whir and clear melodious
    sound
  My raiment sings. And like a wandering
    spirit
  I float unweariedly o'er flood and field.
        (*Translated by Herbert Brougham*)

Sir Patrick Spens

(Anonymous)

This ballad, and the next one, are said to be based loosely on historical events. The king in "Sir Patrick Spens" is said to be a Norwegian king who hired Scottish sailors to take him, his Scottish bride, and her attendants back to Norway.

The king sits in Dumferling town,
    Drinking the blood-red wine:
"O where will I get good sailors
    To sail this ship of mine?"

Up and spoke an old knight,   5
    Sat at the king's right knee:
"Sir Patrick Spens is the best sailor
    That sails upon the sea."

The king has written a broad letter,
    And signed it with his hand,   10
And sent it to Sir Patrick Spens,
    Was walking on the sand.

The first line that Sir Patrick read
    A loud laugh laughed he:
The next line that Sir Patrick read,   15
    A tear blinded his ee.

"O who is this has done this deed,
    This ill deed done to me,
To send me out this time of the year
    To sail upon the sea?   20

"Make haste, make haste, my merry men all,
    Our good ship sails at morn."
"O say not so, my master dear,
    For I fear a deadly storm.

"Late, late last night I saw the new moon   25
    With the old moon in her arm,
And I fear, I fear, my master dear,
    That we will come to harm."

This version of "Sir Patrick Spens" is from *How Does a Poem Mean?* by John Ciardi.

O our Scots nobles were right loth
  To wet their cork-heeled shoon;   30
But long ere all the play was played,
  Their hats they swam aboon.

O long, long will their ladies sit
  With their fans into their hand,
Before they see Sir Patrick Spens   35
  Come sailing to the land.

O long, long will the ladies stand
  With their gold combs in their hair,
Waiting for their own dear lords,
  For they'll see them no mair.   40

Half-o'er, half-o'er to Abadour
  'Tis fifty fathoms deep,
And there lies good Sir Patrick Spens
  With the Scots lords at his feet.

Johnny Armstrong

(Anonymous)

There dwelt a man in fair Westmorland,
  Johnny Armstrong men did him call,
He had neither lands nor rents coming in,
  Yet he kept eight score men in his hall.

He had horse and harness for them all,   5
  Goodly steeds were all milk-white;
O the golden bands about their necks,
  And their weapons, they were all alike.

News then was brought unto the king
  That there was such a one as he,   10
That lived like a bold outlaw,
  And robbed all the north country.

The king he wrote out a letter then,
  A letter which was large and long;
He signed it with his own/hand,   15
  And he promised to do him no wrong.

When this letter came Johnny unto,
   His heart it was as blithe as birds on the tree.
"Never was I sent for before any king,
   My father, my grandfather, nor none but me.   20

"And if we go the king before,
   I would we went most orderly;
Every man of you shall have his scarlet cloak,
   Laced with silver laces three.

"Every one of you shall have his velvet coat,   25
   Laced with silver lace so white;
O the golden bands about your necks,
   Black hats, white feathers, all alike."

By the morrow morning at ten of the clock,
   Toward Edinborough gone was he,   30
And with him all his eight score men;
   Good Lord, it was a goodly sight for to see!

When Johnny came before the king,
   He fell down on his knee,
"O pardon, my sovereign liege," he said,   35
   "O pardon my eight score men and me!"

"Thou shalt have no pardon, thou traitor strong,
   For thy eight score men nor thee;
For tomorrow morning by ten of the clock,
   Both thou and them shall hang on the gallows tree."   40

But Johnny looked over his left shoulder,
   Good Lord, what a grievous look looked he!
Saying, "Asking grace of a graceless face—
   Why there is none for you nor me."

But Johnny had a bright sword by his side,   45
   And it was made of the metal so free,
That had not the king stepped his foot aside,
   He had smitten his head from his fair body.

Saying, "Fight on, my merry men all,
   And see that none of you be ta'en;   50
For rather than men shall say we were hanged,
   Let them report how we were slain."

Then, God wot, fair Edinborough rose,
   And so beset poor Johnny round,
That fourscore and ten of Johnny's best men   55
   Lay gasping all upon the ground.

Then like a mad man Johnny laid about,
  And like a mad man then fought he,
Until a false Scot came Johnny behind,
  And run him through the fair body.   60

Saying, "Fight on, my merry men all,
  And see that none of you be ta'en;
For I will stand by and bleed but awhile,
  And then I will come and fight again."

News then was brought to young Johnny Armstrong,   65
  As he stood by his nurse's knee,
Who vowed if e'er he lived for to be a man,
  On the treacherous Scots revenged he'd be.

The Two Sisters

(Anonymous)

There were two sisters sat in a bower;
  Binnorie, O Binnorie;
There came a knight to be their wooer;
  By the bonny milldams of Binnorie.

He courted the eldest with gloves and rings,   5
But he loved the youngest above all things.

The eldest was vexèd to despair,
And much she envied her sister fair.

The eldest said to the youngest one,
"Will ye see our father's ships come in?"   10

She's taken her by the lily-white hand,
And led her down to the river strand.

The youngest stood upon a stone;
The eldest came and pushed her in.

"O sister, sister, reach your hand,   15
And you shall be heir of half my land.

"O sister, reach me but your glove
And sweet William shall be all your love."

"Sink on, nor hope for hand or glove!
Sweet William shall surely be my love."   20

Sometimes she sank, sometimes she swam,
Until she came to the mouth of the dam.

Out then came the miller's son
And saw the fair maid swimming in.

"O father, father, draw your dam!   25
Here's either a mermaid or a swan."

The miller hasted and drew his dam,
And there he found a drowned womàn.

You could not see her middle small
Her girdle was so rich withal.   30

You could not see her yellow hair
For the gold and pearls that clustered there.

And by there came a harper fine
Who harped to nobles when they dine.

And when he looked that lady on,   35
He sighed and made a heavy moan.

He's made a harp of her breastbone,
Whose sounds would melt a heart of stone.

He's taken three locks of her yellow hair
And with them strung his harp so rare.   40

He went into her father's hall
To play his harp before them all.

But as he laid it on a stone,
The harp began to play alone.

And soon the harp sang loud and clear,   45
"Farewell, my father and mother dear.

"Farewell, farewell, my brother Hugh,
Farewell, my William, sweet and true."

And then as plain as plain could be,
  Binnorie, O Binnorie   50
"There sits my sister who drownèd me
  By the bonny milldams of Binnorie!"

The Conquest of Alhama

(Retold by George Gordon, Lord Byron)

Byron's poem is probably a combination of three or more ballads which are included in a volume called *Guerras Civiles de Granada,* published in 1595. Byron romantically claims that the Moors were forbidden to sing the ballad in Granada on pain of death.

The Moorish king rides up and down,
Through Granada's royal town;
From Elvira's gates to those
Of Bivarambla on he goes.
     Woe is me, Alhama!   5

Letters to the monarch tell
How Alhama's city fell:
In the fire the scroll he threw
And the messenger he slew.
     Woe is me, Alhama!   10

He quits his mule and mounts his horse,
And through the street directs his course;
Through the street of Zacatin
To the Alhambra spurring in.
     Woe is me, Alhama!   15

When the Alhambra walls he gained
On the moment he ordained
That the trumpet straight should sound
With the silver clarion round.
     Woe is me, Alhama!   20

And when the hollow drums of war
Beat the loud alarm afar,
That the Moors of town and plain
Might answer to the martial strain.
     Woe is me, Alhama!   25

Then the Moors, by this aware,
That bloody Mars recalled them there,
One by one, and two by two,
To a mighty squadron grew.
     Woe is me, Alhama!   30

Out then spake an aged Moor
In these words the king before,

"Wherefore call on us, O King?
What may mean this gathering?"
     Woe is me, Alhama!   35

"Friends! ye have, alas! to know
Of a most disastrous blow;
That the Christians, stern and bold,
Have obtained Alhama's hold."
     Woe is me, Alhama!   40

Out then spake old Alfaqui,
With his beard so white to see,
"Good King! thou art justly served,
Good King! this thou hast deserved.
     Woe is me, Alhama!   45

"By thee were slain, in evil hour,
The Abencerrage, Granada's flower;
And strangers were received by thee
Of Cordova the Chivalry.
     Woe is me, Alhama!   50

"And for this, O King! is sent
On thee a double chastisement:
Thee and thine, thy crown and realm,
One last wreck shall overwhelm.
     Woe is me, Alhama!   55

"He who hold no laws in awe,
He must perish by the law;
And Granada must be won,
And thyself with her undone."
     Woe is me, Alhama!   60

Fire flashed from out the old Moor's eyes;
The monarch's wrath began to rise,
Because he answered, and because
He spake exceeding well of laws.
     Woe is me, Alhama!   65

"There is no law to say such things
As may disgust the ear of kings:"—
Thus, snorting with his choler, said
The Moorish king and doomed him dead.
     Woe is me, Alhama!   70

Moor Alfaqui! Moor Alfaqui!
Though thy beard so hoary be,
The king hath sent to have thee seized,
For Alhama's loss displeased.
     Woe is me, Alhama!   75

And to fix thy head upon
High Alhambra's loftiest stone;
That this for thee should be the law,
And others tremble when they saw.
   Woe is me, Alhama!   80

"Cavalier! and man of worth!
Let these words of mine go forth!
Let the Moorish monarch know,
That to him I nothing owe.
   Woe is me, Alhama!   85

"But on my soul Alhama weighs,
And on my inmost spirit preys;
And if the king his land hath lost,
Yet others may have lost the most.
   Woe is me, Alhama!   90

"Sires have lost their children,—wives,
Their lords,—and valiant men, their lives!
One what best his love might claim
Hath lost,—another, wealth or fame.
   Woe is me, Alhama!   95

"I lost a damsel in that hour,
Of all the land the loveliest flower;
Doubloons a hundred I would pay,
And think her ransom cheap that day."
   Woe is me, Alhama!   100

And as these things the old Moor said,
They severed from the trunk his head;
And to the Alhambra's wall with speed
'Twas carried, as the king decreed.
   Woe is me, Alhama!   105

And men and infants therein weep
Their loss, so heavy and so deep;
Granada's ladies, all she rears
Within her walls, burst into tears.
   Woe is me, Alhama!   110

And from the windows o'er the walls
The sable web of mourning falls;
The king weeps as a woman o'er
His loss—for it is much and sore.
   Woe is me, Alhama!   115

1. The action in "Sir Patrick Spens" and "Johnnie Armstrong" is initiated by the sending of a letter. What other similarities do you find in the plots of the two stories?

2. When sung, "The Two Sisters" would have a refrain for the second and fourth lines of each stanza, although the refrain is printed in the text only for the first and final stanzas. This is one kind of repetition used in this ballad. Another is the repetition of certain words or patterns of expression. Find examples of such repetition in this ballad. Why would repetition in so many forms appear in literature of the oral tradition?

3. The translation of the Moorish ballad "Alhama" by the poet Byron (1788–1824) contains language more typical of a literary ballad than of an authentic folk ballad. An example is the allusion to "bloody Mars" in line 27. Find other examples. What is their effect on the ballad?

4. Folk ballads are characteristically direct in their storytelling. They omit details of characterization, moralizing, and background information. How is "Sir Patrick Spens" a good example of such directness? Compare it with the more literary "Alhama." What stanza would probably be omitted from the latter if it were in the oral tradition? Why?

5. Both "Johnnie Armstrong" and "Alhama" say something about the relationship between the common people and their rulers. How are the comments similar? Do they differ in any way?

6. How do the various kinds of songs popular today compare in subject matter and structure with these medieval ballads?

FIGURES OF SPEECH

Typically, the language of folk ballads is full of commonplace figures of speech. Locate the stock figures of speech used in the first three ballads. What colors are used time after time? Can you find any especially vivid figures of speech used at all?

Any language is full of images that were once bright and original and that become dull and commonplace with use. English examples that come immediately to mind might include "dead as a doornail," "stone-deaf," "blind as a bat." Make a list of at least twenty-five such stock figures of speech. How effective are they? Can they ever serve a useful purpose in writing or speech? If so, what? What is their

effect in the ballads? Discuss their use in the songs and ballads popular today.

COMPARING BALLAD VERSIONS

"The Two Sisters" is based on the stock theme of the love triangle. Does the ballad take sides in the issue, or is the story told without passing judgment? In considering this question, compare the version in the text with the following American version, sung today in the southern Appalachian Mountains:

There was an old lord by the Northern Sea,
And he had daughters one, two, three.

A young man he came a-courting there,
And he did choose the young and fair.

He gave his love a gay, gold ring;
Her sister thought it a horrid thing.

He gave his love a beaver hat;
Her ugly sister thought hard of that.

The sisters walked down by the water's brim,
The ugly one pushed the fair one in.

She floated down where the miller sat,
He took her ring and her beaver hat.

The ugly sister was burned at the stake,
The miller was hanged for what he taked.
—ANONYMOUS

What words make the American version more judgmental? What has become of the supernatural element in the trans-Atlantic crossing? What does this tell you about the place of the supernatural in medieval culture as compared to its place in American culture? What cultural difference is suggested in the emphasis on the punishment of the ugly sister and the miller in the American version?

FOR COMPOSITION

Review the characteristics of the ballads, then write a ballad about some sensational or tragic incident of modern times. See if you can eliminate from your ballad all those details that would be eliminated if it had been preserved in the oral tradition. Choose your refrain with care. The typical ballad stanza consists of four lines, with the second and fourth lines rhyming; try to imitate these typical structures.

THE

RENAISSANCE

c. 1300 – c. 1650

I N THE FIFTEENTH and sixteenth centuries, from the time that Portuguese navigators began probing along the shorelines of Africa, voyaging was about the most exciting thing that was happening in the world. Voyages of discovery probably did more than any other single factor to bring about the tremendous changes that affected Europe during this period.

Europe had been trading with the East since the times of the Crusades, in the eleventh and twelfth centuries. The demand for the exotic spices and woods and cloths of the East had brought great prosperity to traders and merchant-speculators, especially to those living in Venice and other Italian towns situated between the East and the rest of Europe. But the capture of Constantinople by the Turks in 1453 temporarily barred the Mediterranean as a route to the East. As a consequence, the Portuguese and Spaniards, who had looked enviously at the growing wealth and splendor of the Italians, set out to find their own way to the East. The effort was more successful than anyone could have dreamed, for it led not only to a route East around the tip of Africa, but to the discovery of the hitherto unknown continents of the Americas, with their untold riches. Nor was booty the whole story, nor even the opening of the vast territories. The first step had been taken in a process that would bring about the involvement, for good or for ill, of all men with all. From this period on, to an ever-increasing degree, the history of any nation or of any region would find its place in the global history of mankind.

The lure of voyaging is reflected in the following account written by Richard Hakluyt (1552–1616). Hakluyt tells of his first fascination with voyaging, which probably seemed to him at least as fantastic and wondrous as space explorations seem to our own age.

● I do remember that being a youth, and one of her Majesties scholars at Westminster that fruitfull nurserie, it was my happe to visit the chamber of M. Richard Hakluyt my cosin, a Gentleman of the Middle Temple, well knowen unto you, at a time when I found lying open upon his boord certeine bookes of Cosmographie, with an universall Mappe: he seeing me somewhat curious in the view thereof, began to instruct my ignorance, by shewing me the division of the earth into three parts after the olde account, and then according to the latter, & better distribution, into more: he pointed with his wand to all the knowen Seas, Gulfs, Bayes, Straights, Capes, Rivers, Empires, Kingdomes, Dukedomes, and Territories of ech part, with declaration also of their speciall commodities, & particular wants, which by the benefit of traffike, & entercourse of merchants, are plentifully supplied. From the Mappe he brought me to the Bible, and turning to the 107 Psalme, directed mee to the 23 & 24 verses, where I read, that they which go downe to the sea in ships, and occupy by the great waters, they see the works of the Lord, and his woonders in the deepe, &c. Which words of the Prophet together with my cousin's discourse (things of high and rare delight to my yong nature) tooke in me so deepe an impression, that I constantly resolved, if ever I were preferred to the University, where better time, and more convenient place might be ministred for these studies, I would by God's assistance prosecute that knowledge and kinde of literature, the doores whereof (after a sort) were so happily opened before me.—RICHARD HAKLUYT

Commercial centers all over Europe prospered as a result of the rich trade that voyages of exploration made possible. The life of one of the most important of these centers, Antwerp in Belgium, was described in detail by Ludovico Guicciardini (1523–1589), a courtier in the service of the Medici family of Florence, who published in 1567 an account of his journey through the Low Countries.

● The second of the notable advantages which have made the city of Antwerp so great, rich, and famous, began about the year 1503–1504, when the Portuguese, by marvelous and amazing navigation and with warlike equipment, having, just before, occupied Calicut, made a treaty with the king of that region. They began to transport spices and drugs from India to Portugal and then to carry them from Portugal to the fairs in this city. . . .

The inhabitants of this city are for the most part engaged in commerce, and indeed they are great merchants and very rich, some here being worth two hundred thousand, others up to four hundred thousand crowns a man, and more. They are courteous, civil, ingenious, quick to imitate foreigners, and to intermarry with them. They are capable of dwelling and carrying on business throughout the world. Most of them, and even the women (though they may not have been out of the country), know how to speak three or four languages, not to mention those who speak five and six and seven; this is something to marvel at as well as a great advantage. They have artisans proficient in every kind of art and craft, for they work so well that they sell their products even before these are finished, and, as everyone knows, continual work brings perfection.

Now as to the kind and number of crafts exercised in this city, one can almost say in a single word—all. For here they make cloth, linens of every kind, tapestry, Turkish carpets and fustians; armor and all other munitions of war; they carry on tanning, painting, dyeing, color-making, gilding, silvering, glassmaking in the Venetian style; they make every kind of mercery, of gold, of silver, of silk, of thread, of wool, and small wares of metals of all kinds and other things beyond number. They also make here all kinds of silk cloth, such as velvet, satin, damask, sarsenet, taffeta, and others; but what is more, from their own silkworms, and contrary almost to nature and to the climate of this country, they produce and weave silk itself, although in small quantity. This, in addition to what comes to them from outside (which is of inestimable value), they work up in all ways and manners. They refine in quantity, with great industry and skill, metals, wax, sugar, and other merchandise. And it is only here that vermilion, which we call cinnabar, is made.—LUDOVICO GUICCIARDINI

HUMANISM AND THE NEW LEARNING

These exciting times of prosperity and discovery stirred the imaginations of artists and challenged the traditional ideas of medieval philosophers and scientists. The new commerce was attracting people away from the land and was changing the old feudal order. All of these challenges and changes seemed radical enough and consistent enough to be thought of as a movement, a bold self-assertive movement that called for new intellectual freedom from the great medieval traditions. This movement began in Italy in the fourteenth century. It spread north and west gradually, until it finally reached England in the sixteenth century, just when her geographic location was becoming crucially advantageous in the fierce competition to acquire territories and riches in America.

This movement has come to be called the Renaissance, "rebirth." Scholars today question whether we should use such a term at all. The name seems to imply an unfair slighting of the preceding medieval centuries. Such scholars prefer to emphasize the continuity of culture by view-

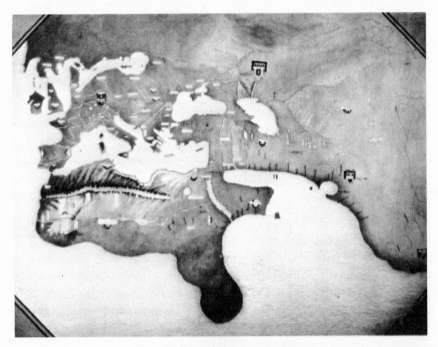

A fifteenth-century map. At bottom is the cartographer's concept of Africa.

ing the achievements of the great scientists and philosophers and artists of the fourteenth and following centuries as outgrowths of the achievements of less well-known men of the twelfth and thirteenth centuries.

Nevertheless, we can detect a spirit in this "renaissance" movement that may justify marking it off. The sense of wonder and excitement that struck Hakluyt when he looked at his cousin's global map seemed to be everywhere in this period. To the men of the Renaissance, the world was suddenly bigger and more varied than it had seemed before. The explorations revealed rich continents where they had thought only raging seas prevailed. The discoveries of exotic people with strange ways did something toward shaking the complacency and self-interest of Europeans. Men felt that new ways were opening in all directions, that the world was beginning afresh to meet—and this time to conquer—its ancient ills. In the following poem, "The Philosophic Flight," the Italian philosopher and poet Giordano Bruno (1548–1600) expresses this sense of intellectual adventure.

● Now that these wings to speed my wish ascend,
    The more I feel vast air beneath my feet,
    The more toward boundless air on pinions fleet,
    Spurning the earth, soaring to heaven, I tend:
    Nor makes them stoop their flight the direful end

"The Philosophic Flight" by Giordano Bruno, translated by John Addington Symonds.

Of Daedal's son; but upward still they beat.
What life the while with this death could compete,
  If dead to earth at last I must descend?
My own heart's voice in the void air I hear.
  Where wilt thou bear me, O rash man! Recall
  Thy daring will! This boldness waits on fear!
Dread not, I answer, that tremendous fall:
  Strike through the clouds, and smile when death is near,
  If death so glorious be our doom at all!

—GIORDANO BRUNO

Many important discoveries began to be made by new scientists, men who sought information about the universe, about the workings of the human body, about the causes of disease, about mechanics. In the Middle Ages, people had assumed that whatever ancient writers like Aristotle and Galen had set down about the physical world was true, and what they hadn't set down was not worth knowing. In general, medieval churchmen feared that new discoveries by science would threaten Christian theology. In what was often dangerous opposition to this tradition, men of the new science replaced the authority of Aristotle with the methods of Aristotle: to observe, record, classify, and finally theorize.

Andreas Vesalius (1514–1564), for one notable example, wrote a new and complete account of human anatomy which is a landmark in the history of medicine. Vesalius, who had to defend his findings against the age-old authority of the Greek physician Galen, pointed out that medical knowledge was in a state of darkness because progress was hampered by old taboos. To study anatomy, Vesalius had to fight the notion that the practice of dissecting corpses was the work of the devil, a notion that arose from the Christians' respect for the body and their faith in its ultimate resurrection. Men before Vesalius had, in fact, liberated themselves and had learned most of what Vesalius now published; but it was left to Vesalius to defend publicly the practice of dissection as scientifically necessary.

But the most far-reaching theories were advanced by Nicholas Copernicus (1473–1543), a Polish physician and astronomer who had studied in Italy. He provided the mathematical basis for the conclusion that the heavenly bodies revolved around the sun, *not* around the earth. Copernicus's conclusions frightened many religious people, since these theories seemed to contradict the Bible. Churchmen had looked upon the "fact" that the earth was the hub of the universe as upholding the Christian concept that man was the climax of creation and the chief concern of God.

Perhaps the richest store of Renaissance scientific speculation is in the notebooks of Leonardo da Vinci (1452–1519). One of the greatest of Renaissance artists, da Vinci was also the most productive and versatile experimenter and inventor. His notebooks were compiled mostly between

1482 and 1498, a period when he was in the service of the Sforza family at the court of Milan, where he produced his famous painting of the Last Supper. The entries in his notebooks, ranging in length from a sentence or two to whole essays, explore just about every aspect of natural science and many aspects of mechanics, including plans for airplanes and submarines. The notes are profusely illustrated and include precise anatomical drawings, which Leonardo made from scientific curiosity and as studies for his painting and sculpture. The following passage, in which he considers explanations offered for the appearance of spots on the moon, is a good example of Leonardo's observation and reasoning.

● Some have said that vapors are given off from the moon after the manner of clouds, and are interposed between the moon and our eyes. If this were the case these spots would never be fixed either as to position or shape; and when the moon was seen from different points, even though these spots did not alter their position, they would change their shape, as does a thing which is seen on different sides.

Others have said that the moon is made up of parts, some more, some less transparent, as though one part were after the manner of alabaster, and another like crystal or glass. It would then follow that when the rays of the sun struck the less transparent part, the light would stay on the surface, and consequently the denser part would be illuminated, and the transparent part would reveal the shadows of its obscure depths. Thus then they define the nature of the moon, and this view has found favor with many philosophers, and especially with Aristotle; but nevertheless it is false, since in the different phases which the moon and the sun frequently present to our eyes, we should be seeing these spots vary, and at one time they would appear dark and at another light. They would be dark when the sun is in the west and the moon in the center of the sky, because the transparent hollows would then be in shadow, as far as the tops of their edges, since the sun could not cast its rays into the mouths of these same hollows; and they would appear bright at full moon, when the moon in the east faces the sun in the west; for then the sun would illumine even the lowest depths of these transparent parts, and in consequence, as no shadow was created, the moon would not at such times reveal to us the above-mentioned spots, and so it would be, sometimes more, sometimes less, according to the change in the position of the sun to the moon and of the moon to our eyes, as I have said above.—LEONARDO DA VINCI

In the Renaissance, *scientia* (meaning "knowledge," all kinds of knowledge) was inextricably bound to *philosophia*, the "love of wisdom." Without being less concerned for man's soul and his eternal life, the writers and thinkers of the Renaissance were also concerned with the perfectibility of

From *The Notebooks of Leonardo da Vinci*, translated and edited by Edward MacCurdy. Reprinted by permission of Harcourt, Brace & World, Inc.

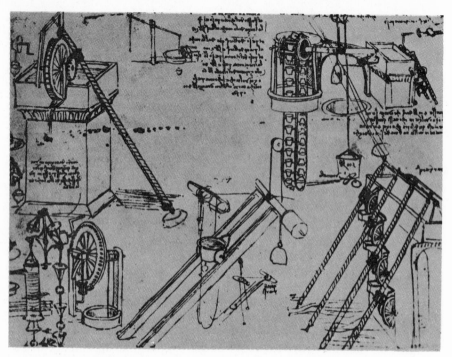

Hydraulic machinery designed by da Vinci. Note his famous mirror handwriting.

man and society in this world. They looked on the ancient Greeks and Romans as potent examples of how human reason had helped men wisely conduct their affairs without the aid of divine revelation (that is, without the help of the Hebrew and Christian Bible).

Thus scholars were recovering and reexamining old texts, particularly those by the ancient Roman writers, and the process of printing by movable type was making these classics widely available. Education based upon a solid knowledge of classical Latin and a competence in Greek—though not neglecting the study of Christian doctrine—became the road to wisdom, and wisdom would help men live together in harmony, with justice.

Desiderius Erasmus (1466–1536), a Dutch priest and scholar, was recognized throughout Europe as the leader of the new "humanism," a philosophy which had originated among the classical scholars of the Italian academies a century before. Erasmus was unquestionably the most influential intellectual in Europe in his time. He moved about Europe among scholars and princes; he wrote textbooks in Greek and Latin; he made a new Latin translation of the Greek text of the New Testament. He was a sharp critic of abuses in the Church and an effective advocate of radical reform, but he had no intention of challenging the fundamental authority of the Church. He annoyed the militant Protestants by refusing to join Martin Luther, but this fidelity was cold comfort to his friend the Dutch Pope Adrian VI, who made some attempts at internal reform but was not spared the sting of Erasmus' criticisms.

Erasmus did more than anyone else to propagate the new humanism, which was characterized by a belief in developing and exalting the "whole man"—his body as well as his spirit. The humanists revived the study of the classic writings in Greek and Latin, not in an attempt to make them conform to Christian doctrine, but in a new attempt to understand them in their own right. It is easy to understand why the literatures of Greece and Rome appealed to the humanists. Like them, the people of the ancient cultures believed in the perfectibility of man, in the pleasures of the world of here and now, and in personal freedom. In line with their emphasis on free inquiry, the humanists believed in a rational examination of religious doctrines, and this frequently led to a new critical attitude toward the Church.

The new educational philosophy of the humanists was also described and advocated by François Rabelais (1495–1553), in one of the most remarkable and yet characteristic literary works of the period. Rabelais wrote a series of stories, collectively called *Gargantua and Pantagruel,* concerning a line of gigantic rulers of a mythical kingdom. In these stories, Rabelais parodies the France of his day and expresses his own ideals of law, government, and religion. *Gargantua and Pantagruel* expresses tremendous gusto for life. Gargantua, for example, is born crying for drink and is promptly mollified with great casks of wine. Gargantua's appetite is Rabelais's symbol of an unquenchable thirst for all experience, all the pleasures of mind and body, and as such it is a fair symbol of the Renaissance.

Rabelais puts his views on education into his account of the education of Gargantua, which was first carried on under the old monastic regimen of the Middle Ages, and then under the enlightened classical education of the New Learning. Gargantua, the humanist-educated king, in turn gives advice to his son Pantagruel, who has gone off to Paris to study. "Learn all languages perfectly," he says; that is, Greek and Latin in the purest style of the ancients, and Hebrew, Chaldaic, and Arabic, "for the sake of Holy Scriptures." He prescribes cosmography and astronomy, geometry, arithmetic, and music, civil law and philosophy.

● As for a knowledge of the facts of nature, I would have you apply yourself to this study with such curiosity that there should be no sea, river, or stream of which you do not know the fish; you should likewise be familiar with all the birds of the air, all the trees, shrubs, and thickets of the forest, all the grasses of the earth, all the metals hidden in the bellies of the abysses, and the precious stones of all the East and South: let nothing be unknown to you.

From "Gargantua and Pantagruel" from *The Portable Rabelais,* translated by Samuel Putnam. Reprinted by permission of Crown Publishers, Inc.

Then, very carefully, go back to the books of the Greek, Arabic, and Latin physicians, not disdaining the Talmudists and the Cabalists, and by means of frequent dissections, see to it that you acquire a perfect knowledge of that other world which is man. And at certain hours of the day, form the habit of spending some time with the Holy Scriptures. First in Greek, the New Testament and the Epistles of the Apostles; and then, in Hebrew, the Old Testament.

In short, let me see you an abysm of science, for when you shall have become a full-grown man, you will have to forsake your quiet life and leisurely studies, to master the art of knighthood and of arms, in order to be able to defend my household and to succor my friends in all their undertakings against the assaults of evildoers.

—FRANÇOIS RABELAIS

THE REFORMATION

The new emphasis on free inquiry and secular learning was quick to affect what had been central to life in medieval Europe—the one, unified Church. Traditional Christian teachings were being challenged by the humanists, who, in their efforts to free men's minds from the dogma of the medieval Church, were propagating new respect for the pagan classics. These writings, they felt, contained ideas that were as worthy of consideration and allegiance as were those of traditional Christian teaching.

This intellectual challenge of humanism came at a time when the ideals and the dominance of the Church were being attacked by other forces as well. With the rise of world trade, a wealthy merchant class was coming into power. Its love of luxury and material goods was out of harmony with the Church's ideals of asceticism and otherworldliness. Adventurers on the high seas and traders at the world marketplaces were not interested in simplicity, austerity, and self-denial. Luxury was both the reward of their enterprises and the proof of their success. The new middle-class morality which began to develop exalted the ideal of hard work for profit. This desire for luxury and worldly sophistication affected the papacy and hierarchy of the Church as much as it did anyone else.

The immense temporal power of the Church was being seriously challenged by the new kings and nobility, who engaged in deadly struggles with the Church for territory and allegiance. One by-product of these power struggles was that they tended to attract into the Church's hierarchy ambitious men who had little interest in the Church's spiritual mission. Thus the Church as an institution became as vulnerable to corruption as any secular institution.

Throughout the later Middle Ages, reformers arose who sought to hold the Church to its role as the spiritual authority for men. Many of these demands for change resulted in the movement called the Reformation. The movement began in 1517 when the German monk Martin Luther (see page 502) tacked onto the door of the church in Wittenberg his protest against the sale of indulgences to raise money for the building of St. Peter's in Rome. Subsequently, because of intense papal persecution, Luther broke completely from the Church of Rome and established a national German church. His example was swiftly followed by reformist leaders in Switzerland and the Netherlands. Quarrels between Henry VIII of England and the Roman Pope soon brought England into fraternity with these countries of northern Europe, which became strongholds of Protestantism against the loyalist Catholic countries of France, Spain, and Italy.

The Reformation divided Europe and divided nations internally. For over a century it caused ideological and political ferment which frequently erupted into violence and war.

POLITICS AND SOCIETY

The Renaissance can be seen in the magnificent public buildings and private houses that were designed and decorated by what may be the greatest assemblage of artists and artisans in any period of history. It can be seen in its busy, vigorous cities, such as the Antwerp described by Guicciardini, which were growing all over Europe and becoming wealthy centers of trade. The Renaissance can be seen in the ambition and daring that moved both the explorers and those who, like Hakluyt, read accounts of the explorers' adventures and the wonders they saw in new lands. The Renaissance can also be seen in the vigorous intellectual life of men whose thoughts ranged over the whole universe and all the affairs of men. But it must be seen, too, in its unlovely side.

In the spring of 1348, the devastating plague which had moved from Asia all across Europe struck Florence. In a frame story for the tales of *Decameron* (see page 507), Giovanni Boccaccio (1313–1375) describes Florence as the plague hit. The strongest impression of Boccaccio's description is of chaos, created by the special circumstances of plague, to be sure; but it is well to remember that the man of the Renaissance, in high station or low, was always aware that disaster of some sort—rampant disease or famine or war—was never far off.

● What I am going to relate is indeed a strange thing to hear—a thing that I should hardly have dared believe and much less write about, though I had heard it from a trustworthy witness, had I not seen it with my own eyes, and in the presence of many others. So active, I say, was the virulence of the plague in communicating itself from one person to another, that not only did it affect human beings, but, what is more strange, it very often proceeded in an extraordinary way. If an article belonging to one sick of the plague or who had died of it was touched by an animal outside of the human species, the creature was not only

An excerpt from "Preface to the Ladies" from Boccaccio's *Decameron*, The Limited Editions Club edition, translated by Frances Winwar. Reprinted by permission of The George Macy Companies, Inc. and Frances Winwar.

infected, but in a very short time it died of the disease—a fact which among others I observed one day with my own eyes, as I said before. The rags of a poor fellow who had died of the plague had been thrown into the public street. Two hogs came across them and, according to their habit, first they went for them with their snouts and then, taking them in their teeth, began shaking them about their jaws. A little while later, after rolling round and round as though they had swallowed poison, both of them fell down dead upon the rags they had found to their misfortune.

Because of such happenings and many others of a like sort, various fears and superstitions arose among the survivors, almost all of which tended toward one end—to flee from the sick and whatever had belonged to them. In this way each man thought to be safeguarding his own health. Some among them were of the opinion that by living temperately and guarding against excess of all kinds, they could do much toward avoiding the danger; and forming a band they lived away from the rest of the world. Gathering in those houses where no one had been ill and living was more comfortable, they shut themselves in. They ate moderately of the best that could be had and drank excellent wines, avoiding all luxuriousness. With music and whatever other delights they could have, they lived together in this fashion, allowing no one to speak to them and avoiding news either of death or sickness from the outer world.

Others, arriving at a contrary conclusion, held that plenty of drinking and enjoyment, singing and free living and the gratification of the appetite in every possible way, letting the devil take the hindmost, was the best preventative of such a malady; and as far as they could, they suited the action to the word. Day and night they went from one tavern to another, drinking and carousing unrestrainedly. At the least inkling of something that suited them, they ran wild in other people's houses, and there was no one to prevent them, for everyone had abandoned all responsibility for his belongings as well as for himself, considering his days numbered. Consequently most of the houses had become common property, and strangers would make use of them at will whenever they came upon them, even as the rightful owners might have done. Following this uncharitable way of thinking, they did their best to run away from the infected.

Meanwhile, in the midst of the affliction and misery that had befallen the city, even the reverend authority of divine and human law had almost crumbled and fallen into decay, for its ministers and executors, like other men, had either died or sickened or had been left so entirely without assistants that they were unable to attend to their duties. As a result everyone had leave to do as he saw fit.—GIOVANNI BOCCACCIO

If life was hard for the poor in these times, it was full of other dangers for the wealthy. The consolidation of cities and states under single powerful

God separating the waters, by Michelangelo (1512), from the Sistine chapel.

rulers was ending the petty fighting among the feudal nobility which had made every house a fortress and had made travel without armed escort unthinkable. But the intrigues that now took place in the courts of powerful princes and popes were deadly games that no man with any pretensions to wealth or power could avoid playing. National monarchies were arising, and there was an accompanying scramble for power. The breakup of the feudal stability of the Middle Ages and the rivalries created by the new trade gave a new importance to these national powers. At the same time a sense of national identity was replacing the medieval sense of identity with the one Church.

These conditions produced a ferment in the political structure of Europe. Seeing the anarchy and turmoil caused by new conditions and hoping to bring a better world out of this period of change, many men turned their thoughts to questions about commonwealth, about the conduct of rulers, about the responsibilities of the individual. At their most profound, these men were examining anew, as men in every age must, the ultimate questions of man's identity, of his position in his own world and in the universal scheme of things.

It was within these conditions that Niccolo Machiavelli (1469–1527) offered his own cold-blooded, pragmatic advice on the conduct of a ruler. Machiavelli's discourse, called *The Prince,* followed a conventional pattern. Each of its twenty-six brief essays or chapters treated a conventional topic: the ruler's boldness in war, his generosity toward his subjects, his care for his honor, his avoidance of flatterers, etc. But Machiavelli's advice was not conventional. Believing that gentle means and easy solutions could not produce a strong central government that could keep order, he gave hardheaded—some would say cynical—advice on how to acquire and solidify control. He argued shocking positions, as in the consideration of the question: Is it better for a ruler to be loved than feared, or the reverse?

● The answer is that it would be desirable to be both but, since that is difficult, it is much safer to be feared than to be loved, if one must choose. For on men in general this observation may be made: They are ungrateful, fickle, and deceitful, eager to avoid dangers, and avid for gain, and while you are useful to them they are all with you, offering you their blood, their property, their lives, and their sons so long as danger is remote, as we noted above, but when it approaches, they turn on you. Any prince, trusting only in their words and having no other preparations made, will fall to his ruin, for friendships that are bought at a price and not by greatness and nobility of soul are paid for indeed, but they are not owned and cannot be called upon in time of need. Men have less hesitation in offending a man who is loved than one who is feared, for love is held by a bond of obligation which, as men are wicked, is broken whenever personal advantage suggests it, but fear is accompanied by the dread of punishment which never relaxes.—NICCOLO MACHIAVELLI

He pointed to the dictator Cesare Borgia, the unscrupulous and ruthless right arm of his father, Pope Alexander VI, as the model of a ruler who did not hesitate to shift his principles in order to keep his power. (Borgia had built a short-lived empire in central Italy by murdering his enemies.) Thus the word *Machiavellian* has come to mean "unscrupulously cunning and self-seeking," and the philosophy familiarly associated with Machiavelli's name is that "the ends justify the means," with the implication being that the means are vile and the ends not much more than a tolerable pretense of good. Even in his own times, Machiavelli's name became a household word for all that is monstrous and evil, especially outside of Italy, where he quickly became more a legend than a philosopher.

Yet Machiavelli's intention was to show men the way to a just and harmonious state for the benefit of all citizens. For his own time, he felt that this meant realistically facing the fact that disunity was destructive and that only if a strong man took control and enforced unity could peace and justice be restored. Machiavelli may not have distinguished the true good of the state from the selfish purposes of the tyrant. And he may not have recognized how difficult it would be to persuade the strong man to give up his power once it was no longer needed. But we need to ask, when we condemn Machiavelli's remedies as cynical and ruthless, if we must also condemn the diseases in civil life for which he prescribed them.

From *The Prince* by Machiavelli, translated by Thomas G. Bergin. Reprinted by permission of Appleton-Century-Crofts, educational division of Meredith Corporation.

Literature received inspiration from the exciting, far-ranging intellectual ferment of the Renaissance and encouragement from two new developments which created a larger audience for writers—the invention of printing and the spread of education. The court and wealthy aristocrats were still the chief patrons of secular literature, but the prosperous middle class was making itself felt as readers of printed books and as audiences for the public theaters, where even the poorer classes became, in a sense, patrons of the arts. As a consequence, the professional writer emerged as a new phenomenon in this period, and fiction and drama in particular were enriched by the influences of popular culture.

Poetry was still the chief of the literary arts, and the period produced an astonishing number of very competent poets as well as a high quota of truly great ones. The key to the approach of the Renaissance poets to their art is craftsmanship. The writing of poetry in Latin on classical models, as well as the translation into English of classical Latin poetry, was a prominent part of the training in the schools. Poetry became an accomplishment which anyone of education and culture would acquire, at least as a hobby. For example, both Henry VIII of England and his daughter Elizabeth have left a few tolerable poems; even the hardheaded, cold-eyed Machiavelli wrote poems and a verse drama; and the artist Michelangelo wrote a number of sonnets that earn him the name of poet.

Among the great variety and great quantity of lyric poems produced by the Renaissance, the sonnet is easily the most conspicuous. The Italian humanist-poet Francesco Petrarca (1304–1374) (see page 491), known in English as Petrarch, was the inspiration for its wide popularity, though Dante and others had used the form before him. In its demand for poetic craft, the sonnet is perhaps the most characteristic form of Renaissance poetry. It is a form that has set up for itself very restricting rules of the game, and it consequently challenges the poet to express himself within certain rigid bounds. The Renaissance poets confined the subject matter of the sonnet to secular topics, usually a lover's thoughts about a lady, or, in the case of most of Shakespeare's sonnets (see page 494), about a friend. Although the sonneteers worked endless variations on this theme, their skill was not in the originality of ideas but in the originality of expression, which came from conceiving the old idea in a new image. The pose of the sonneteer is frankly and deliberately artificial, and what he creates is an image of perfection. There may never be a lady so perfect in beauty and virtue as the one imagined by a sonneteer, but all imperfect ladies are reflected in this perfect creature and are themselves glorified in her.

Prose fiction in the Renaissance was moving in the direction of what we know today as the novel. Many of Boccaccio's stories show a skill in the development of the narrative that is lacking in even the best of the medieval tales and romances. The plot is enriched by parallel situations or subplots. Characters and setting are presented with a realism of detail that was new to storytelling.

Two other great pieces of Renaissance fiction make a further step in the direction of the novel by developing continuous plot lines that extend over a long sequence of events. Rabelais's *Gargantua and Pantagruel* and Cervantes' *Don Quixote* (see page 513) are both episodic—that is, the relationship between the incidents is loose and often slight. But these works showed that it was possible to explore through one central plot and one set of characters a great variety of themes. The novel becomes a little world that mirrors the real world as the writer sees it.

The Renaissance produced a revival of drama, a form which had been popular but little respected in the Middle Ages. Indeed, play-acting had been suspect as a frivolous and immoral occupation, in spite of the fact that the plays shown were almost always Bible stories or allegories teaching moral lessons. Drama survived into the sixteenth century as little more than a lively subliterary tradition, popular among common folk. But this tradition now came into the hands of young writers who had read the ancient Greek and Roman dramas. These writers produced vigorous plays with exciting plots constructed to draw the audience's attention from crisis to climax. They used all the resources of stage, spectacle, and acting at their disposal. Their plays were both serious and comic, and, though often based on classical plots or on ancient legends or events, they dealt with the problems of human society and the experiences of the human spirit.

The theater flourished as box-office business and as literature, especially in Spain and England. A host of bright young men—many of them university-educated and none of them aristocrats—tried to earn a living by writing for the public theaters. Many of their plays can still hold the stage today. Perhaps even more important, these writers created the conditions under which the greatest talents could come to fulfillment in the late 1500's and early 1600's: in England, Shakespeare (see page 541) and Ben Jonson; in Spain, the incredibly prolific Lope de Vega and, somewhat later, Calderón. The best, of course, was Shakespeare, whose plays after four centuries still seem the richest poetry, the most thoughtful literature, and the most stageworthy drama that has been produced at any time, in any language.

PETRARCH

In church on Good Friday, April 6, 1327, Francesco Petrarca (1304–1374) fell in love with a lady whom he called Laura. Petrarch dedicated over 300 sonnets to Laura, with whom he apparently had a respectful but not intimate relationship. In these poems, Petrarch traces the course of his passion, from his first meeting with Laura to her death from the plague in 1348.

Sonnet 42

The spring returns, the spring wind softly blowing
Sprinkles the grass with gleam and glitter of showers,
Powdering pearl and diamond, dripping with flowers,
Dropping wet flowers, dancing the winter's going;
The swallow twitters, the groves of midnight are glowing   5
With nightingale music and madness; the sweet fierce powers
Of love flame up through the earth; the seed-soul towers
And trembles; nature is filled to overflowing . . .
The spring returns, but there is no returning
Of spring for me. O heart with anguish burning!   10
She that unlocked all April in a breath
Returns not . . . And these meadows, blossoms, birds,
These lovely gentle girls—words, empty words,
As bitter as the black estates of death!

Sonnet 126

In what bright realm, what sphere of radiant thought
Did nature find the model whence she drew
That delicate dazzling image where we view
Here on this earth what she in heaven wrought?
What fountain-haunting nymph, what dryad, sought   5
In groves, such golden tresses ever threw
Upon the gust? What heart such virtues knew?—
Though her chief virtue with my death is fraught.
He looks in vain for heavenly beauty, he
Who never looked upon her perfect eyes,   10
The vivid blue orbs turning brilliantly—
He does not know how love yields and denies;
He only knows, who knows how sweetly she
Can talk and laugh, the sweetness of her sighs.

"Sonnet XLII (The spring returns)" and "Sonnet CXXVI (In what bright realm)" from *The Sonnets of Petrarch*, translated by Joseph Auslander (Longmans, Green & Company, 1932). Reprinted by permission of David McKay Company, Inc.

PIERRE DE RONSARD

A favorite of the French court, Ronsard (1524–1585) belonged to a group of poets dedicated to establishing a French school of poetry equal to the ancients. Ronsard's greatest poetry is in his sonnets, the last series of which he dedicated to Hélène de Surgères, a maid of honor at court. They were written in the last ten years of his life, after the relationship with Hélène had ended.

Of His Lady's Old Age

When you are very old, at evening
  You'll sit and spin beside the fire, and say,
Humming my songs, "Ah well, ah well-a-day.
When I was young, of me did Ronsard sing."
None of your maidens that doth hear the thing,   5
  Albeit with her weary task foredone,
  But wakens at my name, and calls you one
Blest, to be held in long remembering.

I shall be low beneath the earth and laid
On sleep, a phantom in the myrtle shade,   10
  While you beside the fire, a grande dame gray,
My love, your pride, remember and regret;
Ah, love me, love, we may be happy yet,
  And gather roses, while 'tis called today.

"Of His Lady's Old Age" by Pierre de Ronsard, translated by Andrew Lang.

EDMUND SPENSER

In his sequence of sonnets called *Amoretti,* English poet and civil servant Edmund Spenser (1552–1599) records the history of his courtship with his second wife, Elizabeth Boyle. Spenser's great poem is the long allegorical *Faerie Queene.* In spite of its flattering allusions to Queen Elizabeth, it won for Spenser more praise than solid reward at court.

Sonnet 62

The weary year his race now having run,
The new begins his compassed course anew:
With show of morning mild he hath begun,
Betokening peace and plenty to ensue.
So let us, which this change of weather view, 5
Change eeke° our minds and former lives amend;
The old year's sins forepast let us eschew,
And fly the faults with which we did offend.
Then shall the new year's joy forth freshly send
Into the glooming world his gladsome ray; 10
And all these storms, which now his beauty blend,
Shall turn to calms and timely clear away.
So likewise, love, cheer you your heavy spright,°
And change old year's annoy to new delight.

> 6. **eeke:** also. 13. **spright:** spirit.

Sonnet 79

Men call you fair, and you do credit it,
For that your self ye daily such do see;
But the true fair, that is the gentle wit
And virtuous mind, is much more praised of me.
For all the rest, how ever fair it be, 5
Shall turn to nought and lose that glorious hue:
But only that is permanent and free
From frail corruption, that doth flesh ensue.°
That is true beauty; that doth argue you
To be divine and born of heavenly seed, 10
Derived from that fair spirit° from whom all true
And perfect beauty did at first proceed.
He only fair, and what he fair hath made;
All other fair, like flowers, untimely fade.

> 8. **ensue:** exit after, survive. 11. **spirit:** pronounced as "sprite."

WILLIAM SHAKESPEARE

For an account of Shakespeare (1564–1616) as a playwright, see page 541. Shakespeare's greatest non-dramatic poetry is in a group of 154 sonnets, which are without rival as the highpoint of the outpouring of sonnets in Elizabethan England. In addition to their richness of language and imagery, Shakespeare's sonnets have an unusual depth of thought and feeling, ranging beyond the conventional subject of love to a contemplation of the beauty of life and the mortality of man. In his first 126 sonnets, Shakespeare celebrates his devoted friendship with a young man, which he presents as a higher, less selfish relationship than his passionate love for a woman, which is the subject of the remaining 28 sonnets. The identity of the young man and of the "dark lady," to whom the sonnets are addressed, has never been determined with certainty.

Sonnet 30

When to the sessions of sweet silent thought
I summon up remembrance of things past,
I sigh the lack of many a thing I sought,
And with old woes new wail my dear times' waste:
Then can I drown an eye, unused to flow,   5
For precious friends hid in death's dateless night,
And weep afresh love's long since canceled woe,
And moan the expense of many a vanished sight:
Then can I grieve at grievances foregone,
And heavily from woe to woe tell o'er   10
The sad account of forebemoanèd moan,
Which I new pay as if not paid before.
  But if the while I think on thee, dear friend,
  All losses are restored and sorrows end.

Sonnet 64

When I have seen by Time's fell hand defaced
The rich proud cost of outworn buried age;
When sometime lofty towers I see down-razed,
And brass eternal slave to mortal rage;
When I have seen the hungry ocean gain   5
Advantage on the kingdom of the shore,
And the firm soil win of the watery main,
Increasing store with loss, and loss with store;
When I have seen such interchange of state,
Or state itself confounded to decay;   10
Ruin hath taught me thus to ruminate—
That Time will come and take my love away.
  This thought is as a death, which cannot choose
  But weep to have that which it fears to lose.

PETRARCH: SONNET 42

1. Lines 1–4 personify the spring wind. What kind of person is implied by the personification? Who is "she" in line 11?

2. What idea about the processes of nature is expressed by the last phrase of line 6 and by lines 7–8?

PETRARCH: SONNET 126

In creating his idea of love, Petrarch had in mind the teaching of Plato that all things of this world are dim reflections and partial imitations of a complete and perfect world of ideas. Which terms in lines 1–4 are particularly suggestive of Plato's theory? Which terms suggest the infusion of Judeo-Christian ideas about creation (see page 20)?

RONSARD: OF HIS LADY'S OLD AGE

1. Describe the scene created in the octave. What is the significance of the inclusion of the old lady's young handmaidens in the scene?

2. How does the image described in the sestet contrast with the image in the octave?

3. Paraphrase lines 12–13 so as to be sure you understand their syntax and meaning.

SPENSER: SONNET 62

What exactly is the "change in weather" mentioned in line 5? What are the several ways, stated and implied, in which a change in weather is appropriate as a comparison to a change in spirit?

SPENSER: SONNET 79

1. Do you find in Spenser's distinction between the "fair" and the "true fair" an echo of the Platonic doctrine mentioned in connection with Petrarch's Sonnet 126? Explain your answer. How is the Christian idea of God the Creator adapted to the Platonic idea?

2. How would you account for differences in feeling and tone between these poems by Spenser, which are very similar in thought?

SHAKESPEARE: SONNET 30

1. Point out where Shakespeare makes use of the repetition of sounds. How do these sound effects support the meaning of the poem?

2. In what other ways, when you read the poem aloud, do the sounds and rhythms of the words give a slow and heavy feeling?

SHAKESPEARE: SONNET 64

1. Line 2 could be rephrased "The proud, costly monuments of a past age." Why is the poetic line more effective than this one?

2. What is striking about the pattern of words in line 8? How is that pattern echoed in the pattern of words and in the meaning of lines 9–10?

3. Notice the pattern of sounds in line 11. Do you see similar patterns in any other lines?

THE SONNET

A sonnet consists of fourteen lines of ten syllables each (eleven, if there is an extra unstressed syllable at the end of the line, as there usually is in Italian). The lines are rhymed in groups, and the units of meaning usually coincide with these groupings. In the most common form used by Petrarch—the form that has come to be called the Italian or Petrarchan sonnet—the sonnet falls into two main parts, an octave and a sestet. The octave has two rhyme sounds in the pattern *abba abba,* which subdivides into two groups; the sestet has two or three rhyme sounds in any pattern, so that it may or may not fall into subgroupings.

The other form of the sonnet is called the English or, more commonly, the Shakespearean. Although Petrarch and others had used this form occasionally, it became the usual form in England, where it had a tremendous vogue in the 1590's. The Shakespearean sonnet is less restrictive than the Italian only to the extent that it allows more rhymes. It falls into four parts—three quatrains and a concluding couplet. The three quatrains contain two rhyme sounds in each, in the pattern *abab cdcd efef.* The concluding couplet introduces a new rhyme sound, *gg.*

Both of these sonnet forms are subject to deliberate variation, and at times the poet may, for special effect, make the units of meaning conflict with the rhyme groups instead of coinciding with them. Such variation is part of the sonnet game that intrigued the Renaissance poets.

1. Which of these sonnets are written in the Italian pattern? In each one, how do the octave and sestet define two main sense units as well as rhyme groups? Does the octave subdivide into a sense unit for each quatrain? Are there any subgroupings in the sestet? Explain.

2. Which of these sonnets are written in the English pattern? In each one, how is the couplet set off in meaning from the rest of the poem? What is the distinctive sense unit of each quatrain? What is the progression of meaning through these units? Where is the climactic point?

3. What variations on the basic rhyme pattern are made by Spenser in his two sonnets? Do you notice any special effect achieved by these variations? Explain.

4. Examine the imagery of each sonnet with these questions in mind: Does a dominating image run through the poem? What relationship do the images of the poem have to one another? Is there any relationship established between the images and the direct statements? Support your answers with references to specific passages in the poem.

FOR COMPOSITION

From the evidence presented by the sonnets themselves, define the idea of love and friendship that underlies them. Consider these questions in particular: What connection does the sonneteer see between physical beauty and spiritual beauty (virtue)? How does love or friendship ennoble the speaker? Why does his contemplation of the person he is addressing bring to his mind the passing of time and the decay of all mortal things?

GIL VICENTE

Sometimes called the Portuguese Shakespeare, Vicente (c. 1465–1536?) wrote lyric poems and plays for the court but always spoke to the heart of the Portuguese people.

Song

If thou art sleeping, maiden,
  Awake and open thy door.
'Tis the break of day, and we must away
  O'er meadow, and mount, and moor.

Wait not to find thy slippers,
  But come with thy naked feet;
We shall have to pass through the dewy grass
  And waters wide and fleet.

"Song" by Gil Vicente, translated by Henry W. Longfellow. Reprinted by permission of Houghton Mifflin Company.

JOACHIM DU BELLAY

A friend of Ronsard, Du Bellay (c. 1522–1560) was also a member of the group of poets who hoped to properly cultivate the French language and bring it on a level with Latin and Greek. The following poem, in fact, is Du Bellay's French version of a Latin poem.

Elegy on His Cat

I have not lost my rings, my purse,
My gold, my gems—my loss is worse,
One that the stoutest heart must move.
My pet, my joy, my little love,
My tiny kitten, my Belaud,   5
I lost, alas, three days ago.
O little friend, adieu, adieu!
Would that I too were dead like you!
Dame Nature never shaped a cat
So sleek as you, so soft to pat,   10
So sweetly bred, so midget-sized,
So fit to be immortalized.
    His like in France you will not meet,
But only in a Roman street.°
Gray was his coat, yet not all gray,   15
But streaked with many a silver ray,
All satin-smooth; and down his spine
In little billows argentine
It rose and fell, then vanished quite
Beneath a belly ermine-white.   20
Tiny his head and small his joints,
And short his ears, with pinkish points;
Under his nostrils coraline
A little muzzle leonine,
And all around it, bristling bright,   25
Twice seven whiskers, silver white.
Cruel death has struck at him
And has chilled each furry limb.

Death, alas, had never seen
Belaud frolic on the green,   30
Seen him leap, and run, and scratch,
Or with lightning motion catch
Some poor mouse which scurried past,
Catch him, loose him, hold him fast.
Oh, how soft would Belaud climb   35
On my couch at napping-time,
Or with sudden impulse shrewd
Ravish from my lips the food,
Or with frenzied jerk and bound
Like a wheel spin round and round,   40
Following the speeding trail
Of his own revolving tail,
Or, displaying all the fur
Of his ermine stomacher,°
On his velvet haunches perch   45
Like some Doctor of the Church.
    Sweet Belaud, you cunning actor,
You were sure no malefactor!
E'en your sins did halfway please.
It was you who stole my cheese,   50
You, alas, who killed my linnet,
Wrecked the cage with birdie in it,
Feeling sure you did no wrong
Since it irked you with its song.
I forgive you, little pet.   55
I, too, am not perfect yet.

14. **Roman street:** Cats were held in special esteem in ancient Rome; the allusion suggests a particularly noble and imperious cat. 44. **stomacher:** a decorative panel worn over the front of a gown.

"Elegy on His Cat" by Joachim du Bellay from *French Lyrics in English Verse,* translated and edited by William Frederic Giese. Published by The University of Wisconsin Press, 1946. Reprinted by permission of the Regents of the University of Wisconsin.

PIERRE DE RONSARD

This lyric appears in a group of sonnets which Ronsard (1524–1585) wrote about his fruitless love for a young noblewoman named Cassandra. Unlike the sonnet on page 492, this lyric was written when Ronsard was a young man in his late twenties.

The Rose

See, Mignonne, hath not the rose,
That this morning did unclose
  Her purple mantle to the light,
Lost before the day be dead,
The glory of her raiment red,   5
  Her color, bright as yours is bright?

Ah, Mignonne, in how few hours
The petals of her purple flowers
  All have faded, fallen, died;
Sad nature, mother ruinous,   10
That seest thy fair child perish thus
  Twixt matin song and eventide.

Hear me, my darling, speaking sooth,°
Gather the fleet flower of your youth,
  Take ye your pleasure at the best;   15
Be merry ere your beauty flit,
For length of days will tarnish it
  Like roses that were loveliest.

13. **sooth:** truth.

"The Rose" by Pierre de Ronsard, translated by Andrew Lang.

THOMAS NASHE

Nashe (1567–1601) was a well-known English journalist with a keen sense of the ridiculous. He had a hard time making a living by writing, and he once complained that the "seven liberal sciences and a good leg will scarce get a scholar bread and cheese." His finest poem, which follows, is in a dark mood. In 1592–93 there were violent outbreaks of the bubonic plague in London, and Nashe appears to have fled the city. In those two years, the epidemic claimed 22,000 lives.

Litany in Time of Plague

Adieu, farewell earth's bliss,
This world uncertain is;
Fond° are life's lustful joys,
Death proves them all but toys,
None from his darts can fly.   5
I am sick, I must die.
    Lord, have mercy on us!

Rich men, trust not in wealth,
Gold cannot buy you health;
Physic° himself must fade,   10
All things to end are made.
The plague full swift goes by;
I am sick, I must die.
    Lord, have mercy on us!

Beauty is but a flower   15
Which wrinkles will devour:
Brightness falls from the air,
Queens have died young and fair,
Dust hath closed Helen's eye.
I am sick, I must die.   20
    Lord, have mercy on us!

Strength stoops unto the grave,
Worms feed on Hector brave,
Swords may not fight with fate.
Earth still holds ope her gate;   25
Come! come! the bells do cry.
I am sick, I must die.
    Lord, have mercy on us!

Wit with his wantonness
Tasteth death's bitterness;   30
Hell's executioner
Hath no ears for to hear
What vain art can reply.
I am sick, I must die.
    Lord, have mercy on us!   35

Haste, therefore, each degree,
To welcome destiny.
Heaven is our heritage,
Earth but a player's stage;
Mount we unto the sky.   40
I am sick, I must die.
    Lord, have mercy on us!

3. **Fond:** foolish. 10. **Physic:** healing.

BEN JONSON

Shakespeare's friendly rival, Ben Jonson (1572–1637), worked for restraint and polish in his writing. The following familiar song should be read in a light spirit. It is a charming, clever compliment to a lady and displays Jonson's wit rather than his deep feelings.

Song to Celia

Drink to me only with thine eyes,
    And I will pledge with mine;
Or leave a kiss but in the cup,
    And I'll not look for wine.
The thirst that from the soul doth rise   5
    Doth ask a drink divine;
But might I of Jove's nectar sup,
    I would not change for thine.

I sent thee late a rosy wreath,
    Not so much honoring thee   10
As giving it a hope that there
    It could not withered be.
But thou thereon didst only breathe,
    And sent'st it back to me;
Since when it grows, and smells, I swear,   15
    Not of itself but thee.

MARTIN LUTHER

Luther (1483–1546), who split from the Roman Church to establish a national German church, also translated the Bible into the German vernacular and wrote hymns, such as the following, to enrich his reformed worship, in which Latin was replaced by the German language.

A Mighty Fortress Is Our God

A mighty fortress is our God,
A bulwark never failing,
Our helper he, amid the flood
Of mortal ill prevailing;
For still our ancient foe   5
Doth seek to work us woe,
His craft and power are great,
And armed with cruel hate,
On earth is not his equal.

Did we in our strength confide,   10
Our striving would be losing,
Were not the right man on our side,
The man of God's own choosing.
Dost ask who that may be?
Christ Jesus, it is he,   15
Lord Sabaoth° his name,
From age to age the same,
And he must win the battle.

And though this world, with devils filled,
Should threaten to undo us,   20
We will not fear, for God hath willed
His truth to triumph through us.
The Prince of Darkness grim,
We tremble not at him,
His rage we can endure,   25
For lo! his doom is sure,
Our little word shall fell him.

That word above all earthly powers—
No thanks for them—abideth;
The spirit and the gift is ours,   30
Through him who with us sideth.
Let goods and kindred go,
This mortal life also;
The body they may kill,
God's truth abideth still,   35
His kingdom is forever.

16. **Lord Sabaoth:** Lord of armies. *Sabaoth* is from a Hebrew word for "armies" or "hosts of peoples."

"A Mighty Fortress Is Our God" by Martin Luther, translated by F. H. Hedge.

TERESA OF AVILA

A Carmelite nun from Avila in Spain, Teresa Sánchez Cepeda Dávila y Ahumada (1515–1582) was a vigorous and commonsensical reformer who worked from within the Roman Church. Teresa expressed her mystical experiences in poetry, often through the use of homely metaphors.

If, Lord, Thy Love for Me Is Strong

If, Lord, thy love for me is strong
As this which binds me unto thee,
What holds me from thee, Lord, so long,
What holds thee, Lord, so long from me?

O soul, what then desirest thou? 5
—Lord, I would see thee, who thus choose thee.
What fears can yet assail thee now?
—All that I fear is but to lose thee.

Love's whole possession I entreat,
Lord, make my soul thine own abode, 10
And I will build a nest so sweet
It may not be too poor for God.

O soul in God hidden from sin,
What more desires for thee remain,
Save but to love, and love again, 15
And, all on flame with love within,
Love on, and turn to love again?

"If, Lord, Thy Love for Me Is Strong" by St. Teresa of Avila from *Poems* by Arthur Symons. Reprinted by permission of William Heinemann Ltd. and Dodd, Mead & Company, Inc.

JOHN DONNE

John Donne (1572–1631), who became an Anglican minister at the age of forty-three, is noted for the complex, intellectual way in which he expresses emotion. At the same time, however, Donne writes with heart and passion. Both these qualities are evident in the poems which follow. The second poem, one of Donne's most famous, is one of nineteen so-called "Holy Sonnets," composed after the death of his wife in 1617.

A Lecture upon the Shadow

Stand still, and I will read to thee
A lecture, love, in Love's philosophy.
    These three hours that we have spent,
    Walking here, two shadows went
Along with us, which we ourselves produced;   5
But, now the sun is just above our head,
    We do those shadows tread,
    And to brave clearness all things are reduced.
  So whilst our infant loves did grow,
  Disguises did, and shadows, flow,   10
From us, and our cares;° but, now 'tis not so.

That love hath not attained the highest degree
Which is still diligent lest others see.

Except our loves at this noon stay,
We shall new shadows make the other way.   15
    As the first were made to blind
    Others, these which come behind
Will work upon ourselves and blind our eyes.
If our loves faint and westwardly decline,
    To me thou, falsely, thine,   20
    And I to thee mine actions shall disguise.
  The morning shadows wear away,
  But these grow longer all the day.
  But oh, love's day is short if love decay.

Love is a growing, or full constant light;   25
And his first minute after noon is night.

---

11. **cares:** that is, cares not to let others see we are in love.

Holy Sonnet 10

Death be not proud, though some have called thee
Mighty and dreadful, for thou art not so;
For those whom thou think'st thou dost overthrow
Die not, poor Death; nor yet canst thou kill me.
From Rest and Sleep, which but thy picture be,   5
Much pleasure; then from thee much more must flow;
And soonest our best men with thee do go—
Rest of their bones and souls' delivery!

Thou'rt slave to Fate, chance, kings, and desperate men,
And dost with poison, war, and sickness dwell;   10
And poppy or charms can make us sleep as well
And better than thy stroke. Why swell'st thou then?
One short sleep past, we wake eternally,
And Death shall be no more; Death, thou shalt die!

FOR STUDY AND DISCUSSION

VICENTE: SONG

There is very little subject matter in the poem by Gil Vicente; it only has poetry. What makes it poetic? In arriving at your conclusions, consider the qualities of other poems you have been reading.

DU BELLAY: ELEGY ON HIS CAT

Why do the phrases in a series in lines 10–12 produce a humorous effect? Point out instances where the translator has used rhyme for humorous effect. Point out instances where the translator has chosen words with humorous suggestion. Try to explain the source of humor for each one.

RONSARD: THE ROSE

The word *mignonne* in French means "delicate, pretty." It can also refer to a flower, a scarlet variety of pear blossom. What is added to the basic comparison between the lady and the rose by the idea that she herself is a flower, and that her youth is a flower to be gathered?

NASHE: LITANY IN TIME OF PLAGUE

1. Nashe's litany deals with the impermanence of worldly things against the inevitability of death. How would you characterize the tone of this poem? Can you identify any elements of form or imagery that might explain the total effect of the poem? For example, is the speaker directly involved in the poem? What is the effect of his references to Helen and to Hector? What characteristics of a litany are adapted to the poem?

2. Do you see any contrasts in attitude and tone between Nashe's poem and the poem by the ancient Greek writer Semonides on page 106?

JONSON: SONG TO CELIA

Toasting ("pledging") in wine and sending roses ("a rosy wreath") are ordinary expressions of favor or compliment. How does the poet refine these ordinary expressions into special and extravagant compliments?

LUTHER: A MIGHTY FORTRESS IS OUR GOD

1. How does the thought of this poem reflect the Protestant emphasis upon personal faith as the means of salvation, over and above good works and the sacraments of the Church?

2. What images dominate this poem? What is their significance? How do they compare with the image used in the third stanza of the religious lyric by Teresa of Avila?

3. How does the image of Christ in Luther's poem differ from a characteristic medieval image, such as the one in the following fifteenth-century English carol.

● I sing of a maiden
   That is makeles [matchless];
King of all kings
   To her son she ches [chose].

He came al so still
   There his mother was,
As dew in April
   That falleth on the grass.

He came al so still
   To his mother's bour,
As dew in April
   That falleth on the flour.

He came al so still
   There his mother lay,
As dew in April
   That falleth on the spray.

Mother and maiden
   Was never none but she;
Well may such a lady
   Goddes mother be.
               —ANONYMOUS

TERESA: IF, LORD, THY LOVE FOR ME

1. The poem sets up a dialogue between the soul and the Lord. Which parts are spoken by which speaker?

2. St. Teresa assumes, of course, a Trinitarian deity: God the Father, God the Son, and God the Holy Spirit. Which aspect of the divine being is she addressing here? How is her use of the images of a bird and a flame a clue to the answer to this question?

3. What human relationship does the relationship here between soul and Lord most resemble? How does that relationship distinguish St. Teresa's religious emotion and experience from Martin Luther's?

DONNE: A LECTURE UPON THE SHADOW

1. Principal evidence of Donne's poetic style is his elaborately developed images, which as metaphors often make unusual and striking comparisons. In this poem, trace the detailed development of the image of the shadow and the progression of meanings attached to it. It will be helpful to note that the speaker begins the poem at noon and that the first stanza recalls the morning hours, whereas the second long stanza anticipates the afternoon and evening. It is important to notice in which direction the lovers are facing.

2. How does the image of the sun support and expand the meanings of the image of the shadow throughout the poem?

3. The couplets following each long stanza have the quality of epigrams. Why is this effect appropriate to a "lecture," as the poem pretends to be?

4. Explain the full meaning that the final couplet takes on, in the light of what has been said in the rest of the poem.

5. Another aspect of Donne's style is his complex and often unconventional sentence structures. For example, in lines 20–21 "actions" is the noun that both "thine" and "mine" modify. Paraphrase lines 20–21. Point out other instances of unusual syntax. In each case, can you see any effect that would *not* be achieved by the more normal or expected wording?

DONNE: HOLY SONNET 10

1. Identify the three arguments (in lines 3–4, 5–6, and 7–8) by which the poet proves that death is not "mighty and dreadful." What are the two further proofs in lines 9–10 and 11–12? How do these latter arguments differ from the previous ones? How do the language and form of the poem mark the division between the two phases of argumentation?

2. How do the references to sleep unify the poem?

3. Explain the paradox of the last statement in the poem.

THE TRANSLATION

Here is the first stanza of Luther's hymn in the original German. Note in the English translation the elements of language—the length of vowels, the quality of consonants, and the placing of emphases in words—which support the impression of forceful statement and sturdy faith. Does the translator's language have qualities similar to those of the original?

  ● Ein' feste Burg ist unser Gott,
    Ein' gute Wehr und Waffen,
    Er hilft uns frei aus aller Noth,
    Die uns jetzt hat betroffen.
    Der alt' böse Feind
    Mit Ernst er's jetzt meint;
    Gross' Macht und viel List
    Sein' grausam' Rüstung ist,
    Auf Erd'n ist nicht sein's Gleichen.
              —MARTIN LUTHER

FOR COMPOSITION

Write a composition describing the differences in imagery, tone, and effect among the poems about death: Ronsard's (pages 492 and 499), Shakespeare's (page 494), Nashe's (page 500), and Donne's (page 505).

The Decameron

GIOVANNI BOCCACCIO

Giovanni Boccaccio (1313–1375), the son of a Florentine merchant, was born in France and lived in Naples in his young manhood. One of the first who could be called a professional man of letters, he was an admirer of Dante and Petrarch and an advocate of the new kind of literature and learning that they heralded.

In 1348 the appalling plague, the Black Death, struck Florence. Three out of every five persons died, and life came to such a standstill that grass literally grew in the streets. This calamity provided the setting for Boccaccio's principal and most famous work, the *Decameron*, a collection of stories grouped loosely within a frame story about ten young Florentines who have fled to a country villa in the hills above Florence, while the plague rages in the city. To pass the time, they decide that for each of ten days (*decameron* is derived from the Greek words for "ten" and "day"), a "king" or "queen" chosen from their number will set a topic, about which each member must tell a story.

The hundred stories of the *Decameron* range from short anecdotes to stories involving many episodes within a complex plot; some are merry jokes and some soberly or wittily teach moral lessons. Their settings together make up a picture of the European world of the time. The themes of the stories cover a variety of human experiences and worldly problems, but the dominant themes are love and the misdeeds of monks and friars. The satiric tale presented here belongs in the latter category. This is the tenth story told on the sixth day of the retreat.

Friar Onion

Now THAT EACH of the company had told a story, Dioneo knew his turn had come; so without waiting for a formal invitation, he began when the rest, who were still praising Guido's pregnant answer, were silent:

Enchanting ladies, although it is my privilege to speak on whatever strikes my fancy, today, however, I don't intend to depart from the subject all of you have so ably treated. No, I shall follow in your footsteps and show you how skillfully one of the little brothers of Saint Anthony applied his nimble wit to avoid the trap two young rogues had set at his feet. You won't be bored, I hope, if I enlarge somewhat upon the story to do it justice, for see, the sun is still high in the heavens.

Now, then! Certaldo, as you must have heard, is a hamlet of Val d'Elsa in our own section of the country, and though a tiny place, it was once inhabited by noble and prosperous gentlemen. It was a field of plentiful harvest for a certain little monk of the order of Saint Anthony, and for a long time he had made it a practice to visit it once a year and garner the fruits which

"The Story of Friar Onion" from Boccaccio's *Decameron*, The Limited Editions Club edition, translated by Frances Winwar. Reprinted by permission of The George Macy Companies, Inc. and Frances Winwar.

the simple of soul gave to him and the rest of his brotherhood. He was called Friar Onion and was a very welcome figure there, perhaps no less by virtue of his name as for more spiritual reasons; for, as you know, the soil of that part of the country yields onions that are famous all over Tuscany. He was a meager little person, was Friar Onion, carrot-haired and jolly-faced, and the merriest scamp in the world. Moreover, despite the gaps in his education, he was so eloquent and witty a talker, that anyone who did not know him well might have thought him not only an accomplished rhetorician, but a Tully—even Quintilian [1] himself! In fine, there was not a soul in the whole district for whose children he had not acted as godfather, or to whom he was not bound by ties of friendship and sympathy.

One fine Sunday morning in the month of August, he visited the town as usual, and when all the good gossips and gaffers had gathered from the villages round about to hear mass, he stepped forward at the proper moment and addressed them:

"Sisters and brethren, you all know it's customary every year to send an offering of your grain and oats to the poor folks of our master Saint Anthony. Some of you send a great deal, and some a few handfuls, according to your means and devotion, in return for the protection the blessed Saint Anthony gives your oxen and your asses, your pigs and your sheep. Over and above this, all of you, especially those who are registered in our holy company, pay the little trifle you are scheduled to pay, once a year. It's for the collection of these dues that I've been sent among you by my chief, that is, by my master, the abbot, so—may the good Lord lay his blessing upon you!—when you hear the little bells tinkling this afternoon, come and meet me outside the church,

[1] **Tully ... Quintilian:** Tully refers to Cicero (Marcus Tullius Cicero). To the Renaissance, he and the rhetorician Quintilian represented Latin prose at its most correct and elegant (see page 194).

where I'll preach to you as usual, and give you the cross to kiss. There's one special attraction besides. Since I know you're all faithful followers of our master Saint Anthony, I'm going to reward you by a special favor, and show you a most wonderful holy relic that I brought back myself from the Holy Land across the sea. It is a feather of the Angel Gabriel, my friends, one of those he dropped in the Virgin Mary's room, when he came to make the Annunciation to her in Nazareth."

Then, his message delivered, he was silent and continued with the mass.

While he was speaking, there happened to be among his numerous flock in the church two very clever rogues, one called Giovanni del Bragoniera and the other Biagio Pizzini. For some time they laughed together at this relic of Friar Onion's, but then, though they were his friends and boon companions, they decided to play him a trick through this precious feather. That afternoon, they knew, the friar was to lunch with a friend of his at the hamlet. Accordingly, when they thought he must be at table, they slipped into the street and went to the hostelry where he had his lodgings, intending that while Biagio engaged Friar Onion's servant in conversation, Giovanni was to ransack the holy man's trappings in search of his feather, whatever it was, and take it away. The fun would come when the friar tried to explain the loss of his relic to the faithful.

Now Friar Onion had as servant, a fellow who had as many attributes as he had nicknames—Guccio the Whale was one, Guccio Greaser another, and some even called him Guccio the Pig. So mischievous and errant a rascal was he that even the notorious Lippo Topo couldn't have held a candle to him. Indeed, Friar Onion would sometimes expatiate upon his virtues to his friends and say, "I have a servant, my friends, who has nine such qualities, that if the least of them had been in Solomon, Aristotle, or Seneca, it would have been enough to discount all their goodness, wisdom, and piety. Think what a marvel my man must be, who possesses the whole nine of them, and not an ounce of goodness, wisdom, or piety!"

Sometimes, when he was asked what these nine qualities were, he would answer, enumerating them in doggerel: "What are they, you ask? I'll tell you. He is lazy, dirty, thoughtless; ill-bred, foul-tongued, careless; lazy, crack-brained, heedless—not to mention other little flaws which I had better suppress. But the funniest thing about him is that wherever he may be, he's forever anxious to get himself a wife and go into housekeeping, thinking he's so handsome and irresistible with his thick, greasy beard, that all the women who clap eyes on him immediately fall victim to his charms. Really, if he were left to his own devices, he'd lose his belt strap, chasing after them. He's useful enough to me, though, to be truthful, for no matter how confidentially anybody wants to speak to me, Guccio must be there to get an earful. If I should ever be asked a question, he's so afraid I won't know how to answer, that he immediately blurts out Yes, or No, as he sees fit."

This was the gentleman Friar Onion had left at the inn, with the explicit command to see that nobody tampered with his belongings, especially his saddlebags, that contained his most sacred possessions. But Guccio Greaser hankered more after the kitchen than does the nightingale after the green arbor, especially when he scented some jolly slut about, and as it was, he had made a find in mine host's kitchen. A fat, dumpy, clumsy wench she was, with . . . a sweaty, oily, sooty mug that was a match for the Baronci's. Upon making his discovery, Guccio had swooped down upon her in the kitchen like a vulture on his carrion, leaving Friar Onion's room and baggage under the custody of heaven. Though it was August, he sat hugging the hearth and struck up conversation with my lady Nuta, telling her he was a gentleman, he was, and had piles and piles of money, all belonging to him in his own right, plus what he had for other

folks, which was even more than he owned himself. Yes, and he could do lots of things and had as clever a tongue in his head as anyone, the Lord knows. Indeed, regardless of his hood, that was larded with more grease than would have served to baste Altopascio's caldron, despite his patched cloak, that hung in tatters and shone with sweat about the collar and armpits and was adorned, besides, with more spots and splashes than any plaid or India weave, unmindful of his shoes, all down at the heel and torn, and his yawning socks, he pursued her with a grandeur that would have done honor to a Sire de Chatillon. "I'll dress you up and set you up fine, I will, girl," said he. "Indeed, I'll get you out of slavin' for others and give you hopes of better fortune, even if you have no dowry or anything."

He made her many other grandiloquent promises; but for all his magnificent delivery, wind were his words, and wind they remained, like most of his undertakings.

Well, the two scamps found Guccio the Pig mighty busy courting Nuta, which gave them no little satisfaction, seeing that half their trouble was then over. No one stood in their way, so slipping into Friar Onion's room, the door of which was open, they made for his saddlebags, which contained the precious feather. When they spread them open before them, they came upon a clumsy bundle of silk, inside of which they discovered a small box. They opened it quickly and found— a feather of a parrot's tail, the very feather, they were sure, that Friar Onion had promised to show his faithful at Certaldo.

In his day, it would have been easy for the friar to make the people believe his trumpery. The luxuries of the Orient had made but small headway into Tuscany, though since then they have been introduced with a vengeance, to the ruin of all Italy. But if these eastern refinements were known anywhere in Italy, they were certainly unfamiliar to the people of that hamlet. Indeed, the primitive honesty of the ancients was still so much alive that the inhabitants had never heard of parrots, much less set eyes on such creatures at all.

Now the youths, overjoyed at their find, spirited away the feather, and not to leave the case empty, filled it with a few coals, that lay in a corner of the room. Closing it again and rearranging everything as before, they went away unperceived with their prize, all impatience to hear what Friar Onion would have to say on finding the coals instead of the feather.

Meanwhile, the good folk, on hearing that they were to be shown a feather of the Angel Gabriel in the afternoon, betook themselves to their homes after mass. By the time they had had their dinner and the information had passed from goodman to goodman and gossip to gossip, so vast a crowd had flocked to the hamlet to be shown this marvelous feather that there wasn't room enough left to admit a fly. Friar Onion, too, had had a good meal, after which he took a short nap. On rising in the afternoon and hearing the hubbub of the multitude of peasants swarming for a sight of the feather, he sent Guccio Greaser to fetch the bells and saddlebags. It was a great struggle for the amorous fellow to wrench himself away from Nuta and the kitchen, but he went with the necessary paraphernalia to the place his master had indicated, puffing and panting mightily, for the gallons of water he had drunk had swelled his bowels considerably. Once at the church, he stationed himself in front of the door and set up a vigorous jangling of the bells. The parish folk had gathered to a man, whereupon Friar Onion, unaware that anything had been tampered with, plunged into his sermon, with many a covert hint of his own personal needs. Soon the time came for the unveiling of Angel Gabriel's feather. With a solemn voice, he began by intoning the service; then, after two torches had been lighted, he uncovered his head, carefully undid the silken wrapper, and produced the box. Before thinking of opening it, however, he delivered himself of a few words in praise of the Angel Gabriel

and his relic, and then pulled up the lid of the coffer. It was full of coals. At the revelation, he did not dream of suspecting Guccio the Whale—the fellow was not clever enough to have thought of it; nor did he curse him for not preventing others from playing the trick. No, he cursed himself inwardly for committing the scapegrace to the care of his belongings, knowing him as he did to be negligent, disobedient, crack-brained, and heedless. Outwardly, he did not even change color, however, but raising his face and his hands to heaven, exclaimed loud enough for everyone to hear: "Almighty God, may thy might be praised forever!" after which, closing the casket and turning to the populace, he said:

"Sisters and brothers, you must know that while I was still a mere youth, I was sent by my superior to those far lands where the sun rises and was expressly commissioned to look for the dispensations for making porcelain, which, though they're cheap enough to seal, are more useful to others than to us. Well, setting out on this enterprise, I left Venice and journeyed through the Borgo de' Greci. From there, I rode through the kingdom of Algarve and Baldacca, until I came to Parione, out of which, not without a dry gullet, I arrived in Sardinia. But why should I mention all the lands I traveled? After I had passed the Strait of Saint George, I landed in Truffle and Buffle, great regions, both of them teeming with folk; from there I came to the land of Trumpery, where I found many of our brethren and monks of other orders, all of them going about freely and easily, avoiding annoyance for the good Lord's sake, and caring not a whit for other people's woes, provided their own gains were assured. No coin did they spend, but what was unminted.

"From this territory, I passed into the district of Abruzzi, where men and women clatter about the mountains on wooden pattens, and dress the pigs in the pigs' own gut-skins. Still farther, I came across people who carried bread in staves and wine in bags. Then, from those regions, I reached the mountains of the Baschi, where all the streams run perpendicularly. In short, I got entangled so far inland, that I traveled as far as India Pastinaca, where —and I swear to the truth of this by the gown I'm wearing—I even saw feathered creatures fly, a wonder too strange to be believed by those who have not seen it! But Maso del Saggio will support my statement—Maso, whom I found established as a powerful merchant there, cracking nuts and carrying on a retail business in the shells.

"However, since I couldn't find what I was looking for, and as from that point on it is only possible to travel by water, I retraced my steps and came to those holy lands where, in the summer of the year, stale bread is worth four pence a loaf and the warm can be had for nothing. It's here that I met the venerable Father Blame-notme Ifyouplease, the most worshipful patriarch of Jerusalem, who, out of respect for the gown of my master Saint Anthony's order, which I have always worn, insisted on showing me all the precious relics he had collected. What a wealth of them! There were so many, that if I were to enumerate them, I'd have to talk for days before I reached the end of the tale! But I don't want to disappoint you, my friends, so I shall tell you about a few of them. First, he showed me the finger of the Holy Ghost, as perfect and solid as you please, a ringlet of the seraph who appeared to Saint Francis, and one of the fingernails of the cherubim. Yes, he also let me see a rib of the Verbum Caro Look-out-of-the-Window, and the clothes of the Holy Catholic Faith, a number of rays of the star that shone for the three Magi in the East, and a bottle containing the sweat shed by Saint Michael when he fought with the devil. Besides, he showed me the jawbone of Saint Lazarus' Death, and many, many other wonderful things. Well, after that, because I told him a lot of things gratuitously in our dialect, about the slopes of Mount Moretto, and recited to him a few chapters

of the Caprezio, which he had long been seeking, high and low, he divided his holy relics with me. He gave me one of the teeth of the Holy Cross, an echo of the bells of Solomon's temple, shut up in a tiny bottle, the feather of the Angel Gabriel which I've already told you about, and one of the clods of Saint Gerard of Villa Magna. That relic, however, I presented to Gerard of Bonsi in Florence a little while ago, for his great devotion to that saint. Among other things, the patriarch also gave me some of the coals on which the blessed martyr Saint Lawrence was roasted, and all these treasures I faithfully brought back with me. In fact, I have them, each and every one.

"Now, to tell the truth, I must inform you that my superior never allowed me to display them, until he had made sure whether they were the real article or not. Recently, because of certain miracles that have been performed by their virtue, and because of some certificates sent by the Patriarch of Jerusalem, he's been convinced of their authenticity and has given me permission to exhibit them. However, in my nervousness over entrusting them to others, I always carry them about with me—the feather of the Angel Gabriel, in a box by itself, so that it won't be ruffled, and the coals that roasted Saint Lawrence in another. Now these two boxes are so much alike that I've often mistaken one for the other, which is now the case, for thinking I had brought you the casket containing the feather, I find it's the one that holds the coals.

"I'm convinced it was no error that created the confusion. Indeed, I verily believe it was the manifest will of God that guided my hand to the coals, for now that I think of it, the feast of Saint Lawrence will be around in two days. Yes, it was the Lord's will. He intended me to show you the coals on which the blessed martyr was roasted, that I might rekindle in your souls the devotion you ought to feel for that saint. Therefore, it was not the feather he let me take, as I had intended, but the blessed coals, quenched by the agonized sweat of that holiest of bodies. Take off your hats now, O my blessed children, as you approach to gaze upon these coals. But first, I'd like you to know that whoever has the sign of the cross marked on him by one of these coals may rest easy all through the year that no fire will touch him, but he'll feel the sting of it."

His harangue over, he intoned a *laud* in honor of Saint Lawrence and opened the box, revealing the coals to the throng. Awed at the wonder of them, the sheepish multitude stared wide-eyed at the lumps and flocked about Friar Onion, begging him, for a more generous consideration than usual, to mark them with the relics. Obligingly, the friar took the coals in his hand and began scratching the biggest crosses he could on the men's white shirts and jerkins and the women's veils, re-assuring them the while that though the lumps were used up in the marking, they always grew again in the box, as he had often had occasion to observe.

In this fashion, he decorated the good folks of Certaldo, much to his own advantage, and so with nimble cunning he played a prank on those who had sought to embarrass him by stealing his feather. As for the two rogues, they had been present at his sermon. So amused were they at his novel and far-fetched expedient, and at the style of his harangue, that they laughed almost to the point of lockjaw. But later, when the crowd had dispersed, they hilariously confessed to him what they had done, and gave him back his feather, which profited him as much the following year, as the lumps of coal had done that day.

FOR STUDY AND DISCUSSION

1. Point out the words and statements that describe the physical appearance and manner of Friar Onion and of Guccio. What do these details suggest about the character or nature of each of them?

2. Satire pictures its subject as significantly different from what it pretends to be or, in the view of the satirist, ought to be. In this satiric tale, what is the implied "norm" of appropriate conduct for a friar and his servant?

3. In Boccaccio's time, the Church had a great deal of secular power as well as spiritual power and was therefore an important center for intellectual and political activity. Many men took holy orders who today would go into professional life as teachers, scholars, lawyers, politicians, civil servants. In what ways does Boccaccio's story reflect such conditions? To what extent do such conditions explain his criticism?

4. Besides the friar and his servant, who and what are the objects of Boccaccio's satire?

5. Divide the tale into what you consider its main parts. Define the function of each part in advancing the tale toward its climax. (Is there an anticlimactic section? If so, what purpose does it serve?) How are the transitions marked from one part to the next?

6. At what point in the story do you know that the crucial moment will come when Friar Onion offers to show the crowd the feather? At what point do you know (or have a fairly good idea) that Friar Onion will outsmart the tricksters? How does Boccaccio hold your interest, even if you have guessed what the outcome is going to be?

7. What similarities are established between the friar and his servant? How does the parallel between them contribute to our understanding of Boccaccio's purpose and to our interest in the story?

FOR COMPOSITION

1. (Before class discussion.) Write a short essay in which you define the character of Guccio. Show the means by which Boccaccio reveals this character, and explain the use he makes of him, other than his role in the plot itself.

2. (After class discussion.) Write a short tale to expose the folly that you think a specific kind of person (teachers, teen-age boys, city people, etc.) is especially prone to. Try to make clear that it is the folly you are satirizing, not the individual person.

Don Quixote

MIGUEL DE CERVANTES

The pride and consolation of Cervantes' life (1547–1616), which was a long tale of poverty and imprisonment, was that he had fought with distinction at the Battle of Lepanto, the naval battle in which the Christian forces under Don John of Austria won a stunning victory over the Turks. Other than that, in order to scrape together a living, Cervantes wrote some indifferent plays, tolerable romances, excellent short stories, and what has been called "the wisest and most splendid book in the world"— *The Ingenious Gentleman Don Quixote de la Mancha.*

Cervantes initially created Don Quixote to make fun of the knights in popular romances, who performed incredible deeds with intolerable self-assurance. In the opening episode of his book, Cervantes describes the hero and his trappings in the manner of simple caricature. In his first few adventures, the knight performs ludicrous capers in the midst of commonplace situations. After his friends have tricked him into returning home, where they try to cure him of his madness by burning the romances he has been reading, Don Quixote sets off again, in spite of them, accompanied this time by a peasant neighbor, Sancho Panza, who has been persuaded to act as his squire. Already Don Quixote has taken on much more complexity than the parody he started out to be, and the addition of Sancho as his earthy "commonsensical" foil enriches the character of Quixote immeasurably.

The episode of the windmills is the most famous episode in *Don Quixote.* More than any other, it defines the term *quixotic,* as it is commonly used. "To tilt at windmills" or to be "quixotic" is to make a gallant but inept attempt to do battle against a reality that any sensible man would leave alone. Sancho Panza, Don Quixote's "squire," represents the earthy, sensible man, and the conversation between the two after the "battle" defines the differences in their points of view.

It is apparent, however, that the difference is not really as simple as a matter of the "sensible" against the "imaginative," or of the "realistic" against the "idealistic," much less of the "sane" against the "crazy." Which is the more "realistic"—the man who permits trials to defeat him, or the man who rises from defeat to attempt new adventures? Can you prove that the encounter is only with windmills, as Sancho says, or is it with giants-become-windmills, as Don Quixote sees it?

The following passages give only a brief glimpse into Cervantes' long, leisurely, episodic novel. It is a book which should be read slowly and lived with. To do so is to come to know these characters better than oneself, and to feel the gallantry and pathos of being a small human who must cope with a great and wonderful and terrible world.

CHAPTER 1

*Which treats of the station in life
and the pursuits of the famous
gentleman, Don Quixote de la Mancha.*

I N A VILLAGE of La Mancha,[1] the name
of which I have no desire to recall, there
lived not so long ago one of those gentlemen who always have a lance in the rack,
an ancient buckler, a skinny nag, and a
greyhound for the chase. A stew with
more beef than mutton in it, chopped meat
for his evening meal, scraps for a Saturday, lentils on Friday, and a young pigeon
as a special delicacy for Sunday went to
account for three quarters of his income.
The rest of it he laid out on a broadcloth
greatcoat and velvet stockings for feast
days, with slippers to match, while the
other days of the week he cut a figure in
a suit of the finest homespun. Living with
him were a housekeeper in her forties, a
niece who was not yet twenty, and a lad
of the field and market place who saddled
his horse for him and wielded the pruning
knife.

This gentleman of ours was close on to
fifty, of a robust constitution but with little
flesh on his bones and a face that was lean
and gaunt. He was noted for his early
rising, being very fond of the hunt. They
will try to tell you that his surname was
Quijada or Quesada [2]—there is some
difference of opinion among those who
have written on the subject—but according to the most likely conjectures we
are to understand that it was really Que-
jana. But all this means very little so far
as our story is concerned, providing that

in the telling of it we do not depart one
iota from the truth.

You may know, then, that the afore-
said gentleman, on those occasions when
he was at leisure, which was most of the
year around, was in the habit of reading
books of chivalry with such pleasure and
devotion as to lead him almost wholly to
forget the life of a hunter and even the administration of his estate. So great was his
curiosity and infatuation in this regard
that he even sold many acres of tillable
land in order to be able to buy and read
the books that he loved, and he would
carry home with him as many of them as
he could obtain.

Of all those that he thus devoured, none
pleased him so well as the ones that had
been composed by the famous Feliciano
de Silva,[3] whose lucid prose style and
involved conceits were as precious to him
as pearls; especially when he came to
read those tales of love and amorous challenges that are to be met with in many
places, such a passage as the following,
for example: "The reason of the unreason
that afflicts my reason, in such a manner
weakens my reason that I with reason
lament me of your comeliness." And he
was similarly affected when his eyes fell
upon such lines as these: ". . . the high
heaven of your divinity divinely fortifies
you with the stars and renders you deserving of that desert your greatness doth
deserve."

The poor fellow used to lie awake nights
in an effort to disentangle the meaning and
make sense out of passages such as these,
although Aristotle himself would not have
been able to understand them, even if he
had been resurrected for that sole purpose. He was not at ease in his mind over
those wounds that Don Belianís gave and
received; for no matter how great the
surgeons who treated him, the poor fel-

---

[1] **La Mancha:** a province of south-central Spain,
a poor plateau land lying alongside the mountains
called Sierra Morena. To Cervantes, La Mancha
represented a poor, backward area in the middle of
nowhere.

[2] **Quijada** (kē·hä′dä) **or Quesada** (kä·sä′dä): distinguished Spanish family names.

From *The Ingenious Gentleman Don Quixote de la Mancha* by
Miguel de Cervantes Saavedra, translated by Samuel Putnam, copyright 1949 by The Viking Press, Inc. Reprinted by permission of the
publisher.

[3] **Feliciano de Silva:** The names of authors and
characters and the titles of stories in the following
paragraphs belong to romances that were more or
less well known to Cervantes' audience. It is not
necessary to know the stories to understand what
Cervantes thought of them.

low must have been left with his face and his entire body covered with marks and scars. Nevertheless, he was grateful to the author for closing the book with the promise of an interminable adventure to come; many a time he was tempted to take up his pen and literally finish the tale as had been promised, and he undoubtedly would have done so, and would have succeeded at it very well, if his thoughts had not been constantly occupied with other things of greater moment.

He often talked it over with the village curate, who was a learned man, a graduate of Sigüenza,[1] and they would hold long discussions as to who had been the better knight, Palmerin of England or Amadis of Gaul; but Master Nicholas, the barber of the same village, was in the habit of saying that no one could come up to the Knight of Phoebus, and that if anyone *could* compare with him it was Don Galaor, brother of Amadis of Gaul, for Galaor was ready for anything—he was none of your finical knights who went around whimpering as his brother did, and in point of valor he did not lag behind him.

In short, our gentleman became so immersed in his reading that he spent whole nights from sundown to sunup and his days from dawn to dusk in poring over his books, until, finally, from so little sleeping and so much reading, his brain dried up and he went completely out of his mind. He had filled his imagination with everything that he had read, with enchantments, knightly encounters, battles, challenges, wounds, with tales of love and its torments, and all sorts of impossible things, and as a result had come to believe that all these fictitious happenings were true; they were more real to him than anything else in the world. He would remark that the Cid Ruy Díaz had been a very good knight, but there was no comparison between him and the Knight of the Flaming Sword, who with a single backward

[1] **Sigüenza:** a minor Spanish university that signified a neglible education in joking references.

stroke had cut in half two fierce and monstrous giants. He preferred Bernardo del Carpio, who at Roncesvalles had slain Roland despite the charm the latter bore, availing himself of the stratagem which Hercules employed when he strangled Antaeus, the son of Earth, in his arms.

He had much good to say for Morgante who, though he belonged to the haughty, overbearing race of giants, was of an affable disposition and well brought up. But, above all, he cherished an admiration for Rinaldo of Montalbán, especially as he beheld him sallying forth from his castle to rob all those that crossed his path, or when he thought of him overseas stealing the image of Mohammed which, so the story has it, was all of gold. And he would have liked very well to have had his fill of kicking that traitor Galalón, a privilege for which he would have given his housekeeper with his niece thrown into the bargain.

At last, when his wits were gone beyond repair, he came to conceive the strangest idea that ever occurred to any madman in this world. It now appeared to him fitting and necessary, in order to win a greater amount of honor for himself and serve his country at the same time, to become a knight errant and roam the world on horseback, in a suit of armor; he would go in quest of adventures, by way of putting into practice all that he had read in his books; he would right every manner of wrong, placing himself in situations of the greatest peril such as would redound to the eternal glory of his name. As a reward for his valor and the might of his arm, the poor fellow could already see himself crowned Emperor of Trebizond at the very least; and so, carried away by the strange pleasure that he found in such thoughts as these, he at once set about putting his plan into effect.

The first thing he did was to burnish up some old pieces of armor, left him by his great-grandfather, which for ages had lain in a corner, moldering and forgotten. He polished and adjusted them as best he could, and then he noticed that one very important thing was lacking: there was no closed helmet, but only a morion, or visorless headpiece, with turned-up brim of the kind foot soldiers wore. His ingenuity, however, enabled him to remedy this, and he proceeded to fashion out of cardboard a kind of half-helmet, which, when attached to the morion, gave the appearance of a whole one. True, when he went to see if it was strong enough to withstand a good slashing blow, he was somewhat disappointed; for when he drew his sword and gave it a couple of thrusts, he succeeded only in undoing a whole week's labor. The ease with which he had hewed it to bits disturbed him no little, and he decided to make it over. This time he placed a few strips of iron on the inside, and then, convinced that it was strong enough, refrained from putting it to any further test; instead, he adopted it then and there as the finest helmet ever made.

After this, he went out to have a look at his nag; and although the animal had more *cuartos,* or cracks, in its hoof than there are quarters in a real,[1] and more blemishes than Gonela's [2] steed which *tantum pellis et ossa fuit,*[3] it nonetheless looked to its master like a far better horse than Alexander's Bucephalus or the Babieca of the Cid. He spent all of four days in trying to think up a name for his mount; for—so he told himself—seeing that it belonged to so famous and worthy a knight, there was no reason why it should not have a name of equal renown. The kind of name he wanted was one that would at once indicate what the nag had been before it came to belong to a knight errant and what its present status was; for it stood to reason that, when the master's wordly condition changed, his horse also ought to have a famous, high-sounding appellation, one suited to the new order of things and the new profession that it was to follow.

After he in his memory and imagination had made up, struck out, and discarded many names, now adding to and now subtracting from the list, he finally hit upon "Rocinante," [4] a name that impressed him as being sonorous and at the same time indicative of what the steed had been when it was but a hack, whereas now it was nothing other than the first and foremost of all the hacks in the world.

Having found a name for his horse that pleased his fancy, he then desired to do as much for himself, and this required another week, and by the end of that period he had made up his mind that he was henceforth to be known as Don Quixote,[5] which, as has been stated, has led the authors of this veracious history to assume that his real name must undoubtedly have been Quijada, and not Quesada as others would have it. But remembering that the valiant Amadis was not content to call himself that and nothing more, but added the name of his kingdom and fatherland that he might make it famous also, and thus came to take the name Amadis of Gaul, so our good knight chose to add his place of origin and become "Don Quixote de la Mancha"; for by this means, as he saw it, he was making very plain his lineage and was conferring honor upon his country by taking its name as his own.[6]

And so, having polished up his armor and made the morion over into a closed helmet, and having given himself and his horse a name, he naturally found but one thing lacking still: he must seek out a lady of whom he could become enamored; for a knight errant without a ladylove was like a tree without leaves or fruit, a body without a soul.

"If," he said to himself, "as a punishment for my sins or by a stroke of fortune I should come upon some giant hereabouts, a thing that very commonly

[1] **real** (rä·äl'): an old Spanish coin, something like a nickel; a quarter was one eighth of a real.

[2] **Gonela:** a fifteenth-century court jester of Italy.

[3] ***tantum pellis et ossa fuit:*** "was nothing but skin and bones" (Latin).

[4] **Rocinante** (rō'sē·nän'tā): coined from the word *rocin,* "a nag" or "hack."

[5] **Quixote:** the name for a piece of armor which covers the thigh.

[6] If a man named Smith from Wichita called himself Lord Smythe of Kansas, the effect might be something like this.

happens to knights errant, and if I should slay him in a hand-to-hand encounter or perhaps cut him in two, or, finally, if I should vanquish and subdue him, would it not be well to have someone to whom I may send him as a present, in order that he, if he is living, may come in, fall upon his knees in front of my sweet lady, and say in a humble and submissive tone of voice, 'I, lady, am the giant Caraculiambro, lord of the island Malindrania, who has been overcome in single combat by that knight who never can be praised enough, Don Quixote de la Mancha, the same who sent me to present myself before your Grace that your Highness may dispose of me as you see fit'?"

Oh, how our good knight reveled in this speech, and more than ever when he came to think of the name that he should give his lady! As the story goes, there was a very good-looking farm girl who lived near by, with whom he had once been smitten, although it is generally believed that she never knew or suspected it. Her name was Aldonza Lorenzo, and it seemed to him that she was the one upon whom he should bestow the title of mistress of his thoughts. For her he wished a name that should not be incongruous with his own and that would convey the suggestion of a princess or a great lady; and accordingly, he resolved to call her "Dulcinea del Toboso," she being a native of that place. A musical name to his ears, out of the ordinary and significant, like the others he had chosen for himself and his appurtenances.

FROM CHAPTER 2

Which treats of the first sally that the ingenious Don Quixote made from his native heath.

HAVING, THEN, made all these preparations, he did not wish to lose any time in putting his plan into effect, for he could not but blame himself for what the world was losing by his delay, so many were the wrongs that were to be righted, the grievances to be redressed, the abuses to be done away with, and the duties to be performed. Accordingly, without informing anyone of his intention and without letting anyone see him, he set out one morning before daybreak on one of those very hot days in July. Donning all his armor, mounting Rocinante, adjusting his ill-contrived helmet, bracing his shield on his arm, and taking up his lance, he sallied forth by the back gate of his stable yard into the open countryside. It was with great contentment and joy that he saw how easily he had made a beginning toward the fulfillment of his desire.

No sooner was he out on the plain, however, than a terrible thought assailed him, one that all but caused him to abandon the enterprise he had undertaken. This occurred when he suddenly remembered that he had never formally been dubbed a knight, and so, in accordance with the law of knighthood, was not permitted to bear arms against one who had a right to that title. And even if he had been, as a novice knight he would have had to wear white armor, without any device on his shield, until he should have earned one by his exploits. These thoughts led him to waver in his purpose, but, madness prevailing over reason, he resolved to have himself knighted by the first person he met, as many others had done if what he had read in those books that he had at home was true. And so far as white armor was concerned, he would scour his own the first chance that offered until it shone whiter than any ermine. With this he became more tranquil and continued on his way, letting his horse take whatever path it chose, for he believed that therein lay the very essence of adventures. . . .

[Don Quixote gets himself "knighted" by a bewildered innkeeper, who marvels at such an extraordinary variety of madness, but he is finally tricked by his friends and brought home, where he is treated as a lunatic. His family deprives him of the dangerous books, and they hope that the madness will pass.]

*Of the second sally of our good
knight, Don Quixote de la Mancha.*

... He remained at home very tranquilly for a couple of weeks, without giving sign of any desire to repeat his former
madness. During that time he had the
most pleasant conversations with his two
old friends, the curate and the barber,
on the point he had raised to the effect
that what the world needed most was
knights errant and a revival of chivalry.
The curate would occasionally contradict
him and again would give in, for it was
only by means of this artifice that he could
carry on a conversation with him at all.

In the meanwhile Don Quixote was
bringing his powers of persuasion to bear
upon a farmer who lived near by, a good
man—if this title may be applied to one
who is poor—but with very few wits in
his head. The short of it is, by pleas and
promises, he got the hapless rustic to
agree to ride forth with him and serve him
as his squire. Among other things, Don
Quixote told him that he ought to be more
than willing to go, because no telling what
adventure might occur which would win
them an island, and then he (the farmer)
would be left to be the governor of it.
As a result of these and other similar
assurances, Sancho Panza forsook his
wife and children and consented to take
upon himself the duties of squire to his
neighbor.

Next, Don Quixote set out to raise
some money, and by selling this thing and
pawning that and getting the worst of the
bargain always, he finally scraped together
a reasonable amount. He also asked a
friend of his for the loan of a buckler and
patched up his broken helmet as well as
he could. He advised his squire, Sancho,
of the day and hour when they were to
take the road and told him to see to laying
in a supply of those things that were most
necessary, and, above all, not to forget the
saddlebags. Sancho replied that he would
see to all this and added that he was also
thinking of taking along with him a very

good ass that he had, as he was not much
used to going on foot.

With regard to the ass, Don Quixote
had to do a little thinking, trying to recall
if any knight errant had ever had a squire
thus asininely mounted. He could not
think of any, but nevertheless he decided
to take Sancho with the intention of providing him with a nobler steed as soon as
occasion offered; he had but to appropriate the horse of the first discourteous
knight he met. Having furnished himself
with shirts and all the other things that
the innkeeper had recommended, he and
Panza rode forth one night unseen by
anyone and without taking leave of wife
and children, housekeeper or niece. They
went so far that by the time morning came
they were safe from discovery had a hunt
been started for them.

Mounted on his ass, Sancho Panza rode
along like a patriarch, with saddlebags
and flask, his mind set upon becoming
governor of that island that his master
had promised him. Don Quixote determined to take the same route and road
over the Campo de Montiel that he had
followed on his first journey; but he was
not so uncomfortable this time, for it was
early morning and the sun's rays fell upon
them slantingly and accordingly did not
tire them too much.

"Look, Sir Knight errant," said Sancho,
"your Grace should not forget that island
you promised me; for no matter how big
it is, I'll be able to govern it right enough."

"I would have you know, friend Sancho
Panza," replied Don Quixote, "that
among the knights errant of old it was a
very common custom to make their
squires governors of the islands or the
kingdoms that they won, and I am resolved that in my case so pleasing a usage
shall not fall into desuetude. I even mean
to go them one better; for they very often,
perhaps most of the time, waited until
their squires were old men who had had
their fill of serving their masters during
bad days and worse nights, whereupon
they would give them the title of count,
or marquis at most, of some valley or
province more or less. But if you live

and I live, it well may be that within a week I shall win some kingdom with others dependent upon it, and it will be the easiest thing in the world to crown you king of one of them. You need not marvel at this, for all sorts of unforeseen things happen to knights like me, and I may readily be able to give you even more than I have promised."

"In that case," said Sancho Panza, "if by one of those miracles of which your Grace was speaking I should become king, I would certainly send for Juana Gutiérrez, my old lady, to come and be my queen, and the young ones could be infantes." [1]

"There is no doubt about it," Don Quixote assured him.

"Well, I doubt it," said Sancho, "for I think that even if God were to rain kingdoms upon the earth, no crown would sit well on the head of Mari Gutiérrez,[2] for I am telling you, sir, as a queen she is not worth two maravedis. She would do better as a countess, God help her."

"Leave everything to God, Sancho," said Don Quixote, "and he will give you whatever is most fitting; but I trust you will not be so pusillanimous as to be content with anything less than the title of viceroy."

"That I will not," said Sancho Panza, "especially seeing that I have in your Grace so illustrious a master who can give me all that is suitable to me and all that I can manage."

FROM CHAPTER 8

Of the good fortune which the valorous Don Quixote had in the terrifying and never-before-imagined adventure of the windmills, along with other events that deserve to be suitably recorded.

AT THIS POINT they caught sight of thirty or forty windmills which were

---

[1] **infantes** (in·fän′täz): a term used to designate the daughters of a Spanish king.

[2] **Mari Gutiérrez:** Sancho's wife, who appears under several names during the course of the story.

---

standing on the plain there, and no sooner had Don Quixote laid eyes upon them than he turned to his squire and said, "Fortune is guiding our affairs better than we could have wished; for you see there before you, friend Sancho Panza, some thirty or more lawless giants with whom I mean to do battle. I shall deprive them of their lives, and with the spoils from this encounter we shall begin to enrich ourselves; for this is righteous warfare, and it is a great service to God to remove so accursed a breed from the face of the earth."

"What giants?" said Sancho Panza.

"Those that you see there," replied his master, "those with the long arms, some of which are as much as two leagues in length."

"But look, your Grace, those are not giants but windmills, and what appear to be arms are their wings which, when whirled in the breeze, cause the millstone to go."

"It is plain to be seen," said Don Quixote, "that you have had little experience in this matter of adventures. If you are afraid, go off to one side and say your prayers while I am engaging them in fierce, unequal combat."

Saying this, he gave spurs to his steed Rocinante, without paying any heed to Sancho's warning that these were truly windmills and not giants that he was riding forth to attack. Nor even when he was close upon them did he perceive what they really were, but shouted at the top of his lungs, "Do not seek to flee, cowards and vile creatures that you are, for it is but a single knight with whom you have to deal!"

At that moment a little wind came up and the big wings began turning.

"Though you flourish as many arms as did the giant Briareus," said Don Quixote when he perceived this, "you still shall have to answer to me."

He thereupon commended himself with all his heart to his lady Dulcinea, beseeching her to succor him in this peril; and, being well covered with his shield and with his lance at rest, he bore down upon them at a full gallop and fell upon the first mill that stood in his way, giving a thrust at the wing, which was whirling at such a speed that his lance was broken into bits and both horse and horseman went rolling over the plain, very much battered indeed. Sancho upon his donkey came hurrying to his master's assistance as fast as he could, but when he reached the spot, the knight was unable to move, so great was the shock with which he and Rocinante had hit the ground.

"God help us!" exclaimed Sancho, "did I not tell your Grace to look well, that those were nothing but windmills, a fact which no one could fail to see unless he had other mills of the same sort in his head?"

"Be quiet, friend Sancho," said Don Quixote. "Such are the fortunes of war, which more than any other are subject to constant change. What is more, when I come to think of it, I am sure that this must be the work of that magician Frestón, the one who robbed me of my study and my books, and who has thus changed the giants into windmills in order to deprive me of the glory of overcoming them, so great is the enmity that he bears me; but in the end his evil arts shall not prevail against this trusty sword of mine."

"May God's will be done," was Sancho Panza's response. And with the aid of his squire the knight was once more mounted on Rocinante, who stood there with one shoulder half out of joint. And so, speaking of the adventure that had just befallen them, they continued along the Puerto Lápice highway; for there, Don Quixote said, they could not fail to find many and varied adventures, this being a much-traveled thoroughfare. The only thing was, the knight was exceedingly downcast over the loss of his lance.

"I remember," he said to his squire, "having read of a Spanish knight by the name of Diego Pérez de Vargas, who, having broken his sword in battle, tore from an oak a heavy bough or branch and with it did such feats of valor that day, and pounded so many Moors, that he

came to be known as Machuca,[1] and he and his descendants from that day forth have been called Vargas y Machuca. I tell you this because I, too, intend to provide myself with just such a bough as the one he wielded, and with it I propose to do such exploits that you shall deem yourself fortunate to have been found worthy to come with me and behold and witness things that are almost beyond belief."

"God's will be done," said Sancho. "I believe everything that your Grace says; but straighten yourself up in the saddle a little, for you seem to be slipping down on one side, owing, no doubt, to the shaking up that you received in your fall."

"Ah, that is the truth," replied Don Quixote, "and if I do not speak of my sufferings, it is for the reason that it is not permitted knights errant to complain of any wound whatsoever, even though their bowels may be dropping out."

"If that is the way it is," said Sancho, "I have nothing more to say; but, God knows, it would suit me better if your Grace did complain when something hurts him. I can assure you that I mean to do so, over the least little thing that ails me—that is, unless the same rule applies to squires as well."

Don Quixote laughed long and heartily over Sancho's simplicity, telling him that he might complain as much as he liked and where and when he liked, whether he had good cause or not; for he had read nothing to the contrary in the ordinances of chivalry. Sancho then called his master's attention to the fact that it was time to eat. The knight replied that he himself had no need of food at the moment, but his squire might eat whenever he chose. Having been granted this permission, Sancho seated himself as best he could upon his beast, and, taking out from his saddlebags the provisions that he had stored there, he rode along leisurely behind his master, munching his victuals and taking a good, hearty swig now and then at the leather flask in a manner that might

---

[1] **Machuca** (mä·choo′kä): literally, "the pounder."

well have caused the biggest-bellied tavernkeeper of Málaga to envy him. Between draughts he gave not so much as a thought to any promise that his master might have made him, nor did he look upon it as any hardship, but rather as good sport, to go in quest of adventures however hazardous they might be.

The short of the matter is, they spent the night under some trees, from one of which Don Quixote tore off a withered bough to serve him as a lance, placing it in the lance head from which he had removed the broken one. He did not sleep all night long for thinking of his lady Dulcinea; for this was in accordance with what he had read in his books, of men of arms in the forest or desert places who kept a wakeful vigil, sustained by the memory of their ladies fair. Not so with Sancho, whose stomach was full, and not with chicory water. He fell into a dreamless slumber, and had not his master called him, he would not have been awakened either by the rays of the sun in his face or by the many birds who greeted the coming of the new day with their merry song.

Upon arising, he had another go at the flask, finding it somewhat more flaccid than it had been the night before, a circumstance which grieved his heart, for he could not see that they were on the way to remedying the deficiency within any very short space of time. Don Quixote did not wish any breakfast; for, as has been said, he was in the habit of nourishing himself on savorous memories. They then set out once more along the road to Puerto Lápice, and around three in the afternoon they came in sight of the pass that bears that name.

"There," said Don Quixote as his eyes fell upon it, "we may plunge our arms up to the elbow in what are known as adventures. But I must warn you that even though you see me in the greatest peril in the world, you are not to lay hand upon your sword to defend me, unless it be that those who attack me are rabble and men of low degree, in which case you

may very well come to my aid; but if they be gentlemen, it is in no wise permitted by the laws of chivalry that you should assist me until you yourself shall have been dubbed a knight."

"Most certainly, sir," replied Sancho, "your Grace shall be very well obeyed in this; all the more so for the reason that I myself am of a peaceful disposition and not fond of meddling in the quarrels and feuds of others. However, when it comes to protecting my own person, I shall not take account of those laws of which you speak, seeing that all laws, human and divine, permit each one to defend himself whenever he is attacked."

"I am willing to grant you that," assented Don Quixote, "but in this matter of defending me against gentlemen you must restrain your natural impulses."

"I promise you I shall do so," said Sancho. "I will observe this precept as I would the Sabbath day."

. . .

FOR STUDY AND DISCUSSION

1. Clearly Cervantes wants you to laugh at Don Quixote as he prepares himself for his preposterous undertaking. But what else does he want you to feel about him? What in the details and in the style of presentation conveys all these attitudes to you?

2. How does Don Quixote go about creating the character of Dulcinea? What does this tell you about Don Quixote's approach to his adventures? Do you find any evidence here or elsewhere that Don Quixote is deliberately assuming his "madness," knowing very well how he appears to other people? If so, why do you suppose Cervantes usually "pretends" to the reader that he, as narrator, takes Don Quixote seriously?

3. In the episode of the windmills, who wins? What does he win? Who loses? What does he lose?

4. Trace precisely the sequence of reactions of Don Quixote and of Sancho to their encounter with the windmills. How do their attitudes interact upon each other?

5. Define precisely the relationships in this story among the reader, the narrator, and Don Quixote.

SATIRIC AND COMIC EFFECTS

Parody, burlesque, and caricature are imitations made for comic or satiric effect. Parody makes the characteristics of someone or something seem ridiculous by transferring them to a ridiculous subject. Burlesque makes someone or something seem ridiculous by treating it with mock seriousness. Caricature picks out one or two characteristics of someone or something and submits them to ridiculous exaggeration.

1. Which of these methods does Cervantes most often use in mocking the old romances?

2. Does Boccaccio use any of these methods in his story of Friar Onion? If so, does he use them for satiric or only for comic effect?

3. What characteristics of style does Cervantes satirize in the fourth and fifth paragraphs of the first episode? What other characteristics of knightly romances does he satirize?

FOR COMPOSITION

1. Write an essay which first gives a thoughtful definition of the term *quixotic,* so far as you can derive it from these passages.

Then consider in what ways you admire and can sympathize with the quixotic character in Cervantes' story. What do you think of this sort of character when you have to deal with him in your own life?

2. Write an explanation of the following poem, "Parable," by the modern American poet Richard Wilbur, which takes up the idea expressed in the last sentence of the last paragraph on page 517. Show how the poem supports and reflects the idea.

I read how Quixote in his random ride
Came to a crossing once, and lest he lose
The purity of chance, would not decide

Whither to fare, but wished his horse to
  choose.
For glory lay wherever he might turn.
His head was light with pride, his horse's
  shoes

Were heavy, and he headed for the barn.
                    —RICHARD WILBUR

"Parable" from *Ceremony And Other Poems,* copyright 1948, 1949, 1950 by Richard Wilbur. Reprinted by permission of Harcourt, Brace & World, Inc.

The Essays

MICHEL DE MONTAIGNE

Montaigne (1533–1592) referred to his *Essays* as "an integral part of my life." Though he seldom speaks about himself in the essays, Montaigne does speak of all he has thought and felt and experienced about a wide range of topics. In fact, Montaigne is considered the inventor of the modern essay. This medium was ideal for Montaigne. A purely personal and conversational piece of writing, with no pretensions to authority, the essay permitted Montaigne to digress as he loved to do. It also permitted him to quote frequently from his favorite authors, the writers of ancient Greece and Rome.

The essays are most directly the fruit of Montaigne's retirement at the age of thirty-eight from his occupations as lawyer and civil counselor in the French city of Bordeaux. Montaigne intended to live a quiet scholarly life on his modest country estate, but his retirement was, in fact, often broken, particularly by a period of four years when he served as mayor of Bordeaux. This position was a sensitive one. Bordeaux, as capital of the French province bordering the northern Spanish province of Navarre, stood critically between the Catholic king of France and the Protestant heir-presumptive, who was king of Navarre. Montaigne, himself a Catholic, apparently served in a position of unique trust between these opposing political and religious factions, so that he played an important diplomatic role in the events that led to the conversion of Henry of Navarre to Catholicism and his succession to the French throne as Henry IV.

Most of the essays were written in the early years of Montaigne's retirement, but Montaigne continued adding and revising, and an expanded edition saw the light in his own lifetime. Shakespeare became acquainted with the essays in an English translation made by John Florio, which was published in 1603.

In "Of Cannibals" Montaigne talks about the primitive natives of the New World, some of whom were taken back to Europe as prisoners of the voyagers. Europeans were fascinated by these "natural" men.

Of Cannibals

WHEN KING PYRRHUS[1] passed over into Italy, after he had reconnoitered the formation of the army that the Romans were sending to meet him, he said: "I do not know what barbarians these are" (for so the Greeks called all foreign nations), "but the formation of this army that I see is not at all barbarous." The Greeks said as much of the army that Flamininus brought into their country, and so did Philip, seeing from a knoll the order and distribution of the Roman camp, in his kingdom, under Publius Sulpicius Galba. Thus we should beware of clinging to vulgar opinions, and judge things by reason's way, not by popular say.

I had with me for a long time a man who

[1] **King Pyrrhus:** of a district in Greece. He fought the Romans in 280 B.C.

had lived for ten or twelve years in that other world which has been discovered in our century, in the place where Villegaignon landed and which he called Antarctic France.[1] This discovery of a boundless country seems worthy of consideration. I don't know if I can guarantee that some other such discovery will not be made in the future, so many personages greater than ourselves having been mistaken about this one. I am afraid we have eyes bigger than our stomachs, and more curiosity than capacity. We embrace everything, but we clasp only wind.

Plato brings in Solon,[2] telling how he had learned from the priests of the city of Saïs in Egypt that in days of old, before the Flood, there was a great island named Atlantis, right at the mouth of the Strait of Gibraltar, which contained more land than Africa and Asia put together, and that the kings of that country, who not only possessed that island but had stretched out so far on the mainland that they held the breadth of Africa as far as Egypt and the length of Europe as far as Tuscany, undertook to step over into Asia and subjugate all the nations that border on the Mediterranean, as far as the Black Sea; and for this purpose crossed the Spains, Gaul, Italy, as far as Greece, where the Athenians checked them; but that some time after, both the Athenians and themselves and their island were swallowed up by the Flood.

It is quite likely that that extreme devastation of waters made amazing changes in the habitations of the earth, as people maintain that the sea cut off Sicily from Italy—

> 'Tis said an earthquake once asunder tore
> These lands with dreadful havoc, which before
> Formed but one land, one coast
> [VIRGIL]

[1] **Antarctic France:** Brazil. Villegaignon landed there in 1557. *Antarctic* here would mean "in the southern hemisphere."

[2] **Solon:** lawmaker of ancient Athens (638 B.C.?– 559 B.C.?).

—Cyprus from Syria, the island of Euboea from the mainland of Boeotia; and elsewhere joined lands that were divided, filling the channels between them with sand and mud:

> A sterile marsh, long fit for rowing, now
> Feeds neighbor towns, and feels the heavy plow.
> [HORACE]

But there is no great likelihood that that island was the new world which we have just discovered; for it almost touched Spain, and it would be an incredible result of a flood to have forced it away as far as it is, more than twelve hundred leagues; besides, the travels of the moderns have already almost revealed that it is not an island but a mainland connected with the East Indies on one side and elsewhere with the lands under the two poles; or, if it is separated from them, it is by so narrow a strait and interval that it does not deserve to be called an island on that account.

It seems that there are movements, some natural, others feverish, in these great bodies, just as in our own. When I consider the inroads that my river, the Dordogne, is making in my lifetime into the right bank in its descent, and that in twenty years it has gained so much ground and stolen away the foundations of several buildings, I clearly see that this is an extraordinary disturbance; for if it had always gone at this rate, or was to do so in the future, the face of the world would be turned topsy-turvy. But rivers are subject to changes: now they overflow in one direction, now in another, now they keep to their course. I am not speaking of the sudden inundations whose causes are manifest. In Médoc, along the seashore, my brother, the sieur d'Arsac, can see an estate of his buried under the sands that the sea spews forth; the tops of some buildings are still visible; his farms and domains have changed into very thin pasturage. The inhabitants say that for some time the sea has been pushing toward them so hard that they have lost four leagues of land. These sands are its harbingers; and we see great dunes of moving sand that march half a league ahead of it and keep conquering land.

The other testimony of antiquity with which some would connect this discovery is in Aristotle, at least if that little book *Of Unheard-of Wonders* is by him. He there relates that certain Carthaginians, after setting out upon the Atlantic Ocean from the Strait of Gibraltar and sailing a long time, at last discovered a great fertile island, all clothed in woods and watered by great deep rivers, far remote from any mainland; and that they, and others since, attracted by the goodness and fertility of the soil, went there with their wives and children and began to settle there. The lords of Carthage, seeing that their country was gradually becoming depopulated, expressly forbade anyone to go there any more, on pain of death, and drove out these new inhabitants, fearing, it is said, that in course of time they might come to multiply so greatly as to supplant their former masters and ruin their state. This story of Aristotle does not fit our new lands any better than the other.

This man I had was a simple, crude fellow—a character fit to bear true witness; for clever people observe more things and more curiously, but they interpret them; and to lend weight and conviction to their interpretation, they cannot help altering history a little. They never show you things as they are, but bend and disguise them according to the way they have seen them; and to give credence to their judgment and attract you to it, they are prone to add something to their matter, to stretch it out and amplify it. We need a man either very honest, or so simple that he has not the stuff to build up false inventions and give them plausibility; and wedded to no theory. Such was my man; and besides this, he at various times brought sailors and merchants, whom he had known on that trip, to see me. So I content myself with his informa-

tion, without inquiring what the cosmographers say about it.

We ought to have topographers who would give us an exact account of the places where they have been. But because they have over us the advantage of having seen Palestine, they want to enjoy the privilege of telling us news about all the rest of the world. I would like everyone to write what he knows, and as much as he knows, not only in this, but in all other subjects; for a man may have some special knowledge and experience of the nature of a river or a fountain, who in other matters knows only what everybody knows. However, to circulate this little scrap of knowledge, he will undertake to write the whole of physics. From this vice spring many great abuses.

Now, to return to my subject, I think there is nothing barbarous and savage in that nation, from what I have been told, except that each man calls barbarism whatever is not his own practice; for indeed it seems we have no other test of truth and reason than the example and pattern of the opinions and customs of the country we live in. *There* is always the perfect religion, the perfect government, the perfect and accomplished manners in all things. Those people are wild, just as we call wild the fruits that nature has produced by herself and in her normal course; whereas really it is those that we have changed artificially and led astray from the common order, that we should rather call wild. The former retain alive and vigorous their genuine, their most useful and natural virtues and properties, which we have debased in the latter in adapting them to gratify our corrupted taste. And yet for all that, the savor and delicacy of some uncultivated fruits of those countries is quite as excellent, even to our taste, as that of our own. It is not reasonable that art should win the place of honor over our great and powerful Mother Nature. We have so overloaded the beauty and richness of her works by our inventions that we have quite smothered her. Yet wherever her purity shines forth, she wonderfully puts to shame our vain and frivolous attempts:

> Ivy comes readier without our
> care;
> In lonely caves the arbutus grows
> more fair;
> No art with artless bird song can
> compare.
>
> [PROPERTIUS]

All our efforts cannot even succeed in reproducing the nest of the tiniest little bird, its contexture, its beauty and convenience; or even the web of the puny spider. All things, says Plato, are produced by nature, by fortune, or by art; the greatest and most beautiful by one or the other of the first two, the least and most imperfect by the last.

These nations, then, seem to me barbarous in this sense, that they have been fashioned very little by the human mind and are still very close to their original naturalness. The laws of nature still rule them, very little corrupted by ours; and they are in such a state of purity that I am sometimes vexed that they were unknown earlier, in the days when there were men able to judge them better than we. I am sorry that Lycurgus[1] and Plato did not know of them; for it seems to me that what we actually see in these nations surpasses not only all the pictures in which poets have idealized the golden age and all their inventions in imagining a happy state of man, but also the conceptions and the very desire of philosophy. They could not imagine a naturalness so pure and simple as we see by experience; nor could they believe that our society could be maintained with so little artifice and human solder. This is a nation, I should say to Plato, in which there is no sort of traffic, no knowledge of letters, no science of numbers, no name for a magistrate or for political superiority, no custom of

servitude, no riches or poverty, no contracts, no successions, no partitions, no occupations but leisure ones, no care for any but common kinship, no clothes, no agriculture, no metal, no use of wine or wheat. The very words that signify lying, treachery, dissimulation, avarice, envy, belittling, pardon—unheard of. How far from this perfection would he find the republic that he imagined: *Men fresh sprung from the gods* [Seneca].

These manners nature first ordained.

[VIRGIL]

For the rest, they live in a country with a very pleasant and temperate climate, so that according to my witnesses it is rare to see a sick man there; and they have assured me that they never saw one palsied, bleary-eyed, toothless, or bent with age. They are settled along the sea and shut in on the land side by great high mountains, with a stretch about a hundred leagues wide in between. They have a great abundance of fish and flesh which bear no resemblance to ours, and they eat them with no other artifice than cooking. The first man who rode a horse there, though he had had dealings with them on several other trips, so horrified them in this posture that they shot him dead with arrows before they could recognize him.

Their buildings are very long, with a capacity of two or three hundred souls; they are covered with the bark of great trees, the strips reaching to the ground at one end and supporting and leaning on one another at the top, in the manner of some of our barns, whose covering hangs down to the ground and acts as a side. They have wood so hard that they cut with it and make of it their swords and grills to cook their food. Their beds are of a cotton weave, hung from the roof like those in our ships, each man having his own; for the wives sleep apart from their husbands.

[MONTAIGNE CONTINUES ON
PAGE 535]

---

[1] **Lycurgus:** lawmaker of ancient Sparta in the ninth century B.C.

Art in the Renaissance

During the fourteenth and fifteenth centuries, there gradually spread throughout Europe a sense of a bright new world. This feeling was strongest in Italy, where the growth of towns had made the feudal system outmoded. During this period scientists and navigators began systematically to explore the world around them, and scholars and writers began to revive the literature and art of ancient Greece and Rome. It was largely because of this revival that the period came to be known as the "Renaissance."

This new spirit was expressed in many Italian paintings of the period. A charming example is the *Abduction of Helen by Paris* (PLATE 1), by a follower of Fra Angelico, a Florentine artist often identified as Benozzo Gozzoli. Depicting an episode from an ancient Greek legend, the artist displayed his classical learning by including a small antique statue inside a Roman building, but he clothed the figures in Renaissance costumes, giving the picture what must have seemed a smart, modern look. Also, making the receding lines of the building converge toward a single vanishing point, he demonstrated the new science of perspective. The bright colors and flat silhouettes, though, remind us of medieval manuscript illustrations of a century earlier (see page 429).

Most fifteenth-century Italian artists painted in *egg tempera,* a fast-drying opaque watercolor paint especially suited for rendering sharp outlines and crisp details. After about 1450, however, many Italian painters began to use oil paint, a new medium developed in Flanders. Because oil dries very slowly, artists could blend colors in soft tonal gradations. Look at the subtle effects of light and shade in Antonello da Messina's *St. Jerome in His Study* (PLATE 2). Notice too how effectively Antonello has handled the perspective, using the converging lines to create an overall feeling of order. All the many details—even the lion at the right (St. Jerome's symbol)—are skillfully arranged to lead us to the impressive figure of the great scholar in the composition.

The outstanding Northern Renaissance artist was German painter, goldsmith, and engraver named Albrecht Dürer. Many of his paintings reveal an engraver's eye for minute detail. Note, for example, in his *Self-Portrait*

(PLATE 3) the linear treatment of the pleats of the shirt and the strands of hair. The idea of posing a figure next to a window with a landscape view was something Dürer learned from Florentine painters, but the hard, angular modeling of the face and clothing is characteristic of German style.

The High Renaissance began with the sixteenth century, when a number of Florentine artists were developing a new style of great expressive power. One of the younger masters of this style was Raphael, who painted a series of wall frescoes for the Pope's apartments in the Vatican. A masterpiece in this series is *The School of Athens* (PLATE 4), showing the great philosophers of ancient Greece assembled within a majestic Roman architectural setting. In the center are the figures of Aristotle (right) and Plato (left). To represent some of these philosophers, Raphael used the features of his own contemporaries. The figure of Plato is a portrait of the venerable Leonardo da Vinci, and the brooding figure of Heraclitus in the center foreground looks like Raphael's rival, Michelangelo. The forms in this picture are heavy and monumental, arranged in planes parallel to the picture's surface. The graceful poses of the figures, however, help to relieve the massiveness of the arches and at the same time harmonize with them in a unified design of grand proportions.

Raphael's classic style influenced Italian art for many generations. Compare, for instance, *The School of Athens* with *The Family of Darius Before Alexander* (PLATE 5), a large oil on canvas painted about half a century later by the Venetian artist Paolo Veronese. In Veronese's painting we see, once again, figures and architecture arranged in planes parallel to the picture's surface. But notice that Veronese's design is asymmetrical, with the main figures grouped off-center at the right, balanced only by the small figure of a monkey on the parapet at the left. Particularly compelling is the richness of color and texture of the sumptuous costumes—an effect that is typically Venetian, quite different from the harder, more sculptural effects of Florentine painting.

Michelangelo, Raphael's famous contemporary, is known mainly for the immense fresco that he painted for Pope Julius II on the ceiling of the Sistine Chapel in Rome. Yet Michelangelo considered himself basically a sculptor. To him, the Sistine Ceiling commission was an interruption of a project he had begun a few years earlier—a three-story marble tomb for the Pope. Michelangelo never completed the tomb, but he did produce several magnificent statues for it. The most famous is *Moses* (PLATE 6). This huge, awesome figure, intended for display from the second story, was designed to be seen from below. But even seeing it at eye-level we can sense its tremendous energy and power. This is expressed through the opposing gestures of the arms, leg, and head. Notice how the long beard and the billowing folds of the clothing heighten this effect, dramatizing the wrathful look in the old prophet's eyes.

PLATE 1. Follower of Fra Angelico (Florentine, 15th century): *The Abduction of Helen by Paris.* About 1450. Tempera on wood, 20 x 24 inches. (Reproduced by courtesy of the Trustees, The National Gallery, London)

PLATE 2. ANTONELLO DA MESSINA (Sicilian, about 1430–1479): *St. Jerome in His Study.*
Oil on lime, 18 x 14¼ inches. (Reproduced by courtesy of the Trustees, The National Gallery,
London)

PLATE 3. ALBRECHT DÜRER (German, 1471–1528): *Self-Portrait*. 1498. Oil on canvas, 20½ x 16⅛ inches. (Prado, Madrid)

PLATE 4. RAPHAEL (Umbrian, 1483–1520): *The School of Athens*. 1509–10. Fresco, width: 25 feet 3⅜ inches. (Stanza della Segnatura, Vatican, Rome)

PLATE 6. MICHELANGELO (Florentine, 1475–1564): *Moses*. 1514–16. Statue for the tomb of Pope Julius II. Marble, height: 7 feet 8¾ inches. (Vatican, Rome)

They get up with the sun and eat immediately upon rising, to last them through the day; for they take no other meal than that one. Like some other Eastern peoples, of whom Suidas [1] tells us, who drank apart from meals, they do not drink then; but they drink several times a day, and to capacity. Their drink is made of some root and is of the color of our claret wines. They drink it only lukewarm. This beverage keeps only two or three days; it has a slightly sharp taste, is not at all heady, is good for the stomach, and has a laxative effect upon those who are not used to it; it is a very pleasant drink for anyone who is accustomed to it. In place of bread they use a certain white substance like preserved coriander. I have tried it; it tastes sweet and a little flat.

The whole day is spent in dancing. The younger men go to hunt animals with bows. Some of the women busy themselves meanwhile with warming their drink, which is their chief duty. Some one of the old men, in the morning before they begin to eat, preaches to the whole barnful in common, walking from one end to the other and repeating one single sentence several times until he has completed the circuit (for the buildings are fully a hundred paces long). He recommends to them only two things: valor against the enemy and love for their wives. And they never fail to point out this obligation, as their refrain, that it is their wives who keep their drink warm and seasoned.

There may be seen in several places, including my own house, specimens of their beds, of their ropes, of their wooden swords and the bracelets with which they cover their wrists in combats, and of the big canes, open at one end, by whose sound they keep time in their dances. They are close shaven all over and shave themselves much more cleanly than we, with nothing but a wooden or stone razor. They believe that souls are immortal and that those who have deserved well of the gods are lodged in that part of heaven where the sun rises, and the damned in the west.

They have some sort of priests and prophets, but they rarely appear before the people, having their home in the mountains. On their arrival there is a great feast and solemn assembly of several villages—each barn, as I have described it, makes up a village, and they are about one French league from each other. The prophet speaks to them in public, exhorting them to virtue and their duty; but their whole ethical science contains only these two articles: resoluteness in war and affection for their wives. He prophesies to them things to come and the results they are to expect from their undertakings, and urges them to war or holds them back from it; but this is on the condition that when he fails to prophesy correctly, and if things turn out otherwise than he has predicted, he is cut into a thousand pieces if they catch him and condemned as a false prophet. For this reason, the prophet who has once been mistaken is never seen again.

Divination is a gift of God; that is why its abuse should be punished as imposture. Among the Scythians,[2] when the soothsayers failed to hit the mark, they were laid, chained hand and foot, on carts full of heather and drawn by oxen, on which they were burned. Those who handle matters subject to the control of human capacity are excusable if they do the best they can. But these others, who come and trick us with assurances of an extraordinary faculty that is beyond our ken, should they not be punished for not making good their promise and for the temerity of their imposture?

They have their wars with the nations

---

[1] **Suidas:** author of a combination dictionary-encyclopedia, probably of the tenth century.

[2] **Scythians:** an ancient nomadic people who lived along the Black Sea.

beyond the mountains, further inland, to which they go quite naked, with no other arms than bows or wooden swords ending in a sharp point, in the manner of the tongues of our boar spears. It is astonishing what firmness they show in their combats, which never end but in slaughter and bloodshed; for as to routs and terror, they know nothing of either.

Each man brings back as his trophy the head of the enemy he has killed and sets it up at the entrance to his dwelling. After they have treated their prisoners well for a long time with all the hospitality they can think of, each man who has a prisoner calls a great assembly of his acquaintances. He ties a rope to one of the prisoner's arms, by the end of which he holds him, a few steps away, for fear of being hurt, and gives his dearest friend the other arm to hold in the same way; and these two, in the presence of the whole assembly, kill him with their swords. This done, they roast him and eat him in common and send some pieces to their absent friends. This is not, as people think, for nourishment, as of old the Scythians used to do; it is to betoken an extreme revenge. And the proof of this came when they saw the Portuguese, who had joined forces with their adversaries, inflict a different kind of death on them when they took them prisoner, which was to bury them up to the waist, shoot the rest of their body full of arrows, and afterward hang them. They thought that these people from the other world, being men who had sown the knowledge of many vices among their neighbors and were much greater masters than themselves in every sort of wickedness, did not adopt this sort of vengeance without some reason, and that it must be more painful than their own; so they began to give up their old method and to follow this one.

I am not sorry that we notice the barbarous horror of such acts, but I am heartily sorry that, judging their faults rightly, we should be so blind to our own. I think there is more barbarity in eating a man alive than in eating him dead; and in tearing by tortures and the rack a body still full of feeling, in roasting a man bit by bit, in having him bitten and mangled by dogs and swine (as we have not only read but seen within fresh memory, not among ancient enemies, but among neighbors and fellow citizens, and what is worse, on the pretext of piety and religion), than in roasting and eating him after he is dead.

Indeed, Chrysippus and Zeno,[1] heads of the Stoic sect, thought there was nothing wrong in using our carcasses for any purpose in case of need and getting nourishment from them; just as our ancestors, when besieged by Caesar in the city of Alesia, resolved to relieve their famine by eating old men, women, and other people useless for fighting.

> The Gascons once, 'tis said, their
> life renewed
> By eating of such food.
> [JUVENAL]

And physicians do not fear to use human flesh in all sorts of ways for our health, applying it either inwardly or outwardly. But there never was any opinion so disordered as to excuse treachery, disloyalty, tyranny, and cruelty, which are our ordinary vices.

So we may well call these people barbarians, in respect to the rules of reason, but not in respect to ourselves, who surpass them in every kind of barbarity.

Their warfare is wholly noble and generous, and as excusable and beautiful as this human disease can be; its only basis among them is their rivalry in valor. They are not fighting for the conquest of new lands, for they still enjoy that natural abundance that provides them without toil and trouble with all necessary things in such profusion that they have no wish to enlarge their boundaries. They are still in that happy state of desiring only as much as their natural needs demand; anything beyond that is superfluous to them.

[1] **Chrysippus and Zeno:** philosophers of ancient Greece.

They generally call those of the same age brothers; those who are younger, children; and the old men are fathers to all the others. These leave to their heirs in common the full possession of their property, without division or any other title at all than just the one that nature gives to her creatures in bringing them into the world.

If their neighbors cross the mountains to attack them and win a victory, the gain of the victor is glory and the advantage of having proved the master in valor and virtue; for apart from this they have no use for the goods of the vanquished, and they return to their own country, where they lack neither anything necessary nor that great thing, the knowledge of how to enjoy their condition happily and be content with it. These men of ours do the same in their turn. They demand of their prisoners no other ransom than that they confess and acknowledge their defeat. But there is not one in a whole century who does not choose to die rather than to relax a single bit, by word or look, from the grandeur of an invincible courage; not one who would not rather be killed and eaten than so much as ask not to be. They treat them very freely, so that life may be all the dearer to them, and usually entertain them with threats of their coming death, of the torments they will have to suffer, the preparations that are being made for that purpose, the cutting up of their limbs, and the feast that will be made at their expense. All this is done for the sole purpose of extorting from their lips some weak or base word, or making them want to flee, so as to gain the advantage of having terrified them and broken down their firmness. For indeed, if you take it the right way, it is in this point alone that true victory lies:

It is no victory
Unless the vanquished foe
admits your mastery.
[CLAUDIAN]

The Hungarians, very bellicose fighters, did not in olden times pursue their ad-vantage beyond putting the enemy at their mercy. For having wrung a confession from him to this effect, they let him go unharmed and unransomed, except, at most, for exacting his promise never again to take up arms against them.

We win enough advantages over our enemies which are borrowed advantages, not really our own. It is the quality of a porter, not of valor, to have sturdier arms and legs; agility is a dead and corporeal quality; it is a stroke of luck to make our enemy stumble, or dazzle his eyes by the sunlight; it is a trick of art and technique, which may be found in a worthless cow-ard, to be an able fencer. The worth and value of a man is in his heart and his will; there lies his real honor. Valor is the strength, not of legs and arms, but of heart and soul; it consists not in the worth of our horse or our weapons, but in our own. He who falls obstinate in his courage, *if he has fallen, he fights on his knees* [Seneca]. He who relaxes none of his assurance, no matter how great the dan-ger of imminent death; who, giving up his soul, still looks firmly and scornfully at his enemy—he is beaten not by us, but by fortune; he is killed, not conquered.

The most valiant are sometimes the most unfortunate. Thus there are triumphant defeats that rival victories. Nor did those four sister victories, the fairest that the sun ever set eyes on—Salamis, Plataea, Mycale, and Sicily [1]—ever dare match all their combined glory against the glory of the annihilation of King Leonidas and his men at the pass of Thermopylae.[2]

Who ever hastened with more glorious and ambitious desire to win a battle than Captain Ischolas to lose one? Who ever secured his safety more ingeniously and painstakingly than he did his destruction?

[1] **Salamis, Plataea, Mycale, and Sicily:** references to great battles of ancient Greece. The first three were sites of victories for the Athenians in their wars against Persia. The last refers to the utter defeat of the Athenians in their attempt to subject Sicily in 415 B.C.

[2] **Thermopylae:** see page 119.

He was charged to defend a certain pass in the Peloponnesus against the Arcadians. Finding himself wholly incapable of doing this, in view of the nature of the place and the inequality of the forces, he made up his mind that all who confronted the enemy would necessarily have to remain on the field. On the other hand, deeming it unworthy both of his own virtue and magnanimity and of the Lacedaemonian name to fail in his charge, he took a middle course between these two extremes, in this way. The youngest and fittest of his band he preserved for the defense and service of their country and sent them home; and with those whose loss was less important, he determined to hold this pass and by their death to make the enemy buy their entry as dearly as he could. And so it turned out. For he was presently surrounded on all sides by the Arcadians, and after slaughtering a large number of them, he and his men were all put to the sword. Is there a trophy dedicated to victors that would not be more due to these vanquished? The role of true victory is in fighting, not in coming off safely; and the honor of valor consists in combating, not in beating.

To return to our story. These prisoners are so far from giving in, in spite of all that is done to them, that on the contrary, during the two or three months that they are kept, they wear a gay expression; they urge their captors to hurry and put them to the test; they defy them, insult them, reproach them with their cowardice and the number of battles they have lost to the prisoners' own people.

I have a song composed by a prisoner which contains this challenge, that they should all come boldly and gather to dine off him, for they will be eating at the same time their own fathers and grandfathers, who have served to feed and nourish his body. "These muscles," he says, "this flesh and these veins are your own, poor fools that you are. You do not recognize that the substance of your ancestors' limbs is still contained in them. Savor them well; you will find in them the taste of your own flesh." An idea that certainly does not smack of barbarity. Those that paint these people dying, and who show the execution, portray the prisoner spitting in the face of his slayers and scowling at them. Indeed, to the last gasp they never stop braving and defying their enemies by word and look. Truly here are real savages by our standards; for either they must be thoroughly so, or we must be; there is an amazing distance between their character and ours.

The men there have several wives, and the higher their reputation for valor the more wives they have. It is a remarkably beautiful thing about their marriages that the same jealousy our wives have to keep us from the affection and kindness of other women, theirs have to win this for them. Being more concerned for their husbands' honor than for anything else, they strive and scheme to have as many companions as they can, since that is a sign of their husbands' valor. . . .

And lest it be thought that all this is done through a simple and servile bondage to usage and through the pressure of the authority of their ancient customs, without reasoning or judgment, and because their minds are so stupid that they cannot take any other course, I must cite some examples of their capacity. Besides the warlike song I have just quoted, I have another, a love song, which begins in this vein: "Adder, stay; stay, adder, that from the pattern of your coloring my sister may draw the fashion and the workmanship of a rich girdle that I may give to my love; so may your beauty and your pattern be forever preferred to all other serpents." This first couplet is the refrain of the song. Now I am familiar enough with poetry to be a judge of this: not only is there nothing barbarous in this fancy, but it is altogether Anacreontic.[1] Their language, moreover, is a soft language, with an agreeable sound, somewhat like Greek in its endings.

Three of these men,[2] ignorant of the

[1] **Anacreontic:** like the poetry of Anacreon (563 B.C.?–478 B.C.?), a Greek love poet.

[2] **these men:** the cannibals.

price they will pay some day, in loss of repose and happiness, for gaining knowledge of the corruptions of this side of the ocean; ignorant also of the fact that of this intercourse will come their ruin (which I suppose is already well advanced: poor wretches, to let themselves be tricked by the desire for new things, and to have left the serenity of their own sky to come and see ours!)—three of these men were at Rouen, at the time the late King Charles IX [1] was there. The king talked to them for a long time; they were shown our ways, our splendor, the aspect of a fine city. After that, someone asked their opinion and wanted to know what they had found most amazing. They mentioned three things, of which I have forgotten the third, and I am very sorry for it; but I still remember two of them. They said that in the first place they thought it very strange that so many grown men, bearded, strong, and armed, who were around the king (it is likely that they were talking about the Swiss of his guard), should submit to obey a child and that one of them was not chosen to command instead. Second (they have a way in their language of speaking of men as halves of one another), they had noticed that there were among us men full and gorged with all sorts of good things and that their other halves were beggars at their doors, emaciated with hunger and poverty; and they thought it strange that these needy halves could endure such an injustice, and did not take the others by the throat or set fire to their houses.

I had a very long talk with one of them; but I had an interpreter who followed my meaning so badly and who was so hindered by his stupidity in taking in my ideas that I could get hardly any satisfaction from the man. When I asked him what profit he gained from his superior position among his people (for he was a captain, and our sailors called him king), he told me that it was to march foremost

[1] **King Charles IX:** who was twelve years old at the time, in 1562.

in war. How many men followed him? He pointed to a piece of ground, to signify as many as such a space could hold; it might have been four or five thousand men. Did all his authority expire with the war? He said that this much remained, that when he visited the villages dependent on him, they made paths for him through the underbrush by which he might pass quite comfortably.

All this is not too bad—but what's the use? They don't wear breeches.

FOR STUDY AND DISCUSSION

1. How are the allusions made in the first paragraph relevant to the essay as a whole?

2. In what way do the last two paragraphs return to the subject of the introductory section of the essay? Why is the last paragraph effective?

3. What does the second paragraph reveal about the author's attitude? Do you find this impression confirmed elsewhere in the essay? Where?

4. The ninth paragraph begins, "Now, to return to my subject . . ." What is the subject? Trace the path of Montaigne's digression from that subject. Does one subject naturally lead to the next? How does Montaigne keep the connections clear?

5. From what is said and implied in this essay, what are the essential differences between the barbarians' ideas of religion and European Christianity, as Montaigne sees them?

LOGICAL ANALYSIS

In his essay, Montaigne is trying to persuade you, through logical argument, to accept certain conclusions about the essential goodness of primitive people and their moral superiority to Europeans. Read critically and try to evaluate the logic of his argument.

1. By what principle does Montaigne justify his conclusion in the seventh paragraph that his "simple, crude" traveler was a more reliable witness than a "clever" person would be? Do you agree with this principle? What facts can you offer to support your opinion?

2. On what basis are you expected to believe the information in paragraphs fourteen through sixteen? Can you disprove anything in these paragraphs?

3. In the nineteenth paragraph, by what process of argument does Montaigne arrive at the conclusions that the cannibals eat their enemies as a symbolic act of revenge? Why does Montaigne mention the conclusion which he rejects: that they (like the Scythians) commit cannibalism for nourishment?

4. Plato's statement, which is paraphrased at the end of the ninth paragraph, is a generalization offered without evidence. Can you provide evidence from your own observation to support it? Would it ever be possible to gather enough evidence to support it?

5. How does Montaigne define *barbarous* in the tenth paragraph? How does this definition differ from the meanings commonly attached to the word, as it is used, for example, in the first paragraph? How do confusion and error in argument arise from such differences in definition?

The Tempest

WILLIAM SHAKESPEARE

William Shakespeare (1564–1616) was a wealthy and famous man when in 1611, at the age of forty-seven, he completed *The Tempest* and retired to his native Stratford-on-Avon in Warwickshire, England, for the five years that remained of his life. The wealth undoubtedly came primarily from his joint ownership of an acting company, called by that time the King's Men (under the honorary patronage of James I), and of its theater, the Globe. But the company's success and Shakespeare's fame came from the plays he had written for the company and had sometimes acted in. Thirty-six plays spanned a career of not much more than twenty years. Not all of the plays are of equal quality, of course; but all are distinctive as the work of a true poet and dramatist, and the better half of them are incomparable.

We do not know when, under what circumstances, or for what purpose Shakespeare initially left Stratford. He was the son of a well-to-do tradesman and must have been educated in the excellent grammar school of the town. By the time he turned twenty-one he had a wife and three children. Some time thereafter he must have left Stratford and gone to London; but nothing is known of the next seven years until, in a pamphlet printed in London in 1592, Shakespeare was attacked as an upstart actor who was having unmerited success as a playwright. This success had infuriated the author of the pamphlet, a slightly senior rival named Robert Greene. By 1598 Shakespeare was prominent enough to be singled out by an amateur critic, Francis Meres, as "most excellent" among English playwrights. By this time he had written *Romeo and Juliet, Henry IV, The Merchant of Venice,* and *A Midsummer Night's Dream,* among other plays, as well as two long narrative poems and many, if not all, of his sonnets (see page 494), although these were published later. Still, this "most excellent" of playwrights had yet to write the most excellent of his plays, since he produced his most mature works in the years following 1598: *As You Like It, Twelfth Night, Othello, Macbeth, Hamlet, King Lear.*

The last few years of Shakespeare's career are marked by a change of tone and pace to a romantic, lyrical kind of play that is neither tragic nor comic but partly both. Many reasons have been offered for this change, but perhaps it is wisest simply to allow that Shakespeare was finished with uproarious comedy, had said all he had to say in tragedy, and was ready for a different kind of expression. In any case, the last plays—*Pericles, The Winter's Tale, Cymbeline,* and *The Tempest*—make a fitting and harmonious conclusion to the brilliant array of Shakespeare's literary creations.

No complete source for the story of *The Tempest* has been found, but it seems obvious that Shakespeare had at hand John Florio's translation of Montaigne's essay "Of Cannibals" (see page 523) when he was writing the play.

Dramatis Personae

ALONSO, *King of Naples*
SEBASTIAN, *his brother*
PROSPERO, *the right Duke of Milan*
ANTONIO, *his brother, the usurping Duke of Milan*
FERDINAND, *son to the King of Naples*
GONZALO, *an honest old councilor*
ADRIAN ⎫
FRANCISCO ⎬ *lords*
CALIBAN, *a savage and deformed slave*
TRINCULO, *a jester*
STEPHANO, *a drunken butler*

MASTER *of a ship*
BOATSWAIN
MARINERS
MIRANDA, *daughter to Prospero*
ARIEL, *an airy spirit*
IRIS ⎫
CERES ⎪
JUNO ⎬ *presented by spirits*
NYMPHS ⎪
REAPERS ⎭
OTHER SPIRITS, *attending on Prospero*

SCENES—*A ship at sea and an uninhabited island.*

ACT I

SCENE I. *On a ship at sea. A tempestuous noise of thunder and lightning heard.*

[*Enter a* SHIPMASTER *and a* BOATSWAIN.]

MASTER. Boatswain!
BOATSWAIN. Here, master. What cheer?
MASTER. Good,° speak to the mariners! Fall to't yarely,° or we run ourselves aground. Bestir, bestir!   [*Exit.*]

[*Enter* MARINERS.]

BOATSWAIN. Heigh, my hearts! Cheerly, cheerly, my hearts! Yare, yare!   5
Take in the topsail. Tend to the master's whistle. Blow till thou burst thy wind, if room enough!

[*Enter* ALONSO, SEBASTIAN, ANTONIO, FERDINAND, GONZALO, *and* LORDS.]

ALONSO. Good boatswain, have care. Where's the master? Play the men.°
BOATSWAIN. I pray now, keep below.
ANTONIO. Where is the master, boatswain?   10
BOATSWAIN. Do you not hear him? You mar our labor. Keep your cabins.
You do assist the storm.
GONZALO. Nay, good, be patient.
BOATSWAIN. When the sea is. Hence! What cares these roarers for the name of king? To cabin. Silence! Trouble us not!   15
GONZALO. Good, yet remember whom thou hast aboard.
BOATSWAIN. None that I more love than myself. You are a councilor. If
you can command these elements to silence, and work the peace of

3. **Good:** my good man.   **yarely:** quickly, smartly.   8. **Play the men:** act like men.

the present,° we will not hand a rope more. Use your authority. If
you cannot, give thanks you have lived so long, and make your- 20
self ready in your cabin for the mischance of the hour, if it so hap.
Cheerly, good hearts! Out of our way, I say.   [*Exit.*]

GONZALO. I have great comfort from this fellow. Methinks he hath no
drowning mark upon him, his complexion is perfect gallows.° Stand
fast, good Fate, to his hanging. Make the rope of his destiny our 25
cable, for our own doth little advantage. If he be not born to be
hanged, our case is miserable.   [*Exeunt.*]

[*Reenter* BOATSWAIN.]

BOATSWAIN. Down with the topmast! Yare! Lower, lower! Bring her to
try with main course. [*A cry within.*] A plague upon this howling!
They are louder than the weather or our office.°   30

[*Reenter* SEBASTIAN, ANTONIO, *and* GONZALO.]

Yet again! What do you here? Shall we give o'er, and drown? Have
you a mind to sink?

SEBASTIAN. A pox o' your throat, you bawling, blasphemous, incharitable
dog!

BOATSWAIN. Work you, then!   35

ANTONIO. Hang, cur! Hang, you insolent noisemaker. We are less afraid
to be drowned than thou art.

GONZALO. I'll warrant him for drowning,° though the ship were no stronger
than a nutshell.

BOATSWAIN. Lay her ahold, ahold! Set her two courses.° Off to sea 40
again, lay her off!

[*Enter* MARINERS, *wet.*]

MARINERS. All lost! To prayers, to prayers! All lost!

BOATSWAIN. What, must our mouths be cold?°

GONZALO. The king and prince at prayers! Let's assist them,
     For our case is as theirs.

SEBASTIAN.   I'm out of patience.   45

ANTONIO. We are merely cheated of our lives by drunkards.
     This wide-chapped° rascal—would thou mightst lie drowning
     The washing of ten tides!°

GONZALO.   He'll be hanged yet,
     Though every drop of water swear against it
     And gape at widest to glut° him.   50

[*A confused noise within:* "Mercy on us!"—"We split, we split!"—"Farewell, my wife and children!"—"Farewell, brother!"—"We split, we split,
we split!"]

19. **work the peace of the present:** end the storm at once.   24. **his complexion is perfect
gallows:** According to an old proverb, someone destined to be hanged will never be drowned.
30. **office:** work.   38. **warrant him for drowning:** guarantee he won't drown. Gonzalo again
refers to his joke that the boatswain is marked only for hanging.   40. **courses:** sails.   43. **cold:**
with prayers, instead of warm with liquor, as he is now making his own mouth.   47. **wide-
chapped:** full-cheeked (with liquor).   48. **ten tides:** Antonio wishes upon the boatswain a
worse punishment than that given to pirates, who were hanged on the shore and left until three
high tides had washed over them.   50. **glut:** swallow.

ANTONIO. Let's all sink with the king.

SEBASTIAN. Let's take leave of him.   [*Exeunt* ANTONIO *and* SEBASTIAN.]

GONZALO. Now would I give a thousand furlongs of sea for an acre of barren ground, long heath, brown furze, anything. The wills above be done! But I would fain die a dry death.   [*Exeunt.*] 55

SCENE II. *The island. Before* PROSPERO'S *cell.*

[*Enter* PROSPERO *and* MIRANDA.]

MIRANDA. If by your art, my dearest father, you have
            Put the wild waters in this roar, allay them.
            The sky, it seems, would pour down stinking pitch
            But that the sea, mounting to the welkin's° cheek,
            Dashes the fire out. Oh, I have suffered   5
            With those that I saw suffer! A brave vessel,
            Who had no doubt some noble creature in her,
            Dashed all to pieces. Oh, the cry did knock
            Against my very heart! Poor souls, they perished!
            Had I been any god of power, I would   10
            Have sunk the sea within the earth or ere
            It should the good ship so have swallowed and
            The fraughting souls° within her.

PROSPERO.   Be collected.
            No more amazement. Tell your piteous heart
            There's no harm done.

MIRANDA.   Oh, woe the day!

PROSPERO.   No harm.   15
            I have done nothing but in care of thee,
            Of thee, my dear one, thee, my daughter, who
            Art ignorant of what thou art, naught knowing
            Of whence I am, nor that I am more better
            Than Prospero, master of a full poor cell,   20
            And thy no greater father.

MIRANDA.   More to know
            Did never meddle with my thoughts.

PROSPERO.   'Tis time
            I should inform thee farther. Lend thy hand,
            And pluck my magic garment from me.—So.

                                                      [*Lays down his mantle.*]
            Lie there, my art.° Wipe thou thine eyes, have comfort.   25
            The direful spectacle of the wreck, which touched
            The very virtue of compassion in thee,
            I have with such provision° in mine art
            So safely ordered that there is no soul,
            No, not so much perdition° as a hair,   30
            Betid° to any creature in the vessel

---

4. **welkin's:** sky's.   13. **fraughting souls:** the souls (people) who were her freight.   25. **my art:** Prospero has worn a special cloak for working the magic that produced the tempest. 28. **provision:** foresight.   30. **perdition:** loss.   31. **betid:** befallen.

Which thou heard'st cry, which thou saw'st sink. Sit down,
For thou must now know farther.
MIRANDA.   You have often
Begun to tell me what I am, but stopped,
And left me to a bootless inquisition,°   35
Concluding "Stay, not yet."
PROSPERO.   The hour's now come,
The very minute bids thee ope thine ear.
Obey, and be attentive. Canst thou remember
A time before we came unto this cell?
I do not think thou canst, for then thou wast not   40
Out three years old.
MIRANDA.   Certainly, sir, I can.
PROSPERO. By what? By any other house or person?
Of anything the image tell me that
Hath kept with thy remembrance.
MIRANDA.   'Tis far off,
And rather like a dream than an assurance   45
That my remembrance warrants. Had I not
Four or five women once that tended me?
PROSPERO. Thou hadst, and more, Miranda. But how is it
That this lives in thy mind? What seest thou else
In the dark backward and abysm of time?   50
If thou remember'st aught ere thou camest here,
How thou camest here thou mayst.
MIRANDA.   But that I do not.
PROSPERO. Twelve year since, Miranda, twelve year since,
Thy father was the Duke of Milan, and
A prince of power.
MIRANDA.   Sir, are not you my father?   55
PROSPERO. Thy mother was a piece of virtue, and
She said thou wast my daughter, and thy father
Was Duke of Milan, and his only heir
A princess, no worse issued.
MIRANDA.   Oh, the Heavens!
What foul play had we that we came from thence?   60
Or blessèd was't we did?
PROSPERO.   Both, both, my girl.
By foul play, as thou say'st, were we heaved thence,
But blessedly holp° hither.
MIRANDA.   Oh, my heart bleeds
To think o' the teen° that I have turned you to,
Which is from my remembrance! Please you, farther.   65
PROSPERO. My brother, and thy uncle, called Antonio—
I pray thee mark me—that a brother should
Be so perfidious!—he whom, next thyself,
Of all the world I loved, and to him put
The manage of my state—as at that time   70

35. **bootless inquisition:** futile question.   63. **holp:** helped.   64. **teen:** grief.

Through all the signories° it was the first,
And Prospero the prime duke, being so reputed
In dignity, and for the liberal arts
Without a parallel, those being all my study—
The government I cast upon my brother,   75
And to my state grew stranger, being transported
And rapt in secret studies. Thy false uncle—
Dost thou attend me?

MIRANDA.   Sir, most heedfully.

PROSPERO. Being once perfected how to grant suits,
How to deny them, who to advance, and who   80
To trash for overtopping,° new-created
The creatures that were mine, I say, or changed 'em,
Or else new-formed 'em—having both the key
Of officer and office, set all hearts i' the state
To what tune pleased his ear, that now he was   85
The ivy which had hid my princely trunk,
And sucked my verdure out on't. Thou attend'st not.

MIRANDA. Oh, good sir, I do.

PROSPERO.   I pray thee, mark me.
I, thus neglecting worldly ends, all dedicated
To closeness and the bettering of my mind   90
With that which, but by being so retired,
O'erprized all popular rate,° in my false brother
Awaked an evil nature. And my trust,
Like a good parent, did beget of him
A falsehood in its contrary as great   95
As my trust was, which had indeed no limit,
A confidence sans° bound. He being thus lorded,
Not only with what my revenue yielded,
But what my power might else exact, like one
Who having into truth, by telling of it,   100
Made such a sinner of his memory,
To credit his own lie, he did believe
He was indeed the duke—out o' the substitution,
And executing the outward face of royalty,
With all prerogative.—Hence his ambition growing—   105
Dost thou hear?

MIRANDA.   Your tale, sir, would cure deafness.

PROSPERO. To have no screen between this part he played
And him he played it for, he needs will be
Absolute Milan.° Me, poor man, my library
Was dukedom large enough. Of temporal royalties°   110
He thinks me now incapable; confederates,°
So dry° he was for sway, wi' the King of Naples

71. **signories:** dukedoms.   81. **trash for overtopping:** check for running ahead.   91–92. **that
which . . . rate:** In other words, except for keeping him so secluded, the learning was worth
more than popular opinion recognized.   97. **sans:** without (French).   109. **Absolute Milan:**
Duke of Milan in fact.   110. **temporal royalties:** worldly rule.   111. **confederates:** conspires.
112. **dry:** thirsty (eager).

To give him annual tribute, do him homage,
Subject his coronet to his crown,° and bend
The dukedom, yet unbowed—alas, poor Milan!—   115
To most ignoble stooping.
MIRANDA.   Oh, the Heavens!
PROSPERO. Mark his condition, and event, then tell me
      If this might be a brother.
MIRANDA.   I should sin
      To think but nobly of my grandmother.
      Good wombs have borne bad sons.
PROSPERO.   Now the condition.   120
      This King of Naples, being an enemy
      To me inveterate, hearkens my brother's suit.
      Which was that he, in lieu o' the premises,°
      Of homage, and I know not how much tribute,
      Should presently extirpate me and mine   125
      Out of the dukedom, and confer fair Milan,
      With all the honors, on my brother. Whereon,   .
      A treacherous army levied, one midnight
      Fated to the purpose did Antonio open
      The gates of Milan, and, i' the dead of darkness   130
      The ministers for the purpose hurried thence
      Me and thy crying self.
MIRANDA.   Alack, for pity!
      I, not remembering how I cried out then,
      Will cry it o'er again. It is a hint°
      That wrings mine eyes to't.
PROSPERO.   Hear a little further,   135
      And then I'll bring thee to the present business
      Which now's upon 's, without the which this story
      Were most impertinent.
MIRANDA.   Wherefore did they not
      That hour destroy us?
PROSPERO.   Well demanded, wench.
      My tale provokes that question. Dear, they durst not,   140
      So dear the love my people bore me, nor set
      A mark so bloody on the business, but
      With colors fairer painted their foul ends.
      In few, they hurried us aboard a bark,
      Bore us some leagues to sea, where they prepared   145
      A rotten carcass of a butt, not rigged,
      Nor tackle, sail, nor mast. The very rats
      Instinctively have quit it. There they hoist us,
      To cry to the sea that roared to us, to sigh
      To the winds, whose pity, sighing back again,   150
      Did us but loving wrong.

---

114. **Subject his coronet to his crown:** pay homage to him (the King of Naples) as his king.
The coronet was worn by rulers like dukes who were lower than the king.   123. **in lieu o' the
premises:** in return for these terms.   134. **hint:** occasion.

MIRANDA.   Alack, what trouble
     Was I then to you!
PROSPERO.   Oh, a cherubin
     Thou wast that did preserve me. Thou didst smile,
     Infusèd with a fortitude from Heaven,
     When I have decked the sea with drops full salt.   155
     Under my burden groaned, which raised in me
     An undergoing stomach° to bear up
     Against what should ensue.
MIRANDA.   How came we ashore?
PROSPERO. By Providence divine.
     Some food we had, and some fresh water, that   160
     A noble Neapolitan, Gonzalo,
     Out of his charity, who being then appointed
     Master of this design, did give us, with
     Rich garments, linens, stuffs, and necessaries,
     Which since have steaded much. So, of his gentleness,   165
     Knowing I loved my books, he furnished me
     From mine own library with volumes that
     I prize above my dukedom.
MIRANDA.   Would I might
     But ever see that man!
PROSPERO.   Now I arise.   [Resumes his mantle.]
     Sit still, and hear the last of our sea sorrow.   170
     Here in this island we arrived, and here
     Have I, thy schoolmaster, made thee more profit
     Than other princes can that have more time
     For vainer hours, and tutors not so careful.
MIRANDA. Heavens thank you for't! And now I pray you, sir,   175
     For still 'tis beating in my mind, your reason
     For raising this sea storm?
PROSPERO.   Know thus far forth.°
     By accident most strange, bountiful Fortune,
     Now my dear lady,° hath mine enemies
     Brought to this shore. And by my prescience°   180
     I find my zenith doth depend upon
     A most auspicious star, whose influence
     If now I court not, but omit, my fortunes
     Will ever after droop.° Here cease more questions.
     Thou art inclined to sleep, 'tis a good dullness,   185
     And give it away. I know thou canst not choose.
                              [MIRANDA sleeps.]
     Come away, servant, come. I am ready now.
     Approach, my Ariel, come.

               [Enter ARIEL.]

     157. stomach: courage. The stomach was supposedly the source of courage.   177. thus
far forth: this much more.   179. Now my dear lady: now kind to me (as once Fortune was
against me).   180. prescience: foreknowledge.   184. my zenith . . . will ever after droop: to
achieve the height of my good fortune, I must take advantage of a favorable star that is now
in the ascendant in my horoscope; if I neglect it, I will never have good fortune again.

ARIEL. All hail, great master! Grave sir, hail! I come
　　　To answer thy best pleasure, be 't to fly,　　　　　　　190
　　　To swim, to dive into the fire, to ride
　　　On the curled clouds, to thy strong bidding, task°
　　　Ariel and all his quality.°
PROSPERO.　　　　　　　　　　Hast thou, spirit,
　　　Performed to point the tempest that I bade thee?
ARIEL. To every article.　　　　　　　　　　　　　　　195
　　　I boarded the King's ship. Now on the beak,
　　　Now in the waist, the deck, in every cabin,
　　　I flamed amazement.° Sometime I'd divide,
　　　And burn in many places; on the topmast,
　　　The yards and bowsprit, would I flame distinctly,　　200
　　　Then meet and join. Jove's lightnings, the precursors
　　　O' the dreadful thunderclaps, more momentary
　　　And sight-outrunning were not. The fire and cracks
　　　Of sulfurous roaring the most mighty Neptune
　　　Seem to besiege, and make his bold waves tremble—　205
　　　Yea, his dread trident shake.
PROSPERO.　　　　　　　　　　My brave spirit!
　　　Who was so firm, so constant, that this coil°
　　　Would not infect his reason?
ARIEL.　　　　　　　　　　Not a soul
　　　But felt a fever of the mad° and played
　　　Some tricks of desperation. All but mariners　　　　210
　　　Plunged in the foaming brine, and quit the vessel,
　　　Then all afire with me. The King's son, Ferdinand,
　　　With hair upstaring—then like reeds, not hair—
　　　Was the first man that leaped, cried, "Hell is empty,
　　　And all the devils are here."
PROSPERO.　　　　　　　　　　Why, that's my spirit!　215
　　　But was not this nigh shore?
ARIEL.　　　　　　　　　　Close by, my master.
PROSPERO. But are they, Ariel, safe?
ARIEL.　　　　　　　　　　Not a hair perished,
　　　On their sustaining° garments not a blemish,
　　　But fresher than before. And, as thou badest me,
　　　In troops I have dispersed them 'bout the isle.　　　220
　　　The king's son have I landed by himself,
　　　Whom I left cooling of the air with sighs
　　　In an odd angle of the isle, and sitting
　　　His arms in this sad knot.
PROSPERO.　　　　　　　　　　Of the king's ship,
　　　The mariners, say how thou hast disposed,　　　　　225
　　　And all the rest o' the fleet.
ARIEL.　　　　　　　　　　Safely in harbor

---

192. **task:** put to work.　193. **quality:** other spirits of Ariel's band.　198. **flamed amaze-ment:** caused amazement by appearing as fire. The following description indicates that Ariel took the form of the phenomenon called St. Elmo's fire, sometimes seen on a ship during a storm.　207. **coil:** confusion.　209. **of the mad:** like madness.　218. **sustaining:** buoyant.

Is the king's ship—in the deep nook where once
Thou call'dst me up at midnight to fetch dew
From the still-vexed Bermoothes,° there she's hid.
The mariners all under hatches stowed,   230
Who, with a charm joined to their suffered labor,
I have left asleep. And for the rest o' the fleet,
Which I dispersed, they all have met again,
And are upon the Mediterranean flote,
Bound sadly home for Naples,   235
Supposing that they saw the king's ship wrecked
And his great person perish.
PROSPERO.   Ariel, thy charge
Exactly is performed. But there's more work.
What is the time o' the day?
ARIEL.   Past the midseason.
PROSPERO. At least two glasses.° The time 'twixt six and now   240
Must by us both be spent most preciously.
ARIEL. Is there more toil? Since thou dost give me pains,
Let me remember thee what thou hast promisèd,
Which is not yet performed me.
PROSPERO.   How now? Moody?
What is't thou canst demand?
ARIEL.   My liberty.   245
PROSPERO. Before the time be out? No more!
ARIEL.   I prithee
Remember I have done thee worthy service,
Told thee no lies, made thee no mistakings, served
Without or grudge or grumblings. Thou didst promise
To bate me° a full year.
PROSPERO.   Dost thou forget   250
From what a torment I did free thee?
ARIEL.   No.
PROSPERO. Thou dost, and think'st it much to tread the ooze
Of the salt deep,
To run upon the sharp wind of the North,
To do me business in the veins o' the earth   255
When it is baked with frost.
ARIEL.   I do not, sir.
PROSPERO. Thou liest, malignant thing! Hast thou forgot
The foul witch Sycorax, who with age and envy
Was grown into a hoop? Hast thou forgot her?
ARIEL. No, sir.
PROSPERO.   Thou hast. Where was she born? Speak, tell me.   260
ARIEL. Sir, in Argier.°
PROSPERO.   Oh, was she so? I must
Once in a month recount what thou hast been,
Which thou forget'st. This damned witch Sycorax,
For mischiefs manifold and sorceries terrible

---

229. **Bermoothes:** Bermudas.   240. **two glasses:** two turns of the hourglass.   250. **bate me:** shorten my time of service.   261. **Argier:** Algiers.

To enter human hearing, from Argier,   265
Thou know'st, was banished. For one thing she did
They would not take her life. Is not this true?
ARIEL. Aye, sir.
PROSPERO. This blue-eyed° hag was hither brought with child,
And here was left by the sailors. Thou, my slave,   270
As thou report'st thyself, wast then her servant.
And, for thou wast a spirit too delicate
To act her earthy and abhorred commands,
Refusing her grand hests, she did confine thee,
By help of her more potent ministers   275
And in her most unmitigable rage,
Into a cloven pine. Within which rift
Imprisoned thou didst painfully remain
A dozen years. Within which space she died,
And left thee there, where thou didst vent thy groans   280
As fast as mill wheels strike. Then was this island—
Save for the son that she did litter here,
A freckled whelp hag-born—not honored with
A human shape.
ARIEL.   Yes, Caliban her son.
PROSPERO. Dull thing, I say so, he, that Caliban   285
Whom now I keep in service. Thou best know'st
What torment I did find thee in. Thy groans
Did make wolves howl and penetrate the breasts
Of ever-angry bears. It was a torment
To lay upon the damned, which Sycorax   290
Could not again undo. It was mine art,
When I arrived and heard thee, that made gape
The pine and let thee out.
ARIEL.   I thank thee, master.
PROSPERO. If thou more murmur'st, I will rend an oak
And peg thee in his knotty entrails till   295
Thou hast howled away twelve winters.
ARIEL.   Pardon, master.
I will be correspondent to command,
And do my spiriting gently.
PROSPERO.   Do so, and after two days
I will discharge thee.
ARIEL.   That's my noble master!
What shall I do? Say what. What shall I do?   300
PROSPERO. Go make thyself like a nymph o' the sea.
Be subject to no sight but thine and mine, invisible
To every eyeball else. Go take this shape,
And hither come in't. Go, hence with diligence!   [*Exit* ARIEL.]
Awake, dear heart, awake! Thou hast slept well.   305
Awake!
MIRANDA.   The strangeness of your story put
Heaviness in me.

269. **blue-eyed:** eyes blue with circles, from her pregnancy.

PROSPERO.   Shake it off. Come on,
    We'll visit Caliban my slave, who never
    Yields us kind answer.
MIRANDA.   'Tis a villain, sir,
    I do not love to look on.
PROSPERO.   But, as 'tis,   310
    We cannot miss° him. He does make our fire,
    Fetch in our wood, and serves in offices
    That profit us. What ho! Slave! Caliban!
    Thou earth,° thou! Speak.
CALIBAN.   [Within] There's wood enough within.
PROSPERO. Come forth, I say! There's other business for thee.   315
    Come, thou tortoise! When?

                [Reenter ARIEL, like a water nymph.]

    Fine apparition! My quaint Ariel,
    Hark in thine ear.
ARIEL.   My lord, it shall be done.   [Exit.]
PROSPERO. Thou poisonous slave, got by the Devil himself
    Upon thy wicked dam, come forth!   320

                    [Enter CALIBAN.]

CALIBAN. As wicked dew as e'er my mother brushed
    With raven's feather from unwholesome fen
    Drop on you both! A southwest blow on ye
    And blister you all o'er!
PROSPERO. For this, be sure, tonight thou shalt have cramps,   325
    Side stitches that shall pen thy breath up. Urchins°
    Shall, for that vast of night that they may work,
    All exercise on thee. Thou shalt be pinched
    As thick as honeycomb, each pinch more stinging
    Than bees that made 'em.
CALIBAN.   I must eat my dinner.   330
    This island's mine, by Sycorax my mother,
    Which thou takest from me. When thou camest first,
    Thou strokedst me, and madest much of me, wouldst give me
    Water with berries in't. And teach me how
    To name the bigger light, and how the less,   335
    That burn by day and night. And then I loved thee,
    And showed thee all the qualities o' th' isle,
    The fresh springs, brine pits, barren place and fertile.
    Cursèd be I that did so! All the charms
    Of Sycorax, toads, beetles, bats, light on you!   340
    For I am all the subjects that you have,
    Which first was mine own king. And here you sty me
    In this hard rock whiles you do keep from me
    The rest o' th' island.
PROSPERO.   Thou most lying slave,

    311. **miss:** do without.   314. **earth:** lump of dirt.   326. **Urchins:** goblins in the shape of
hedgehogs.

Whom stripes may move, not kindness! I have used thee,   345
Filth as thou art, with human care, and lodged thee
In mine own cell till thou didst seek to violate
The honor of my child.
CALIBAN. Oh ho, oh ho! Would 't had been done!
Thou didst prevent me. I had peopled else   350
This isle with Calibans.
PROSPERO.   Abhorrèd slave,
Which any print of goodness wilt not take,
Being capable of all ill! I pitied thee,
Took pains to make thee speak, taught thee each hour
One thing or other. When thou didst not, savage,   355
Know thine own meaning, but wouldst gabble like
A thing most brutish, I endowed thy purposes
With words that made them known. But thy vile race,
Though thou didst learn, had that in't which good natures
Could not abide to be with. Therefore wast thou   360
Deservedly confined into this rock,
Who hadst deserved more than a prison.
CALIBAN. You taught me language, and my profit on't
Is I know how to curse. The red plague rid you
For learning me your language!
PROSPERO.   Hagseed, hence!   365
Fetch us in fuel, and be quick, thou'rt best,
To answer other business. Shrug'st thou, malice?
If thou neglect'st, or dost unwillingly
What I command, I'll rack thee with old° cramps,
Fill all thy bones with aches, make thee roar   370
That beasts shall tremble at thy din.
CALIBAN.   No, pray thee.
[Aside] I must obey. His art is of such power
It would control my dam's god, Setebos,
And make a vassal of him.
PROSPERO.   So, slave. Hence!   [Exit CALIBAN.]

[Reenter ARIEL with other SPIRITS, all invisible, playing and singing;
FERDINAND follows.]

ARIEL. [Sings.]
"Come unto these yellow sands,   375
    And then take hands.
Curtsied when you have and kissed
    The wild waves whist,°
Foot it featly° here and there,
And, sweet sprites, the burden° bear."   380
SPIRITS. [Dispersedly°] "Hark, hark!" "Bowwow."
ARIEL. "The watchdogs bark."
SPIRITS.   [Dispersedly] "Bowwow."
ARIEL. "Hark, hark! I hear

369. **old:** great.   378. **whist:** silent.   379. **featly:** smartly.   380. **burden:** refrain.
381. **s.d. dispersedly:** from different sides.

The strain of strutting chanticleer
Cry cock-a-diddle-dow.'' 385
FERDINAND. Where should this music be? I' th' air or th' earth?
It sounds no more, and, sure, it waits upon
Some god o' th' island. Sitting on a bank,
Weeping again the king my father's wreck,
This music crept by me upon the waters, 390
Allaying both their fury and my passion
With its sweet air. Thence I have followed it,
Or it hath drawn me rather. But 'tis gone.
No, it begins again.
ARIEL. [*Sings.*]
    "Full fathom five thy father lies, 395
        Of his bones are coral made,
    Those are pearls that were his eyes.
        Nothing of him that doth fade
    But doth suffer a sea change
    Into something rich and strange. 400
    Sea nymphs hourly ring his knell."
SPIRITS.   "Dingdong."
ARIEL. "Hark! Now I hear them.—Dingdong, bell."
FERDINAND. The ditty does remember my drowned father.
    This is no mortal business, nor no sound
    That the earth owes.°—I hear it now above me. 405
PROSPERO. The fringèd curtains of thine eye advance,°
    And say what thou seest yond.
MIRANDA.   What is't? A spirit?
    Lord, how it looks about! Believe me, sir,
    It carries a brave form. But 'tis a spirit.
PROSPERO. No, wench, it eats and sleeps and hath such senses 410
    As we have, such. This gallant which thou seest
    Was in the wreck, and but he's something stained
    With grief, that's beauty's canker, thou mightst call him
    A goodly person. He hath lost his fellows,
    And strays about to find 'em.
MIRANDA.   I might call him 415
    A thing divine, for nothing natural
    I ever saw so noble.
PROSPERO.   [*Aside*] It goes on,° I see,
    As my soul prompts it. Spirit, fine spirit! I'll free thee
    Within two days for this.
FERDINAND.   Most sure, the goddess
    On whom these airs attend! Vouchsafe my prayer 420
    May know if you remain upon this island,
    And that you will some good instruction give
    How I may bear me here. My prime request,
    Which I do last pronounce, is, O you wonder!
    If you be maid or no?
MIRANDA.   No wonder, sir, 425
    But certainly a maid.

405. **owes:** owns.   406. **advance:** raise.   417. **It goes on:** The plan goes as it should.

FERDINAND.   My language! Heavens!
    I am the best of them° that speak this speech,
    Were I but where 'tis spoken.
PROSPERO.   How? The best?
    What wert thou if the King of Naples heard thee?
FERDINAND. A single thing, as I am now, that wonders   430
    To hear thee speak of Naples. He does hear me,
    And that he does I weep. Myself am Naples,
    Who with mine eyes, never since at ebb, beheld
    The King my father wrecked.
MIRANDA.   Alack, for mercy!
FERDINAND. Yes, faith, and all his lords, the Duke of Milan   435
    And his brave son being twain.
PROSPERO.   [*Aside*] The Duke of Milan
    And his more braver daughter could control thee,
    If now 'twere fit to do't. At the first sight
    They have changed eyes.° Delicate Ariel,
    I'll set thee free for this. [*To* FERDINAND] A word, good sir.   440
    I fear you have done yourself some wrong. A word.
MIRANDA. Why speaks my father so ungently? This
    Is the third man that e'er I saw, the first
    That e'er I sighed for. Pity move my father
    To be inclined my way!
FERDINAND.   Oh, if a virgin,   445
    And your affection not gone forth, I'll make you
    The Queen of Naples.
PROSPERO.   Soft, sir! One word more.
    [*Aside*] They are both in either's powers. But this swift business
    I must uneasy make, lest too light winning
    Make the prize light. [*To* FERDINAND] One word more. I charge thee
    That thou attend me. Thou dost here usurp   451
    The name thou owest not, and hast put thyself
    Upon this island as a spy, to win it
    From me, the lord on 't.
FERDINAND.   No, as I am a man.
MIRANDA. There's nothing ill can dwell in such a temple.   455
    If the ill spirit have so fair a house,
    Good things will strive to dwell with 't.
PROSPERO.   Follow me.
    Speak not you for him, he's a traitor. Come,
    I'll manacle thy neck and feet together.
    Sea water shalt thou drink, thy food shall be   460
    The fresh-brook mussels, withered roots, and husks
    Wherein the acorn cradled. Follow.
FERDINAND.   No.
    I will resist such entertainment till
    Mine enemy has more power.
                 [*Draws, and is charmed from moving.*]

427. **the best of them:** highest in rank. Ferdinand thinks his father is drowned and that he is now King of Naples.   439. **changed eyes:** exchanged looks of love.

MIRANDA.   O dear Father,
Make not too rash a trial of him, for   465
He's gentle, and not fearful.
PROSPERO.   What! I say,
My foot my tutor?° Put thy sword up, traitor,
Who makest a show but darest not strike, thy conscience
Is so possessed with guilt. Come from thy ward,°
For I can here disarm thee with this stick   470
And make thy weapon drop.
MIRANDA.   Beseech you, Father.
PROSPERO. Hence! Hang not on my garments.
MIRANDA.   Sir, have pity.
I'll be his surety.
PROSPERO.   Silence! One word more
Shall make me chide thee, if not hate thee. What!
An advocate for an impostor! Hush!   475
Thou think'st there is no more such shapes as he,
Having seen but him and Caliban. Foolish wench!
To the most of men this is a Caliban,
And they to him are angels.
MIRANDA.   My affections
Are, then, most humble. I have no ambition   480
To see a goodlier man.
PROSPERO.   Come on, obey.
Thy nerves are in their infancy again,
And have no vigor in them.
FERDINAND.   So they are.
My spirits, as in a dream, are all bound up.
My father's loss, the weakness which I feel,   485
The wreck of all my friends, nor this man's threats,
To whom I am subdued, are but light to me
Might I but through my prison once a day
Behold this maid. All corners else o' th' earth
Let liberty make use of, space enough   490
Have I in such a prison.
PROSPERO.   [*Aside*] It works.
                              [*To* FERDINAND] Come on.
[*To* ARIEL] Thou hast done well, fine Ariel!
                              [*To* FERDINAND] Follow me.
[*To* ARIEL] Hark what thou else shalt do me.
MIRANDA.   Be of comfort.
My father's of a better nature, sir,
Than he appears by speech. This is unwonted   495
Which now came from him.
PROSPERO.   Thou shalt be as free
As mountain winds. But then exactly do
All points of my command.
ARIEL.   To the syllable.
PROSPERO. Come, follow. Speak not for him.   [*Exeunt.*]

467. **My foot my tutor:** "My foot" refers to Miranda, subordinate to her father, yet here
ordering him about.   469. **ward:** defensive position.

ACT II

SCENE I. *Another part of the island.*

[*Enter* ALONSO, SEBASTIAN, ANTONIO, GONZALO, ADRIAN, *and* FRANCISCO.]

GONZALO. Beseech you, sir, be merry. You have cause.
    So have we all, of joy, for our escape
    Is much beyond our loss. Our hint of° woe
    Is common. Every day some sailor's wife,
    The masters of some merchant,° and the merchant,   5
    Have just our theme of woe. But for the miracle—
    I mean our preservation—few in millions
    Can speak like us. Then wisely, good sir, weigh
    Our sorrow with our comfort.
ALONSO.   Prithee, peace.
SEBASTIAN. He receives comfort like cold porridge.   10
ANTONIO. The visitor will not give him o'er so.°
SEBASTIAN. Look, he's winding up the watch of his wit.
    By and by it will strike.
GONZALO. Sir—
SEBASTIAN. One. Tell.   15
GONZALO. When every grief is entertained that's offered,
    Comes to the entertainer—
SEBASTIAN. A dollar.
GONZALO. Dolor comes to him, indeed. You have spoken truer than you
    purposed.   20
SEBASTIAN. You have taken it wiselier than I meant you should.
GONZALO. Therefore, my lord—
ANTONIO. Fie, what a spendthrift is he of his tongue!
ALONSO. I prithee, spare.
GONZALO. Well, I have done. But yet—   25
SEBASTIAN. He will be talking.
ANTONIO. Which, of he or Adrian, for a good wager, first begins to crow?
SEBASTIAN. The old cock.
ANTONIO. The cockerel.°
SEBASTIAN. Done. The wager?   30
ANTONIO. A laughter.°
SEBASTIAN. A match!
ADRIAN. Though this island seem to be desert—
SEBASTIAN. Ha, ha, ha!—So, you're paid.
ADRIAN. Uninhabitable, and almost inaccessible—   35
SEBASTIAN. Yet—
ADRIAN. Yet—
ANTONIO. He could not miss 't.
ADRIAN. It must needs be of subtle, tender, and delicate temperance.
ANTONIO. Temperance was a delicate wench.   40

---

3. **hint of:** occasion for.   5. **merchant:** merchant ship.   11. **The visitor will not give him o'er so:** Gonzalo will not be put off from giving advice.   29. **cockerel:** young rooster, i.e., Adrian, the old one being Gonzalo.   31. **A laughter:** The winner gets the laugh.

SEBASTIAN. Aye, and a subtle, as he most learnedly delivered.°
ADRIAN. The air breathes upon us here most sweetly.
SEBASTIAN. As if it had lungs, and rotten ones.
ANTONIO. Or as 'twere perfumed by a fen.
GONZALO. Here is everything advantageous to life. 45
ANTONIO. True—save means to live.
SEBASTIAN. Of that there's none, or little.
GONZALO. How lush and lusty the grass looks! How green!
ANTONIO. The ground indeed is tawny.
SEBASTIAN. With an eye of green in't. 50
ANTONIO. He misses not much.
SEBASTIAN. No, he doth but mistake the truth totally.
GONZALO. But the rarity of it is—which is indeed almost beyond credit—
SEBASTIAN. As many vouched° rarities are.
GONZALO. That our garments, being, as they were, drenched in the sea, 55
    hold notwithstanding their freshness and glosses, being rather new-
    dyed than stained with salt water.
ANTONIO. If but one of his pockets could speak, would it not say he lies?
SEBASTIAN. Aye, or very falsely pocket up his report.
GONZALO. Methinks our garments are now as fresh as when we put 60
    them on first in Afric, at the marriage of the king's fair daughter
    Claribel to the King of Tunis.
SEBASTIAN. 'Twas a sweet marriage, and we prosper well in our return.
ADRIAN. Tunis was never graced before with such a paragon to their queen.
GONZALO. Not since Widow Dido's° time. 65
ANTONIO. Widow! A pox o' that! How came that widow in? Widow Dido!
SEBASTIAN. What if he had said "Widower Aeneas" too? Good Lord, how
    you take it!
ADRIAN. "Widow Dido," said you? You make me study of that. She was of
    Carthage, not of Tunis. 70
GONZALO. This Tunis, sir, was Carthage.
ADRIAN. Carthage?
GONZALO. I assure you, Carthage.
ANTONIO. His word is more than the miraculous harp.°
SEBASTIAN. He hath raised the wall, and houses too. 75
ANTONIO. What impossible matter will he make easy next?
SEBASTIAN. I think he will carry this island home in his pocket, and give it
    his son for an apple.
ANTONIO. And, sowing the kernels of it in the sea, bring forth more islands.
GONZALO. Aye.
ANTONIO. Why, in good time. 80
GONZALO. Sir, we were talking that our garments seem now as fresh as
    when we were at Tunis at the marriage of your daughter, who is
    now queen.

---

41. **delivered:** pronounced. 54. **vouched:** guaranteed. 65. **Widow Dido:** In the *Aeneid*,
before Aeneas came to Carthage (near modern Tunis), Dido, Queen of Carthage, had been
widowed. Aeneas had also been widowed when his wife was lost in the flight from burning
Troy. Dido, of course, fell in love with Aeneas, though he abandoned her. 74. **the miraculous harp:** According to the legends told by Ovid, the walls of Thebes arose to the music of a
harp. Gonzalo has just "created" a whole city (Carthage) of Tunis.

ANTONIO. And the rarest that e'er came there. 85

SEBASTIAN. Bate,° I beseech you, Widow Dido.

ANTONIO. Oh, Widow Dido! Aye, Widow Dido.

GONZALO. Is not, sir, my doublet as fresh as the first day I wore it? I mean,
    in a sort.

ANTONIO. That sort was well fished for. 90

GONZALO. When I wore it at your daughter's marriage?

ALONSO. You cram these words into mine ears against
    The stomach of my sense. Would I had never
    Married my daughter there! For, coming thence,
    My son is lost and, in my rate,° she too 95
    Who is so far from Italy removed
    I ne'er again shall see her. O thou mine heir
    Of Naples and of Milan, what strange fish
    Hath made his meal on thee?

FRANCISCO.   Sir, he may live.
    I saw him beat the surges under him,
    And ride upon their backs. He trod the water, 100
    Whose enmity he flung aside, and breasted
    The surge most swoln that met him. His bold head
    'Bove the contentious waves he kept, and oared
    Himself with his good arms in lusty stroke 105
    To the shore, that o'er his wave-worn basis° bowed,
    As stooping to relieve him. I not doubt
    He came alive to land.

ALONSO. No, no, he's gone.

SEBASTIAN. Sir, you may thank yourself for this great loss, 110
    That would not bless our Europe with your daughter,
    But rather lose her to an African,
    Where she, at least, is banished from your eye
    Who hath cause to wet° the grief on 't.

ALONSO.   Prithee, peace.

SEBASTIAN. You were kneeled to, and importuned otherwise, 115
    By all of us, and the fair soul herself
    Weighed between loathness° and obedience, at
    Which end o' the beam should bow. We have lost your son,
    I fear, forever. Milan and Naples have
    More widows in them of this business' making 120
    Than we bring men to comfort them.
    The fault's your own.

ALONSO.   So is the dear'st o' the loss.

GONZALO. My lord Sebastian,
    The truth you speak doth lack some gentleness,
    And time to speak it in. You rub the sore 125
    When you should bring the plaster.

SEBASTIAN.   Very well.

ANTONIO. And most chirurgeonly.°

---

    86. Bate: except.   **95. rate:** opinion.   **106. basis:** sandy edge.   **114. wet the grief:** weep
for sorrow.   **117. loathness:** reluctance. (The marriage was arranged by her father.)   **127. chirurgeonly:** like a good surgeon.

GONZALO. It is foul weather in us all, good sir,
    When you are cloudy.
SEBASTIAN.   Foul weather?
ANTONIO.   Very foul.
GONZALO. Had I plantation° of this isle, my lord—   130
ANTONIO. He'd sow 't with nettle seed.
SEBASTIAN.   Or docks, or mallows.
GONZALO. And were the king on 't, what would I do?
SEBASTIAN. 'Scape being drunk for want of wine.
GONZALO. I' the commonwealth I would by contraries°
    Execute all things, for no kind of traffic°   135
    Would I admit, no name of magistrate.
    Letters should not be known; riches, poverty,
    And use of service,° none; contract, succession,
    Bourn,° bound of land, tilth,° vineyard, none;
    No use of metal,° corn, or wine, or oil;   140
    No occupation—all men idle, all;
    And women too, but innocent and pure;
    No sovereignty—
SEBASTIAN.   Yet he would be king on't.
ANTONIO. The latter end of his commonwealth forgets the beginning.
GONZALO. All things in common nature should produce   145
    Without sweat or endeavor. Treason, felony,
    Sword, pike, knife, gun, or need of any engine°
    Would I not have. But Nature should bring forth,
    Of its own kind, all foison,° all abundance,
    To feed my innocent people.   150
SEBASTIAN. No marrying 'mong his subjects?
ANTONIO. None, man—all idle knaves.
GONZALO. I would with such perfection govern, sir,
    To excel the Golden Age.
SEBASTIAN.   'Save His Majesty!
ANTONIO. Long live Gonzalo!
GONZALO.   And—do you mark me, sir?   155
ALONSO. Prithee, no more. Thou dost talk nothing to me.
GONZALO. I do well believe your Highness, and did it to minister occasion°
    to these gentlemen, who are of such sensible° and nimble lungs that
    they always use to laugh at nothing.
ANTONIO. 'Twas you we laughed at.   160
GONZALO. Who in this kind of merry fooling am nothing to you. So you
    may continue and laugh at nothing still.
ANTONIO. What a blow was there given!
SEBASTIAN. An° it had not fallen flat-long.°

---

130. **plantation:** colonization, but Antonio takes it in the sense of "planting." 134. **by
contraries:** in ways opposite to what is customary. 135. **traffic:** trade. 138. **service:** servants. 139. **Bourn:** boundaries (therefore, no private property). **tilth:** farming. 140. **metal:**
money. 147. **engine:** weapon of war. 149. **foison:** abundance. 157. **minister occasion:**
give opportunity (for laughter). 158. **sensible:** sensitive. 164. **An:** if. **flat-long:** on the flat
side of the sword.

GONZALO. You are gentlemen of brave mettle, you would lift the moon   165
    out of her sphere if she would continue in it five weeks without
    changing.

[*Enter* ARIEL, *invisible, playing solemn music.*]

SEBASTIAN. We would so, and then go a-batfowling.°
ANTONIO. Nay, good my lord, be not angry.
GONZALO. No, I warrant you, I will not adventure my discretion so   170
    weakly.° Will you laugh me asleep, for I am very heavy?
ANTONIO. Go sleep, and hear us.

[*All sleep except* ALONSO, SEBASTIAN, *and* ANTONIO.]

ALONSO. What, all so soon asleep! I wish mine eyes
    Would, with themselves, shut up my thoughts. I find   175
    They are inclined to do so.
SEBASTIAN.   Please you, sir,
    Do not omit the heavy offer of it.°
    It seldom visits sorrow. When it doth,
    It is a comforter.
ANTONIO.   We two, my lord,
    Will guard your person while you take your rest,   180
    And watch your safety.
ALONSO.   Thank you.—Wondrous heavy.

[ALONSO *sleeps. Exit* ARIEL.]

SEBASTIAN. What a strange drowsiness possesses them!
ANTONIO. It is the quality o' the climate.
SEBASTIAN.   Why
    Doth it not then our eyelids sink? I find not
    Myself disposed to sleep.
ANTONIO.   Nor I. My spirits are nimble.   185
    They fell together all, as by consent,
    They dropped as by a thunderstroke. What might,
    Worthy Sebastian?—Oh, what might?—No more.—
    And yet methinks I see it in thy face,
    What thou shouldst be. The occasion speaks thee,° and   190
    My strong imagination sees a crown
    Dropping upon thy head.
SEBASTIAN.   What, art thou waking?
ANTONIO. Do you not hear me speak?
SEBASTIAN.   I do, and surely
    It is a sleepy language, and thou speak'st
    Out of thy sleep. What is it thou didst say?   195
    This is a strange repose, to be asleep
    With eyes wide open—standing, speaking, moving,
    And yet so fast asleep.
ANTONIO.   Noble Sebastian,

---

168. **a-batfowling:** hunting for birds at night with a stick and a lantern (here, the full moon).
170–71. **adventure my discretion so weakly:** risk my reputation as a sensible man by getting
angry at anything so feeble.   177. **omit the heavy offer of it:** miss this good chance to sleep.
190. **occasion speaks thee:** opportunity calls you.

Thou let'st thy fortune sleep—die, rather—wink'st
Whiles thou art waking.

SEBASTIAN.   Thou dost snore distinctly.   200
There's meaning in thy snores.

ANTONIO. I am more serious than my custom. You
Must be so too, if heed me, which to do
Trebles thee o'er.°

SEBASTIAN.   Well, I am standing water.°

ANTONIO. I'll teach you how to flow.°

SEBASTIAN.   Do so. To ebb   205
Hereditary sloth instructs me.

ANTONIO.   Oh,
If you but knew how you the purpose cherish
Whiles thus you mock it! How, in stripping it,
You more invest it! Ebbing men, indeed,
Most often do so near the bottom run   210
By their own fear or sloth.

SEBASTIAN.   Prithee, say on.
The setting° of thine eye and cheek proclaim
A matter° from thee, and a birth, indeed,
Which throes° thee much to yield.

ANTONIO.   Thus, sir.
Although this lord of weak remembrance, this,°   215
Who shall be of as little memory
When he is earthed, hath here almost persuaded—
For he's a spirit of persuasion, only
Professes to persuade—the king his son's alive,
'Tis as impossible that he's undrowned   220
As he that sleeps here swims.

SEBASTIAN.   I have no hope
That he's undrowned.

ANTONIO.   Oh, out of that "no hope"
What great hope have you! No hope that way is
Another way so high a hope that even
Ambition cannot pierce a wink beyond,   225
But doubt discovery there. Will you grant with me
That Ferdinand is drowned?

SEBASTIAN.   He's gone.

ANTONIO.   Then tell me,
Who's the next heir of Naples?

SEBASTIAN.   Claribel.

ANTONIO. She that is Queen of Tunis, she that dwells
Ten leagues beyond man's life,° she that from Naples   230
Can have no note, unless the sun were post°—
The man i' the moon's too slow—till newborn chins

---

204. **Trebles thee o'er:** will make you three times what you now are in wealth and power.
standing water: between the flow and ebb of the tide. 205. **flow:** advance. 212. **setting:**
expression. 213. **A matter:** a serious concern. 214. **throes:** pains. 215. **this:** obviously
Gonzalo, though it was actually Francisco who claimed that Ferdinand is alive. 230. **Ten
leagues beyond man's life:** like saying "a hundred miles from nowhere." 231. **post:** messenger.

Be rough and razorable. She that from whom
We all were sea-swallowed, though some cast again,
And by that destiny, to perform an act   235
Whereof what's past is prologue, what to come,
In yours and my discharge.

SEBASTIAN.   What stuff is this! How say you?
'Tis true, my brother's daughter's Queen of Tunis,
So is she heir of Naples, 'twixt which regions
There is some space.

ANTONIO.   A space whose every cubit   240
Seems to cry out, "How shall that Claribel
Measure us back° to Naples? Keep° in Tunis,
And let Sebastian wake." Say this were death
That now hath seized them—why, they were no worse
Than now they are. There be that can rule Naples   245
As well as he that sleeps, lords that can prate
As amply and unnecessarily
As this Gonzalo. I myself could make
A chough° of as deep chat.° Oh, that you bore
The mind that I do! What a sleep were this   250
For your advancement! Do you understand me?

SEBASTIAN. Methinks I do.

ANTONIO.   And how does your content
Tender your own good fortune?

SEBASTIAN.   I remember
You did supplant your brother Prospero.

ANTONIO.   True.
And look how well my garments sit upon me,   255
Much feater° than before. My brother's servants
Were then my fellows, now they are my men.°

SEBASTIAN. But—for your conscience.

ANTONIO. Aye, sir, where lies that? If 'twere a kibe,°
'Twould put me to° my slipper. But I feel not   260
This deity in my bosom. Twenty consciences,
That stand 'twixt me and Milan, candied be they,
And melt ere they molest!° Here lies your brother,
No better than the earth he lies upon
If he were that which now he's like, that's dead.   265
Whom I, with this obedient steel, three inches of it,
Can lay to bed forever whiles you, doing thus,
To the perpetual wink° for aye might put
This ancient morsel, this Sir Prudence who
Should not upbraid our course. For all the rest,   270
They'll take suggestion as a cat laps milk,

---

242. **Measure us back:** travel the distance (the cubits) back. **Keep:** let her stay.
249. **chough** (pronounced "chuff"): a jackdaw, sometimes taught to speak. **deep chat:** profound conversation. 256. **feater:** more appropriately. 257. **men:** servants. 259. **kibe:** sore on the heel. 260. **'Twould put me to:** it would make me wear. 262–63. **candied be they, and melt ere they molest:** I would sugar them and eat them before I would let them disturb me. 268. **wink:** sleep.

WILLIAM SHAKESPEARE   563

They'll tell the clock to° any business that
We say befits the hour.
SEBASTIAN.   Thy case, dear friend,
Shall be my precedent. As thou got'st Milan,
I'll come by Naples. Draw thy sword. One stroke   275
Shall free thee from the tribute which thou payest,
And I the king shall love thee.
ANTONIO.   Draw together,
And when I rear my hand, do you the like,
To fall it on Gonzalo.
SEBASTIAN.   Oh, but one word. [*They talk apart.*]

[*Reenter* ARIEL, *invisible.*]

ARIEL. My master through his art foresees the danger   280
That you, his friend, are in, and sends me forth—
For else his project dies—to keep them living.
                              [*Sings in* GONZALO'S *ear.*]
    "While you here do snoring lie,
      Open-eyed conspiracy
        His time° doth take.   285
    If of life you keep a care,
    Shake off slumber, and beware.
        Awake, awake!"
ANTONIO. Then let us both be sudden.
GONZALO.   Now, good angels
    Preserve the king!   [*They wake.*] 290
ALONSO. Why, how now? Ho, awake!—Why are you drawn?
    Wherefore this ghastly looking?
GONZALO.   What's the matter?
SEBASTIAN. Whiles we stood here securing your repose,
    Even now, we heard a hollow burst of bellowing
    Like bulls, or rather lions. Did 't not wake you?   295
    It struck mine ear most terribly.
ALONSO.   I heard nothing.
ANTONIO. Oh, 'twas a din to fright a monster's ear,
    To make an earthquake! Sure, it was the roar
    Of a whole herd of lions.
ALONSO.   Heard you this, Gonzalo?
GONZALO. Upon mine honor, sir, I heard a humming,   300
    And that a strange one too, which did awake me.
    I shaked you, sir, and cried. As mine eyes opened
    I saw their weapons drawn.—There was a noise,
    That's verily. 'Tis best we stand upon our guard,
    Or that we quit this place. Let's draw our weapons.   305
ALONSO. Lead off this ground, and let's make further search
    For my poor son.
GONZALO.   Heavens keep him from these beasts!
    For he is sure i' th' island.

272. **tell the clock to:** say it's time for. 285. **time:** opportunity.

ALONSO.   Lead away.
ARIEL. Prospero my lord shall know what I have done.
    So, King, go safely on to seek thy son.   [*Exeunt.*] 310

SCENE II. *Another part of the island.*

[*Enter* CALIBAN *with a burden of wood. A noise of thunder heard.*]

CALIBAN. All the infections that the sun sucks up
    From bogs, fens, flats, on Prosper fall, and make him
    By inchmeal° a disease! His spirits hear me,
    And yet I needs must curse. But they'll nor pinch,
    Fright me with urchin shows, pitch me i' the mire,   5
    Nor lead me, like a firebrand,° in the dark
    Out of my way, unless he bid 'em. But
    For every trifle are they set upon me—
    Sometime like apes, that mow° and chatter at me,
    And after bite me; then like hedgehogs, which   10
    Lie tumbling in my barefoot way and mount
    Their pricks at my footfall. Sometime am I
    All wound with adders, who with cloven tongues
    Do hiss me into a madness.

[*Enter* TRINCULO.]

                    Lo, now, lo!
    Here comes a spirit of his, and to torment me   15
    For bringing wood in slowly. I'll fall flat.
    Perchance he will not mind me.
TRINCULO. Here's neither bush nor shrub to bear off any weather at all,
    and another storm brewing, I hear it sing i' the wind. Yond same
    black cloud, yond huge one, looks like a foul bombard° that   20
    would shed his liquor. If it should thunder as it did before, I know not
    where to hide my head. Yond same cloud cannot choose but fall by
    pailfuls. What have we here? A man or a fish? Dead or alive? A fish—
    he smells like a fish, a very ancient and fishlike smell, a kind of not
    of the newest Poor John.° A strange fish! Were I in England   25
    now, as once I was, and had but this fish painted,° not a holiday fool
    there but would give a piece of silver. There would this monster
    make a man°—any strange beast there makes a man. When they will
    not give a doit° to relieve a lame beggar, they will lay out ten to see
    a dead Indian. Legged like a man! And his fins like arms! Warm,   30
    o' my troth! I do now let loose my opinion, hold it no longer—this
    is no fish, but an islander that hath lately suffered by a thunderbolt.
    [*Thunder.*] Alas, the storm is come again! Best way is to creep under
    his gaberdine, there is no other shelter hereabout. Misery acquaints

3. **By inchmeal:** inch by inch.   6. **firebrand:** will-o'-the-wisp.   9. **mow:** make faces.
20. **bombard:** leather jug.   25. **Poor John:** name of a kind of dried fish.   26. **painted:** painted
on a signboard for a booth at a fair.   28. **make a man:** make a man's fortune.   29. **doit:** small
coin, about a cent.

a man with strange bedfellows. I will here shroud° till the dregs 35
of the storm be past. [TRINCULO *crawls under the cloak with* CALIBAN.]

[*Enter* STEPHANO, *singing, a bottle in his hand.*]

STEPHANO. "I shall no more to sea, to sea,
      Here shall I die ashore—"
This is a very scurvy° tune to sing at a man's funeral.°
Well, here's my comfort.   [*Drinks. Sings.*] 40
"The master, the swabber, the boatswain, and I,
    The gunner, and his mate,
  Loved Mall, Meg, and Marian, and Margery,
    But none of us cared for Kate.
      For she had a tongue with a tang, 45
    Would cry to a sailor, Go hang!
  She loved not the savor of tar nor of pitch,
Yet a tailor might scratch her where'er she did itch.
    Then, to sea, boys, and let her go hang!"
This is a scurvy tune too, but here's my comfort.   [*Drinks.*] 50
CALIBAN. Do not torment me.—Oh!
STEPHANO. What's the matter? Have we devils here? Do you put tricks
upon 's with salvages and men of Ind,° ha? I have not 'scaped drown-
ing to be afeard now of your four legs, for it hath been said, As proper
a man as ever went on four legs cannot make him give ground. 55
And it shall be said so again while Stephano breathes at nostrils.
CALIBAN. The spirit torments me.—Oh!
STEPHANO. This is some monster of the isle with four legs, who hath got,
as I take it, an ague.° Where the devil should he learn our language?
I will give him some relief, if it be but for that. If I can recover 60
him, and keep him tame, and get to Naples with him, he's a present
for any emperor that ever trod on neat's leather.°
CALIBAN. Do not torment me, prithee, I'll bring my wood home faster.
STEPHANO. He's in his fit now, and does not talk after the wisest. He shall
taste of my bottle. If he have never drunk wine afore, it will go 65
near to remove his fit. If I can recover him, and keep him tame, I will
not take too much for him. He shall pay for him that hath him, and
that soundly.
CALIBAN. Thou dost me yet but little hurt, thou wilt anon, I know it by
thy trembling.° Now Prosper works upon thee. 70
STEPHANO. Come on your ways. Open your mouth, here is that which
will give language to you, cat.° Open your mouth, this will shake
your shaking, I can tell you, and that soundly. You cannot tell who's
your friend. Open your chaps again.
TRINCULO. I should know that voice. It should be—but he is drowned, 75
and these are devils.—Oh, defend me!

---

    35. **shroud:** cover myself.   39. **scurvy:** lousy. **funeral:** Stephano is mourning, after his
fashion, the "death" of Trinculo.   53. **Ind:** India.   59. **ague:** fever with chills (Caliban is
trembling with fear).   62. **neat's leather:** cowhide (shoes).   70. **thy trembling:** Trinculo is
trembling now, thinking that Stephano's voice must be that of a ghost. Caliban does not distinguish between the new voice (Stephano's) and the voice of the person who crawled under
the cloak with him (Trinculo's).   72. **cat:** alluding to a proverb that says that liquor can make
a cat speak.

STEPHANO. Four legs and two voices—a most delicate monster! His forward voice, now, is to speak well of his friend, his backward voice is to utter foul speeches and to detract. If all the wine in my bottle will recover him, I will help his ague. Come,—Amen! I will pour some 80 in thy other mouth.

TRINCULO. Stephano!

STEPHANO. Doth thy other mouth call me? Mercy, mercy! This is a devil and no monster. I will leave him, I have no long spoon.°

TRINCULO. Stephano! If thou beest Stephano, touch me, and speak to 85 me for I am Trinculo—be not afeard—thy good friend Trinculo.

STEPHANO. If thou beest Trinculo, come forth. I'll pull thee by the lesser legs. If any be Trinculo's legs, these are they. Thou art very Trinculo indeed! How camest thou to be the siege° of this mooncalf?° Can he vent Trinculos? 90

TRINCULO. I look him to be killed with a thunderstroke. But art thou not drowned, Stephano? I hope, now, thou art not drowned. Is the storm overblown? I hid me under the dead mooncalf's gaberdine for fear of the storm. And art thou living, Stephano? O Stephano, two Neapolitans 'scaped! 95

STEPHANO. Prithee do not turn me about, my stomach is not constant.

CALIBAN. [Aside] These be fine things, an if° they be not sprites.
    That's a brave god, and bears celestial liquor.
    I will kneel to him.

STEPHANO. How didst thou 'scape? How camest thou hither? Swear, 100 by this bottle, how thou camest hither. I escaped upon a butt of sack,° which the sailors heaved o'erboard, by this bottle, which I made of the bark of a tree with mine own hands, since I was cast ashore.

CALIBAN. I'll swear upon that bottle to be thy true subject, for the liquor is not earthly. 105

STEPHANO. Here, swear, then, how thou escapedst.

TRINCULO. Swam ashore, man, like a duck. I can swim like a duck, I'll be sworn.

STEPHANO. Here, kiss the book.° Though thou canst swim like a duck, thou art made like a goose. 110

TRINCULO. O Stephano, hast any more of this?

STEPHANO. The whole butt, man. My cellar is in a rock by the seaside, where my wine is hid. How now, mooncalf! How does thine ague?

CALIBAN. Hast thou not dropped from Heaven?

STEPHANO. Out o' the moon, I do assure thee. I was the man i' the 115 moon when time was.°

CALIBAN. I have seen thee in her, and I do adore thee. My mistress showed me thee, and thy dog, and thy bush.°

STEPHANO. Come, swear to that, kiss the book. I will furnish it anon with new contents. Swear. 120

---

84. **long spoon:** A proverb says that he who eats with the Devil must have a long spoon, a reference from a time when people ate from a common dish. The long spoon would help avoid the claws of the Devil. 89. **siege:** excrement. **mooncalf:** misshapen creature. 97. **an if:** if. 101. **butt of sack:** barrel of Spanish wine. 109. **book:** bottle. 116. **when time was:** once upon a time. 118. **thee, and thy dog, and thy bush:** The man in the moon was supposed to have a dog and carry a thornbush.

TRINCULO. By this good light, this is a very shallow monster! I afeard of
    him! A very weak monster! The man i' the moon! A most poor
    credulous monster! Well drawn,° monster, in good sooth!°
CALIBAN. I'll show thee every fertile inch o' th' island. And I will kiss thy
    foot. I prithee be my god.   125
TRINCULO. By this light, a most perfidious and drunken monster! When's
    god's asleep, he'll rob his bottle.
CALIBAN. I'll kiss thy foot, I'll swear myself thy subject.
STEPHANO. Come on, then, down, and swear.
TRINCULO. I shall laugh myself to death at this puppyheaded monster.   130
    A most scurvy monster! I could find in my heart to beat him—
STEPHANO. Come, kiss.
TRINCULO. But that the poor monster's in drink. An abominable monster!
CALIBAN. I'll show thee the best springs, I'll pluck thee berries,
    I'll fish for thee, and get thee wood enough.   135
    A plague upon the tyrant that I serve!
    I'll bear him no more sticks, but follow thee,
    Thou wondrous man.
TRINCULO. A most ridiculous monster, to make a wonder of a poor drunkard!
CALIBAN. I prithee let me bring thee where crabs° grow.   140
    And I with my long nails will dig thee pignuts.
    Show thee a jay's nest, and instruct thee how
    To snare the nimble marmoset. I'll bring thee
    To clustering filberts, and sometimes I'll get thee
    Young scamels° from the rock. Wilt thou go with me?   145
STEPHANO. I prithee now, lead the way, without any more talking. Trinculo,
    the king and all our company else being drowned, we will inherit
    here. Here, bear my bottle, fellow Trinculo, we'll fill him by and by
    again.
CALIBAN. [Sings drunkenly.]
    "Farewell, master, farewell, farewell!"   150
TRINCULO. A howling monster, a drunken monster!
CALIBAN. "No more dams I'll make for fish.
        Nor fetch in firing
        At requiring,
        Nor scrape trencher,° nor wash dish.   155
        'Ban, 'Ban, Cacaliban
        Has a new master.—Get a new man."
    Freedom, heyday! Heyday, freedom! Freedom, heyday, freedom!
STEPHANO. O brave monster! Lead the way.   [Exeunt.]

    123. **drawn:** drunk. **in good sooth:** truly. 140. **crabs:** crab apples. 145. **scamels:** prob-
ably seabirds. 155. **trencher:** wooden plate.

ACT III

SCENE I. *Before* PROSPERO'S *cell.*

[*Enter* FERDINAND, *bearing a log.*]

FERDINAND. There be some spots are painful, and their labor
    Delight in them sets off. Some kinds of baseness
    Are nobly undergone, and most poor matters
    Point to rich ends. This my mean task
    Would be as heavy to me as odious, but   5
    The mistress which I serve quickens° what's dead
    And makes my labors pleasures. Oh, she is
    Ten times more gentle than her father's crabbèd,
    And he's composed of harshness. I must remove
    Some thousands of these logs, and pile them up,   10
    Upon a sore injunction.° My sweet mistress
    Weeps when she sees me work, and says such baseness
    Had never like executor. I forget.
    But these sweet thoughts do even refresh my labors,
    Most busy lest when I do it.°

[*Enter* MIRANDA *and* PROSPERO, *who is at a distance, unseen by* MIRANDA *and* FERDINAND.]

MIRANDA.   Alas, now, pray you   15
    Work not so hard. I would the lightning had
    Burned up those logs that you are enjoined to pile!
    Pray set it down and rest you. When this burns,
    'Twill weep° for having wearied you. My father
    Is hard at study, pray now, rest yourself.   20
    He's safe for these three hours.
FERDINAND.   O most dear mistress,
    The sun will set before I shall discharge
    What I must strive to do.
MIRANDA.   If you'll sit down,
    I'll bear your logs the while. Pray give me that,
    I'll carry it to the pile.
FERDINAND.   No, precious creature,   25
    I had rather crack my sinews, break my back,
    Than you should such dishonor undergo
    While I sit lazy by.
MIRANDA.   It would become me
    As well as it does you. And I should do it
    With much more ease, for my goodwill is to it,   30
    And yours it is against.

---

    6. quickens: enlivens.   **11. sore injunction:** stern command.   **15. Most busy lest when I do it:** least overburdened with work when I am laboring; most busy when I am thinking sweet thoughts of Miranda.   **19. weep:** Miranda is being poetic and comparing the sap oozing from a burning log to tears.

PROSPERO.   Poor worm, thou art infected!
         This visitation shows it.
MIRANDA.   You look wearily.
FERDINAND. No, noble mistress, 'tis fresh morning with me
         When you are by at night. I do beseech you—
         Chiefly that I might set it in my prayers—   35
         What is your name?
MIRANDA.   Miranda.—O my father,
         I have broke your hest° to say so!
FERDINAND.   Admired° Miranda!
         Indeed the top of admiration! Worth
         What's dearest to the world! Full many a lady
         I have eyed with best regard, and many a time   40
         The harmony of their tongues hath into bondage
         Brought my too diligent ear. For several virtues
         Have I liked several women, never any
         With so full soul but some defect in her
         Did quarrel with the noblest grace she owed,°   45
         And put it to the foil.° But you, oh, you,
         So perfect and so peerless, are created
         Of every creature's best!
MIRANDA.   I do not know
         One of my sex, no woman's face remember
         Save, from my glass, mine own. Nor have I seen   50
         More that I may call men than you, good friend,
         And my dear father. How features are abroad,
         I am skill-less° of. But, by my modesty,
         The jewel in my dower, I would not wish
         Any companion in the world but you,   55
         Nor can imagination form a shape
         Besides yourself to like of.° But I prattle
         Something too wildly, and my father's precepts
         I therein do forget.
FERDINAND.   I am, in my condition,
         A prince, Miranda, I do think, a king—   60
         I would not so!—and would no more endure
         This wooden slavery° than to suffer
         The flesh fly blow° my mouth. Hear my soul speak.
         The very instant that I saw you did
         My heart fly to your service, there resides,   65
         To make me slave to it, and for your sake
         Am I this patient logman.
MIRANDA.   Do you love me?
FERDINAND. O Heaven, O earth, bear witness to this sound,
         And crown what I profess with kind event°
         If I speak true! If hollowly, invert   70

37. **hest:** command.   **Admired.** The name Miranda means "one to be admired," in Latin.
45. **owed:** owned.   46. **put it to the foil:** canceled it out.   53. **skill-less:** ignorant.   57. **like of:** compare to.   62. **wooden slavery:** the forced labor of carrying wood.   63. **blow:** lay eggs in.
69. **kind event:** favorable outcome.

What best is boded° me to mischief! I,
Beyond all limit of what else i' the world,
Do love, prize, honor you.

MIRANDA.   I am a fool
To weep at what I am glad of.

PROSPERO.   Fair encounter
Of two most rare affections! Heavens rain grace   75
On that which breeds between 'em!

FERDINAND.   Wherefore weep you?

MIRANDA. At mine unworthiness, that dare not offer
What I desire to give, and much less take
What I shall die to want.° But this is trifling,
And all the more it seeks to hide itself,   80
The bigger bulk it shows. Hence, bashful cunning!
And prompt me, plain and holy innocence!
I am your wife, if you will marry me.
If not, I'll die your maid. To be your fellow°
You may deny me, but I'll be your servant,   85
Whether you will or no.

FERDINAND.   My mistress, dearest,
And I thus humble ever.

MIRANDA.   My husband, then?

FERDINAND. Aye, with a heart as willing
As bondage e'er of freedom. Here's my hand.

MIRANDA. And mine, with my heart in 't. And now farewell   90
Till half an hour hence.

FERDINAND.   A thousand thousand!°

        [Exeunt FERDINAND and MIRANDA severally.°]

PROSPERO. So glad of this as they I cannot be,
Who are surprised with all, but my rejoicing
At nothing can be more. I'll to my book,
For yet ere suppertime must I perform   95
Much business appertaining.   [Exit.]

SCENE II.   Another part of the island.

[Enter CALIBAN, STEPHANO, and TRINCULO.]

STEPHANO. Tell not me.—When the butt is out, we will drink water, not
    a drop before. Therefore bear up, and board 'em.° Servant-monster,
    drink to me.

TRINCULO. Servant-monster! The folly° of this island! They say there's
    but five upon this isle. We are three of them. If th' other two be   5
    brained like us, the state totters.

STEPHANO. Drink, servant-monster, when I bid thee. Thy eyes are almost
    set° in thy head.

---

71. **boded:** prophesied. 79. **to want:** for lack of. 84. **fellow:** equal or wife. 91. **thousand:** i.e., farewells. **s.d. *severally*:** by different exits.
    2. **bear up, and board 'em:** drink up! 4. **folly:** freak. 8. **set:** closed (with drunkenness).

TRINCULO. Where should they be set else? He were a brave monster indeed
    if they were set in his tail.   10
STEPHANO. My man-monster hath drowned his tongue in sack. For my part,
    the sea cannot drown me. I swam, ere I could recover the shore,
    five-and-thirty leagues off and on. By this light, thou shalt be my
    lieutenant, monster, or my standard.°
TRINCULO. Your lieutenant, if you list.° He's no standard.   15
STEPHANO. We'll not run, Monsieur Monster.
TRINCULO. Nor go neither, but you'll lie, like dogs, and yet say nothing
    neither.
STEPHANO. Mooncalf, speak once in thy life, if thou beest a good mooncalf.
CALIBAN. How does thy honor? Let me lick thy shoe. I'll not serve him,   20
    he is not valiant.
TRINCULO. Thou liest, most ignorant monster. I am in case° to jostle a con-
    stable. Why, thou deboshed fish thou, was there ever man a coward
    that hath drunk so much sack as I today? Wilt thou tell a monstrous
    lie, being but half a fish and half a monster?   25
CALIBAN. Lo, how he mocks me! Wilt thou let him, my lord?
TRINCULO. "Lord," quoth he! That a monster should be such a natural!°
CALIBAN. Lo, lo, again! Bite him to death, I prithee.
STEPHANO. Trinculo, keep a good tongue in your head. If you prove a
    mutineer—the next tree! The poor monster's my subject, and he   30
    shall not suffer indignity.
CALIBAN. I thank my noble lord. Wilt thou be pleased to hearken once again
    to the suit I made to thee?
STEPHANO. Marry, will I. Kneel and repeat it. I will stand, and so shall
    Trinculo.   35

[Enter ARIEL, *invisible.]*

CALIBAN. As I told thee before, I am subject to a tyrant, a sorcerer, that by
    his cunning hath cheated me of the island.
ARIEL. Thou liest.
CALIBAN. Thou liest, thou jesting monkey thou.
    I would my valiant master would destroy thee!   40
    I do not lie.
STEPHANO. Trinculo, if you trouble him any more in 's tale, by this hand,
    I will supplant some of your teeth.
TRINCULO. Why, I said nothing.
STEPHANO. Mum, then, and no more. Proceed.   45
CALIBAN. I say, by sorcery he got this isle.
    From me he got it. If thy greatness will
    Revenge it on him—for I know thou darest,
    But this thing dare not—
STEPHANO. That's most certain.   50
CALIBAN. Thou shalt be lord of it, and I'll serve thee.
STEPHANO. How now shall this be compassed? Canst thou bring me to the
    party?

14. **standard:** standard-bearer. 15. **list:** like. 22. **in case:** in condition. 27. **natural:**
idiot.

CALIBAN. Yea, yea, my lord. I'll yield him thee asleep,
      Where thou mayst knock a nail into his head.   55
ARIEL. Thou liest, thou canst not.
CALIBAN. What a pied° ninny's this! Thou scurvy patch!°
      I do beseech thy greatness, give him blows,
      And take his bottle from him. When that's gone,
      He shall drink naught but brine, for I'll not show him   60
      Where the quick freshes are.
STEPHANO. Trinculo, run into no further danger. Interrupt the monster
      one word further and, by this hand, I'll turn my mercy out o' doors
      and make a stockfish° of thee.
TRINCULO. Why, what did I? I did nothing. I'll go farther off.   65
STEPHANO. Didst thou not say he lied?
ARIEL. Thou liest.
STEPHANO. Do I so? Take thou that. [*Beats him.*] As you like this, give me
      the lie° another time.
TRINCULO. I did not give the lie. Out o' your wits, and hearing too? A   70
      pox o' your bottle! This can sack and drinking do. A murrain° on your
      monster, and the devil take your fingers!
CALIBAN. Ha, ha, ha!
STEPHANO. Now, forward with your tale.—Prithee, stand farther off.
CALIBAN. Beat him enough. After a little time   75
      I'll beat him too.
STEPHANO.   Stand farther.—Come, proceed.
CALIBAN. Why, as I told thee, 'tis a custom with him
      I' th' afternoon to sleep. There thou mayst brain him,
      Having first seized his books, or with a log
      Batter his skull, or paunch him° with a stake,   80
      Or cut his weasand° with thy knife. Remember
      First to possess his books, for without them
      He's but a sot, as I am, nor hath not
      One spirit to command. They all do hate him
      As rootedly as I. Burn but his books.   85
      He has brave utensils°—for so he calls them—
      Which, when he has a house, he'll deck withal.
      And that most deeply to consider is
      The beauty of his daughter. He himself
      Calls her a nonpareil. I never saw a woman   90
      But only Sycorax my dam and she,
      But she as far surpasseth Sycorax
      As great'st does least.
STEPHANO.   Is it so brave a lass?
CALIBAN. Aye, lord, she will become thy bed, I warrant,
      And bring thee forth brave brood.   95
STEPHANO. Monster, I will kill this man. His daughter and I will be king

---

57. **pied:** varicolored, referring to the colorful jester costume that Trinculo wears.   **patch:**
clown.   64. **stockfish:** dried cod, which is tenderized by being beaten.   69. **give me the lie:**
call me a liar.   71. **murrain:** plague.   80. **paunch him:** stab him in the belly.   81. **weasand:**
windpipe.   86. **brave utensils:** rich furnishings.

and queen—save our Graces!—and Trinculo and thyself shall be
viceroys. Dost thou like the plot, Trinculo?

TRINCULO. Excellent.

STEPHANO. Give me thy hand. I am sorry I beat thee, but while thou   100
livest keep a good tongue in thy head.

CALIBAN. Within this half-hour will he be asleep.
Wilt thou destroy him then?

STEPHANO.   Aye, on mine honor.

ARIEL. This will I tell my master.

CALIBAN. Thou makest me merry, I am full of pleasure.   105
Let us be jocund. Will you troll the catch°
You taught me but whilere?°

STEPHANO. At thy request, monster, I will do reason,° any reason.—Come
on, Trinculo, let us sing. [*Sings.*]
"Flout 'em and scout 'em,   110
And scout 'em and flout 'em.
Thought is free."

CALIBAN. That's not the tune. [ARIEL *plays the tune on a tabor and pipe.*]

STEPHANO. What is this same?

TRINCULO. This is the tune of our catch, played by the picture of No-   115
body.°

STEPHANO. If thou beest a man, show thyself in thy likeness. If thou beest
a devil, take 't as thou list.°

TRINCULO. Oh, forgive me my sins!

STEPHANO. He that dies pays all debts. I defy thee. Mercy upon us!   120

CALIBAN. Art thou afeard?

STEPHANO. No, monster, not I.

CALIBAN. Be not afeard. The isle is full of noises,
Sounds and sweet airs that give delight and hurt not.
Sometimes a thousand twangling instruments   125
Will hum about mine ears, and sometime voices
That, if I then had waked after long sleep,
Will make me sleep again. And then, in dreaming,
The clouds methought would open and show riches
Ready to drop upon me, that when I waked,   130
I cried to dream again.

STEPHANO. This will prove a brave kingdom to me, where I shall have my
music for nothing.

CALIBAN. When Prospero is destroyed.

STEPHANO. That shall be by and by. I remember the story.   135

TRINCULO. The sound is going away. Let's follow it, and after do our work.

STEPHANO. Lead, monster, we'll follow. I would I could see this taborer,
he lays it on.

TRINCULO. Wilt come? I'll follow, Stephano.   [*Exeunt.*]

---

106. **troll the catch:** sing the song.   107. **whilere:** recently.   108. **reason:** anything within
reason.   115–16. **picture of Nobody:** something like the little man who wasn't there. A 1606
printing of a play, called *Nobody and Some-body,* shows a picture of Nobody, with a huge
head and no body.   118. **take 't as thou list:** do as you like.

SCENE III. *Another part of the island.*

[*Enter* ALONSO, SEBASTIAN, ANTONIO, GONZALO, ADRIAN, *and* FRANCISCO.]

GONZALO. By'r Lakin,° I can go no further, sir,
    My old bones ache. Here's a maze trod, indeed,
    Through forthrights and meanders! By your patience,
    I needs must rest me.
ALONSO.   Old lord, I cannot blame thee,
    Who am myself attached with weariness,   5
    To the dulling of my spirits. Sit down and rest.
    Even here I will put off my hope, and keep it
    No longer for my flatterer. He is drowned
    Whom thus we stray to find, and the sea mocks
    Our frustrate search on land. Well, let him go.   10
ANTONIO. [*Aside to* SEBASTIAN] I am right glad that he's so out of hope.
    Do not, for one repulse, forgo the purpose
    That you resolved to effect.
SEBASTIAN.   [*Aside to* ANTONIO] The next advantage
    Will we take thoroughly.
ANTONIO. [*Aside to* SEBASTIAN] Let it be tonight.
    For now they are oppressed with travel, they   15
    Will not, nor cannot, use such vigilance
    As when they are fresh.
SEBASTIAN. [*Aside to* ANTONIO] I say tonight. No more.
                    [*Solemn and strange music.*]
ALONSO. What harmony is this?—My good friends, hark!
GONZALO. Marvelous sweet music!

[*Enter* PROSPERO *above, invisible. Enter several* SPIRITS *in strange shapes, bringing in a banquet. They dance about it with gentle actions of salutation, and, inviting the king, etc., to eat, they depart.*]

ALONSO. Give us kind keepers, Heavens!—What were these?   20
SEBASTIAN. A living drollery!° Now I will believe
    That there are unicorns, that in Arabia
    There is one tree, the phoenix' throne, one phoenix
    At this hour reigning there.
ANTONIO.   I'll believe both,
    And what does else want credit, come to me   25
    And I'll be sworn 'tis true! Travelers ne'er did lie,
    Though fools at home condemn 'em.
GONZALO.   If in Naples
    I should report this now, would they believe me?
    If I should say I saw such islanders—
    For, certes,° these are people of the island—   30
    Who, though they are of monstrous shape, yet note
    Their manners are more gentle-kind than of

---

1. **By'r Lakin:** an oath (by our Ladykin, "little Lady," i.e., the Virgin). 21. **drollery:** puppet show. 30. **certes:** surely.

Our human generation you shall find
Many—nay, almost any.
PROSPERO.   [*Aside*] Honest lord,
Thou hast said well, for some of you there present   35
Are worse than devils.
ALONSO.   I cannot too much muse°
Such shapes, such gesture, and such sound, expressing—
Although they want the use of tongue—a kind
Of excellent dumb discourse.
PROSPERO.   [*Aside*] Praise in departing.°
FRANCISCO. They vanished strangely.
SEBASTIAN.   No matter, since   40
They have left their viands behind, for we have stomachs.—
Will 't please you taste of what is here?
ALONSO.   Not I.
GONZALO. Faith, sir, you need not fear. When we were boys,
Who would believe that there were mountaineers
Dewlapped° like bulls, whose throats had hanging at 'em   45
Wallets of flesh? Or that there were such men
Whose heads stood in their breasts?° Which now we find
Each putter-out of five for one° will bring us
Good warrant° of.
ALONSO.   I will stand to and feed,
Although my last. No matter, since I feel   50
The best is past. Brother, my lord the duke,
Stand to, and do as we.

[*Thunder and lightning. Enter* ARIEL, *like a harpy,° claps his wings upon
the table, and, with a quaint device,° the banquet vanishes.*]

ARIEL. You are three men of sin, whom Destiny—
That hath to instrument this lower world
And what is in 't—the never-surfeited sea   55
Hath caused to belch up you. And on this island,
Where man doth not inhabit—you 'mongst men
Being most unfit to live. I have made you mad,
And even with suchlike valor men hang and drown
Their proper selves.   [ALONSO, SEBASTIAN, *etc., draw their swords.*]
                    You fools! I and my fellows   60
Are ministers of Fate. The elements
Of whom your swords are tempered may as well
Wound the loud winds, or with bemocked-at stabs
Kill the still-closing waters, as diminish

---

36. **muse:** wonder at.   39. **Praise in departing:** a reference to a proverb that says to hold
your praise until you see how your entertainment turns out.   45. **Dewlapped:** having folds of
loose skin hanging from the throat.   47. **men whose heads stood in their breasts:** as reported
by the famous voyager Sir Walter Raleigh, in his account of a trip to Guiana in 1595.
48. **putter-out of five for one:** In those days, voyagers to remote lands often left money with
the merchant they were traveling for, under the condition that they would receive five times
the amount if they returned home safely.   49. **warrant:** testimony.   **s.d. harpy:** a disgusting
winged woman of mythology, who appeared in the *Aeneid* to befoul and steal Aeneas' food.
quaint device: ingenious piece of machinery.

One dowle° that's in my plume. My fellow ministers   65
Are like invulnerable. If you could hurt,
Your swords are now too massy° for your strengths,
And will not be uplifted. But remember—
For that's my business to you—that you three
From Milan did supplant good Prospero,   70
Exposed unto the sea, which hath requit° it,
Him and his innocent child. For which foul deed
The powers, delaying not forgetting, have
Incensed the seas and shores—yea, all the creatures—
Against your peace. Thee of thy son, Alonso,   75
They have bereft, and do pronounce by me
Lingering perdition°—worse than any death
Can be at once—shall step by step attend
You and your ways. Whose wraths to guard you from—
Which here, in this most desolate isle, else falls   80
Upon your heads—is nothing but heart sorrow
And a clear life ensuing.°

[ARIEL *vanishes in thunder; then, to soft music, enter the* SPIRITS *in various*
shapes again, and dance, with mocks and mows,° and carry out the table.]

PROSPERO. Bravely the figure of this harpy hast thou
　　　Performed, my Ariel, a grace it had, devouring.°
　　　Of my instruction hast thou nothing bated°   85
　　　In what thou hadst to say. So, with good life°
　　　And observation strange,° my meaner ministers°
　　　Their several kinds° have done. My high charms work,
　　　And these mine enemies are all knit up°
　　　In their distractions.° They now are in my power,   90
　　　And in these fits I leave them while I visit
　　　Young Ferdinand—whom they suppose is drowned—
　　　And his and mine loved darling.   [*Exit above.*]
GONZALO. I' the name of something holy, sir, why stand you
　　　In this strange stare?
ALONSO.　　　　　　　　Oh, it is monstrous, monstrous!   95
　　　Methought the billows spoke, and told me of it,
　　　The winds did sing it to me, and the thunder,
　　　That deep and dreadful organ pipe, pronounced
　　　The name of Prosper. It did bass my trespass.°
　　　Therefore my son i' th' ooze is bedded, and   100
　　　I'll seek him deeper than e'er plummet sounded,
　　　And with him there lie mudded.   [*Exit.*]

---

　　65. **dowle:** pin feather.　67. **massy:** heavy.　71. **requit it:** taken revenge for your deed.
77. **perdition:** destruction.　82. **is nothing but heart sorrow and a clear life ensuing:** only repentance and a clean life hereafter (can guard you from the wraths of the powers Ariel serves).
s.d. *mocks and mows:* mocking gestures and grimaces.　84. **a grace it had, devouring:** The
disgusting ways of the harpy were made graceful in Ariel's performance.　85. **bated:** left out.
86. **good life:** realism.　87. **observation strange:** unusual care.　**meaner ministers:** lesser servants.　88. **several kinds:** various tasks.　89. **knit up:** enmeshed.　90. **distractions:** perplexi-
ties.　99. **bass my trespass:** provide the bass part to (i.e., give an ominous sound to) my crime.

SEBASTIAN.   But one fiend at a time,
    I'll fight their legions o'er.
ANTONIO.   I'll be thy second.

                              [Exeunt SEBASTIAN *and* ANTONIO.]

GONZALO. All three of them are desperate. Their great guilt,
    Like poison given to work a great time after,   105
    Now 'gins to bite the spirits. I do beseech you
    That are of suppler joints, follow them swiftly,
    And hinder them from what this ecstasy°
    May now provoke them to.
ADRIAN.   Follow, I pray you.   *[Exeunt.]*

ACT IV

SCENE I. *Before* PROSPERO'S *cell.*

[Enter PROSPERO, FERDINAND, *and* MIRANDA.]

PROSPERO. If I have too austerely punished you,
    Your compensation makes amends. For I
    Have given you here a third° of mine own life,
    Or that for which I live, who once again
    I tender° to thy hand. All thy vexations   5
    Were but my trials of thy love, and thou
    Hast strangely° stood the test. Here, afore Heaven,
    I ratify this my rich gift. O Ferdinand,
    Do not smile at me that I boast her off,
    For thou shalt find she will outstrip all praise   10
    And make it halt behind her.
FERDINAND.   I do believe it
    Against an oracle.°
PROSPERO. Then, as my gift, and thine own acquisition
    Worthily purchased, take my daughter. But
    If thou dost break her virgin knot before   15
    All sanctimonious ceremonies may
    With full and holy rite be ministered,
    No sweet aspersion° shall the Heavens let fall
    To make this contract grow;° but barren hate,
    Sour-eyed disdain, and discord shall bestrew   20
    The union of your bed with weeds so loathly
    That you shall hate it both. Therefore take heed,
    As Hymen's° lamps shall light you.
FERDINAND.   As I hope
    For quiet days, fair issue, and long life,

108. **ecstasy:** fit of madness.
   3. **a third:** i.e., his heart (his mind and his power perhaps being the other two thirds). 5. **tender:** give over. 7. **strangely:** unusually well. 12. **Against an oracle:** even if an oracle should deny it. 18. **aspersion:** sprinkling (i.e., blessing). 19. **grow:** bear fruit. 23. **Hymen:** god of marriage.

With such love as 'tis now, the murkiest den,   25
The most opportune place, the strong'st suggestion°
Our worser genius can,° shall never melt
Mine honor into lust, to take away
The edge of that day's celebration
When I shall think or° Phoebus' steeds are foundered,   30
Or Night kept chained below.°
PROSPERO.   Fairly spoke.
Sit, then, and talk with her, she is thine own.
What, Ariel! My industrious servant, Ariel!

[*Enter* ARIEL.]

ARIEL. What would my potent master? Here I am.
PROSPERO. Thou and thy meaner fellows your last service   35
Did worthily perform, and I must use you
In such another trick. Go bring the rabble,
O'er whom I give thee power, here to this place.
Incite them to quick motion, for I must
Bestow upon the eyes of this young couple   40
Some vanity° of mine art. It is my promise,
And they expect it from me.
ARIEL.   Presently?
PROSPERO. Aye, with a twink.
ARIEL. Before you can say, "come," and "go,"
And breathe twice and cry, "so, so,"   45
Each one, tripping on his toe,
Will be here with mop° and mow.
Do you love me, master? No?
PROSPERO. Dearly, my delicate Ariel. Do not approach
Till thou dost hear me call.
ARIEL.   Well, I conceive.°   [*Exit.*] 50
PROSPERO. Look thou be true. Do not give dalliance°
Too much the rein. The strongest oaths are straw
To the fire i' the blood. Be more abstemious,
Or else, good night your vow!
FERDINAND.   I warrant you, sir,
The white cold virgin snow upon my heart   55
Abates the ardor of my liver.°
PROSPERO.   Well.
Now come, my Ariel! Bring a corollary°
Rather than want a spirit. Appear, and pertly!
No tongue! All eyes! Be silent.   [*Soft music.*]

[*Enter* IRIS.°]

---

26. **suggestion:** temptation.   27. **worser genius can:** bad angel can make.   30. **or:** either.
31. **Phoebus' steeds are foundered, or Night kept chained below:** i.e., night will seem never to come on his wedding day. (Phoebus is the mythological god whose horses carry the sun across the sky each day.)   41. **vanity:** display.   47. **mop:** antic.   50. **conceive:** understand.   51. **dalliance:** fondling.   56. **liver:** the liver was regarded as the source of sexual passion.   57. **corollary:** extra one.   **s.d. Iris:** messenger of the gods, personified as the rainbow.

IRIS. Ceres,° most bounteous lady, thy rich leas 60
      Of wheat, rye, barley, vetches, oats, and pease;
      Thy turfy mountains, where live nibbling sheep,
      And flat meads thatched with stover,° them to keep;
      Thy banks with pioned and twilled brims,°
      Which spongy April at thy hest betrims 65
      To make cold nymphs chaste crowns; and thy broom° groves,
      Whose shadow the dismissed bachelor loves,
      Being lasslorn; thy pole-clipped vineyard;
      And thy sea marge, sterile and rocky-hard,
      Where thou thyself dost air—the Queen o' the Sky,° 70
      Whose watery arch° and messenger am I,
      Bids thee leave these, and with her sovereign grace,
      Here on this grassplot, in this very place,
      To come and sport.—Her peacocks fly amain.°
      Approach, rich Ceres, her to entertain. 75

[Enter CERES.]

CERES. Hail, many-colored messenger, that ne'er
      Dost disobey the wife of Jupiter;
      Who, with thy saffron wings, upon my flowers
      Diffusest honey drops, refreshing showers,
      And with each end of thy blue bow dost crown 80
      My bosky° acres and my unshrubbed down,°
      Rich scarf to my proud earth.—Why hath thy queen
      Summoned me hither, to this short-grassed green?
IRIS. A contract of true love to celebrate,
      And some donation freely to estate° 85
      On the blest lovers.
CERES.   Tell me, heavenly bow,
      If Venus or her son, as thou dost know,
      Do now attend the queen? Since they did plot
      The means that dusky Dis° my daughter got,
      Her and her blind boy's° scandaled company 90
      I have forsworn.
IRIS.   Of her society
      Be not afraid. I met Her Deity
      Cutting the clouds towards Paphos, and her son
      Dove-drawn with her. Here thought they to have done
      Some wanton charm upon this man and maid, 95
      Whose vows are, that no bedright shall be paid
      Till Hymen's torch be lighted. But in vain,
      Mars's hot minion° is returned again.

---

60. **Ceres:** goddess of corn and plenty. 63. **stover:** grass. 64. **pioned and twilled brims:** dug and heaped up with high banks, probably. 66. **broom:** a shrub with yellow flowers. 70. **Queen o' the Sky:** the goddess Juno, wife of Jupiter. 71. **watery arch:** rainbow. 74. **amain:** swiftly. 81. **bosky:** wooded. **down:** rolling, open country. 85. **estate:** bestow. 89. **dusky Dis:** dark Pluto, god of Hades. Venus, goddess of love, had her son Cupid fire an arrow into Pluto's heart. Sick with love, he seized Ceres' daughter Proserpine and took her to live with him as Queen of Hades. 90. **blind boy's:** Cupid's. 98. **Mars's hot minion:** i.e., Venus, beloved of Mars.

Her waspish-headed° son has broke his arrows,
Swears he will shoot no more, but play with sparrows,   100
And be a boy right out.

CERES.   High'st queen of state,
Great Juno, comes. I know her by her gait.

[*Enter* JUNO.]

JUNO. How does my bounteous sister? Go with me
To bless this twain, that they may prosperous be,
And honored in their issue.   105

[*They sing.*]

JUNO. "Honor, riches, marriage blessing,
Long continuance, and increasing,
Hourly joys be still upon you!
Juno sings her blessings on you."

CERES. "Earth's increase, foison plenty,   110
Barns and garners never empty,
Vines with clustering bunches growing,
Plants with goodly burden bowing,
Spring come to you at the farthest
In the very end of harvest!   115
Scarcity and want shall shun you,
Ceres' blessing so is on you."

FERDINAND. This is a most majestic vision, and
Harmonious charmingly. May I be bold
To think these spirits?

PROSPERO.   Spirits which by mine art   120
I have from their confines called to enact
My present fancies.

FERDINAND.   Let me live here ever.
So rare a wondered father and a wise
Makes this place Paradise.

[JUNO *and* CERES *whisper, and send* IRIS *on employment.*]

PROSPERO.   Sweet, now silence!
Juno and Ceres whisper seriously,   125
There's something else to do. Hush, and be mute,
Or else our spell is marred.

IRIS. You nymphs, called Naiads, of the windring° brooks,
With your sedged crowns and ever-harmless looks,
Leave your crisp channels, and on this green land   130
Answer your summons. Juno does command.
Come, temperate nymphs, and help to celebrate
A contract of true love. Be not too late.

[*Enter certain* NYMPHS.]

You sunburned sicklemen, of August weary,
Come hither from the furrow, and be merry.   135

---

99. **waspish-headed:** quick-tempered.   128. **windring:** winding.

Make holiday, your rye-straw hats put on,
And these fresh nymphs encounter every one
In country footing.

[*Enter certain* REAPERS, *properly habited.° They join with the* NYMPHS *in a graceful dance, toward the end whereof* PROSPERO *starts suddenly and speaks. After which, to a strange, hollow, and confused noise, they heavily° vanish.*]

PROSPERO.   [*Aside*]   I had forgot that foul conspiracy
    Of the beast Caliban and his confederates   140
    Against my life. The minute of their plot
    Is almost come. [*To the* SPIRITS] Well done! Avoid,° no more!
FERDINAND. This is strange. Your father's in some passion
    That works him strongly.
MIRANDA.   Never till this day
    Saw I him touched with anger so distempered.   145
PROSPERO. You do look, my son, in a movèd sort,
    As if you were dismayed. Be cheerful, sir.
    Our revels now are ended. These our actors,
    As I foretold you, were all spirits, and
    Are melted into air, into thin air.   150
    And, like the baseless fabric of this vision,
    The cloud-capped towers, the gorgeous palaces,
    The solemn temples, the great globe itself—
    Yea, all which it inherit—shall dissolve
    And, like this insubstantial pageant faded,   155
    Leave not a rack° behind. We are such stuff
    As dreams are made on, and our little life
    Is rounded with a sleep. Sir, I am vexed.
    Bear with my weakness, my old brain is troubled.
    Be not disturbed with my infirmity.   160
    If you be pleased, retire into my cell,
    And there repose. A turn or two I'll walk,
    To still my beating mind.
FERDINAND and MIRANDA.   We wish your peace.   [*Exeunt.*]
PROSPERO. Come with a thought. I thank thee, Ariel. Come.

[*Enter* ARIEL.]

ARIEL. Thy thoughts I cleave to. What's thy pleasure?
PROSPERO.   Spirit,   165
    We must prepare to meet with Caliban.
ARIEL. Aye, my commander. When I presented Ceres,
    I thought to have told thee of it, but I feared
    Lest I might anger thee.
PROSPERO. Say again, where didst thou leave these varlets?   170
ARIEL. I told you, sir, they were red-hot with drinking,
    So full of valor that they smote the air
    For breathing in their faces, beat the ground
    For kissing of their feet, yet always bending

    s.d. *habited*: costumed.   ***heavily*:** sorrowfully.   **142. Avoid:** Be gone.   **156. rack:** cloud.

Toward their project. Then I beat my tabor. 175
At which, like unbacked° colts, they pricked their ears,
Advanced their eyelids, lifted up their noses
As they smelt music. So I charmed their ears,
That, calflike, they my lowing followed through
Toothed briers, sharp furzes, pricking goss,° and thorns 180
Which entered their frail shins. At last I left them
I' the filthy-mantled pool beyond your cell,
There dancing up to the chins, that the foul lake
O'erstunk their feet.
PROSPERO.   This was well done, my bird.
Thy shape invisible retain thou still. 185
The trumpery° in my house, go bring it hither,
For stale° to catch these thieves.
ARIEL.   I go, I go.   [*Exit.*]
PROSPERO. A devil, a born devil, on whose nature
Nurture° can never stick, on whom my pains,
Humanely taken, all, all lost, quite lost. 190
And as with age his body uglier grows,
So his mind cankers.° I will plague them all,
Even to roaring.

[*Reenter* ARIEL, *loaden with glistering apparel, etc.*]

Come, hang them on this line.°

[PROSPERO *and* ARIEL *remain, invisible. Enter* CALIBAN, STEPHANO, *and*
TRINCULO, *all wet.*]

CALIBAN. Pray you, tread softly, that the blind mole may not
Hear a footfall. We now are near his cell. 195
STEPHANO. Monster, your fairy, which you say is a harmless fairy, has done
little better than played the jack° with us.
TRINCULO. Monster, I do smell all horse piss, at which my nose is in great
indignation.
STEPHANO. So is mine. Do you hear, monster? If I should take a dis- 200
pleasure against you, look you—
TRINCULO. Thou wert but a lost monster.
CALIBAN. Good my lord, give me thy favor still.
Be patient, for the prize I'll bring thee to
Shall hoodwink this mischance.° Therefore speak softly. 205
All's hushed as midnight yet.
TRINCULO. Aye, but to lose our bottles in the pool—
STEPHANO. There is not only disgrace and dishonor in that, monster, but
an infinite loss.
TRINCULO. That's more to me than my wetting. Yet this is your harm- 210
less fairy, monster.
STEPHANO. I will fetch off° my bottle, though I be o'er ears° for my labor.

176. **unbacked:** never ridden. 180. **goss:** gorse. 186. **trumpery:** trifles that these fools
would consider valuables. 187. **stale:** decoy. 189. **Nurture:** education, refinement.
192. **cankers:** grows malignant. 193. **line:** linden tree. 197. **jack:** knave. 205. **hoodwink
this mischance:** i.e., make us forget this accident. 212. **fetch off:** recover. **o'er ears:** i.e., in
that pond.

CALIBAN. Prithee, my king, be quiet. See'st thou here,
    This is the mouth o' the cell. No noise, and enter.
    Do that good mischief which may make this island   215
    Thine own forever, and I, thy Caliban,
    For aye thy footlicker.
STEPHANO. Give me thy hand. I do begin to have bloody thoughts.
TRINCULO. O King Stephano! O peer! O worthy Stephano! Look what a
    wardrobe here is for thee!   220
CALIBAN. Let it alone, thou fool, it is but trash.
TRINCULO. Oh ho, monster! We know what belongs to a frippery.° O King
    Stephano!
STEPHANO. Put off that gown, Trinculo. By this hand, I'll have that gown.
TRINCULO. Thy Grace shall have it.   225
CALIBAN. The dropsy drown this fool! What do you mean
    To dote thus on such luggage? Let 's alone,
    And do the murder first. If he awake
    From toe to crown he'll fill our skins with pinches,
    Make us strange stuff.   230
STEPHANO. Be you quiet, monster. Mistress line, is not this my jerkin? Now
    is the jerkin under the line. Now, jerkin, you are like to lose your
    hair and prove a bald jerkin.°
TRINCULO. Do, do. We steal by line and level, an 't like your Grace.
STEPHANO. I thank thee for that jest—here's a garment for 't. Wit shall   235
    not go unrewarded while I am king of this country. "Steal by line
    and level" is an excellent pass of pate°—there's another garment
    for 't.
TRINCULO. Monster, come, put some lime° upon your fingers, and away
    with the rest.   240
CALIBAN. I will have none on 't. We shall lose our time,
    And all be turned to barnacles, or to apes
    With foreheads villainous low.
STEPHANO. Monster, lay to your fingers. Help to bear this away where my
    hogshead of wine is, or I'll turn you out of my kingdom. Go to,   245
    carry this.
TRINCULO. And this.
STEPHANO. Aye, and this.

[*A noise of hunters heard. Enter divers* SPIRITS, *in shapes of dogs and
    hounds, hunting them about, with* PROSPERO *and* ARIEL *setting them on.*]

PROSPERO. Hey, Mountain, hey!
ARIEL. Silver! There it goes, Silver!   250
PROSPERO. Fury, Fury! There, Tyrant, there! Hark, hark!
               [CALIBAN, STEPHANO, *and* TRINCULO *are driven out.*]
    Go charge my goblins that they grind their joints
    With dry convulsions. Shorten up their sinews

---

222. **frippery:** old-clothes shop (conversely, they know good stuff when they see it).
233. This speech and the next one contain elaborate Elizabethan jokes that have mystified
editors. Stephano is making a pun in saying that the jerkin is "under the line," since "under
the line" also means south of the equator. There tropical diseases caused voyagers' hair to fall
out. 237. **pass of pate:** show of wit. 239. **lime:** birdlime, to make them sticky, for Caliban
keeps dropping the clothes in disgust.

With agèd cramps,° and more pinch-spotted make them
Then pard° or cat-o'-mountain.°
ARIEL.   Hark, they roar!   255
PROSPERO. Let them be hunted soundly. At this hour
Lie at my mercy all mine enemies.
Shortly shall all my labors end, and thou
Shalt have the air at freedom. For a little
Follow, and do me service.   [*Exeunt.*]   260

ACT V

SCENE I. *Before the cell of* PROSPERO.

[*Enter* PROSPERO *in his magic robes, and* ARIEL.]

PROSPERO. Now does my project gather to a head.
My charms crack° not, my spirits obey, and Time
Goes upright with his carriage.° How's the day?
ARIEL. On the sixth hour, at which time, my lord,
You said our work should cease.
PROSPERO.   I did say so   5
When first I raised the tempest. Say, my spirit,
How fares the king and 's followers?
ARIEL.   Confined together
In the same fashion as you gave in charge,
Just as you left them—all prisoners, sir,
In the line grove which weather-fends° your cell.   10
They cannot budge till your release. The king,
His brother, and yours abide all three distracted,
And the remainder mourning over them,
Brimful of sorrow and dismay. But chiefly
Him that you termed, sir, "The good old lord, Gonzalo."   15
His tears run down his beard like winter's drops
From eaves of reeds. Your charm so strongly works 'em
That if you now beheld them, your affections
Would become tender.
PROSPERO.   Dost thou think so, spirit?
ARIEL. Mine would, sir, were I human.
PROSPERO.   And mine shall.   20
Hast thou, which art but air, a touch, a feeling
Of their afflictions, and shall not myself,
One of their kind, that relish all as sharply,
Passion° as they, be kindlier moved than thou art?
Though with their high wrongs I am struck to the quick,   25
Yet with my nobler reason 'gainst my fury

---

254. **agèd cramps:** pains of old age.   255. **pard:** leopard.   **cat-o'-mountain:** wildcat.
2. **crack:** fail.   3. **Goes upright with his carriage:** stands upright under his burden (i.e., moves quickly).   10. **weather-fends:** protects from the weather.   24. **Passion:** feel through the emotions.

Do I take part. The rarer action is
In virtue than in vengeance. They being penitent,
The sole drift of my purpose doth extend
Not a frown further. Go release them, Ariel.   30
My charms I'll break, their senses I'll restore,
And they shall be themselves.

ARIEL.   I'll fetch them, sir.   [*Exit.*]

PROSPERO. Ye elves of hills, brooks, standing lakes, and groves,
And ye that on the sands with printless foot
Do chase the ebbing Neptune and do fly him   35
When he comes back; you demipuppets° that
By moonshine do the green sour ringlets° make,
Whereof the ewe not bites; and you whose pastime
Is to make midnight mushrooms° that rejoice
To hear the solemn curfew,° by whose aid—   40
Weak masters though ye be—I have bedimmed
The noontide sun, called forth the mutinous winds,
And 'twixt the green sea and the azured vault
Set roaring war. To the dread rattling thunder
Have I given fire, and rifted° Jove's stout oak   45
With his own bolt. The strong-based promontory
Have I made shake, and by the spurs° plucked up
The pine and cedar. Graves at my command
Have waked their sleepers, oped, and let 'em forth
By my so potent art. But this rough magic   50
I here abjure, and when I have required
Some heavenly music—which even now I do—
To work mine end upon their senses, that
This airy charm is for, I'll break my staff,
Bury it certain fathoms in the earth,   55
And deeper than did ever plummet sound
I'll drown my book.   [*Solemn music.*]

[*Reenter* ARIEL *before; then* ALONSO, *with a frantic gesture, attended by*
GONZALO; SEBASTIAN *and* ANTONIO *in like manner, attended by* ADRIAN
and FRANCISCO. *They all enter the circle which* PROSPERO *had made, and
there stand charmed, which* PROSPERO *observing, speaks:*]

A solemn air, and the best comforter
To an unsettled fancy, cure thy brains,
Now useless, boiled within thy skull! There stand,   60
For you are spell-stopped.
Holy Gonzalo, honorable man,
Mine eyes, even sociable to the show of thine,°
Fall fellowly drops. The charm dissolves apace,°
And as the morning steals upon the night,   65
Melting the darkness, so their rising senses

36. **demipuppets:** tiny creatures.   37. **green sour ringlets:** circles of dark green, bitter grass,
supposedly made by dancing fairies and avoided by sheep.   39. **midnight mushrooms:** Mushrooms sprout in one night and were thought to be grown by fairies.   40. **curfew:** rung at 9 P.M.
After people are indoors, fairies are free to do their work.   45. **rifted:** split.   47. **spurs:** roots.
63. **sociable to the show of thine:** in sympathy with your tears.   64. **apace:** quickly.

Begin to chase the ignorant fumes that mantle
Their clearer reason. O good Gonzalo,
My true preserver, and a loyal sir
To him thou follow'st! I will pay thy graces   70
Home° both in word and deed. Most cruelly
Didst thou, Alonso, use me and my daughter.
Thy brother was a furtherer in the act.
Thou art pinched for 't now, Sebastian. Flesh and blood,
You, brother mine, that entertained ambition,   75
Expelled remorse and nature, who with Sebastian—
Whose inward pinches therefore are most strong—
Would here have killed your king, I do forgive thee,
Unnatural though thou art. Their understanding
Begins to swell, and the approaching tide   80
Will shortly fill the reasonable shore°
That now lies foul and muddy. Not one of them
That yet looks on me, or would know me. Ariel,
Fetch me the hat and rapier in my cell.
I will discase° me, and myself present   85
As I was sometime Milan.° Quickly, spirit.
Thou shalt ere long be free.

ARIEL. [*Sings and helps to attire him.*]
 "Where the bee sucks, there suck I.
  In a cowslip's bell I lie,
  There I couch when owls do cry.   90
  On the bat's back I do fly
  After summer merrily.
 Merrily, merrily shall I live now
 Under the blossom that hangs on the bough."

PROSPERO. Why, that's my dainty Ariel! I shall miss thee,   95
 But yet thou shalt have freedom. So, so, so.
 To the king's ship, invisible as thou art.
 There shalt thou find the mariners asleep
 Under the hatches. The master and the boatswain
 Being awake, enforce them to this place,   100
 And presently, I prithee.

ARIEL. I drink the air before me, and return
 Or ere your pulse twice beat.   [*Exit.*]

GONZALO. All torment, trouble, wonder, and amazement
 Inhabits here. Some heavenly power guide us   105
 Out of this fearful country!

PROSPERO.   Behold, Sir King,
 The wrongèd Duke of Milan, Prospero.
 For more assurance that a living prince
 Does now speak to thee, I embrace thy body,
 And to thee and thy company I bid   110
 A hearty welcome.

---

71. **pay thy graces home:** repay you fully for your virtuous service. 81. **reasonable shore:** shore of reason (i.e., sanity is returning). 85. **discase:** take off the magic robe. 86. **sometime Milan:** formerly Duke of Milan.

ALONSO. Whether thou be'st he or no,
Or some enchanted trifle to abuse me,
As late I have been, I not know. Thy pulse
Beats, as of flesh and blood, and since I saw thee,
The affliction of my mind amends, with which,   115
I fear, a madness held me. This must crave—
An if this be at all°—a most strange story.
Thy dukedom I resign, and do entreat
Thou pardon me my wrongs.—But how should Prospero
Be living and be here?
PROSPERO. First, noble friend,   120
Let me embrace thine age, whose honor cannot
Be measured or confined.
GONZALO. Whether this be
Or be not, I'll not swear.
PROSPERO. You do yet taste
Some subtilties o' the isle, that will not let you
Believe things certain. Welcome, my friends all!   125
[Aside to SEBASTIAN and ANTONIO] But you, my brace of lords, were
    I so minded,
I here could pluck His Highness' frown upon you,
And justify you traitors. At this time
I will tell no tales.
SEBASTIAN. [Aside] The Devil speaks in him.
PROSPERO. No.
For you, most wicked sir, whom to call brother   130
Would even infect my mouth, I do forgive
Thy rankest fault—all of them—and require
My dukedom of thee, which perforce I know
Thou must restore.
ALONSO. If thou be'st Prospero,
Give us particulars of thy preservation—   135
How thou hast met us here, who three hours since
Were wrecked upon this shore, where I have lost—
How sharp the point of this remembrance is!—
My dear son Ferdinand.
PROSPERO. I am woe° for't, sir.
ALONSO. Irreparable is the loss, and patience   140
Says it is past her cure.
PROSPERO. I rather think
You have not sought her help of whose soft grace
For the like loss I have her sovereign aid,
And rest myself content.
ALONSO. You the like loss!
PROSPERO. As great to me as late, and, supportable   145
To make the dear loss, have I means much weaker
Than you may call to comfort you, for I
Have lost my daughter.

117. **An if this be at all:** if this be real.   139. **woe:** sorry.

ALONSO.   A daughter?
     O Heavens, that they were living both in Naples,
     The king and queen there! That they were, I wish   150
     Myself were mudded in that oozy bed
     Where my son lies. When did you lose your daughter?
PROSPERO. In this last tempest. I perceive these lords
     At this encounter do so much admire°
     That they devour their reason, and scarce think   155
     Their eyes do offices of truth,° their words
     Are natural breath. But howsoe'er you have
     Been jostled from your senses, know for certain
     That I am Prospero, and that very Duke
     Which was thrust forth of Milan, who most strangely   160
     Upon this shore where you were wrecked was landed,
     To be the lord on 't. No more yet of this,
     For 'tis a chronicle of day by day,
     Not a relation for a breakfast, nor
     Befitting this first meeting. Welcome, sir.   165
     This cell's my court. Here have I few attendants,
     And subjects none abroad. Pray you look in.
     My dukedom since you have given me again,
     I will requite° you with as good a thing,
     At least bring forth a wonder to content ye   170
     As much as me my dukedom.

[Here PROSPERO discovers° FERDINAND and MIRANDA playing at chess.]

MIRANDA. Sweet lord, you play me false.
FERDINAND.   No, my dear'st love,
     I would not for the world.
MIRANDA. Yes, for a score of kingdoms you should wrangle,
     And I would call it fair play.
ALONSO.   If this prove   175
     A vision of the island, one dear son
     Shall I twice lose.
SEBASTIAN.   A most high miracle!
FERDINAND. Though the seas threaten, they are merciful.
     I have cursed them without cause.   [Kneels.]
ALONSO.   Now all the blessings
     Of a glad father compass thee about!   180
     Arise, and say how thou camest here.
MIRANDA.   Oh, wonder!
     How many goodly creatures are there here!
     How beauteous mankind is! Oh, brave new world,
     That has such people in 't!
PROSPERO.   'Tis new to thee.
ALONSO. What is this maid with whom thou wast at play?   185
     Your eld'st° acquaintance cannot be three hours.

---

154. **admire:** wonder.   156. **do offices of truth:** i.e., see truly.   169. **requite:** repay.
s.d. discovers: pulls back a curtain to reveal them to the audience.   186. **eld'st:** longest.

Is she the goddess that hath severed us,
And brought us thus together?

FERDINAND.   Sir, she is mortal,
But by immortal providence she's mine.
I chose her when I could not ask my father   190
For his advice, nor thought I had one. She
Is daughter to this famous Duke of Milan,
Of whom so often I have heard renown
But never saw before, of whom I have
Received a second life, and second father   195
This lady makes him to me.

ALONSO.   I am hers.
But oh, how oddly will it sound that I
Must ask my child° forgiveness!

PROSPERO.   There, sir, stop.
Let us not burden our remembrances with
A heaviness that's gone.

GONZALO.   I have inly wept,   200
Or should have spoke ere this. Look down, you gods,
And on this couple drop a blessèd crown!
For it is you that have chalked forth the way
Which brought us hither.

ALONSO.   I say Amen, Gonzalo!

GONZALO. Was Milan thrust from Milan, that his issue   205
Should become kings of Naples? Oh, rejoice
Beyond a common joy! And set it down
With gold on lasting pillars. In one voyage
Did Claribel her husband find at Tunis
And Ferdinand, her brother, found a wife   210
Where he himself was lost, Prospero his dukedom
In a poor isle, and all of us ourselves
When no man was his own.

ALONSO. [*To* FERDINAND *and* MIRANDA] Give me your hands.
Let grief and sorrow still° embrace his heart
That doth not wish you joy!

GONZALO.   Be it so! Amen!   215

[*Reenter* ARIEL, *with the* MASTER *and* BOATSWAIN *amazedly following.*]

Oh, look, sir, look, sir! Here is more of us.
I prophesied if a gallows were on land,
This fellow could not drown. Now, blasphemy,°
That swear'st grace o'erboard,° not an oath on shore?
Hast thou no mouth by land? What is the news?   220

BOATSWAIN. The best news is that we have safely found
Our king and company. The next, our ship—
Which, but three glasses since, we gave out split—

---

198. **my child:** i.e., Miranda, his new daughter-in-law.   214. **still:** forever.   218. **blas-phemy:** Gonzalo applies the word to the boatswain as a name.   219. **swear'st grace o'erboard:** by your swearing you drive away heavenly protection from the ship.

Is tight and yare and bravely rigged as when
We first put out to sea.
ARIEL.   [*Aside to* PROSPERO] Sir, all this service   225
    Have I done since I went.
PROSPERO.   [*Aside to* ARIEL] My tricksy spirit!
ALONSO. These are not natural events, they strengthen
    From strange to stranger. Say, how came you hither?
BOATSWAIN. If I did think, sir, I were well awake,
    I'd strive to tell you. We were dead of sleep,   230
    And—how we know not—all clapped under hatches,
    Where, but even now, with strange and several noises
    Of roaring, shrieking, howling, jingling chains,
    And more diversity of sounds, all horrible,
    We were awaked, straightway at liberty.   235
    Where we, in all her trim, freshly beheld
    Our royal, good, and gallant ship, our master
    Capering to eye her.—On a trice, so please you,
    Even in a dream, were we divided from them,
    And were brought moping hither.
ARIEL.   [*Aside to* PROSPERO] Was 't well done?   240
PROSPERO. [*Aside to* ARIEL] Bravely, my diligence. Thou shalt be free.
ALONSO. This is as strange a maze as e'er men trod,
    And there is in this business more than nature
    Was ever conduct of.° Some oracle
    Must rectify° our knowledge.
PROSPERO.   Sir, my liege,   245
    Do not infest your mind with beating on
    The strangeness of this business. At picked leisure
    Which shall be shortly, single I'll resolve° you,
    Which to you shall seem probable, of every
    These happened accidents. Till when, be cheerful,   250
    And think of each thing well. [*Aside to* ARIEL] Come hither, spirit.
    Set Caliban and his companions free,
    Untie the spell. [*Exit* ARIEL.] How fares my gracious sir?
    There are yet missing of your company
    Some few odd lads that you remember not.   255

[*Reenter* ARIEL, *driving in* CALIBAN, STEPHANO, *and* TRINCULO, *in their
    stolen apparel.*]

STEPHANO. Every man shift for all the rest, and let no man take care for him-
    self, for all is but fortune.—Coragio,° bully-monster, coragio!
TRINCULO. If these be true spies which I wear in my head, here's a goodly
    sight.
CALIBAN. Oh, Setebos, these be brave spirits indeed!   260
    How fine my master is! I am afraid
    He will chastise me.

---

244. **was ever conduct of:** ever brought about.   245. **rectify:** set straight (by filling out and
explaining).   248. **resolve:** inform.   257. **Coragio:** courage.

SEBASTIAN. Ha, ha!
What things are these, my lord Antonio?
Will money buy 'em?
ANTONIO. Very like. One of them
Is a plain fish, and no doubt marketable. 265
PROSPERO. Mark but the badges° of these men, my lords,
Then say if they be true. This misshapen knave,
His mother was a witch, and one so strong
That could control the moon, make flows and ebbs,
And deal in her command, without her power.° 270
These three have robbed me, and this demidevil—
For he's a bastard one—had plotted with them
To take my life. Two of these fellows you
Must know and own, this thing of darkness I
Acknowledge mine.
CALIBAN. I shall be pinched to death. 275
ALONSO. Is not this Stephano, my drunken butler?
SEBASTIAN. He is drunk now. Where had he wine?
ALONSO. And Trinculo is reeling ripe. Where should they
Find this grand liquor that hath gilded 'em?—
How camest thou in this pickle? 280
TRINCULO. I have been in such a pickle since I saw you last that I fear me
will never out of my bones. I shall not fear flyblowing.°
SEBASTIAN. Why, how now, Stephano!
STEPHANO. Oh, touch me not.—I am not Stephano, but a cramp.
PROSPERO. You'd be king o' the isle, sirrah? 285
STEPHANO. I should have been a sore one, then.
ALONSO. This is a strange thing as e'er I looked on. [*Pointing to* CALIBAN.]
PROSPERO. He is as disproportioned in his manners
As in his shape. Go, sirrah, to my cell.
Take with you your companions. As you look 290
To have my pardon, trim° it handsomely.
CALIBAN. Aye, that I will, and I'll be wise hereafter,
And seek for grace. What a thrice-double ass
Was I to take this drunkard for a god
And worship this dull fool!
PROSPERO. Go to, away! 295
ALONSO. Hence, and bestow your luggage where you found it.
SEBASTIAN. Or stole it, rather.

[*Exeunt* CALIBAN, STEPHANO, *and* TRINCULO.]
PROSPERO. Sir, I invite your Highness and your train
To my poor cell, where you shall take your rest
For this one night. Which, part of it, I'll waste 300
With such discourse as I not doubt shall make it
Go quick away—the story of my life,
And the particular accidents° gone by

266. **badges:** emblems of the master worn by the servants. 270. **deal in her command, without her power:** perform the moon's function (control tides) without the moon's power. 282. **not fear flyblowing:** i.e., so well pickled that he cannot be spoiled by maggots. 291. **trim:** tidy. 303. **accidents:** events.

Since I came to this isle. And in the morn
I'll bring you to your ship, and so to Naples,   305
Where I have hope to see the nuptial
Of these our dear belovèd solemnized,
And thence retire me to my Milan, where
Every third thought shall be my grave.
ALONSO.   I long
To hear the story of your life, which must   310
Take the ear strangely.
PROSPERO.   I'll deliver all,
And promise you calm seas, auspicious gales,
And sail so expeditious that shall catch
Your royal fleet far off. [*Aside to* ARIEL] My Ariel, chick,
That is thy charge. Then to the elements   315
Be free, and fare thou well! Please you, draw near.   [*Exeunt.*]

Epilogue

SPOKEN BY PROSPERO

Now my charms are all o'erthrown,
And what strength I have's mine own,
Which is most faint. Now, 'tis true,
I must be here confined by you,
Or sent to Naples. Let me not,   5
Since I have my dukedom got,
And pardoned the deceiver, dwell
In this bare island by your spell,
But release me from my bands
With the help of your good hands.°   10
Gentle breath° of yours my sails
Must fill, or else my project fails,
Which was to please. Now I want°
Spirits to enforce, art to enchant,
And my ending is despair   15
Unless I be relieved by prayer
Which pierces so that it assaults
Mercy itself, and frees all faults.
As you from crimes would pardoned be,
Let your indulgence set me free.   20

10. **good hands:** applause.   11. **breath:** comments.   13. **want:** lack.

The Tempest and Shakespeare's
Vision of the World

In *The Tempest,* critics have seen Shakespeare acting out his own career as a playwright and saying farewell to it. The idea is an attractive one. Prospero-Shakespeare, the magician-artist, manipulates his characters through the mazes of terror and joy created by life and their own natures. Finally, he brings them through to reconciliation and bids farewell to his special powers, which could not last forever, in a mixed spirit of regret and satisfaction:

> Our revels now are ended. These our actors,
> As I foretold you, were all spirits, and
> Are melted into the air, into thin air.
> And, like the baseless fabric of this vision,
> The cloud-capped towers, the gorgeous palaces,
> The solemn temples, the great globe itself—
> Yea, all which it inherit—shall dissolve
> And, like this insubstantial pageant faded,
> Leave not a rack behind. We are such stuff
> As dreams are made on, and our little life
> Is rounded with a sleep.

The Tempest is the last of Shakespeare's own plays (he later collaborated on a few plays) and the words are too appropriate a valedictory to be denied. Nevertheless, this idea that Prospero represents Shakespeare is at most only one element—and probably the most incidental one—in a play of such richness that all attempts to interpret it allegorically are more or less misleading.

Instead, we will see the play most fully and clearly if we take it as presenting a complex situation in a fantastic world. In the process, it might reveal or hint at Shakespeare's most profound thoughts about our own world and how we live in it— and how we could live in it if we made it and ourselves better than we are.

The Tempest is set on an island that is obviously off-course from the route between Naples and Tunis. At the same time, however, Shakespeare seemed to model this island after the remote islands of the Americas that were being discovered by voyagers of the time. The island is its own world; Prospero's enchantment has imposed its rule on this island and on the island creatures. By his magic, Prospero brings into this enchanted world a group of people from the world of Naples and Milan, which had formerly been his domain. His purpose is not merely to restore this corrupt world to its former state (Prospero admits that he had been less than perfect as a ruler of Milan) but to bring about the condition of harmony that his magic has achieved on the island. By bitter experience Prospero has gained knowledge of the world; by study and contemplation he has gained the wisdom to control it. The island has benefited, but he has yet to use his power in the real world of men.

Prospero has to contend with greed and violence and lust. These vices are epitomized in the monstrous figure of Caliban, the "natural" man unimproved by knowledge and discipline; they are embodied more realistically in Alonso and Antonio and Sebastian. He must also contend with the naiveté of Gonzalo and Ferdinand, since innocence is not sturdy enough to prevail in a corrupt world. Tests and ordeals serve to bring both the corrupt and the naive into the light. But there are those who will remain forever in the dark, who, in a harmonious world, must be subjected to rigid control. Caliban is the most notable example, but controls must also be placed on Antonio, who never admits the error of his ways, but recognizes only his failure this time to get what he wanted. Finally we behold Prospero's vision of a restored world, which is presumably Shakespeare's own, when Prospero sets all to rights.

Above all, Prospero brings together Ferdinand and Miranda. Their meeting is the principal purpose of the magic shipwreck at the beginning of the play; their declaration of love is the pivotal scene; and Prospero's revelation of the pair to the rest of the characters is the climactic point of the play. Love; the continuity of life; a wise, instructed innocence; youth and beauty—these are the constituents of the world's harmony.

To understand Shakespeare's vision of harmony and understand its relevance to our own experience, we must recognize that the assumptions he makes are not necessarily ours, or even easy for us to accept provisionally. While the play lasts, however, we must accept the world as Shakespeare and other men of his time saw it. For example, we must allow that men are created unequal: Shakespeare sees a difference between Caliban and Miranda that Prospero's training cannot touch; indeed, Prospero has learned that Caliban can only be controlled, not persuaded or educated, whereas Miranda's nature, as well as her "nurture," shows in her purity and intelligence and beauty. Accordingly, Shakespeare's vision of harmony is based upon a hierarchy that is fundamental to the views of his time. The dukedom is Prospero's by absolute right, not only in law and justice. There is an absolute distinction between ruler and ruled, between an aristocratic class whose intellectual and moral virtues are high, and a servant class whose virtues, at best, are passive. In this hierarchy, men are higher than beasts; fathers are the rulers of their children; the mind is superior to the body; and a providence or destiny rules over all. To apply modern ideas of natural equality and individual worth here would be to misunderstand why Prospero treats Caliban more harshly and Stephano more contemptuously than he does Antonio or Alonso.

If we enter imaginatively into the world of *The Tempest* and see it just as Shakespeare shows it to us, we do not need to strain for meanings through allegory in order to find a rich texture of profound and subtle insights. As readers, however, we are presented with only one element of the play: the words upon the page. The whole play is words spoken on a stage, accompanied by gesture and movement, expression of face and voice, costumes and scenery, lights and sound, music and dance. These elements not only make the whole play more appealing, but they are part of the dramatist's conception of his work, just as much as are the words. Even the audience, with its interrupting laughter and its tensions, is part of the playwright's conception. Consequently, we can get a wrong or limited notion of the play if we forget that it was designed to be presented by actors in front of an audience.

For *The Tempest,* in particular, we must remember that its thought-provoking speeches and situations occur in a context of fantasy, comedy, and spectacle. Stephano and Trinculo wear ridiculous costumes and indulge in slapstick even when bent on murder. The comic drunkenness of the boatswain in the first scene alleviates what could otherwise be a scene of horror. All the resources of the stage are involved in the masque for the betrothal scene and in the masquelike elements that run throughout the play: the flights of Ariel and his songs, the dances of his attendants, the fantastic costuming of all these airy creatures and, in a different mood, of

Caliban as well. While it deals with somber themes of corruption and chastisement and reconciliation, *The Tempest* also speaks of love, and its pervasive mood is lyric and comic.

THE TEMPEST AND THE RENAISSANCE

The Tempest is full of the English Renaissance. Its setting on an "uninhabited island" calls up the excitement associated in the 1500's with discoveries of new lands across remote and dangerous seas. The figure of Caliban reflects contemporary interest in the "savages" which the explorers were telling about. The strange ways of these savages—as reported in accounts that were often highly romanticized—invited critical comparison with European civilization. Some Europeans, like Montaigne, tended to view the New World natives as "noble savages," unspoiled by the false values of civilized society. Shakespeare, however, shows Caliban, the "natural man," as a near-brute who needs the restraints and the ideals that reason and the accumulated wisdom of civilization show to men.

Like the famous Utopia (1516) of Sir Thomas More, *The Tempest* creates in an exotic and untouched land an image of ideal human society. In the play's story greedy men bring ugliness and unhappiness into a world made for man's sustenance and delight, but forces of love and benevolent authority overcome and reform them. This optimistic estimate of man's potentialities is characteristic of the Renaissance, and the inquiry into how the principles of universal order can be used to achieve perfect harmony among men was a concern central to many humanistic philosophers of the Renaissance.

Shakespeare presents these serious ideas in *The Tempest* in the exuberant and colorful manner that we associate with Renaissance "style." The speeches show the soaring lyricism and verbal richness typical of the best Renaissance poetry, and the heroine presents an ideal of beauty and purity such as was imagined by sonneteers from Petrarch on (see pages 491–494). The earthy comedy of Stephano and Trinculo, the pageantry, and the whole atmosphere of gaiety reflect the popular side of Renaissance vitality in Elizabethan London.

FOR STUDY AND DISCUSSION

ACT I

1. How would you describe the mood of the opening scene? What does this scene lead you to expect about the play to come?

2. What attitudes toward the tempest are taken by various characters in the first scene? How do these attitudes contrast with one another?

3. Summarize these situations that occur before the opening of the play: the rebellion in Milan, Prospero's and Miranda's voyage to the island, the life stories of Caliban and of Ariel. What devices does Shakespeare use to explain these earlier situations to the audience?

4. What elements of fantasy are introduced in the first act? How does the fantasy affect the mood of the play?

5. What are the unique conditions of Miranda's upbringing? How do they make her different from ordinary girls? Is Miranda like the heroines of fantasy and fairy-tale literature? Explain.

6. In what different ways does Prospero treat Miranda, Ariel, and Caliban? What does this tell you about Prospero?

7. Compare and contrast Caliban and Ariel. What is the significance and effectiveness of the contrast between them? Visually, how would these two characters contrast?

8. Why is it important for the audience to know that Prospero planned the meeting of Ferdinand and Miranda? What motives does Prospero have for doing so? Why does he then treat Ferdinand badly?

ACT II

1. What does the rescue of Alonso and his company from shipwreck tell about Prospero's intentions?

2. What do you learn about the characters

of Antonio and Sebastian when you see how they treat Gonzalo?

3. Gonzalo discourses on the ideal commonwealth he would like to create. What new theme in the play does this speech bring to your attention? Shakespeare was familiar with Montaigne's essay "Of Cannibals" (see page 523). What passage in the essay is remarkably like this speech of Gonzalo?

4. Why does Prospero egg on Antonio and Sebastian and then frustrate their scheme? Why does Shakespeare introduce this twist into the plot?

5. What makes the scene between Caliban, Trinculo, and Stephano so funny? How is this comic scene relevant to the main action of the play?

ACT III

1. In Scene ii of this act, how does Shakespeare keep the low comedy from losing its comic tone when the characters' thoughts turn to murder and abduction? Compare the handling of this scene with the handling of the tempest in the first act.

2. Clearly Caliban's complaints to Stephano about the tyranny of Prospero are not justified. Why not? On the other hand, in what ways does Shakespeare allow a degree of sympathy for Caliban?

3. In what ways is the third scene of this act parallel to the scene that precedes it? What is the significance of this? How is it dramatically effective?

4. What might be the symbolism of the magic banquet and of Ariel's appearance as a harpy?

ACT IV

1. What is Prospero's argument for chastity in the first scene of this act? How does this idea fit in with the whole idea of harmony in human life?

2. The brief masque, or entertainment, which Ariel and his spirits present not only honored the lovers of the play, Ferdinand and Miranda, but it also honored King James's daughter and her bridegroom, for whom *The Tempest* was presented in February 1613. What is the tone and mood of this brief entertainment?

3. What is the significance and the dramatic effectiveness of breaking off the masque, in the first scene of this act, with a recollection of Caliban's conspiracy? Why is Caliban men-

tioned and not Stephano? Why is this plot mentioned instead of Antonio's?

4. What changes have taken place in Caliban's behavior, in the first scene of this act, as compared with his earlier behavior in the presence of Trinculo and Stephano?

ACT V

1. How does Ariel's song, in the first scene of this act, help to establish his feeling of release and to explain why he felt thwarted even by Prospero's benevolent rule? Why must Prospero, instead of being free like Ariel, resume the duties of his dukedom?

2. What differences in character between Alonso and Antonio are revealed by the way they react to Prospero's revelations in the final act? (Note that Antonio's reactions have to be inferred from his presence in the scene; he has almost no lines to speak.)

3. Prospero shows unusual charity toward those who have wronged him. Why do you think he acts this way? What does his attitude contribute toward the theme of the play?

THE ELIZABETHAN THEATER

The Elizabethan stage was essentially a bare platform projecting out into an enclosed courtyard, under open sky. Important use was made of secondary acting areas "within"— that is, in a curtained area at the rear of the main platform—and "above"—that is, on galleries or on second- and third-story platforms, also at the rear of the main platform. When, for example, Prospero reveals Ferdinand and Miranda to Alonso (Act V, Scene i), he pulls back the curtain of the inner stage, after which they come forward to join the rest of the scene on the main platform. When Ariel watches the shipwrecked party and casts a spell of sleep on some of them (Act II, Scene i), he is standing on the upper stage, wrapped in a cloak to signify his invisibility. Furthermore, at one place in Act III, Scene iii, the stage direction indicates that Prospero appears at yet a third level ("above"), on a gallery otherwise used by the musicians who accompanied the singing and dancing and at times provided incidental music.

This stage was extremely flexible and allowed quick passage from scene to scene, since one group of characters simply left one area as another group entered elsewhere. By the same token, however, it made little provision for realistic stage sets or scenery.

Varied properties took the place of scenery. Servants carrying torches might indicate a nighttime scene, although the torches were carried in broad daylight. Simple furniture— a stool, a table—could be brought onto the main platform to suggest a tavern, and somewhat more elaborate properties—a bedstead, a king's throne, Prospero's cave—could be set up behind the curtains of the inner stage. But at most, even the properties could only suggest settings and be minimally useful.

Though stage sets were not used and though there was no light but daylight, there was much sound and color and spectacle on the stage. Stage machinery permitted a character, such as a ghost, to sink through a trap door below the level of the platform and, like Ariel, to "fly" through the air, though always straight up or straight down. Cannons were shot off, fog was created by smoke, and flashes of gunpowder simulated lightning. There were lavish costumes, a lot of music, and even bags of real blood made murder scenes realistic.

Shakespeare makes a sort of apology for the limitations in realistic stage sets in the prologue to *Henry V*. Since the stage cannot "hold the vasty fields of France" on which the battles of that play are fought, he asks his audience to let the actors

On your imaginary forces work . . .
Think when we talk of horses that you see
    them
Printing their proud hoofs i' the receiving
    earth.

Thus, in the Elizabethan theater it was usually the dialogue itself that had to convey almost all the visual impressions. Today, painted sets and sophisticated lighting techniques can re-create realistically almost any setting at all—a battlefield at dawn, a sunny mountain meadow, the kitchen of a city apartment—but when Shakespeare needed a moonlit night, he had to use poetry to create one, and then he had to rely on his audience to keep their "imaginary forces" actively at work.

1. Keeping in mind the conditions of the Elizabethan stage, examine carefully the opening scene of *The Tempest*. What stage effects would be used to suggest a tempest at sea? How would the actors convey the impression that they were in the midst of a tempest? What specific impressions of a storm do the words themselves suggest?

2. Describe completely the presentation of one scene of the play. Indicate first the kind of stage you have in mind (an Elizabethan stage, a modern proscenium stage, or a modern arena stage) and describe whatever setting, properties, or special effects you would provide for it. Describe in detail the costuming and make-up of the characters. Indicate where each character would enter and leave and describe the important movements and actions he would make onstage.

DRAMATIC STRUCTURE

There are so many ways of putting together a play that perhaps no better generalization can be made about dramatic structure than that all plays are put together in some way (and some contemporary experimental drama —"happenings" and the like—seem to challenge even that one). Shakespeare's plays are difficult to categorize because of the great flexibility with which he created structural patterns to suit his immediate dramatic purpose.

The Tempest was written and presented as nine scenes and an epilogue, which followed one another without a break. Only the departure of one group of characters through one exit and the arrival of another group from elsewhere marked a new scene, and nothing divided the scenes into acts. The act divisions are the additions of the editors of the first folio of 1623, who were essentially imitating printed editions of Roman plays. The original effect of a Shakespearean play was more like that of a modern movie than like that of a modern play, in which the curtain is dropped between scenes and the spectator can leave his seat between acts.

The traditional formula for plot—exposition, inciting action, development, climax, and resolution—is somewhat more applicable to a play of Shakespeare's. But it, too, draws our attention away from the more intricate climaxes and parallels of scenes that comprise the play's real structure. One of the fascinations in seeing different productions of a Shakespearean play results from the fact that each director can, within limits, choose to emphasize the climaxes and parallels that mean something to him.

Consider the structure of *The Tempest* in the following ways:

1. Trace the plot lines that involve the three distinct groups of characters in *The Tempest:* Prospero, Ferdinand, and Miranda; Alonso and his party; Caliban, Trinculo, and Stephano. In what order are the three plots initiated and advanced? What direct connections are there among these plot lines? What parallels? What is the dramatic sequence in the last scene, in which all the plot lines are brought to a climax? (How, for example, would the effect be different if the sailors and Caliban were brought in first instead of last?)

2. Midway in the play, in Act III, Scene i, is the declaration of love between Ferdinand and Miranda. Can this scene be regarded dramatically or thematically as a pivot on which the whole direction of the play turns? If so, has a problem been developed in the first half? Is there a change of direction, toward its solution, in the latter half? What is the effect of having this scene preceded and followed by the principal low-comedy scenes?

3. Where in the sequence of scenes is use made of comedy, of song, of special stage effects, and of episodes of conflict and tension? From this examination, construct the pattern of emotions through which Shakespeare leads his audience. What satisfactions should the audience be made to feel at the end?

4. For what dramatic reasons do you suppose Shakespeare chose to begin the play with the shipwreck, making necessary the long exposition of earlier events in Act I, Scene ii? What significant difference in dramatic impact would be caused if the play had begun with a scene showing Antonio usurping Prospero's dukedom? with Gonzalo providing for the embarkation of Prospero and Miranda? with the arrival of Prospero and Miranda on the island?

FOR COMPOSITION

1. Examine all parts of the play in which one of the secondary characters appears (perhaps Sebastian, Gonzalo, Ariel, Caliban, Trinculo, or Stephano). Write an analysis of the character such as a director might give to an actor who is to play the part. Describe what the character's motives are, what his importance is to the rest of the play, what he should look like, what kind of voice and manner he should have, how he would be costumed. Is there a contemporary actor whom you can visualize in the part?

2. In a brief essay, explain how the love scenes—especially those at the end of Act I and at the beginning of Act III—differ from those of a modern play or movie (a) in the way love is revealed, (b) in the ideals of love that are suggested, and (c) in the attitudes of the lovers toward each other. Tell which, in your view, gives a truer picture of love: the modern work or *The Tempest*. In what ways would each be dramatically effective?

3. If you came upon a pleasant, fertile, untouched island, would you react as Gonzalo does (see Act II, Scene i)? In a brief essay, explain the kind of society you would try to create if you could start afresh and how you would bring it about. In dealing with this topic, take into consideration the ideas of the characters in the play. Are their ideas on how the world should be run still prevalent today? Are any of Gonzalo's ideas common today? Would you adopt any of them?

4. Reread the scenes which present Ariel's songs and dances. Explain whether these musical effects fit into the action of the play or whether they are simply pleasant diversions that could be omitted without damaging the plot. In your essay, compare the use of musical effects in this play with the use of songs and dances in a contemporary musical comedy.

THE AGE OF RATIONALISM

c. 1650 – c. 1800

I N THE SEVENTEENTH AND EIGHTEENTH centuries, the outlines of the modern world began to appear. Science advanced in giant strides, and men began to use it to examine and manipulate the physical world. Sea power and commerce rapidly established worldwide dominance of England, France, and Spain, with the result that European culture has since been the inevitable reference point for the cultures of the Western world. Most political and social systems of modern times are founded on the revolutionary ideas formulated by philosophers of these centuries. Far-reaching intellectual battles raged on, as men, hostile to the hand of religious authority, inquired into new rational and scientific systems of thought that would replace the medieval religious authoritarianism already challenged by the Renaissance.

The age called itself the Age of Enlightenment, and it appeared to be a time of optimism and confidence. Ignorant of the terrors that science would later produce and unaware of the bloody wars that would put a violent end to the period, men of this age were certain that the day would soon come when science and reason would be used to develop the perfect society. No longer were ancient Greece and Rome looked back to as perfect ages. The perfect age was coming.

RATIONALISM

A philosophy called rationalism dominated the age. The basic theory of the rationalists is that men can arrive at truth solely through reason—by rational, logical thinking. In general, the rationalists cherished one widely accepted belief: that the universe and every aspect of man's experience, complex as it might be, is ordered according to a logical plan that can be discovered through observation and reasoning. The massive and influential French *Encyclopédie* was a landmark of rationalism and preached the radical belief that man could improve his lot by replacing faith with reason. Compiled between 1751 and 1772 by a group of French intellectuals, the *Encyclopédie* attempted to popularize and spread the new doctrines of the Enlightenment. The following remarks by Denis Diderot, its principal editor, reflect the rationalists' philosophy.

● Both the real universe and the world of ideas have an infinite number of aspects by which they may be made comprehensible, and the number of possible "systems of human knowledge" is as large as the number of these points of view. The only system that would be free from all arbitrariness is . . . the one that must have existed from all eternity in the mind of God. . . . [Therefore,] let us . . . take hold of those things that are bound up with our human condition, being content to make our way upward from them toward some more general notions. The more elevated the point of view from which we approach our subject, the more territory it will reveal to us, the grander and more instructive will be the prospect we shall survey. It follows that the order must be simple, for there is rarely any grandeur without simplicity; it must be clear and easy to grasp, not a tortuous maze in which one goes astray. . . . —DENIS DIDEROT

This line of reasoning had been earlier developed by the German mathematician and philosopher Gottfried Wilhelm von Leibnitz (1646–1716), who argued that God is a rational being and that the universe he created must therefore be a rational one. A rational universe, says Leibnitz, is one in which everything has a place and a useful purpose. It follows, then, that even evil has its necessary place in God's plan—man would see the purpose of evil if he could but know God's plan fully and rightly.

Not all the rationalists accepted this corollary. The French intellectual and writer Voltaire (1694–1778), in his tale *Candide* (see page 616), lampooned this easy optimism. But Voltaire's contempt for such blind complacency in the face of contradictory evidence is just as typical of rationalism as is the optimists' belief in the world's goodness. Voltaire, a disillusioned optimist himself, underscored his beliefs by intervening in cases in which he saw injustice and tyranny at work, as in the notorious Calas case of the 1760's. A Huguenot merchant, Jean Calas had been tortured and executed for the alleged murder of his son, supposedly because the son had planned to renounce his Protestantism. Voltaire undertook a vigorous and ultimately successful campaign to clear the name of the Calas family,

From *Diderot: Rameau's Nephew and Other Works,* translated by Jacques Barzun and Ralph Bowen. Reprinted by permission of Doubleday & Company, Inc.

An illustration from the industry section of the *Encyclopédie*. The artist gives a tidy picture of an iron forge. One must imagine intense heat, noise, and curses from the men when things did not go as smoothly as depicted here.

restore its position, and expose the bigotry and intolerance of the Catholic-dominated legal system which had brought about the execution of the father.

RELIGIOUS STRIFE

The Calas case was one symptom of a chronic condition of bitter religious rivalry which broke out sporadically in large-scale purges and persecutions. Conflicts caused by different theologies and by different allegiances—to the papacy, to various national churches, to individual consciences—provided grounds for many arguments waged with words and with swords. The Thirty Years' War in Germany (1618–1648) was essentially a struggle between Catholics and Protestants. The notorious Spanish Inquisition, originally directed against Moors and Jews, now turned against Protestants. The French persecution of Protestant Huguenots was revived in 1685 when Louis XIV revoked the Edict of Nantes. This act of toleration had been made earlier by the once-Protestant Henry IV, who converted to Catholicism for political expediency, supposedly with the words "Paris is well worth a Mass." On the other hand, there was persecution of Catholics in England, and the brutal treatment of Catholic Ireland by the troops of Oliver Cromwell is still remembered in the bitterness between the Orange and the Green. Protestants and Catholics alike persecuted the

Anabaptists, a group of fundamentalist sects who rejected all temporal allegiances and were often troublesome as conscientious objectors to taxation and military service.

Conflicts over religious toleration and political liberty culminated in the American and French revolutions. The advances eventually made toward guaranteeing individual freedom and equality before the law are perhaps the most valuable contributions made by this age to later times.

ABSOLUTISM

Most of Europe was dominated during these centuries by strong monarchies. In France, Louis XIV and his great-grandson who succeeded him, Louis XV, spanned most of the seventeenth and eighteenth centuries as "absolute" monarchs. Frederick William I and his son, Frederick II, established Prussian dominance over the fragmented states of Germany and made it a force in the dynastic wars which accompanied this period of strong monarchies. In this period also, Russia was brought into the political and intellectual community of Europe by her Westernizing despot Peter I, a seven-foot giant with immense energy, who proclaimed himself Emperor of All Russia in 1721. Peter's efforts to Westernize Russia's court life and expand Russia's territories were carried on in the subsequent reign of Catherine II, the wife of Peter's incompetent grandson who died mysteriously after only a six months' rule.

PRESSURES FOR POLITICAL CHANGE

It is symptomatic of the attitudes of the monarchs of this age that several of them were self-styled "the Great"—Frederick II of Prussia, Peter I and Catherine II of Russia—and Louis XIV pictured himself as the "Sun King." Yet pressures undermining the absolutism of kings and governments were strong, in the long run stronger than the monarchies themselves. In part, the pressures for change were economic ones. The middle classes, enriched by world trade, wanted more power and less restriction from monarchs whose first allegiance was not to them but to the old hierarchy, dominated by an aristocracy of landowners. The large numbers of the lower classes, long ignored, were gaining strength in the growing, crowded cities, and the poor of both city and farm were becoming increasingly restive with their miserable lot in the midst of prosperity and ostentatious extravagance. These pressures first erupted in the English civil wars that began in 1642. All of Europe was profoundly shaken when, in 1649, an anointed king, Charles I, was beheaded by the victorious forces of a Puritan Parliament. Although the Commonwealth government, headed by Cromwell, ultimately failed and Charles II was peaceably invited by Parliament to reclaim the throne, the power of the English monarchy was sharply diminished. England had made a major step in the direction of constitutional monarchy, the first of the European nations to move toward democracy.

The American Revolution (1775–1783) a century later was in many ways an echo of the English civil wars. The middle-class merchants in America were protesting taxation and regulation by a monarch and insisting upon their right to be governed by their own representatives. As before, these middle-class leaders were supported by laborers and farmers who saw in representative government a better chance for a fair share of the economy. The French Revolution (1789–1795), inspired to a degree by its American counterpart, had similar origins and purposes, though they were overshadowed and even overwhelmed later when the lower classes were unleashed. They struck out savagely against the repressions and deprivations imposed upon them by the ruinous insensitivity of the Bourbon monarchy.

The French Revolution failed in the short run to establish the ideal government which its advocates had envisioned once the aristocratic rascals should be thrown out. But the autocratic government of Napoleon, which in 1799 came to restore order out of the chaos into which the revolutionary movement had degenerated, was not absolute in the sense that the Bourbon monarchy had been. In any case, Napoleon confirmed the shift of political power to the bourgeoisie, a broader base, at least, for government than the old aristocracy had been. The American Revolution was more successful in supplanting the old order with a stable, broadly representative government. The American Constitution, in fact, and its first ten amendments, the so-called Bill of Rights, may be thought of as the culminating achievement of liberal thought and activity in the seventeenth and eighteenth centuries.

PHILOSOPHERS AND THE SPREAD OF IDEAS

Philosophers were responsible for giving ideological impetus to the movements toward democratic government, limited monarchy, religious toleration, and other civil liberties. Probably in no period since the fifth and fourth centuries B.C. in Athens have philosophers carried such prestige and influence. One of the earliest and most eloquent voices raised in England in the cause of personal freedom was that of the Puritan philosopher and poet, John Milton (1608–1674), who sacrificed work on his major poetic epic (see page 629) in middle age to serve as spokesman for the democratic ideals of the Commonwealth. Another Englishman, the philosopher John Locke (1632–1704), championed the idea that men had certain natural rights which a ruler was obliged to observe and protect, or suffer popular overthrow. Locke's writings were far-reaching, influencing Thomas Paine, Thomas Jefferson, and Benjamin Franklin in America. Just as influential were the writings of the Baron de Montesquieu (1689–1755) (see page 612), whose studies of governments had a great influence on the formation of limited monarchies in Europe, and those of Jean-Jacques Rousseau (1712–1778), who claimed that man is "naturally" good and innocent and becomes corrupted only because of the vices of his environment, government, and education.

But it was the philosopher-author Voltaire who dominated the Age of Rationalism. With volumes of writings that showed a keen mind and a tart humor, he tried to purge his age of superstition, dogmatism, tyranny, and sentimentality. Voltaire became the high priest of tolerance, and, like Erasmus in an earlier age, he disseminated liberal ideas and stimulated controversy throughout Europe and England. But Voltaire's tolerance wavered on the subject of society's lower classes, who were for the most part illiterate, burdened with disease, and exploited. These people, Voltaire remarked caustically, will always spend their time going from Mass to the tavern and back, because there is singing in both places.

"ENLIGHTENMENT"

Ironically, it was not only the revolutionaries and liberal philosophers who brought about the vast political and social changes in these centuries. Several of the strong monarchs considered themselves "enlightened" and exercised their power to effect liberal reforms which ultimately weakened or destroyed their own positions. Frederick of Prussia was influenced by French liberal ideas through his virtually life-long correspondence with Voltaire, and at various times he drew Voltaire and other intellectuals to his court. Catherine of Russia was also a correspondent of Voltaire, but the legal reforms she instituted early in her reign were more specifically indebted to Montesquieu. The timid and piecemeal reforms permitted by Louis XVI of France, out of necessity rather than understanding or conviction, opened a gate to the revolution that was already imminent; and France's costly support of the American Revolution (motivated, to be sure,

A satiric drawing labeled "inhuman satisfaction." Voltaire is at right. His famous grin illustrates a "self-righteous sneer."

as much by rivalry against England as by liberal sentiment) aggravated the financial crisis that sped the French Revolution.

The common inspiration of all this philosophical and political activity was the emergence of modern science and the scientific method. Enthusiasm for scientific investigation that had begun in the Renaissance fully dominated the Age of Rationalism, with ever-widening scope. Research was spurred by the invention of important new instruments, such as the microscope, telescope, and thermometer.

The heliocentric theory of the sixteenth-century astronomer Copernicus was extended by the discoveries of Galileo, Johannes Kepler, and Sir Isaac Newton. Important discoveries concerning the physical and chemical nature of matter were made in the seventeenth century by the English scientist Robert Boyle (called the father of modern chemistry) and by Benjamin Franklin and his French contemporary, Antoine Laurent Lavoisier, in the eighteenth century. Sir William Harvey's description of the circulation of the blood was a striking new piece of knowledge about the human body. Clinical medicine was notably advanced by Thomas Sydenham in England and Benjamin Rush in America, and botany became a science when the Swedish scholar Linnaeus established the classification of plants.

But of all the scientific developments of the period, probably the most fundamentally important was that of mathematical science. The experimental method, still called Cartesian, was defined by René Descartes, and the invention of calculus (independently by Newton and Leibnitz) made mathematics the tool and language of this method. Descartes, in fact, proposed that the only certain way to truth in any field was through the deductive method used in mathematics. Certainly the most influential single work of the period was Newton's demanding masterpiece, *The Mathematical Principles of Natural Philosophy* (1687), which describes the universe as a kind of mathematical machine, which is orderly, logical, and governed by absolute laws that can be discovered by human reason and described mathematically. Newton's theories were the chief authority for the idea that similar order could be discovered in the fields of religion, politics, literature, and even morality, using the same kind of rational, logical examination. For example, the title of a major work by Scottish philosopher David Hume shows how scientific thought, specifically Newton's, influenced even the study of human behavior: *A Treatise of Human Nature—an Attempt to Introduce the Experimental Method of Reasoning into Moral Subjects.*

This kind of rational, science-oriented philosophy, characterized by a skepticism toward past authority and a suspicion of anything that the senses might reveal, had a profound effect on theology and on religious institutions themselves. Rationalism was a complicating element indeed in the religious turbulence of these post-Reformation centuries. For one thing, rationalism raised questions about the supernatural basis of Christianity, and churchmen and freethinkers felt compelled to reinterpret traditional theology so as to prove, in the words of Locke's essay, "The Reasonableness of Christianity." The most eloquent spokesman and defender of Christianity was the French mathematician and mystic Blaise Pascal. He appealed to his fellow scientists to restrict their mathematical inquiries to the world of science. A mere philosophy, he said, cannot be expected to solve the mysteries of life.

DEISM

Nevertheless, for many thinkers, rationalism gave rise to deism. The deists conceived of a mechanistic universe set in motion by a rational deity, something like a master mechanic, who then left it to run according to its mathematical laws. Such a deity would never, having set up such a system, interfere with its workings by performing miracles. Furthermore, this deity planted in all men's hearts certain ethical and moral laws, which every man can know through his reason, without any need for church interpretation. Deism left no place for the ceremonies of religion, nor for its mysteries, nor for the priesthood, nor for the teaching authority of a church. Nor did it see the need for special revelation of truth through divine texts or prophets, nor, ultimately, for the special mission of Jesus Christ. The deists' concept of an aloof, intellectual deity was fundamentally different from the traditional Christian concept of a loving, fatherly God.

Deism, despite its philosophically unstable and contradictory beliefs, had great appeal among intellectuals, though not all were willing to follow it to its most radical implications. Many deists, like Thomas Jefferson in America, believed in maintaining orthodox religious beliefs and observances on the grounds that the common man was not prepared to understand the subtleties of deism, nor able to govern himself through his own reason; ordinary men, he felt, needed the moral pressures of an organized church and of a disciplinary deity. "If God did not exist," remarked Voltaire with characteristic irony, "it would be necessary to invent him."

ELEGANCE AS A STYLE OF LIFE

Though the seventeenth and eighteenth centuries seem preoccupied with wars and controversies, the aristocrats of the time enjoyed a mode of life unparalleled in richness, elegance, taste, and manners. Whatever was going on in the background, the façade was sumptuous. In all the great capitals of Europe, ladies and gentlemen, dressed in silks, powdered and pomaded, were carried in ornamented sedan chairs through the squalid and

Prussia's king, "the great Fritz," performs with the flute at Sans Souci.

noisy streets by liveried attendants. Louis XIV's palace at Versailles was an overcrowded rabbit warren of courtiers scrambling for position and seeking favors, but its apartments and grounds were magnificent on a scale never before seen in Europe. Life at the court of the Sun King was as regimented as that of an army camp; every act of the king's day was performed with ritual and attended formally by large numbers of eager courtiers. All this splendor, pomp, and ceremony gave grandeur to the entire life of the court and enhanced its king as a godlike symbol of power and majesty.

Almost as glorious as Versailles were many other ornate palaces and stately homes newly built in Europe and England: Sans Souci, Frederick the Great's palace at Potsdam; the Schönbrunn palace in Vienna; and the Nymphenburg castle at Munich. Peter the Great of Russia constructed a whole new city, St. Petersburg, to provide a suitable setting for his imperial dignity and for the new era that his reign was bringing into existence. Queen Anne of England built Blenheim Palace in the new style and in royal dimensions as the nation's gift to its great military hero, John Churchill, Duke of Marlborough.

The fashionable architecture was neoclassic, with qualities of balance, serenity, and spaciousness harking back to the public architecture of ancient Greece and Rome. Buildings were enhanced by elaborate formal gardens and by wide parks, planned to look unplanned. Interior decoration was similarly rich and elegant. Rooms were lighter and more cheerful than they had been before, with many-paned windows and crystal chandeliers, although glass was still an item of luxury. Walls were painted or covered with stretched silk. Furniture acquired new lightness and new grace, for this was the age of the great English cabinetmakers—Sheraton, Chippendale, and Hepplewhite. World trade now made available exotic woods, fabrics, and art objects, especially from China. All fashionable houses sought such fads from the Orient, called *chinoiserie:* imported porcelain bowls and plates, carved wood, silk hangings, and wallpaper were everywhere.

The palaces of kings and the estates of noblemen were, of course, the principal showpieces of the new refinement and luxury, but the wealthy merchants also penetrated court society and adopted its tastes, often so slavishly that they gave rise to the kind of ridicule that the French playwright Molière (1622–1673) leveled at the upstart man of means. Nevertheless, much of the beauty of London, Paris, and Vienna is attributable to the townhouses and theaters, business establishments and clubs, coffee houses and fashionable shops built by and serving the affluent bourgeoisie. The wealthy middle class also shared with kings and their courts the patronage of the arts. Molière, for example, was protected by Louis XIV and rewarded for acting before the court, but his success and livelihood were achieved in the public theater, which was as fashionable among the merchants as it was among the aristocrats.

THE BAROQUE IN THE ARTS

The leading role that Italy had played in the Renaissance was now taken over by France. Although England took an important lead in scientific and political thinking, all Europe looked to France as the source of ideas and as the model of style, in nearly everything from literature to dress. In art, architecture, and music the favored fashion was baroque, a style distinguished by a lavish complexity that is unified and controlled by strict and balanced forms; thus the baroque is characterized by conflicting qualities of irregularity and balance, of ornateness and simplicity, of emotionalism and formality, of energy and order. It is probably not too far-fetched to relate this style to the philosophy of rationalism itself, which asserted the logical orderliness of a universe that yet had infinite variety and complexity. The baroque style appears in the disciplined complexities of Bach's music, in the swirling stone of Bernini's sculptures, and in the ornate formalism of the palace of Versailles.

The modern age of music began in the eighteenth century. The giants of music of this so-called baroque period were the German composer Johann Sebastian Bach and the Austrian composers Joseph Haydn and Wolfgang Amadeus Mozart. To this vigorous period of rich harmonies and brilliant effects also belong Domenico Scarlatti and Antonio Vivaldi of Italy, Henry

Purcell and the German-born George Frederick Handel of England, and Jean-Baptiste Lully and François Couperin of France. Opera had begun in 1607 with the *Orfeo* of Claudio Monteverdi, but with the production of another *Orfeo* in 1762, German composer Christoph Gluck moved opera into its period of greatest development by enriching the dramatic possibilities of the form.

LITERARY TRENDS

As the German philosopher Immanuel Kant observed, his age might give high value to "reason" and "enlightenment," but it was not a reasonable and enlightened age. Many literary spokesmen, therefore, found voice in satire. Their favorite targets were the pretentiousness, hypocrisy, and materialism of the wealthy bourgeoisie. Satire is evident in the shrewd didactic *Fables* (see page 626) of Jean de la Fontaine (1621–1695). It is evident in the humorous plays of Molière (see page 686), which hold up for laughter the behavior of the French of his day. Satire characterizes Voltaire's novel *Candide,* which not only ridicules optimism as a way of viewing the world, but also parodies the absurd styles of popular romance and adventure stories. Perhaps the most scathing satire of the age was written by Irish-born Jonathan Swift (1667–1745); his novel *Gulliver's Travels,* read by children as a delightful fantasy, reflects bitter outrage at the corruption that Swift saw in every British institution and at the cocksureness of the times.

Something of the scientific spirit of the age showed itself in literary criticism. Writers worried themselves about the nature of literature, about the subjects appropriate to each kind of literature, and about the elements of proper style. There was general agreement that there must be some logical, discoverable laws that govern literary propriety and excellence, though there was little actual agreement as to what those laws might be. Nevertheless, such stern critics as John Dryden and Samuel Johnson in England became ponderous dictators of taste and excellence in literature.

The theater flourished, particularly in France. Here writers in the seventeenth century imitated classical Greek dramas, which still had enormous literary prestige. Neoclassical tragedy was brought to a point of excellence by Pierre Corneille (1606–1684) and Jean Racine (1639–1699), and the comedies of Molière attained similar preeminence. In England the theaters were closed in 1642 by Cromwell and his Puritans, and they remained closed until Charles II was restored to the throne in 1660. Charles and his court had spent their exile in France, and they sailed back to England with a taste for things French, including French comedy. The subsequent revival of the drama in England gave to literature what is called Restoration comedy, witty and brilliantly made satires, like William Congreve's *Way of the World* (1700) and Richard Sheridan's *The Rivals* (1775) and *School for Scandal* (1777). It was Dublin-born Sheridan who created such delicious caricatures of London society as Lydia Languish, Anthony Absolute, and Benjamin Backbite.

The seventeenth and eighteenth centuries have often been called, somewhat contemptuously, the Age of Prose and Reason. It is true that no great lyric poets appear during this time, but when the romantic imagination is generally suspect, this is not surprising. Critics prominent during this age looked back in disapproval at the irregularities in form and language used by poets of previous centuries. Voltaire, for example, felt that Shakespeare was too "irregular" to be fully appreciated, and though Voltaire was too intelligent not to recognize Shakespeare's talent, he called him a barbarian.

Generally, in the Age of Reason, the didactic or satiric poem became preeminent. It is usually witty and displays the kind of ornamental diction strictly prescribed for poetry and never spoken by anyone.

But these poems were too formal and too classical in style to suit popular taste. The bourgeois public, whose hankering after culture had been ridiculed by Molière some years earlier, was becoming more literate, and in the eighteenth century this public found another literary form much to their liking: the novel. What attracted most of these people to the novel was sentimentality, which they could not find in neoclassical poetry. Installments of melodramatic and meandering novels like Samuel Richardson's *Clarissa* (1744–1748), about a young lady who dies of shame when a contemptuous rake attempts to ruin her virtue, were bought and borrowed and wept over copiously. (Samuel Johnson told readers: "If you were to read Richardson for the story, your impatience would be so much fretted that you'd hang yourself. But you must read him for the sentiment.") However, novels did not remain sentimental. Henry Fielding, also an Englishman, despised Richardson's moralizing, and in 1749 he wrote his own greatest novel, *Tom Jones,* a lively, funny, and realistic story which, for all its gusto, does not ignore the harsher side of eighteenth-century life.

German literature in this period was not remarkable and not free from French models until the latter part of the eighteenth century, when three of Germany's greatest writers lived: the eloquent critic Gotthold Lessing (1729–1781), who urged Germans to develop a literature of their own; the Romantic Friedrich von Schiller (1759–1805), poet and dramatist (he wrote the ever-popular *William Tell)*; and Schiller's close friend Johann von Goethe (1749–1832), who was the giant among them. Goethe's great hero, Faust (see page 676), is a man who encompasses all knowledge and all experience in an effort to fulfill his own best nature. Faust finds his fulfillment at last in unselfish devotion to the creation of a brave, new world, where all men can find freedom from tyranny and need. Goethe's own long and many-faceted career is seen both as culminating the Age of Enlightenment and as heralding the new Romantic Age, which was being formed by the political, social, and industrial revolutions that were closing the eighteenth century.

Persian Letters

CHARLES DE MONTESQUIEU

Charles Louis de Secondat, Baron de la Brède et de Montesquieu (1689–1755),
was a lawyer and philosopher who lived most of his life under the long rule of
Louis XV. He was born a hundred years after the death of Montaigne, and his life
bears some coincidental and some significant resemblances to his predecessor. Like
Montaigne, Montesquieu was involved in the legal and civic affairs of the provincial capital of Bordeaux. Like Montaigne, he retired while still in his thirties to his
estate (which, in Montesquieu's case, was a considerable one), in order to devote his
life to study and thought. Like Montaigne's, Montesquieu's writings embody his
mature reflections upon a wide range of experience and learning.

Montesquieu is most famous for his *Spirit of Laws,* in which he examines many
forms of government, both ancient and modern. In an age dominated by one of the
most absolute dynasties that Europe has ever known—the Bourbon kings of France
—Montesquieu made a strong case for republican government. His ideas encouraged the political unrest that was to culminate in popular revolutions in France and
America before the century was over. Montesquieu's ideas are also embodied in
the system of government established by the American Constitution, especially in
the provisions for mutual control among several branches of government.

In his own time, Montesquieu was also famous for a work he had written when
he was in his twenties and published when he was thirty-two. *Persian Letters* is the
title of a wide-ranging and miscellaneous group of essays, written as if they were
letters from three Persian travelers, telling friends about their impressions of European life. (Usbek and Rica are in Paris, Rhedi in Venice, Mirza in Ispahan, a city
in Iran.) The letters are loosely held together by a sequence of minor events. They
are occasionally interspersed with letters from Persia, which capitalize on European
curiosity about life in exotic lands, especially in the fabled harems of the East.

But clearly the purpose of the *Persian Letters* is to comment satirically upon
European manners and institutions, by exposing them to the scrutiny of characters
whose vision is not clouded by European smugness and prejudice. The fiction allows
Montesquieu to disguise references and to evade censorship by putting unpopular
opinions in the mouths of foreigners and infidels.

Letters 86 and 106 follow. Letter 86 implicitly attacks Louis XIV's revocation
in 1685 of the Edict of Nantes, a concession of religious toleration for Protestants,
which had been hard-won in the religious wars of the last half of the sixteenth century. In spite of a ban on emigration that accompanied the revocation, nearly 52,000
Protestant families escaped to Switzerland. Many of them were artisans, and they
had constituted a large part of the artisan class in France.

Letter 86

USBEK TO MIRZA, AT ISPAHAN

You know, Mirza, that some ministers of Shah Soliman formed the design of obliging all the Armenians of Persia to quit the kingdom or become Mohammedans, in the belief that our empire will continue polluted as long as it retains within its bosom these infidels. If, on that occasion, bigotry had carried the day, there would have been an end to the greatness of Persia.

It is not known how the matter dropped. Neither those who made the proposition, nor those who rejected it, realized the consequences of their acts; chance performed the office of reason and of policy and saved the empire from jeopardy greater than that which would have been entailed by a defeat in the field and the loss of two cities. It is understood that the proscription of the Armenians would have extirpated in a single day all the merchants and almost all the artisans in the kingdom. I am sure that the great Shah Abbas [1] would rather have lost both his arms than have signed such an order; in sending to the Mogul and to the other kings of Ind the most industrious of his subjects, he would have felt that he was giving away the half of his dominions.

The persecution of the Guebres by our zealous Mohammedans has obliged them to fly in crowds into the Indies [2] and has deprived Persia of that nation which labored so heartily that it alone, by its toil, was in a fair way to overcome the sterility of our land. Only one thing remained for bigotry to do, and that was to destroy industry, with the result that the empire fell of itself, carrying along with it as a necessary consequence that very religion which they wished to advance.

If unbiased discussion were possible, I am not sure, Mirza, that it would not be a good thing for a state to have several religions. It is worthy of note that those who profess tolerated creeds usually prove more useful to their country than those who profess the established faith, because, being excluded from all honors and unable to distinguish themselves except by wealth and its shows, they are led to acquire riches by their labor and to embrace the most toilsome of occupations.

Besides, as all religions contain some precepts advantageous to society, it is well that they should be zealously observed. Now, could there be a greater incitement to zeal than a multiplicity of religions? They are rivals who never forgive anything. Jealousy descends to individuals: each one stands upon his guard, afraid of doing anything that may dishonor his party and of exposing it to the contempt and unpardonable censures of the opposite side. It has also been remarked that a new sect introduced into a state was always the surest means of correcting the abuses of the old faith.

It is sophistry to say that it is against the interest of the prince to tolerate many religions in his kingdom: though all the sects in the world were to gather together into one state, it would not be in the least detrimental to it, because there is no creed which does not ordain obedience and preach submission. I acknowledge that history is full of religious wars, but we

[1] **Shah Abbas:** Abbas I, surnamed "the Great" (1587–1629), had a glowing reputation in later generations, which may have been enhanced by the line of dissolute rulers who followed him. The reigning Shah referred to in the opening sentence, Soliman II (or Suleiman), was one of these.

Letters 86 and 106 by Charles de Montesquieu from *Persian Letters*, translated by John Davidson. Reprinted by permission of Routledge & Kegan Paul, Ltd.

[2] The Guebres (or Ghebers) were Zoroastrian in religion, the Persians Mohammedan (see page 311). Apparently this refers to the migration in the eighth century A.D. of a group of Zoroastrians to the region of Bombay in India.

must distinguish. It is not the multiplicity of religions which has produced wars; it is the intolerant spirit animating that which believed itself in the ascendant.

This is the spirit of proselytism which the Jews caught from the Egyptians and which passed from them like an epidemic disease to the Mohammedans and the Christians. It is, in short, that capricious mood which in its progress can be compared only to a total eclipse of human reason.

In conclusion, even if there were no inhumanity in distressing the consciences of others, even if there did not result from such a course any of the evil effects which do spring from it in thousands, it would still be foolish to advise it. He who would have me change my religion is led to that, without doubt, because he would not change his own, although force were employed; and yet he finds it strange that I will not do a thing which he himself would not do, perhaps for the empire of the world.

Paris, the 26th of the first moon of Gemmadi, 1715.

Letter 106

RHEDI TO USBEK, AT PARIS

IN ONE of your letters you said much to me about the arts and sciences cultivated in the West. You are inclined to regard me as a barbarian; but I am not certain that the profit derived from them recompenses men for the bad use to which they are put every day. I have heard it said that the invention of bombs alone has deprived all the nations of Europe of freedom. The princes, being no longer able to trust the guardianship of towns to the citizens, who would surrender them at the first bomb, have made it a pretext for keeping large bodies of regular troops, whom they have since used to oppress their subjects.

You know that since the invention of gunpowder no place is impregnable; that is to say, Usbek, that there is no longer upon the earth a refuge from injustice and violence. I dread always lest they should at last discover some secret which will furnish them with a briefer method of destroying men, by killing them off wholesale in tribes and nations.

You have read the historians; think of them seriously. Almost all monarchies have been founded upon ignorance of the arts and have been destroyed by their overcultivation. The ancient empire of Persia may furnish us with an example at our own doors.

I have not been long in Europe, yet I have heard sensible people talk of the ravages of alchemy. It seems to be a fourth plague, which ruins men, destroying them one by one, but continually; while war, pestilence, and famine destroys them in the mass, but at intervals.

Of what advantage has the invention of the mariner's compass been to us and the discovery of so many nations who have given us more diseases than wealth? Gold and silver have been established by a general agreement as the means of purchasing all goods and as a pledge of their value, because these metals are rare and useless for any other purpose. Of what consequence was it to us, then, that they should become more common, and that to mark the value of any commodity we should have two or three signs in place of one? This was only more inconvenient.

But, on the other hand, this invention has been hurtful to the countries of the New World. Entire nations have been destroyed, and those who have escaped death have been reduced to a slavery so dreadful that the description of it makes even a Mussulman shudder.

Happy in their ignorance are the children of Mohammed! Their amiable simplicity, so dear to our holy Prophet, perpetually recalls to me the artlessness of the olden time and the peace which reigned in the hearts of our first fathers.

Venice, the 5th of the moon of Rhamazan, 1717.

FOR STUDY AND DISCUSSION

1. In what ways does Montesquieu's defense of religious toleration in Letter 86 go beyond the usual argument that everyone has a right to his own beliefs?

2. What do Montesquieu's arguments imply about the nature of religious truth?

3. How can you tell which conclusion Montesquieu wants the reader to draw from Letter 106: that the investigations of science are valuable, or that they should be stopped?

LOGICAL ANALYSIS

The plan of argument in Letter 86 can be described in the following stages:

(a) Proposition examined and rejected
(b) Counterproposition offered and supported
(c) Arguments against the counterproposition refuted
(d) Climactic argument made for the counterproposition

1. Identify these stages and define in one brief sentence the proposition and the counterproposition.

2. How are the examples of the Armenians and the Guebres pertinent to criticism of the revocation of the Treaty of Nantes?

3. How does Montesquieu refute the objection that he supposes would be made against his counter-proposition?

4. How is the climactic argument different from the arguments offered earlier in support of the counterproposition?

5. What is the effectiveness of this plan of argument? Note that more of the essay is devoted to refuting what Montesquieu believes is wrong than to presenting arguments for what he thinks is right. Remember that Montesquieu was writing during a time when France was dominated by the arrogant Bourbon monarchy, which rejected even the limited toleration offered by the Edict of Nantes; how might this situation have affected the way Montesquieu presents his argument?

FOR COMPOSITION

The problem Montesquieu deals with in Letter 106 is still raised today, with respect to space exploration, for example. Write an essay in which you present arguments and draw conclusions about some contemporary manifestation of this problem.

Candide

VOLTAIRE

"Voltaire" was the penname of François-Marie Arouet (1694–1778). The pen was the sharpest and the name the most famous (or infamous, depending on your viewpoint) during the whole Age of Reason. Through great numbers of pamphlets, letters, poems, plays, and stories, Voltaire swayed public opinion on nearly all the prominent questions and issues discussed during his time.

Voltaire saw himself as a relentless seeker after justice, an assailant of political tyranny and religious authoritarianism, and an exposer of humbug. His keen satiric criticism spared no institution and no person, not even the Church and the king. "Crush the infamous thing!" was his battle cry, and he hurled it at all the forces that threatened the new "enlightenment" as he saw it. He was a passionate admirer of the political philosophy of John Locke and was an intellectual forerunner of the great revolutions that later broke out in America and France. A deist who rejected the authority of the Church he was born into, Voltaire espoused the rationalistic, science-oriented philosophy of Sir Isaac Newton, whom he once selected as the greatest man in the world. In theory and action, Voltaire advocated the rationalistic philosophy that looked at the world just as it is, with common sense, without hypocrisy, prejudice, self-deception, or sentiment.

Many of his pamphlets and stories he published anonymously to avoid prosecution, though their authorship was always well known. *Candide,* which he called "a philosophical tale," was one such work. Though it was probably not of special significance to its author, it has endured longer than most of Voltaire's works, many of which have by this time lost their significance, as the issues that inspired them have faded.

A short comic novel, *Candide* is the odyssey of an engaging innocent, who has been schooled by one of the superficial devotees of Leibnitz's optimistic philosophy to believe that everything that happens in the world is for the best. "All is for the best in this best of all possible worlds" is the teaching of his tutor, the unrealistic Doctor Pangloss, and Candide clings doggedly to this slogan through a series of disastrous adventures, which range from the terrifying to the disgusting.

Candide was brought up in the household of the Baron Thunder-ten-tronckh, "one of the most powerful lords in Westphalia, for his castle possessed a door and windows." Candide's first love was the Baron's daughter, Cunegonde, for which presumption he was thrown out of the castle. As he is tossed from country to country by circumstances of the most dire sort, always he holds before himself the hope of being reunited with Mlle. Cunegonde. He does come upon her eventually, held prisoner by the Grand Inquisitor, a misfortune that had occurred after she was taken as booty by the Bulgarians, who had ravaged her father's most agreeable of all castles. Candide kills the Grand Inquisitor and sails with Cunegonde for South America, where they hope to find the best of all possible worlds and lasting happiness. But Candide loses Cunegonde for the sake of the immediate happiness of the governor of Buenos Aires, and again the sweet-natured youth is forced to run, along with his new footman Cacambo. In their flight, they are nearly skewered and boiled by cannibals, the Oreillons, but Cacambo exhibits his clear-headedness by talking the savages out of their dinner plans.

17

The arrival of Candide and his man at the country of Eldorado

WHEN THEY HAD REACHED the frontiers of the Oreillons, Cacambo said to Candide, "You see now that this part of the world is not one pin better than the other. Take a fool's advice for once, and let us return to Europe as fast as ever we can." "How is that possible?" said Candide. "And pray what part of it would you have us go to? If I go to my own country, the Bulgarians and Abarians kill all they meet with there; if I return to Portugal, I am sure I shall be burnt alive; if we stay in this country, we run the hazard of being roasted every moment. And again, how can I think of leaving that part of the globe where Miss Cunegonde lives?"

"Why, then, let us take our course towards Cayenne," said Cacambo. "We shall meet with some Frenchmen there, for you know they are to be met with all over the globe; perhaps they will give us some relief, and God may have pity upon us."

It was no easy matter for them to go to Cayenne, as they did not know whereabouts it lay; besides, mountains, rivers, precipices, banditti, and savages were difficulties they were sure to encounter in their journey. Their horses died with fatigue, and their provisions were soon consumed. After having lived a whole month on the wild fruits, they found themselves on the banks of a small river which was bordered by cocoa trees, which both pre-

served their lives and kept up their hopes.

Cacambo, who was on all occasions as good a counselor as the old woman,[1] said to Candide, "We can hold out no longer; we have walked enough already, and here's an empty canoe upon the shore. Let's fill it with cocoa, then get on board, and let it drift with the stream. A river always runs to some inhabited place. If we don't meet with what we like, we are sure to meet with something new." "Why, what you say is very right, e'en let us go," said Candide, "and recommend ourselves to the care of Providence."

They rowed some leagues between the two banks, which were enameled with flowers in some places, in others barren, in some parts level, and in others very steep. The river grew broader as they proceeded and at last lost itself in a vault of frightful rocks, which reached as high as the clouds. Our two travelers still had the courage to trust themselves to the stream. The river now growing narrower drove them along with such rapidity and noise as filled them with the utmost horror. In about four and twenty hours, they got sight of daylight again, but their canoe was dashed in pieces against the breakers. They were obliged to crawl from one rock to another for a whole league; after which they came in sight of a spacious plain, bounded with inaccessible mountains. The country was highly cultivated, both for pleasure and profit; the useful and the ornamental were most agreeably blended. The roads were covered or, more properly speaking, were adorned with carriages, whose figure and materials were very bril-

[1] The old woman had traveled with Candide and his beloved to the New World. She knew everything of life, having survived the most horrendous misfortunes. Kidnapped by pirates and enslaved in Morocco, she caught the plague in Algiers and was disfigured by the Turks before entering Cunegonde's service.

liant. They were full of men and women of an extraordinary beauty and were drawn with great swiftness by large red sheep, which for fleetness surpassed the finest horses of Andalusia, Tetuan, or Mequinez.

"This certainly," said Candide, "is a better country than Westphalia." He and Cacambo got on shore near the first village they came to. The very children of the village were dressed in gold brocades, all tattered, playing at quoits at the entrance of the town. Our two travelers from the other world amused themselves with looking at them. The quoits were made of large round pieces, yellow, red, and green, and cast a surprising light. Our travelers' hands itched prodigiously to be fingering some of them; for they were almost certain that they were either gold, emeralds, or rubies, the least of which would have been no small ornament to the throne of the Great Mogul. "To be sure," said Cacambo, "these must be the children of the king of the country, diverting themselves at quoits." The master of the village came at that instant to call them to school. "That's the preceptor to the royal family," cried Candide.

The little brats immediately quitted their play, leaving their quoits and other playthings behind them. Candide picked them up, ran to the schoolmaster, and presented them to him with a great deal of humility, acquainting him, by signs, that their Royal Highnesses had forgot their gold and jewels. The master of the village smiled and flung them upon the ground, and having stared at Candide with some degree of surprise, walked off.

Our travelers did not fail immediately to pick up the gold, rubies, and emeralds. "Where have we got to now?" cried Candide. "The princes of the blood must certainly be well educated here, since they are taught to despise both gold and jewels." Cacambo was as much surprised as Candide. At length they drew near to the first house in the village, which was built like one of our European palaces. There was a vast crowd of people at the door

and still a greater within. They heard very good music, and their nostrils were saluted by a most refreshing smell from the kitchen.

Cacambo went up to the door and heard them speaking the Peruvian language, which was his mother tongue, for every one of my readers knows that Cacambo was born at Tucuman, a village where they make use of no other language. "I'll be your interpreter, master," cried Cacambo, in the greatest rapture. "This is a tavern, in with you, in with you."

Immediately, two waiters and two maids that belonged to the house, dressed in clothes of gold tissue and having their hair tied back with ribbons, invited them to sit down to table with the landlord. They served up four soups, each garnished with two parakeets, a boiled vulture that weighed about two hundred pounds, two apes roasted, of an excellent taste, three hundred hummingbirds in one plate, and six hundred flybirds in another; together with exquisite ragouts, and the most delicious tarts, all in plates of a species of rock-crystal. After which, the lads and lasses served them with a great variety of liquors made from the sugar cane.

The guests were mostly tradesmen and carriers, all extremely polite, who asked some questions of Cacambo, with the greatest discretion and circumspection, and received satisfactory answers.

When the repast was ended, Cacambo and Candide thought to discharge their reckoning by putting down two of the large pieces of gold which they had picked up. But the landlord and landlady burst into a loud fit of laughing and could not restrain it for some time. When they had recovered themselves at last, the landlord said, "Gentlemen, we can see pretty well that you are strangers; we are not much used to such guests here. Pardon us for laughing when you offered us the stones of our highways in discharge of your reckoning. It is plain, you have got none of the money of this kingdom; but there is no occasion for it, in order to dine here. All the inns, which are established for the conveniency of trade, are maintained by the government. You have had but a sorry entertainment here, because this is but a poor village; but anywhere else, you will be sure to be received in a manner suitable to your merit."

Cacambo explained the host's speech to Candide, who heard it with as much astonishment and wonder as his friend Cacambo interpreted it. "What country can this be," said they to each other, "which is unknown to the rest of the world and of so different a nature from ours? It is probably that country where everything really is for the best; for it is absolutely necessary that there should be one of that sort. And in spite of all Doctor Pangloss's arguments, I could not help thinking that things were very bad in Westphalia."

18

What they saw in the country of Eldorado

CACAMBO COULD NOT conceal his curiosity from his landlord. "For my part," said the latter to him, "I am very ignorant, and I am well aware of it; but we have an old man here, who has retired from court, and is reckoned both the wisest and most communicative person in the kingdom." So saying, without any more ado, he conducted Cacambo to the old man's house. Candide acted now only the second personage and followed his servant. They entered into a very plain house, for the door was nothing but silver, and the ceilings nothing but gold, but finished with so much taste that the handsomest ceilings of Europe did not surpass them. The antechamber was indeed only covered with rubies and emeralds, but the order in which everything was arranged made amends for this great simplicity.

The old gentleman received the two strangers on a sofa stuffed with the feathers of hummingbirds, and ordered them to be served with liquors in vessels of diamond, after which he satisfied their curiosity in the following manner.

"I am now in my hundred and seventy-second year, and I have heard my deceased father, who was groom to his Majesty, mention the surprising revolutions of Peru, of which he was an eyewitness. The kingdom we are in at present is the ancient country of the Incas, who left it very indiscreetly in order to conquer one part of the world; instead of doing which, they themselves were all destroyed by the Spaniards.

"The princes of their family who remained in their native country were more wise; they made a law, by the unanimous consent of their whole nation, that none of our inhabitants should ever go out of our little kingdom; and it is owing to this that we have preserved both our innocence and our happiness. The Spaniards have had some confused idea of this country, and have called it *Eldorado;* and an Englishman, named Sir *Walter Raleigh,* has been on our coasts, above a hundred years ago; but as we are surrounded by inaccessible rocks and precipices, we have hitherto been sheltered from the rapacity of the European nations, who are inspired with an insensate rage for the stones and dirt of our land; to possess these, I verily believe they would not hesitate a moment to murder us all."

The conference between Candide and the old man was pretty long and turned upon the form of government, the manners, the women, the public amusements, and the arts of Eldorado. At last, Candide, who had always a taste for metaphysics, bid Cacambo ask if there was any religion in that country.

The old gentleman said, reddening a little, "How is it possible that you should question it? Do you take us for ungrateful wretches?" Cacambo then humbly asked him what the religion of Eldorado was. This made the old gentleman redden again. "Can there be more religions than one?" said he. "We profess, I believe, the religion of the whole world; we worship the deity from evening to morning." "Do you worship one God?" said Cacambo, who still acted as interpreter in explaining Candide's doubts. "You may be sure we do," said the old man, "since it is evident there can be neither two, nor three, nor four. I must say that the people of your world propose very odd questions." Candide was not yet wearied in interrogating the good old man; he wanted to know how they prayed to God in Eldorado. "We never pray at all," said the respectable sage; "we have nothing to ask of him; he has given us all we need, and we incessantly return him thanks."

Candide had a curiosity to see their priests, and bid Cacambo ask where they were. This made the old gentleman smile. "My friends," said he, "we are all of us priests; the king and the heads of each family sing their songs of thanksgiving every morning, accompanied by five or six thousand musicians." "What!" said Cacambo, "have you no clerics to preach, to dispute, to tyrannize, to set people together by the ears, and to get those burnt who are not of the same opinions as themselves?" "We must be very great fools indeed if we had," said the old gentleman; "we are all of us of the same opinion, here, and we don't understand what you mean by clerics."

Candide was in an ecstasy during all this discourse, and said to himself, "This place is vastly different from Westphalia, and my lord the baron's castle. If our friend Pangloss had seen Eldorado, he would never have maintained that nothing upon earth could surpass the castle of Thunder-ten-tronckh. It is plain that everybody should travel."

After this long conversation was finished, the good old man ordered a coach and six sheep to be got ready, and twelve of his domestics to conduct the travelers to the court. "Excuse me," says he to them, "if my age deprives me of the honor of attending you. The king will receive you in a manner that you will not be displeased with, and you will, I doubt not, make allowance for the customs of the country if you should meet with anything that you disapprove of."

Candide and Cacambo got into the coach, and the six sheep were so fleet that in less than four hours they reached the king's palace, which was situated at one end of the metropolis. The gate was two hundred and twenty feet high and one hundred broad; it is impossible to describe the materials it was composed of. But one may easily guess that it must have prodigiously surpassed those stones and the sand which we call gold and jewels.

Candide and Cacambo, on their alighting from the coach, were received by twenty maids of honor, of an exquisite beauty, who conducted them to the baths and presented them with robes made of the down of hummingbirds; after which, the great officers and their ladies introduced them into his Majesty's apartment, between two rows of musicians, consisting of a thousand in each, according to the custom of the country.

When they approached the foot of the throne, Cacambo asked one of the great officers in what manner they were to behave when they went to pay their respects to his Majesty; whether they were to fall down on their knees or their bellies; whether they were to put their hands upon their heads or upon their backs; whether they were to lick up the dust of the room; and, in a word, what the ceremony was. "The custom is," said the great officer, "to embrace the king, and kiss him on both cheeks." Candide and Cacambo accordingly clasped his Majesty round the neck, who received them in the most polite manner imaginable and very genteelly invited them to sup with him.

In the interim, they showed them the city: the public edifices that seemed almost to touch the clouds; the market places embellished with a thousand columns; fountains of pure water, besides others of rose water and the liquors that are extracted from the sugar canes, which played continually in the squares, which were paved with a kind of precious stone that diffused a fragrance like that of cloves or cinnamon. Candide asked them to show them their courts of justice and their parliament house, and they told him they had none and that they were strangers to lawsuits. He then inquired if they had any prisons and was told they had not. What surprised him most and gave him the greatest pleasure was the palace of sciences, in which he saw a gallery two thousand paces in length, full of mathematical instruments and scientific apparatus.

After having spent the afternoon in going over about a thousandth part of the city, they were reconducted to the palace. Candide seated himself at table with his Majesty, his valet Cacambo, and a great many ladies. Never was there a better entertainment; and never was more wit shown at table than what his Majesty displayed. Cacambo interpreted the king's repartees to Candide, and though they were translated, they appeared excellent repartees still; a thing which surprised Candide about as much as anything else.

They spent a whole month in this hospitable manner, Candide continually remarking to Cacambo, "I must say it again and again, my friend, that the castle where I was born was nothing in comparison to the country where we are now; but yet Miss Cunegonde is not here, and without doubt, you have left a sweetheart behind you in Europe. If we stay where we are, we shall be looked upon only as other folks; whereas, if we return to our own world, only with twelve sheep loaded with pebbles of Eldorado, we shall be richer than all the kings put together; we shall have no need to be afraid of the inquisitors and we may easily recover Miss Cunegonde."

This proposal was extremely agreeable to Cacambo. So fond are we of running about, of making a figure among our countrymen, of telling our exploits and what we have seen in our travels, that these two really happy men resolved to be no longer so and accordingly asked his Majesty's leave to depart.

"You are very foolish," said his Majesty to them. "I am not ignorant that my country is a small affair, but when one is well off it's best to keep so. I certainly have no right to detain strangers; it is a degree of tyranny inconsistent with our customs and laws; all men are free. You may depart when you please, but you cannot get away without the greatest difficulty. It is impossible to go against the current up the rapid river which runs under the rocks; your passage hither was a kind of miracle. The mountains which surround my kingdom are a thousand feet high and as steep as a wall; they are at least ten leagues over, and their descent is a succession of precipices. However, since you seem determined to leave us, I will immediately give orders to the constructors of my machines to make one to transport you comfortably. When they have conveyed you to the other side of the mountains, no one must attend you, because my subjects have made a vow never to pass beyond them, and they are too wise to break it. There is nothing else you can ask of me which shall not be granted." "We ask your Majesty," said Cacambo, very eagerly, "only a few sheep loaded with provisions, together with some of the common stones and dirt of your country."

The king laughed heartily; "I cannot," said he, "conceive what pleasure you Europeans find in our yellow clay; but you are welcome to take as much of it as you please, and much good may it do you."

He gave immediate orders to his engineers to construct a machine to hoist up and transport these two extraordinary persons out of his kingdom. Three thousand able mechanics set to work, and in a fortnight's time the machine was completed, which cost no more than twenty millions sterling of their currency.

Candide and Cacambo were both placed on the machine, together with two large red sheep bridled and saddled for them to ride on when they were over the mountains, twenty sheep of burden loaded with provisions, thirty with the greatest curiosities of the country, by way of present, and fifty with gold, precious stones, and diamonds. The king, after tenderly embracing the two vagabonds, took his leave of them.

It was a very fine spectacle to see them depart and the ingenious manner in which they and the sheep were hoisted over the mountains. The contrivers of the machine took their leave of them, after having got them safe over, and now Candide had no other desire and no other aim than to go to present his sheep to Miss Cunegonde. "We have now got enough," said he, "to pay for the ransom of Miss Cunegonde, no matter what price the governor of Buenos Aires puts upon her. Let us march toward Cayenne, there take shipping, and then we will determine what kingdom to make a purchase of."

19

What happened to them at Surinam, and how Candide became acquainted with Martin

THE FIRST DAY'S journey of our two travelers was very agreeable, they being elated with the idea of finding themselves masters of more treasure than Asia, Europe, or Africa could scrape together. Candide was so transported that he carved the name of Cunegonde upon almost every tree that he came to. The second day, two of their sheep sunk in a morass and were lost, with all that they carried; two others died of fatigue a few days after; seven or eight died at once of want, in a desert; and some few days after, some others fell down a precipice. In short, after a march of one hundred days, their whole flock amounted to no more than two sheep.

"My friend," said Candide to Cacambo, "you see how perishable the riches of this world are; there is nothing durable, nothing to be depended on but virtue and the happiness of once more seeing Miss Cunegonde." "I grant it," said Cacambo;

"but we have still two sheep left, besides more treasure than ever the king of Spain was master of; and I see a town a good way off, that I take to be Surinam, belonging to the Dutch. We are at the end of our troubles, and at the beginning of our happiness."

As they drew nigh to the city, they saw a Negro stretched on the ground, more than half naked, having only a pair of drawers of blue cloth; the poor fellow had lost his left leg and his right hand. "Good God!" said Candide to him, in Dutch, "what do you here, in this terrible condition?" "I am waiting for my master, Mynheer Vanderdendur, the great merchant," replied the Negro. "And was it Mynheer Vanderdendur that used you in this manner?" said Candide. "Yes sir," said the Negro, "it is the custom of the country. They give us a pair of linen drawers for our whole clothing twice a year. If we should chance to have one of our fingers caught in the mill as we are working in the sugar-houses, they cut off our hand; if we offer to run away, they cut off one of our legs; and I have had the misfortune to be found guilty of both these offenses. Such are the conditions on which you eat sugar in Europe! Yet when my mother sold me for ten crowns at Patagonia on the coast of Guinea, she said to me, 'My dear boy, bless our fetishes, adore them always, they will make you live happily. You have the honor to be a slave to our lords, the whites, and will by that means be in a way of making the fortunes both of your father and your mother.' Alas! I do not know whether I have made their fortunes, but I am sure they have not made mine. The dogs, monkeys, and parrots are a thousand times less wretched than we. The Dutch missionaries who converted me told me every Sunday that we all are sons of Adam, both blacks and whites. I am not a genealogist, myself, but if these preachers speak the truth, we are all cousins-german; and you must own that it is a shocking thing to use one's relations in this barbarous manner."

"Ah! Pangloss," cried Candide, "you

never dreamed of such an abominable piece of cruelty and villainy! There is an end of the matter; I see I must at last renounce your optimism." "What do you mean by optimism?" said Cacambo. "Why," said Candide, "it is the folly of maintaining that everything is right, when it is wrong." He then looked upon the Negro with tears in his eyes and entered Surinam weeping.

Their first business was to inquire whether there was any vessel in the harbor wherein they could hire a passage for Buenos Aires. The person they applied to was no other than a Spanish commander, who offered to make an honorable bargain with them. He appointed to meet them at an inn, whither Candide and the faithful Cacambo went to wait for him with their two sheep.

Candide, whose heart was always on his lips, told the Spaniard his adventures and confessed that he was determined to run away with Miss Cunegonde. "I shall take care how I carry you to Buenos Aires, if that is the case," said the captain; "for I should be hanged, and so would you. The fair Cunegonde is my lord's favorite mistress."

This was a thunderclap to Candide; he wept a long time, but at last, drawing Cacambo aside: "I will tell you, my dear friend," said he, "what I would have you do. We have each of us about five or six millions of diamonds in our pocket; and as you are smarter at a bargain than I am, go you and fetch Miss Cunegonde from Buenos Aires. If the governor should make any objection, give him a million diamonds; if that does not succeed, give him two millions. As you did not murder the inquisitor, they will have no complaint against you; in the meantime, I will fit out another vessel and go and wait for you at Venice; that is a safe place, and I need not be afraid there of Bulgarians, Abares, or inquisitors." Cacambo applauded this sage resolution. He was, indeed, under great concern at leaving so good a master who used him like a familiar friend; but the pleasure of being serviceable to

him soon got the better of the sorrow he felt in parting with him.

They took leave of each other with tears, Candide recommending to him at the same time not to forget their good old woman. The same day Cacambo set sail. This Cacambo was a very honest fellow.

Candide stayed some time at Surinam, waiting for another vessel to carry him and the two remaining sheep to Italy. He hired servants and purchased everything necessary for so long a voyage; at last, Mynheer Vanderdendur, the master of a large vessel, came and offered his service. "What will you charge," said he to the Dutchman, "for carrying me, my servants, goods, and the two sheep you see here directly to Venice?" The master of the vessel asked ten thousand piasters; Candide made no objection.

"Oh, oh," said the crafty Vanderdendur to himself, after he had left him, "if this stranger can give ten thousand piasters without any words about it, he must be immensely rich." Returning a few minutes after, he let him know that he could not go for less than twenty thousand. "Well, you shall have twenty thousand then," said Candide.

"Odso," said the captain with a low voice, "this man makes no more of twenty thousand piasters than he did of ten!" He then returned a second time and said that he could not carry him to Venice for less than thirty thousand piasters. "You shall have thirty thousand then," replied Candide.

"Oh, oh," said the Dutch trader again to himself, "this man makes nothing of thirty thousand piasters; no doubt but the two sheep are loaded with immense treasures; let us stand out no longer; let us, however, finger the thirty thousand piasters first, and then we shall see."

Candide sold two small diamonds, the least of which was worth more than what the captain had asked. He advanced him the money. The two sheep were put aboard the vessel. Candide followed in a small wherry, intending to join the vessel in the road. But the captain improved his opportunity, unfurled sails, and unmoored. The wind being favorable, Candide, distracted and out of his wits, soon lost sight of him. "Ah!" cried he, "this is a trick worthy of the old world." He returned on shore, overwhelmed with sorrow, for he had lost more than would have made the fortunes of twenty princes.

He ran immediately to the Dutch judge, and as he hardly knew what he was about, knocked very loud at the door; he went in, told his case, and raised his voice a little higher than became him. The judge began by making him pay ten thousand piasters for the noise he had made; after which he heard him very patiently and promised to examine into the affair as soon as ever the trader should return, at the same time making him pay ten thousand piasters more for the expense of hearing his case.

This proceeding made Candide stark mad. He had indeed experienced misfortunes a thousand times more affecting, but the coolness of the judge and the knavish trick of the master of the vessel who had robbed him fired his spirits and plunged him into a profound melancholy. The villainy of mankind presented itself to his mind in all its deformity, and he dwelt upon nothing but the most dismal ideas. At last, a French vessel was ready to sail for Bordeaux, and as he had no sheep loaded with diamonds to carry with him, he paid the common price as a cabin passenger and ordered the crier to give notice all over the city that he would pay the passage and board of any honest man that would go the voyage with him, and give him two thousand piasters besides on condition that he would make it appear that he was the most disgusted with his condition and the most wretched person in that province.

A vast multitude of candidates presented themselves, enough to have manned a fleet. Candide selected twenty from among them, who seemed to have the best pretensions and to be the most sociable. But as every one of them thought the preference due to himself, he invited them all to his inn and gave them a supper, on condition that each one of them should take an oath that he would relate his adventures faithfully, promising to choose that person who seemed to be the greatest object of pity and had the greatest reason to be dissatisfied with his lot, and to give a small present to the rest as a recompense for their trouble.

The assembly continued till four o'clock the next morning. As Candide was employed in hearing their adventures, he could not help recollecting what the old woman had told him during their voyage to Buenos Aires, and the bet she had made, that there was not a single person in the ship that had not experienced some terrible misfortune. He thought of Pangloss at every adventure that was related. "That Pangloss," said he, "would be hard put to it to defend his system now. I wish he was but here. Indeed, if everything is ordered for the best, it must be at Eldorado, but nowhere else on earth." At last, he decided in favor of a poor scholar, who had written ten years for the booksellers at Amsterdam. For he thought there could not be a more disagreeable employment in the world.

This scholar,[1] though in other respects a good sort of a man, had been robbed by his wife, beat by his son, and abandoned by his daughter, who got a Portuguese to run away with her; had been stripped of a small employment, which was all he had to subsist on and was persecuted by the clerics at Surinam because they took him for a Socinian.[2]

It must indeed be confessed that most of the other candidates were as unhappy as he; but he met with a preference, because Candide thought that a scholar was best calculated to amuse him during the voyage. All his competitors thought that

[1] Martin.
[2] **Socinian:** a heretic, follower of the sixteenth-century rationalistic theologians named Socinus, who, among other things, denied the divinity of Christ.

Candide did them a great piece of injustice; but he appeased them by giving each of them a hundred piasters.

FOR STUDY AND DISCUSSION

1. The swiftness with which Voltaire tells his story is frequently commented upon. For example, in a single speech near the beginning of this episode, Candide and Cacambo decide their destination; how many sentences are used to narrate their difficult journey? What is the particular effect of this kind of narration? How does it compare with the technique used by Cervantes in *Don Quixote* (see page 514)? How does it compare with the technique used in a modern novel you have read?

2. In what ways is Candide a reflector—directly or by contrast—of Voltaire's attitudes? How does Cacambo function as a foil to Candide? In this use of character, how does Cervantes compare with Voltaire?

3. Up to this time, Candide has very diligently followed Pangloss's example of interpreting every event and circumstance optimistically. What is the effect, then, of Candide's remark at the end of Chapter 17: "in spite of all Doctor Pangloss's arguments, I could not help thinking that things were very bad in Westphalia"?

4. What are the significant characteristics of Eldorado? Summarize Voltaire's views, as you infer them from this episode, on organized religion, on government, and on wealth.

5. From the contrast he draws between Surinam and Eldorado, what does Voltaire imply are the root causes of evil in the world?

FOR COMPOSITION

1. Cacambo suggests that they let themselves drift with the current, saying "If we don't meet with what we like, we are sure to meet with something new." Candide agrees and adds that they should recommend themselves to the care of Providence. Don Quixote let his horse "take whatever path it chose, for he believed that therein lay the very essence of adventures." Use these details in writing a composition in which you compare and contrast the attitudes and purposes of Candide and Don Quixote.

2. From your observation of Eldorado and Surinam, of Candide and Martin, what do you conclude that Eldorado represents: an ideal toward which men should strive? an ideal which can inspire men even though they can never attain it? a false ideal that is so far from reality that only a fool like Candide would believe it? In a composition, explain and justify your conclusion, and take account of the alternatives you reject.

3. Find passages of Voltaire's story which obviously parody far-fetched stories of adventure and romance. What other parodies have you read, or viewed, which poke fun at a certain type of story, movie, or TV show? Write a brief story or script in which you parody the style of some type of story, TV show, or movie which you dislike.

Fables

JEAN DE LA FONTAINE

The name of Jean de la Fontaine (1621–1695) is practically synonymous with verse fables. Fontaine derived his beast stories from a variety of sources, mostly ancient, but he pointed them with wry, satiric wit at human affairs in seventeenth-century France. The morality of the fables is utilitarian, and many have found their philosophy uncongenial. Nineteenth-century French poet Alphonse de Lamartine said flatly, "They are poison." However, the fables are memorized by French school-children and have long been regarded by the French as tiny masterpieces, as models of perfect style. Therein, perhaps, lies one reason for their great popularity.

The Heifer, the Goat, and the Sheep, in Company with the Lion

The heifer, the goat, and their sister the sheep,
Compacted their earnings in common to keep,
'Tis said, in time past, with a lion, who swayed
Full lordship o'er neighbors, of whatever grade.
The goat, as it happened, a stag having snared,   5
Sent off to the rest, that the beast might be shared.
All gathered; the lion first counts on his claws,
And says, "We'll proceed to divide with our paws
The stag into pieces, as fixed by our laws."
    This done, he announces part first as his own;   10
    " 'Tis mine," he says, "truly, as lion alone.
    To such a decision there's nought to be said,
    As he who has made it is doubtless the head.
Well, also, the second to me should belong;
'Tis mine, be it known, by the right of the strong.   15
Again, as the bravest, the third must be mine.
To touch but the fourth whoso maketh a sign,

    I'll choke him to death
    In the space of a breath."

"The Heifer, the Goat, and the Sheep, in Company with the Lion," "The Cock and the Fox," and "The Council Held by the Rats" by Jean de la Fontaine, translated by Elizur Wright.

The Cock and the Fox

Upon a tree there mounted guard
  A veteran cock, adroit and cunning;
When to the roots a fox up running
  Spoke thus, in tones of kind regard:
"Our quarrel, brother, 's at an end;   5
  Henceforth I hope to live your friend;
    For peace now reigns
    Throughout the animal domains.
I bear the news. Come down, I pray,
And give me the embrace fraternal;   10
  And please, my brother, don't delay:
So much the tidings do concern all,
  That I must spread them far today.
Now you and yours can take your walks
Without a fear or thought of hawks;   15
And should you clash with them or others,
In us you'll find the best of brothers—
    For which you may, this joyful night,
    Your merry bonfires light.
      But, first, let's seal the bliss   20
      With one fraternal kiss."
"Good friend," the cock replied, "upon my word,
A better thing I never heard;
    And doubly I rejoice
    To hear it from your voice: 25
And, really, there must be something in it,
  For yonder come two greyhounds, which, I flatter
  Myself, are couriers on this very matter:
They come so fast, they'll be here in a minute.
  I'll down, and all of us will seal the blessing   30
  With general kissing and caressing."
    "Adieu," said Fox, "my errand's pressing;
    I'll hurry on my way,
    And we'll rejoice some other day."
So off the fellow scampered, quick and light,   35
To gain the foxholes of a neighboring height—
Less happy in his stratagem than flight.
  The cock laughed sweetly in his sleeve—
  'Tis doubly sweet deceiver to deceive.

The Council Held by the Rats

  Old Rodilard, a certain cat,
    Such havoc of the rats had made,
  'Twas difficult to find a rat
    With nature's debt unpaid.

The few that did remain,   5
    To leave their holes afraid,
From usual food abstain,
    Not eating half their fill.
    And wonder no one will,
That one who made on rats his revel,   10
With rats passed not for cat, but devil.
Now, on a day, this dread rat eater,
Who had a wife, went out to meet her;
And while he held his caterwauling,
The unkilled rats, their chapter calling,   15
Discussed the point, in grave debate,
How they might shun impending fate.
    Their dean, a prudent rat,
Thought best, and better soon than late,
    To bell the fatal cat;   20
That, when he took his hunting round,
The rats, well cautioned by the sound,
Might hide in safety under ground;
    Indeed he knew no other means.
    And all the rest   25
    At once confessed
Their minds were with the dean's.
No better plan, they all believed,
Could possibly have been conceived.
No doubt the thing would work right well,   30
If anyone would hang the bell.
    But, one by one, said every rat,
    I'm not so big a fool as that.
The plan, knocked down in this respect,
The council closed without effect,   35
And many a council I have seen,
Or reverend chapter with its dean,
    That, thus resolving wisely,
    Fell through like this precisely.

    To argue or refute   40
        Wise counselors abound;
    The man to execute
        Is harder to be found.

FOR STUDY AND DISCUSSION

1. Identify the human situations and the types of people satirized by each fable. What sort of attitude toward life is expressed in these fables? Do they urge people to be kindly, complacent, suspicious, shrewd? Explain.

2. How is each verse fable given a final turn, or "punch line"?

3. Point out particular poetic techniques that the translator uses for comic or for satiric effects. Why might he deliberately have created a singsong rhythm in "The Heifer, the Goat, and the Sheep . . ."?

Paradise Lost

JOHN MILTON

Paradise Lost was for John Milton (1608–1674) the goal and purpose of his life. When scarcely more than a boy, he decided that his destiny was to write a great poem for the glory of God. He prepared himself by wide and intensive study, and he learned the craft of poetry in both English and Latin. In the 1640's Milton was already known as a poet, but with some misgivings he let himself be deflected from literature to answer the call of civic and religious duty. When the English civil wars began, Milton served the Puritans, whom he hoped would overthrow the double tyranny of national Church and of monarchy, to establish a purer religion and a true, free, Christian republic. However, after several years' service in an important diplomatic post in Cromwell's government, Milton became disillusioned with the new orthodoxy, for it seemed as oppressive as the old. Moreover, he was afflicted by rapidly failing eyesight, and by the time he was in his early forties, he had become totally blind.

The restoration of the Stuart monarchy in 1660 destroyed all that Milton had worked and hoped for. Blind and in defeat, permitted by his enemies to live in obscurity in a country cottage twenty miles from London, Milton now completed the poem he had long felt God wanted from him. His great learning, his religious convictions, and his poetic genius poured out in some ten thousand verses of poetry, all dictated aloud to his daughters. After the completion of *Paradise Lost,* Milton went on to write the other major works of his later years: a short epic about Christ's temptation and sacrifice, *Paradise Regained,* and a classical tragedy on the Old Testament story, *Samson Agonistes (agonistes* is a Greek word for "champion"). In Samson, Milton might have seen some reflections of himself. Samson, blinded and enslaved by his inferiors, made a last great effort to destroy tyranny and confound the enemies of truth.

Milton's purpose in *Paradise Lost* is to "assert Eternal Providence and justify God's ways to man." After his profound disillusionment in public life, yet with a deeper and purer religious faith than he had ever had before, Milton wished to show that God provides all things for man's good and that his ways are just. *Paradise Lost* tells the story of Satan's rebellion in heaven and of his fall into hell, where thoughts of lost happiness eternally torment him. Milton shows that God brings good out of this evil by creating the race of men, who in time may merit the heaven that Satan has rejected. But man, like Satan, is capable of freely choosing between good or evil. Foreknowing that he will choose the evil—but not ordaining it—God voluntarily provides for man's redemption through his son, Christ, the agent of love. Thus, even man's choice of evil results in an increase of good, for it produces the great redemptive act of Christ, which restores to man the "blissful seat" in paradise.

Book 9 is about the crucial encounter of innocence with evil, the heart of *Paradise Lost*. In the preceding books, Satan, determined to work against God's good by causing the downfall of man, leaves his brimstone lake and flies to Eden, where he takes the shape of a bird and sits on the highest tree in the Garden. From there the Prince of Darkness, suddenly filled with grief, catches his first sight of Adam and Eve walking in the Garden, "the loveliest pair that ever since in love's embrace met." Overhearing their conversation, Satan learns that the fruit of the Tree of Knowledge is forbidden to them, under penalty of death. He determines to use the tree to seduce the "gentle pair" to sin.

The presence of evil in Paradise has been discovered. The angel Raphael comes to Eden as a messenger from God to warn Adam and Eve that Satan has determined to continue his rebellion by corrupting God's new creation. Raphael tells the first man and woman of God's provision for their welfare and reminds them of their duties as children of God, so that when the test of Satan's temptation comes they will be prepared. But Adam's and Eve's wills are free. If they chose ill, it will be their own doing, not determined by God. As Book 9 opens, Raphael returns to Heaven, and the stage is left to Adam and Eve, on Earth.

Milton preceded each book by a summary. In the selection that follows, the summary has been split up and placed before the various episodes it describes.

Book 9

No more of talk where God or angel guest
With man, as with his friend, familiar used
To sit indulgent, and with him partake
Rural repast, permitting him the while
Venial discourse unblamed. I now must change   5
Those notes to tragic; foul distrust, and breach
Disloyal on the part of man, revolt,
And disobedience; on the part of Heaven
Now alienated, distance and distaste,
Anger and just rebuke, and judgment given,   10
That brought into this world a world of woe,
Sin and her shadow Death, and misery,
Death's harbinger. Sad task, yet argument
Not less but more heroic than the wrath
Of stern Achilles on his foe° pursued   15
Thrice fugitive about Troy wall; or rage
Of Turnus for Lavinia disespoused;°
Or Neptune's ire or Juno's, that so long
Perplexed the Greek and Cytherea's son;°
If answerable style I can obtain   20
Of my celestial patroness,° who deigns
Her nightly visitation unimplored,

15. **his foe:** Hector (see the *Iliad*, page 55). In the following lines, Milton compares his story of God's wrath to ancient stories about the ire of various mythological figures.   17. **rage of Turnus for Lavinia disespoused:** a reference to an episode in the *Aeneid*. To win Italy, Aeneas defeated Turnus and married Turnus's betrothed, Lavinia.   19. **the Greek and Cytherea's son:** Odysseus is the Greek and Aeneas is the son of Venus, or Cytherea. The gods Neptune and Juno were hostile to both these heroes.   21. **my celestial patroness:** the "heavenly Muse," Urania, whose inspiration Milton invokes in the opening lines of *Paradise Lost*.

And dictates to me slumbering, or inspires
Easy my unpremeditated verse,
Since first this subject for heroic song   25
Pleased me long choosing, and beginning late;°
Not sedulous by nature to indite
Wars, hitherto the only argument
Heroic deemed, chief mastery to dissect
With long and tedious havoc fabled knights   30
In battles feigned (the better fortitude
Of patience and heroic martyrdom
Unsung), or to describe races and games,
Or tilting furniture, emblazoned shields,
Impresses quaint,° caparisons and steeds,   35
Bases and tinsel trappings, gorgeous knights
At joust and tournament; then marshaled feast
Served up in hall with sewers and seneschals;
The skill of artifice or office mean,
Not that which justly gives heroic name   40
To person or to poem. Me of these
Nor skilled nor studious, higher argument
Remains, sufficient of itself to raise
That name, unless an age too late, or cold
Climate, or years damp my intended wing   45
Depressed, and much they may, if all be mine,
Not hers who brings it nightly to my ear.

Satan, having compassed the Earth, with meditated guile returns as a mist by
night into Paradise; enters into the Serpent sleeping. [Lines 48–191]

The sun was sunk, and after him the star
Of Hesperus, whose office is to bring
Twilight upon the earth, short arbiter   50
'Twixt day and night, and now from end to end
Night's hemisphere had veiled the horizon round,
When Satan, who late fled before the threats
Of Gabriel out of Eden, now improved
In meditated fraud and malice, bent   55
On man's destruction, maugre° what might hap
Of heavier on himself, fearless returned.
By night he fled, and at midnight returned
From compassing the earth, cautious of day,
Since Uriel, regent of the sun, descried   60
His entrance, and forewarned the Cherubim
That kept their watch; thence full of anguish driven,
The space of seven continued nights he rode
With darkness, thrice the equinoctial line
He circled, four times crossed the car of Night   65

26. **beginning late:** Milton felt that his main task had been sadly delayed by his involvement in the Puritan Revolution.   35. **Impresses quaint:** intricately drawn emblems on shields.
56. **maugre:** in spite of.

From pole to pole, traversing each colure;°
On the eighth returned, and on the coast averse°
From entrance or Cherubic watch, by stealth
Found unsuspected way. There was a place—
Now not, though sin, not time, first wrought the change—   70
Where Tigris at the foot of Paradise
Into a gulf shot under ground, till part
Rose up a fountain by the Tree of Life;
In with the river sunk, and with it rose
Satan, involved in rising mist, then sought   75
Where to lie hid; sea he had searched and land
From Eden over Pontus,° and the pool
Maeotis, up beyond the river Ob;°
Downward as far antarctic; and in length
West from Orontes° to the ocean barred   80
At Darien,° thence to the land where flows
Ganges and Indus. Thus the orb he roamed
With narrow search, and with inspection deep
Considered every creature, which of all
Most opportune might serve his wiles, and found   85
The serpent subtlest beast of all the field.
Him after long debate, irresolute
Of thoughts revolved, his final sentence chose
Fit vessel, fittest imp of fraud, in whom
To enter, and his dark suggestions hide   90
From sharpest sight; for in the wily snake,
Whatever sleights none would suspicious mark,
As from his wit and native subtlety
Proceeding, which, in other beasts observed,
Doubt° might beget of diabolic power   95
Active within beyond the sense of brute.
Thus he resolved, but first from inward grief
His bursting passion into plaints thus poured:
    "O Earth, how like to Heaven, if not preferred
More justly, seat worthier of gods, as built   100
With second thoughts, reforming what was old!
For what God after better worse would build?
Terrestrial Heaven, danced round by other heavens
That shine, yet bear their bright officious lamps,
Light above light, for thee alone, as seems,   105
In thee concentring all their precious beams
Of sacred influence! As God in Heaven
Is center, yet extends to all, so thou
Centring receivest from all those orbs; in thee,
Not in themselves, all their known virtue appears   110

66. **each colure:** two imaginary circles drawn around the globe, at right angles to each other.
67. **averse:** opposite. 77. **Pontus:** the Black Sea. The geographical names in the next few
lines represent distant points in all directions from Eden, traditionally located in the Tigris-
Euphrates Valley. 78. **Ob:** in Siberia. 80. **Orontes:** a river in Syria. 81. **Darien:** Isthmus
of Panama. 95. **Doubt:** suspicion.

Productive in herb, plant, and nobler birth
Of creatures animate with gradual life
Of growth, sense, reason,° all summed up in man.
With what delight could I have walked thee round,
If I could joy in aught, sweet interchange   115
Of hill and valley, rivers, woods, and plains,
Now land, now sea, and shores with forest crowned,
Rocks, dens, and caves; but I in none of these
Find place or refuge; and the more I see
Pleasures about me, so much more I feel   120
Torment within me, as from the hateful siege
Of contraries; all good to me becomes
Bane, and in Heaven much worse would be my state.
But neither here seek I, no nor in Heaven
To dwell, unless by mastering Heaven's Supreme;   125
Nor hope to be myself less miserable
By what I seek, but others to make such
As I, though thereby worse to me redound.
For only in destroying I find ease
To my relentless thoughts; and him destroyed,   130
Or won to what may work his utter loss,
For whom all this was made, all this will soon
Follow, as to him linked in weal or woe;
In woe then, that destruction wide may range.
To me shall be the glory sole among   135
The infernal Powers, in one day to have marred
What he, Almighty styled, six nights and days
Continued making, and who knows how long
Before had been contriving? Though perhaps
Not longer than since I in one night freed   140
From servitude inglorious well-nigh half
The angelic name, and thinner left the throng
Of his adorers. He to be avenged,
And to repair his numbers thus impaired,
Whether such virtue spent of old now failed   145
More angels to create, if they at least
Are his created, or to spite us more,
Determined to advance into our room
A creature formed of earth, and him endow,
Exalted from so base original,   150
With heavenly spoils, our spoils. What he decreed
He effected; man he made, and for him built
Magnificent this world, and earth his seat,
Him lord pronounced, and, O indignity!
Subjected to his service angel wings,   155
And flaming ministers to watch and tend
Their earthy charge. Of these the vigilance
I dread, and to elude, thus wrapped in mist
Of midnight vapor glide obscure, and pry

113. **growth, sense, reason:** the powers of vegetable, animal, and human life, respectively.

In every bush and brake, where hap may find 160
The serpent sleeping, in whose mazy folds
To hide me, and the dark intent I bring.
O foul descent! that I who erst contended
With Gods to sit the highest, am now constrained
Into a beast, and mixed with bestial slime, 165
This essence to incarnate and imbrute,
That to the height of deity aspired;
But what will not ambition and revenge
Descend to? Who aspires must down as low
As high he soared, obnoxious° first or last 170
To basest things. Revenge, at first though sweet,
Bitter ere long back on itself recoils;
Let it; I reck not, so it light well aimed,
Since higher I fall short, on him who next
Provokes my envy, this new favorite 175
Of Heaven, this man of clay, son of despite,°
Whom us the more to spite his Maker raised
From dust: spite then with spite is best repaid."
   So saying, through each thicket dank or dry,
Like a black mist low creeping, he held on 180
His midnight search, where soonest he might find
The serpent. Him fast sleeping soon he found
In labyrinth of many a round self-rolled,
His head the midst, well stored with subtle wiles;
Not yet in horrid shade or dismal den, 185
Nor nocent° yet, but on the grassy herb
Fearless, unfeared, he slept. In at his mouth
The Devil entered, and his brutal sense,
In heart or head, possessing soon inspired
With act intelligential, but his sleep 190
Disturbed not, waiting close the approach of morn.

Adam and Eve in the morning go forth to their labors, which Eve proposes to divide in several places, each laboring apart. Adam consents not, alleging the danger lest that enemy, of whom they were forewarned, should attempt her found alone. Eve, loth to be thought not circumspect or firm enough, urges her going apart, the rather desirous to make trial of her strength; Adam at last yields. [Lines 192–411]

   Now whenas sacred light began to dawn
In Eden on the humid flowers, that breathed
Their morning incense, when all things that breathe
From the earth's great altar send up silent praise 195
To the Creator, and his nostrils fill
With grateful smell, forth came the human pair
And joined their vocal worship to the choir
Of creatures wanting voice; that done, partake
The season,° prime for sweetest scents and airs; 200

170. **obnoxious:** exposed (now obsolete in this sense).   176. **despite:** scorn, hatred (now archaic).   186. **nocent:** harmful (opposite of innocent).   200. **partake the season:** take in (enjoy) the morning.

Then cómmune how that day they best may ply
Their growing work; for much their work outgrew
The hands' dispatch of two gardening so wide.
And Eve first to her husband thus began:
   "Adam, well may we labor still to dress   205
This garden, still to tend plant, herb, and flower,
Our pleasant task enjoined, but till more hands
Aid us, the work under our labor grows,
Luxurious by restraint; what we by day
Lop overgrown, or prune, or prop, or bind,   210
One night or two with wanton growth derides,
Tending to wild. Thou therefore now advise
Or hear what to my mind first thoughts present:
Let us divide our labors, thou where choice
Leads thee, or where most needs, whether to wind   215
The woodbine round this arbor, or direct
The clasping ivy where to climb, while I
In yonder spring of roses intermixed
With myrtle, find what to redress till noon.
For while so near each other thus all day   220
Our task we choose, what wonder if so near
Looks intervene and smiles, or object new
Casual discourse draw on, which intermits
Our day's work, brought to little, though begun
Early, and the hour of supper comes unearned."   225
   To whom mild answer Adam thus returned:
"Sole Eve, associate sole, to me beyond
Compare above all living creatures dear,
Well hast thou mentioned, well thy thoughts employed
How we might best fulfill the work which here   230
God hath assigned us, nor of me shalt pass
Unpraised; for nothing lovelier can be found
In woman, than to study household good,
And good works in her husband to promote.
Yet not so strictly hath our Lord imposed   235
Labor, as to debar us when we need
Refreshment, whether food, or talk between,
Food of the mind, or this sweet intercourse
Of looks and smiles, for smiles from reason flow,
To brute denied, and are of love the food,   240
Love not the lowest end of human life.
For not to irksome toil, but to delight
He made us, and delight to reason joined.
These paths and bowers doubt not but our joint hands
Will keep from wilderness with ease, as wide   245
As we need walk, till younger hands ere long
Assist us. But if much convérse perhaps
Thee satiate, to short absence I could yield.
For solitude sometimes is best society,
And short retirement urges sweet return.   250
But other doubt possesses me, lest harm

Befall thee severed from me; for thou knowest
What hath been warned us, what malicious foe,
Envying our happiness, and of his own
Despairing, seeks to work us woe and shame   255
By sly assault; and somewhere nigh at hand
Watches, no doubt, with greedy hope to find
His wish and best advantage, us asunder,
Hopeless to circumvent us joined, where each
To other speedy aid might lend at need;   260
Whether his first design be to withdraw
Our fealty from God, or to disturb
Conjugal love, than which perhaps no bliss
Enjoyed by us excites his envy more;
Or this, or worse, leave not the faithful side   265
That gave thee being, still shades thee and protects.
The wife, where danger or dishonor lurks,
Safest and seemliest by her husband stays,
Who guards her, or with her the worst endures."
    To whom the virgin° majesty of Eve,   270
As one who loves, and some unkindness meets,
With sweet austere composure thus replied:
    "Offspring of Heaven and Earth, and all Earth's lord,
That such an enemy we have, who seeks
Our ruin, both by thee informed I learn,   275
And from the parting angel overheard
As in a shady nook I stood behind,
Just then returned at shut of evening flowers.
But that thou shouldst my firmness therefore doubt
To God or thee, because we have a foe   280
May tempt it, I expected not to hear.
His violence thou fearest not, being such
As we, not capable of death or pain,
Can either not receive, or can repel.
His fraud is then thy fear, which plain infers   285
Thy equal fear that my firm faith and love
Can by his fraud be shaken or seduced;
Thoughts, which how found they harbor in thy breast,
Adam, misthought of her to thee so dear?"
    To whom with healing words Adam replied: 290
"Daughter of God and man, immortal Eve,
For such thou art, from sin and blame entire;°
Not diffident of thee do I dissuade
Thy absence from my sight, but to avoid
The attempt itself, intended by our foe.   295
For he who tempts, though in vain, at least asperses
The tempted with dishonor foul, supposed
Not incorruptible of faith, not proof
Against temptation. Thou myself with scorn
And anger wouldst resent the offered wrong,   300

270. **virgin:** innocent, sinless.   292. **entire:** free, untouched.

Though ineffectual found. Misdeem not then,
If such affront I labor to avert
From thee alone, which on us both at once
The enemy, though bold, will hardly dare,
Or daring, first on me the assault shall light.   305
Nor thou his malice and false guile contemn;
Subtle he needs must be, who could seduce
Angels, nor think superfluous others' aid.
I from the influence of thy looks receive
Access° in every virtue, in thy sight   310
More wise, more watchful, stronger, if need were
Of outward strength; while shame, thou looking on,
Shame to be overcome or overreached,
Would utmost vigor raise, and raised unite.
Why shouldst not thou like sense within thee feel   315
When I am present, and thy trial choose
With me, best witness of thy virtue tried?"
   So spake domestic Adam in his care
And matrimonial love; but Eve, who thought
Less° attribúted to her faith sincere,   320
Thus her reply with accent sweet renewed:
   "If this be our condition, thus to dwell
In narrow circuit straitened by a foe,
Subtle or violent, we not endued
Single with like defense, wherever met,   325
How are we happy, still in fear of harm?
But harm precedes not sin: only our foe
Tempting affronts us with his foul esteem
Of our integrity; his foul esteem
Sticks no dishonor on our front, but turns   330
Foul on himself; then wherefore shunned or feared
By us? Who rather double honor gain
From his surmise proved false, find peace within,
Favor from Heaven, our witness, from the event.
And what is faith, love, virtue, unassayed   335
Alone, without exterior help sustained?
Let us not then suspect our happy state
Left so imperfect by the Maker wise
As not secure to single or combined.°
Frail is our happiness, if this be so,   340
And Eden were no Eden thus exposed."
   To whom thus Adam fervently replied:
"O woman, best are all things as the will
Of God ordained them; his creating hand
Nothing imperfect or deficient left   345
Of all that he created, much less man,
Or aught that might his happy state secure,
Secure from outward force: within himself

---

310. **Access:** increase (a rare usage).   320. **Less:** too little.   339. **secure to single or combined:** safe for us together or alone.

The danger lies, yet lies within his power;
Against his will he can receive no harm. 350
But God left free the will, for what obeys
Reason is free, and reason he made right,
But bid her well beware, and still erect,°
Lest by some fair appearing good surprised
She dictate false, and misinform the will 355
To do what God expressly hath forbid.
Not then mistrust, but tender love enjoins,
That I should mind° thee oft, and mind thou me.
Firm we subsist, yet possible to swerve,
Since reason not impossibly may meet 360
Some specious object by the foe suborned,
And fall into deception unaware,
Not keeping strictest watch, as she was warned.
Seek not temptation then, which to avoid
Were better, and most likely if from me 365
Thou sever not; trial will come unsought.
Wouldst thou approve° thy constancy, approve
First thy obedience; the other who can know,
Not seeing thee attempted, who attest?
But if thou think trial unsought may find 370
Us both securer° than thus warned thou seemest,
Go; for thy stay, not free, absents thee more;
Go in thy native innocence, rely
On what thou hast of virtue, summon all,
For God toward thee hath done his part, do thine." 375
    So spake the patriarch of mankind, but Eve
Persisted; yet submiss,° though last, replied:
    "With thy permission then, and thus forewarned,
Chiefly by what thy own last reasoning words
Touched only, that our trial, when least sought, 380
May find us both perhaps far less prepared,
The willinger I go, nor much expect
A foe so proud will first the weaker seek;
So bent, the more shall shame him his repulse."
Thus saying, from her husband's hand her hand 385
Soft she withdrew, and like a wood-nymph light,
Oread or Dryad, or of Delia's° train,
Betook her to the groves, but Delia's self
In gait surpassed and goddesslike deport,°
Though not as she with bow and quiver armed, 390
But with such gardening tools as art yet rude,
Guiltless of fire had formed, or angels brought.
To Pales,° or Pomona,° thus adorned,

---

353. **erect:** alert. 358. **mind:** remind. 367. **approve:** prove. 371. **securer:** more unguarded. 377. **submiss:** submissively. 387. **Delia's:** Diana (called Delia because she was
born on Delos), the virgin goddess of the hunt. 389. **deport:** deportment. 393. **Pales:** Roman
goddess of pastures. **Pomona:** Roman goddess of fruit, loved by Vertumnus, the god of fruit,
who wooed Pomona in many guises.

Likest she seemed, Pomona when she fled
Vertumnus, or to Ceres° in her prime,   395
Yet virgin of Proserpina from Jove.
Her long with ardent look his eye pursued
Delighted, but desiring more her stay.
Oft he to her his charge of quick return
Repeated, she to him as oft engaged   400
To be returned by noon amid the bower,
And all things in best order to invite
Noontide repast, or afternoon's repose.
O much deceived, much failing, hapless Eve,
Of thy presumed return! event perverse!   405
Thou never from that hour in Paradise
Foundest either sweet repast or sound repose;
Such ambush hid among sweet flowers and shades
Waited with hellish rancor imminent
To intercept thy way, or send thee back   410
Despoiled of innocence, of faith, of bliss.

The Serpent finds Eve alone: his subtle approach, first gazing, then speaking,
with much flattery extolling Eve above all other creatures. [Lines 412–548]

For now, and since first break of dawn the Fiend,
Mere serpent in appearance, forth was come,
And on his quest, where likeliest he might find
The only two of mankind, but in them   415
The whole included race, his purposed prey.
In bower and field he sought, where any tuft
Of grove or garden plot more pleasant lay,
Their tendance or plantation for delight;
By fountain or by shady rivulet   420
He sought them both, but wished his hap might find
Eve separate; he wished, but not with hope
Of what so seldom chanced, when to his wish,
Beyond his hope, Eve separate he spies,
Veiled in a cloud of fragrance, where she stood,   425
Half spied, so thick the roses bushing round
About her glowed, oft stooping to support
Each flower of slender stalk, whose head though gay
Carnation, purple, azure, or specked with gold,
Hung drooping unsustained; them she upstays   430
Gently with myrtle band, mindless the while,
Herself, though fairest unsupported flower,
From her best prop so far, and storm so nigh.
Nearer he drew, and many a walk traversed
Of stateliest covert, cedar, pine, or palm,   435
Then voluble° and bold, now hid, now seen

395. **Ceres:** goddess of earth and grain, who had a daughter, Proserpina, by the god Jove.
436. **voluble:** undulating as he moves.

Among thick-woven arborets and flowers
Imbordered on each bank, the hand° of Eve;

. . .

Much he the place admired, the person more.
As one who long in populous city pent,   445
Where houses thick and sewers annoy the air,
Forth issuing on a summer's morn to breathe
Among the pleasant villages and farms
Adjoined, from each thing met conceives delight,
The smell of grain, or tedded grass,° or kine,   450
Or dairy, each rural sight, each rural sound;
If chance with nymphlike step fair virgin pass,
What pleasing seemed, for her now pleases more,
She most, and in her look sums all delight:
Such pleasure took the Serpent to behold   455
This flowery plot, the sweet recess of Eve
Thus early, thus alone; her heavenly form
Angelic, but more soft and feminine,
Her graceful innocence, her every air
Of gesture or least action overawed   460
His malice, and with rapine sweet bereaved
His fierceness of the fierce intent it brought.
That space the Evil One abstracted stood
From his own evil, and for the time remained
Stupidly good,° of enmity disarmed,   465
Of guile, of hate, of envy, of revenge;
But the hot hell that always in him burns,
Though in mid-Heaven, soon ended his delight,
And tortures him now more, the more he sees
Of pleasure not for him ordained; then soon   470
Fierce hate he recollects, and all his thoughts
Of mischief, gratulating, thus excites:
    "Thoughts, whither have ye led me, with what sweet
Compulsion thus transported to forget
What hither brought us? Hate, not love, nor hope   475
Of Paradise for Hell, hope here to taste
Of pleasure, but all pleasure to destroy,
Save what is in destroying; other joy
To me is lost. Then let me not let pass
Occasion which now smiles: behold alone   480
The woman, opportune to all attempts,
Her husband, for I view far round, not nigh,
Whose higher intellectual more I shun,
And strength, of courage haughty, and of limb
Heroic built, though of terrestrial mold,   485
Foe not informidable, exempt from wound,

---

238. **hand:** handiwork. 450. **tedded grass:** hay spread out to dry. 465. **Stupidly good:**
Satan is not capable of good, but he is momentarily kept from evil by his stupefaction at the
beauty of Eve.

I not; so much hath Hell debased, and pain
Enfeebled me, to what I was in Heaven.
She fair, divinely fair, fit love for gods,
Not terrible, though terror be in love   490
And beauty, not approached by stronger hate,
Hate stronger, under show of love well feigned,
The way which to her ruin now I tend."
    So spake the Enemy of mankind, enclosed
In serpent, inmate bad, and toward Eve   495
Addressed his way, not with indented wave,
Prone on the ground, as since, but on his rear,
Circular base of rising folds, that towered
Fold above fold a surging maze; his head
Crested aloft, and carbuncle his eyes;   500
With burnished neck of verdant gold, erect
Amidst his circling spires, that on the grass
Floated redundant.° Pleasing was his shape,
And lovely, never since of serpent kind
Lovelier; . . .
                              With tract oblique°   510
At first, as one who sought accéss, but feared
To interrupt, sidelong he works his way.
As when a ship by skillful steersman wrought
Nigh river's mouth or foreland, where the wind
Veers oft, as oft so steers, and shifts her sail,   515
So varied he, and of his tortuous train
Curled many a wanton wreath in sight of Eve,
To lure her eye; she busied heard the sound
Of rustling leaves, but minded not, as used
To such disport before her through the field   520
From every beast, more duteous at her call
Than at Circean call the herd disguised.°
He bolder now, uncalled before her stood,
But as in gaze admiring. Oft he bowed
His turret crest, and sleek enameled neck,   525
Fawning, and licked the ground whereon she trod.
His gentle dumb expression turned at length
The eye of Eve to mark his play; he glad
Of her attention gained, with serpent tongue
Organic, or impulse of vocal air,°   530
His fraudulent temptation thus began:
    "Wonder not, sovereign mistress, if perhaps
Thou canst, who art sole wonder, much less arm
Thy looks, the heaven of mildness, with disdain,
Displeased that I approach thee thus, and gaze   535

503. **redundant:** with a wavy motion.   510. **tract oblique:** indirect path.   521–22. **more duteous at her call than at Circean call the herd disguised:** an allusion to an episode in the *Odyssey,* when the victims of the enchantress Circe were turned into swine and made obedient to her call.   530. **with serpent tongue organic, or impulse of vocal air:** either by using his tongue as an organ of speech or by making the vibration of the air sound like speech.

Insatiate, I thus single, nor have feared
Thy awful brow, more awful thus retired.
Fairest resemblance of thy Maker fair,
Thee all things living gaze on, all things thine
By gift, and thy celestial beauty adore,   540
With ravishment beheld, there best beheld
Where universally admired; but here
In this enclosure wild, these beasts among,
Beholders rude, and shallow to discern
Half what in thee is fair, one man except,   545
Who sees thee? (and what is one?) who shouldst be seen
A goddess among gods, adored and served
By angels numberless, thy daily train."

Eve, wondering to hear the Serpent speak, asks how he attained to human speech
and such understanding, not till now; the Serpent answers that by tasting of a certain tree in the garden he attained both to speech and reason, till then void of both.
[Lines 549–612]

So glozed° the Tempter, and his proem° tuned;
Into the heart of Eve his words made way,   550
Though at the voice much marveling; at length
Not unamazed she thus in answer spake:
    "What may this mean? Language of man pronounced
By tongue of brute, and human sense expressed?
The first at least of these I thought denied   555
To beasts, whom God on their creation day
Created mute to all articulate sound;
The latter I demur, for in their looks
Much reason, and in their actions oft appears.
Thee, Serpent, subtlest beast of all the field   560
I knew, but not with human voice endowed;
Redouble then this miracle, and say,
How camest thou speakable of° mute, and how
To me so friendly grown above the rest
Of brutal kind, that daily are in sight?   565
Say, for such wonder claims attention due."
    To whom the guileful Tempter thus replied:
"Empress of this fair world, resplendent Eve,
Easy to me it is to tell thee all
What thou commandest, and right thou shouldst be obeyed.   570
I was at first as other beasts that graze
The trodden herb, of abject thoughts and low,
As was my food, nor aught but food discerned
Or sex, and apprehended nothing high:
Till on a day roving the field, I chanced   575
A goodly tree far distant to behold,
Loaden with fruit of fairest colors mixed,
Ruddy and gold. I nearer drew to gaze;

549. **glozed:** flattered.   **proem:** preface.   563. **of:** from being.

When from the boughs a savory odor blown,
Grateful to appetite, more pleased my sense   580
Than smell of sweetest fennel or the teats
Of ewe or goat dropping with milk at even',
Unsucked of lamb or kid, that tend their play.
To satisfy the sharp desire I had
Of tasting those fair apples, I resolved   585
Not to defer; hunger and thirst at once,
Powerful persuaders, quickened at the scent
Of that alluring fruit, urged me so keen.
About the mossy trunk I wound me soon,
For high from ground the branches would require   590
Thy utmost reach or Adam's: round the tree
All other beasts that saw, with like desire
Longing and envying stood, but could not reach.
Amid the tree now got, where plenty hung
Tempting so nigh, to pluck and eat my fill   595
I spared not, for such pleasure till that hour
At feed or fountain never had I found.
Sated at length, ere long I might perceive
Strange alteration in me, to degree
Of reason in my inward powers, and speech   600
Wanted not long, though to this shape retained.
Thenceforth to speculations high or deep
I turned my thoughts, and with capacious mind
Considered all things visible in Heaven,
Or earth, or middle, all things fair and good;   605
But all that fair and good in thy divine
Semblance, and in thy beauty's heavenly ray
United I beheld; no fair to thine
Equivalent or second, which compelled
Me thus, though importune perhaps, to come   610
And gaze, and worship thee of right declared
Sovereign of creatures, universal dame.''°

Eve requires him to bring her to that tree, and finds it to be the Tree of Knowledge forbidden. [Lines 613–63]

So talked the spirited sly Snake; and Eve
Yet more amazed unwary thus replied:
"Serpent, thy overpraising leaves in doubt   615
The virtue of that fruit, in thee first proved.°
But say, where grows the tree, from hence how far?
For many are the trees of God that grow
In Paradise, and various, yet unknown
To us; in such abundance lies our choice   620
As leaves a greater store of fruit untouched,
Still hanging incorruptible, till men

612. **universal dame:** mistress of the universe.   616. **proved:** tested.

Grow up to their provision, and more hands
Help to disburden Nature of her bearth."°
    To whom the wily Adder, blithe and glad: 625
"Empress, the way is ready, and not long,
Beyond a row of myrtles, on a flat,
Fast by a fountain, one small thicket past
Of blowing myrrh and balm; if thou accept
My conduct, I can bring thee thither soon."   630
    "Lead then," said Eve. He leading swiftly rolled
In tangles, and made intricate seem straight,
To mischief swift. Hope elevates, and joy
Brightens his crest, as when a wandering fire,
Compact of unctuous vapor, which the night   635
Condenses, and the cold environs round,
Kindled through agitation to a flame,
Which oft, they say, some evil Spirit attends,
Hovering and blazing with delusive light,
Misleads the amazed night wanderer from his way   640
To bogs and mires, and oft through pond or pool,
There swallowed up and lost, from succor far.
So glistered the dire Snake, and into fraud
Led Eve our credulous mother, to the tree
Of prohibition, root of all our woe;   645
Which when she saw, thus to her guide she spake:
    "Serpent, we might have spared our coming hither,
Fruitless to me, though fruit be here to excess,
The credit of whose virtue rest with thee,°
Wondrous indeed, if cause of such effects.   650
But of this tree we may not taste nor touch;
God so commanded, and left that command
Sole daughter of his voice; the rest, we live
Law to ourselves, our reason is our law."
    To whom the Tempter guilefully replied: 655
"Indeed? Hath God then said that of the fruit
Of all these garden trees ye shall not eat,
Yet lords declared of all in earth or air?"
    To whom thus Eve yet sinless: "Of the fruit
Of each tree in the garden we may eat,   660
But of the fruit of this fair tree amidst
The garden, God hath said, 'Ye shall not eat
Thereof, nor shall ye touch it, lest ye die.' "

The Serpent, now grown bolder, with many wiles and arguments induces her at
length to eat. [Lines 664–792]

    She scarce had said, though brief, when now more bold
The Tempter, but with show of zeal and love   665
To man, and indignation at his wrong,

624. **bearth:** fruit (what she bears).   649. **The credit of whose virtue rest with thee:** the
proof of whose virtue will have to stop with you (because I cannot try it myself).

New part puts on, and as to passion moved,
Fluctuates disturbed, yet comely, and in act
Raised, as of some great matter to begin.
As when of old some orator renowned   670
In Athens or free Rome, where eloquence
Flourished, since mute, to some great cause addressed,
Stood in himself collected, while each part,
Motion, each act won audience ere the tongue,
Sometimes in highth began, as no delay   675
Of preface brooking through his zeal of right:
So standing, moving, or to highth upgrown,
The Tempter all impassioned thus began:
    "O sacred, wise, and wisdom-giving Plant,
Mother of science,° now I feel thy power   680
Within me clear, not only to discern
Things in their causes, but to trace the ways
Of highest agents, deemed however wise.
Queen of this universe, do not believe
Those rigid threats of death; ye shall not die: 685
How should ye? By the fruit? It gives you life
To° knowledge; by the Threatener? Look on me,
Me who have touched and tasted, yet both live,
And life more perfect have attained than Fate
Meant me, by venturing higher than my lot.   690
Shall that be shut to man, which to the beast
Is open? Or will God incense his ire
For such a petty trespass, and not praise
Rather your dauntless virtue, whom the pain
Of death denounced,° whatever thing death be,   695
Deterred not from achieving what might lead
To happier life, knowledge of good and evil?
Of good, how just? Of evil, if what is evil
Be real, why not known, since easier shunned?
God therefore cannot hurt ye, and be just;   700
Not just, not God; not feared then, nor obeyed:
Your feat itself of death removes the fear.
Why then was this forbid? Why but to awe,
Why but to keep ye low and ignorant,
His worshipers? He knows that in the day   705
Ye eat thereof, your eyes that seem so clear,
Yet are but dim, shall perfectly be then
Opened and cleared, and ye shall be as gods,
Knowing both good and evil as they know.
That ye should be as gods, since I as man,   710
Internal man, is but proportion meet,
I of brute human, ye of human gods.
So ye shall die perhaps, by putting off
Human, to put on gods, death to be wished,
Though threatened, which no worse than this can bring. 715

680. **science:** knowledge. 687. **To:** as well as. 695. **denounced:** threatened.

And what are gods that man may not become
As they, participating godlike food?
The gods are first, and that advantage use
On our belief, that all from them proceeds;
I question it, for this fair earth I see,   720
Warmed by the sun, producing every kind,
Them nothing. If they all things, who enclosed
Knowledge of good and evil in this tree,
That whoso eats thereof, forthwith attains
Wisdom without their leave? And wherein lies   725
The offense, that man should thus attain to know?
What can your knowledge hurt him, or this tree
Impart against his will, if all be his?
Or is it envy, and can envy dwell
In heavenly breasts? These, these and many more   730
Causes import your need of this fair fruit.
Goddess humane, reach then, and freely taste!"
    He ended, and his words replete with guile
Into her heart too easy entrance won.
Fixed on the fruit she gazed, which to behold   735
Might tempt alone, and in her ears the sound
Yet rung of his persuasive words, impregned
With reason, to her seeming, and with truth;
Meanwhile the hour of noon drew on, and waked
An eager appetite, raised by the smell   740
So savory of that fruit, which with desire,
Inclinable now grown to touch or taste,
Solicited her longing eye; yet first
Pausing a while, thus to herself she mused:
    "Great are thy virtues, doubtless best of fruits,   745
Though kept from man, and worthy to be admired,
Whose taste, too long forborne, at first assay
Gave elocution to the mute, and taught
The tongue not made for speech to speak thy praise.
Thy praise he also who forbids thy use   750
Conceals not from us, naming thee the Tree
Of Knowledge, knowledge both of good and evil;
Forbids us then to taste, but his forbidding
Commends thee more, while it infers the good
By thee communicated, and our want;   755
For good unknown sure is not had, or had
And yet unknown, is as not had at all.
In plain,° then, what forbids he but to know,
Forbids us good, forbids us to be wise?
Such prohibitions bind not. But if Death   760
Bind us with afterbands, what profits then
Our inward freedom? In the day we eat
Of this fair fruit, our doom is, we shall die.
How dies the Serpent? He hath eaten and lives,

758. **In plain:** in plain terms.

And knows, and speaks, and reasons, and discerns,   765
Irrational till then. For us alone
Was death invented? Or to us denied
This intellectual food, for beasts reserved?
For beasts it seems; yet that one beast which first
Hath tasted, envies not, but brings with joy   770
The good befallen him, author unsuspect,°
Friendly to man, far from deceit or guile.
What fear I, then, rather what know to fear
Under this ignorance of good and evil,
Of God or death, of law or penalty?   775
Here grows the cure of all, this fruit divine,
Fair to the eye, inviting to the taste,
Of virtue to make wise; what hinders then
To reach, and feed at once both body and mind?"
    So saying, her rash hand in evil hour   780
Forth reaching to the fruit, she plucked, she eat.°
Earth felt the wound, and Nature from her seat
Sighing through all her works gave signs of woe,
That all was lost. Back to the thicket slunk
The guilty Serpent, and well might, for Eve   785
Intent now wholly on her taste, naught else
Regarded; such delight till then, as seemed,
In fruit she never tasted, whether true
Or fancied so, through expectation high
Of knowledge, nor was Godhead from her thought.   790
Greedily she engorged without restraint,
And knew not eating° death.

Eve, pleased with the taste, deliberates a while whether to impart thereof to Adam or not; at last brings him of the fruit; relates what persuaded her to eat thereof. [Lines 792–885]

                Satiate at length,
And heightened as with wine, jocund and boon,°
Thus to herself she pleasingly began:
    "O sovereign, virtuous, precious of all trees   795
In Paradise, of operation blest
To sapience, hitherto obscured, infamed,°
And thy fair fruit let hang, as to no end
Created; but henceforth my early care,
Not without song, each morning, and due praise,   800
Shall tend thee, and the fertile burden ease
Of thy full branches offered free to all;
Till dieted by thee I grow mature
In knowledge, as the gods who all things know;
Though others envy what they cannot give;   805
For had the gift been theirs, it had not here
Thus grown. Experience, next to thee I owe,

771. **author unsuspect:** unquestionable authority.   781. **eat:** pronounced "et," still good British usage as the past tense. (American usage would be "ate.")   792. **knew not eating:** knew not that she was eating.   793. **boon:** blithe.   797. **infamed:** maligned, defamed.

Best guide; not following thee, I had remained
In ignorance; thou openest wisdom's way,
And givest accéss, though secret she retire.   810
And I perhaps am secret; Heaven is high,
High and remote to see from thence distinct
Each thing on earth; and other care perhaps
May have diverted from continual watch
Our great Forbidder, safe with all his spies   815
About him. But to Adam in what sort
Shall I appear? Shall I to him make known
As yet my change, and give him to partake
Full happiness with me, or rather not,
But keep the odds of knowledge in my power   820
Without copartner? So to add what wants
In female sex, the more to draw his love,
And render me more equal, and perhaps,
A thing not undesirable, sometime
Superior; for inferior who is free?   825
This may be well. But what if God have seen,
And death ensue? Then I shall be no more,
And Adam wedded to another Eve
Shall live with her enjoying, I extinct;
A death to think. Confirmed then I resolve,   830
Adam shall share with me in bliss or woe.
So dear I love him, that with him all deaths
I could endure, without him live no life."
    So saying, from the tree her step she turned,
But first low reverence done, as to the power   835
That dwelt within, whose presence had infused
Into the plant sciential° sap, derived
From nectar, drink of gods. Adam the while
Waiting desirous her return, had wove
Of choicest flowers a garland to adorn   840
Her tresses, and her rural labors crown,
As reapers oft are wont their harvest queen.
Great joy he promised to his thoughts, and new
Solace in her return, so long delayed;
Yet oft his heart, divine of° something ill,   845
Misgave him; he the faltering measure felt;
And forth to meet her went, the way she took
That morn when first they parted. By the Tree
Of Knowledge he must pass; there he her met,
Scarce from the tree returning; in her hand   850
A bough of fairest fruit that downy smiled,
New gathered, and ambrosial smell diffused.
To him she hasted; in her face excuse
Came prologue, and apology to prompt,
Which with bland words at will she thus addressed: 855
    "Hast thou not wondered, Adam, at my stay?

837. **sciential:** knowledge-giving. 845. **divine of:** sensing.

Thee I have missed, and thought it long, deprived
Thy presence, agony of love till now
Not felt, nor shall be twice, for never more
Mean I to try what rash untried I sought,   860
The pain of absence from thy sight. But strange
Hath been the cause, and wonderful to hear:
This tree is not as we are told, a tree
Of danger tasted, nor to evil unknown
Opening the way, but of divine effect   865
To open eyes, and make them gods who taste;
And hath been tasted such. The Serpent wise,
Or not restrained as we, or not obeying,
Hath eaten of the fruit, and is become
Not dead, as we are threatened, but thenceforth   870
Endued with human voice and human sense,
Reasoning to admiration, and with me
Persuasively hath so prevailed, that I
Have also tasted, and have also found
The effects to correspond, opener mine eyes,   875
Dim erst, dilated spirits, ampler heart,
And growing up to Godhead; which for thee
Chiefly I sought, without thee can despise.
For bliss, as thou hast part, to me is bliss;
Tedious, unshared with thee, and odious soon.   880
Thou therefore also taste, that equal lot
May join us, equal joy, as equal love;
Lest thou not tasting, different degree
Disjoin us, and I then too late renounce
Deity for thee, when fate will not permit."   885

Adam, at first amazed, but perceiving her lost, resolves through vehemence of
love to perish with her, and, extenuating the trespass, eats also of the fruit. [Lines
886–1011]

Thus Eve with countenance blithe her story told;
But in her cheek distemper flushing glowed.
On the other side, Adam, soon as he heard
The fatal trespass done by Eve, amazed,
Astonied° stood and blank, while horror chill   890
Ran through his veins, and all his joints relaxed;
From his slack hand the garland wreathed for Eve
Down dropped, and all the faded roses shed.
Speechless he stood and pale, till thus at length
First to himself he inward silence broke: 895
    "O fairest of creation, last and best
Of all God's works, creature in whom excelled
Whatever can to sight or thought be formed,
Holy, divine, good, amiable, or sweet!
How art thou lost, how on a sudden lost,   900

890. **Astonied:** stupefied.

Defaced, deflowered, and now to death devote!
Rather how hast thou yielded to transgress
The strict forbiddance, how to violate
The sacred fruit forbidden! Some cursèd fraud
Of enemy hath beguiled thee, yet unknown,   905
And me with thee hath ruined, for with thee
Certain my resolution is to die;
How can I live without thee, how forgo
Thy sweet converse and love so dearly joined,
To live again in these wild woods forlorn?   910
Should God create another Eve, and I
Another rib afford, yet loss of thee
Would never from my heart; no, no! I feel
The link of nature draw me: flesh of flesh,
Bone of my bone thou art, and from thy state   915
Mine never shall be parted, bliss or woe."
   So having said, as one from sad dismay
Recomforted, and after thoughts disturbed
Submitting to what seemed remédiless,
Thus in calm mood his words to Eve he turned: 920
   "Bold deed thou hast presumed, adventurous Eve,
And peril great provoked, who thus hast dared
Had it been only coveting to eye
That sacred fruit, sacred to abstinence,
Much more to taste it under ban to touch.   925
But past who can recall, or done undo?
Not God omnipotent, nor Fate. Yet so
Perhaps thou shalt not die; perhaps the fact
Is not so heinous now, foretasted fruit,
Profaned first by the Serpent, by him first   930
Made common and unhallowed ere our taste,
Nor yet on him found deadly; he yet lives,
Lives, as thou saidst, and gains to live as man
Higher degree of life, inducement strong
To us, as likely tasting to attain   935
Proportional ascent, which cannot be
But to be gods, or angels, demigods.
Nor can I think that God, Creator wise,
Though threatening, will in earnest so destroy
Us his prime creatures, dignified so high,   940
Set over all his works, which in our fall,
For us created, needs with us must fail,
Dependent made; so God shall uncreate,
Be frustrate, do, undo, and labor lose,
Not well conceived of God, who though his power   945
Creation could repeat, yet would be loth
Us to abolish, lest the Adversary
Triumph and say: 'Fickle their state whom God
Most favors, who can please him long? Me first
He ruined, now mankind; whom will he next?'   950
Matter of scorn not to be given the Foe;

650   THE AGE OF RATIONALISM

However, I with thee have fixed my lot,
Certain to undergo like doom: if death
Consort with thee, death is to me as life;
So forcible within my heart I feel   955
The bond of nature draw me to my own,
My own in thee, for what thou art is mine;
Our state cannot be severed; we are one,
One flesh; to lose thee were to lose myself."
    So Adam, and thus Eve to him replied: 960
"O glorious trial of exceeding love,
Illustrious evidence, example high!
Engaging me to emulate, but short
Of thy perfection, how shall I attain,
Adam? From whose dear side I boast me sprung,   965
And gladly of our union hear thee speak,
One heart, one soul in both; whereof good proof
This day affords, declaring thee resolved,
Rather than death or aught than death more dread
Shall separate us, linked in love so dear,   970
To undergo with me one guilt, one crime,
If any be, of tasting this fair fruit,
Whose virtue (for of good still good proceeds,
Direct, or by occasion) hath presented
This happy trial of thy love, which else   975
So eminently never had been known.
Were it I thought death menaced would ensue
This my attempt, I would sustain alone
The worst, and not persuade thee, rather die
Deserted, than oblige° thee with a fact   980
Pernicious to thy peace, chiefly assured
Remarkably so late of thy so true,
So faithful love unequaled; but I feel
Far otherwise the event, not death, but life
Augmented, opened eyes, new hopes, new joys,   985
Taste so divine, that what of sweet before
Hath touched my sense, flat seems to this and harsh.
On my experience, Adam, freely taste,
And fear of death deliver to the winds."
    So saying, she embraced him, and for joy   990
Tenderly wept, much won that he his love
Had so ennobled, as of choice to incur
Divine displeasure for her sake, or death.
In recompense (for such compliance bad
Such recompense best merits) from the bough   995
She gave him of that fair enticing fruit
With liberal hand. He scrupled not to eat
Against his better knowledge, not deceived,
But fondly overcome with female charm.
Earth trembled from her entrails, as again   1000

980. **oblige:** implicate.

In pangs, and Nature gave a second groan;
Sky lowered and, muttering thunder, some sad drops
Wept at completing of the mortal sin
Original; while Adam took no thought,
Eating his fill, nor Eve to iterate   1005
Her former trespass feared, the more to soothe
Him with her loved society, that now
As with new wine intoxicated both
They swim in mirth, and fancy that they feel
Divinity within them breeding wings   1010
Wherewith to scorn the earth.

    The effects thereof in them both; they seek to cover their nakedness; then fall
to variance and accusation of one another. [Lines 1011–1189]

                                 But that false fruit
Far other operation first displayed,
Carnal desire inflaming: he on Eve
Began to cast lascivious eyes, she him
As wantonly repaid; in lust they burn,   1015
Till Adam thus 'gan Eve to dalliance move:
    "Eve, now I see thou art exact of taste,
And elegant, of sapience no small part;
Since to each meaning savor we apply,
And palate call judicious; I the praise   1020
Yield thee, so well this day thou hast purveyed.
Much pleasure we have lost, while we abstained
From this delightful fruit, nor known till now
True, relish, tasting; if such pleasure be
In things to us forbidden, it might be wished   1025
For this one tree had been forbidden ten.
But come, so well refreshed, now let us play,
As meet is, after such delicious fare;
For never did thy beauty since the day
I saw thee first and wedded thee, adorned   1030
With all perfections, so inflame my sense
With ardor to enjoy thee,° fairer now
Than ever, bounty of this virtuous tree."
    So said he, and forbore not glance or toy°
Of amorous intent, well understood   1035
Of Eve, whose eye darted contagious fire.
Her hand he seized, and to a shady bank,
Thick overhead with verdant roof embowered,
He led her nothing loth; flowers were the couch,
Pansies, and violets, and asphodel,   1040
And hyacinth, earth's freshest softest lap.
There they their fill of love and love's disport
Took largely, of their mutual guilt the seal,
The solace of their sin, till dewy sleep

    1032. **enjoy thee:** This underscores the change in Adam's attitude toward sex. By using a
phrase like "enjoy thee," Adam degrades both himself and Eve.   1034. **toy:** caress.

Oppressed them, wearied with their amorous play.   1045
Soon as the force of that fallacious fruit,
That with exhilarating vapor bland
About their spirits had played, and inmost powers
Made err, was now exhaled, and grosser sleep
Bred of unkindly° fumes, with conscious dreams   1050
Encumbered, now had left them, up they rose
As from unrest, and each the other viewing,
Soon found their eyes how opened, and their minds
How darkened; innocence, that as a veil
Had shadowed them from knowing ill, was gone;   1055
Just confidence, and native righteousness,
And honor from about them, naked left
To guilty Shame; he° covered, but his robe
Uncovered more. So rose the Danite strong,°
Herculean Samson, from the harlot-lap   1060
Of Philistean Dalilah, and waked
Shorn of his strength, they destitute and bare
Of all their virtue. Silent, and in face
Confounded, long they sat, as strucken mute,
Till Adam, though not less than Eve abashed,   1065
At length gave utterance to these words constrained:
    "O Eve, in evil hour thou didst give ear
To that false worm, of whomsoever taught
To counterfeit man's voice, true in our fall,
False in our promised rising; since our eyes   1070
Opened we find indeed, and find we know
Both good and evil, good lost and evil got,
Bad fruit of knowledge, if this be to know,
Which leaves us naked thus, of honor void,
Of innocence, of faith, of purity,   1075
Our wonted ornaments now soiled and stained,
And in our faces evident the signs
Of foul concupiscence; whence evil store,
Even shame, the last of evils; of the first
Be sure then. How shall I behold the face   1080
Henceforth of God or angel, erst with joy
And rapture so oft beheld? Those heavenly shapes
Will dazzle now this earthly, with their blaze
Insufferably bright. O might I here
In solitude live savage, in some glade   1085
Obscured, where highest woods impenetrable
To star or sunlight, spread their umbrage broad
And brown as evening! Cover me, ye pines,
Ye cedars, with innumerable boughs
Hide me, where I may never see them° more.   1090
But let us now, as in bad plight, devise
What best may for the present serve to hide

1050. **unkindly:** unnatural.   1058. **he:** Shame.   1059. **Danite strong:** a reference to Samson, a descendant of Dan.   1090. **them:** the heavenly shapes.

The parts of each from other that seem most
To shame obnoxious, and unseemliest seen,
Some tree whose broad smooth leaves together sewed,   1095
And girded on our loins, may cover round
Those middle parts, that this newcomer, Shame,
There sit not, and reproach us as unclean."
    So counseled he, and both together went
Into the thickest wood; there soon they chose   1100
The fig tree, not that kind for fruit renowned,
But such as at this day to Indians known
In Malabar or Deccan spreads her arms
Branching so broad and long, that in the ground
The bended twigs take root, and daughters grow   1105
About the mother tree, a pillared shade
High overarched, and echoing walks between;
There oft the Indian herdsman shunning heat
Shelters in cool, and tends his pasturing herds
At loopholes cut through thickest shade. Those leaves   1110
They gathered, broad as Amazonian targe,°
And with what skill they had, together sewed,
To gird their waist, vain covering if to hide
Their guilt and dreaded shame, O how unlike
To that first naked glory! Such of late   1115
Columbus found the American so girt
With feathered cincture, naked else and wild
Among the trees on isles and woody shores.
Thus fenced, and as they thought, their shame in part
Covered, but not at rest or ease of mind,   1120
They sat them down to weep; nor only tears
Rained at their eyes, but high winds worse within
Began to rise, high passions, anger, hate,
Mistrust, suspicion, discord, and shook sore
Their inward state of mind, calm region once   1125
And full of peace, now tossed and turbulent;
For understanding ruled not, and the will
Heard not her lore, both in subjection now
To sensual appetite, who from beneath
Usurping over sovereign reason claimed   1130
Superior sway. From thus distempered breast,
Adam, estranged in look and altered style,
Speech intermitted thus to Eve renewed:
    "Would thou hadst hearkened to my words, and stayed
With me, as I besought thee, when that strange   1135
Desire of wandering this unhappy morn,
I know not whence possessed thee; we had then
Remained still happy, not as now, despoiled
Of all our good, shamed, naked, miserable.
Let none henceforth seek needless cause to approve°   1140

1111. **Amazonian targe:** shield of the giant Amazon women of classical mythology.
1140. **approve:** prove, test.

The faith they owe;° when earnestly they seek
Such proof, conclude they then begin to fail."
   To whom, soon moved with touch of blame, thus Eve:
"What words have passed thy lips, Adam severe!
Imputest thou that to my default, or will   1145
Of wandering, as thou callest it, which who knows
But might as ill have happened thou being by,
Or to thyself perhaps? Hadst thou been there,
Or here the attempt, thou couldst not have discerned
Fraud in the Serpent, speaking as he spake;   1150
No ground of enmity between us known
Why he should mean me ill, or seek to harm.
Was I to have never parted from thy side?
As good have grown there still a lifeless rib.
Being as I am, why didst not thou, the head,   1155
Command me absolutely not to go,
Going into such danger as thou saidst?
Too facile then, thou didst not much gainsay,
Nay didst permit, approve, and fair dismiss.
Hadst thou been firm and fixed in thy dissent,   1160
Neither had I transgressed, nor thou with me."
   To whom then first incensed Adam replied:
"Is this the love, is this the recompense
Of mine to thee, ingrateful Eve, expressed
Immutable when thou wert lost, not I,   1165
Who might have lived and joyed immortal bliss,
Yet willingly chose rather death with thee?
And am I now upbraided, as the cause
Of thy transgressing? Not enough severe,
It seems, in thy restraint. What could I more?   1170
I warned thee, I admonished thee, foretold
The danger, and the lurking enemy
That lay in wait; beyond this had been force,
And force upon free will hath here no place.
But confidence then bore thee on, secure   1175
Either to meet no danger, or to find
Matter of glorious trial; and perhaps
I also erred in overmuch admiring
What seemed in thee so perfect, that I thought
No evil durst attempt thee, but I rue   1180
That error now, which is become my crime,
And thou the accuser. Thus it shall befall
Him who to worth in women overtrusting
Lets her will rule; restraint she will not brook,
And left to herself, if evil thence ensue,   1185
She first his weak indulgence will accuse."
   Thus they in mutual accusation spent
The fruitless hours, but neither self-condemning,
And of their vain contest appeared no end.

1141. **owe:** own, have.

1. At two points (lines 6–13 and 404–11) Milton tells the reader about the dire consequences of the calamity that is to come. What is the dramatic effectiveness of his doing so? Why do you think these anticipations are placed where they are?

2. According to Milton (lines 13–47), why is his own epic superior to the great epics of ancient literatures? On the other hand, Milton clearly follows classical examples; what quality is given to the poem by his use of epic similes, of classical allusions, and of the classical epic form (see page 104)?

3. What impression does Milton give of Satan in the description of his journey to Eden (lines 62–69), and of his search for a disguise (lines 76–86)? Compare this impression with that of the description of Satan as the serpent (lines 494–531). In what specific ways is the contrast ironic?

4. Why does Satan choose the snake as his disguise?

5. Satan reveals an awareness that he has chosen the worse (lines 163–67), and he shows some appreciation of beauty and goodness in his praise of God's world (lines 99–107, 114–25) and in his awe at the sight of the innocent Eve (lines 455–70). What is the dramatic effect of Satan's candor?

6. What does Satan reveal (lines 126–39) of his motives for destroying the innocence of Adam and Eve? In your opinion, do comparable satisfactions take the place of real happiness in human reality? Explain.

7. Assuming, as Milton does, the absolute perfection of God, what is the flaw in Satan's reasoning (lines 102–13) about the creation of the world and man? Because Satan's exaltation of man is fallacious, does it follow that Milton rejects the humanist view of man's capabilities? Explain.

8. Satan's account of God's purpose in creating the world and man is factually true, but his interpretation is fallacious. Distinguish between the true and false in this passage (lines 139–51).

9. How would Milton explain God's provision of "flaming ministers" (line 156) to guard Paradise, on the one hand, and Satan's ability to elude them, on the other?

10. What is the dramatic appropriateness of the change of scene at line 192?

11. What are Adam's views on women and marriage (lines 227–34)? on reason and free will (lines 343–56)? In the light of these ideas, what is the dilemma posed to Adam by Eve's argument that she should be free and independent in Eden? How does he resolve the dilemma? Do you believe his solution wrong, since it leads to an evil conclusion? Explain.

12. How does Eve, beginning at line 273, get around Adam's arguments? How does she put him on the defensive? In what ways do her manner and method here foreshadow her later rebellion?

13. Eve is described (lines 385–411) as she leaves Adam and again (lines 424–62) as she appears to Satan. What is the dramatic purpose of this extensive attention to Eve's appearance at this point? Does the second passage give any significantly different impressions of Eve? Explain. What is the effect of the extended simile beginning at line 445?

14. Trace these dramatic steps by which the serpent brings Eve to eat the fruit: How does Satan first ingratiate himself to Eve, beginning at line 532? What is the effect of his false humility (lines 534–35)? What misconception of Heaven does Satan insinuate (lines 546–48)? What is Eve's reaction to the serpent's speaking? What temptations to Eve are hidden in the serpent's testimonial to the virtues of the fruit (lines 571–612)? What is the effect of Satan's sudden address to the tree (lines 679–83)?

15. Summarize the effect that Satan has had upon Eve by the time he makes his direct attack upon what she has been taught, beginning at line 684.

16. Examine Satan's final argument, and distinguish in it elements of truth, of half-truth, of falsehood, and of false reasoning. What arguments given by Satan are especially attractive and persuasive to man?

17. What are the several factors that bring Eve finally to eat the fruit? To what extent is her last speech (lines 745–79) before eating the fruit a recapitulation of Satan's arguments?

18. How does Eve show the immediate effects of her fall? What motivates her to involve Adam in her sin?

19. What is the dramatic irony of lines 838–44?

20. Compare Eve's approach to Adam and her words to him, beginning at line 853, with Satan's approach and words to her. Why is Adam not taken in as she was? How does Adam's reasoning in lines 896–916 differ

from Eve's? How does his reasoning in lines 921–59 differ from Satan's? What finally determines Adam's choice?

21. Beginning at the thousandth line, how does Milton describe the effects of the fall on nature and on Adam and Eve?

22. What happened to the serpent?

23. Are there any parallels in human reality to Adam's sinful loyalty to Eve? Consider for an example the slogan, "My country, right or wrong." Does such loyalty show faulty reasoning? Explain.

MILTON'S POETIC STYLE

Choose a complete passage of fifteen to twenty lines that you found difficult to follow at first reading. Then examine the passage in the following ways:

1. Milton was proficient in Latin and aware of the original Latin meaning of many English words. Pick out the words you found difficult in the passage and look in the dictionary for their meanings. How many of them are of Latin origin and how many of Anglo-Saxon (Germanic) origin? How many of them make a distinctly sensory suggestion? How many are abstractions? Do any of the words carry uncommon meanings?

2. Pick out the words, phrases, or clauses in the passage which are placed where you would not expect them to be placed in a standard prose sentence. Are any words understood but not directly stated? Do such unusual structures constitute a high proportion of the passage?

3. Read the passage aloud. Note how Milton inserts pauses in the rhythm which mark distinct units of meaning. These units often flow on from a pause in one line to a pause in another. Observe that stress falls on the most important words and reinforces the sense of the lines.

4. Paraphrase the passage, using different words and rearranging sentence patterns so that the meaning becomes immediately clearer to you. (Change the passage as little as necessary to accomplish this, however.) Compare your paraphrase with the original, and explain what qualities are added to the passage by Milton's diction, sentence structures, and rhythms.

FOR COMPOSITION

1. Write a concise narrative summarizing the changing thoughts and feelings of Eve throughout her encounter with evil and her recognition of her loss of innocence. Show how Milton makes Eve and her situation seem human, dramatic, and touching, rather than like a didactic tale of temptation, ambition, and deceit. Explain how Milton's poem compares with "The Fall of Man" from Genesis (see page 22), from which he drew material.

2. In a carefully organized essay, amply supported by quotation from and reference to Book 9, explain Milton's answer to the question: Why is there evil and suffering in a world created by a perfect God?

3. Explain how Milton's assertion of God's providence in *Paradise Lost* differs from Candide's credo: "All is for the best in this best of all possible worlds"?

4. According to *Paradise Lost,* man's present unhappiness has been caused by an original calamity, a sin of pride, in which man violated the law of love in order to exalt self. In a brief essay, explain your own attitude toward this idea. Give strong evidence to support your belief.

Essay on Man

ALEXANDER POPE

Alexander Pope (1688–1744) was a dominating figure of the literary and intellectual salons of eighteenth-century London. Deformed, crippled, and in constant pain from tuberculosis of the spine, he often showed a waspish disposition. But it is difficult to say how much this manner was created by his physical troubles and how much by the fashion of an age which was fiercely critical and rudely intolerant in its arguments over the state of society, the truths of religion, the worth of the ancient writers, and the standards of taste. Certainly it is true that Pope was capable of loyalty, and he formed warm friendships with many people, including some of the ablest political leaders and literary wits of his day.

Pope was generally recognized as the chief poet of his time. His poetry was intellectual, usually about man in general; it was not emotional and not about himself. The poems on which Pope's reputation primarily rest reflect what his rational age most valued in literature. The *Essay on Criticism* is a 744-line pronouncement on the standards of literary taste and judgment. *The Rape of the Lock* is a witty satire about a quarrel that had caused some excitement in Pope's day, over the snipping of a curl from a Miss Arabella Fermor's head. The *Essay on Man* is a philosophical poem defining the nature of man and his place in a Newtonian universe.

As poetry, this last is a model of compressed and vivid poetic argument. As philosophy, it is a useful compendium of ideas that had gained currency among the more advanced intellectuals of the day, who were influenced by the political philosophy of Locke and the scientific philosophy of Newton. Pope offers in the poem not his own original ideas, but a summary of the thought of his time. To be sure, there was nothing like thorough agreement among eighteenth-century philosophers, but Pope usually chose a middle ground, so that his poem can be taken as a kind of common denominator of the new philosophy.

The poetic essay was written in four "epistles" addressed to Henry St. John, Viscount Bolingbroke, a friend of Voltaire and a vigorous and effective exponent of liberal thought. Pope's purpose was in a sense like Milton's: to show that God's ways are just and benevolent. But Pope goes further than Milton toward the view that all things, even apparent evils when properly understood, have a necessary place in God's perfect plan for the universe. "Whatever is, is right," a famous line from Pope's poem, expresses a viewpoint like the one Voltaire satirized in *Candide*.

In Epistle 1, Pope writes about the nature and state of man with respect to the universe; in Epistle 2, with respect to man himself, as an individual.

Epistle 3

Of the nature and state of man with respect to society

Here then we rest: "The Universal Cause
Acts to one end, but acts by various laws."
In all the madness of superfluous health,
The trim of pride, the impudence of wealth,
Let this great truth be present night and day;   5
But most be present, if we preach or pray.

   I. Look round our world; behold the chain of love
Combining all below and all above.
See plastic Nature° working to this end,
The single atoms each to other tend,   10
Attract, attracted to, the next in place
Formed and impelled its neighbor to embrace.
See matter next, with various life endued,
Press to one center still, the general good.
See dying vegetables life sustain,   15
See life dissolving vegetate again:
All forms that perish other forms supply
(By turns we catch the vital breath, and die),
Like bubbles on the sea of matter born,
They rise, they break, and to that sea return.   20
Nothing is foreign: parts relate to whole;
One all-extending, all-preserving Soul
Connects each being, greatest with the least;
Made beast in aid of man, and man of beast;
All served, all serving: nothing stands alone;   25
The chain holds on, and where it ends, unknown.
   Has God, thou fool! worked solely for thy good,
Thy joy, thy pastime, thy attire, thy food?
Who for thy table feeds the wanton fawn,
For him as kindly spread the flowery lawn.   30
Is it for thee the lark ascends and sings?
Joy tunes his voice, joy elevates his wings.
Is it for thee the linnet pours his throat?
Loves of his own and raptures swell the note.
The bounding steed you pompously bestride,   35
Shares with his lord the pleasure and the pride.
Is thine alone the seed that strews the plain?
The birds of heaven shall vindicate their grain.
Thine the full harvest of the golden year?
Part pays, and justly, the deserving steer: 40
The hog, that plows not nor obeys thy call,
Lives on the labors of this lord of all.
   Know, Nature's children all divide her care;
The fur that warms a monarch, warmed a bear.

9. **plastic Nature:** creative Nature.

While man exclaims, "See all things for my use!"   45
"See man for mine!" replies a pampered goose:
And just as short of reason he must fall,
Who thinks all made for one, not one for all.
    Grant that the powerful still the weak control;
Be man the wit° and tyrant of the whole: 50
Nature that tyrant checks; he only knows,
And helps, another creature's wants and woes.
Say, will the falcon, stooping from above,
Smit with her varying plumage, spare the dove?
Admires the jay the insect's gilded wings?   55
Or hears the hawk when Philomela° sings?
Man cares for all: to birds he gives his woods,
To beasts his pastures, and to fish his floods;
For some his interest prompts him to provide,
For more his pleasure, yet for more his pride: 60
All feed on one vain patron, and enjoy
The extensive blessing of his luxury.
That very life his learnèd hunger craves,
He saves from famine, from the savage° saves;
Nay, feasts the animal he dooms his feast,   65
And, till he ends the being, makes it blest;
Which sees no more the stroke, or feels the pain,
Than favored man by touch ethereal° slain.
The creature had his feast of life before;
Thou too must perish, when thy feast is o'er!   70
    To each unthinking being, Heaven a friend,
Gives not the useless knowledge of its end:
To man imparts it; but with such a view
As, while he dreads it, makes him hope it too:
The hour concealed, and so remote the fear,   75
Death still draws nearer, never seeming near.
Great standing miracle! that Heaven assigned
Its only thinking thing this turn of mind.

    II. Whether with reason, or with instinct blest,°
Know, all enjoy that power which suits them best;   80
To bliss alike by that direction tend,
And find the means proportioned to their end.
Say, where full instinct is the unerring guide,
What pope or council can they need beside?
Reason, however able, cool at best,   85
Cares not for service, or but serves when pressed,
Stays till we call, and then not often near;
But honest Instinct comes a volunteer,
Sure never to o'ershoot, but just to hit;

---

    50. **the wit:** the only intellectual creature in the universe. 56. **Philomela:** a poetic name for the nightingale. 64. **the savage:** savage beast. 68. **touch ethereal:** lightning, a reference to an ancient belief that men struck by lightning were favored by heaven. 79. **Whether with reason, or with instinct blest:** whether blessed with reason, as men are, or with instinct, as animals are.

While still too wide or short is human wit;   90
Sure by quick Nature happiness to gain,
Which heavier reason labors at in vain,
This too serves always, reason never long;
One must go right, the other may go wrong.
See then the acting and comparing powers   95
One in their nature, which are two in ours;
And reason raise o'er instinct as you can,
In this 'tis God directs, in that 'tis man.
   Who taught the nations of the field and wood
To shun their poison, and to choose their food?   100
Prescient, the tides or tempests to withstand,
Build on the wave,° or arch beneath the sand?
Who made the spider parallels design,
Sure as Demoivre,° without rule or line?
Who bid the stork, Columbus-like, explore   105
Heavens not his own, and worlds unknown before?
Who calls the council, states the certain day,
Who forms the phalanx, and who points the way?

   III. God in the nature of each being founds
Its proper bliss, and sets its proper bounds: 110
But as he framed a whole, the whole to bless,
On mutual wants built mutual happiness:
So from the first, eternal order ran,
And creature linked to creature, man to man.
Whate'er of life all-quickening ether keeps,   115
Or breathes through air, or shoots beneath the deeps,
Or pours profuse on earth, one nature feeds
The vital flame, and swells the genial° seeds.
Not man alone, but all that roam the wood,
Or wing the sky, or roll along the flood,   120
Each loves itself, but not itself alone,
Each sex desires alike, till two are one.
Nor ends the pleasure with the fierce embrace;
They love themselves, a third time, in their race.
Thus beast and bird their common charge attend,   125
The mothers nurse it, and the sires defend;
The young dismissed to wander earth or air,
There stops the instinct, and there ends the care;
The link dissolves, each seeks a fresh embrace,
Another love succeeds, another race.   130
A longer care man's helpless kind demands;
That longer care contracts more lasting bands:
Reflection, reason, still the ties improve,
At once extend the interest, and the love;
With choice we fix, with sympathy we burn;   135
Each virtue in each passion takes its turn;

102. **Build on the wave:** the legendary halcyon bird is said to build his nest on the sea.
104. **Demoivre:** Abraham de Moivre (1667–1754), a French mathematician, originator of a
theorem in trigonometry.   118. **genial:** generative.

And still new needs, new helps, new habits rise,
That graft benevolence on charities.
Still as one brood, and as another rose,
These natural love maintained, habitual those: 140
The last, scarce ripened into perfect man,
Saw helpless him from whom their life began:
Memory and forecast just returns engage,
That pointed back to youth, this on to age;
While pleasure, gratitude, and hope, combined,   145
Still spread the interest, and preserved the kind.

    IV. Nor think, in Nature's state they blindly trod;°
The state of Nature was the reign of God:
Self-love and social at her° birth began,
Union the bond of all things, and of man.   150
Pride then was not; nor arts,° that pride to aid;
Man walked with beast, joint tenant of the shade;
The same his table, and the same his bed;
No murder clothed him, and no murder fed.
In the same temple, the resounding wood,   155
All vocal beings hymned their equal God:
The shrine with gore unstained, with gold undressed,
Unbribed, unbloody, stood the blameless priest:
Heaven's attribute was universal care,
And man's prerogative to rule, but spare.   160
Ah! how unlike the man of times to come!
Of half that live the butcher and the tomb;°
Who, foe to Nature, hears the general groan,
Murders their species, and betrays his own.
But just disease to luxury° succeeds,   165
And every death its own avenger breeds;
The fury-passions from that blood began,
And turned on man a fiercer savage, man.
    See him from Nature rising slow to art!
To copy instinct then was reason's part;   170
Thus then to man the voice of Nature spake —
"Go, from the creatures thy instructions take:
Learn from the birds what food the thickets yield;
Learn from the beasts the physic of the field;
Thy arts of building from the bee receive;   175
Learn of the mole to plow, the worm to weave;
Learn of the little nautilus to sail,
Spread the thin oar, and catch the driving gale.

[POPE CONTINUES ON PAGE 671]

    147. Nor think, in Nature's state they blindly trod: Pope is contradicting the idea that man's
natural state is savage, without law or order.   **149. her:** Nature's.   **151. arts:** here, as elsewhere, used in the general sense to mean knowledge and skills.   **162. the tomb:** by eating
flesh, man entombs it in his body.   **165. luxury:** gluttony and lust.

Seventeenth-Century Painting

Toward the close of the sixteenth century, the well of inspiration in Italian art seemed to be running dry. Paintings by leading artists of the time tended to be highly mannered and overly decorative. Fresh talent and a wholly new point of view was badly needed. Fortunately, both were soon abundantly supplied by a young artist who arrived in Rome about 1591. He was known as "Caravaggio," from the name of his birthplace in northern Italy.

What set Caravaggio's paintings apart from those of his contemporaries was his uncompromising, down-to-earth realism. Even in pictures with religious subjects, commissioned as altarpieces for churches, Caravaggio included likenesses of ordinary people he had observed in the streets. Equally startling was his dramatic use of light and shadow—what the Italians call *chiaroscuro* ("light-dark"). In his portrait of Alof de Wignacourt (PLATE 1), you can see how sharp contrasts of brilliant light and deep shadows enliven what otherwise might have seemed merely a routine portrait. The suit of armor is itself such a superb piece of realistic painting that it almost steals the show from the main subject of the portrait—the elderly gentleman who is posed in his costume of Grand Master of an order of knights in Malta.

Caravaggio's unusual style particularly impressed a young Flemish painter named Peter Paul Rubens, who had come to Rome in 1600 to study the masterpieces of the Renaissance. By the time Rubens returned to Antwerp, eight years later, he had blended into his own style the best qualities of both Italian and Flemish painting. Some of his most exciting subjects are pictures of the chase, such as *Boar Hunt* (PLATE 2), in which the powerful forces of nature become part of the overall theme. Notice that Rubens' method of composition is very different from the classic one used by Raphael in his *School of Athens* (page 532). For here the hunters, dogs, and horses are arranged not in a series of planes parallel to the picture's surface, but in a sort of semicircle swinging back into depth. The charging horses and riders at the lower right lead us into space in a diagonal path toward the action of the other animals and hunters and the twisting forms of a fallen tree. This diagonal plunge into deep space was one of the characteristics of a dramatic new style which came to be known as the *Baroque*.

Another painter strongly influenced by Caravaggio's dramatic chiaroscuro was the Spaniard Diego Velásquez. In his later works, however, such as *The Carpet Weavers* (PLATE 3), Velásquez gave up theatrical contrasts for more subtle visual effects. He is concerned here with the blurring effect of the spokes on a rapidly turning spinning wheel. He makes us more aware of light falling on surfaces than of the solidity of the objects themselves. The action is suggested mainly by the movement of light into the right foreground and across the back room from an unseen window at the left.

One of the most extraordinary demonstrations of Baroque chiaroscuro and movement can be found in *The Night Watch* (PLATE 4), a huge group portrait of a Dutch military company by Holland's greatest painter, Rembrandt van Rijn. Unlike routine group portraits, in which the figures are placed side by side, this one is extremely complex in design. Rembrandt has placed some of the figures in deep shadow and concentrated the lighting wherever it seemed best for the composition. The result is an elaborate interplay of opposing currents of action. No sooner are we pulled inward by bursts of light than we are forced outward again by gestures and movements of the figures. Naturally, some of the officers portrayed were unhappy that Rembrandt had obscured their likenesses, but we can only be grateful that he made such a daring experiment.

Another master of Baroque composition was one of Rembrandt's younger Dutch contemporaries, Jan Vermeer of Delft. Vermeer leads us deep into the space of his pictures, but in a much more quiet, orderly way than most other Baroque painters. For example, in *The Artist and His Studio* (PLATE 5), as we move past the furniture at the left, we pause to examine certain objects revealed by light from a window. Then we come to the artist, to the picture he is painting, and finally to his "subject"—a young woman wearing a laurel wreath, holding a trumpet in one hand and a large book in the other. Most important here is the way Vermeer has handled the light, both on the woman's figure and also as it moves in diffused tones across the back wall and over the textures of the parchment map.

The Death of Germanicus (PLATE 6), by the French artist Nicolas Poussin, might seem at first to have been painted during the Renaissance rather than the Baroque era. The subject is classical (Germanicus was a Roman general under Augustus Caesar), and the distribution of figures straight across the picture is reminiscent of both Raphael's and Veronese's style of composition (pages 532 and 533). But the figures are more crowded together and their gestures more lively than in most Renaissance paintings. Flickering lights and broad shadows interrupt the larger forms as they sweep across the picture, reaching a climax in the white toga and pillow silhouetting the dying man.

PLATE 1. CARAVAGGIO (Italian, 1573–1610) : *Portrait of Alof de Wignacourt*. 1607–08. **Oil on** canvas, 76¾ x 52¾ inches. (Musée du Louvre, Paris)

665

PLATE 2. PETER PAUL RUBENS (Flemish, 1577–1640): *Boar Hunt*. 1618–20. Oil on canvas, 53$\frac{18}{16}$ x 66$\frac{3}{8}$ inches. (Staatliche Kunstsammlung, Dresden)

PLATE 3. DIEGO VELÁSQUEZ (Spanish, 1599–1660): *The Carpet Weavers (Las Hilanderas).*
About 1657. Oil on canvas, 7 feet 2½ inches by 9 feet 5¾ inches. (Prado, Madrid)

PLATE 4. REMBRANDT VAN RIJN (Dutch, 1606–1669): *The Night Watch*. 1642. Oil on canvas, 11 feet 9$\frac{5}{16}$ inches by 14 feet 4$\frac{7}{16}$ inches. (Rijksmuseum, Amsterdam)

PLATE 5. JAN VERMEER (Dutch, 1632–1675): *The Artist and His Studio*. 1665–70. Oil on canvas, 47¼ x 39⅜ inches. (Kunsthistorisches Museum, Vienna)

PLATE 6. NICOLAS POUSSIN (French, 1594–1665): *The Death of Germanicus.* 1627–31. Oil on canvas, 58¼ x 77⅞ inches. (The Minneapolis Institute of Arts)

Here too all forms of social union find,
And hence let reason, late, instruct mankind: 180
Here subterranean works and cities° see;
There towns aerial° on the waving tree.
Learn each small people's genius, policies,
The ant's republic, and the realm of bees;
How those in common all their wealth bestow,   185
And anarchy without confusion know;
And these forever, though a monarch reign,
Their separate cells and properties maintain.
Mark what unvaried laws preserve each state,
Laws wise as Nature, and as fixed as fate.   190
In vain thy reason finer webs shall draw,
Entangle justice in her net of law,
And right, too rigid, harden into wrong;
Still for the strong too weak, the weak too strong.
Yet go! and thus o'er all the creatures sway,   195
Thus let the wiser make the rest obey;
And, for those arts mere instinct could afford,
Be crowned as monarchs, or as gods adored."

    V. Great Nature spoke; observant men obeyed;
Cities were built, societies were made: 200
Here rose one little state; another near
Grew by like means, and joined, through love or fear.
Did here the trees with ruddier burdens bend,
And there the streams in purer rills descend?
What war could ravish, commerce could bestow,   205
And he returned a friend, who came a foe.
Converse and love mankind might strongly draw,
When love was liberty, and Nature law.
Thus states were formed; the name of king unknown,
Till common interest placed the sway in one.   210
'Twas virtue only (or in arts or arms,
Diffusing blessings, or averting harms)
The same which in a sire the sons obeyed,
A prince the father of a people made.

    VI. Till then, by Nature crowned, each patriarch sate,   215
King, priest, and parent of his growing state;
On him, their second Providence, they hung,
Their law his eye, their oracle his tongue.
He from the wondering furrow called the food,
Taught to command the fire, control the flood,   220
Draw forth the monsters of the abyss profound,
Or fetch the aerial eagle to the ground.
Till drooping, sickening, dying they began
Whom they revered as God to mourn as man:

181. **subterranean works and cities:** ant colonies.   182. **towns aerial:** beehives.

Then, looking up from sire to sire, explored   225
One great first father, and that first adored.
Or plain tradition that this ALL begun,
Conveyed unbroken faith from sire to son;
The worker from the work distinct was known,
And simple reason never sought but one:°   230
Ere wit oblique° had broke that steady light,°
Man, like his Maker, saw that all was right;
To virtue, in the paths of pleasure, trod,
And owned a Father when he owned a God.
Love all the faith, and all the allegiance then;   235
For Nature knew no right divine in men,
No ill could fear in God: and understood
A sovereign being but a sovereign good.
True faith, true policy, united ran,
That was but love of God, and this of man.   240
    Who first taught souls enslaved, and realms undone,
The enormous faith of many made for one;
That proud exception to all Nature's laws,
To invert the world, and counterwork its Cause?
Force first made conquest, and that conquest, law;   245
Till Superstition taught the tyrant awe,
Then shared the tyranny, then lent it aid,
And gods of conquerors, slaves of subjects made:
She,° midst the lightning's blaze, and thunder's sound,
When rocked the mountains, and when groaned the ground,   250
She taught the weak to bend, the proud to pray,
To Power unseen, and mightier far than they:
She, from the rending earth and bursting skies,
Saw gods descend, and fiends infernal rise:
Here fixed the dreadful, there the blest abodes;   255
Fear made her devils, and weak hope her gods;
Gods partial, changeful, passionate, unjust,
Whose attributes were rage, revenge, or lust;
Such as the souls of cowards might conceive,
And, formed like tyrants, tyrants would believe.   260
Zeal then, not charity, became the guide;
And hell was built on spite, and heaven on pride.
Then sacred seemed the ethereal vault no more;
Altars grew marble then, and reeked with gore:
Then first the flamen° tasted living food;   265
Next his grim idol smeared with human blood;
With Heaven's own thunders shook the world below,
And played the god an engine° on his foe.
    So drives self-love, through just and through unjust,
To one man's power, ambition, lucre, lust: 270
The same self-love, in all, becomes the cause
Of what restrains him, government and laws.

230. **but one:** one God.   231. **oblique:** here suggesting something distorted.   **light:** of
reason.   249. **She:** superstition.   265. **flamen:** pagan priest.   268. **engine:** weapon.

For, what one likes if others like as well,
What serves one will, when many wills rebel?
How shall he keep, what, sleeping or awake,   275
A weaker may surprise, a stronger take?
His safety must his liberty restrain:
All join to guard what each desires to gain.
Forced into virtue thus by self-defense,
Even kings learned justice and benevolence: 280
Self-love forsook the path it first pursued,
And found the private in the public good.
 'Twas then, the studious head or generous mind,
Follower of God or friend of humankind,
Poet or patriot, rose but to restore   285
The faith and moral, Nature gave before;
Relumed her ancient light, not kindled new;
If not God's image, yet his shadow drew:
Taught power's due use to people and to kings,
Taught nor to slack, nor strain its tender strings,   290
The less, or greater, set so justly true,
That touching one must strike the other too;
Till jarring interests of themselves create
The according music of a well-mixed state.
Such is the world's great harmony, that springs   295
From order, union, full consent of things:
Where small and great, where weak and mighty, made
To serve, not suffer, strengthen, not invade;
More powerful each as needful to the rest,
And, in proportion as it blesses, blest;   300
Draw to one point, and to one center bring
Beast, man, or angel, servant, lord, or king.
 For forms of government let fools contest;
Whate'er is best administered is best:
For modes of faith let graceless zealots fight;   305
His can't be wrong whose life is in the right:
In faith and hope the world will disagree,
But all mankind's concern is charity:
All must be false that thwart this one great end;
And all of God, that bless mankind or mend.   310
 Man, like the generous vine, supported lives;
The strength he gains is from the embrace he gives.
On their own axis as the planets run,
Yet make at once their circle round the sun;
So two consistent motions act the soul;   315
And one regards itself, and one the whole.
 Thus God and Nature linked the general frame,
And bade self-love and social be the same.

1. Pope could expect that the image of the "chain of love" (lines 7–8) would bring to his readers' minds a common image usually referred to as "the great chain of Being." This latter image is used to describe life as a continuous, interdependent series of creations, ascending from the mineral through the animal and human to the angelic. How is Pope's "chain of love" image relevant to this "chain of Being" image? What ideas and what qualities does the "sea of matter" image (line 19) add to the chain images? How does Pope make use of the chain image again in lines 109–14?

2. In lines 27–42 Pope cites a number of animal examples to prove that the creations of nature have not been made solely for the benefit of man (and that, conversely, man is intended to serve other creatures). From his examples, what can you infer about God's purposes for nature, other than "for thy [man's] good"?

3. What is the logical error made by the "pampered goose" (line 46)? What is the knowledge that the goose lacks which might correct his thinking? What are the implications for man?

4. What do lines 53–70 imply are the human qualities that animals do not share? What qualities does man share with the animals?

5. By the time he comes to Section II, the alert reader will probably recognize the imperative ("Know"), with which it begins, as a characteristic rhetorical device in this poem, and the rhetorical question in lines 83–84 will also seem typical. Pick out the uses of these devices in Section I. What do such devices suggest about the author's attitude? What tone or quality do they give to the poem? How does the device of personification, which Pope uses frequently, add to this impression? What similarity can you find between the impression created by these devices and the poetic effect of the couplet form?

6. What does Pope attribute to instinct and what to reason in lines 79–108 and 169–98? What implications are made for man's trusting his own instincts?

7. What virtues does Pope ascribe to primitive society in lines 152–98? By implication, what vices does he ascribe to civilized society? When he speaks in line 190 of the bees and ants having "laws wise as Nature, and as fixed as Fate," what does he imply about human laws?

8. How are the primitive virtues reflected in the early development of civilized society (lines 199–240)? How does Pope explain the corruption of civilized society (lines 241–82)? Is civilization therefore to be deplored, according to Pope? Do you think he advocates a return to a primitive life? Explain.

9. From the context, what do you think Pope means by *zeal* (line 261)? What brings about self-love's change of direction (the passage beginning at line 269)? What is the connection between zeal and self-love?

THE HEROIC COUPLET

Pope is generally considered to be the master of the form called the heroic couplet or closed couplet: "heroic" because it was considered especially suitable for long poems on elevated, heroic themes, such as the epic; and "closed" because its chief characteristic is that each two-line rhyme unit (couplet) encapsules a complete unit of thought. The heroic couplet is a very formal sort of form, one which emphasizes artfully, with relatively little concession to naturalness in language.

In addition to being a closed unit of meaning, the heroic couplet tends to be symmetrical within itself. For example, the first line may be a dependent clause and the second a main clause, the two together forming a sentence. Furthermore, each line normally falls into two balanced parts. The first epistle of the *Essay on Man* ends with a famous couplet:

And, spite of pride, in erring reason's spite,
One truth is clear, Whatever is, is right.

The first line is divided into two parallel phrases. The second line is the main statement of the sentence, and it is divided between the main clause itself and the quoted statement in apposition to it. (You might note also that the phrases of the first line are mirror images of each other, a device echoed in the quoted statement.)

This kind of subdivision and careful parallelism is typical of the heroic couplet and gives it its particular quality. But a series of couplets which slavishly followed this form would become monotonous and mechanical. Indeed, we can readily find examples of second-rate poets who produced just such regimented verse. A good poet like Pope, on the other hand, uses the form with flexibility and ease. Actually, Pope writes very few couplets which exactly fit the description given above.

Examine about a dozen consecutive couplets, asking the following questions about each one:

1. Is the couplet a complete sense-unit?

2. Is each line a distinct subunit of thought? Is each line completely self-contained or is there a run-on between the lines?

3. Are there further parallel subunits within each line? Does the division or pause come in the middle of the line, early in the line, or toward the end of the line?

4. Summarize Pope's use of the heroic couplet form from the samples you have examined. Discuss whether Pope has produced a sense of both freedom and discipline in his verse.

FOR COMPOSITION

1. Montaigne (see page 523), Milton (see page 630), and Pope, with distinct differences, all try to convey an idea of what man was or would be in a natural state. All wrote in ages that were pre-Darwin, pre-Freud, pre-Einstein. In an essay, discuss the relevance of each writer's ideas to contemporary life. Are all their ideas necessarily out of date today, because of what we have subsequently learned from anthropology and psychology? What are your own views on what these earlier writers have said?

2. In a carefully organized essay, explain the views on society expressed in Pope's poem. Trace the stages of social evolution he describes, from God's original creation to the future ideal that Pope urges men to aspire to. What creative and what destructive forces conflict in this evolution? What is the basis of Pope's confidence that the creative forces will win out?

3. In the chain image expressed in lines 213–14, and in the passage beginning at line 295, Pope draws analogies among the organization of the universe under God, of society under the monarch, and of the family under the father. In an essay, explain and criticize these analogies.

Faust

JOHANN WOLFGANG VON GOETHE

(Translated by Louis MacNeice)

Johann Wolfgang von Goethe (1749–1832) is unquestionably the colossus of German literature and, like Leonardo da Vinci, a truly "universal man." He was trained as a lawyer, and for ten years, from the age of twenty-six to thirty-six, he served as chief minister of state to the duchy of Saxe-Weimar, where he brought about important political reforms under the liberal Duke Charles Augustus. As a serious student of biology, Goethe made some perceptive suggestions concerning the nature of matter and some observations that strikingly anticipated Darwin's theory of evolution. He was an amateur but accomplished cellist, a painter, and a fine athlete. But it was as a writer that he found himself idolized everywhere in Europe when, in 1774, he published *The Sorrows of Young Werther,* an emotional novel of thwarted love that leads to suicide.

Goethe's accomplishments as a writer range through all kinds of literature. He wrote numerous lyric poems about his turbulent love affairs, and two epic poems; he wrote other fiction in addition to *Werther;* he wrote a book of criticism, a travel account, and an autobiography. His first notable work, written at the age of twenty-three, about two years before *Werther,* was a drama, and during his years in Weimar he served as director of the state theater and continued to write plays.

The great work of his life is *Faust.* He cast the story in dramatic form, though its poetic qualities are more notable than its theatrical ones. Published in two parts—the first in 1808 and the second after his death—the play occupied in one way or another Goethe's entire life. The earliest draft had been written before he went to Weimar, and Part II was finished very shortly before his death fifty-odd years later. Consequently, *Faust* is a large work in every sense, reflecting all of Goethe's diverse and intensely felt experiences, his wide learning, and his probing thought. The two early scenes presented here can reveal only Goethe's conception of the focal character and the nature of the quest which comprises the rest of the poem.

The historical Faust was a quack scholar-magician of the early sixteenth century, who became a legend in his own time. The popular English play *Doctor Faustus,* written by Christopher Marlowe, gave the German legend wide currency, and many other literary and subliterary treatments elaborated on it. Goethe owes to the legend little more than a few details and incidents and the core idea of a man whose restless search for truth leads him beyond the ordinary bounds of knowledge and morality into a compact with the Devil. Faust's complex, symbolic odyssey through doubt and error, which is the concern of Goethe's play, is Goethe's own creation, and the ideas that it signifies are the fruit of Goethe's own wisdom. Most particularly, the salvation that Faust achieves at the end of his quest is Goethe's startling alteration of the traditional moral of the legend, which has Faust carried off by demons as punishment for his impudence and sin. This striking characteristic of Goethe's Faust is announced in the Prologue in Heaven and is fulfilled at the end of Part II. Faust's errors will be justified and he will find the fulfillment he seeks, not in spite of but because of his refusal to accept man's lot in passive obedience to a higher power.

The Prologue in Heaven

[*Enter the* LORD *and the* HEAVENLY HOSTS, *with* MEPHISTOPHELES *following. The three* ARCHANGELS *step forward.*]

RAPHAEL. The chanting sun, as ever, rivals
 The chanting of his brother spheres
 And marches round his destined circuit—
 A march that thunders in our ears.
 His aspect cheers the Hosts of Heaven   5
 Though what his essence none can say;
 These inconceivable creations
 Keep the high state of their first day.
GABRIEL. And swift, with inconceivable swiftness,
 The earth's full splendor rolls around,   10
 Celestial radiance alternating
 With a dread night too deep to sound;
 The sea against the rocks' deep bases
 Comes foaming up in far-flung force,
 And rock and sea go whirling onward   15
 In the swift spheres' eternal course.
MICHAEL. And storms in rivalry are raging
 From sea to land, from land to sea,
 In frenzy forge the world a girdle
 From which no inmost part is free.   20
 The blight of lightning flaming yonder
 Marks where the thunderbolt will play;
 And yet Thine envoys, Lord, revere
 The gentle movement of Thy day.
CHOIR OF ANGELS. Thine aspect cheers the Hosts of Heaven 25
 Though what Thine essence none can say,
 And all Thy loftiest creations
 Keep the high state of their first day.

[MEPHISTOPHELES *steps forward.*]

MEPHISTOPHELES. Since you, O Lord, once more approach and ask
 If business down with us be light or heavy—   30
 And in the past you've usually welcomed me—
 That's why you see me also at your levee.
 Excuse me, I can't manage lofty words—
 Not though your whole court jeer and find me low;
 My pathos certainly would make you laugh   35

From *Goethe's Faust,* translated by Louis MacNeice, copyright 1951 by Louis MacNeice. Reprinted by permission of Oxford University Press, Inc. and Faber & Faber Ltd.

Had you not left off laughing long ago.
Your suns and worlds mean nothing much to me;
How men torment themselves, that's all I see.
The little god of the world, one can't reshape, reshade him;
He is as strange today as that first day you made him.   40
His life would be not so bad, not quite,
Had you not granted him a gleam of Heaven's light;
He calls it Reason, uses it not the least
Except to be more beastly than any beast.
He seems to me—if your Honor does not mind—   45
Like a grasshopper—the long-legged kind—
That's always in flight and leaps as it flies along
And then in the grass strikes up its same old song.
I could only wish he confined himself to the grass!
He thrusts his nose into every filth, alas.   50

LORD. Mephistopheles, have you no other news?
Do you always come here to accuse?
Is nothing ever right in your eyes on earth?

MEPHISTOPHELES. No, Lord! I find things there as downright bad as ever.
I am sorry for men's days of dread and dearth;   55
Poor things, *my* wish to plague 'em isn't fervent.

LORD. Do you know Faust?

MEPHISTOPHELES.   The Doctor?

LORD.   Aye, my servant.

MEPHISTOPHELES. Indeed! He serves you oddly enough, I think.
The fool has no earthly habits in meat and drink.
The ferment in him drives him wide and far,   60
That he is mad he too has almost guessed;
He demands of heaven each fairest star
And of earth each highest joy and best,
And all that is new and all that is far
Can bring no calm to the deep-sea swell of his breast.   65

LORD. Now he may serve me only gropingly,
Soon I shall lead him into the light.
The gardener knows when the sapling first turns green
That flowers and fruit will make the future bright.

MEPHISTOPHELES. What do you wager? You will lose him yet,   70
Provided *you* give *me* permission
To steer him gently the course I set.

LORD. So long as he walks the earth alive,
So long you may try what enters your head;
Men make mistakes as long as they strive.   75

MEPHISTOPHELES. I thank you for that; as regards the dead,
The dead have never taken my fancy.
I favor cheeks that are full and rosy-red;
No corpse is welcome to my house;
I work as the cat does with the mouse.   80

LORD. Very well; you have my full permission.
Divert this soul from its primal source
And carry it, if you can seize it,
Down with you upon your course—

And stand ashamed when you must needs admit: 85
A good man with his groping intuitions
Still knows the path that is true and fit.
MEPHISTOPHELES. All right—but it won't last for long.
I'm not afraid my bet will turn out wrong.
And, if my aim prove true and strong,   90
Allow me to triumph wholeheartedly.
Dust shall be eaten—and greedily—
Like my cousin the Snake renowned in tale and song.
LORD. That too you are free to give a trial;
I have never hated the likes of you.   95
Of all the spirits of denial
The joker is the last that I eschew.
Man finds relaxation too attractive—
Too fond too soon of unconditional rest;
Which is why I am pleased to give him a companion   100
Who lures and thrusts and must, as devil, be active.
But ye, true sons of Heaven, it is your duty
To take your joy in the living wealth of beauty.
The changing Essence which ever works and lives
Wall you around with love, serene, secure!   105
And that which floats in flickering appearance
Fix ye it firm in thoughts that must endure.
CHOIR OF ANGELS. Thine aspect cheers the Hosts of Heaven
Though what Thine essence none can say,
And all Thy loftiest creations   110
Keep the high state of their first day.

[*Heaven closes.*]

MEPHISTOPHELES *(alone)*. I like to see the Old One now and then
And try to keep relations on the level.
It's really decent of so great a person
To talk so humanely even to the Devil.   115

The Pact with the Devil

[In the previous scenes, Faust has become disillusioned with human knowledge. A doctor of philosophy, he has explored to the limits of his reason all areas of learning, yet they have yielded him no answers about the ultimate purpose of life. Faust has even turned in frustration to "white magic." But when he uses it to summon up the powerful Earth Spirit, he finds that it won't reveal any more than his reason does. In despair, Faust decides on suicide. But a cup of poison is pulled from his lips by the bells and choruses of Easter, which are celebrating the resurrection of Christ and the springtime renewal of life.

This brings Faust back to the world of simple enjoyment. On a walk in the countryside, he feels the comforts of earth and air, and he observes the ordinary burghers content with this moment of respite from the rigors of their lives. He thinks that he may find in simple acceptance a solution to his questions, but it is at that moment that he becomes susceptible to the influence of Mephistopheles.

JOHANN WOLFGANG VON GOETHE   679

Back in his study, Faust is in turmoil as Mephistopheles tries to persuade him to try the Devil's way, the way of sensual pleasures, without thought for the why's or the consequences. Faust is in despair again. He cries a curse on love, on hope, on faith, and on patience.]

.   .   .

MEPHISTOPHELES. Stop playing with your grief which battens
    Like a vulture on your life, your mind!
    The worst of company would make you feel
    That you are a man among mankind.
    Not that it's really my proposition   5
    To shove you among the common men;
    Though I'm not one of the Upper Ten,
    If you would like a coalition
    With me for your career through life,
    I am quite ready to fit in,   10
    I'm yours before you can say knife.
    I am your comrade;
    If you so crave,
    I am your servant, I am your slave.
FAUST. And what have I to undertake in return?   15
MEPHISTOPHELES. Oh it's early days to discuss what that is.
FAUST. No, no, the devil is an egoist
    And ready to do nothing gratis
    Which is to benefit a stranger.
    Tell me your terms and don't prevaricate!   20
    A servant like you in the house is a danger.
MEPHISTOPHELES. I will bind myself to your service in this world,
    To be at your beck and never rest nor slack;
    When we meet again on the other side,
    In the same coin you shall pay me back.   25
FAUST. The other side gives me little trouble;
    First batter this present world to rubble,
    Then the other may rise—if that's the plan.
    This earth is where my springs of joy have started,
    And this sun shines on me when brokenhearted;   30
    If I can first from them be parted,
    Then let happen what will and can!
    I wish to hear no more about it—
    Whether there too men hate and love
    Or whether in those spheres too, in the future,   35
    There is a Below or an Above.
MEPHISTOPHELES. With such an outlook you can risk it.
    Sign on the line! In these next days you will get
    Ravishing samples of my arts;
    I am giving you what never man saw yet.   40
FAUST. Poor devil, can *you* give anything ever?
    Was a human spirit in its high endeavor
    Even once understood by one of your breed?
    Have you got food which fails to feed?
    Or red gold which, never at rest,   45

Like mercury runs away through the hand?
A game at which one never wins?
A girl who, even when on my breast,
Pledges herself to my neighbor with her eyes?
The divine and lovely delight of honor   50
Which falls like a falling star and dies?
Show me the fruits which, before they are plucked, decay
And the trees which day after day renew their green!
MEPHISTOPHELES. Such a commission doesn't alarm me,
I have such treasures to purvey.   55
But, my good friend, the time draws on when we
Should be glad to feast at our ease on something good.
FAUST. If ever I stretch myself on a bed of ease,
Then I am finished! Is that understood?
If ever your flatteries can coax me   60
To be pleased with myself, if ever you cast
A spell of pleasure that can hoax me—
Then let *that* day be my last!
That's my wager!
MEPHISTOPHELES.   Done!
FAUST.   Let's shake!
If ever I say to the passing moment   65
"Linger a while! Thou art so fair!"
Then you may cast me into fetters,
I will gladly perish then and there!
Then you may set the death-bell tolling,
Then from my service you are free,   70
The clock may stop, its hand may fall,
And that be the end of time for me!
MEPHISTOPHELES. Think what you're saying, we shall not forget it.
FAUST. And you are fully within your rights;
I have made no mad or outrageous claim.   75
If I stay as I am, I am a slave—
Whether yours or another's, it's all the same.
MEPHISTOPHELES. I shall this very day at the College Banquet
Enter your service with no more ado,
But just one point—As a life-and-death insurance   80
I must trouble you for a line or two.
FAUST. So you, you pedant, you too like things in writing?
Have you never known a man? Or a man's word? Never?
Is it not enough that my word of mouth
Puts all my days in bond for ever?   85
Does not the world rage on in all its streams
And shall a promise hamper *me?*
Yet this illusion reigns within our hearts
And from it who would be gladly free?
Happy the man who can inwardly keep his word;   90
Whatever the cost, he will not be loath to pay!
But a parchment, duly inscribed and sealed,
Is a bogey from which all wince away.
The word dies on the tip of the pen

JOHANN WOLFGANG VON GOETHE   681

And wax and leather lord it then.   95
What do you, evil spirit, require?
Bronze, marble, parchment, paper?
Quill or chisel or pencil of slate?
You may choose whichever you desire.
MEPHISTOPHELES. How can you so exaggerate   100
With such a hectic rhetoric?
Any little snippet is quite good—
And you sign it with one little drop of blood.
FAUST. If that is enough and is some use,
One may as well pander to your fad.   105
MEPHISTOPHELES. Blood is a very special juice.
FAUST. Only do not fear that I shall break this contract.
What I promise is nothing more
Than what all my powers are striving for.
I have puffed myself up too much, it is only   110
Your sort that really fits my case.
The great Earth Spirit has despised me
And Nature shuts the door in my face.
The thread of thought is snapped asunder,
I have long loathed knowledge in all its fashions.   115
In the depths of sensuality
Let us now quench our glowing passions!
And at once make ready every wonder
Of unpenetrated sorcery!
Let us cast ourselves into the torrent of time,   120
Into the whirl of eventfulness,
Where disappointment and success,
Pleasure and pain may chop and change
As chop and change they will and can;
It is restless action makes the man.   125
MEPHISTOPHELES. No limit is fixed for you, no bound;
If you'd like to nibble at everything
Or to seize upon something flying round—
Well, may you have a run for your money!
But seize your chance and don't be funny!   130
FAUST. I've told you, it is no question of happiness.
The most painful joy, enamored hate, enlivening
Disgust—I devote myself to all excess.
My breast, now cured of its appetite for knowledge,
From now is open to all and every smart,   135
And what is allotted to the whole of mankind
That will I sample in my inmost heart,
Grasping the highest and lowest with my spirit,
Piling men's weal and woe upon my neck,
To extend myself to embrace all human selves   140
And to founder in the end, like them, a wreck.
MEPHISTOPHELES. O believe *me*, who have been chewing
These iron rations many a thousand year,
No human being can digest
This stuff, from the cradle to the bier.   145

This universe—believe a devil—
Was made for no one but a god!
He exists in eternal light
But *us* he has brought into the darkness
While *your* sole portion is day and night.   150
FAUST. I will all the same!
MEPHISTOPHELES.   That's very nice.
There's only one thing I find wrong;
Time is short, art is long.
You could do with a little artistic advice.
Confederate with one of the poets   155
And let him flog his imagination
To heap all virtues on your head,
A head with such a reputation:
Lion's bravery,
Stag's velocity,   160
Fire of Italy,
Northern tenacity.
Let *him* find out the secret art
Of combining craft with a noble heart
And of being in love like a young man,   165
Hotly, but working to a plan.
Such a person—*I'd* like to meet him;
"Mr. Microcosm" is how I'd greet him.°
FAUST. What am I then if fate must bar
My efforts to reach that crown of humanity   170
After which all my senses strive?
MEPHISTOPHELES. You are in the end . . . what you are.
You can put on full-bottomed wigs with a million locks,
You can put on stilts instead of your socks,
You remain forever what you are.   175
FAUST. I feel my endeavors have not been worth a pin
When I raked together the treasures of the human mind,
If at the end I but sit down to find
No new force welling up within.
I have not a hair's breadth more of height,   180
I am no nearer the Infinite.
MEPHISTOPHELES. My very good sir, you look at things
Just in the way that people do;
We must be cleverer than that
Or the joys of life will escape from you.   185
Hell! You have surely hands and feet,
Also a head and you-know-what;
The pleasures I gather on the wing,
Are they less mine? Of course they're not!
Suppose I can afford six stallions,   190
I can add that horsepower to my score
And dash along and be a proper man
As if my legs were twenty-four.

168. In other words, that man would be the epitome, or microcosm, of the whole universe.

So good-by to thinking! On your toes!
The world's before us. Quick! Here goes!   195
I tell you, a chap who's intellectual
Is like a beast on a blasted heath
Driven in circles by a demon
While a fine green meadow lies round beneath.
FAUST. How do we start?
MEPHISTOPHELES.   We just say go—and skip.   200
But please get ready for this pleasure trip.   [*Exit* FAUST.]
Only look down on knowledge and reason,
The highest gifts that men can prize,
Only allow the spirit of lies
To confirm you in magic and illusion,   205
And then I have you body and soul.
Fate has given this man a spirit
Which is always pressing onward, beyond control,
And whose mad striving overleaps
All joys of the earth between pole and pole.   210
Him shall I drag through the wilds of life
And through the flats of meaninglessness,
I shall make him flounder and gape and stick
And to tease his insatiableness
Hang meat and drink in the air before his watering lips;   215
In vain he will pray to slake his inner thirst,
And even had he not sold himself to the devil
He would be equally accursed.

FOR STUDY AND DISCUSSION

1. Raphael's first speech describes the movement of planets and stars in the universe; Gabriel's speech describes the whirling of the earth within the larger pattern; and Michael's speech further narrows the focus to the violent motions of storms upon earth. How has the translator tried to reflect, through rhythm and diction, contrasting impressions of these three views?

2. Raphael's view is that of the philosopher contemplating the total meaning of life; Gabriel's is that of the scientist examining the physical world; and Michael's is that of ordinary man directly experiencing his world. What attitudes toward life are suggested by these three viewpoints?

3. How does Mephistopheles' view of life contrast with all of these? What criticisms does he make of the world as God has made it? Is his an erroneous view of life or only a limited one? Explain.

4. Mephistopheles is obviously surprised that the Lord singles out Faust as "my ser-vant." What does the Lord explain to him about the nature of man and of God? What is Mephistopheles' misunderstanding about these things?

5. Mephistopheles clearly expects to tempt Faust into serious sin, as the serpent did Eve. How does the Lord's interpretation of the bargain indicate that Goethe's conception of sin is very different from Milton's?

6. How do the final statements of the angels and Mephistopheles comment upon the inadequacy of Mephistopheles' understanding (and thereby foreshadow his failure)?

7. What are Faust's reasons for denying any concern about whom he might have to serve in the next world? What does he later reveal (in his speech beginning in Part I, line 65) about his idea of hell, the worst that could possibly happen to a man?

8. Faust indicates by his sarcastic rhetorical questions (beginning in Part I, at line 41) that he knows the kind of dissatisfaction that comes with the pleasures Mephistopheles can offer. What is the difference between that kind of

dissatisfaction and the kind he implies is his salvation, when he says (lines 58–59):

If ever I stretch myself on a bed of ease,
Then I am finished!

9. To prepare Faust for "this pleasure trip," Mephistopheles in a later scene has him rejuvenated. From what you know of Mephistopheles' promises, what trap does he hope to catch Faust in with this transformation?

10. To what extent are the attitudes expressed by Faust in this scene endorsed by the principles earlier stated by the Lord?

11. What specific stylistic characteristics in the speeches of Faust and Mephistopheles contribute to their characterization? How does Mephistopheles' style and tone change in the last speech of the Pact scene?

12. What are the important differences in personality between Goethe's Mephistopheles and Milton's Satan? What significance do you find in these differences?

FOR COMPOSITION

1. In an essay, explain how the views of man and God held by Milton (see page 630), Pope (see page 659), and Goethe would provide different bases for morality. What argument would each make, for example, against the killing of an enemy or against uninhibited sensual indulgence? Would they condone or condemn disobedience to authority? Which view do you feel would be the truest basis for morality? Give reasons for your answer.

2. In the Book of Job in the Bible, God also makes a pact with Satan. Read the Book of Job (it is brief) and then think about these pacts between God and Satan. In an essay, describe the terms of the two pacts and the reasons they were made. What implications are made by each writer about the purposes of human existence and the reasons for mental and physical suffering? What implications does each writer make about worldly standards for happiness and righteousness?

The Misanthrope

MOLIÈRE

(Translated by Richard Wilbur)

Jean Baptiste Poquelin (1622–1673) was the son of a solidly respectable Parisian bourgeois who was a successful furniture merchant. He was given a good education by the Jesuits and was destined to follow in his father's business or perhaps to enter the law. Instead, in the best tradition of wayward sons, he fell in love with the theater and joined a traveling troupe of players—a shocking move in a time when actors were bohemians, denied Christian burial and considered anything but solid and respectable. In his new life as Molière, the young man endured many years of hardship, but his experiences gave him valuable theatrical training. By 1658 Molière had emerged in Paris as a successful playwright and actor, favored by the powerful Louis XIV, who even protected the writer from the attacks of those offended by his plays.

There were many who were offended. Molière was devastating in his witty exposures of the frivolity of court life and of the greed and hypocrisy of the respected middle class. He reserved a special bitterness for the professions of law and medicine; in his day, doctors and lawyers were given to pretentiousness, and Molière had unfortunate encounters with both professions. He maintained a decent caution about any reflections upon the king himself, and Louis was amused as Molière lampooned the society of which Louis himself was both cause and symptom.

Molière's plays have the classic simplicity and clarity that his age admired in all forms of expression. In *The Misanthrope* his writing is especially austere. The plot is slight, consisting of complications upon a basic situation involving suitor and coquette. Action in the play is limited, so that little use is made of suspense over its outcome. There are no interludes of music or pageantry or low comedy. Today we would imagine the visual effects of costuming and scenery as beautiful and elaborate, but Molière used these effects to provide a neutral background for the action; the costumes would simply be varieties of the fashionable dress of the period, and the setting throughout would be an undifferentiated room, its specific locale being unimportant.

Even the characters' gestures and movements would call little attention to themselves. Instead, all of the attention of Molière's play is focussed on the words and on the dramatic structures within which the words are spoken.

The central issue of honesty versus worldly hypocrisy is established at the beginning of the play, and as each character is introduced, a distinct element is added to the dramatic pattern. The play is written in strong, formal couplets, but the language is plain and straightforward, and each character's speech is subtly varied to express his distinctive habits of thought and feeling. Thus by the simplest dramatic and linguistic devices, Molière creates a rich comment upon the foibles of mankind. The play is at moments hilarious and often witty, but its pervasive tone is one of deep and sober amusement that is not far from the borders of tragedy.

Characters

ALCESTE (al·sest′), *in love with Célimène*
PHILINTE (fē·laṅt′), *Alceste's friend*
ORONTE (ô·rôṅt′), *in love with Célimène*
CÉLIMÈNE (sā·lē·men′), *Alceste's beloved*
ÉLIANTE (ā·lē·äṅt′), *Célimène's cousin*
ARSINOÉ (ar·sē·nō·ā′), *a friend of Célimène*
ACASTE (a·kast′)   ⎱ *marquesses*
CLITANDRE (klē·täṅdr′) ⎰
BASQUE (bask), *Célimène's servant*
A GUARD *of the Marshalsea*
DUBOIS (dü·bwä′), *Alceste's valet*

The scene throughout is in Célimène's house at Paris.

ACT I

[*Enter* PHILINTE *and* ALCESTE.]

PHILINTE. Now, what's got into you?
ALCESTE *(seated).*   Kindly leave me alone.
PHILINTE. Come, come, what is it? This lugubrious tone . . .
ALCESTE. Leave me, I said; you spoil my solitude.
PHILINTE. Oh, listen to me, now, and don't be rude.
ALCESTE. I choose to be rude, sir, and to be hard of hearing.   5
PHILINTE. These ugly moods of yours are not endearing;
    Friends though we are, I really must insist . . .
ALCESTE *(abruptly rising).* Friends? Friends, you say? Well, cross me off
    your list.
    I've been your friend till now, as you well know;
    But after what I saw a moment ago   10
    I tell you flatly that our ways must part.
    I wish no place in a dishonest heart.
PHILINTE. Why, what have I done, Alceste? Is this quite just?
ALCESTE. My God, you ought to die of self-disgust.
    I call your conduct inexcusable, sir,   15
    And every man of honor will concur.
    I see you almost hug a man to death,
    Exclaim for joy until you're out of breath,
    And supplement these loving demonstrations

With endless offers, vows, and protestations;   20
Then when I ask you "Who was that?" I find
That you can barely bring his name to mind!
Once the man's back is turned, you cease to love him,
And speak with absolute indifference of him!
By God, I say it's base and scandalous   25
To falsify the heart's affections thus;
If I caught myself behaving in such a way,
I'd hang myself for shame, without delay.
PHILINTE. It hardly seems a hanging matter to me;
I hope that you will take it graciously   30
If I extend myself a slight reprieve,
And live a little longer, by your leave.
ALCESTE. How dare you joke about a crime so grave?
PHILINTE. What crime? How else are people to behave?
ALCESTE. I'd have them be sincere, and never part   35
With any word that isn't from the heart.
PHILINTE. When someone greets us with a show of pleasure,
It's but polite to give him equal measure,
Return his love the best that we know how,
And trade him offer for offer, vow for vow.   40
ALCESTE. No, no, this formula you'd have me follow,
However fashionable, is false and hollow,
And I despise the frenzied operations
Of all these barterers of protestations,
These lavishers of meaningless embraces,   45
These utterers of obliging commonplaces,
Who court and flatter everyone on earth
And praise the fool no less than the man of worth.
Should you rejoice that someone fondles you,
Offers his love and service, swears to be true,   50
And fills your ears with praises of your name,
When to the first damned fop he'll say the same?
No, no: no self-respecting heart would dream
Of prizing so promiscuous an esteem;
However high the praise, there's nothing worse   55
Than sharing honors with the universe.
Esteem is founded on comparison:
To honor all men is to honor none.
Since you embrace this indiscriminate vice,
Your friendship comes at far too cheap a price;   60
I spurn the easy tribute of a heart
Which will not set the worthy man apart:
I choose, sir, to be chosen; and in fine,
The friend of mankind is no friend of mine.
PHILINTE. But in polite society, custom decrees   65
That we show certain outward courtesies. . . .
ALCESTE. Ah, no! we should condemn with all our force
Such false and artificial intercourse.
Let men behave like men; let them display
Their inmost hearts in everything they say;   70

Let the heart speak, and let our sentiments
Not mask themselves in silly compliments.
PHILINTE. In certain cases it would be uncouth
And most absurd to speak the naked truth;
With all respect for your exalted notions,   75
It's often best to veil one's true emotions.
Wouldn't the social fabric come undone
If we were wholly frank with everyone?
Suppose you met with someone you couldn't bear;
Would you inform him of it then and there?   80
ALCESTE. Yes.
PHILINTE.   Then you'd tell old Emilie it's pathetic
The way she daubs her features with cosmetic
And plays the gay coquette at sixty-four?
ALCESTE. I would.
PHILINTE.   And you'd call Dorilas a bore,
And tell him every ear at court is lame   85
From hearing him brag about his noble name?
ALCESTE. Precisely.
PHILINTE.   Ah, you're joking.
ALCESTE.   *Au contraire:*
In this regard there's none I'd choose to spare.
All are corrupt; there's nothing to be seen
In court or town but aggravates my spleen.   90
I fall into deep gloom and melancholy
When I survey the scene of human folly,
Finding on every hand base flattery,
Injustice, fraud, self-interest, treachery....
Ah, it's too much; mankind has grown so base,   95
I mean to break with the whole human race.
PHILINTE. This philosophic rage is a bit extreme;
You've no idea how comical you seem;
Indeed, we're like those brothers in the play
Called *School for Husbands,*° one of whom was prey ...   100
ALCESTE. Enough, now! None of your stupid similes.
PHILINTE. Then, let's have no more tirades, if you please.
The world won't change, whatever you say or do;
And since plain speaking means so much to you,
I'll tell you plainly that by being frank   105
You've earned the reputation of a crank,
And that you're thought ridiculous when you rage
And rant against the manners of the age.
ALCESTE. So much the better; just what I wish to hear.
No news could be more grateful to my ear.   110
All men are so detestable in my eyes,
I should be sorry if they thought me wise.
PHILINTE. Your hatred's very sweeping, is it not?
ALCESTE. Quite right: I hate the whole degraded lot.
PHILINTE. Must all poor human creatures be embraced,   115

100. *School for Husbands:* an earlier comedy by Molière.

Without distinction, by your vast distaste?
Even in these bad times, there are surely a few . . .
ALCESTE. No, I include all men in one dim view:
    Some men I hate for being rogues; the others
    I hate because they treat the rogues like brothers,   120
    And, lacking a virtuous scorn for what is vile,
    Receive the villain with a complaisant smile.
    Notice how tolerant people choose to be
    Toward that bold rascal who's at law with me.
    His social polish can't conceal his nature;   125
    One sees at once that he's a treacherous creature;
    No one could possibly be taken in
    By those soft speeches and that sugary grin.
    The whole world knows the shady means by which
    The lowbrow's grown so powerful and rich,   130
    And risen to a rank so bright and high
    That virtue can but blush, and merit sigh.
    Whenever his name comes up in conversation,
    None will defend his wretched reputation;
    Call him knave, liar, scoundrel, and all the rest,   135
    Each head will nod, and no one will protest.
    And yet his smirk is seen in every house,
    He's greeted everywhere with smiles and bows,
    And when there's any honor that can be got
    By pulling strings, he'll get it, like as not.   140
    My God! It chills my heart to see the ways
    Men come to terms with evil nowadays;
    Sometimes, I swear, I'm moved to flee and find
    Some desert land unfouled by humankind.
PHILINTE. Come, let's forget the follies of the times   145
    And pardon mankind for its petty crimes;
    Let's have an end of rantings and of railings,
    And show some leniency toward human failings.
    This world requires a pliant rectitude;
    Too stern a virtue makes one stiff and rude;   150
    Good sense views all extremes with detestation,
    And bids us to be noble in moderation.
    The rigid virtues of the ancient days
    Are not for us; they jar with all our ways
    And ask of us too lofty a perfection.   155
    Wise men accept their times without objection,
    And there's no greater folly, if you ask me,
    Than trying to reform society.
    Like you, I see each day a hundred and one
    Unhandsome deeds that might be better done,   160
    But still, for all the faults that meet my view,
    I'm never known to storm and rave like you.
    I take men as they are, or let them be,
    And teach my soul to bear their frailty;
    And whether in court or town, whatever the scene,   165
    My phlegm's as philosophic as your spleen.

ALCESTE. This phlegm which you so eloquently commend,
  Does nothing ever rile it up, my friend?
  Suppose some man you trust should treacherously
  Conspire to rob you of your property,   170
  And do his best to wreck your reputation?
  Wouldn't you feel a certain indignation?
PHILINTE. Why, no. These faults of which you so complain
  Are part of human nature, I maintain,
  And it's no more a matter for disgust   175
  That men are knavish, selfish, and unjust,
  Than that the vulture dines upon the dead,
  And wolves are furious, and apes ill-bred.
ALCESTE. Shall I see myself betrayed, robbed, torn to bits,
  And not . . . Oh, let's be still and rest our wits.   180
  Enough of reasoning, now. I've had my fill.
PHILINTE. Indeed, you would do well, sir, to be still.
  Rage less at your opponent, and give some thought
  To how you'll win this lawsuit that he's brought.
ALCESTE. I assure you I'll do nothing of the sort.   185
PHILINTE. Then who will plead your case before the court?
ALCESTE. Reason and right and justice will plead for me.
PHILINTE. Oh, Lord. What judges do you plan to see?
ALCESTE. Why, none. The justice of my cause is clear.
PHILINTE. Of course, man; but there's politics to fear. . . .   190
ALCESTE. No, I refuse to lift a hand. That's flat.
  I'm either right or wrong.
PHILINTE.   Don't count on that.
ALCESTE. No, I'll do nothing.
PHILINTE.   Your enemy's influence
  Is great, you know . . .
ALCESTE.   That makes no difference.
PHILINTE. It will; you'll see.
ALCESTE.   Must honor bow to guile?   195
  If so, I shall be proud to lose the trial.
PHILINTE. Oh, really . . .
ALCESTE.   I'll discover by this case
  Whether or not men are sufficiently base
  And impudent and villainous and perverse
  To do me wrong before the universe.   200
PHILINTE. What a man!
ALCESTE.   Oh, I could wish, whatever the cost,
  Just for the beauty of it, that my trial were lost.
PHILINTE. If people heard you talking so, Alceste,
  They'd split their sides. Your name would be a jest.
ALCESTE. So much the worse for jesters.
PHILINTE.   May I inquire   205
  Whether this rectitude you so admire,
  And these hard virtues you're enamored of
  Are qualities of the lady whom you love?
  It much surprises me that you, who seem
  To view mankind with furious disesteem,   210

Have yet found something to enchant your eyes
Amid a species which you so despise.
And what is more amazing, I'm afraid,
Is the most curious choice your heart has made.
The honest Éliante is fond of you;   215
Arsinoé, the prude, admires you too;
And yet your spirit's been perversely led
To choose the flighty Célimène instead,
Whose brittle malice and coquettish ways
So typify the manners of our days.   220
How is it that the traits you most abhor
Are bearable in this lady you adore?
Are you so blind with love that you can't find them?
Or do you contrive, in her case, not to mind them?

ALCESTE. My love for that young widow's not the kind   225
I see her faults, despite my ardent love,
I see her faults, despite my ardent love,
And all I see I fervently reprove.
And yet I'm weak; for all her falsity,
That woman knows the art of pleasing me,   230
And though I never cease complaining of her,
I swear I cannot manage not to love her.
Her charm outweighs her faults; I can but aim
To cleanse her spirit in my love's pure flame.

PHILINTE. That's no small task; I wish you all success.   235
You think then that she loves you?
ALCESTE.   Heavens, yes!
I wouldn't love her did she not love me.
PHILINTE. Well, if her taste for you is plain to see,
Why do these rivals cause you such despair?
ALCESTE. True love, sir, is possessive and cannot bear   240
To share with all the world. I'm here today
To tell her she must send that mob away.
PHILINTE. If I were you, and had your choice to make,
Éliante, her cousin, would be the one I'd take;
That honest heart, which cares for you alone,   245
Would harmonize far better with your own.
ALCESTE. True, true: each day my reason tells me so;
But reason doesn't rule in love, you know.
PHILINTE. I fear some bitter sorrow is in store;
This love . . .

                    [*Enter* ORONTE.]

ORONTE (*to* ALCESTE). The servants told me at the door   250
That Éliante and Célimène were out,
But when I heard, dear sir, that you were about,
I came to say, without exaggeration,
That I hold you in the vastest admiration,
And that it's always been my dearest desire   255
To be the friend of one I so admire.
I hope to see my love of merit requited,

And you and I in friendship's bond united.
I'm sure you won't refuse—if I may be frank—
A friend of my devotedness—and rank.   260

[*During this speech of* ORONTE, ALCESTE *is abstracted and seems unaware that he is being spoken to. He only breaks off his reverie when* ORONTE *says:*]

    It was for you, if you please, that my words were intended.
ALCESTE. For me, sir?
ORONTE.   Yes, for you. You're not offended?
ALCESTE. By no means. But this much surprises me. . . .
    The honor comes most unexpectedly. . . .
ORONTE. My high regard should not astonish you;   265
    The whole world feels the same. It is your due.
ALCESTE. Sir . . .
ORONTE.   Why, in all the state there isn't one
    Can match your merits; they shine, sir, like the sun.
ALCESTE. Sir . . .
ORONTE.   You are higher in my estimation
    Than all that's most illustrious in the nation.   270
ALCESTE. Sir . . .
ORONTE.   If I lie, may heaven strike me dead!
    To show you that I mean what I have said,
    Permit me, sir, to embrace you most sincerely,
    And swear that I will prize our friendship dearly.
    Give me your hand. And now, sir, if you choose,   275
    We'll make our vows.
ALCESTE.   Sir . . .
ORONTE.   What! You refuse?
ALCESTE. Sir, it's a very great honor you extend:
    But friendship is a sacred thing, my friend;
    It would be profanation to bestow
    The name of friend on one you hardly know.   280
    All parts are better played when well-rehearsed;
    Let's put off friendship, and get acquainted first.
    We may discover it would be unwise
    To try to make our natures harmonize.
ORONTE. By heaven! You're sagacious to the core;   285
    This speech has made me admire you even more.
    Let time, then, bring us closer day by day;
    Meanwhile, I shall be yours in every way.
    If, for example, there should be anything
    You wish at court, I'll mention it to the king.   290
    I have his ear, of course; it's quite well known
    That I am much in favor with the throne.
    In short, I am your servant. And now, dear friend,
    Since you have such fine judgment, I intend
    To please you, if I can, with a small sonnet   295
    I wrote not long ago. Please comment on it,
    And tell me whether I ought to publish it.

ALCESTE. You must excuse me, sir; I'm hardly fit
　　To judge such matters.
ORONTE.　　　　　　　　Why not?
ALCESTE.　　　　　　　　　　　I am, I fear,
　　Inclined to be unfashionably sincere.　　　　　　　　　　300
ORONTE. Just what I ask; I'd take no satisfaction
　　In anything but your sincere reaction.
　　I beg you not to dream of being kind.
ALCESTE. Since you desire it, sir, I'll speak my mind.
ORONTE. "Sonnet." It's a sonnet. . . . "Hope" . . . The poem's addressed　305
　　To a lady who wakened hopes within my breast.
　　"Hope" . . . this is not the pompous sort of thing,
　　Just modest little verses, with a tender ring.
ALCESTE. Well, we shall see.
ORONTE.　　　　　　　　"Hope" . . . I'm anxious to hear
　　Whether the style seems properly smooth and clear,　　　　310
　　And whether the choice of words is good or bad.
ALCESTE. We'll see, we'll see.
ORONTE.　　　　　　　　Perhaps I ought to add
　　That it took me only a quarter-hour to write it.
ALCESTE. The time's irrelevant, sir. Kindly recite it.
ORONTE (reading). "Hope comforts us awhile, 'tis true,　　　　315
　　　　　　　Lulling our cares with careless laughter,
　　　　　　　And yet such joy is full of rue,
　　　　　　　My Phyllis, if nothing follows after."
PHILINTE. I'm charmed by this already; the style's delightful.
ALCESTE (in a low voice, to PHILINTE). How can you say that? Why, the
　　thing is frightful.　　　　　　　　　　　　　　　　320
ORONTE. "Your fair face smiled on me awhile,
　　　But was it kindness so to enchant me?
　　　'Twould have been fairer not to smile,
　　　If hope was all you meant to grant me."
PHILINTE. What a clever thought! How handsomely you phrase it!　325
ALCESTE (in a low voice, to PHILINTE). You know the thing is trash. How
　　dare you praise it?
ORONTE. "If it's to be my passion's fate
　　Thus everlastingly to wait,
　　Then death will come to set me free:
　　For death is fairer than the fair;　　　　　　　　　　330
　　Phyllis, to hope is to despair
　　When one must hope eternally."
PHILINTE. The close is exquisite—full of feeling and grace.
ALCESTE (in a low voice, aside). Oh, blast the close; you'd better close your
　　face
　　Before you send your lying soul to hell.　　　　　　　335
PHILINTE. I can't remember a poem I've liked so well.
ALCESTE (in a low voice, aside). Good Lord!
ORONTE (to PHILINTE).　　　　　　　　I fear you're flattering me a bit.
PHILINTE. Oh, no!
ALCESTE (in a low voice, aside). What else d'you call it, you hypocrite?

ORONTE (*to* ALCESTE). But you, sir, keep your promise now: don't shrink
    From telling me sincerely what you think.   340
ALCESTE. Sir, these are delicate matters; we all desire
    To be told that we've the true poetic fire.
    But once, to one whose name I shall not mention,
    I said, regarding some verse of his invention,
    That gentlemen should rigorously control   345
    That itch to write which often afflicts the soul;
    That one should curb the heady inclination
    To publicize one's little avocation;
    And that in showing off one's works of art
    One often plays a very clownish part.   350
ORONTE. Are you suggesting in a devious way
    That I ought not . . .
ALCESTE.   Oh, that I do not say.
    Further, I told him that no fault is worse
    Than that of writing frigid, lifeless verse,
    And that the merest whisper of such a shame   355
    Suffices to destroy a man's good name.
ORONTE. D'you mean to say my sonnet's dull and trite?
ALCESTE. I don't say that. But I went on to cite
    Numerous cases of once-respected men
    Who came to grief by taking up the pen.   360
ORONTE. And am I like them? Do I write so poorly?
ALCESTE. I don't say that. But I told this person, "Surely
    You're under no necessity to compose;
    Why you should wish to publish, heaven knows.
    There's no excuse for printing tedious rot   365
    Unless one writes for bread, as you do not.
    Resist temptation, then, I beg of you;
    Conceal your pastimes from the public view;
    And don't give up, on any provocation,
    Your present high and courtly reputation,   370
    To purchase at a greedy printer's shop
    The name of silly author and scribbling fop."
    These were the points I tried to make him see.
ORONTE. I sense that they are also aimed at me:
    But now—about my sonnet—I'd like to be told . . .   375
ALCESTE. Frankly, that sonnet should be pigeonholed.
    You've chosen the worst models to imitate.
    The style's unnatural. Let me illustrate:

        For example, "Your fair face smiled on me awhile,"
        Followed by "'Twould have been fairer not to smile!"   380
        Or this: "such joy is full of rue";
        Or this: "For death is fairer than the fair";
        Or, "Phyllis, to hope is to despair
            When one must hope eternally!"

    This artificial style, that's all the fashion,   385
    Has neither taste, nor honesty, nor passion;

It's nothing but a sort of wordy play,
And nature never spoke in such a way.
What, in this shallow age, is not debased?
Our fathers, though less refined, had better taste;   390
I'd barter all that men admire today
For one old love song I shall try to say:

    "If the king had given me for my own
      Paris, his citadel,
    And I for that must leave alone   395
      Her whom I love so well,
    I'd say then to the Crown,
    Take back your glittering town;
    My darling is more fair, I swear,
    My darling is more fair."   400

The rhyme's not rich, the style is rough and old,
But don't you see that it's the purest gold
Beside the tinsel nonsense now preferred,
And that there's passion in its every word?

    "If the king had given me for my own   405
      Paris, his citadel,
    And I for that must leave alone
      Her whom I love so well,
    I'd say then to the Crown,
    Take back your glittering town;   410
    My darling is more fair, I swear,
    My darling is more fair."

There speaks a loving heart. *(To* PHILINTE*)* You're laughing, eh?
Laugh on, my precious wit. Whatever you say,
I hold that song's worth all the bibelots   415
That people hail today with ah's and oh's.
ORONTE. And I maintain my sonnet's very good.
ALCESTE. It's not at all suprising that you should.
    You have your reasons; permit me to have mine
    For thinking that you cannot write a line.   420
ORONTE. Others have praised my sonnet to the skies.
ALCESTE. I lack their art of telling pleasant lies.
ORONTE. You seem to think you've got no end of wit.
ALCESTE. To praise your verse, I'd need still more of it.
ORONTE. I'm not in need of your approval, sir.   425
ALCESTE. That's good; you couldn't have it if you were.
ORONTE. Come now, I'll lend you the subject of my sonnet;
    I'd like to see you try to improve upon it.
ALCESTE. I might, by chance, write something just as shoddy;
    But then I wouldn't show it to everybody.   430
ORONTE. You're most opinionated and conceited.
ALCESTE. Go find your flatterers, and be better treated.
ORONTE. Look here, my little fellow, pray watch your tone.
ALCESTE. My great big fellow, you'd better watch your own.

PHILINTE *(stepping between them)*. Oh, please, please, gentlemen! This will
  never do.   435
ORONTE. The fault is mine, and I leave the field to you.
  I am your servant, sir, in every way.
ALCESTE. And I, sir, am your most abject valet.   *[Exit* ORONTE.]
PHILINTE. Well, as you see, sincerity in excess
  Can get you into a very pretty mess;   440
  Oronte was hungry for appreciation. . . .
ALCESTE. Don't speak to me.
PHILINTE.   What?
ALCESTE.   No more conversation.
PHILINTE. Really, now . . .
ALCESTE.   Leave me alone.
PHILINTE.   If I . . .
ALCESTE.   Out of my sight!
PHILINTE. But what . . .
ALCESTE.   I won't listen.
PHILINTE.   But . . .
ALCESTE.   Silence!
PHILINTE.   Now, is it polite . . .
ALCESTE. By heaven, I've had enough. Don't follow me.   445
PHILINTE. Ah, you're just joking. I'll keep you company. *[Exeunt.]*

ACT II

[Enter ALCESTE *and* CÉLIMÈNE.]

ALCESTE. Shall I speak plainly, madam? I confess
  Your conduct gives me infinite distress,
  And my resentment's grown too hot to smother.
  Soon, I foresee, we'll break with one another.
  If I said otherwise, I should deceive you;   5
  Sooner or later, I shall be forced to leave you,
  And if I swore that we shall never part,
  I should misread the omens of my heart.
CÉLIMÈNE. You kindly saw me home, it would appear,
  So as to pour invectives in my ear.   10
ALCESTE. I've no desire to quarrel. But I deplore
  Your inability to shut the door
  On all these suitors who beset you so.
  There's what annoys me, if you care to know.
CÉLIMÈNE. Is it my fault that all these men pursue me?   15
  Am I to blame if they're attracted to me?
  And when they gently beg an audience,
  Ought I to take a stick and drive them hence?
ALCESTE. Madam, there's no necessity for a stick;
  A less responsive heart would do the trick.   20
  Of your attractiveness I don't complain;
  But those your charms attract, you then detain

By a most melting and receptive manner,
And so enlist their hearts beneath your banner.
It's the agreeable hopes which you excite   25
That keep these lovers round you day and night;
Were they less liberally smiled upon,
That sighing troop would very soon be gone.
But tell me, madam, why it is that lately
This man Clitandre interests you so greatly?   30
Because of what high merits do you deem
Him worthy of the honor of your esteem?
Is it that your admiring glances linger
On the splendidly long nail of his little finger?
Or do you share the general deep respect   35
For the blond wig he chooses to affect?
Are you in love with his embroidered hose?
Do you adore his ribbons and his bows?
Or is it that this paragon bewitches
Your tasteful eye with his vast German breeches?   40
Perhaps his giggle, or his falsetto voice,
Makes him the latest gallant of your choice?

CÉLIMÈNE. You're much mistaken to resent him so.
Why I put up with him you surely know:
My lawsuit's very shortly to be tried,   45
And I must have his influence on my side.

ALCESTE. Then lose your lawsuit, madam, or let it drop;
Don't torture me by humoring such a fop.

CÉLIMÈNE. You're jealous of the whole world, sir.

ALCESTE.   That's true,
Since the whole world is well received by you.   50

CÉLIMÈNE. That my good nature is so unconfined
Should serve to pacify your jealous mind;
Were I to smile on one and scorn the rest,
Then you might have some cause to be distressed.

ALCESTE. Well, if I mustn't be jealous, tell me, then,   55
Just how I'm better treated than other men.

CÉLIMÈNE. You know you have my love. Will that not do?

ALCESTE. What proof have I that what you say is true?

CÉLIMÈNE. I would expect, sir, that my having said it
Might give the statement a sufficient credit.   60

ALCESTE. But how can I be sure that you don't tell
The selfsame thing to other men as well?

CÉLIMÈNE. What a gallant speech! How flattering to me!
What a sweet creature you make me out to be!
Well then, to save you from the pangs of doubt,   65
All that I've said I hereby cancel out;
Now, none but yourself shall make a monkey of you:
Are you content?

ALCESTE.   Why, why am I doomed to love you?
I swear that I shall bless the blissful hour
When this poor heart's no longer in your power!   70
I make no secret of it: I've done my best

To exorcise this passion from my breast;
But thus far all in vain; it will not go;
It's for my sins that I must love you so.
CÉLIMÈNE. Your love for me is matchless, sir; that's clear.   75
ALCESTE. Indeed, in all the world it has no peer;
Words can't describe the nature of my passion,
And no man ever loved in such a fashion.
CÉLIMÈNE. Yes, it's a brand-new fashion, I agree:
You show your love by castigating me,   80
And all your speeches are enraged and rude.
I've never been so furiously wooed.
ALCESTE. Yet you could calm that fury, if you chose.
Come, shall we bring our quarrels to a close?
Let's speak with open hearts, then, and begin . . .   85

[*Enter* BASQUE.]

CÉLIMÈNE. What is it?
BASQUE.   Acaste is here.
CÉLIMÈNE.   Well, send him in.   [*Exit* BASQUE.]
ALCESTE. What! Shall we never be alone at all?
You're always ready to receive a call,
And you can't bear, for ten ticks of the clock,
Not to keep open house for all who knock.   90
CÉLIMÈNE. I couldn't refuse him: he'd be most put out.
ALCESTE. Surely that's not worth worrying about.
CÉLIMÈNE. Acaste would never forgive me if he guessed
That I consider him a dreadful pest.
ALCESTE. If he's a pest, why bother with him then?   95
CÉLIMÈNE. Heavens! One can't antagonize such men;
Why, they're the chartered gossips of the court,
And have a say in things of every sort.
One must receive them, and be full of charm;
They're no great help, but they can do you harm,   100
And though your influence be ever so great,
They're hardly the best people to alienate.
ALCESTE. I see, dear lady, that you could make a case
For putting up with the whole human race;
These friendships that you calculate so nicely . . .   105

[*Enter* BASQUE.]

BASQUE. Madam, Clitandre is here as well.
ALCESTE.   Precisely.
CÉLIMÈNE. Where are you going?
ALCESTE.   Elsewhere.
CÉLIMÈNE.   Stay.
ALCESTE.   No, no.
CÉLIMÈNE. Stay, sir.
ALCESTE.   I can't.
CÉLIMÈNE.   I wish it.

ALCESTE.   No, I must go.
    I beg you, madam, not to press the matter;
    You know I have no taste for idle chatter.   110
CÉLIMÈNE. Stay. I command you.
ALCESTE.   No, I cannot stay.
CÉLIMÈNE. Very well; you have my leave to go away.

         [*Enter* ÉLIANTE, PHILINTE, ACASTE, *and* CLITANDRE.]

ÉLIANTE (*to* CÉLIMÈNE). The marquesses have kindly come to call.
    Were they announced?
CÉLIMÈNE.   Yes. Basque, bring chairs for all.
                [BASQUE *provides the chairs, and exits.*]
(*To* ALCESTE) You haven't gone?
ALCESTE.   No; and I shan't depart   115
    Till you decide who's foremost in your heart.
CÉLIMÈNE. Oh, hush.
ALCESTE.   It's time to choose; take them, or me.
CÉLIMÈNE. You're mad.
ALCESTE.   I'm not, as you shall shortly see.
CÉLIMÈNE. Oh?
ALCESTE.   You'll decide.
CÉLIMÈNE.   You're joking now, dear friend.
ALCESTE. No, no; you'll choose; my patience is at an end.   120
CLITANDRE. Madam, I come from court, where poor Cléonte
    Behaved like a perfect fool, as is his wont.
    Has he no friend to counsel him, I wonder,
    And teach him less unerringly to blunder?
CÉLIMÈNE. It's true, the man's a most accomplished dunce;   125
    His gauche behavior charms the eye at once;
    And every time one sees him, on my word,
    His manner's grown a trifle more absurd.
ACASTE. Speaking of dunces, I've just now conversed
    With old Damon, who's one of the very worst;   130
    I stood a lifetime in the broiling sun
    Before his dreary monologue was done.
CÉLIMÈNE. Oh, he's a wondrous talker and has the power
    To tell you nothing hour after hour:
    If, by mistake, he ever came to the point,   135
    The shock would put his jawbone out of joint.
ÉLIANTE (*to* PHILINTE). The conversation takes its usual turn,
    And all our dear friends' ears will shortly burn.
CLITANDRE. Timante's a character, madam.
CÉLIMÈNE.   Isn't he, though?
    A man of mystery from top to toe,   140
    Who moves about in a romantic mist
    On secret missions which do not exist.
    His talk is full of eyebrows and grimaces;
    How tired one gets of his momentous faces;
    He's always whispering something confidential   145
    Which turns out to be quite inconsequential;

Nothing's too slight for him to mystify;
He even whispers when he says good-by.
ACASTE. Tell us about Géralde.
CÉLIMÈNE.   That tiresome ass.
    He mixes only with the titled class,   150
    And fawns on dukes and princes and is bored
    With anyone who's not at least a lord.
    The man's obsessed with rank, and his discourses
    Are all of hounds and carriages and horses;
    He uses Christian names with all the great,   155
    And the word *milord,* with him, is out of date.
CLITANDRE. He's very taken with Bélise, I hear.
CÉLIMÈNE. She is the dreariest company, poor dear.
    Whenever she comes to call, I grope about
    To find some topic which will draw her out,   160
    But, owing to her dry and faint replies,
    The conversation wilts, and droops, and dies.
    In vain one hopes to animate her face
    By mentioning the ultimate commonplace;
    But sun or shower, even hail or frost   165
    Are matters she can instantly exhaust.
    Meanwhile her visit, painful though it is,
    Drags on and on through mute eternities,
    And though you ask the time, and yawn, and yawn,
    She sits there like a stone and won't be gone.   170
ACASTE. Now for Adraste.
CÉLIMÈNE.   Oh, that conceited elf
    Has a gigantic passion for himself;
    He rails against the court and cannot bear it
    That none will recognize his hidden merit;
    All honors given to others give offense   175
    To his imaginary excellence.
CLITANDRE. What about young Cléon? His house, they say,
    Is full of the best society, night and day.
CÉLIMÈNE. His cook has made him popular, not he:
    It's Cléon's table that people come to see.   180
ÉLIANTE. He gives a splendid dinner, you must admit.
CÉLIMÈNE. But must he serve himself along with it?
    For my taste, he's a most insipid dish
    Whose presence sours the wine and spoils the fish.
PHILINTE. Damis, his uncle, is admired no end.   185
    What's your opinion, madam?
CÉLIMÈNE.   Why, he's my friend.
PHILINTE. He seems a decent fellow, and rather clever.
CÉLIMÈNE. He works too hard at cleverness, however.
    I hate to see him sweat and struggle so
    To fill his conversation with *bons mots.*°   190
    Since he's decided to become a wit

190. *bons mots:* clever sayings.

His taste's so pure that nothing pleases it;
He scolds at all the latest books and plays,
Thinking that wit must never stoop to praise,
That finding fault's a sign of intellect,   195
That all appreciation is abject,
And that by damning everything in sight
One shows oneself in a distinguished light.
He's scornful even of our conversations:
Their trivial nature sorely tries his patience;   200
He folds his arms and stands above the battle,
And listens sadly to our childish prattle.

ACASTE. Wonderful, madam! You've hit him off precisely.

CLITANDRE. No one can sketch a character so nicely.

ALCESTE. How bravely, sirs, you cut and thrust at all   205
These absent fools, till one by one they fall:
But let one come in sight, and you'll at once
Embrace the man you lately called a dunce,
Telling him in a tone sincere and fervent
How proud you are to be his humble servant.   210

CLITANDRE. Why pick on us? Madam's been speaking, sir,
And you should quarrel, if you must, with her.

ALCESTE. Go on, dear lady, mock me as you please;
You have your audience in ecstasies.

PHILINTE. But what she says is true: you have a way   215
Of bridling at whatever people say;
Whether they praise or blame, your angry spirit
Is equally unsatisfied to hear it.

ALCESTE. Men, sir, are always wrong, and that's the reason
That righteous anger's never out of season;   220
All that I hear in all their conversation
Is flattering praise or reckless condemnation.

CÉLIMÈNE. But . . .

ALCESTE.   No, no, madam, I am forced to state
That you have pleasures which I deprecate,
And that these others, here, are much to blame   225
For nourishing the faults which are your shame.

CLITANDRE. I shan't defend myself, sir; but I vow
I'd thought this lady faultless until now.

ALCESTE. No, no, by God, the fault is yours, because
You lead her on with laughter and applause,   230
And make her think that she's the more delightful
The more her talk is scandalous and spiteful.
Oh, she would stoop to malice far, far less
If no such claque approved her cleverness.
It's flatterers like you whose foolish praise   235
Nourishes all the vices of these days.

PHILINTE. But why protest when someone ridicules
Those you'd condemn, yourself, as knaves or fools?

[MOLIÈRE CONTINUES ON PAGE 711]

MASTERPIECES OF WORLD ART

Eighteenth-Century Painting

In France, during the second half of the seventeenth century, the vigorous style of the Baroque had developed into a grandiose courtly art centered around the magnificent "Sun King," Louis XIV. Then as the aging king's long reign drew to a close, the severely formal disciplines he had imposed on his court gradually gave way to a more carefree attitude which found expression in a new, lively decorative style called Rococo.

Among the most charming examples of Rococo art are Antoine Watteau's pictures of actors in a traveling Italian repertory company known as the Commedia del'Arte. *Gilles* (PLATE 1), for example, shows the clown Pierrot standing in an idyllic grove, with other members of the cast behind him. Watteau is said to have painted this large canvas as a signboard advertising the opening of a new theater in Paris. Unfortunately, though, he died—at the age of only thirty-seven—a week before this event took place. Within his short lifetime, Watteau helped to create a delightful new style, in which delicacy, grace, and elegance replaced the powerful forms of the Baroque. His paintings lead us into an enchanted world of gentle pleasures and make-believe, a world to which the highly sophisticated French court became passionately devoted.

The Rococo soon developed into an international style. In Italy, its leading master was Giovanni Domenico Tiepolo, a Venetian who worked in a rich decorative tradition dating back to the sixteenth century. In *The Trojan Horse* (PLATE 2), we can see certain resemblances to Veronese's sumptuous style (see page 533), particularly in the asymmetrical way Tiepolo has balanced a large mass of figures on one side with smaller ones on the other. The diagonal thrust of the wall into deep space, however, reminds us of the Baroque, but it is more exaggerated. Also Tiepolo's forms are more fluid and his colors lighter and more lively than those of most Baroque paintings. Here again, as in Watteau's picture, we seem to be looking in on a theatrical world of make-believe.

During the eighteenth century, pictures of famous cities were in such vogue that certain artists specialized in painting them to order. Canaletto's views of Venice were among the most popular, particularly those of the beautiful Square of St. Mark's. In PLATE 3 Canaletto shows strollers conversing with one another or peering into small canopied stalls. Beyond is the magnificent Byzantine church of St. Mark's, and off to the right is the Palace of the Doges, with its richly ornamented Gothic arcade. Notice how strategically Canaletto has placed the figures, booths, and accents of light and color to guide us through this detailed, yet remarkably spacious, composition.

French Rococo art of the later eighteenth century often showed a tendency toward mere prettiness, which only a few artists managed to avoid. One was Jean Honoré Fragonard, whose portrait of a lovely young woman is shown in PLATE 4. Fragonard's lively brushwork and firm contours express not merely the femininity of his young model, but also her robust, youthful vitality. Notice how he has echoed her pert profile in the bow on her hair, the gestures of her fingers, the frills of her collar and bodice, the flounces of her sleeve, and finally in the wrinkles of the pillow behind her. Note also the wide range of colors, from hot orange reds in the shadows to pearl-grays and chalky off-whites in the highlights of her flesh.

In PLATE 5 we see a very different kind of portrait; a young aristocrat and his pets, by Fragonard's Spanish contemporary, Goya. The little boy stands absolutely expressionless and transfixed, like a doll or an image in a dream. This trancelike mood is intensified by the three cats shown staring at the magpie in front of them. Goya's brushwork is extremely delicate, especially in his rendering of the tiny birds in the cage and the soft tones of the child's face. Yet surrounding these passages are bold contrasts of tone and color, dominated by the brilliant red of the boy's suit.

In the years leading up to the French Revolution of 1789, Rococo art began to seem outmoded, for the spirit of the times demanded a return to the ideal of self-sacrifice. This attitude was expressed through a revival of interest in ancient Greece and Rome. Jacques-Louis David's painting *The Death of Socrates* (PLATE 6), for instance, shows the great Greek philosopher in prison about to drink the poison forced upon him for his criticisms of Athenian institutions. Surrounding Socrates are his grief-stricken disciples and family. Solemn as a classical frieze on a Greek temple, each disciple is represented in a different attitude expressive of his own feelings. Both in subject matter and composition, this painting makes an interesting comparison with Poussin's *Death of Germanicus* (see page 670). David's "neoclassic" style was to dominate French art throughout the Revolutionary period and into the early nineteenth century.

PLATE 1. ANTOINE WATTEAU (French, 1684–1721): *Gilles*. 1721. Oil on canvas, 72⅝ x 66¾ inches. (Musée du Louvre, Paris)

PLATE 2. DOMENICO TIEPOLO (Venetian, 1727–1804) : *The Trojan Horse*. Oil on canvas, 15¼ x
26¼ inches. (Reproduced by courtesy of the Trustees, The National Gallery, London)

PLATE 3. CANALETTO (Venetian, 1697–1768): *The Square of St. Mark's*. About 1740. Oil on canvas, 45 x 60½ inches. (National Gallery of Art, Washington, D.C., Gift of Mrs. Barbara Hutton)

PLATE 4. JEAN HONORE FRAGONARD (French, 1732–1806): *A Young Girl Reading*. About 1776. Oil on canvas, 32 x 25½ inches. (National Gallery of Art, Washington, D.C., Gift of Mrs. Mellon Bruce in memory of her father, Andrew Mellon)

PLATE 5. FRANCISCO DE GOYA (Spanish, 1746–1828): *Don Manuel Osorio de Zuñiga*. 1784. Oil on canvas, 50 x 40 inches. (The Metropolitan Museum of Art, New York, The Jules S. Bache Collection, 1949)

PLATE 6. JACQUES-LOUIS DAVID (French, 1748–1825): *The Death of Socrates*. 1780. Oil on canvas, 51 x 77¼ inches. (The Metropolitan Museum of Art, New York, Wolfe Fund, 1931)

CÉLIMÈNE. Why, sir? Because he loves to make a fuss.
  You don't expect him to agree with us,   240
  When there's an opportunity to express
  His heaven-sent spirit of contrariness?
  What other people think, he can't abide;
  Whatever they say, he's on the other side;
  He lives in deadly terror of agreeing;   245
  'Twould make him seem an ordinary being.
  Indeed, he's so in love with contradiction,
  He'll turn against his most profound conviction
  And with a furious eloquence deplore it,
  If only someone else is speaking for it.   250
ACASTE. I see her charms and graces, which are many;
  But as for faults, I've never noticed any.
ALCESTE. I see them, sir; and rather than ignore them,
  I strenuously criticize her for them.
  The more one loves, the more one should object   255
  To every blemish, every least defect.
  Were I this lady, I would soon get rid
  Of lovers who approved of all I did,
  And by their slack indulgence and applause
  Endorsed my follies and excused my flaws.   260
CÉLIMÈNE. If all hearts beat according to your measure,
  The dawn of love would be the end of pleasure;
  And love would find its perfect consummation
  In ecstasies of rage and reprobation.
ÉLIANTE. Love, as a rule, affects men otherwise,   265
  And lovers rarely love to criticize.
  They see their lady as a charming blur,
  And find all things commendable in her.
  If she has any blemish, fault, or shame,
  They will redeem it by a pleasing name.   270
  The pale-faced lady's lily-white, perforce;
  The swarthy one's a sweet brunette, of course;
  The spindly lady has a slender grace;
  The fat one has a most majestic pace;
  The plain one, with her dress in disarray,   275
  They classify as *beauté négligée;*
  The hulking one's a goddess in their eyes,
  The dwarf, a concentrate of Paradise;
  The haughty lady has a noble mind;
  The mean one's witty, and the dull one's kind;   280
  The chatterbox has liveliness and verve;
  The mute one has a virtuous reserve.
  So lovers manage, in their passion's cause,
  To love their ladies even for their flaws.
ALCESTE. But I still say . . .
CÉLIMÈNE.   I think it would be nice   285

To stroll around the gallery once or twice.
What! You're not going, sirs?
CLITANDRE and ACASTE.   No, madam, no.
ALCESTE. You seem to be in terror lest they go.
Do what you will, sirs; leave, or linger on,
But I shan't go till after you are gone.   290
ACASTE. I'm free to linger, unless I should perceive
Madam is tired and wishes me to leave.
CLITANDRE. And as for me, I needn't go today
Until the hour of the king's *coucher.*°
CÉLIMÈNE *(to ALCESTE).* You're joking, surely?
ALCESTE.   Not in the least; we'll see   295
Whether you'd rather part with them, or me.

[*Enter* BASQUE.]

BASQUE *(to ALCESTE).* Sir, there's a fellow here who bids me state
That he must see you and that it can't wait.
ALCESTE. Tell him that I have no such pressing affairs.
BASQUE. It's a long tailcoat that this fellow wears,   300
With gold all over.
CÉLIMÈNE *(to ALCESTE).* You'd best go down and see.
Or—have him enter.   [*Exit* BASQUE.]

[*Enter a* GUARD.]

ALCESTE *(confronting the GUARD).* Well, what do you want with me?
Come in, sir.
GUARD.   I've a word, sir, for your ear.
ALCESTE. Speak it aloud, sir; I shall strive to hear.
GUARD. The marshals° have instructed me to say   305
You must report to them without delay.
ALCESTE. Who? Me, sir?
GUARD.   Yes, sir; you.
ALCESTE.   But what do they want?
PHILINTE *(to ALCESTE).* To scotch your silly quarrel with Oronte.
CÉLIMÈNE *(to PHILINTE).* What quarrel?
PHILINTE.   Oronte and he have fallen out
Over some verse he spoke his mind about;   310
The marshals wish to arbitrate the matter.
ALCESTE. Never shall I equivocate or flatter!
PHILINTE. You'd best obey their summons; come, let's go.
ALCESTE. How can they mend our quarrel, I'd like to know?
Am I to make a cowardly retraction,   315
And praise those jingles to his satisfaction?
I'll not recant; I've judged that sonnet rightly.
It's bad.
PHILINTE.   But you might say so more politely. . . .
ALCESTE. I'll not back down; his verses make me sick.

---

294. **the king's *coucher*:** a formal ceremony of the king's preparations for bed, attended by officials and favor-seekers.   305. **marshals:** a tribunal established to settle petty quarrels, in order to discourage duelling.

PHILINTE. If only you could be more politic!   320
    But come, let's go.
ALCESTE.   I'll go, but I won't unsay
    A single word.
PHILINTE.   Well, let's be on our way.
ALCESTE. Till I am ordered by my lord the king
    To praise that poem, I shall say the thing
    Is scandalous, by God, and that the poet   325
    Ought to be hanged for having the nerve to show it.
    (*To* CLITANDRE *and* ACASTE, *who are laughing*) By heaven, sirs, I
      really didn't know
    That I was being humorous.
CÉLIMÈNE.   Go, sir, go;
    Settle your business.
ALCESTE.   I shall, and when I'm through,
    I shall return to settle things with you.   [*Exit.*] 330

ACT III

[*Enter* CLITANDRE *and* ACASTE.]

CLITANDRE. Dear Marquess, how contented you appear;
    All things delight you, nothing mars your cheer.
    Can you, in perfect honesty, declare
    That you've a right to be so debonair?
ACASTE. By Jove, when I survey myself, I find   5
    No cause whatever for distress of mind.
    I'm young and rich; I can in modesty
    Lay claim to an exalted pedigree;
    And owing to my name and my condition
    I shall not want for honors and position.   10
    Then as to courage, that most precious trait,
    I seem to have it, as was proved of late
    Upon the field of honor, where my bearing,
    They say, was very cool and rather daring.
    I've wit, of course; and taste in such perfection   15
    That I can judge without the least reflection,
    And at the theater, which is my delight,
    Can make or break a play on opening night,
    And lead the crowd in hisses or bravos,
    And generally be known as one who knows.   20
    I'm clever, handsome, gracefully polite;
    My waist is small, my teeth are strong and white;
    As for my dress, the world's astonished eyes
    Assure me that I bear away the prize.
    I find myself in favor everywhere,   25
    Honored by men and worshiped by the fair;
    And since these things are so, it seems to me
    I'm justified in my complacency.
CLITANDRE. Well, if so many ladies hold you dear,
    Why do you press a hopeless courtship here?   30

ACASTE. Hopeless, you say? I'm not the sort of fool
    That likes his ladies difficult and cool.
    Men who are awkward, shy, and peasantish
    May pine for heartless beauties, if they wish,
    Grovel before them, bear their cruelties,   35
    Woo them with tears and sighs and bended knees,
    And hope by dogged faithfulness to gain
    What their poor merits never could obtain.
    For men like me, however, it makes no sense
    To love on trust, and foot the whole expense.   40
    Whatever any lady's merits be,
    I think, thank God, that I'm as choice as she;
    That if my heart is kind enough to burn
    For her, she owes me something in return;
    And that in any proper love affair   45
    The partners must invest an equal share.
CLITANDRE. You think, then, that our hostess favors you?
ACASTE. I've reason to believe that that is true.
CLITANDRE. How did you come to such a mad conclusion?
    You're blind, dear fellow. This is sheer delusion.   50
ACASTE. All right, then: I'm deluded and I'm blind.
CLITANDRE. Whatever put the notion in your mind?
ACASTE. Delusion.
CLITANDRE.   What persuades you that you're right?
ACASTE. I'm blind.
CLITANDRE.   But have you any proofs to cite?
ACASTE. I tell you I'm deluded.
CLITANDRE.   Have you, then,   55
    Received some secret pledge from Célimène?
ACASTE. Oh, no: she scorns me.
CLITANDRE.   Tell me the truth, I beg.
ACASTE. She just can't bear me.
CLITANDRE.   Ah, don't pull my leg.
    Tell me what hope she's given you, I pray.
ACASTE. I'm hopeless, and it's you who win the day.   60
    She hates me thoroughly, and I'm so vexed
    I mean to hang myself on Tuesday next.
CLITANDRE. Dear Marquess, let us have an armistice
    And make a treaty. What do you say to this?
    If ever one of us can plainly prove   65
    That Célimène encourages his love,
    The other must abandon hope, and yield,
    And leave him in possession of the field.
ACASTE. Now, there's a bargain that appeals to me;
    With all my heart, dear Marquess, I agree.   70
    But hush.

[*Enter* CÉLIMÈNE.]

CÉLIMÈNE.   Still here?
CLITANDRE.   'Twas love that stayed our feet.

CÉLIMÈNE. I think I heard a carriage in the street.
 Whose is it? D'you know?

[*Enter* BASQUE.]

BASQUE.   Arsinoé is here,
 Madam.
CÉLIMENE.   Arsinoé, you say? Oh, dear.
BASQUE. Éliante is entertaining her below.   [*Exit.*]   75
CÉLIMÈNE. What brings the creature here, I'd like to know?
ACASTE. They say she's dreadfully prudish, but in fact
 I think her piety . . .
CÉLIMÈNE.   It's all an act.
 At heart she's worldly, and her poor success
 In snaring men explains her prudishness.   80
 It breaks her heart to see the beaux and gallants
 Engrossed by other women's charms and talents,
 And so she's always in a jealous rage
 Against the faulty standards of the age.
 She lets the world believe that she's a prude   85
 To justify her loveless solitude,
 And strives to put a brand of moral shame
 On all the graces that she cannot claim.
 But still she'd love a lover; and Alceste
 Appears to be the one she'd love the best.   90
 His visits here are poison to her pride;
 She seems to think I've lured him from her side;
 And everywhere, at court or in the town,
 The spiteful, envious woman runs me down.
 In short, she's just as stupid as can be,   95
 Vicious and arrogant in the last degree,
 And . . .

[*Enter* ARSINOÉ.]

CÉLIMÈNE.   Ah! What happy chance has brought you here?
 I've thought about you ever so much, my dear.
ARSINOÉ. I've come to tell you something you should know.
CÉLIMÈNE. How good of you to think of doing so!   100
                 [CLITANDRE *and* ACASTE *exit, laughing.*]
ARSINOÉ. It's just as well those gentlemen didn't tarry.
CÉLIMÈNE. Shall we sit down?
ARSINOÉ.   That won't be necessary.
 Madam, the flame of friendship ought to burn
 Brightest in matters of the most concern,
 And as there's nothing which concerns us more   105
 Than honor, I have hastened to your door
 To bring you, as your friend, some information
 About the status of your reputation.
 I visited, last night, some virtuous folk,
 And, quite by chance, it was of you they spoke;   110
 There was, I fear, no tendency to praise
 Your light behavior and your dashing ways.

The quantity of gentlemen you see
And your by now notorious coquetry
Were both so vehemently criticized   115
By everyone, that I was much surprised.
Of course, I needn't tell you where I stood;
I came to your defense as best I could,
Assured them you were harmless, and declared
Your soul was absolutely unimpaired.   120
But there are some things, you must realize,
One can't excuse, however hard one tries,
And I was forced at last into conceding
That your behavior, madam, is misleading,
That it makes a bad impression, giving rise   125
To ugly gossip and obscene surmise,
And that if you were more *overtly* good,
You wouldn't be so much misunderstood.
Not that I think you've been unchaste—no! no!
The saints preserve me from a thought so low!   130
But mere good conscience never did suffice:
One must avoid the outward show of vice.
Madam, you're too intelligent, I'm sure,
To think my motives anything but pure
In offering you this counsel—which I do   135
Out of a zealous interest in you.
CÉLIMÈNE. Madam, I haven't taken you amiss;
I'm very much obliged to you for this;
And I'll at once discharge the obligation
By telling you about *your* reputation.   140
You've been so friendly as to let me know
What certain people say of me, and so
I mean to follow your benign example
By offering you a somewhat similar sample.
The other day, I went to an affair   145
And found some most distinguished people there
Discussing piety, both false and true.
The conversation soon came round to you.
Alas! Your prudery and bustling zeal
Appeared to have a very slight appeal.   150
Your affectation of a grave demeanor,
Your endless talk of virtue and of honor,
The aptitude of your suspicious mind
For finding sin where there is none to find,
Your towering self-esteem, that pitying face   155
With which you contemplate the human race,
Your sermonizings and your sharp aspersions
On people's pure and innocent diversions—
All these were mentioned, madam, and, in fact,
Were roundly and concertedly attacked.   160
"What good," they said, "are all these outward shows,
When everything belies her pious pose?
She prays incessantly; but then, they say,

She beats her maids and cheats them of their pay;
She shows her zeal in every holy place,   165
But still she's vain enough to paint her face;
She holds that nudity in art is vicious,
But views it with a pulse rate that's suspicious."
Of course, I said to everybody there
That they were being viciously unfair;   170
But still they were disposed to criticize you,
And all agreed that someone should advise you
To leave the morals of the world alone,
And worry rather more about your own.
They felt that one's self-knowledge should be great   175
Before one thinks of setting others straight;
That one should learn the art of living well
Before one threatens other men with hell,
And that the Church is best equipped, no doubt,
To guide our souls and root our vices out.   180
Madam, you're too intelligent, I'm sure,
To think my motives anything but pure
In offering you this counsel—which I do
Out of a zealous interest in you.

ARSINOÉ. I dared not hope for gratitude, but I   185
Did not expect so acid a reply;
I judge, since you've been so extremely tart,
That my good counsel pierced you to the heart.

CÉLIMÈNE. Far from it, madam. Indeed, it seems to me
We ought to trade advice more frequently.   190
One's vision of oneself is so defective
That it would be an excellent corrective.
If you are willing, madam, let's arrange
Shortly to have another frank exchange
In which we'll tell each other, *entre nous,*   195
What you've heard tell of me, and I of you.

ARSINOÉ. Oh, people never censure you, my dear;
It's me they criticize. Or so I hear.

CÉLIMÈNE. Madam, I think we either blame or praise
According to our taste and length of days.   200
There is a time of life for coquetry,
And there's a season, too, for prudery.
When all one's charms are gone, it is, I'm sure,
Good strategy to be devout and pure:
It makes one seem a little less forsaken.   205
Some day, perhaps, I'll take the road you've taken:
Time brings all things. But I have time aplenty,
And see no cause to be a prude at twenty.

ARSINOÉ. You give your age in such a gloating tone
That one would think I was an ancient crone;   210
We're not so far apart, in sober truth,
That you can mock me with a boast of youth!
Madam, you baffle me. I wish I knew
What moves you to provoke me as you do.

CÉLIMÈNE. For my part, madam, I should like to know   215
    Why you abuse me everywhere you go.
    Is it my fault, dear lady, that your hand
    Is not, alas, in very great demand?
    If men admire me, if they pay me court
    And daily make me offers of the sort   220
    You'd dearly love to have them make to you,
    How can I help it? What would you have me do?
    If what you want is lovers, please feel free
    To take as many as you can from me.
ARSINOÉ. Oh, come. D'you think the world is losing sleep   225
    Over that flock of lovers which you keep,
    Or that we find it difficult to guess
    What price you pay for their devotedness?
    Surely you don't expect us to suppose
    Mere merit could attract so many beaux?   230
    It's not your virtue that they're dazzled by;
    Nor is it virtuous love for which they sigh.
    You're fooling no one, madam; the world's not blind;
    There's many a lady heaven has designed
    To call men's noblest, tenderest feelings out,   235
    Who has no lovers dogging her about;
    From which it's plain that lovers nowadays
    Must be acquired in bold and shameless ways,
    And only pay one court for such reward
    As modesty and virtue can't afford.   240
    Then don't be quite so puffed up, if you please,
    About your tawdry little victories;
    Try, if you can, to be a shade less vain,
    And treat the world with somewhat less disdain.
    If one were envious of your amours,   245
    One soon could have a following like yours;
    Lovers are no great trouble to collect
    If one prefers them to one's self-respect.
CÉLIMÈNE. Collect them then, my dear; I'd love to see
    You demonstrate that charming theory;   250
    Who knows, you might . . .
ARSINOÉ.   Now, madam, that will do;
    It's time to end this trying interview.
    My coach is late in coming to your door,
    Or I'd have taken leave of you before.
CÉLIMÈNE. Oh, please don't feel that you must rush away;   255
    I'd be delighted, madam, if you'd stay.
    However, lest my conversation bore you,
    Let me provide some better company for you;
    This gentleman, who comes most apropos,
    Will please you more than I could do, I know.   260

[*Enter* ALCESTE.]

    Alceste, I have a little note to write
    Which simply must go out before tonight;

Please entertain *madame;* I'm sure that she
Will overlook my incivility.   [*Exit.*]
ARSINOÉ. Well, sir, our hostess graciously contrives   265
For us to chat until my coach arrives;
And I shall be forever in her debt
For granting me this little *tête-à-tête.*
We women very rightly give our hearts
To men of noble character and parts,   270
And your especial merits, dear Alceste,
Have roused the deepest sympathy in my breast.
Oh, how I wish they had sufficient sense
At court, to recognize your excellence!
They wrong you greatly, sir. How it must hurt you   275
Never to be rewarded for your virtue!
ALCESTE. Why, madam, what cause have I to feel aggrieved?
What great and brilliant thing have I achieved?
What service have I rendered to the king
That I should look to him for anything?   280
ARSINOÉ. Not everyone who's honored by the state
Has done great services. A man must wait
Till time and fortune offer him the chance.
Your merit, sir, is obvious at a glance,
And . . .
ALCESTE.   Ah, forget my merit; I'm not neglected.   285
The court, I think, can hardly be expected
To mine men's souls for merit, and unearth
Our hidden virtues and our secret worth.
ARSINOÉ. *Some* virtues, though, are far too bright to hide;
Yours are acknowledged, sir, on every side.   290
Indeed, I've heard you warmly praised of late
By persons of considerable weight.
ALCESTE. This fawning age has praise for everyone,
And all distinctions, madam, are undone.
All things have equal honor nowadays,   295
And no one should be gratified by praise.
To be admired, one only need exist,
And every lackey's on the honors list.
ARSINOÉ. I only wish, sir, that you had your eye
On some position at court, however high;   300
You'd only have to hint at such a notion
For me to set the proper wheels in motion;
I've certain friendships I'd be glad to use
To get you any office you might choose.
ALCESTE. Madam, I fear that any such ambition   305
Is wholly foreign to my disposition.
The soul God gave me isn't of the sort
That prospers in the weather of a court.
It's all too obvious that I don't possess
The virtues necessary for success.   310
My one great talent is for speaking plain;
I've never learned to flatter or to feign;

And anyone so stupidly sincere
Had best not seek a courtier's career.
Outside the court, one must dispense   315
With honors, privilege, and influence;
But still one gains the right, foregoing these,
Not to be tortured by the wish to please.
One needn't live in dread of snubs and slights,
Nor praise the verse that every idiot writes,   320
Nor humor silly marquesses, nor bestow
Politic sighs on Madam So-and-So.
ARSINOÉ. Forget the court, then; let the matter rest.
But I've another cause to be distressed
About your present situation, sir.   325
It's to your love affair that I refer.
She whom you love, and who pretends to love you,
Is, I regret to say, unworthy of you.
ALCESTE. Why, madam! Can you seriously intend
To make so grave a charge against your friend?   330
ARSINOÉ. Alas, I must. I've stood aside too long
And let that lady do you grievous wrong;
But now my debt to conscience shall be paid:
I tell you that your love has been betrayed.
ALCESTE. I thank you, madam; you're extremely kind.   335
Such words are soothing to a lover's mind.
ARSINOÉ. Yes, though she *is* my friend, I say again
You're very much too good for Célimène.
She's wantonly misled you from the start.
ALCESTE. You may be right; who knows another's heart?   340
But ask yourself if it's the part of charity
To shake my soul with doubts of her sincerity.
ARSINOÉ. Well, if you'd rather be a dupe than doubt her,
That's your affair. I'll say no more about her.
ALCESTE. Madam, you know that doubt and vague suspicion   345
Are painful to a man in my position;
It's most unkind to worry me this way
Unless you've some real proof of what you say.
ARSINOÉ. Sir, say no more: all doubt shall be removed,
And all that I've been saying shall be proved.   350
You've only to escort me home, and there
We'll look into the heart of this affair.
I've ocular evidence which will persuade you
Beyond a doubt that Célimène's betrayed you.
Then, if you're saddened by that revelation,   355
Perhaps I can provide some consolation.   [*Exeunt.*]

ACT IV

[*Enter* ÉLIANTE *and* PHILINTE.]

PHILINTE. Madam, he acted like a stubborn child;
I thought they never would be reconciled;

In vain we reasoned, threatened, and appealed;
He stood his ground and simply would not yield.
The marshals, I feel sure, have never heard   5
An argument so splendidly absurd.
"No, gentlemen," said he, "I'll not retract.
His verse is bad: extremely bad, in fact.
Surely it does the man no harm to know it.
Does it disgrace him, not to be a poet?   10
A gentleman may be respected still,
Whether he writes a sonnet well or ill.
That I dislike his verse should not offend him;
In all that touches honor, I commend him;
He's noble, brave, and virtuous—but I fear   15
He can't in truth be called a sonneteer.
I'll gladly praise his wardrobe; I'll endorse
His dancing, or the way he sits a horse;
But, gentlemen, I cannot praise his rhyme.
In fact, it ought to be a capital crime   20
For anyone so sadly unendowed
To write a sonnet and read the thing aloud."
At length he fell into a gentler mood
And, striking a concessive attitude,
He paid Oronte the following courtesies: 25
"Sir, I regret that I'm so hard to please,
And I'm profoundly sorry that your lyric
Failed to provoke me to a panegyric."
After these curious words, the two embraced,
And then the hearing was adjourned—in haste.   30
ÉLIANTE. His conduct has been very singular lately;
Still, I confess that I respect him greatly.
The honesty in which he takes such pride
Has—to my mind—its noble, heroic side.
In this false age, such candor seems outrageous;   35
But I could wish that it were more contagious.
PHILINTE. What most intrigues me in our friend Alceste
Is the grand passion that rages in his breast.
The sullen humors he's compounded of
Should not, I think, dispose his heart to love;   40
But since they do, it puzzles me still more
That he should choose your cousin to adore.
ÉLIANTE. It does, indeed, belie the theory
That love is born of gentle sympathy,
And that the tender passion must be based   45
On sweet accords of temper and of taste.
PHILINTE. Does she return his love, do you suppose?
ÉLIANTE. Ah, that's a difficult question, sir. Who knows?
How can we judge the truth of her devotion?
Her heart's a stranger to its own emotion.   50
Sometimes it thinks it loves, when no love's there;
At other times it loves quite unaware.
PHILINTE. I rather think Alceste is in for more
Distress and sorrow than he's bargained for;

Were he of my mind, madam, his affection   55
Would turn in quite a different direction,
And we would see him more responsive to
The kind regard which he receives from you.
ÉLIANTE. Sir, I believe in frankness, and I'm inclined,
In matters of the heart, to speak my mind.   60
I don't oppose his love for her; indeed,
I hope with all my heart that he'll succeed,
And were it in my power, I'd rejoice
In giving him the lady of his choice.
But if, as happens frequently enough   65
In love affairs, he meets with a rebuff—
If Célimène should grant some rival's suit—
I'd gladly play the role of substitute;
Nor would his tender speeches please me less
Because they'd once been made without success.   70
PHILINTE. Well, madam, as for me, I don't oppose
Your hopes in this affair; and heaven knows
That in my conversations with the man
I plead your cause as often as I can.
But if those two should marry and so remove   75
All chance that he will offer you his love,
Then I'll declare my own and hope to see
Your gracious favor pass from him to me.
In short, should you be cheated of Alceste,
I'd be most happy to be second best.   80
ÉLIANTE. Philinte, you're teasing.
PHILINTE.   Ah, madam, never fear;
No words of mine were ever so sincere,
And I shall live in fretful expectation
Till I can make a fuller declaration.

[*Enter* ALCESTE.]

ALCESTE. Avenge me, madam! I must have satisfaction,   85
Or this great wrong will drive me to distraction!
ÉLIANTE. Why, what's the matter? What's upset you so?
ALCESTE. Madam, I've had a mortal, mortal blow.
If chaos repossessed the universe,
I swear I'd not be shaken any worse.   90
I'm ruined. . . . I can say no more. . . . My soul . . .
ÉLIANTE. Do try, sir, to regain your self-control.
ALCESTE. Just heaven! Why were so much beauty and grace
Bestowed on one so vicious and so base?
ÉLIANTE. Once more, sir, tell us. . . .
ALCESTE.   My world has gone to wrack;   95
I'm—I'm betrayed; she's stabbed me in the back:
Yes, Célimène (who would have thought it of her?)
Is false to me, and has another lover.
ÉLIANTE. Are you quite certain? Can you prove these things?
PHILINTE. Lovers are prey to wild imaginings   100
And jealous fancies. No doubt there's some mistake. . . .

ALCESTE. Mind your own business, sir, for heaven's sake.
　　(*To* ÉLIANTE) Madam, I have the proof that you demand
　　Here in my pocket, penned by her own hand.
　　Yes, all the shameful evidence one could want　　　　　　105
　　Lies in this letter written to Oronte—
　　Oronte! whom I felt sure she couldn't love,
　　And hardly bothered to be jealous of.
PHILINTE. Still, in a letter, appearances may deceive;
　　This may not be so bad as you believe.　　　　　　　　110
ALCESTE. Once more I beg you, sir, to let me be;
　　Tend to your own affairs; leave mine to me.
ÉLIANTE. Compose yourself; this anguish that you feel . . .
ALCESTE. Is something, madam, you alone can heal.
　　My outraged heart, beside itself with grief,　　　　　　115
　　Appeals to you for comfort and relief.
　　Avenge me on your cousin, whose unjust
　　And faithless nature has deceived my trust;
　　Avenge a crime your pure soul must detest.
ÉLIANTE. But how, sir?
ALCESTE. 　　　　　　Madam, this heart within my breast　　120
　　Is yours; pray take it; redeem my heart from her,
　　And so avenge me on my torturer.
　　Let her be punished by the fond emotion,
　　The ardent love, the bottomless devotion,
　　The faithful worship which this heart of mine　　　　　　125
　　Will offer up to yours as to a shrine.
ÉLIANTE. You have my sympathy, sir, in all you suffer;
　　Nor do I scorn the noble heart you offer;
　　But I suspect you'll soon be mollified,
　　And this desire for vengeance will subside.　　　　　　130
　　When some beloved hand has done us wrong
　　We thirst for retribution—but not for long;
　　However dark the deed that she's committed,
　　A lovely culprit's very soon acquitted.
　　Nothing's so stormy as an injured lover,　　　　　　　135
　　And yet no storm so quickly passes over.
ALCESTE. No, madam, no—this is no lovers' spat;
　　I'll not forgive her; it's gone too far for that;
　　My mind's made up; I'll kill myself before
　　I waste my hopes upon her any more.　　　　　　　　140
　　Ah, here she is. My wrath intensifies.
　　I shall confront her with her tricks and lies,
　　And crush her utterly, and bring you then
　　A heart no longer slave to Célimène. [*Exeunt* ÉLIANTE *and* PHILINTE.]

　　　　　　　[*Enter* CÉLIMÈNE.]

　　(*Aside*) Sweet heaven, help me to control my passion.　　145
CÉLIMÈNE (*aside, to* ALCESTE). Oh, Lord. Why stand there staring in that
　　　fashion?
　　And what d'you mean by those dramatic sighs,
　　And that malignant glitter in your eyes?

ALCESTE. I mean that sins which cause the blood to freeze
      Look innocent beside your treacheries;   150
      That nothing hell's or heaven's wrath could do
      Ever produced so bad a thing as you.
CÉLIMÈNE. Your compliments were always sweet and pretty.
ALCESTE. Madam, it's not the moment to be witty.
      No, blush and hang your head; you've ample reason,   155
      Since I've the fullest evidence of your treason.
      Ah, this is what my sad heart prophesied;
      Now all my anxious fears are verified;
      My dark suspicion and my gloomy doubt
      Divined the truth, and now the truth is out.   160
      For all your trickery, I was not deceived;
      It was my bitter stars that I believed.
      But don't imagine that you'll go scot-free;
      You shan't misuse me with impunity.
      I know that love's irrational and blind;   165
      I know the heart's not subject to the mind,
      And can't be reasoned into beating faster;
      I know each soul is free to choose its master;
      Therefore had you but spoken from the heart,
      Rejecting my attentions from the start,   170
      I'd have no grievance, or at any rate
      I could complain of nothing but my fate.
      Ah, but so falsely to encourage me—
      That was a treason and a treachery
      For which you cannot suffer too severely,   175
      And you shall pay for that behavior dearly.
      Yes, now I have no pity, not a shred;
      My temper's out of hand; I've lost my head;
      Shocked by the knowledge of your double-dealings,
      My reason can't restrain my savage feelings;   180
      A righteous wrath deprives me of my senses,
      And I won't answer for the consequences.
CÉLIMÈNE. What does this outburst mean? Will you please explain?
      Have you, by any chance, gone quite insane?
ALCESTE. Yes, yes, I went insane the day I fell   185
      A victim to your black and fatal spell,
      Thinking to meet with some sincerity
      Among the treacherous charms that beckoned me.
CÉLIMÈNE. Pooh. Of what treachery can you complain?
ALCESTE. How sly you are, how cleverly you feign!   190
      But you'll not victimize me any more.
      Look: here's a document you've seen before.
      This evidence, which I acquired today,
      Leaves you, I think, without a thing to say.
CÉLIMÈNE. Is this what sent you into such a fit?   195
ALCESTE. You should be blushing at the sight of it.
CÉLIMÈNE. Ought I to blush? I truly don't see why.
ALCESTE. Ah, now you're being bold as well as sly;
      Since there's no signature, perhaps you'll claim . . .

CÉLIMÈNE. I wrote it, whether or not it bears my name. 200
ALCESTE. And you can view with equanimity
 This proof of your disloyalty to me!
CÉLIMÈNE. Oh, don't be so outrageous and extreme.
ALCESTE. You take this matter lightly, it would seem.
 Was it no wrong to me, no shame to you, 205
 That you should send Oronte this *billet doux?*°
CÉLIMÈNE. Oronte! Who said it was for him?
ALCESTE.   Why, those
 Who brought me this example of your prose.
 But what's the difference? If you wrote the letter
 To someone else, it pleases me no better. 210
 My grievance and your guilt remain the same.
CÉLIMÈNE. But need you rage, and need I blush for shame,
 If this was written to a *woman* friend?
ALCESTE. Ah! Most ingenious. I'm impressed no end;
 And after that incredible evasion 215
 Your guilt is clear. I need no more persuasion.
 How dare you try so clumsy a deception?
 D'you think I'm wholly wanting in perception?
 Come, come, let's see how brazenly you'll try
 To bolster up so palpable a lie: 220
 Kindly construe this ardent closing section
 As nothing more than sisterly affection!
 Here, let me read it. Tell me, if you dare to,
 That this is for a woman . . .
CÉLIMÈNE.   I don't care to.
 What right have you to badger and berate me, 225
 And so highhandedly interrogate me?
ALCESTE. Now, don't be angry; all I ask of you
 Is that you justify a phrase or two . . .
CÉLIMÈNE. No, I shall not. I utterly refuse,
 And you may take those phrases as you choose. 230
ALCESTE. Just show me how this letter could be meant
 For a woman's eyes, and I shall be content.
CÉLIMÈNE. No, no, it's for Oronte; you're perfectly right.
 I welcome his attentions with delight,
 I prize his character and his intellect, 235
 And everything is just as you suspect.
 Come, do your worst now; give your rage free rein;
 But kindly cease to bicker and complain.
ALCESTE *(aside).* Good God! Could anything be more inhuman?
 Was ever a heart so mangled by a woman? 240
 When I complain of how she has betrayed me,
 She bridles, and commences to upbraid me!
 She tries my tortured patience to the limit;
 She won't deny her guilt; she glories in it!
 And yet my heart's too faint and cowardly 245
 To break these chains of passion and be free,

206. *billet doux:* love letter, literally a "sweet note."

To scorn her as it should and rise above
This unrewarded, mad, and bitter love.
(To CÉLIMÈNE*)* Ah, traitress, in how confident a fashion
You take advantage of my helpless passion,   250
And use my weakness for your faithless charms
To make me once again throw down my arms!
But do at least deny this black transgression;
Take back that mocking and perverse confession;
Defend this letter and your innocence,   255
And I, poor fool, will aid in your defense.
Pretend, pretend, that you are just and true,
And I shall make myself believe in you.

CÉLIMÈNE. Oh, stop it. Don't be such a jealous dunce,
Or I shall leave off loving you at once.   260
Just why should I *pretend?* What could impel me
To stoop so low as that? And kindly tell me
Why, if I loved another, I shouldn't merely
Inform you of it, simply and sincerely!
I've told you where you stand, and that admission   265
Should altogether clear me of suspicion;
After so generous a guarantee,
What right have you to harbor doubts of me?
Since women are (from natural reticence)
Reluctant to declare their sentiments,   270
And since the honor of our sex requires
That we conceal our amorous desires,
Ought any man for whom such laws are broken
To question what the oracle has spoken?
Should he not rather feel an obligation   275
To trust that most obliging declaration?
Enough, now. Your suspicions quite disgust me;
Why should I love a man who doesn't trust me?
I cannot understand why I continue,
Fool that I am, to take an interest in you.   280
I ought to choose a man less prone to doubt,
And give you something to be vexed about.

ALCESTE. Ah, what a poor enchanted fool I am;
These gentle words, no doubt, were all a sham;
But destiny requires me to entrust   285
My happiness to you, and so I must.
I'll love you to the bitter end, and see
How false and treacherous you dare to be.

CÉLIMÈNE. No, you don't really love me as you ought.

ALCESTE. I love you more than can be said or thought; 290
Indeed, I wish you were in such distress
That I might show my deep devotedness.
Yes, I could wish that you were wretchedly poor,
Unloved, uncherished, utterly obscure;
That fate had set you down upon the earth   295
Without possessions, rank, or gentle birth;
Then, by the offer of my heart, I might

Repair the great injustice of your plight;
I'd raise you from the dust, and proudly prove
The purity and vastness of my love.   300
CÉLIMÈNE. This is a strange benevolence indeed!
God grant that I may never be in need. . . .
Ah, here's Monsieur Dubois, in quaint disguise.

[*Enter* DUBOIS.]

ALCESTE. Well, why this costume? Why those frightened eyes?
What ails you?
DUBOIS.   Well, sir, things are most mysterious.   305
ALCESTE. What do you mean?
DUBOIS.   I fear they're very serious.
ALCESTE. What?
DUBOIS.   Shall I speak more loudly?
ALCESTE.   Yes. Speak out.
DUBOIS. Isn't there someone here, sir?
ALCESTE.   Speak, you lout!
Stop wasting time.
DUBOIS.   Sir, we must slip away.
ALCESTE. How's that?
DUBOIS.   We must decamp without delay.   310
ALCESTE. Explain yourself.
DUBOIS.   I tell you we must fly.
ALCESTE. What for?
DUBOIS.   We mustn't pause to say good-by.
ALCESTE. Now what d'you mean by all of this, you clown?
DUBOIS. I mean, sir, that we've got to leave this town.
ALCESTE. I'll tear you limb from limb and joint from joint   315
If you don't come more quickly to the point.
DUBOIS. Well, sir, today a man in a black suit,
Who wore a black and ugly scowl to boot,
Left us a document scrawled in such a hand
As even Satan couldn't understand.   320
It bears upon your lawsuit, I don't doubt;
But all hell's devils couldn't make it out.
ALCESTE. Well, well, go on. What then? I fail to see
How this event obliges us to flee.
DUBOIS. Well, sir, an hour later, hardly more,   325
A gentleman who's often called before
Came looking for you in an anxious way.
Not finding you, he asked me to convey
(Knowing I could be trusted with the same)
The following message. . . . Now, what *was* his name?   330
ALCESTE. Forget his name, you idiot. What did he say?
DUBOIS. Well, it was one of your friends, sir, anyway.
He warned you to begone, and he suggested
That if you stay, you may well be arrested.
ALCESTE. What? Nothing more specific? Think, man, think!   335
DUBOIS. No, sir. He had me bring him pen and ink,

And dashed you off a letter which, I'm sure,
Will render things distinctly less obscure.
ALCESTE. Well—let me have it!
CÉLIMÈNE.   What *is* this all about?
ALCESTE. God knows; but I have hopes of finding out.   340
How long am I to wait, you blitherer?
DUBOIS *(after a protracted search for the letter).* I must have left it on your
table, sir.
ALCESTE. I ought to . . .
CÉLIMÈNE.   No, no, keep your self-control;
Go find out what's behind his rigmarole.
ALCESTE. It seems that fate, no matter what I do,   345
Has sworn that I may not converse with you;
But, madam, pray permit your faithful lover
To try once more before the day is over.   [*Exeunt.*]

ACT V

[*Enter* ALCESTE *and* PHILINTE.]

ALCESTE. No, it's too much. My mind's made up, I tell you.
PHILINTE. Why should this blow, however hard, compel you . . .
ALCESTE. No, no, don't waste your breath in argument;
Nothing you say will alter my intent;
This age is vile, and I've made up my mind   5
To have no further commerce with mankind.
Did not truth, honor, decency, and the laws
Oppose my enemy and approve my cause?
My claims were justified in all men's sight;
I put my trust in equity and right;   10
Yet, to my horror and the world's disgrace,
Justice is mocked, and I have lost my case!
A scoundrel whose dishonesty is notorious
Emerges from another lie victorious!
Honor and right condone his brazen fraud,   15
While rectitude and decency applaud!
Before his smirking face, the truth stands charmed,
And virtue conquered, and the law disarmed!
His crime is sanctioned by a court decree!
And not content with what he's done to me,   20
The dog now seeks to ruin me by stating
That I composed a book now circulating,
A book so wholly criminal and vicious
That even to speak its title is seditious!
Meanwhile Oronte, my rival, lends his credit   25
To the same libelous tale and helps to spread it!
Oronte! a man of honor and of rank,
With whom I've been entirely fair and frank;
Who sought me out and forced me, willy-nilly,
To judge some verse I found extremely silly;   30

And who, because I properly refused
To flatter him, or see the truth abused,
Abets my enemy in a rotten slander!
There's the reward of honesty and candor!
The man will hate me to the end of time   35
For failing to commend his wretched rhyme!
And not this man alone, but all humanity
Do what they do from interest and vanity;
They prate of honor, truth, and righteousness,
But lie, betray, and swindle nonetheless.   40
Come then: man's villainy is too much to bear;
Let's leave this jungle and this jackal's lair.
Yes! treacherous and savage race of men,
You shall not look upon my face again.

PHILINTE. Oh, don't rush into exile prematurely;   45
Things aren't as dreadful as you make them, surely.
It's rather obvious, since you're still at large,
That people don't believe your enemy's charge.
Indeed, his tale's so patently untrue
That it may do more harm to him than you.   50

ALCESTE. Nothing could do that scoundrel any harm:
His frank corruption is his greatest charm,
And, far from hurting him, a further shame
Would only serve to magnify his name.

PHILINTE. In any case, his bald prevarication   55
Has done no injury to your reputation,
And you may feel secure in that regard.
As for your lawsuit, it should not be hard
To have the case reopened, and contest
This judgment. . . .

ALCESTE.   No, no, let the verdict rest.   60
Whatever cruel penalty it may bring,
I wouldn't have it changed for anything.
It shows the times' injustice with such clarity
That I shall pass it down to our posterity
As a great proof and signal demonstration   65
Of the black wickedness of this generation.
It may cost twenty thousand francs; but I
Shall pay their twenty thousand and gain thereby
The right to storm and rage at human evil,
And send the race of mankind to the devil.   70

PHILINTE. Listen to me. . . .

ALCESTE.   Why? What can you possibly say?
Don't argue, sir; your labor's thrown away.
Do you propose to offer lame excuses
For men's behavior and the times' abuses?

PHILINTE. No, all you say I'll readily concede: 75
This is a low, dishonest age indeed;
Nothing but trickery prospers nowadays,
And people ought to mend their shabby ways.
Yes, man's a beastly creature; but must we then

Abandon the society of men? 80
Here in the world, each human frailty
Provides occasion for philosophy,
And this is virtue's noblest exercise;
If honesty shone forth from all men's eyes,
If every heart were frank and kind and just, 85
What could our virtues do but gather dust
(Since their employment is to help us bear
The villainies of men without despair)?
A heart well-armed with virtue can endure. . . .
ALCESTE. Sir, you're a matchless reasoner, to be sure; 90
Your words are fine and full of cogency;
But don't waste time and eloquence on me.
My reason bids me go, for my own good.
My tongue won't lie and flatter as it should;
God knows what frankness it might next commit, 95
And what I'd suffer on account of it.
Pray let me wait for Célimène's return
In peace and quiet. I shall shortly learn,
By her response to what I have in view,
Whether her love for me is feigned or true. 100
PHILINTE. Till then, let's visit Éliante upstairs.
ALCESTE. No, I am too weighed down with somber cares.
Go to her, do; and leave me with my gloom
Here in the darkened corner of this room.
PHILINTE. Why, that's no sort of company, my friend; 105
I'll see if Éliante will not descend. [*Exit.*]

[*Enter* CÉLIMÈNE *and* ORONTE.]

ORONTE. Yes, madam, if you wish me to remain
Your true and ardent lover, you must deign
To give me some more positive assurance.
All this suspense is quite beyond endurance. 110
If your heart shares the sweet desires of mine,
Show me as much by some convincing sign;
And here's the sign I urgently suggest:
That you no longer tolerate Alceste,
But sacrifice him to my love, and sever 115
All your relations with the man forever.
CÉLIMÈNE. Why do you suddenly dislike him so?
You praised him to the skies not long ago.
ORONTE. Madam, that's not the point. I'm here to find
Which way your tender feelings are inclined. 120
Choose, if you please, between Alceste and me,
And I shall stay or go accordingly.
ALCESTE (*emerging from the corner*). Yes, madam, choose; this gentle-
man's demand
Is wholly just, and I support his stand.
I too am true and ardent; I too am here 125
To ask you that you make your feelings clear.

No more delays, now; no equivocation;
The time has come to make your declaration.
ORONTE. Sir, I've no wish in any way to be
An obstacle to your felicity. 130
ALCESTE. Sir, I've no wish to share her heart with you;
That may sound jealous, but at least it's true.
ORONTE. If, weighing us, she leans in your direction . . .
ALCESTE. If she regards you with the least affection . . .
ORONTE. I swear I'll yield her to you there and then. 135
ALCESTE. I swear I'll never see her face again.
ORONTE. Now, madam, tell us what we've come to hear.
ALCESTE. Madam, speak openly and have no fear.
ORONTE. Just say which one is to remain your lover.
ALCESTE. Just name one name, and it will all be over. 140
ORONTE. What! Is it possible that you're undecided?
ALCESTE. What! Can your feelings possibly be divided?
CÉLIMÈNE. Enough: this inquisition's gone too far:
How utterly unreasonable you are!
Not that I couldn't make the choice with ease; 145
My heart has no conflicting sympathies;
I know full well which one of you I favor,
And you'd not see me hesitate or waver.
But how can you expect me to reveal
So cruelly and bluntly what I feel? 150
I think it altogether too unpleasant
To choose between two men when both are present;
One's heart has means more subtle and more kind
Of letting its affections be divined,
Nor need one be uncharitably plain 155
To let a lover know he loves in vain.
ORONTE. No, no speak plainly; I for one can stand it.
I beg you to be frank.
ALCESTE.   And I demand it.
The simple truth is what I wish to know,
And there's no need for softening the blow. 160
You've made an art of pleasing everyone,
But now your days of coquetry are done:
You have no choice now, madam, but to choose,
For I'll know what to think if you refuse;
I'll take your silence for a clear admission 165
That I'm entitled to my worst suspicion.
ORONTE. I thank you for this ultimatum, sir,
And I may say I heartily concur.
CÉLIMÈNE. Really, this foolishness is very wearing:
Must you be so unjust and overbearing? 170
Haven't I told you why I must demur?
Ah, here's Éliante; I'll put the case to her.

[*Enter* ÉLIANTE *and* PHILINTE.]

Cousin, I'm being persecuted here
By these two persons, who, it would appear,

Will not be satisfied till I confess   175
Which one I love the more, and which the less,
And tell the latter to his face that he
Is henceforth banished from my company.
Tell me, has ever such a thing been done?
ÉLIANTE. You'd best not turn to me; I'm not the one   180
To back you in a matter of this kind:
I'm all for those who frankly speak their mind.
ORONTE. Madam, you'll search in vain for a defender.
ALCESTE. You're beaten, madam, and may as well surrender.
ORONTE. Speak, speak, you must; and end this awful strain.   185
ALCESTE. Or don't, and your position will be plain.
ORONTE. A single word will close this painful scene.
ALCESTE. But if you're silent, I'll know what you mean.

[*Enter* ARSINOÉ, ACASTE, *and* CLITANDRE.]

ACASTE (*to* CÉLIMÈNE). Madam, with all due deference, we two
Have come to pick a little bone with you.   190
CLITANDRE (*to* ORONTE *and* ALCESTE). I'm glad you're present, sirs; as you'll soon learn,
Our business here is also your concern.
ARSINOÉ (*to* CÉLIMÈNE). Madam, I visit you so soon again
Only because of these two gentlemen,
Who came to me indignant and aggrieved   195
About a crime too base to be believed.
Knowing your virtue, having such confidence in it,
I couldn't think you guilty for a minute,
In spite of all their telling evidence;
And, rising above our little difference,   200
I've hastened here in friendship's name to see
You clear yourself of this great calumny.
ACASTE. Yes, madam, let us see with what composure
You'll manage to respond to this disclosure.
You lately sent Clitandre this tender note.   205
CLITANDRE. And this one, for Acaste, you also wrote.
ACASTE (*to* ORONTE *and* ALCESTE). You'll recognize this writing, sirs, I think;
The lady is so free with pen and ink
That you must know it all too well, I fear.
But listen: this is something you should hear: 210

"How absurd you are to condemn my lightheartedness in society
and to accuse me of being happiest in the company of others. Nothing could be more unjust; and if you do not come to me instantly and
beg pardon for saying such a thing, I shall never forgive you as long
as I live. Our big bumbling friend the viscount"—   215

What a shame that he's not here.—

"Our big bumbling friend the viscount, whose name stands first in
your complaint, is hardly a man to my taste; and ever since the day
I watched him spend three quarters of an hour spitting into a well, so
as to make circles in the water, I have been unable to think   220
highly of him. As for the little marquess"—

In all modesty, gentlemen, that is I.—

"As for the little marquess, who sat squeezing my hand for such a
long while yesterday, I find him in all respects the most trifling creature alive; and the only things of value about him are his cape   225
and his sword. As for the man with the green ribbons"—

(*To* ALCESTE). It's your turn now, sir.—

"As for the man with the green ribbons, he amuses me now and
then with his bluntness and his bearish ill-humor; but there are many
times indeed when I think him the greatest bore in the world.   230
And as for the sonneteer"—

(*To* ORONTE). Here's your helping.—

"And as for the sonneteer, who has taken it into his head to be
witty, and insists on being an author in the teeth of opinion, I simply
cannot be bothered to listen to him, and his prose wearies me   235
quite as much as his poetry. Be assured that I am not always so well
entertained as you suppose; that I long for your company, more than
I dare to say, at all these entertainments to which people drag me;
and that the presence of those one loves is the true and perfect sea-
soning to all one's pleasures."   240

CLITANDRE. And now for me:

"Clitandre, whom you mention, and who so pesters me with his
saccharine speeches, is the last man on earth for whom I could feel
any affection. He is quite mad to suppose that I love him, and so are
you, to doubt that you are loved. Do come to your senses; ex-   245
change your suppositions for his; and visit me as often as possible,
to help me bear the annoyance of his unwelcome attentions."—

It's a sweet character that these letters show,
And what to call it, madam, you well know.
Enough. We're off to make the world acquainted   250
With this sublime self-portrait that you've painted.   [*Exit.*]

ACASTE. Madam, I'll make you no farewell oration;
No, you're not worthy of my indignation.
Far choicer hearts than yours, as you'll discover,
Would like this little marquess for a lover.   [*Exit.*]   255

ORONTE. So! After all those loving letters you wrote,
You turn on me like this, and cut my throat!
And your dissembling, faithless heart, I find,
Has pledged itself by turns to all mankind!
How blind I've been! But now I clearly see;   260
I thank you, madam, for enlightening me.
My heart is mine once more, and I'm content;
The loss of it shall be your punishment.
(*To* ALCESTE). Sir, she is yours; I'll seek no more to stand
Between your wishes and this lady's hand.   [*Exit.*]   265

ARSINOÉ (*to* CÉLIMÈNE). Madam, I'm forced to speak. I'm far too stirred
To keep my counsel, after what I've heard.
I'm shocked and staggered by your want of morals.
It's not my way to mix in others' quarrels;

But really, when this fine and noble spirit, 270
This man of honor and surpassing merit,
Laid down the offering of his heart before you,
How *could* you . . .

ALCESTE.   Madam, permit me, I implore you,
To represent myself in this debate.
Don't bother, please, to be my advocate. 275
My heart, in any case, could not afford
To give your services their due reward;
And if I chose, for consolation's sake,
Some other lady, 'twould not be you I'd take.

ARSINOÉ. What makes you think you could, sir? And how dare you 280
Imply that I've been trying to ensnare you?
If you can for a moment entertain
Such flattering fancies, you're extremely vain.
I'm not so interested as you suppose
In Célimène's discarded gigolos. 285
Get rid of that absurd illusion, do.
Women like me are not for such as you.
Stay with this creature, to whom you're so attached;
I've never seen two people better matched.   [*Exit.*]

ALCESTE (*to* CÉLIMÈNE). Well, I've been still throughout this exposé, 290
Till everyone but me has said his say.
Come, have I shown sufficient self-restraint?
And may I now . . .

CÉLIMÈNE.   Yes, make your just complaint.
Reproach me freely, call me what you will;
You've every right to say I've used you ill. 295
I've wronged you, I confess it; and in my shame
I'll make no effort to escape the blame.
The anger of those others I could despise;
My guilt toward you I sadly recognize.
Your wrath is wholly justified, I fear; 300
I know how culpable I must appear,
I know all things bespeak my treachery,
And that, in short, you've grounds for hating me.
Do so; I give you leave.

ALCESTE.   Ah, traitress—how,
How should I cease to love you, even now? 305
Though mind and will were passionately bent
On hating you, my heart would not consent.
(*To* ÉLIANTE *and* PHILINTE) Be witness to my madness, both of you;
See what infatuation drives one to;
But wait; my folly's only just begun, 310
And I shall prove to you before I'm done
How strange the human heart is, and how far
From rational we sorry creatures are.
(*To* CÉLIMÈNE) Woman, I'm willing to forget your shame,
And clothe your treacheries in a sweeter name; 315
I'll call them youthful errors, instead of crimes,
And lay the blame on these corrupting times.

My one condition is that you agree
To share my chosen fate, and fly with me
To that wild, trackless, solitary place   320
In which I shall forget the human race.
Only by such a course can you atone
For those atrocious letters; by that alone
Can you remove my present horror of you,
And make it possible for me to love you.   325

CÉLIMÈNE. What! *I* renounce the world at my young age,
And die of boredom in some hermitage?

ALCESTE. Ah, if you really loved me as you ought,
You wouldn't give the world a moment's thought;
Must you have me, and all the world beside?   330

CÉLIMÈNE. Alas, at twenty one is terrified
Of solitude. I fear I lack the force
And depth of soul to take so stern a course.
But if my hand in marriage will content you,
Why, there's a plan which I might well consent to,   335
And . . .

ALCESTE.   No, I detest you now. I could excuse
Everything else, but since you thus refuse
To love me wholly, as a wife should do,
And see the world in me, as I in you,
Go! I reject your hand, and disenthrall   340
My heart from your enchantments, once for all.   [*Exit* CÉLIMÈNE.]
(*To* ÉLIANTE.) Madam, your virtuous beauty has no peer;
Of all this world, you only are sincere;
I've long esteemed you highly, as you know;
Permit me ever to esteem you so,   345
And if I do not now request your hand,
Forgive me, madam, and try to understand.
I feel unworthy of it; I sense that fate
Does not intend me for the married state,
That I should do you wrong by offering you   350
My shattered heart's unhappy residue,
And that in short . . .

ÉLIANTE.   Your argument's well taken:
Nor need you fear that I shall feel forsaken.
Were I to offer him this hand of mine,
Your friend Philinte, I think, would not decline.   355

PHILINTE. Ah, madam, that's my heart's most cherished goal,
For which I'd gladly give my life and soul.

ALCESTE (*to* ÉLIANTE *and* PHILINTE). May you be true to all you now pro-
    fess,
And so deserve unending happiness.
Meanwhile, betrayed and wronged in everything,   360
I'll flee this bitter world where vice is king,
And seek some spot unpeopled and apart
Where I'll be free to have an honest heart.

PHILINTE. Come, madam, let's do everything we can
To change the mind of this unhappy man.   [*Exeunt*.] 365

ACT I

1. Define the contrast made between Alceste and Philinte in the opening scene. How does Molière suggest the attitude he wants his audience to have toward each of them? Which is the more attractive character? How does Molière make it clear that Alceste is the "main character," the one who should be the focus of the audience's attention?

2. How does Molière establish the impression that the characters in this play will be "types" and that the play will be a commentary on the ways of society? If the characters are "types," how are they also individualized?

3. How is Oronte characterized by the words "and rank" in his first speech (line 260)? What is the comic effect of his next line? What attitude is the audience to have toward Oronte?

4. In criticizing Oronte's verse, Alceste indicates (beginning at line 385) that he favors the old ballad over the fashionable love sonnet. In what ways is his taste appropriate to his character? What indicates that Molière might be parodying both types of poetry?

5. In the opening scene, Alceste bluntly advocates telling "old Emilie" her coquetry is pathetic. How does his performance in telling Oronte his verse is bad (beginning with line 341) differ from what he had advocated earlier? Does Alceste's honesty accomplish the purpose it is intended to serve? Explain. How does his first scene with Oronte, then, complicate our impression of him?

ACT II

1. How does the introduction of Célimène's suitors (beginning with line 113) influence our attitude toward the quarrel between Alceste and Célimène at the beginning of the act?

2. Beginning with line 125, Célimène puts on a performance for the amusement of Clitandre and Acaste. What is Molière satirizing here? Identify the types of people that Célimène makes fun of.

3. What is funny about the arrest of Alceste?

ACT III

1. Why do you think Arsinoé is introduced at this late and central point in the play (beginning at line 73)? What does she add to the cast of types already presented? What function does she serve in the plot? Why is she a special trap to Alceste?

2. What is the main source of comedy in the character of Arsinoé? How does Célimène top her in their scene together (beginning at line 137)? What new light does this scene throw on the character of Célimène?

ACT IV

What is funny about the quarrel between Alceste and Célimène (beginning at line 146)? How does this scene affect the audience's impressions of the two characters?

ACT V

1. In the opening scene of Act II, Célimène had explained to Alceste why she put up with several of her suitors. At that time, how did she seem to feel about Alceste? At the end of the play, what seems to have been the reason she put up with Alceste?

2. In your opinion, why does Éliante choose Philinte instead of Alceste?

3. How does the ending of the play affect your feelings toward Alceste and Célimène? What comment upon the theme of the play is made by this ending? What characters in the play seem to have Molière's approval, and why?

GENERAL

1. Montaigne (see page 523) represents the society of the cannibals as not even having words for "lying, treachery, dissimulation . . . belittling . . ." Does Montaigne make the same implications that Molière does upon the causes of falsity in civilized society? Do you think their assumptions are valid? Explain your answers.

2. Do people like Alceste ever "change" society? Do people like Philinte and Éliante? Why or why not? How could the outlook expressed in "Courage and Moderation" (page 105), "Arete" (page 111), and "The Golden Mean" (page 206) be applied to Alceste's failure?

3. Molière wrote this serious comedy in 1666. Discuss the appropriateness of its theme to contemporary life. What kinds of criticisms are leveled at society today? Through what artistic forms is such criticism expressed?

4. Are any of Molière's character types seen on the contemporary screen, on TV

comedies, on soap operas, on the legitimate stage? How have they changed? Someone has said that we take pleasure in comedy because we feel superior to the people involved in the action. Do you agree? If not, how would you explain the pleasure that comedy gives you?

5. Some translations of *The Misanthrope* are in prose, but Richard Wilbur, the translator of the version in the text and a well-known modern poet (see also page 522), put the lines in couplets, as Molière did. What is the effect of having the characters speak in couplets? Does the style of the writing seem to suit the play? Explain.

DRAMATIC STRUCTURE

A playwright can convey meaning through the placement of scenes which invite comparison or contrast with one another. Observe the way Molière uses parallel scenes, and discuss how this technique adds meaning to the play.

1. What are the differences in tone between the scenes that open and close Act I? What explains the change in Alceste? The scene ending Act II is comic; how does it relate to the ending of Act I? How is it similar to that scene?

2. Compare the end of Act III with the end of Act. I. How is Alceste affected in this later scene?

3. Compare the end of Act IV with the end of Act II. How does the comedy of these scenes differ?

4. Compare Alceste as he appears in the last scene of the play with Alceste in the last scene of Act I. Has his situation changed? Has his attitude changed? Did you hope at the beginning that he would come to such a position at the end? Explain your answers.

5. The beginning of Act V reminds us of the first scene of the play. What is the purpose of this echo? What new tones and significances does the situation now have?

6. How does Célimène's witty performance in Act II anticipate the final scene of the play? How does this contrast affect your feelings about Célimène in the climax of the play?

Meaning is also lent to the play through the pairing and contrasting of characters. We partly understand what one character *is* by seeing what he is *not* in another character; or, conversely, by seeing him reflected, perhaps unexpectedly, in another character.

What meanings can you find in comparing or contrasting the characters in each group that follows?

(a) Alceste and Éliante
(b) Célimène and Arsinoé
(c) Oronte, Clitandre, and Acaste
(d) Alceste and Célimène
(e) Alceste and Philinte

FOR COMPOSITION

1. The title of this play comes from two Greek words meaning "to hate mankind." Write a full assessment of the character of Alceste, the misanthrope. Show in at least two paragraphs how Molière makes him simultaneously an admirable and a foolish person. In a final paragraph, explain as fully as possible why Alceste became a misanthrope.

2. It is often observed that as people grow older they lose whatever of Alceste's zeal they once had and they come to accept the advice of Philinte. What reasons can you offer for such a change in people? Is this a good thing? Argue the case that it is good or that it is not, in an essay. Use specific evidence from your own observations of life and literature, particularly keeping in mind the causes of Alceste's defeat in *The Misanthrope*. In making your case, do not ignore evidence for the opposite conclusion, and make whatever concessions to it you think are just.

ROMANTICISM AND REALISM

1798–1914

A S THE NINETEENTH CENTURY began, people wondered if they were listening to the death rattle of the old order or witnessing the turbulent beginnings of a bright new world. Could this old order—the *ancien régime* of absolute monarchy in France and its counterparts in other countries— be defeated? Without the stability of this old order, would society collapse into ruin? Could the forces destroying the old order build a new society out of the wreckage of the old? In the collision between old and new, armies marched, men's lives were consumed like chaff on a bonfire, and anointed monarchs trembled on their thrones.

A quarter-century past, in 1775, when news of the American Revolution reached Europe, it had aroused both fears and hopes. While kings and princelings disapproved, the discontented middle classes began to see violent upheaval as the means of escape from government restrictions on trade and on personal liberty. Hope stirred even among the peasants and the propertyless, so that when, in 1789, the French Revolution broke out, the lower classes added reckless fury to the purposeful aggression of the merchants and intellectuals. Thus the forces released against the entrenched powers of monarchy and aristocracy were themselves often in conflict. As a consequence, in little more than sixty years, France alone experienced in startling succession the Revolution of 1789, which set up a republic and guillotined Louis XVI and Marie Antoinette; the dictatorship of Napoleon, which set itself in place of the new republic; an autocratic regime, which deposed Napoleon; a liberal revolution in midcentury, which set up Napoleon's nephew as president; and the crafty nephew's reestablishment of imperial rule, with himself as Emperor Napoleon III.

To all of Europe, the French Revolution and the ensuing shifts in political power revealed how fragile were the very bases of society, bases which hitherto had been accepted as part of the natural ordering of things. It is no surprise that, henceforward, no ruling group could ever feel sure that it would hold sway forever.

THE NAPOLEON YEARS

Napoleon Bonaparte (1769–1821), who at first seemed no more than an upstart general in the French army, rose to become at one and the same time heir and liquidator of the French Revolution. Power fell into his hands through a *coup* in 1799, and to the dismay of revolutionists everywhere, he went on to make himself dictator of continental Europe. Until their disastrous advance into the vastness of Russia in 1812, his armies celebrated one military success after another. Napoleon literally bled Europe white, conscripting and sacrificing the lives of the young men not only of France but of every country where his henchmen could enforce his edicts. Ever onward he pushed, stimulating antagonisms that longed for a day of reckoning. That day came. A coalition of England, Prussia, and Russia wrote *finis* to his career in 1815, on the Flemish plain of Waterloo. Napoleon spent the remaining years of his life as a prisoner of the English on the desolate island of St. Helena in the South Atlantic Ocean.

But the "Napoleonic epic" had laid successful siege to men's minds. To British poet Lord Byron (1788–1824), Napoleon was the very embodiment of the Romantic ideal of the restless man of extraordinary spirit, who cannot accept the limitations set by lesser, cautious men. In one portion of his semiautobiographical poem *Childe Harold's Pilgrimage,* Byron looks upon the field of Waterloo and reflects on the man imprisoned on St. Helena.

> ●There sunk the greatest, nor the worst of men,
> Whose Spirit, antithetically mixed,
> One moment of the mightiest, and again
> On little objects with like firmness fixed;
> Extreme in all things! hadst thou been betwixt,
> Thy throne had still been thine, or never been;
> For Daring made thy rise as fall: thou seek'st
> Even now to reassume the imperial mien,
> And shake again the world, the Thunderer of the scene!
>
> —GEORGE GORDON, LORD BYRON

The cataclysmic effect of the Napoleonic wars upon Russia is one of the themes of the great Russian novel *War and Peace* by Leo Tolstoy (1828–1910) (see his story on page 804). The poem by Victor Hugo (1802–1885) (see page 758), on the Grand Army's humiliating retreat from Moscow, is often standard memorization fare for students of French literature. Napoleon was the inspiration for the Third Symphony of the German composer Ludwig van Beethoven (1770–1827). (However, Beethoven, in fury,

Bonaparte gathers crowds as he rides to seize rule of France, October 1799.

tore off the original dedication page upon learning that Napoleon, once looked on as the great liberator of Europe, had crowned himself emperor. The symphony was published under the title by which it is now known, the *Eroica,* or "heroic," with the sub-title: "To the memory of a great man." The Napoleon whom Beethoven had admired was "dead.")

The fascination with Napoleon did not end with his own times. "All of us," declared André Malraux, the French novelist and art historian, and cabinet minister under De Gaulle, "have felt the coolness and haze of the morning of Austerlitz" (where Napoleon won a great victory in 1805, over the combined armies of Russia and Austria).

The consequences of this historic upheaval—the French Revolution followed by the Empire of Napoleon—were of great complexity. Napoleon had forcibly borne in upon people that politics extended far beyond the parish pump. The upheaval proved to all men that they were caught up in far-reaching multiple interrelationships and shared a common destiny in a universe common to all. Ordinary men had seen that kings by supposed "divine right" could be cowed, insulted, and evicted. Plunged in extraordinary circumstances, these ordinary men themselves proved to be capable of extraordinary actions.

But the notion of universal brotherhood, of freedom for all men, suffered a serious limitation and perversion under Napoleon's despotic rule. When Napoleon was exiled in 1815, Europe was stabilized by a reactionary move which restored the monarchies that had existed before the Revolution.

Though a long period of general peace did ensue after 1815, it was costly in terms of what it did to the movements for reform. And as the spread of industry enhanced the possibilities for personal enrichment, it seemed for a while that the impotence of those beautiful, humanitarian dreams had been demonstrated once and for all.

THE AGE OF PROGRESS

For good reason the nineteenth century is often labeled the Age of Progress. The steady acceleration of scientific study which began then has not yet abated; by our own times it has become so rapid and intense that we even speak of "explosions" of knowledge. In the nineteenth century, as today, much of this scientific knowledge was put to the service of technology, to produce in rapid succession inventions which now seem crude but which implemented a breakthrough toward the technologically dominated culture of the twentieth century. The steam engine, the process for making steel and aluminum, the electric dynamo—all helped in radically transforming and expanding industry and commerce, to the extent that every aspect of life in western Europe and America has been affected.

As significant as the scientific and technological achievements themselves were the attitudes they inspired. Officially, the Age of Progress produced a faith in progress that was not limited to a certainty that transportation and factory production would be improved. Among the dominant middle class, at least, there existed a smug assumption that material progress would lead to universal well-being and happiness, to the greatest culture the world had ever seen, and to a moral and spiritual regeneration that would complete the utopian prospect.

The optimism was not, of course, universally shared. The poor saw little cause for hope in the development of sprawling industrial slums and in the neglect of those living from the land. These views were largely unheard by officialdom, but the plight of the masses of the poor was a factor in the polarization of economic theory, between laissez-faire capitalism and the scientific socialism of the revolutionary Karl Marx (1818–1883).

Oddly enough, the principal development in theoretical science—Charles Darwin's formulation of a theory of evolution, published in the *Origin of Species* (1859)—cut two ways in its effect upon philosophical attitudes. On the one hand, Darwin's theory demonstrated a process of biological selection which assured not only constant change but also the inexorable improvement of all species. As individual species improved, so did nature as a whole; and this looked like progress. On the other hand, the theory gave a depressing picture of man as only one species of animal among many, a species also subject to the impersonal processes of selection and discard.

As the century of progress wore on, the ills caused by industrialization increased. The gaps widened between the affluent bourgeoisie and the impoverished factory laborers and peasants, between the rich and powerful nations of western Europe and the subject people of their colonial empires. The liberal political reforms begun by the revolutions of the late eighteenth century had not brought about an era of justice, but in many cases seemed only to have encouraged dangerous impulses toward nationalism and racism. The English reveled in their "Englishness," and the Germans in their "Germanness." France and England stretched out their tentacles over the earth and established colonies. Italy, unified in 1861, and Germany, unified in 1871, arrived late on the colonial scene and were all the more impatient because of the power and wealth they had lost. As a consequence of all this, international diplomacy, ever an intriguing game for those who practiced it at the highest level, now resembled a desperate game for high stakes, whose participants teetered on the brink of an abyss. The Franco-Prussian War (1870–71), the climax of the long series of conflicts that had torn France, was an especially disillusioning experience, not only to the French, who were reduced from empire to occupation, but to others who saw in the military dictatorship of Otto von Bismarck a new form of the autocracy which had been thrown out with the *ancien régime.*

Steadily, the level of armaments and the number of men under arms increased, until finally, with the assassination of an Austrian archduke in the Balkan town of Sarajevo in 1914, the nations of Europe fell into the maelstrom of World War I.

THE ROMANTIC REVOLT IN LITERATURE

As the eighteenth century had progressed, rumblings of discontent with the *ancien régime* of literary dogmatism grew more frequent. On the continent of Europe, French literary dogmas, laying down the particular "rules" to be observed in writing of each literary type, had long been accepted almost without challenge. English writers were more fortunate than their continental colleagues, for in England the prescribed rules had never been so despotically imposed. Yet in England, in the late eighteenth century, the limits of what was found officially acceptable began to strike some writers as constricting.

Shortly before the century's close, there occurred the birth—though this was scarcely realized at the time—of a new movement and a fresh sensibility in literature. It did not happen in France, which was enjoying enormous prestige from its cultural imperialism, but in the misty German-speaking states and in England. The initiators of this movement were fired by anticlassical, anti-"French" tastes. The English sponsors were poets William Wordsworth (1770–1850) (see page 750) and Samuel Taylor Coleridge (1772–1834), who ushered in the movement in 1798 with a volume of poetry entitled *Lyrical Ballads,* on which they collaborated. The movement in literature with which their names are associated has come to be known as Romanticism.

When the *Lyrical Ballads* came out during its authors' absence in Germany, Mrs. Coleridge reported with devastating cheerfulness that the poems "are not liked at all by any." Fortunately, she was not entirely right. Though conservative critics were horrified at what they considered trivial subject matter and prosy verse, other readers and writers were sympathetic and receptive.

This may be said about the new movement. The Romantic writers thought that they were undertaking something new. Negatively, they rebelled against the established literary rules. Positively, they favored "inspiration" (a term as hard to define as any other), the expression of their own emotions, originality, the free play of imagination, and, in general, the right to individual expression, despite society's constraints.

Many Romantic writers came to see themselves, in fact, as rebels, at odds with the unheroic, complacent present and passionately devoted to personal freedom. In a reaction against their own times, which were steadily becoming more commercialized and uglier, many Romantic writers used as background for their works some simpler or more mysterious epoch of the past, especially the Middle Ages, or some more picturesque and exotic faraway country.

Along with the Romantic writers' longing to escape from the present to other times and other places often went a dissatisfaction with anything existent, if not, indeed, with anything that could exist. For the regret or nostalgia which has so often been noted in Romantic writing is usually a thirst for something unattainable. The result is a vague, uneasy feeling that pro-

In an 1871 cartoon a gorilla complains to the founder of the SPCA that Darwin has insulted him by claiming to be his descendant.

duces inescapable melancholy and sudden, unstable progressions from despair to joy, from joy to despair.

LYRIC POETRY

Within literature, the sensitivity of the Romantic seemed to find its readiest expression in lyric poetry. The label "Romantic" does not mean that this poetry was preoccupied with love; love as a subject for poetry may even be less prominent in the nineteenth century than it was in the seventeenth. The general impression that nineteenth-century poetry is "romantic" in the amorous sense probably arises from two circumstances. In the first place, this poetry tends to be more personal and more intensely emotional than the artful, playful poetry of the Renaissance and the witty, satiric poetry exalted by the Age of Reason. In the second place, the private amours of several prominent poets—Lord Byron in England and Victor Hugo in France, for two sensational examples—were unusually flamboyant and well publicized, as was the romantic elopement in 1846 of English poets Robert Browning (see page 761) and Elizabeth Barrett.

If any subject dominates Romantic poetry, it is nature in all its manifestations, from its most commonplace and fleeting details to its most monumental and spectacular. External nature continually appears in the poetry of the Romantics, sometimes as the subject upon which feeling is expended, sometimes as the basis of imagery and metaphor. Some poets, like Wordsworth, turned to nature with the conviction that God himself might be seen behind or in it.

The Romantic poet's reflection on nature leads him easily to an interest in the simple peasant who lives close to nature. This interest often has social and political overtones, as the virtuous simplicity of the peasant is exalted above the decadence of the aristocracy. Though the nineteenth-century lyric is seldom a vehicle for the direct expression of political ideas—as it becomes in the twentieth century—many of these lyrics do reflect the revolutionist's sympathy with the simple man and scorn for the wielders of power.

Wordsworth defined poetry as "the spontaneous overflow of powerful emotion," and these qualities of spontaneity and emotion became especially valued in the poetry of the Romantics. Accordingly, lyric poetry became the dominant and characteristic kind. But Wordsworth's definition has misled some to think that these poems were natural effusions, easily produced during a peak moment of emotion. This is not true; at best, these lyrics are too carefully written to have been produced in a spurt of inspiration.

Nevertheless, it is significant that the Romantic poet thought of himself as following his unique inspiration rather than conforming to established standards of taste, and Wordsworth's Preface to the *Lyrical Ballads* was looked on as a declaration of independence from the neoclassical tastes that had dominated the eighteenth century.

In the next generation after Wordsworth and Coleridge appeared a great and controversial trio of English Romantic poets. Lord Byron, Percy Bysshe Shelley (1792–1822), and John Keats (1795–1821) (see page 751) produced intensely emotional and personal poetry which inflamed conservative critics, who regarded the poets as dangerous radicals. The counterparts of these English Romantics on the continent included the Italian count Giacomo Leopardi (1798–1837) (see page 756), and the dashing Russian Alexander Pushkin (1799–1837) (see page 753). The careers of these five poets were brilliant and brief. They all died young, no doubt by simple coincidence, but there is an appropriateness in the fact. All were touched with melancholy over the unattainable and transitory, and beauty caught for one, fleeting moment is a common theme of their poetry.

Two famous poets prominent in Victorian England, who were boys when Byron, Shelley, and Keats died, were Alfred, Lord Tennyson (1809–1892) and Robert Browning (1812–1889). Though the Victorian poets had certain characteristics of their own, in general they did not react violently against the style set by their Romantic predecessors. Tennyson might have turned out official poetry that satisfied the public's demand for earnest moralizing and optimism, but in the poetry he wrote for himself he showed the sensuousness and melancholy of the Romantics (see page 760). Browning did indeed write many dramatic poems that were objective and realistic in situation and in language (one critic noted that Browning put into poetry such things as corsetstrings and aching corns), but a large body of his work is clearly Romantic in outlook (see page 761).

The generation of poets prominent in the second half of the nineteenth century and up to the period before the first World War can be looked on as Romanticism's second wave. Romantic in such aspects as their sensuousness and occasional mystic leanings, many of these poets were nevertheless defiantly critical of the stereotyped imagery and empty wordiness that characterized some poetry of earlier Romantics. Some, like the influential Charles Baudelaire (1821–1867) (see page 762), abandoned attempts at making forthright statements in poetry and aimed instead at achieving an art of suggestion. Correspondingly, a close kinship developed between poetry and the nuances and modulations of music, rather than with the plastic values of the visual arts. This new movement, under the somewhat misleading name of Symbolism, had a worldwide impact which has lasted until our own day.

ROMANTICISM AND REALISM IN THE NOVEL

Before the nineteenth century, the novel had been regarded as an inferior literary genre. Critics, so generous with advice and rules for writers of other forms of literature, did not lay down the law to mere novelists, who could do whatever they liked. Thus, the novel offered the writer the wonderful opportunity to develop a form already immensely popular with readers both rich and poor.

The one novelist who dominated the scene in the early nineteenth century was Sir Walter Scott (1771–1832). His historical romances, such as *Ivanhoe,* lavish with meticulous descriptions of natural scenery, costumes, and customs, filled his contemporaries with a sense of rewarded expectation. Scott brought alive for them the figures and conflicts, the very trappings and utensils, of the faraway Middle Ages. Scott came at the outset of what proved to be the novel's great age.

Though England produced its share of prominent novelists, official Victorian prudery eventually imposed on English novelists limitations that their continental brethren could ignore. William Makepeace Thackeray (1811–1863) knew more of the ways of the man about town than he dared relate, and the low life depicted by Charles Dickens (1812–1870) was carefully purged of its grosser and morally offensive aspects. Neither of these British novelists can rival the vision of society that was vigorously conjured up by the Frenchman Honoré de Balzac (1799–1850), in the long series of novels which, in conscious contrast to Dante's *Divine Comedy,* he called the *Human Comedy.*

The novel in France, and especially the work of Balzac, confronts us with the problem, sometimes left unexplained and even unmentioned, of where all the Romantics went and where the writers who cultivated Realism and Naturalism came from. How did the tender, emotional idealism of Romanticism yield to an outlook that some people would characterize as hard and pessimistic? The answer lies, perhaps, both in the fact that opposites attract each other and in the fact that social awareness increased as the century went on. However, the transformation that took place in literature affected subject matter more than it affected the writers' basic attitudes and approaches. An exact re-creation of all the details of medieval life, as in the novels of Sir Walter Scott, required the same sort of research that was later directed, just as easily, to the investigation of contemporary slum conditions, alcholism, or crime, as in the Naturalistic novels of Émile Zola (1840–1902) (see his story on page 772).

In date, Balzac certainly belonged to the Romantic era. He began his career by writing shockers and he never entirely shook off the lurid preoccupations of those early days. Thus one of his characters, "the illustrious Vautrin," is an escaped convict who, at one point, masquerades as a Spanish monsignor and later rises to be head of the Paris police. Yet critics, for many years, classified Balzac as a writer of Realistic novels. Other non-Realistic aspects of Honoré de Balzac were his acceptance of the doctrine of occultism and his belief in his own powers of divination; with one piercing glance, Balzac could, he asserted, tell a man's age, profession, maladies, vices, and everything else of importance about him. Balzac's novels, we

An earthy Balzac grins, and an effete Byron kicks off the dust of England.

must conclude, while they have elements of Realism, also have other elements that are anything but Realistic.

These remarks have tried to suggest that Romanticism was intimately bound up with and reacted upon by the goals of Realism. The moral of all this may be that any literary work at all worthy of our attention transcends and makes a mockery of all labels—"Classicism," "Romanticism," "Realism," "Naturalism," or whatever. Labels have their uses, especially on medicine bottles, but they cannot adequately inform us of the richly human, hence contradictory, qualities that distinguish great literature.

REALISM IN DRAMA

Since it is the most public of all the literary forms, requiring a building for its enactment and the physical presence of an audience to make it most meaningful, the drama poses a tough problem for revolutionaries. Furthermore, since words spoken from a stage make a greater impact than words that lie inert upon a page, the fury that can be aroused by the shockingly new in drama may call up powers of suppression that would be less likely used against a slim, little-read volume of verse. In the highly centralized French state, the supreme test was, and is, the "capture" of one of the two

Paris theaters, not only subsidized but actually run by the central government. This victory was won by the French Romantics in 1830, at the opening night of Victor Hugo's revolutionary Romantic play *Hernani*. The young generation, the Romantic writers and artists, sat in the cheaper seats and cheered and countercheered the indignant whistles and shouts of the older generation, the bourgeoisie, who were entrenched in classical tastes and in the more expensive sections of the theater. After the "battle of *Hernani*," Romanticism was thought for a time to have won a solid position on the stage.

However, the sense of theater possessed by the Romantic writers proved to be deficient. Hugo's plays were monstrous melodramas which heaped extravagant language on improbable situations. As a consequence, the theater remained the preserve of more conventional plays which gave bourgeois audiences a flattering and soothing image of bourgeois life. For many years, the theater, in France and every other country, continued to be a botched, shabby, and emotionally turgid business—a place of entertainment, beyond a doubt, but scarcely a temple of art.

Late in the nineteenth century, the drama began to come once more into its own. The greatest and most influential dramatist of the time was Henrik Ibsen (1828–1906) (see page 823). Though scarcely a handful of foreigners could read Dano-Norwegian, Ibsen's plays nevertheless found their way into translations and to the stage in one country after another, arousing strong admiration and no less strong antipathies. "Problem plays"—this was the term invented to categorize them. Some lesser playwrights did write plays that were no more than this, taking up the problems of unemployment or the exploitation of wet nurses, but Ibsen himself was a genuine artist and a creator of unforgettable characters. What the theater needed, seemingly, in order to get off to a fresh start, was a stern dose of the real, even of the uncomfortably real. Ibsen's plays were of startling originality precisely because they were enmeshed in everyday reality.

FIN DE SIÈCLE

In the eighteenth century, society had still left at least a niche that the man of letters, the painter, and the musician could occupy as his own. The writer had had his small literate audience to speak to and his wealthy patron to protect and support him. But by the nineteenth century, though more people were literate, the educational level of the literate audience had fallen, and the writer began to be alienated from the majority of readers. Besides this, aristocratic patrons were not so wealthy or powerful as they had once been, and the new industrialists who took over their wealth did not, in general, take over their concern with the arts. Nor did the industrialists, the politicians, and the bankers share the writers' outlooks. Consequently, the artist began to be separated from the utilitarian world of commerce and politics.

The wielders of power, as well as the middle class, struck the artist as crass, unspiritual, and little concerned with beauty. The artist felt, too, that the age's materialistic triumphs were backed up and given a clear conscience by materialistic philosophies and by a mechanistic interpretation of the very structure of the cosmos. Indeed, it seemed to the artist that the spirit had no home and no place to hide. Close to the century's end, the English poet A. E. Housman thought of himself as

> . . . a stranger and afraid
> In a world I never made.

The image of the artist as a "bohemian"—as a rebel against the establishment which misunderstands him and lets him starve in a garret—was a product of this time. The picture reflected reality to a considerable extent, and for many artists it was (and is) a proud symbol of their superiority.

By the century's end, the Romantic melancholy which had characterized the work of earlier writers had intensified into a feeling appropriately labeled *fin de siècle*—the "end-of-the-century" sickness, a malaise of spirit caused by the final degeneration of enthusiasm and idealism into disillusionment and bewilderment.

The century that saw the births of Darwin, Marx, and Freud—that is one way of summing up the nineteenth century. By the end of the century, the effects of these men began to be felt, and these effects signal our arrival in the modern world. Darwin's theories of evolution, if accepted, appeared to place man within the animal kingdom to a greater degree than popular beliefs had yet contemplated. These theories, together with the notion that the universe was slowing down and growing ever colder, struck many who believed in them as anything but cheering. The works of Karl Marx, which attributed primary importance not to man but to the economic organization of society, seemed to be another step in denying man his autonomy as a free soul, showing him to have no more control over his destiny than has a rolling billiard ball. Viennese physician Sigmund Freud (1856–1939), to cap it all, invaded what many considered the last bastion of man's freedom, his inner fantasy world; Freud's publication in 1920 of *A General Introduction to Psychoanalysis* suggested that a study of the subconscious also exemplified how man was the victim of the blind play of inexorable forces. The bleak outlook that resulted from all these theories could be summed up in the four title words of a book by English author Wynwood Reade: *The Martyrdom of Man*. It would lead us beyond the scope of this introduction to relate that, proving the rule that nothing lasts forever, this pessimism did not last. Freedom, men would once more come to believe, is not necessarily an illusion.

WILLIAM WORDSWORTH

In his youth, Wordsworth (1770–1850) was an idealistic partisan of the 1789 Revolution in France, but he became disillusioned as the struggle for a new, just world turned to terror and bloodletting. In his long verse autobiography, *The Prelude,* subtitled "The Growth of a Poet's Mind," he tells, among other things, of how he rediscovered balance and tranquillity in the beautiful natural surroundings which had molded his childhood and youth. By developing a close sympathy with nature, Wordsworth claimed, man could tap his innate and indestructible sense of harmony and joy.

The lines titled "There Was a Boy" were first published as a separate poem. Later, Wordsworth incorporated them into *The Prelude,* as part of Book V on education. Of lines 24–25 of this poem, Coleridge remarked, ". . . had I met these lines running wild in the deserts of Arabia, I should have instantly screamed out, 'Wordsworth!' "

There Was a Boy

There was a boy; ye knew him well, ye cliffs
And islands of Winander!° many a time
At evening, when the earliest stars began
To move along the edges of the hills,
Rising or setting, would he stand alone   5
Beneath the trees or by the glimmering lake,
And there, with fingers interwoven, both hands
Pressed closely palm to palm, and to his mouth
Uplifted, he, as through an instrument,
Blew mimic hootings to the silent owls,   10
That they might answer him; and they would shout
Across the watery vale, and shout again,
Responsive to his call, with quivering peals,
And long halloos and screams, and echoes loud,
Redoubled and redoubled, concourse wild   15
Of jocund din; and, when a lengthened pause
Of silence came and baffled his best skill,
Then sometimes, in that silence while he hung
Listening, a gentle shock of mild surprise
Has carried far into his heart the voice   20
Of mountain torrents; or the visible scene
Would enter unawares into his mind,
With all its solemn imagery, its rocks,
Its woods, and that uncertain heaven, received
Into the bosom of the steady lake.   25

---

2. **Winander:** one of the lakes in the Lake District, in the north of England, where Wordsworth grew up and spent most of his adult life.

This boy was taken from his mates, and died
In childhood, ere he was full twelve years old,
Fair is the spot, most beautiful the vale
Where he was born; the grassy churchyard hangs
Upon a slope above the village school,   30
And through that churchyard when my way has led
On summer evenings, I believe that there
A long half hour together I have stood
Mute, looking at the grave in which he lies!

The World Is Too Much with Us

The world is too much with us; late and soon,
Getting and spending, we lay waste our powers:
Little we see in Nature that is ours;
We have given our hearts away, a sordid boon!
The Sea that bares her bosom to the moon;   5
The winds that will be howling at all hours,
And are up-gathered now like sleeping flowers;
For this, for everything, we are out of tune;
It moves us not.—Great God! I'd rather be
A Pagan suckled in a creed outworn;   10
So might I, standing on this pleasant lea,
Have glimpses that would make me less forlorn;
Have sight of Proteus rising from the sea;
Or hear old Triton° blow his wreathed horn.

13–14. **Proteus . . . Triton:** sons of Neptune, god of the sea. Proteus tended the herd of seals and could change his shape; Triton was a messenger who used a conch shell as a trumpet.

JOHN KEATS

The multi-sensuous images created by John Keats (1795–1821) have been widely imitated and painstakingly analyzed. Critic Douglas Bush writes that Keats "makes us simultaneously see, touch, smell, and almost hear 'hushed, cool-rooted flowers, fragrant eyed.' " Keats wrote the following ode on September 19, 1819. A few days after he had finished it, he wrote to a friend: "I never liked stubble fields so much as now—Aye, better than the chilly green of the spring. Somehow a stubble field looks warm—in the same way that some pictures look warm. This struck me so much in my Sunday's walk that I composed upon it."

To Autumn

1

Season of mists and mellow fruitfulness,
   Close bosom-friend of the maturing sun;
Conspiring with him how to load and bless
   With fruit the vines that round the thatch-eaves run;
To bend with apples the mossed cottage-trees,   5
   And fill all fruit with ripeness to the core;
      To swell the gourd, and plump the hazel shells
With a sweet kernel; to set budding more,
And still more, later flowers for the bees,
Until they think warm days will never cease,   10
      For Summer has o'er-brimmed their clammy cells.

2

Who hath not seen thee oft amid thy store?
   Sometimes whoever seeks abroad may find
Thee sitting careless on a granary floor,
   Thy hair soft-lifted by the winnowing wind;   15
Or on a half-reaped furrow sound asleep,
   Drowsed with the fume of poppies, while thy hook
      Spares the next swath and all its twinèd flowers.
And sometimes like a gleaner thou dost keep
   Steady thy laden head across a brook;   20
   Or by a cider-press, with patient look,
      Thou watchest the last oozings hours by hours.

3

Where are the songs of Spring? Ay, where are they?
   Think not of them, thou hast thy music too—
While barred clouds bloom the soft-dying day,   25
   And touch the stubble-plains with rosy hue;
Then in a wailful choir the small gnats mourn
   Among the river sallows, borne aloft
      Or sinking as the light wind lives or dies;
And full-grown lambs loud bleat from hilly bourn;   30
   Hedge-crickets sing; and now with treble soft
   The red-breast whistles from a garden-croft;
      And gathering swallows twitter in the skies.

ALEXANDER PUSHKIN

Pushkin (1799–1837) holds a preeminent place in Russian literature, like the place accorded Shakespeare in English, Goethe in German, Dante in Italian. In the Romantic tradition, Pushkin was an individualist, passionately devoted to writing, deeply responsive to nature, restless and rebellious. He was exiled to Siberia for a time because of the revolutionary tone of some of his writings, but a new czar brought him back to be the literary lion of the court. Pushkin married a beautiful but harebrained woman who was totally engrossed in the glitter of the St. Petersburg court and not in Pushkin's work. Because of her and his delicate honor, Pushkin became involved in a duel with a Frenchman and was, tragically, dead at thirty-eight.

In addition to his lyrics, Pushkin is famous for many longer works. *Eugene Onegin,* a novel in verse, and *Boris Godunov,* a historical drama, have been interpreted into music by Tchaikovsky and Moussorgsky, respectively.

FROM *Autumn*

October at last has come! The thicket has shaken
The last leaf lingering down from the naked branch.
Autumn is breathing cold, the road is frozen—
The brook still runs with a murmur behind the mill,
But the pond is still; my neighbor is up and away   5
With a hunt, away to the farthest dreaming field,
Where the winter wheat will suffer from his mad sport,
And the bark of dogs will startle the forest oaks.

It is my time now! I never could love the spring,
The dragging thaw, the mud, the stench—I am sick   10
In spring: my blood's astray, my mind is oppressed
With a yearning pain. Winter is better for me.
I love the serious snow fields under the moon!
How the light run of the sled is swift and free,
And the hand of a love down under the sables warm!   15

And Oh the fun, to be shod with the sharpened steel,
And glide on the glassy face of the standing river!
The shining alarm of a winter holiday!
But still there's a limit in things!—A half year's snow—
Even at last to the old cave-dweller, the bear,   20
It is long enough! You can not forever and ever

Slide in a sled with the beautiful young Armida,
Or sulk behind double glass by a friendly stove.

. . .

They commonly scold the last days of autumn: to me,
My reader and friend, they are dear; their beauty is quiet,   25
Their modesty brilliant; they draw me to them like a child
Whom the family does not love. I will tell you frankly:
Of all the seasons of time I can love but one;
I find in her—I am not a vainglorious lover,
Though willful of fancy—I find in my love much good.   30

How shall I tell you? She ravishes me
As a dying virgin, perhaps, might ravish you.
Condemned, and bending meekly, and murmuring not.
Not angry—a smile on the fading lips—
She does not perceive the abysmal opening mouth   35
Of the tomb—the purplish light on her features, plays—
Today she is here—she lives—and tomorrow not.

Sweet mournful days, charm of the dreaming eyes,
Your beauty is dear to me that says farewell!
I love the sumptuous decline of nature's life,   40
The tents of the forest adorned with purple and gold,
And loud with the sound of the faster breath of the wind,
A billowy curtain of fog concealing the sky,
And the sun's rare beam, and the early frost,
And the threat of the gray-head winter standing off!   45

With every autumn that comes I bloom again;
It is good for my health, it is good, this Russian cold;
I fall afresh in love with the habit of being;
Sleep flies early, and hunger is in its place,
The blood romps joyfully through my heart,   50
Desire seethes up—I laugh again, I am young,
I am living life—such is my organism
(If you will excuse me, please, the prosaism).

So saddle my horse; and into the plentiful open
With fluttering mane he will carry me flying, and under   55
His body his glittering hoofs will ring like a tune
Through the frozen valley, will crackle and crash on the ice—
Till the brief day dies! And then the chimney, forgotten,
Will waken again with fire—will pour sharp light,
Or dimly glow, while I sit reading long,   60
And nourishing the long thoughts in my soul.

. . .

HEINRICH HEINE

Like many other Romantics, the German poet Heinrich Heine (1797–1856) felt ill at ease with autocratic governments. Drawn to the artistic center of bohemian Paris, he made his permanent home in France—a move which subjected him to charges of disloyalty to Germany. Nevertheless, Heine is the greatest lyricist to write in the German language since Goethe. Often he uses the simple meters of folk songs, and his *lieder* ("songs")—about his passion for his cousin—have been set to music by such famous composers as Schubert, Mendelssohn, and Franz. A less popular, more obviously cynical side of Heine's artistic personality is seen in the second poem that follows, one of a group of three lyrics about his dying in Paris. (Heine was bedridden for eight years, on a "mattress grave," with a spinal disease.)

Song

O dearest, canst thou tell me why
 The rose should be so pale?
And why the azure violet
 Should wither in the vale?

And why the lark should in the cloud
 So sorrowfully sing?   5
And why from loveliest balsam buds
 A scent of death should spring?

And why the sun upon the mead
 So chillingly should frown?   10
And why the earth should, like a grave,
 Be moldering and brown?

And why it is that I myself
 So languishing should be?
And why it is, my heart of hearts,   15
 That thou forsakest me?

My Departure

Every idle desire has died in my breast;
even hatred of evil things, even my feeling
for my own and other men's distress.
What lives in me is death.
The curtain falls, the play is done;   5
my dear German public is goosestepping home, yawning.
They are no fools, these good people:
they are slurping their dinners quite happily,
bear-hugging beer mugs—singing and laughing.

That fellow in Homer's book was quite right: 10
he said: the meanest little Philistine living
in Stukkert-am-Neckar is luckier
than I, the golden-haired Achilles, the dead lion,
glorious shadow-king of the underworld.

GIACOMO LEOPARDI

Sick all his life, often in intense pain, half blind, unable to sleep—it is little wonder that Count Leopardi (1798–1837) is called gloomy. Nevertheless, he was a gentle man, an excellent and productive scholar, and Italy's finest lyric poet since Petrarch. Leopardi was intensely patriotic, and the shame of Italy's failure to rise to a republican revolution undoubtedly contributed to his pessimism. He often showed a Romantic death wish, but essentially Leopardi was too intelligent to become either sentimental or decadent. Leopardi's epitaph could be these lines, from a poem he addressed to himself:

> ". . . weary bitterness
> Is life, naught else, and ashes is the world.
> Be now at peace. . . ."

Saturday Night in the Village

The day
is ready to close;
the girl takes the downward
path homeward from the vineyard,
and jumps from crevice to crevice   5
like a goat, as she holds a swath
of violets and roses
to decorate her hair and bodice
tomorrow as usual for the Sabbath.

Her grandmother sits,   10
facing the sun going out,
and spins and starts to reason
with the neighbors, and renew the day,
when she used to dress herself for the holiday
and dance away   15
the nights—still quick and healthy,
with the boys, companions of her fairer season.

Once again the landscape is brown,
the sky drains to a pale blue,
shadows drop from mountain and thatch,   20
the young moon whitens.
As I catch
the clatter of small bells,
sounding in the holiday,
I can almost say   25
my heart takes comfort in the sound.

Children place their pickets
and sentinels,
and splash round and round
the village fountain.   30
They jump like crickets,
and make a happy sound.
The field hand,
who lives on nothing,
marches home whistling,   35
and gorges on the day of idleness at hand.

Then all's at peace;
the lights are out;
I hear the rasp of shavings,
and the rapping hammer   40
of the carpenter, working all night
by lanternlight—
hurrying and straining himself
to increase his savings
before the whitening day.   45

This is the most kind
of the seven days; tomorrow, you will wait
and pray for Sunday's boredom and anguish
to be extinguished
in the workdays' grind   50
you anticipate.

Lively boy,
the only age you are alive
is like this day of joy,
a clear and breathless Saturday   55
that heralds life's holiday.
Rejoice, my child,
this is the untroubled instant.
Why should I undeceive you?
Let it not grieve you,   60
if the following day is slow to arrive.

VICTOR HUGO

Undoubtedly, Victor Hugo (1802–1885) was the greatest Romantic writer in nineteenth-century France. He was a legend, adored in his own time. English poet Charles Swinburne compared one of Hugo's books to the effort of God creating springtime. Outside of France, Hugo became famous with his great "protest" novel *Les Misérables,* which the American public eagerly read in installments during the days of the Civil War. But Hugo is most prominent to his countrymen as a lyricist.

The following lines, adapted by American poet Robert Lowell from Hugo's longer poem called *The Expiation,* refer to Napoleon's winter retreat from Moscow in 1812. Napoleon had reached and "captured" Moscow on September 15. Expecting to find shelter and food for his troops, he instead found that the Russians had fled the city and stripped it of supplies. On October 19, 1812, Napoleon turned his Grand Army around and began the tragic retreat across the frozen plains of Russia, leaving behind him Moscow in flames.

Russia 1812

The snow fell, and its power was multiplied.
For the first time the Eagle° bowed its head—
dark days! Slowly the Emperor returned—
behind him Moscow! Its onion domes still burned.
The snow rained down in blizzards—rained and froze.   5
Past each white waste a further white waste rose.
None recognized the captains or the flags.
Yesterday the Grand Army, today its dregs!
No one could tell the vanguard from the flanks.
The snow! The hurt men struggled from the ranks,   10
hid in the bellies of dead horses, in stacks
of shattered caissons. By the bivouacs,
one saw the picket dying at his post,
still standing in his saddle, white with frost,
the stone lips frozen to the bugle's mouth!   15
Bullets and grapeshot mingled with the snow,
that hailed . . . The Guard, surprised at shivering, march
in a dream now; ice rimes the gray mustache.
The snow falls, always snow! The driving mire
submerges; men, trapped in that white empire,   20
have no more bread and march on barefoot—gaps!
They were no longer living men and troops,
but a dream drifting in a fog, a mystery,
mourners parading under the black sky.
The solitude, vast, terrible to the eye,   25

2. **Eagle:** the standard of Napoleon's armies and a nickname for Napoleon himself.

"Russia 1812" (from *The Expiation*) by Victor Hugo from *Imitations* by Robert Lowell, copyright © 1958, 1959, 1960, 1961 by Robert Lowell. Reprinted by permission of Farrar, Straus & Giroux, Inc.

was like a mute avenger everywhere,
as snowfall, floating through the quiet air,
buried the huge army in a huge shroud.
Could anyone leave this kingdom? A crowd—
each man, obsessed with dying, was alone.   30
Men slept—and died! The beaten mob sludged on,
ditching the guns to burn their carriages.
Two foes. The North, the Czar. The North was worse.
In hollows where the snow was piling up,
one saw whole regiments fallen asleep.   35
Attila's dawn, Cannaes of Hannibal!°
The army marching to its funeral!
Litters, wounded, the dead, deserters—swarms,
crushing the bridges down to cross a stream.
They went to sleep ten thousand, woke up four.   40
Ney,° bringing up the former army's rear,
hacked his horse loose from three disputing Cossacks . . .
All night, the *qui vive?*° The alert! Attacks;
retreats! White ghosts would wrench away our guns,
or we would see dim, terrible squadrons,   45
circles of steel, whirlpools of savages,
rush sabering through the camp like dervishes.
And in this way, whole armies died at night.

The Emperor was there, standing—he saw.
This oak already trembling from the axe,   50
watched his glories drop from him branch by branch:
chiefs, soldiers. Each one had his turn and chance—
they died! Some lived. These still believed his star,
and kept their watch. They loved the man of war,
this small man with his hands behind his back,   55
whose shadow, moving to and fro, was black
behind the lighted tent. Still believing, they
accused their destiny of *lèse-majesté*.°
His misfortune had mounted on their back.
The man of glory shook. Cold stupefied   60
him, then suddenly he felt terrified.
Being without belief, he turned to God:
"God of armies, is this the end?" he cried.
And then at last the expiation came,
as he heard some one call him by his name,   65
some one half-lost in shadow, who said, "No,
Napoleon." Napoleon understood,
restless, bareheaded, leaden, as he stood
before his butchered legions in the snow.

36. **Attila's dawn, Cannaes of Hannibal:** Attila, leader of the barbaric Huns, was finally
defeated when he attacked Gaul in 451 A.D. Hannibal, a Carthaginian general, destroyed the
Roman army at Cannae, but it was his last victory before the tide turned against him.   41. **Ney:**
marshal of the French army, in charge of the defense of the rear in the retreat from Moscow.
43. *qui vive?:* a sentry's challenge; literally, "who lives?"   58. *lèse-majesté:* treason;
literally, "injured majesty."

ALFRED, LORD TENNYSON

Because of his official position as England's poet laureate, Tennyson (1809–1892) produced some popular patriotic verses, but his greatest poetry is found in his personal lyrics. Troubled by questions that scientific skepticism was raising about man and God, Tennyson wrote lyrics which show a passion for the past and which give voice to a formless, nameless feeling of sadness for something that is lost forever. The two poems that follow are among the eleven short lyrics interspersed in a long poem called *The Princess*. The first one was inspired by a boatman's bugle echoing over the lakes of Killarney, which the poet visited on his honeymoon.

The Splendor Falls

The splendor falls on castle walls
  And snowy summits old in story:
The long light shakes across the lakes,
  And the wild cataract leaps in glory.
Blow, bugle, blow, set the wild echoes flying,   5
Blow, bugle; answer, echoes, dying, dying, dying.

O hark, O hear! how thin and clear,
  And thinner, clearer, farther going!
O sweet and far from cliff and scar
  The horns of Elfland faintly blowing!   10
Blow, let us hear the purple glens replying:
Blow, bugle; answer, echoes, dying, dying, dying.

O love, they die in yon rich sky,
  They faint on hill or field or river:
Our echoes roll from soul to soul,   15
  And grow forever and forever.
Blow, bugle, blow, set the wild echoes flying,
And answer, echoes, answer, dying, dying, dying.

Tears, Idle Tears

Tears, idle tears, I know not what they mean,
Tears from the depth of some divine despair
Rise in the heart, and gather to the eyes,
In looking on the happy autumn fields,
And thinking of the days that are no more.   5

Fresh as the first beam glittering on a sail,
That brings our friends up from the underworld,
Sad as the last which reddens over one
That sinks with all we love below the verge;
So sad, so fresh, the days that are no more.   10

Ah, sad and strange as in dark summer dawns
The earliest pipe of half-awakened birds
To dying ears, when unto dying eyes
The casement slowly grows a glimmering square;
So sad, so strange, the days that are no more.   15

Dear as remembered kisses after death,
And sweet as those by hopeless fancy feigned
On lips that are for others; deep as love,
Deep as first love, and wild with all regret;
O Death in Life, the days that are no more.   20

ROBERT BROWNING

Some of the most popular and original of the poems by Robert Browning (1812–1889) are psychological character studies of murderers. The other substantial portion of Browning's work is about the love between men and women. Browning had little faith in the intellect, and he felt that love—divine and human—is the prime motivating force in the world. The following poems appeared in 1845, the year before Browning and Elizabeth Barrett made their romantic elopement to Italy.

Meeting at Night

The gray sea and the long black land;
And the yellow half-moon large and low;
And the startled little waves that leap
In fiery ringlets from their sleep,
As I gain the cove with pushing prow,   5
And quench its speed i' the slushy sand.

Then a mile of warm sea-scented beach;
Three fields to cross till a farm appears;
A tap at the pane, the quick sharp scratch
And blue spurt of a lighted match,   10
And a voice less loud, through its joys and fears,
Than the two hearts beating each to each!

Parting at Morning

Round the cape of a sudden came the sea,
And the sun looked over the mountain's rim:
And straight was a path of gold for him,
And the need of a world of men for me.

CHARLES BAUDELAIRE

Although French Symbolist Baudelaire (1812–1867) claimed to be in revolt against Romantic traditions, he was still in bondage to his emotions and his macabre imagination. His poetry, like that of the American Edgar Allan Poe, with whom he felt a mystic kinship, exaggerates Romantic traits by dwelling obsessively on melancholy, spiritual weariness, and physical decay. His collection of poems, *Flowers of Evil,* brought Baudelaire to trial on charges of moral offenses, and before the books were released for sale, six poems had to be literally snipped out of them. In character, Baudelaire was a man of conflicts, a sensualist who desired purity, a Catholic who was also a Satanist. He liked to shock the bourgeoisie, and when he once found some regarding him with horror, he told them that he had killed and eaten his father, to horrify them even more. But, Baudelaire's character aside, his poetry is still a vital influence on writers, who imitate its exquisite sounds, its imagery, and its rich suggestive language. The following poem is one of Baudelaire's few happy lyrics. The "kind land" of dreams that he evokes is Holland, as he imagined it to be from the Dutch paintings he had seen.

Invitation to the Voyage

My child, my sister, dream
How sweet all things would seem
Were we in that kind land to live together
And there love slow and long,
There love and die among   5
Those scenes that image you, that sumptuous weather.
Drowned suns that glimmer there
Through cloud-disheveled air
Move me with such a mystery as appears
Within those other skies   10
Of your treacherous eyes
When I behold them shining through their tears.

"Invitation to the Voyage" by Charles Baudelaire, translated by Richard Wilbur, © 1956 by Richard Wilbur. Reprinted from his volume *Things of This World* by permission of Harcourt, Brace & World, Inc.

There, there is nothing else but grace and measure,
Richness, quietness, and pleasure.

Furniture that wears   15
The luster of the years
Softly would glow within our glowing chamber,
Flowers of rarest bloom
Proffering their perfume
Mixed with the vague fragrances of amber;   20
Gold ceilings would there be,
Mirrors deep as the sea,
The walls all in an Eastern splendor hung—
Nothing but should address
The soul's loneliness,   25
Speaking her sweet and secret native tongue.

There, there is nothing else but grace and measure,
Richness, quietness, and pleasure.

See, sheltered from the swells
There in the still canals   30
Those drowsy ships that dream of sailing forth;
It is to satisfy
Your least desire, they ply
Hither through all the waters of the earth.
The sun at close of day   35
Clothes the fields of hay,
Then the canals, at last the town entire
In hyacinth and gold:
Slowly the land is rolled
Sleepward under a sea of gentle fire.   40

There, there is nothing else but grace and measure,
Richness, quietness, and pleasure.

PAUL VERLAINE

Paul Verlaine (1844–1896), the leading poet of the second half of the century in France, presents a decadent echo of the flamboyant lives of earlier Romantic poets. He spent two years in prison for shooting his young protégé, Arthur Rimbaud, and his addiction to liquor nearly wrecked his career and his life. Verlaine was a Symbolist and his intention in poetry was not to state an idea but to suggest an impression or mood through sound. The musical quality which Verlaine achieved with the French language cannot be reproduced, even in the best of translations.

Autumn Song

Long sobbing winds,
The violins
  Of autumn drone,
Wounding my heart
With languorous smart   5
  In monotone.

Choking and pale,
When on the gale
  The hour sounds deep,
I call to mind   10
Dead years behind,
  And I weep.

And I, going,
Borne by blowing
  Winds and grief,   15
Flutter, here—there,
As on the air
  The dying leaf.

The Sky Is Just Beyond the Roof

The sky is just beyond the roof
  So blue, so calm;
A treetop just beyond the roof
  Rocks its slow palm.

The chime in the sky that I see   5
  Distantly rings;
A bird on the tree that I see
  Plaintively sings.

My God, my God, but life is there,
  Tranquil and sweet;   10
This peaceful murmur that I hear
  Comes from the street!

What have you done, you who stand here,
  In tears and ruth?
Say, what have you done, you who are here,   15
  With your lost youth?

"Autumn Song" and "The Sky Is Just Beyond the Roof" by Paul Verlaine, translated by Bergen Applegate.

ARTHUR RIMBAUD

By the time he was twenty-one years old, Rimbaud (1854–1891) had written all his poetry, escaped from a tyrannical mother, lived as a vagabond, and served time in jail. Some time after Verlaine emerged from prison, after trying to murder him, Rimbaud knocked the older poet out, left him on a river bank, and vanished. It is now known that after many wanderings, he became a trader, gun-running and possibly slave-trading in and around Indonesia and Africa. His poetry was later published by Verlaine, who thought his protégé dead. But while the startling new poems were causing a literary sensation in Paris, their rebellious young author was living in a palm-leaf hut in Abyssinia. Rimbaud returned to Paris to die, admitting that his desperate, passionate search for experience, knowledge, and truth was a failure.

The Sleeper of the Valley

There's a green hollow where a river sings
Silvering the torn grass in its glittering flight,
And where the sun from the proud mountain flings
Fire—and the little valley brims with light.

A soldier young, with open mouth, bare head,   5
Sleeps with his neck in dewy water cress,
Under the sky and on the grass his bed,
Pale in the deep green and the light's excess.

He sleeps amid the iris and his smile
Is like a sick child's slumbering for a while.   10
Nature, in thy warm lap his chilled limbs hide!

The perfume does not thrill him from his rest.
He sleeps in sunshine, hand upon his breast,
Tranquil—with two red holes in his right side.

JOSÉ-MARIA DE HEREDIA

Heredia (1842–1905), born near Santiago de Cuba, joined the group of writers in Paris who were rebelling against the extravagances of Romanticism and trying to repress the revelation of personal feelings in their poems. Heredia, who used the French language, wrote little and published less, but he is admired for the precision of his sonnets, each of which presents one striking picture, in flawless language, polished like a gem.

The Bath

As might a centaur, man and beast in one,
  Into the surf they plunge, naked and free;
  Powdered with golden mist, they seem to be
Athletes of bronze aglow beneath the sun.
The rustic rider and wild stallion   5
  Breathe in the briny odor thirstily,
  And as they meet the chill surge of the sea
Through flesh and mane delicious shivers run.
The wave swells, rushes, rises like a wall,
  Then breaks in foam. The bathers shout and neigh,   10
  And from the stallion's tail blue showers fly;
Mane streaming wild, he rears against the sky,
Then dark breasts cleave the billows as they fall
  Whipped into frothing cataracts of spray.

"The Bath" by José-Maria de Heredia, translated by John Hervey.

ANTÓNIO NOBRE

The Portuguese poet António Nobre (1867–1900) was another foreigner who was drawn for a time to the Paris literary scene.

Sonnet

You never noticed? In the town, the way
Is lined with rows of telegraphic wires
Where all day long the birds are perched in choirs,
And in the night, if moonlight copies day.

Along the dipping cables where they sway,   5
What torture wings, what anguish of desires!
A worried soul from overseas inquires,
The scheming statesman risks another play.

—Revolt!—No use.—Fear seventy are dead,
A hundred injured.—Love.—No hope ahead.   10
—Success at last!—?—!—Despairing.—Come to me.

And much the worthy birds pay heed to that!
They never cease their cheerful chirping chat.
And so, António, you too should be.

GEORG TRAKL

Georg Trakl (1887–1914), Austrian by birth, was strongly influenced by the French Symbolist poets contemporary with him. He was a pharmacist in a military hospital when he died, probably a suicide in despair over the war.

Untergang

Over the white pond
the wild birds have flown away.
From our stars blows in the evening an icy
wind.

"Sonnet" by António Nobre, translated by Jean R. Longland from *Music of the Mind: 1000 Years of European Poetry*, edited by Richard McLaughlin and Howard E. Slack, copyright © 1963 by Richard McLaughlin and Howard E. Slack. Reprinted by permission of the publisher, Grosset & Dunlap, Inc.
"Untergang" by Georg Trakl from *Twenty German Poets*, translated and edited by Walter Kaufman, © copyright 1962 by Random House, Inc. Reprinted by permission of the publisher.

Over our graves
the broken brow of night bends down.
Under oak trees we rock in a silver
skiff.   5

Always the white walls of the town resound.
Under bows of thorns   10
O my brother, we climb, blind hands, toward
midnight.

FOR STUDY AND DISCUSSION

THERE WAS A BOY

1. Pick out the details that make the boy
seem a harmonious part of external nature.
2. The death of a child could easily be
treated sentimentally. Has Wordsworth shown
his emotion at the end to be justifiable, and not
merely a stock sentimental response to a sad
situation? Explain.

THE WORLD IS TOO MUCH WITH US

1. What do Wordsworth's allusions to mythology signify? Finish the idea left to your
inference: I'd rather be / A Pagan than . . .
2. The poem changes tone twice. Define
the different tones and identify the poetic
elements that create them.
3. After you have read the poem, what
should "the world" and "Nature" mean to
you? Explain what Wordsworth means by
saying we are too much "with" the world.

TO AUTUMN

1. Keats's poem is not only descriptive,
it is evocative. What kinds of details about
autumn has he chosen to include? What kinds
has he avoided? Has he evoked the feeling of
warmth? Explain.
2. How many words in the first stanza suggest the quality of fullness? To what extent
does the imagery of the other two stanzas
contribute to this impression? What other
impressions stand out in these stanzas? What
patterns can you see in the development of
these three stanzas?
3. When Keats addresses autumn in the
second stanza, he personifies the season as a
harvester. What does this personification add
to the evocation of autumn? How is the personification anticipated in the first stanza?
How is it developed in the last stanza?

AUTUMN

1. Compare the images Pushkin uses in the
first three stanzas to make the reader react
more favorably toward winter than toward
spring. How do these images prepare you for
the images of autumn, the subject of praise in
the poem?
2. How do Pushkin's images of autumn
compare with Keats's? How do the poems differ in descriptive technique?
3. Paraphrase the topic of each of the last
five stanzas. What is the effect of the final
turn in the poem?

SONG

1. The question device in this poem is not
itself remarkable, but the extent of its use is.
What other rhetorical pattern is carried out
consistently through the poem?
2. How does the last question tie together
all the others?

MY DEPARTURE

1. Is the speaker being ironic when he says
in line 7, "They are no fools"? Explain.
2. What is the significance of the allusion
to Achilles in the last stanza?
3. How is the paradoxical statement in
line 4 indicative of the speaker's attitude
toward life and death?

SATURDAY NIGHT IN THE VILLAGE

1. In what ways are the girl and her grandmother different and in what ways similar?
What idea suggested by these contrasting
images could be applied to the village life in
general?
2. What is the point of the contrast made
between the field hand and the carpenter?
3. Why is Saturday the "most kind of the
seven days"? Examine the irony in this stanza
(lines 46–51). Why is Sunday a day of "anguish"?

4. Interpret the moral given in the last stanza. What is the irony in its being addressed to a "lively boy"?

RUSSIA 1812

1. Winter is an important fact about Napoleon's retreat from Moscow. But how does Hugo's use of winter go beyond the recording of literal fact?
2. Point out the images and metaphors that describe Napoleon himself. What attitude toward Napoleon is conveyed by Hugo's choice of words?
3. What is "the expiation" (line 64)? Consider the connotations of the word in giving your answer.
4. Examine the ironies in lines 1, 4, 8, 13–15, 17, 18, 20, 35, 43. Analyze the last section of the poem in terms of its ironic picture of Napoleon.
5. The relationship between man and nature in Pushkin's "Autumn" is not ironic, as it is in Hugo's "Russia 1812." What creates the differences in effect?

THE SPLENDOR FALLS

1. This poem relies on sound for its effect perhaps as completely as it is possible to do. What qualities of vowels and consonants differentiate the impression of continuous motion for the light (line 3), from the impression of abrupt movement for the cataract (line 4)? How does the rhythmic difference between these two lines contribute to these impressions? What vowel and consonant sounds tie the two lines together?
2. Lines 7 and 8 are both metrically regular; that is, in a normal reading of each line, each second syllable would be more heavily stressed. Yet the two lines are quite different in effect. What metrical elements create the difference?
3. The repeated lines obviously create an echo effect. How many other uses of repeated patterns of sound can you find in the poem?

TEARS, IDLE TEARS

1. Define precisely the feelings evoked by the images of this poem. What might Tennyson mean by "some divine despair"? (See the selection from *Paradise Lost,* page 630.)
2. Find at least three verses from Fitzgerald's translation of Omar Khayyam's *Rubaiyat* (see page 334) that show other ways of looking at the situation that causes Tennyson such anguish.

MEETING AT NIGHT; PARTING AT MORNING

1. How does the impression of the land change in the first poem? What significance does this suggest for the phrase "a world of men" in the second poem?
2. How does the impression of the sea change from the first poem, in which the view is landward from the sea, to the second poem, in which the view is reversed?
3. "Meeting" and "Parting" clearly intend to use images to evoke more than they state; but if the poet had wanted to convey more details about the images—such as specifying the relationship of the two people—he presumably would have done so. Can you identify the thoughts and feelings evoked by the images in these poems, without falling into the trap of writing an addition to what Browning says?

INVITATION TO THE VOYAGE

1. How is the idea expressed in the refrain developed in the details of the imagery? What distinguishes the imagery of the third stanza; of the second?
2. What does the poem imply about Baudelaire's concept of the nature of love?
3. What additional idea about love is conveyed through the comparison of the dream world (the "kind land") with the world that appears in the lover's tear-filled eyes?
4. How does this poem express the idea that romantic love may offer an escape from life? How does Baudelaire's attitude contrast or compare with Browning's?

AUTUMN SONG

1. How do the images used here contrast with those in Keats's poem? What does this difference suggest about the way each poet feels about autumn? How do the effects of the poems differ? What accounts for the difference?
2. Here is the poem Verlaine wrote:

●Les sanglots longs
    Des violons
        De l'automne
    Blessent mon cœur
    D'une langueur
        Monotone.

Tout suffocant
Et blême, quand
   Sonne l'heure,
Je me souviens
Des jours anciens
   Et je pleure.

Et je m'en vais
Au vent mauvais
   Qui m'emporte
Deci, delà,
Pareil à la
   Feuille morte.

—PAUL VERLAINE

Listen to a good reading of the French. How would you describe the impressions made by its sounds? Does the English version convey the same general impression? Do you notice any differences? In examining the two versions, do you find any significant differences in the handling of rhymes, in the pauses, or in the number and stress of syllables in a line?

THE SKY IS JUST BEYOND THE ROOF

1. What is the vantage point of the speaker? How do you picture what he sees?
2. Who is the "you" in the last stanza? Why is he in tears?
3. Compare the attitude expressed in this poem with that in Heine's "My Departure."

THE SLEEPER OF THE VALLEY

1. The poem is built upon a surprising twist: Why are we unprepared for the bullet holes? Do you find this last line effective? Why or why not? Is it still effective when you read the poem a second time and know how it will end?
2. Explain the irony created by the words and imagery in the poem. How does the sonnet form help emphasize the irony?

THE BATH

1. An identity between man and nature is suggested by the image of the centaur. Are any human qualities exalted by the identification of man with horse? Explain.
2. What details of the image seem particularly effective, both in creating the picture itself and in making metaphoric suggestions?
3. Where does the translator attempt to reinforce the image by the sounds and rhythms of the words?

SONNET

1. What is the main image created by the poem? What contrasts between contemporary life and the birds are created in the image?
2. What is the effect of the opening line? What do you think of the poet's advice to himself in the last line? What is the tone of the poem?

UNTERGANG

1. The poem seems at first an image of night, but eventually it reveals itself as an allegory of life. What is added by the detail of the "wild birds," who are not in the present scene? Which details hint that the poem intends to do more than evoke an impression of night?
2. Explore the full significance of the fact that it is midnight (rather than dawn) toward which "we" are climbing.
3. *Untergang* literally means "going down." In what various ways is the title appropriate?

FOR COMPOSITION

1. In a short poem or a paragraph describe your impression of a season of the year or a time of the day. In an accompanying brief essay, explain the impression you were trying for. Point out the descriptive details (imagery) you chose and tell why you made that selection. What feelings or interests are revealed by your choice of imagery?
2. The awareness that time brings about change and that the past cannot be recovered is expressed in one way or another in the poems by Wordsworth, Pushkin, Leopardi, Tennyson, Baudelaire, and Verlaine. In an essay, distinguish precisely what each poet seems to yearn for and cite the ways in which he gives individual expression to a sense of loss.
3. The sonnets by Wordsworth, Heredia, and Nobre reveal certain attitudes toward the natural world. Write an essay defining precisely the attitude evident in each poem. Are any attitudes expressed in common? How do the sonnets differ in attitude and in imagery? To what extent do any or all of the views speak to you?
4. In an essay comment on the similarities or differences you observe between the philosophy underlying the Wordsworth poems and that underlying the Zen anecdotes (see page 301).

The Short Story in the Nineteenth Century

The short story as a distinct and important kind of literature is a development of the nineteenth century. There are many earlier examples of short prose fiction, but the "tale" was usually a piece of didactic folk literature or a light literary diversion; seldom was it undertaken by an important writer. When the tale was taken seriously, as by Boccaccio and Chaucer (see pages 507 and 435), it was usually used for satire or for moralizing, but storytelling for its own pleasures, usually for comic delight, remained the chief purpose of such tales.

By the nineteenth century, Edgar Allan Poe (1809–1849) in America, Guy de Maupassant (1850–1893) in France, and Anton Chekhov (1860–1904) in Russia were turning the tale into a more complex and comprehensive literary form by developing its dramatic and analytic potential. (It remained for writers of the twentieth century to exploit the poetic capabilities of the short story; in fact, an examination of the full resources of the genre may best be undertaken by reading the stories of more recent writers.) Many nineteenth-century stories have a richness and solidity that may lead us to think of them as miniature novels, but they are both more and less than novels. Their length gives them an intensity of suspense that is not found in the longer novel form. It is significant, in fact, that the first of the modern short stories were suspense tales of mystery and terror, including the first detective story, Edgar Allan Poe's "Murders in the Rue Morgue." Poe and Maupassant developed, as a capstone to the suspense, a technique that for a long time became a hallmark of the short story: the sharp and unexpected twist at the end, which makes a dramatic and usually ironic climax.

In the nineteenth century, the short story, like the novel, was characteristically a vehicle for making critical observations on men and society. Toward the end of the century, French writer Émile Zola (1840–1902) argued an extremely clinical, scientific role for the writer of fiction. His long essay *The Experimental Novel* refers not to any experiments upon the form of the novel, but to the use of the novel (or story) as a kind of experimental laboratory for dissecting the human species. Zola sees the function of the novelist explicitly as an extension of the function of the physiologist and psychologist.

Zola and his followers called themselves Naturalists, and they felt that the word was appropriate to describe a literature which showed that life is really a Darwinian struggle, in which the weak are ruthlessly crushed by such social evils as alcoholism, poverty, and mental disease. "We are looking for the causes of social evil," wrote Zola. "We study the anatomy of classes and individuals to explain the derangements which are produced in society and in man." Though there were many criticisms leveled at the Naturalists—they were accused, for one thing, of dwelling on the sordid side of life and ignoring the spiritual qualities of man—still, important influences came from the movement. Writers ever since have been concerned with facing the truth about the sufferings of people, especially of the poor and exploited, and they have insisted on the freedom to express themselves in realistic language—even if it be shocking. And Zola and his followers did not want merely to shock; they exposed the unpleasant and ugly facts of life so that "everything may be healed."

The Attack on the Mill

ÉMILE ZOLA

Émile Zola (1840–1902) is famous for his gallant gesture of 1898, when he put his considerable prestige at stake in making a public defense of Alfred Dreyfus, a military man who had been imprisoned on a false accusation of selling information to the Germans. In his famous letter "I Accuse!" Zola denounced the corruption and anti-Semitism in the French military that was being concealed by the trumped-up charges against Dreyfus.

Zola's principal work is a series of Naturalistic novels, *The Rougons and Mac-quarts,* which explore in minute, realistic detail the history of two branches of a family, the legitimate branch and the illegitimate branch. The family is tainted with alcoholism and mental disease, and the novels are set in such locales as Paris slums, poverty-stricken farms, and sordid coal-mining communities. Zola aims to show how the evil effects of heredity and environment are worked out through four unfortunate generations of offspring.

"The Attack on the Mill" appeared in a collection of stories of various writers in 1880. Like other works by Zola, it shows the tragic impotence of a lone human will. The setting of the story is in the province of Lorraine, on France's northern border with Germany. The year is 1870. In that year, the French Emperor Napoleon III made a bumbling effort to bolster support among his subjects. The French were traditionally hostile to Germany, so Napoleon announced his opposition to the unification of the German states taking place under Bismarck. Though Napoleon had not intended to fight, Bismarck tricked him into declaring war, a war which Bismarck knew he could easily win. On August 4, Prussian troops invaded France at Wissembourg, in the border province of Alsace, neighboring Lorraine to the east. This story opens on July 24.

1

IT WAS HIGH HOLIDAY at Father Merlier's mill on that pleasant summer afternoon. Three tables had been brought out into the garden and placed end to end in the shade of the great elm, and now they were awaiting the arrival of the guests. It was known throughout the length and

The Attack on the Mill by Émile Zola, translated by E. P. Robins.

breadth of the land that that day was to witness the betrothal of old Merlier's daughter, Françoise, to Dominique, a young man who was said to be not over-fond of work, but whom never a woman for three leagues of the country around could look at without sparkling eyes, such a well-favored young fellow was he.

That mill of Father Merlier's was truly a very pleasant spot. It was situated right in the heart of Rocreuse, at the place where the main road makes a sharp bend. The village has but a single street, bordered on either side by a row of low, whitened cottages, but just there, where the road curves, there are broad stretches of meadowland, and huge trees, which follow the course of the Morelle, cover the low grounds of the valley with a most delicious shade. All Lorraine has no more charming bit of nature to show. To right and left dense forests, great monarchs of the wood, centuries old, rise from the gentle slopes and fill the horizon with a sea of waving, trembling verdure, while away toward the south extends the plain, of wondrous fertility and checked almost to infinity with its small enclosures, divided off from one another by their live hedges. But what makes the crowning glory of Rocreuse is the coolness of this verdurous nook, even on the hottest days of July and August. The Morelle comes down from the woods of Gagny, and it would seem as if it gathered to itself on the way all the delicious freshness of the foliage beneath which it glides for many a league; it brings down with it the murmuring sounds, the glacial, solemn shadows of the forest. And that is not the only source of coolness; there are running waters of all sorts singing among the copses; one cannot take a step without coming on a gushing spring, and as he makes his way along the narrow paths, he seems to be treading above subterrane lakes that seek the air and sunshine through the moss above and profit by every smallest crevice, at the roots of trees or among the chinks and crannies of the rocks, to burst forth in fountains of crystalline clearness. So numerous and so loud are the whispering voices of these streams that they silence the songs of the bullfinches. It is as if one were in an enchanted park, with cascades falling and flashing on every side.

The meadows below are never athirst. The shadows beneath the gigantic chestnut trees are of inky blackness, and along the edges of the fields long rows of poplars stand like walls of rustling foliage. There is a double avenue of huge plane trees ascending across the fields toward the an-

cient castle of Gagny, now gone to rack and ruin. In the region, where drought is never known, vegetation of all kinds is wonderfully rank; it is like a flower garden down there in the low ground between those two wooded hills, a natural garden, where the lawns are broad meadows and the giant trees represent colossal beds. When the noonday sun pours down his scorching rays, the shadows lie blue upon the ground, vegetation slumbers in the genial warmth, while every now and then a breath of almost icy coldness rustles the foliage.

Such was the spot where Father Merlier's mill enlivened nature run riot with its cheerful clack. The building itself, constructed of wood and plaster, looked as if it might be coeval with our planet. Its foundations were in part laved by the Morelle, which here expands into a clear pool. A dam, a few feet in height, afforded sufficient head of water to drive the old wheel, which creaked and groaned as it revolved, with the asthmatic wheezing of a faithful servant who has grown old in her place. Whenever Father Merlier was advised to change it, he would shake his head and say that like as not a young wheel would be lazier and not so well acquainted with its duties, and then he would set to work and patch up the old one with anything that came to hand, old hogshead staves, bits of rusty iron, zinc, or lead. The old wheel only seemed the gayer for it, with its odd, round countenance, all plumed and feathered with tufts of moss and grass, and when the water poured over it in a silvery tide, its gaunt black skeleton was decked out with a gorgeous display of pearls and diamonds.

That portion of the mill which was bathed by the Morelle had something of the look of a Moorish arch that had been dropped down there by chance. A good half of the structure was built on piles; the water came in under the floor, and there were deep holes, famous throughout the whole country for the eels and the huge crawfish that were to be caught there. Below the fall the pool was as clear as a looking glass, and when it was not clouded by foam from the wheel one could see great fish swimming about in it with the slow, majestic movements of a fleet. There was a broken stairway leading down to the stream, near a stake to which a boat was fastened, and over the wheel was a gallery of wood. Such windows as there were were arranged without any attempt at order. The whole was a quaint conglomeration of nooks and corners, bits of wall, additions made here and there as afterthoughts, beams and roofs, which gave the mill the aspect of an old dismantled citadel, but ivy and all sorts of creeping plants had grown luxuriantly and kindly covered up such crevices as were too unsightly, casting a mantle of green over the old dwelling. Young ladies who passed that way used to stop and sketch Father Merlier's mill in their albums.

The side of the house that faced the road was less irregular. A gateway in stone afforded access to the principal courtyard, on the right and left hand of which were sheds and stables. Beside a well stood an immense elm that threw its shade over half the court. At the farther end, opposite the gate, stood the house, surmounted by a dovecote, the four windows of its first floor symmetrically aligned. The only manifestation of pride that Father Merlier ever allowed himself was to paint this façade every ten years. It had just been freshly whitened at the time of our story, and dazzled the eyes of all the village when the sun lighted it up in the middle of the day.

For twenty years had Father Merlier been mayor of Rocreuse. He was held in great consideration on account of his fortune; he was supposed to be worth something like eighty thousand francs, the result of patient saving. When he married Madeleine Guilliard, who brought him the mill as her dowry, his entire capital lay in his two strong arms, but Madeleine had never repented of her choice, so manfully had he conducted their joint affairs. Now his wife was dead, and he was left a widower with his daughter Françoise.

Doubtless he might have sat himself down to take his rest and suffered the old mill wheel to sleep among its moss, but he would have found the occupation too irksome and the house would have seemed dead to him, so he kept on working still, for the pleasure of it. In those days Father Merlier was a tall old man, with a long, unspeaking face, on which a laugh was never seen, but beneath which there lay, nonetheless, a large fund of good humor. He had been elected mayor on account of his money, and also for the impressive air that he knew how to assume when it devolved on him to marry a couple.

Françoise Merlier had just completed her eighteenth year. She was small, and for that reason was not accounted one of the beauties of the country. Until she reached the age of fifteen she was even homely; the good folks of Rocreuse could not see how it was that the daughter of Father and Mother Merlier, such a hale, vigorous couple, had such a hard time of it in getting her growth. When she was fifteen, however, though still remaining delicate, a change came over her and she took on the prettiest little face imaginable. She had black eyes, black hair, and was red as a rose withal; her little mouth was always graced with a charming smile, there were delicious dimples in her cheeks, and a crown of sunshine seemed to be ever resting on her fair, candid forehead. Although small as girls went in that region she was far from being slender; she might not have been able to raise a sack of wheat to her shoulder, but she became quite plump with age and gave promise of becoming eventually as well rounded and appetizing as a partridge. Her father's habits of taciturnity had made her reflective while yet a young girl; if she always had a smile on her lips, it was in order to give pleasure to others. Her natural disposition was serious.

As was no more than to be expected, she had every young man in the countryside at her heels as a suitor, more even for her money than for her attractiveness, and she had made a choice at last, a choice that had been the talk and scandal of the entire neighborhood. On the other side of the Morelle lived a strapping young fellow who went by the name of Dominique Penquer. He was not to the manor born; ten years previously he had come to Rocreuse from Belgium to receive the inheritance of an uncle who had owned a small property on the very borders of the forest of Gagny, just facing the mill and distant from it only a few musket shots. His object in coming was to sell the property, so he said, and return to his own home again; but he must have found the land to his liking for he made no move to go away. He was seen cultivating his bit of a field and gathering the few vegetables that afforded him an existence. He hunted, he fished; more than once he was near coming in contact with the law through the intervention of the keepers. This independent way of living, of which the peasants could not very clearly see the resources, had in the end given him a bad name. He was vaguely looked on as nothing better than a poacher. At all events he was lazy, for he was frequently found sleeping in the grass at hours when he should have been at work. Then, too, the hut in which he lived, in the shade of the last trees of the forest, did not seem like the abode of an honest young man; the old women would not have been surprised at any time to hear that he was on friendly terms with the wolves in the ruins of Gagny. Still, the young girls would now and then venture to stand up for him, for he was altogether a splendid specimen of manhood, was this individual of doubtful antecedents, tall and straight as a young poplar, with a milk-white skin and ruddy hair and beard that seemed to be of gold when the sun shone on them. Now one fine morning it came to pass that Françoise told Father Merlier that she loved Dominique and that never, never would she consent to marry any other young man.

It may be imagined what a knockdown blow it was that Father Merlier received that day! As was his wont, he said never a word; his countenance wore its usual re-flective look, only the fun that used to bubble up from within no longer shone in his eyes. Françoise, too, was very serious, and for a week father and daughter scarcely spoke to each other. What troubled Father Merlier was to know how that rascal of a poacher had succeeded in bewitching his daughter. Dominique had never shown himself at the mill. The miller played the spy a little, and was rewarded by catching sight of the gallant, on the other side of the Morelle, lying among the grass and pretending to be asleep. Françoise could see him from her chamber window. The thing was clear enough; they had been making sheep's eyes at each other over the old mill wheel, and so had fallen in love.

A week slipped by; Françoise became more and more serious. Father Merlier still continued to say nothing. Then, one evening, of his own accord, he brought Dominique to the house, without a word. Françoise was just setting the table. She made no demonstration of surprise; all she did was to add another plate, but her laugh had come back to her and the little dimples appeared again upon her cheeks. Father Merlier had gone that morning to look for Dominique at his hut on the edge of the forest, and there the two men had had a conference, with closed doors and windows, that lasted three hours. No one ever knew what they said to each other; the only thing certain is that when Father Merlier left the hut he already treated Dominique as a son. Doubtless the old man had discovered that he whom he had gone to visit was a worthy young man, even though he did lie in the grass to gain the love of young girls.

All Rocreuse was up in arms. The women gathered at their doors and could not find words strong enough to characterize Father Merlier's folly in thus receiving a ne'er-do-well into his family. He let them talk. Perhaps he thought of his own marriage. Neither had he possessed a penny to his name at the time when he married Madeleine and her mill, and yet that had not prevented him from being a good husband to her. Moreover, Dominique put an end to their tittle-tattle by setting to work in such strenuous fashion that all the countryside was amazed. It so happened just then that the boy of the mill drew an unlucky number and had to go for a soldier, and Dominique would not hear to their engaging another. He lifted sacks, drove the cart, wrestled with the old wheel when it took an obstinate fit and refused to turn, and all so pluckily and cheerfully that people came from far and near merely for the pleasure of seeing him. Father Merlier laughed his silent laugh. He was highly elated that he had read the youngster aright. There is nothing like love to hearten up young men.

In the midst of all that laborious toil, Françoise and Dominique fairly worshiped each other. They had not much to say, but their tender smiles conveyed a world of meaning. Father Merlier had not said a word thus far on the subject of their marriage, and they had both respected his silence, waiting until the old man should see fit to give expression to his will. At last, one day along toward the middle of July, he had had three tables laid in the courtyard, in the shade of the big elm, and had invited his friends of Rocreuse to come that afternoon and drink a glass of wine with him. When the courtyard was filled with people and everyone there had a full glass in his hand, Father Merlier raised his own high above his head and said:

"I have the pleasure of announcing to you that Françoise and this stripling will be married in a month from now, on St. Louis's feast day."

Then there was a universal touching of glasses, attended by a tremendous uproar; everyone was laughing. But Father Merlier, raising his voice above the din, again spoke:

"Dominique, kiss your wife that is to be. It is no more than customary."

And they kissed, very red in the face, both of them, while the company laughed louder still. It was a regular fete; they emptied a small cask. Then, when only the intimate friends of the house remained, conversation went on in a calmer strain. Night had fallen, a starlit night and very clear. Dominique and Françoise sat on a bench, side by side, and said nothing. An old peasant spoke of the war that the emperor had declared against Prussia. All the lads of the village were already gone off to the army. Troops had passed through the place only the night before. There were going to be hard knocks.

"Bah!" said Father Merlier, with the selfishness of a man who is quite happy, "Dominique is a foreigner, he won't have to go—and if the Prussians come this way, he will be here to defend his wife."

The idea of the Prussians coming there seemed to the company an exceedingly good joke. The army would give them one good, conscientious thrashing and the affair would be quickly ended.

"I have seen them, I have seen them," the old peasant repeated in a low voice.

There was silence for a little, then they all touched glasses once again. Françoise and Dominique had heard nothing; they had managed to clasp hands behind the bench in such a way as not to be seen by the others, and this condition of affairs seemed so beatific to them that they sat there, mute, their gaze lost in the darkness of the night.

What a magnificent, balmy night! The village lay slumbering on either side of the white road as peacefully as a little child. The deep silence was undisturbed save by the occasional crow of a cock in some distant barnyard, acting on a mistaken impression that dawn was at hand. Perfumed breaths of air, like long-drawn sighs, almost, came down from the great woods that lay around and above, sweeping softly over the roofs, as if caressing them. The meadows, with their black intensity of shadow, took on a dim, mysterious majesty of their own, while all the springs, all the brooks and water courses that gurgled and trickled in the darkness, might have been taken for the cool and rhythmical breathing of the sleeping country. Every now and then the old dozing mill wheel, like a watchdog that barks uneasily in his slumber, seemed to be dreaming as if it were endowed with some strange form of life; it creaked, it groaned, it talked to itself, rocked by the fall of the Morelle, whose current gave forth the deep, sustained music of an organ pipe. Never was there a more charming or happier nook, never did more entire or deeper peace come down to cover it.

2

One month later to a day, on the eve of the feast of St. Louis, Rocreuse was in a state of alarm and dismay. The Prussians had beaten the emperor and were advancing on the village by forced marches. For a week past, people passing along the road had brought tidings of the enemy: "They are at Lormières, they are at Novelles"; and by dint of hearing so many stories of the rapidity of their advance, Rocreuse woke up every morning in the full expectation of seeing them swarming down out of Gagny wood. They did not come, however, and that only served to make the fright the greater. They would certainly fall upon the village in the nighttime and put every soul to the sword.

There had been an alarm the night before, a little before daybreak. The inhabitants had been aroused by a great noise of men tramping upon the road. The women were already throwing themselves upon their knees and making the sign of the cross when someone, to whom it happily occurred to peep through a half-opened window, caught sight of red trousers. It was a French detachment. The captain forthwith asked for the mayor, and, after a long conversation with Father Merlier, had remained at the mill.

The sun rose bright and clear that morning, giving promise of a warm day. There was a golden light floating over the woodland, while in the low grounds white mists were rising from the meadows. The pretty village, so neat and trim, awoke in the cool dawning, and the country, with its stream and its fountains, was as gracious as a freshly plucked bouquet. But the beauty of the day brought gladness to the face of no one; the villagers had watched the captain and seen him circle round and round the old mill, examine the adjacent houses, then pass to the other bank of the Morelle and from thence scan the country with a field glass; Father Merlier, who accompanied him, appeared to be giving explanations. After that the captain had posted some of his men behind walls, behind trees, or in hollows. The main body of the detachment had encamped in the courtyard of the mill. So there was going to be a fight, then? And when Father Merlier returned, they questioned him. He spoke no word, but slowly and sorrowfully nodded his head. Yes, there was going to be a fight.

Françoise and Dominique were there in the courtyard, watching him. He finally took his pipe from his lips and gave utterance to these few words:

"Ah! my poor children, I shall not be able to marry you tomorrow!"

Dominique, with lips tight set and an angry frown upon his forehead, raised himself on tiptoe from time to time and stood with eyes bent on Gagny wood, as if he would have been glad to see the Prussians appear and end the suspense they were in. Françoise, whose face was grave and very pale, was constantly passing back and forth, supplying the needs of the soldiers. They were preparing their soup in a corner of the courtyard, joking and chaffing one another while awaiting their meal.

The captain appeared to be highly pleased. He had visited the chambers and the great hall of the mill that looked out on the stream. Now, seated beside the well, he was conversing with Father Merlier.

"You have a regular fortress here," he was saying. "We shall have no trouble in holding it until evening. The bandits are late; they ought to be here by this time."

The miller looked very grave. He saw his beloved mill going up in flame and smoke, but uttered no word of remonstrance or complaint, considering that it would be useless. He only opened his mouth to say:

"You ought to take steps to hide the boat; there is a hole behind the wheel fitted to hold it. Perhaps you may find it of use to you."

The captain gave an order to one of his men. This captain was a tall, fine-looking man of about forty, with an agreeable expression of countenance. The sight of Dominique and Françoise seemed to afford him much pleasure; he watched them as if he had forgotten all about the approaching conflict. He followed Françoise with his eyes as she moved about the courtyard, and his manner showed clearly enough that he thought her charming. Then, turning to Dominique:

"You are not with the army, I see, my boy?" he abruptly asked.

"I am a foreigner," the young man replied.

The captain did not seem particularly pleased with the answer; he winked his eyes and smiled. Françoise was doubtless a more agreeable companion than a musket would have been. Dominique, noticing his smile, made haste to add:

"I am a foreigner, but I can lodge a rifle bullet in an apple at five hundred yards. See, there's my rifle behind you."

"You may find use for it," the captain dryly answered.

Françoise had drawn near; she was trembling a little, and Dominique, regardless of the bystanders, took and held firmly clasped in his own the two hands that she held forth to him, as if committing herself to his protection. The captain smiled again, but said nothing more. He remained seated, his sword between his legs, his eyes fixed on space, apparently lost in a dreamy reverie.

It was ten o'clock. The heat was already oppressive. A deep silence prevailed. The soldiers had sat down in the shade of the sheds in the courtyard and begun to eat their soup. Not a sound came from the village, where the inhabitants had all barricaded their houses, doors and windows. A dog, abandoned by his master, howled mournfully upon the road. From the woods and the nearby meadows, that lay fainting in the heat, came a long-drawn, whispering, soughing sound, produced by the union of what wandering breaths of air there were. A cuckoo sang. Then the silence became deeper still.

And all at once, upon that lazy, sleepy air, a shot rang out. The captain rose quickly to his feet, the soldiers left their half-emptied plates. In a few seconds all were at their posts; the mill was occupied from top to bottom. And yet the captain, who had gone out through the gate, saw nothing; to right and left the road stretched away, desolate and blindingly white in the fierce sunshine. A second report was heard, and still nothing to be seen, not even so much as a shadow; but just as he was turning to reenter he chanced to look over toward Gagny and there beheld a little puff of smoke, floating away on the tranquil air, like thistledown. The deep peace of the forest was apparently unbroken.

"The rascals have occupied the wood," the officer murmured. "They know we are here."

Then the firing went on, and became more and more continuous, between the French soldiers posted about the mill and the Prussians concealed among the trees. The bullets whistled over the Morelle without doing any mischief on either side. The firing was irregular; every bush seemed to have its marksman, and nothing was to be seen save those bluish smoke wreaths that hung for a moment on the wind before they vanished. It lasted thus for nearly two hours. The officer hummed a tune with a careless air. Françoise and Dominique, who had remained in the courtyard, raised themselves to look out over a low wall. They were more particularly interested in a little soldier who had his post on the bank of the Morelle, behind the hull of an old boat; he would lie face downward on the ground, watch his chance, deliver his fire, then slip back into a ditch a few steps in his rear to reload, and his movements were so comical, he displayed such cunning and activity, that it was difficult for anyone watching him to refrain from smiling. He must have caught sight of a Prussian, for he rose quickly and brought his piece to the shoulder, but before he could discharge it he uttered a loud cry, whirled completely around in his tracks and fell backward into the ditch, where for an instant his legs moved convulsively, just as the claws of a fowl do when it is beheaded. The little soldier had received a bullet directly through his heart. It was the first casualty of the day. Françoise instinctively seized Dominique's hand and held it tight in a convulsive grasp.

"Come away from there," said the captain. "The bullets reach us here."

As if to confirm his words a slight, sharp sound was heard up in the old elm, and the end of a branch came to the ground, turning over and over as it fell, but the two young people never stirred, riveted to the spot as they were by the interest of the spectacle. On the edge of the wood a Prussian had suddenly emerged from behind a tree, as an actor comes upon the stage from the wings, beating the air with his arms and falling over upon his back. And beyond that there was no movement; the two dead men appeared to be sleeping in the bright sunshine; there was not a soul to be seen in the fields on which the heat lay heavy. Even the sharp rattle of the musketry had ceased. Only the Morelle kept on whispering to itself with its low, musical murmur.

Father Merlier looked at the captain with an astonished air, as if to inquire whether that were the end of it.

"Here comes their attack," the officer murmured. "Look out for yourself! Don't stand there!"

The words were scarcely out of his mouth when a terrible discharge of musketry ensued. The great elm was riddled, its leaves came eddying down as thick as snowflakes. Fortunately, the Prussians had aimed too high. Dominique dragged,

almost carried Françoise from the spot, while Father Merlier followed them, shouting:

"Get into the small cellar, the walls are thicker there!"

But they paid no attention to him; they made their way to the main hall, where ten or a dozen soldiers were silently waiting, watching events outside through the chinks of the closed shutters. The captain was left alone in the courtyard, where he sheltered himself behind the low wall, while the furious fire was maintained uninterruptedly. The soldiers whom he had posted outside only yielded their ground inch by inch; they came crawling in, however, one after another, as the enemy dislodged them from their positions. Their instructions were to gain all the time they could, taking care not to show themselves, in order that the Prussians might remain in ignorance of the force they had opposed to them. Another hour passed, and as a sergeant came in, reporting that there were now only two or three men left outside, the officer took his watch from his pocket, murmuring:

"Half past two. Come, we must hold out for four hours yet."

He caused the great gate of the courtyard to be tightly secured and everything was made ready for an energetic defense. The Prussians were on the other side of the Morelle; consequently there was no reason to fear an assault at the moment. There was a bridge, indeed, a mile and a quarter away, but they were probably unaware of its existence, and it was hardly to be supposed that they would attempt to cross the stream by fording. The officer therefore simply caused the road to be watched; the attack, when it came, was to be looked for from the direction of the fields.

The firing had ceased again. The mill appeared to lie there in the sunlight, void of all life. Not a shutter was open, not a sound came from within. Gradually, however, the Prussians began to show themselves at the edge of Gagny wood. Heads were protruded here and there;

they seemed to be mustering up their courage. Several of the soldiers within the mill brought up their pieces to an aim, but the captain shouted:

"No, no; not yet; wait. Let them come nearer."

They displayed a great deal of prudence in their advance, looking at the mill with a distrustful air; they seemed hardly to know what to make of the old structure, so lifeless and gloomy, with its curtains of ivy. Still, they kept on advancing. When there were fifty of them or so in the open, directly opposite, the officer uttered one word:

"Now!"

A crashing, tearing discharge burst from the position, succeeded by an irregular, dropping fire. Françoise, trembling violently, involuntarily raised her hands to her ears. Dominique, from his position behind the soldiers, peered out upon the field, and when the smoke drifted away a little, counted three Prussians extended on their backs in the middle of the meadow. The others had sought shelter among the willows and the poplars. And then commenced the siege.

For more than an hour the mill was riddled with bullets; they beat and rattled on its old walls like hail. The noise they made was plainly audible as they struck the stonework, were flattened, and fell back into the water; they buried themselves in the woodwork with a dull thud. Occasionally a creaking sound would announce that the wheel had been hit. Within the building the soldiers husbanded their ammunition, firing only when they could see something to aim at. The captain kept consulting his watch every few minutes, and as a ball split one of the shutters in halves and lodged in the ceiling:

"Four o'clock," he murmured. "We shall never be able to hold the position."

The old mill, in truth, was gradually going to pieces beneath that terrific fire. A shutter that had been perforated again and again until it looked like a piece of lace fell off its hinges into the water and had to be replaced by a mattress. Every moment, almost, Father Merlier exposed himself to the fire in order to take account of the damage sustained by his poor wheel, every wound of which was like a bullet in his own heart. Its period of usefulness was ended this time, for certain; he would never be able to patch it up again. Dominique had besought Françoise to retire to a place of safety, but she was determined to remain with him; she had taken a seat behind a great oaken clothespress, which afforded her protection. A ball struck the press, however, the sides of which gave out a dull, hollow sound, whereupon Dominique stationed himself in front of Françoise. He had as yet taken no part in the firing, although he had his rifle in his hand; the soldiers occupied the whole breadth of the windows, so that he could not get near them. At every discharge the floor trembled.

"Look out! look out!" the captain suddenly shouted.

He had just descried a dark mass emerging from the wood. As soon as they gained the open they set up a telling platoon fire. It struck the mill like a tornado. Another shutter parted company and the bullets came whistling in through the yawning aperture. Two soldiers rolled upon the floor; one lay where he fell and never moved a limb; his comrades pushed him up against the wall because he was in their way. The other writhed and twisted, beseeching some one to end his agony, but no one had ears for the poor wretch; the bullets were still pouring in and everyone was looking out for himself and searching for a loophole whence he might answer the enemy's fire. A third soldier was wounded; that one said not a word, but with staring, haggard eyes sank down beneath a table. Françoise, horror-stricken by the dreadful spectacle of the dead and dying men, mechanically pushed away her chair and seated herself on the floor, against the wall; it seemed to her that she would be smaller there and less exposed. In the meantime men had gone and secured all the mattresses in the house; the opening of the window was partially closed again. The hall was filled with debris of every description, broken weapons, dislocated furniture.

"Five o'clock," said the captain. "Stand fast, boys. They are going to make an attempt to pass the stream."

Just then Françoise gave a shriek. A bullet had struck the floor and, rebounding, grazed her forehead on the ricochet. A few drops of blood appeared. Dominique looked at her, then went to the window and fired his first shot, and from that time kept on firing uninterruptedly. He kept on loading and discharging his piece mechanically, paying no attention to what was passing at his side, only pausing from time to time to cast a look at Françoise. He did not fire hurriedly or at random, moreover, but took deliberate aim. As the captain had predicted, the Prussians were skirting the belt of poplars and attempting the passage of the Morelle, but each time that one of them showed himself he fell with one of Dominique's bullets in his brain. The captain, who was watching the performance, was amazed; he complimented the young man, telling him that he would like to have many more marksmen of his skill. Dominique did not hear a word he said. A ball struck him in the shoulder, another raised a contusion on his arm. And still he kept on firing.

There were two more deaths. The mattresses were torn to shreds and no longer availed to stop the windows. The last volley that was poured in seemed as if it would carry away the mill bodily, so fierce it was. The position was no longer tenable. Still, the officer kept repeating:

"Stand fast. Another half hour yet."

He was counting the minutes, one by one, now. He had promised his commanders that he would hold the enemy there until nightfall, and he would not budge a hair's breadth before the moment that he had fixed on for his withdrawal. He maintained his pleasant air of good humor, smiling at Françoise by way of reassuring her. He had picked up the musket of one of the dead soldiers and was firing away with the rest.

There were but four soldiers left in the room. The Prussians were showing themselves en masse on the other bank of the Morelle, and it was evident that they might now pass the stream at any moment. A few moments more elapsed; the captain was as determined as ever and would not give the order to retreat, when a sergeant came running into the room, saying:

"They are on the road; they are going to take us in the rear."

The Prussians must have discovered the bridge. The captain drew out his watch again.

"Five minutes more," he said. "They won't be here within five minutes."

Then exactly at six o'clock, he at last withdrew his men through a little postern that opened on a narrow lane, whence they threw themselves into the ditch and in that way reached the forest of Sauval. The captain took leave of Father Merlier with much politeness, apologizing profusely for the trouble he had caused. He even added:

"Try to keep them occupied for a while. We shall return."

While this was occurring Dominique had remained alone in the hall. He was still firing away, hearing nothing, conscious of nothing; his sole thought was to defend Françoise. The soldiers were all gone and he had not the remotest idea of the fact; he aimed and brought down his man at every shot. All at once there was a great tumult. The Prussians had entered the courtyard from the rear. He fired his last shot, and they fell upon him with his weapon still smoking in his hand.

It required four men to hold him; the rest of them swarmed about him, vociferating like madmen in their horrible dialect. Françoise rushed forward to intercede with her prayers. They were on the point of killing him on the spot, but an officer came in and made them turn the prisoner over to him. After exchanging a few words in German with his men he turned to Dominique and said to him roughly, in very good French:

"You will be shot in two hours from now."

3

It was the standing regulation, laid down by the German staff, that every Frenchman, not belonging to the regular army, taken with arms in his hands, should be shot. Even the *compagnies franches* were not recognized as belligerants. It was the intention of the Germans, in making such terrible examples of the peasants who attempted to defend their firesides, to prevent a rising en masse, which they greatly dreaded.

The officer, a tall, spare man about fifty years old, subjected Dominique to a brief examination. Although he spoke French fluently, he was unmistakably Prussian in the stiffness of his manner.

"You are a native of this country?"

"No, I am a Belgian."

"Why did you take up arms? These are matters with which you have no concern."

Dominique made no reply. At this moment the officer caught sight of Françoise where she stood listening, very pale; her slight wound had marked her white forehead with a streak of red. He looked from one to the other of the young people and appeared to understand the situation; he merely added:

"You do not deny having fired on my men?"

"I fired as long as I was able to do so," Dominique quietly replied.

The admission was scarcely necessary, for he was black with powder, wet with sweat, and the blood from the wound in his shoulder had trickled down and stained his clothing.

"Very well," the officer repeated. "You will be shot two hours hence."

Françoise uttered no cry. She clasped her hands and raised them above her head in a gesture of mute despair. Her action was not lost upon the officer. Two soldiers had led Dominique away to an adjacent room where their orders were to guard him and not lose sight of him. The girl had sunk upon a chair; her strength had failed her, her legs refused to support her; she was denied the relief of tears, it seemed as if her emotion was strangling her. The officer continued to examine her attentively and finally addressed her:

"Is that young man your brother?" he inquired.

She shook her head in negation. He was as rigid and unbending as ever, without the suspicion of a smile on his face. Then, after an interval of silence, he spoke again:

"Has he been living in the neighborhood long?"

She answered yes, by another motion of the head.

"Then he must be well acquainted with the woods about here?"

This time she made a verbal answer. "Yes, sir," she said, looking at him with some astonishment.

He said nothing more, but turned on his heel, requesting that the mayor of the village should be brought before him. But Françoise had risen from her chair, a faint tinge of color on her cheeks, believing that she had caught the significance of his questions, and with renewed hope she ran off to look for her father.

As soon as the firing had ceased, Father Merlier had hurriedly descended by the wooden gallery to have a look at his wheel. He adored his daughter and had a strong feeling of affection for Dominique, his son-in-law who was to be; but his wheel also occupied a large space in his heart. Now that the two little ones, as he called them, had come safe and sound out of the fray, he thought of his other love, which must have suffered sorely, poor thing, and bending over the great wooden skeleton he was scrutinizing its wounds with a heartbroken air. Five of the buckets were reduced to splinters, the central framework was honeycombed. He was thrusting his fingers into the cavities that the bullets had made to see how deep they were, and reflecting how he was ever to repair all that damage. When Françoise found him, he was already plugging up the crevices with moss and such debris as he could lay hands on.

"They are asking for you, Father," said she.

And at last she wept as she told him what she had just heard. Father Merlier shook his head. It was not customary to shoot people like that. He would have to look into the matter. And he reentered the mill with his usual placid, silent air. When the officer made his demand for supplies for his men, he answered that the people of Rocreuse were not accustomed to be ridden roughshod and that nothing would be obtained from them through violence; he was willing to assume all the responsibility, but only on condition that he was allowed to act independently. The officer at first appeared to take umbrage at this easy way of viewing matters, but finally gave way before the old man's brief and distinct representations. As the latter was leaving the room the other recalled him to ask:

"Those woods there, opposite, what do you call them?"

"The woods of Sauval."

"And how far do they extend?"

The miller looked him straight in the face. "I do not know," he replied.

And he withdrew. An hour later the subvention in money and provisions that the officer had demanded was in the courtyard of the mill. Night was closing in; Françoise followed every movement of the soldiers with an anxious eye. She never once left the vicinity of the room in which Dominique was imprisoned. About seven o'clock she had a harrowing emotion; she saw the officer enter the prisoner's apartment and for a quarter of an hour heard their voices raised in violent discussion. The officer came to the door for a moment and gave an order in German which she did not understand, but when twelve men came and formed in the courtyard with shoul-

dered muskets, she was seized with a fit of trembling and felt as if she should die. It was all over, then; the execution was about to take place. The twelve men remained there ten minutes; Dominique's voice kept rising higher and higher in a tone of vehement denial. Finally the officer came out, closing the door behind him with a vicious bang and saying:

"Very well; think it over. I give you until tomorrow morning."

And he ordered the twelve men to break ranks by a motion of his hand. Françoise was stupefied. Father Merlier, who had continued to puff away at his pipe while watching the platoon with a simple, curious air, came and took her by the arm with fatherly gentleness. He led her to her chamber.

"Don't fret," he said to her; "try to get some sleep. Tomorrow it will be light and we shall see more clearly."

He locked the door behind him as he left the room. It was a fixed principle with him that women are good for nothing and that they spoil everything whenever they meddle in important matters. Françoise did not retire to her couch, however; she remained a long time seated on her bed, listening to the various noises in the house. The German soldiers quartered in the courtyard were singing and laughing; they must have kept up their eating and drinking until eleven o'clock, for the riot never ceased for an instant. Heavy footsteps resounded from time to time through the mill itself, doubtless the tramp of the guards as they were relieved. What had most interest for her was the sounds that she could catch in the room that lay directly under her own; several times she threw herself prone upon the floor and applied her ear to the boards. That room was the one in which they had locked up Dominique. He must have been pacing the apartment, for she could hear for a long time his regular, cadenced tread passing from the wall to the window and back again; then there was a deep silence; doubtless he had seated himself. The other sounds ceased, too; everything was still. When it seemed to her that the house was sunk in slumber she raised her window as noiselessly as possible and leaned out.

Without, the night was serene and balmy. The slender crescent of the moon, which was just setting behind Sauval wood, cast a dim radiance over the landscape. The lengthening shadows of the great trees stretched far athwart the fields in bands of blackness, while in such spots as were unobscured the grass appeared of a tender green, soft as velvet. But Françoise did not stop to consider the mysterious charm of night. She was scrutinizing the country and looking to see where the Germans had posted their sentinels. She could clearly distinguish their dark forms outlined along the course of the Morelle. There was only one stationed opposite the mill, on the far bank of the stream, by a willow whose branches dipped in the water. Françoise had an excellent view of him; he was a tall young man, standing quite motionless with face up-turned toward the sky, with the meditative air of a shepherd.

When she had completed her careful inspection of localities she returned and took her former seat upon the bed. She remained there an hour, absorbed in deep thought. Then she listened again; there was not a breath to be heard in the house. She went again to the window and took another look outside, but one of the moon's horns was still hanging above the edge of the forest and this circumstance doubtless appeared to her unpropitious, for she resumed her waiting. At last the moment seemed to have arrived; the night was now quite dark; she could no longer discern the sentinel opposite her, the landscape lay before her black as a sea of ink. She listened intently for a moment, then formed her resolve. Close beside her window was an iron ladder made of bars set in the wall, which ascended from the mill wheel to the granary at the top of the building and had formerly served the miller as a means of inspecting certain portions of the gearing, but a change having been made in the machinery, the ladder had long since become lost to sight beneath the thick ivy that covered all that side of the mill.

Françoise bravely climbed over the balustrade of the little balcony in front of her window, grasped one of the iron bars and found herself suspended in space. She commenced the descent; her skirts were a great hindrance to her. Suddenly a stone became loosened from the wall and fell into the Morelle with a loud splash. She stopped, benumbed with fear, but reflection quickly told her that the waterfall, with its continuous roar, was sufficient to deaden any noise that she could make, and then she descended more boldly, putting aside the ivy with her foot, testing each round of her ladder. When she was on a level with the room that had been converted into a prison for her lover, she stopped. An unforeseen difficulty came near depriving her of all her courage: the window of the room beneath was not situated directly under the window of her bedroom, there was a wide space between it and the ladder, and when she extended her hand it only encountered the naked wall.

Would she have to go back the way she came and leave her project unaccomplished? Her arms were growing very tired, the murmuring of the Morelle, far down below, was beginning to make her dizzy. Then she broke off bits of plaster from the wall and threw them against Dominique's window. He did not hear; perhaps he was asleep. Again she crumbled fragments from the wall, until the skin was peeled from her fingers. Her strength was exhausted, she felt that she was about to fall backward into the stream, when at last Dominique softly raised his sash.

"It is I," she murmured. "Take me quick; I am about to fall." Leaning from the window he grasped her and drew her into the room, where she had a paroxysm of weeping, stifling her sobs in order that she might not be heard. Then, by a supreme effort of the will, she overcame her emotion.

"Are you guarded?" she asked, in a low voice.

Dominique, not yet recovered from his stupefaction at seeing her there, made answer by simply pointing toward his door. There was a sound of snoring audible on the outside; it was evident that the sentinel had been overpowered by sleep and had thrown himself upon the floor close against the door in such a way that it could not be opened without arousing him.

"You must fly," she contined earnestly. "I came here to bid you fly and say farewell."

But he seemed not to hear her. He kept repeating:

"What, is it you, is it you? Oh, what a fright you gave me! You might have killed yourself." He took her hands, he kissed them again and again. "How I love you, Françoise! You are as courageous as you are good. The only thing I feared was that I might die without seeing you again, but you are here, and now they may shoot me when they will. Let me but have a quarter of an hour with you and I am ready."

He had gradually drawn her to him; her head was resting on his shoulder. The peril that was so near at hand brought them closer to each other, and they forgot everything in that long embrace.

"Ah, Françoise!" Dominique went on in low, caressing tones, "today is the feast of St. Louis, our wedding day, that we have been waiting for so long. Nothing has been able to keep us apart, for we are both here, faithful to our appointment, are we not? It is now our wedding morning."

"Yes, yes," she repeated after him, "it is now our wedding morning."

They shuddered as they exchanged a kiss. But suddenly she tore herself from his arms: the terrible reality arose before her eyes.

"You must fly, you must fly," she murmured breathlessly. "There is not a moment to lose." And as he stretched out his arms in the darkness to draw her to him again, she went on in tender, beseeching tones: "Oh! listen to me, I entreat you. If you die, I shall die. In an hour it will be daylight. Go, go at once; I command you to go."

Then she rapidly explained her plan to him. The iron ladder extended downward to the wheel; once he had got that far he could climb down by means of the buckets and get into the boat, which was hidden in a recess. Then it would be an easy matter for him to reach the other bank of the stream and make his escape.

"But are there no sentinels?" said he.

"Only one, directly opposite here, at the foot of the first willow."

"And if he sees me, if he gives the alarm?"

Françoise shuddered. She placed in his hand a knife that she had brought down with her. They were silent.

"And your father—and you?" Dominique continued. "But no, it is not to be thought of; I must not fly. When I am no longer here those soldiers are capable of murdering you. You do not know them. They offered to spare my life if I would guide them into Sauval forest. When they discover that I have escaped, their fury will be such that they will be ready for every atrocity."

The girl did not stop to argue the question. To all the considerations that he adduced, her one simple answer was: "Fly. For love of me, fly. If you love me, Dominique, do not linger here a single moment longer."

She promised that she would return to her bedroom; no one should know that she had assisted him. She concluded by folding him in her arms and smothering him with kisses, in an extravagant outburst of passion. He was vanquished. He put only one more question to her:

"Will you swear to me that your father knows what you are doing and that he counsels my flight?"

"It was my father who sent me to you," Françoise unhesitatingly replied.

She told a falsehood. At that moment she had but one great, overmastering longing, to know that he was in safety, to escape from the horrible thought that the morning's sun was to be the signal for his death. When he should be far away, then calamity and evil might burst upon her head; whatever fate might be in store for her would seem endurable, so that only his life might be spared. Before and above all other considerations, the selfishness of her love demanded that he should be saved.

"It is well," said Dominique; "I will do as you desire."

No further word was spoken. Dominique went to the window to raise it again. But suddenly there was a noise that chilled them with fright. The door was shaken violently; they thought that someone was about to open it; it was evidently a party going the rounds who had heard their voices. They stood by the window, close locked in each other's arms, awaiting the event with anguish unspeakable. Again there came the rattling at the door, but it did not open. Each of them drew a deep sigh of relief; they saw how it was; the soldier lying across the threshold had turned over in his sleep. Silence was restored, indeed, and presently the snoring commenced again, sounding like sweet music in their ears.

Dominique insisted that Françoise should return to her room first of all. He took her in his arms, he bade her a silent farewell, then assisted her to grasp the ladder, and himself climbed out on it in turn. He refused to descend a single step, however, until he knew that she was in her chamber. When she was safe in her room she let fall, in a voice scarce louder than the whispering breeze, the words:

"*Au revoir*, I love you!"

She kneeled at the window, resting her elbows on the sill, straining her eyes to follow Dominique. The night was still very dark. She looked for the sentinel, but could see nothing of him; the willow alone was dimly visible, a pale spot upon the surrounding blackness. For a moment she heard the rustling of the ivy as Dominique descended, then the wheel creaked, and there was a faint splash which told that the young man had found the boat. This was confirmed when, a minute later, she descried the shadowy outline of the skiff on the gray bosom of the Morelle. Then a horrible feeling of dread seemed to clutch her by the throat and deprive her of power to breathe; she momently expected to hear the sentry give the alarm; every faintest sound among the dusky shadows seemed to her over-wrought imagination to be the hurrying tread of soldiers, the clash of steel, the click of musket locks. The seconds slipped by, however; the landscape still preserved its solemn peace. Dominique must have landed safely on the other bank. Françoise no longer had eyes for anything. The silence was oppressive. And she heard the sound of trampling feet, a hoarse cry, the dull thud of a heavy body falling. This was followed by another silence, even deeper than that which had gone before. Then, as if conscious that Death had passed that way, she became very cold in presence of the impenetrable night.

4

At early daybreak the repose of the mill was disturbed by the clamor of angry voices. Father Merlier had gone and unlocked Françoise's door. She descended to the courtyard, pale and very calm, but when there could not repress a shudder upon being brought face to face with the body of a Prussian soldier that lay on the ground beside the well, stretched out upon a cloak.

Soldiers were shouting and gesticulating angrily about the corpse. Several of them shook their fists threateningly in the direction of the village. The officer had just sent a summons to Father Merlier to appear before him in his capacity as mayor of the commune.

"Here is one of our men," he said, in a voice that was almost unintelligible from anger, "who was found murdered on the bank of the stream. The murderer must be found, so that we may make a salutary example of him, and I shall expect you to cooperate with us in finding him."

"Whatever you desire," the miller replied, with his customary impassiveness. "Only it will be no easy matter."

The officer stooped down and drew aside the skirt of the cloak which concealed the dead man's face, disclosing as he did so a frightful wound. The sentinel had been struck in the throat and the weapon had not been withdrawn from the wound. It was a common kitchen knife, with a black handle.

"Look at that knife," the officer said to Father Merlier. "Perhaps it will assist us in our investigation."

The old man had started violently, but recovered himself at once; not a muscle of his face moved as he replied:

"Everyone about here has knives like that. Like enough your man was tired of fighting and did the business himself. Such things have happened before now."

"Be silent!" the officer shouted in a fury. "I don't know what it is that keeps me from applying the torch to the four corners of your village."

His rage fortunately kept him from noticing the great change that had come over Françoise's countenance. Her feelings had compelled her to sit down upon the stone bench beside the well. Do what she would, she could not remove her eyes from the body that lay stretched upon the ground, almost at her feet. He had been a tall, handsome young man in life, very like Dominique in appearance, with blue eyes and golden hair. The resemblance went to her heart. She thought that perhaps the dead man had left behind him in his German home some loved one who would weep for his loss. And she recognized her knife in the dead man's throat. She had killed him.

The officer, meantime, was talking of visiting Rocreuse with some terrible punishment, when two or three soldiers came running in. The guard had just that moment ascertained the fact of Dominique's escape. The agitation caused by the tidings was extreme. The officer went to inspect the locality, looked out through the still open window, saw at once how the event had happened, and returned in a state of exasperation.

Father Merlier appeared greatly vexed by Dominique's flight. "The idiot!" he murmured; "he has upset everything."

Françoise heard him and was in an agony of suffering. Her father, moreover, had no suspicion of her complicity. He shook his head, saying to her in an undertone:

"We are in a nice box, now!"

"It was that scoundrel! it was that scoundrel!" cried the officer. "He has got away to the woods; but he must be found, or by ——, the village shall stand the consequences." And addressing himself to the miller: "Come, you must know where he is hiding?"

Father Merlier laughed in his silent way and pointed to the wide stretch of wooded hills.

"How can you expect to find a man in that wilderness?" he asked.

"Oh! there are plenty of hiding places that you are acquainted with. I am going to give you ten men; you shall act as guide to them."

"I am perfectly willing. But it will take a week to beat up all the woods of the neighborhood."

The old man's serenity enraged the officer; he saw, indeed, what a ridiculous proceeding such a hunt would be. It was at that moment that he caught sight of Françoise where she sat, pale and trembling, on her bench. His attention was aroused by the girl's anxious attitude. He was silent for a moment, glancing suspiciously from father to daughter and back again.

"Is not this man," he at last coarsely asked the old man, "your daughter's lover?"

Father Merlier's face became ashly pale, and he appeared for a moment as if about to throw himself on the officer and throttle him. He straightened himself up and made no reply. Françoise had hidden her face in her hands.

"Yes, that is how it is," the Prussian continued; "you or your daughter have assisted him to escape. You are his accomplices. For the last time, will you surrender him?"

The miller did not answer. He had turned away and was looking at the distant landscape with an air of supreme indifference, just as if the officer were talking to some other person. That put the finishing touch to the latter's wrath.

"Very well, then!" he declared, "you shall be shot in his stead."

And again he ordered out the firing party. Father Merlier was as imperturbable as ever. He scarcely did so much as to shrug his shoulders; the whole drama appeared to him to be in very doubtful taste. He probably believed that they would not take a man's life in that unceremonious manner. When the platoon was on the ground he gravely said:

"So, then, you are in earnest?—Very well, I am willing it should be so. If you feel you must have a victim, it may as well be I as another."

But Françoise arose, greatly troubled, stammering: "Have mercy, good sir; do not harm my father. Take my life instead of his. It was I who assisted Dominique to escape; I am the only guilty one."

"Hold your tongue, my girl," Father Merlier exclaimed. "Why do you tell such a falsehood? She passed the night locked in her room, monsieur; I assure you that she does not speak the truth."

"I *am* speaking the truth," the girl eagerly replied. "I left my room by the window, I incited Dominique to fly. It is the truth, the whole truth."

The old man's face was very white. He could read in her eyes that she was not lying, and her story terrified him. Ah, those children, those children! how they spoiled everything, with their hearts and feelings! Then he said angrily:

"She is crazy; do not listen to her. It is a lot of trash she is giving you. Come, let us get through with this business."

She persisted in her protestations; she kneeled, she raised her clasped hands in supplication. The officer stood tranquilly by and watched the harrowing scene.

"Mon Dieu," he said at last, "I take your father because the other has escaped me. Bring me back the other man and your father shall have his liberty."

She looked at him for a moment with eyes dilated by the horror which his proposal inspired in her.

"It is dreadful," she murmured. "Where can I look for Dominique now? He is gone; I know nothing beyond that."

"Well, make your choice between them, him or your father."

"Oh! my God! how can I choose? Even if I knew where to find Dominique, I could not choose. You are breaking my heart. I would rather die at once. Yes, it would be more quickly ended thus. Kill me, I beseech you, kill me—"

The officer finally became weary of this scene of despair and tears. He cried:

"Enough of this! I wish to treat you kindly. I will give you two hours. If your lover is not here within two hours, your father shall pay the penalty that he has incurred."

And he ordered Father Merlier away to the room that had served as a prison for Dominique. The old man asked for tobacco and began to smoke. There was no trace of emotion to be descried on his impassive face. Only when he was alone he wept two big tears that coursed slowly down his cheeks as he smoked his solitary pipe. His poor, dear child, what a fearful trial she was enduring!

Françoise remained in the courtyard. Prussian soldiers passed back and forth, laughing. Some of them addressed her with coarse pleasantries which she did not understand. Her gaze was bent upon the door through which her father had disappeared, and with a slow movement she raised her hand to her forehead, as if to keep it from bursting. The officer turned sharply and said to her:

"You have two hours. Try to make good use of them."

She had two hours. The words kept buzzing, buzzing in her ears. Then she went forth mechanically from the courtyard; she walked straight ahead with no definite end. Where was she to go? what was she to do? She did not even endeavor to arrive at any decision, for she felt how utterly useless were her efforts. And yet she would have liked to see Dominique; they could have come to some understanding together, perhaps they might have hit on some plan to extricate them from their difficulties. And so, amid the confusion of her whirling thoughts, she took her way downward to the bank of the Morelle, which she crossed below the dam by means of some steppingstones which were there. Proceeding onward, still involuntarily, she came to the first willow, at the corner of the meadow, and stooping down, beheld a sight that made her grow deathly pale—a pool of blood. It was the spot. And she followed the trace that Dominique had left in the tall grass; it was evident that he had run, for the footsteps that crossed the meadow in a diagonal line were separated from one another by wide intervals. Then, beyond that point, she lost the trace, but thought she had discovered it again in an adjoining field. It led her onward to the border of the forest, where the trail came abruptly to an end.

Though conscious of the futility of the proceeding, Françoise penetrated into the wood. It was a comfort to her to be alone. She sat down for a moment, then, reflecting that time was passing, rose again to her feet. How long was it since she left the mill? Five minutes? or a half hour? She had lost all idea of time. Perhaps Dominique had sought concealment in a clearing that she knew of, where they had gone together one afternoon and eaten hazel nuts. She directed her steps toward the clearing; she searched

it thoroughly. A blackbird flew out, whistling his sweet and melancholy note; that was all. Then she thought that he might have taken refuge in a hollow among the rocks where he went sometimes with his gun to secure a bird or a rabbit, but the spot was untenanted. What use was there in looking for him? She would never find him, and little by little the desire to discover his hiding place became a passionate longing. She proceeded at a more rapid pace. The idea suddenly took possession of her that he had climbed into a tree, and thenceforth she went along with eyes raised aloft and called him by name every fifteen or twenty steps, so that he might know she was near him. The cuckoos answered her; a breath of air that rustled the leaves made her think that he was there and was coming down to her. Once she even imagined that she saw him; she stopped, with a sense of suffocation, with a desire to run away. What was she to say to him? Had she come there to take him back with her and have him shot? Oh! no, she would not mention those things; she would tell him that he must fly, that he must not remain in the neighborhood. Then she thought of her father awaiting her return, and the reflection caused her most bitter anguish. She sank upon the turf, weeping hot tears, crying aloud:

"My God! My God! why am I here!"

It was a mad thing for her to have come. And as if seized with sudden panic, she ran hither and thither; she sought to make her way out of the forest. Three times she lost her way, and had begun to think she was never to see the mill again, when she came out into a meadow, directly opposite Rocreuse. As soon as she caught sight of the village she stopped. Was she going to return alone?

She was standing there when she heard a voice calling her by name, softly:

"Françoise! Françoise!"

And she beheld Dominique, raising his head above the edge of a ditch. Just God! she had found him!

Could it be, then, that Heaven willed his death? She suppressed a cry that rose to her lips and slipped into the ditch beside him.

"You were looking for me?" he asked.

"Yes," she replied bewilderedly, scarce knowing what she was saying.

"Ah! what has happened?"

She stammered, with eyes downcast: "Why, nothing; I was anxious, I wanted to see you."

Thereupon, his fears alleviated, he went on to tell her how it was that he had remained in the vicinity. He was alarmed for them. Those rascally Prussians were not above wreaking their vengeance on women and old men. All had ended well, however, and he added, laughing:

"The wedding will be deferred for a week, that's all."

He became serious, however, upon noticing that her dejection did not pass away.

"But what is the matter? You are concealing something from me."

"No, I give you my word I am not. I am tired; I ran all the way here."

He kissed her, saying it was imprudent for them both to remain there longer, and was about to climb out of the ditch in order to return to the forest. She stopped him; she was trembling violently.

"Listen, Dominique; perhaps it will be as well for you to remain here, after all. There is no one looking for you; you have nothing to fear."

"Françoise, you are concealing something from me," he said again.

Again she protested that she was concealing nothing. She only liked to know that he was near her. And there were other reasons still that she gave in stammering accents. Her manner was so strange that no consideration could now have induced him to go away. He believed, moreover, that the French would return presently. Troops had been seen over toward Sauval.

"Ah! let them make haste; let them come as quickly as possible," she murmured fervently.

At that moment the clock of the church at Rocreuse struck eleven; the strokes reached them, clear and distinct. She arose in terror; it was two hours since she had left the mill.

"Listen," she said, with feverish rapidity, "should we need you I will go up to my room and wave my handkerchief from the window."

And she started off homeward on a run, while Dominique, greatly disturbed in mind, stretched himself at length beside the ditch to watch the mill. Just as she was about to enter the village, Françoise encountered an old beggarman, Father Bontemps, who knew everyone and everything in that part of the country. He saluted her; he had just seen the miller, he said, surrounded by a crowd of Prussians; then, making numerous signs of the cross and mumbling some inarticulate words, he went his way.

"The two hours are up," the officer said, when Françoise made her appearance.

Father Merlier was there, seated on the bench beside the well. He was smoking still. The young girl again proffered her supplication, kneeling before the officer and weeping. Her wish was to gain time. The hope that she might yet behold the return of the French had been gaining strength in her bosom, and amid her tears and sobs she thought she could distinguish in the distance the cadenced tramp of an advancing army. Oh! if they would but come and deliver them all from their fearful trouble!

"Hear me, sir; grant us an hour, just one little hour. Surely you will not refuse to grant us an hour!"

But the officer was inflexible. He even ordered two men to lay hold of her and take her away, in order that they might proceed undisturbed with the execution of the old man. Then a dreadful conflict took place in Françoise's heart. She could not allow her father to be murdered in that manner; no, no, she would die in company with Dominique rather, and she was just darting away in the direction of her room in order to signal her fiancé, when Dominique himself entered the courtyard.

The officer and his soldiers gave a great shout of triumph, but he, as if there had been no soul there but Françoise, walked straight up to her; he was perfectly calm, and his face wore a slight expression of sternness.

"You did wrong," he said. "Why did you not bring me back with you? Had it not been for Father Bontemps, I should have known nothing of all this. Well, I am here, at all events."

5

It was three o'clock. The heavens were piled high with great black clouds, the tail end of a storm that had been raging somewhere in the vicinity. Beneath the coppery sky and ragged scud, the valley of Rocreuse, so bright and smiling in the sunlight, became a grim chasm, full of sinister shadows. The Prussian officer had done nothing with Dominique beyond placing him in confinement, giving no indication of his ultimate purpose in regard to him. Françoise, since noon, had been suffering unendurable agony; notwithstanding her father's entreaties she would not leave the courtyard. She was waiting for the French troops to appear, but the hours slipped by, night was approaching, and she suffered all the more since it appeared as if the time thus gained would have no effect on the final result.

About three o'clock, however, the Prussians began to make their preparations for departure. The officer had gone to Dominique's room and remained closeted with him for some minutes, as he had done the day before. Françoise knew that the young man's life was hanging in the balance; she clasped her hands and put up fervent prayers. Beside her sat Father Merlier, rigid and silent, declining, like the true peasant he was, to attempt any interference with accomplished facts.

"Oh! my God! my God!" Françoise exclaimed, "they are going to kill him!"

The miller drew her to him and took her on his lap as if she had been a little child. At this juncture the officer came from the room, followed by two men conducting Dominque between them.

"Never, never!" the latter exclaimed. "I am ready to die."

"You had better think the matter over," the officer replied. "I shall have no trouble in finding someone else to render us the service which you refuse. I am generous with you; I offer you your life. It is simply a matter of guiding us across the forest to Montredom; there must be paths."

Dominique made no answer.

"Then you persist in your obstinacy?"

"Shoot me, and have done with the matter," he replied.

Françoise, in the distance, entreated her lover with clasped hands; she was forgetful of all considerations save one; she would have had him commit a treason. But Father Merlier seized her hands that the Prussians might not see the wild gestures of a woman whose mind was disordered by her distress.

"He is right," he murmured, "it is best for him to die."

The firing party was in readiness. The officer still had hopes of bringing Dominique over and was waiting to see him exhibit some signs of weakness. Deep silence prevailed. Heavy peals of thunder were heard in the distance; the fields and woods lay lifeless beneath the sweltering heat. And it was in the midst of this oppressive silence that suddenly the cry arose:

"The French! the French!"

It was a fact; they were coming. The line of red trousers could be seen advancing along the Sauval road, at the edge of the forest. In the mill the confusion was extreme; the Prussian soldiers ran to and fro, giving vent to guttural cries. Not a shot had been fired as yet.

"The French! the French!" cried Françoise, clapping her hands for joy. She was like a woman possessed. She had escaped from her father's embrace and was laughing boisterously, her arms raised high in air. They had come at last, then, and had come in time, since Dominique was still there, alive!

A crash of musketry that rang in her ears like a thunderclap caused her to suddenly turn her head. The officer had muttered: "We will finish this business first," and with his own hands pushing Dominique up against the wall of a shed, had given the command to the squad to fire. When Françoise turned, Dominique was lying on the ground, pierced by a dozen bullets.

She did not shed a tear, she stood there like one suddenly rendered senseless. Her eyes were fixed and staring, and she went and seated herself beneath the shed, a few steps from the lifeless body. She looked at it wistfully; now and then she would make a movement with her hand in an aimless, childish way. The Prussians had seized Father Merlier as a hostage.

It was a pretty fight. The officer, perceiving that he could not retreat without being cut to pieces, rapidly made the best disposition possible of his men; it was as well to sell their lives dearly. The Prussians were now the defenders of the mill and the French were the attacking party. The musketry fire began with unparalleled fury; for half an hour there was no lull in the storm. Then a deep report was heard and a ball carried away a large branch of the old elm. The French had artillery; a battery, in position just beyond the ditch where Dominique had concealed himself, commanded the main street of Rocreuse. The conflict could not last long after that.

Ah! the poor old mill! The cannon balls raked it from wall to wall. Half the roof was carried away; two of the walls fell in. But it was on the side toward the Morelle that the damage was greatest. The ivy, torn from the tottering walls, hung in tatters, debris of every description floated away upon the bosom of the stream, and through a great breach Françoise's chamber was visible with its little bed, the snow-white curtains of which were carefully drawn. Two balls struck the old wheel in quick succession and it gave one parting groan; the buckets were carried away downstream, the frame was crushed into a shapeless mass. It was the soul of the stout old mill, parting from the body.

Then the French came forward to carry the place by storm. There was a mad hand-to-hand conflict with the bayonet. Under the dull sky the pretty valley became a huge slaughter pen; the broad meadows looked on in fright, with their great isolated trees and their rows of poplars, dotting them with shade, while to right and left the forest was like the walls of a tilting ground enclosing the combatants, and in nature's universal panic the gentle murmur of the springs and watercourses sounded like sobs and wails.

Françoise had not stirred from the shed, where she remained hanging over Dominique's body. Father Merlier had met his death from a stray bullet. Then the French captain, the Prussians being exterminated and the mill on fire, entered the courtyard at the head of his men. It was the first success that he had gained since the breaking out of the war, so all afire with enthusiasm, drawing himself up to the full height of his lofty stature, he laughed pleasantly, as a handsome cavalier like him might laugh, and perceiving poor idiotic Françoise where she crouched between the corpses of her father and her husband, among the smoking ruins of the mill, he saluted her gallantly with his sword and shouted:

"Victory! victory!"

FOR STUDY AND DISCUSSION

1. The story begins with an extensive and detailed description of its setting. What are the principal subjects of the description? What atmosphere and emotions are called up by the words and the images?

2. What is the general effect of beginning the story with this description of setting and of making the description so fully detailed? To answer this question, it might be helpful to speculate on the impression the story would

make if it began, for example, with a crucial moment in the middle of the action (say, for example, Dominique's escape).

3. Compare the descriptions of the mill and countryside in Part 1 with their descriptions in Parts 3 and 5. What are the principal differences in detail and in atmosphere? How important, then, does setting seem to be in this story?

4. What are you led to expect of each character in the story from his or her physical appearance and from the brief history given of his or her past life? Are you led to anticipate any outcome that is different from what does later occur? Explain.

5. Why are you inclined from the beginning to feel sympathetic toward Françoise, certainly, and toward Dominique, perhaps with some hesitation? What keeps you from feeling hostile to Father Merlier when he opposes them?

6. Is there any significant development of your understanding of the characters or of your feelings toward them? Do they themselves change in the course of the story? Explain.

7. Is any one person the central character in the story? Give reasons for your answer.

8. Define the main action in each section of the story. What are the time relationships among the sections? What parts of the plot are treated more extensively than others? What are the principal climaxes?

9. How much meaning can be read into the contrast that exists between the scene that begins the story and that which ends it? How much can be read into the contrast between the betrothal party and the soldiers' party?

10. How is the mill wheel occasionally personified? Does the personification have any special significance or effect? Explain.

11. Are there any recurrent impressions created by images prominent throughout the story? Explain.

12. The plot is concerned with love and with war. What issues are being raised in this story? What ideas or attitudes about the issues does Zola lead the reader to take?

Two Friends

GUY DE MAUPASSANT

Guy de Maupassant (1850–1893) was a literary disciple and friend of the pioneering Realistic novelist, Gustave Flaubert. He is also often presented as a Naturalist, and indeed he was one of the literary group who used to gather at Zola's house on Sunday afternoons in the suburbs of Paris. After serving in the Franco-Prussian War, Maupassant held minor government posts while he pursued his writing, using a craftsmanlike manner in emulation of Flaubert. Unlike Flaubert, Maupassant was prolific; he published thirty volumes of stories and several novels in his short lifetime. More than any other writer represented here, he gave new shape and direction to the short story. The emphasis upon a few accurate and significant details and the use of an unexpected plot twist at the end to reveal the whole meaning of the story are marks that Maupassant put upon the form. His stories are true to the attitude of the time, the *maladie de fin de siècle;* Maupassant, who knew for several years that he was going insane, was a moral and intellectual nihilist, hard on middle-class respectability, sentimentality, reactionaries, and women.

Among the things he admired was friendship maintained to death, as is shown in the following story, set during the Franco-Prussian War. After the French defeat on September 1, 1870, at Sedan, during which Emperor Napoleon III himself was captured by the Germans, Bismarck's armies moved on Paris and laid siege on September 19. Paris, under a provisional republican government that deposed the captured emperor, held out until January 28, 1871. Maupassant sets his story in that January, when the city was desperate after months of famine and was on the verge of capitulation.

PARIS WAS BLOCKADED, starved, in its death agony. Sparrows were becoming scarcer and scarcer on the rooftops and the sewers were being depopulated. One ate whatever one could get.

As he was strolling sadly along the outer boulevard one bright January morning, his hands in his trousers pockets and his stomach empty, M. Morissot, watchmaker by trade but local militiaman for the time being, stopped short before a fellow militiaman whom he recognized as a

"Two Friends" by Guy de Maupassant, translated by Gordon R. Silber.

friend. It was M. Sauvage, a riverside acquaintance.

Every Sunday, before the war, Morissot left at dawn, a bamboo pole in his hand, a tin box on his back. He would take the Argenteuil railroad, get off at Colombes, and walk to Marante Island. As soon as he arrived at this ideal spot he would start to fish; he fished until nightfall.

Every Sunday he would meet a stout, jovial little man, M. Sauvage, a haberdasher in Rue Notre-Dame-de-Lorette, another ardent fisherman. Often they spent half a day side by side, line in hand and feet dangling above the current. Inevitably they had struck up a friendship.

Some days they did not speak. Sometimes they did; but they understood one another admirably without saying anything because they had similar tastes and responded to their surroundings in exactly the same way.

On a spring morning, toward ten o'clock, when the young sun was drawing up from the tranquil stream wisps of haze which floated off in the direction of the current and was pouring down its vernal warmth on the backs of the two fanatical anglers, Morissot would sometimes say to his neighbor, "Nice, isn't it?" and M. Sauvage would answer, "There's nothing like it." And that was enough for them to understand and appreciate each other.

On an autumn afternoon, when the sky, reddened by the setting sun, cast reflections of its scarlet clouds on the water, made the whole river crimson, lighted up the horizon, made the two friends look as ruddy as fire, and gilded the trees which were already brown and beginning to tremble with a wintery shiver, M. Sauvage would look at Morissot with a smile and say, "Fine sight!" And Morissot, awed, would answer, "It's better than the city, isn't it?" without taking his eyes from his float.

As soon as they recognized one another they shook hands energetically, touched at meeting under such changed circumstances. M. Sauvage, with a sigh, grumbled, "What goings-on!" Morissot groaned dismally, "And what weather! This is the first fine day of the year."

The sky was, in fact, blue and brilliant.

They started to walk side by side, absent-minded and sad. Morissot went on, "And fishing! Ah! Nothing but a pleasant memory."

"When'll we get back to it?" asked M. Sauvage.

They went into a little café and had an absinthe, then resumed their stroll along the sidewalks.

Morissot stopped suddenly. "How about another, eh?" M. Sauvage agreed, "If you want." And they entered another wine shop.

On leaving they felt giddy, muddled, as one does after drinking on an empty stomach. It was mild. A caressing breeze touched their faces.

The warm air completed what the absinthe had begun. M. Sauvage stopped. "Suppose we went?"

"Went where?"

"Fishing, of course."

"But where?"

"Why, on our island. The French outposts are near Colombes. I know Colonel Dumoulin; they'll let us pass without any trouble."

Morissot trembled with eagerness: "Done! I'm with you." And they went off to get their tackle.

An hour later they were walking side by side on the highway. They reached the villa which the Colonel occupied. He smiled at their request and gave his consent to their whim. They started off again, armed with a pass.

Soon they passed the outposts, went through the abandoned village of Colombes, and reached the edge of the little vineyards which slope toward the Seine. It was about eleven.

Opposite, the village of Argenteuil seemed dead. The heights of Orgemont and Sannois dominated the whole countryside. The broad plain which stretches as far as Nanterre was empty, absolutely empty, with its bare cherry trees and its colorless fields.

Pointing up to the heights, M. Sauvage murmured, "The Prussians are up there!" And a feeling of uneasiness paralyzed the two friends as they faced this deserted region.

"The Prussians!" They had never seen any, but for months they had felt their presence—around Paris, ruining France, pillaging, massacring, starving the country, invisible and all-powerful. And a kind of superstitious terror was superimposed on the hatred which they felt for this unknown and victorious people.

Morissot stammered, "Say, suppose we met some of them?"

His Parisian jauntiness coming to the

surface in spite of everything, M. Sauvage answered, "We'll offer them some fish."

But they hesitated to venture into the country, frightened by the silence all about them.

Finally M. Sauvage pulled himself together: "Come on! On our way! But let's go carefully." And they climbed over into a vineyard, bent double, crawling, taking advantage of the vines to conceal themselves, watching, listening.

A stretch of bare ground had to be crossed to reach the edge of the river. They began to run, and when they reached the bank they plunged down among the dry reeds.

Morissot glued his ear to the ground and listened for sounds of anyone walking in the vicinity. He heard nothing. They were indeed alone, all alone.

Reassured, they started to fish.

Opposite them Marante Island, deserted, hid them from the other bank. The little building which had housed a restaurant was shut up and looked as if it had been abandoned for years.

M. Sauvage caught the first gudgeon, Morissot got the second, and from then on they pulled in their lines every minute or two with a silvery little fish squirming on the end, a truly miraculous draught.

Skillfully they slipped the fish into a sack made of fine net which they had hung in the water at their feet. And happiness pervaded their whole being, the happiness which seizes upon you when you regain a cherished pleasure of which you have long been deprived.

The good sun was pouring down its warmth on their backs. They heard nothing more; they no longer thought about anything at all; they forgot about the rest of the world—they were fishing!

But suddenly a dull sound which seemed to come from under ground made the earth tremble. The cannon were beginning.

Morissot turned and saw, over the bank to the left, the great silhouette of Mount Valérien wearing a white plume on its brow, powdersmoke which it had just spit out.

And almost at once a second puff of smoke rolled from the summit, and a few seconds after the roar still another explosion was heard.

Then more followed, and time after time the mountain belched forth death-dealing breath, breathed out milky-white vapor which rose slowly in the calm sky and formed a cloud above the summit.

M. Sauvage shrugged his shoulders. "There they go again," he said.

As he sat anxiously watching his float bob up and down, Morissot was suddenly seized by the wrath which a peace-loving man will feel toward madmen who fight, and grumbled, "Folks sure are stupid to kill one another like that."

M. Sauvage answered, "They're worse than animals."

And Morissot, who had just pulled in a bleak, went on, "And to think that it will always be like this as long as there are governments."

M. Sauvage stopped him: "The Republic wouldn't have declared war—"

Morissot interrupted: "Under kings you have war abroad; under the Republic you have war at home."

And they started a leisurely discussion, unraveling great political problems with the sane reasonableness of easy-going, limited individuals, and found themselves in agreement on the point that men would never be free. And Mount Valérien thundered unceasingly, demolishing French homes with its cannon, crushing out lives, putting an end to the dreams which many had dreamt, the joys which many had been waiting for, the happiness which many had hoped for, planting in wives' hearts, in maidens' hearts, in mothers' hearts, over there, in other lands, sufferings which would never end.

"That's life for you," opined M. Sauvage.

"You'd better say 'That's death for you,'" laughed Morissot.

But they shuddered in terror when they

realized that someone had just come up behind them, and looking around they saw four men standing almost at their elbows, four tall men, armed and bearded, dressed like liveried servants, with flat caps on their heads, pointing rifles at them.

The two fish lines dropped from their hands and floated off down stream.

In a few seconds they were seized, trussed up, carried off, thrown into a rowboat and taken over to the island.

And behind the building which they had thought deserted they saw a score of German soldiers.

A kind of hairy giant who was seated astride a chair smoking a porcelain pipe asked them in excellent French: "Well, gentlemen, have you had good fishing?"

Then a soldier put down at the officer's feet the sack full of fish which he had carefully brought along. The Prussian smiled: "Aha! I see that it didn't go badly. But we have to talk about another little matter. Listen to me and don't get excited.

"As far as I am concerned, you are two spies sent to keep an eye on me. I catch you and I shoot you. You were pretending to fish in order to conceal your business. You have fallen into my hands, so much the worse for you. War is like that.

"But—since you came out past the outposts you have, of course, the password to return. Tell me that password and I will pardon you."

The two friends, side by side, pale, kept silent. A slight nervous trembling shook their hands.

The officer went on: "No one will ever know. You will go back placidly. The secret will disappear with you. If you refuse, it is immediate death. Choose."

They stood motionless, mouths shut.

The Prussian quietly went on, stretching out his hand toward the stream: "Remember that within five minutes you will be at the bottom of that river. Within five minutes! You have relatives, of course?"

Mount Valérien kept on thundering.

The two fishermen stood silent. The German gave orders in his own language.

Then he moved his chair so as not to be near the prisoners and twelve men took their places, twenty paces distant, rifles grounded.

The officer went on: "I give you one minute, not two seconds more."

Then he rose suddenly, approached the two Frenchmen, took Morissot by the arm, dragged him aside, whispered to him, "Quick, the password? Your friend won't know. I'll pretend to relent."

Morissot answered not a word.

The Prussian drew M. Sauvage aside and put the same question.

M. Sauvage did not answer.

They stood side by side again.

And the officer began to give commands. The soldiers raised their rifles.

Then Morissot's glance happened to fall on the sack full of gudgeons which was lying on the grass a few steps away.

A ray of sunshine made the little heap of still squirming fish gleam. And he almost weakened. In spite of his efforts his eyes filled with tears.

He stammered, "Farewell, Monsieur Sauvage."

M. Sauvage answered, "Farewell, Monsieur Morissot."

They shook hands, trembling from head to foot with a shudder which they could not control.

The officer shouted, "Fire!"

The twelve shots rang out together.

M. Sauvage fell straight forward, like a log. Morissot, who was taller, tottered, half turned, and fell crosswise on top of his comrade, face up, as the blood spurted from his torn shirt.

The German gave more orders.

His men scattered, then returned with rope and stones which they tied to the dead men's feet. Then they carried them to the bank.

Mount Valérien continued to roar, its summit hidden now in a mountainous cloud of smoke.

Two soldiers took Morissot by the head and the feet, two others seized M. Sauvage. They swung the bodies for a moment then let go. They described an arc and plunged into the river feet first, for the weights made them seem to be standing upright.

There was a splash, the water trembled, then grew calm, while tiny wavelets spread to both shores.

A little blood remained on the surface.

The officer, still calm, said in a low voice: "Now the fish will have their turn."

And he went back to the house.

And all at once he caught sight of the sack of gudgeons in the grass. He picked it up, looked at it, smiled, shouted, "Wilhelm!"

A soldier in a white apron ran out. And the Prussian threw him the catch of the two and said: "Fry these little animals right away while they are still alive. They will be delicious."

Then he lighted his pipe again.

FOR STUDY AND DISCUSSION

1. How much of the story is devoted to giving exact locations? What is the effect of this device and of the use of real place names?

2. Why do Morissot and Sauvage feel a "superstitious terror" for the Prussians? How does Maupassant carry out their impression in his treatment of the Prussians? What is the significance of the comparison of the Prussians to "liveried servants"? What details support this impression of the Prussians? What does the image of the officer as a "hairy giant" contribute to the impression?

3. What is the relevance of the views of Morissot and Sauvage on republics and monarchies?

4. Morissot comments on the irony of Sauvage's cliché, "That's life for you." What is the irony of Morissot's own rejoinder?

5. When the Prussian officer says, "I catch you and I shoot you. . . . You have fallen into my hands, so much the worse for you," we may think of the fish who have been falling into the hands of the fishermen. Is this ironic similarity a critical comment on war or on fishing or on both? Explain. What other ironic use does Maupassant make of the "caught fishermen"?

6. What is the effect of the suddenness and of the lack of detail with which the climax of the story is treated?

FOR COMPOSITION

In an essay, summarize the ways in which Maupassant contrasts the innocent and private and peaceful with the violent and predatory. What comment does Maupassant make upon the relationship of the two types of behavior? You may want to expand this topic by comparing the ways in which the same conflict is treated by Zola (see page 772).

The Siege of Berlin

ALPHONSE DAUDET

Alphonse Daudet (1840–1897) was born in southern France, and although he did not write in Provençal, his most typical stories are realistic and humorous tales of provincial life. In many ways, Daudet resembles Charles Dickens, by whom he was undoubtedly influenced. Like Dickens, Daudet writes with a lively pace, draws appealing characters, and brings his readers quickly to tears or to laughter.

This story covers the six-month span of the Franco-Prussian War, a major catastrophe for the French. Under the inept leadership of Napoleon III, a nephew of the first Napoleon, France entered into war with Germany. Unfortunately for the French, the man directing German foreign policy at the time was Otto von Bismarck, a most capable diplomat, who viewed Napoleon III as the "greatest unrecognized mediocrity in Europe."

Old Colonel Jouve in Daudet's story had been in his youth a cuirassier, a cavalry officer, in the armies of the first Napoleon, who had set up the First Empire (1804–1815). The Colonel's first attack of apoplexy occurs during Napoleon III's Second Empire, on August 4, 1870, the day the news reached Paris of the first French defeat by Bismarck at Wissembourg in Alsace. His fatal attack occurs on the day the Germans entered Paris, after the French surrender of January 28, 1871.

WE WERE GOING up the Champs Élysées with Doctor V—, gathering from the walls pierced by shell, the pavement plowed by grapeshot, the history of besieged Paris, when just before reaching the Place de l'Étoile, the doctor stopped and pointed out to me one of those large corner houses, so pompously grouped around the Arc de Triomphe.

"Do you see," said he, "those four closed windows on the balcony up there? In the beginning of August, that terrible month of August of '70, so laden with storm and disaster, I was summoned there to attend a case of apoplexy. The sufferer was Colonel Jouve, an old cuirassier of the First Empire, full of enthusiasm for glory and patriotism, who, at the commencement of the war, had taken an apartment with a balcony in the Champs Élysées—for what do you think? To witness the triumphal entry of our troops! Poor old man! The news of Wissembourg arrived as he was rising from table. On reading the name of Napoleon at the foot of that bulletin of defeat he fell senseless!

"I found the old cuirassier stretched upon the floor, his face bleeding and inert as from the blow of a club. Standing, he would have been very tall; lying down he looked immense, with fine features, beautiful teeth, and white curling hair, carrying his eighty years as though they had been sixty. Beside him knelt his granddaughter in tears. She resembled him. Seeing them side by side, I was reminded of two Greek medallions stamped with

"The Siege of Berlin" from *Selected Stories of Alphonse Daudet*, edited by J. I. Rodale. Reprinted by permission of A. S. Barnes & Company, Inc.

the same impress, only the one was antique, earth-stained, its outlines somewhat worn; the other beautiful and clear, in all the luster of freshness.

"The child's sorrow touched me. Daughter and granddaughter of soldiers, for her father was on MacMahon's staff,[1] the sight of this old man stretched before her evoked in her mind another vision no less terrible. I did my best to reassure her, though in reality I had but little hope. We had to contend with hemoptysis, from which at eighty there is small chance of recovery.

"For three days the patient remained in the same condition of immobility and stupor. Meanwhile came the news of Reichshofen—you remember how strangely? Till the evening, we all believed in a great victory—20,000 Prussians killed, the Crown Prince prisoner.[2]

"I cannot tell by what miracle, by what magnetic current, an echo of this national joy can have reached our poor invalid, hitherto deaf to all around him; but that evening, on approaching the bed, I found a new man. His eye was almost clear, his speech less difficult, and he had the strength to smile and to stammer:

" 'Victory, victory!'

" 'Yes, Colonel, a great victory.' And as I gave the details of MacMahon's splendid success I saw his features relax and his countenance brighten.

"When I went out his granddaughter was waiting for me, pale and sobbing.

" 'But he is saved,' said I, taking her hands.

"The poor child had hardly courage to answer me. The true Reichshofen had just been announced, MacMahon a fugitive, the whole army crushed. We looked at each other in consternation, she anxious

at the thought of her father, I trembling for the grandfather. Certainly he would not bear this new shock. And yet what could we do? Let him enjoy the illusion which had revived him? But then we should have to deceive him.

" 'Well then, I will deceive him!' said the brave girl, and hastily wiping away her tears she reentered her grandfather's room with a beaming face.

"It was a hard task she had set herself. For the first few days it was comparatively easy, as the old man's head was weak, and he was as credulous as a child. But with returning health came clearer ideas. It was necessary to keep him *au courant* with the movements of the army and to invent military bulletins. It was pitiful to see that beautiful girl bending night and day over her map of Germany, marking it with little flags, forcing herself to combine the whole of a glorious campaign—Bazaine on the road to Berlin, Frossard in Bavaria, MacMahon on the Baltic. In all this she asked my counsel, and I helped her as far as I could, but it was the grandfather who did the most for us in this imaginary invasion. He had conquered Germany so often during the First Empire! He knew all the moves beforehand: 'Now they should go there. This is what they will do,' and his anticipations were always realized, not a little to his pride. Unfortunately, we might take towns and gain battles, but we never went fast enough for the Colonel. He was insatiable. Every day I was greeted with a fresh feat of arms:

" 'Doctor, we have taken Mayence,' said the young girl, coming to meet me with a heart-rending smile, and through the door I heard a joyous voice crying:

" 'We are getting on, we are getting on! In a week we shall enter Berlin!'

"At that moment the Prussians were but a week from Paris. At first we thought it might be better to move to the provinces, but once out of doors, the state of the country would have told him all, and I thought him still too weak, too enervated, to know the truth. It was therefore de-

---

[1] **MacMahon's staff:** MacMahon and Bazaine were marshals of the French army. Bazaine was defeated at Wissembourg.

[2] Rumor had the French believing that they had won the battle at Reichshofen, but MacMahon was defeated, driven back across Lorraine, and cut off from Bazaine. In an attempt to rejoin forces, MacMahon was decisively beaten on September 1, 1870, at Sedan, and Paris was left unprotected.

cided that they should stay where they were.

"On the first day of the invasion, I went to see my patient—much agitated, I remember, and with that pang in my heart which we all felt at knowing that the gates of Paris were shut, that the war was under our walls, that our suburbs had become our frontiers.

"I found the old man jubilant and proud.

"'Well,' said he, 'the siege has begun!'

"I looked at him stupefied.

"'How, Colonel, you know?'

"His granddaughter turned to me, 'Oh yes, Doctor, it is great news. The siege of Berlin has commenced.'

"She said this composedly, while drawing out her needle. How could he suspect anything? He could not hear the cannon nor see that unhappy Paris, so sullen and disorderly. All that he saw from his bed was calculated to keep up his delusion. Outside was the Arc de Triomphe, and in the room quite a collection of souvenirs of the First Empire. Portraits of marshals, engravings of battles, the King of Rome [1] in his baby robes; the stiff consoles, ornamented with trophies in brass, were covered with Imperial relics, medals, bronzes; a stone from St. Helena [2] under a glass shade; miniatures, all representing the same becurled lady with light eyes, in ball dress, in a yellow gown with leg-of-mutton sleeves; and all—the consoles, the King of Rome, the medals, the yellow ladies with short waists and sashes under their arms in that style of awkward stiffness which was the grace of 1806.—Good Colonel! it was this atmosphere of victory and conquest, rather than all we could say, which made him believe so naively in the siege of Berlin.

"From that day our military operations became much simpler. Taking Berlin was

[1] **the King of Rome:** Napoleon I's son, given this title at birth.

[2] **St. Helena:** the island in the Atlantic west of Africa, where Napoleon I spent his last exile. Note that the picture of this desolate place is "under a glass shade," as if it were a souvenir of a holiday resort.

merely a matter of patience. Every now and then, when the old man was tired of waiting, a letter from his son was read to him—an imaginary letter of course, as nothing could enter Paris, and as, since Sedan, MacMahon's aide-de-camp had been sent to a German fortress. Can you not imagine the despair of the poor girl, without tidings of her father, knowing him to be a prisoner, deprived of all comforts, perhaps ill, and yet obliged to make him speak in cheerful letters, somewhat short, as from a soldier in the field, always advancing in a conquered country. Sometimes, when the invalid was weaker than usual, weeks passed without fresh news. But was he anxious and unable to sleep, suddenly a letter arrived from Germany which she read gaily at his bedside, struggling hard with her tears. The Colonel listened religiously, smiling with an air of superiority, approving, criticizing, explaining; but it was in the answers to his son that he was at his best. 'Never forget that you are a Frenchman,' he wrote; 'be generous to those poor people. Do not make the invasion too hard for them.' His advice was never ending: edifying sermons about respect of property, the politeness due to ladies, in short, quite a code of military honor for the use of conquerors. With all this he put in some general reflections on politics and the conditions of the peace to be imposed on the vanquished. With regard to the latter, I must say he was not exacting:

"'The war indemnity and nothing else. It is no good to take provinces. Can one turn Germany into France?'

"He dictated this with so firm a voice, and one felt so much sincerity in his words, so much patriotic faith, that it was impossible to listen to him unmoved.

"Meanwhile the siege went on—not the siege of Berlin, alas! We were at the worst period of cold, of bombardment, of epidemic, of famine. But, thanks to our care, and the indefatigable tenderness which surrounded him, the old man's serenity was never for a moment disturbed. Up to the end I was able to procure white bread and fresh meat for him, but for him only. You could not imagine anything more touching than those breakfasts of the grandfather, so innocently egotistic, sitting up in bed, fresh and smiling, the napkin tied under his chin, at his side his granddaughter, pale from her privations, guiding his hands, making him drink, helping him to eat all these good forbidden things. Then, revived by the repast, in the comfort of his warm room, with the wintry wind shut out and the snow eddying about the window, the old cuirassier would recall his northern campaigns and would relate to us that disastrous retreat in Russia where there was nothing to eat but frozen biscuit and horseflesh.

"'Can you understand that, little one? We ate horseflesh.'

"I should think she did understand it. For two months she had tasted nothing else. As convalescence approached, our task increased daily in difficulty. The numbness of the Colonel's senses, as well as of his limbs, which had hitherto helped us so much, was beginning to pass away. Once or twice already, those terrible volleys at the Porte Maillot had made him start and prick up his ears like a war horse; we were obliged to invent a recent victory of Bazaine's before Berlin and salvoes fired from the Invalides [1] in honor of it. Another day (the Thursday of Buzenval I think it was) his bed had been pushed to the window, whence he saw some of the National Guard massed upon the Avenue de la Grande Armée.

"'What soldiers are those?' he asked, and we heard him grumbling beneath his teeth:

"'Badly drilled, badly drilled.'

"Nothing came of this, but we understood that henceforth greater precautions were necessary. Unfortunately we were not careful enough.

"One evening I was met by the child in much trouble.

"'It is tomorrow they make their entry,' she said.

"Could the grandfather's door have been open? In thinking of it since, I remember that all the evening his face wore an extraordinary expression. Probably he had overheard us; only we spoke of the Prussians and he thought of the French, of the triumphal entry he had so long expected, MacMahon descending the Avenue amidst flowers and flourish of trumpets, his own son riding beside the marshal, and he himself on his balcony, in full uniform as at Lützen,[2] saluting the ragged colors and the eagles blackened by powder.

"Poor Colonel Jouve! He no doubt imagined that we wished to prevent his taking part in the defile of our troops, lest the emotion should prove too much for him, and therefore took care to say nothing to us; but the next day, just at the time the Prussian battalions cautiously entered the long road leading from the Porte Maillot to the Tuileries, the window up there was softly opened and the Colonel appeared on the balcony with his helmet, his sword, all his long unused but glorious apparel of Milhaud's Cuirassiers.

"I often ask myself what supreme effort of will, what sudden impulse of fading vitality had placed him thus erect in harness.

"All we know is that he was there, standing at the railing, wondering to find the wide avenues so silent, the shutters all closed, Paris like a great lazaret, flags everywhere, but such strange ones, white with red crosses, and no one to meet our soldiers.

"For a moment he may have thought himself mistaken.

"But no! there, behind the Arc de Triomphe, there was a confused sound, a black line advancing in the growing daylight—then, little by little, the spikes of the helmets glisten, the little drums of Jena begin to beat, and under the Arc de

---

[1] **Invalides:** the military hospital in Paris, where Napoleon I is buried.

[2] **Lützen:** a town in Prussia where, in 1813, Napoleon I won a notable victory.

l'Étoile, accompanied by the heavy tramp of the troops, by the clatter of sabers, bursts forth Schubert's *Triumphal March*.

"In the dead silence of the streets was heard a cry, a terrible cry:

"'To arms!—to arms!—the Prussians.' And the four uhlans [1] of the advanced guard might have seen up there, on the balcony, a tall old man stagger, wave his arms, and fall. This time Colonel Jouve was dead."

[1] **uhlans:** cavalrymen in the German army.

FOR STUDY AND DISCUSSION

1. Show how Colonel Jouve is used to symbolize France itself during the Napoleonic era.

2. In what various ways is an ironic contrast established between reality as it exists in the old cuirassier's mind and reality as it is reported by the narrator? How is the irony used as the basis for suspense in the story?

3. What comment does the story make, especially through its irony, upon the character of the old Colonel? upon Napoleon and the First Empire? upon old soldiers? upon victory and defeat?

4. In what other ways might the story of the siege of Paris have been told? What effect does Daudet achieve with the unusual point of view he uses here?

FOR COMPOSITION

Through the ages, in all cultures, there has persisted a literary form which creates an uncomplicated world. Characters are all good or all bad; heroines are pure and beautiful; heroes are brave and handsome; villains are bad and often physically unattractive. Write an essay telling if Daudet's story fits in any ways this description of a stock romance. How about Maupassant's story (page 794) and *The Tempest* (page 542)?

How Much Land Does a Man Need?

a parable - how a man should live

LEO TOLSTOY

Count Leo Nikolayevich Tolstoy (1828–1910) is considered by many to be the giant of Russian literature. Wealthy and talented, he was nevertheless restless and dissatisfied with himself and his society. Although he wished to believe in the innate goodness of man, he found himself as disgusted with the ignorance and petty greed of the peasants as he was with the artificiality of the aristocracy. During his most tranquil years, Tolstoy wrote his two great Realistic novels, *War and Peace* and *Anna Karenina*. Soon after these triumphs, however, his inner conflict between the lure of a "natural life" and the restraining dictates of reason and moral law came to a head, and he began to crave a religious justification of his life. Thus, when Tolstoy was about fifty, he evolved his own brand of Christianity, which was a kind of ethical humanism. The aim of man, as Tolstoy now saw it, was to do right, to love all men, and to free oneself from greed, anger, and lust. The ownership of property is thus evil, because it is the gratification of greed and asserts a single man's monopoly over something that belongs to all. After this "conversion," Tolstoy tried to give away his wealth and live simply, as a peasant. He died in an obscure railway station as he was running away from intolerable conditions at home, brought on by Countess Tolstoy's desperate opposition to her husband's radical new way of life.

AN ELDER SISTER came to visit her younger sister in the country. The elder was married to a shopkeeper in town, the younger to a peasant in the village. As the sisters sat over their tea talking, the elder began to boast of the advantages of town life, saying how comfortably they lived there, how well they dressed, what fine clothes her children wore, what good things they ate and drank, and how she went to the theater, promenades, and entertainments.

The younger sister was piqued, and in turn disparaged the life of a shopkeeper, and stood up for that of a peasant.

"I wouldn't change my way of life for yours," said she. "We may live roughly, but at least we're free from worry. You live in better style than we do, but though you often earn more than you need, you're very likely to lose all you have. You know the proverb, 'Loss and gain are brothers twain.' It often happens that people who're wealthy one day are begging their bread the next. Our way is safer. Though a peasant's life is not a rich one, it's long. We'll never grow rich, but we'll always have enough to eat."

The elder sister said sneeringly:

"Enough? Yes, if you like to share with the pigs and the calves! What do you

"How Much Land Does a Man Need?" by Leo Tolstoy, translated by Louise and Aylmer Maude. Published in *Twenty-Three Tales* by Oxford University Press. Reprinted by permission of the publisher.

know of elegance or manners! However much your good man may slave, you'll die as you live—in a dung heap—and your children the same."

"Well, what of that?" replied the younger sister. "Of course our work is rough and hard. But on the other hand, it's sure, and we need not bow to anyone. But you, in your towns, are surrounded by temptations; today all may be right, but tomorrow the Evil One may tempt your husband with cards, wine, or women, and all will go to ruin. Don't such things happen often enough?"

Pahom, the master of the house, was lying on the top of the stove[1] and he listened to the women's chatter.

"It is perfectly true," thought he. "Busy as we are from childhood tilling mother earth, we peasants have no time to let any nonsense settle in our heads. Our only trouble is that we haven't land enough. If I had plenty of land, I shouldn't fear the Devil himself!"

The women finished their tea, chatted a while about dress, and then cleared away the tea things and lay down to sleep.

But the Devil had been sitting behind the stove and had heard all that had been said. He was pleased that the peasant's wife had led her husband into boasting and that he had said that if he had plenty of land he would not fear the Devil himself.

"All right," thought the Devil. "We'll have a tussle. I'll give you land enough; and by means of the land I'll get you into my power."

2

Close to the village there lived a lady, a small landowner who had an estate of about three hundred acres. She had always lived on good terms with the peasants until she engaged as her manager an old soldier, who took to burdening the people with fines. However careful Pahom tried to be, it happened again and again that now a horse of his got among the lady's oats, now a cow strayed into her garden, now his calves found their way into her meadows—and he always had to pay a fine.

Pahom paid up, but grumbled, and, going home in a temper, was rough with his family. All through that summer Pahom had much trouble because of this manager, and he was actually glad when winter came and the cattle had to be stabled. Though he grudged the fodder when they could no longer graze on the pasture land, at least he was free from anxiety about them.

In the winter the news got about that the lady was going to sell her land and that the keeper of the inn on the high road was bargaining for it. When the peasants heard this they were very much alarmed.

"Well," thought they, "if the innkeeper gets the land, he'll worry us with fines worse than the lady's manager. We all depend on that estate."

So the peasants went on behalf of their village council and asked the lady not to sell the land to the innkeeper, offering her a better price for it themselves. The lady agreed to let them have it. Then the peasants tried to arrange for the village council to buy the whole estate, so that it might be held by them all in common. They met twice to discuss it, but could not settle the matter; the Evil One sowed discord among them and they could not agree. So they decided to buy the land individually, each according to his means; and the lady agreed to this plan as she had to the other.

Presently Pahom heard that a neighbor of his was buying fifty acres, and that the lady had consented to accept one half in cash and to wait a year for the other half. Pahom felt envious.

"Look at that," thought he, "the land

[1] **lying on the top of the stove:** A brick or tile oven would be a feature of any Russian room of the period, but its use in this story as a principal item of furniture marks the house as a poor one, where warmth is not easy to come by.

is all being sold, and I'll get none of it."
So he spoke to his wife.

"Other people are buying," said he, "and we must also buy twenty acres or so. Life is becoming impossible. That manager is simply crushing us with his fines."

So they put their heads together and considered how they could manage to buy it. They had one hundred rubles laid by. They sold a colt and one half of their bees, hired out one of their sons as a farm hand and took his wages in advance, borrowed the rest from a brother-in-law, and so scraped together half the purchase money.

Having done this, Pahom chose a farm of forty acres, some of it wooded, and went to the lady to bargain for it. They came to an agreement, and he shook hands with her upon it and paid her a deposit in advance. Then they went to town and signed the deeds, he paying half the price down, and undertaking to pay the remainder within two years.

So now Pahom had land of his own. He borrowed seed and sowed it on the land he had bought. The harvest was a good one, and within a year he had managed to pay off his debts both to the lady and to his brother-in-law. So he became a landowner, plowing and sowing his own land, making hay on his own land, cutting his own trees, and feeding his cattle on his own pasture. When he went out to plow his fields, or to look at his growing corn, or at his grass meadows, his heart would fill with joy. The grass that grew and the flowers that bloomed there seemed to him unlike any that grew elsewhere. Formerly, when he had passed by that land, it had appeared the same as any other land, but now it seemed quite different.

3

So Pahom was well contented, and everything would have been right if the neighboring peasants would only not have trespassed on his wheatfields and mead-

ows. He appealed to them most civilly, but they still went on: now the herdsmen would let the village cows stray into his meadows, then horses from the night pasture would get among his corn. Pahom turned them out again and again, and forgave their owners, and for a long time he forbore to prosecute anyone. But at last he lost patience and complained to the District Court. He knew it was the peasants' want of land, and no evil intent on their part, that caused the trouble, but he thought:

"I can't go on overlooking it, or they'll destroy all I have. They must be taught a lesson."

So he had them up, gave them one lesson, and then another, and two or three of the peasants were fined. After a time Pahom's neighbors began to bear him a grudge for this, and would now and then let their cattle on to his land on purpose. One peasant even got into Pahom's wood at night and cut down five young lime trees for their bark. Pahom, passing through the wood one day, noticed something white. He came nearer and saw the stripped trunks lying on the ground, and close by stood the stumps where the trees had been. Pahom was furious.

"If he'd only cut one here and there it would have been bad enough," thought Pahom, "but the rascal has actually cut down a whole clump. If I could only find out who did this, I'd get even with him."

He racked his brains as to who it could be. Finally he decided: "It must be Simon—no one else could have done it." So he went to Simon's homestead to have a look around, but he found nothing and only had an angry scene. However, he now felt more certain than ever that Simon had done it, and he lodged a complaint. Simon was summoned. The case was tried, and retried, and at the end of it all Simon was acquitted, there being no evidence against him. Pahom felt still more aggrieved, and let his anger loose upon the Elders and the Judges.

"You let thieves grease your palms," said he. "If you were honest folk yourselves you wouldn't let a thief go free."

So Pahom quarreled with the judges and with his neighbors. Threats to burn his hut began to be uttered. So though Pahom had more land, his place in the community was much worse than before.

About this time a rumor got about that many people were moving to new parts.

"There's no need for me to leave my land," thought Pahom. "But some of the others may leave our village and then there'd be more room for us. I'd take over their land myself and make my estates somewhat bigger. I could then live more at ease. As it is, I'm still too cramped to be comfortable."

One day Pahom was sitting at home when a peasant, passing through the village, happened to drop in. He was allowed to stay the night, and supper was given him. Pahom had a talk with this peasant and asked him where he came from. The stranger answered that he came from beyond the Volga, where he had been working. One word led to another, and the man went on to say that many people were settling in those parts. He told how some people from his village had settled there. They had joined the community there and had had twenty-five acres per man granted them. The land was so good, he said, that the rye sown on it grew as high as a horse, and so thick that five cuts of a sickle made a sheaf. One peasant, he said, had brought nothing with him but his bare hands, and now he had six horses and two cows of his own.

Pahom's heart kindled with desire. "Why should I suffer in this narrow hole, if one can live so well elsewhere?" he thought. "I'll sell my land and my homestead here, and with the money I'll start afresh over there and get everything new. In this crowded place one is always having trouble. But I must first go and find out all about it myself."

Toward summer he got ready and started out. He went down the Volga on a steamer to Samara, then walked another three hundred miles on foot, and at last reached the place. It was just as the stranger had said. The peasants had plenty of land: every man had twenty-five acres of communal land given him for his use, and anyone who had money could buy, besides, at a ruble and a half an acre, as much good freehold land as he wanted.

Having found out all he wished to know, Pahom returned home as autumn came on, and began selling off his belongings. He sold his land at a profit, sold his homestead and all his cattle, and withdrew from membership in the village. He only waited till the spring, and then started with his family for the new settlement.

4

As soon as Pahom and his family reached their new abode, he applied for admission into the council of a large village. He stood treat to the Elders and obtained the necessary documents. Five shares of communal land were given him for his own and his sons' use: that is to say—125 acres (not all together, but in different fields) besides the use of the communal pasture. Pahom put up the buildings he needed and bought cattle. Of the communal land alone he had three times as much as at his former home, and the land was good wheat land. He was ten times better off than he had been. He had plenty of arable land and pasturage, and could keep as many head of cattle as he liked.

At first, in the bustle of building and settling down, Pahom was pleased with it all, but when he got used to it he began to think that even here he hadn't enough land. The first year he sowed wheat on his share of the communal land and had a good crop. He wanted to go on sowing wheat, but had not enough communal land for the purpose, and what he had already used was not available, for in those parts wheat is sown only on virgin soil or on fallow land. It is sown for one or two years, and then the land lies fallow till it is again overgrown with steppe grass.

There were many who wanted such land, and there was not enough for all, so that people quarreled about it. Those who were better off wanted it for growing wheat, and those who were poor wanted it to let to dealers, so that they might raise money to pay their taxes. Pahom wanted to sow more wheat, so he rented land from a dealer for a year. He sowed much wheat and had a fine crop, but the land was too far from the village—the wheat had to be carted more than ten miles. After a time Pahom noticed that some peasant dealers were living on separate farms and were growing wealthy, and he thought:

never satisfied

"If I were to buy some freehold land and have a homestead on it, it would be a different thing altogether. Then it would all be fine and close together."

The question of buying freehold land recurred to him again and again.

He went on in the same way for three years, renting land and sowing wheat. The seasons turned out well and the crops were good, so that he began to lay by money. He might have gone on living contentedly, but he grew tired of having to rent other people's land every year and having to scramble for it. Wherever there was good land to be had, the peasants would rush for it and it was taken up at once, so that unless you were sharp about it, you got none. It happened in the third year that he and a dealer together rented a piece of pasture land from some peasants, and they had already plowed it up, when there was some dispute and the peasants went to law about it, and things fell out so that the labor was all lost.

"If it were my own land," thought Pahom, "I should be independent, and there wouldn't be all this unpleasantness."

So Pahom began looking out for land which he could buy, and he came across a peasant who had bought thirteen hundred acres, but having got into difficulties was willing to sell again cheap. Pahom bargained and haggled with him, and at last they settled the price at fifteen hundred rubles, part in cash and part to be

paid later. They had all but clinched the matter when a passing dealer happened to stop at Pahom's one day to get feed for his horses. He drank tea with Pahom, and they had a talk. The dealer said that he was just returning from the land of the Bashkirs,[1] far away, where he had bought thirteen thousand acres of land, all for a thousand rubles. Pahom questioned him further, and the dealer said:

"All one has to do is to make friends with the chiefs. I gave away about one hundred rubles' worth of silk robes and carpets, besides a case of tea, and I gave wine to those who would drink it; and I got the land for less than three kopecks an acre." And he showed Pahom the title deed, saying:

"The land lies near a river, and the whole steppe is virgin soil."

Pahom plied him with questions, and the dealer said:

"There's more land there than you could cover if you walked a year, and it all belongs to the Bashkirs. They're as simple as sheep, and land can be got almost for nothing."

"There, now," thought Pahom, "with my one thousand rubles, why should I get only thirteen hundred acres, and saddle myself with a debt besides? If I take it out there, I can get more than ten times as much for my money."

5

Pahom inquired how to get to the place, and as soon as the grain dealer had left him, he prepared to go there himself. He left his wife to look after the homestead, and started on his journey, taking his hired man with him. They stopped at a town on their way and bought a case of

[1] **the Bashkirs:** nomads who live on the vast Russian steppes. Tolstoy found their way of life invigorating and was taken with its simplicity. Many times, for physical and spiritual refreshment, Tolstoy traveled to the Bashkirs for a "kumiss treatment," kumiss being a fermented drink made by the Bashkirs and highly esteemed in Russia as a tonic.

tea, some wine, and other presents, as the grain dealer had advised.

On and on they went until they had gone more than three hundred miles, and on the seventh day they came to a place where the Bashkirs had pitched their round tents. It was all just as the dealer had said. The people lived on the steppe, by a river, in felt-covered tents. They neither tilled the ground nor ate bread. Their cattle and horses grazed in herds on the steppe. The colts were tethered behind the tents, and the mares were driven to them twice a day. The mares were milked, and from the milk kumiss was made. It was the women who prepared the kumiss, and they also made cheese. As far as the men were concerned, drinking kumiss and tea, eating mutton, and playing on their pipes was all they cared about. They were all stout and merry, and all the summer long they never thought of doing any work. They were quite ignorant, and knew no Russian, but were good-natured enough.

As soon as they saw Pahom, they came out of their tents and gathered around the visitor. An interpreter was found, and Pahom told them he had come about some land. The Bashkirs seemed very glad; they took Pahom and led him into one of the best tents, where they made him sit on some down cushions placed on a carpet, while they sat around him. They gave him some tea and kumiss, and had a sheep killed, and gave him mutton to eat. Pahom took presents out of his cart and distributed them among the Bashkirs, and divided the tea amongst them. The Bashkirs were delighted. They talked a great deal among themselves and then told the interpreter what to say.

"They wish to tell you," said the interpreter, "that they like you and that it's our custom to do all we can to please a guest and to repay him for his gifts. You have given us presents, now tell us which of the things we possess please you best, that we may present them to you."

"What pleases me best here," answered Pahom, "is your land. Our land is crowded and the soil is worn out, but you have plenty of land, and it is good land. I never saw the likes of it."

The interpreter told the Bashkirs what Pahom had said. They talked among themselves for a while. Pahom could not understand what they were saying, but saw they they were much amused and heard them shout and laugh. Then they were silent and looked at Pahom while the interpreter said:

"They wish me to tell you that in return for your presents they will gladly give you as much land as you want. You have only to point it out with your hand and it is yours."

The Bashkirs talked again for a while and began to dispute. Pahom asked what they were disputing about, and the interpreter told him that some of them thought they ought to ask their chief about the land and not act in his absence, while others thought there was no need to wait for his return. *further & further...*

6

While the Bashkirs were disputing, a man in a large fox-fur cap appeared on the scene. They all became silent and rose to their feet. The interpreter said: "This is our chief himself."

Pahom immediately fetched the best dressing gown and five pounds of tea, and offered these to the chief. The chief accepted them and seated himself in the place of honor. The Bashkirs at once began telling him something. The chief listened for a while, then made a sign with his head for them to be silent, and addressing himself to Pahom, said in Russian:

"Well, so be it. Choose whatever piece of land you like; we have plenty of it."

"How can I take as much as I like?" thought Pahom. "I must get a deed to make it secure, or else they may say: 'It is yours,' and afterward may take it away again."

"Thank you for your kind words," he

said aloud. "You have much land, and I only want a little. But I should like to be sure which portion is mine. Could it not be measured and made over to me? Life and death are in God's hands. You good people give it to me, but your children might wish to take it back again."

"You are quite right," said the chief. "We will make it over to you."

"I heard that a dealer had been here," continued Pahom, "and that you gave him a little land, too, and signed title deeds to that effect. I should like to have it done in the same way."

The chief understood.

"Yes," replied he, "that can be done quite easily. We have a scribe, and we will go to town with you and have the deed properly sealed."

"And what will be the price?" asked Pahom.

"Our price is always the same: one thousand rubles a day."

Pahom did not understand.

"A day? What measure is that? How many acres would that be?"

"We do not know how to reckon it out," said the chief. "We sell it by the day. As much as you can go around on your feet in a day is yours, and the price is one thousand rubles a day."

Pahom was surprised.

"But in a day you can get around a large tract of land," he said.

The chief laughed.

"It will all be yours!" said he. "But there is one condition: If you don't return on the same day to the spot whence you started, your money is lost."

"But how am I to mark the way that I have gone?"

"Why, we shall go to any spot you like and stay there. You must start from that spot and make your round, taking a spade with you. Wherever you think necessary, make a mark. At every turning, dig a hole and pile up the turf; then afterward we will go around with a plow from hole to hole. You may make as large a circuit as you please, but before the sun sets you must return to the place you started from.

All the land you cover will be yours."

Pahom was delighted. It was decided to start early next morning. They talked a while, and after drinking some more kumiss and eating some more mutton, they had tea again, and then the night came on. They gave Pahom a feather bed to sleep on, and the Bashkirs dispersed for the night, promising to assemble the next morning at daybreak and ride out before sunrise to the appointed spot.

7

Pahom lay on the feather bed, but could not sleep. He kept thinking about the land.

"What a large tract I'll mark off!" thought he, "I can easily do thirty-five miles in a day. The days are long now, and within a circuit of thirty-five miles what a lot of land there will be! I'll sell the poorer land or let it to peasants, but I'll pick out the best and farm it myself. I'll buy two ox teams and hire two more laborers. About a hundred and fifty acres shall be plowland, and I'll pasture cattle on the rest."

Pahom lay awake all night and dozed off only just before dawn. Hardly were his eyes closed when he had a dream. He thought he was lying in that same tent and heard somebody chuckling outside. He wondered who it could be, and rose and went out, and he saw the Bashkir chief sitting in front of the tent holding his sides and rolling about with laughter. Going nearer to the chief, Pahom asked: "What are you laughing at?" But he saw that it was no longer the chief but the grain dealer who had recently stopped at his house and had told him about the land. Just as Pahom was going to ask: "Have you been here long?" he saw that it was not the dealer, but the peasant who had come up from the Volga long ago, to Pahom's old home. Then he saw that it was not the peasant either, but the Devil himself with hoofs and horns, sitting there and chuckling, and before him lay a man, prostrate on the ground, barefooted, with only trousers and a shirt on. And Pahom dreamed that he looked more attentively to see what sort of man it was lying there, and he saw that the man was dead, and that it was himself. Horror-struck, he awoke.

prophetic

"What things one dreams about!" thought he.

Looking around he saw through the open door that the dawn was breaking.

"It's time to wake them up," thought he. "We ought to be starting."

He got up, roused his man (who was sleeping in his cart), bade him harness, and went to call the Bashkirs.

"It's time to go to the steppe to measure the land," he said.

The Bashkirs rose and assembled, and the chief came, too. Then they began drinking kumiss again, and offered Pahom some tea, but he would not wait.

"If we are to go, let's go. It's high time," said he.

8

The Bashkirs got ready and they all started; some mounted on horses and some in carts. Pahom drove in his own small cart with his servant and took a spade with him. When they reached the steppe, the red dawn was beginning to kindle. They ascended a hillock (called by the Bashkirs a *shikhan*) and, dismounting from their carts and their horses, gathered in one spot. The chief came up to Pahom and, stretching out his arm toward the plain:

"See," said he, "all this, as far as your eye can reach, is ours. You may have any part of it you like."

Pahom's eyes glistened: it was all virgin soil, as flat as the palm of your hand, as black as the seed of a poppy, and in the hollows different kinds of grasses grew breast-high.

The chief took off his fox-fur cap, placed it on the ground, and said:

"This will be the mark. Start from here, and return here again. All the land you go around shall be yours."

Pahom took out his money and put it on the cap. Then he took off his outer coat, remaining in his sleeveless undercoat. He unfastened his girdle and tied it tight below his stomach, put a little bag of bread into the breast of his coat, and, tying a flask of water to his girdle, he drew up the tops of his boots, took the spade from his man, and stood ready to start. He considered for some moments which way he had better go—it was tempting everywhere.

"No matter," he concluded, "I'll go toward the rising sun."

He turned his face to the east, stretched himself, and waited for the sun to appear above the rim.

"I must lose no time," he thought, "and it's easier walking while it's still cool."

The sun's rays had hardly flashed above the horizon when Pahom, carrying the spade over his shoulder, went down into the steppe.

Pahom started walking neither slowly nor quickly. After having gone a thousand yards he stopped, dug a hole, and placed pieces of turf one on another to make it more visible. Then he went on; and now that he had walked off his stiffness he quickened his pace. After a while he dug another hole.

Pahom looked back. The hillock could be distinctly seen in the sunlight, with the people on it, and the glittering iron rims of the cartwheels. At a rough guess Pahom concluded that he had walked three miles. It was growing warmer; he took off his undercoat, slung it across his shoulder, and went on again. It had grown quite warm now; he looked at the sun—it was time to think of breakfast.

"The first shift is done, but there are four in a day, and it's too soon yet to turn. But I'll just take off my boots," said he to himself.

He sat down, took off his boots, stuck them into his girdle, and went on. It was easy walking now.

"I'll go on for another three miles,"

thought he, "and then turn to the left. This spot is so fine that it would be a pity to lose it. The further one goes, the better the land seems."

He went straight on for a while, and when he looked around, the hillock was scarcely visible and the people on it looked like black ants, and he could just see something glistening there in the sun.

"Ah," thought Pahom, "I have gone far enough in this direction; it's time to turn. Besides, I'm in a regular sweat, and very thirsty."

He stopped, dug a large hole, and heaped up pieces of turf. Next he untied his flask, had a drink, and then turned sharply to the left. He went on and on; the grass was high, and it was very hot.

Pahom began to grow tired: he looked at the sun and saw that it was noon.

"Well," he thought, "I must have a rest."

He sat down, and ate some bread and drank some water; but he did not lie down, thinking that if he did he might fall asleep. After sitting a little while, he went on again. At first he walked easily; the food had strengthened him; but it had become terribly hot and he felt sleepy. Still he went on, thinking: "An hour to suffer, a lifetime to live."

He went a long way in this direction also, and was about to turn to the left again, when he perceived a damp hollow: "It would be a pity to leave that out," he thought. "Flax would do well there." So he went on past the hollow and dug a hole on the other side of it before he made a sharp turn. Pahom looked toward the hillock. The heat made the air hazy: it seemed to be quivering, and through the haze the people on the hillock could scarcely be seen.

"Ah," thought Pahom, "I have made the sides too long; I must make this one shorter." And he went along the third side, stepping faster. He looked at the sun: it was nearly halfway to the horizon, and he had not yet done two miles of the third side of the square. He was still ten miles from the goal.

"No," he thought, "though it will make my land lopsided, I must hurry back in a straight line now. I might go too far, and as it is I have a great deal of land."

So Pahom hurriedly dug a hole and turned straight toward the hillock.

9

Pahom went straight toward the hillock, but he now walked with difficulty. He was exhausted from the heat, his bare feet were cut and bruised, and his legs began to fail. He longed to rest, but it was impossible if he meant to get back before sunset. The sun waits for no man, and it was sinking lower and lower.

"Oh, Lord," he thought, "if only I have not blundered trying for too much! What if I am too late?"

He looked toward the hillock and at the sun. He was still far from his goal, and the sun was already near the rim of the sky.

Pahom walked on and on; it was very hard walking, but he went quicker and quicker. He pressed on, but was still far from the place. He began running, threw away his coat, his boots, his flask, and his cap, and kept only the spade which he used as a support.

"What am I to do?" he thought again. "I've grasped too much and ruined the whole affair. I can't get there before the sun sets."

And this fear made him still more breathless. Pahom kept on running; his soaking shirt and trousers stuck to him, and his mouth was parched. His breast was working like a blacksmith's bellows, his heart was beating like a hammer, and his legs were giving way as if they did not belong to him. Pahom was seized with terror lest he should die of the strain.

Though afraid of death, he could not stop.

"After having run all that way they will call me a fool if I stop now," thought he.

And he ran on and on, and drew near and heard the Bashkirs yelling and shouting to him, and their cries inflamed his heart still more. He gathered his last strength and ran on.

The sun was close to the rim of the sky and, cloaked in mist, looked large, and red as blood. Now, yes, now, it was about to set! The sun was quite low, but he was also quite near his goal. Pahom could already see the people on the hillock waving their arms to make him hurry. He could see the fox-fur cap on the ground and the money in it, and the chief sitting on the ground holding his sides. And Pahom remembered his dream.

"There's plenty of land," thought he, "but will God let me live on it? I have lost my life, I have lost my life! Never will I reach that spot!"

Pahom looked at the sun, which had reached the earth: one side of it had already disappeared. With all his remaining strength he rushed on, bending his body forward so that his legs could hardly follow fast enough to keep him from falling. Just as he reached the hillock it suddenly grew dark. He looked up—the sun had already set!

He gave a cry: "All my labor has been in vain," thought he, and was about to stop, but he heard the Bashkirs still shouting and remembered that though to him, from below, the sun seemed to have set, they on the hillock could still see it. He took a long breath and ran up the hillock. It was still light there. He reached the top and saw the cap. Before it sat the chief, laughing and holding his sides. Again Pahom remembered his dream, and he uttered a cry: his legs gave way beneath him, he fell forward and reached the cap with his hands.

"Ah, that's a fine fellow!" exclaimed the chief. "He has gained much land!"

Pahom's servant came running up and tried to raise him, but he saw that blood was flowing from his mouth. Pahom was dead.

The Bashkirs clicked their tongues to show their pity.

His servant picked up the spade and dug a grave long enough for Pahom to lie in, and buried him in it.

Six feet from his head to his heels was all he needed.

FOR STUDY AND DISCUSSION

1. Examine the blending of allegory and realism in this story. How would this same story differ in effect if it was told in one mode or the other?

2. What means does Tolstoy use to maintain suspense through his long and somewhat repetitious story?

3. Explain the irony of the ending. This ending is neither subtle nor totally unexpected, but what makes it appropriate and satisfying?

4. The main story is told within a "frame." How is the frame story relevant to the action and themes of the principal story?

5. What is the significance of the contrast made between city life and peasant life?

6. In *The Canterbury Tales,* the Pardoner tells an allegorical tale about greed (see page 447). Compare and contrast the techniques used by Tolstoy and the Pardoner. Which story is more effective, and why? Is the purpose of each story the same? Explain.

7. Having a character make a pact with the devil is a common literary device. How did the German writer Goethe use this technique (see page 677)? What characteristics do Goethe's Devil and Faust have in common with Tolstoy's Devil and Pahom? Is this "devil-pact" device used in literature today? Do modern writers use the Devil, or do they use something else to represent evil? Explain why this might be so.

So Much for the King

GIOVANNI VERGA

Giovanni Verga (1840–1922) was a Sicilian writer who until recent years was not well known outside Italy, even though one of his stories provided the libretto for a popular opera, Mascagni's *Cavalleria Rusticana*. Verga's earliest works were rather empty Romantic novels; but around 1880 he returned from northern Italy to his native Sicily and began writing novels and stories about peasant life. In a strong, distinctive style, he made detached and realistic exposures of the common-place tragedies of peasant life, especially as it was being affected by the remote and incomprehensible world of politics and progress.

NEIGHBOR COSIMO, the litter driver,[1] had dressed down his mules, lengthened the halters a bit for the night, spread a handful of bedding under the feet of the bay mare, who had slipped twice on the wet cobblestones of the narrow street of Grammichele, after the heavy rain there had been, and then he'd gone to stand in the stable doorway with his hands in his pockets, to yawn in the face of all the people who had come to see the king, for there was such a thronging that day in the streets of Caltagirone that you'd have thought it was the festival of San Giacomo; at the same time he kept his ears open and his eye on his cattle, which were steadily munching their barley, so that nobody should come and steal them from him.

Just at that moment they came to tell him that the king wanted to speak to

[1] A litter was like a large sedan chair carried by two mules, one behind and one in front, used in all the inland roads of Sicily a hundred years ago.

him. Or rather it wasn't the king who wanted to speak to him, because the king never speaks to anybody, but one of those through whose mouth the king speaks, when he has something to say; and they told him that His Majesty wanted his litter, next day at dawn, to go to Catania, because he didn't want to be obliged, neither to the bishop nor to the lieutenant, but preferred to pay out of his own pocket, like anybody else.

Neighbor Cosimo ought to have been pleased, because it was his business to drive people in his litter, and at that very time he was waiting for somebody to come and hire his conveyance, and the king isn't one to stand and haggle for a dime more or less, like so many folks. But he would rather have gone back to Grammichele with his litter empty, it bothered him so much to have to carry the king in his litter, that the holiday all turned to poison for him at the mere thought of it, and he couldn't enjoy the illuminations any more, nor the band that was playing in the marketplace, nor the triumphal car that was going round the streets, with the picture of the king and queen, nor the church of San Giacomo all lit up, so that it was spitting out flames, and the Host was exposed inside, and the bells ringing for the king.

The grander the festival, the more frightened did he become of having to take the actual king in his litter, and all those squibs,[1] that crowd, those illuminations and that clash of bells simply went to his stomach, so that he couldn't close his eyes all night, but he spent it in examining the shoes of the bay mare, currycombing his mules, and stuffing them up to their throats with barley, to get their strength up, as if the king weighed twice as much as anybody else. The stables were full of cavalry soldiers, with huge spurs on their heels, which they didn't take off even when they threw themselves down to sleep on the planks, and on all the nails of the stable-posts were hung sabers and pistols so that it seemed to poor Uncle Cosimo that they were there to cut off his head, if by bad luck one of the mules should go and slip on the wet stones of the narrow street while he was carrying the king; and really there had poured such quantities of water out of the sky just on those particular days that the people must have been crazy mad to see the king, to come all the way to Caltagirone in such weather. For himself, sure as God's above, he'd rather have been in his own poor little house, where the mules were pinched for room in the stable, but where you could hear them munching their barley not far from the bed-head, and he'd willingly have paid the five-dollar piece which the king was due to fork out, to find himself in his own bed, with the door shut, and lying with his nose under the blankets, his wife busying herself around with the lamp in her hand, to settle up the house for the night.

At dawn the bugle of the soldiers ringing like a cock that knows the time made him start from his doze, and put the stables into a turmoil. The wagoners raised their heads from the pole they had laid down for a pillow, the dogs barked, and

[1] **squibs:** firecrackers.

the hostess put in an appearance from the hayloft, heavy with sleep, scratching her head. It was still dark as midnight, but people were going up and down the street as if it was Christmas night, and the hucksters near the fire, with their little paper lanterns in front of them, banged their knives on their benches to sell their almond-rock. Ah, how all the people who were buying toffee must be enjoying themselves at their festival, trailing round the streets tired and sleepy, waiting for the king, and as they saw the litter go by with its collar bells jingling and its woolen tassels, they opened their eyes and envied Neighbor Cosimo who had seen the king face to face, while nobody else had had so much luck up till then, not in all the forty-eight hours that the crowd had been waiting day and night in the streets, with the rain coming down as God sent it. The church of San Giacomo was still spitting fire and flame, at the top of the steps that there was no end to, waiting for the king to wish him Godspeed, and all its bells were ringing to tell him it was time for him to be going. Were they never going to put out those lights; and had the sexton an arm of iron, to keep on ringing day and night? Meanwhile in the flatlands of San Giacomo the ashen dawn had hardly come, and the valley was a sea of mist; and yet the crowd was thick as flies, with their noses in their cloaks, and the moment they saw the litter coming they wanted to suffocate Neighbor Cosimo and his mules, thinking the king was inside.

But the king kept them waiting a good bit still; perhaps at that moment he was pulling on his breeches, or drinking his little glass of brandy, to clear his throat, a thing that Neighbor Cosimo hadn't even thought of that morning, for all his throat felt so tight. An hour later arrived the cavalry with unsheathed sabers, and made way. Behind the cavalry rolled another wave of people, and then the band, and then again some gentlemen, and ladies in little hats, their noses red with cold; and even the hucksters came running up, with their little benches on their heads, to set up shop again; to try to sell a bit more almond toffee; so that in the big square you couldn't have got a pin in, and the mules wouldn't even have been able to shake the flies off, if the cavalry hadn't been there to make space; and so if you please the cavalry brought along with them a cloud of horseflies, those flies that send the mules in a litter right off their heads, so that Neighbor Cosimo commended himself to God and to the souls in purgatory every one he caught under the belly of his cattle.

At last the ringing was heard twice as loud, as if the bells had gone mad, and then the loud banging of crackers let off for the king, another flood of people came running up, and the carriage of the king appeared in sight, seeming to swim on the heads of the people in the midst of all that crowd. Then resounded the trumpets and drums, and the crackers began to explode again, till the mules, God save us, threatened to break the harness and everything, lashing out kicks; the soldiers drew their sabers, having sheathed them again, and the crowd shouted: "The queen, the queen! That little body there, beside her husband, you'd never believe it!"

But the king was a fine-built man, large and stout, with red trousers and a saber hanging at his stomach; and he drew behind him the bishop, the mayor, the lieutenant, and another bunch of gentlemen in gloves and white handkerchiefs folded around their necks, and dressed in black so that they must have felt spiders running in their bones, in that bit of a north wind that was sweeping the mist from the plain of San Giacomo. Now the king, before he mounted his horse, and while his wife was getting into the litter, was talking first to one then to another, as if it was no matter to him, and coming up to Neighbor Cosimo he clapped him on the shoulder, and told him just like this, in his Neapolitan way of talking, "Remember you are carrying your queen!" —so that Neighbor Cosimo felt his legs sinking back into his belly, the more so

that at that moment a frenzied cry was heard, the crowd swayed like a sea of ripe corn, and a young girl, still dressed like a nun and very pale, was seen to throw herself at the feet of the king and cry, "Pardon!" She was asking pardon for her father, who had been one of those who had had a hand in trying to pull the king down from the throne, and had been condemned to have his head cut off. The king spoke a word to one of those near him, and that was enough for them not to cut off the head of the girl's father. And so she rose quite happy, and then they had to carry her away in a faint, she was so glad.

Which was as good as saying that the king with one word could have anybody's head he liked cut off, even Neighbor Cosimo's, if a mule in the litter should chance to stumble and throw out his wife, bit of a thing as she was.

Poor Neighbor Cosimo had all this before his eyes as he walked beside his bay mule with his hand on the shaft, and a bit of Madonna's dress between his lips, recommending himself to God as if he was at death's door, while all the caravan, with king, queen, and soldiers, had started off on the journey amid the shouting and bell ringing, and the banging of the cannon cracker which you could still hear away down on the plain; and when they had come right down in the valley, on the top of the hill they could still see the black crowd teeming in the sun as if it was the cattle fair in the plain of San Giacomo.

But what good did Neighbor Cosimo get from the sun and the fine day? If his heart was blacker than a thundercloud, and he didn't dare raise his eyes from the cobblestones on which the mules put down their feet as if they were walking on eggs; nor could he look round to see how the corn was coming on, nor enjoy seeing the clusters of olives hanging along the hedges, nor think of what a lot of good all the last week's rain had done, while his heart was beating like a hammer at the mere thought that the torrent might be swollen, and they had got to cross the ford! He didn't dare to seat himself straddle-legs on the shafts, as he always did when he wasn't carrying his queen, and snatch forty winks under that fine sun and on that level road that the mules could have followed with their eyes shut; whilst the mules, who had no understanding and didn't know what they were carrying, were enjoying the dry level road, the mild sun, and the green country, wagging their hindquarters and shaking the collar bells cheerfully, and for two pins they would have started trotting, so that Neighbor Cosimo had his heart in his mouth with fright merely seeing his creatures growing lively, without a thought in the world neither for the queen nor anything.

The queen, for her part, kept up a chatter with another lady, whom they'd put in the litter to while away the time with her, in a language of which nobody understood a single damn; she looked round at the country with her eyes blue as flax flowers, and she rested a little hand on the window frame, so little that it seemed made on purpose to have nothing to do; and it certainly wasn't worth while having stuffed the mules with barley to carry that scrap of a thing, queen though she was! But she could have people's heads cut off with a single word, small though she might be, and the mules, who had no sense in them, what with that light load, and all that barley in their bellies, felt strongly tempted to start dancing and jumping along the road, and so get Neighbor Cosimo's head taken off for him.

So that the poor devil did nothing all the way but recite paternosters and ave marias between his teeth, and beseech the souls of his own dead, those whom he knew and those whom he didn't know, until they got to Zia Lisa, where a great crowd had gathered to see the king, and in front of every hole of a tavern there was their own side of pork skinned and hung up for the feast. When he got home at last, after having delivered the queen safe and sound, he couldn't believe it was true, and he kissed the edge of the manger as he tied up his mules, then he went to bed without eating or drinking, and didn't even want to see the queen's money, but would have left it in his jacket pocket for who knows how long, if it hadn't been for his wife who went and put it at the bottom of the stocking under the straw mattress.

His friends and acquaintances, curious to know how the king and queen were made, came to ask him about the journey, pretending they had come to inquire if he had caught malaria. But he wouldn't tell them anything, feeling himself in a fever again at the very mention of it, and the doctor came morning and evening, and charged him about half of that money from the queen.

Only many years later, when they came to seize his mules in the name of the king, because he couldn't pay his debts, Neighbor Cosimo couldn't rest for thinking that those were the very mules which had brought his wife safe and sound— the king's wife, that is—poor beasts; and in those days there were no carriage roads, so the queen would have broken her neck if it hadn't been for his litter, and people said that the king and queen had come to Sicily on purpose to make the roads, and still there weren't any yet, which was a dirty shame. But in those days litter drivers could make a living, and Neighbor Cosimo would have been able to pay his debts, and they wouldn't have seized his mules, if the king and queen hadn't come to make the high-roads.

And later, when they took away his Orazio, whom they called Turk, because he was so swarthy and strong, to make him an artilleryman, and that poor old woman of a wife of his wept like a fountain, there came to his mind again that girl who had come to throw herself at the feet of the king crying, "Pardon!"— and the king had sent her away happy with one word. Nor could you make him understand that there was another king now, and that they'd kicked out the old one. He said that if the king had been there, he'd have sent him away happy, him and his wife, because he had patted him on the shoulder, and he knew him and had seen him face to face, with his red trousers and his saber hung at his stomach, and with a word he could have people's heads cut off, and send to seize mules into the bargain, if anyone didn't pay his debts, and take the sons for soldiers, just as he pleased.

FOR STUDY AND DISCUSSION

1. What contrasts are set up among the three ways of life that come together at the festival: the daily, commonplace life of Cosimo; the festival life of the village; and the life of the king?

2. Is the clemency for the young nun's father an indication of the king's magnanimity? Explain.

3. What effect does the king have on the village? on Cosimo?

4. What is the significance of the king's costume? Why does Verga emphasize the queen's size?

5. What does the story say about Cosimo, the peasantry, the king, the monarchy, and the social order?

6. Whose "voice" seems to be telling this story? Is the point of view Cosimo's, or someone else's? Explain. How effective is this viewpoint in giving force to the story?

FOR COMPOSITION

The stories by Verga and Zola (see page 772) show people who are destroyed by forces they cannot control. In each case, what is the nature of these forces, and to what extent does the nature of the victim make him vulnerable to these forces? Are any of these characters more the victims of themselves than of outside circumstances? From your consideration of these questions, infer each author's idea of human nature and of the environment in which man has to find his way. In an essay, compare and contrast these writers' views.

Misery

ANTON CHEKHOV

To say that Anton Pavlovich Chekhov (1860–1904) was a prolific writer is an understatement, since he published over a thousand stories, as well as the five major plays from which his reputation mainly derives. A Russian, the grandson of a serf, Chekhov was trained as a doctor but soon gave up medicine in favor of writing. Like Maupassant, by whom he was influenced, Chekhov played a considerable part in the development of the short story. His principal contribution was the subtle and precise exploration of a mood or of a psychological state, often presented indirectly through a character's outward behavior. It has been said that Chekhov's writings apply, better than those of anyone else, to the words of critic Anatole France: "Russian fiction is largely the account of the undoing of human life, rather than of its shaping."

"To whom shall I tell my grief?"

THE TWILIGHT of the evening. Big flakes of wet snow are whirling lazily about the street lamps, which have just been lighted, and lying in a thin soft layer on roofs, horses' backs, shoulders, caps. Iona Potapov, the sledge driver, is all white like a ghost. He sits on the box without stirring, bent as double as the living body can be bent. If a regular snowdrift fell on him it seems as though even then he would not think it necessary to shake it off. . . . His little mare is white and motionless, too. Her stillness, the angularity of her lines, and the sticklike straightness of her legs make her look like a halfpenny gingerbread horse. She is probably lost in thought. Anyone who has been torn away from the plow, from the familiar gray landscapes, and cast into this slough, full of monstrous lights, of unceasing uproar and hurrying people, is bound to think.

It is a long time since Iona and his nag have budged. They came out of the yard before dinnertime, and not a single fare yet. But now the shades of evening are falling on the town. The pale light of the street lamps changes to a vivid color, and the bustle of the street grows noisier.

"Sledge to Vyborgskaya!" Iona hears. "Sledge!"

Iona starts, and through his snow-plastered eyelashes sees an officer in a military overcoat with a hood over his head.

"To Vyborgskaya," repeats the officer. "Are you asleep? To Vyborgskaya!"

In token of assent Iona gives a tug at the reins which sends cakes of snow flying from the horse's back and shoulders. The officer gets into the sledge. The sledge driver clicks to the horse, cranes his neck like a swan, rises in his seat, and more from habit than necessity brandishes his whip. The mare cranes her neck, too, crooks her sticklike legs, and hesitatingly sets off. . . .

"Where are you shoving, you devil?" Iona immediately hears shouts from the dark mass shifting to and fro before him. "Where the devil are you going? Keep to the r-right!"

"You don't know how to drive! Keep to the right," says the officer angrily.

A coachman driving a carriage swears at him; a pedestrian crossing the road and brushing the horse's nose with his shoulder looks at him angrily and shakes the snow off his sleeve. Iona fidgets on the box as though he were sitting on thorns, jerks his elbows, and turns his eyes about like one possessed, as though he did not know where he was or why he was there.

"What rascals they all are!" says the officer jocosely. "They are simply doing their best to run up against you or fall under the horse's feet. They must be doing it on purpose."

Iona looks at his fare and moves his lips. . . . Apparently he means to say something, but nothing comes but a sniff.

"What?" inquires the officer.

Iona gives a wry smile, and straining his throat, brings out huskily: "My son . . . er . . . my son died this week, sir."

"H'm! What did he die of?"

Iona turns his whole body round to his fare, and says:

"Who can tell! It must have been from fever. . . . He lay three days in the hospital and then he died. . . . God's will."

"Turn round, you devil!" comes out of the darkness. "Have you gone cracked, you old dog? Look where you are going!"

"Drive on! drive on! . . ." says the officer. "We shan't get there till tomorrow, going on like this. Hurry up!"

The sledge driver cranes his neck again, rises in his seat, and with heavy grace swings his whip. Several times he looks round at the officer, but the latter keeps his eyes shut and is apparently disinclined to listen. Putting his fare down at Vyborgskaya, Iona stops by a restaurant, and again sits huddled up on the box. . . .

Again the wet snow paints him and his horse white. One hour passes, and then another. . . .

Three young men, two tall and thin, one short and hunchbacked, come up, railing at each other and loudly stamping on the pavement with their galoshes.

"Cabby, to the Police Bridge!" the hunchback cries in a cracked voice. "The three of us . . . twenty kopecks!"

Iona tugs at the reins and clicks to his horse. Twenty kopecks is not a fair price, but he has no thoughts for that. Whether it is a ruble or whether it is five kopecks does not matter to him now so long as he has a fare. . . . The three young men, shoving each other and using bad language, go up to the sledge, and all three try to sit down at once. The question remains to be settled: Which are to sit down and which one is to stand? After a long altercation, ill-temper, and abuse, they come to the conclusion that the hunchback must stand because he is the shortest.

"Well, drive on," says the hunchback in his cracked voice, settling himself and breathing down Iona's neck. "Cut along! What a cap you've got, my friend! You wouldn't find a worse one in all Petersburg. . . ."

"He-he! . . . he-he! . . ." laughs Iona. "It's nothing to boast of!"

"Well, then, nothing to boast of, drive on! Are you going to drive like this all the way? Eh? Shall I give you one in the neck?"

"My head aches," says one of the tall ones. "At the Dukmasovs' yesterday Vaska and I drank four bottles of brandy between us."

"I can't make out why you talk such stuff," says the other tall one angrily. "You lie like a brute."

"Strike me dead, it's the truth! . . ."

"It's about as true as that a louse coughs."

"He-he!" grins Iona. "Me-er-ry gentlemen!"

"Tfoo! the devil take you!" cries the hunchback indignantly. "Will you get on, you old plague, or won't you? Is that the way to drive? Give her one with the whip. Hang it all! give it her well."

Iona feels behind his back the jolting person and quivering voice of the hunchback. He hears abuse addressed to him, he sees people, and the feeling of loneliness begins little by little to be less heavy on his heart. The hunchback swears at him, till he chokes over some elaborately whimsical string of epithets and is overpowered by his cough. His tall companions begin talking of a certain Nadyezhda Petrovna. Iona looks round at them. Waiting till there is a brief pause, he looks round once more and says:

"This week . . . er . . . my . . . er . . . son died!"

"We shall all die, . . ." says the hunchback with a sigh, wiping his lips after coughing. "Come, drive on! drive on! My friends, I simply cannot stand crawling like this! When will he get us there?"

"Well, you give him a little encouragement . . . one in the neck!"

"Do you hear, you old plague? I'll make you smart. If one stands on ceremony with fellows like you, one may as well walk. Do you hear, you old dragon? Or don't you care a hang what we say?"

And Iona hears rather than feels a slap on the back of his neck.

"He-he! . . ." he laughs. "Merry gentlemen . . . God give you health!"

"Cabman, are you married?" asks one of the tall ones.

"I? He-he! Me-er-ry gentlemen. The only wife for me now is the damp earth. . . . He-ho-ho! . . . The grave that is! . . . Here my son's dead and I am alive. . . . It's a strange thing, death has come in at the wrong door. . . . Instead of coming for me it went for my son. . . ."

And Iona turns round to tell them how his son died, but at that point the hunchback gives a faint sigh and announces that, thank God! they have arrived at last. After taking his twenty kopecks, Iona gazes for a long while after the revelers, who disappear into a dark entry. Again he is alone and again there is silence for him.

. . . The misery which has been for a brief space eased comes back again and tears his heart more cruelly than ever. With a look of anxiety and suffering Iona's eyes stray restlessly among the crowds moving to and fro on both sides of the street: can he not find among those thousands someone who will listen to him? But the crowds flit by heedless of him and his misery. . . . His misery is immense, beyond all bounds. If Iona's heart were to burst and his misery to flow out, it would flood the whole world, it seems, but yet it is not seen. It has found a hiding place in such an insignificant shell that one would not have found it with a candle by daylight. . . .

Iona sees a house porter with a parcel and makes up his mind to address him.

"What time will it be, friend?" he asks.

"Going on for ten. . . . Why have you stopped here? Drive on!"

Iona drives a few paces away, bends himself double, and gives himself up to his misery. He feels it is no good to appeal to people. But before five minutes have passed he draws himself up, shakes his head as though he feels a sharp pain, and tugs at the reins. . . . He can bear it no longer.

"Back to the yard!" he thinks. "To the yard!"

And his little mare, as though she knew his thoughts, falls to trotting. An hour and a half later Iona is sitting by a big dirty stove. On the stove, on the floor, and on the benches are people snoring. The air is full of smells and stuffiness. Iona looks at the sleeping figures, scratches himself, and regrets that he has come home so early. . . .

"I have not earned enough to pay for the oats, even," he thinks. "That's why I am so miserable. A man who knows how to do his work . . . who has had enough to eat, and whose horse has had enough to eat, is always at ease. . . ."

In one of the corners a young cabman gets up, clears his throat sleepily, and makes for the water bucket.

"Want a drink?" Iona asks him.

"Seems so."

"May it do you good.... But my son is dead, mate.... Do you hear? This week in the hospital.... It's a queer business...."

Iona looks to see the effect produced by his words, but he sees nothing. The young man has covered his head over and is already asleep. The old man sighs and scratches himself.... Just as the young man had been thirsty for water, he thirsts for speech. His son will soon have been dead a week, and he has not really talked to anybody yet.... He wants to talk of it properly, with deliberation.... He wants to tell how his son was taken ill, how he suffered, what he said before he died, how he died.... He wants to describe the funeral, and how he went to the hospital to get his son's clothes. He still has his daughter Anisya in the country.... And he wants to talk about her, too.... Yes, he has plenty to talk about now. His listener ought to sigh and exclaim and lament.... It would be even better to talk to women. Though they are silly creatures, they blubber at the first word.

"Let's go out and have a look at the mare," Iona thinks. "There is always time for sleep.... You'll have sleep enough, no fear...."

He puts on his coat and goes into the stables where his mare is standing. He thinks about oats, about hay, about the weather.... He cannot think about his son when he is alone.... To talk about him with someone is possible, but to think of him and picture him is insufferable anguish....

"Are you munching?" Iona asks his mare, seeing her shining eyes. "There, munch away, munch away.... Since we have not earned enough for oats, we will eat hay.... Yes... I have grown too old to drive.... My son ought to be driving, not I.... He was a real cabman.... He ought to have lived...."

Iona is silent for a while, and then he goes on:

"That's how it is, old girl.... Kuzma Ionitch is gone.... He said good-by to me.... He went and died for no reason.... Now, suppose you had a little colt, and you were own mother to that little colt.... And all at once that same little colt went and died.... You'd be sorry, wouldn't you?..."

The little mare munches, listens, and breathes on her master's hands. Iona is carried away and tells her all about it.

FOR STUDY AND DISCUSSION

1. How is the initial image of the man and the horse significant to the rest of the story? How is it complemented by the closing image of the story?

2. The narrator remarks at the beginning: "Anyone who has been torn away from the plow, from the familiar gray landscapes, and cast into this slough, full of monstrous lights, of unceasing uproar and hurrying people, is bound to think." What has the contrast between country and city to do with the theme of the story?

3. What is the effect of one of the passengers' being a hunchback? What is significant in the way the three passengers behave toward one another and toward the cabdriver?

4. Trace the development of Iona's attempts to share his grief. What significance is attached to his final solution at the end of the story?

5. Is there any evidence that Chekhov intends to suggest certain attitudes toward the classes to which several individuals in the story belong? Explain. How does this story compare or contrast with Verga's in this respect?

6. Is there any evidence that Chekhov felt that Iona should have stood up more manfully or more bravely to the misfortune that had come into his life? Explain. What attitude toward life and toward sensitive individuals is found beneath the surface of this story?

FOR COMPOSITION

Many selections in this anthology deal with sorrow. Write an essay in which you compare or contrast the sorrow expressed in Tu Fu's poem "Loneliness" (page 278), the sorrow expressed in Tennyson's poem "Tears, Idle Tears" (page 760), and the sorrow expressed by Chekhov in "Misery." What images drawn from nature does each writer associate with sorrow?

An Enemy of the People

HENRIK IBSEN

"The righteous heard of him with creepy shudders," wrote American critic H. L. Mencken; "there was bold talk of denying him the use of the mails." The man who caused all this uproar in a distant and more proper era was Norwegian dramatist Henrik Ibsen (1828–1906).

Most of the plays that made Ibsen famous date from the 1880's, when he was in his fifties. But he had been associated with the theater since he was twenty-three, when he went to the northern provincial town of Bergen to be stage manager and resident playwright for the state theater. Like Shakespeare and Molière, Ibsen had thorough training in all aspects of the theater, both at Bergen and later in the national capital (then Christiania, now Oslo).

Most of his early work *(Peer Gynt,* as the best example) had taken its subject matter from the Romantic legends of Norway's ancient past, but Ibsen found his real style when he turned away from romance and from Norway itself. In 1864, irritated by the political controversy that had brought about the failure of the Christiania theater and disgusted with the smug bourgeois society of his country, Ibsen went to the more cosmopolitan city of Rome. To Ibsen, this contact with the larger world of Europe was a liberation, and here he began to write a new kind of drama to raise critical questions about the problems of society.

Ibsen had long been interested in the movements for social reform which were taking place all across Europe, in the psychology of the subconscious, which would later take the name Freudian, and in the Darwinian concepts of the evolution of life and of social organization. All these new ideas informed Ibsen's analysis of society and of individuals, and he revolutionized drama to give expression to this analysis. Ibsen abandoned the artificial tricks used by other dramatists to make their complicated plots work out smoothly. Rather than let a story be carefully told by "couriers and prattling chambermaids" (in Mencken's words), Ibsen let his story reveal itself. Utterly Realistic in situations, speech, and sets, Ibsen's plays didn't soothe the audience; they shocked. They weren't diverting entertainments; they were life itself. Ibsen's style became the dominant one for dramatists of the twentieth century; it is only in recent years, in fact, that the theater has, in any important way, turned away from it.

Ibsen's new kind of Realistic, "problem" play made a distinct impact with *A Doll's House,* a play in which the heroine rebels against the degrading and wasteful role in which bourgeois society entraps women. The play that culminated Ibsen's career was *Hedda Gabler.* This play, too, is about a woman who refuses to accept her passive role, and out of frustration she is driven into complex psychological distortions which result in the destruction of the lives of those around her and finally of herself.

An Enemy of the People was written partly as a retort to the shower of abuse heaped on Ibsen for his play *Ghosts,* which not only deals with the taboo subject of venereal disease, but also shows that "respectable" society tolerates a hypocritical moral code. In *An Enemy of the People,* the hero's conflict with the townspeople is like Ibsen's battle with a public which refused to face reality.

Characters

DR. THOMAS STOCKMANN, *medical officer of the municipal baths*
MRS. STOCKMANN, *his wife*
PETRA, *their daughter, a teacher*
EJLIF
MORTEN } *their sons (aged thirteen and ten respectively)*
PETER STOCKMANN, *the doctor's elder brother; mayor of the town and chief constable, a chairman of the Baths' Committee, etc., etc.*
MORTEN KIIL, *a tanner (*MRS. STOCKMANN'S *adoptive father)*
HOVSTAD, *editor of the* People's Messenger
BILLING, *subeditor*
CAPTAIN HORSTER
ASLAKSEN, *a printer*
MEN *of various conditions and occupations, some few* WOMEN, *and a troop of* SCHOOLBOYS—*the audience at a public meeting*

The action takes place in a coast town in southern Norway.

ACT I

SCENE: *Dr. Stockmann's sitting room. It is evening. The room is plainly but neatly appointed and furnished. In the right-hand wall are two doors; the farther leads out to the hall, the nearer to the doctor's study. In the left-hand wall, opposite the door leading to the hall, is a door leading to the other rooms occupied by the family. In the middle of the same wall stands the stove, and, further forward, a couch with a looking glass hanging over it and an oval table in front of it. On the table is a lighted lamp, with a lampshade. At the back of the room, an open door leads to the dining room.* BILLING *is seen sitting at the dinner table, on which a lamp is burning. He has a napkin tucked under his chin, and* MRS. STOCKMANN *is standing by the table handing him a large plateful of roast beef. The other places at the table are empty, and the table somewhat in disorder, a meal having evidently recently been finished.*

From *Ghosts, An Enemy of the People, The Warriors at Helgeland* by Henrik Ibsen, translated by R. Farquharson Sharp. Everymans' Library Edition. Reprinted by permission of E. P. Dutton & Co., Inc., and J. M. Dent & Sons Ltd., Publishers.

MRS. STOCKMANN. You see, if you come an hour late, Mr. Billing, you have to put up with cold meat.

BILLING *(as he eats).* It is uncommonly good, thank you—remarkably good.

MRS. STOCKMANN. My husband makes such a point of having his meals punctually, you know—

BILLING. That doesn't affect me a bit. Indeed, I almost think I enjoy a meal all the better when I can sit down and eat all by myself and undisturbed.

MRS. STOCKMANN. Oh, well, as long as you are enjoying it— *(Turns to the hall door, listening.)* I expect that is Mr. Hovstad coming, too.

BILLING. Very likely.

[PETER STOCKMANN *comes in. He wears an overcoat and his official hat, and carries a stick.*]

PETER STOCKMANN. Good evening, Katherine.

MRS. STOCKMANN *(coming forward into the sitting room).* Ah, good evening—is it you? How good of you to come up and see us!

PETER STOCKMANN. I happened to be passing, and so— *(Looks into the dining room.)* But you have company with you, I see.

MRS. STOCKMANN *(a little embarrassed)*. Oh, no—it was quite by chance he came in. *(Hurriedly.)* Won't you come in and have something, too?

PETER STOCKMANN. I! No, thank you. Good gracious—hot meat at night! Not with my digestion.

MRS. STOCKMANN. Oh, but just once in a way—

PETER STOCKMANN. No, no, my dear lady; I stick to my tea and bread and butter. It is much more wholesome in the long run—and a little more economical, too.

MRS. STOCKMANN *(smiling)*. Now you mustn't think that Thomas and I are spendthrifts.

PETER STOCKMANN. Not you, my dear; I would never think that of you. *(Points to the doctor's study.)* Is he not at home?

MRS. STOCKMANN. No, he went out for a little turn after supper—he and the boys.

PETER STOCKMANN. I doubt if that is a wise thing to do. *(Listens.)* I fancy I hear him coming now.

MRS. STOCKMANN. Now, I don't think it is he. *(A knock is heard at the door.)* Come in! (HOVSTAD *comes in from the hall.)* Oh, it is you, Mr. Hovstad!

HOVSTAD. Yes, I hope you will forgive me, but I was delayed at the printer's. Good evening, Mr. Mayor.

PETER STOCKMANN *(bowing a little distantly)*. Good evening. You have come on business, no doubt.

HOVSTAD. Partly. It's about an article for the paper.

PETER STOCKMANN. So I imagined. I hear my brother has become a prolific contributor to the *People's Messenger*.

HOVSTAD. Yes, he is good enough to write in the *People's Messenger* when he has any home truths to tell.

MRS. STOCKMANN *(to HOVSTAD)*. But won't you—? *(Points to the dining room.)*

PETER STOCKMANN. Quite so, quite so. I don't blame him in the least, as a writer, for addressing himself to the quarters where he will find the readiest sympathy. And, besides that, I personally have no reason to bear any ill will to your paper, Mr. Hovstad.

HOVSTAD. I quite agree with you.

PETER STOCKMANN. Taking one thing with another, there is an excellent spirit of toleration in the town—an admirable municipal spirit. And it all springs from the fact of our having a great common interest to unite us—an interest that is in an equally high degree the concern of every rightminded citizen—

HOVSTAD. The baths, yes.

PETER STOCKMANN. Exactly—our fine, new, handsome baths. Mark my words, Mr. Hovstad—the baths will become the focus of our municipal life! Not a doubt of it!

MRS. STOCKMANN. That is just what Thomas says.

PETER STOCKMANN. Think how extraordinarily the place has developed within the last year or two! Money has been flowing in, and there is some life and some business doing in the town. Houses and landed property are rising in value every day.

HOVSTAD. And unemployment is diminishing.

PETER STOCKMANN. Yes, that is another thing. The burden of the poor rates has been lightened, to the great relief of the propertied classes; and that relief will be even greater if only we get a really good summer this year, and lots of visitors—plenty of invalids, who will make the baths talked about.

HOVSTAD. And there is a good prospect of that, I hear.

PETER STOCKMANN. It looks very promising. Inquiries about apartments and that sort of thing are reaching us every day.

HOVSTAD. Well, the doctor's article will come in very suitably.

PETER STOCKMANN. Has he been writing something just lately?

HOVSTAD. This is something he wrote in the winter; a recommendation of the baths—an account of the excellent sanitary conditions here. But I held the article over, temporarily.

PETER STOCKMANN. Ah—some little difficulty about it, I suppose?

HOVSTAD. No, not at all; I thought it would be better to wait till the spring, because it is just at this time that people begin to think seriously about their summer quarters.

PETER STOCKMANN. Quite right; you were perfectly right, Mr. Hovstad.

HOVSTAD. Yes, Thomas is really indefatigable when it is a question of the baths.

PETER STOCKMAN. Well—remember, he is the medical officer to the baths.

HOVSTAD. Yes, and what is more, they owe their existence to him.

PETER STOCKMANN. To him? Indeed! It is true I have heard from time to time that some people are of that opinion. At the same time I must say I imagined that I took a modest part in the enterprise.

MRS. STOCKMANN. Yes, that is what Thomas is always saying.

HOVSTAD. But who denies it, Mr. Stockmann? You set the thing going and made a practical concern of it; we all know that. I only meant that the idea of it came first from the doctor.

PETER STOCKMANN. Oh, ideas—yes! My brother has had plenty of them in his time—unfortunately. But when it is a question of putting an idea into practical shape, you have to apply to a man of different mettle, Mr. Hovstad. And I certainly should have thought that in this house at least—

MRS. STOCKMANN. My dear Peter—

HOVSTAD. How can you think that—?

MRS. STOCKMANN. Won't you go in and have something, Mr. Hovstad? My husband is sure to be back directly.

HOVSTAD. Thank you, perhaps just a morsel.   [*Goes into the dining room.*]

PETER STOCKMANN (*lowering his voice a little*). It is a curious thing that these farmers' sons never seem to lose their want of tact.

MRS. STOCKMANN. Surely it is not worth bothering about! Cannot you and Thomas share the credit as brothers?

PETER STOCKMANN. I should have thought so; but apparently some people are not satisfied with a share.

MRS. STOCKMANN. What nonsense! You and Thomas get on so capitally together. (*Listens.*) There he is at last, I think.

[*Goes out and opens the door leading to the hall.*]

DR. STOCKMANN (*laughing and talking outside*). Look here—here is another guest for you, Katherine. Isn't that jolly! Come in, Captain Horster; hang your coat up on this peg. Ah, you don't wear an overcoat. Just think, Katherine; I met him in the street and could hardly persuade him to come up! (CAPTAIN HORSTER *comes into the room and greets* MRS. STOCKMANN. *He is followed by* DR. STOCKMANN.) Come along in, boys. They are ravenously hungry again, you know. Come along, Captain Horster; you must have a slice of beef.

[*Pushes* HORSTER *into the dining room.* EJLIF *and* MORTEN *go in after them.*]

MRS. STOCKMANN. But, Thomas, don't you see—?

DR. STOCKMANN (*turning in the doorway*). Oh, is it you, Peter? (*Shakes hands with him.*) Now that is very delightful.

PETER STOCKMANN. Unfortunately I must go in a moment—

DR. STOCKMANN. Rubbish! There is some toddy just coming in. You haven't forgotten the toddy, Katherine?

MRS. STOCKMANN. Of course not; the water is boiling now.

[*Goes into the dining room.*]

PETER STOCKMANN. Toddy too!

DR. STOCKMANN. Yes, sit down and we will have it comfortably.

PETER STOCKMANN. Thanks, I never care about an evening's drinking.

DR. STOCKMANN. But this isn't an evening's drinking.

PETER STOCKMANN. It seems to me— (*Looks toward the dining room.*) It is extraordinary how they can put away all that food.

DR. STOCKMANN (*rubbing his hands*). Yes, isn't it splendid to see young people eat? They have always got an appetite, you know! That's as it should be. Lots of food—to build up their strength! They are the people who are going to stir up the fermenting forces of the future, Peter.

PETER STOCKMANN. May I ask what they will find here to "stir up," as you put it?

DR. STOCKMANN. Ah, you must ask the young people that—when the time comes. We shan't be able to see it, of course. That stands to reason—two old fogies, like us—

PETER STOCKMANN. Really, really! I must say that is an extremely odd expression to—

DR. STOCKMANN. Oh, you mustn't take me too literally, Peter. I am so heartily happy and contented, you know. I think it is such an extraordinary piece of good fortune to be in the middle of all this growing, germinating life. It is a splendid time to live in! It is as if a whole new world were being created around one.

PETER STOCKMANN. Do you really think so?

DR. STOCKMANN. Ah, naturally you can't appreciate it as keenly as I. You have lived all your life in these surroundings, and your impressions have got blunted. But I, who have been buried all these years in my little corner up north, almost without ever seeing a stranger who might bring new ideas with him—well, in my case it has just the same effect as if I had been transported into the middle of a crowded city.

PETER STOCKMANN. Oh, a city—!

DR. STOCKMANN. I know, I know; it is all cramped enough here, compared with many other places. But there is life here—there is promise—there are innumerable things to work for and fight for; and that is the main thing. (Calls.) Katherine, hasn't the postman been here?

MRS. STOCKMANN (from the dining room). No.

DR. STOCKMANN. And then to be comfortably off, Peter! That is something one learns to value, when one has been on the brink of starvation, as we have.

PETER STOCKMANN. Oh, surely—

DR. STOCKMANN. Indeed I can assure you we have often been very hard put to it, up there. And now to be able to live like a lord! Today, for instance, we had roast beef for dinner—and, what is more, for supper too. Won't you come and have a little bit? Or let me show it you, at any rate? Come here—

PETER STOCKMANN. No, no—not for worlds!

DR. STOCKMANN. Well, but just come here then. Do you see, we have got a table cover?

PETER STOCKMANN. Yes, I noticed it.

DR. STOCKMANN. And we have got a lampshade too. Do you see? All out of Katherine's savings! It makes the room so cozy. Don't you think so? Just stand here for a moment—no, no, not there—just here, that's it! Look now, when you get the light on it altogether—I really think it looks very nice, doesn't it?

PETER STOCKMANN. Oh, if you can afford luxuries of this kind—

DR. STOCKMANN. Yes, I can afford it now. Katherine tells me I earn almost as much as we spend.

PETER STOCKMANN. Almost—yes!

DR. STOCKMANN. But a scientific man must live in a little bit of style. I am quite sure an ordinary civil servant spends more in a year than I do.

PETER STOCKMANN. I dare say. A civil servant—a man in a well-paid position—

DR. STOCKMANN. Well, any ordinary merchant, then! A man in that position spends two or three times as much as—

PETER STOCKMANN. It just depends on circumstances.

DR. STOCKMANN. At all events I assure you I don't waste money unprofitably. But I can't find it in my heart to deny myself the pleasure of entertaining my friends. I need that sort of thing, you know. I have lived for so long shut out of it all, that it is a necessity of life to me to mix with young, eager, ambitious men, men of liberal and active minds; and that describes every one of those fellows who are enjoying their supper in there. I wish you knew more of Hovstad—

PETER STOCKMANN. By the way, Hovstad was telling me he was going to print another article of yours.

DR. STOCKMANN. An article of mine?

PETER STOCKMANN. Yes, about the baths. An article you wrote in the winter.

DR. STOCKMANN. Oh, that one! No, I don't intend that to appear just for the present.

PETER STOCKMANN. Why not? It seems to me that this would be the most opportune moment.

DR. STOCKMANN. Yes, very likely—under normal conditions.

[Crosses the room.]

PETER STOCKMANN (following him with his eyes). Is there anything abnormal about the present conditions?

DR. STOCKMANN (standing still). To tell you the truth, Peter, I can't say just at this moment—at all events not tonight. There may be much that is very abnormal about the present conditions—and it is possible there may be nothing abnormal about them at all. It is quite possible it may be merely my imagination.

PETER STOCKMANN. I must say it all sounds most mysterious. Is there something going on that I am to be kept in ignorance of? I should have imagined that I, as chairman of the governing body of the baths—

DR. STOCKMANN. And I should have imagined that I— Oh, come, don't let us fly out at one another, Peter.

PETER STOCKMANN. Heaven forbid! I am not in the habit of flying out at people, as you call it. But I am entitled to request most emphatically that all arrangements shall be made in a businesslike manner, through the proper channels, and shall be dealt with by the legally constituted authorities. I can allow no going behind our backs by any roundabout means.

DR. STOCKMANN. Have I ever at any time tried to go behind your backs!

PETER STOCKMANN. You have an in-grained tendency to take your own way, at all events; and that is almost equally inadmissible in a well-ordered community. The individual ought undoubtedly to acquiesce in subordinating himself to the community—or, to speak more accurately, to the authorities who have the care of the community's welfare.

DR. STOCKMANN. Very likely. But what the deuce has all this got to do with me?

PETER STOCKMANN. That is exactly what you never appear to be willing to learn, my dear Thomas. But, mark my words, some day you will have to suffer for it—sooner or later. Now I have told you. Good-by.

DR. STOCKMANN. Have you taken leave of your senses? You are on the wrong scent altogether.

PETER STOCKMANN. I am not usually that. You must excuse me now if I— (Calls into the dining room.) Good night, Katherine. Good night, gentlemen.

[Goes out.]

MRS. STOCKMANN (coming from the dining room). Has he gone?

DR. STOCKMANN. Yes, and in such a bad temper.

MRS. STOCKMANN. But dear Thomas, what have you been doing to him again?

DR. STOCKMANN. Nothing at all. And, anyhow, he can't oblige me to make my report before the proper time.

MRS. STOCKMANN. What have you got to make a report to him about?

DR. STOCKMANN. Hm! Leave that to me, Katherine. —It is an extraordinary thing that the postman doesn't come.

[HOVSTAD, BILLING, and HORSTER have got up from the table and come into the sitting room. EJLIF and MORTEN come in after them.]

BILLING (stretching himself). Ah!—one feels a new man after a meal like that.

HOVSTAD. The mayor wasn't in a very sweet temper tonight, then.

DR. STOCKMANN. It is his stomach; he has a wretched digestion.

HOVSTAD. I rather think it was us two of

the *People's Messenger* that he couldn't digest.

MRS. STOCKMANN. I thought you came out of it pretty well with him.

HOVSTAD. Oh yes; but it isn't anything more than a sort of truce.

BILLING. That is just what it is! That word sums up the situation.

DR. STOCKMANN. We must remember that Peter is a lonely man, poor chap. He has no home comforts of any kind; nothing but everlasting business. And all that infernal weak tea wash that he pours into himself! Now then, my boys, bring chairs up to the table. Aren't we going to have that toddy, Katherine?

MRS. STOCKMANN (*going into the dining room*). I am just getting it.

DR. STOCKMANN. Sit down here on the couch beside me, Captain Horster. We so seldom see you— Please sit down, my friends.

[*They sit down at the table. MRS. STOCK-MANN brings a tray, with a spirit lamp, glasses, bottles, etc., upon it.*]

MRS. STOCKMANN. There you are! This is arrack, and this is rum, and this one is the brandy. Now everyone must help himself.

DR. STOCKMANN (*taking a glass*). We will. (*They all mix themselves some toddy.*) And let us have the cigars. Ejlif, you know where the box is. And you, Morten, can fetch my pipe. (*The two boys go into the room on the right.*) I have a suspicion that Ejlif pockets a cigar now and then!—but I take no notice of it. (*Calls out.*) And my smoking cap too, Morten. Katherine, you can tell him where I left it. Ah, he has got it. (*The boys bring the various things.*) Now, my friends. I stick to my pipe, you know. This one has seen plenty of bad weather with me up north. (*Touches glasses with them*). Your good health! Ah! it is good to be sitting snug and warm here.

MRS. STOCKMANN (*who sits knitting*). Do you sail soon, Captain Horster?

HORSTER. I expect to be ready to sail next week.

MRS. STOCKMANN. I suppose you are going to America?

HORSTER. Yes, that is the plan.

MRS. STOCKMANN. Then you won't be able to take part in the coming election.

HORSTER. Is there going to be an election?

BILLING. Didn't you know?

HORSTER. No, I don't mix myself up with those things.

BILLING. But do you not take an interest in public affairs?

HORSTER. No, I don't know anything about politics.

BILLING. All the same, one ought to vote, at any rate.

HORSTER. Even if one doesn't know anything about what is going on?

BILLING. Doesn't know! What do you mean by that? A community is like a ship; everyone ought to be prepared to take the helm.

HORSTER. Maybe that is all very well on shore; but on board ship it wouldn't work.

HOVSTAD. It is astonishing how little most sailors care about what goes on on shore.

BILLING. Very extraordinary.

DR. STOCKMANN. Sailors are like birds of passage; they feel equally at home in any latitude. And that is only an additional reason for our being all the more keen, Hovstad. Is there to be anything of public interest in tomorrow's *Messenger?*

HOVSTAD. Nothing about municipal affairs. But the day after tomorrow I was thinking of printing your article—

DR. STOCKMANN. Ah, devil take it— my article! Look here, that must wait a bit.

HOVSTAD. Really? We had just got convenient space for it, and I thought it just the opportune moment—

DR. STOCKMANN. Yes, yes, very likely you are right; but it must wait all the same. I will explain to you later.

[PETRA *comes in from the hall, in hat and cloak and with a bundle of exercise books under her arm.*]

PETRA. Good evening.

DR. STOCKMANN. Good evening, Petra; come along.

[*Mutual greetings;* PETRA *takes off her things and puts them down on a chair by the door.*]

PETRA. And you have all been sitting here enjoying yourselves, while I have been out slaving!

DR. STOCKMANN. Well, come and enjoy yourself too!

BILLING. May I mix a glass for you?

PETRA (*coming to the table*). Thanks, I would rather do it; you always mix it too strong. But I forgot, Father—I have a letter for you.

[*Goes to the chair where she has laid her things.*]

DR. STOCKMANN. A letter? From whom?

PETRA (*looking in her coat pocket*). The postman gave it to me just as I was going out—

DR. STOCKMANN (*getting up and going to her*). And you only give to me now!

PETRA. I really had not time to run up again. There it is!

DR. STOCKMANN (*seizing the letter*). Let's see, let's see, child! (*Looks at the address.*) Yes, that's all right!

MRS. STOCKMANN. Is it the one you have been expecting so anxiously, Thomas?

DR. STOCKMANN. Yes, it is. I must go to my room now and— Where shall I get a light, Katherine? Is there no lamp in my room again?

MRS. STOCKMANN. Yes, your lamp is already lit on your desk.

DR. STOCKMANN. Good, good. Excuse me for a moment— [*Goes into his study.*]

PETRA. What do you suppose it is, Mother?

MRS. STOCKMANN. I don't know; for the last day or two he has always been asking if the postman has not been.

BILLING. Probably some country patient.

PETRA. Poor old Dad!—he will over-

work himself soon. (*Mixes a glass for herself.*) There, that will taste good!

HOVSTAD. Have you been teaching in the evening school again today?

PETRA (*sipping from her glass*). Two hours.

BILLING. And four hours of school in the morning—

PETRA. Five hours.

MRS. STOCKMANN. And you have still got exercises to correct, I see.

PETRA. A whole heap, yes.

HORSTER. You are pretty full up with work too, it seems to me.

PETRA. Yes—but that is good. One is so delightfully tired after it.

BILLING. Do you like that?

PETRA. Yes, because one sleeps so well then.

MORTEN. You must be dreadfully wicked, Petra.

PETRA. Wicked?

MORTEN. Yes, because you work so much. Mr. Rörlund says work is a punishment for our sins.

EJLIF. Pooh, what a duffer you are, to believe a thing like that!

MRS. STOCKMANN. Come, come, Ejlif!

BILLING (*laughing*). That's capital!

HOVSTAD. Don't you want to work as hard as that, Morten?

MORTEN. No, indeed I don't.

HOVSTAD. What do you want to be, then?

MORTEN. I should like best to be a Viking.

EJLIF. You would have to be a pagan then.

MORTEN. Well, I could become a pagan, couldn't I?

BILLING. I agree with you, Morten! My sentiments, exactly.

MRS. STOCKMANN (*signaling to him*). I am sure that is not true, Mr. Billing.

BILLING. Yes, I swear it is! I am a pagan, and I am proud of it. Believe me, before long we shall all be pagans.

MORTEN. And then shall be allowed to do anything we like?

BILLING. Well, you see, Morten—

MRS. STOCKMANN. You must go to your

room now, boys; I am sure you have some lessons to learn for tomorrow.

EJLIF. I should like so much to stay a little longer—

MRS. STOCKMANN. No, no; away you go, both of you.

[*The boys say good night and go into the room on the left.*]

HOVSTAD. Do you really think it can do the boys any harm to hear such things?

MRS. STOCKMANN. I don't know; but I don't like it.

PETRA. But you know, Mother, I think you really are wrong about it.

MRS. STOCKMANN. Maybe, but I don't like it—not in our own home.

PETRA. There is so much falsehood both at home and at school. At home one must not speak, and at school we have to stand and tell lies to the children.

HORSTER. Tell lies?

PETRA. Yes, don't you suppose we have to teach them all sorts of things that we don't believe?

BILLING. That is perfectly true.

PETRA. If only I had the means I would start a school of my own, and it would be conducted on very different lines.

BILLING. Oh, bother the means—!

HORSTER. Well if you are thinking of that, Miss Stockmann, I shall be delighted to provide you with a schoolroom. The great big old house my father left me is standing almost empty; there is an immense dining room downstairs—

PETRA (*laughing*). Thank you very much; but I am afraid nothing will come of it.

HOVSTAD. No, Miss Petra is much more likely to take to journalism, I expect. By the way, have you had time to do anything with that English story you promised to translate for us?

PETRA. No, not yet; but you shall have it in good time.

[DR. STOCKMANN *comes in from his room with an open letter in his hand.*]

DR. STOCKMANN (*waving the letter*).

Well, now the town will have something new to talk about, I can tell you!

BILLING. Something new?

MRS. STOCKMANN. What is this?

DR. STOCKMANN. A great discovery, Katherine.

HOVSTAD. Really?

MRS. STOCKMANN. A discovery of yours?

DR. STOCKMANN. A discovery of mine. (*Walks up and down.*) Just let them come saying, as usual, that it is all fancy and a crazy man's imagination! But they will be careful what they say this time, I can tell you!

PETRA. But, Father, tell us what it is.

DR. STOCKMANN. Yes, yes—only give me time, and you shall know all about it. If only I had Peter here now! It just shows how we men can go about forming our judgments, when in reality we are as blind as any moles—

HOVSTAD. What are you driving at, Doctor?

DR. STOCKMANN (*standing still by the table*). Isn't it the universal opinion that our town is a healthy spot?

HOVSTAD. Certainly.

DR. STOCKMANN. Quite an unusually healthy spot, in fact—a place that deserves to be recommended in the warmest possible manner either for invalids or for people who are well—

MRS. STOCKMANN. Yes, but my dear Thomas—

DR. STOCKMANN. And we have been recommending it and praising it—I have written and written, both in the *Messenger* and in pamphlets—

HOVSTAD. Well, what then?

DR. STOCKMANN. And the baths—we have called them the "main artery of the town's life-blood," the "nerve center of our town," and the devil knows what else—

BILLING. "The town's pulsating heart" was the expression I once used on an important occasion—

DR. STOCKMANN. Quite so. Well, do you know what they really are, these great, splendid, much-praised baths, that have cost so much money—do you know what they are?

HOVSTAD. No, what are they?

MRS. STOCKMANN. Yes, what are they?

DR. STOCKMANN. The whole place is a pesthouse!

PETRA. The baths, Father?

MRS. STOCKMANN (at the same time). Our baths!

HOVSTAD. But, Doctor—

BILLING. Absolutely incredible!

DR. STOCKMANN. The whole bath establishment is a whited, poisoned sepulcher, I tell you—the gravest possible danger to the public health! All the nastiness up at Mölledal, all that stinking filth, is infecting the water in the conduit pipes leading to the reservoir; and the same cursed, filthy poison oozes out on the shore too—

HORSTER. Where the bathing place is?

DR. STOCKMANN. Just there.

HOVSTAD. How do you come to be so certain of all this, Doctor?

DR. STOCKMANN. I have investigated the matter most conscientiously. For a long time past I have suspected something of the kind. Last year we had some very strange cases of illness among the visitors—typhoid cases, and cases of gastric fever—

MRS. STOCKMANN. Yes, that is quite true.

DR. STOCKMANN. At the time, we supposed the visitors had been infected before they came; but later on, in the winter, I began to have a different opinion; and so I set myself to examine the water, as well as I could.

MRS. STOCKMANN. Then that is what you have been so busy with?

DR. STOCKMANN. Indeed I have been busy, Katherine. But here I had none of the necessary scientific apparatus; so I sent samples, both of the drinking water and of the sea water, up to the university, to have an accurate analysis made by a chemist.

HOVSTAD. And have you got that?

DR. STOCKMANN (showing him the letter). Here it is! It proves the presence of decomposing organic matter in the water—it is full if infusoria. The water is absolutely dangerous to use, either internally or externally.

MRS. STOCKMANN. What a mercy you discovered it in time.

DR. STOCKMANN. You may well say so.

HOVSTAD. And what do you propose to do now, Doctor?

DR. STOCKMANN. To see the matter put right—naturally.

HOVSTAD. Can that be done?

DR. STOCKMANN. It must be done. Otherwise the baths will be absolutely useless and wasted. But we need not anticipate that; I have a very clear idea what we shall have to do.

MRS. STOCKMANN. But why have you kept this all so secret, dear?

DR. STOCKMANN. Do you suppose I was going to run about the town gossiping about it, before I had absolute proof? No, thank you. I am not such a fool.

PETRA. Still, you might have told us—

DR. STOCKMANN. Not a living soul. But tomorrow you may run round to the old badger—

MRS. STOCKMANN. Oh, Thomas! Thomas!

DR. STOCKMANN. Well, to your grandfather, then. The old boy will have something to be astonished at! I know he thinks I am cracked—and there are lots of other people think so too, I have noticed. But now these good folks shall see—they shall just see—! (Walks about, rubbing his hands.) There will be a nice upset in the town, Katherine; you can't imagine what it will be. All the conduit pipes will have to be relaid.

HOVSTAD (getting up). All the conduit pipes—?

DR. STOCKMANN. Yes, of course. The intake is too low down; it will have to be lifted to a position much higher up.

PETRA. Then you were right after all.

DR. STOCKMANN. Ah, you remember, Petra—I wrote opposing the plans before the work was begun. But at that time no one would listen to me. Well, I am going to let them have it, now! Of course I have prepared a report for the Baths Committee; I have had it ready for a week, and was only waiting for this to come. *(Shows the letter.)* Now it shall go off at once. *(Goes into his room and comes back with some papers.)* Look at that! Four closely written sheets!—and the letter shall go with them. Give me a bit of paper, Katherine—something to wrap them up in. That will do! Now give it to—to—*(stamps his foot)*—what the deuce is her name?—give it to the maid, and tell her to take it at once to the mayor.

[MRS. STOCKMANN *takes the packet and goes out through the dining room.*]

PETRA. What do you think Uncle Peter will say, Father?

DR. STOCKMANN. What is there for him to say? I should think he would be very glad that such an important truth has been brought to light.

HOVSTAD. Will you let me print a short note about your discovery in the *Messenger?*

DR. STOCKMANN. I shall be very much obliged if you will.

HOVSTAD. It is very desirable that the public should be informed of it without delay.

DR. STOCKMANN. Certainly.

MRS. STOCKMANN *(coming back)*. She has just gone with it.

BILLING. Upon my soul, Doctor, you are going to be the foremost man in the town!

DR. STOCKMANN *(walking about happily)*. Nonsense! As a matter of fact I have done nothing more than my duty. I have only made a lucky find—that's all. Still, all the same—

BILLING. Hovstad, don't you think the town ought to give Dr. Stockmann some sort of testimonial?

HOVSTAD. I will suggest it, anyway.

BILLING. And I will speak to Aslaksen about it.

DR. STOCKMANN. No, my good friends, don't let us have any of that nonsense. I won't hear of anything of the kind.

And if the Baths Committee should think of voting me an increase of salary, I will not accept it. Do you hear, Katherine?—I won't accept it.

MRS. STOCKMANN. You are quite right, Thomas.

PETRA *(lifting her glass)*. Your health, Father!

HOVSTAD and BILLING. Your health, Doctor! Good health!

HORSTER *(touches glasses with* DR. STOCKMANN*)*. I hope it will bring you nothing but good luck.

DR. STOCKMANN. Thank you, thank you, my dear fellows! I feel tremendously happy! It is a splendid thing for a man to be able to feel that he has done a service to his native town and to his fellow citizens. Hurrah, Katherine!

[*He puts his arms round her and whirls her round and round, while she protests with laughing cries. They all laugh, clap their hands, and cheer the doctor. The boys put their heads in at the door to see what is going on.*]

ACT II

SCENE: *The same. The door into the dining room is shut. It is morning.* MRS. STOCKMANN, *with a sealed letter in her hand, comes in from the dining room, goes to the door of the doctor's study, and peeps in.*

MRS. STOCKMANN. Are you in, Thomas?

DR. STOCKMANN *(from within his room)*. Yes, I have just come in. *(Comes into the room.)* What is it?

MRS. STOCKMANN. A letter from your brother.

DR. STOCKMANN. Aha, let us see! *(Opens the letter and reads:)* "I return herewith the manuscript you sent me"— *(Reads on in a low murmur.)* Hm!—

MRS. STOCKMANN. What does he say?

DR. STOCKMANN *(putting the papers in his pocket)*. Oh, he only writes that he will come up here himself about midday.

MRS. STOCKMANN. Well, try and remember to be at home this time.

DR. STOCKMANN. That will be all right; I have got through all my morning visits.

MRS. STOCKMANN. I am extremely curious to know how he takes it.

DR. STOCKMANN. You will see he won't like it's having been I, and not he, that made the discovery.

MRS. STOCKMANN. Aren't you a little nervous about that?

DR. STOCKMANN. Oh, he really will be pleased enough, you know. But, at the same time, Peter is so confoundedly afraid of anyone's doing any service to the town except himself.

MRS. STOCKMANN. I will tell you what, Thomas—you should be good-natured, and share the credit of this with him. Couldn't you make out that it was he who set you on the scent of this discovery?

DR. STOCKMANN. I am quite willing. If only I can get the thing set right. I—

[MORTEN KIIL *puts his head in through the door leading from the hall, looks round in an inquiring manner, and chuckles.*]

MORTEN KIIL *(slyly)*. Is it—is it true?

MRS. STOCKMANN *(going to the door)*. Father!—is it you?

DR. STOCKMANN. Ah, Mr. Kiil—good morning, good morning!

MRS. STOCKMANN. But come along in.

MORTEN KIIL. If it is true, I will; if not, I am off.

DR. STOCKMANN. If what is true?

MORTEN KIIL. This tale about the water supply. Is it true?

DR. STOCKMANN. Certainly it is true. But how did you come to hear it?

MORTEN KIIL *(coming in)*. Petra ran in on her way to the school—

DR. STOCKMANN. Did she?

MORTEN KIIL. Yes; and she declares that— I thought she was only making a fool of me, but it isn't like Petra to do that.

DR. STOCKMANN. Of course not. How could you imagine such a thing!

MORTEN KIIL. Oh well, it is better never to trust anybody; you may find you have been made a fool of before you know where you are. But it is really true, all the same?

DR. STOCKMANN. You can depend upon it that it is true. Won't you sit down? *(Settles him on the couch.)* Isn't it a real bit of luck for the town—

MORTEN KIIL *(suppressing his laughter)*. A bit of luck for the town?

DR. STOCKMANN. Yes, that I made the discovery in good time.

MORTEN KIIL *(as before)*. Yes, yes, yes!—But I should never have thought you the sort of man to pull your own brother's leg like this!

DR. STOCKMANN. Pull his leg!

MRS. STOCKMANN. Really, Father dear—

MORTEN KIIL *(resting his hands and his chin on the handle of his stick and winking slyly at the doctor)*. Let me see, what was the story? Some kind of beast that had got into the water pipes, wasn't it?

DR. STOCKMANN. Infusoria—yes.

MORTEN KIIL. And a lot of these beasts had got in, according to Petra—a tremendous lot.

DR. STOCKMANN. Certainly; hundreds of thousands of them, probably.

MORTEN KIIL. But no one can see them —isn't that so?

DR. STOCKMANN. Yes; you can't see them.

MORTEN KIIL *(with a quiet chuckle)*. Damn—it's the finest story I have ever heard!

DR. STOCKMANN. What do you mean?

MORTEN KIIL. But you will never get the mayor to believe a thing like that.

DR. STOCKMANN. We shall see.

MORTEN KIIL. Do you think he will be fool enough to—?

DR. STOCKMANN. I hope the whole town will be fools enough.

MORTEN KIIL. The whole town! Well, it wouldn't be a bad thing. It would just serve them right, and teach them a lesson. They think themselves so much cleverer than we old fellows. They hounded me out of the council; they did, I tell you—

they hounded me out. Now they shall pay for it. You pull their legs too, Thomas!

DR. STOCKMANN. Really, I—

MORTEN KIIL. You pull their legs! (*Gets up.*) If you can work it so that the mayor and his friends all swallow the same bait, I will give ten pounds to a charity—like a shot!

DR. STOCKMANN. That is very kind of you.

MORTEN KIIL. Yes, I haven't got much money to throw away, I can tell you; but if you can work this, I will give five pounds to a charity at Christmas.

[HOVSTAD *comes in by the hall door.*]

HOVSTAD. Good morning! (*Stops.*) Oh, I beg your pardon—

DR. STOCKMANN. Not at all; come in.

MORTEN KIIL (*with another chuckle*). Oho!—is he in this too?

HOVSTAD. What do you mean?

DR. STOCKMANN. Certainly he is.

MORTEN KIIL. I might have known it! It must get into the papers. You know how to do it, Thomas! Set your wits to work. Now I must go.

DR. STOCKMANN. Won't you stay a little while?

MORTEN KIIL. No, I must be off now. You keep up this game for all it is worth; you won't repent it, I'm damned if you will!

[*He goes out;* MRS. STOCKMANN *follows him into the hall.*]

DR. STOCKMANN (*laughing*). Just imagine—the old chap doesn't believe a word of all this about the water supply.

HOVSTAD. Oh that was it, then?

DR. STOCKMANN. Yes, that was what we were talking about. Perhaps it is the same thing that brings you here?

HOVSTAD. Yes, it is. Can you spare me a few minutes, Doctor?

DR. STOCKMANN. As long as you like, my dear fellow.

HOVSTAD. Have you heard from the mayor yet?

DR. STOCKMANN. Not yet. He is coming here later.

HOVSTAD. I have given the matter a great deal of thought since last night.

DR. STOCKMANN. Well?

HOVSTAD. From your point of view, as a doctor and a man of science, this affair of the water supply is an isolated matter. I mean, you do not realize that it involves a great many other things.

DR. STOCKMANN. How, do you mean?— Let us sit down, my dear fellow. No, sit here on the couch. (HOVSTAD *sits down on the couch,* DR. STOCKMANN *on a chair on the other side of the table.*) Now then. You mean that—?

HOVSTAD. You said yesterday that the pollution of the water was due to impurities in the soil.

DR. STOCKMANN. Yes, unquestionably it is due to that poisonous morass up at Mölledal.

HOVSTAD. Begging your pardon, Doctor, I fancy it is due to quite another morass altogether.

DR. STOCKMANN. What morass?

HOVSTAD. The morass that the whole life of our town is built on and is rotting in.

DR. STOCKMANN. What the deuce are you driving at, Hovstad?

HOVSTAD. The whole of the town's interests have, little by little, got into the hands of a pack of officials.

DR. STOCKMANN. Oh, come!—they are not all officials.

HOVSTAD. No, but those that are not officials are at any rate the officials' friends and adherents; it is the wealthy folk, the old families in the town, that have got us entirely in their hands.

DR. STOCKMANN. Yes, but after all they are men of ability and knowledge.

HOVSTAD. Did they show any ability or knowledge when they laid the conduit pipes where they are now?

DR. STOCKMANN. No, of course that was a great piece of stupidity on their part. But that is going to be set right now.

HOVSTAD. Do you think that will be all such plain sailing?

DR. STOCKMANN. Plain sailing or no, it has got to be done, anyway.

HOVSTAD. Yes, provided the press takes up the question.

DR. STOCKMANN. I don't think that will be necessary, my dear fellow, I am certain my brother—

HOVSTAD. Excuse me, Doctor; I feel bound to tell you I am inclined to take the matter up.

DR. STOCKMANN. In the paper?

HOVSTAD. Yes. When I took over the *People's Messenger* my idea was to break up this ring of self-opinionated old fossils who had got hold of all the influence.

DR. STOCKMANN. But you know you told me yourself what the result had been; you nearly ruined your paper.

HOVSTAD. Yes, at the time we were obliged to climb down a peg or two, it is quite true; because there was a danger of the whole project of the baths coming to nothing if they failed us. But now the scheme has been carried through, and we can dispense with these grand gentlemen.

DR. STOCKMANN. Dispense with them, yes; but we owe them a great debt of gratitude.

HOVSTAD. That shall be recognized ungrudgingly. But a journalist of my democratic tendencies cannot let such an opportunity as this slip. The bubble of official infallibility must be pricked. This superstition must be destroyed, like any other.

DR. STOCKMANN. I am wholeheartedly with you in that, Mr. Hovstad; if it is a superstition, away with it!

HOVSTAD. I should be very reluctant to bring the mayor into it, because he is your brother. But I am sure you will agree with me that truth should be the first consideration.

DR. STOCKMANN. That goes without saying. *(With sudden emphasis.)* Yes, but—but—

HOVSTAD. You must not misjudge me. I am neither more self-interested nor more ambitious than most men.

DR. STOCKMANN. My dear fellow— who suggests anything of the kind?

HOVSTAD. I am of humble origin, as you know; and that has given me opportunities of knowing what is the most crying need in the humbler ranks of life. It is that they should be allowed some part in the direction of public affairs, Doctor. That is what will develop their faculties and intelligence and self-respect—

DR. STOCKMANN. I quite appreciate that. ·

HOVSTAD. Yes—and in my opinion a journalist incurs a heavy responsibility if he neglects a favorable opportunity of emancipating the masses—the humble and oppressed. I know well enough that in exalted circles I shall be called an agitator, and all that sort of thing; but they may call what they like. If only my conscience doesn't reproach me, then—

DR. STOCKMANN. Quite right! Quite right, Mr. Hovstad. But all the same— devil take it! *(A knock is heard at the door.)* Come in!

[ASLAKSEN *appears at the door. He is poorly but decently dressed, in black, with a slightly crumpled white neckcloth; he wears gloves and has a felt hat in his hand.*]

ASLAKSEN *(bowing)*. Excuse my taking the liberty, Doctor—

DR. STOCKMANN *(getting up)*. Ah, it is you, Aslaksen!

ASLAKSEN. Yes, Doctor.

HOVSTAD *(standing up)*. Is it me you want, Aslaksen?

ASLAKSEN. No; I didn't know I should find you here. No, it was the doctor I—

DR. STOCKMANN. I am quite at your service. What is it?

ASLAKSEN. Is what I heard from Mr. Billing true, sir—that you mean to improve our water supply?

DR. STOCKMANN. Yes, for the baths.

ASLAKSEN. Quite so, I understand. Well, I have come to say that I will back that up by every means in my power.

HOVSTAD *(to the DOCTOR)*. You see!

DR. STOCKMANN. I shall be very grateful to you, but—

ASLAKSEN. Because it may be no bad thing to have us small tradesmen at your back. We form, as it were, a compact majority in the town—if we choose. And it is always a good thing to have the majority with you, Doctor.

DR. STOCKMANN. That is undeniably true; but I confess I don't see why such unusual precautions should be necessary in this case. It seems to me that such a plain, straightforward thing—

ASLAKSEN. Oh, it may be very desirable, all the same. I know our local authorities so well; officials are not generally very ready to act on proposals that come from other people. That is why I think it would not be at all amiss if we made a little demonstration.

HOVSTAD. That's right.

DR. STOCKMANN. Demonstration, did you say? What on earth are you going to make a demonstration about?

ASLAKSEN. We shall proceed with the greatest moderation, Doctor. Moderation is always my aim; it is the greatest virtue in a citizen—at least, I think so.

DR. STOCKMANN. It is well known to be a characteristic of yours, Mr. Aslaksen.

ASLAKSEN. Yes, I think I may pride myself on that. And this matter of the water supply is of the greatest importance to us small tradesmen. The baths promise to be a regular gold mine for the town. We shall all make our living out of them, especially those of us who are householders. That is why we will back up the project as strongly as possible. And as I am at present chairman of the Householders' Association—

DR. STOCKMANN. Yes—?

ASLAKSEN. And, what is more, local secretary of the Temperance Society—you know, sir, I suppose, that I am a worker in the temperance cause?

DR. STOCKMANN. Of course, of course.

ASLAKSEN. Well, you can understand that I come into contact with a great many people. And as I have the reputation of a temperate and law-abiding citizen—like yourself, Doctor—I have a certain influence in the town, a little bit of power, if I may be allowed to say so.

DR. STOCKMANN. I know that quite well, Mr. Aslaksen.

ASLAKSEN. So you see it would be an easy matter for me to set on foot some testimonial, if necessary.

DR. STOCKMANN. A testimonial?

ASLAKSEN. Yes, some kind of an address of thanks from the townsmen for your share in a matter of such importance to the community. I need scarcely say that it would have to be drawn up with the greatest regard to moderation, so as not to offend the authorities—who, after all, have the reins in their hands. If we pay strict attention to that, no one can take it amiss, I should think!

HOVSTAD. Well, and even supposing they didn't like it—

ASLAKSEN. No, no, no; there must be no discourtesy to the authorities, Mr. Hovstad. It is no use falling foul of those upon whom our welfare so closely depends. I have done that in my time, and no good ever comes of it. But no one can take exception to a reasonable and frank expression of a citizen's views.

DR. STOCKMANN (shaking him by the hand). I can't tell you, dear Mr. Aslaksen, how extremely pleased I am to find such hearty support among my fellow citizens. I am delighted—delighted! Now, you will take a small glass of sherry, eh?

ASLAKSEN. No, thank you; I never drink alcohol of that kind.

DR. STOCKMANN. Well, what do you say to a glass of beer, then?

ASLAKSEN. Nor that either, thank you, Doctor. I never drink anything as early as this. I am going into town now to talk this over with one or two householders, and prepare the ground.

DR. STOCKMANN. It is tremendously kind of you, Mr. Aslaksen; but I really cannot understand the necessity for all these precautions. It seems to me that the thing should go of itself.

ASLAKSEN. The authorities are somewhat slow to move, Doctor. Far be it from me to seem to blame them—

HOVSTAD. We are going to stir them up in the paper tomorrow, Aslaksen.

ASLAKSEN. But not violently, I trust, Mr. Hovstad. Proceed with moderation, or you will do nothing with them. You may take my advice; I have gathered my experience in the school of life. Well, I must say good-by, Doctor. You know now that we small tradesmen are at your back at all events, like a solid wall. You have the compact majority on your side, Doctor.

DR. STOCKMANN. I am very much obliged, dear Mr. Aslaksen. *(Shakes hands with him.)* Good-by, good-by.

ASLAKSEN. Are you going my way, toward the printing office, Mr. Hovstad?

HOVSTAD. I will come later; I have something to settle up first.

ASLAKSEN. Very well.

[*Bows and goes out;* STOCKMANN *follows him into the hall.*]

HOVSTAD (*as* STOCKMANN *comes in again*). Well, what do you think of that, Doctor? Don't you think it is high time we stirred a little life into all this slackness and vacillation and cowardice?

DR. STOCKMANN. Are you referring to Aslaksen?

HOVSTAD. Yes, I am. He is one of those who are floundering in a bog—decent fellow though he may be, otherwise. And most of the people here are in just the same case—seesawing and edging first to one side and then to the other, so overcome with caution and scruple that they never dare to take any decided step.

DR. STOCKMANN. Yes, but Aslaksen seemed to me so thoroughly well intentioned.

HOVSTAD. There is one thing I esteem higher than that; and that is for a man to be self-reliant and sure of himself.

DR. STOCKMANN. I think you are perfectly right there.

HOVSTAD. That is why I want to seize this opportunity, and try if I cannot manage to put a little virility into these well intentioned people for once. The idol of Authority must be shattered in this town. This gross and inexcusable blunder about the water supply must be brought home to the mind of every municipal voter.

DR. STOCKMANN. Very well; if you are of opinion that it is for the good of the community, so be it. But not until I have had a talk with my brother.

HOVSTAD. Anyway, I will get a leading article ready; and if the mayor refuses to take the matter up—

DR. STOCKMANN. How can you suppose such a thing possible?

HOVSTAD. It is conceivable. And in that case—

DR. STOCKMANN. In that case I promise you— Look here, in that case you may print my report—every word of it.

HOVSTAD. May I? Have I your word for it?

DR. STOCKMANN (*giving him the manuscript*). Here it is; take it with you. It can do no harm for you to read it through, and you can give it me back later on.

HOVSTAD. Good, good! That is what I will do. And now good-by, Doctor.

DR. STOCKMANN. Good-by, good-by. You will see everything will run quite smoothly, Mr. Hovstad—quite smoothly.

HOVSTAD. Hm!—we shall see.

[*Bows and goes out.*]

DR. STOCKMANN (*opens the dining-room door and looks in*). Katherine! Oh, you are back, Petra?

PETRA (*coming in*). Yes, I have just come from the school.

MRS. STOCKMANN (*coming in*). Has he not been here yet?

DR. STOCKMANN. Peter? No. But I have had a long talk with Hovstad. He is quite excited about my discovery. I find it has a much wider bearing than I at first imagined. And he has put his paper at my disposal if necessity should arise.

MRS. STOCKMANN. Do you think it will?

DR. STOCKMANN. Not for a moment. But at all events it makes me feel proud to know that I have the liberal-minded, independent press on my side. Yes, and—just imagine—I have had a visit from the chairman of the Householders' Association!

[IBSEN CONTINUES ON PAGE 847]

MASTERPIECES OF WORLD ART
Nineteenth-Century Painting

Most new developments in nineteenth-century painting took place in France. They gained recognition, though, only after bitter struggles against the powerful opposition of the press and the Academy of Fine Arts. The Academy insisted that all painters obey the rules of "classical" art established by David, and that they limit their subjects to portraits and lofty historical, mythological, or Biblical themes.

During the 1830's, a group of artists in Paris launched a countermovement known as Romanticism, which declared the right of every artist to express his own emotions however seemed most appropriate. Their leader, Eugène Delacroix, is represented here by a painting called *Tiger Hunt* (PLATE 1). Unlike the statuesque and smoothly painted pictures of David, this little canvas fairly explodes in a violent swirl of twisting shapes, sudden color contrasts, and lively, sketchy brushstrokes. The action builds up from the background to a frenzied climax in the struggle between the hunter and the tiger. Such themes of adventure in faraway exotic lands greatly appealed to the romantic imagination.

After Delacroix's death in 1863, young progressive painters in Paris found a new leader in a wealthy, cultivated Parisian named Édouard Manet. To them, Manet was a "realist," for unlike the classicists of the Academy and romanticists like Delacroix, he usually chose his subjects from everyday life. A good example of his later work is a rather large canvas called *Boating* (PLATE 2), which despite its size, creates the effect of an intimate close-up. Note the sketchiness of Manet's technique, particularly in depicting the woman's dress, where different tones and colors are used side by side to approximate the shimmer of sunlight.

This "broken-color" technique was also used by several of Manet's younger friends. One of them, Claude Monet, had worked alongside him during the summer of 1874, sketching views near the town of Argenteuil. Monet usually completed his pictures on the spot, for he believed that an artist could not capture the true colors of outdoor light unless he actually painted outdoors. Concerned mainly with recording his general impression of a scene, Monet was willing to sacrifice many details. In his picture of the Argenteuil bridge (PLATE 3), notice that he has indicated the figures on the bridge and the landscape on the far shore by only a few sketchy brush-strokes. Monet makes us look at the composition as a whole because of the way he has unified it in light and color. The lack of detail in the paintings of Monet and his friends led a hostile critic to condemn these artists as mere "impressionists." Nevertheless, they soon adopted this term themselves, and so they have been known ever since.

Edgar Degas was another type of Impressionist. More interested in painting human figures than landscapes, he sought out people in all kinds of situations—jockeys on horseback, people in cafés, women in millinery shops. Unlike Monet, Degas made many preparatory sketches, yet he managed to preserve much of their original spontaneity in his finished pictures. This spontaneity is present even in his pictures of the ballet, the most formal of all theater arts; for Degas often viewed his subjects from unusual angles, much like modern photographers. In *Dancer Bowing with Flowers* (PLATE 4), for instance, the main figure is seen from above and placed off-center, while others are cut off by the left edge of the picture. But the composition is held together with the strong vertical accents of two orange parasols, the one on the left continuing downward through the dancer and providing the main axis for the whole design.

In the 1880's when Impressionism had finally become popular, several artists were already abandoning it because they felt that it was too concerned with surface effects and not enough with clarity and solidity of form. Paul Cézanne, for example, attempted to adapt the Impressionist shimmer of broken colors to a more rugged, structural style. In pictures such as *On the Bank of a River* (PLATE 5), Cézanne transformed sky, foliage, and reflection into broad patches of color that seem to shift and interlock like the facets of a precious stone.

Among the many foreign artists attracted to French Impressionism was the Dutch painter Vincent van Gogh. After two years in Paris, however, Van Gogh began to work toward an altogether different style, which he developed further in the small town of Arles in southern France. There he painted with bold outlines and large, flat areas of color, directly expressing his inner drives and emotions. Look, for example, at his painting of his house in Arles (PLATE 6). The pale, eerie harmony of pink, yellow, and faded green buildings here seems unusually disquieting against such a dark blue sky, and the dark accents of the three front windows and door of the corner house seem somehow mysterious and threatening.

Cézanne and Van Gogh, with their vastly different styles, were to become the two most important single influences on the development of modern art in the twentieth century.

PLATE 1. EUGÈNE DELACROIX (French, 1798–1863): *Tiger Hunt*. 1856. Oil on canvas, 28⅛ x 36⁷⁄₁₆ inches. (Musée du Louvre, Paris)

PLATE 2. ÉDOUARD MANET (French, 1832–1883): *Boating*. 1874. Oil on canvas, 38¼ x 51¼ inches. (The Metropolitan Museum of Art, New York, Bequest of Mrs. H. O. Havemeyer, 1929; The H. O. Havemeyer Collection)

PLATE 3. CLAUDE MONET (French, 1840–1926): *Bridge over the Seine at Argenteuil.* Oil on canvas, 22¹⁸⁄₁₈ x 31½ inches. (Bayerischen Staatsgemäldesammlungen, Munich)

PLATE 4. EDGAR DEGAS (French, 1834–1917): *Dancer Bowing with Flowers*. 1878. Pastel on *papier collé* on canvas, 28⅔ x 30½ inches. (Musée du Louvre, Paris)

PLATE 5. PAUL CÉZANNE (French, 1839–1906): *On the Bank of a River*. About 1904. Oil on canvas, 23¾ x 29 inches. (Museum of Art, Rhode Island School of Design, Providence)

PLATE 6. VINCENT VAN GOGH (Dutch, 1853–1890): *Vincent's House at Arles*. 1888. Oil on canvas, 28¾ x 36¼ inches. (Collection, Vincent van Gogh Foundation, Amsterdam)

MRS. STOCKMANN. Oh! What did he want?

DR. STOCKMANN. To offer me his support, too. They will support me in a body if it should be necessary. Katherine—do you know what I have got behind me?

MRS. STOCKMANN. Behind you? No, what have you got behind you?

DR. STOCKMANN. The compact majority.

MRS. STOCKMANN. Really? Is that a good thing for you, Thomas?

DR. STOCKMANN. I should think it was a good thing. *(Walks up and down rubbing his hands.)* By Jove, it's a fine thing to feel this bond of brotherhood between oneself and one's fellow citizens!

PETRA. And to be able to do so much that is good and useful, Father!

DR. STOCKMANN. And for one's own native town into the bargain, my child!

MRS. STOCKMANN. That was a ring at the bell.

DR. STOCKMANN. It must be he, then. *(A knock is heard at the door.)* Come in!

PETER STOCKMANN *(comes in from the hall).* Good morning.

DR. STOCKMANN. Glad to see you, Peter!

MRS. STOCKMANN. Good morning, Peter. How are you?

PETER STOCKMANN. So-so, thank you. *(To* DR. STOCKMANN.*)* I received from you yesterday, after office hours, a report dealing with the condition of the water at the baths.

DR. STOCKMANN. Yes. Have you read it?

PETER STOCKMANN. Yes, I have.

DR. STOCKMANN. And what have you to say to it?

PETER STOCKMANN *(with a sidelong glance).* Hm!—

MRS. STOCKMANN. Come along, Petra.

[*She and* PETRA *go into the room on the left.*]

PETER STOCKMANN *(after a pause).* Was it necessary to make all these investigations behind my back?

DR. STOCKMANN. Yes, because until I was absolutely certain about it—

PETER STOCKMANN. Then you mean that you are absolutely certain now?

DR. STOCKMANN. Surely you are convinced of that.

PETER STOCKMANN. Is it your intention to bring this document before the Baths Committee as a sort of official communication?

DR. STOCKMANN. Certainly. Something must be done in the matter—and that quickly.

PETER STOCKMANN. As usual, you employ violent expressions in your report. You say, amongst other things, that what we offer visitors in our baths is a permanent supply of poison.

DR. STOCKMANN. Well, can you describe it any other way, Peter? Just think—water that is poisonous, whether you drink it or bathe in it! And this we offer to the poor sick folk who come to us trustfully and pay us at an exorbitant rate to be made well again!

PETER STOCKMANN. And your reasoning leads you to this conclusion, that we must build a sewer to draw off the alleged impurites from Mölledal and must relay the water conduits.

DR. STOCKMANN. Yes. Do you see any other way out of it? I don't.

PETER STOCKMANN. I made a pretext this morning to go and see the town engineer and, as if only half seriously, broached the subject of these proposals as a thing we might perhaps have to take under consideration some time later on.

DR. STOCKMANN. Some time later on!

PETER STOCKMANN. He smiled at what he considered to be my extravagance, naturally. Have you taken the trouble to consider what your proposed alterations would cost? According to the information I obtained, the expenses would probably mount up to fifteen or twenty thousand pounds.

DR. STOCKMANN. Would it cost so much?

PETER STOCKMANN. Yes; and the worst part of it would be that the work would take at least two years.

DR. STOCKMANN. Two years? Two whole years?

PETER STOCKMANN. At least. And what are we to do with the baths in the meantime? Close them? Indeed we should be obliged to. And do you suppose anyone would come near the place after it had got about that the water was dangerous?

DR. STOCKMANN. Yes, but, Peter, that is what it is.

PETER STOCKMANN. And all this at this juncture—just as the baths are beginning to be known. There are other towns in the neighborhood with qualifications to attract visitors for bathing purposes. Don't you suppose they would immediately strain every nerve to divert the entire stream of strangers to themselves? Unquestionably they would; and then where should we be? We should probably have to abandon the whole thing, which has cost us so much money—and then you would have ruined your native town.

DR. STOCKMANN. I—should have ruined—!

PETER STOCKMANN. It is simply and solely through the baths that the town has before it any future worth mentioning. You know that just as well as I.

DR. STOCKMANN. But what do you think ought to be done, then?

PETER STOCKMANN. Your report has not convinced me that the condition of the water at the baths is as bad as you represent it to be.

DR. STOCKMANN. I tell you it is even worse!—or at all events it will be in summer, when the warm weather comes.

PETER STOCKMANN. As I said, I believe you exaggerate the matter considerably. A capable physician ought to know what measures to take—he ought to be capable of preventing injurious influences or of remedying them if they become obviously persistent.

DR. STOCKMANN. Well? What more?

PETER STOCKMANN. The water supply for the baths is now an established fact, and in consequence must be treated as such. But probably the committee, at its discretion, will not be disinclined to consider the question of how far it might be possible to introduce certain improvements consistently with a reasonable expenditure.

DR. STOCKMANN. And do you suppose that I will have anything to do with such a piece of trickery as that?

PETER STOCKMAN. Trickery!!

DR. STOCKMANN. Yes, it would be a trick—a fraud, a lie, a downright crime toward the public, toward the whole community!

PETER STOCKMANN. I have not, as I remarked before, been able to convince myself that there is actually any imminent danger.

DR. STOCKMANN. You have! It is impossible that you should not be convinced. I know I have represented the facts absolutely truthfully and fairly. And you know it very well, Peter, only you won't acknowledge it. It was owing to your action that both the baths and the water conduits were built where they are; and that is what you won't acknowledge—that damnable blunder of yours. Pooh!—do you suppose I don't see through you?

PETER STOCKMANN. And even if that were true? If I perhaps guard my reputation somewhat anxiously, it is in the interests of the town. Without moral authority I am powerless to direct public affairs as seems, to my judgment, to be best for the common good. And on that account—and for various other reasons, too—it appears to me to be a matter of importance that your report should not be delivered to the committee. In the interests of the public, you must withhold it. Then, later on, I will raise the question and we will do our best, privately; but nothing of this unfortunate affair—not a single word of it—must come to the ears of the public.

DR. STOCKMANN. I am afraid you will not be able to prevent that now, my dear Peter.

PETER STOCKMANN. It must and shall be prevented.

DR. STOCKMANN. It is no use, I tell you. There are too many people that know about it.

PETER STOCKMANN. That know about it? Who? Surely you don't mean those fellows on the *People's Messenger?*

DR. STOCKMANN. Yes, they know. The liberal-minded, independent press is going to see that you do your duty.

PETER STOCKMANN (*after a short pause*). You are an extraordinarily independent man, Thomas. Have you given no thought to the consequences this may have for yourself?

DR. STOCKMANN. Consequences?—for me?

PETER STOCKMANN. For you and yours, yes.

DR. STOCKMANN. What the deuce do you mean?

PETER STOCKMANN. I believe I have always behaved in a brotherly way to you—have always been ready to oblige or to help you?

DR. STOCKMANN. Yes, you have, and I am grateful to you for it.

PETER STOCKMANN. There is no need. Indeed, to some extent I was forced to do so—for my own sake. I always hoped that, if I helped to improve your financial position, I should be able to keep some check on you.

DR. STOCKMANN. What!! Then it was only for your own sake!—

PETER STOCKMANN. Up to a certain point, yes. It is painful for a man in an official position to have his nearest relative compromising himself time after time.

DR. STOCKMANN. And do you consider that I do that?

PETER STOCKMANN. Yes, unfortunately, you do, without even being aware of it. You have a restless, pugnacious, rebellious disposition. And then there is that disastrous propensity of yours to want to write about every sort of possible and impossible thing. The moment an idea comes into your head, you must needs go and write a newspaper article or a whole pamphlet about it.

DR. STOCKMANN. Well, but is it not the duty of a citizen to let the public share in any new ideas he may have?

PETER STOCKMANN. Oh, the public doesn't require any new ideas. The public is best served by the good, old-established ideas it already has.

DR. STOCKMANN. And that is your honest opinion?

PETER STOCKMANN. Yes, and for once I must talk frankly to you. Hitherto I have tried to avoid doing so, because I know how irritable you are; but now I must tell you the truth, Thomas. You have no conception what an amount of harm you do yourself by your impetuosity. You complain of the authorities, you even complain of the government—you are always pulling them to pieces; you insist that you have been neglected and persecuted. But what else can such a cantankerous man as you expect?

DR. STOCKMANN. What next! Cantankerous, am I?

PETER STOCKMANN. Yes, Thomas, you are an extremely cantankerous man to work with—I know that to my cost. You disregard everything that you ought to have consideration for. You seem completely to forget that it is me you have to thank for your appointment here as medical officer to the baths—

DR. STOCKMANN. I was entitled to it as a matter of course!—I and nobody else! I was the first person to see that the town could be made into a flourishing watering place, and I was the only one who saw it at that time. I had to fight single-handed in support of the idea for many years; and I wrote and wrote—

PETER STOCKMANN. Undoubtedly. But things were not ripe for the scheme then—though, of course, you could not judge of that in your out-of-the-way corner up north. But as soon as the opportune moment came I—and the others—took the matter into our hands—

DR. STOCKMANN. Yes, and made this mess of all my beautiful plan. It is pretty obvious now what clever fellows you were!

PETER STOCKMANN. To my mind the whole thing only seems to mean that you are seeking another outlet for your combativeness. You want to pick a quarrel with your superiors—an old habit of yours. You cannot put up with any authority over you. You look askance at anyone who occupies a superior official position; you regard him as a personal enemy, and then any stick is good enough to beat him with. But now I have called your attention to the fact that the town's interests are at stake—and, incidentally, my own too. And therefore I must tell you, Thomas, that you will find me inexorable with regard to what I am about to require you to do.

DR. STOCKMANN. And what is that?

PETER STOCKMANN. As you have been so indiscreet as to speak of this delicate matter to outsiders, despite the fact that you ought to have treated it as entirely official and confidential, it is obviously impossible to hush it up now. All sorts of rumors will get about directly, and everybody who has a grudge against us will take care to embellish these rumors. So it will be necessary for you to refute them publicly.

DR. STOCKMANN. I! How? I don't understand.

PETER STOCKMANN. What we shall expect is that, after making further investigations, you will come to the conclusion that the matter is not by any means as dangerous or as critical as you imagined in the first instance.

DR. STOCKMANN. Oho!—so that is what you expect!

PETER STOCKMANN. And, what is more, we shall expect you to make public profession of your confidence in the committee and in their readiness to consider fully and conscientiously what steps may be necessary to remedy any possible defects.

DR. STOCKMANN. But you will never be able to do that by patching and tinkering at it—never! Take my word for it, Peter; I mean what I say, as deliberately and emphatically as possible.

PETER STOCKMANN. As an officer under the committee, you have no right to any individual opinion.

DR. STOCKMANN (amazed). No right?

PETER STOCKMANN. In your official capacity, no. As a private person, it is quite another matter. But as a subordinate member of the staff of the baths, you have no right to express any opinion which runs contrary to that of your superiors.

DR. STOCKMANN. This is too much! I, a doctor, a man of science, have no right to—!

PETER STOCKMANN. The matter in hand is not simply a scientific one. It is a complicated matter, and has its economic as well as its technical side.

DR. STOCKMANN. I don't care what it is! I intend to be free to express my opinion on any subject under the sun.

PETER STOCKMANN. As you please—but not on any subject concerning the baths. That we forbid.

DR. STOCKMANN (shouting). You forbid—! You! A pack of—

PETER STOCKMANN. I forbid it—I, your chief; and if I forbid it, you have to obey.

DR. STOCKMANN (controlling himself). Peter—if you were not my brother—

PETRA (throwing open the door). Father, you shan't stand this!

MRS. STOCKMANN (coming in after her). Petra, Petra!

PETER STOCKMANN. Oh, so you have been eavesdropping.

MRS. STOCKMANN. You were talking so loud, we couldn't help—

PETRA. Yes, I was listening.

PETER STOCKMANN. Well, after all, I am very glad—

DR. STOCKMANN (going up to him). You were saying something about forbidding and obeying?

PETER STOCKMANN. You obliged me to take that tone with you.

DR. STOCKMANN. And so I am to give myself the lie, publicly?

PETER STOCKMANN. We consider it

absolutely necessary that you should make some such public statement as I have asked for.

DR. STOCKMANN. And if I do not—obey?

PETER STOCKMANN. Then we shall publish a statement ourselves to reassure the public.

DR. STOCKMANN. Very well; but in that case I shall use my pen against you. I stick to what I have said; I will show that I am right and that you are wrong. And what will you do then?

PETER STOCKMANN. Then I shall not be able to prevent your being dismissed.

DR. STOCKMANN. What—?

PETRA. Father—dismissed!

MRS. STOCKMANN. Dismissed!

PETER STOCKMANN. Dismissed from the staff of the baths. I shall be obliged to propose that you shall immediately be given notice, and shall not be allowed any further participation in the baths' affairs.

DR. STOCKMANN. You would dare to do that!

PETER STOCKMANN. It is you that are playing the daring game.

PETRA. Uncle, that is a shameful way to treat a man like Father!

MRS. STOCKMANN. Do hold your tongue, Petra!

PETER STOCKMANN (looking at PETRA). Oh, so we volunteer our opinions already, do we? Of course. (To MRS. STOCKMANN.) Katherine, I imagine you are the most sensible person in this house. Use any influence you may have over your husband, and make him see what this will entail for his family as well as—

DR. STOCKMANN. My family is my own concern and nobody else's!

PETER STOCKMANN. For his own family, as I was saying, as well as for the town he lives in.

DR. STOCKMANN. It is I who have the real good of the town at heart! I want to lay bare the defects that sooner or later must come to the light of day. I will show whether I love my native town.

PETER STOCKMANN. You, who in your blind obstinacy want to cut off the most important source of the town's welfare?

DR. STOCKMANN. The source is poisoned, man! Are you mad? We are making our living by retailing filth and corruption! The whole of our flourishing municipal life derives its sustenance from a lie!

PETER STOCKMANN. All imagination—or something even worse. The man who can throw out such offensive insinuations about his native town must be an enemy of our community.

DR. STOCKMANN (going up to him). Do you dare to—!

MRS. STOCKMANN (throwing herself between them). Thomas!

PETRA (catching her father by the arm). Don't lose your temper, Father!

PETER STOCKMANN. I will not expose myself to violence. Now you have had a warning; so reflect on what you owe to yourself and your family. Goodby.   [Goes out.]

DR. STOCKMANN (walking up and down). Am I to put up with such treatment as this? In my own house, Katherine! What do you think of that!

MRS. STOCKMANN. Indeed it is both shameful and absurd, Thomas—

PETRA. If only I could give uncle a piece of my mind—

DR. STOCKMANN. It is my own fault. I ought to have flown out at him long ago!—shown my teeth!—bitten! To hear him call me an enemy to our community! Me! I shall not take that lying down, upon my soul!

MRS. STOCKMANN. But, dear Thomas, your brother has power on his side—

DR. STOCKMANN. Yes, but I have right on mine, I tell you.

MRS. STOCKMANN. Oh yes, right—right. What is the use of having right on your side if you have not got might?

PETRA. Oh, Mother!—how can you say such a thing!

DR. STOCKMANN. Do you imagine that in a free country it is no use having right on your side? You are absurd, Katherine. Besides, haven't I got the liberal-minded, independent press to lead the way, and the compact majority behind me? That is might enough, I should think!

MRS. STOCKMANN. But, good heavens, Thomas, you don't mean to—?

DR. STOCKMANN. Don't mean to what?

MRS. STOCKMANN. To set yourself up in opposition to your brother.

DR. STOCKMANN. In God's name, what else do you suppose I should do but take my stand on right and truth?

PETRA. Yes, I was just going to say that.

MRS. STOCKMANN. But it won't do you any earthly good. If they won't do it, they won't.

DR. STOCKMANN. Oho, Katherine! Just give me time and you will see how I will carry the war into their camp.

MRS. STOCKMANN. Yes, you carry the war into their camp, and you get your dismissal—that is what you will do.

DR. STOCKMANN. In any case I shall have done my duty toward the public— toward the community. I, who am called its enemy!

MRS. STOCKMANN. But toward your family, Thomas? Toward your own home! Do you think that is doing your duty toward those you have to provide for?

PETRA. Ah, don't think always first of us, Mother.

MRS. STOCKMANN. Oh, it is easy for you to talk; you are able to shift for yourself, if need be. But remember the boys, Thomas; and think a little, too, of yourself, and of me—

DR. STOCKMANN. I think you are out of your senses, Katherine! If I were to be such a miserable coward as to go on my knees to Peter and his damned crew, do you suppose I should ever know an hour's peace of mind all my life afterward?

MRS. STOCKMANN. I don't know anything about that; but God preserve us from the peace of mind we shall have, all the same, if you go on defying him! You will find yourself again without the means of subsistence, with no income to count upon. I should think we had had enough of that in the old days. Remember that,

Thomas; think what that means.

DR. STOCKMANN (collecting himself with a struggle and clenching his fists). And this is what this slavery can bring upon a free, honorable man! Isn't it horrible, Katherine?

MRS. STOCKMANN. Yes, it is sinful to treat you so, it is perfectly true. But, good heavens, one has to put up with so much injustice in this world.—There are the boys. Thomas! Look at them! What is to become of them? Oh, no, no, you can never have the heart—

[EJLIF and MORTEN have come in while she was speaking, with their school books in their hands.]

DR. STOCKMANN. The boys—! (Recovers himself suddenly.) No, even if the whole world goes to pieces, I will never bow my neck to this yoke!

[Goes toward his room.]

MRS. STOCKMANN (following him). Thomas—what are you going to do!

DR. STOCKMANN (at his door). I mean to have the right to look my sons in the face when they are grown men.

[Goes into his room.]

MRS. STOCKMANN (bursting into tears). God help us all!

PETRA. Father is splendid! He will not give in.

[The boys look on in amazement; PETRA signs to them not to speak.]

ACT III

SCENE: The editorial office of the People's Messenger. The entrance door is on the left-hand side of the back wall; on the right-hand side is another door with glass panels through which the printing room can be seen. Another door in the right-hand wall. In the middle of the room is a large table covered with papers, newspapers, and books. In the foreground on the left a window, before which stand a desk and a high stool. There are a couple of easy chairs by the *table, and other chairs standing along the wall. The room is dingy and uncomfortable; the furniture is old, the chairs stained and torn. In the printing room the compositors are seen at work, and a printer is working a hand press.* HOVSTAD *is sitting at the desk, writing.* BILLING *comes in from the right with Dr. Stockmann's manuscript in his hand.*

BILLING. Well, I must say!

HOVSTAD *(still writing)*. Have you read it through?

BILLING *(laying the manuscript on the desk)*. Yes, indeed I have.

HOVSTAD. Don't you think the doctor hits them pretty hard?

BILLING. Hard? Bless my soul, he's crushing! Every word falls like—how shall I put it?—like the blow of a sledge hammer.

HOVSTAD. Yes, but they are not the people to throw up the sponge at the first blow.

BILLING. That is true; and for that reason we must strike blow upon blow until the whole of this aristocracy tumbles to pieces. As I sat in there reading this, I almost seemed to see a revolution in being.

HOVSTAD *(turning round)*. Hush!—Speak so that Aslaksen cannot hear you.

BILLING *(lowering his voice)*. Aslaksen is a chicken-hearted chap, a coward; there is nothing of the man in him. But this time you will insist on your own way, won't you? You will put the doctor's article in?

HOVSTAD. Yes, and if the mayor doesn't like it—

BILLING. That will be the devil of a nuisance.

HOVSTAD. Well, fortunately we can turn the situation to good account, whatever happens. If the mayor will not fall in with the doctor's project, he will have all the small tradesmen down on him—the whole of the Householders' Association and the rest of them. And if he does fall in with it, he will fall out with the whole crowd of large share-holders in the baths, who up to now have been his most valuable supporters—

BILLING. Yes, because they will certainly have to fork out a pretty penny—

HOVSTAD. Yes, you may be sure they will. And in this way the ring will be broken up, you see, and then in every issue of the paper we will enlighten the public on the mayor's incapability on one point and another, and make it clear that all the positions of trust in the town, the whole control of municipal affairs, ought to be put in the hands of the liberals.

BILLING. That is perfectly true! I see it coming—I see it coming; we are on the threshold of a revolution!

[A knock is heard at the door.]

HOVSTAD. Hush! *(Calls out.)* Come in! (DR. STOCKMANN *comes in by the street door.* HOVSTAD *goes to meet him.)* Ah, it is you, Doctor! Well?

DR. STOCKMANN. You may set to work and print it, Mr. Hovstad!

HOVSTAD. Has it come to that, then?

BILLING. Hurrah!

DR. STOCKMANN. Yes, print away. Undoubtedly it has come to that. Now they must take what they get. There is going to be a fight in the town, Mr. Billing!

BILLING. War to the knife, I hope! We will get our knives to their throats, Doctor!

DR. STOCKMANN. This article is only a beginning. I have already got four or five more sketched out in my head. Where is Aslaksen?

BILLING *(calls into the printing room)*. Aslaksen, just come here for a minute!

HOVSTAD. Four or five more articles, did you say? On the same subject?

DR. STOCKMANN. No—far from it, my dear fellow. No, they are about quite another matter. But they all spring from the question of the water supply and the drainage. One thing leads to another, you know. It is like beginning to pull down an old house, exactly.

BILLING. Upon my soul, it's true; you

find you are not done till you have pulled all the old rubbish down.

ASLAKSEN (coming in). Pulled down? You are not thinking of pulling down the baths surely, Doctor?

HOVSTAD. Far from it; don't be afraid.

DR. STOCKMANN. No, we meant something quite different. Well, what do you think of my article, Mr. Hovstad?

HOVSTAD. I think it is simply a masterpiece—

DR. STOCKMANN. Do you really think so? Well, I am very pleased, very pleased.

HOVSTAD. It is so clear and intelligible. One need have no special knowledge to understand the bearing of it. You will have every enlightened man on your side.

ASLAKSEN. And every prudent man too, I hope?

BILLING. The prudent and the imprudent—almost the whole town.

ASLAKSEN. In that case we may venture to print it.

DR. STOCKMANN. I should think so!

HOVSTAD. We will put it in tomorrow morning.

DR. STOCKMANN. Of course—you must not lose a single day. What I wanted to ask you, Mr. Aslaksen, was if you would supervise the printing of it yourself.

ASLAKSEN. With pleasure.

DR. STOCKMANN. Take care of it as if it were a treasure! No misprints—every word is important. I will look in again a little later; perhaps you will be able to let me see a proof. I can't tell you how eager I am to see it in print, and see it burst upon the public—

BILLING. Burst upon them—yes, like a flash of lightning!

DR. STOCKMANN. And to have it submitted to the judgment of my intelligent fellow townsmen. You cannot imagine what I have gone through today. I have been threatened first with one thing and then with another; they have tried to rob me of my most elementary right as a man—

BILLING. What! Your rights as a man!

DR. STOCKMANN. They have tried to degrade me, to make a coward of me, to force me to put personal interests before my most sacred convictions—

BILLING. That is too much—I'm damned if it isn't.

HOVSTAD. Oh, you mustn't be surprised at anything from that quarter.

DR. STOCKMANN. Well, they will get the worst of it with me; they may assure themselves of that. I shall consider the *People's Messenger* my sheet-anchor now, and every single day I will bombard them with one article after another, like bombshells—

ASLAKSEN. Yes, but—

BILLING. Hurrah!—it is war, it is war!

DR. STOCKMANN. I shall smite them to the ground—I shall crush them—I shall break down all their defenses, before the eyes of the honest public! That is what I shall do!

ASLAKSEN. Yes, but in moderation, Doctor—proceed with moderation—

BILLING. Not a bit of it, not a bit of it! Don't spare the dynamite!

DR. STOCKMANN. Because it is not merely a question of water supply and drains now, you know. No—it is the whole of our social life that we have got to purify and disinfect—

BILLING. Spoken like a deliverer!

DR. STOCKMANN. All the incapables must be turned out, you understand—and that in every walk of life! Endless vistas have opened themselves to my mind's eye today. I cannot see it all quite clearly yet, but I shall in time. Young and vigorous standard bearers—those are what we need and must seek, my friends; we must have new men in command at all our outposts.

BILLING. Hear, hear!

DR. STOCKMANN. We only need to stand by one another, and it will all be perfectly easy. The revolution will be launched like a ship that runs smoothly off the stocks. Don't you think so?

HOVSTAD. For my part I think we have now a prospect of getting the municipal authority into the hands where it should lie.

ASLAKSEN. And if only we proceed with moderation, I cannot imagine that there will be any risk.

DR. STOCKMANN. Who the devil cares whether there is any risk or not! What I am doing, I am doing in the name of truth and for the sake of my conscience.

HOVSTAD. You are a man who deserves to be supported, Doctor.

ASLAKSEN. Yes, there is no denying that the doctor is a true friend to the town—a real friend to the community, that he is.

BILLING. Take my word for it, Aslaksen, Dr. Stockmann is a friend of the people.

ASLAKSEN. I fancy the Householders' Association will make use of that expression before long.

DR. STOCKMANN (affected, grasps their hands). Thank you, thank you, my dear staunch friends. It is very refreshing to me to hear you say that; my brother called me something quite different. By Jove, he shall have it back, with interest! But now I must be off to see a poor devil— I will come back, as I said. Keep a very careful eye on the manuscript, Aslaksen, and don't for worlds leave out any of my notes of exclamation! Rather put one or two more in! Capital, capital! Well, good-by for the present—good-by, good-by!

[*They show him to the door, and bow him out.*]

HOVSTAD. He may prove an invaluably useful man to us.

ASLAKSEN. Yes, so long as he confines himself to this matter of the baths. But if he goes further afield, I don't think it would be advisable to follow him.

HOVSTAD. Hm!—that all depends—

BILLING. You are so infernally timid, Aslaksen!

ASLAKSEN. Timid? Yes, when it is a question of the local authorities, I am timid, Mr. Billing; it is a lesson I have learnt in the school of experience, let me tell you. But try me in higher poli-tics, in matters that concern the government itself, and then see if I am timid.

BILLING. No, you aren't, I admit. But this is simply contradicting yourself.

ASLAKSEN. I am a man with a conscience, and that is the whole matter. If you attack the government, you don't do the community any harm, anyway; those fellows pay no attention to attacks, you see—they go on just as they are, in spite of them. But *local* authorities are different; they *can* be turned out, and then perhaps you may get an ignorant lot into office who may do irreparable harm to the householders and everybody else.

HOVSTAD. But what of the education of citizens by self-government—don't you attach any importance to that?

ASLAKSEN. When a man has interests of his own to protect, he cannot think of everything, Mr. Hovstad.

HOVSTAD. Then I hope I shall never have interests of my own to protect!

BILLING. Hear, hear!

ASLAKSEN (with a smile). Hm! (Points to the desk.) Mr. Sheriff Stensgaard was your predecessor at that editorial desk.

BILLING (spitting). Bah! That turncoat.

HOVSTAD. I am not a weathercock—and never will be.

ASLAKSEN. A politician should never be too certain of anything, Mr. Hovstad. And as for you, Mr. Billing, I should think it is time for you to be taking in a reef or two in your sails, seeing that you are applying for the post of secretary to the Bench.

BILLING. I—!

HOVSTAD. Are you, Billing?

BILLING. Well, yes—but you must clearly understand I am doing it only to annoy the bigwigs.

ASLAKSEN. Anyhow, it is no business of mine. But if I am to be accused of timidity and of inconsistency in my principles, this is what I want to point out: my political past is an open book. I have never changed, except perhaps to become a little more moderate, you see. My heart is still with the people; but I don't deny that my reason has a certain bias toward the authorities—the local ones, I mean.

[*Goes into the printing room.*]

BILLING. Oughtn't we to try and get rid of him, Hovstad?

HOVSTAD. Do you know anyone else who will advance the money for our paper and printing bill?

BILLING. It is an infernal nuisance that we don't possess some capital to trade on.

HOVSTAD (*sitting down at his desk*). Yes, if we only had that, then—

BILLING. Suppose you were to apply to Dr. Stockmann?

HOVSTAD (*turning over some papers*). What is the use? He has got nothing.

BILLING. No, but he has got a warm man in the background, old Morten Kiil— the Badger, as they call him.

HOVSTAD (*writing*). Are you so sure *he* has got anything?

BILLING. Good Lord, of course he has! And some of it must come to the Stockmanns. Most probably he will do something for the children, at all events.

HOVSTAD (*turning half round*). Are you counting on that?

BILLING. Counting on it? Of course I am not counting on anything.

HOVSTAD. That is right. And I should not count on the secretaryship to the Bench either, if I were you; for I can assure you—you won't get it.

BILLING. Do you think I am not quite aware of that? My object is precisely *not* to get it. A slight of that kind stimulates a man's fighting power—it is like getting a supply of fresh bile—and I am sure one needs that badly enough in a hole-and-corner place like this, where it is so seldom anything happens to stir one up.

HOVSTAD (*writing*). Quite so, quite so.

BILLING. Ah, I shall be heard of yet!— Now I shall go and write the appeal to the Householders' Association.

[*Goes into the room on the right.*]

HOVSTAD (*sitting at his desk, biting his penholder, says slowly*). Hm!—that's it, is it? (*A knock is heard.*) Come in! (PETRA *comes in by the outer door.* HOVSTAD *gets up.*) What, you!—here?

PETRA. Yes, you must forgive me—

HOVSTAD (*pulling a chair forward*). Won't you sit down?

PETRA. No, thank you; I must go again in a moment.

HOVSTAD. Have you come with a message from your father, by any chance?

PETRA. No, I have come on my own account. (*Takes a book out of her coat pocket.*) Here is the English story.

HOVSTAD. Why have you brought it back?

PETRA. Because I am not going to translate it.

HOVSTAD. But you promised me faithfully—

PETRA. Yes, but then I had not read it. I don't suppose you have read it either?

HOVSTAD. No, you know quite well I don't understand English; but—

PETRA. Quite so. That is why I wanted to tell you that you must find something else. (*Lays the book on the table.*) You can't use this for the *People's Messenger*.

HOVSTAD. Why not?

PETRA. Because it conflicts with all your opinions.

HOVSTAD. Oh, for that matter—

PETRA. You don't understand me. The burden of this story is that there is a supernatural power that looks after the so-called good people in this world and makes everything happen for the best in their case—while all the so-called bad people are punished.

HOVSTAD. Well, but that is all right. That is just what our readers want.

PETRA. And are you going to be the one to give it to them? For myself, I do not believe a word of it. You know quite well that things do not happen so in reality.

HOVSTAD. You are perfectly right; but an editor cannot always act as he would prefer. He is often obliged to bow to the wishes of the public in unimportant matters. Politics are the most important thing in life—for a newspaper, anyway; and if I want to carry my public with me on the path that leads to liberty and progress, I must not frighten them away. If they find a moral tale of this sort in the serial at the bottom of the page, they will be all the more ready to read what is printed above it; they feel more secure, as it were.

PETRA. For shame! You would never go and set a snare like that for your readers; you are not a spider!

HOVSTAD (smiling). Thank you for having such a good opinion of me. No; as a matter of fact that is Billing's idea and not mine.

PETRA. Billing's!

HOVSTAD. Yes; anyway he propounded that theory here one day. And it is Billing who is so anxious to have that story in the paper; I don't know anything about the book.

PETRA. But how can Billing, with his emancipated views—

HOVSTAD. Oh, Billing is a many-sided man. He is applying for the post of secretary to the Bench, too, I hear.

PETRA. I don't believe it, Mr. Hovstad. How could he possibly bring himself to do such a thing?

HOVSTAD. Ah, you must ask him that.

PETRA. I should never have thought it of him.

HOVSTAD (looking more closely at her). No? Does it really surprise you so much?

PETRA. Yes. Or perhaps not altogether. Really, I don't quite know—

HOVSTAD. We journalists are not much worth, Miss Stockmann.

PETRA. Do you really mean that?

HOVSTAD. I think so sometimes.

PETRA. Yes, in the ordinary affairs of everyday life, perhaps; I can understand that. But now, when you have taken a weighty matter in hand—

HOVSTAD. This matter of your father's, you mean?

PETRA. Exactly. It seems to me that now you must feel you are a man worth more than most.

HOVSTAD. Yes, today I do feel something of that sort.

PETRA. Of course you do, don't you? It is a splendid vocation you have chosen —to smooth the way for the march of unappreciated truths, and new and courageous lines of thought. If it were nothing more than because you stand fearlessly in the open and take up the cause of an injured man—

HOVSTAD. Especially when that injured man is—ahem!—I don't rightly know how to—

PETRA. When that man is so upright and so honest, you mean?

HOVSTAD (more gently). Especially when he is your father, I meant.

PETRA (suddenly checked). That?

HOVSTAD. Yes, Petra—Miss Petra.

PETRA. Is it that that is first and foremost with you? Not the matter itself? Not the truth?—Not my father's big generous heart?

HOVSTAD. Certainly—of course—that too.

PETRA. No, thank you; you have betrayed yourself, Mr. Hovstad, and now I shall never trust you again in anything.

HOVSTAD. Can you really take it so amiss in me that it is mostly for your sake —?

PETRA. What I am angry with you for is for not having been honest with my father. You talked to him as if the truth and the good of the community were what lay nearest to your heart. You have made fools of both my father and me. You are not the man you made yourself out to be. And that I shall never forgive you— never!

HOVSTAD. You ought not to speak so bitterly, Miss Petra—least of all now.

PETRA. Why not now, especially?

HOVSTAD. Because your father cannot do without my help.

PETRA (looking him up and down). Are you that sort of man, too? For shame!

HOVSTAD. No, no, I am not. This came upon me so unexpectedly—you must believe that.

PETRA. I know what to believe. Goodby.

ASLAKSEN (coming from the printing room, hurriedly and with an air of mystery). Damnation, Hovstad!—(Sees PETRA.) Oh, this is awkward—

PETRA. There is the book; you must give it to someone else.

[*Goes toward the door.*]

HOVSTAD (*following her*). But, Miss Stockmann—

PETRA. Good-by.   [*Goes out.*]

ASLAKSEN. I say—Mr. Hovstad—

HOVSTAD. Well, well!—what is it?

ASLAKSEN. The mayor is outside in the printing room.

HOVSTAD. The mayor, did you say?

ASLAKSEN. Yes, he wants to speak to you. He came in by the back door—didn't want to be seen, you understand.

HOVSTAD. What can he want? Wait a bit—I will go myself. (*Goes to the door of the printing room, opens it, bows, and invites* PETER STOCKMANN *in.*) Just see, Aslaksen, that no one—

ASLAKSEN. Quite so.

[*Goes into the printing room.*]

PETER STOCKMANN. You did not expect to see me here, Mr. Hovstad?

HOVSTAD. No, I confess I did not.

PETER STOCKMANN (*looking round*). You are very snug in here—very nice indeed.

HOVSTAD. Oh—

PETER STOCKMANN. And here I come, without any notice, to take up your time!

HOVSTAD. By all means, Mr. Mayor. I am at your service. But let me relieve you of your— (*Takes* STOCKMANN'S *hat and stick and puts them on a chair.*) Won't you sit down?

PETER STOCKMANN (*sitting down by the table*). Thank you. (HOVSTAD *sits down.*) I have had an extremely annoying experience today, Mr. Hovstad.

HOVSTAD. Really? Ah well, I expect with all the various business you have to attend to—

PETER STOCKMANN. The medical officer of the baths is responsible for what happened today.

HOVSTAD. Indeed? The doctor?

PETER STOCKMANN. He has addressed a kind of report to the Baths Committee on the subject of certain supposed defects in the baths.

HOVSTAD. Has he indeed?

PETER STOCKMANN. Yes—has he not told you? I thought he said—

HOVSTAD. Ah, yes—it is true he did mention something about—

ASLAKSEN (*coming from the printing room*). I ought to have that copy—

HOVSTAD (*angrily*). Ahem!—there it is on the desk.

ASLAKSEN (*taking it*). Right.

PETER STOCKMANN. But look there—that is the thing I was speaking of!

ASLAKSEN. Yes, that is the doctor's article, Mr. Mayor.

HOVSTAD. Oh, is *that* what you were speaking about?

PETER STOCKMANN. Yes, that is it. What do you think of it?

HOVSTAD. Oh, I am only a layman—and I have only taken a very cursory glance at it.

PETER STOCKMANN. But you are going to print it?

HOVSTAD. I cannot very well refuse a distinguished man—

ASLAKSEN. I have nothing to do with editing the paper, Mr. Mayor—

PETER STOCKMANN. I understand.

ASLAKSEN. I merely print what is put into my hands.

PETER STOCKMANN. Quite so.

ASLAKSEN. And so I must—

[*Moves off toward the printing room.*]

PETER STOCKMANN. No, but wait a moment, Mr. Aslaksen. You will allow me, Mr. Hovstad?

HOVSTAD. If you please, Mr. Mayor.

PETER STOCKMANN. You are a discreet and thoughtful man, Mr. Aslaksen.

ASLAKSEN. I am delighted to hear you think so, sir.

PETER STOCKMANN. And a man of very considerable influence.

ASLAKSEN. Chiefly among the small tradesmen, sir.

PETER STOCKMANN. The small taxpayers are the majority — here as everywhere else.

ASLAKSEN. That is true.

PETER STOCKMANN. And I have no doubt you know the general trend of opinion among them, don't you?

ASLAKSEN. Yes, I think I may say I do, Mr. Mayor.

PETER STOCKMANN. Yes. Well, since there is such a praiseworthy spirit of self-sacrifice among the less wealthy citizens of our town—

ASLAKSEN. What?

HOVSTAD. Self-sacrifice?

PETER STOCKMANN. It is pleasing evidence of a public-spirited feeling, extremely pleasing evidence. I might almost say I hardly expected it. But you have a closer knowledge of public opinion than I.

ASLAKSEN. But, Mr. Mayor—

PETER STOCKMANN. And indeed it is no small sacrifice that the town is going to make.

HOVSTAD. The town?

ASLAKSEN. But I don't understand. Is it the baths—?

PETER STOCKMANN. At a provisional estimate, the alterations that the medical officer asserts to be desirable will cost somewhere about twenty thousand pounds.

ASLAKSEN. That is a lot of money, but—

PETER STOCKMANN. Of course it will be necessary to raise a municipal loan.

HOVSTAD (getting up). Surely you never mean that the town must pay—?

ASLAKSEN. Do you mean that it must come out of the municipal funds?—out of the ill-filled pockets of the small tradesmen?

PETER STOCKMANN. Well, my dear Mr. Aslaksen, where else is the money to come from?

ASLAKSEN. The gentlemen who own the baths ought to provide that.

PETER STOCKMANN. The proprietors of the baths are not in a position to incur any further expense.

ASLAKSEN. Is that absolutely certain, Mr. Mayor?

PETER STOCKMANN. I have satisfied myself that it is so. If the town wants these very extensive alterations, it will have to pay for them.

ASLAKSEN. But, damn it all—I beg your pardon—this is quite another matter, Mr. Hovstad!

HOVSTAD. It is, indeed.

PETER STOCKMANN. The most fatal part of it is that we shall be obliged to shut the baths for a couple of years.

HOVSTAD. Shut them? Shut them altogether?

ASLAKSEN. For two years?

PETER STOCKMANN. Yes, the work will take as long as that—at least.

ASLAKSEN. I'm damned if we will stand that, Mr. Mayor! What are we householders to live upon in the meantime?

PETER STOCKMANN. Unfortunately, that is an extremely difficult question to answer, Mr. Aslaksen. But what would you have us do? Do you suppose we shall have a single visitor in the town, if we go about proclaiming that our water is polluted, that we are living over a plague spot, that the entire town—

ASLAKSEN. And the whole thing is merely imagination?

PETER STOCKMANN. With the best will in the world, I have not been able to come to any other conclusion.

ASLAKSEN. Well then I must say it is absolutely unjustifiable of Dr. Stockmann —I beg your pardon, Mr. Mayor—

PETER STOCKMANN. What you say is lamentably true, Mr. Aslaksen. My brother has, unfortunately, always been a headstrong man.

ASLAKSEN. After this, do you mean to give him your support, Mr. Hovstad?

HOVSTAD. Can you suppose for a moment that I—?

PETER STOCKMANN. I have drawn up a short résumé of the situation as it appears from a reasonable man's point of view. In it I have indicated how certain possible defects might suitably be remedied without outrunning the resources of the Baths Committee.

HOVSTAD. Have you got it with you, Mr. Mayor?

PETER STOCKMANN (fumbling in his pocket). Yes, I brought it with me in case you should—

ASLAKSEN. Good Lord, there he is!

PETER STOCKMANN. Who? My brother?

HOVSTAD. Where? Where?

ASLAKSEN. He has just gone through the printing room.

PETER STOCKMANN. How unlucky! I don't want to meet him here, and I had still several things to speak to you about.

HOVSTAD (*pointing to the door on the right*). Go in there for the present.

PETER STOCKMANN. But—?

HOVSTAD. You will only find Billing in there.

ASLAKSEN. Quick, quick, Mr. Mayor— he is just coming.

PETER STOCKMANN. Yes, very well; but see that you get rid of him quickly.

[*Goes out through the door on the right, which* ASLAKSEN *opens for him and shuts after him.*]

HOVSTAD. Pretend to be doing something, Aslaksen.

[*Sits down and writes.* ASLAKSEN *begins foraging among a heap of newspapers that are lying on a chair.*]

DR. STOCKMANN (*coming in from the printing room*). Here I am again.
          [*Puts down his hat and stick.*]

HOVSTAD (*writing*). Already, Doctor? Hurry up with what we were speaking about, Aslaksen. We are very pressed for time today.

DR. STOCKMANN (*to* ASLAKSEN). No proof for me to see yet, I hear.

ASLAKSEN (*without turning round*). You couldn't expect it yet, Doctor.

DR. STOCKMANN. No, no; but I am impatient, as you can understand. I shall not know a moment's peace of mind till I see it in print.

HOVSTAD. Hm!—it will take a good while yet, won't it, Aslaksen?

ASLAKSEN. Yes, I am almost afraid it will.

DR. STOCKMANN. All right, my dear friends; I will come back. I do not mind coming back twice if necessary. A matter of such great importance—the welfare of the town at stake—it is no time to shirk trouble. (*Is just going, but stops and comes back.*) Look here—there is one thing more I want to speak to you about.

HOVSTAD. Excuse me, but could it not wait till some other time?

DR. STOCKMANN. I can tell you in half a dozen words. It is only this. When my article is read tomorrow and it is realized that I have been quietly working the whole winter for the welfare of the town—

HOVSTAD. Yes, but, Doctor—

DR. STOCKMANN. I know what you are going to say. You don't see how on earth it was any more than my duty—my obvious duty as a citizen. Of course it wasn't; I know that as well as you. But my fellow citizens, you know—! Good Lord, think of all the good souls who think so highly of me—!

ASLAKSEN. Yes, our townsfolk have had a very high opinion of you so far, Doctor.

DR. STOCKMANN. Yes, and that is just why I am afraid they— Well, this is the point; when this reaches them, especially the poorer classes, and sounds in their ears like a summons to take the town's affairs into their own hands for the future—

HOVSTAD (*getting up*). Ahem! Doctor, I won't conceal from you the fact—

DR. STOCKMANN. Ah!—I knew there was something in the wind! But I won't hear a word of it. If anything of that sort is being set on foot—

HOVSTAD. Of what sort?

DR. STOCKMANN. Well, whatever it is— whether it is a demonstration in my honor, or a banquet, or a subscription list for some presentation to me—whatever it is, you must promise me solemnly and faithfully to put a stop to it. You too, Mr. Aslaksen; do you understand?

HOVSTAD. You must forgive me, Doctor, but sooner or later we must tell you the plain truth—

[*He is interrupted by the entrance of* MRS. STOCKMANN, *who comes in from the street door.*]

MRS. STOCKMANN (*seeing her husband*). Just as I thought!

HOVSTAD (*going toward her*). You too, Mrs. Stockmann?

DR. STOCKMANN. What on earth do *you* want here, Katherine?

MRS. STOCKMANN. I should think you know very well what I want.

HOVSTAD. Won't you sit down? Or perhaps—

MRS. STOCKMANN. No, thank you; don't trouble. And you must not be offended at my coming to fetch my husband; I am the mother of three children, you know.

DR. STOCKMANN. Nonsense!—We know all about that.

MRS. STOCKMANN. Well, one would not give you credit for much thought for your wife and children today; if you had had that, you would not have gone and dragged us all into misfortune.

DR. STOCKMANN. Are you out of your senses, Katherine! Because a man has a wife and children, is he not to be allowed to proclaim the truth—is he not to be allowed to be an actively useful citizen—is he not to be allowed to do a service to his native town!

MRS. STOCKMANN. Yes, Thomas—in reason.

ASLAKSEN. Just what I say. Moderation is everything.

MRS. STOCKMANN. And that is why you wrong us, Mr. Hovstad, in enticing my husband away from his home and making a dupe of him in all this.

HOVSTAD. I certainly am making a dupe of no one—

DR. STOCKMANN. Making a dupe of me! Do you suppose *I* should allow myself to be duped!

MRS. STOCKMANN. It is just what you do. I know quite well you have more brains than anyone in the town, but you are extremely easily duped, Thomas. *(To* HOVSTAD.*)* Please do realize that he loses his post at the baths if you print what he has written—

ASLAKSEN. What!

HOVSTAD. Look here, Doctor—

DR. STOCKMANN *(laughing).* Ha—ha!— just let them try! No, no—they will take good care not to. I have got the compact majority behind me, let me tell you!

MRS. STOCKMANN. Yes, that is just the worst of it—your having any such horrid thing behind you.

DR. STOCKMANN. Rubbish, Katherine! —Go home and look after your house and leave me to look after the community. How can you be so afraid, when I am so confident and happy? *(Walks up and down, rubbing his hands.)* Truth and the People will win the fight, you may be certain! I see the whole of the broad-minded middle class marching like a victorious army—! *(Stops beside a chair.)* What the deuce is that lying there?

ASLAKSEN. Good Lord!

HOVSTAD. Ahem!

DR. STOCKMANN. Here we have the topmost pinnacle of authority!

[*Takes the mayor's official hat carefully between his fingertips and holds it up in the air.*]

MRS. STOCKMANN. The mayor's hat!

DR. STOCKMANN. And here is the staff of office too. How in the name of all that's wonderful—?

HOVSTAD. Well, you see—

DR. STOCKMANN. Oh, I understand. He has been here trying to talk you over. Ha! —ha!—he made rather a mistake there! And as soon as he caught sight of me in the printing room— *(Bursts out laughing.)* Did he run away, Mr. Aslaksen?

ASLAKSEN *(hurriedly).* Yes, he ran away, Doctor.

DR. STOCKMANN. Ran away without his stick or his— Fiddlesticks! Peter doesn't run away and leave his belongings behind him. But what the deuce have you done with him? Ah!—in there, of course. Now you shall see, Katherine.

MRS. STOCKMANN. Thomas—please don't—!

ASLAKSEN. Don't be rash, Doctor.

[DR. STOCKMANN *has put on the mayor's hat and taken his stick in his hand. He goes up to the door, opens it, and stands with his hand to his hat at the salute.* PETER STOCKMANN *comes in, red with anger.* BILLING *follows him.*]

PETER STOCKMANN. What does this tomfoolery mean?

DR. STOCKMANN. Be respectful, my good Peter. I am the chief authority in the town now.   [*Walks up and down.*]

MRS. STOCKMANN (*almost in tears*). Really, Thomas!

PETER STOCKMANN (*following him about*). Give me my hat and stick.

DR. STOCKMANN (*in the same tone as before*). If you are chief constable, let me tell you that I am the mayor—I am the master of the whole town, please understand!

PETER STOCKMANN. Take off my hat, I tell you. Remember it is part of an official uniform.

DR. STOCKMANN. Pooh! Do you think the newly awakened lionhearted people are going to be frightened by an official hat? There is going to be a revolution in the town tomorrow, let me tell you. You thought you could turn me out; but now I shall turn you out—turn you out of all your various offices. Do you think I cannot? Listen to me. I have triumphant social forces behind me. Hovstad and Billing will thunder in the *People's Messenger,* and Aslaksen will take the field at the head of the whole Householders' Association—

ASLAKSEN. That I won't, Doctor.

DR. STOCKMANN. Of course you will—

PETER STOCKMANN. Ah!—may I ask then if Mr. Hovstad intends to join this agitation?

HOVSTAD. No, Mr. Mayor.

ASLAKSEN. No, Mr. Hovstad is not such a fool as to go and ruin his paper and himself for the sake of an imaginary grievance.

DR. STOCKMANN (*looking round him*). What does this mean?

HOVSTAD. You have represented your case in a false light, Doctor, and therefore I am unable to give you my support.

BILLING. And after what the mayor was so kind as to tell me just now, I—

DR. STOCKMANN. A false light! Leave that part of it to me. Only print my article; I am quite capable of defending it.

HOVSTAD. I am not going to print it. I

cannot and will not and dare not print it.

DR. STOCKMANN. You dare not? What nonsense!—you are the editor; and an editor controls his paper, I suppose!

ASLAKSEN. No, it is the subscribers, Doctor.

PETER STOCKMANN. Fortunately, yes.

ASLAKSEN. It is public opinion—the enlightened public — householders and people of that kind; they control the newspapers.

DR. STOCKMANN (*composedly*). And I have all these influences against me?

ASLAKSEN. Yes, you have. It would mean the absolute ruin of the community if your article were to appear.

DR. STOCKMANN. Indeed.

PETER STOCKMANN. My hat and stick, if you please. (DR. STOCKMANN *takes off the hat and lays it on the table with the stick.* PETER STOCKMANN *takes them up.*) Your authority as mayor has come to an untimely end.

DR. STOCKMANN. We have not got to the end yet. (*To* HOVSTAD.) Then it is quite impossible for you to print my article in the *People's Messenger?*

HOVSTAD. Quite impossible—out of regard for your family as well.

MRS. STOCKMANN. You need not concern yourself about his family, thank you, Mr. Hovstad.

PETER STOCKMANN (*taking a paper from his pocket*). It will be sufficient, for the guidance of the public, if this appears. It is an official statement. May I trouble you?

HOVSTAD (*taking the paper*). Certainly; I will see that it is printed.

DR. STOCKMANN. But not mine. Do you imagine that you can silence me and stifle the truth! You will not find it so easy as you suppose. Mr. Aslaksen, kindly take my manuscript at once and print it as a pamphlet—at my expense. I will have four hundred copies—no, five— six hundred.

ASLAKSEN. If you offered me its weight in gold, I could not lend my press for any such purpose, Doctor. It would be flying in the face of public opinion. You will not get it printed anywhere in the town.

DR. STOCKMANN. Then, give it back to me.

HOVSTAD (giving the manuscript). Here it is.

DR. STOCKMANN (taking his hat and stick). It shall be made public all the same. I will read it out at a mass meeting of the townspeople. All my fellow citizens shall hear the voice of truth!

PETER STOCKMANN. You will not find any public body in the town that will give you the use of their hall for such a purpose.

ASLAKSEN. Not a single one, I am certain.

BILLING. No, I'm damned if you will find one.

MRS. STOCKMANN. But this is too shameful! Why should every one turn against you like that?

DR. STOCKMANN (angrily). I will tell you why. It is because all the men in this town are old women—like you; they all think of nothing but their families, and never of the community.

MRS. STOCKMANN (putting her arm into his). Then I will show them that an—an old woman can be a man for once. I am going to stand by you, Thomas!

DR. STOCKMANN. Bravely said, Katherine! It shall be made public—as I am a living soul! If I can't hire a hall, I shall hire a drum, and parade the town with it and read it at every street corner.

PETER STOCKMANN. You are surely not such an arrant fool as that!

DR. STOCKMANN. Yes, I am.

ASLAKSEN. You won't find a single man in the whole town to go with you.

BILLING. No, I'm damned if you will.

MRS. STOCKMANN. Don't give in, Thomas. I will tell the boys to go with you.

DR. STOCKMANN. That is a splendid idea!

MRS. STOCKMANN. Morten will be delighted; and Ejlif will do whatever he does.

DR. STOCKMANN. Yes, and Petra!—and you too, Katherine!

MRS. STOCKMANN. No, I won't do that; but I will stand at the window and watch you, that's what I will do.

DR. STOCKMANN (puts his arms round her and kisses her). Thank you, my dear! Now you and I are going to try a fall, my fine gentlemen! I am going to see whether a pack of cowards can succeed in gagging a patriot who wants to purify society!

[He and his wife go out by the street door.]

PETER STOCKMANN (shaking his head seriously). Now he has sent her out of her senses, too.

ACT IV

SCENE: *A big old-fashioned room in Captain Horster's house. At the back folding doors, which are standing open, lead to an anteroom. Three windows in the left-hand wall. In the middle of the opposite wall a platform has been erected. On this is a small table with two candles, a water bottle and glass, and a bell. The room is lit by lamps placed between the windows. In the foreground on the left there is a table with candles and a chair. To the right is a door and some chairs standing near it. The room is nearly filled with a crowd of townspeople of all sorts, a few women and schoolboys being among them. People are still streaming in from the back, and the room is soon filled.*

FIRST CITIZEN (meeting another). Hullo, Lamstad! You here too?

SECOND CITIZEN. I go to every public meeting, I do.

THIRD CITIZEN. Brought your whistle too, I expect!

SECOND CITIZEN. I should think so. Haven't you?

THIRD CITIZEN. Rather! And old Evensen said he was going to bring a cowhorn, he did.

SECOND CITIZEN. Good old Evensen!

[Laughter among the crowd.]

FOURTH CITIZEN (coming up to them).

I say, tell me what is going on here to-night.

SECOND CITIZEN. Dr. Stockmann is going to deliver an address attacking the mayor.

FOURTH CITIZEN. But the mayor is his brother.

FIRST CITIZEN. That doesn't matter; Dr. Stockmann's not the chap to be afraid.

THIRD CITIZEN. But he is in the wrong; it said so in the *People's Messenger*.

SECOND CITIZEN. Yes, I expect he must be in the wrong this time, because neither the Householders' Association nor the Citizens' Club would lend him their hall for his meeting.

FIRST CITIZEN. He couldn't even get the loan of the hall at the baths.

SECOND CITIZEN. No, I should think not.

FIRST MAN (*in another part of the crowd*). I say—who are we to back up in this?

SECOND MAN (*beside him*). Watch Aslaksen, and do as he does.

BILLING (*pushing his way through the crowd, with a writing case under his arm*). Excuse me, gentlemen—do you mind letting me through? I am reporting for the *People's Messenger*. Thank you very much!

[*He sits down at the table on the left.*]

FIRST WORKMAN. Who was that?

SECOND WORKMAN. Don't you know him? It's Billing, who writes for Aslaksen's paper.

[CAPTAIN HORSTER *brings in* MRS. STOCKMANN *and* PETRA *through the door on the right.* EJLIF *and* MORTEN *follow them in.*]

HORSTER. I thought you might all sit here; you can slip out easily from here, if things get too lively.

MRS. STOCKMANN. Do you think there will be a disturbance?

HORSTER. One can never tell—with such a crowd. But sit down, and don't be uneasy.

MRS. STOCKMANN (*sitting down*). It was extremely kind of you to offer my husband the room.

HORSTER. Well, if nobody else would—

PETRA (*who has sat down beside her mother*). And it was a plucky thing to do, Captain Horster.

HORSTER. Oh, it is not such a great matter as all that.

[HOVSTAD *and* ASLAKSEN *make their way through the crowd.*]

ASLAKSEN (*going up to* HORSTER). Has the doctor not come yet?

HORSTER. He is waiting in the next room.

[*Movement in the crowd by the door at the back.*]

HOVSTAD. Look—here comes the mayor!

BILLING. Yes, I'm damned if he hasn't come after all!

[PETER STOCKMANN *makes his way gradually through the crowd, bows courteously, and takes up a position by the wall on the left. Shortly afterward* DR. STOCKMANN *comes in by the right-hand door. He is dressed in a black frock-coat, with a white tie. There is a little feeble applause which is hushed down. Silence is obtained.*]

DR. STOCKMANN (*in an undertone*). How do you feel, Katherine?

MRS. STOCKMANN. All right, thank you. (*Lowering her voice.*) Be sure not to lose your temper, Thomas.

DR. STOCKMANN. Oh, I know how to control myself. (*Looks at his watch, steps on to the platform, and bows.*) It is a quarter past—so I will begin.

[*Takes his manuscript out of his pocket.*]

ASLAKSEN. I think we ought to elect a chairman first.

DR. STOCKMANN. No, it is quite unnecessary.

SOME OF THE CROWD. Yes—yes!

PETER STOCKMANN. I certainly think,

too, that we ought to have a chairman.

DR. STOCKMANN. But I have called this meeting to deliver a lecture, Peter.

PETER STOCKMANN. Dr. Stockmann's lecture may possibly lead to a considerable conflict of opinion.

VOICES IN THE CROWD. A chairman! A chairman!

HOVSTAD. The general wish of the meeting seems to be that a chairman should be elected.

DR. STOCKMANN (restraining himself). Very well—let the meeting have its way.

ASLAKSEN. Will the mayor be good enough to undertake the task?

THREE MEN (clapping their hands). Bravo! Bravo!

PETER STOCKMANN. For various reasons, which you will easily understand, I must beg to be excused. But fortunately we have amongst us a man who I think will be acceptable to you all. I refer to the president of the Householders' Association, Mr. Aslaksen.

SEVERAL VOICES. Yes—Aslaksen! Bravo Aslaksen!

[DR. STOCKMANN takes up his manuscript and walks up and down the platform.]

ASLAKSEN. Since my fellow citizens choose to entrust me with this duty, I cannot refuse.

[Loud applause. ASLAKSEN mounts the platform.]

BILLING (writing). "Mr. Aslaksen was elected with enthusiasm."

ASLAKSEN. And now, as I am in this position, I should like to say a few brief words. I am a quiet and peaceable man, who believes in discreet moderation, and—and—in moderate discretion. All my friends can bear witness to that.

SEVERAL VOICES. That's right! That's right, Aslaksen!

ASLAKSEN. I have learnt in the school of life and experience that moderation is the most valuable virtue a citizen can possess—

PETER STOCKMANN. Hear, hear!

ASLAKSEN. And moreover that discre-

tion and moderation are what enable a man to be of most service to the community. I would therefore suggest to our esteemed fellow citizen, who has called this meeting, that he should strive to keep strictly within the bounds of moderation.

A MAN (by the door). Three cheers for the Moderation Society!

A VOICE. Shame!

SEVERAL VOICES. Sh!—Sh!

ASLAKSEN. No interruptions, gentlemen, please! Does anyone wish to make any remarks?

PETER STOCKMANN. Mr. Chairman.

ASLAKSEN. The mayor will address the meeting.

PETER STOCKMANN. In consideration of the close relationship in which, as you all know, I stand to the present medical officer of the baths, I should have preferred not to speak this evening. But my official position with regard to the baths and my solicitude for the vital interests of the town compel me to bring forward a motion. I venture to presume that there is not a single one of our citizens present who considers it desirable that unreliable and exaggerated accounts of the sanitary condition of the baths and the town should be spread abroad.

SEVERAL VOICES. No, no! Certainly not! We protest against it!

PETER STOCKMANN. Therefore I should like to propose that the meeting should not permit the medical officer either to read or to comment on his proposed lecture.

DR. STOCKMANN (impatiently). Not permit—! What the devil—!

MRS. STOCKMANN (coughing). Ahem! —ahem!

DR. STOCKMANN (collecting himself). Very well. Go ahead!

PETER STOCKMANN. In my communication to the *People's Messenger,* I have put the essential facts before the public in such a way that every fair-minded citizen can easily form his own opinion. From it you will see that the main result of the medical officer's proposals—

apart from their constituting a vote of censure on the leading men of the town—would be to saddle the ratepayers with an unnecessary expenditure of at least some thousands of pounds.

[*Sounds of disapproval among the audience, and some catcalls.*]

ASLAKSEN (*ringing his bell*). Silence, please, gentlemen! I beg to support the mayor's motion. I quite agree with him that there is something behind this agitation started by the doctor. He talks about the baths; but it is a revolution he is aiming at—he wants to get the administration of the town put into new hands. No one doubts the honesty of the doctor's intentions—no one will suggest that there can be any two opinions as to that. I myself am a believer in self-government for the people, provided it does not fall too heavily on the ratepayers. But that would be the case here; and that is why I will see Dr. Stockmann damned —I beg your pardon—before I go with him in the matter. You can pay too dearly for a thing sometimes; that is my opinion.

[*Loud applause on all sides.*]

HOVSTAD. I, too, feel called upon to explain my position. Dr. Stockmann's agitation appeared to be gaining a certain amount of sympathy at first, so I supported it as impartially as I could. But presently we had reason to suspect that we had allowed ourselves to be misled by misrepresentation of the state of affairs—

DR. STOCKMANN. Misrepresentation—!

HOVSTAD. Well, let us say a not entirely trustworthy representation. The mayor's statement has proved that. I hope no one here has any doubt as to my liberal principles; the attitude of the *People's Messenger* toward important political questions is well known to everyone. But the advice of experienced and thoughtful men has convinced me that in purely local matters a newspaper ought to proceed with a certain caution.

ASLAKSEN. I entirely agree with the speaker.

HOVSTAD. And, in the matter before us, it is now an undoubted fact that Dr. Stockmann has public opinion against him. Now, what is an editor's first and most obvious duty, gentlemen? Is it not to work in harmony with his readers? Has he not received a sort of tacit mandate to work persistently and assiduously for the welfare of those whose opinions he represents? Or is it possible I am mistaken in that?

VOICES FROM THE CROWD. No, no! You are quite right!

HOVSTAD. It has cost me a severe struggle to break with a man in whose house I have been lately a frequent guest—a man who till today has been able to pride himself on the undivided goodwill of his fellow citizens—a man whose only, or at all events whose essential, failing is that he is swayed by his heart rather than his head.

A FEW SCATTERED VOICES. That is true! Bravo, Stockmann!

HOVSTAD. But my duty to the community obliged me to break with him. And there is another consideration that impels me to oppose him, and, as far as possible, to arrest him on the perilous course he has adopted; that is, consideration for his family—

DR. STOCKMANN. Please stick to the water supply and drainage!

HOVSTAD. Consideration, I repeat, for his wife and his children for whom he has made no provision.

MORTEN. Is that us, Mother?

MRS. STOCKMANN. Hush!

ASLAKSEN. I will now put the mayor's proposition to the vote.

DR. STOCKMANN. There is no necessity! Tonight I have no intention of dealing with all that filth down at the baths. No; I have something quite different to say to you.

PETER STOCKMANN (*aside*). What is coming now?

A DRUNKEN MAN (*by the entrance door*). I am a ratepayer! And therefore

I have a right to speak too! And my entire—firm—inconceivable opinion is—

A NUMBER OF VOICES. Be quiet, at the back there!

OTHER VOICES. He is drunk! Turn him out!

[*They turn him out.*]

DR. STOCKMANN. Am I allowed to speak?

ASLAKSEN (*ringing his bell*). Dr. Stockmann will address the meeting.

DR. STOCKMANN. I should like to have seen anyone, a few days ago, dare to attempt to silence me as has been done tonight! I would have defended my sacred rights as a man, like a lion! But now it is all one to me; I have something of even weightier importance to say to you.

[*The crowd presses nearer to him,* MORTEN KIIL *conspicuous among them.*]

DR. STOCKMANN (*continuing*). I have thought and pondered a great deal these last few days—pondered over such a variety of things that in the end my head seemed too full to hold them—

PETER STOCKMANN (*with a cough*). Ahem!

DR. STOCKMANN. But I got them clear in my mind at last, and then I saw the whole situation lucidly. And that is why I am standing here tonight. I have a great revelation to make to you, my fellow citizens! I will impart to you a discovery of a far wider scope than the trifling matter that our water supply is poisoned and our medicinal baths are standing on pestiferous soil.

A NUMBER OF VOICES (*shouting*). Don't talk about the baths! We won't hear you! None of that!

DR. STOCKMANN. I have already told you that what I want to speak about is the great discovery I have made lately —the discovery that all the sources of our *moral* life are poisoned and that the whole fabric of our civic community is founded on the pestiferous soil of falsehood.

VOICES OF DISCONCERTED CITIZENS. What is that he says?

PETER STOCKMANN. Such an insinuation—!

ASLAKSEN (*with his hand on his bell*). I call upon the speaker to moderate his language.

DR. STOCKMANN. I have always loved my native town as a man only can love the home of his youthful days. I was not old when I went away from here; and exile, longing, and memories cast, as it were, an additional halo over both the town and its inhabitants. (*Some clapping and applause.*) And there I stayed, for many years, in a horrible hole far away up north. When I came into contact with some of the people that lived scattered about among the rocks, I often thought it would have been more service to the poor half-starved creatures if a veterinary doctor had been sent up there, instead of a man like me.

[*Murmurs among the crowd.*]

BILLING (*laying down his pen*). I'm damned if I have ever heard—!

HOVSTAD. It is an insult to a repectable population!

DR. STOCKMANN. Wait a bit! I do not think anyone will charge me with having forgotten my native town up there. I was like one of the eider ducks brooding on its nest, and what I hatched was—the plans for these baths. (*Applause and protests.*) And then when fate at last decreed for me the great happiness of coming home again—I assure you, gentlemen, I thought I had nothing more in the world to wish for. Or rather, there was one thing I wished for—eagerly, untiringly, ardently —and that was to be able to be of service to my native town and the good of the community.

PETER STOCKMANN (*looking at the ceiling*). You chose a strange way of doing it—ahem!

DR. STOCKMANN. And so, with my eyes blinded to the real facts, I reveled in happiness. But yesterday morning—no, to be precise, it was yesterday afternoon

—the eyes of my mind were opened wide, and the first thing I realized was the colossal stupidity of the authorities—

[*Uproar, shouts and laughter.* MRS. STOCKMANN *coughs persistently.*]

PETER STOCKMANN. Mr. Chairman!

ASLAKSEN (*ringing his bell*). By virtue of my authority—!

DR. STOCKMANN. It is a petty thing to catch me up on a word, Mr. Aslaksen. What I mean is only that I got scent of the unbelievable piggishness our leading men had been responsible for down at the baths. I can't stand leading men at any price!—I have had enough of such people in my time. They are like billy goats in a young plantation; they do mischief everywhere. They stand in a free man's way, whichever way he turns, and what I should like best would be to see them exterminated like any other vermin—

[*Uproar.*]

PETER STOCKMANN. Mr. Chairman, can we allow such expressions to pass?

ASLAKSEN (*with his hand on his bell*). Doctor—!

DR. STOCKMANN. I cannot understand how it is that I have only now acquired a clear conception of what these gentry are, when I had almost daily before my eyes in this town such an excellent specimen of them—my brother Peter—slow-witted and hidebound in prejudice—

[*Laughter, uproar, and hisses.* MRS. STOCKMANN *sits coughing assiduously.* ASLAKSEN *rings his bell violently.*]

THE DRUNKEN MAN (*who has got in again*). Is it me he is talking about? My name's Petersen, all right—devil take me if I—

ANGRY VOICES. Turn out that drunken man! Turn him out.

       [*He is turned out again.*]

PETER STOCKMANN. Who was that person?

FIRST CITIZEN. I don't know who he is, Mr. Mayor.

SECOND CITIZEN. He doesn't belong here.

THIRD CITIZEN. I expect he is a worker from over at— (*The rest is inaudible.*)

ASLAKSEN. He had obviously had too much beer.—Proceed, Doctor; but please strive to be moderate in your language.

DR. STOCKMANN. Very well, gentlemen, I will say no more about our leading men. And if anyone imagines, from what I have just said, that my object is to attack these people this evening, he is wrong—absolutely wide of the mark. For I cherish the comforting conviction that these parasites—all these venerable relics of a dying school of thought—are most admirably paving the way for their own extinction; they need no doctor's help to hasten their end. Nor is it folk of that kind who constitute the most pressing danger to the community. It is not they who are most instrumental in poisoning the sources of our moral life and infecting the ground on which we stand. It is not they who are the most dangerous enemies of truth and freedom among us.

VOICES (*shouting from all sides*). Who then? Who is it? Name! Name!

DR. STOCKMANN. You may depend upon it I shall name them! That is precisely the great discovery I made yesterday. (*Raises his voice.*) The most dangerous enemy of truth and freedom among us is the compact majority—yes, the damned compact liberal majority—that is it! Now you know!

[*Tremendous uproar. Most of the crowd are shouting, stamping, and hissing. Some of the older men among them exchange stolen glances and seem to be enjoying themselves.* MRS. STOCKMANN *gets up, looking anxious.* EJLIF *and* MORTEN *advance threateningly upon some schoolboys who are playing pranks.* ASLAKSEN *rings his bell and begs for silence.* HOVSTAD *and* BILLING *both talk at once, but are inaudible. At last quiet is restored.*]

ASLAKSEN. As chairman, I call upon the speaker to withdraw the ill-considered expressions he has just used.

DR. STOCKMANN. Never, Mr. Aslaksen! It is the majority in our community that denies me my freedom and seeks to prevent my speaking the truth.

HOVSTAD. The majority always has right on its side.

BILLING. And truth too, by God!

DR. STOCKMANN. The majority *never* has right on its side. Never, I say! That is one of these social lies against which an independent, intelligent man must wage war. Who is it that constituted the majority of the population in a country? Is it the clever folk or the stupid? I don't imagine you will dispute the fact that at present the stupid people are in an absolutely overwhelming majority all the world over. But, good Lord!—you can never pretend that it is right that the stupid folk should govern the clever ones! *(Uproar and cries.)* Oh, yes—you can shout me down. I know! but you cannot answer me. The majority has *might* on its side—unfortunately; but *right* it has *not.* I am in the right—I and a few other scattered individuals. The minority is always in the right.

[*Renewed uproar.*]

HOVSTAD. Aha!—So Dr. Stockmann has become an aristocrat since the day before yesterday!

DR. STOCKMANN. I have already said that I don't intend to waste a word on the puny, narrow-chested, short-winded crew whom we are leaving astern. Pulsating life no longer concerns itself with them. I am thinking of the few, the scattered few among us, who have absorbed new and vigorous truths. Such men stand, as it were, at the outposts, so far ahead that the compact majority has not yet been able to come up with them; and there they are fighting for truths that are too newly-born into the world of consciousness to have any considerable number of people on their side as yet.

HOVSTAD. So the doctor is a revolutionary now!

DR. STOCKMANN. Good heavens—of course I am, Mr. Hovstad! I propose to raise a revolution against the lie that the majority has the monopoly of the truth. What sort of truths are they that the majority usually supports? They are truths that are of such advanced age that they are beginning to break up. And if a truth is as old as that, it is also in a fair way to become a lie, gentlemen. *(Laughter and mocking cries.)* Yes, believe me or not, as you like; but truths are by no means as long-lived as Methuselah—as some folk imagine. A normally constituted truth lives, let us say, as a rule seventeen or eighteen, or at most twenty years; seldom longer. But truths as aged as that are always worn frightfully thin, and nevertheless it is only then that the majority recognizes them and recommends them to the community as wholesome moral nourishment. There is no great nutritive value in that sort of fare, I can assure you; and, as a doctor, I ought to know. These "majority truths" are like last year's cured meat—like rancid, tainted ham; and they are the origin of the moral scurvy that is rampant in our communities.

ASLAKSEN. It appears to me that the speaker is wandering a long way from his subject.

PETER STOCKMANN. I quite agree with the chairman.

DR. STOCKMANN. Have you gone clean out of your senses, Peter? I am sticking as closely to my subject as I can; for my subject is precisely this, that it is the masses, the majority—this infernal compact majority—that poisons the sources of our moral life and infects the ground we stand on.

HOVSTAD. And all this because the great, broad-minded majority of the people is prudent enough to show deference only to well-ascertained and well-approved truths?

DR. STOCKMANN. Ah, my good Mr. Hovstad, don't talk nonsense about well-ascertained 'truths! The truths of which the masses now approve are the very truths that the fighters at the outposts held to in the days of our grandfathers. We fighters at the outposts nowadays no longer approve of them; and I do not believe there is any other well-ascertained truth except this, that no community can live a healthy life if it is nourished only on such old marrowless truths.

HOVSTAD. But instead of standing there using vague generalities, it would be interesting if you would tell us what these old marrowless truths are, that we are nourished on.

[*Applause from many quarters.*]

DR. STOCKMANN. Oh, I could give you a hole string of such abominations; but to begin with I will confine myself to one well-approved truth, which at bottom is a foul lie, but upon which nevertheless Mr. Hovstad and the *People's Messenger* and all the *Messenger's* supporters are nourished.

HOVSTAD. And that is—?

DR. STOCKMANN. That is, the doctrine you have inherited from your forefathers and proclaim thoughtlessly far and wide —the doctrine that the public, the crowd, the masses are the essential part of the population—that they constitute the People—that the common folk, the ignorant and incomplete element in the community, have the same right to pronounce judgment and to approve, to direct and to govern, as the isolated, intellectually superior personalities in it.

BILLING. Well, damn me if ever I—

HOVSTAD (*at the same time, shouting out*). Fellow citizens, take good note of that!

A NUMBER OF VOICES (*angrily*). Oho!— we are not the People! Only the superior folks are to govern, are they!

FIRST WORKMAN. Turn the fellow out, for talking such rubbish!

SECOND WORKMAN. Out with him!

THIRD WORKMAN (*calling out*). Blow your horn, Evensen!

[*A horn is blown loudly, amidst hisses and an angry uproar.*]

DR. STOCKMANN (*when the noise has somewhat abated*). Be reasonable! Can't you stand hearing the voice of truth for once? I don't in the least expect you to agree with me all at once; but I must say I did expect Mr. Hovstad to admit I was right, when he had recovered his composure a little. He claims to be a freethinker—

VOICES (*in murmurs of astonishment*). Freethinker, did he say? Is Hovstad a freethinker?

HOVSTAD (*shouting*). Prove it, Dr. Stockmann! When have I said so in print?

DR. STOCKMANN (*reflecting*). No, confound it, you are right! —you have never had the courage to. Well, I won't put you in a hole, Mr. Hovstad. Let us say it is I that am the freethinker, then. I am going to prove to you, scientifically, that the *People's Messenger* leads you by the nose in a shameful manner when it tells you that you—that the common people, the crowd, the masses are the real essence of the People. That is only a newspaper lie, I tell you! The common people are nothing more than the raw material of which a People is made. (*Groans, laughter, and uproars.*) Well, isn't that the case? Isn't there an enormous difference between a well-bred and an ill-bred strain of animals? Take, for instance, a common barnyard hen. What sort of eating do you get from a shriveled-up old scrag of a fowl like that? Not much, do you? And what sort of eggs does it lay? A fairly good crow or a raven can lay pretty nearly as good an egg. But take a well-bred Spanish or Japanese hen, or a good pheasant or a turkey—then you will see the difference. Or take the case of dogs, with whom we humans are on such intimate terms. Think first of an ordinary common cur—I mean one of the horrible, coarse-haired, low-bred curs that do nothing but run about the streets and befoul the walls of the houses. Compare one of these curs with a poodle whose sires for many generations have been bred in a gentleman's house, where they have had the best of food and had the opportunity of hearing soft voices and music. Do you not think that the poodle's brain is developed to quite a different degree from that of the cur? Of course it is. It is puppies of well-bred poodles like that that showmen train to do incredibly clever tricks—things that a common cur could never learn to do even if it stood on its head.

[*Uproar and mocking cries.*]

FIRST CITIZEN (*calls out*). Are you going to make out we are dogs, now?

SECOND CITIZEN. We are not animals, Doctor!

DR. STOCKMANN. Yes, but, bless my soul, we *are*, my friend! It is true we are the finest animals anyone could wish for; but, even among us, exceptionally fine animals are rare. There is a tremendous difference between poodle-men and cur-men. And the amusing part of it is that Mr. Hovstad quite agrees with me as long as it is a question of four-footed animals—

HOVSTAD. Yes, it is true enough as far as they are concerned.

DR. STOCKMANN. Very well. But as soon as I extend the principle and apply it to two-legged animals, Mr. Hovstad stops short. He no longer dares to think independently or to pursue his ideas to their logical conclusion; so he turns the whole theory upside down and proclaims in the *People's Messenger* that it is the barnyard hens and street curs that are the finest specimens in the menagerie. But that is always the way, as long as a man retains the traces of common origin and has not worked his way up to intellectual distinction.

HOVSTAD. I lay no claim to any sort of distinction. I am the son of humble countryfolk, and I am proud that the stock I come from is rooted deep among the common people he insults.

VOICES. Bravo, Hovstad! Bravo! Bravo!

DR. STOCKMANN. The kind of common people I mean are not only to be found low down in the social scale; they crawl and swarm all around us—even in the highest social positions. You have only to look at your own fine, distinguished mayor! My brother Peter is every bit as plebeian as anyone that walks in two shoes—

[*Laughter and hisses.*]

PETER STOCKMANN. I protest against personal allusions of this kind.

DR. STOCKMANN (*imperturbably*). And that, not because he is, like myself, descended from some old rascal of a pirate from Pomerania or thereabouts—because that is who we are descended from—

PETER STOCKMANN. An absurd legend. I deny it!

DR. STOCKMANN. But because he thinks what his superiors think and holds the same opinions as they. People who do that are, intellectually speaking, common people; and that is why my magnificent brother Peter is in reality so very far from any distinction—and consequently also so far from being liberal-minded.

PETER STOCKMANN. Mr. Chairman—

HOVSTAD. So it is only the distinguished men that are liberal-minded in this country? We are learning something quite new!

[*Laughter.*]

DR. STOCKMANN. Yes, that is part of my new discovery too. And another part of it is that broad-mindedness is almost precisely the same thing as morality. That is why I maintain that it is absolutely inexcusable in the *People's Messenger* to proclaim, day in and day out, the false doctrine that it is the masses, the crowd, the compact majority that have the monopoly of broad-mindedness and morality—and that vice and corruption and every kind of intellectual depravity are the result of culture, just as all the filth that is draining into our baths is the result of the tanneries up at Möl-ledal! (*Uproar and interruptions.* DR. STOCKMANN *is undisturbed, and goes on, carried away by his ardor, with a smile.*) And yet this same *People's Messenger* can go on preaching that the masses ought to be elevated to higher conditions of life! But, bless my soul, if the *Messenger's* teaching is to be depended upon, this very raising up of the masses would mean nothing more or less than setting them straightway upon the paths of depravity! Happily the theory that culture demoralizes is only an old falsehood that our forefathers believed in and we have inherited. No, it is ignorance, poverty, ugly conditions of life that do the devil's work! In a house which does not get aired and swept every day—my wife Katherine maintains that the floor ought to be scrubbed as well, but that is a debatable question—in such a house, let me tell you, people will lose within two or three years the power of thinking or acting in a moral manner. Lack of oxygen weakens the conscience. And there must be a plentiful lack of oxygen in very many houses in this town, I should think, judging from the fact that the whole compact majority can be unconscientious enough to wish to build the town's prosperity on a quagmire of falsehood and deceit.

ASLAKSEN. We cannot allow such a grave accusation to be flung at a citizen community.

A CITIZEN. I move that the chairman direct the speaker to sit down.

VOICES (*angrily*). Hear, hear! Quite right! Make him sit down!

DR. STOCKMANN (*losing his self-control*). Then I will go and shout the truth at every street corner! I will write it in other towns' newspapers! The whole country shall know what is going on here!

HOVSTAD. It almost seems as if Dr. Stockmann's intention were to ruin the town.

DR. STOCKMANN. Yes, my native town is so dear to me that I would rather ruin it than see it flourishing upon a lie.

ASLAKSEN. This is really serious.

[*Uproar and catcalls.* MRS. STOCKMANN *coughs, but to no purpose; her husband does not listen to her any longer.*]

HOVSTAD (*shouting above the din*). A man must be a public enemy to wish to ruin a whole community!

DR. STOCKMANN (*with growing fervor*). What does the destruction of a community matter, if it lives on lies! It ought to be razed to the ground, I tell you! All who live by lies ought to be exterminated like vermin! You will end by infecting the whole country; you will bring about such a state of things that the whole country will deserve to be ruined. And if things come to that pass, I shall say from the bottom of my heart: Let the whole country perish, let all these people be exterminated!

VOICES FROM THE CROWD. That is talking like an out-and-out enemy of the people!

BILLING. There sounded the voice of the people, by all that's holy!

THE WHOLE CROWD (*shouting*). Yes, yes! He is an enemy of the people! He hates his country! He hates his own people!

ASLAKSEN. Both as a citizen and as an individual, I am profoundly disturbed by what we have had to listen to. Dr. Stockmann has shown himself in a light I should never have dreamed of. I am unhappily obliged to subscribe to the opinion which I have just heard my estimable fellow citizens utter; and I propose that we should give expression to that opinion in a resolution. I propose a resolution as follows: "This meeting declares that it considers Dr. Thomas Stockmann, medical officer of the baths, to be an enemy of the people."

[*A storm of cheers and applause. A number of men surround the* DOCTOR *and hiss him.* MRS. STOCKMANN *and* PETRA *have got up from their seats.* MORTEN *and* EJLIF *are fighting the other school-*

boys for hissing; some of their elders separate them.]

DR. STOCKMANN *(to the men who are hissing him).* Oh, you fools! I tell you that—

ASLAKSEN *(ringing his bell).* We cannot hear you now, Doctor. A formal vote is about to be taken; but, out of regard for personal feelings, it shall be by ballot and not verbal. Have you any clean paper, Mr. Billing?

BILLING. I have both blue and white here.

ASLAKSEN *(going to him).* That will do nicely; we shall get on more quickly that way. Cut it up into small strips—yes, that's it. *(To the meeting.)* Blue means no; white means yes. I will come round myself and collect votes.

[PETER STOCKMANN *leaves the hall.* ASLAKSEN *and one or two others go round the room with the slips of paper in their hats.*]

FIRST CITIZEN *(to* HOVSTAD*).* I say, what has come to the doctor? What are we to think of it?

HOVSTAD. Oh, you know how headstrong he is.

SECOND CITIZEN *(to* BILLING*).* Billing, you go to their house—have you ever noticed if the fellow drinks?

BILLING. Well I'm hanged if I know what to say. There are always spirits on the table when you go.

THIRD CITIZEN. I rather think he goes quite off his head sometimes.

FIRST CITIZEN. I wonder if there is any madness in his family?

BILLING. I shouldn't wonder if there were.

FOURTH CITIZEN. No, it is nothing more than sheer malice; he wants to get even with somebody for something or other.

BILLING. Well certainly he suggested a rise in his salary on one occasion lately, and did not get it.

THE CITIZENS *(together).* Ah!—then it is easy to understand how it is!

THE DRUNKEN MAN *(who has got among the audience again).* I want a blue one, I do! And I want a white one too!

VOICES. It's that drunken chap again! Turn him out!

MORTEN KIIL *(going up to* DR. STOCKMANN*).* Well, Stockmann, do you see what these monkey tricks of yours lead to?

DR. STOCKMANN. I have done my duty.

MORTEN KIIL. What was that you said about the tanneries at Mölledal?

DR. STOCKMANN. You heard well enough. I said they were the source of all the filth.

MORTEN KIIL. My tannery too?

DR. STOCKMANN. Unfortunately your tannery is by far the worst.

MORTEN KIIL. Are you going to put that in the papers?

DR. STOCKMANN. I shall conceal nothing.

MORTEN KIIL. That may cost you dear, Stockmann.   [*Goes out.*]

A STOUT MAN *(going up to* CAPTAIN HORSTER, *without taking any notice of the ladies).* Well, Captain, so you lend your house to enemies of the people?

HORSTER. I imagine I can do what I like with my own possessions, Mr. Vik.

THE STOUT MAN. Then you can have no objection to my doing the same with mine.

HORSTER. What do you mean, sir?

THE STOUT MAN. You shall hear from me in the morning.

[*Turns his back on him and moves off.*]

PETRA. Was that not your owner, Captain Horster?

HORSTER. Yes, that was Mr. Vik the shipowner.

ASLAKSEN *(with the voting papers in his hands, gets up onto the platform and rings his bell).* Gentlemen, allow me to announce the result. By the votes of everyone here except one person—

A YOUNG MAN. That is the drunk chap!

ASLAKSEN. By the votes of every one here except a tipsy man, this meeting of citizens declares Dr. Thomas Stockmann to be an enemy of the people. *(Shouts and applause.)* Three cheers for our ancient and honorable citizen community! (Renewed applause.) Three cheers for our able and energetic mayor, who has so loyally suppressed the promptings of family feeling! (Cheers.) The meeting is dissolved.   [Gets down.]

· BILLING. Three cheers for the chairman!

THE WHOLE CROWD. Three cheers for Aslaksen! Hurrah!

DR. STOCKMANN. My hat and coat, Petra! Captain, have you room on your ship for passengers to the New World?

HORSTER. For you and yours we will make room, Doctor.

DR. STOCKMANN (as PETRA helps him into his coat). Good. Come, Katherine! Come, boys!

MRS. STOCKMANN (in an undertone). Thomas, dear, let us go out by the back way.

DR. STOCKMANN. No back ways for me, Katherine. (Raising his voice.) You will hear more of this enemy of the people, before he shakes the dust off his shoes upon you! I am not so forgiving as a certain Person; I do not say: "I forgive you, for ye know not what ye do."

ASLAKSEN (shouting). That is a blasphemous comparison, Dr. Stockmann!

BILLING. It is, by God! It's dreadful for an earnest man to listen to.

A COARSE VOICE. Threatens us now, does he!

OTHER VOICES (excitedly). Let's go and break his windows! Duck him in the fjord!

ANOTHER VOICE. Blow your horn, Evensen! Pip, pip!

[Horn-blowing, hisses, and wild cries. DR. STOCKMANN goes out through the hall with his family, HORSTER elbowing a way for them.]

THE WHOLE CROWD (howling after them as they go). Enemy of the people! Enemy of the people!

BILLING (as he puts his papers together). Well, I'm damned if I go and drink toddy with the Stockmanns tonight!

[The crowd press toward the exit. The uproar continues outside; shouts of "Enemy of the people!" are heard from without.]

ACT V

SCENE: Dr. Stockmann's study. Bookcases and cabinets containing specimens line the walls. At the back is a door leading to the hall; in the foreground on the left, a door leading to the sitting room. In the right-hand wall are two windows, of which all the panes are broken. The doctor's desk, littered with books and papers, stands in the middle of the room, which is in disorder. It is morning. DR. STOCKMANN in dressing-gown, slippers, and a smoking cap, is bending down and raking with an umbrella under one of the cabinets. After a little while he rakes out a stone.

DR. STOCKMANN (calling through the open sitting room door). Katherine, I have found another one.

MRS. STOCKMANN (from the sitting room). Oh, you will find a lot more yet, I expect.

DR. STOCKMANN (adding the stone to a heap of others on the table). I shall treasure these stones as relics. Ejlif and Morten shall look at them every day, and when they are grown up they shall inherit them as heirlooms. (Rakes about under a bookcase.) Hasn't—what the deuce is her name?—the girl, you know—hasn't she been to fetch the glazier yet?

MRS. STOCKMANN (coming in). Yes, but he said he didn't know if he would be able to come today.

DR. STOCKMANN. You will see he won't dare to come.

MRS. STOCKMANN. Well, that is just what Randine thought—that he didn't dare to, on account of the neighbors. (Calls into the sitting room.) What is it you want, Randine? Give it to me. (Goes in, and comes out again directly.) Here is a letter for you, Thomas.

DR. STOCKMANN. Let me see it. (*Opens and reads it.*) Ah!—of course.

MRS. STOCKMANN. Who is it from?

DR. STOCKMANN. From the landlord. Notice to quit.

MRS. STOCKMANN. Is it possible? Such a nice man—

DR. STOCKMANN (*looking at the letter*). Does not dare do otherwise, he says. Doesn't like doing it, but dare not do otherwise—on account of his fellow citizens—out of regard for public opinion. Is in a dependent position—dare not offend certain influential men—

MRS. STOCKMANN. There, you see, Thomas!

DR. STOCKMANN. Yes, yes, I see well enough; the whole lot of them in the town are cowards; not a man among them dares do anything for fear of the other. (*Throws the letter on to the table.*) But it doesn't matter to us, Katherine. We are going to sail away to the New World, and—

MRS. STOCKMANN. But, Thomas, are you sure we are well advised to take this step?

DR. STOCKMANN. Are you suggesting that I should stay here, where they have pilloried me as an enemy of the people—branded me—broken my windows! And just look here, Katherine—they have torn a great rent in my black trousers too!

MRS. STOCKMANN. Oh, dear!—and they are the best pair you have got!

DR. STOCKMANN. You should never wear your best trousers when you go out to fight for freedom and truth. It is not that I care so much about the trousers, you know; you can always sew them up again for me. But that the common herd should dare to make this attack on me, as if they were my equals—that is what I cannot, for the life of me, swallow!

MRS. STOCKMANN. There is no doubt they have behaved very ill to you, Thomas; but is that sufficient reason for our leaving our native country for good and all?

DR. STOCKMANN. If we went to another town, do you suppose we should not find the common people just as insolent as they are here? Depend upon it, there is not much to choose between them. Oh, well, let the curs snap—that is not the worst part of it. The worst is that, from one end of this country to the other, every man is the slave of his party. Although, as far as that goes, I daresay it is not much better in the free West either; the compact majority, and liberal public opinion, and all that infernal old bag of tricks are probably rampant there, too. But there things are done on a larger scale, you see. They may kill you, but they won't put you to death by slow torture. They don't squeeze a free man's soul in a vice, as they do here. And, if need be, one can live in solitude. (*Walks up and down.*) If only I knew where there was a virgin forest or a small South Sea island for sale, cheap—

MRS. STOCKMANN. But think of the boys, Thomas.

DR. STOCKMANN (*standing still*). What a strange woman you are, Katherine! Would you prefer to have the boys grow up in a society like this? You saw for yourself last night that half the population are out of their minds; and if the other half have not lost their senses, it is because they are mere brutes, with no sense to lose.

MRS. STOCKMANN. But, Thomas dear, the imprudent things you said had something to do with it, you know.

DR. STOCKMANN. Well, isn't what I said perfectly true? Don't they turn every idea topsy-turvy? Don't they make a regular hodge-podge of right and wrong? Don't they say that the things I know are true are lies? The craziest part of it all is the fact of these "liberals," men of full age, going about in crowds imagining that they are the broad-minded party! Did you ever hear anything like it, Katherine!

MRS. STOCKMANN. Yes, yes, it's mad enough of them, certainly; but—(PETRA *comes in from the sitting room*). Back from school already?

PETRA. Yes. I have been given notice of dismissal.

MRS. STOCKMANN. Dismissal?

DR. STOCKMANN. You too?

PETRA. Mrs. Busk gave me my notice; so I thought it was best to go at once.

DR. STOCKMANN. You were perfectly right, too!

MRS. STOCKMANN. Who would have thought Mrs. Busk was a woman like that!

PETRA. Mrs. Busk isn't a bit like that, Mother; I saw quite plainly how it hurt her to do it. But she didn't dare do otherwise, she said; and so I got my notice.

DR. STOCKMANN (laughing and rubbing his hands). She didn't dare do otherwise, either! It's delicious!

MRS. STOCKMANN. Well, after the dreadful scenes last night—

PETRA. It was not only that. Just listen to this, Father!

DR. STOCKMANN. Well?

PETRA. Mrs. Busk showed me no less than three letters she received this morning—

DR. STOCKMANN. Anonymous, I suppose?

PETRA. Yes.

DR. STOCKMANN. Yes, because they didn't dare to risk signing their names, Katherine!

PETRA. And two of them were to the effect that a man, who has been our guest here, was declaring last night at the club that my views on various subjects are extremely emancipated—

DR. STOCKMANN. You did not deny that, I hope?

PETRA. No, you know I wouldn't. Mrs. Busk's own views are tolerably emancipated, when we are alone together; but now that this report about me is being spread, she dare not keep me on any longer.

MRS. STOCKMANN. And someone who had been a guest of ours! That shows you the return you get for your hospitality, Thomas!

DR. STOCKMANN. We won't live in such a disgusting hole any longer. Pack up as quickly as you can, Katherine; the sooner we can get away, the better.

MRS. STOCKMANN. Be quiet—I think I hear someone in the hall. See who it is, Petra.

PETRA (opening the door). Oh, it's you, Captain Horster! Do come in.

HORSTER (coming in). Good morning. I thought I would just come in and see how you were.

DR. STOCKMANN (shaking his hand). Thanks—that is really kind of you.

MRS. STOCKMANN. And thank you, too, for helping us through the crowd, Captain Horster.

PETRA. How did you manage to get home again?

HORSTER. Oh, somehow or other. I am fairly strong and there is more sound than fury about these folk.

DR. STOCKMANN. Yes, isn't their swinish cowardice astonishing? Look here, I will show you something! There are all the stones they have thrown through my windows. Just look at them! I'm hanged if there are more than two decently large bits of hardstone in the whole heap; the rest are nothing but gravel—wretched little things. And yet they stood out there bawling and swearing that they would do me some violence; but as for *doing* anything—you don't see much of that in this town.

HORSTER. Just as well for you this time, Doctor!

DR. STOCKMANN. True enough. But it makes one angry all the same; because if some day it should be a question of a national fight in real earnest, you will see that public opinion will be in favor of taking to one's heels, and the compact majority will turn tail like a flock of sheep, Captain Horster. That is what is so mournful to think of; it gives me so much concern, that— No, devil take it, it is ridiculous to care about it! They have called me an enemy of the people, so an enemy of the people let me be!

MRS. STOCKMANN. You will never be that, Thomas.

DR. STOCKMANN. Don't swear to that, Katherine. To be called an ugly name may have the same effect as a pin-scratch in the lung. And that hateful name—I can't get quit of it. It is sticking here in the pit of my stomach, eating into me like a corrosive acid. And no magnesia will remove it.

PETRA. Bah!—You should only laugh at them, Father.

HORSTER. They will change their minds some day, Doctor.

MRS. STOCKMANN. Yes, Thomas, as sure as you are standing here.

DR. STOCKMANN. Perhaps, when it is too late. Much good may it do them! They may wallow in their filth then and rue the day when they drove a patriot into exile. When do you sail, Captain Horster?

HORSTER. Hm!—That was just what I had come to speak about—

DR. STOCKMANN. Why, has anything gone wrong with the ship?

HORSTER. No; but what has happened is that I am not to sail in it.

PETRA. Do you mean that you have been dismissed from your command?

HORSTER (smiling). Yes, that's just it.

PETRA. You too.

MRS. STOCKMANN. There, you see, Thomas!

DR. STOCKMANN. And that for the truth's sake! Oh, if I had thought such a thing possible—

HORSTER. You mustn't take it to heart; I shall be sure to find a job with some shipowner or other, elsewhere.

DR. STOCKMANN. And that is this man Vik—a wealthy man, independent of everyone and everything—! Shame on him!

HORSTER. He is quite an excellent fellow otherwise; he told me himself he would willingly have kept me on, if only he had dared—

DR. STOCKMANN. But he didn't dare? No, of course not.

HORSTER. It is not such an easy matter, he said, for a party man—

DR. STOCKMANN. The worthy man spoke the truth. A party is like a sausage machine; it mashes up all sorts of heads together into the same mincemeat—fatheads and blockheads, all in one mash!

MRS. STOCKMANN. Come, come, Thomas dear!

PETRA (to HORSTER). If only you had not come home with us, things might not have come to this pass.

HORSTER. I do not regret it.

PETRA (holding out her hand to him). Thank you for that!

HORSTER (to DR. STOCKMANN). And so what I came to say was that if you are determined to go away, I have thought of another plan—

DR. STOCKMANN. That's splendid!—if only we can get away at once.

MRS. STOCKMANN. Hush!—wasn't that someone knocking?

PETRA. That is Uncle, surely.

DR. STOCKMANN. Aha! (Calls out.) Come in!

MRS. STOCKMANN. Dear Thomas, promise me definitely—

[PETER STOCKMANN comes in from the hall.]

PETER STOCKMANN. Oh, you are engaged. In that case, I will—

DR. STOCKMANN. No, no, come in.

PETER STOCKMANN. But I wanted to speak to you alone.

MRS. STOCKMANN. We will go into the sitting room in the meanwhile.

HORSTER. And I will look in again later.

DR. STOCKMANN. No, go in there with them, Captain Horster; I want to hear more about—

HORSTER. Very well, I will wait, then.

[He follows MRS. STOCKMANN and PETRA into the sitting room.]

DR. STOCKMANN. I dare say you find it rather drafty here today. Put your hat on.

PETER STOCKMANN. Thank you, if I may. (Does so.) I think I caught cold last night; I stood and shivered—

DR. STOCKMANN. Really? I found it warm enough.

PETER STOCKMANN. I regret that it was not in my power to prevent those excesses last night.

DR. STOCKMANN. Have you anything particular to say to me besides that?

PETER STOCKMANN (*taking a big letter from his pocket*). I have this document for you, from the Baths Committee.

DR. STOCKMANN. My dismissal?

PETER STOCKMANN. Yes, dating from today. (*Lays the letter on the table.*) It gives us pain to do it; but, to speak frankly, we dared not do otherwise on account of public opinion.

DR. STOCKMANN (*smiling*). Dared not? I seem to have heard that word before, today.

PETER STOCKMANN. I must beg you to understand your position clearly. For the future you must not count on any practice whatever in the town.

DR. STOCKMANN. Devil take the practice! But why are you so sure of that?

PETER STOCKMANN. The Householders' Association is circulating a list from house to house. All right-minded citizens are being called upon to give up employing you; and I can assure you that not a single head of a family will risk refusing his signature. They simply dare not.

DR. STOCKMANN. No, no; I don't doubt it. But what then?

PETER STOCKMANN. If I might advise you, it would be best to leave the place for a little while—

DR. STOCKMANN. Yes, the propriety of leaving the place *has* occurred to me.

PETER STOCKMANN. Good. And then, when you have had six months to think things over, if, after mature consideration, you can persuade yourself to write a few words of regret, acknowledging your error—

DR. STOCKMANN. I might have my appointment restored to me, do you mean?

PETER STOCKMANN. Perhaps. It is not at all impossible.

DR. STOCKMANN. But what about public opinion, then? Surely you would not dare to do it on account of public feeling.

PETER STOCKMANN. Public opinion is an extremely mutable thing. And, to be quite candid with you, it is a matter of great importance to us to have some admission of that sort from you in writing.

DR. STOCKMANN. Oh, that's what you are after, is it! I will just trouble you to remember what I said to you lately about foxy tricks of that sort!

PETER STOCKMANN. Your position was quite different then. At that time you had reason to suppose you had the whole town at your back—

DR. STOCKMANN. Yes, and now I feel I have the whole town *on* my back— (*Flaring up.*) I would not do it if I had the devil and his dam on my back—! Never— never, I tell you!

PETER STOCKMANN. A man with a family has no right to behave as you do. You have no right to do it, Thomas.

DR. STOCKMANN. I have no right! There is only one single thing in the world a free man has no right to do. Do you know what that is?

PETER STOCKMANN. No.

DR. STOCKMANN. Of course you don't, but I will tell you. A free man has no right to soil himself with filth; he has no right to behave in a way that would justify his spitting in his own face.

PETER STOCKMANN. This sort of thing sounds extremely plausible, of course; and if there were no other explanation for your obstinacy— But as it happens that there is—

DR. STOCKMANN. What do you mean?

PETER STOCKMANN. You understand very well what I mean. But, as your brother and as a man of discretion, I advise you not to build too much upon expectations and prospects that may so very easily fail you.

DR. STOCKMANN. What in the world is all this about?

PETER STOCKMANN. Do you really ask me to believe that you are ignorant of the terms of Mr. Kiil's will?

DR. STOCKMANN. I know that the small amount he possesses is to go to an institution for indigent old working people. How does that concern me?

PETER STOCKMANN. In the first place, it is by no means a small amount that is in question. Mr. Kiil is a fairly wealthy man.

DR. STOCKMANN. I had no notion of that!

PETER STOCKMANN. Hm!—hadn't you really? Then I suppose you had no notion, either, that a considerable portion of his wealth will come to your children, you and your wife having a life-rent of the capital. Has he never told you so?

DR. STOCKMANN. Never, on my honor! Quite the reverse; he has consistently done nothing but fume at being so unconscionably heavily taxed. But are you perfectly certain of this, Peter?

PETER STOCKMANN. I have it from an absolutely reliable source.

DR. STOCKMANN. Then, thank God, Katherine is provided for—and the children too! I must tell her this at once— (Calls out.) Katherine, Katherine!

PETER STOCKMANN (restraining him). Hush, don't say a word yet!

MRS. STOCKMANN (opening the door). What is the matter?

DR. STOCKMANN. Oh, nothing, nothing; you can go back. (She shuts the door. DR. STOCKMANN walks up and down in his excitement.) Provided for!—Just think of it, we are all provided for! And for life! what a blessed feeling it is to know one is provided for!

PETER STOCKMANN. Yes, but that is just exactly what you are not. Mr. Kiil can alter his will any day he likes.

DR. STOCKMANN. But he won't do that, my dear Peter. The Badger is much too delighted at my attack on you and your wise friends.

PETER STOCKMANN (starts and looks intently at him). Ah, that throws a light on various things.

DR. STOCKMANN. What things?

PETER STOCKMANN. I see that the whole thing was a combined maneuver on your part and his. These violent, reckless attacks that you have made against the leading men of the town, under the pretense that it was in the name of truth—

DR. STOCKMANN. What about them?

PETER STOCKMANN. I see that they were nothing else than the stipulated price for that vindictive old man's will.

DR. STOCKMANN (almost speechless). Peter—you are the most disgusting plebeian I have ever met in all my life.

PETER STOCKMANN. All is over between us. Your dismissal is irrevocable—we have a weapon against you now.

[Goes out.]

DR. STOCKMANN. For shame! For shame! (Calls out.) Katherine, you must have the floor scrubbed after him! Let—what's her name—devil take it, the girl who has always got soot on her nose—

MRS. STOCKMANN (in the sitting room). Hush, Thomas, be quiet!

PETRA (coming to the door). Father, Grandfather is here asking if he may speak to you alone.

DR. STOCKMANN. Certainly he may. (Going to the door.) Come in, Mr. Kiil. (MORTEN KIIL comes in. DR. STOCKMANN shuts the door after him.) What can I do for you? Won't you sit down?

MORTEN KIIL. I won't sit. (Looks around.) You look very comfortable here today, Thomas.

DR. STOCKMANN. Yes, don't we!

MORTEN KIIL. Very comfortable—plenty of fresh air. I should think you have got enough today of that oxygen you were talking about yesterday. Your conscience must be in splendid order today, I should think.

DR. STOCKMANN. It is.

MORTEN KIIL. So I should think. (Taps his chest.) Do you know what I have got here?

DR. STOCKMANN. A good conscience, too, I hope.

MORTEN KIIL. Bah!—No, it is something better than that.

[He takes a thick pocketbook from his breast pocket, opens it, and displays a packet of papers.]

DR. STOCKMANN (looking at him in astonishment). Shares in the baths?

MORTEN KIIL. They were not difficult to get today.

DR. STOCKMANN. And you have been buying—?

MORTEN KIIL. As many as I could pay for.

DR. STOCKMANN. But, my dear Mr. Kiil—consider the state of the baths' affairs!

MORTEN KIIL. If you behave like a reasonable man, you can soon set the baths on their feet again.

DR. STOCKMANN. Well, you can see for yourself that I have done all I can, but— They are all mad in this town!

MORTEN KIIL. You said yesterday that the worst of this pollution came from my tannery. If that is true, then my grandfather and my father before me, and I myself, for many years past, have been poisoning the town like three destroying angels. Do you think I am going to sit quiet under that reproach?

DR. STOCKMANN. Unfortunately, I am afraid you will have to.

MORTEN KIIL. No, thank you. I am jealous of my name and reputation. They call me the Badger, I am told. A badger is a kind of pig, I believe; but I am not going to give them the right to call me that. I mean to live and die a clean man.

DR. STOCKMANN. And how are you going to set about it?

MORTEN KIIL. You shall cleanse me, Thomas.

DR. STOCKMANN. I!

MORTEN KIIL. Do you know what money I have bought these shares with? No, of course you can't know—but I will tell you. It is the money that Katherine and Petra and the boys will have when I am gone. Because I have been able to save a little bit after all, you know.

DR. STOCKMANN (flaring up). And you have gone and taken Katherine's money for *this!*

MORTEN KIIL. Yes, the whole of the money is invested in the baths now. And now I just want to see whether you are quite stark, staring mad, Thomas! If you still make out that these animals and other nasty things of that sort come from my tannery, it will be exactly as if you were to flay broad strips of skin from Katherine's body, and Petra's, and the boys'; and no decent man would do that —unless he were mad.

DR. STOCKMANN (walking up and down). Yes, but I *am* mad; I *am* mad!

MORTEN KIIL. You cannot be so absurdly mad as all that, when it is a question of your wife and children.

DR. STOCKMANN (standing still in front of him). Why couldn't you consult me about it, before you went and bought all that trash?

MORTEN KIIL. What is done cannot be undone.

DR. STOCKMANN (walks about uneasily). If only I were not so certain about it—! But I am absolutely convinced that I am right.

MORTEN KIIL (weighing the pocketbook in his hand). If you stick to your mad idea, this won't be worth much, you know.

[Puts the pocketbook in his pocket.]

DR. STOCKMANN. But, hang it all! it might be possible for science to discover some prophylactic, I should think—or some antidote of some kind—

MORTEN KIIL. To kill these animals, do you mean?

DR. STOCKMANN. Yes, or to make them innocuous.

MORTEN KIIL. Couldn't you try some ratsbane?

DR. STOCKMANN. Don't talk nonsense! They all say it is only imagination, you know. Well, let it go at that! Let them have their own way about it! Haven't the ignorant, narrow-minded curs reviled me as an enemy of the people?—and haven't they been ready to tear the clothes off my back, too?

MORTEN KIIL. And broken all your windows to pieces!

DR. STOCKMANN. And then there is my duty to my family. I must talk it over with Katherine; she is great on those things.

MORTEN KIIL. That is right; be guided by a reasonable woman's advice.

DR. STOCKMANN (advancing toward him). To think you could do such a preposterous thing! Risking Katherine's money in this way, and putting me in such a horribly painful dilemma! When I look at you, I think I see the devil himself—

MORTEN KIIL. Then I had better go. But I must have an answer from you before two o'clock—yes or no. If it is no, the shares go to a charity, and that this very day.

DR. STOCKMANN. And what does Katherine get?

MORTEN KIIL. Not a halfpenny. (*The door leading to the hall opens, and* HOVSTAD *and* ASLAKSEN *make their appearance.*) Look at those two!

DR. STOCKMANN (*staring at them*). What the devil!—have *you* actually the face to come into my house?

HOVSTAD. Certainly.

ASLAKSEN. We have something to say to you, you see.

MORTEN KIIL (*in a whisper*). Yes or no—before two o'clock.

ASLAKSEN (*glancing at* HOVSTAD). Aha!   [MORTEN KIIL *goes out.*]

DR. STOCKMANN. Well, what do you want with me? Be brief.

HOVSTAD. I can quite understand that you are annoyed with us for our attitude at the meeting yesterday—

DR. STOCKMANN. Attitude, do you call it? Yes, it was a charming attitude! I call it weak, womanish—damnably shameful!

HOVSTAD. Call it what you like, we could not do otherwise.

DR. STOCKMANN. You *dared* not do otherwise—isn't that it?

HOVSTAD. Well, if you like to put it that way.

ASLAKSEN. But why did you not let us have word of it beforehand?—just a hint to Mr. Hovstad or to me?

DR. STOCKMANN. A hint? Of what?

ASLAKSEN. Of what was behind it all.

DR. STOCKMANN. I don't understand you in the least.

ASLAKSEN (*with a confidential nod*). Oh, yes, you do, Dr. Stockmann.

HOVSTAD. It is no good making a mystery of it any longer.

DR. STOCKMANN (*looking first at one of them and then at the other*). What the devil do you both mean?

ASLAKSEN. May I ask if your father-in-law is not going round the town buying up all the shares in the baths?

DR. STOCKMANN. Yes, he has been buying baths' shares today; but—

ASLAKSEN. It would have been more prudent to get someone else to do it—someone less nearly related to you.

HOVSTAD. And you should not have let your name appear in the affair. There was no need for anyone to know that the attack on the baths came from you. You ought to have consulted me, Dr. Stockmann.

DR. STOCKMANN (*looks in front of him; then a light seems to dawn on him and he says in amazement:*) Are such things conceivable? Are such things possible?

ASLAKSEN (*with a smile*). Evidently they are. But it is better to use a little finesse, you know.

HOVSTAD. And it is much better to have several persons in a thing of that sort; because the responsibility of each individual is lessened, when there are others with him.

DR. STOCKMANN (*composedly*). Come to the point, gentlemen. What do you want?

ASLAKSEN. Perhaps Mr. Hovstad had better—

HOVSTAD. No, you tell him, Aslaksen.

ASLAKSEN. Well, the fact is that, now we know the bearings of the whole affair, we think we might venture to put the *People's Messenger* at your disposal.

DR. STOCKMANN. Do you dare do that now? What about public opinion? Are you not afraid of a storm breaking upon our heads?

HOVSTAD. We will try to weather it.

ASLAKSEN. And you must be ready to go off quickly on a new tack, Doctor. As soon as your invective has done its work—

DR. STOCKMANN. Do you mean, as soon as my father-in-law and I have got hold of the shares at a low figure?

HOVSTAD. Your reasons for wishing to get the control of the baths are mainly scientific, I take it.

DR. STOCKMANN. Of course; it was for scientific reasons that I persuaded the old Badger to stand in with me in the matter. So we will tinker at the conduit pipes a little, and dig up a little bit of the shore, and it shan't cost the town a sixpence. That will be all right—eh?

HOVSTAD. I think so—if you have the *People's Messenger* behind you.

ASLAKSEN. The press is a power in a free community, Doctor.

DR. STOCKMANN. Quite so. And so is public opinion. And you, Mr. Aslaksen—I suppose you will be answerable for the Householders' Association?

ASLAKSEN. Yes, and for the Temperance Society. You may rely on that.

DR. STOCKMANN. But, gentlemen—I really am ashamed to ask the question—but, what return do you—?

HOVSTAD. We should prefer to help you without any return whatever, believe me. But the *People's Messenger* is in rather a shaky condition; it doesn't go really well; and I should be very unwilling to suspend the paper now, when there is so much work to do here in the political way.

DR. STOCKMANN. Quite so; that would be a great trial to such a friend of the people as you are. (*Flares up.*) But I am an enemy of the people, remember! (*Walks about the room.*) Where have I put my stick? Where the devil is my stick?

HOVSTAD. What's that?

ASLAKSEN. Surely you never mean—?

DR. STOCKMANN (*standing still*). And suppose I don't give you a single penny of all I get out of it? Money is not very easy to get out of us rich folk, please to remember!

HOVSTAD. And you please to remember that this affair of the shares can be represented in two ways!

DR. STOCKMANN. Yes, and you are just the man to do it. If I don't come to the rescue of the *People's Messenger,* you will certainly take an evil view of the affair; you will hunt me down, I can well imagine—pursue me—try to throttle me as a dog does a hare.

HOVSTAD. It is a natural law; every animal must fight for its own livelihood.

ASLAKSEN. And get its food where it can, you know.

DR. STOCKMANN (*walking about the room*). Then you go and look for yours in the gutter; because I am going to show you which is the strongest animal of us three! (*Finds an umbrella and brandishes it above his head.*) Ah, now—!

HOVSTAD. You are surely not going to use violence!

ASLAKSEN. Take care what you are doing with that umbrella.

DR. STOCKMANN. Out of the window with you, Mr. Hovstad.

HOVSTAD (*edging to the door*). Are you quite mad!

DR. STOCKMANN. Out of the window, Mr. Aslaksen! Jump, I tell you! You will have to do it, sooner or later.

ASLAKSEN (*running round the writing table*). Moderation, Doctor—I am a delicate man—I can stand so little— (*Calls out.*) Help, help!

[MRS. STOCKMANN, PETRA, *and* HORSTER *come in from the sitting room.*]

MRS. STOCKMANN. Good gracious, Thomas! What is happening?

DR. STOCKMANN (*brandishing the umbrella*). Jump out, I tell you! Out into the gutter!

HOVSTAD. An assault on an unoffending man! I call you to witness, Captain Horster. [*Hurries out through the hall.*]

ASLAKSEN (*irresolutely*). If only I knew the way about here—

[*Steals out through the sitting room.*]

MRS. STOCKMANN (*holding her husband back*). Control yourself, Thomas!

DR. STOCKMANN (*throwing down the umbrella*). Upon my soul, they have escaped after all.

MRS. STOCKMANN. What did they want you to do?

DR. STOCKMANN. I will tell you later on; I have something else to think about now. (*Goes to the table and writes something on a calling card.*) Look there, Katherine; what is written there?

MRS. STOCKMANN. Three big No's; what does that mean?

DR. STOCKMANN. I will tell you that too, later on. *(Holds out the card to* PETRA.) There, Petra; tell sooty-face to run over to the Badger's with that, as quickly as she can. Hurry up!

[PETRA *takes the card and goes out to the hall.*]

DR. STOCKMANN. Well, I think I have had a visit from every one of the devil's messengers today! But now I am going to sharpen my pen till they can feel its point; I shall dip it in venom and gall; I shall hurl my inkpot at their heads!

MRS. STOCKMANN. Yes, but we are going away, you know, Thomas.

[PETRA *comes back.*]

DR. STOCKMANN. Well?

PETRA. She has gone with it.

DR. STOCKMANN. Good.—Going away, did you say? No, I'll be hanged if we are going away! We are going to stay where we are, Katherine!

PETRA. Stay here?

MRS. STOCKMANN. Here, in the town?

DR. STOCKMANN. Yes, here. This is the field of battle—this is where the fight will be. This is where I shall triumph! As soon as I have had my trousers sewn up I shall go out and look for another house. We must have a roof over our heads for the winter.

HORSTER. That you shall have in my house.

DR. STOCKMANN. Can I?

HORSTER. Yes, quite well. I have plenty of room, and I am almost never at home.

MRS. STOCKMANN. How good of you, Captain Horster!

PETRA. Thank you!

DR. STOCKMANN *(grasping his hand).* Thank you, thank you! That is one trouble over! Now I can set to work in earnest at once. There is an endless amount of things to look through here, Katherine! Luckily I shall have all my time at my disposal; because I have been dismissed from the baths, you know.

MRS. STOCKMANN *(with a sigh).* Oh, yes, I expected that.

DR. STOCKMANN. And they want to take my practice away from me, too. Let them! I have got the poor people to fall back upon, anyway—those that don't pay anything, and, after all, they need me most, too. But, by Jove, they will have to listen to me; I shall preach to them in season and out of season, as it says somewhere.

MRS. STOCKMANN. But, dear Thomas, I should have thought events had showed you what use it is to preach.

DR. STOCKMANN. You are really ridiculous, Katherine. Do you want me to let myself be beaten off the field by public opinion and the compact majority and all that devilry? No, thank you! And what I want to do is so simple and clear and straightforward. I only want to drum into the heads of these curs the fact that the liberals are the most insidious enemies of freedom—that party programs strangle every young and vigorous truth—that considerations of expediency turn morality and justice upside down—and that they will end by making life here unbearable. Don't you think, Captain Horster, that I ought to be able to make people understand that?

HORSTER. Very likely; I don't know much about such things myself.

DR. STOCKMANN. Well, look here—I will explain! It is the party leaders that must be exterminated. A party leader is like a wolf, you see—like a voracious wolf. He requires a certain number of smaller victims to prey upon every year, if he is to live. Just look at Hovstad and Aslaksen! How many smaller victims have they not put an end to—or at any rate maimed and mangled until they are fit for nothing except to be householders or subscribers to the *People's Messenger!* *(Sits down on the edge of the table.)* Come here, Katherine—look how beautifully the sun shines today! And this lovely spring air I am drinking in!

MRS. STOCKMANN. Yes, if only we could live on sunshine and spring air, Thomas.

DR. STOCKMANN. Oh, you will have to pinch and save a bit—then we shall get along. That gives me very little concern. What is much worse is that I know of no one who is liberal-minded and high-minded enough to venture to take up my work after me.

PETRA. Don't think about that, Father; you have plenty of time before you— Hullo, here are the boys already!

[EJLIF *and* MORTEN *come in from the sitting room.*]

MRS. STOCKMANN. Have you got a holiday?

MORTEN. No; but we were fighting with the other boys between lessons—

EJLIF. That isn't true; it was the other boys were fighting with us.

MORTEN. Well, and then Mr. Rörlund said we had better stay at home for a day or two.

DR. STOCKMANN (*snapping his fingers and getting up from the table*). I have it! I have it, by Jove! You shall never set foot in the school again!

THE BOYS. No more school!

MRS. STOCKMANN. But, Thomas—

DR. STOCKMANN. Never, I say. I will educate you myself; that is to say, you shan't learn a blessed thing—

MORTEN. Hooray!

DR. STOCKMANN. But I will make liberal-minded and high-minded men of you. You must help me with that, Petra.

PETRA. Yes, Father, you may be sure I will.

DR. STOCKMANN. And my school shall be in the room where they insulted me and called me an enemy of the people. But we are too few as we are; I must have at least twelve boys to begin with.

MRS. STOCKMANN. You will certainly never get them in this town.

DR. STOCKMANN. We shall. (*To the boys.*) Don't you know any street urchins—regular ragamuffins—?

MORTEN. Yes, Father, I know lots!

DR. STOCKMANN. That's capital! Bring me some specimens of them. I am going to experiment with curs, just for once; there may be some exceptional heads among them.

MORTEN. And what are we going to do, when you have made liberal-minded and high-minded men of us?

DR. STOCKMANN. Then you shall drive all the wolves out of the country, my boys!

[EJLIF *looks rather doubtful about it;* MORTEN *jumps about crying* "Hurrah!"]

MRS. STOCKMANN. Let us hope it won't be the wolves that will drive you out of the country, Thomas.

DR. STOCKMANN. Are you out of your mind, Katherine? Drive me out! Now— when I am the strongest man in the town!

MRS. STOCKMANN. The strongest—now?

DR. STOCKMANN. Yes, and I will go so far as to say that now I am the strongest man in the whole world.

MORTEN. I say!

DR. STOCKMANN (*lowering his voice*). Hush! You mustn't say anything about it yet; but I have made a great discovery.

MRS. STOCKMANN. Another one?

DR. STOCKMANN. Yes. (*Gathers them round him, and says confidentially:*) It is this, let me tell you—that the strongest man in the world is he who stands most alone.

MRS. STOCKMANN (*smiling and shaking her head*). Oh, Thomas, Thomas!

PETRA (*encouragingly, as she grasps her father's hands*). Father!

FOR STUDY AND DISCUSSION

1. In Act I, how do Mayor Stockmann's manner and attitudes immediately characterize him?

2. How does Ibsen prepare the audience to side with Dr. Stockmann before the major problem in the play is presented?

3. What is the significance of the doctor's inability to remember the name of the housemaid? What attitude does Ibsen want the audience to take toward the doctor's scorn of "the mob" in Act V? How do you feel about the doctor's attitude?

4. As the play progresses, what characteristics of Dr. Stockmann emerge and complicate the audience's feelings about him? Are there any comparable complexities in the other characterizations?

5. What elements of society are represented by the characters of the play? In general, do Ibsen's characters seem to be merely representations of certain attitudes or vices in society, or are they real, humanized characters? Explain.

6. In Act I, when the mayor rebukes his brother for his "ingrained tendency" to take his own way, he states this principle: "The individual ought undoubtedly to acquiesce in subordinating himself to the community—or, to speak more accurately, to the authorities who have care of the community's welfare." Is this only one principle, as the mayor implies, or is it two? If two, what is the difference between them? How is either or both of these principles crucial to the major issue of the play?

7. The major problem of the play is introduced almost casually in Act I, among trivial or seemingly trivial details. Its importance is not made apparent until Act II, and the conflict is not actually joined until Act III. This crucial point itself is similarly understated by the deceptive quietness of Dr. Stockmann's reaction to the desertion of Hovstad, Aslaksen, and Billing. In what different ways are the inciting action and the major crisis presented in *Antigone* (see page 140) and *The Tempest* (see page 542)? How does the dramatic effect of Ibsen's technique differ from that of the earlier plays?

8. Through what techniques does Ibsen create an on-stage image of the public as a herd of sheep? Granting that Ibsen uses the drunken man in Act IV for comic relief, tell what other significance the drunken man has in the scene.

9. In Act III, what is the point of Petra's objection to translating a story which claims that "there is a supernatural power that looks after all the so-called good people . . . while all the so-called bad people are punished?" What does she mean by "so-called good" and "so-called bad"? What is the connection between Petra's attitude toward this idea of God and the attitudes she shares with her father?

10. In Act II, Hovstad says that the poison causing the trouble in town is not merely coming from the refuse from the tanneries, but also from the people who created the situation. For dramatic reasons we recognize that his point is probably true, but it is characteristic of Hovstad's unreliability that his reasoning is emotional. What emotionally loaded words does he use to imply conclusions that at this point have not been proved? What emotionally loaded words does the mayor use in his speech at the public meeting in Act IV, to imply his own integrity and his brother's recklessness? On the other hand, are the doctor's arguments strictly logical? ("Dr. Stockmann . . . has a more muddled head on his shoulders than I have, and he has besides certain characteristics which will permit people to tolerate various things from his lips which they might not so readily if they had issued from mine . . ." wrote Ibsen about the hero of his play.) How does the doctor's emotionalism complicate the dramatic conflict in this play?

11. Would you call the doctor an insufferable intellectual snob? Why or why not?

12. Do you agree with the doctor's position that the majority does not have right on its side (see Act IV)? Explain. Is this position a threat to the American philosophy of majority rule? Explain.

THE REALISTIC STAGE

Ibsen set a new direction for the drama by showing how the indoor "box" stage could be used to achieve an illusion of reality. Before Ibsen, the theatrical experience had been treated by playwrights and directors as frankly illusory and artificial; the extensive use of pageantry, stylized acting, and soliloquies contributed to this effect. Audiences came to the theater to see the dramatization of an event that was not supposed to be like life. Both as a playwright and as a stage manager, Ibsen tried to make the audience forget that what it was watching was imaginary, not real. He treated the stage as if it were a room in which real events were actually taking place, with the difference being that one wall was removed so that an audience on the outside could see and hear what was going on. Until very recent years, dramatists and directors followed Ibsen's style, both in the writing and staging of new plays and in the re-staging of earlier ones. The movies, until very recently, have been a further extension of Ibsen's principle.

The stage in Molière's day had been a single, generalized set, for which simple daylight or candlelight gave illumination. When a curtain was drawn across the front of this type of stage, however, it became possible to change the scenery and the props, so that one setting could be changed for another. With gas lamps, lighting became more flexible, so that it could be used to indicate different times of day, to suggest moods, and to create special effects. (At the end of Ibsen's *Ghosts,* the growing light of the sun is used to produce a terrible irony, as the hero realizes the onset of his blindness.) Furthermore, Ibsen capitalized on the relative intimacy of the indoor theater and had his actors use voice modulations and gestures to add meaning to what they said.

Ibsen wrote his plays, then, with the expectation that the stage and the actors would help interpret his lines to the audience, and he indicated what effects he sought by writing detailed descriptions of the settings and often by adding to a speech a clue ("a little embarrassed," "laughing," etc.) telling how it should be spoken. Elaborate stage directions of this kind, virtually nonexistent in earlier plays, have become today as much a part of a play as the characters' speeches themselves.

1. In *An Enemy of the People,* what does Ibsen reveal about the characters, their personal situations, and the society they live in from his stage directions?

2. Follow Ibsen's stage directions and imagine the purely visual impressions of the play, without speeches or actions. What atmosphere would be suggested by each of the four sets? (Acts I and II have the same location.) How would each set be lighted? What kinds of movement would dominate each of the acts?

3. In what ways do these visual impressions enhance the impressions made by the actions and speeches of each act? What is the dramatic pattern created by the five acts?

FOR COMPOSITION

1. Critic Eric Bentley, in writing of Ibsen, pro and con, makes the following statement about *An Enemy of the People:* "An Enemy is one-sided, a play of moral blacks and whites. To read it as a subtle study in self-righteousness, like *Le Misanthrope,* would be to conceive another play. Stockmann is an Alceste taken pretty much at his own valuation." Review *The Misanthrope* (see page 687), and write an essay in which you first explain what Bentley means in his statement, and then tell whether you agree with him or not. Cite reasons for your opinion.

2. What evidences can you find in the play that Dr. Stockmann's thinking is influenced by the ideas that man is a member of the animal kingdom and that he has evolved from lower forms of life? Write a statement summarizing the doctor's concept of man's nature and destiny, taking account of what he says about the individual and about the majority. Tell whether you feel that his concept puts man in a more degraded and ignoble position than does the mayor's concept of man.

3. Trace the social and economic pressures that move each of these individuals or groups to act against Dr. Stockmann: Mayor Stockmann; Hovstad; Aslaksen; Mrs. Busk (Petra's employer); the members of the Home-owners' Association; the Stockmanns' landlord; Vik (the owner of Captain Horster's ship). Is there any source of pressure which is a prime mover, that is, which is not itself under pressure from another source? Explain clearly the connections among these pressures, and comment upon Dr. Stockmann's final "discovery" about this situation: that "the strongest man in the world is he who stands most alone."

PART 4

MODERN EUROPE
AND AFRICA

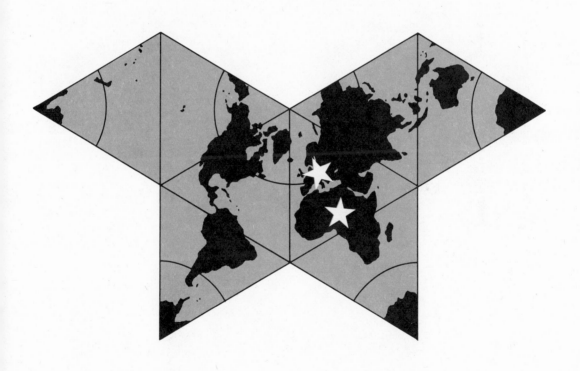

MODERN EUROPE AND AFRICA

1914–1960's

THE EXPERIENCES which an artist describes and the values which he defines have been called at various times matters of the "spirit," "soul," "heart," "imagination," or, perhaps, "aesthetic sense." Whatever they are called, it is certain that these experiences and values do not lend themselves to scientific analysis. They cannot be weighed or measured, analyzed structurally, or charted into wavelengths. Nor can these experiences and values be submitted to the tests of utility or marketability. They have no measurable cash value, teach no skills, offer no short cuts to worldly success. Yet through the ages, the artist, by addressing himself to these experiences and values, has defined for man his humanness, his essential reality, and his place in the larger, complex world around him. Traditionally, the artist has offered this definition out of an historical continuity of cultural experience and out of firmly established personal and social values, which both he and his audience accepted confidently as the accumulated wisdom of mankind.

But what happens when the historical continuity of a culture appears to be sharply broken off and when traditional personal and social values are brought sharply into question? What happens when the values of the artist seem to be no longer those of his audience, indeed, when society appears to reject as irrelevant the artist's traditional role as interpreter of experience? To answer these questions is to describe, in part at least, the role of the artist in the modern world.

The Industrial Revolution set the direction for the modern world. As early as the mid-eighteenth century, writers like Oliver Goldsmith (in his poem "The Deserted Village") had warned that materialism and industrialization were catastrophes which would dehumanize man; the old ways—which had seen most men working the soil and living in close harmony with nature—would be disrupted, and men would lose their secure social and cultural roots. The Romantic poets of the next era also decried the evils of industrialization and materialism and looked to nature for reaffirmation of the values and meanings they saw threatened. But in the Romantic period there was still the appearance of a choice. A Wordsworth could still find in England's Lake District the old ways going on as they always had, could still believe that by an act of will a nation could turn its back on industrialism and materialism and return to its ancient heritage.

But by some time late in the nineteenth century, men had ceased to hold such illusions. The Technological Age had succeeded the Industrial Age, and for millions of people life changed rapidly. Vast, sprawling cities inhabited by heterogeneous, transient populations became the centers of the world, and the sense of community, so strong in rural and village life, where all individuals were important and productive, was disappearing. In a few decades, science and industry gave people the automobile, the telephone, the radio, electricity, central heating, sanitation, movies, mass-produced books and magazines, better food, and new drugs to cure old diseases. The most admired men of the early modern age bore names like Carnegie and Rockefeller, Edison and Bell, Ford and McCormick, Rutherford and Curie, and their counterparts have continued to be celebrated by succeeding generations. These are the scientists, technologists, and practical men of business; they are not poets and painters and musicians. How to increase production and how to acquire wealth had become the most important questions—not those asking to what end production should be put, or what is the proper use of wealth. It is little wonder that, to the modern artist, the world has seemed to be in the condition of the lost motorist who said, "I don't know where I'm going, but I'm sure making good time."

Further, compelling discoveries had changed the way men thought about themselves. Social applications which Charles Darwin had never suggested were drawn from his concept of "the survival of the fittest." These applications appeared to give license to unrestrained aggressiveness in politics, in economics, and in many other areas of life once subject, at least in theory, to the restraints of a Judeo-Christian ethic. Another significant intellectual development of the nineteenth century which helped to shape the modern mind was Karl Marx's theory of economic determinism, which claims that human history is shaped by scientifically inevitable economic laws. Taken over and modified by the socialist and revolutionist Lenin (1870–1924), Marxism formed the economic and philosophic basis of what we know today as Russian Communism. Sigmund Freud's discoveries in psychoanalysis, indicating that individual lives are molded by unconscious influences stemming from experiences in infancy and early childhood, continued to whittle away even more at the notion that men had the power to shape their own lives and destinies. Meanwhile, discoveries in the physical sciences were indicating the immensity and complexity of the universe and making man's place in it seem ever smaller and less and less significant. Far from being at the center of the universe, man's home, the Earth, was pictured as a mere speck of dust in a remote corner of a minor galaxy. Finally, the anthropological sciences had begun to show that many of man's cherished institutions and beliefs draw their significance from a particular culture and, far from representing absolute truth, might have neither relevance nor validity outside their particular frameworks.

In the face of this deluge of scientific information and theorizing, the concepts of human freedom and human dignity were brought into serious question. The old definitions of the meaning and purpose of human existence no longer satisfied many persons. The result was introspection of a sort and intensity not known in previous ages, introspection which affected both the

Masked diplomats make futile attempts at peace talks. From German choreographer Kurt Jooss's satiric ballet *The Green Table*, presented in 1932.

artist and his audience. Accompanying it was anxiety, derived from a loss of confidence in the stability of human institutions and values.

A SEARCH FOR MEANING

The single historical event which more than any other capped this ferment was World War I, a war characterized by a savagery that the world thought it had outgrown. Whatever was left of the optimistic doctrine that human history was a record of slow but certain human progress seemed to perish with the young men on Verdun's bloody fields. To the artist, already disgusted with a civilization which appeared increasingly materialistic, self-destructive, and antihuman, World War I seemed to call for a total rejection of modern society. American poet Ezra Pound (1885–   ) spoke for many of his contemporary artists when he wrote of young men dying in World War I:

● There died a myriad,
And of the best, among them,
For an old bitch gone in the teeth,
For a botched civilization.
—EZRA POUND

And the years following World War I, the war fought "to make the world safe for democracy," saw totalitarianism take hold again, in Italy, Russia, Germany, Japan, and elsewhere. The economic collapse which became the Great Depression of the '30's was the painful backdrop before which other tragedies were acted out—the inhuman anti-Jewish pogroms in Germany, the vast political purges in Russia, the bloody civil war in Spain, and, ultimately, World War II and the terrifying nuclear explosions with which it ended. "Gone is the heart of man," mourned poet Edith Sitwell in August of 1945, and there were many who agreed with her.

But it was not only hatred of this "botched civilization" with which the artist had to contend. If he were to speak—as the artist traditionally had—of those experiences and values which define the nature of man to men, he had to contend with an apparent decay of meaning. The old ideals of love, religion, morality, patriotism, and beauty were being submitted to the tests of a society interested more in utility than abstraction. What could be measured or tested was important; what could not was not to be taken seriously. Traditions must stand the test of utility or be discarded. Nature was to be controlled and put to use, not admired and emulated. Nothing could be expected to last, once something newer and apparently better was offered as a substitute. This applied as much to values as to automobiles and washing machines. Materialism's cycle of invention, utility, obsolescence, and re-

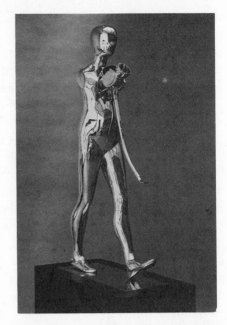

The glittering towers of skyscrapers, and an artist's concept of modern man, faceless, with a machine where his heart should be (by Ernest Trova, 1965).

jection overshadowed nature's slower order of birth, life, death, and rebirth. Even when artists have written of nature, they have seemed to see in it evidence of the decay of meaning. Thus, American poet Robert Frost (1874–1963) has described the artist's sense of the impermanence of all human experience in a poem called "Nothing Gold Can Stay."

> ●Nature's first green is gold,
> Her hardest hue to hold.
> Her early leaf's a flower;
> But only so an hour.
> Then leaf subsides to leaf.
> So Eden sank to grief,
> So dawn goes down to day.
> Nothing gold can stay.
> —ROBERT FROST

It has thus been in an atmosphere of introspection, anxiety, change, and alienation from society that the modern artists have approached their work. They have strongly sensed that their own age has not developed from the past but has broken from it, and this has denied them a cultural continuity on which to build their work. Inevitably, artists have come to that work in

"Nothing Gold Can Stay" from *Complete Poems of Robert Frost,* copyright 1923 by Holt, Rinehart and Winston, Inc., copyright 1951 by Robert Frost. Reprinted by permission of the publisher.

their distinctively personal ways. Deliberate obscurantism or private symbolisms have been the choices of some; Ezra Pound has suggested that a modern poet should never expect really to be understood by more than thirty people. Nostalgic re-creation of the past has been the direction of others. Still others have searched endlessly through the complexities of modern life for the threads of continuity from the past which they were sure must exist. Whatever the direction they have chosen, nearly all have spoken in a new voice, different from any that had been heard before.

The most characteristic element of this new voice is a diction that utilizes the ordinary idiom of the modern world. The tradition of having a literary language, a kind of elevated, high-class language used by the literary artist, has not disappeared entirely, but the major writers of modern literature have abandoned it. In poetry, one characteristic of the new diction is an effort to use images drawn from commonplace aspects of modern life and to state them in ordinary speech. Thus, T. S. Eliot (1888–1965) (see page 905) pictures an evening sky, not in the Romantic nature images we might have learned to expect from an earlier poet like William Wordsworth, but in these words:

> ●Let us go then, you and I,
> When the evening is spread out against the sky
> Like a patient etherized upon a table;
>
> —T. S. ELIOT

And the Russian poet Vladimir Mayakovski (1893–1930) records the end of a romance (see page 919) by saying:

> ●Love's boat has smashed against the daily grind.
> Now you and I are quits.
>
> —VLADIMIR MAYAKOVSKI

Think of the patriotic way the battle scene is described in *The Song of Roland* (see page 377), and read what American poet Randall Jarrell (1914–1965) says about aerial warfare in World War II:

> ●In bombers named for girls, we burned
> The cities we had learned about in school—
> Till our lives wore out; our bodies lay among
> The people we had killed and never seen.
> When we lasted long enough they gave us medals;
> When we died they said, "Our casualties were low."
>
> —RANDALL JARRELL

Lines by T. S. Eliot from "The Love Song of J. Alfred Prufrock," from *Collected Poems* by T. S. Eliot. Reprinted by permission of Harcourt, Brace & World, Inc., and Faber and Faber Ltd.
Lines by Vladimir Mayakovski from "Past One O'clock," from *The Bedbug and Selected Poetry* by Vladimir Mayakovski, translated by Max Hayward and George Reavy, edited by Patricia Blake, copyright © 1960 by The World Publishing Company. Reprinted by permission of the publisher.
Lines by Randall Jarrell from "Losses," from *Little Friend, Little Friend* by Randall Jarrell. Reprinted by permission of Mrs. Randall Jarrell.

Though most strikingly noticeable in poetry, a new diction has been sought by prose writers, too; American Ernest Hemingway (1898–1961), for example, developed a style that was terse and deceptively simple, but which was convincingly articulate. *Ulysses,* the major novel of Irish writer James Joyce (1882–1941) (see his story on page 972), presents its whole content through a series of internal monologues which must inevitably be in the idiom of the characters' own speech. This use of the internal monologue, which is called stream of consciousness, has reflected, too, the modern writer's interest in psychology and the general modern trend toward introspection.

Having found his new idiom, however, each writer still has had to decide what he would say with it. On this there has been no general agreement. In examining the attitudes expressed by various writers, British poet Stephen Spender (1909–   ) has made a useful distinction between those whom he calls "moderns" and those whom he calls "contemporaries." By the "moderns" he means those artists who find themselves unable to accept the values of their world; they are the alienated, the expatriates, the haters of "a botched civilization." The "contemporaries," on the other hand, do not accept their world without question, but they remain a part of it; they accept the values of science and progress and the historic forces they see at work in the world. The "contemporary" artist might struggle hard to channel the forces and energies of his world to reform the human condition, but he accepts those forces and energies and seeks to work with them. The "modern" rejects those forces and energies and seeks to conserve the lost values of the past, from which he believes his world has severed itself. T. S. Eliot, for example, returned to the values of a traditional religion, which many people had discarded because they saw it as meaningless in the light of modern urban culture.

Some of the most significant "modern" writers have sought to demonstrate the profound ways in which their world has alienated itself from cultures of the past. In their quest, they have confronted the present with the past, and the most influential works of the "moderns" do this with considerable success. James Joyce in *Ulysses* attempts to create the whole of contemporary experience in following one character through one day (June 16, 1904), but he sets this commonplace day's odyssey in the framework of the classical journey taken by Ulysses. T. S. Eliot writes in *The Waste Land* of existence in a modern urban desert, devoid of meaning or vitality, but he sets this wasteland within the structure of the medieval myth of the search for the Holy Grail.

Both of these works experiment extensively with traditional patterns and forms. Some degree of distortion characterizes each, as each artist presents his subjective response to the modern distortion of historic traditions. There is a kind of distortion by selection, too. The artists seemed to ask themselves which modern details and which ancient details could be set side by side to suggest most strikingly the profound changes in the modern world. For example, T. S. Eliot uses many allusions to the works of earlier writers. To describe the flow of humanity on a crowded city street, he borrows a line from Dante's *Divine Comedy,* a line in which Dante describes his amazement at the number of souls in hell. By the selection of such a detail, Eliot is able to suggest not only the quantity but the quality of people who live in his urban wasteland.

Most writers, however, have not found the solution in such a confrontation of present with past. Aware of the decay of meaning, many artists earlier in this century simply turned to concentrate on their art instead of on what they had to communicate. In fact, some wanted their art judged solely on the success or lack of success of its technique, without consideration of whether it communicated anything or not. Technique became even further divorced from meaning as many artists became almost neurotically introspective and personal; thus a movement toward antirationalism began to characterize some poetry and painting. The extreme exponents of this movement were the Dadaists, nihilists who repudiated and jested at everything: society, war, religion, literature, language, reason itself. (One Dada poem consisted solely of the letter W.) Less extreme than the Dadaists were

Dada art (by Swiss artist Meret Oppenheim, 1936). Incongruous objects like this were meant to shock observers out of complacency into new awareness.

the Surrealists who repudiated common sense and the social establishment, but who also, in a more positive vein, proposed a program: to change art and find the "more real than real world" through examination of the subconscious and dreams. The method of the Surrealists was the free association of ideas, and they drew heavily from the works of Freud. Searching the subconscious for their images and symbols, the Surrealist artists and poets shocked the bourgeoisie with nightmarish productions.

But there was no place to go with this approach to literature, even though it produced some valuable technical innovations and freshness. The inescapable fact is that the vehicle of literature is words, and words either have meanings which are communicable, or they cease to be words and become private symbols. Some writers, as well as artists, feeling that they had gone as far with this approach as was possible, quit their art entirely. They could find no meaning in the world which was expressible or worth expressing. Dada painter Marcel Duchamp (1887–1968), for the most notable example, gave up painting for chess; and for one reason or another, poet Paul Valéry (1871–1945) (see page 912) renounced writing for twenty years to pursue higher mathematics and philosophy.

But most writers, of course, though they might see no meaning in the world, have continued writing anyway. Some, by bringing society's values into question, have demanded that society reexamine its assumptions of meaning. Others have placed the responsibility on man to create his own meanings. Many, of course, have recorded life without comment, without requirement of meaning, suggesting that the interest of the writing lies in the situation itself, whether it has meaning or not. (This is usually appearance only, however, for by his very selection of the details to record, the writer interprets and gives a hint of the meaning of what he has observed.)

The "contemporaries" of whom Stephen Spender speaks have different motivations and artistic problems. As indicated, these are the writers who can accept the modern world with its industrial strength, its scientific enthusiasm, and its materialism, yet still want to make it a better, more humane place. It is to this group that the reform writers of the different decades belong. American writer Upton Sinclair (1898–1968), for example, did not reject the material progress of the United States; he wanted it to develop toward humane goals. The Socialist writers of the thirties did not despise the economic strength or the scientific achievements of Western society; they simply wanted them carried out under public rather than private ownership. This is one kind of "contemporary."

The outlook of yet another kind is represented in a story like "The Little Shoemakers" (see page 983). Isaac Singer (1904–   ) clearly does not deny the value of modern progress; the sons in the story emigrate from Poland and make their fortunes in America, and this change is presented as a good thing. Yet among their luxuries and new values, Singer suggests, cer-

United Nations scene, 1966. The delegates are from Nigeria, Japan, and Mali.

tain old values are still relevant, and these are represented in the character of the war-weary old father. To work skillfully with one's hands is still a good thing for a man to do, even when need no longer requires him to. To be aware of his heritage and of the ancient values of that heritage is also a good thing for a man, even when he accepts a new culture and new values.

THE "NEW" NATIONS

Though Spender's classifications of "modern" and "contemporary" usefully describe much of modern literature in Europe and North America, there are yet other dimensions of modern literature which do not lend themselves so readily to his classifications. These are the literatures of the "new" nations.

The end of World War II signalled the imminent end of colonialism as it had been practiced by European powers since the days of the Renaissance explorations, and especially since the days of the nineteenth century. Long-subject peoples of Asia, Latin America, and Africa demanded independence and self government. With fervent nationalism and new cultural pride, they threw off the domination of their colonial masters, and, in a process that is still continuing, assumed their proper places among the independent nations of the world.

Though many of the new states were not technologically advanced, they were often repositories of rich pre-colonial cultures. Inspired by the heady exuberance accompanying their new independence, many of these nations encouraged native artists to rediscover and reinterpret their ancient traditions. From Ghana to Indonesia, from Swaziland to Tonga, painters, sculptors, poets, storytellers, dancers, and musicians brought twentieth century insights to bear on the folk materials and on the more sophisticated achievements of their ancestors. The result has been a tremendous thrust of artistic vitality and creativity in the "new" nations, a creativity of such variety as to defy simple classifications. Much of it is too new and, in some instances, too exotic for Western tastes to be able yet to evaluate. But there is no doubt that the literatures of the new nations are among the most exciting developments of the modern period.

Some of the most involved writers of modern times have come from black Africa. A number of these writers are politicians themselves and lead their own political parties. Others have protested powerfully against colonialism, inspiring those working for nationhood and warning those watching from the outside. For their writings and actions, some of these men have served long and brutal prison terms.

Like modern life itself, then, modern literature is varied and complex. It cannot be adequately summarized in so brief an introduction. But despite the natural conservatism of the arts, literature has clearly been changing at the same rapid rate that the society has changed. The artist's ability to interpret the modern age and to state the values of our culture is still open to question. But no computer yet invented can pose the moral question or offer the crucial definition or speak the truth which will tell modern man who he is and what he is and why he is. The artist still has this task to perform.

GERARD MANLEY HOPKINS

"To seem the stranger lies my lot . . ." writes Hopkins (1844–1889) in one of his sonnets, and this English-born poet did indeed live a good part of his life in spiritual and geographical exile. He converted to Roman Catholicism while living in a Protestant country, and later, after he was ordained a Jesuit priest, he left friends and family in England to take up a teaching assignment in Dublin, a city he never grew to like. Hopkins met with difficulties in trying to publish his unusual poems, so he wrote for an audience of one—Robert Bridges, a fellow poet and friend.

To express the special essence of everything—what he calls inscape—Hopkins developed a unique combination of syntax, metaphor, diction, and rhythm. His syntax often employs wrenched word order and ellipsis. His metaphors are frequently charged with multiple meanings and ambiguities, and he often puts words in original contexts, experiments with new compounds of words, and revives words no longer commonly used. His rhythm, adapted from Anglo-Saxon verse forms, relies heavily on alliteration and breaks sharply from the tradition of using a fixed number of syllables in each line; in fact, Hopkins frequently marks with accents the words he wants stressed. All of these innovations had great appeal to twentieth-century poets searching for new forms of expression.

Hopkins's poetry went practically unread until Robert Bridges published it in 1918, almost thirty years after his friend's death.

Spring and Fall:

to a young child

Márgarét, are you gríeving
Over Goldengrove unleaving?
Leáves, líke the things of man, you
With your fresh thoughts care for, can you?
Áh! ás the heart grows older   5
It will come to such sights colder
By and by, nor spare a sigh
Though worlds of wanwood leafmeal lie;
And yet you *will* weep and know why.
Now no matter, child, the name: 10
Sórrow's spríngs áre the same.
Nor mouth had, no nor mind, expressed
What heart heard of, ghost guessed:
It iś the blight man was born for,
It is Margaret you mourn for.   15

God's Grandeur

The world is charged with the grandeur of God.
  It will flame out, like shining from shook foil;
  It gathers to a greatness, like the ooze of oil
Crushed. Why do men then now not reck his rod?
Generations have trod, have trod, have trod;   5
  And all is seared with trade; bleared, smeared with toil;
  And wears man's smudge and shares man's smell: the soil
Is bare now, nor can foot feel, being shod.

And for all this, nature is never spent;
  There lives the dearest freshness deep down things;   10
And though the last lights off the black West went
  Oh, morning, at the brown brink eastward, springs—
Because the Holy Ghost over the bent
  World broods with warm breast and with ah! bright wings.

THOMAS HARDY

When he was over fifty-five, Thomas Hardy (1840–1928) turned from his career as a successful prose writer (he had published eleven novels and three collections of short stories) to his first love—poetry. During the last years of his long life, Hardy emerged as a versatile poet who is considered to have bridged the gap between the conventionally phrased sentiments of popular Victorian poetry and the compressed, individualized expressions of twentieth-century poets. Both his novels and his poetry show a love for the wild Wessex countryside and an ironic view of man caught in the grip of forces too powerful for him to control. Many of his best poems are written in the Wessex dialect—simple, homely language that undercuts a man's pretensions. The *Collected Poems of Thomas Hardy*, which runs to eight hundred pages, contains only a handful of outstanding poems, yet these few poems can hold their own with the best modern verse in English.

The Man He Killed

"Had he and I but met
  By some old ancient inn,
We should have sat us down to wet
  Right many a nipperkin!°

4. **nipperkin:** a liquor container that holds about a half pint.

"But ranged as infantry,   5
  And staring face to face,
I shot at him as he at me,
  And killed him in his place.

"I shot him dead because—
  Because he was my foe,   10
Just so: my foe of course he was;
  That's clear enough; although

"He thought he'd 'list, perhaps,
  Off-hand like—just as I—
Was out of work—had sold his traps—   15
  No other reason why.

"Yes; quaint and curious war is!
  You shoot a fellow down
You'd treat if met where any bar is,
  Or help to half a crown."   20

In Time of "The Breaking of Nations"

1

Only a man harrowing clods
  In a slow silent walk
With an old horse that stumbles and nods
  Half asleep as they stalk.

2

Only thin smoke without flame   5
  From the heaps of couch-grass;°
Yet this will go onward the same
  Though dynasties pass.

3

Yonder a maid and her wight
  Come whispering by: 10
War's annals will fade into night
  Ere their story die.

6. **couch-grass:** coarse grasses that spread rapidly by creeping.

WILLIAM BUTLER YEATS

The early poems of William Butler Yeats (1865–1939), one of the giants of modern poetry, reflect a Romantic, nostalgic interest in the Celtic past and in the countryside of Western Ireland, where Yeats spent much of his childhood. But in his maturity, a significant change occurred. Yeats abandoned his earlier Romanticism, stripped his poetry of its dreamy images and poetic diction, and sought, as Wordsworth had sought a century earlier, a terse colloquial style which would still permit his words to sing. In so doing, Yeats was one of the first to break completely with the poetic conventions of the 1890's, which had esteemed prettiness and regularity in poetry, over strength and individuality. By now Yeats had also developed his strange, unintellectual interest in the occult, and for his poetry he used a personal set of symbols; a "tower," for example, might represent the contemplative life, and a "gyre" the spinning of an era to its close. Deceptively simple though the language of his mature poems may be, the lines are rich in allusions and in suggestive symbolic meaning. In writing poetry, Yeats liked to think that he heeded Aristotle's advice: to think like the wise man but to express himself like the common people.

The first poem that follows was written when Yeats heard of the death of Major Gregory, the son of his friend Lady Gregory. The young Irish pilot, a member of England's Royal Flying Corps, was killed in action in an air battle in January 1918.

The second poem reflects Yeats's theory that civilizations begin in violence, establish order in maturity, and end in violence, in two-thousand-year cycles. For Yeats, one such civilization began with the Christian era. Brutality and bloodshed, then, are inescapable as this cycle now draws to a close. The "second coming" of the title recalls paradoxically the Christian prophecy of the second coming of the Messiah, which would mark the end of this world and the establishment of Christ's kingdom on earth. Yeats stated that he believed this poem, published in 1919, prophesied the rise of totalitarianism, which would result in World War II.

An Irish Airman Foresees His Death

I know that I shall meet my fate
Somewhere among the clouds above;
Those that I fight I do not hate,
Those that I guard I do not love;
My country is Kiltartan Cross,   5
My countrymen Kiltartan's poor,
No likely end could bring them loss
Or leave them happier than before.
Nor law, nor duty bade me fight,
Nor public men, nor cheering crowds,   10
A lonely impulse of delight
Drove to this tumult in the clouds;

I balanced all, brought all to mind,
The years to come seemed waste of breath,
A waste of breath the years behind   15
In balance with this life, this death.

The Second Coming

Turning and turning in the widening gyre
The falcon cannot hear the falconer;
Things fall apart; the center cannot hold;
Mere anarchy is loosed upon the world,
The blood-dimmed tide is loosed, and everywhere   5
The ceremony of innocence is drowned;
The best lack all conviction, while the worst
Are full of passionate intensity.

Surely some revelation is at hand;
Surely the Second Coming is at hand.   10
The Second Coming! Hardly are those words out
When a vast image out of *Spiritus Mundi*°
Troubles my sight: somewhere in sands of the desert
A shape with lion body and the head of a man,
A gaze blank and pitiless as the sun,   15
Is moving its slow thighs, while all about it
Reel shadows of the indignant desert birds.
The darkness drops again; but now I know
That twenty centuries of stony sleep
Were vexed to nightmare by a rocking cradle,   20
And what rough beast, its hour come round at last,
Slouches towards Bethlehem to be born?

12. *Spiritus Mundi:* for Yeats, the "soul of the world," the collective memory of man,
from which spring the dream images of the race.

T. S. ELIOT

Along with Yeats, Thomas Stearns Eliot (1888–1965) is recognized as the most significant force in shaping the direction of modern poetry. Eliot's revolutionary approach to poetry was strongly influenced by the French Symbolists of the nineteenth century. Concerned with the sterility of society and with the boredom, disillusionment, and triviality in people's lives, he rejected the poetic conventions of the past, claiming that they could not possibly express the problems and complexities of the modern world. Consequently, relying on revelation and suggestion rather than on explanation, he chose to use a rapid series of sense impressions to convey thoughts, to make use of the free association of ideas, and to do this in the natural rhythms of the speech spoken in his own day. ("Every revolution in poetry," observed Eliot in regard to this last innovation, "is apt to be, and sometimes announces itself as, a return to common speech. That is the revolution which Wordsworth announced in his prefaces . . .")

Eliot, who was educated at Harvard, the Sorbonne, and Oxford, revered the great traditions of other eras; he saw man, in fact, as not only involved in the immensities and trivialities of modern life, but also as subject to a sense of the more beautiful and serene past, a sense which underlines his awareness of the hollowness of contemporary life. Thus Eliot incorporates in his poetry references to certain classics—to Dante, to the Elizabethan dramatists, to the metaphysical poets of the seventeenth century—even freely echoing lines from them. He also arbitrarily draws from several less well-known fields of interest (from the *Upanishads,* for example), so that some of his symbols and imagery are obscure. Although some have claimed that all these techniques make Eliot's poems too intellectual, his finest poems are actually emotionally charged.

The poetry Eliot wrote after the late 1920's reflects his conversion to an active Anglo-Catholicism and an acceptance of the Church as an institution where men can communicate with the present and with the past. From then on his major works portray a hopefulness in expressing the soul's struggle for renewal, despite the emptiness of an emotionally impoverished, materialistic world. Of the poems that follow, the "Preludes" (1917) exemplify the first period of Eliot's creativity, while "Journey of the Magi" (1927) embodies his later religious feeling.

Preludes

I

The winter evening settles down
With smell of steaks in passageways.
Six o'clock.
The burnt-out ends of smoky days.
And now a gusty shower wraps   5
The grimy scraps
Of withered leaves about your feet
And newspapers from vacant lots;
The showers beat
On broken blinds and chimney-pots,   10
And at the corner of the street
A lonely cab-horse steams and stamps.

And then the lighting of the lamps.

II

The morning comes to consciousness
Of faint stale smells of beer   15
From the sawdust-trampled street
With all its muddy feet that press
To early coffeestands.

With the other masquerades
That time resumes,   20
One thinks of all the hands
That are raising dingy shades
In a thousand furnished rooms.

III

You tossed a blanket from the bed,
You lay upon your back and waited; 25
You dozed, and watched the night
    revealing

The thousand sordid images
Of which your soul was constituted;
They flickered against the ceiling.
And when all the world came back   30
And the light crept up between the shutters
And you heard the sparrows in the gutters,
You had such a vision of the street
As the street hardly understands;
Sitting along the bed's edge, where   35
You curled the papers from your hair,
Or clasped the yellow soles of feet
In the palms of both soiled hands.

IV

His soul stretched tight across the skies
That fade behind a city block,   40
Or trampled by insistent feet
At four and five and six o'clock;
And short square fingers stuffing pipes,
And evening newspapers, and eyes
Assured of certain certainties,   45
The conscience of a blackened street
Impatient to assume the world.

I am moved by fancies that are curled
Around these images, and cling;
The notion of some infinitely gentle   50
Infinitely suffering thing.

Wipe your hand across your mouth, and
    laugh;
The worlds revolve like ancient women
Gathering fuel in vacant lots.

Journey of the Magi

"A cold coming we had of it,
Just the worst time of the year
For a journey, and such a long journey:
The ways deep and the weather sharp,
The very dead of winter."   5
And the camels galled, sore-footed, refractory,
Lying down in the melting snow.
There were times we regretted
The summer palaces on slopes, the terraces,
And the silken girls bringing sherbet.   10
Then the camel men cursing and grumbling
And running away, and wanting their liquor and women,
And the night-fires going out, and the lack of shelters,
And the cities hostile and the towns unfriendly
And the villages dirty and charging high prices: 15
A hard time we had of it.
At the end we preferred to travel all night,
Sleeping in snatches,
With the voices singing in our ears, saying
That this was all folly.   20

Then at dawn we came down to a temperate valley,
Wet, below the snow line, smelling of vegetation,
With a running stream and a water-mill beating the darkness,
And three trees on the low sky.
And an old white horse galloped away in the meadow.   25
Then we came to a tavern with vine-leaves over the lintel,
Six hands at an open door dicing for pieces of silver,
And feet kicking the empty wine-skins.
But there was no information, and so we continued
And arrived at evening, not a moment too soon   30
Finding the place; it was (you may say) satisfactory.

All this was a long time ago, I remember,
And I would do it again, but set down
This set down
This: were we led all that way for   35
Birth or Death? There was a Birth, certainly,
We had evidence and no doubt. I had seen birth and death,
But had thought they were different; this Birth was
Hard and bitter agony for us, like Death, our death.
We returned to our places, these Kingdoms,   40
But no longer at ease here, in the old dispensation,
With an alien people clutching their gods.
I should be glad of another death.

DYLAN THOMAS

Welsh-born poet Dylan Thomas (1914–1953) became well known in the 1940's with poems that turned away from economics, the machine age, and politics and returned English poetry to a personal, lyrical Romanticism. His poetic style is characterized by the Surrealistic use of free association and dreamlike images, and by the use of half-rhymes and consonant chime so typical of Hopkins's poetry. Thomas's dynamic exuberance and intense emotional tone result from a complex use of language—from a profusion of alliteration, puns, and imaginative symbolism; he has been accused, in fact, of being obsessed with the sounds of words rather than with their intellectual content. He draws principally from childhood memories and is moved by the primitive forces of generation, life, and death.

Fern Hill

Now as I was young and easy under the apple boughs
About the lilting house and happy as the grass was green,
    The night above the dingle starry,
        Time let me hail and climb
      Golden in the heydays of his eyes,   5
And honored among wagons I was prince of the apple towns
And once below a time I lordly had the trees and leaves
        Trail with daisies and barley
    Down the rivers of the windfall light.

And as I was green and carefree, famous among the barns   10
About the happy yard and singing as the farm was home,
    In the sun that is young once only,
        Time let me play and be
      Golden in the mercy of his means,
And green and golden I was huntsman and herdsman, the calves   15
Sang to my horn, the foxes on the hills barked clear and cold,
        And the sabbath rang slowly
    In the pebbles of the holy streams.

All the sun long it was running, it was lovely, the hay
Fields high as the house, the tunes from the chimneys, it was air   20
      And playing, lovely and watery
        And fire green as grass.
      And nightly under the simple stars
As I rode to sleep the owls were bearing the farm away,

All the moon long I heard, blessed among stables, the nightjars°   25
    Flying with the ricks, and the horses
        Flashing into the dark.

And then to awake, and the farm, like a wanderer white
With the dew, come back, the cock on his shoulder: it was all
    Shining, it was Adam and maiden,   30
        The sky gathered again
And the sun grew round that very day.
So it must have been after the birth of the simple light
In the first, spinning place, the spellbound horses walking warm
    Out of the whinnying green stable   35
        On to the fields of praise.

And honored among foxes and pheasants by the gay house
Under the new made clouds and happy as the heart was long,
    In the sun born over and over,
        I ran my heedless ways,   40
    My wishes raced through the house high hay
And nothing I cared, at my sky blue trades, that time allows
In all his tuneful turning so few and such morning songs
    Before the children green and golden
        Follow him out of grace,   45

Nothing I cared, in the lamb white days, that time would take me
Up to the swallow thronged loft by the shadow of my hand,
    In the moon that is always rising,
        Nor that riding to sleep
    I should hear him fly with the high fields   50
And wake to the farm forever fled from the childless land.
Oh as I was young and easy in the mercy of his means,
    Time held me green and dying
    Though I sang in my chains like the sea.

25. **nightjars:** nighthawks.

FOR STUDY AND DISCUSSION

SPRING AND FALL

1. The word *unleaving* (line 2), invented by Hopkins, means "losing leaves." How is the name *Goldengrove* appropriate to both the literal and figurative meaning of the poem? How would you put lines 3 and 4 into normal English word order? What does "such sights" (line 6) refer to?

2. The word *wan* means "pale, gloomy, dismal." What does "worlds of wanwood" (line 8) mean? The word *leafmeal,* invented by Hopkins, is an adverb; what might it mean? How does Hopkins's stress on the word *will* (line 9) affect the meaning of the line?

3. What are "sorrow's springs," according to the poem?

4. What does the word *ghost* (line 13) mean? Paraphrase lines 12 and 13, in normal English word order. What several meanings does the word *fall* have in the poem? What is the "blight man was born for"?

5. Discuss the ways in which the title "Spring and Fall" relates to the subject of the poem.

GOD'S GRANDEUR

1. What are the denotations and connotations of the word *charged* (line 1)? How do these meanings relate to those of *spent* (line 9)? The similes in lines 2 and 3 illustrate the

ways the essence, or inscape, of things is revealed. Explain these two similes. "Reck his rod" means "heed his power." How do lines 5–8 explain the ways that man ignores God's power?

2. The phrase "deep down things" (line 10) means "deep down in things." Does the omission of the word in change the meaning of the line? Explain. How does the image in lines 11 and 12 clarify the statement that "nature is never spent"? The words black and brown (lines 11 and 12) are not usually used to describe a sunset or sunrise. What does Hopkins's choice of these colors imply?

3. Hopkins expects the reader to know that the traditional symbol for the Holy Spirit is a dove. Why is the world bent (line 13)? What does the word broods (line 14) suggest here? How do the words warm and bright (line 14) refer back to the similes in lines 2 and 3?

4. Both this poem and Wordsworth's "The World Is Too Much with Us" (see page 751) are sonnets and deal with similar subjects. What comparable idea is stated in the octet of each poem? In the sestet, how do the poets disagree in their resolution of the problem? How do the meters and vocabularies differ?

THE MAN HE KILLED

1. What can we learn from the poem about the man who is speaking—his station in life, his attitude toward war, his thoughts?

2. Why does Hardy repeat certain words in verse 3? How does Hardy use contrast of situation for added effect? What irregular rhyme patterns does Hardy use? for what purpose?

3. What does the poem say about the rationality of war? Is this an oversimplification of the problem? How does the viewpoint in this poem compare with that expressed in the ancient Chinese poems on pages 271 and 273?

4. How effective is this poem as poetry? Are there any jingly rhymes or awkward rhythms? Can their use be justified or is this a bad poem? Explain.

IN TIME OF "THE BREAKING OF NATIONS"

1. "The Breaking of Nations" refers to the quotation from Jeremiah (51:20): "Thou art my battle axe and weapons of war: for with thee will I break in pieces the nations, and with thee will I destroy kingdoms." What is the relation of the title to the content of the poem? How are the three examples of un-changing values related? What do they represent?

2. What added impact results from Hardy's repetition of the word only to start stanzas 1 and 2? To what does the word this (line 7) refer?

AN IRISH AIRMAN FORESEES HIS DEATH

1. What is the airman's motive for engaging in combat? Would you consider this a subjective or an objective reaction to war? Explain.

2. Why is it understandable that an Irishman serving in 1918 in the British army would express the thoughts found in lines 3–8?

3. A key statement in the poem is "I balanced all" (line 13). What does this mean? What "pairs" of things are mentioned in the poem? How is each pair "balanced"?

4. In what way is this airman's reaction to war similar to that of Hardy's soldier in "The Man He Killed"? In what way is the airman's feeling completely different? Which seems to you the better poem—Yeats's or Hardy's—and why?

THE SECOND COMING

1. In the first stanza, distinguish between Yeats's images and his direct statements. What lines in the first verse express directly Yeats's attitude toward contemporary man? Discuss the implications of these lines in view of the rise of totalitarianism.

2. What images in the first stanza indicate a loss of purpose and order in the world? What kind of bird is the falcon? What is its natural relation to the falconer? How does its present behavior symbolize the state of civilization? What contrasts in imagery are set up in lines 5–6?

3. What images in the second stanza are used to describe a vision or a dream? What line best expresses the nature of the creature in the dream?

4. The "Second Coming" (line 10) recalls, of course, the prophecy of the Messiah. How does this add irony to the poem? What other allusions in the second stanza contribute to this ironic contrast between Christian tradition and Yeats's dismal vision? Why might Yeats's concept of a new era be so pessimistic?

PRELUDES

1. What impressions of city life does Eliot project through the images in parts I and II? What images seem to carry a symbolic mean-

ing? Does any line in part I seem to carry a symbolic meaning? Does any line in part I seem to express a note of hope? If so, is it sustained throughout the rest of the poem? What time period elapses during the course of the poem? In what various ways does "morning come to consciousness"? Does morning seem to bring renewed hope to "all the hands" mentioned? Explain. What "masquerades" are resumed each day?

2. How does the change of pronoun in part III intensify the emotion? What details emphasize the "sordid images"? What reaction does the "you" of part III seem to be experiencing toward her own life and toward the city and society?

3. What time of day is evoked by the images in part IV? Has the change in time brought reassurance or comfort? What does the image in the first line of part IV mean? What certainties should an individual feel beyond the evening newspaper? How does the conscience of the blackened street "assume the world"? What effect might this have on the individual?

4. Does the viewpoint of the speaker vary in part IV? Explain why this might have been done. What does the speaker conclude in lines 48–51 about how the kind of life described in the poem affects the human spirit?

5. What change in the speaker's tone occurs abruptly in the last three lines? What idea is suggested by the image of "ancient women gathering fuel in vacant lots"? What might the "vacant lots" symbolize?

6. Eliot felt that the meaning of a poem should not be directly stated so much as it should be experienced. Summarize the experience of city life as it is set forth in this poem. What values, both personal and communal, can be lost in such an environment?

JOURNEY OF THE MAGI

1. Who is the speaker in the poem? At what point in time is he speaking, in relation to the events described? How does this supposedly eyewitnessed description of the events compare with the familiar biblical story (Matthew 2:1–2), in fact and in mood?

2. What is the speaker's tone in lines 1–20? Think of one word that best reflects the speaker's personal reactions toward the journey here described. What hardships, physical and emotional, did the travelers encounter?

3. How does the tempo of the poem shift in lines 21–31? What images might be used symbolically here to convey an idea of new life? What symbolic references point to forthcoming tragedy and death? What images here are reminders of the crucifixion of Christ? When the destination is finally reached, what is the impact as the speaker describes the moment as "satisfactory"?

4. Is this restrained reaction explained in lines 32–43? Does the speaker question the truth of his experience? Explain your answers. What made it a painful and ambiguous experience? How is this ambiguity foreshadowed by the symbolism in lines 21–31? What has happened to the wise man to make him feel lonely upon returning to his own land? What does he mean by "another" death?

5. The quotation at the beginning of the poem is from a Nativity sermon preached in 1622 by Lancelot Andrews, an Anglican bishop. Do we need this information to understand the poem? What characteristic of Eliot's poetic technique does the use of the quotation illustrate?

FERN HILL

1. Who is the speaker and what feeling does he recapture in this poem? What colors does he associate with this feeling?

2. With what force is youth in conflict? How is a reminder of this force woven into the context of each verse? Why is the central symbol of the farm so appropriate? In the first three verses, what role does the child play in relation to the world and life?

3. How is the biblical event alluded to in the fourth stanza related to the way the child awakens to a new day? What change of tone occurs during the fifth and sixth verses? How would you explain the image in lines 53–54?

4. Time, which is personified throughout the poem, seems to be described as the Pied Piper in lines 42–45. Why is this a fitting figure of speech? What word might be substituted for *grace* in line 45? Thomas has a charming talent for shifting the wording of clichés slightly so that they are endowed with fresh meaning. Point out where such shifts occur in lines 2, 6, 7, 19, 38.

5. Part of the poem's music is due to the use of half-rhymes. Identify some of the words that come close to rhyming. What words or phrases definitely convey their effect more by sound than sense?

PAUL VALÉRY

In his youth, Valéry (1871–1945) was a follower of the poet Stéphane Mallarmé, who, as master of the French Symbolist movement, formed elusive poems around a central symbol which would suggest or evoke subtle emotions, states of mind, or mysteries. Following the death of Mallarmé, Valéry wrote less and less, and eventually devoted himself to studying mathematics and philosophy. But on the urging of his friend André Gide, he yielded again to poetry. Still bearing signs of the Symbolist influence, Valéry had become more interested in lucidity and precision of thought. He was devoted to the intellect, distrusted spontaneity, emotion, and sentiment, and declared, without regret, that love is vanishing. ("The last lover will be classed as a sexual maniac.") Although he demanded absolute logic in poetry, Valéry's thought often confuses the average reader. But by 1925 his reputation had spread so widely that he was voted the foremost poet in France, even by those who had renounced all effort to understand him. In theme, his poems often depict the tension between man's conflicting natures, between his active involvement with life and the inward-turning contemplative existence of the spirit.

Asides

What do you do? Why, everything.
What are you worth? Worth, well,
The worth of mastery and disgust,
Presentiment and trial . . .
What are you worth? Worth, well . . .   5
What do you want? Nothing, all.

What do you know? Boredom.
What can you do? Dream.
And with the power of the mind
Can turn the morning into night.   10
What can you do? Dream,
And so drive boredom from the mind.

What do you want? My own good.
What must you do? Learn.
Learn and master and foresee,   15
All, of course, to no good.
What do you fear? The will.
Who are you? Nothing, nothing at all.

Where are you going? To death.
What will you do there? Die;   20
Nor ever return to this rotten game,
Forever and ever and ever the same.
Where are you going? To die.
What will you do there? Be dead.

"Asides" by Paul Valéry, translated by William Jay Smith from *Anthology of French Poetry* (Anchor Books), edited by Angel Flores. Reprinted by permission of Angel Flores.

Caesar

Caesar, serene Caesar, your foot on all,
The hard fists in the beard, and the gloomy eyes
Pregnant with eagles and battles of foreseen fall,
Your heart swells, feeling itself omnipotent cause.

In vain the lake trembles, licking its rosy bed,   5
Vainly glistens the gold of the young wheat straws.
You harden in the knots of your gathered body
The word which must finally rive your tight-clenched jaws.

The spacious world, beyond the immense horizon,
The Empire awaits the torch, the order, the lightning   10
Which will turn the evening to a furious dawn.

Happily there on the waves, and cradled in hazard,
A lazy fisherman is drifting and singing,
Not knowing what thunder collects in the center of Caesar.

"Caesar" by Paul Valéry, translated by C. F. MacIntyre, reprinted by permission of the publisher, The Devin-Adair Company, from *War and the Poet,* edited by Richard Eberhart and Selden Rodman. Copyright 1945 by The Devin-Adair Company.

JACQUES PRÉVERT

One of the most popular of twentieth-century French poets, Prévert (1900–) writes verse in language of crystalline clarity, which often abounds in wit, dead-pan humor, and wild fancy. Prévert's poems have so delighted the French public that they have been sung in night clubs and recited over the radio. Prévert, whose techniques were influenced by the Surrealists, uses his verse to protest practically everything.

To Paint the Portrait of a Bird

Paint first a cage
with an open door
paint then
something pretty
something simple   5
something handsome
something useful
for the bird
then place the canvas against a tree
in a garden   10
in a wood
or in a forest
hide behind the tree
silently
motionless   15
Sometimes the bird arrives at once
but it may also take many years
before making up its mind
Do not be discouraged
wait   20
wait if need be many years
a speedy or a delayed arrival
bears no relation
to the success of the portrait
When the bird arrives   25
if it arrives

observe the most profound silence
wait until the bird enters the cage
and when it has entered
close the door gently with a stroke of the brush   30
then
paint out one by one all the bars of the cage
taking care to touch none of the bird's feathers
Paint then the portrait of a tree
choosing the loveliest of its branches   35
for the bird
paint too the green foliage and the fresh wind
the dust of the sun
and the noise of insects in the grass in the summer heat
and then wait for the bird to sing   40
If the bird does not sing
it is a bad sign
a sign that the picture is bad
but if it sings it is a good sign
a sign that you can sign   45
So you pluck gently then
one of the bird's feathers
and you write your name in a corner of the portrait.

RAINER MARIA RILKE

The most respected German lyric poet of modern times, Rilke (1875–1926) combines the German genius for expressing abstract thought, with innovations in the use of the German language which give his poetry an unusual musical quality. Rilke traveled widely throughout Europe and felt closely akin to the French Symbolists, who strongly influenced his poetic style. His life was a task in almost every way, and his works reflect a long religious search for the meaning of life and for the clarification of man's role in the world. As he became increasingly saddened by the inhumanity of World War I, by his own marital problems, by the death of his friend (the sculptor Rodin), and by constant fear of losing his poetic gifts, Rilke slowly withdrew into solitude. The action is significant, because the theme of some of his greatest poems is reconciliation through withdrawal.

Among Rilke's last works are the ten *Duino Elegies* (named for a castle he once retreated to in Switzerland), which are laments for man. In one of these elegies, Rilke gives voice to what might be the climax of his long search for meaning and purpose—he expresses confidence in the importance of literature as the explanation of the earth, as the means of making transitory things endure forever.

Rilke suffered for years from a form of leukemia. He died after he was pricked by a thorn from the roses he was gathering to give to a young friend.

The Merry-Go-Round

Jardin du Luxembourg

Under the roof and the roof's shadow turns
this train of painted horses for a while
in this bright land that lingers
before it perishes. In what brave style
they prance—though some pull wagons.   5
And there burns
a wicked lion red with anger . . .
and now and then a big white elephant.

Even a stag runs here, as in the wood,
save that he bears a saddle where, upright,   10
a little girl in blue sits, buckled tight.

And on the lion whitely rides a young
boy who clings with little sweaty hands,
the while the lion shows his teeth and tongue.

And now and then a big white elephant.   15

And on the horses swiftly going by
are shining girls who have outgrown this play;
in the middle of the flight they let their eyes
glance here and there and near and far away—

and now and then a big white elephant.   20

And all this hurries toward the end, so fast,
whirling futilely, evermore the same.
A flash of red, of green, of gray, goes past,
and then a little scarce-begun profile.
And oftentimes a blissful dazzling smile   25
vanishes in this blind and breathless game.

"The Merry-Go-Round" from *Selected Poems* by Rilke, translated by C. F. MacIntyre. Reprinted by permission of University of California Press.

Two Translations of "Self-Portrait"

(Adapted by Robert Lowell)

The bone-build of the eyebrows has a mule's
or Pole's noble and narrow steadfastness.
A scared blue child is peering through the eyes,
and there's a kind of weakness, not a fool's,
yet womanish—the gaze of one who serves.   5
The mouth is just a mouth . . . untidy curves,
quite unpersuasive, yet it says its *yes,*
when forced to act. The forehead cannot frown,
and likes the shade of dumbly looking down.

A still life, *nature morte*—hardly a whole!   10
It has done nothing worked through or alive,
in spite of pain, in spite of comforting . . .
Out of this distant and disordered thing
something in earnest labors to unroll.

(Translated by M. D. Herter Norton)

The old long-noble generation's
steadfastness in the eyebrow's build.
In the glance still childhood's fear and blue
and humility here and there, not of a servile sort,
yet of one who serves and of a woman.   5
The mouth made as a mouth, large and defined,
not persuasive, but in a just behalf
affirmative. The forehead without guile,
liking the shade of quiet downward-gazing.

This, as assembled whole, only just sensed;   10
never yet in sorrow or success
gathered to enduring attainment,
yet such as though from afar with scattered things
something serious, real were being planned.

HERMANN HESSE

Hermann Hesse (1877–1962), German-born novelist and poet, was "not susceptible to nationalistic sentiments." After 1912 he moved to Switzerland and later took out Swiss citizenship. During World War I Hesse suffered public denouncement because he spoke out against the terrible bloodshed and hatred. In his writings, he displays a meditative bent, an interest in psychoanalysis and in Christian as well as Indian mysticism. His novels and poems, always melodic and often ironic, are haunted by his vision of man's spiritual loneliness.

Alone

They stretch across this earth-ball:
roads without number or name,
but all are alike:
their goal is the same.

You can ride, you can travel   5
with a friend of your own;
the final step
you must walk alone.

No wisdom is better
than this, when known: 10
that every hard thing
is done alone.

"Alone" by Hermann Hesse from *Twentieth-Century German Verse*, edited and translated by Herman Salinger. Reprinted by permission of Princeton University Press.

VLADIMIR MAYAKOVSKI

Vladimir Mayakovski (1893–1930) emerged from his youthful experiences as a political prisoner and an advocate of revolution to become literary spokesman of the Soviet Union in the 1920's. As his country had attempted to rid itself of pre-war social and political traditions, so did Mayakovski propose a violent break with established poetic conventions. He became an enthusiastic follower of the school of Futurism, which demanded that poetry be stripped of logical form and content and use startling new words, dialect expressions, and even vulgarities to give expression to such aspects of life as speed, machinery, and revolution.

Mayakovski was preoccupied with two major forces in his poetry—the Revolution and himself. Sometimes he had difficulty in subordinating his vision of his own importance as an individual to the service of his country. But in the last decade of his life, this poet so dedicated himself to the new culture that many of his poems are obviously public utterances—meant to be shouted from platforms or used as propaganda. At the same time, however, he was savagely critical of the growing bureaucracy and corruption in the Communist Party. In 1930, disappointed in love and no longer able to satisfy the changing demands of new Soviet policies, he committed suicide.

The following poem was found in Mayakovski's pocket after he had shot himself. It was part of a larger poem he was working on at the time.

Past One O'clock . . .

Past one o'clock. You must have gone to bed.
The Milky Way streams silver through the night.
I'm in no hurry; with lightning telegrams
I have no cause to wake or trouble you,
And, as they say, the incident is closed.   5
Love's boat has smashed against the daily grind.
Now you and I are quits. Why bother then
to balance mutual sorrows, pains, and hurts.
Behold what quiet settles on the world.
Night wraps the sky in tribute from the stars.   10
In hours like these, one rises to address
The ages, history, and all creation.

BORIS PASTERNAK

Pasternak (1890–1960), a Russian poet and novelist, is highly esteemed in the Western world, in part because he overcame the limitations of Communist ideology to develop personal genius in his own way. He was not opposed to the Revolution, which he saw as an inevitable natural force, but unlike his friend Mayakovski, he never permitted his talent to be exploited for propaganda purposes. Although he approved of the Futurist demand for language reform and from the Imagists learned to create striking metaphors, Pasternak belongs to no school of poetry. His sensitive poems are primarily devoted to love, nature, religious values, and childhood memories. Although he shows the eye of a painter and the ear of a musician in his poetry, Pasternak is primarily a philosopher; his exuberant observations of the concrete world are manifestations of a deeply meditative mind.

Pasternak's novel *Dr. Zhivago,* which was smuggled out of Russia in 1957, displeased Soviet officials because of its obvious weariness with revolution. In 1958 Pasternak was awarded the Nobel prize for this novel, but the violent reaction of his own government caused him to refuse the award.

In Everything I Strive

In everything I strive to reach
The very kernel:
In work and in exploring ways,
In pangs of heart.

Down to the essence of spent days,   5
Their very cause,
Foundations, deepest roots,
The very core.

And grasping at the thread of acts
And destinies,   10
To live, think, feel and love, and make
Discoveries.

O if I only could explain,
Or even partly,
I'd write a couple of quatrains   15
On passion's traits.

On lawlessness and sin,
Pursuits, escapes,
The consequence of chance and haste,
And elbows, palms.   20

Of passion I'd evolve the law
And very principle,
Repeat the first initials of
Its various names.

Like garden soil I'd break up verse.   25
With all their veins
A-quiver, lindens there would blossom,
In Indian file.

To verse I'd bring the breath of roses,
The breath of mint,   30
The scent of sedge, mown hay, and
   meadows,
And peals of thunder.

Thus once upon a time Chopin,
In his *Études,*   34
Of groves and parks, estates and graves,
The wonder introduced.

The play and trial of elation
Thus achieved,
Is like the bowstring, tightly drawn,
Of a stubborn bow.   40

UMBERTO SABA

Because of his devotion to his native city, Saba (1883–1957) is closely associated with Trieste, where he lived most of his life. Some of his most personal poems reflect the tensions of his half-Jewish ancestry, which forced him into hiding in Florence during World War II. Saba rejected the obscure and difficult poetic style that was used by many Italian writers. His lyrics are spontaneous, natural, and conversational. Nevertheless, his artless manner has often resulted in lines rich in subtlety and symbolism.

Ulysses

From days of youth I remember sailing
past the Dalmatian shore; the rugged islets
came forth from the waves. On them, but rarely,
sea birds, intent on prey, would alight; the beaches,
Kelp-encrusted, gave slippery footing. Under   5
the sun they sparkled, bright as emeralds.
The tide rising or the dark blotting them out,
barks bearing leeward gave them wide berth,
fleeing their treachery. And now my kingdom
is that land of No-man. The harbor kindles   10
its light for others. I turn out to sea,
once more impelled by heart untamed and love,
laden with sorrow, of the life of man.

"Ulysses" by Umberto Saba, translated by Thomas G. Bergin from *Italian Sampler: An Anthology of Italian Verse*. Montreal, Mario Casalini Ltd., 1964. Reprinted by permission of Thomas G. Bergin.

SALVATORE QUASIMODO

After the totalitarian blackout of the Mussolini regime, Quasimodo (1901–1968), an Italian poet, expressed directly his passionate and often nonconformist involvement with the life of his times, with the fate of his country and of mankind in the world today. Before this, he had already gained a reputation for more abstract (and often obscure) poetry, and for his excellent translations of ancient Greek lyrics and English drama into Italian. Although his interests underwent a significant change because of the war, his poetry never became political. His style still reflects the careful and spare craftsmanship of a classical mind.

Snow

Evening descends: again you leave us,
o dear images of the earth, trees,
animals, poor people enclosed
in the cloaks of the soldiers, mothers
with insides made barren by tears.   5
And the snow lights us from the meadows
like moonlight. Oh, these dead. Beat
on the forehead, strike deep to the heart.
Let someone at least cry out in silence,
in this white circle of the entombed.   10

"Snow" by Salvatore Quasimodo, translated by William Weaver from *The Promised Land and Other Poems*, edited by Sergio Pacifici, © Sergio Pacifici, 1957. Reprinted by permission of the editor.

FEDERICO GARCÍA LORCA

The tragic murder of Lorca (1898–1936) in the early days of the Spanish Civil War made him a symbol of those soon to be victimized, not only by the years of bitter fighting in Spain, but also by the horrors of the larger war in Europe. Prophetically, Lorca's poems and poetic dramas show violent emotions and a preoccupation with blood and death. His "Lament for Ignacio Sánchez Mejías," written about the death of the famed Spanish bullfighter and hailed as the greatest elegy in modern Spanish poetry, expresses a dread, hypnotic fascination with agony, death, and decay, and Lorca cannot forget the bullfighter's spilt blood.

Lorca's distaste for urban life led him to turn for relief and subject matter to the folklore and music of the rural people and gypsies of Andalusia, his native region. The spontaneous music of his poetry reflects the rhythms of the Andalusian folk songs, which Lorca enjoyed singing in public. A friend of the Spanish Surrealist painter Salvador Dali, Lorca experimented with Surrealistic techniques in his poetry, often freely using a startling juxtaposition of multisensory images.

The Guitar

Now begins the cry
Of the guitar,
Breaking the vaults
Of dawn.
Now begins the cry   5
Of the guitar.
Useless
To still it.
Impossible
To still it.   10
It weeps monotonously
As weeps the water,
As weeps the wind
Over snow.
Impossible   15
To still it.
It weeps
For distant things,
Warm southern sands
Desiring white camelias.   20
It mourns the arrow without a target,
The evening without morning.
And the first bird dead
Upon a branch.
O guitar!   25
A wounded heart,
Wounded by five swords.

"The Guitar" by Lorca, translated by Elizabeth du Gué Trapier from *Translations from Hispanic Poets*, 1938, Hispanic Society of America, New York. Reprinted by permission of the publisher.

JUAN RAMÓN JIMÉNEZ

From Andalusia, in southern Spain, Jiménez (1881–1958) was not involved in politics, but the Spanish Civil War forced him into self-imposed exile from which he never returned. His early work, characterized by a colorful and delicate lyricism, romanticizes his native region. Later he abandoned conventional form and sentimentality and sought expression in concentrated images and condensed language that often reveal pessimism. His most famous work, *Platero and I,* a prose-poem about a donkey of Andalusia, has been called "one of the two or three books capable of giving back to people their childhood soul."

Vigil

Night departs, a black bull—
full flesh of mourning, terror, mystery—
roaring with vast horror
at the sweating dread of all the slain;
and day comes in, a young child   5
begging trust, love, laughter,
a child in the remote
arcana
where ends and beginnings meet,
playing a moment   10
on some kind of field
of light and shadow
with the fleeing bull.

CONSTANTINE P. CAVAFY

The great poet of Alexandria, Egypt, Konstantinos Kabaphēs (1863–1933), better known as Cavafy in the non-Greek world, used a combination of the pure literary Greek language and the idiomatic speech of the common people. The settings of his unique poems are rarely contemporary. One of his favorite historical periods is the time when the ancient Greek kingdoms were set up as satellites of Rome; the other is the era when the Christian Emperor Constantine ruled the Empire. In his vignettes and anecdotes of these times, his tone is usually ironic, never sentimental. Even his personal lyrics are marked by an objective viewpoint and a straightforward style: Cavafy never uses imagery or any ornamentation of language.

Waiting for the Barbarians

What are we waiting for, gathered in the marketplace?

    The barbarians are to arrive today.

Why so little activity in the Senate?
Why do the Senators sit there without legislating?

    Because the barbarians will arrive today.   5
    Why should the Senators bother with laws now?
    The barbarians, when they come, will do the lawmaking.

Why has our emperor risen so early,
and why does he sit at the largest gate of the city
on the throne, in state, wearing the crown?   10

    Because the barbarians will arrive today.
    And the emperor is waiting to receive
    their leader. He has even prepared
    a parchment for him. There
    he has given him many titles and names.   15

Why did our two consuls and our praetors go out
today in the scarlet, the embroidered togas?
Why did they wear bracelets with so many amethysts,
and rings with brilliant sparkling emeralds?
Why today do they carry precious staves   20
splendidly inlaid with silver and gold?

"Waiting for the Barbarians" from *The Poems of C. P. Cavafy*, translated by John Mavrogodato. Reprinted by permission of the Author's Literary Estate and The Hogarth Press Ltd.

Because the barbarians will arrive today;
and such things dazzle barbarians.

And why don't the worthy orators come as always
to make their speeches, say what they have to say?   25

Because the barbarians will arrive today;
and they are bored by eloquence and public speaking.

What does this sudden uneasiness mean,
and this confusion? (How grave the faces have become!)
Why are the streets and squares rapidly emptying,   30
and why is everyone going back home so lost in thought?

Because it is night and the barbarians have not come.
And some men have arrived from the frontiers
and they say that there are no barbarians any longer.

And now, what will become of us without barbarians?   35
Those people were a kind of solution.

GEORGE SEFERIS

The writings of Greek poet and statesman Geōrgios Sepheriadēs (1900–   ), whose penname is George Seferis, show an engagement with contemporary politics, a responsiveness to the ancient Greek past, and an awareness of the long tradition to which his work belongs. In awarding him the Nobel prize for literature in 1963, the Swedish Academy spoke of his poetry as symbolizing "all that is indestructible in the Hellenic acceptance of life." His poems are written in free verse that is precise and rhythmic; his attitude toward his subject matter is usually restrained, understated, and ironic. His most frequent themes reflect the loneliness of contemporary man in exile from a more glorious past, and the decay of modern life as he sees it.

The Return of the Exile

"Old friend, what are you looking for?
After those many years abroad you come
With images you tended
Under foreign skies
Far away from your own land."   5

"I look for my old garden;
The trees come only to my waist,
The hills seem low as terraces;
Yet when I was a child
I played there on the grass   10
Underneath great shadows
And used to run across the slopes
For hours and hours, breathless."

"My old friend, rest a little.
You will soon get used to it.   15
Together we will climb
The hill paths that you know;
Together we will sit and rest
Underneath the plane trees' dome;
Little by little they'll come back to you,   20
Your garden and your slopes."

"I look for my old house,
The house with the tall windows
Darkened by the ivy,
And for that ancient column   25
The landmark of the sailor."

"The Return of the Exile" from *Poems* by George Seferis, translated by Rex Warner, English translation © Rex Warner, 1960. Reprinted by permission of Atlantic-Little, Brown and Company and the Bodley Head.

How can I get into this hutch?
The roof's below my shoulders
And however far I look
I see men on their knees;   30
You'd say that they were praying."

"My old friend, can't you hear me?
You will soon get used to it.
Here is your house in front of you,
And at this door will soon come knocking   35
Your friends and your relations
To give you a fine welcome."

"Why is your voice so far away?
Raise your head a little higher
That I may grasp the words you say,   40
For as you speak you seem to grow
Shorter still and shorter
As though you were sinking down into the ground."

"My old friend, just think a little.
You will soon get used to it;   45
Your homesickness has built for you
A nonexistent land with laws
Outside the earth and man."

"Now I hear nothing—not a sound.
My last friend too has sunk and gone.   50
How strange it is, this leveling
All around from time to time:
They pass and mow here
Thousands of scythe-bearing chariots."

LÉOPOLD SÉDAR–SENGHOR

In 1960, Léopold Senghor—university professor, statesman, and the most famous lyricist of French-speaking Africa—was elected first President of his country, Senegal. Senghor was born in Senegal in 1906, attended the Sorbonne in Paris, taught in Paris, and served for twelve years as the Senegal deputy to the French National Assembly. As a poet, Senghor has been a leading exponent of *la négritude,* a word coined by black writers living outside Africa to describe their protest against the colonization of Africa and their positive assertion of the values of black African culture. Expression of immediate personal experience has not been of primary importance to the *négritude* poets; they write to promote black Africa itself, to express those traits which they hope will be unifying, self-identifying forces for all black men, not Africans alone. In his famous accolade to Senghor's anthology of French-African poetry, Jean Paul Sartre writes that the *négritude* poets remind him of Orpheus stirring to reclaim Eurydice from the underworld.

We Delighted, My Friend

We delighted, my friend, in an African presence:
Furniture from Guinea and the Congo,
Heavy and polished, dark and light.
Primitive and pure masks on distant walls yet so near.
Taborets of honor for the hereditary hosts,   5
The princes from the high country.
Wild and proud perfumes from the thick tresses of silence,
Cushions of shadow and leisure like quiet wells running.
Eternal words and the distant alternating chant
As in the loin cloth from the Sudan.   10
But then the friendly light of your blue kindness
Will soften the obsession of this presence in
Black, white, and red, O red like the soil of Africa.

JAMES D. RUBADIRI

Rubadiri, a teacher and poet, was born in 1930 in the beautiful country of Nyasaland, which lies like a teardrop among the larger countries of Zambia, Tanzania, and Mozambique in central Africa. In 1964, when it achieved independence from Britain, Nyasaland was renamed Malawi, a name which commemorates an old African empire of the region. In the following poem, Rubadiri, who had agitated for independence, describes the arduous journey begun in October 1874 by British explorer-journalist Henry Morton Stanley. Starting from the east African coast, Stanley worked his way inland to the court of the great black king Mutesa, in Buganda in central Africa. Rubadiri's visualization of this historic event is based deliberately on T. S. Eliot's visualization of the journey of the Magi (see Eliot's poem on page 907). Stanley's visit to Mutesa's court proved to be the first step in bringing the region of the Nile's sources under the "protection" of Britain. By the end of his monumental three-year expedition, Stanley and a handful of surviving African carriers had reached Africa's west coast. One result of Stanley's expedition was the partition of vast, rich regions of Africa among the states of Europe.

Stanley Meets Mutesa

Such a time of it they had;
The heat of the day
The chill of the night
And the mosquitoes that followed.
Such was the time and   5
They bound for a kingdom.

The thin weary line of carriers
With tattered dirty rags to cover their backs;
The battered bulky chests
That kept on falling off their shaven heads.   10
Their tempers high and hot
The sun fierce and scorching
With it rose their spirits
With its fall their hopes
As each day sweated their bodies dry and   15
Flies clung in clumps on their sweat scented backs.
Such was the march
And the hot season just breaking.

"Stanley Meets Mutesa" by James D. Rubadiri from *Darkness and Light: An Anthology of African Writing,* edited by Peggy Rutherford. Reprinted by permission of The Faith Press Limited, London, and Drum Publications, Africa.

Each day a weary pony dropped,
Left for the vultures on the plains;   20
Each afternoon a human skeleton collapsed,
Left for the Masai on the plains;
But the march trudged on
Its khaki leader in front
He the spirit that inspired.   25
He the light of hope.

Then came the afternoon of a hungry march,
A hot and hungry march it was;
The Nile and the Nyanza
Lay like two twins   30
Azure across the green countryside.
The march leapt on chanting
Like young gazelles to a water hole.
Hearts beat faster
Loads felt lighter   35
As the cool water lapt their sore feet.
No more the dread of hungry hyenas
But only tales of valor when
At Mutesa's court fires are lit.
No more the burning heat of the day   40
But song, laughter, and dance.

The village looks on behind banana groves,
Children peer behind reed fences.
Such was the welcome
No singing women to chant a welcome   45
Or drums to greet the white ambassador;
Only a few silent nods from aged faces
And one rumbling drum roll
To summon Mutesa's court to parley
For the country was not sure.   50

The gate of reeds is flung open,
There is silence
But only a moment's silence—
A silence of assessment.
The tall black king steps forward,   55
He towers over the thin bearded white man,
Then grabbing his lean white hand
Manages to whisper
"Mtu mweupe karibu"
White man you are welcome.   60
The gate of polished reed closes behind them
And the West is let in.

WOLE SOYINKA

This Nigerian poet and playwright, one of Africa's outstanding writers, has had plays produced off-Broadway in New York and has won many international literary awards. Some African critics feel that Soyinka is able to describe more fully than the *négritude* poets the nuances of the human situation in Africa. Soyinka, who was born in Nigeria in 1935, taught drama at Ibadan University in eastern Nigeria until 1967. In August of that year, he made a visit to the rebel Biafran leader in an attempt to end the civil war. As a result, he was seized by the federal Nigerians and placed in solitary confinement, without trial, in a northern Nigerian prison. In a letter smuggled out of prison, dated December 20, 1967, Soyinka wrote: "Since I am not an idealist only in theory, I did all I could to bring the war to a rapid halt." In a later letter, he remarked wryly, "Beyond a certain limit, evil passes beyond human capacity. Surely!?"

Civilian and Soldier

My apparition rose from the fall of lead,
Declared, "I'm a civilian." It only served
To aggravate your fright. For how could I
Have risen, a being of this world, in that hour
Of impartial death! And I thought also: nor is   5
Your quarrel of this world.
                              You stood still
For both eternities, and oh I heard the lesson
Of your training sessions, cautioning—
Scorch earth behind you, do not leave
A dubious neutral to the rear. Reiteration   10
Of my civilian quandary, burrowing earth
From the lead festival of your more eager friends
Worked the worse on your confusion, and when
You brought the gun to bear on me, and death
Twitched me gently in the eye, your plight   15
And all of you came clear to me.
                              I hope some day
Intent upon my trade of living, to be checked
In stride by *your* apparition in a trench,
Signalling, I am a soldier. No hesitation then
But I shall shoot you clean and fair   20
With meat and bread, a gourd of wine
A bunch of breasts from either arm, and that
Lone question—do you, friend, even now, know
What it is all about?

"Civilian and Soldier" and "Dedication" from *Idanre and Other Poems* by Wole Soyinka, © Wole Soyinka 1967. Reprinted by permission of Hill and Wang, Inc. and Methuen & Co. Ltd., London.

Dedication

for Moremi, 1963

Earth will not share the rafter's envy; dung floors
Break, not the gecko's slight skin, but its fall
Taste this soil for death and plumb her deep for life

As this yam, wholly earthed, yet a living tuber
To the warmth of waters, earthed as springs   5
As roots of baobab, as the hearth.

The air will not deny you. Like a top
Spin you on the navel of the storm, for the hoe
That roots the forests plows a path for squirrels.

Be ageless as dark peat, but only that rain's   10
Fingers, not the feet of men, may wash you over.
Long wear the sun's shadow; run naked to the night.

Peppers green and red—child—your tongue arch
To scorpion tail, spit straight return to danger's threats
Yet coo with the brown pigeon, tendril dew between your lips.   15

Shield you like the flesh of palms, skyward held
Cuspids in thorn nesting, insealed as the heart of kernel—
A woman's flesh is oil—child, palm oil on your tongue

Is suppleness to life, and wine of this gourd
From self-same timeless run of runnels as refill   20
Your podlings, child, weaned from yours we embrace

Earth's honeyed milk, wine of the only rib.
Now roll your tongue in honey till your cheeks are
Swarming honeycombs—your world needs sweetening, child.

Camwood round the heart, chalk for flight   25
Of blemish—see? it dawns!—antimony beneath
Armpits like a goddess, and leave this taste

Long on your lips, of salt, that you may seek
None from tears. This, rain-water, is the gift
Of gods—drink of its purity, bear fruits in season.   30

Fruits then to your lips: haste to repay
The debt of birth. Yield man-tides like the sea
And ebbing, leave a meaning of the fossilled sands.

ASIDES

1. What is the use of the dramatic device known as "asides" in a play? Is this dialogue between two different people or does it express internal conflict? Explain.

2. From the kind of questions asked, describe the attitude of the questioner toward life. Is he interested in the values of the active life or of the philosophical spirit? Explain. What would you say is the pervasive mood of the entire poem?

3. Are the answers given in concrete or abstract terms? What attitude do the replies express?

4. What is suggested by the word *presentiment?* Are the last two words in the first stanza contradictory or paradoxical? Explain.

5. What kind of person experiences knowing as boredom and doing as dreaming? What is the implication of using the mind to turn morning into night?

6. Is the spirit which wants its own good necessarily self-centered? Explain. Why does the introspective man fear the will?

7. Why is the last verse shocking when it expresses, except for the last two words, an idea we all accept?

8. Are any of the questions answered to your satisfaction? Why or why not?

CAESAR

1. Do you think Caesar in this poem represents a specific man or a generic term? Explain. What contradictory words describe Caesar in the first stanza? How can they be applicable to one person? What does the phrase "pregnant with eagles" imply?

2. What is the reaction of the natural world to the thoughts of Caesar?

3. If *rive* means "to tear apart or rend," what impression of Caesar at this moment do lines 7–8 convey?

4. As the scene enlarges in the third stanza, does the Empire seem to play an active or passive part in the moment of decision? Explain. How can an evening be changed into a "furious dawn"?

5. What is the contrast between the figure of Caesar and that of the fisherman? In what respect is the fisherman "cradled in hazard," instead of rocking in a boat? What do the words *drifting* and *singing* suggest about the desires of ordinary man? What will be the effect of Caesar's decision on common humanity as represented by the fisherman?

TO PAINT THE PORTRAIT OF A BIRD

1. Why does the speaker say "paint first a cage" and not the bird? What might the cage suggest as the beginning of some process of expression?

2. The speaker says to choose "something pretty / something simple" etc., to paint "for the bird." What might these generalities represent?

3. What should your attitude be as you await the arrival of the bird? How does the speaker describe the possible encounter with the bird? What should you do then? What do you think this means?

4. What does the action of plucking one of the bird's feathers mean?

5. What does the poem imply about the relationship between art and life? between the artist and his subject?

6. What is the tone of the speaker in the poem?

THE MERRY-GO-ROUND

1. What kind of motion is expressed in this poem? What tempo? Before answering, identify the different figures who flash by but once. What do these riders represent? What different reactions do they reflect? What is their attitude toward the situation?

2. What does the big elephant represent? Why is the line about the elephant repeated?

3. Do such phrases as "lingers before it perishes," "whirling futilely," "scarce-begun profile," and "blind and breathless game" tell you anything about what the merry-go-round might symbolize? Explain.

4. The poet has captured a picture of movement in a moment of time. What does this show about the role of the reader in modern poetry?

SELF-PORTRAIT

1. Suggest a synonym to describe the appearance of the eyebrows, as described in the first two lines of Lowell's adaptation. What do "noble and narrow" suggest in this context? Is there a hint given here regarding who the hero of modern life might be? Explain. In Lowell's adaptation, what does the speaker say about his forehead, eyes, mouth? Why does he emphasize the eyes and lips? What do these features tell us of the speaker's

nature? What contradictory qualities are apparent? What limitations of personality are implied in the description of the forehead?

2. How does the presentation of the subject in the first nine lines of Lowell's adaptation differ from that in the last five? Do the details of the portrait suggest a universal man's portrait, not a self-portrait at all? Is the portrait (line 10) real? Is it complete? Explain your answer. What is the speaker suggesting he must do in order to achieve a whole personality? How does the speaker suggest the idea of present man and man of the past? Out of the rational and irrational elements of man, what hope does the speaker hold?

3. Compare the almost literal translation done by Norton with Lowell's freer adaptation. Remember, as you read, that the literal translation is not meant to be fluent English poetry; it is merely a guide to the German of the original. Lowell has taken many liberties with Rilke's poem. How has he changed wording and imagery? Has he kept the effect? Has Lowell made Rilke's poem better, worse, or merely different? Explain your answer by citing specific lines.

4. Here is the second part of the poem in German. Listen to it read aloud. Is it rhymed? What is its tempo? How do the two translations compare with the original German in musical quality?

● Das, als Zusammenhang, erst nur geahnt;
noch nie im Leiden oder im Gelingen
zusammgefasst zu dauerndem Durchdringen,
doch so, als wäre mit zerstreuten Dingen
von fern ein Ernstes, Wirkliches geplant.
— RAINER MARIA RILKE

ALONE

1. What are the two attitudes that the poet presents about life in stanzas one and two?

2. What is the poet saying about the nature of man in lines 5–6?

3. By what poetic device does the poet emphasize his most significant concept?

4. What "hard" things besides death must man accomplish alone?

PAST ONE O'CLOCK

1. What mood does the first line set? Do you think the speaker is pitying himself? Quote lines to support your answer. What, is he suggesting, can dispel the enchantment of love?

2. What is the relation of time to the subject of the poem? What does the poet suggest about the universality of his experience?

3. What contrasting images are presented in the poem? What is their effect?

IN EVERYTHING I STRIVE

1. Essentially, what is the speaker striving for? How would you interpret the word *kernel* in line 2? How much of the remainder of the poem is the speaker's explanation of the various aspects of "kernel"? Is the poem limited to a consideration of artistic expression or can it be deepened to include man's whole experience? Explain. In each verse of lines 5–24, what different elements is the speaker seeking?

2. If the speaker finds the answer to his striving, how will his poetry be affected? What two things must be fused if poetry is to be life itself, rather than a mirror of life?

3. What two processes are involved in the "play and trial of elation" (line 37)? What is the significance of the tension implied in the final image?

ULYSSES

1. How do the memories expressed in the first nine lines describe a youthful attitude toward life and nature?

2. Recall the story of Ulysses and the Cyclops and explain the double meaning that the word "No-man" (line 10) suggests.

3. Why does the harbor kindle its light for others and not for the speaker? Explain the significance of the phrase "heart untamed." Paraphrase the last sentence in the poem.

4. What images and phrases in the poem would seem especially significant to apply to Ulysses? What or who does the figure of Ulysses represent here?

SNOW

1. What tone and mood does the poem convey? Point out the images that contribute most strongly to this tone and mood.

2. What grief, other than that caused by death, is suggested in the first five lines? What kinds of death may be implied, besides physical?

3. Using an imperative tone in the last two lines, what does the poet suggest may be the only answer to this grief he has evoked?

THE GUITAR

1. How does the translator convey the tone and tempo of the guitar music and what mood does the poem create? For what specific things does the guitar weep? What might these specific things represent?

2. How would you explain the image used in line 21? What is suggested by the images in lines 22–24?

3. Explain how the details of the image in lines 26–27 are appropriate to describe this guitar. Why is its "heart" described as "wounded"?

VIGIL

1. What may the bull represent, besides night? What attitude toward his subject does the poet reveal in using the image of a bull here? How does his attitude compare or contrast with Quasimodo's in "Snow"?

2. Describe the manner in which night departs. Do these images appeal most strongly to the mind or to the senses? Explain. How is alliteration used to reinforce the impact of the words in the first four lines?

3. What may the child represent, besides day? Is the figure of the child described visually or conceptually? Explain.

4. *Arcana* means "secret or mysterious knowledge, known only to certain initiates." The word is in the plural form here. Why is this word placed alone on a line?

5. Substitute for the phrase "some kind" (line 11) a more specific description of the nature of the "field."

6. What is the bull fleeing from? What does the title signify?

WAITING FOR THE BARBARIANS

1. What picture is conveyed by the question-answer pattern established in the first two lines? What tone is established for the poem? How is this tone sustained through the successive pattern of questions and answers?

2. What do we find out about the barbarians through hearing the reactions of those waiting for them? What does the dialogue tell us about the state of mind of those who are waiting? How do they plan to receive the barbarians? What do the barbarians represent to these people?

3. Why are the people disillusioned when the barbarians do not come? For what problem were the barbarians "a kind of solution"?

4. Do you think the last line works? By making a direct, although abstract statement about the poem's theme, does the last line, in your opinion, destroy the mood of the poem, or does it add a new element to the poem? Explain your answers.

THE RETURN OF THE EXILE

1. Who are the characters in this poetic dialogue and how do their points of view differ?

2. In the second and fourth stanzas, what views, common to most people returning home after long absence, are expressed by the exile?

3. What is happening to the exile in stanzas 6 and 8?

4. Why does the friend repeat the phrase "you will soon get used to it"? Tell if this refrain is meant to be cynical or reassuring. How does the friend explain what has happened to the exile?

5. Why does the reality of his remembered homeland become less and less vivid to the exile? Why has this reality existed solely for him? Would it ever be possible for the exile to find his homeland as he expected it to be upon his return?

6. In the last verse, is the exile making some kind of statement about illusion and reality? Explain the significance of the "scythe-bearing chariots" image.

7. The figure of Odysseus, often evoked by just an image, prevails in Seferis's poetry as a symbol of the wandering exile of all ages. What images reminiscent of the ancient Greek voyager do you find in this poem?

WE DELIGHTED, MY FRIEND

1. For the *négritude* poets, Africa is a Paradise lost, and in themselves they try to discover traits or attitudes derived from long-forgotten African culture. Does this theme find reflection in Senghor's poem? Explain.

2. How are images of house furnishings used in this poem? Explain the metaphor in lines 7–8. List the contrasting words and images and tell what effect is conveyed by this recurrent use of opposites.

3. What tone or feeling has the translator created by her choice of words?

STANLEY MEETS MUTESA

1. Reread Eliot's "Journey of the Magi" (page 907) and comment on the significance of the distinctions between his use of cold and Rubadiri's use of heat.

2. What are the moods of the travelers in Eliot's and in Rubadiri's poems, as they approach their destinations? Like the journey described by Eliot, does Rubadiri's journey also result in a birth and a death?

3. Why must each poem reflect a different point of view? Does point of view alter the emotional impact of each poem?

4. Discuss the ironies in Rubadiri's poem, particularly in lines 25–26 and 60. What larger irony may be implied in considering the changes brought about by each journey?

CIVILIAN AND SOLDIER

1. Who is the speaker? What is his conflict with the soldier? How will he treat the soldier when their positions are reversed? What does the speaker's "lone question" refer to?

2. Compare Soyinka's poem with Hardy's "The Man He Killed" (page 901) and with Rimbaud's "The Sleeper of the Valley" (page 765), in regard to the attitudes expressed toward the ways man behaves in his wars.

3. Discuss the effectiveness of the phrases "fall of lead," "impartial death," "dubious neutral," "lead festival," and "trade of living."

DEDICATION

1. It has been said that the traditional African religious scheme can be interpreted in terms of "dynamism," or of power. Traditionally, the supreme value to an African has been to live a vital, forceful life and to assure its continuity in his descendants. Is this life view revealed in "Dedication"? Explain. With what elemental forces does the speaker wish the child to identify?

2. What is the speaker's attitude toward life and death?

3. What images does Soyinka use as metaphors for various aspects of the human condition? How do they compare with the images in Dylan Thomas's poem (page 908)? Compare the tone, cadence, and imagery of Soyinka's poem with those of Psalm 104 (page 32).

The Modern Short Story

Literature and poetry used to be virtually synonymous, but for the past century and more, prose has been encroaching upon the province of poetry. Undoubtedly many factors have brought about this shift in literary taste, but a decline in the quality of poetry is certainly not one of them. There is as much good poetry written today as at any time in the past, and nearly every serious writer in any genre has trained himself in part by writing poetry. Nevertheless, poetry has lost out to prose in popularity with the widest reading public, and some of the most significant and influential literary statements in this century have been made in the forms of fiction.

The short story form took on particular prominence earlier in this century, especially through the great proliferation of wide-circulation magazines. Perhaps this was a symptom of the times: not only had people become dubious of broad, comprehensive views of life, but they had also become impatient of sustained reading over long periods of time. Be that as it may, the short story came to be a medium for the kind of careful and inventive craftsmanship that Renaissance writers devoted to lyric poetry. And modern writers found many ways, more or less radical, of changing the traditional method of telling a story. No longer did events have to be witnessed from the outside and then related in chronological sequence. Katherine Mansfield (1888–1923) and James Joyce (1882–1941), for example, take the reader inside a character's consciousness, in order to describe the world from a unique point of view and to explore the psychology of a character as he copes with that world (see their stories on pages 958 and 972). Using another narrative method, Albert Camus (1913–1960) attempts to expose the inmost reality of a character by detailing his most commonplace actions (see page 998). Even plot, which had been thought of as the element that makes a story a story, was shown to be dispensable. Though Thomas Mann (1875–1955), in "The Infant Prodigy" (see page 962), creates significant activity in describing the interior reactions of people to a concert, this activity remains motionless, since nothing of any importance happens outwardly.

In modern short stories we also find reflected the significant concerns of the time. The importance that modern psychology, since the time of Freud, has attached to the subconscious is reflected by the inward focus of the Joyce and Mansfield stories. The idea of "absurdity" as a way of looking at modern life—an idea loosely identified with existentialism—is distinguished in the stories of Eugène Ionesco (1912–   ) (see page 1015) and of Camus: the characters in "Rhinoceros" and "The Guest" must make fundamental choices about their own lives and their own identities, in a world that offers no absolute principles to guide them, no clear models to serve as precedents, and no certain rewards or punishments to motivate them.

Amy Foster

JOSEPH CONRAD

It was Conrad's remarkable achievement not only to become a writer in a language other than his own but to win wide acclaim as a subtle and versatile stylist. Born in Russian Poland, Jósef Teodor Konrad Korzeniowski (1857–1924) was the son of a Polish poet and nationalist who was sent into exile in Russia for revolutionary activities. After the death of his parents, young Jósef was brought up by an uncle, who sent him off with a tutor on a tour of Europe when he was fifteen. But a year later, Conrad abandoned his studies and went to sea with the French merchant marine. French thus became Conrad's second language; but when much later he turned to writing, he wrote in his third language, English, which he had begun to learn while studying in England to be a ship's master. For sixteen years, Conrad was an officer on various English ships, mostly in trade with the Orient, and this long experience with the sea provided subject matter when he started writing in 1889. He spent most of the rest of his life in England, painstakingly writing his novels, novellas, and short stories. Among his best-known novels are *Lord Jim, Heart of Darkness,* and *Victory.* "Amy Foster" was one of a group of stories that appeared in 1903.

Conrad stands at the opening of the twentieth century and is one of the first of the modern voices. He is a psychological writer to the extent that he probes into human hopes and illusions and shows how man can be wrecked or helped by them. Not overly optimistic, Conrad almost always warns us that if our dreams do not reach out to include others we lose our humanity.

KENNEDY IS A country doctor, and lives in Colebrook, on the shores of Eastbay. The high ground rising abruptly behind the red roofs of the little town crowds the quaint High Street against the wall which defends it from the sea. Beyond the sea wall there curves for miles in a vast and regular sweep the barren beach of shingle, with the village of Brenzett standing out darkly across the water, a spire in a clump of trees; and still farther out the perpendicular column of a lighthouse, looking in the distance no bigger than a lead pencil, marks the vanishing point of the land. The country at the back of Brenzett is low and flat; but the bay is fairly well sheltered from the seas, and occasionally a big ship, windbound or through stress of weather, makes use of the anchoring ground a mile and a half due north from you as you stand at the back door of the Ship Inn in Brenzett. A dilapidated windmill nearby, lifting its shattered arms from a mount no loftier than a rubbish heap, and a Martello tower squatting at the water's edge half a mile to the south of the Coastguard cottages are familiar to the skippers of small craft. These are the official seamarks for the patch of trustworthy bottom represented on the Admiralty charts by an irregular oval of dots enclosing several figure sixes, with a tiny anchor engraved among them, and the legend "mud and shells" over all.

The brow of the upland overtops the square tower of the Colebrook Church. The slope is green and looped by a white road. Ascending along this road, you open a valley broad and shallow, a wide green trough of pastures and hedges merging inland into a vista of purple tints and flowing lines closing the view.

In this valley down to Brenzett and Colebrook and up to Darnford, the market town fourteen miles away, lies the practice of my friend Kennedy. He had begun life as surgeon in the Navy, and afterward had been the companion of a famous traveler, in the days when there were continents with unexplored interiors. His papers on the fauna and flora made him known to scientific societies. And now he had come to a country practice—from choice. The penetrating power of his mind, acting like a corrosive fluid, had destroyed his ambition, I fancy. His intelligence is of a scientific order, of an investigating habit, and of that unappeasable curiosity which believes that there is a particle of a general truth in every mystery.

A good many years ago now, on my return from abroad, he invited me to stay with him. I came readily enough, and as he could not neglect his patients to keep me company, he took me on his rounds—thirty miles or so of an afternoon, sometimes. I waited for him on the roads; the horse reached after the leafy twigs, and, sitting high in the dogcart, I could hear Kennedy's laugh through the half-open door of some cottage. He had a big, hearty laugh that would have fitted a man twice his size, a brisk manner, a bronzed face, and a pair of gray, profoundly attentive eyes. He had the talent of making people talk to him freely, and an inexhaustible patience in listening to their tales.

One day, as we trotted out of a large village into a shady bit of road, I saw on our left hand a low, black cottage, with diamond panes in the windows, a creeper on the end wall, a roof of shingle, and some roses climbing on the rickety trellis-work of the tiny porch. Kennedy pulled up to a walk. A woman, in full sunlight, was throwing a dripping blanket over a line stretched between two old apple trees. And as the bobtailed, long-necked chestnut, trying to get his head, jerked the left hand, covered by a thick dogskin glove, the doctor raised his voice over the hedge: "How's your child, Amy?"

I had time to see her dull face, red, not with a mantling blush, but as if her flat cheeks had been vigorously slapped, and to take in the squat figure, the scanty, dusty brown hair drawn into a tight knot at the back of the head. She looked quite young. With a distinct catch in her breath, her voice sounded low and timid.

"He's well, thank you."

We trotted again. "A young patient of yours," I said; and the doctor, flicking the chestnut absently, muttered, "Her husband used to be."

"She seems a dull creature," I remarked, listlessly.

"Precisely," said Kennedy. "She is very passive. It's enough to look at the red hands hanging at the end of those short arms, at those slow, prominent brown eyes, to know the inertness of her mind—an inertness that one would think made it everlastingly safe from all the surprises of imagination. And yet which of us is safe? At any rate, such as you see her, she had enough imagination to fall in love. She's the daughter of one Isaac Foster, who from a small farmer has sunk into a shepherd; the beginning of his misfortunes dating from his runaway marriage with the cook of his widowed father—a well-to-do, apoplectic grazier, who passionately struck his name off his will, and had been heard to utter threats against his life. But this old affair, scandalous enough to serve as a motive for a Greek tragedy, arose from the similarity of their characters. There are other tragedies, less scandalous and of a subtler poignancy, arising from irreconcilable differences and from that fear of the Incomprehensible that hangs over all our heads—over all our heads. . . ."

The tired chestnut dropped into a walk; and the rim of the sun, all red in a speckless sky, touched familiarly the smooth top of a plowed rise near the road as I had seen it times innumerable touch the distant horizon of the sea. The uniform brownness of the harrowed field glowed with a rose tinge, as though the powdered clods had sweated out in minute pearls of blood the toil of uncounted plowmen. From the edge of a copse a wagon with two horses was rolling gently along the ridge. Raised above our heads upon the skyline, it loomed up against the red sun, triumphantly big, enormous, like a chariot of giants drawn by two slow-stepping steeds of legendary proportions. And the clumsy figure of the man plodding at the head of the leading horse projected itself on the background of the Infinite with a heroic uncouthness. The end of his carter's whip quivered high up in the blue. Kennedy discoursed.

"She's the eldest of a large family. At the age of fifteen they put her out to service at the New Barns Farm. I attended Mrs. Smith, the tenant's wife, and saw that girl there for the first time. Mrs. Smith, a genteel person with a sharp nose, made her put on a black dress every afternoon. I don't know what induced me to notice her at all. There are faces that call your attention by a curious want of definiteness in their whole aspect, as, walking in a mist, you peer attentively at a vague shape which, after all, may be nothing more curious or strange than a signpost. The only peculiarity I perceived in her was a slight hesitation in her utterance, a sort of preliminary stammer which passes away with the first word. When sharply spoken to, she was apt to lose her head at once; but her heart was of the kindest. She had never been heard to express a dislike for a single human being, and she was tender to every living creature. She was devoted to Mrs. Smith, to

Mr. Smith, to their dogs, cats, canaries; and as to Mrs. Smith's gray parrot, its peculiarities exercised upon her a positive fascination. Nevertheless, when that outlandish bird, attacked by the cat, shrieked for help in human accents, she ran out into the yard stopping her ears, and did not prevent the crime. For Mrs. Smith this was another evidence of her stupidity; on the other hand, her want of charm, in view of Smith's well-known frivolousness, was a great recommendation. Her shortsighted eyes would swim with pity for a poor mouse in a trap, and she had been seen once by some boys on her knees in the wet grass helping a toad in difficulties. If it's true, as some German fellow has said, that without phosphorus there is no thought, it is still more true that there is no kindness of heart without a certain amount of imagination. She had some. She had even more than is necessary to understand suffering and to be moved by pity. She fell in love under circumstances that leave no room for doubt in the matter; for you need imagination to form a notion of beauty at all, and still more to discover your ideal in an unfamiliar shape.

"How this aptitude came to her, what it did feed upon, is an inscrutable mystery. She was born in the village, and had never been farther away from it than Colebrook or perhaps Darnford. She lived for four years with the Smiths. New Barns is an isolated farmhouse a mile away from the road, and she was content to look day after day at the same fields, hollows, rises; at the trees and the hedgerows; at the faces of the four men about the farm, always the same—day after day, month after month, year after year. She never showed a desire for conversation, and, as it seemed to me, she did not know how to smile. Sometimes of a fine Sunday afternoon she would put on her best dress, a pair of stout boots, a large gray hat trimmed with a black feather (I've seen her in that finery), seize an absurdly slender parasol, climb over two stiles, tramp over three fields and along two hundred yards of road—never farther. There stood Foster's cottage. She would help her mother to give their tea to the younger children, wash up the crockery, kiss the little ones, and go back to the farm. That was all. All the rest, all the change, all the relaxation. She never seemed to wish for anything more. And then she fell in love. She fell in love silently, obstinately —perhaps helplessly. It came slowly, but when it came it worked like a powerful spell; it was love as the ancients understood it: an irresistible and fateful impulse—a possession! Yes, it was in her to become haunted and possessed by a face, by a presence, fatally, as though she had been a pagan worshiper of form under a joyous sky—and to be awakened at last from that mysterious forgetfulness of self, from that enchantment, from that transport, by a fear resembling the unaccountable terror of a brute. . . ."

With the sun hanging low on its western limit, the expanse of the grasslands framed in the counterscarps of the rising ground took on a gorgeous and somber aspect. A sense of penetrating sadness, like that inspired by a grave strain of music, disengaged itself from the silence of the fields. The men we met walked past, slow, unsmiling, with downcast eyes, as if the melancholy of an overburdened earth had weighted their feet, bowed their shoulders, borne down their glances.

"Yes," said the doctor to my remark, "one would think the earth is under a curse, since of all her children these that cling to her the closest are uncouth in body and as leaden of gait as if their very hearts were loaded with chains. But here on this same road you might have seen among these heavy men a being lithe, supple and long-limbed, straight like a pine, with something striving upward in his appearance as though the heart within him had been buoyant. Perhaps it was only the force of the contrast, but when he was passing one of these villagers here, the soles of his feet did not seem to me to touch the dust of the road. He vaulted over the stiles, paced these slopes with

a long elastic stride that made him noticeable at a great distance, and had lustrous black eyes. He was so different from the mankind around that, with his freedom of movement, his soft—a little startled— glance, his olive complexion and graceful bearing, his humanity suggested to me the nature of a woodland creature. He came from there."

The doctor pointed with his whip, and from the summit of the descent seen over the rolling tops of the trees in a park by the side of the road, appeared the level sea far below us, like the floor of an immense edifice inlaid with bands of dark ripple, with still trails of glitter, ending in a belt of glassy water at the foot of the sky. The light blur of smoke, from an invisible steamer, faded on the great clearness of the horizon like the mist of a breath on a mirror; and, inshore, the white sails of a coaster, with the appearance of disentangling themselves slowly from under the branches, floated clear of the foliage of the trees.

"Shipwrecked in the bay?" I said.

"Yes; he was a castaway. A poor emigrant from Central Europe bound to America and washed ashore here in a storm. And for him, who knew nothing of the earth, England was an undiscovered country. It was some time before he learned its name; and for all I know he might have expected to find wild beasts or wild men here, when, crawling in the dark over the sea wall, he rolled down the other side into a dike, where it was another miracle he didn't get drowned. But he struggled instinctively like an animal under a net, and this blind struggle threw him out into a field. He must have been, indeed, of a tougher fiber than he looked to withstand without expiring such buffetings, the violence of his exertions, and so much fear. Later on, in his broken English that resembled curiously the speech of a young child, he told me himself that he put his trust in God, believing he was no longer in this world. And truly —he would add—how was he to know? He fought his way against the rain and the gale on all fours, and crawled at last among some sheep huddled close under the lee of a hedge. They ran off in all directions, bleating in the darkness, and he welcomed the first familiar sound he heard on these shores. It must have been two in the morning then. And this is all we know of the manner of his landing, though he did not arrive unattended by any means. Only his grisly company did not begin to come ashore till much later in the day. . . ."

The doctor gathered the reins, clicked his tongue; we trotted down the hill. Then turning, almost directly, a sharp corner into High Street, we rattled over the stones and were home.

Late in the evening Kennedy, breaking a spell of moodiness that had come over him, returned to the story. Smoking his pipe, he paced the long room from end to end. A reading lamp concentrated all its light upon the papers on his desk; and, sitting by the open window, I saw, after the windless, scorching day, the frigid splendor of a hazy sea lying motionless under the moon. Not a whisper, not a splash, not a stir of the shingle, not a footstep, not a sigh came up from the earth below—never a sign of life but the scent of climbing jasmine; and Kennedy's voice, speaking behind me, passed through the wide casement, to vanish outside in a chill and sumptuous stillness.

". . . The relations of shipwrecks in the olden times tell us of much suffering. Often the castaways were only saved from drowning to die miserably from starvation on a barren coast; others suffered violent death or else slavery, passing through years of precarious existence with people to whom their strangeness was an object of suspicion, dislike, or fear. We read about these things, and they are very pitiful. It is indeed hard upon a man to find himself a lost stranger, helpless, incomprehensible, and of a mysterious origin, in some obscure corner of the earth. Yet among all the adventurers shipwrecked in all the wild parts of the world, there is not one, it seems to me,

that ever had to suffer a fate so simply tragic as the man I am speaking of, the most innocent of adventurers cast out by the sea in the bight [1] of this bay, almost within sight from this very window.

"He did not know the name of his ship. Indeed, in the course of time we discovered he did not even know that ships had names—'like Christian people'; and when, one day, from the top of Talfourd Hill, he beheld the sea lying open to his view, his eyes roamed afar, lost in an air of wild surprise, as though he had never seen such a sight before. And probably he had not. As far as I could make out, he had been hustled together with many others on board an emigrant ship at the mouth of the Elbe, too bewildered to take note of his surroundings, too weary to see anything, too anxious to care. They were driven below into the 'tween-deck and battened down from the very start. It was a low timber dwelling—he would say—with wooden beams overhead, like the houses in his country, but you went into it down a ladder. It was very large, very cold, damp and somber, with places in the manner of wooden boxes where people had to sleep one above another, and it kept on rocking all ways at once all the time. He crept into one of these boxes and lay down there in the clothes in which he had left his home many days before, keeping his bundle and his stick by his side. People groaned, children cried, water dripped, the lights went out, the walls of the place creaked, and everything was being shaken so that in one's little box one dared not lift one's head. He had lost touch with his only companion (a young man from the same valley, he said), and all the time a great noise of wind went on outside and heavy blows fell—boom! boom! An awful sickness overcame him, even to the point of making him neglect his prayers. Besides, one could not tell whether it was morning or evening. It seemed always to be night in that place.

"Before that he had been traveling a

[1] **bight:** curve.

long, long time on the iron track. He looked out of the window, which had a wonderfully clear glass in it, and the trees, the houses, the fields, and the long roads seemed to fly round and round about him till his head swam. He gave me to understand that he had on his passage beheld uncounted multitudes of people—whole nations—all dressed in such clothes as the rich wear. Once he was made to get out of the carriage, and slept through a night on a bench in a house of bricks with his bundle under his head; and once for many hours he had to sit on a floor of flat stones, dozing, with his knees up and with his bundle between his feet. There was a roof over him, which seemed made of glass, and was so high that the tallest mountain pine he had ever seen would have had room to grow under it. Steam machines rolled in at one end and out at the other. People swarmed more than you can see on a feast day round the miraculous Holy Image in the yard of the Carmelite Convent down in the plains where, before he left his home, he drove his mother in a wooden cart—a pious old woman who wanted to offer prayers and make a vow for his safety. He could not give me an idea of how large and lofty and full of noise and smoke and gloom, and clang of iron, the place was, but someone had told him it was called Berlin. Then they rang a bell, and another steam machine came in, and again he was taken on and on through a land that wearied his eyes by its flatness without a single bit of a hill to be seen anywhere. One more night he spent shut up in a building like a good stable with a litter of straw on the floor, guarding his bundle among a lot of men, of whom not one could understand a single word he said. In the morning they were all led down to the stony shores of an extremely broad muddy river, flowing not between hills but between houses that seemed immense. There was a steam machine that went on the water, and they all stood upon it packed tight, only now there were with them many women and children who made much noise. A cold rain fell, the wind blew in his face; he was wet through, and his teeth chattered. He and the young man from the same valley took each other by the hand.

"They thought they were being taken to America straight away, but suddenly the steam machine bumped against the side of a thing like a great house on the water. The walls were smooth and black, and there uprose, growing from the roof as it were, bare trees in the shape of crosses, extremely high. That's how it appeared to him then, for he had never seen a ship before. This was the ship that was going to swim all the way to America. Voices shouted, everything swayed; there was a ladder dipping up and down. He went up on his hands and knees in mortal fear of falling into the water below, which made a great splashing. He got separated from his companion, and when he descended into the bottom of that ship his heart seemed to melt suddenly within him.

"It was then also, as he told me, that he lost contact for good and all with one of those three men who the summer before had been going about through all the little towns in the foothills of his country. They would arrive on market days driving in a peasant's cart, and would set up an office in an inn or some other house. There were three of them, of whom one with a long beard looked venerable; and they had red cloth collars round their necks and gold lace on their sleeves like government officials. They sat proudly behind a long table; and in the next room, so that the common people shouldn't hear, they kept a cunning telegraph machine, through which they could talk to the Emperor of America. The fathers hung about the door, but the young men of the mountains would crowd up to the table asking many questions, for there was work to be got all the year round at three dollars a day in America, and no military service to do.

"But the American Kaiser would not take everybody. Oh, no! He himself had great difficulty in getting accepted, and the venerable man in uniform had to go out of the room several times to work the telegraph on his behalf. The American Kaiser engaged him at last at three dollars, he being young and strong. However, many able young men backed out, afraid of the great distance; besides, those only who had some money could be taken. There were some who sold their huts and their land because it cost a lot of money to get to America; but then, once there, you had three dollars a day, and if you were clever you could find places where true gold could be picked up on the ground. His father's house was getting overfull. Two of his brothers were married and had children. He promised to send money home from America by post twice a year. His father sold an old cow, a pair of piebald mountain ponies of his own raising, and a cleared plot of fair pasture land on the sunny slope of a pine-clad pass to an innkeeper, in order to pay the people of the ship that took men to America to get rich in a short time.

"He must have been a real adventurer at heart, for how many of the greatest enterprises in the conquest of the earth had for their beginning just such a bargaining away of the paternal cow for the mirage or true gold far away! I have been telling you more or less in my own words what I learned fragmentarily in the course of two or three years, during which I seldom missed an opportunity of a friendly chat with him. He told me this story of his adventure with many flashes of white teeth and lively glances of black eyes, at first in a sort of anxious baby talk, then, as he acquired the language, with great fluency, but always with that singing, soft, and at the same time vibrating intonation that instilled a strangely penetrating power into the sound of the most familiar English words, as if they had been the words of an unearthly language. And he always would come to an end, with many emphatic shakes of his head, upon that awful sensation of his heart melting within him directly he set foot on board that ship. Afterward there seemed to come for him a period of blank ignorance, at any rate as to facts. No doubt he must have been abominably seasick and abominably unhappy—this soft and passionate adventurer, taken thus out of his knowledge, and feeling bitterly as he lay in his emigrant bunk his utter loneliness; for his was a highly sensitive nature. The next thing we know of him for certain is that he had been hiding in Hammond's pig-pound by the side of the road to Norton, six miles, as the crow flies, from the sea. Of these experiences he was unwilling to speak: they seemed to have seared into his soul a somber sort of wonder and indignation. Through the rumors of the countryside, which lasted for a good many days after his arrival, we know that the fishermen of West Colebrook had been disturbed and startled by heavy knocks against the walls of weatherboard cottages, and by a voice crying piercingly strange words in the night. Several of them turned out even, but, no doubt, he had fled in sudden alarm at their rough angry tones hailing each other in the darkness. A sort of frenzy must have helped him up the steep Norton hill. It was he, no doubt, who early the following morning had been seen lying (in a swoon, I should say) on the roadside grass by the Brenzett carrier, who actually got down to have a nearer look, but drew back, intimidated by the perfect immobility, and by something queer in the aspect of that tramp, sleeping so still under the showers. As the day advanced, some children came dashing into school at Norton in such a fright that the schoolmistress went out and spoke indignantly to a 'horrid-looking man' on the road. He edged away, hanging his head, for a few steps, and then suddenly ran off with extraordinary fleetness. The driver of Mr. Bradley's milk cart made no secret of it that he had lashed with his whip at a hairy sort of gypsy fellow who, jumping up at a turn of the road by the Vents, made a snatch at the pony's bridle. And he caught him a good one, too, right over the face, he said, that made him drop down in the mud a jolly sight quicker than he had jumped up; but it was a good half a mile before he could stop the pony. Maybe that in his desperate endeavors to get help, and in his need to get in touch with someone, the poor devil had tried to stop the cart. Also three boys confessed afterward to throwing stones at a funny tramp, knocking about all wet and muddy, and, it seemed, very drunk, in the narrow deep lane by the limekilns. All this was the talk of three villages for days; but we have Mrs. Finn's (the wife of Smith's wagoner) unimpeachable testimony that she saw him get over the low wall of Hammond's pigpound and lurch straight at her, babbling aloud in a voice that was enough to make one die of fright. Having the baby with her in a perambulator, Mrs. Finn called out to him to go away, and as he persisted in coming nearer, she hit him courageously with her umbrella over the head, and, without once looking back, ran like the wind with the perambulator as far as the first house in the village. She stopped then, out of breath, and spoke to old Lewis, hammering there at a heap of stones; and the old chap, taking off his immense black wire goggles, got up on his shaky legs to look where she pointed. Together they followed with their eyes the figure of the man running over a field; they saw him fall down, pick himself up, and run on again, staggering and waving his long arms above his head, in the direction of the New Barns Farm. From that moment he is plainly in the toils of his obscure and touching destiny. There is no doubt after this of what happened to him. All is certain now: Mrs. Smith's intense terror; Amy Foster's stolid conviction held against the other's nervous attack, that the man 'meant no harm'; Smith's exasperation (on his return from Darnford Market) at finding the dog barking himself into a fit, the back door locked, his wife in hysterics; and all for an unfortunate dirty tramp, supposed to be even then lurking in his stackyard. Was he? He would teach him to frighten women.

"Smith is notoriously hot-tempered, but the sight of some nondescript and miry creature sitting cross-legged among a lot of loose straw, and swinging itself to and fro like a bear in a cage, made him pause. Then this tramp stood up silently before him, one mass of mud and filth from head to foot. Smith, alone among his stacks with this apparition, in the stormy twilight ringing with the infuriated barking of the dog, felt the dread of an inexplicable strangeness. But when that being, parting with his black hands the long matted locks that hung before his face, as you part the two halves of a curtain, looked out at him with glistening, wild, black and white eyes, the weirdness of this silent encounter fairly staggered him. He has admitted since (for the story has been a legitimate subject of conversation about here for years) that he made more than one step backward. Then a sudden burst of rapid, senseless speech persuaded him at once that he had to do with an escaped lunatic. In fact, that impression never wore off completely. Smith has not in his heart given up his secret conviction of the man's essential insanity to this very day.

"As the creature approached him, jabbering in a most discomposing manner, Smith (unaware that he was being addressed as 'gracious lord,' and adjured in God's name to afford food and shelter) kept on speaking firmly but gently to it, and retreating all the time into the other yard. At last, watching his chance, by a sudden charge he bundled him headlong into the wood-lodge, and instantly shot the bolt. Thereupon he wiped his brow, though the day was cold. He had done his duty to the community by shutting up a wandering and probably dangerous maniac. Smith isn't a hard man at all, but he had room in his brain only for that one idea of lunacy. He was not imaginative enough to ask himself whether the man might not be perishing with cold and hunger. Meantime, at first, the maniac made a great deal of noise in the lodge. Mrs. Smith was screaming upstairs, where she had locked herself in her bedroom; but Amy Foster sobbed piteously at the kitchen door, wringing her hands and muttering, 'Don't! don't!' I dare say Smith had a rough time of it that evening with one noise and another, and this insane, disturbing voice crying obstinately through the door only added to his irritation. He couldn't possibly have connected this troublesome lunatic with the sinking of a ship in Eastbay, of which there had been a rumor in the Darnford marketplace. And I dare say the man inside had been very near to insanity on that night. Before his excitement collapsed and he became unconscious, he was throwing himself violently about in the dark, rolling on some dirty sacks, and biting his fists with rage, cold, hunger, amazement, and despair.

"He was a mountaineer of the eastern range of the Carpathians, and the vessel sunk the night before in Eastbay was the Hamburg emigrant ship *Herzogin Sophia-Dorothea,* of appalling memory.

"A few months later we could read in the papers the accounts of the bogus 'Emigration Agencies' among the Slavic peasantry in the more remote provinces of Austria. The object of these scoundrels was to get hold of the poor ignorant people's homesteads, and they were in league with the local usurers. They exported their victims through Hamburg mostly. As to the ship, I had watched her out of this very window, reaching close-hauled under short canvas into the bay on a dark, threatening afternoon. She came to an anchor, correctly by the chart, off the Brenzett Coastguard station. I remember before the night fell looking out again at the outlines of her spars and rigging that stood out dark and pointed on a background of ragged, slaty clouds like another and a slighter spire to the left of the Brenzett churchtower. In the evening the wind rose. At midnight I could hear in my bed the terrific gusts and the sounds of a driving deluge.

"About that time the Coastguardsmen thought they saw the lights of a steamer over the anchoring ground. In a moment they vanished; but it is clear that another vessel of some sort had tried for shelter in the bay on that awful, blind night, had rammed the German ship amidships ('a breach'—as one of the divers told me afterward—'that you could sail a Thames barge through'), and then had gone out either scatheless or damaged, who shall say; but had gone out, unknown, unseen, and fatal, to perish mysteriously at sea. Of her nothing ever came to light, and yet the hue and cry that was raised all over the world would have found her out if she had been in existence anywhere on the face of the waters.

"A completeness without a clue, and a stealthy silence as of a neatly executed crime, characterize this murderous disaster, which, as you remember, had its gruesome celebrity. The wind would have prevented the loudest outcries from reaching the shore; there had been evidently no time for signals of distress. It was death without any sort of fuss. The Hamburg ship, filling all at once, capsized as she sank, and at daylight there was not even the end of a spar to be seen above water. She was missed, of course, and at first the Coastguardsmen surmised that she had either dragged her anchor or parted her cable sometime· during the night, and had been blown out to sea. Then, after the tide turned, the wreck must have shifted a little and released some of the bodies, because a child—a little fair-haired child in a red frock—came ashore abreast of the Martello tower. By the afternoon you could see along three miles of beach dark figures with bare legs dashing in and out of the tumbling foam, and rough-looking men, women with hard faces, children, mostly fair-haired, were being carried, stiff and dripping, on stretchers, on wattles, on ladders, in a long procession past the door of the Ship Inn, to be laid out in a row under the north wall of the Brenzett Church.

"Officially, the body of the little girl in the red frock is the first thing that came ashore from that ship. But I have patients among the seafaring population of West Colebrook, and, unofficially, I am informed that very early that morning two brothers, who went down to look after their cobble hauled up on the beach, found a good way from Brenzett, an ordinary ship's hencoop, lying high and dry on the shore, with eleven drowned ducks inside. Their families ate the birds, and the hencoop was split into firewood with a hatchet. It is possible that a man (supposing he happened to be on deck at the time of the accident) might have floated ashore on that hencoop. He might. I admit it is improbable, but there was the man—and for days, nay, for weeks—it didn't enter our heads that we had among us the only living soul that had escaped from that disaster. The man himself, even when he learned to speak intelligibly, could tell us very little. He remembered he had felt better (after the ship had anchored, I suppose), and that the darkness, the wind, and the rain took his breath away. This looks as if he had been on deck sometime during that night. But we mustn't forget he had been taken out of his knowledge, that he had been seasick and battened down below for four days, that he had no general notion of a ship or of the sea, and therefore could have no definite idea of what was happening to him. The rain, the wind, the darkness he knew; he understood the bleating of the sheep, and he remembered the pain of his wretchedness and misery, his heartbroken astonishment that it was neither seen nor understood, his dismay at finding all the men angry and all the women fierce. He had approached them as a beggar, it is true, he said; but in his country, even if they gave nothing, they spoke gently to beggars. The children in his country were not taught to throw stones at those who asked for compassion. Smith's strategy overcame him completely. The wood-lodge presented the horrible aspect of a dungeon. What would be done to him next? ... Now wonder that Amy Foster appeared to his eyes with the aureole of an angel of light. The girl had not been able to sleep for thinking of the poor man, and

in the morning, before the Smiths were up, she slipped out across the back yard. Holding the door of the wood-lodge ajar, she looked in and extended to him half a loaf of white bread—'such bread as the rich eat in my country,' he used to say.

"At this he got up slowly from among all sorts of rubbish, stiff, hungry, trembling, miserable, and doubtful. 'Can you eat this?' she asked in her soft and timid voice. He must have taken her for a 'gracious lady.' He devoured ferociously, and tears were falling on the crust. Suddenly he dropped the bread, seized her wrist, and imprinted a kiss on her hand. She was not frightened. Through his forlorn condition she had observed that he was good-looking. She shut the door and walked back slowly to the kitchen. Much later on, she told Mrs. Smith, who shuddered at the bare idea of being touched by that creature.

"Through this act of impulsive pity he was brought back again within the pale of human relations with his new surroundings. He never forgot it—never.

"That very same morning old Mr. Swaffer (Smith's nearest neighbor) came over to give his advice, and ended by carrying him off. He stood, unsteady on his legs, meek, and caked over in half-dried mud, while the two men talked around him in an incomprehensible tongue. Mrs. Smith had refused to come downstairs till the madman was off the premises; Amy Foster, far from within the dark kitchen, watched through the open back door; and he obeyed the signs that were made to him to the best of his ability. But Smith was full of mistrust. 'Mind, sir! It may be all his cunning,' he cried repeatedly in a tone of warning. When Mr. Swaffer started the mare, the deplorable being sitting humbly by his side, through weakness, nearly fell out over the back of the high two-wheeled cart. Swaffer took him straight home. And it is then that I come upon the scene.

"I was called in by the simple process of the old man beckoning to me with his forefinger over the gate of his house as I happened to be driving past. I got down, of course.

"'I've got something here,' he mumbled, leading the way to an outhouse at a little distance from his other farm buildings.

"It was there that I saw him first, in a long, low room taken upon the space of of that sort of coach-house. It was bare and whitewashed, with a small square aperture glazed with one cracked, dusty pane at its further end. He was lying on his back upon a straw pallet; they had given him a couple of horse blankets, and he seemed to have spent the remainder of his strength in the exertion of cleaning himself. He was almost speechless; his quick breathing under the blankets pulled up to his chin, his glittering, restless black eyes reminded me of a wild bird caught in a snare. While I was examining him, old Swaffer stood silently by the door, passing the tips of his fingers along his shaven upper lip. I gave some directions, promised to send a bottle of medicine, and naturally made some inquiries.

"'Smith caught him in the stackyard at New Barns,' said the old chap in his deliberate, unmoved manner, and as if the other had been indeed a sort of wild animal. 'That's how I came by him. Quite a curiosity, isn't he? Now tell me, doctor —you've been all over the world—don't you think that's a bit of Hindoo we've got hold of here?'

"I was greatly surprised. His long black hair scattered over the straw bolster contrasted with the olive pallor of his face. It occurred to me he might be a Basque. It didn't necessarily follow that he should understand Spanish; but I tried him with the few words I know, and also with some French. The whispered sounds I caught by bending my ear to his lips puzzled me utterly. That afternoon the young ladies from the rectory (one of them read Goethe with a dictionary, and the other had struggled with Dante for years), coming to see Miss Swaffer, tried their German and

Italian on him from the doorway. They retreated, just the least bit scared by the flood of passionate speech which, turning on his pallet, he let out at them. They admitted that the sound was pleasant, soft, musical—but, in conjunction with his looks perhaps, it was startling—so excitable, so utterly unlike anything one had ever heard. The village boys climbed up the bank to have a peep through the little square aperture. Everybody was wondering what Mr. Swaffer would do with him.

"He simply kept him.

"Swaffer would be called eccentric were he not so much respected. They will tell you that Mr. Swaffer sits up as late as ten o'clock at night to read books, and they will tell you also that he can write a check for two hundred pounds without thinking twice about it. He himself would tell you that the Swaffers had owned land between this and Darnford for these three hundred years. He must be eighty-five today, but he does not look a bit older than when I first came here. He is a great breeder of sheep, and deals extensively in cattle. He attends market days for miles around in every sort of weather, and drives sitting bowed low over the reins, his lank gray hair curling over the collar of his warm coat, and with a green plaid rug round his legs. The calmness of advanced age gives a solemnity to his manner. He is clean shaved; his lips are thin and sensitive; something rigid and monachal [1] in the set of his features lends a certain elevation to the character of his face. He has been known to drive miles in the rain to see a new kind of rose in somebody's garden, or a monstrous cabbage grown by a cottager. He loves to hear tell or to be shown something that he calls 'outlandish.' Perhaps it was just that outlandishness of the man which influenced old Swaffer. Perhaps it was only and inexplicable caprice. All I know is that at the end of three weeks I caught sight of Smith's lunatic digging in Swaf-

[1] **monachal:** monklike.

fer's kitchen garden. They had found out he could use a spade. He dug barefooted.

"His black hair flowed over his shoulders. I suppose it was Swaffer who had given him the striped old cotton shirt; but he wore still the national brown cloth trousers (in which he had been washed ashore) fitting to the leg almost like tights; was belted with a broad leather belt studded with little brass discs; and had never yet ventured into the village. The land he looked upon seemed to him kept neatly, like the grounds round a landowner's house; the size of the cart horses struck him with astonishment; the roads resembled garden walks, and the aspect of the people, especially on Sundays, spoke of opulence. He wondered what made them so hardhearted and their children so bold. He got his food at the back door, carried it in both hands, carefully, to his outhouse, and, sitting alone on his pallet, would make the sign of the cross before he began. Beside the same pallet, kneeling in the early darkness of the short days, he recited aloud the Lord's Prayer before he slept. Whenever he saw old Swaffer he would bow with veneration from the waist, and stand erect while the old man, with his fingers over his upper lip, surveyed him silently. He bowed to Miss Swaffer, who kept house frugally for her father—a broad-shouldered, big-boned woman of forty-five, with the pocket of her dress full of keys, and a gray, steady eye. She was Church—as people said (while her father was one of the trustees of the Baptist Chapel) [1]—and wore a little steel cross at her waist. She dressed severely in black, in memory of one of the innumerable Bradleys of the neighborhood, to whom she had been engaged some twenty-five years ago—a young farmer who broke his neck out hunting on the eve of the wedding day. She had the unmoved countenance of the deaf, spoke very seldom, and her lips,

[1] In the British Isles, the word *chapel* is usually used to refer to any denomination that is not the established Church of England; the word *church* is usually restricted to the established Church.

thin like her father's, astonished one sometimes by a mysteriously ironic curl.

"These were the people to whom he owed allegiance, and an overwhelming loneliness seemed to fall from the leaden sky of that winter without sunshine. All the faces were sad. He could talk to no one, and had no hope of ever understanding anybody. It was as if these had been the faces of people from the other world— dead people—he used to tell me years afterward. Upon my word, I wonder he did not go mad. He didn't know where he was. Somewhere very far from his mountains—somewhere over the water. Was this America, he wondered?

"If it hadn't been for the steel cross at Miss Swaffer's belt he would not, he confessed, have known whether he was in a Christian country at all. He used to cast stealthy glances at it and feel comforted. There was nothing here the same as in his country! The earth and the water were different; there were no images of the Redeemer by the roadside. The very grass was different, and the trees. All the trees but the three old Norway pines on the bit of lawn before Swaffer's house, and these reminded him of his country. He had been detected once, after dusk, with his forehead against the trunk of one of them, sobbing, and talking to himself. They had been like brothers to him at that time, he affirmed. Everything else was strange. Conceive you the kind of an existence overshadowed, oppressed, by the everyday material appearances, as if by the visions of a nightmare. At night, when he could not sleep, he kept on thinking of the girl who gave him the first piece of bread he had eaten in this foreign land. She had been neither fierce nor angry, nor frightened. Her face he remembered as the only comprehensible face among all these faces that were as closed, as mysterious, and as mute as the faces of the dead who are possessed of a knowledge beyond the comprehension of the living. I wonder whether the memory of her compassion prevented him from cutting his throat. But there! I suppose I am an old sentimentalist, and forget the instinctive love of life which it takes all the strength of an uncommon despair to overcome.

"He did the work which was given him with an intelligence which surprised old Swaffer. By and by it was discovered that he could help at the plowing, could milk the cows, feed the bullocks in the cattle-yard, and was of some use with the sheep. He began to pick up words, too, very fast; and suddenly, one fine morning in spring, he rescued from an untimely death a grandchild of old Swaffer.

"Swaffer's younger daughter is married to Willcox, a solicitor and the town clerk of Colebrook. Regularly twice a year they come to stay with the old man for a few days. Their only child, a little girl not three years old at the time, ran out of the house alone in her little white pinafore, and, toddling across the grass of a terraced garden, pitched herself over a low wall head first into the horsepond in the yard below.

"Our man was out with the wagoner and the plow in the field nearest to the house, and as he was leading the team round to begin a fresh furrow, he saw, through the gap of a gate, what for anybody else would have been a mere flutter of something white. But he had straight-glancing, quick, far-reaching eyes, that only seemed to flinch and lose their amazing power before the immensity of the sea. He was barefooted, and looking as outlandish as the heart of Swaffer could desire. Leaving the horses on the turn, to the inexpressible disgust of the wagoner he bounded off, going over the plowed ground in long leaps, and suddenly appeared before the mother, thrust the child into her arms, and strode away.

"The pond was not very deep; but still, if he had not had such good eyes, the child would have perished—miserably suffocated in the foot or so of sticky mud at the bottom. Old Swaffer walked out slowly into the field, waited till the plow came over to his side, had a good look at him, and without saying a word went back to the house. But from that time they laid out his meals on the kitchen table; and at first, Miss Swaffer, all in black and with an inscrutable face, would come and stand in the doorway of the living room to see him make a big sign of the cross before he fell to. I believe that from that day, too, Swaffer began to pay him regular wages.

"I can't follow step by step his development. He cut his hair short, was seen in the village and along the road going to and fro to his work like any other man. Children ceased to shout after him. He became aware of social differences, but remained for a long time surprised at the bare poverty of the churches among so much wealth. He couldn't understand either why they were kept shut up on weekdays. There was nothing to steal in them. Was it to keep people from praying too often? The rectory took much notice of him about that time, and I believe the young ladies attempted to prepare the ground for his conversion. They could not, however, break him of his habit of crossing himself, but he went so far as to take off the string with a couple of brass medals the size of a sixpence, a tiny metal cross, and a square sort of scapulary which he wore round his neck. He hung them on the wall by the side of his bed, and he was still to be heard every evening reciting the Lord's Prayer, in incomprehensible words and in a slow, fervent tone, as he had heard his old father do at the head of all the kneeling family, big and little, on every evening of his life. And though he wore corduroys at work, and a shop-made pepper-and-salt suit on Sundays, strangers would turn round to look after him on the road. His foreignness had a peculiar and indelible stamp. At last people became used to seeing him. But they never became used to him. His rapid, skimming walk; his swarthy complexion, his hat cocked on the left ear; his habit, on warm evenings, of wearing his coat over one shoulder, like a hussar's dolman; his manner of leaping over the stiles, not as a feat of agility, but in the ordinary course of progression—all these peculiarities were, as one may say, so many causes of scorn and offense to the inhabitants of the village. *They* wouldn't in their dinner hour lie flat on their backs on the grass to stare at the sky. Neither did they go about the fields screaming dismal tunes. Many times I have heard his high-pitched voice from behind the ridge of some sloping sheep-walk, a voice light and soaring, like a lark's, but with a melancholy human note, over our fields that hear only the song of birds. And I would be startled myself. Ah! He was different; innocent of heart, and full of good will, which nobody wanted, this castaway, that, like a man transplanted into another planet, was separated by an immense space from his past and by an immense ignorance from his future. His quick, fervent utterance positively shocked everybody. 'An excitable devil,' they called him. One evening, in the taproom of the Coach and Horses (having drunk some whisky), he upset them all by singing a love song of his country. They hooted him down, and he was pained; but Preble, the lame wheelwright, and Vincent, the fat blacksmith, and the other notables, too, wanted to drink their evening beer in peace. On another occasion he tried to show them how to dance. The dust rose in clouds from the sanded floor; he leaped straight up among the deal tables, struck his heels together, squatted on one heel in front of old Preble, shooting out the other leg, uttered wild and exulting cries, jumped up to whirl on one foot, snapping his fingers above his head—and a strange carter who was having a drink in there began to swear and cleared out with his half-pint in his hand into the bar. But when suddenly he sprang upon a table and continued to dance among the glasses, the landlord interfered. He didn't want any 'acrobat tricks in the taproom.' They laid their hands on him. Having had a glass or two, Mr. Swaffer's foreigner tried to expostulate: was ejected forcibly: got a black eye.

"I believe he felt the hostility of his human surroundings. But he was tough—tough in spirit, too, as well as in body. Only the memory of the sea frightened him, with that vague terror that is left by a bad dream. His home was far away; and he did not want now to go to America. I had often explained to him that there is no place on earth where true gold can be found lying ready and to be got for the trouble of the picking up. How, then, he asked, could he ever return home with empty hands when there had been sold a cow, two ponies, and a bit of land to pay for his going? His eyes would fill with tears, and averting them from the immense shimmer of the sea, he would throw himself face down on the grass. But sometimes, cocking his hat with a little conquering air, he would defy my wisdom. He had found his bit of true gold. That was Amy Foster's heart; which was 'a golden heart, and soft to people's misery,' he would say in the accents of overwhelming conviction.

"He was called Yanko. He had explained that this meant Little John; but as he would also repeat very often that he was a mountaineer (some word sounding in the dialect of his country like Goorall), he got it for his surname. And this is the only trace of him that the succeeding ages may find in the marriage register of the parish. There it stands—Yanko Goorall—in the rector's handwriting. The crooked cross made by the castaway, a cross whose tracing no doubt seemed to him the most solemn part of the whole ceremony, is all that remains now to perpetuate the memory of his name.

"His courtship had lasted some time—ever since he got his precarious footing in the community. It began by his buying for Amy Foster a green satin ribbon in Darnford. This was what you did in his country. You bought a ribbon at a stall on a fair-day. I don't suppose the girl knew what to do with it, but he seemed to think that his honorable intentions could not be mistaken.

"It was only when he declared his purpose to get married that I fully understood how, for a hundred futile and inappreciable reasons, how—shall I say odious?—he was to all the countryside. Every old woman in the village was up in arms. Smith, coming upon him near the farm, promised to break his head for him if he found him about again. But he twisted his little black mustache with such a bellicose air and rolled such big, black fierce eyes at Smith that this promise came to nothing. Smith, however, told the girl that she must be mad to take up with a man who was surely wrong in his head. All the same, when she heard him in the gloaming whistle from beyond the orchard a couple of bars of a weird and mournful tune, she would drop whatever she had in her hand—she would leave Mrs. Smith in the middle of a sentence—and she would run out to his call. Mrs. Smith called her a shameless hussy. She answered nothing. She said nothing at all to anybody, and went on her way as if she had been deaf. She and I alone in all the land, I fancy, could see his very real beauty. He was very good-looking, and most graceful in his bearing, with that something wild as of a woodland creature in his aspect. Her mother moaned over her dismally whenever the girl came to see her on her day out. The father was surly, but pretended not to know; and Mrs. Finn once told her plainly that 'this man, my dear, will do you some harm some day yet.' And so it went on. They could be seen on the roads, she tramping stolidly in her finery—gray dress, black feather, stout boots, prominent white cotton gloves that caught your eye a hundred yards away; and he, his coat slung picturesquely over one shoulder, pacing by her side, gallant of bearing and casting tender glances upon the girl with the golden heart. I wonder whether he saw how plain she was. Perhaps among types so different from what he had ever seen, he had not the power to judge; or perhaps he was seduced by the divine quality of her pity.

"Yanko was in great trouble meantime. In his country you get an old man for an ambassador in marriage affairs. He did not know how to proceed. However, one day in the midst of sheep in a field (he was now Swaffer's undershepherd with Foster) he took off his hat to the father and declared himself humbly. 'I dare say she's fool enough to marry you,' was all Foster said. 'And then,' he used to relate, 'he puts his hat on his head, looks black at me as if he wanted to cut my throat, whistles the dog, and off he goes, leaving me to do the work.' The Fosters, of course, didn't like to lose the wages the girl earned: Amy used to give all her money to her mother. But there was in Foster a very genuine aversion to that match. He contended that the fellow was very good with sheep, but was not fit for any girl to marry. For one thing, he used to go along the hedges muttering to himself like a dam' fool; and then, these foreigners behave very queerly to women sometimes. And perhaps, he would want to carry her off somewhere—or run off himself. It was not safe. He preached it to his daughter that the fellow might ill use her in some way. She made no answer. It was, they said in the village, as if the man had done something to her. People discussed the matter. It was quite an excitement, and the two went on 'walking out' together in the face of opposition. Then something unexpected happened.

"I don't know whether old Swaffer ever understood how much he was regarded in the light of a father by his foreign retainer. Anyway the relation was curiously feudal. So when Yanko asked formally for an interview—'and the Miss, too' (he called the severe, deaf Miss Swaffer simply *Miss*)—it was to obtain their permission to marry. Swaffer heard him unmoved, dismissed him by a nod, and then shouted the intelligence into Miss Swaffer's best ear. She showed no surprise, and only remarked grimly, in a veiled blank voice, 'He certainly won't get any other girl to marry him.'

"It is Miss Swaffer who has all the credit for the munificence: but in a very few days it came out that Mr. Swaffer had presented Yanko with a cottage (the cottage you've seen this morning) and something like an acre of ground—had made it over to him in absolute property. Willcox expedited the deed, and I remember him telling me he had a great pleasure in making it ready. It recited: 'In consideration of saving the life of my beloved grandchild, Bertha Willcox.'

"Of course, after that no power on earth could prevent them from getting married.

"Her infatuation endured. People saw her going out to meet him in the evening. She stared with unblinking, fascinated eyes up the road where he was expected to appear, walking freely, with a swing from the hip, and humming one of the love tunes of his country. When the boy was born, he got elevated at the Coach and Horses, essayed again a song and a dance, and was again ejected. People expressed their commiseration for a woman married to that jack-in-the-box. He didn't care. There was a man now (he told me boastfully) to whom he could sing and talk in the language of his country and show how to dance by and by.

"But I don't know. To me he appeared to have grown less springy of step, heavier in body, less keen of eye. Imagination, no doubt; but it seems to me now as if the net of fate had been drawn closer round him already.

"One day I met him on the footpath over the Talfourd Hill. He told me that 'women were funny.' I had heard already of domestic differences. People were saying that Amy Foster was beginning to find out what sort of man she had married. He looked upon the sea with indifferent, unseeing eyes. His wife had snatched the child out of his arms one day as he sat on the doorstep crooning to it a song such as the mothers sing to babies in his mountains. She seemed to think he was doing it some harm. Women are funny. And she had objected to him praying aloud in the evening. Why? He expected the boy to repeat the prayer aloud after him by and by, as he used to do after his old father when

he was a child—in his own country. And I discovered he longed for their boy to grow up so that he could have a man to talk with in that language that to our ears sounded so disturbing, so passionate, and so bizarre. Why his wife should dislike the idea he couldn't tell. But that would pass, he said. And tilting his head knowingly, he tapped his breastbone to indicate that she had a good heart: not hard, not fierce, open to compassion, charitable to the poor!

"I walked away thoughtfully; I wondered whether his difference, his strangeness, were not penetrating with repulsion that dull nature they had begun by irresistibly attracting. I wondered. . . ."

The doctor came to the window and looked out at the frigid splendor of the sea, immense in the haze, as if enclosing all the earth with all the hearts lost among the passions of love and fear.

"Physiologically, now," he said, turning away abruptly, "it was possible. It was possible."

He remained silent. Then went on—

"At all events, the next time I saw him he was ill—lung trouble. He was tough, but I dare say he was not acclimatized as well as I had supposed. It was a bad winter; and, of course, these mountaineers do get fits of homesickness; and a state of depression would make him vulnerable. He was lying half dressed on a couch downstairs.

"A table covered with a dark oilcloth took up all the middle of the little room. There was a wicker cradle on the floor, a kettle spouting steam on the hob, and some child's linen lay drying on the fender. The room was warm, but the door opens right into the garden, as you noticed perhaps.

"He was very feverish, and kept on muttering to himself. She sat on a chair and looked at him fixedly across the table with her brown, blurred eyes. 'Why don't you have him upstairs?' I asked. With a start and a confused stammer she said, 'Oh! ah! I couldn't sit with him upstairs, sir.'

"I gave her certain directions; and going outside, I said again that he ought to be in bed upstairs. She wrung her hands. 'I couldn't. I couldn't. He keeps on saying something—I don't know what.' With the memory of all the talk against the man that had been dinned into her ears, I looked at her narrowly. I looked into her short-sighted eyes, at her dumb eyes that once in her life had seen an enticing shape, but seemed, staring at me, to see nothing at all now. But I saw she was uneasy.

"'What's the matter with him?' she asked in a sort of vacant trepidation. 'He doesn't look very ill. I never did see anybody look like this before. . . .'

"'Do you think,' I asked indignantly, 'he is shamming?'

"'I can't help it, sir,' she said, stolidly. And suddenly she clapped her hands and looked right and left. 'And there's the baby. I am so frightened. He wanted me just now to give him the baby. I can't understand what he says to it.'

"'Can't you ask a neighbor to come in tonight?' I asked.

"'Please, sir, nobody seems to care to come,' she muttered, dully resigned all at once.

"I impressed upon her the necessity of the greatest care, and then had to go. There was a good deal of sickness that winter. 'Oh, I hope he won't talk!' she exclaimed softly just as I was going away.

"I don't know how it is I did not see—but I didn't. And yet, turning in my trap, I saw her lingering before the door, very still, and as if meditating a flight up the miry road.

"Toward the night his fever increased.

"He tossed, moaned, and now and then muttered a complaint. And she sat with the table between her and the couch, watching every movement and every sound, with the terror, the unreasonable terror, of that man she could not understand creeping over her. She had drawn the wicker cradle close to her feet. There was nothing in her now but the maternal instinct and that unaccountable fear.

"Suddenly coming to himself, parched, he demanded a drink of water. She did not move. She had not understood, though he may have thought he was speaking in English. He waited, looking at her, burning with fever, amazed at her silence and immobility, and then he shouted impatiently, 'Water! Give me water!'

"She jumped to her feet, snatched up the child, and stood still. He spoke to her, and his passionate remonstrances only increased her fear of that strange man. I believe he spoke to her for a long time, entreating, wondering, pleading, ordering, I suppose. She says she bore it as long as she could. And then a gust of rage came over him.

"He sat up and called out terribly one word—some word. Then he got up as though he hadn't been ill at all, she says. And as in fevered dismay, indignation, and wonder he tried to get to her round the table, she simply opened the door and ran out with the child in her arms. She heard him call twice after her down the road in a terrible voice—and fled. . . . Ah! but you should have seen stirring behind the dull, blurred glance of those eyes the specter of the fear which had haunted her on that night three miles and a half to the door of Foster's cottage! I did the next day.

"And it was I who found him lying face down and his body in a puddle, just outside the little wicker gate.

"I had been called out that night to an urgent case in the village, and on my way home at daybreak passed by the cottage. The door stood open. My man helped me to carry him in. We laid him on the couch. The lamp smoked, the fire was out, the chill of the stormy night oozed from the cheerless yellow paper on the wall. 'Amy!' I called aloud, and my voice seemed to lose itself in the emptiness of this tiny house as if I had cried in a desert. He opened his eyes. 'Gone!' he said, distinctly. 'I had only asked for water—only for a little water. . . .'

"He was muddy. I covered him up and stood waiting in silence, catching a painfully gasped word now and then. They were no longer in his own language. The fever had left him, taking with it the heat of life. And with his panting breast and lustrous eyes he reminded me again of a wild creature under the net; of a bird caught in a snare. She had left him. She had left him—sick—helpless—thirsty. The spear of the hunter had entered his very soul. 'Why?' he cried, in the penetrating and indignant voice of a man calling to a responsible Maker. A gust of wind and a swish of rain answered.

"And as I turned away to shut the door he pronounced the word 'Merciful!' and expired.

"Eventually I certified heart failure as the immediate cause of death. His heart must have indeed failed him, or else he might have stood this night of storm and exposure, too. I closed his eyes and drove away. Not very far from the cottage I met Foster walking sturdily between the dripping hedges with his collie at his heels.

" 'Do you know where your daughter is?' I asked.

" 'Don't I!' he cried. 'I am going to talk to him a bit. Frightening a poor woman like this.'

" 'He won't frighten her any more,' I said. 'He is dead.'

"He struck with his stick at the mud.

" 'And there's the child.'

"Then, after thinking deeply for a while—

" 'I don't know that it isn't for the best.'

"That's what he said. And she says nothing at all now. Not a word of him. Never. Is his image as utterly gone from her mind as his lithe and striding figure, his caroling voice are gone from our fields? He is no longer before her eyes to excite her imagination into a passion of love or fear; and his memory seems to have vanished from her dull brain as a shadow passes away upon a white screen. She lives in the cottage and works for Miss Swaffer. She is Amy Foster for everybody, and the child is 'Amy Foster's boy.' She calls him Johnny—which means Little John.

"It is impossible to say whether this name recalls anything to her. Does she ever think of the past? I have seen her hanging over the boy's cot in a very passion of maternal tenderness. The little fellow was lying on his back, a little frightened at me, but very still, with his big black eyes, with his fluttered air of a bird in a snare. And looking at him I seemed to see again the other one—the father, cast out mysteriously by the sea to perish in the supreme disaster of loneliness and despair."

FOR STUDY AND DISCUSSION

1. What kind of impression do you have of the setting of this story? What details produce this impression? How does Conrad contrast seascape and landscape?

2. The first character who is mentioned—Kennedy, a doctor—turns out to be the narrator of most of the story. Exactly what are you told about him? How are these details relevant to the role he plays in the story?

3. How are the two main characters in the story introduced? How is your attention directed especially to them? How does the way you are told about Kennedy differ in method and effect from the way you are told about Amy and Yanko?

4. Which other characters are developed with some degree of individuality? To what extent are they revealed by their dress and appearance? their manner? their words and actions?

5. How does Yanko change in the course of the story? How are the changes made apparent? What causes the change?

6. To what extent is Amy changed in the story? In what ways does she remain constant?

7. The death of Yanko is, clearly, the story's main climax, that is, the event toward which we feel everything has been leading and which brings to a conclusion all the problems in the story. What events make up the main plot, those leading *directly* to this climax?

8. What do the parts of the story that follow the death of Yanko add to the main plot? Is there an anticlimax? Explain.

9. Does Conrad make notable use of suspense in the plot structure? Does he at any point lead you to expect, perhaps hope for, any outcome other than the one which does occur? Explain.

10. How are the elements of sea and land used as contrasting images, beyond their use as setting for the story? How does Conrad as-

sociate Yanko with the sea and Amy with the land?

11. What other imagery is associated with Yanko? How do these images differentiate him from the images used to describe the natives of Colebrook?

12. Conrad implies near the beginning that the story will be a tragedy, "arising from irreconcilable differences and from that fear of the Incomprehensible that hangs over all our heads." What are the "irreconcilable differences" in the story? What attitude does Conrad suggest toward them? What is "the incomprehensible" to Yanko? to Amy? to the other people of Colebrook? Does Conrad suggest that some ways of dealing with the incomprehensible are better than others? Explain. In what ways is this theme of broader significance than simply the problem of strangers unable to understand one another?

13. Yanko and Amy are both victims of many things. What victimizes each of them? What does Conrad seem to regard as the ultimate causes of their victimization? Are they unable to avoid disaster? Explain.

POINT OF VIEW

Although our attention is usually focused on the events and characters of a story, we sometimes become aware that a story is being told to us by someone. This voice we hear may be that of a nameless and invisible narrator or it may be that of an identified character. The author's choice of a narrator has a considerable effect upon the structure of a story, and it can be a vital force in conveying tone and meaning. The voice of an unidentified, impersonal, detached narrator is heard telling about outward events in Zola's "Attack on the Mill" (see page 772); this point of view is appropriate, since Zola saw fiction as a medium for making a detached, clinical examination of the forces that determine human life. The unidentified voice telling Chekhov's story "Misery" (see page 819), on the other hand, is not only clearly sympathetic toward the main character, but also is clearly able to reveal the old man's inner experiences and moods. Neither of these narrators, as we have said, is identified.

When a story is related by an identified person—like Kennedy in "Amy Foster"—stricter limitations are imposed upon what he can tell us directly. Actions that this narrator could not have seen, words he could not have heard, and the thoughts of other characters which he could not know must be conveyed indirectly if they are conveyed at all.

"Amy Foster" is particularly interesting because Conrad actually uses several points of view, skillfully moving from one to another without inconsistency. While most of the story is told by Kennedy, who knew Amy and her husband, Conrad adds the fiction that Kennedy is passing on his account to an unidentified friend, who is passing it on to us. Furthermore, parts of the stories of Amy and of Yanko could not have been observed firsthand by Kennedy, so that at times he in turn becomes an intermediary by passing on parts of the story which are told essentially from yet another person's point of view.

1. What characteristics of Kennedy are pointed out by his friend or revealed by Kennedy himself? Clearly Kennedy has virtually no influence upon the events of the story, but how does he affect the impression the story makes upon the reader?

2. Why might Conrad use the unnamed friend as a voice which frames Kennedy's narration?

3. Where does Conrad break off the story of Amy and Yanko to return to the two narrators? Why might he have done this?

4. In what ways does Kennedy's account of Yanko's past life in Europe actually reflect Yanko's point of view? When Conrad moves into and out of this part of the story on pages 943–45), how does he make the transition credible?

5. What point of view lies behind Kennedy's account on pages 945–47 of Yanko's first hours after being washed ashore? How does he manage to convey Yanko's view of the same events?

6. These last considerations indicate that Conrad's method of narration created a difficulty for him: how to tell all parts of the story that needed to be told. He could have avoided these difficulties by using an unidentified, impersonal, omniscient narrator. What do you suppose Conrad felt he could gain by using the more complicated method?

FOR COMPOSITION

Write an essay in which you explain, with supporting reference to the story itself, the view of life that Conrad conveys in this story. Consider how it is like and how it differs from the view expressed in the ancient drama *Antigone* (see page 140). Do you find one more true or more moving than the other?

The Wind Blows

KATHERINE MANSFIELD

Katherine Mansfield (1888–1923) is the only writer represented here who is most accurately labeled a short story writer. It is probably that even if her life had been longer, this genre would have remained her characteristic medium, for it suits her sensitive, introspective mind. "The Wind Blows," which appeared in 1920 in her best collection of stories, reflects her own feelings as a girl in New Zealand, where she was born Kathleen Mansfield Beauchamp, the daughter of a successful banker and industrialist. In 1903 she was sent with her brother to London for schooling and trained as a cellist. She had written stories since childhood, and when she was allowed to return to London after an unhappy period at home, she turned to writing as a profession. In 1911, after several years of coping with some unhappy love affairs and with dreary ill luck in looking for professional recognition, she met critic John Middleton Murry, whom she was able to marry seven years later. Murry became her principal guide and support through her most productive years, which were also years of constant illness. Miss Mansfield died of tuberculosis in a sanitarium near Paris.

Katherine Mansfield's "unusual" stories appeared at a time when people were accustomed to the well-made story with a beginning, a middle, and an end that often held a clever surprise for the reader—the kind of story popularized by Maupassant (see page 794). Miss Mansfield abandoned this technique entirely and concentrated less on events of plot than on atmosphere. She was concerned with essentials, especially with the fragments of situations and moments that are ordinary only on the surface. The most important thing, she felt, was to find out and give out the truth.

SUDDENLY—DREADFULLY—she wakes up. What has happened? Something dreadful has happened. No—nothing has happened. It is only the wind shaking the house, rattling the windows, banging a piece of iron on the roof, and making her bed tremble. Leaves flutter past the window, up and away; down in the avenue a whole newspaper wags in the air like a lost kite and falls, spiked on a pine tree.

It is cold. Summer is over—it is autumn—everything is ugly. The carts rattle by, swinging from side to side; two Chinamen lollop along under their wooden yokes with the straining vegetable baskets—their pigtails and blue blouses fly out in the wind. A white dog on three legs yelps past the gate. It is all over! What is? Oh, everything! And she begins to plait her hair with shaking fingers, not daring to look in the glass. Mother is talking to Grandmother in the hall.

"A perfect idiot! Imagine leaving anything out on the line in weather like this. . . . Now my best little Teneriffe-work tea-cloth is simply in ribbons. *What* is that extraordinary smell? It's the porridge burning. Oh, heavens—this wind!"

She has a music lesson at ten o'clock. At the thought, the minor movement of the Beethoven begins to play in her head, the trills long and terrible like little rolling drums. . . . Marie Swainson runs into the garden next door to pick the "chrysanths" before they are ruined. Her skirt flies up above her waist; she tries to beat it down, to tuck it between her legs while she stoops, but it is no use—up it flies. All the trees and bushes beat about her. She picks as quickly as she can, but she is quite distracted. She doesn't mind what she does—she pulls the plants up by the roots and bends and twists them, stamping her foot and swearing.

"For heaven's sake, keep the front door shut! Go round to the back," shouts someone. And then she hears Bogey:

"Mother, you're wanted on the telephone. Telephone, Mother. It's the butcher."

How hideous life is—revolting, simply revolting. . . . And now her hat elastic's snapped. Of course it would. She'll wear her old tam and slip out the back way. But Mother has seen.

"Matilda. Matilda. Come back im-mediately! What on earth have you got on your head? It looks like a tea cosy. And why have you got that mane of hair on your forehead?"

"I can't come back, Mother. I'll be late for my lesson."

"Come back immediately!"

She won't. She won't. She hates Mother. "Go to hell," she shouts, running down the road.

In waves, in clouds, in big round whirls the dust comes stinging, and with it little bits of straw and chaff and manure. There is a loud roaring sound from the trees in the gardens, and standing at the bottom of the road outside Mr. Bullen's gate she can hear the sea sob: "Ah! . . . Ah! . . . Ah-h!" But Mr. Bullen's drawing room is as quiet as a cave. The windows are closed, the blinds half pulled, and she is not late. The-girl-before-her has just started playing MacDowell's "To an Iceberg." Mr. Bullen looks over at her and half smiles.

"Sit down," he says. "Sit over there in the sofa corner, little lady."

How funny he is. He doesn't exactly laugh at you . . . but there is just something. . . . Oh, how peaceful it is here. She likes this room. It smells of art serge and stale smoke and chrysanthemums . . . there is a big vase of them on the mantelpiece behind the pale photograph of Rubinstein . . . *à mon ami Robert Bullen.* . . . Over the black glittering piano hangs "Solitude"—a dark tragic woman draped in white, sitting on a rock, her knees crossed, her chin on her hands.

"No, no!" says Mr. Bullen, and he leans over the other girl, puts his arms over her shoulders, and plays the passage for her. The stupid—she's blushing! How ridiculous!

Now the-girl-before-her has gone; the front door slams. Mr. Bullen comes back and walks up and down, very softly, waiting for her. What an extraordinary thing. Her fingers tremble so that she can't undo the knot in the music satchel. It's the wind. . . . And her heart beats so hard she feels it must lift her blouse up and down. Mr. Bullen does not say a word. The shabby red piano seat is long enough for two people to sit side by side. Mr. Bullen sits down by her.

"Shall I begin with scales?" she asks, squeezing her hands together. "I had some arpeggios, too."

But he does not answer. She doesn't believe he even hears . . . and then suddenly his fresh hand with the ring on it reaches over and opens Beethoven.

"Let's have a little of the old master," he says.

But why does he speak so kindly—so awfully kindly—and as though they had known each other for years and years and knew everything about each other.

He turns the page slowly. She watches his hand—it is a very nice hand and always looks as though it had just been washed.

"Here we are," says Mr. Bullen.

Oh, that kind voice—Oh, that minor movement. Here come the little drums. . . .

"Shall I take the repeat?"

"Yes, dear child."

His voice is far, far too kind. The crotchets and quavers [1] are dancing up and down the stave like little black boys on a fence. Why is he so . . . She will not cry—she has nothing to cry about. . . .

"What is it, dear child?"

Mr. Bullen takes her hands. His shoulder is there—just by her head. She leans on it ever so little, her cheek against the springy tweed.

"Life is so dreadful," she murmurs, but she does not feel it's dreadful at all. He says something about "waiting" and "marking time" and "that rare thing, a woman," but she does not hear. It is so comfortable . . . forever . . .

Suddenly the door opens and in pops Marie Swainson, hours before her time.

"Take the allegretto a little faster," says Mr. Bullen, and gets up and begins to walk up and down again.

"Sit in the sofa corner, little lady," he says to Marie.

The wind, the wind. It's frightening to be here in her room by herself. The bed, the mirror, the white jug and basin gleam like the sky outside. It's the bed that is frightening. There it lies, sound asleep. . . . Does Mother imagine for one moment that she is going to darn all those stockings knotted up on the quilt like a coil of snakes? She's not. No, Mother. I do not see why I should. . . . The wind—the wind! There's a funny smell of soot blowing down the chimney. Hasn't anyone written poems to the wind? . . . "I bring fresh flowers to the leaves and showers." . . . What nonsense.

"Is that you, Bogey?"

"Come for a walk round the esplanade, Matilda. I can't stand this any longer."

"Right-o. I'll put on my ulster. Isn't it

an awful day!" Bogey's ulster is just like hers. Hooking the collar she looks at herself in the glass. Her face is white, they have the same excited eyes and hot lips. Ah, they know those two in the glass. Good-by, dears; we shall be back soon.

"This is better, isn't it?"

"Hook on," says Bogey.

They cannot walk fast enough. Their heads bent, their legs just touching, they stride like one eager person through the town, down the asphalt zigzag where the fennel grows wild and on to the esplanade. It is dusky—just getting dusky. The wind is so strong that they have to fight their way through it, rocking like two old drunkards. All the poor little pahutukawas on the esplanade are bent to the ground.

"Come on! Come on! Let's get near."

Over by the breakwater the sea is very high. They pull off their hats and her hair blows across her mouth, tasting of salt. The sea is so high that the waves do not break at all; they thump against the rough stone wall and suck up the weedy, dripping steps. A fine spray skims from the water right across the esplanade. They are covered with drops; the inside of her mouth tastes wet and cold.

Bogey's voice is breaking. When he speaks he rushes up and down the scale. It's funny—it makes you laugh—and yet it just suits the day. The wind carries their voices—away fly the sentences like little narrow ribbons.

"Quicker! Quicker!"

It is getting very dark. In the harbor the coal hulks show two lights—one high on a mast, and one from the stern.

"Look, Bogey. Look over there."

A big black steamer with a long loop of smoke streaming, with the portholes lighted, with lights everywhere, is putting out to sea. The wind does not stop her; she cuts through the waves, making for the open gate between the pointed rocks that leads to . . . It's the light that makes her look so awfully beautiful and mysterious. . . . They are on board leaning over the rail arm in arm.

"... Who are they?"

"... Brother and sister."

"Look, Bogey, there's the town. Doesn't it look small? There's the post office clock chiming for the last time. There's the esplanade where we walked that windy day. Do you remember? I cried at my music lesson that day—how many years ago! Good-by, little island, good-by...."

Now the dark stretches a wing over the tumbling water. They can't see those two any more. Good-by, good-by. Don't forget.... But the ship is gone, now.

The wind—the wind.

FOR STUDY AND DISCUSSION

1. Although the voice narrating this story is impersonal, it is restricted to presenting the point of view of the principal character only. Describe how the point of view shifts in the last few paragraphs. What does this shift accomplish? That is, what new or different light does it throw on the preceding events as you think of them in retrospect?

2. What "cinematic" technique indicates the passage of time? How would you define the emotional effect of this technique as used in the story? What is the effect of the similar technique used in a film?

3. What is the effect of the use of the present tense throughout the story?

4. How does the selection of certain details give a coherent impression of the setting? How is the selection of details appropriate to the girl's experience?

5. This story has little that can properly be called plot. How is it held together? Why is most of the story taken up with narrating the episode of the music lesson?

6. How does the image of the wind unify the story? What might the wind symbolize in this story?

7. How does the narrator characterize the girl by revealing her attitudes toward other people?

8. How does the narrator manage to convey both the girl's view of Mr. Bullen and another, somewhat different view?

FOR COMPOSITION

1. Write a story, no longer than "The Wind Blows," in which the focal character is Robert Bullen and one of the events in the story is that Marie Swainson comments upon the departure of Matilda and her brother for study in England. Make a deliberate decision on whether you will imitate Miss Mansfield's method and style.

2. Tell Conrad's story of Amy Foster using the narrative method of "The Wind Blows." Follow the structure and keep to the length of Miss Mansfield's story.

The Infant Prodigy

THOMAS MANN

Thomas Mann (1875–1955) came from a well-to-do merchant family of Lübeck, a German port on the Baltic Sea. His mother was a Brazilian of Portuguese-Creole lineage, and to his Latin blood, Mann, like Goethe before him, attributed the artistic leanings that conflicted with his bourgeois German heritage. This conflict, which he describes in an autobiographical story called *Tonio Kröger,* was resolved in favor of the artistic leanings. At the age of twenty-five, Mann produced a long novel, *Buddenbrooks,* a family saga which reflects his own background, but whose real significance lies in its portrayal of the defeat of the old order by the opportunistic, materialistic civilization of the twentieth century. Until it was burned and banned by Hitler, *Buddenbrooks* had sold over a million copies in Germany alone, and it has been translated into almost every modern language. Another of Mann's major masterpieces is a long novel called *The Magic Mountain* which was completed in 1924. This book, set in a tuberculosis sanitarium, was the fruit of Mann's spiritual travail during the war years, and it depicts a decaying Europe on the brink of World War I.

Mann was comfortably established as Germany's most distinguished writer when, in 1936, he publicly denounced the Nazi regime and was deprived of his citizenship. He came to the United States in 1938, taught for a time at Princeton University, and became an American citizen. He left America in 1952, however, and lived in Zurich for the last few years of his life.

THE INFANT PRODIGY entered. The hall became quiet.

It became quiet and then the audience began to clap, because somewhere at the side a leader of mobs, a born organizer, clapped first. The audience had heard nothing yet, but they applauded; for a mighty publicity organization had heralded the prodigy and people were already hypnotized, whether they knew it or not.

The prodigy came from behind a splendid screen embroidered with Empire garlands and great conventionalized flowers, and climbed nimbly up the steps to the platform, diving into the applause as into a bath; a little chilly and shivering, but yet as though into a friendly element. He advanced to the edge of the platform and smiled as though he were about to be photographed; he made a shy, charming gesture of greeting, like a little girl.

He was dressed entirely in white silk, which the audience found enchanting. The little white jacket was fancifully cut, with a sash underneath it, and even his shoes were made of white silk. But against the white socks his bare little legs stood out quite brown; for he was a Greek boy.

He was called Bibi Saccellaphylaccas.

And such indeed was his name. No one knew what Bibi was the pet name for, nobody but the impresario, and he regarded it as a trade secret. Bibi had smooth black hair reaching to his shoulders; it was parted on the side and fastened back from the narrow domed forehead by a little silk bow. His was the most harmless childish countenance in the world, with an unfinished nose and guileless mouth. The area beneath his pitch-black mouselike eyes was already a little tired and visibly lined. He looked as though he were nine years old but was really eight and given out for seven. It was hard to tell whether to believe this or not. Probably everybody knew better and still believed it, as happens about so many things. The average man thinks that a little falseness goes with beauty. Where should we get any excitement out of our daily life if we were not willing to pretend a bit? And the average man is quite right, in his average brains!

The prodigy kept on bowing until the applause died down, then he went up to the grand piano, and the audience cast a last look at its programs. First came a *Marche solennelle,* then a *Rêverie,* and then *Le Hibou et les moineaux* [1]—all by Bibi Saccellaphylaccas. The whole program was by him, they were all his compositions. He could not score them, of course, but he had them all in his extraordinary little head and they possessed real artistic significance, or so it said, seriously and objectively, in the program. The program sounded as though the impresario had wrested these concessions from his critical nature after a hard struggle.

The prodigy sat down upon the revolving stool and felt with his feet for the pedals, which were raised by means of a clever device so that Bibi could reach them. It was Bibi's own piano; he took it everywhere with him. It rested upon wooden trestles and its polish was somewhat marred by the constant transporta-

---

[1] *Le Hibou et les moineaux:* the owl and the sparrows.

tion—but all that only made things more interesting.

Bibi put his silk-shod feet on the pedals; then he made an artful little face, looked straight ahead of him, and lifted his right hand. It was a brown, childish little hand; but the wrist was strong and unlike a child's, with well-developed bones.

Bibi made his face for the audience because he was aware that he had to entertain them a little. But he had his own private enjoyment in the thing too, an enjoyment which he could never convey to anybody. It was that prickling delight, that secret shudder of bliss, which ran through him every time he sat at an open piano—it would always be with him. And here was the keyboard again, these seven black and white octaves, among which he had so often lost himself in abysmal and thrilling adventures—and yet it always looked as clean and untouched as a newly washed blackboard. This was the realm of music that lay before him. It lay spread out like an inviting ocean, where he might plunge in and blissfully swim, where he might let himself be borne and carried away, where he might go under in night and storm, yet keep the mastery: control, ordain—he held his right hand poised in the air.

A breathless stillness reigned in the room—the tense moment before the first note came.... How would it begin? It began so. And Bibi, with his index finger, fetched the first note out of the piano, a quite unexpectedly powerful first note in the middle register, like a trumpet blast. Others followed, an introduction developed—the audience relaxed.

The concert was held in the palatial hall of a fashionable first-class hotel. The walls were covered with mirrors framed in gilded arabesques, between frescoes of the rosy and fleshly school. Ornamental columns supported a ceiling that displayed a whole universe of electric bulbs, in clusters darting a brilliance far brighter than day and filling the whole space with thin, vibrating golden light. Not a seat was unoccupied, people were standing in the side aisles and at the back. The front seats cost twelve marks; for the impresario believed that anything worth having was worth paying for. And they were occupied by the best society, for it was in the upper classes, of course, that the greatest enthusiasm was felt. There were even some children, with their legs hanging down demurely from their chairs and their shining eyes staring at their gifted little white-clad contemporary.

Down in front on the left side sat the prodigy's mother, an extremely obese woman with a powdered double chin and a feather on her head. Beside her was the impresario, a man of oriental appearance with large gold buttons on his conspicuous cuffs. The princess was in the middle of the front row—a wrinkled, shriveled little old princess but still a patron of the arts, especially everything full of sensibility. She sat in a deep, velvet-upholstered armchair, and a Persian carpet was spread before her feet. She held her hands folded over her gray striped-silk breast, put her head on one side, and presented a picture of elegant composure as she sat looking up at the performing prodigy. Next her sat her lady-in-waiting, in a green striped-silk gown. Being only a lady-in-waiting she had to sit up very straight in her chair.

Bibi ended in a grand climax. With what power this wee manikin belabored the keyboard! The audience could scarcely trust its ears. The march theme, an infectious, swinging tune, broke out once more, fully harmonized, bold and showy; with every note Bibi flung himself back from the waist as though he were marching in a triumphal procession. He ended *fortissimo,* bent over, slipped sideways off the stool, and stood with a smile awaiting the applause.

And the applause burst forth, unanimously, enthusiastically; the child made his demure little maidenly curtsy and people in the front seat thought: "Look what slim little hips he has! Clap, clap! Hurrah, bravo, little chap, Saccophylax or whatever your name is! Wait, let me take off my gloves—what a little devil of a chap he is!"

Bibi had to come out three times from behind the screen before they would stop. Some latecomers entered the hall and moved about looking for seats. Then the concert continued. Bibi's *Rêverie* murmured its numbers, consisting almost entirely of arpeggios, above which a bar of melody rose now and then, weakwinged. Then came *Le Hibou et les moineaux.* This piece was brilliantly successful, it made a strong impression; it was an effective childhood fantasy, remarkably well envisaged. The bass represented the owl, sitting morosely rolling his filmy eyes; while in the treble the impudent, half-frightened sparrows chirped. Bibi received an ovation when he finished, he was called out four times. A hotel page with shiny buttons carried up three great laurel wreaths onto the stage and proffered them from one side while Bibi nodded and expressed his thanks. Even the princess shared in the applause, daintily and noiselessly pressing her palms together.

Ah, the knowing little creature understood how to make people clap! He stopped behind the screen; they had to wait for him; he lingered a little on the steps of the platform, admired the long streamers on the wreaths—although actually such things bored him stiff by now. He bowed with the utmost charm, he gave the audience plenty of time to rave itself out, because applause is valuable and must not be cut short. "*Le Hibou* is my drawing card," he thought—this expression he had learned from the impresario. Now I will play the fantasy, it is a lot better than *Le Hibou,* of course, especially the C-sharp passage. But you idiots dote on the *Hibou,* though it is the first and the silliest thing I wrote. He continued to bow and smile.

Next came a *Méditation* and then an *Étude*—the program was quite comprehensive. The *Méditation* was very like the *Rêverie*—which was nothing against it—and the *Étude* displayed all of Bibi's virtuosity, which naturally fell a little short of his inventiveness. And then the *Fantaisie*. This was his favorite; he varied it a little each time, giving himself free rein and sometimes surprising even himself, on good evenings, by his own inventiveness.

He sat and played, so little, so white and shining, against the great black grand piano, elect and alone, above that confused sea of faces, above the heavy, insensitive mass soul, upon which he was laboring to work with his individual, differentiated soul. His lock of soft black hair with the white silk bow had fallen over his forehead, his trained and bony little wrists pounded away, the muscles stood out visibly on his brown childish cheeks.

Sitting there he sometimes had moments of oblivion and solitude, when the gaze of his strange little mouselike eyes with the big rings beneath them would lose itself and stare through the painted stage into space that was peopled with strange vague life. Then out of the corner of his eye he would give a quick look back into the hall and be once more with his audience.

"Joy and pain, the heights and the depths—that is my *Fantaisie*," he thought lovingly. "Listen, here is the C-sharp passage." He lingered over the approach, wondering if they would notice anything. But no, of course not, how should they? And he cast his eyes up prettily at the ceiling so that at least they might have something to look at.

All these people sat there in their regular rows, looking at the prodigy and thinking all sorts of things in their regular brains. An old gentleman with a white beard, a seal ring on his finger, and a bulbous swelling on his bald spot, a growth if you like, was thinking to himself: "Really, one ought to be ashamed." He had never got any further than "Ah, thou dearest Augustin" on the piano, and here he sat now, a gray old man, looking on while this little hop-o'-my-thumb performed miracles. Yes, yes, it is a gift of

God, we must remember that. God grants his gifts, or he withholds them, and there is no shame in being an ordinary man. Like with the Christ child.—Before a child one may kneel without feeling ashamed. Strange that thoughts like these should be so satisfying—he would even say so sweet, if it was not too silly for a tough old man like him to use the word. That was how he felt, anyhow.

Art . . . the business man with the parrot-nose was thinking. "Yes, it adds something cheerful to life, a little good white silk and a little tumty-ti-ti-tum. Really he does not play so badly. Fully fifty seats, twelve marks apiece, that makes six hundred marks—and everything else besides. Take off the rent of the hall, the lighting, and the programs, you must have fully a thousand marks profit. That is worthwhile."

That was Chopin he was just playing, thought the piano teacher, a lady with a pointed nose; she was of an age when the understanding sharpens as the hopes decay. "But not very original—I will say that afterward; it sounds well. And his hand position is entirely amateur. One must be able to lay a coin on the back of the hand—I would use a ruler on him."

Then there was a young girl, at that self-conscious and chlorotic time of life when the most ineffable ideas come into the mind. She was thinking to herself: "What is it he is playing? It is expressive of passion, yet he is a child. If he kissed me it would be as though my little brother kissed me—no kiss at all. Is there such a thing as passion all by itself, without any earthly object, a sort of child's-play of passion? What nonsense! If I were to say such things aloud they would just be at me with some more cod-liver oil. Such is life."

An officer was leaning against a column. He looked on at Bibi's success and thought: "Yes, you are something and I am something, each in his own way." So he clapped his heel together and paid to the prodigy the respect which he felt to be due to all the powers that be.

Then there was a critic, an elderly man in a shiny black coat and turned-up trousers splashed with mud. He sat in his free seat and thought: "Look at him, this young beggar of a Bibi. As an individual he has still to develop, but as a type he is already quite complete, the artist *par excellence*. He has in himself all the artist's exaltation and his utter worthlessness, his charlatanry and his sacred fire, his burning contempt and his secret raptures. Of course I can't write all that, it is too good. Of course, I should have been an artist myself if I had not seen through the whole business so clearly."

Then the prodigy stopped playing and a perfect storm arose in the hall. He had to come out again and again from behind his screen. The man with the shiny buttons carried up more wreaths: four laurel wreaths, a lyre made of violets, a bouquet of roses. He had not arms enough to convey all these tributes; the impresario himself mounted the stage to help him. He hung a laurel wreath round Bibi's neck, he tenderly stroked the black hair— and suddenly as though overcome he bent down and gave the prodigy a kiss, a resounding kiss, square on the mouth. And then the storm became a hurricane. That kiss ran through the room like an electric shock, it went direct to peoples' marrow and made them shiver down their backs. They were carried away by a helpless compulsion of sheer noise. Loud shouts mingled with the hysterical clapping of hands. Some of Bibi's commonplace little friends down there waved their handkerchiefs. But the critic thought: "Of course that kiss had to come—it's a good old gag. Yes, good Lord, if only one did not see through everything quite so clearly—"

And so the concert drew to a close. It began at half past seven and finished at half past eight. The platform was laden with wreaths and two little pots of flowers stood on the lamp stands of the piano. Bibi played as his last number his *Rhapsodie grecque,* which turned into the Greek national hymn at the end. His fellow countrymen in the audience would gladly have sung it with him if the company had not been so august. They made up for it with a powerful noise and hullabaloo, a hot-blooded national demonstration. And the aging critic was thinking: "Yes, the hymn had to come too. They have to exploit every vein—publicity cannot afford to neglect any means to its end. I think I'll criticize that as inartistic. But perhaps I am wrong, perhaps that is the most artistic thing of all. What is the artist? A jack-in-the-box. Criticism is on a higher plane. But I can't say that." And away he went in his muddy trousers.

After being called out nine or ten times the prodigy did not come any more from behind the screen but went to his mother and the impresario down in the hall. The audience stood about among the chairs and applauded and pressed forward to see Bibi close at hand. Some of them wanted to see the princess too. Two dense circles formed, one round the prodigy, the other round the princess, and you could actually not tell which of them was receiving more homage. But the court lady was commanded to go over to Bibi; she smoothed down his silk jacket a bit to make it look suitable for a court function, led him by the arm to the princess, and solemnly indicated to him that he was to kiss the royal hand. "How do you do it, child?" asked the princess. "Does it come into your head of itself when you sit down?" "*Oui, madame,*" answered Bibi. To himself he thought: "Oh, what a stupid old princess!" Then he turned round shyly and uncourtier-like and went back to his family.

Outside in the cloakroom there was a crowd. People held up their numbers and received with open arms furs, shawls, and galoshes. Somewhere among her acquaintances the piano teacher stood making her critique. "He is not very original," she said audibly and looked about her.

In front of one the great mirrors an elegant young lady was being arrayed in her evening cloak and fur shoes by her brothers, two lieutenants. She was exquisitely beautiful, with her steel-blue eyes and her clean-cut, well-bred face. A really noble dame. When she was ready she stood waiting for her brothers. "Don't stand so long in front of the glass, Adolf," she said softly to one of them, who could not tear himself away from the sight of his simple, good-looking young features. But Lieutenant Adolf thinks: What cheek! He would button his overcoat in front of the glass, just the same. Then they went out on the street where the arc lights gleamed cloudily through the white mist. Lieutenant Adolf struck up a little dance on the frozen snow to keep warm, with his hands in his slanting overcoat pockets and his collar turned up.

A girl with untidy hair and swinging arms, accompanied by a gloomy-faced youth, came out just behind them. A child! she thought. A charming child. But in there he was an awe-inspiring . . . and aloud in a toneless voice she said: "We are all infant prodigies, we artists."

"Well, bless my soul!" thought the old gentleman who had never got further than Augustin on the piano, and whose boil was now concealed by a top hat. "What does all that mean? She sounds very oracular." But the gloomy youth understood. He nodded his head slowly.

Then they were silent and the untidy-haired girl gazed after the brothers and sister. She rather despised them, but she looked after them until they had turned the corner.

FOR STUDY AND DISCUSSION

1. Throughout the story Mann describes in detail the concert hall and the people in it. Why is the setting so important?

2. Examine the particular details which Mann selects to describe the appearance of certain characters. How do these details control the attitude Mann wants to establish toward each person?

3. What attitude toward Bibi does Mann build up at the beginning of the story? Does he give you reason to change your opinion of Bibi later? Is Bibi a true musician or is he a figment of publicity and promotion? Explain your answers.

4. Consider the people whom Mann selects as a cross section of the audience. What attitudes do they represent? What is the particular role of the princess, whose thoughts during the concert are not given? Does any person seem to express the judgment Mann wants you to make? Explain your answers.

5. What are the problems of the artist which are posed by this story of a prodigy? The untidy-haired girl says, "We are all infant prodigies, we artists." What does she mean?

The Cat, a Goldfinch, and the Stars

LUIGI PIRANDELLO

Pirandello (1867–1936) was born in Sicily, the son of the wealthy sulfur mine owner. A linguist, he received a doctorate from the University of Bonn in Germany. At the same time he was writing verse and fiction and making translations from German into Italian. As a writer, he was influenced and personally encouraged by the famous Sicilian novelist, Giovanni Verga (see page 814). Fairly late in life, Pirandello turned to playwriting. Two of his plays which have received wide attention in United States theaters are *Right You Are If You Think You Are* and *Six Characters in Search of an Author*.

Over the course of his life, Pirandello became increasingly introspective and concerned with death, old age, and insanity—themes drawn from his experiences with an insane wife, whose company he endured for fourteen years, until her death. After the first World War, another theme emerged in his writings: the conflict between reality and illusion. Behind the mirage that was life, Pirandello tried to reveal the nature of the real world. Characteristic of Pirandello's attitude toward life are his last instructions for his funeral: "The hearse, the horse, the driver, and—*basta!*"

A STONE. Another stone. Man passes and sees the two lying side by side. But what does this stone know of the one beside it? Or what does the water know of the drain in which it flows? Man sees the water and the drain; he sees the water running in the drain, and he comes to fancy that the water, as it goes, may be confiding to the drain—who knows what secrets?

Ah, what a starry night over the roofs of this little mountain hamlet! Looking up at the sky from these roofs, one would swear that those brightly shining orbs beheld nothing else.

"The Cat, a Goldfinch, and the Stars" from *Horse In The Moon: Twelve Short Stories* by Luigi Pirandello, translated by Samuel Putnam, copyright 1932, renewed © 1960 by E. P. Dutton & Co., Inc. Reprinted by permission of the publisher.

Yet the stars do not even know there is an earth.

Those mountains? It is possible that they are not aware of this little hamlet which has nestled between them since time immemorial? Their names are known: Monte Corno; Monte Moro; and yet, can it be, they do not even know they are mountains? And it is possible that that house over there, the oldest in the village, does not know that it came to be there on account of the road that runs by it, which is the oldest of all roads? Can it, really, be?

And supposing that it *is* so?

Go ahead and believe, then, if you like, that the stars see nothing but the roofs of your little mountain hamlet.

I once knew an old couple who had a goldfinch. And the question, certainly, never occurred to them as to how their faces, its cage, the house with its old-fashioned furnishings might look to the goldfinch, or what the latter might think of all the care and caresses lavished upon it; for they were sure that, when the goldfinch came to alight upon one of their shoulders and began pecking at their wrinkled necks or the lobes of their ears— they were sure that it knew very well that this was a shoulder upon which it had alighted, and that the shoulder or the ear belonged to one of them and not to the other. Was it possible that it did not know them both very well, that it did not know that this was Grandpa and this Grandma? Or that it was not very well aware that the reason they both loved it so was because it had been their little dead grand-daughter's goldfinch, and it was she who had trained it so nicely to come perch upon her shoulder and peck at her ear, and to leave its cage and fly about the house?

For the goldfinch's cage, between the curtains, upon the window shelf, was its home only at night; by day, it spent but a few moments there, pecking at its millet seed or cunningly throwing back its head to swallow a tiny drop of water. The cage, in short, was its palace, while the house was its boundless realm. And oftentimes, it would alight upon the shade of the hanging lamp in the dining room or upon the back of Grandfather's chair, and there it would sit and trill, or—well, you know what goldfinches are!

"Nasty thing!" the old lady would scold, when she caught sight of it doing this. And she would come running with the dust-cloth, always ready to clean up after it, just as if there were a baby in the house that simply could not learn to do certain things in a certain time and place. And as she did so, the old lady would think of her granddaughter, little angel, and of how, for more than a year, she had given her this task to do, until—

"You remember, eh?"

And the old man—did he remember? He could still see her running through the house, such a tiny little mite! And he would shake his head, long and sadly.

The old couple had been left with this orphan on their hands, and she had grown up in the house with them. They had hoped that she might be the joy of their old age; but instead, when she was fifteen — But her memory had remained alive, in the trilling and the fluttering of that goldfinch. It was strange they had not thought of it sooner! But in the depths of despair into which they had fallen after their great grief, how were they ever to have thought of a goldfinch? Upon their bent shoulders, shaking with sobs, it, the goldfinch—yes, the goldfinch—had come to alight, moving its little head from side to side; and then it had stretched out its neck and, with its little beak, had pecked at their ears, as if to say—yes, it was something of hers, something alive— something that was alive still, and which still had need of their care, need of the same love that they had shown her.

Ah, how the old lady had trembled as she took it in her hand and showed it to her aged husband, sobbing all the while! What kisses they had showered upon its little head, upon its beak! It did not like to be held a prisoner in the hand, but had struggled with its tiny feet and head and had returned the old couple's kisses with sharp little pecks.

The old lady was as sure as could be that, when the goldfinch trilled, it was calling for its lost mistress, and that, when it flew here and there through the rooms of the house, it was searching for her, searching for her ceaselessly, and that it was inconsolable at not finding her; she was certain, too, that all those prolonged trills were for her—questions that spoke plainer than words, questions repeated three and four times in succession, the bird waiting for an answer and displaying its anger at not receiving one.

What did this mean, she would like to know, if not that the goldfinch knew all about death? But did the goldfinch really know whom it was calling, who it was from whom it awaited a response to those questions that spoke louder than words?

Ah, good heavens, it was a goldfinch after all! Now it called for her, now it wept for her. How, after all, could anyone doubt that, at this moment, for example, sitting there all huddled up on the perch of its cage, with its little head tucked in and its beak sticking up and its eyes half-closed—how could anyone doubt that it was thinking of her, the dead? At such times, it would let out a few submissive cheeps, which were obvious proof that it was thinking of her, weeping for her, lamenting her absence. They were a torture, those cheeps.

The old man did not contradict his wife. For he was as certain of it as she! He would get up on a chair as if to whisper a few words of comfort to this poor little distressed soul; and scarcely letting himself see what he did, he would open once more the door of the cage.

"There he goes! There he goes! the little rascal!" he would exclaim, turning upon the chair to watch it with a smile in his eyes, his two hands up in front of his face as if to ward it off. And then, Grandpa and Grandma would have a quarrel; for the reason that she, time and time again, had told him that he should leave it alone when it was like that, and not disturb it in its sorrow.

"It's singing," the old man would say.

"What do you mean, it's singing!" the old lady would snap back at him, with a shrug of her shoulders. "You are talking nonsense! It's fairly frantic!"

And she would come running up to soothe it. But how was she to soothe it? It would flutter away disdainfully, first in one direction and then in the other; and quite right it was in so doing, for it must have thought that they had no consideration for it whatsoever at such a time as that.

And lo, the old man not only took all these scoldings from his wife, without telling her that the cage door had been shut, and that it was, possibly, on account of this that the goldfinch had been cheeping so pitifully; but he even wept at her words—wept and shook his head.

"That's right, poor little thing! That's right, poor little thing! He feels that we aren't considerate!"

He knew what it meant, the old man did, not to have consideration shown one. For the old couple were the talk of their neighbors, who severely criticized them for living the way they did, all wrapped up in that goldfinch, and with their windows all the time closed. The old man no longer so much as stuck his nose out of the door; for after all, he was an old man; and so, he stayed at home crying like a baby. But all the same, there were no flies on him; and if anyone in the street should have had the bad taste to crack a joke about him, his life (but what did his life mean to him now?)—his life would not have meant anything to him—it would have meant nothing at all, had he felt that he was an object of ridicule. Yes, sir, on account of that goldfinch there, if anyone had had the bad taste to say anything— Three times, when he was a young fellow, he had been within a hair's breadth—give him liberty or give him death! Ah, it no longer meant much to him, if his blind old eyes went out!

Every once in a while, these violent impulses would boil up in the old man, and he would rise and go, often with the goldfinch on his shoulder, to gaze with truculent eyes through the windowpane at the windows of the house across the way.

Of the reality of those houses across the way, those windows with the fancy panes, those balustrades, those vases of flowers and everything, or of the reality of those roofs, tiles, and chimneys up above, the old man could not doubt, since he knew well enough to whom they belonged, who lived there, and how they lived. But the sad part is, he never once put to himself the question what either his own house or those others opposite could mean to the goldfinch upon his shoulder; and then, there was that big white tabby cat, crouching and sunning itself on the window sill directly facing him. Windows? panes? roofs? tiles? my house? your house? What was my house, your house for that big white cat, sleeping there in the sun? All houses were its houses, all that it could enter. What houses? Wherever it could find something to filch, wherever it could doze comfortably, or pretend to doze.

Did the old couple believe that, by thus keeping their doors and windows always shut, a cat, if it wanted to, could not find some other means of getting in to eat their goldfinch?

Was it too much to assume that the cat knew all about that goldfinch, knew that it was the very breath of life to that old couple, for the reason that it had belonged to their little granddaughter who was dead, and who had trained it so nicely to come out of its cage and fly around the house? And who could have foretold that the old man, once having caught the cat peering intently through the closed panes at the goldfinch it its heedless flight about the room, would go to warn the cat's mistress that—woe, woe, if he caught that cat there another time? There? Where? How was that? The cat's mistress—the old couple—the window—? the goldfinch?

And so, one day, it did eat it—yes, ate that goldfinch which, for it, might very well have been another. Entering the old couple's house, no one could say from where or how, the cat proceeded to eat the goldfinch up. It was near evening, and all the old lady heard was a little anguished peep and a moan. The old man came running in and caught a glimpse of a white object scampering away through the kitchen and, on the floor, a few delicate little white feathers which, as he opened the door, fluttered over the carpet. What a scream he let out! Despite the old lady's attempts to restrain him, he seized a weapon and ran like a madman to the house across the way. No, it was not the neighbor woman, but the cat—it was the cat that the old man wanted to kill, there, under her very eyes; and so, he fired into the dining room, for he had caught sight of the cat there, quietly perched on the cupboard; he fired one, two, three times, and there was a great crashing of pottery. Then the neighbor's son came running

out; he was armed, too, and he fired on the old man.

A tragedy. Weeping and screaming, the old man was taken back to his own house, in a dying condition; he had been shot through the lungs, and they carried him home to his aged wife.

The neighbor's son fled the country. A catastrophe in two homes; the whole countryside in an uproar for a night.

As for the cat, it scarcely remembered, a moment later, having eaten the goldfinch, any goldfinch; and it is doubtful if it understood that the old man was firing at it. It had taken a quick and nimble leap and escaped; and now—there it was, all white against the black roof, gazing up at the stars which, from the darkening depths of interplanetary space, saw—and of this we may be quite certain—nothing whatsoever of the humble roofs of this mountain hamlet; and yet, so brilliantly did they shine up there, one would have sworn that they beheld nothing else that night.

FOR COMPOSITION

1. At the beginning of the story, Pirandello poses a metaphysical problem, that is, one that concerns the essential nature of reality. He asks a challenging question: Is the universe indifferent and meaningless?

What is the relevance of the story to this question? Does the story challenge any assumptions that you usually make about this question? Does Pirandello urge upon you a particular conclusion by the way he tells the story and the ending he gives it?

Write an essay arguing your conclusions about this question of the indifference of the universe and its meaning to man's life. At an appropriate place in your essay, explain how you would interpret the situation in Pirandello's story; make clear the points of difference, if there are any, between your interpretation and the author's.

2. Write an essay in which you compare or contrast the attitude expressed in Pirandello's story with the attitude expressed in Psalm 104 (page 321) and in the selections from the *Upanishads* (page 240). In what ways does Pirandello's story comment on the philosophy implicit in Wordsworth's poem (page 750)?

Araby

JAMES JOYCE

James Joyce (1882–1941) has had a great deal to do with giving contemporary literature its habit of radical innovation in language and in form. Joyce's greatest work, the long novel *Ulysses,* created one of the most violent literary storms of the century, and its importation into the United States in 1939 was the occasion of a landmark judicial decision. His last major work, *Finnegans Wake,* went even further than *Ulysses* in the eccentric use of language to suggest the free flow and association of ideas, the use of what has come to be called the stream of consciousness.

Joyce never wrote anything of any consequence that did not deal with Dublin; he describes the experiences of his Dublin boyhood in his earliest novel, *Portrait of the Artist as a Young Man; Dubliners* is the title he gave his collection of short stories, which includes "Araby"; and Dublin is the setting of both of his major novels. "... If I can get to the heart of Dublin, I can get to the heart of all the cities of the world," Joyce said. Nevertheless, he spent most of his adult life in what he considered the more congenial literary atmosphere of Trieste, Zurich, and Paris, and at the time of his death in Zurich he had not set foot in Ireland for nearly thirty years.

NORTH RICHMOND STREET, being blind, was a quiet street except at the hour when the Christian Brothers' School set the boys free. An uninhabited house of two stories stood at the blind end, detached from its neighbors in a square ground. The other houses of the street, conscious of decent lives within them, gazed at one another with brown imperturbable faces.

The former tenant of our house, a priest, had died in the back drawing room. Air, musty from having been long enclosed, hung in all the rooms, and the waste room behind the kitchen was littered with old useless papers. Among these I found a few paper-covered books, the pages of which were curled and damp:

The Abbot, by Walter Scott, *The Devout Communicant,* and *The Memoirs of Vidocq.* I liked the last best because its leaves were yellow. The wild garden behind the house contained a central apple tree and a few straggling bushes, under one of which I found the late tenant's rusty bicycle pump. He had been a very charitable priest; in his will he had left all his money to institutions and the furniture of his house to his sister.

When the short days of winter came dusk fell before we had well eaten our dinners. When we met in the street the houses had grown somber. The space of sky above us was the color of ever-changing violet and toward it the lamps of the street lifted their feeble lanterns. The cold air stung us and we played till our bodies glowed. Our shouts echoed in the silent street. The career of our play brought us through the dark muddy lanes behind the houses where we ran the gantlet of the rough tribes from the cottages, to the back doors of the dark dripping gardens where odors arose from the ashpits, to the dark odorous stables where a coachman smoothed and combed the horse or shook music from the buckled harness. When we returned to the street, light from the kitchen windows had filled the areas. If my uncle was seen turning the corner we hid in the shadow until we had seen him safely housed. Or if Mangan's sister came out on the doorstep to call her brother in to his tea we watched her from our shadow peer up and down the street. We waited to see whether she would remain or go in and, if she remained, we left our shadow and walked up to Mangan's steps resignedly. She was waiting for us, her figure defined by the light from the half-opened door. Her brother always teased her before he obeyed and I stood by the railings looking at her. Her dress swung as she moved her body and the soft rope of her hair tossed from side to side.

Every morning I lay on the floor in the front parlor watching her door. The blind was pulled down to within an inch of the sash so that I could not be seen. When she came out on the doorstep my heart leaped. I ran to the hall, seized my books, and followed her. I kept her brown figure always in my eye and, when we came near the point at which our ways diverged, I quickened my pace and passed her. This happened morning after morning. I had never spoken to her, except for a few casual words, and yet her name was like a summons to all my foolish blood.

Her image accompanied me even in places the most hostile to romance. On Saturday evenings when my aunt went marketing I had to go to carry some of the parcels. We walked through the flaring streets, jostled by drunken men and bargaining women, amid the curses of laborers, the shrill litanies of shop boys who stood on guard by the barrels of pigs' cheeks, the nasal chanting of street singers, who sang a *come-all-you* about

O'Donovan Rossa,[1] or a ballad about the troubles in our native land. These noises converged in a single sensation of life for me: I imagined that I bore my chalice safely through a throng of foes. Her name sprang to my lips at moments in strange prayers and praises which I myself did not understand. My eyes were often full of tears (I could not tell why) and at times a flood from my heart seemed to pour itself out into my bosom. I thought little of the future. I did not know whether I would ever speak to her or not or, if I spoke to her, how I could tell her of my confused adoration. But my body was like a harp and her words and gestures were like fingers running upon the wires.

One evening I went into the back drawing room in which the priest had died. It was a dark rainy evening and there was no sound in the house. Through one of the broken panes I heard the rain impinge upon the earth, the fine incessant needles of water playing in the sodden beds. Some distant lamp or lighted window gleamed below me. I was thankful that I could see so little. All my senses seemed to desire to veil themselves and, feeling that I was about to slip from them, I pressed the palms of my hands together until they trembled, murmuring: *O love! O love!* many times.

At last she spoke to me. When she addressed the first words to me I was so confused that I did not know what to answer. She asked me was I going to *Araby*. I forget whether I answered yes or no. It would be a splendid bazaar, she said; she would love to go.

—And why can't you? I asked.

While she spoke she turned a silver bracelet round and round her wrist. She could not go, she said, because there would be a retreat that week in her convent. Her brother and two other boys were fighting for their caps and I was

---

[1] "Come all you" is the opening of many rousing Irish ballads (for example, "Come all you young rebels, and list while I sing. . ."). O'Donovan Rossa (1831–1915) was a hero of the Irish Fenian movement.

alone at the railings. She held one of the spikes, bowing her head toward me. The light from the lamp opposite our door caught the white curve of her neck, lit up her hair that rested there and, falling, lit up the hand upon the railing. It fell over one side of her dress and caught the white border of a petticoat, just visible as she stood at ease.

—It's well for you, she said.

—If I go, I said, I will bring you something.

What innumerable follies laid waste my waking and sleeping thoughts after that evening! I wished to annihilate the tedious intervening days. I chafed against the work of school. At night in my bedroom and by day in the classroom her image came between me and the page I strove to read. The syllables of the word *Araby* were called to me through the silence in which my soul luxuriated and cast an Eastern enchantment over me. I asked for leave to go to the bazaar on Saturday night. My aunt was surprised and hoped it was not some Freemason affair. I answered few questions in class. I watched my master's face pass from amiability to sternness; he hoped I was not beginning to idle. I could not call my wandering thoughts together. I had hardly any patience with the serious work of life which, now that it stood between me and my desire, seemed to me child's play, ugly monotonous child's play.

On Saturday morning I reminded my uncle that I wished to go to the bazaar in the evening. He was fussing at the hall stand, looking for the hat brush, and answered me curtly:

—Yes, boy, I know.

As he was in the hall I could not go into the front parlor and lie at the window. I left the house in bad humor and walked slowly toward the school. The air was pitilessly raw and already my heart misgave me.

When I came home to dinner my uncle had not yet been home. Still it was early. I sat staring at the clock for some time and, when its ticking began to irritate me,

I left the room. I mounted the staircase and gained the upper part of the house. The high cold empty gloomy rooms liberated me and I went from room to room singing. From the front window I saw my companions playing below in the street. Their cries reached me weakened and indistinct and, leaning my forehead against the cool glass, I looked over at the dark house where she lived. I may have stood there for an hour, seeing nothing but the brown-clad figure cast by my imagination, touched discreetly by the lamplight at the curved neck, at the hand upon the railings and at the border below the dress.

When I came downstairs again I found Mrs. Mercer sitting at the fire. She was an old garrulous woman, a pawnbroker's widow, who collected used stamps for some pious purpose. I had to endure the gossip of the tea table. The meal was prolonged beyond an hour and still my uncle did not come. Mrs. Mercer stood up to go: she was sorry she couldn't wait any longer, but it was after eight o'clock and she did not like to be out late, as the night air was bad for her. When she had gone I began to walk up and down the room, clenching my fists. My aunt said:

—I'm afraid you may put off your bazaar for this night of Our Lord.

At nine o'clock I heard my uncle's latchkey in the hall door. I heard him talking to himself and heard the hall stand rocking when it had received the weight of his overcoat. I could interpret these signs. When he was midway through his dinner I asked him to give me the money to go to the bazaar. He had forgotten.

—The people are in bed and after their first sleep now, he said.

I did not smile. My aunt said to him energetically:

—Can't you give him the money and let him go? You've kept him late enough as it is.

My uncle said he was very sorry he had forgotten. He said he believed in the old saying: *All work and no play makes Jack a dull boy.* He asked me where I was going and, when I had told him a second time, he asked me did I know *The Arab's Farewell to his Steed*. When I left the kitchen he was about to recite the opening lines of the piece to my aunt.

I held a florin tightly in my hand as I strode down Buckingham Street toward the station. The sight of the streets thronged with buyers and glaring with gas recalled to me the purpose of my journey. I took my seat in a third-class carriage of a deserted train. After an intolerable delay the train moved out of the station slowly. It crept onward among ruinous houses and over the twinkling river. At Westland Row Station a crowd of people pressed to the carriage doors; but the porters moved them back, saying that it was a special train for the bazaar. I remained alone in the bare carriage. In a few minutes the train drew up beside the improvised wooden platform. I passed out on to the road and saw by the lighted dial of a clock that it was ten minutes to ten. In front of me was a large building which displayed the magical name.

I could not find any sixpenny entrance and, fearing that the bazaar would be closed, I passed in quickly through a turnstile, handing a shilling to a weary looking man. I found myself in a big hall girdled at half its height by a gallery. Nearly all the stalls were closed and the greater part of the hall was in darkness. I recognized a silence like that which pervades a church after a service. I walked into the center of the bazaar timidly. A few people were gathered about the stalls which were still open. Before a curtain, over which the words *Café Chantant* were written in colored lamps, two men were counting money on a salver. I listened to the fall of the coins.

Remembering with difficulty why I had come I went over to one of the stalls and examined porcelain vases and flowered tea sets. At the door of the stall a young lady was talking and laughing with two young gentlemen. I remarked their English accents and listened vaguely to their conversation.

—O, I never said such a thing!

—O, but you did!

—O, but I didn't!

—Didn't she say that?

—Yes. I heard her.

—O, there's a . . . fib!

Observing me, the young lady came over and asked me did I wish to buy anything. The tone of her voice was not encouraging; she seemed to have spoken to me out of a sense of duty. I looked humbly at the great jars that stood like eastern guards at either side of the dark entrance to the stall and murmured:

—No, thank you.

The young lady changed the position of one of the vases and went back to the two young men. They began to talk of the same subject. Once or twice the young lady glanced at me over her shoulder.

I lingered before her stall, though I knew my stay was useless, to make my interest in her wares seem the more real. Then I turned away slowly and walked down the middle of the bazaar. I allowed the two pennies to fall against the sixpence in my pocket. I heard a voice call from one end of the gallery that the light was out. The upper part of the hall was now completely dark.

Gazing up into the darkness I saw myself as a creature driven and derided by vanity; and my eyes burned with anguish and anger.

FOR STUDY AND DISCUSSION

1. It can be said that this story is so completely told from one narrator's point of view that the characters, the surroundings, and the weather are colored by his feelings. How do you suppose North Richmond Street, the boy's house, Mangan's sister, and the bazaar would look to a detached observer? Does Joyce hint that there is another point of view? If so, how does he do it?

2. How does the narrator's description of the house, the street, and the weather reflect his attitude toward them? What might this setting reveal about the emotional lives of the characters? What do the references to the former tenant of the house add to the story?

3. What common element relates Mangan's sister and the bazaar in the boy's mind? Ex-

plain the experience in the bazaar as a symbol of the boy's quest and his disillusionment.

4. What does the last sentence of the story signify? Does it alter your thinking about the story as you consider it in retrospect? Explain. In what ways was the boy a victim of vanity?

5. The odor of ashpits hovers over this story of Joyce's Dublin (he said that this was not his fault). Find the images in "Araby" that give definite shape to a certain kind of world. What colors predominate? Describe the kind of world Joyce has created with his art. Does it make any difference whether or not it is faithful to the "real" Dublin? Why? Compare the world shaped by Joyce with that created by Dylan Thomas in "Fern Hill" (page 908).

FOR COMPOSITION

Explain in an essay how "Araby" and "The Wind Blows" (see page 958) are stories of typical adolescent experiences. What insights do they give into immaturity and into the processes of maturing? What comments do they make upon the child's world and upon the adult's world?

Bees and People

MIKHAIL ZOSHCHENKO

Mikhail Zoshchenko (1895–1958) was a prolific Russian writer of satirical sketches. Although he had been born into an affluent and cultured family of St. Petersburg, where czarist sentiment was strong, and had been an officer of the Czar's army in World War I, Zoshchenko served in Kerensky's provisional government set up after the abdication of the Czar in 1917. Later he volunteered for the Red Army in the Bolshevik Revolution of 1917. After a few years of miscellaneous and rather trivial jobs, he took up writing as a member of a group whose members were sympathetic to the Revolution but aloof from the Communist Party and its discipline. In spite of the greater control imposed by the Party in the thirties, Zoshchenko continued to write in his light, satiric vein until 1946, when he was denounced by a party functionary and expelled from the Union of Soviet Writers.

A RED ARMY SOLDIER arrived at a certain collective farm on a visit, and he brought a jar of flower honey as a present for his relatives.

Everyone liked the honey so much that the collective farmers decided to begin keeping bees.

But there weren't any beekeepers in the area, and the farmers had to start from scratch—making hives and moving bees from the woods into these new apartments.

Realizing that this would be a long process, the collective farmers got discouraged. "That'll take forever," they said. "By the time we do this, that, and the other thing, the summer will be over, and we won't see any honey till next year. But we need it now."

Among the members of the *kolkhoz*

there was a splendid person, a certain Ivan Panfilich, who was an elderly man of about seventy-two. In his youth he had been a beekeeper.

And so he said, "If we want to drink tea with honey this year, we'll have to go some place where they keep bees and buy the object of our dreams from them."

The farmers said, "Our collective is worth a million. We won't let expense stand in its way. Let's buy a stock of bees in full swing, with the bees already in the hives. Otherwise, if we get bees from the woods they may turn out to be no good. They might start making some kind of terrible honey like linden-tree honey. And we want flower honey."

So they gave Ivan Panfilich some money and sent him to the town of Tambov.

He arrived in Tambov, and there they told him, "You did well to come to us. Three of our villages have been resettled in the Far East, and we have an extra apiary left over. We can give you this apiary for almost nothing. Only, how you are going to transport the bees—that's a question for us to think about. The merchandise is, you might say, easily scattered—winged. The least little thing and it'll fly away in all directions. We're afraid that you'll arrive at your destination with only the little beehives and the larvae."

Panfilich said, "I'll get them there somehow. I know bees. I've been around bees all my life."

And so he brought sixteen beehives to the station on two carts. At the station he wangled a flatcar. He put his beehives on the car and covered them with a tarpaulin.

In a little while the freight train started moving. And our flatcar started rolling.

Panfilich stood solemnly on the flatcar and conversed with his bees . . . "It's all right, little fellows," he told them. "We'll get there! Just be patient in the dark a little while, and then I'll let you out in the flowers again. And there, I think, you'll get what you want. The main thing is not to get upset that I'm transporting you in the dark. I put the tarpaulin over you on purpose, so you wouldn't get silly and fly out while the train was moving. In that case, I don't think you'd manage to hop back on the train."

The train traveled on for a day. And it traveled for another day.

On the third day Panfilich began to get a little worried. The train was going slowly. It stopped at every station. It stood a long time. And it wasn't clear when it would arrive at his destination.

At the station "Polya" Panfilich got down from his car and addressed the stationmaster. He asked, "Tell me, honored sir, will the train be stopping long at your station?"

The stationmaster answered, "To tell you the truth, I don't know. It might even stop till evening."

Panfilich said, "If it's till evening, I'll take off the tarpaulin and let my little bees out in your fields. Why, they're exhausted from traveling. It's the third day they've been sitting under the tarpaulin. They're starving. They haven't eaten or drunk, and they're not feeding the larvae."

The stationmaster said, "Do what you want! What do I care about your winged passengers! I've got enough to do without them. And now I'm supposed to worry about your larvae. What kind of nonsense is that!"

Panfilich returned to his platform and removed the tarpaulin.

The weather was splendid. A blue sky. The July sun shining. Fields all around. Flowers growing. A chestnut grove in bloom.

So Panfilich took the tarpaulin off the flatcar, and at once a whole army of bees rose skyward. The bees circled, looked around, and set out for the fields and woods.

Passengers crowded around the car. Panfilich stood on it and delivered them a lecture on the usefulness of bees. But during the lecture the stationmaster came out on the platform and began signaling the engineer to start the train.

Panfilich gasped in horror when he saw these signals. In agitation he said to the stationmaster, "Honored sir, don't start the train. All my bees are out."

The stationmaster said, "You'd better whistle to them to come back in a hurry! I can't hold the train longer than three minutes."

Panfilich said, "I beg you, hold the train till sunset! At sunset the bees will return to their places. At least uncouple my flatcar! I can't leave without my bees. There are only a thousand left here; fifteen thousand are in the fields. Understand my situation! Don't be indifferent to a misfortune like this!"

The stationmaster said, "This isn't a health resort for bees, it's a railroad. Just imagine, his bees flew away! On the next train they'll say the flies flew away. Or the fleas, they'll say, jumped out of the sleeping car. So do I have to hold up the train for that? Don't make me laugh!"

At this point the stationmaster again signaled to the engineer.

And so the train began to move.

Panfilich, white as a sheet, stood on his flatcar. He threw up his hands, looked on all sides, and trembled from outraged feelings.

And the train moved along.

Well, a certain number of bees did manage to hop on after the train was in motion. But the majority remained in the fields and groves.

The train disappeared from sight.

The stationmaster returned to the station and got down to work. He was writing something in his records and drinking tea with lemon.

Suddenly he heard a kind of noise in the station.

He opened the window to see what had happened, and he saw that the waiting passengers were in an uproar, running and bustling about.

The stationmaster asked, "What happened?"

They answered, "Some bees have stung three passengers. And now they're attacking the rest. There are so many of them that they darken the sky."

Then the stationmaster saw that a whole cloud of bees was swirling around his station.

Naturally, they were looking for their flatcar. But the car wasn't there. It had gone. And so they were attacking people and everything else around.

The stationmaster was just about to move away from the window to go out into the station when a swarm of enraged bees flew in through the window. He grabbed a towel and started waving it around to chase the bees out of the room.

But apparently this was his downfall.

Two bees stung him on the neck. A third, on the ear. And a fourth stung him on the forehead.

Wrapping the towel around him, the stationmaster lay down on the sofa and began to emit piteous groans.

Soon his assistant ran in and said, "You're not the only one. The bees have stung the telegrapher on duty on the cheek, and now he refuses to work."

The stationmaster, lying on the sofa, said, "Oh, what shall we do?"

Then another employee ran in and told the stationmaster, "The ticket seller, that is, your wife, Klavdia Ivanovna, got stung

on the nose just this minute. Now her looks are completely spoiled."

The stationmaster groaned more loudly and said, "We'll have to get back that flatcar with the crazy beekeeper as soon as we can."

He leaped from the sofa and called on the telephone. And from the next station they answered, "All right. We'll uncouple the flatcar right away. But we don't have an engine to deliver it to you with."

The stationmaster shouted, "We'll send an engine. Hurry up and uncouple the flatcar. The bees have already stung my spouse. My station, 'Polya,' is empty. All the passengers are hiding in a barn. There are only bees flying around here. And I refuse to go out; I don't care if there's a wreck!"

And so the flatcar was quickly returned. Everyone sighed with relief when they saw the flatcar with Panfilich standing on it.

Panfilich ordered them to put the flatcar in the same place where it had been standing before. And when they saw the flatcar, the bees instantly flew over to it.

There were so many bees and they were in such a hurry to get to their places that there was a terrible crush. Such a rumbling and buzzing sound arose among them that a dog began to howl and some pigeons flew skyward.

Panfilich stood on the platform, saying, "Calmly, little fellows, don't hurry! There's time. Take your places according to your tickets!"

In ten minutes everything was quiet.

Having assured himself that everything was in order, Panfilich climbed down from his car.

The people at the station applauded him, and Panfilich, like an actor, began bowing to them. He said, "Turn your collars back down. Unveil your faces! And stop trembling for your fate—no further beestings will take place."

After saying this, Panfilich went to the stationmaster.

The stationmaster, swathed in a towel, was still lying on the sofa. He was gasping and groaning. But he groaned even harder when Panfilich entered the room.

Panfilich said, "I greatly regret, honored sir, that my bees stung you. But it is your own fault. You can't be so indifferent about things, whether they are great or small. Bees will not stand for that. They'll sting people for that without further ado."

The stationmaster groaned even harder, and Panfilich continued, "Bees absolutely cannot tolerate bureaucracy or indifference to their fate. Why, you treated them the way you probably treat people—and there's your reward."

Panfilich looked out the window and added, "The sun has set. My traveling companions have taken their places. I have the honor to bid you farewell! We're ready to leave."

The stationmaster nodded weakly, as if to say, Leave as soon as possible! And he whispered softly, "Are you sure you caught all the bees? Look sharp you don't leave any of them with us!"

Panfilich said, "Even if two or three bees remain with you, that will be for your own good. They'll remind you of this occurrence with their buzzing."

With these words Panfilich left the premises.

Toward evening of the following day our glorious Panfilich arrived at his destination with his live merchandise.

The collective farmers greeted him with music.

FOR STUDY AND DISCUSSION

1. This story is little more than an anecdote. Compare it with the anecdotes in the Chinese-Japanese unit (see page 298). How are the sources of humor similar? Toward what purposes is the humor used? How are the anecdotes structured?

2. How do the manner and attitude of Panfilich add to the humor of the situation? What devices of slapstick comedy does the author use?

3. We can assume that the author's purpose is not to suggest that trains ought to be held up for bees. What, then, is he suggesting about Soviet bureaucracy, as it is represented here?

4. Do the bees in any significant ways mimic the people of the story? In certain eighteenth-century writings, bees were pointed to as an example of an efficient and harmonious society. Does that idea recur here in any way? Explain.

5. Does this story satirize people and situations that are uniquely Russian? Explain. Is the author's purpose to destroy or change conditions, or is the satire benevolent? How can you tell the difference?

6. Do you believe that the drawing of the moral toward the end is necessary? Why or why not?

The Princess and All the Kingdom

PÄR LAGERKVIST

During World War I, Lagerkvist (1891–) emerged as one of Sweden's major writers. In the 1930's he became an eloquent and demanding critic of totalitarianism and called for a society based on humanitarian ideals. Some of Lagerkvist's most powerful works are brief, realistic allegories, often set in remote times and places. His short novel *The Dwarf,* for example, is an allegory of evil, set in the household of a Renaissance prince and narrated by a depraved dwarf.

The following story appeared in 1924.

ONCE UPON A TIME there was a prince, who went out to fight in order to win the princess whose beauty was greater than all others' and whom he loved above everything. He dared his life, he battled his way step by step through the country, ravaging it; nothing could stop him. He bled from his wounds but merely cast himself from one fight to the next, the most valiant nobleman to be seen and with a shield as pure as his own young features. At last he stood outside the city where the princess lived in her royal castle. It could not hold out against him and had to beg for mercy. The gates were thrown open; he rode in as conqueror.

When the princess saw how proud and handsome he was and thought of how he had dared his life for her sake, she could not withstand his power but gave him her hand. He knelt and covered it with ardent

kisses. "Look, my bride, now I have won you!" he exclaimed, radiant with happiness. "Look, everything I have fought for, now I have won it!"

And he commanded that their wedding should take place this same day. The whole city decked itself out for the festival and the wedding was celebrated with rejoicing, pomp, and splendor.

When in the evening he went to enter the princess's bed chamber, he was met outside by the aged chancellor, a venerable man. Bowing his snow-white head, he tendered the keys of the kingdom and the crown of gold and precious stones to the young conqueror.

"Lord, here are the keys of the kingdom which open the treasuries where everything that now belongs to you is kept."

The prince frowned.

"What is that you say, old man? I do not want your keys. I have not fought for sordid gain. I have fought merely to win her whom I love, to win that which for me is the only costly thing on earth."

The old man replied, "This, too, you have won, lord. And you cannot set it aside. Now you must administer and look after it."

"Do you not understand what I say? Do you not understand that one can fight, can conquer, without asking any reward other than one's happiness—not fame and gold, not land and power on earth? Well, then, I have conquered but ask for nothing, only to live happily with what, for me, is the only thing of value in life."

"Yes, lord, you have conquered. You have fought your way forward as the bravest of the brave, you have shrunk from nothing, the land lies ravaged where you have passed by. You have won your happiness. But, lord, others have been robbed of theirs. You have conquered, and therefore everything now belongs to you. It is a big land, fertile and impoverished, mighty and laid waste, full of riches and need, full of joy and sorrow, and all is now yours. For he who has won the princess and happiness, to him also belongs this land where she was born; he shall govern and cherish it."

The prince stood there glowering and fingering the hilt of his sword uneasily.

"I am the prince of happiness, nothing else!" he burst out. "Don't want to be anything else. If you get in my way, then I have my trusty sword."

But the old man put out his hand soothingly and the young man's arm sank. He looked at him searchingly, with a wise man's calm.

"Lord, you are no longer a prince," he said gently. "You are a king."

And lifting the crown with his aged hands, he put it on the other's head.

When the young ruler felt it on his brow he stood silent and moved, more erect than before. And gravely, with his head crowned for power on earth, he went in to his beloved to share her bed.

FOR STUDY AND DISCUSSION

1. How can you tell that this story is an imitation "fairy tale" rather than an authentic folk tale? What are the characteristics of fairy tales that Lagerkvist imitates? Why does he adopt this style?

2. Clearly the situation and the contrasting attitudes of the prince and the old chancellor are intended to point a moral about something other than the problems of kingship. What is the basic theme or principle that the story deals with? What specific situations can you think of that this story could appropriately be applied to?

The Little Shoemakers

ISAAC BASHEVIS SINGER

Isaac Bashevis Singer (1904–   ) was born in a Jewish ghetto in Poland when that country was still part of the Russian Empire. For seven generations, his ancestors had been Chassidic rabbis, men of great learning and piety who were widely sought out for their knowledge of the Torah, the Jewish code of law. But, as his elder brother Israel had already done, Isaac broke from the ancient Chassidic tradition, left the rabbinical seminary in Warsaw, and eventually took up writing. In 1935 he came to the United States to be a writer for the *Jewish Daily Forward,* to which Israel was already a regular contributor.

In Yiddish, a language spoken less and less these days, Singer writes of the Jews of Eastern Europe whose three-millennia-old culture almost totally vanished in Hitler's concentration camps. In many ways, his marvelous stories reflect the conflict between the traditional pieties of the old and new worldliness of the young. Aware of the frailties of man and of the profound emptiness of some aspects of modern life, Singer feels that bridging the abyss requires the most delicate balance between past and present, between what is known and what is unknown. His stories have a moral quality—though without being didactic—that transcends their limited setting. In the words of critic Albert H. Friedlander, Singer's characters "are always individual and not paradigms of the Jew or non-Jew." Singer "does not mourn for them as a type that has been annihilated by the Nazis; he recalls each one as a human being containing a spark of divinity and deserving of his own memorial prayer."

1

THE SHOEMAKERS AND THEIR FAMILY TREE

THE FAMILY of the little shoemakers was famous not only in Frampol but in the outlying district—in Yonev, Kreshev, Bilgoray, and even in Zamoshoh. Abba Shuster, the founder of the line, appeared in Frampol some time after Chmielnitzki's

pogroms.[1] He bought himself a plot of ground on the stubby hill behind the butcher stalls, and there he built a house that remained standing until just the other day. Not that it was in such fine condition —the stone foundation settled, the small windows warped, and the shingled roof turned a moldy green and was hung with swallows' nests. The door, moreover, sank into the ground; the banisters became bowlegged; and instead of stepping up onto the threshold, one was obliged to

[1] **Chmielnitzki's pogroms:** In 1648–49 Bogdan Zinovi Chmielnitzki incited the Cossacks and peasants in the Ukraine to rise against Jews, who served as administrators and leaseholders of his estates. In the pogrom 300,000 Jews were tortured and massacred.

step down. All the same, it did survive the innumerable fires that devastated Frampol in the early days. But the rafters were so rotten that mushrooms grew on them, and when wood dust was needed to staunch the blood of a circumcision, one had only to break off a piece of the outer wall and rub it between one's fingers. The roof, pitched so steeply that the chimney-sweep was unable to climb onto it to look after the chimney, was always catching fire from the sparks. It was only by the grace of God that the house was not overtaken by disaster.

The name of Abba Shuster is recorded, on parchment, in the annals of the Frampol Jewish community. It was his custom to make six pairs of shoes every year for distribution among widows and orphans; in recognition of his philanthropy the synagogue called him to the reading of the Torah under the honorific title, *Murenu,* meaning "our teacher."

His stone in the old cemetery had vanished, but the shoemakers knew a sign for the grave—nearby grew a hazelnut tree. According to the old wives, the tree sprang from Reb [1] Abba's beard.

Reb Abba had five sons; they settled, all but one, in the neighboring towns; only Getzel remained in Frampol. He continued his father's charitable practice of making shoes for the poor, and he too was active in the gravediggers' brotherhood.

The annals go on to say that Getzel had a son, Godel, and that to Godel was born Treitel, and to Treitel, Gimpel. The shoemaker's art was handed down from one generation to the next. A principle was fast established in the family, requiring the eldest son to remain at home and succeed his father at the workbench.

The shoemakers resembled one another. They were all short, sandy-haired, and sound, honest workmen. The people of Frampol believed that Reb Abba, the head of the line, had learned shoemaking from a master of the craft in Brod, who

---

[1] **Reb:** a Yiddish honorific, like "master."

divulged to him the secret of strenthening leather and making it durable. In the cellar of their house the little shoemakers kept a vat for soaking hides. God knows what strange chemicals they added to the tanning fluid. They did not disclose the formula to outsiders, and it was handed on from father to son.

As it is not our business to deal with all the generations of the little shoemakers, we will confine ourselves to the last three. Reb Lippe remained without heir till his old age, and it was taken for a certainty that the line would end with him. But when he was in his late sixties his wife died and he married a milkmaid, who bore him six children. The eldest son, Feivel, was quite well to do. He was prominent in community affairs, attended all the important meetings, and for years served as sexton of the tailors' synagogue. It was the custom in this synagogue to select a new sexton every Simchath Torah. The man so selected was honored by having a pumpkin placed on his head; the pumpkin was set with lighted candles, and the lucky fellow was led about from house to house and refreshed at each stop with wine and strudel or honeycakes. However, Reb Feivel happened to die on Simchath Torah, the day of rejoicing over the Law, while dutifully making these rounds; he fell flat in the marketplace, and there was no reviving him. Because Feivel had been a notable philanthropist, the rabbi who conducted his services declared that the candles he had borne on his head would light his way to paradise. The will found in his strongbox requested that when he was carried to the cemetery, a hammer, an awl, and a last should be laid on the black cloth over his coffin, in sign of the fact that he was a man of peaceful industry who never cheated his customers. His will was done.

Feivel's eldest son was called Abba, after the founder, Like the rest of his stock, he was short and thickset, with a broad yellow beard, and a high forehead lined with wrinkles, such as only rabbis and shoemakers have. His eyes were also yellow, and the overall impression he created was that of a sulky hen. Nevertheless he was a clever workman, charitable like his forebears, and unequaled in Frampol as a man of his word. He would never make a promise unless he was sure he could fulfill it; when he was not sure he said: who knows, God willing, or maybe. Furthermore he was a man of some learning. Every day he read a chapter of the Torah in Yiddish translation and occupied his free time with chapbooks. Abba never missed a single sermon of the traveling preachers who came to town, and he was especially fond of the biblical passages which were read in the synagogue during the winter months. When his wife, Pesha, read to him, of a Sabbath, from the Yiddish translation of the stories in the Book of Genesis, he would imagine that he was Noah, and that his sons were Shem, Ham, and Japheth. Or else he would see himself in the image of Abraham, Isaac, or Jacob. He often thought that if the Almighty were to call on him to sacrifice his eldest son, Gimpel, he would rise early in the morning and carry out his commands without delay. Certainly he would have left Poland and the house of his birth and gone wandering over the earth where God sent him. He knew the story of Joseph and his brothers by heart, but he never tired of reading it over again. He envied the ancients because the King of the Universe revealed himself to them and performed miracles for their sake, but consoled himself by thinking that from him, Abba, to the Patriarchs, there stretched an unbroken chain of generations—as if he too were part of the Bible. He sprang from Jacob's loins; he and his sons were of the seed whose number had become like the sand and the stars. He was living in exile because the Jews of the Holy Land had sinned, but he awaited the Redemption, and he would be ready when the time came.

Abba was by far the best shoemaker in Frampol. His boots were always a perfect fit, never too tight or too roomy.

People who suffered from chilblains, corns, or varicose veins were especially pleased with his work, claiming that his shoes relieved them. He despised the new styles, the gimcrack boots and slippers with fancy heels and poorly stitched soles that fell apart with the first rain. His customers were respectable burghers of Frampol or peasants from the surrounding villages, and they deserved the best. He took their measurements with a knotted string, as in the old days. Most of the Frampol women wore wigs, but his wife, Pesha, covered her head with a bonnet as well. She bore him seven sons, and he named them after his forefathers—Gimpel, Getzel, Treitel, Godel, Feivel, Lippe, and Chananiah. They were all short and sandy-haired like their father. Abba predicted that he would turn them into shoemakers, and as a man of his word he let them look on at the workbench while they were still quite young, and at times taught them the old maxim—good work is never wasted.

He spent sixteen hours a day at the bench, a sack spread on his knees, gouging holes with the awl, sewing with a wire needle, tinting and polishing the leather or scraping it with a piece of glass; and while he worked he hummed snatches from the canticles of the Days of Awe. Usually the cat huddled nearby and watched the proceedings as though she were looking after him. Her mother and grandmother had caught mice, in their time, for the little shoemakers. Abba could look down the hill through the window and see the whole town and a considerable distance beyond, as far as the road to Bilgoray and the pine woods. He observed the groups of matrons who gathered every morning at the butcher stalls and the young men and idlers who went in and out of the courtyard of the synagogue; the girls going to the pump to draw water for tea, and the women hurrying at dusk to the ritual bath.

Evenings, when the sun was setting, the house would be pervaded by a dusky glow. Rays of light danced in the corners, flicked across the ceiling, and set Abba's beard gleaming with the color of spun gold. Pesha, Abba's wife, would be cooking *kasha* and soup in the kitchen, the children would be playing, neighboring women and girls would go in and out of the house. Abba would rise from his work, wash his hands, put on his long coat, and go off to the tailors' synagogue for evening prayers. He knew that the wide world was full of strange cities and distant lands, that Frampol was actually no bigger than a dot in a small prayer book; but it seemed to him that his little town was the navel of the universe and that his own house stood at the very center. He often thought that when the Messiah came to lead the Jews to the land of Israel, he, Abba, would stay behind in Frampol, in his own house, on his own hill. Only on the Sabbath and on Holy Days would he step into a cloud and let himself be flown to Jerusalem.

2

ABBA AND HIS ELEVEN SONS

SINCE GIMPEL was the eldest, and therefore destined to succeed his father, he came foremost in Abba's concern. He sent him to the best Hebrew teachers and even hired a tutor who taught him the elements of Yiddish, Polish, Russian, and arithmetic. Abba himself led the boy down into the cellar and showed him the formula for adding chemicals and various kinds of bark to the tanning fluid. He revealed to him that in most cases the right foot is larger than the left, and that the source of all trouble in the fitting of shoes is usually to be found in the big toes. Then he taught Gimpel the principles for cutting soles and inner soles, snub-toed and pointed shoes, high heels and low; and for fitting customers with flat feet, bunions, hammer toes, and calluses.

On Fridays, when there was always a rush of work to get out, the older boys would leave *cheder* at ten in the morning and help their father in the shop. Pesha baked *chalah* and prepared their lunch. She would grasp the first loaf and carry it, hot from the oven, blowing on it all the while and tossing it from hand to hand, to show it to Abba, holding it up, front and back, till he nodded approval. Then she would return with a ladle and let him sample the fish soup or ask him to taste a crumb of freshly baked cake. Pesha valued his judgment. When she went to buy cloth for herself or the children she brought home swatches for him to choose. Even before going to the butcher she asked his opinion—what should she get, breast or roast, flank or ribs? She consulted him not out of fear or because she had no mind of her own, but simply because she had learned that he always knew what he was talking about. Even when she was sure he was wrong, he would turn out to be right, after all. He never browbeat her, but merely cast a glance to let her know when she was being a fool. This was also the way he handled the children. A strap hung on the wall, but he seldom made use of it; he had his way by kindness. Even strangers respected him. The merchants sold him hides at a fair price and presented no objections when he asked for credit. His own customers trusted him and paid his prices without a murmur. He was always called sixth to the reading of the Torah in the tailors' synagogue—a considerable honor—and when he pledged or was assessed for money, it was never necessary to remind him. He paid up, without fail, right after the Sabbath. The town soon learned of his virtues, and though he was nothing but a plain shoemaker and, if the truth be told, something of an ignoramus, they treated him as they would a distinguished man.

When Gimpel turned thirteen, Abba girded the boy's loins in sackcloth and put him to work at the bench. After Gimpel, Getzel, Treitel, Godel, and Feivel became apprentices. Though they were his own sons and he supported them out of his earnings, he nevertheless paid them a wage. The two youngest boys, Lippe and Chananiah, were still attending the elementary *cheder,* but they too lent a hand at hammering pegs. Abba and Pesha were proud of them. In the morning the six workers trooped into the kitchen for breakfast, washed their six pairs of hands with the appropriate benediction, and their six mouths chewed the roasted groats and corn bread.

Abba loved to place his two youngest boys one on each knee, and sing an old Frampol song to them:

"A mother had
Ten little boys,
Oh, Lord, ten little boys!

The first one was Avremele,
The second one was Beréle,
The third one was called Gimpele,
The fourth one was called Dovid'l,
The fifth one was called Hershele . . ."

And all the boys came in on the chorus:

"Oh, Lord, Hershele!"

Now that he had apprentices, Abba turned out more work, and his income grew. Living was cheap in Frampol, and since the peasants often made him a present of a measure of corn or a roll of butter, a sack of potatoes or a pot of honey, a hen or a goose, he was able to save some money on food. As their prosperity increased, Pesha began to talk of rebuilding the house. The rooms were too narrow, the ceiling was too low. The floor shook underfoot. Plaster was peeling off the walls, and all sorts of maggots and worms crawled through the woodwork. They lived in constant fear that the ceiling would fall on their heads. Even though they kept a cat, the place was infested with mice. Pesha insisted that they tear down this ruin and build a larger house.

Abba did not immediately say no. He told his wife he would think it over. But after doing so, he expressed the opinion that he would rather keep things as they were. First of all, he was afraid to tear down the house, because this might bring bad luck. Second, he feared the evil eye —people were grudging and envious enough. Third, he found it hard to part with the home in which his parents and grandparents, and the whole family, stretching back for generations, had lived and died. He knew every corner of the house, each crack and wrinkle. When one layer of paint peeled off the wall, another, of a different color, was exposed; and behind this layer, still another. The walls were like an album in which the fortunes of the family had been recorded. The attic was stuffed with heirlooms—tables and chairs, cobbler's benches and lasts, whetstones and knives, old clothes, pots, pans, bedding, salting boards, cradles. Sacks full of torn prayer books lay spilled on the floor.

Abba loved to climb up to the attic on a hot summer's day. Spiders spun great webs, and the sunlight filtering in through cracks fell upon the threads in rainbows. Everything lay under a thick coat of dust. When he listened attentively he would hear a whispering, a murmuring and soft scratching, as of some unseen creature engaged in endless activity, conversing in an unearthly tongue. He was sure that the souls of his forefathers kept watch over the house. In much the same way he loved the ground on which it stood. The weeds were as high as a man's head. There was a dense growth of hairy and brambly vegetation all about the place— the very leaves and twigs would catch hold of one's clothing as though with teeth and claws. Flies and midges swarmed in the air and the ground crawled with worms and snakes of all description. Ants had raised their hills in this thicket; field mice had dug their holes. A pear tree grew in the midst of this wilderness; every year, at the time of the Feast of the Tabernacle, it yielded small fruit with the taste and hardness of wood. Birds and bees flew over this jungle, great big golden-bellied flies. Toadstools sprang up after each rain. The ground was unkept, but an unseen hand guarded its fertility.

When Abba stood here looking up at

the summer sky, losing himself in contemplation of the clouds, shaped like sailboats, flocks of sheep, brooms, and elephant herds, he felt the presence of God, his providence and his mercy. He could virtually see the Almighty seated on his throne of glory, the earth serving him as a footstool. Satan was vanquished; the angels sang hymns. The Book of Memory in which were recorded all the deeds of men lay open. From time to time, at sunset, it even seemed to Abba that he saw the river of fire in the nether world. Flames leaped up from the burning coals; a wave of fire rose, flooding the shores. When he listened closely he was sure he heard the muffled cries of sinners and the derisive laughter of the evil host.

No, this was good enough for Abba Shuster. There was nothing to change. Let everything stand as it had stood for ages, until he lived out his allotted time and was buried in the cemetery among his ancestors, who had shod the sacred community and whose good name was preserved not only in Frampol but in the surrounding district.

3

GIMPEL EMIGRATES TO AMERICA

THEREFORE THE PROVERB SAYS: Man proposes, God disposes.

One day while Abba was working on a boot, his eldest son, Gimpel, came into the shop. His freckled face was heated, his sandy hair disheveled under the skullcap. Instead of taking his place at the bench, he stopped at his father's side, regarded him hesitantly, and at last said, "Father, I must tell you something."

"Well, I'm not stopping you," replied Abba.

"Father," he cried, "I'm going to America."

Abba dropped his work. This was the last thing he expected to hear, and up went his eyebrows.

"What happened? Did you rob someone? Did you get into a fight?"

"No, Father."

"Then why are you running away?"

"There's no future for me in Frampol."

"Why not? You know a trade. God willing, you'll marry some day. You have everything to look forward to."

"I'm sick of small towns; I'm sick of the people. This is nothing but a stinking swamp."

"When they get around to draining it," said Abba, "there won't be any more swamp."

"No, Father, that's not what I mean."

"Then what do you mean?" cried Abba angrily. "Speak up!"

The boy spoke up, but Abba couldn't understand a word of it. He laid into synagogue and state with such venom, Abba could only imagine that the poor soul was possessed: the Hebrew teachers beat the children; the women empty their slop pails right outside the door; the shopkeepers loiter in the streets; there are no toilets anywhere, and the public relieves itself as it pleases, behind the bathhouse or out in the open, encouraging epidemics and plagues. He made fun of Ezreal the Healer and of Mecheles the Marriage Broker, nor did he spare the rabbinical court and the bath attendant, the washerwoman and the overseer of the poorhouse, the professions and the benevolent societies.

At first Abba was afraid that the boy had lost his mind, but the longer he continued his harangue, the clearer it became that he had strayed from the path of righteousness. Jacob Reifman, the atheist, used to hold forth in Shebreshin, not far from Frampol. A pupil of his, a detractor of Israel, was in the habit of visiting an aunt in Frampol and had gathered quite a following among the good-for-nothings. It had never occurred to Abba that his Gimpel might fall in with this gang.

"What do you say, Father?" asked Gimpel.

Abba thought it over. He knew that there was no use arguing with Gimpel, and he remembered the proverb: A rotten apple spoils the barrel. "Well," he replied, "what can I do? If you want to go, go. I won't stop you."

And he resumed his work.

But Pesha did not give in so easily. She begged Gimpel not to go so far away; she wept and implored him not to bring shame on the family. She even ran to the cemetery, to the graves of her forefathers, to seek the intercession of the dead. But she was finally convinced that Abba was right: it was no use arguing. Gimpel's face had turned hard as leather, and a mean light showed in his yellow eyes. He had become a stranger in his own home. He spent that night out with friends, and returned in the morning to pack his prayer shawl and phylacteries, a few shirts, a blanket, and some hard-boiled eggs—and he was all set to go. He had saved enough money for passage. When his mother saw that it was settled, she urged him to take at least a jar of preserves, a bottle of cherry juice, bedding, pillows. But Gimpel refused. He was going to steal over the border into Germany, and he stood a better chance if he traveled light. In short, he kissed his mother, said good-by to his brothers and friends, and off he went. Abba, not wanting to part with his son in anger, took him in the wagon to the station at Reivetz. The train arrived in the middle of the night with a hissing and whistling, a racket and din. Abba took the headlights of the locomotive for the eyes of a hideous devil, and shied away from the funnels with their columns of sparks and smoke and their clouds of steam. The blinding lights only intensified the darkness. Gimpel ran around with his baggage like a madman, and his father ran after him. At the last moment the boy kissed his father's hand, and Abba called after him, into the darkness, "Good luck! Don't forsake your religion!"

The train pulled out, leaving a smell of smoke in Abba's nostrils and a ringing in his ears. The earth trembled under his feet. As though the boy had been dragged off by demons! When he returned home and Pesha fell on him, weeping, he said to her, "The Lord gave and the Lord has taken away. . . ."

Months passed without word from Gimpel. Abba knew that this was the way with young men when they leave home— they forget their dearest ones. As the proverb says: Out of sight, out of mind. He doubted that he would ever hear from him, but one day a letter came from America. Abba recognized his son's handwriting. Gimpel wrote that he crossed the border safely, that he saw many strange cities and spent four weeks on board ship, living on potatoes and herring because he did not want to touch improper food. The ocean was very deep and the waves as high as the sky. He saw flying fish but no mermaids or mermen, and he did not hear them singing. New York is a big city, the houses reach into the clouds. The trains go over the roofs. The Gentiles speak English. No one walks with his eyes on the ground; everybody holds his head high. He met a lot of his countrymen in New York; they all wear short coats. He too. The trade he learned at home has come in very handy. He is *all right;* he is earning a living. He will write again, a long letter. He kisses his father and mother and his brothers, and sends regards to his friends.

A friendly letter after all.

In his second letter Gimpel announced that he had fallen in love with a girl and bought her a diamond ring. Her name is Bessie; she comes from Rumania; and she works *at dresses*. Abba put on his spectacles with the brass frames and spent a long time puzzling this out. Where did the boy learn so many English words? The third letter stated that he was married and that *a reverend* had performed the service. He enclosed a snapshot of himself and wife.

Abba could not believe it. His son was wearing a gentleman's coat and a high hat. The bride was dressed like a countess in a white dress, with train and veil; she held a bouquet of flowers in her hand.

Pesha took one look at the snapshot and began to cry. Gimpel's brothers gaped. Neighbors came running, and friends from all over town; they could have sworn that Gimpel had been spirited away by magic to a land of gold, where he had taken a princess to wife—just as in the storybooks the pack merchants brought to town.

To make a long story short, Gimpel induced Getzel to come to America, and Getzel brought over Treitel; Godel followed Treitel, and Feivel, Godel; and all five brothers brought the young Lippe and Chananiah across. Pesha lived only for the mail. She fastened a charity box to the doorpost, and whenever a letter came she dropped a coin through the slot. Abba worked all alone. He no longer needed apprentices because he now had few expenses and could afford to earn less; in fact, he could have given up work altogether, as his sons sent him money from abroad. Nevertheless he rose at his usual early hour and remained at the bench until late in the evening. His hammer sounded away, joined by the cricket on the hearth, the mouse in its hole, the shingles crackling on the roof. But his mind reeled. For generations the little shoemakers had lived in Frampol. Suddenly the birds had flown the coop. Was this a punishment, a judgment, on him? Did it make sense?

Abba bored a hole, stuck in a peg, and murmured, "So—you, Abba, know what you're doing and God does not? Shame on you, fool! His will be done. Amen!"

4

THE SACK OF FRAMPOL

Almost forty years went by. Pesha had long since died of cholera, during the Austrian occupation. And Abba's sons had grown rich in America. They wrote every week, begging him to come and join them, but he remained in Frampol, in the same house on the stubby hill. His own grave lay ready, next to Pesha's, among the little shoemakers; the stone had already been raised; only the date was missing. Abba put up a bench by the side of her grave, and on the eve of Rosh Hashonah or during fasts, he went there to pray and read Lamentations. He loved it in the cemetery. The sky was so much clearer and loftier than in town, and a great, meaningful silence rose from the consecrated ground and the old gravestone overgrown with moss. He loved to sit and look at the tall white birches, which trembled even when no breeze blew, and at the crows balancing in the branches, like black fruit. Before she died, Pesha made him promise that he would not remarry and that he would come regularly to her grave with news of the children. He kept his promise. He would stretch out alongside the mound and whisper into her ear, as if she were still alive, "Gimpel has another grandchild. Getzel's youngest daughter is engaged, thank God. . . ."

The house on the hill was nearly in ruins. The beams had rotted away, and the roof had to be supported by stone posts. Two of the three windows were boarded over because it was no longer possible to fit glass to the frames. The floor ·was all but gone, and the bare ground lay exposed to the feet. The pear tree in the garden had withered; the trunk and branches were covered with scales. The garden itself was now overgrown with poisonous berries and grapes, and there was a profusion of the burrs that children throw about on Tishe b'Av. People swore they saw strange fires burning there at night and claimed that the attic was full of bats which fly into girls' hair. Be that as it may, an owl certainly did hoot somewhere near the house. The neighbors repeatedly warned Abba to move out of this ruin before it was too late—the least wind might knock it over. They pleaded with him to give up working—his sons were showering him with money. But Abba stubbornly rose at dawn and continued at the shoemaker's bench. Although yellow hair does not readily change color, Abba's beard had turned completely white, and the white, staining, had turned yellow again. His brows had sprouted like brushes and hid his eyes, and his high forehead was like a piece of yellow parchment. But he had not lost his touch. He could still turn out a stout shoe with a broad heel, even if it did take a little longer. He bored holes with the awl, stitched with the needle, hammered his pegs, and in a hoarse voice sang the old shoemaker's song:

> "A mother bought a billy goat,
> The shochet killed the billy goat,
> Oh, Lord, the billy goat!
> Avremele took its ears,
> Berele took its lung,
> Gimpele took the gullet
> And Dovid'l took the tongue,
> Hershele took the neck. . . ."

As there was no one to join him, he now sang the chorus alone:

> "Oh, Lord, the billy goat!"

His friends urged him to hire a servant, but he would not take a strange woman into the house. Occasionally one of the neighbor women came in to sweep and dust, but even this was too much for him. He got used to being alone. He learned to cook for himself and would prepare soup on the tripod and on Fridays even put up the pudding for the Sabbath. Best of all, he liked to sit alone at the bench and follow the course of his thoughts, which had become more and more tangled with the years. Day and night he carried on conversations with himself. One voice asked questions, the other answered. Clever words came to his mind, sharp, timely expressions full of the wisdom of age, as though his grandfathers had come to life again and were conducting their endless disputations inside his head on matters pertaining to this world and the next. All his thoughts ran on one theme: What is life and what is death, what is time that goes on without stopping, and how far away is America? His eyes would close;

the hammer would fall out of his hand; but he would still hear the cobbler's characteristic rapping—a soft tap, a louder one, and a third, louder still—as if a ghost sat at his side, mending unseen shoes. When one of the neighbors asked him why he did not go to join his sons, he would point to the heap on the bench and say, "Nu, and the shoes? Who will mend them?"

Years passed, and he had no idea how or where they vanished. Traveling preachers passed through Frampol with disturbing news of the outside world. In the tailors' synagogue, which Abba still attended, the young men spoke of war and anti-Semitic decrees, of Jews flocking to Palestine. Peasants who had been Abba's customers for years suddenly deserted him and took their trade to Polish shoemakers. And one day the old man heard that a new world war was imminent. Hitler—may his name vanish!—had raised his legions of barbarians and was threatening to grab up Poland. This scourge of Israel had expelled the Jews from Germany, as in the days of Spain. The old man thought of the Messiah and became terribly excited. Who knows? Perhaps this was the battle of Gog and Magog? Maybe the Messiah really was coming and the dead would rise again! He saw the graves opening and the little shoemakers stepping forth—Abba, Getzel, Treitel, Gimpel, his grandfather, his own father. He called them all into his house and set out brandy and cakes. His wife, Pesha, was ashamed to find the house in such condition, but "Never mind," he assured her, "we'll get someone to sweep up. As long as we're all together!" Suddenly a cloud appears, envelops the town of Frampol—synagogue, House of Study, ritual bath, all the Jewish homes, his own among them—and carries the whole settlement off to the Holy Land. Imagine his amazement when he encounters his sons from America. They fall at his feet, crying, "Forgive us, Father!"

When Abba pictured this event his hammer quickened in tempo. He saw the little shoemakers dress for the Sabbath in silks and satins, in flowing robes with broad sashes, and go forth rejoicing in Jerusalem. They pray in the Temple of Solomon, drink the wine of paradise, and eat of the mighty steer and Leviathan. The ancient Jochanan the Shoemaker, renowned for his piety and wisdom, greets the family and engages them in a discussion of Torah and shoemaking. Sabbath over, the whole clan returns to Frampol, which has become part of the Land of Israel, and reenters the old home. Even though the house is as small as ever, it has miraculously grown roomy enough, like the hide of a deer, as it is written in the Book. They all work at one bench, Abbas, Gimpels, Getzels, Godels, the Treitels and the Lippes, sewing golden sandals for the daughters of Zion and lordly boots for the sons. The Messiah himself calls on the little shoemakers and has them take his measure for a pair of silken slippers.

One morning, while Abba was wandering among his thoughts, he heard a tremendous crash. The old man shook in his bones: the blast of the Messiah's trumpet! He dropped the boot he had been working on and ran out in ecstasy. But it was not Elijah the Prophet proclaiming the Messiah. Nazi planes were bombing Frampol. Panic spread through the town. A bomb fell near the synagogue, so loud that Abba felt his brain shudder in his skull. Hell opened before him. There was a blaze of lightning, followed by a blast that illuminated all of Frampol. A black cloud rose over the courtyard of the synagogue. Flocks of birds flapped about in the sky. The forest was burning. Looking down from his hill, Abba saw the orchards under great columns of smoke. The apple trees were blossoming and burning. Several men who stood near him threw themselves down on the ground and shouted to him to do the same. He did not hear them; they were moving their lips in dumbshow. Shaking with fright, his knees knocking together, he reentered the house and packed a sack with his prayer shawl and phylacteries, a shirt, his shoe-

maker's tools, and the paper money he had put away in the straw mattress. Then he took up a stick, kissed the *mezzuzah*, and walked out the door. It was a miracle that he was not killed; the house caught fire the moment he left. The roof swung out like a lid, uncovering the attic with its treasures. The walls collapsed. Abba turned about and saw the shelf of sacred books go up in flames. The blackened pages turned in the air, glowing with fiery letters like the Torah given the Jews on Mount Sinai.

5

ACROSS THE OCEAN

FROM THAT DAY ON, Abba's life was transformed beyond recognition—it was like a story he had read in the Bible, a fantastic tale heard from the lips of a visiting preacher. He had abandoned the house of his forefathers and the place of his birth and, staff in hand, gone wandering into the world like the Patriarch Abraham. The havoc in Frampol and the surrounding villages brought Sodom and Gomorrah to mind, burning like a fiery furnace. He spent his nights in the cemetery together with the other Jews, lying with his head on a gravestone—he too, as Jacob did at Beth-El, on the way from Beer Sheba to Haran.

On Rosh Hashonah the Frampol Jews held services in the forest, with Abba leading the most solemn prayer of the Eighteen Benedictions because he was the only one with a prayer shawl. He stood under a pine tree, which served as an altar, and in a hoarse voice intoned the litany of the Days of Awe. A cuckoo and a woodpecker accompanied him, and all the birds roundabout twittered, whistled, and screeched. Late summer gossamers wafted through the air and trailed onto Abba's beard. From time to time a lowing sounded through the forest, like a blast on the ram's horn. As the Day of Atonement drew near, the Jews of Frampol rose at midnight to say the prayer for forgiveness, reciting it in fragments, whatever they could remember. The horses in the surrounding pastures whinnied and neighed, frogs croaked in the cool night. Distant gunfire sounded intermittently; the clouds shone red. Meteors fell; flashes of lightning played across the sky. Half-starved little children, exhausted from crying, took sick and died in their mothers' arms. There were many burials in the open fields. A woman gave birth.

Abba felt he had become his own great-great-grandfather, who had fled Chmielnitzki's pogroms, and whose name is recorded in the annals of Frampol. He was ready to offer himself in Sanctification of the Name. He dreamed of priests and Inquisitions, and when the wind blew among the branches he heard martyred Jews crying out, "Hear, O Israel, the Lord our God, the Lord is One!"

Fortunately Abba was able to help a good many Jews with his money and shoemaker's tools. With the money they hired wagons and fled south, toward Rumania; but often they had to walk long distances, and their shoes gave out. Abba would stop under a tree and take up his tools. With God's help, they surmounted danger and crossed the Rumanian frontier at night. The next morning, the day before Yom Kippur, an old widow took Abba into her house. A telegram was sent to Abba's sons in America, informing them that their father was safe.

You may be sure that Abba's sons moved heaven and earth to rescue the old man. When they learned of his whereabouts they ran to Washington and with great difficulty obtained a visa for him; then they wired a sum of money to the consul in Bucharest, begging him to help their father. The consul sent a courier to Abba, and he was put on a train to Bucharest. There he was held a week, then transferred to an Italian seaport, where he was shorn and deloused and had his clothes steamed. He was put on board the last ship for the United States.

It was a long and severe journey. The train from Rumania to Italy dragged on, uphill and down, for thirty-six hours. He was given food, but for fear of touching anything ritually unclean he ate nothing at all. His phylacteries and prayer shawl got lost, and with them he lost all track of time and could no longer distinguish between Sabbath and weekdays. Apparently he was the only Jewish passenger on board. There was a man on the ship who spoke German, but Abba could not understand him.

It was a stormy crossing. Abba spent almost the whole time lying down, and frequently vomited gall, though he took nothing but dry crusts and water. He would doze off and wake to the sound of the engines throbbing day and night, to the long, threatening signal blasts, which reeked of fire and brimstone. The door of his cabin was constantly slamming to and fro, as though an imp were swinging on it. The glassware in the cupboard trembled and danced; the walls shook; the deck rocked like a cradle.

During the day Abba kept watch at the porthole over his bunk. The ship would leap up as if mounting the sky, and the torn sky would fall as though the world were returning to original chaos. Then the ship would plunge back into the ocean, and once again the firmament would be divided from the waters, as in the Book of Genesis. The waves were a sulfurous yellow and black. Now they would sawtooth out to the horizon like a mountain range, reminding Abba of the Psalmist's words: "The mountains skipped like rams, the little hills like lambs." Then they would come heaving back, as in the miraculous Parting of the Waters. Abba had little learning, but biblical references ran through his mind, and he saw himself as the prophet Jonah, who fled before God. He too lay in the belly of a whale and, like Jonah, prayed to God for deliverance. Then it would seem to him that this was not ocean but limitless desert, crawling with serpents, monsters, and dragons, as it is written in Deuteronomy. He hardly slept a wink at night. When he got up to relieve himself, he would feel faint and lose his balance. With great difficulty he would regain his feet and, his knees buckling under, go wandering, lost, down the narrow, winding corridor, groaning and calling for help until a sailor led him back to the cabin. Whenever this happened he was sure that he was dying. He would not even receive decent Jewish burial, but be dumped in the ocean. And he made his confession, beating his knotty fist on his chest and exclaiming, "Forgive me, Father!"

Just as he was unable to remember when he began his voyage, so he was unaware when it came to an end. The ship had already been made fast to the dock in New York harbor, but Abba hadn't the vaguest notion of this. He saw huge buildings and towers, but mistook them for the pyramids of Egypt. A tall man in a white hat came into the cabin and shouted something at him, but he remained motionless. At last they helped him dress and led him out on deck, where his sons and daughters-in-law and grandchildren were waiting. Abba was bewildered; a crowd of Polish landowners, counts and countesses, Gentile boys and girls, leaped at him, hugged him, and kissed him, crying out in a strange language, which was both Yiddish and not Yiddish. They half led, half carried him away, and placed him in a car. Other cars arrived, packed with Abba's kinfolk, and they set out, speeding like shot arrows over bridges, rivers, and roofs. Buildings rose up and receded, as if by magic, some of the buildings touching the sky. Whole cities lay spread out before him; Abba thought of Pithom and Rameses. The car sped so fast, it seemed to him the people in the streets were moving backward. The air was full of thunder and lightning; a banging and trumpeting, it was a wedding and a conflagration at once. The nations had gone wild, a heathen festival . . .

His sons were crowding around him. He saw them as in a fog and did not know them. Short men with white hair. They

shouted, as if he were deaf.
"I'm Gimpel!"
"Getzel!"
"Feivel!"

The old man closed his eyes and made no answer. Their voices ran together; everything was turning pell-mell, topsy-turvy. Suddenly he thought of Jacob arriving in Egypt, where he was met by Pharaoh's chariots. He felt he had lived through the same experience in a previous incarnation. His beard began to tremble; a hoarse sob rose from his chest. A forgotten passage from the Bible stuck in his gullet.

Blindly he embraced one of his sons and sobbed out, "Is this you? Alive?"

He had meant to say: "Now let me die, since I have seen thy face, because thou art yet alive."

6

THE AMERICAN HERITAGE

Abba's sons lived on the outskirts of a town in New Jersey. Their seven homes, surrounded by gardens, stood on the shore of a lake. Every day they drove to the shoe factory, owned by Gimpel, but on the day of Abba's arrival they took a holiday and prepared a feast in his honor. It was to be held in Gimpel's house, in full compliance with the dietary laws. Gimpel's wife, Bessie, whose father had been a Hebrew teacher in the old country, remembered all the rituals and observed them carefully, going so far as to cover her head with a kerchief. Her sisters-in-law did the same, and Abba's sons put on the skullcaps they had once worn during Holy Days. The grandchildren and great-grandchildren, who did not know a word of Yiddish, actually learned a few phrases. They had heard the legends of Frampol and the little shoemakers and the first Abba of the family line. Even the gentiles in the neighborhood were fairly well acquainted with this history. In the ads Gimpel published in the papers, he had proudly disclosed that his family belonged to the shoemaking aristocracy:

Our experience dates back three hundred years to the Polish city of Brod, where our ancestor, Abba, learned the craft from a local master. The community of Frampol, in which our family worked at its trade for fifteen generations, bestowed on him the title of Master in recognition of his charitable services. This sense of public responsibility has always gone hand in hand with our devotion to the highest principles of the craft and our strict policy of honest dealing with our customers.

The day Abba arrived, the papers in Elizabeth carried a notice to the effect that the seven brothers of the famous shoe company were welcoming their father from Poland. Gimpel received a mass of congratulatory telegrams from rival manufacturers, relatives, and friends.

It was an extraordinary feast. Three tables were spread in Gimpel's dining room; one for the old man, his sons, and daughters-in-law, another for the grandchildren, and the third for the great-grandchildren. Although it was broad daylight, the tables were set with candles —red, blue, yellow, green—and their flames were reflected from the dishes and silverware, the crystal glasses and the wine cups; the decanters reminiscent of the Passover seder. There was an abundance of flowers in every available corner. To be sure, the daughters-in-law would have preferred to see Abba properly dressed for the occasion, but Gimpel put his foot down, and Abba was allowed to spend his first day in the familiar long coat, Frampol style. Even so, Gimpel hired a photographer to take pictures of the banquet—for publication in the newspapers—and invited a rabbi and a cantor to the feast to honor the old man with traditional song.

Abba sat in an armchair at the head of the table. Gimpel and Getzel brought in a bowl and poured water over his hands for the benediction before eating. The food was served on silver trays. Fruit juices and salads were set before the old man, sweet brandies, cognac, caviar. But Pharaoh, Joseph, Potiphar's wife, the Land of Goshen, the chief baker, and the chief butler spun round and round in his head. His hands trembled so that he was unable to feed himself, and Gimpel had to help him. No matter how often his sons spoke to him, he still could not tell them apart. Whenever the phone rang he jumped— the Nazis were bombing Frampol. The entire house was whirling round and round like a carousel; the tables were standing on the ceiling and everyone sat upside down. His face was sickly pale in the light of the candles and the electric bulbs. He fell asleep soon after the soup course, while the chicken was being served. Quickly they led him to the bedroom, undressed him, and called a doctor.

He spent several weeks in bed, in and out of consciousness, fitfully dozing as in a fever. He even lacked the strength to say his prayers. There was a nurse at his bedside day and night. Eventually he recovered enough to take a few steps outdoors, in front of the house, but his senses remained disordered. He would walk into clothes closets, lock himself into the bathroom and forget how to come out; the doorbell and the radio frightened him; and he suffered constant anxiety because of the cars that raced past the house. One day Gimpel brought him to a synagogue ten miles away, but even here he was bewildered. The sexton was clean-shaven; the candelabra held electric lights; there was no courtyard, no faucet for washing one's hands, no stove to stand around. The cantor, instead of singing like a cantor should, babbled and croaked. The congregation wore tiny little prayer shawls, like scarves around their necks. Abba was sure he had been hauled into church to be converted. . . .

When spring came and he was no better, the daughters-in-law began to hint that it wouldn't be such a bad idea to put him in a home. But something unforeseen took place. One day, as he happened to open a closet, he noticed a sack lying on the floor which seemed somehow familiar. He looked again and recognized his shoemaker's equipment from Frampol: last, hammer and nails, his knife and pliers, the file and the awl, even a broken-down shoe. Abba felt a tremor of excitement; he could hardly believe his eyes. He sat down on a footstool and began to poke about with fingers grown clumsy and stale. When Bessie came in and found him playing with a dirty old shoe, she burst out laughing.

"What are you doing, Father? Be careful, you'll cut yourself, God forbid!"

That day Abba did not lie in bed dozing. He worked busily till evening and even ate his usual piece of chicken with greater appetite. He smiled at the grandchildren when they came in to see what he was doing. The next morning, when Gimpel told his brothers how their father had returned to his old habits, they laughed and thought nothing more of it—but the activity soon proved to be the old man's salvation. He kept at it day after day without tiring, hunting up old shoes in the clothes closets and begging his sons to supply him with leather and tools. When they gave in, he mended every last pair of shoes in the house—man, woman, and child's. After the Passover holidays the brothers got together and decided to build a little hut in the yard. They furnished it with a cobbler's bench, a stock of leather soles and hides, nails, dyes, brushes— everything remotely useful in the craft.

Abba took on new life. His daughters-in-law cried, he looked fifteen years younger. As in the Frampol days, he now rose at dawn, said his prayers, and got right to work. Once again he used a knotted string as a measuring tape. The first pair of shoes, which he made for Bessie, became the talk of the neighborhood. She had always complained of her feet, but this pair, she insisted, were the most comfortable shoes she had ever worn. The other girls soon followed her example and

also had themselves fitted. Then came the grandchildren. Even some of the gentile neighbors came to Abba when they heard that in sheer joy of the work he was turning out custom-made shoes. He had to communicate with them, for the most part, in gestures, but they got along very well. As for the younger grandchildren and the great-grandchildren, they had long been in the habit of standing at the door to watch him work. Now he was earning money, and he plied them with candies and toys. He even whittled a stylus and began to instruct them in the elements of Hebrew and piety.

One Sunday, Gimpel came into the workshop and, no more than half in earnest, rolled up his sleeves and joined Abba at the bench. The other brothers were not to be outdone, and on the following Sunday eight work stools were set up in the hut. Abba's sons spread sackcloth aprons on their knees and went to work, cutting soles and shaping heels, boring holes and hammering pegs, as in the good old days. The women stood outside, laughing, but they took pride in their men, and the children were fascinated. The sun streamed in through the windows, and motes of dust danced in the light. In the high spring sky, lofting over the grass and the water, floated clouds in the form of brooms, sailboats, flocks of sheep, herds of elephants. Birds sang; flies buzzed; butterflies fluttered about.

Abba raised his dense eyebrows, and his sad eyes looked around at his heirs, the seven shoemakers: Gimpel, Getzel, Treitel, Godel, Feivel, Lippe, and Chananiah. Their hair was white, though yellow streaks remained. No, praise God, they had not become idolaters in Egypt. They had not forgotten their heritage, nor had they lost themselves among the unworthy. The old man rattled and bumbled deep in his chest, and suddenly began to sing in a stifled, hoarse voice:

> "A mother had
> Ten little boys,
> Oh, Lord, ten little boys!

The sixth one was called Velvele,
The seventh one was Zeinvele,
The eighth one was called Chenele,
The ninth one was called Tevele,
The tenth one was called Judele . . ."

And Abba's sons came in on the chorus:

"Oh, Lord, Judele!"

FOR STUDY AND DISCUSSION

1. What are you told about the appearance of Frampol and of Abba Shuster's house? about the family lineage of Abba Shuster? about the customs and daily life of the family and the community? What is the purpose of all this detail?

2. What are the most distinctive qualities of this family and of their way of life? Why is Gimpel's departure a mortal blow; in other words, why can they not continue essentially unchanged even though one member of the family lives elsewhere?

3. How does Singer manage to show that these people are persecuted? What effect does persecution have upon their way of life?

4. What qualities of life in America are described in contrast to qualities of life in the old country? Does Singer imply that one way is better than the other? Does Abba's acceptance of his situation at the end amount to an endorsement of the new way of life? Explain your answers.

5. What emotional tone does Singer give to the story? How does this tone affect your attitude toward the way of life he is re-creating?

6. Clearly, one purpose of "The Little Shoemakers" is to make the reader know and feel what life was like for a pious Jewish family living in a central European town, from the turn of the century up to the outbreak of World War II. Compare Singer's purpose in his story with the purpose of Katherine Mansfield in "The Wind Blows" and of James Joyce in "Araby." Do these two stories depend on a specific time and setting for their effects? Explain. Could Singer's story have been set in another time and place and still have achieved its effect? Explain.

The Guest

ALBERT CAMUS

"For more than twenty years of absolutely insane history, lost hopelessly like all those of my age in the convulsions of the epoch, I derived comfort from the vague impression that writing was an honor today because it obligated a man, obligated him to more than just writing. It obligated me in particular, such as I was, to bear—along with all the others living the same history—the tribulation and hope we shared." Camus (1913–1960) spoke these words at his acceptance of the Nobel prize for literature in 1957. As might be expected, his whole life—his writings and his actions—was a response to the anxieties that have characterized the generations living in a "century of fear."

Camus is world-famous as a novelist, though he considered himself primarily a man of the theater, as actor, director, and playwright. He was born in Algiers, and French North Africa is the setting for his earliest fictional sketches and for his two major novels, *The Stranger* and *The Plague*. During the German occupation of France in World War II, Camus was a vigorous worker in the underground resistance movement. For twenty years he was deeply concerned with the problems of Algeria, and as the struggle became more fanatical on both sides—French and Algerian—Camus spoke out, warning, suggesting, protesting. Yet, scandalized as he might be, Camus felt that the artist's task is always to reconcile: "No great work of genius," he wrote, "has ever been founded on hatred or contempt."

Camus died instantly when a car driven by a friend crashed into a tree on a road to Paris.

THE ABSURD

Camus' name has been associated with a way of viewing what he calls the "absurdity" of man's existence. In general, Camus' outlook, modified over the course of his life, was an answer to the outlook of the French existentialists, inheritors of the pessimism and skepticism of the *fin de siècle*. These existential thinkers had destroyed the façade of orderliness with which previous rational philosophies had viewed life, and most of them were left with the conviction that life had no meaning, so it mattered little how man lived it.

In reaction to these nihilistic attitudes, Camus sought his own answers to the Why, which, he said, one day appears in a man's life. Camus did affirm that the mind cannot answer this Why. Hence, existence is absurd because life remains meaningless; man is a lonely stranger in the universe, an exile from a lost home which he cannot even remember. However, Camus also concluded that since man's only certainty is life, he must respond positively to the summons to live and even to struggle. To be a man, to live, is what counts, and to be a man involves choice, responsibility, and action.

One of Camus' famous heroes is Sisyphus. In mythology, Sisyphus was condemned by the gods to roll a huge boulder to the top of a mountain, but the rock always rolled back down as soon as it reached the summit. Camus, in an essay called "The Myth of Sisyphus" (1943), sees Sisyphus, pursuing a hopeless task, as an image of man; because he accepts his meaningless struggle toward a never-to-be-achieved summit, perhaps even scorns it, Sisyphus is happy. "His rock is his thing," says Camus. He does not allow it to lie inert at the bottom of the slope. To extend the analogy, Camus says that life is our thing. What matters most is that we do something with it.

THE SCHOOLMASTER was watching the two men climb toward him. One was on horseback, the other on foot. They had not yet tackled the abrupt rise leading to the schoolhouse built on the hillside. They were toiling onward, making slow progress in the snow, among the stones, on the vast expanse of the high, deserted plateau. From time to time, the horse stumbled. Without hearing anything yet, he could see the breath issuing from the horse's nostrils. One of the men, at least, knew the region. They were following the trail although it had disappeared days ago under a layer of dirty white snow. The schoolmaster calculated that it would take them half an hour to get onto the hill. It was cold; he went back into the school to get a sweater.

He crossed the empty, frigid classroom. On the blackboard the four rivers of France, drawn with four different colored chalks, had been flowing toward their estuaries for the past three days. Snow had suddenly fallen in mid-October after eight months of drought without the transition of rain, and the twenty pupils, more or less, who lived in the villages scattered over the plateau had stopped coming. With fair weather they would return. Daru now heated only the single room that was his lodging, adjoining the classroom and giving also onto the plateau to the east. Like the class windows, his window looked to the south too. On that side the school was a few kilometers from the point where the plateau began to slope

toward the south. In clear weather could be seen the purple mass of the mountain range where the gap opened onto the desert.

Somewhat warmed, Daru returned to the window from which he had first seen the two men. They were no longer visible. Hence they must have tackled the rise. The sky was not so dark, for the snow had stopped falling during the night. The morning had opened with a dirty light which had scarcely become brighter as the ceiling of clouds lifted. At two in the afternoon it seemed as if the day were merely beginning. But still this was better than those three days when the thick snow was falling amid unbroken darkness with little gusts of wind that rattled the double door of the classroom. Then Daru had spent long hours in his room, leaving it only to go to the shed and feed the chickens or get some coal. Fortunately the delivery truck from Tadjid, the nearest village to the north, had brought his supplies two days before the blizzard. It would return in forty-eight hours.

Besides, he had enough to resist a siege, for the little room was cluttered with bags of wheat that the administration left as a stock to distribute to those of his pupils whose families had suffered from the drought. Actually they had all been victims because they were all poor. Every day Daru would distribute a ration to the children. They had missed it, he knew, during these bad days. Possibly one of the fathers or big brothers would come this afternoon and he could supply them with grain. It was just a matter of carrying them over to the next harvest. Now shiploads of wheat were arriving from France and the worst was over. But it would be hard to forget that poverty, that army of ragged ghosts wandering in the sunlight, the plateaus burned to a cinder month after month, the earth shriveled up little by little, literally scorched, every stone bursting into dust under one's foot. The sheep had died then by thousands and even a few men, here and there, sometimes without anyone's knowing.

In contrast with such poverty, he who lived almost like a monk in his remote schoolhouse, nonetheless satisfied with the little he had and with the rough life, had felt like a lord with his whitewashed walls, his narrow couch, his unpainted shelves, his well, and his weekly provision of water and food. And suddenly this snow, without warning, without the foretaste of rain. This is the way the region was, cruel to live in, even without men—who didn't help matters either. But Daru had been born here. Everywhere else, he felt exiled.

He stepped out onto the terrace in front of the schoolhouse. The two men were now halfway up the slope. He recognized the horseman as Balducci, the old gendarme he had known for a long time. Balducci was holding on the end of a rope an Arab who was walking behind him with hands bound and head lowered. The gendarme waved a greeting to which Daru did not reply, lost as he was in contemplation of the Arab dressed in a faded blue jellaba,[1] his feet in sandals but covered with socks of heavy raw wool, his head surmounted by a narrow, short *chèche*.[2] They were approaching. Balducci was holding back his horse in order not to hurt the Arab, and the group was advancing slowly.

Within earshot, Balducci shouted: "One hour to do the three kilometers from El Ameur!" Daru did not answer. Short and square in his thick sweater, he watched them climb. Not once had the Arab raised his head. "Hello," said Daru when they got up onto the terrace. "Come in and warm up." Balducci painfully got down from his horse without letting go the rope.

[1] **jellaba:** a loose woolen garment with a hood.
[2] **chèche:** a brimless cap.

From under his bristling mustache he smiled at the schoolmaster. His little dark eyes, deep-set under a tanned forehead, and his mouth surrounded with wrinkles made him look attentive and studious. Daru took the bridle, led the horse to the shed, and came back to the two men, who were now waiting for him in the school. He led them into his room. "I am going to heat up the classroom," he said. "We'll be more comfortable there." When he entered the room again, Balducci was on the couch. He had undone the rope tying him to the Arab, who had squatted near the stove. His hands still bound, the *chèche* pushed back on his head, he was looking toward the window. At first Daru noticed only his huge lips, fat, smooth, almost Negroid; yet his nose was straight, his eyes were dark and full of fever. The *chèche* revealed an obstinate forehead and, under the weathered skin now rather discolored by the cold, the whole face had a restless and rebellious look that struck Daru when the Arab, turning his face toward him, looked him straight in the eyes. "Go into the other room," said the schoolmaster, "and I'll make you some mint tea." "Thanks," Balducci said. "What a chore! How I long for retirement." And addressing his prisoner in Arabic: "Come on, you." The Arab got up and, slowly, holding his bound wrists in front of him, went into the classroom.

With the tea, Daru brought a chair. But Balducci was already enthroned on the nearest pupil's desk and the Arab had squatted against the teacher's platform facing the stove, which stood between the desk and the window. When he held out the glass of tea to the prisoner, Daru hesitated at the sight of his bound hands. "He might perhaps be untied." "Sure," said Balducci. "That was for the trip." He started to get to his feet. But Daru, setting the glass on the floor, had knelt beside the Arab. Without saying anything, the Arab watched him with his feverish eyes. Once his hands were free, he rubbed his swollen wrists against each other, took the glass of tea, and sucked up the burning liquid in swift little sips.

"Good," said Daru. "And where are you headed?"

Balducci withdrew his mustache from the tea. "Here, son."

"Odd pupils! And you're spending the night?"

"No. I'm going back to El Ameur. And you will deliver this fellow to Tinguit. He is expected at police headquarters."

Balducci was looking at Daru with a friendly little smile.

"What's this story?" asked the schoolmaster. "Are you pulling my leg?"

"No, son. Those are the orders."

"The orders? I'm not . . ." Daru hesitated, not wanting to hurt the old Corsican. "I mean, that's not my job."

"What! What's the meaning of that? In wartime people do all kinds of jobs."

"Then I'll wait for the declaration of war!"

Balducci nodded.

"O.K. But the orders exist and they concern you too. Things are brewing, it appears. There is talk of a forthcoming revolt. We are mobilized, in a way."

Daru still had his obstinate look.

"Listen, son," Balducci said. "I like you and you must understand. There's only a dozen of us at El Ameur to patrol throughout the whole territory of a small department and I must get back in a hurry. I was told to hand this guy over to you and return without delay. He couldn't be kept there. His village was beginning to stir; they wanted to take him back. You must take him to Tinguit tomorrow before the day is over. Twenty kilometers shouldn't faze a husky fellow like you. After that, all will be over. You'll come back to your pupils and your comfortable life."

Behind the wall the horse could be heard snorting and pawing the earth. Daru was looking out the window. Decidedly, the weather was clearing and the light was increasing over the snowy plateau. When all the snow was melted, the sun would take over again and once more would burn the fields of stone. For days, still, the unchanging sky would shed its dry light on the solitary expanse where nothing had any connection with man.

"After all," he said, turning around toward Balducci, "what did he do?" And, before the gendarme had opened his mouth, he asked: "Does he speak French?"

"No, not a word. We had been looking for him for a month, but they were hiding him. He killed his cousin."

"Is he against us?"

"I don't think so. But you can never be sure."

"Why did he kill?"

"A family squabble, I think. One owed the other grain, it seems. It's not at all clear. In short, he killed his cousin with a billhook. You know, like a sheep, *kreezk!*"

Balducci made the gesture of drawing a blade across his throat and the Arab, his attention attracted, watched him with a sort of anxiety. Daru felt a sudden wrath against the man, against all men with their rotten spite, their tireless hates, their blood lust.

But the kettle was singing on the stove. He served Balducci more tea, hesitated, then served the Arab again, who, a second time, drank avidly. His raised arms made the jellaba fall open and the schoolmaster saw his thin, muscular chest.

"Thanks, kid," Balducci said. "And now, I'm off."

He got up and went toward the Arab, taking a small rope from his pocket.

"What are you doing?" Daru asked dryly.

Balducci, disconcerted, showed him the rope.

"Don't bother."

The old gendarme hesitated. "It's up to you. Of course, you are armed?"

"I have my shotgun."

"Where?"

"In the trunk."

"You ought to have it near your bed."

"Why? I have nothing to fear."

"You're crazy, son. If there's an uprising, no one is safe, we're all in the same boat."

"I'll defend myself. I'll have time to see them coming."

Balducci began to laugh, then suddenly the mustache covered the white teeth.

"You'll have time? O.K. That's just what I was saying. You have always been a little cracked. That's why I like you, my son was like that."

At the same time he took out his revolver and put it on the desk.

"Keep it; I don't need two weapons from here to El Ameur."

The revolver shone against the black paint of the table. When the gendarme turned toward him, the schoolmaster caught the smell of leather and horse-flesh.

"Listen, Balducci," Daru said suddenly, "every bit of this disgusts me, and first of all your fellow here. But I won't hand him over. Fight, yes, if I have to. But not that."

The old gendarme stood in front of him and looked at him severely.

"You're being a fool," he said slowly. "I don't like it either. You don't get used to putting a rope on a man even after years of it, and you're even ashamed—yes, ashamed. But you can't let them have their way."

"I won't hand him over," Daru said again.

"It's an order, son, and I repeat it."

"That's right. Repeat to them what I've said to you: I won't hand him over."

Balducci made a visible effort to reflect. He looked at the Arab and at Daru. At last he decided.

"No, I won't tell them anything. If you want to drop us, go ahead; I'll not denounce you. I have an order to deliver the prisoner and I'm doing so. And now you'll just sign this paper for me."

"There's no need. I'll not deny that you left him with me."

"Don't be mean with me. I know you'll tell the truth. You're from hereabouts and you are a man. But you must sign, that's the rule."

Daru opened his drawer, took out a little square bottle of purple ink, the red wooden penholder with the "sergeant-major" pen he used for making models of penmanship, and signed. The gendarme carefully folded the paper and put it into his wallet. Then he moved toward the door.

"I'll see you off," Daru said.

"No," said Balducci. "There's no use being polite. You insulted me."

He looked at the Arab, motionless in the same spot, sniffed peevishly, and turned away toward the door. "Good-by, son," he said. The door shut behind him. Balducci appeared suddenly outside the window and then disappeared. His footsteps were muffled by the snow. The horse stirred on the other side of the wall and several chickens fluttered in fright. A moment later Balducci reappeared outside the window leading the horse by the bridle. He walked toward the little rise without turning around and disappeared from sight with the horse following him. A big stone could be heard bouncing down. Daru walked back toward the prisoner, who, without stirring, never took his eyes off him. "Wait," the schoolmaster said in Arabic and went toward the bedroom. As he was going through the door, he had a second thought, went to the desk, took the revolver, and stuck it in his pocket. Then, without looking back, he went into his room.

For some time he lay on his couch watching the sky gradually close over, listening to the silence. It was this silence that had seemed painful to him during the first days here, after the war. He had requested a post in the little town at the base of the foothills separating the upper plateaus from the desert. There, rocky walls, green and black to the north, pink and lavender to the south, marked the frontier of eternal summer. He had been named to a post farther north, on the plateau itself. In the beginning, the solitude and the silence had been hard for him on these wastelands peopled only by stones. Occasionally, furrows suggested cultivation, but they had been dug to uncover a certain kind of stone good for building. The only plowing here was to harvest rocks. Elsewhere a thin layer of soil accumulated in the hollows would be scraped out to enrich paltry village gardens. This is the way it was: bare rock covered three quarters of the region. Towns sprang up, flourished, then disappeared; men came by, loved one another or fought bitterly, then died. No one in this desert, neither he nor his guest, mattered. And yet, outside this desert neither of them, Daru knew, could have really lived.

When he got up, no noise came from the classroom. He was amazed at the unmixed joy he derived from the mere thought that the Arab might have fled and that he would be alone with no decision to make. But the prisoner was there. He had merely stretched out between the stove and the desk. With eyes open, he was staring at the ceiling. In that position, his thick lips were particularly noticeable, giving him a pouting look. "Come," said Daru. The Arab got up and followed him. In the bedroom, the schoolmaster pointed to a chair near the table under the window. The Arab sat down without taking his eyes off Daru.

"Are you hungry?"

"Yes," the prisoner said.

Daru set the table for two. He took flour and oil, shaped a cake in a frying-pan, and lighted the little stove that functioned on bottled gas. While the cake was cooking, he went out to the shed to get cheese, eggs, dates, and condensed milk. When the cake was done he set it on the window sill to cool, heated some condensed milk diluted with water, and beat up the eggs into an omelet. In one of his motions he knocked against the revolver stuck in his right pocket. He set the bowl down, went into the classroom, and put the revolver in his desk drawer. When he came back to the room, night was falling. He put on the light and served the Arab. "Eat," he said. The Arab took a piece of the cake, lifted it eagerly to his mouth, and stopped short.

"And you?" he asked.

"After you. I'll eat too."

The thick lips opened slightly. The Arab hesitated, then bit into the cake determinedly.

The meal over, the Arab looked at the schoolmaster. "Are you the judge?"

"No, I'm simply keeping you until tomorrow."

"Why do you eat with me?"

"I'm hungry."

The Arab fell silent. Daru got up and went out. He brought back a folding bed from the shed, set it up between the table and the stove, perpendicular to his own bed. From a large suitcase which, upright in a corner, served as a shelf for papers, he took two blankets and arranged them on the camp bed. Then he stopped, felt useless, and sat down on his bed. There was nothing more to do or to get ready. He had to look at this man. He looked at him, therefore, trying to imagine his face bursting with rage. He couldn't do so. He could see nothing but the dark yet shining eyes and the animal mouth.

"Why did you kill him?" he asked in a voice whose hostile tone surprised him.

The Arab looked away.

"He ran away. I ran after him."

He raised his eyes to Daru again and they were full of a sort of woeful interrogation. "Now what will they do to me?"

"Are you afraid?"

He stiffened, turning his eyes away.

"Are you sorry?"

The Arab stared at him openmouthed. Obviously he did not understand. Daru's annoyance was growing. At the same time he felt awkward and self-conscious with his big body wedged between the two beds.

"Lie down there," he said impatiently. "That's your bed."

The Arab didn't move. He called to Daru:

"Tell me!"

The schoolmaster looked at him.

"Is the gendarme coming back tomorrow?"

"I don't know."

"Are you coming with us?"

"I don't know. Why?"

The prisoner got up and stretched out on top of the blankets, his feet toward the window. The light from the electric bulb shone straight into his eyes and he closed them at once.

"Why?" Daru repeated, standing beside the bed.

The Arab opened his eyes under the

blinding light and looked at him, trying not to blink.

"Come with us," he said.

In the middle of the night, Daru was still not asleep. He had gone to bed after undressing completely; he generally slept naked. But when he suddenly realized that he had nothing on, he hesitated. He felt vulnerable and the temptation came to him to put his clothes back on. Then he shrugged his shoulders; after all, he wasn't a child and, if need be, he could break his adversary in two. From his bed he could observe him, lying on his back, still motionless with his eyes closed under the harsh light. When Daru turned out the light, the darkness seemed to coagulate all of a sudden. Little by little, the night came back to life in the window where the starless sky was stirring gently. The schoolmaster soon made out the body lying at his feet. The Arab still did not move, but his eyes seemed open. A faint wind was prowling around the school-house. Perhaps it would drive away the clouds and the sun would reappear.

During the night the wind increased. The hens fluttered a little and then were silent. The Arab turned over on his side with his back to Daru, who thought he heard him moan. Then he listened for his guest's breathing, become heavier and more regular. He listened to that breath so close to him and mused without being able to go to sleep. In this room where he had been sleeping alone for a year, this presence bothered him. But it bothered him also by imposing on him a sort of brotherhood he knew well but refused to accept in the present circumstances. Men who share the same rooms, soldiers or prisoners, develop a strange alliance as if, having cast off their armor with their clothing, they fraternized every evening, over and above their differences, in the ancient community of dream and fatigue. But Daru shook himself; he didn't like such musings, and it was essential to sleep.

A little later, however, when the Arab stirred slightly, the schoolmaster was still not asleep. When the prisoner made a second move, he stiffened, on the alert. The Arab was lifting himself slowly on his arms with almost the motion of a sleepwalker. Seated upright in bed, he waited motionless without turning his head toward Daru, as if he were listening attentively. Daru did not stir; it had just occurred to him that the revolver was still in the drawer of his desk. It was better to act at once. Yet he continued to observe the prisoner, who, with the same slithery motion, put his feet on the ground, waited again, then began to stand up slowly. Daru was about to call out to him when the Arab began to walk, in a quite natural but extraordinarily silent way. He was heading toward the door at the end of the room that opened into the shed. He lifted the latch with precaution and went out, pushing the door behind him but without shutting it. Daru had not stirred. "He is running away," he merely thought. "Good riddance!" Yet he listened attentively. The hens were not fluttering; the guest must be on the plateau. A faint sound of water reached him, and he didn't know what it was until the Arab again stood framed in the doorway, closed the door carefully, and came back to bed without a sound. Then Daru turned his back on him and fell asleep. Still later he seemed, from the depths of his sleep, to hear furtive steps around the school-house. "I'm dreaming! I'm dreaming!" he repeated to himself. And he went on sleeping.

When he awoke, the sky was clear; the loose window let in a cold, pure air. The Arab was asleep, hunched up under the blankets now, his mouth open, utterly relaxed. But when Daru shook him, he started dreadfully, staring at Daru with wild eyes as if he had never seen him and such a frightened expression that the schoolmaster stepped back. "Don't be afraid. It's me. You must eat." The Arab nodded his head and said yes. Calm had returned to his face, but his expression was vacant and listless.

The coffee was ready. They drank it seated together on the folding bed as they munched their pieces of the cake. Then Daru led the Arab under the shed and showed him the faucet where he washed. He went back into the room, folded the blankets and the bed, made his own bed and put the room in order. Then he went through the classroom and out onto the terrace. The sun was already rising in the blue sky; a soft, bright light was bathing the deserted plateau. On the ridge the snow was melting in spots. The stones were about to reappear. Crouched on the edge of the plateau, the schoolmaster looked at the deserted expanse. He thought of Balducci. He had hurt him, for he had sent him off in a way as if he didn't want to be associated with him. He could still hear the gendarme's farewell and, without knowing why, he felt strangely empty and vulnerable. At that moment, from the other side of the schoolhouse, the prisoner coughed. Daru listened to him almost despite himself and then, furious, threw a pebble that whistled through the air before sinking into the snow. The man's stupid crime revolted him, but to hand him over was contrary to honor. Merely thinking of it made him smart with humiliation. And he cursed at one and the same time his own people who had sent him this Arab and the Arab too who had dared to kill and not managed to get away. Daru got up, walked in a circle on the terrace, waited motionless, and then went back into the schoolhouse.

The Arab, leaning over the cement floor of the shed, was washing his teeth with two fingers. Daru looked at him and said: "Come." He went back into the room ahead of the prisoner. He slipped a hunting jacket on over his sweater and put on walking shoes. Standing, he waited until the Arab had put on his *chèche* and sandals. They went into the classroom and the schoolmaster pointed to the exit, saying: "Go ahead." The fellow didn't budge. "I'm coming," said Daru. The Arab went out. Daru went back into the room and made a package of pieces of rusk, dates, and sugar. In the classroom, before going out, he hesitated a second in front of his desk, then crossed the threshold and locked the door. "That's the way," he said. He started toward the east, followed by the prisoner. But, a short distance from the schoolhouse, he thought he heard a slight sound behind them. He retraced his steps and examined the surroundings of the house; there was no one there. The Arab watched him without seeming to understand. "Come on," said Daru.

They walked for an hour and rested beside a sharp peak of limestone. The snow was melting faster and faster and the sun was drinking up the puddles at once, rapidly cleaning the plateau, which gradually dried and vibrated like the air itself. When they resumed walking, the ground rang under their feet. From time to time a bird rent the space in front of them with a joyful cry. Daru breathed in deeply the fresh morning light. He felt a sort of rapture before the vast familiar expanse, now almost entirely yellow under its dome of blue sky. They walked an hour more, descending toward the south. They reached a level height made up of crumbly rocks. From there on, the plateau sloped down, eastward, toward a low plain where there were a few spindly trees and, to the south, toward outcroppings of rock that gave the landscape a chaotic look.

Daru surveyed the two directions. There was nothing but the sky on the horizon. Not a man could be seen. He turned toward the Arab, who was looking at him blankly. Daru held out the package to him. "Take it," he said. "There are dates, bread, and sugar. You can hold out for two days. Here are a thousand francs too." The Arab took the package and the money but kept his full hands at chest level as if he didn't know what to do with what was being given him. "Now look," the schoolmaster said as he pointed in the direction of the east, "there's the way to Tinguit. You have a two-hour walk. At Tinguit you'll find the administration and the police. They are expecting you." The

Arab looked toward the east, still holding the package and the money against his chest. Daru took his elbow and turned him rather roughly toward the south. At the foot of the height on which they stood could be seen a faint path. "That's the trail across the plateau. In a day's walk from here you'll find pasturelands and the first nomads. They'll take you in and shelter you according to their law." The Arab had now turned toward Daru and a sort of panic was visible in his expression. "Listen," he said. Daru shook his head: "No, be quiet. Now I'm leaving you." He turned his back on him, took two long steps in the direction of the school, looked hesitantly at the motionless Arab, and started off again. For a few minutes he heard nothing but his own step resounding on the cold ground and did not turn his head. A moment later, however, he turned around. The Arab was still there on the edge of the hill, his arms hanging now, and he was looking at the schoolmaster. Daru felt something rise in his throat. But he swore with impatience, waved vaguely, and started off again. He had already gone some distance when he again stopped and looked. There was no longer anyone on the hill.

Daru hesitated. The sun was now rather high in the sky and was beginning to beat down on his head. The schoolmaster retraced his steps, at first somewhat uncertainly, then with decision. When he reached the little hill, he was bathed in sweat. He climbed it as fast as he could and stopped, out of breath, at the top. The rock-fields to the south stood out sharply against the blue sky, but on the plain to the east a steamy heat was already rising. And in that slight haze, Daru, with heavy heart, made out the Arab walking slowly on the road to prison.

A little later, standing before the window of the classroom, the schoolmaster was watching the clear light bathing the whole surface of the plateau, but he hardly saw it. Behind him on the blackboard, among the winding French rivers, sprawled the clumsily chalked-up words he had just read: "You handed over our brother. You will pay for this." Daru looked at the sky, the plateau, and, beyond, the invisible lands stretching all the way to the sea. In this vast landscape he had loved so much, he was alone.

FOR STUDY AND DISCUSSION

1. Daru has an isolated job among half-comprehending, pitiful strangers in a hostile, desert land. How do you know that Camus thinks of Daru's situation as an image of the human condition? How is Daru's condition more like than unlike that of a man who holds a busy and profitable job and lives with his family in a comfortable home?

2. How does the sense that all men are essentially in the same condition affect Daru's feelings and actions? What is Balducci's conflicting attitude?

3. If Daru is representative of a human situation, is he also individualized and distinctive? Explain. How does his individual character create the conflict in the story and affect his resolution of it?

4. What conflicts involving justice and morality are tearing at Daru? Why does he choose as he does? What contrary attitude is shown by the Arab in his choice? Does the ironic ending make Daru's choice seem foolish and wrong? Explain.

5. The story has little plot; one could say that not much "happens" in it. What accounts for the build-up of suspense and movement in the story? Why does Camus dwell upon seemingly trivial details, such as details about what is drawn on the blackboard, details about the Arab's appearance, details about Daru's preparation of a meal, and so on?

6. Who is the narrator of the story? What are the opportunities and limitations presented by this choice of narration? How do both serve the author's purposes in this story?

FOR COMPOSITION

Discuss in an essay how the experiences of Daru in "The Guest" and of the boy in "Araby" (see page 972) reveal something essential about the condition and essence of man. Which of the authors seems to be closer to agreeing with Conrad's views of man and of the causes of human unhappiness (see page 939)?

Abstract Painting

During the twentieth century the artist gradually became less interested in depicting reality. The represented object finally disappeared, and art was completely abstract. By suppressing storytelling in painting and freeing color from its representational role, Manet and the Impressionists had cleared the way for abstract art. Gauguin and Van Gogh carried the trend further toward the abstract by using unorthodox color schemes and distorted forms. It was Cézanne, however, who exerted the strongest influence on early twentieth-century painting.

Cézanne's advice to see nature in terms of the cylinder, the sphere, and the cone was followed by Picasso and Braque. They invented a new style of painting called *Cubism*. In an early Cubist painting (PLATE 1), Picasso reduced the still life—carafe, pitcher, and fruit bowl—to simple geometric forms. He then selected a basic cubic shape that he found in the still life and repeated this shape throughout, thus filling the space with a lively angular design. Picasso said: "I paint objects as I think them, not as I see them."

Later Cubist paintings by Picasso and Braque became less three-dimensional. Instead of composing with cubes, they made elaborate designs with overlapping planes. Some of these later Cubist works were puzzling at first because only fragments of the original subjects are visible. A Cubist portrait of an accordionist by Picasso was once thought to be a landscape. Despite such confusion, Cubism was the main source for advances in painting during the early twentieth century.

To the Cubist study of geometric forms, Robert Delaunay added movement and color. In one of his paintings of the Eiffel Tower (PLATE 2), by breaking, bending, and reassembling, he created poetic images of Parisian vistas as seen through the Tower. After finishing the Eiffel Tower series, Delaunay made studies of the rhythmic play of pure colors. He painted complementary colors of high intensity partly enclosed in circular forms, one of the first examples of nonobjective art in France.

Marc Chagall, gifted with a playful imagination and a pleasing sense of color, used some Cubist techniques in *Paris Through the Window* (PLATE 3). The whole surface is broken into transparent planes of color. Edges of two major planes form an arrow pointing to the man with two faces at the lower right. The human-headed cat, upside-down train, floating people and sprouting flowers are all elements of Chagall's delightful sense of fantasy.

Piet Mondrian came from Holland to Paris in 1910 when Cubism was flourishing. He began transforming his studies of nature into abstract geometric patterns. Curving branches of an apple tree, for example, became a series of curved lines supported by a few horizontals and verticals. In *Color Planes in Oval* (PLATE 4), Mondrian constructed a delicate network of vertical and horizontal lines with only a few diagonals over a background of pastel colors. In later paintings he finally limited himself to the exclusive use of right angles and primary colors. Mondrian and Kandinsky represent two schools of thought in modern art that are still diametrically opposed. Mondrian represents the logical painter, filled with restraint and discipline as he searches for order and structure. Kandinsky in his early paintings represents the romantic painter, passionately devoted to color and applying it in explosive bursts of creative energy. In 1910, while Braque and Picasso were turning still life and people into curves and angles, and Delaunay was rearranging the Eiffel Tower, Kandinsky produced the first truly nonobjective paintings. The painting represented in PLATE 5, however, still has some recognizable figures and landscape. Notice the lightning striking the trees at the upper left and the horse and rider just left of center. It was just a short step from this type of painting to his completely nonobjective canvases of the same period. At last the painter was completely independent of realism and, as Kandinsky said, "Everything is permitted."

The action painters and the tachists of several generations later were the artistic heirs of Kandinsky. For men like Pollock, De Kooning, and Kline, it was the act of painting that counted. The artist engaged in a struggle with his painting. Accidents such as spots or dribbles of paint might show him the way toward the next move in the struggle. The French school of action painting, known as Tachism (*tache* is the French word for *spot*), is related to American action painting, but it evolved independently. The French painter, Pierre Soulages, is an exponent of this movement. Soulages is concerned with space, and he portrays it with great strength and simplicity by opening up small areas of light color in his dark canvases. These small swaths of color also enable us to appreciate the sensual quality of the oily paint. The massive brushstrokes are simple, yet powerful—like steel girders in a modern building. In *April 14, 1958* (PLATE 6), by a strange coincidence, they evoke the architecture of the Guggenheim Museum, one of the most important museums of modern art in this country.

PLATE 1. PABLO PICASSO (Spanish, born 1881): *Still Life (Compotier)*. 1908. Oil on canvas, 28¾ x 25⅞ inches. (The Solomon R. Guggenheim Museum Collection, New York)

PLATE 2. ROBERT DELAUNAY (French, 1885–1941): *Eiffel Tower*. 1911. Oil on canvas, 49½ x 36½ inches. (The Solomon R. Guggenheim Collection, New York)

PLATE 3. MARC CHAGALL (Russian, born 1887): *Paris Through the Window*. 1913. Oil on canvas, 52¾ x 54¾ inches. (The Solomon R. Guggenheim Museum Collection, New York)

PLATE 4. PIET MONDRIAN (Dutch, 1872–1944): *Color Planes in Oval*. 1914?. Oil on canvas, 42⅞ x 31 inches. (Collection, The Museum of Modern Art, New York, Purchase)

PLATE 5. WASSILY KANDINSKY (Russian, 1866–1944): *Study for Composition No. 2*. 1910. Oil on canvas, 38⅝ x 51¾ inches. (The Solomon R. Guggenheim Museum Collection, New York)

PLATE 6. PIERRE SOULAGES (French, born 1919): *14 Avril 1958*. Oil on canvas, 63¾ x 51¼ inches. (The Cleveland Museum of Art, Gift of Katherine White Reswick)

Rhinoceros

EUGÈNE IONESCO

Eugène Ionesco (1912–) is primarily known as a playwright, although most of his full-length plays, including *Rhinoceros* (1960), were written first as short stories. Ionesco was born in Rumania (Ionesco is the Rumanian form of Johnson), but he has lived most of his life in France. An admirer of Albert Camus (see page 998), he has become one of the leading contributors to the so-called theater of the absurd. This movement, also known as the antitheater movement, rejects logic and traditional dramatic structure and concerns itself with representing, among other things, the void behind reality and the way contemporary society has mechanized and brutalized man. Ionesco uses startling and often bewildering combinations of Surrealism, Naturalism, comedy, and tragedy to break through the barriers of communication, to express indirectly something about what he calls "incommunicable reality." Though criticized by some as being obscure and nightmarish, his plays have established Ionesco as an internationally important dramatist who has something to say, even if it is painful to hear.

MY FRIEND JOHN and I were sitting on the terrace of a café, calmly talking about one thing and another, when suddenly from across the street we caught sight of an enormous, powerful, loudly snorting rhinoceros, charging straight ahead down the sidewalk. The pedestrians quickly got out of his path as he brushed along against the shop windows. One housewife yelped with fright and let her shopping basket fall from her hands; a bottle broke and wine began to spread across the pavement; several other people, including an old man, dashed precipitately into the nearest shops. All this lasted no longer than a lightning flash. Then people came out of the stores again and watched the progress of the rhinoceros, which was already far in the distance; after standing around and commenting on the event for a few moments, they went on their way.

My reactions are rather slow. I absent-mindedly registered the image of a running wild animal, without attaching undue importance to it. And besides, my mouth was dry that morning and I felt rather tired—all because of the drinking we had done the night before to celebrate a friend's birthday. John had not been with us, which is why, after the first moment of surprise, he was able to say: "A rhinoceros loose in the city! Doesn't it even surprise you? That kind of thing shouldn't be allowed."

"As a matter of fact," I said, "that hadn't occurred to me until now. It *is* dangerous."

"We must protest to the municipal authorities."

"Maybe it escaped from the zoo," I said.

"You're dreaming!" he replied. "There hasn't been a zoo in this town since all the animals were wiped out by the plague in the seventeenth century."

"Then perhaps it escaped from a circus."

"What circus are you talking about? The authorities have refused all vagrants permission to stay within the city limits. And no circus has passed through here since we were children."

"Maybe the beast has been hiding in the marshy woods hereabouts ever since then," I replied, yawning.

"You're completely fogged by alcoholic fumes—"

"They come up from the stomach—"

"Yes, and they affect the brain. Where have you ever seen marshy woods in these parts? Our province is called Little Castille because it's such a desert."

"Perhaps the creature took shelter under a boulder. Or maybe it built its nest on a dry branch."

"You and your paradoxes are boring. You're incapable of discussing anything seriously."

"Especially today."

"Today as usual."

"Don't get so excited, my friend. Let's not quarrel over anything so trifling as a wild animal . . ."

We changed the subject and got back to talking about the fine weather we'd been enjoying, about the rain which falls so rarely in this part of the country, and about the need to have artificial clouds constructed in the sky, and other banal and unsolvable problems.

Finally we parted. That was a Sunday. I went home to lie down, and slept the rest of the day—another Sunday wasted. On Monday morning I went to the office, solemnly promising myself I would never again get drunk, especially on a Saturday, so as not to ruin the next day, Sunday. Actually I had only one day off each week, and three weeks' vacation in the summer. Instead of drinking and then feeling ill, how much better it would be to feel fresh and fit and use my rare mo-ments of freedom in a more intelligent fashion! I'd go to the museums, read the literary magazines, attend improving lectures. And instead of spending all my available cash on liquor, why not buy theater tickets and see the interesting new plays? I've never really known anything about the avant-garde theater that everyone talks so much about, I've never even seen any plays by Ionesco. Now or never was the time to turn over a new leaf.

The following Sunday I ran into John again, and at the same café.

"I've kept my word," I told him, holding out my hand.

"What word?" he wanted to know.

"I've kept my promise to myself. I've made a vow to stop drinking. Instead of drinking, I've decided to cultivate my mind. Today, my head is clear. This afternoon I'm going to the municipal museum, and this evening to the theater. Would you like to come with me?"

"Let's hope your good intentions will last," John replied. "But I can't go with you. I've promised to meet some friends at a bar."

"Oh, my friend, now you're setting a bad example. You'll only end up by getting drunk!"

"One swallow doesn't make a summer," John said in an irritated tone. "But as for you . . ."

Our conversation was about to take a tiresome turn, when we heard a loud trumpeting, the precipitate sounds of a perissodactyl's hooves, then screams and the meowing of a cat; almost simultaneously we saw appear, then disappear, in the space of a lightning flash, a rhinoceros snorting loudly and charging full speed straight ahead along the sidewalk on the other side of the street.

Immediately after him came a woman, cradling a small, formless and bloody object in her arms. "He's crushed my cat," she wailed. "He's crushed my cat!"

Several people immediately came up to the poor disheveled woman, who appeared to be the very incarnation of desolation, and sympathized with her.

"Isn't that too bad," they said. "Poor little creature!"

John and I got to our feet. In one bound we'd crossed the street and come up to the unhappy woman.

"All cats are mortal," I said stupidly, not quite knowing how to console her.

"That's the one that charged past my shop last week," the grocer recalled.

"It's not the same one," John said. "It's not at all the same one. The one last week had two horns on his snout, he was an Asiatic rhinoceros; and the one today had only one—therefore he must be an African rhinoceros."

"You're talking nonsense," I said impatiently. "How could you make out his horns! The beast moved with such speed we were barely able to see him, let alone have enough time to count his horns."

"At least I'm not wandering around in a fog," John briskly replied. "My mind is clear, and I count quickly."

"He charged with his head lowered."

"Exactly. That made it possible to see better."

"You're only being pretentious, John. A pedant, a pedant who is not sure of his facts. In the first place, it's the Asiatic rhinoceros that has one horn on its snout and the African rhinoceros that has two!"

"You're wrong, it's the other way around."

"Do you want to bet?"

"I won't bet with you. It's you that's got two horns," he cried, red with rage. "You Asiatic!" (John is a bad loser.)

"I don't have any horns. I've never worn any. Nor am I Asiatic. On the other hand, the Asiatics are human like everybody else."

"They're yellow!" he cried, quite beside himself. He turned his back on me and marched off, cursing.

I felt ridiculous. I should have been more conciliatory and less argumentative: I knew he couldn't bear being contradicted. The least objection made him foam at the mouth. That was his only weakness; he had a heart of gold and he'd done me many good turns. Several people were standing around listening to us; now they forgot about the crushed cat and the unfortunate woman. They surrounded me, arguing; some maintained that the Asiatic rhinoceros was in fact one-horned and that therefore I was in the right; others maintained the opposite: that the one-horned rhinoceros was African and that my opponent was right.

"That's not the question," interrupted one gentleman (wearing a straw hat, a small mustache and pince-nez, his head characteristically a logician's) who until then had stood nearby without saying a word. "The argument rests on a problem you've lost sight of. At the outset the question was whether today's rhinoceros was the same as last Sunday's or whether it was another rhinoceros. That's the problem that must be resolved. You could have seen the same one-horned rhinoceros both times, just as you could have seen the same two-horned rhinoceros both times. You could also have seen a one-horned rhinoceros the first time, and then the second time another one with a single horn. And also, you could have seen a two-horned rhinoceros the first time, and then another two-horned rhinoceros the second time, and that would have been no more conclusive. For it is also possible that one and the same rhinoceros lost one of its horns in the course of the past week before it appeared again today. It is also possible that there are two two-horned rhinoceroses and that each has lost one of its horns. If you could prove that the first time you saw a one-horned rhinoceros, whether it was Asiatic or African, and that today you saw a two-horned rhinoceros, no matter what the continent of its origin, then and only then could you conclude that you were dealing with two different rhinoceroses, for it is scarcely possible that a second horn could grow on a rhinoceros' snout in the space of a few days, enough to be visible at any rate; for that would convert an Asiatic or an African rhinoceros into an

African or Asiatic rhinoceros, which is scarcely possible in all good logic, since the same creature cannot have been born in two places at the same time, nor even successively."

"That seems clear to me," I said, "but it hardly resolves the question."

"Obviously," replied the gentleman, smiling with a competent air. "But now at least the problem has been correctly stated."

"That's not the problem either," said the grocer, who appeared to care little for logic because of a passionate temperament. "Can we permit our cats to be crushed before our very eyes by a rhinoceros, whether it has two horns or one and whether it hails from Asia or Africa?"

"He's got something there," everyone exclaimed. "We cannot permit our cats to be crushed by rhinoceroses or by anything else!"

The grocer pointed theatrically to the poor weeping woman who still rocked in her arms the shapeless mass, spotted with blood, that had been her cat.

The next day I read in the newspaper, in the "Crushed Cats" column, a two-line account of the unfortunate creature's death: "Trampled underfoot by a pachyderm," it said, without giving further details.

That Sunday afternoon I did not go to the museums, and in the evening I did not get to the theater. I stayed at home alone, bored to death, bitterly regretting that I had quarreled with John. He is so sensitive, I should have spared him, I said to myself. It's absurd to get upset over such a trifle, over the horns of a rhinoceros that one has never even seen before—an animal originating in Africa or in Asia, far distant continents—how could this have mattered to me? As for John, on the other hand, he was an old friend, to whom I owed so much, and who . . .

In short, while I was promising myself that I would go see John at the earliest opportunity and make my peace with

him, I had managed to drink a whole bottle of cognac without even noticing it. I noticed it the next day, however: my hair was killing me, my throat felt like wood, my conscience was sore, I was really very uncomfortable. But duty before everything—I got to the office on time, or almost. I signed the time sheet just as they came to collect it.

"I suppose you saw rhinoceroses, too?" my boss said to me. (Much to my surprise he was already there in the office.)

"Of course I saw it," I said, taking off my suit coat and putting on an old jacket with worn elbows that I used for work.

"Ah, you saw it! There, you see!" cried Daisy, the stenographer, apparently very moved. (How pretty she was, with her rosy cheeks and her blond hair. She enchanted me. If I could fall in love, it would be with her.) "A one-horned rhinoceros!"

"Two-horned!" corrected my colleague, Émile Dudard, B.L., eminent jurist, assured of a brilliant future in the firm and perhaps in Daisy's heart as well.

"Well, I didn't see it! And I don't believe it!" declared Botard, an ex-teacher who was employed as our archivist. "And no one has ever seen one in this country, except in schoolbooks. These rhinoceroses flourish only in old wives' tales. It's all a myth, like flying saucers."

I was about to remark to Botard that the verb "flourish" applied to one or several rhinoceroses seemed inexact to me when the jurist cried: "In any case there was a cat crushed, and there are witnesses."

"Collective psychosis," replied Botard, who had advanced ideas. "It's like religion, which is the opium of the people!"

"I believe in flying saucers," said Daisy.

The boss cut our discussion short: "All right, all right! Enough of this chatter! Rhinoceros or no rhinoceros, flying saucers or not, there's work to be done!"

The stenographer started to type. I seated myself at my desk and became absorbed in my writing. Émile Dudard began to correct the proofs of a commentary on the law for the repression of alcoholism, while the boss retired into his office, slamming the door.

"It's all a hoax!" Botard was still fuming over Dudard's remarks. "It's your kind of propaganda that gives rise to these rumors!"

"It was not propaganda," I intervened.

"Since I saw it . . ." Daisy said, chiming in with my words.

"You make me laugh," Dudard said to Botard. "Propaganda? For what reason?"

"In any case, *I'm* not in the pay of the Penténégrins!"

"That's an insult!" cried Botard, striking the table with his fist.

The door of the boss's office opened suddenly; he stuck his head out. "Mr. Boeuf hasn't come in today?"

"Obviously, if he's not here," I said.

"I need him badly. Did he call in to say he was sick? If this keeps up much longer, I'm going to fire him."

This was not the first time the boss had made such threats about our colleague.

"Has any of you the key to his desk?" he continued.

At just that moment Mrs. Boeuf came into the office. She seemed frightened.

"I hope you will excuse my husband. He went home to see his family for the weekend. He has a touch of the flu. Here, he explains the whole thing in his telegram. He hopes to be back on Wednesday. Please give me a glass of water . . . and a chair!" she said, collapsing on the bench we brought to her.

"That's very annoying! But still it's no reason for you to go off the deep end!" the boss observed.

"A rhinoceros has been chasing me all the way here from my house," she stammered.

"With one horn or two?" I asked.

"Don't make me laugh!" exclaimed Botard.

"Let her speak!" Dudard said indignantly.

Mrs. Boeuf made a great effort to be more precise. "He was there, downstairs at the entrance. He seemed to want to come up."

At that moment we heard a very loud noise: apparently the stairway was collapsing under a formidable weight. We hurried out onto the landing. And sure enough, among all the debris, its head low, uttering alarmed and alarming trumpetings, there was a rhinoceros, vainly turning round and round. I could see that it had two horns.

"It's an African rhinoceros," I said, ". . . no, I mean Asiatic."

The confusion in my mind was such that I no longer knew whether two-hornedness was a characteristic of the Asiatic rhinoceros or the African, whether one-hornedness was a characteristic of the African or Asiatic rhinoceros, or whether, on the contrary, two-hornedness . . . in short, I was mentally floundering, while Botard was glaring at Dudard.

"It's an infamous plot!" he said, pointing his finger at our jurist like a prosecuting attorney. "It's all your fault!"

"It's yours!" replied the latter.

"Calm down, this is scarcely the time for that!" said Daisy, trying in vain to quiet them.

"For years now I've been telling the management they would have to replace those old worm-eaten stairs with concrete," said the boss. "It was inevitable that something like this would happen. I predicted it, and I was right!"

"As usual," Daisy said ironically. "But how are we going to get down?"

"I'll take you in my arms!" the boss joked amorously, caressing the stenographer's cheek, "and we'll jump together."

"Don't put your coarse old hand on my face, you pachyderm!"

The boss didn't have time to react to that. Mrs. Boeuf, who had got to her feet and joined us, and who for several minutes had been staring closely at the rhinoceros milling around below, uttered a terrible cry: "It's my husband! My poor Boeuf, what's happened to you?"

The rhinoceros, or perhaps Boeuf, responded by a trumpeting that was both violent and tender, while Mrs. Boeuf fainted in my arms, and Botard, lifting his to heaven, fumed: "It's sheer madness! What a lousy system!"

After we had recovered from the first moments of surprise, we telephoned the Fire Department, and the firemen came with their ladders and helped us descend. Mrs. Boeuf, although we tried to dissuade her from it, started off toward the conjugal domicile on her consort's back. She had grounds for divorce (who was at fault?), but she preferred not to desert her husband in his present condition.

At the little café where we all went to lunch (without the Boeufs, of course), we learned that several rhinoceroses had been seen in different parts of the city: seven according to some, seventeen according to others, thirty-two according to someone else. Faced with all these eyewitness accounts, Botard could no longer deny the perissodactylous evidence. But he knew, he said, what it all meant. He would explain it to us one day. There was no question of returning to the office in the afternoon—so much the worse for business. We should have to wait until they had repaired the stairs.

I took advantage of this opportunity to pay a visit to John, intending to effect a reconciliation. He was in bed.

"I don't feel very well!" he said.

"You know, John, we were both right. There are two-horned rhinoceroses in the city, as well as one-horned rhinoceroses. It matters very little what continent they come from. What really counts, as far as I can see, is the existence of the rhinoceros itself."

"I'm not feeling very well," my friend repeated, without listening to me. "I don't feel very well!"

"What's the matter with you? I'm very sorry to hear this!"

"A little fever. Migraine headache."

It happened to be his forehead that hurt him. It felt as though it was throbbing, he said. And there was actually a swelling just above his nose. His complexion was greenish and he was hoarse.

"Have you a sore throat? Maybe it is angina."

I took his pulse. Its rhythm was regular. "This can't be very serious. A few days' rest will see you through. Have you telephoned for a doctor?"

As I was letting go his wrist, I noticed that his veins were becoming distended and very prominent. Looking closer, I saw that the skin was changing color and hardening before my eyes. Perhaps it is more serious than I thought, I said to myself. Aloud I said: "We must call the doctor."

"My pajamas are binding me," he said in a raucous voice.

"What's happening to your skin? It's like leather . . ." Then, looking at him fixedly, I said: "Do you know what's happened to Boeuf? He's turned into a rhinoceros."

"What difference does that make? Worse things than that can happen! After all, rhinoceroses are creatures like you and me, they have as much right to lead their own lives as have we—"

"So long as they don't destroy ours. Have you ever taken into account the difference in mentality?"

"Do you think that ours is preferable?"

"Even so, we have our own morality, which I conceive to be incompatible with that of these animals. We have a philosophy, a system of universal values——"

"Humanism is old hat! You're a ridiculous old sentimentalist. You're boring me with this nonsense."

"I am astonished to hear you say that, my friend! Have you gone out of your mind?"

He really seemed to have gone out of it. A blind rage had disfigured his face, so transforming his voice that I could scarcely comprehend the words that issued from his mouth.

"As for hearing such things from you—" I was going to continue but he didn't give me the chance. He threw back the covers, tore off his pajamas, and rose from his bed stark naked (he! he, who was ordinarily so modest!); he was green with rage from head to foot.

The swelling on his forehead had enlarged; his eyes were fixed, he did not seem to see me any more. Or rather, yes, he saw me very well for he charged straight toward me, his head lowered. I scarcely had time to jump to one side, otherwise he'd have nailed me to the wall.

"You're a rhinoceros!" I shouted.

"I'll trample you! I'll trample you!"

I could still distinguish these words as I rushed through the door.

I descended the stairs four at a time, while the walls shook under the blows of his horn and I heard him uttering frightful trumpetings of rage.

"Call the police! Call the police! You've got a rhinoceros in the building!" I cried as I rushed past the astonished tenants who were standing on the landings and in the doorways of their apartments.

On the ground floor I only just managed to escape a rhinoceros that came out of the superintendent's apartment and tried to charge me; then at last I found myself out on the street, in a sweat, my legs collapsing, at the end of my strength.

Fortunately, a bench was there on the edge of the sidewalk. But I scarcely had time to catch my breath when I saw a whole herd of rhinoceroses rushing down the slope of the avenue. If only they would be content with the middle of the street! But no, there were so many of them that they overflowed onto the sidewalk. I leaped up from the bench and flattened myself against the wall. Puffing, trumpeting, reeking of hot animal flesh and hide, they brushed past me, enveloping me in a cloud of dust. When they had disappeared I could not sit down on the bench again: the beasts had demolished it!

I had considerable difficulty pulling myself together. For a few days I had to stay at home. Daisy came to visit me several times and kept me informed of new developments.

The first to become a rhinoceros was

our boss, to the great indignation of Botard, who nevertheless also became a rhinoceros twenty-four hours later. "One must keep up with the times!" were his last human words.

Botard's case scarcely astonished me, in spite of his seeming obduracy. I understood less well the boss's transformation. But in his case, of course, the change was no doubt involuntary; yet one would have supposed that he had enough will power to resist it.

Daisy recalled how she had pointed out to him that he had coarse hands the very day Boeuf made his appearance as a rhinoceros. This must have made a strong impression on the boss; he seemed to shrug it off at the time, but now it was clear that it had sunk in deep. "If only I had been less brutal, if I had used greater tact, this might never have happened."

"And I should have been more sympathetic with John. I should have shown him more friendship, been more understanding," I said in my turn.

Daisy informed me that Dudard had changed too, as well as a cousin of hers I had not met. And other people had also changed; friends we had in common, as well as people we did not know.

"There are a lot now," she said, "perhaps a fourth of all the inhabitants of the city."

"Nevertheless, they're still in the minority."

"Judging by the way things are going, that won't be the case for long!" she sighed.

"Alas! They're so much more powerful."

Soon everyone got used to seeing herds of rhinoceroses charging through the streets at full speed. Pedestrians took them in their stride, getting out of their way and then going on about their business as though nothing untoward had happened.

How can one be a rhinoceros! It's unthinkable! I would say to myself futilely.

After a while, the authorities proposed

herding them into great stockades. The Society for the Prevention of Cruelty to Animals opposed this measure on humanitarian grounds. And, for reasons easy enough to understand, the fact that everyone had a close relative or a friend among the rhinoceroses made it almost impossible to put the project into effect. Therefore it was abandoned.

The situation grew worse, as can be imagined. At the Ministry of Statistics the statisticians kept a census of the animals, computed approximately according to the daily increase of their number, in terms of percentage of one-horned as well as of two-horned varieties. But before long there were defections among the statisticians themselves. This inevitably resulted in an increase of salary for those that remained.

One day I perceived from my balcony, trumpeting and charging toward a meeting of his comrades, no doubt, a rhinoceros carrying a straw hat impaled on his horn.

The logician! I cried to myself. He too—how is it possible?

At that moment Daisy opened my door.

"The logician has become a rhinoceros!" I said.

She already knew it for she had just seen him on the street. She was carrying a basket of groceries.

"Shall we lunch together?" she asked. "You know, I've had a lot of trouble finding anything at all to eat. The markets have been ruined; they've devoured everything. Most of the other stores are closed down, with signs up saying 'Closed for Alterations.'"

"I love you, Daisy, don't ever leave me."

"Close the window, darling. They make too much noise, and the dust comes in even up here."

"As long as we are together, I fear nothing, and nothing else matters." Then, after closing the window: "I was afraid I would never again be able to fall in love with a woman."

I pressed her very close in my arms.

She responded to my embrace.

"How very much I want to make you happy! Could you be happy with me?"

"Why not? You declare there's nothing to fear and you're afraid of everything!"

"My love, my joy!" I babbled as I kissed her lips with an intense, poignant passion I had not known I possessed.

The ringing of the telephone interrupted us. She disengaged herself from my embrace and went to the phone, picked up the receiver, and uttered a cry: "Listen—"

I put the receiver to my ear. Wild trumpetings could be heard.

"They're playing games with us now!"

"What can be going on?" She was frightened.

We turned on the radio in order to get the news: more trumpetings. She trembled.

"Be calm," I said, "be calm!"

Terrified, she cried: "They've seized the radio stations!"

"Be calm! Be calm!" I repeated, more and more agitated.

The next day, as usual, they were running in all directions along the street. One could watch for hours and never catch sight of a single human being. Our building continually trembled under the hooves of our neighbors, the perissodactyls.

"Let come what may," said Daisy. "What do you think we should do?"

"They've all gone mad. The world is sick."

"It's not for us to cure it."

"One can no longer understand anyone. Do *you* understand them? Do you?"

"We must try to interpret their psychology, to learn their language."

"They haven't got a language."

"What do you know about it?"

"Listen, Daisy," I said, "we will have children, and our children will have children. That will take time, but the two of us will be able to regenerate humanity. All it requires is a little courage—"

"I don't want to have children."

"How do you think you can save the world, then?"

"After all, maybe it is we who need to be saved. Maybe it is we who are abnormal. Do you see any others of our species around?"

"Daisy, I don't like to hear you talk that way!" I looked at her desperately. "It's we who are in the right, Daisy, I assure you."

"What pretensions! There's no such thing as 'right.' It's the way the world is that's right, it's not you or I."

"Yes, Daisy, I know I'm right. The proof is that you understand me and that I love you as much as a man can love a woman."

"I am a little ashamed of what you call love, it's so morbid . . . it can't compare with the magnificent energy that emanates from all these creatures around us."

"Energy? There's energy for you!" I said, putting an end to the argument by giving her a slap.

Then, while she was crying, I said: "I will not abdicate, not I. I will not abdicate."

She got up in tears and threw her perfumed arms around my neck. "I will withstand everything, with you, to the end."

She was not able to keep her word. She became very sad, wasting away before my eyes. One morning she abandoned me without leaving a single word.

The situation became literally untenable for me. It was my fault that Daisy had gone. Who knew what had befallen her? Still another person on my conscience. There was not a soul who could help me find her. I imagined the worst, feeling myself responsible.

And everywhere their trumpetings, their insane charges, the clouds of dust. I tried shutting myself up in my apartment and put cotton in my ears, but I saw them even at night in my dreams.

The only solution was to convert them. But to what? Were the mutations reversible? And to convert them I would have to talk to them. In order to make them relearn my language (which moreover was already getting rusty) I would

have to learn theirs first. And I could not distinguish one trumpeting from another, one rhinoceros from another rhinoceros.

One day, looking at myself in the mirror, I saw how ugly I was with my long face; what I really needed was a horn, if not two, to enhance my sagging features.

I came to see that their trumpetings, albeit a little harsh certainly, did have a certain charm. I tried to trumpet myself, but how weak it was, how lacking in vigor! By dint of a still greater effort, I only managed to howl. Howling is not trumpeting.

I saw clearly that it is not always necessary to be in the swim and that one's own individuality is a good thing to hold onto. However, one must also participate; to distinguish oneself is all right, yes, but—from one's own kind. I no longer looked like anyone, nor anything, with the exception of a few old-fashioned photographs, which no longer bore any relationship to the living.

Every morning I looked at my hands in the hope that the palms might have coarsened during my sleep. The skin remained flabby. I contemplated my too white body, my hairy legs; ah, if only I had a tough hide and that magnificent dark green color, a decent hairless nudity like theirs!

My state of mind grew more and more wretched. I felt I was a monster. Alas, I would never become a rhinoceros. It was impossible for me to change.

I no longer dare look at myself. I am ashamed. And besides, I couldn't, no, I really couldn't.

FOR STUDY AND DISCUSSION

1. What meanings do you attach to the figure of the rhinoceros, as an image of what man can become? How does Ionesco hint that people are on their way to rhinoceroshood even before they begin developing bumps on their foreheads?

2. One theme which we can recognize in Ionesco's fable is that of conformity, as one person after another adopts a style that he had previously deplored. What insights and opin-

ions does Ionesco offer on this subject? Do you agree with his commentary? Explain.

3. Can this story be read as a political satire? Explain. What contemporary political situations could it apply to? What would lead you to think Ionesco had these situations in mind?

4. What part does the narrator play in the events he is telling about? What is the significance of the emphasis on his weaknesses? What is the significance of the love affair that he halfheartedly tries to protect from the trend toward rhinocerosism? Is the narrator heroic? Explain. What do you think will finally happen to him?

5. Like Lagerkvist's "The Princess and All the Kingdom," this story is a fable, but it is more detailed and complicated. Does Ionesco's story manage to say more than Lagerkvist's? Is it more effective as a story? Why?

6. Examine carefully the dialogue in this story. Do the people really communicate their concerns or their affections to one another? Do these people have any reality to you? Are the so-called human beings in the story any different from the rhinoceroses? Explain your answers.

7. "There's no such thing as right," says Daisy. Would your society agree? Explain.

No Witchcraft for Sale

DORIS LESSING

Doris Lessing (1919–) was born in Persia, the daughter of a British banker who subsequently became a planter in Southern Rhodesia. In short stories, novels, and plays, she has written sympathetically of the social and economic problems of black Africans who live in a state that officially sanctions racial prejudice. After spending twenty-five years in Africa, she is now a political exile from Rhodesia and lives in London.

In the preface to her collection called *African Stories,* Mrs. Lessing says that she believes that writers brought up in Africa have many advantages: "—being at the center of a modern battlefield; part of a society in rapid, dramatic change. But in the long run it can also be a handicap: to wake up every morning with one's eyes on a fresh evidence of inhumanity; to be reminded twenty times a day of injustice, and always the same brand of it, can be limiting. There are other things in living besides injustice, even for the victims of it. I know an African short-story writer whose gift is for satirical comedy, and he says that he has to remind himself, when he sits down to write, that 'as a human being he has the right to laugh.' Not only have white sympathizers criticized him for 'making comedy out of oppression,' his compatriots do too. Yet I am sure that one day out of Africa will come a great comic novel to make the angels laugh . . . .

"And while the cruelties of the white man toward the black man are among the heaviest counts in the indictment against humanity, color prejudice is not our original fault, but only one aspect of the atrophy of the imagination that prevents us from seeing ourselves in every creature that breathes under the sun.

"I believe that the chief gift from Africa to writers, white and black, is the continent itself, its presence which for some people is like an old fever, latent always in their blood; or like an old wound throbbing in the bones as the air changes. That is not a place to visit unless one chooses to be an exile ever afterward from an inexplicable majestic silence lying just over the border of memory or of thought. Africa gives you the knowledge that man is a small creature, among other creatures, in a large landscape."

THE FARQUARS had been childless for years when little Teddy was born; and they were touched by the pleasure of their servants, who brought presents of fowls and eggs and flowers to the homestead when they came to rejoice over the baby, exclaiming with delight over his downy golden head and his blue eyes. They congratulated Mrs. Farquar as if she had achieved a very great thing, and she felt that she had—her smile for the lingering, admiring natives was warm and grateful.

Later, when Teddy had his first haircut, Gideon the cook picked up the soft gold tufts from the ground, and held them reverently in his hand. Then he smiled at the little boy and said: "Little Yellow Head." That became the native name for the child. Gideon and Teddy were great friends from the first. When Gideon had finished his work, he would lift Teddy on his shoulders to the shade of a big tree and play with him there, forming curious little toys from twigs and leaves and grass, or shaping animals from wetted soil. When Teddy learned to walk it was often Gideon who crouched before him, clucking encouragement, finally catching him when he fell, tossing him up in the air till they both became breathless with laughter. Mrs. Farquar was fond of the old cook because of his love for her child.

There was no second baby; and one day Gideon said: "Ah, missus, missus, the Lord above sent this one; Little Yellow Head is the most good thing we have in our house." Because of that "we" Mrs. Farquar felt a warm impulse toward her cook; and at the end of the month she raised his wages. He had been with her now for several years; he was one of the few natives who had his wife and children in the compound and never wanted to go home to his kraal,[1] which was some hundreds of miles away. Sometimes a small piccanin [2] who had been born the same time as Teddy could be seen peering from the edge of the bush, staring in awe at the little white boy with his miraculous fair hair and Northern blue eyes. The two little children would gaze at each other with a wide, interested gaze, and once Teddy put out his hand curiously to touch the black child's cheeks and hair.

Gideon, who was watching, shook his head wonderingly, and said: "Ah, missus, these are both children, and one will grow up to be a baas,[3] and one will be a servant;" and Mrs. Farquar smiled and said sadly, "Yes, Gideon, I was thinking the same." She sighed. "It is God's will," said Gideon, who was a mission boy. The Farquars were very religious people; and this shared feeling about God bound servant and masters even closer together.

Teddy was about six years old when he was given a scooter, and discovered the intoxications of speed. All day he would fly around the homestead, in and out of flowerbeds, scattering squawking chickens and irritated dogs, finishing with a wide dizzying arc into the kitchen door. There he would cry: "Gideon, look at me!" And Gideon would laugh and say: "Very clever, Little Yellow Head." Gideon's youngest son, who was now a herdsboy, came especially up from the compound to see the scooter. He was afraid to come near it, but Teddy showed off in front of him. "Piccanin," shouted Teddy, "get out of my way!" And he raced in circles around the black child until he was frightened, and fled back to the bush.

"Why did you frighten him?" asked Gideon, gravely reproachful.

[1] **kraal:** native village, as distinct from the compound, the protected area for white settlers.
[2] **piccanin:** variant of *pickaninny,* a term of Spanish origin (probably from *pequeño* for "small"), used condescendingly to designate African children.
[3] **baas:** a Dutch word, related to the English "boss," used to designate the white settlers in their role as masters to the natives.

Teddy said defiantly: "He's only a black boy," and laughed. Then, when Gideon turned away from him without speaking, his face fell. Very soon he slipped into the house and found an orange and brought it to Gideon, saying: "This is for you." He could not bring himself to say he was sorry; but he could not bear to lose Gideon's affection either. Gideon took the orange unwillingly and sighed. "Soon you will be going away to school, Little Yellow Head," he said wonderingly, "and then you will be grown up." He shook his head gently and said, "And that is how our lives go." He seemed to be putting a distance between himself and Teddy, not because of resentment, but in the way a person accepts something inevitable. The baby had lain in his arms and smiled up into his face: the tiny boy had swung from his shoulders and played with him by the hour. Now Gideon would not let his flesh touch the flesh of the white child. He was kind, but there was a grave formality in his voice that made Teddy pout and sulk away. Also, it made him into a man: with Gideon he was polite, and carried himself formally, and if he came into the kitchen to ask for something, it was in the way a white man uses towards a servant, expecting to be obeyed.

But on the day that Teddy came staggering into the kitchen with his fists to his eyes, shrieking with pain, Gideon dropped the pot full of hot soup that he was holding, rushed to the child, and forced aside his fingers. "A snake!" he exclaimed. Teddy had been on his scooter, and had come to a rest with his foot on the side of a big tub of plants. A tree snake, hanging by its tail from the roof, had spat full into his eyes. Mrs. Farquar came running when she heard the commotion. "He'll go blind," she sobbed, holding Teddy close against her. "Gideon, he'll go blind!" Already the eyes, with perhaps half an hour's sight left in them, were swollen up to the size of fists: Teddy's small white face was distorted by great purple oozing protuberances. Gideon said: "Wait a minute, missus, I'll get some medicine." He ran off into the bush.

Mrs. Farquar lifted the child into the house and bathed his eyes with permanganate. She had scarcely heard Gideon's words; but when she saw that her remedies had no effect at all, and remembered how she had seen natives with no sight in their eyes, because of the spitting of a snake, she began to look for the return of her cook, remembering what she heard of the efficacy of native herbs. She stood by the window, holding the terrified, sobbing little boy in her arms, and peered helplessly into the bush. It was not more than a few minutes before she saw Gideon come bounding back, and in his hand he held a plant.

"Do not be afraid, missus," said Gideon, "this will cure Little Yellow Head's eyes." He stripped the leaves from the plant, leaving a small white fleshy root. Without even washing it, he put the root in his mouth, chewed it vigorously, and then held the spittle there while he took the child forcibly from Mrs. Farquar. He gripped Teddy down between his knees, and pressed the balls of his thumbs into the swollen eyes, so that the child screamed and Mrs. Farquar cried out in protest: "Gideon, Gideon!" But Gideon took no notice. He knelt over the writhing child, pushing back the puffy lids till chinks of eyeball showed, and then he spat hard, again and again, into first one eye, and then the other. He finally lifted Teddy gently into his mother's arms, and said: "His eyes will get better." But Mrs. Farquar was weeping with terror, and she could hardly thank him: it was impossible to believe that Teddy could keep his sight. In a couple of hours the swellings were gone: the eyes were inflamed and tender but Teddy could see. Mr. and Mrs. Farquar went to Gideon in the kitchen and thanked him over and over again. They felt helpless because of their gratitude: it seemed they could do nothing to express it. They gave Gideon presents for his wife and children, and a big increase in wages, but these things could not pay for Teddy's now completely cured eyes. Mrs. Farquar said: "Gideon, God chose you as an instrument for his goodness," and Gideon said: "Yes, missus, God is very good."

Now, when such a thing happens on a farm, it cannot be long before everyone hears of it. Mr. and Mrs. Farquar told their neighbors and the story was discussed from one end of the district to the other. The bush is full of secrets. No one can live in Africa, or at least on the veld, without learning very soon that there is an ancient wisdom of leaf and soil and season —and, too, perhaps most important of all, of the darker tracts of the human mind— which is the black man's heritage. Up and down the district people were telling anecdotes, reminding each other of things that had happened to them.

"But I saw it myself, I tell you. It was a puff-adder bite. The kaffir's [1] arm was swollen to the elbow, like a great shiny black bladder. He was groggy after a half a minute. He was dying. Then suddenly a kaffir walked out of the bush with his hands full of green stuff. He smeared something on the place, and next day my boy was back at work, and all you could see was two small punctures in the skin."

This was the kind of tale they told. And, as always, with a certain amount of exasperation, because while all of them knew that in the bush of Africa are waiting valuable drugs locked in bark, in simple-looking leaves, in roots, it was impossible to ever get the truth about them from the natives themselves.

The story eventually reached town; and perhaps it was at a sundowner party, or some such function, that a doctor, who happened to be there, challenged it. "Nonsense," he said. "These things get exaggerated in the telling. We are always checking up on this kind of story, and we draw a blank every time."

Anyway, one morning there arrived a strange car at the homestead, and out

<hr>

[1] **kaffir:** name to designate a member of any of several Bantu tribes, but used loosely as the equivalent of *native*.

stepped one of the workers from the laboratory in town, with cases full of test tubes and chemicals.

Mr. and Mrs. Farquar were flustered and pleased and flattered. They asked the scientist to lunch, and they told the story all over again, for the hundredth time. Little Teddy was there too, his blue eyes sparkling with health, to prove the truth of it. The scientist explained how humanity might benefit if this new drug could be offered for sale; and the Farquars were even more pleased: they were kind, simple people, who liked to think of something good coming about because of them. But when the scientist began talking of the money that might result, their manner showed discomfort. Their feelings over the miracle (that was how they thought of it) were so strong and deep and religious, that it was distasteful to them to think of money. The scientist, seeing their faces, went back to his first point, which was the advancement of humanity. He was perhaps a trifle perfunctory: it was not the first time he had come salting the tail of a fabulous bush secret.

Eventually, when the meal was over, the Farquars called Gideon into their living room and explained to him that this baas, here, was a Big Doctor from the Big City, and he had come all that way to see Gideon. At this Gideon seemed afraid; he did not understand; and Mrs. Farquar explained quickly that it was because of the wonderful thing he had done with Teddy's eyes that the Big Baas had come.

Gideon looked from Mrs. Farquar to Mr. Farquar, and then at the little boy, who was showing great importance because of the occasion. At last he said grudgingly: "The Big Baas want to know what medicine I used?" He spoke incredulously, as if he could not believe his old friends could so betray him. Mr. Farquar began explaining how a useful medicine could be made out of the root, and how it could be put on sale, and how thousands of people, black and white, up and down the continent of Africa, could be saved by the medicine when that spitting snake filled their eyes with poison. Gideon listened, his eyes bent on the ground, the skin of his forehead puckering in discomfort. When Mr. Farquar had finished he did not reply. The scientist, who all this time had been leaning back in a big chair, sipping his coffee and smiling with skeptical good humor, chipped in and explained all over again, in different words, about the making of drugs and the progress of science. Also, he offered Gideon a present.

There was silence after this further explanation, and then Gideon remarked indifferently that he could not remember the root. His face was sullen and hostile, even when he looked at the Farquars, whom he usually treated like old friends. They were beginning to feel annoyed; and this feeling annulled the guilt that had been sprung into life by Gideon's accusing manner. They were beginning to feel that he was unreasonable. But it was at that moment that they all realized he would never give in. The magical drug would remain where it was, unknown and useless except for the tiny scattering of Africans who had the knowledge, natives who might be digging a ditch for the municipality in a ragged shirt and a pair of patched shorts, but who were still born to healing, hereditary healers, being the nephews or sons of the old witch doctors whose ugly masks and bits of bone and all the uncouth properties of magic were the outward signs of real power and wisdom.

The Farquars might tread on that plant fifty times a day as they passed from house to garden, from cow kraal to mealie field, but they would never know it.

But they went on persuading and arguing, with all the force of their exasperation; and Gideon continued to say that he could not remember, or that there was no such root, or that it was the wrong season of the year, or that it wasn't the root itself, but the spit from his mouth that had cured Teddy's eyes. He said all these things one after another, and seemed not to care they were contradictory. He was rude and stubborn. The Farquars could hardly recognize their gentle, lovable old servant in this ignorant, perversely obstinate African, standing there in front of them with lowered eyes, his hands twitching his cook's apron, repeating over and over whichever one of the stupid refusals that first entered his head.

And suddenly he appeared to give in. He lifted his head, gave a long, blank angry look at the circle of whites, who seemed to him like a circle of yelping dogs pressing around him, and said: "I will show you the root."

They walked single file away from the homestead down a kaffir path. It was a blazing December afternoon, with the sky full of hot rain clouds. Everything was hot: the sun was like a bronze tray whirling overhead, there was a heat shimmer over the fields, the soil was scorching underfoot, the dusty wind blew gritty and thick and warm in their faces. It was a terrible day, fit only for reclining on a verandah with iced drinks, which is where they would normally have been at that hour.

From time to time, remembering that on the day of the snake it had taken ten minutes to find the root, someone asked: "Is it much further, Gideon?" And Gideon would answer over his shoulder, with angry politeness: "I'm looking for the root, baas." And indeed, he would frequently bend sideways and trail his hand among the grasses with a gesture that was insulting in its perfunctoriness. He walked them through the bush along unknown paths for two hours, in that melting destroying heat, so that the sweat trickled coldly down them and their heads ached. They were all quite silent: the Farquars because they were angry, the scientist because he was being proved right again; there was no such plant. His was a tactful silence.

At last, six miles from the house, Gideon suddenly decided they had had enough; or perhaps his anger evaporated at that moment. He picked up, without an attempt at looking anything but casual, a handful of blue flowers from the grass, flowers that had been growing plentifully all down the paths they had come.

He handed them to the scientist without looking at him, and marched off by himself on the way home, leaving them to follow him if they chose.

When they got back to the house, the scientist went to the kitchen to thank Gideon: he was being very polite, even though there was an amused look in his eyes. Gideon was not there. Throwing the flowers casually into the back of his car, the eminent visitor departed on his way back to his laboratory.

Gideon was back in his kitchen in time to prepare dinner, but he was sulking. He spoke to Mr. Farquar like an unwilling servant. It was days before they liked each other again.

The Farquars made inquiries about the root from their laborers. Sometimes they were answered with distrustful stares. Sometimes the natives said: "We do not know. We have never heard of the root." One, the cattle boy, who had been with them a long time, and had grown to trust them a little, said: "Ask your boy in the kitchen. Now, there's a doctor for you. He's the son of a famous medicine man who used to be in these parts, and there's nothing he cannot cure." Then he added politely: "Of course, he's not as good as the white man's doctor, we know that, but he's good for us."

After some time, when the soreness had gone from between the Farquars and Gideon, they began to joke: "When are you going to show us the snakeroot, Gideon?" And he would laugh and shake his head, saying, a little uncomfortably: "But I did show you, missus, have you forgotten?"

Much later, Teddy, as a schoolboy, would come into the kitchen and say:

"You old rascal, Gideon! Do you remember that time you tricked us all by making us walk miles all over the veld for nothing? It was so far my father had to carry me!"

And Gideon would double up with polite laughter. After much laughing, he would suddenly straighten himself up, wipe his old eyes, and look sadly at Teddy, who was grinning mischievously at him across the kitchen: "Ah, Little Yellow Head, how you have grown! Soon you will be grown up with a farm of your own . . ."

FOR STUDY AND DISCUSSION

1. Analyze the complex feelings of servants toward masters, and masters toward servants. What is the significance of the statement in the third paragraph: "Mrs. Farquar felt a warm impulse toward her cook; and at the end of the month she raised his wages"? Where else in the story do you find statements of similar significance?

2. Does the author want you to believe that "witchcraft" is the crucial element in Gideon's remedy? If not, why has modern science been unable to find a remedy to match its effectiveness? What is the scientist's attitude?

3. What interplay of feelings takes place in Gideon after he is asked to identify the plant for the investigator? What do these conflicting feelings reflect about the relationship between masters and servants?

4. Consider the four stories—"Bees and People," "The Princess and All the Kingdom," "The Cat, a Goldfinch, and the Stars," and "No Witchcraft for Sale"—as commentaries upon conditions or principles that are broader than the immediate situations of the stories themselves. To what extent is each story concerned with its subject matter, and to what extent does it have broader applications? Do any authors indicate specifically that they intend larger relevance for their stories? If not, how can you tell that they had such intentions?

Life Is Sweet at Kumansenu

ABIOSEH NICOL

Nicol was born in 1924 in Sierra Leone, one of the smallest and poorest of the west African countries. He received further education in Nigeria and in British universities, and for several years he has been associated with Cambridge University. Nicol is an experienced writer; his stories, poems, and articles have appeared in a number of publications, and in 1952 he received the Margaret Wrong Prize and Medal for Literature in Africa. Nicol's prose style is very much in the English manner, but his stories are robust and show a sharp sense of the dramatic and ironic. In the introduction to a collection of his stories, he states that he began writing because "most of those who wrote about us seldom gave any nobility to their African characters." Most of Nicol's stories are placed in colonial pre-independent Africa, with emphasis on black and white keeping their distances. The following story, however, deals with an old Yoruban (Nigerian) tribal belief. According to this belief, a dead child might creep back into its mother's womb in the form of subsequent babies, and it will haunt its mother by dying again and again, in the death of child after child. To know whether her next child will be Abiku—as the dreaded wanderer is called—a mother will brand a mark on the body of her dead child. If that mark appears on the next child she gives birth to, she knows that the wanderer, Abiku, is calling again.

THE SEA and the wet sand to one side of it; green tropical forest on the other; above it, the slow, tumbling clouds. The clean round blinding disc of sun and the blue sky covered and surrounded the small African village, Kumansenu.

A few square mud houses with roofs like helmets were here thatched, and there covered with corrugated zinc, where the prosperity of cocoa or trading had touched the head of the family.

The widow Bola stirred her palm-oil stew and thought of nothing in particular. She chewed a kola nut rhythmically with her strong toothless jaws, and soon unconsciously she was chewing in rhythm with the skipping of Asi, her granddaughter. She looked idly at Asi, as the seven-year-old brought the twisted palm-leaf rope smartly over her head and jumped over it, counting in English each time the rope struck the ground and churned up a little red dust. Bola herself did not understand English well, but she could easily count up to twenty in English, for market purposes. Asi shouted six and then said nine, ten. Bola called out that after six came seven. And I should know, she sighed. Although now she was old and her womb and breasts were withered, there was a time when she bore children regularly every two years. Six times she had borne a boy child and six times they had died. Some had swollen

"Life Is Sweet at Kumansenu" from *The Truly Married Woman* by Abioseh Nicol. Reprinted by permission of the publisher, Oxford University Press.

up and with weak plaintive cries had faded away. Others had shuddered in sudden convulsions, with burning skins, and had rolled up their eyes and died. They had all died; or rather he had died, Bola thought; because she knew it was one child all the time whose spirit had crept up restlessly into her womb to be born and mock her. The sixth time, Musa, the village magician whom time had now transformed into a respectable Muslim, had advised her and her husband to break the bones of the quiet little corpse and mangle it so that it could not come back to torment them alive again. But she had held on to the child and refused to let them mutilate it. Secretly, she had marked it with a sharp pointed stick at the left buttock before it was wrapped in a mat and taken away. When at the seventh time she had borne a son and the purification ceremonies had taken place, she had turned it surreptitiously to see whether the mark was there. It was. She showed it to the old woman who was the midwife and asked her what it was, and she had forced herself to believe that it was an accidental scratch made while the child was being scrubbed with herbs to remove placental blood. But this child had stayed. Meji, he had been called. And he was now thirty years of age and a second-class clerk in government offices in a town ninety miles away. Asi, his daughter, had been left with her to do the things an old woman wanted a small child for: to run and take messages to the neighbors, to fetch a cup of water from the earthenware pot in the kitchen, to sleep with her, and to be fondled.

She threw the washed and squeezed cassava leaves into the red boiling stew, putting in a finger's pinch of salt, and then went indoors, carefully stepping over the threshold to look for the dried red pepper. She found it and then dropped it, leaning against the wall with a little cry. He turned round from the window and looked at her with a twisted half smile of love and sadness. In his short-sleeved, open-necked white shirt and gray gabardine trousers, gold-plated wrist watch and brown suede shoes, he looked like the picture in African magazines of a handsome clerk who would get to the top because he ate the correct food or regularly took the correct laxative, which was being advertised. His skin was grayish brown and he had a large red handkerchief tied round his neck.

"Meji, God be praised," Bola cried. "You gave me quite a turn. My heart is weak and I can no longer take surprises. When did you come? How did you come? By lorry, by fishing boat? And how did you come into the house? The front door was locked. There are so many thieves nowadays. I'm so glad to see you, so glad," she mumbled and wept, leaning against his breast.

Meji's voice was hoarse, and he said, "I'm glad to see you too, mother," rubbing her back affectionately.

Asi ran in and cried "Papa, Papa," and was rewarded with a lift and a hug.

"Never mind how I came, mother," Meji said, laughing, "I'm here, and that's all that matters."

"We must make a feast, we must have a big feast. I must tell the neighbors at once. Asi, run this very minute to Mr. Addai, the catechist, and tell him your papa is home. Then to Mamie Gbera to ask her for extra provisions, and to Pa Babole for drummers and musicians . . ."

"Stop," said Meji raising his hand. "This is all quite unnecessary. I don't want to see *anyone,* no one at all. I wish to rest quietly and completely. No one is to know I'm here."

Bola looked very crestfallen. She was so proud of Meji and wanted to show him off. The village would never forgive her for concealing such an important visitor. Meji must have sensed this because he held her shoulder comfortingly and said, "They will know soon enough. Let us enjoy one another, all three of us, this time. Life is too short."

Bola turned to Asi, picked up the

packet of pepper and told her to go and drop a little into the boiling pot outside, taking care not to go too near the fire or play with it. After the child had gone, Bola said to her son, "Are you in trouble? Is it the police?"

He shook his head. "No," he said, "it's just that I like returning to you. There will always be this bond of love and affection between us, and I don't wish to share it with others. It is our private affair and that is why I've left my daughter with you." He ended up irrelevantly, "Girls somehow seem to stay with relations longer."

"And don't I know it," said Bola. "But you look pale," she continued, "and you keep scraping your throat. Are you ill?" She laid her hand on his brow. "And you're cold, too."

"It's the cold wet wind," he said, a little harshly. "I'll go and rest now if you can open and dust my room for me. I'm feeling very tired. Very tired indeed. I've travelled very far today and it has not been an easy journey."

"Of course, my son, of course," Bola replied, bustling away hurriedly but happily.

Meji slept all afternoon till evening, and his mother brought his food to his room and, later, took the empty basins away. Then he slept again till morning.

The next day, Saturday, was a busy one, and after further promising Meji that she would tell no one he was about, Bola went off to market. Meji took Asi for a long walk through a deserted path and up into the hills. She was delighted. They climbed high until they could see the village below in front of them, and the sea in the distance, and the boats with their wide white sails. Soon the sun had passed its zenith and was half way towards the west. Asi had eaten all the food, the dried fish and the flat tapioca pancakes and the oranges. Her father said he wasn't hungry, and this had made the day perfect for Asi, who had chattered, eaten, and then

played with her father's fountain pen and other things from his pocket. They soon left for home because he had promised that they would be back before dark; he had carried her down some steep boulders and she had held on to his shoulders because he had said his neck hurt so and she must not touch it. She had said, "Papa, I can see behind you and you haven't got a shadow. Why?"

He had then turned her round facing the sun. Since she was getting drowsy, she had started asking questions and her father had joked with her and humored her. "Papa, why has your watch stopped at twelve o'clock?" "Because the world ends at noon." Asi had chuckled at that. "Papa, why do you wear a scarf always round your neck?" "Because my head will fall off if I don't." She had laughed out loud at that. But soon she had fallen asleep as he bore her homewards.

Just before nightfall, with his mother dressed in her best, they had all three, at her urgent request, gone to his father's grave, taking a secret route and avoiding the main village. It was a small cemetery, not more than twenty years or so old, started when the Rural Health Department had insisted that no more burials were to take place in the backyard of households. Bola took a bottle of wine and a glass and four split halves of kola, each a half sphere, two red and two white. They reached the graveside and she poured some wine into the glass. Then she spoke to her dead husband softly and caressingly. She had brought his son to see him, she said. This son whom God had given success, to the confusion and discomfiture of their enemies. Here he was, a man with a pensionable clerk's job and not a poor farmer, a fisherman, or a simple mechanic. All the years of their married life, people had said she was a witch because her children had died young. But this boy of theirs had shown that she was a good woman. Let her husband answer her now, to show that he was listening. She threw the four kola nuts up into the air and they fell on to the grave. Three fell with the flat face upwards and one with its flat face downwards. She picked them up again and conversed with him once more and threw the kola nuts up again. But still there was an odd one or sometimes two.

They did not fall with all four faces up, or with all four faces down, to show that he was listening and was pleased. She spoke endearingly, she cajoled, she spoke severely. But all to no avail. She then asked Meji to perform. He crouched by the graveside and whispered. Then he threw the kola nuts and they rolled a little, Bola following them eagerly with her sharp old eyes. They all ended up face downwards. Meji emptied the glass of wine on the grave and then said that he felt nearer his father at that moment than he had ever done before in his life.

It was sundown, and they all three went back silently home in the short twilight. That night, going outside the house towards her son's window, she had found, to her sick disappointment, that he had been throwing all the cooked food away out there. She did not mention this when she went to say good night, but she did sniff and say that there was a smell of decay in the room. Meji said that he thought there was a dead rat up in the rafters, and he would clear it away after she had gone to bed.

That night it rained heavily, and sheet lightning turned the darkness into brief silver daylight for one or two seconds at a time. Then the darkness again and the rain. Bola woke soon after midnight and thought she could hear knocking. She went to Meji's room to ask him to open the door, but he wasn't there. She thought he had gone out for a while and had been locked out by mistake. She opened the door quickly, holding an oil lamp upwards. He stood on the veranda, curiously unwet, and refused to come in.

"I have to go away," he said hoarsely, coughing.

"Do come in," she said.

"No," he said, "I have to go, but I wanted to thank you for giving me a chance."

"What nonsense is this?" she said. "Come in out of the rain."

"I did not think I should leave without thanking you."

The rain fell hard, the door creaked, and the wind whistled.

"Life is sweet, mother dear, good-by, and thank you."

He turned round and started running. There was a sudden diffuse flash of silent lightning and she saw that the yard was empty. She went back heavily and fell into a restless sleep. Before she slept she said to herself that she must see Mr. Addai next morning, Sunday, or better still, Monday, and tell him about all this, in case Meji was in trouble. She hoped Meji would not be annoyed. He was such a good son.

But it was Mr. Addai who came instead, on Sunday afternoon, quiet and grave, and met Bola sitting on an old stool in the veranda, dressing Asi's hair in tight thin plaits.

Mr. Addai sat down and, looking away, he said, "The Lord giveth and the Lord taketh away." Soon half the village were sitting round the veranda and in the yard.

"But I tell you, he was here on Friday and left Sunday morning," Bola said. "He couldn't have died on Friday."

Bola had just recovered from a fainting fit after being told of her son's death in town. His wife, Asi's mother, had come with the news, bringing some of his property. She said Meji had died instantly at noon on Friday and had been buried on Saturday at sundown. They would have brought him to Kumansenu for burial. He had always wished that. But they could not do so in time as bodies did not last more than a day in the hot season, and there were no lorries available for hire.

"He was here, he was here," Bola said, rubbing her forehead and weeping.

Asi sat by quietly. Mr. Addai said comfortingly, "Hush, hush, he couldn't have been, because no one in the village saw him."

"He said we were to tell no one," Bola said.

The crowd smiled above Bola's head and shook their heads. "Poor woman," someone said, "she is beside herself with grief."

"He died on Friday," Mrs. Meji repeated, crying. "He was in the office and he pulled up the window to look out and call the messenger. Then the sash broke. The window fell, broke his neck, and the sharp edge almost cut his head off; they say he died at once."

"My papa had a scarf around his neck," Asi shouted suddenly.

"Hush," said the crowd.

Mrs. Meji dipped her hand into her bosom and produced a small gold locket and put it round Asi's neck, to quiet her.

"Your papa had this made last week for your Christmas present. You may as well have it now."

Asi played with it and pulled it this way and that.

"Be careful, child," Mr. Addai said, "it is your father's last gift."

"I was trying to remember how he showed me yesterday to open it," Asi said.

"You have never seen it before," Mrs. Meji said, sharply, trembling with fear mingled with anger.

She took the locket and tried to open it.

"Let me have it," said the village goldsmith, and he tried whispering magic words of incantation. Then he said, defeated, "It must be poor quality gold; it has rusted. I need tools to open it."

"I remember now," Asi said in the flat complacent voice of childhood.

The crowd gathered round quietly and the setting sun glinted on the soft red African gold of the dangling trinket. The goldsmith handed the locket over to Asi and asked in a loud whisper, "How did he open it?"

"Like so," Asi said and pressed a secret catch. It flew open and she spelled out gravely the word inside, "A-S-I."

The silence continued.

"His neck, poor boy," Bola said a little wildly. "This is why he could not eat the lovely meals I cooked for him."

Mr. Addai announced a service of intercession after vespers that evening. The crowd began to leave quietly.

Musa, the magician, was one of the last to leave. He was now very old and bent. In times of grave calamity, it was known that even Mr. Addai did not raise objection to his being consulted.

He bent over further and whispered in Bola's ear, "You should have had his bones broken and mangled thirty-one years ago when he went for the sixth time and then he would not have come back to mock you all these years by pretending to be alive. I told you so. But you women are naughty and stubborn."

Bola stood up, her black face held high, her eyes terrible with maternal rage and pride.

"I am glad I did not," she said, "and that is why he came back specially to thank me before he went for good."

She clutched Asi to her. "I am glad I gave him the opportunity to come back, for life is sweet. I do not expect you to understand why I did so. After all, you are only a man."

FOR STUDY AND DISCUSSION

1. Like the Chinese story "The Cricket Boy" (page 303), this story is based on supernatural happenings. Tell what feelings or thoughts are communicated to you through this story of the restless wanderer child whose mother defies custom to give him a chance for life. Does Nicol's story resemble in any way the story by Doris Lessing (page 1026)? Explain.

2. Some Africans claim that the old tribal values are the quintessence of the African personality, though this point of view is strongly challenged by others. What values, particularly those dealing with the family, are strong in tribal culture? Base your answers on what you read in this story. Compare these

values with those that underlie Singer's story (page 983).

3. Traditionally, Africans have believed that their dead are nearby, not only in the grave, which was usually in the family compound, but also as spirits around them. The dead are consulted in family matters, libations are poured out to assuage their thirst, and nuts are rolled on the ground to discover their will. How does Nicol use these customs in this story? How does he want to make you feel about these people and their old ways? Compare Bola's and Meji's customs in regard to the dead with those of Antigone (page 140). How do they compare with customs in your society?

4. Has Nicol made you feel that the African outlook on life is world-affirming or world-denying? How does this story differ in emotional effect from the stories told by Conrad (page 939) and Camus (page 999)? Must a world-affirming viewpoint necessarily be like the viewpoint traditionally associated with Omar Khayyam (page 334)? Explain.

5. Modern social pressures are breaking down many of the old tribal customs in Africa. What evidence of this do you find in Nicol's story? (Why, for example, has the magician become a Muslim?) Do you see any similarities between this situation and other historical situations involving great change, such as the time when feudal society disintegrated in Europe? What has been the result of such changes in terms of contemporary culture?

FOR COMPOSITION

1. Write an essay commenting on the idea that, in dealing with people different from ourselves, we easily ignore or violate our bond of common humanity. To illustrate your comments, use Mrs. Lessing's story and Conrad's "Amy Foster," as well as any other works of literature you think appropriate.

2. Write an essay commenting on the idea that human speech is an imperfect means for people to understand one another. To illustrate your comments use Ionesco's "Rhinoceros" and Conrad's "Amy Foster," and any other appropriate literary works.

3. Write an essay commenting on the idea that the individual is sometimes caught between his need for other people and society's indifference toward his individuality. To illustrate your points use Singer's "The Little Shoemakers" and Joyce's "Araby," as well as any other stories or any contemporary movies you think appropriate.

4. Reread the story about Gilgamesh (page 13) and in an essay tell whether you believe that the existential problem tormenting Gilgamesh is like or unlike the problems faced by the characters in these modern short stories.

5. Recall a brief but significant episode in your own experience and tell it in three separate ways: as you saw it, as you can imagine another person involved might have seen it, and as an omniscient narrator might have seen it.

6. For the same episode, or for another, write an opening paragraph setting scene and atmosphere. Make your description suggestive of your attitude toward the episode and of the feeling you would like to arouse in your reader.

7. Present your ideas on how the story by Nicol could be dramatized for television. In your presentation include suggestions for stage sets, special effects, music, costumes. What scenes would you divide the story into? What scene would be climactic?

Glossary of Terms

ALLEGORY   A narrative in prose or verse, in which actions, characters, and sometimes settings stand for qualities or ideas outside the story itself (see Dante, page 400).

ALLITERATION   Repetition of the same sound in the stressed syllables of several words within a line or phrase, as in "Oft to the wanderer, weary of exile." Also, repetition of the same initial letter in several words in a group.

ANECDOTE   Usually a brief narrative about an amusing or entertaining incident. Found in literatures of many cultures and often used didactically (see page 298).

BALLAD   Generally, a song which tells a story, using simple stanzas and a refrain. The FOLK BALLAD, or traditional ballad (see pages 467–71), is of unknown authorship and is transmitted orally. The stanza of a typical British folk ballad consists of four lines, of alternating iambic tetrameter and iambic trimeter, rhyming abcb. The LITERARY BALLAD (see page 472) is a conscious imitation of a folk ballad.

BALLADE   A fixed French verse form popular in the fourteenth and fifteenth centuries. It consists either of three eight-line stanzas rhyming ababbcbc and a four-line envoy rhyming bcbc, or of three ten-line stanzas rhyming ababbccdcd and a five-line envoy rhyming ccdcd. The last line of each stanza and of the envoy is the same (see page 463).

BAROQUE   A style that prevailed in European art and music between about 1580 and 1680. The term is often used to describe extravagances in an otherwise classical style and theatricality in effect (see page 609).

BLANK VERSE   Poetry written in lines of unrhymed iambic pentameter. It is the poetic form used by most Elizabethan dramatists, including Shakespeare (see page 542), but it originated in Italy as the form that most closely matched the meter of Greek tragedy.

CAESURA   A break or pause in a poetic line. In Anglo-Saxon verse it was used mechanically to separate a poetic line into two parts having parallel structure (see page 455).

CANTICLE   A nonmetrical hymn, usually for singing in church (see page 459). Dante (page 401) used the term to signify the three major portions of his epic.

CANTO   A subdivision of an epic or long poem (see Dante, page 401).

CHANSONS DE GESTE   From *chanson,* "song," and *geste,* "deeds." Epic poems recited in the Old French vernacular, relating the deeds of Charlemagne or other feudal lords of his era (see *Song of Roland,* page 377).

CLASSICAL or CLASSICISM   In one sense, in the West, *classicism* refers to an adherence to the principles of balance, restraint, dignity, etc., as manifested in the art and literature of ancient Greece and Rome. The term *classical* is also used in opposition to *romantic;* in such usage, *classical* describes a concern for form and craft, and *romantic* describes a concern for personal inspiration and expression of emotion (see page 742 ff.). In any tradition, however, the term *classical* is used generally to describe a period of high literary achievement, when works of great literary merit, called "classics," were produced. Usually these works comprehensively represent the spirit of the culture or nationality they spring from (see page 230 for a discussion of India's "classic" literature).

COMEDY   In one sense, a literary work with a happy ending, in which the hero manages to extricate himself from an obstacle or challenge; in contrast to tragedy, where the hero is defeated. In Dante's time, the term was used to describe a work which not only ended happily but which was written in the vernacular (see page 400).

DADA   A movement that began around 1916 in Europe, which aimed at sweeping the world clean of all the rules of art and literature prevalent at the time. Dadaists eventually ridiculed all the values held by their civilization, feeling that they had merely led the world into a senseless war (see page 896).

DIDACTIC LITERATURE   Writings intended to instruct. Applied to poetry especially, but also to other forms with strong moral elements.

ECLOGUE   A short polished poem, usually pastoral, written in dialogue or soliloquy form.

The term was first applied to Virgil's poems (page 198). The form was widely imitated by Italian poets in the European Renaissance.

ELEGY   A lyric poem, usually formal in tone and diction, lamenting death (see pages 114, 498). In Greek literature, the term referred only to a specific verse form, and to the emotions frequently conveyed by that form.

ENVOY   A short stanza which concludes certain poetic forms. Originally, it served as a postscript dedicating the poem to a patron or another important person (see page 464).

EPIC   In general, a long narrative poem told in an elevated style, about heroic persons and grand events, usually significant to a particular race or nation. Ancient epics, like *Gilgamesh,* the *Iliad,* and the *Mahabharata,* seem to have drawn material from older oral traditions. Virgil's literary epic, the *Aeneid,* however, was a conscious imitation of the *Iliad* and *Odyssey,* and it was written to give Romans a lofty view of their past. Similarly, Dante's and Milton's literary epics (pages 401 and 630) were consciously written in imitation of the classical epics to effect lofty purposes.

EPIGRAM   A brief, witty, and pointed comment, often in verse (see page 213).

EXISTENTIALISM   A philosophic outlook often associated with French writers Sartre and Camus (see page 998). It stresses that man's nature is defined and given meaning by decisive actions, not by latent dispositions. Most existentialists regard man as an alien in an indifferent universe.

FABLE   A brief narrative, often with a stated moral, and often having animals or inanimate objects as characters. Some say India's *Panchatantra* (page 253) is the fountainhead of all European fables; others say the genre rose at the same time in Greece (see page 116).

FIGURE OF SPEECH   An expression that states something that is not literally true in order to achieve a special effect. Most figures of speech (metaphor, simile, and personification) are based on comparisons.

FIN DE SIÈCLE or MALAISE DE FIN DE SIÈCLE   "Disease of the end of the century." In Europe, an outlook characterized by disillusionment and despair, perhaps caused by the shifting of moral and spiritual values as the nineteenth century closed (see page 748).

FOLK LITERATURE   Stories and poems that originate orally among unlettered people, and which are passed on through oral tradition.

FRAME STORY   A literary device in which one story encloses and supports one or more related stories (see page 435).

FUTURISM   A movement that originated around 1910 in Italy and which called for a rejection of traditional literary forms and "sentimental" themes in an effort to portray more directly the dynamism and intensity of contemporary life.

HAIKU   A Japanese verse form which emerged in the sixteenth century. It has 17 syllables in lines of 5, 7, and 5 syllables, respectively. Each haiku includes a reference to a season and is usually restricted to images drawn from nature. Haiku often reflect a Zen-Buddhist outlook (see page 295).

HOMERIC SIMILE or EXTENDED SIMILE   Usually a detailed comparison of one entire action with another (see page 64, lines 10–15). To the Homeric simile, a European tradition of extended simile can be traced (see Dante, page 409, lines 40–43; Milton, page 641, lines 513–17).

HUMANISM   A literary and intellectual movement that began in the mid-fourteenth century in Italy, with a new enthusiastic attitude toward classical Latin poetry, drama, and prose writings. As it spread over Europe, humanism came to be characterized by an intense interest in all human affairs. Humanism was a departure from medieval scholasticism: scholastics restricted their studies to theology and science, and they felt that all learning had to be made to harmonize with Christian doctrine (see pages 478–84). The term HUMANITIES has come to mean specifically the study of classical Latin and Greek literatures, or, more generally, the study of literature, history, fine art, and philosophy, as distinguished from the study of the sciences.

IAMBIC PENTAMETER   A verse pattern consisting of ten syllables in a poetic line; the syllables alternate, unstressed followed by stressed. The term means "five iambs" (an iamb being a pair of syllables, the first unstressed, the second stressed). Iambic pentameter is the most common verse pattern in English poetry.

IMAGE   In literature, words that evoke a mental picture or some other sense experience.

IRONY   Verbal irony is a form of speech in which the speaker means something different from what he says. Dramatic irony is a plot device, in which an action or a situation produces a result different from what is expected. Dramatic irony also refers to a speech or an action in a play, which has greater or different significance to the audience than to the character himself, because the audience knows something that the character does not.

JONGLEUR A medieval musician and reciter of verses, who performed at French and Norman English courts. Originally, the term was applied to acrobats and entertainers in general. For their material, the jongleurs used the *chansons de geste* and the troubadours' lyrics.

KABUKI A Japanese dramatic form that arose in the seventeenth century, based on popular or comic themes and patronized by the merchant class who were dissatisfied with the solemn Nō dramas (see page 263).

KENNING In Anglo-Saxon and other early Germanic poetry, a formulaic metaphor which was substituted for the actual name of a person or thing (see page 372). Kennings were often compound words or phrases. In the best poetry, kennings carried rich suggestive associations.

LYRIC A poem, usually short, which expresses personal emotions or moods, distinguished from dramatic and narrative verse. In general, lyric poetry retains most pronouncedly those elements which give evidence of poetry's origins in musical expressions.

METAPHOR A figure of speech in which one object is identified with another and spoken of as if it actually were that object: "The *Lord* is my *shepherd*." Metaphor also involves association, that is, speaking of something in terms of something else: "My white head is in love with a *green maid*." *"Fire flashed* from out the old Moor's eyes." Some say that metaphor marks off the poetic utterance from the logical or discursive one.

METER The rhythmical arrangement of accented and unaccented syllables in poetry. The impulse to create meter is said by some to be part of the larger human impulse to create order out of chaos.

MNEMONICS Certain devices (such as repetition, rhyme, meter) that appear in literature in the oral tradition, designed to help the oral storyteller's or singer's memory.

MYTH Usually, a story that has a god as a character, and contains some imaginative explanation for the origins of the human and natural words. Some say that myths project subconscious aspects of human existence. Carl Jung speaks of myths as psychic phenomena that reveal the nature of the soul.

NATURALISM A literary movement that arose in the late nineteenth century in France. Naturalists saw literature as a vehicle for dissecting, with scientific exactness, life and the human species (see pages 771 and 772). The Naturalists tended to view life as a Darwinian struggle, in which the weak were crushed by the strong and powerful.

NÉGRITUDE A literary movement that arose among French-speaking black Africans, late in the 1800's, which aimed at affirming the values of black African culture (see page 929).

NEOCLASSICISM "New classicism." An imitation of the style identified with the art and literature of ancient Greece and Rome. The word is usually associated with European art and literature from the mid-1600's through the eighteenth century (see page 610).

NIHILISM From the Latin word "nothing." A doctrine that denies any basis for truth or knowledge.

NŌ The classic Japanese dramatic form, perfected in the fourteenth century. Nō is Zen oriented, and its messages are deeply religio-philosophical.

ODE The most serious and dignified form of lyric, having elevated diction and often written for a special occasion (see page 354).

ONOMATOPOEIA In a broad sense, the use of a word whose sound imitates or suggests its meaning, as *tweet*. The English language preserves a large onomatopoeic element.

ORAL TRADITION Poetry or poetic narratives composed *in* oral performance, whether by individual poets or by the people in a community, and passed on orally from generation to generation (*Gilgamesh*, the *Book of Songs*, the *Iliad*, the *Rig Veda*, etc., drew from oral traditions).

PARALLELISM Repetition of phrases that are symmetrical in structure or similar, opposite, or complementary in meaning (see the Hebrew psalms, page 30).

PASTORAL An old poetic form which presents an artificial and ideal picture of rural life, usually in a Golden Age, in which shepherds and shepherdesses play parts (see page 113).

PASTOURELLE A short, polished poem popular in the Middle Ages in Europe, which relates the amorous encounter of a man of position with a simple maiden (see page 460).

PERSONIFICATION A figure of speech in which something inanimate is given animate qualities, as in the Indian poem on page 235.

ROMANCE (MEDIEVAL) Originally, a term applied to literature in vernacular French (as opposed to Latin), later used to refer to any chivalric or amorous tale of adventure. Two popular romance cycles were those about King Arthur (see page 393) and Alexander the Great.

RUBAI From Persian for "quatrain." A popular Persian verse form. The rubai is usually witty, succinct, and spontaneous, of subtle meter, and usually rhymed aaba. To Persian poets it is an occasional poem, so the impression of continuity conveyed by Fitzgerald's English translation of Khayyam's rubaiyat is misleading (see page 334).

SATIRE In literature, writing that holds human weaknesses or wrongdoings up for ridicule or contempt. Some satiric techniques are irony, sarcasm, wit, exaggeration, mockery, understatement (see Martial, Voltaire, La Fontaine, etc.). The satiric spirit seems to appear in the folklore and literature of all peoples. Some say it derives from the use of derisive language in magic rituals to drive away evil.

SIMILE A figure of speech which describes something by comparing it explicitly with something else. A simile always includes a word of comparison, such as *like* or *as:* "The life of man is like a summer's leaf."

SONNET A short lyric verse form, popular in the West since the Renaissance. It consists of fourteen lines, usually of iambic pentameter. Several variations are allowed in this basic pattern (such as the Italian or English forms) (see page 495).

STOCK EPITHET An adjective or descriptive phrase used repeatedly to describe a person or thing, or to take the place of its name (Homer repeatedly uses the stock epithet *"white-armed* goddess").

SUFIS Members of an Islamic sect, who tend toward asceticism and mysticism. Sufi poets often apply the erotic imagery of human love to the divine-human relationship (see pages 353, 354).

SURREALISM A movement that began in the 1920's in France. It aimed at liberating man from the limitations of logic and freeing his imagination for participation in "surreality,"
which was "beyond" realism. Surrealists, who drew heavily from Freud, were interested in dreams and the subconscious. In literature, Surrealism is often marked by sensory appeals and by incongruous, daring arrangement of details.

SYMBOLISM A literary movement that arose in France toward the end of the nineteenth century. Symbolist poets avoid direct statements of meaning and instead use symbols to suggest meaning or mood. They use words for their magic suggestiveness, and the power of words in their poetry goes far beyond mere denotations (see Baudelaire, page 762).

TANKA A classic Japanese verse form that developed in the seventh century A.D. It has 31 syllables in lines of 5, 7, 5, 7, 7 syllables, respectively. (Five poems on pages 293–94 are tanka, though not so labeled in the text.)

THEATER OF THE ABSURD A twentieth-century movement initiated by dramatists in France, who rejected traditional dramatic structure and dislocated reality in an attempt to portray such things as the void behind the material world and society's brutalization of individual man (see page 1015).

TRAGEDY In broad terms, a literary work which depicts a struggle in which the main character is defeated in some way; despite the defeat and because of his courage, the character emerges as heroic. To the ancient Greeks, tragedy involved a hero who was a great person—such as a king, queen, or warrior—and the cause of his defeat was a flaw in character (see page 168).

TROUBADOURS Lyricists attached to courts in southern France and parts of Spain and Italy, who versified about courtly love in the Provençal language. They flourished from the eleventh to the fourteenth centuries (see page 458).

TROUVÈRES Writers in northern France who wrote about courtly love in vernacular French. They flourished from the eleventh to the fourteenth centuries. Where the troubadours concentrated on polished lyrics, the trouvères also wrote longer romances and *chansons de geste* (see pages 393, 461).

ZEN–BUDDHISM A form of contemplative Buddhism which originated in China around A.D. 500, but which subsequently had great influence on Japanese culture. Zen stresses receptivity for abrupt enlightenment (see pages 301–02).

Index of Fine Art

Index of Authors and Titles

Key: top, *t;* center, *c;* bottom, *b;* left, *l;* right, *r.*

Fine art acknowledgments: pp. 843, 844, 1009, Authorization SPADEM 1969 by French Reproduction Rights, Inc.; pp. 1010, 1011, 1014, Rights Reserved ADAGP Paris.

Fine art photo credits: p. 82, *t,* W. Katz, Photo Researchers, N. Y., *b,* Fritz Henle, Photo Researchers, N. Y.; p. 83, *t,* Scala, Florence; p. 84, *b,* Harbrace; p. 85, Scala, Florence; p. 321, *t,* Editorial Photocolor Archives, N. Y., *b,* American Library Color Slide Co., Inc., N. Y.; pp. 425, 426, 427, 429, Giraudon, Paris; pp. 529, 530, John R. Freeman (Photographers) Ltd., London; pp. 531, 532, Scala, Florence; p. 533, John R. Freeman (Photographers) Ltd., London; p. 534, Scala, Florence; p. 665, Les Musées Nationaux, Versailles; p. 666, Farben-photographie Gerhard Reinhold, Leipzig-Mölkau; p. 667, Scala, Florence; p. 669, Copyright by Photo Meyer, Vienna; p. 705, Les Musées Nationaux, Versailles; p. 706, John R. Freeman (Photographers) Ltd., London; p. 841, Les Musées Nationaux, Versailles; p. 843, Joachim Blauel; p. 844, Les Musées Nationaux, Versailles.

In-text photo credits: p. 6, *l,* Hirmer Fotoarchiv, Munich, *r,* Professor Y. Yadin, Hebrew University, Jerusalem; p. 42, Candia Museum, Crete; p. 47, The British Museum; p. 50, Editorial Photocolor Archives, N. Y.; pp. 171, 176, The Bettmann Archive, Inc., N. Y.; p. 180, Alinari—Art Reference Bureau, Ancram, N. Y.; p. 185, Editorial Photocolor Archives, N. Y.; p. 186, Brogi—Art Reference Bureau,

Ancram, N. Y.; p. 231, The Metropolitan Museum of Art, N. Y., Rogers Fund, 1927; p. 234, Victoria & Albert Museum, London; p. 263, Consulate General of Japan, N. Y.; p. 265, *l,* from Chiang Yee, "Chinese Calligraphy: An Introduction to Its Aesthetic & Technique," Harvard University Press, copyright 1938; p. 266, Segalen, Mission Archeologique; p. 315, The Metropolitan Museum of Art, N. Y., Rogers Fund, 1913; p. 318, The Metropolitan Museum of Art, N. Y., Gift of Horace Havemeyer, 1941, The H. O. Havemeyer Collection; p. 361, Editorial Photocolor Archives, N. Y.; p. 364, with special authorization of the city of Bayeux, photo, Giraudon, Paris; p. 366, Editorial Photocolor Archives, N. Y.; p. 369, Bibliothèque Nationale, Paris, photo by R. J. Ségalat; p. 479, Editorial Photocolor Archives, N. Y.; p. 482, The Bettmann Archive, Inc., N. Y.; p. 487, Alinari—Art Reference Bureau, Ancram, N. Y.; p. 602, Diderot Encyclopedia; pp. 605, 608, The Bettmann Archive, Inc., N. Y.; p. 740, N. Y. Public Library Picture Collection; pp. 743, 747, *l,* The Bettmann Archive, Inc., N. Y.; pp. 747, *r,* 891, N. Y. Public Library Picture Collection; p. 893, *l,* Jim Theologos, *r,* Ernest Trova, *Study from Falling Man Series: Walking Man* (1964), Collection, The Museum of Modern Art, N. Y., Gift of Miss Vicki Laura List; p. 896, Meret Oppenheim, *Object* (1936), Collection, The Museum of Modern Art, N. Y.; p. 898, United Nations. The maps on pages 1, 5, 41, 182, 223, 227, 316, 357, and 887 are Harbrace maps.